A Biographical Encyclopedia

A Biographical Encyclopedia

VOLUME
7
Harr-I

Anne Commire, Editor
Deborah Klezmer, Associate Editor

YORKIN PUBLICATIONS

Yorkin Publications

Anne Commire, *Editor*
Deborah Klezmer, *Associate Editor*
Barbara Morgan, *Assistant Editor*

Eileen O'Pasek, Gail Schermer, Patricia Coombs, James Fox,
Catherine Cappelli, Karen Rikkers, *Editorial Assistants*
Karen Walker, *Assistant for Genealogical Charts*

Special acknowledgment is due to Peg Yorkin who made this project possible.

Thanks also to Karin and John Haag, Bob Schermer, and to
the Gale Group staff, in particular Dedria Bryfonski, Linda Hubbard, John Schmittroth, Cynthia Baldwin,
Tracey Rowens, Randy Bassett, Christine O'Bryan, Rebecca Parks, and especially Sharon Malinowski.

The Gale Group

Sharon Malinowski, *Senior Editor*
Rebecca Parks, *Editor*
Linda S. Hubbard, *Managing Editor, Multicultural Team*

Margaret A. Chamberlain, *Permissions Specialist*
Mary K. Grimes, *Image Cataloger*

Mary Beth Trimper, *Production Director*
Evi Seoud, *Assistant Production Manager*

Cynthia Baldwin, *Product Design Manager*
Tracey Rowens, *Cover and Page Designer*
Michael Logusz, *Graphic Artist*

Barbara Yarrow, *Graphic Services Manager*
Randy Bassett, *Image Database Supervisor*
Robert Duncan, *Imaging Specialist*
Christine O'Bryan, *Graphics Desktop Publisher*
Dan Bono, *Technical Support*

Gale Group, Inc.
27500 Drake Road
Farmington Hills, MI 48331-3535

Library of Congress Catalog Card Number 99-24692
A CIP record is available from the British Library

ISBN 0-7876-4066-2
Printed in the United States of America.

Library of Congress Cataloging-in-Publication Data

Women in world history : a biographical encyclopedia / Anne Commire, editor, Deborah Klezmer, associate editor.
p. cm.
Includes bibliographical references and index.
ISBN 0-7876-3736-X (set). — ISBN 0-7876-4064-6 (v. 5). —
ISBN 0-7876-4065-4 (v. 6) — ISBN 0-7876-4066-2 (v. 7) — ISBN 0-7876-4067-0 (v. 8) — ISBN 0-7876-4068-9 (v. 9)
1. Women—History Encyclopedias.2. Women—Biography Encyclopedias.
I. Commire, Anne. II. Klezmer, Deborah.
HQ1115.W6 1999 99-24692
920.72'03—DC21

10 9 8 7 6 5 4 3 2 1

Harraden, Beatrice (1864–1936)

English novelist and suffragist. *Born on January 24, 1864, in Hampstead, London, England; died on May 5, 1936, in Barton-on-Sea, Hampshire, England; daughter of Samuel and Rosalie (Lindstedt) Harraden; attended Cheltenham Ladies College, Dresden, and Queens College and Bedford College, London; graduated from London University, B.A., 1883.*

Beatrice Harraden showed a streak of individuality at a time when women in a university environment were considered a novelty. Born in Hampstead, London, in 1864, she was educated at Cheltenham Ladies College in Dresden and then progressed to Queens College and Bedford College in London. In 1883, she received her B.A. from London University with honors in the classics and mathematics.

Harraden's earliest publishing accomplishments occurred with the appearance of her short stories in *Blackwood's Magazine*. Her first book, *Things Will Take a Turn* (1891), was a children's story. In 1893, her most successful book, *Ships That Pass in the Night,* was initially rejected by William Blackwood since the publisher considered it too short and felt that it did not have salable qualities. Lawrence & Bullen subsequently purchased the manuscript which was an immediate success upon its release, selling more than a million copies. Her next book, *In Varying Moods* (1894), was a collection of short stories set in numerous locations throughout Europe. Among the books considered her best are *Hilda Stafford* (1897), *Untold Tales of the Past* (1897) and *The Fowler* (1899).

In addition to her literary career, Harraden took an active interest in the women's suffrage movement and became a prominent member of the Women's Social and Political Union. To promote the cause, she frequently marched in parades and spoke at meetings. In 1930, Harraden was granted a civil-list pension for services to literature. She died at Barton-on-Sea in Hampshire, England, on May 5, 1936, at the age of 72.

Judith C. Reveal,
freelance writer, Greensboro, Maryland

Harriet.

Variant of Henrietta.

Harriman, Daisy (1870–1967).

See Harriman, Florence Jaffray.

Harriman, Florence Jaffray (1870–1967)

American social reformer, Democratic Party activist, and U.S. minister to Norway at the time of the Nazi invasion. *Name variations: Daisy Harriman; Mrs. J. Borden Harriman. Born Florence Jaffray Hurst on July 21, 1870, in New York City; died in Washington, D.C., on August 31, 1967; daughter of Francis William Jones Hurst (head of a steamship company) and Caroline Elise Jaffray Hurst; attended classes with Mrs. Lippincott, first at the home of J.P. Morgan, and later on Lexington Avenue; married J(efferson) Borden Harriman, on November 18, 1889 (died 1914); children: one,* ***Ethel Borden Harriman Russell*** *(December 1898–1953).*

Awards: granted the Great Cross of St. Olav, the highest honor of Norway (1942); received the Citation for Distinguished Service, Presidential Medal of Freedom (1963).

Mother died when Daisy was three (1873); lived in house of maternal grandfather, Edward Jaffray; appointed manager of New York State Reformatory for Women at Bedford (1906–18); co-founded Colony Club with Anne Morgan and Elisabeth Marbury, New York's first women's social club, and served as president (1907–16); helped found women's welfare committee of National Civic Federation, and toured South to report on child-labor conditions; served as chair, Women's National Wilson and Marshall Association (1912); was only woman member of Federal Industrial Relations Commission (1913–14); served as chair of Committee of Women in Industry of the Advisory

Committee of the Council of National Defense (1917); organized Red Cross Motor Corps, served as assistant director of transportation in France (1918); was a delegate to Inter-Allied Women's Council (1919); co-founded Women's National Democratic Club (1922), and was president (1922–30); served as Democratic Committeewoman, Washington, D.C. (1924–36); named U.S. minister to Norway (1937–40); appointed vice-chair of White Committee to Defend America by Aiding the Allies (1941).

Selected publications: From Pinafores to Politics *(Henry Holt, 1923);* Mission to the North *(Lippincott, 1941).*

In 1937, President Franklin Roosevelt selected Norway as a posting for Daisy Harriman, a dignified white-haired grandmother, whom he wished to name as the second woman ever to head an American legation. A neutral country, Norway seemed safely removed from the impending European crisis. Three years later, in the early hours of April 9, 1940, at 3:30 AM, the telephone rang beside the bed of Harriman at the American Embassy in Norway; it was the British ambassador alerting her that German warships were coming up the fjord. Harriman's cable to Washington, transmitted via the American Embassy in Sweden, was the first official news of the invasion. By 9:45, she was in her car with her chauffeur, a clerk, a typewriter, and the code book, following the Norwegian king Haakon VII as he fled the occupied capital city of Oslo.

Marbury, Elisabeth. *See de Wolfe, Elsie for sidebar.*

As Harriman trailed the retreating government, evading the Nazi forces through the Norwegian countryside, her military attaché was killed by shrapnel, and the American flag, which they had fixed to the car roof to warn the Germans that the car was an official one from a neutral country, was used to cover his coffin. When Harriman realized that no purpose could be served by following the king into exile, she crossed into Sweden, where, that August, she oversaw the evacuation of hundreds of American dependents from the region.

Florence Jaffray Hurst Harriman, known all her life as Daisy, was born in New York City in 1870, the eldest of two daughters, of Francis William Jones Hurst, head of a steamship company and president of the Yacht Club, and **Caroline Elise Jaffray**. Caroline died of puerperal fever after the birth of a third daughter, and Daisy and her sisters lived with their father in the house of their maternal grandfather, Edward Jaffray. Jaffray, a naturalized American who had been born in England, had connections in both countries; he regaled his granddaughter with stories about British Prime Minister Benjamin Disraeli, while President Chester A. Arthur, John Hay, and Herbert Hoover were among those who dropped in for breakfast or came more formally in the evening to dine. Daisy believed her father, a retired British army officer, had been disappointed to have no sons, and so had reared his daughters to ride horseback, sail, and always maintain an erect military bearing.

Daisy received what she called a "sketchy" education from Mrs. Lippincott, first at the home of J. Pierpont Morgan, and later in a private school on Lexington Avenue. After making her debut in 1888, she married J. Borden Harriman, known as Bordie, who was a banker a few years her senior whom she had known from childhood, and the cousin of E.H. and Averill Harriman. After a number of miscarriages attributed to Daisy's refusal to give up horseback riding sidesaddle, they had a daughter, Ethel, in 1898.

Even as a young society matron, Daisy Harriman "had a vague notion that a woman should be able to do something in the workaday world." In 1906, she was named manager of the New York State Reformatory for Women at Bedford, and served until 1918. Also in 1906, after her husband questioned the propriety of her staying alone in a hotel in New York, she persuaded friends ***Anne Morgan** and **Elisabeth Marbury** to join her in founding the Colony Club, New York's first social club for women, which opened the following year despite criticism from those who claimed it would enable women to "receive clandestine letters," and the more worldly critics who predicted a club could not survive financially without a bar. Daisy was president from 1907 until 1916.

The club gave her access to a number of political movements. Her first contact with Woodrow Wilson, who became her political ideal, occurred at this time, when, as president of Princeton, he was invited to the opening. A speaker at the club from the National Civic Federation (NCF) inspired Daisy to join the women's department which lobbied for better conditions for working women in stores, hotels, and factories. Through the NCF, she toured cotton-mills in the South to inspect child-labor conditions, and in 1911 published articles in *Harper's Weekly* about her findings, "the first money I had ever earned." This earning power would become not only a source of pride but a necessity.

Daisy Harriman also worked for health care, particularly for improved infant mortality and control of tuberculosis. Like many women of the day, she saw direct involvement in elective politics as essential to any wide-reaching reform. Her even-handed treatment of Southern mill owners in her reports had recommended her to Woodrow Wilson, a Southerner, and in 1912, she was appointed head of the Women's Wilson and Marshall Association to campaign for the Democratic ticket. The following year, she campaigned for John Mitchel, the young reform mayor of New York, and was consulted by him on appointments.

Wilson rewarded her efforts on his behalf by naming her to the Federal Industrial Relations Commission, created during the Taft administration to investigate the causes of industrial unrest. Harriman became the first woman ever appointed to a federal commission. Although some felt that a woman with closer ties to working women, or at least with a more extensive background in social work might have been more appropriate, Harriman's executive ability, compelling personality, and connections to the prominent and powerful were seen as real assets. The commission successfully intervened in a threatened railway strike, but Daisy took exception to the final report summarizing the hearings they had conducted, believing that it did not make allowances for the "technical problems of production." While labor leaders like Mother (***Mary Harris**) **Jones** complained that Daisy would betray the workers if she did not sign the report, wealthy Washingtonians like ***Eleanor "Cissy" Patterson** were equally dubious, sniffing, "So you're the dangerous woman who's come down to take all our money away from us?" Seeking a distraction from the tensions of the committee, Harriman visited the Mexican border during their civil war in 1915, volunteering at the hospital where the wounded were brought from the battle of Matamoros and writing about her experiences for *Harper's Weekly.*

War had come to Europe, too. Harriman and her husband had gone to England in 1914 for Daisy to study labor conditions. They had traveled to a spa in Carlsbad where Bordie sought to improve his failing health, undermined by heavy drinking, and were there when war broke out. Borden Harriman died in Washington in December 1914. "Her husband was rich one week and poor the next," Daisy's contemporary, ***Alice Roosevelt Longworth**, noted. "Unfortunately, he died during one of his poor periods, so Daisy wasn't particularly well off."

By April 1917, the U.S. had also been drawn into the conflict. Samuel Gompers appointed Harriman chair of the Committee of Women in

Florence Jaffray Harriman

Industry, part of the Advisory Committee of the Council of National Defense, and she reported on the safety of women workers in munitions mills. She also organized the Red Cross Motor Corps, learning first aid and automobile repair; "the members," reported **Anne Hard**, "looked so snappy in the breeches and Sam Brown belts, Mrs. Harriman looking snappiest of all." She went to France in 1917 to study conditions in munitions factories and hospitals, and again in 1918 as assistant director of transportation, reporting to President Wilson on her return. She attended the Paris peace conference, lobbying for T.E. Lawrence as well as for expedited leave for those in the military whose wives were ill, and was made a delegate to the Inter-Allied Women's Council to consult with committees on issues relating to women and children.

Though Daisy Harriman was a longtime supporter of Woodrow Wilson and his policies, she parted company with him over his opposition to women's suffrage. While president of the Colony Club, she had felt she could not publicly declare her sympathy, but free of that responsibility by 1917, she led a march for women's suffrage in New York City. On the whole, however, she believed that persuasion was more effective than confrontation.

In 1923, Daisy Harriman published *From Pinafores to Politics,* a memoir of women's political activity before suffrage. During the 1920s, when the Republicans were in power, she defended progressive ideas. She saw the Equal Rights Amendment proposed by ***Alice Paul** and the Women's Party as a threat to protective legislation for women, and opposed it as chair of the campaign committee of the Consumers League. She also worked for American membership in the League of Nations and the World Court, as well as for disarmament and the movement to outlaw war.

After the 19th Amendment granting all women the right to vote passed in 1920, Harriman strove to increase support for the Democratic Party among the newly enfranchised women. In 1922, she co-founded the Women's National Democratic Club and served as its first president until 1930, creating a place where Democratic women would feel at home as they often did not in the regular party councils. She was Democratic Committeewoman from Washington, D.C., from 1924 to 1936. But it was as the host of Sunday night supper parties at "Uplands," her house on Foxhall Road overlooking the city, that she became renowned. Originally a gathering to boost the out-of-power Democrats' morale, the parties expanded to include the most stimulating members of Washington society, from ambassadors and senators to left-wing columnists. Daisy created an atmosphere formal enough and diverse enough to provoke "the exchange of healthy home truths" that might not have taken place in smaller, more partisan groups. Cocktails were not served lest they interfere with the diners' mental agility; as her guests were finishing dessert, Harriman would toss out a question for general debate. It was also noted that, unlike other political salons where women were banished to the drawing room, her brilliant gatherings were comprised of equal numbers of women and men; according to journalist Anne Hard, author "***Mary Roberts Rinehart** will stand off Senator Robinson, Senator Walsh, Senator Harrison, Mr. Houston and half-a-dozen distinguished Democrats in a play of wit at once serious and gay."

Daisy Harriman was a delegate to the 1932 Democratic convention, but she was loyal to Newton D. Baker, Woodrow Wilson's secretary of war. When Franklin Roosevelt secured the nomination, she worked for his election, but her failure to support him from the start was held against her for four years. During this bleak period, she amused herself by writing a novel, but feeling that the characters were wooden, destroyed the only copies. Daisy maintained close ties with many in the New Deal, sharing her house with secretary of labor ***Frances Perkins** during the summer of 1933 and entertaining members of the administration at her "tea cup chancellery," even though she sometimes had to supplement her income by interior decorating or renting out her house. She campaigned vigorously for FDR in 1936 and supported his controversial plan in 1937 to expand (or pack) the Supreme Court.

At the start of his first administration in 1933, Roosevelt had appointed ***Ruth Bryan Owen (Rohde)** as his representative to Denmark, the first woman to head a U.S. embassy. She resigned in 1936 after marrying a captain in the Danish Royal Guards, creating an opportunity for Roosevelt to nominate a second female chief of mission. In April 1937, Roosevelt named Daisy Harriman to head the post in Oslo. She was well-suited to diplomatic life, given her interests in politics and reform, her ability to see both sides of a question, and her skill as a host. Tall, erect, and handsome, she made a striking impression with her white hair, blue eyes, and severe dark clothes, and she delighted the athletic Norwegians by swimming in the fjords and taking up skiing. She was a conscientious emissary, entertaining visiting Americans and touring the countryside to learn all she could about her host country, even going out with fishing boats north of the Arctic circle. A Christian Scientist, she worried secretary of state Cordell Hull by refusing medical attention when she fell ill with pneumonia.

Minister Harriman's first international crisis came in November 1939 when an American freighter, *City of Flint,* was seized by a German crew on the pretext that it was carrying contraband to England. Seeking to evade patrolling British warships, the Germans sailed it to the Norwegian port of Bergen. Daisy learned the whereabouts of the ship before the press could, and she negotiated the return of the *City of Flint* to the United States.

Because it was a neutral country, Norway was surprised by the German invasion in April of the following year. Two invading troop ships were sunk in the fjord, enabling King Haakon and his government to flee, with Daisy following behind, sometimes under fire, on roads crowded with refugees, pausing often to telephone reports to the U.S. minister to Sweden, Frederick Sterling. "How are you?" he anxiously asked the 69-year-old woman. "I've never been better in my life," she answered in her usual brisk manner. Secretary of State Hull cabled her: "I congratulate you on the courage, energy, and efficiency with which you are performing your duties under such trying and dangerous conditions. It is in the best traditions of our diplomatic service." Her military attaché, Captain Losey, after arguing strenuously for her to remain behind, had gone north without her to report on the evacuation of American dependents to Sweden, when he was killed. Daisy, who reached the Swedish border by sled after her car became stuck in the snow, waited in Stockholm for news of the whereabouts of the Norwegian government so she could join them.

When King Haakon and his government went into exile in London, they requested Daisy to accompany the Crown Princess ***Martha of Sweden** and her children to the United States, as guests of President Roosevelt, who had met her on an earlier visit to Washington. An American transport was dispatched to Petsamo, in the extreme north of Finland, and Daisy oversaw the evacuation of nearly 900 American women and children.

Harriman campaigned again for Franklin Roosevelt in the 1940 election, served as vice-chair of the White Committee to Defend America by Aiding the Allies, to counter the desire of isolationists to stay out of the European war, and supported a postwar international organization. In 1941, she published a memoir of her experience in Norway, *Mission to the North*. After the war, she resumed entertaining; her political salon was rivaled only by that of Alice Roosevelt Longworth.

In 1953, Harriman's daughter Ethel Harriman Russell died of leukemia. In 1955, at age 84, Daisy Harriman led a parade through Washington, D.C., to protest "taxation without representation" in the nation's capital, whose citizens had no elected members of Congress. "It's time for another Boston tea party," this tireless champion of political rights wrote in a letter to *The New York Times*. In 1963, President John F. Kennedy awarded her the first Citation of Merit for Distinguished Service (the Presidential Medal of Freedom). Florence Harriman died of a stroke in Washington, D.C., at age 97. Throughout her long life, she had enjoyed what she described as "a box seat at the America of my times." It would be more accurate to say that she had been on stage for almost every act.

SOURCES:

Harriman, Florence J. *From Pinafores to Politics*. NY: Henry Holt, 1923.

———. *Mission to the North*. Philadelphia, PA: J.B. Lippincott, 1941.

Ware, Susan. *Beyond Suffrage: Women in the New Deal*. Cambridge, MA: Harvard University Press, 1981.

COLLECTIONS:

Correspondence and papers are located in the Manuscript Division, Library of Congress, Washington, D.C.

Kristie Miller,
author of *Ruth Hanna McCormick: A Life in Politics 1880–1944*
(University of New Mexico Press, 1992)

Harriman, Mrs. J. Borden (1870–1967).

See Harriman, Florence Jaffray.

Harriman, Pamela (1920–1997)

British-born socialite and politician who was U.S. ambassador to France from 1993 to 1997. *Born Pamela Digby on March 20, 1920, in Farnborough, England; died on February 5, 1997, in Paris, France; the eldest of four children, three daughters and a son, of Lord Edward Kenelm, 11th Baron Digby, and Constance Pamela Alice (Bruce) Digby; married Randolph Churchill, in 1939 (divorced 1945); married Leland Hayward (theatrical producer), in 1960 (died 1971); married W. Averell Harriman (governor of New York and presidential advisor), around 1972 (died 1986); children: (first marriage) one son, Winston Churchill (b. 1940).*

Called by some the "century's greatest courtesan," Pamela Harriman gained her wealth and power through the men she acquired, notably three husbands—Winston Churchill's son Randolph, Broadway producer Leland Hayward, and former New York governor and presidential advisor Averell Harriman—and a string of impressive lovers, including Aly Khan, Gianni Agnelli, Elie de Rothschild, and Stavros Niarchos. **Barbara Kanrowitz**, in a review of the biography *Reflected Glory* by **Sally Bedell Smith**, calls Harriman the victim of an era in which women of ambition had limited choices. "Under other circumstances, she might have been a CEO like Paley," she writes. "She certainly had the drive. But given her time, she pursued one of the few available routes to power." Harriman's later years were devoted to politics, and she is credited with helping to put the Democratic Party back on its feet after years of Republican rule. As a major Democratic fund raiser, and a loyal backer of Bill Clinton, Harriman was rewarded with an appointment as ambassador to France, a post she held from 1993 until her death in 1997.

Pamela Harriman

Born into British aristocracy, Pamela Harriman was the daughter of the 11th Baron Digby and **Constance Bruce Digby**, whom Pamela called "a very, very strong woman." A red-headed, chubby-cheeked youngster, Pamela grew up at Minterne, the family's 1,500-acre estate in Dorset. As a debutante, Harriman was said to be low on the list of attractive girls. In 1939, after an unsuccessful social season in London, she took a job in the Foreign Office as part of the prewar effort. A friend introduced her to her first husband Randolph Churchill, a known drinker, gambler, and womanizer, who, she said, swept her off her feet. Friends concur that much of Harriman's attraction to Randolph was the family connection. "She was not educated, but I think she was very cunning," said acquaintance Lady **Mary Dunn** about Harriman's decision to marry Randolph. "The war had started. Randolph got her the Churchill name."

The marriage, a disaster that would officially end in 1945, produced Harriman's only son, Winston, born in 1940. Harriman made the most of the unfortunate union by endearing herself to the Churchill family. Through her father-in-law, who pressed her into service as a hostess (and as an intelligence broker during World War II), she met many important people, including American diplomat and multimillionaire Averell Harriman, who was sent to London by President Franklin Roosevelt in March 1941. At the time, Averell Harriman was 49 and married to his second wife **Marie Norton Whitney**. Something of a philanderer himself, Averell had just concluded a brief romance with ballerina ***Vera Zorina**, who was married to George Balanchine. Pamela's on-again, off-again love affair with Averell Harriman (which did not preclude a fling with CBS newscaster Edward R. Murrow), lasted until 1946, when he replaced Henry Wallace as secretary of commerce, and Pamela went off to Paris. Subsidized by wealthy lovers Agnelli and Rothschild, she spent the 1950s immersed in the art world.

Harriman's second husband was the colorful Leland Hayward, a talent agent, airline executive, and theatrical producer, who brought to Broadway such hits as *South Pacific*, *Gypsy*, and *The Sound of Music*. They met in New York and married in 1960, after Hayward divorced his third wife, **Nancy Keith**. Harriman was devoted to Hayward and nursed him through a series of strokes. When he died in 1971, Pamela entered into a bitter fight over Hayward's modest estate with children from his second marriage to actress ***Margaret Sullavan**. (Daughter **Brooke Hayward** denounced Harriman in her 1977 best-seller, *Haywire*.)

Four months after Hayward's death, at a party given by newspaper publisher ***Katharine Graham**, Harriman reunited with Averell Harriman, now 79 years old and widowed. They married eight weeks later, and, as a gift to her new husband, Harriman became a U.S. citizen. The couple settled in Washington, where Pamela became active as a Democratic fund raiser and a loyal supporter of Bill Clinton. After her husband's death in 1986, she redoubled her efforts to restore to power her adopted Democratic Party. "No one in this country can take greater credit for winning the White House than Pamela," said Speaker of the House Tom Foley.

Seventy-three at the time of her appointment as ambassador to France, Harriman surprised legions of doubters on both sides of the Atlantic by overcoming her image as socialite and dilettante and establishing herself as a powerful and capable American presence in Paris. Serving during a period of strained relations over trade, NATO restructuring, Bosnia, the

Middle East, and CIA spying inside France, Harriman proved to be a skilled mediator and, much to the delight of the French, appeared to have better access to the American president than former ambassadors had enjoyed. Harriman, having spent years living in France and having a perfect command of the language, also used her considerable social acumen to bring together an eclectic mix of politicians, diplomats, artists and intellectuals. In April 1996, French Culture Minister Philippe Douste-Blazy made her a commander of the Order of Arts and Letters and praised her efforts to "intensify French-American cultural links with passion, ardor and intelligence."

Pamela Harriman's tenure as ambassador was cut short by her death in February 1997, less than 48 hours after suffering a stroke. "She was one of the most unusual and gifted people I ever met," said Clinton in tribute. "She was a source of judgment and inspiration to me, a source of constant good humor and charm and real friendship."

SOURCES:

Gleick, Elizabeth, and J.D. Podolsky. "Life of the Party," in *People Weekly.* April 26, 1993, pp. 39–41.

Kantrowitz, Barbara. "A Woman of the World," in *Newsweek.* October 28, 1996, p. 78.

Ogden, Christopher. *Life of the Party.* Boston, MA: Little Brown, 1994.

Rothberg, Donald M. "Charmed life: Harriman's last reward was to serve her country," in *The Day* [New London, CT]. February 6, 1997.

Smith, Sally Bedell. *Reflected Glory: The Life of Pamela Churchill Harriman.* NY: Simon & Schuster, 1996.

Harrington, countess of.

See Foote, Maria (c. 1797–1867).

Harriot.

Variant of Henrietta.

Harris, Barbara (1930—)

African-American suffragan bishop for the Massachusetts Diocese of the Episcopal Church who was the first woman bishop in the history of the Episcopal Church. *Born Barbara Clementine Harris in Philadelphia, Pennsylvania, on June 12, 1930; one of three children, two girls and a boy, of Walter Harris (a steelworker) and Beatrice (Price) Harris (a classical pianist); graduated from Philadelphia High School for Girls, 1948; attended Charles Morris Price School of Advertising and Journalism; attended Villanova University (1977–79); attended Hobart and William Smith College; married and divorced; no children.*

Elected suffragan (assistant) bishop of the Massachusetts diocese of the Episcopal Church in 1988, Barbara Clementine Harris was the first woman ever admitted to the church's hierarchy. "There seem to be fresh winds blowing across the church," she preached around the time of her consecration. "Things thought to be impossible a short time ago are coming to be." Harris came to her position well into her middle years, having served as a corporate executive before entering the priesthood at age 50. "You don't set out in life to be a bishop," she told **Alisa Valdes-Rodriguez** in a 1998 interview for *The Boston Globe.* "At least I didn't." Harris' election to the episcopate was not without controversy. Church traditionalists objected to her gender, her divorced status, and her educational, theological, and ministerial qualifications. Furthermore, her outspoken articles in the liberal and highly controversial publication *The Witness* caused some to view her as a dangerous radical. But since taking office, Harris has silenced most of her detractors. She has also made good her promise to help broaden the scope of the church to meet the needs of more people, "including minorities, women, the incarcerated, the poor and other marginalized groups."

Barbara Harris was born in 1930 in Philadelphia, Pennsylvania, one of three children of an educated black family. She grew up in Germantown, where her father Walter Harris worked at a local steel mill and her mother **Beatrice Price Harris**, a classical pianist, served as the organist and choir director at the neighborhood church. A "cradle Episcopalian," Barbara was baptized and confirmed at St. Barnabas Church and, as a teenager, played the piano for church school and started the Young Adults Group, which at the time was one of the largest youth groups in the city.

After high school, Harris attended Philadelphia's Charles Morris Price School of Advertising and Journalism and, in 1949, took a job with a public-relations firm owned by African-Americans, working her way up to president. In 1968, she joined the Sun Oil Company, where she eventually became a public-relations executive. Continuing to live in Philadelphia, Harris remained active in the church, changing parishes as an adult to follow her religious mentor, the Reverend Paul Washington, who was also known for his political activism. Washington and Harris first worked together as youth counselors during the 1950s. "Church was not something to be played with for Barbara," he said. "She was never someone you could describe as a pew warmer. She was going to get in the midst of things." During the 1960s, Harris worked for African-American and women's rights; she marched with Martin Luther

Barbara Harris

King, Jr., and was a member of the Urban League, among other organizations.

When ordination became a possibility for women, Harris began studying for the ministry, although she says she struggled against her calling for some time, feeling she was not a worthy candidate. "A friend of mine who was a priest and is now a bishop said, 'God does not call those who are worthy; He makes worthy those who are called.' That helped." She was ordained to the diaconate in 1978 and ordained as a priest in 1980. Her eight years of parish experience included a thriving prison ministry. According to Washington, she spent enough time in prison to have nearly served a two-year sentence herself. Harris was interim rector at the Church of the Advocate when she was elected suffragan bishop.

Old friends insist that her lofty position has not changed Harris, who still favors fashionable clothes, high-heeled pumps, and long, painted fingernails. She still cooks, drives her BMW, employs someone to clean her house, and frequently displays her razor-sharp wit. Once, while addressing the church's continued reluctance to recognize the status of women priests and bishops, she remarked: "I could be a combination of the Virgin Mary, ***Lena Horne** and ***Madame Curie** and I would still get clobbered by some." While down-to-earth and accessible, Harris is nonetheless a woman with a mission. **Myrtle Gordon**, a national church consultant on aging and on clergy wives, characterizes Harris as "fiercely strong in her beliefs, loyalties, and concern for people's welfare in relation to the witness of the church; a dynamo in her strong conviction; one motivated and propelled to rectify situations caused by the church's failure to perceive and attend to people's needs."

The position of suffragan bishop is a permanent one, giving Harris the opportunity to prove her "worthiness" many times over. Since her election, four other Episcopal women have become bishops.

SOURCES:

Smith, Jessie Carney, ed. *Notable Black American Women.* Detroit, MI: Gale Research, 1992.

Time. Summer 1990, p. 60.

Valdes-Rodriguez, Alisa. "Former corporate executive answers a higher calling," in *The Day* [New London, CT]. August 22, 1998.

Barbara Morgan,
Melrose, Massachusetts

Harris, Julie (1921—)

British costume designer. *Born in London, England, in 1921; studied at the Chelsea Polytechnic.*

Filmography: Holiday Camp *(1948);* Once Upon a Dream *(1948);* Broken Journey *(1949);* Good Time Girl *(1949);* The Calendar *(1949);* My Brother's Keeper *(1949);* Quartet *(1949);* Under Capricorn *(with Roger Furse, 1950);* Trio *(1951);* The Clouded Yellow *(1951);* Highly Dangerous *(1951);* Traveller's Joy *(1951);* Mr. Drake's Duck *(1951);* Night Without Stars *(with Balmain, 1952);* Hotel Sahara *(1952);* Another Man's Poison *(1952);* Encore *(1952);* So Little Time *(1952);* Something Money Can't Buy *(1953);* South of Algiers *(U.S.,* The Golden Mask, *1953);* Made in Heaven *(1953);* Desperate Moment *(1953);* Turn the Key Softly *(1954);* Always a Bride *(1954);* The Red Beret *(U.S.,* Paratrooper, *1954);* You Know What Sailors Are *(1954);* The Seekers *(U.S.,* Land of Fury, *1955);* Value For Money *(1956);* Cast a Dark Shadow *(1956);* Simon and Laura *(1956);* The March Hare *(1957);* Reach for the Sky *(1957);* It's a Wonderful World *(1957);* House of Secrets *(U.S.,* Triple Deception, *1957);* Miracle in Soho *(1958);* The Story of Costello *(with Jean Louis, 1958);* Seven Thunders *(U.S.,* The Beast of Marseilles, *1958);* The Gypsy and the Gentleman *(1958);* The Sheriff of Fractured Jaw *(1959);* Whirlpool *(1959);* Sapphire *(1960);* North West Frontier *(U.S.,* Flame Over India, *with Yvonne Caffin, 1960);* The Greengage Summer *(U.S.,* Loss of Innocence, *1961);* All Night Long *(1962);* We Joined the Navy *(1963);* The Fat Lady *(1963);* Tamahine *(with Guy Laroche, 1964);* The Chalk Garden *(1964);* Father Came Too *(1964);* Psyche 59 *(1964);* A Hard Day's Night *(1965);* Carry on Cleo *(1965);* Help! *(1965);* Darling *(1965);* The Wrong Box *(1967);* Eye of the Devil *(with John Furness, 1967);* Casino Royale *(with Guy Laroche and Paco Rabanne, 1967);* Deadfall *(1968);* The Whisperers *(1968);* Decline and Fall . . . of a Birdwatcher! *(with Duse, 1969);* Prudence and the Pill *(1969);* Goodbye Mr. Chips *(1970);* The Private Life of Sherlock Holmes *(1972);* Follow Me *(U.S.,* The Public Eye, *1973);* Live and Let Die *(1975);* The Slipper and the Rose *(1976).*

Julie Harris, born in London, England, in 1921, was costume designer for countless films. As a child, she longed to be an actress, but her parents were against the idea. Instead, she attended art school, the Chelsea Polytechnic. She then worked for the court dressmaker Reville, before joining the film industry in 1945, as an assistant in the design department under ***Elizabeth Haffenden** at Gainsborough Studios. In 1965, Harris won an Academy Award for black and white design for the movie *Darling*, starring **Julie Christie**. (Before 1967, awards were given separately for color and black and white films.) She also received Society of Film and Television Arts (SFTA) awards for *Psyche, Help!, The Wrong Box, Casino Royale,* and *The Slipper and the Rose.*

The designer's job is to augment an actor's search for character, writes Harris. "I remember that, in *The Whisperers*, I was set the daunting task of transforming Dame ***Edith Evans** into a shabby, pathetic old-age pensioner. This is even more difficult than it sounds, because there are some people who simply rise above whatever you put them in. I found a dreadful old fur coat for £1 in the Portobello Road, but when Dame Edith put it on, she still looked like Lady Bracknell."

SOURCES:

Leese, Elizabeth. *Costume Design in the Movies.* Foreword by Julie Harris. NY: Dover, 1991.

Harris, Julie (1925—)

American actress, originator of the role of Frankie Addams in* The Member of the Wedding, *who has received an unprecedented ten Tony nominations and five Tony Awards. *Born in Grosse Pointe Park, Michigan, on December 2, 1925; only daughter and one of three children of William Pickett Harris (an investment banker) and Elsie (Smith) Harris; attended the Grosse Point Country Day School; attended Miss Mary C. Wheeler's School, Providence, Rhode Island; attended Miss Hewitt's Classes, New York City; attended Yale University School of Drama, 1944–45; attended The Actors Studio, New York City; married Jay I. Julien (a lawyer and producer), in August 1946 (divorced 1954); married Manning Gurian (a stage manager), on October 21, 1954 (divorced 1967); married William Erwin Carroll (a writer), on April 27, 1977; children: (second marriage) one son, Peter Alston Gurian.*

Selected theater: Atlanta in It's a Gift *(Playhouse Theater, New York City, March 1945); Nelly in* The Playboy of the Western World *(Booth Theater, New York City, October 1946); The White Rabbit in* Alice in Wonderland *(International Theater, New York City, May 1947); Third Witch in* Macbeth *(National Theater, New York City, March 1948); Ida Mae in* Sundown Beach *(Actors Studio Production at the Belasco Theater, New York City, September 1948); Nancy Gear in* The Young and the Fair *(Fulton Theater, New York City, November 1948); Angel Tuttle in* Magnolia Alley *(Mansfield Theater, New York City, April 1949); Felisa in* Montserrat *(Fulton Theater, New York City, October 1949); Frankie Addams in* The Member of the Wedding *(Empire Theater, New York City, January 1950); Sally Bowles in* I Am a Camera *(Empire Theater, New York City, November 1951); Colombe in* Mademoiselle Colombe *(Longacre Theater, New York City, January 1954); Joan in* The Lark *(Longacre Theater, New York City, November 1955); Margery Pinchwife in* The Country Wife *(Adelphi Theater, New York City, November 1957); Ruth Arnold in* The Warm Peninsula *(Helen Hayes Theater, New York City, October 1958); Brigid Mary in* Little Moon of Alban *(Longacre Theater, New York City, December 1960)); Josefa in* A Shot in the Dark *(Booth Theater, New York City, October 1961); June in* Marathon '33 *(ANTA Theater, December 1963); Annie in* Ready When You Are, C.B. *(Brooks Atkinson Theater, New York City December 1964); Georgina in* Skyscraper *(Lunt-Fontanne Theater, New York City, November 1965); Ann Stanley in* Forty Carats *(Morosco Theater, New York City, December 1968); Anna Reardon in* And Miss Reardon Drinks a Little *(Morosco Theater, New York City, February 1971); Claire in* Voices *(Ethel Barrymore Theater, New York City, April 1972); Mary Lincoln in* The Last of Mrs. Lincoln *(ANTA Theater, New York City, December 1972); Mrs. Rogers in* The Au Pair Man *(Vivian Beaumont Theater, December 1973); Lydia Cruttwell in* In Praise of Love *(Morosco Theater, New York Theater, December 1974); Emily Dickinson in* The Belle of Amherst *(Longacre Theater, New York City, April 1976); Gertie Kessel in* Break a Leg *(Palace Theater, New York City, April 1979); Ethel Thayer in* On Golden Pond *(Ahmanson Theater, Los Angeles, February 1980); Isak Dinesen in* Lucifer's Child *(Music Box Theater, New York City, April 1991); Fonsia in a national tour of* The Gin Game *(1999).*

Filmography: The Member of the Wedding *(1952);* East of Eden *(1955);* I Am a Camera *(1955);* The Truth About Women *(U.K., 1958);* Sally's Irish Rogue *(*The Poacher's Daughter, *Ire., 1958);* Requiem for a Heavyweight *(1962);* The Haunting *(U.S./U.K., 1963);* Harper *(1966);* You're a Big Boy Now *(1976);* Reflections in a Golden Eye *(1967);* The Split *(1968);* The People Next Door *(1970);* The Hiding Place *(1975);* Voyage of the Damned *(UK, 1976);* The Bell Jar *(1979);* Gorillas in the Mist *(1988);* The Dark Half *(1991);* Housesitter *(1992).*

Julie Harris was born in 1925, one of three children of William Pickett Harris, an investment banker, and **Elsie Smith Harris**, and grew up in Grosse Pointe Park, Michigan, a wealthy suburb of Detroit. Single-minded in her drive to become an actress, she remembers being a skinny, self-conscious kid, and not much of a student. As a youngster, she was addicted to the movies—she saw *Gone With the Wind* 13 times—and from the age of 10 attended the theater regularly with her parents. At 14, she made her stage debut as a juggler in a school production of *The Juggler of Notre Dame*, after which she convinced her parents to send her to a New York City preparatory school where they offered a course in drama. Asked by a teacher why she wanted to learn to act, she replied, "Acting is my *life*."

Harris began her professional training at a summer acting camp run by **Charlotte Perry** and **Portia Mansfield** in Steamboat Springs, Colorado, which she attended from 1941 to 1943. She enrolled in the Yale University School of Drama in 1944, but took a leave of absence to appear in her first Broadway play, Curt Goetz's *It's a Gift* (1945), which ran for six weeks. Her early training also included four years at the Actors Studio, where she was one of the original students, and a brief stint with the visiting Old Vic Company in 1946, playing walk-ons. At age 25, after winning acclaim in a number of Actors Studio and Broadway productions, Harris was cast by director Harold Clurman as Frankie Addams, the motherless 12-year-old tomboy in ***Carson McCullers**' tender play, *The Member of the Wedding,* which began a long Broadway run on January 5, 1950. "That play was really the beginning of everything big for me," Harris said. Indeed, Brooks Atkinson's review in *The New York Times* fairly glowed: "In the long immensely complicated part of the adolescent girl, Julie Harris, a very gifted young actress, gives an extraordinary performance—vibrant, full of anguish and elation by turns, rumpled, unstable, egotistic, and unconsciously cruel." Harris won the Donaldson Award for her performance and recreated the role in the 1952 movie, for which she won an Academy Award nomination.

Julie Harris (b. 1925)

Harris triumphed again as the sophisticated, hedonistic Sally Bowles in John van Druten's adaptation of Christopher Isherwood's *I Am a Camera* (1951). "Miss Harris's Sally is a frail, alcoholic adolescent with grubby fingers," wrote critic Kenneth Tynan. "She bursts with unrealized affectations, and is for ever latching herself on to a fullrush length cigarette-holder, like a peignoir suspended from a clothes hook. . . . I expect Miss Harris to mature astonishingly and to become, very shortly, one of the nobler ladies of the modern stage." Harris, who won a second Donaldson as well as the first of her five Tony Awards for the role, acknowledged that because of her conservative upbringing, she had a hard time relating to Sally's rather sordid lifestyle. "I never really got it right; in those days we weren't allowed to talk about things like abortion and the script really didn't have a lot in common with what eventually became *Cabaret.* Sally should really have been played all along by **Vanessa Redgrave**: she was a rebel, all I managed was a runaway schoolgirl."

After a two-month run in the critically acclaimed but short-lived *Mademoiselle Colombe* (1954), an adaptation of Jean Anouilh's satire of Parisian backstage life in 1900, Harris tackled another Anouilh play, *The Lark* (1955), concerning the trial of ***Joan of Arc** and adapted this time by ***Lillian Hellman**. As Saint Joan, a role for which Harris prepared prodigiously, even reading the original trial records, she experienced one of those perfect moments on stage, when everything comes together and the actor is one with the audience. "When I started to speak the lines, I couldn't because I was crying. Part of me was trying to pull me out of this emotion so I could speak my line. Another part was saying that what was happening was right for the part, right for this particular moment. Yes, for this is probably what Joan would have done. And the audience knew it and was thrilled by it. For me, it was an almost spiritual moment." For her portrayal of Joan, Harris won her second Tony as Best Actress.

Now established as a remarkable stage technician, Harris further distinguished herself in the range and variety of her roles. She portrayed a nun in *Little Moon of Alban* (1960), a vaudevillian in ◆ **June Havoc**'s autobiographical *Marathon '33* (1963), and a chic 40-year-old divorcee who becomes romantically involved with a man half her age in *Forty Carats* (1968), for which she received another Tony Award. After creating the role of the unstable and frigid Anna Reardon, in *And Miss Reardon Drinks a Little* (1971), she received her fourth Tony and a

◆ ***Havoc, June.*** *See Lee, Gypsy Rose for sidebar.*

Drama Desk Award for her interpretation of *Mary Todd Lincoln in James Prideaux's *The Last of Mrs. Lincoln* (1972). In 1974, yet another Tony nomination came her way for her portrayal of Mrs. Rogers in *The Au Pair Man.*

Harris has always had a fascination with 19th-century American writers, particularly poet and recluse ***Emily Dickinson**. ("I feel akin to certain souls," she told an interviewer for the *Christian Science Monitor* in 1976.) After recording Dickinson's poetry and letters and also giving readings before high school students and other groups, in 1976 she brought Dickinson to the stage in William Luce's one-woman play *The Belle of Amherst,* a performance that Jack Kroll, the critic for *Newsweek*, called "astonishing in its sagacity and passion," and Brooks Atkinson deemed a "masterpiece." The play was recorded on the Pathways of Sound and also brought Harris her fifth Tony, then an all-time record. She toured the show and also made her London debut as Dickinson at the Phoenix Theater in September 1977. She has subsequently brought to the stage other historically significant women, including ***Charlotte Brontë** (*Bronte*) and ***Isak Dinesen** (*Lucifer's Child*).

Harris' movie career began with film versions of *The Member of the Wedding* (1952) and *I Am a Camera* (1955), in which she recreated the roles of Frankie and Sally. Of her subsequent screen characterizations, the most memorable include the sensitive teen-aged Abra in *East of Eden* (1955), the compassionate employment counselor in *Requiem for a Heavyweight* (1962), the neurotic spinster in ***Shirley Jackson**'s *The Haunting* (1963), and the dope addict and night-club performer in *Harper* (1966). On television, Harris has been seen in numerous dramas and won Emmys for two roles on NBC's "Hallmark Hall of Fame" presentations: Brigid Mary in *Little Moon of Alban* (1958) and Queen ***Victoria** in *Victoria Regina* (1961). For seven years during the 1980s, she was regularly seen as Lilimae Clements on the popular series "Knots Landing."

Julie Harris projects a stage presence that belies her slight stature (5'4", about 105 pounds) and delicate features. Off stage, she is said to possess an unpretentious, ladylike demeanor that is unusual in a star of her magnitude. In a 1971 interview with Don Keith for *After Dark*, Harris admitted to sometimes feeling as vulnerable as she appears. "Life really spooks me," she said. "Everything about it: its night times and getting up and deciding things." Harris has been married three times. Her first marriage to Jay Julien, a lawyer and producer, lasted eight years. Soon after a divorce in 1954, she married Peter Gurian, with whom she had a son, Peter Alston, in 1955. "I had to convince myself that I should go back to the theater," she said later. "I found out that I was happy just being a mother." Harris divorced Gurian in 1967 and married writer William Erwin Carroll in 1977.

In 1980, Harris was in Los Angeles to play Ethel Thayer in *On Golden Pond*. In 1989, she toured as Daisy Werthan in Alfred Uhry's Pulitzer Prize-winning *Driving Miss Daisy,* in 1999 as Fonsia in *The Gin Game*. The actress, who once said she had found God in the theater, continues to grace the stage.

SOURCES:

Candee, Marjorie Dent, ed. *Current Biography 1956*. NY: H.W. Wilson, 1956.

Harris, Julie. "Solo," in *World Monitor.* Vol 5, no. 1. January 1992, pp. 14–17.

———, with Barry Tarshis. *Julie Harris Talks to Young Actors*. NY: Lothrop, Lee & Shepard, 1971.

Keith, Don Lee. "Julie Harris is a saint," in *After Dark*. November 1971.

Moritz, Charles, ed. *Current Biography 1977.* NY: H.W. Wilson, 1977.

Morley, Sheridan. *The Great Stage Stars*. London: Angus & Robertson, 1986.

Wilmeth, Don B., and Tice L. Miller, eds. *Cambridge Guide to American Theater*. Cambridge, MA: Cambridge University Press, 1993.

Barbara Morgan,
Melrose, Massachusetts

Harris, Marjorie Silliman

(1890–1976)

American philosopher. *Born June 6, 1890, in Virginia; died in March 1976, in Wethersfield, Connecticut; daughter of George Wells and Elizabeth Silliman Harris; B.A. Mount Holyoke College, 1913; Susan Linn Sage Scholarship in Philosophy and Ph.D., Cornell University, 1921.*

Was an instructor in philosophy, University of Colorado (1921–22); was adjunct professor of philosophy, Randolph-Macon Women's College (1922–25), associate professor (1925–30), professor (1930–58); was professor emeritus and chair of philosophy (1934–58).

Selected works: "If We Have Life, Do We Need Philosophy?" in Journal of Philosophy *(September 15, 1927); "Beauty and the Good" in* Philosophical Review *(September 1930); "Bergson's Conception of Freedom" in* Philosophical Review *(September 1933); "A Transcendent Approach to Philosophy" in* Philosophy and Phenomenological Research *(Vol. 15, 1955);* Francisco Romero on Problems of Philosophy *(1960);*

"Philosophy for Tomorrow" in Philosophy and Phenomenological Research *(Vol. 24, 1964).*

Marjorie Silliman Harris spent most of her career as a professional philosopher at Randolph-Macon Women's College. Eventually she became chair of the department of philosophy and received the honor of Professor Emeritus. Although she was an American scholar, Harris concentrated on the French philosophers, Henri Bergson and August Comte, and on the Argentinean philosopher Francisco Romero. She published many articles in philosophical journals and one book on Romero. Against the background of Romero's thought, she developed a personal vision of the importance of philosophy as an individual pursuit, a type of reflection that makes life meaningful. In her spare time, she enjoyed birdwatching.

Catherine Hundleby, M.A.
Philosophy, University of Guelph

Harris, Mary Belle (1874–1957)

American prison administrator. *Born on August 19, 1874, in Factoryville, Pennsylvania; died on February 22, 1957, in Lewisburg, Pennsylvania; the only daughter of John Howard and Mary Elizabeth (Mace) Harris; graduated from Bucknell University, A.B. in music, 1893, A.M. in Latin, 1894; earned Ph.D. in Sanskrit and Indo-European comparative philology from the University of Chicago, 1900.*

Mary Belle Harris was born in Factoryville, Pennsylvania, the oldest of three children. Her father John Howard was a Baptist minister and president of Bucknell University from 1889 to 1919. Her mother **Mary Mace Harris** died when Mary Belle was only six. John Howard married **Lucy Adelaide Bailey**—a close family friend—a year later. Their family grew by six sons as a result of this second marriage, and Bailey was a much-loved stepmother to Mary Belle. Harris and her brothers received an education at the Keystone Academy, a Baptist secondary school founded by her father.

Harris did not actually start in the career for which she became famous until she was nearly 40. She worked as a scholar and teacher after earning an A.B. in music, an A.M. in Latin at Bucknell University, and a Ph.D. in Sanskrit and Indo-European comparative philology from the University of Chicago. Harris taught Latin in Chicago and Baltimore between 1900 and 1910. In Baltimore, she studied archaeology and numismatics at Johns Hopkins University. In 1912, she traveled to Europe to teach at the American Classical School in Rome.

When Harris returned to America in 1914, a close friend from her years at the University of Chicago, ***Katharine Bement Davis**—now commissioner of corrections in New York City—offered Harris the post of superintendent of women and deputy warden of the Workhouse on Blackwell's Island (now Roosevelt Island), a strip of land in the East River, between Manhattan and Queens. Harris, who had no job prospects, accepted the post, even though she lacked experience in corrections administration. The Workhouse, severely overcrowded with a daily population of 700 women, was known for its grim atmosphere. Harris, who believed that prisons should teach employable skills and rehabilitate, dedicated herself to prison reform. She created a library and permitted card playing and knitting in the women's cells in order to alleviate boredom; she also facilitated daily outdoor exercise by fencing off a section of the prison yard. She quickly earned a reputation for success based on common sense.

Harris remained at the Workhouse for three years. In 1917, the defeat of reform mayor John Mitchel forced her resignation, and, in February of 1918, she assumed the superintendent's position at the State Reformatory for Women in Clinton, New Jersey. She continued her reforms, which included a system of self-government in the cottages and an Exit Club for women preparing for parole.

In September of 1918, Harris was granted a leave of absence to join the War Department's Commission on Training Camp Activities. She became assistant director of the Section on Reformatories and Detention Houses, where she was responsible for dealing with women arrested in camp areas. She set up detention homes and health facilities in various cities in the South, including Florida, South Carolina, Virginia and Georgia.

In May of 1919, Harris became superintendent of the State Home for Girls in Trenton, New Jersey, a juvenile institution notorious for its dangerous inmates. Although plagued with continual problems, Harris was successful in establishing a system of self-government, then resigned from the State Home in 1924. The following year, on March 12, 1925, Harris was sworn in as the first superintendent of the Federal Industrial Institution for Women, a new establishment to be built at Alderson, West Virginia. She worked with the architects, overseeing all aspects of construction to ensure that Alderson would be a place of education for the inmates. It opened November 24, 1928, and, under Harris' direction, became a model institution. The innovative features of the prison included the absence of a large surrounding wall or heavily armed guards, the establishment of farming and other physical activities, a system of self-government, and the promotion of education and vocational training. Despite the relative freedom of the institution, there were few disciplinary problems or escapes.

Following Harris' retirement from Alderson in March 1941, she returned to Pennsylvania and served on the state Board of Parole until it was abolished in 1943. She then settled in Lewisburg, Pennsylvania, served as a trustee for Bucknell University, and lectured and wrote about her activities in the world of female incarceration. In 1953, she began an extended tour of Europe and North Africa, visited her nephew in Cyprus, and inspected two Libyan prisons. She returned to Lewisburg in July of 1954 and died there on February 22, 1957, of a heart attack.

Mildred Harris

Harris was outspoken in her quest for reform in women's penal institutions, emphasizing the need for women to "build within them a wall of self-respect," to learn employable skills which they could use upon their release, and to free themselves from dependency upon the community and/or men. She was considered a tough and powerful administrator and was recognized for her positive contributions to penal reform.

SOURCES:

Sicherman, Barbara, and Carol Hurd Green, eds. *Notable American Women: The Modern Period.* Cambridge, MA: The Belknap Press of Harvard University Press, 1980.

Judith C. Reveal,
freelance writer, Greensboro, Maryland

Harris, Mildred (1901–1944)

American silent-screen star. *Name variations: Mildred Harris Chaplin. Born in Cheyenne, Wyoming, on November 29, 1901 (another source cites April 18); died of pneumonia in Hollywood, California, on July 20, 1944; married Charlie Chaplin (the actor), in 1917 (divorced 1920); married Eldridge F. McGovern (divorced 1929); married William P. Fleckerstein (a Minneapolis brewer); children: (second marriage) one son.*

The blonde, blue-eyed Mildred Harris made her film debut at age nine. At eleven, she was hired by Vitagraph to play children's roles in a number of films, including D.W. Griffith's *Enoch Arden.* By 13, she was starring as Dorothy in the silent film *The Patchwork Girl of Oz.* Harris became the first wife of Charlie Chaplin at 18; the marriage lasted three years. Until she died of pneumonia, at age 43, following abdominal surgery, Harris appeared as a juvenile, ingenue, or bit player in over 40 films, six of them directed by ***Lois Weber**: *The Price of a Good Time, For Husbands Only, The Doctor and the Woman, Borrowed Clothes, Home,* and *Forbidden.*

Harris, Patricia Roberts (1924–1985)

Noted attorney and public servant, first African-American woman to achieve ambassadorial rank, occupant of two Cabinet-level positions in the administration of President Jimmy Carter, and dean of Howard University Law School. *Born on May 31, 1924, in Mattoon, Illinois; died of cancer on March 23, 1985; daughter of Bert Roberts (a railroad waiter) and Chiquita Roberts; spent her early years in Mattoon and Chicago, Illinois, and upon graduation from*

Patricia Roberts Harris

high school had numerous offers of college scholarships; attended Howard University, in Washington, D.C., and graduated summa cum laude; elected to Phi Beta Kappa in 1945; completed graduate work in industrial relations at the University of Chicago; received her J.D. degree from George Washington University Law School, 1960; married William Beasley Harris (a Washington attorney), in 1955; no children.

Raised in Illinois; active in civil-rights campaigns (1940s–1960s); appointed ambassador to Luxemburg (1965); served as professor of law and later dean of the Law School at Howard University; served as secre-

tary of Housing and Urban Development (HUD) and later as secretary of Health, Education, and Welfare in the Carter Administration; held a variety of Democratic Party positions, including temporary chair of the credentials committee (1972); ran unsuccessfully for mayor of the District of Columbia (1982); served as full-time professor at George Washington National Law Center.

Patricia Roberts Harris held two Cabinet positions in the administration of President Jimmy Carter, was the first black woman to serve as an ambassador, and served as dean of Howard Law School. Known for her political savvy, she was also regarded as a tough, productive administrator who had a no-nonsense, demanding management style.

Born Patricia Roberts on May 31, 1924, in Mattoon, Illinois, she counted African-American slaves, Delaware and Cherokee Indians, and English and Irish settlers among her ancestors. Her African-American forebears had been moved from Virginia to Illinois in the early part of the 19th century; there, they bought their freedom through work. Her father was a dining-car waiter for the Illinois Central Railroad, a common profession for African-Americans in the 1920s, and Harris was raised in Mattoon and Chicago.

"I grew up in the Midwest with an awareness of the lack of real relevance of race," said Harris. When she graduated from high school, she had five college scholarships from which to choose and selected the largely black Howard University in Washington, D.C. While there, Harris was concerned with the problems of racial prejudice and was part of the early civil-rights movement. She was vice chair of the student chapter of the National Association for the Advancement of Colored People (NAACP) and joined with other students in an early sit-in demonstration at the Little Palace Cafeteria, a white restaurant located in the heart of a black section of Washington that would not serve blacks. Harris developed the belief that nonviolent action was the best means of fighting discrimination, a belief that she held throughout her life, causing criticism from some quarters for her lack of militancy on civil-rights issues.

Upon completion of her summa cum laude degree at Howard in 1945, Harris returned to Illinois to study industrial relations for two years at the University of Chicago. In the next several years, she held a variety of administrative posts in Chicago and Washington: she was a program director for the YWCA, an assistant director for the American Council on Human Rights, and an executive director of the black sorority Delta Sigma Theta.

In 1955, Patricia Roberts married Washington attorney William Beasley Harris, then a member of the faculty of Howard Law School. A few years later, Harris had her own law degree. "If there is one thing which gives me satisfaction," she noted, "it is law, the last refuge of the generalist, of which there are too few these days." While at George Washington University School of Law, she was honored with the post of associate editor of the *George Washington Law Review* and was awarded the John Bell Larner Prize as the first scholar in her class.

For the next two years, Harris held her first government position, as an attorney in the appeals and research section of the criminal division of the Department of Justice. She resigned for a post at Howard Law School, where she served for a number of years as dean and as a professor of law. Her courses focused on constitutional law and government regulation of business.

In July 1963, Lyndon Johnson tapped Harris for her first presidential appointment, naming her co-chair of the National Women's Committee for civil rights. In this capacity, Harris helped coordinate activities of nearly one-hundred national women's organizations on behalf of civil-rights causes, such as peaceful desegregation. The committee stressed the establishment of avenues of communication between the races. Harris worked tirelessly in this unpaid position, convinced that peaceful demonstrations and democratic process could secure rights for African-Americans. Major civil-rights legislation was before Congress at this time, so the efforts of this committee were significant. In 1964, Johnson appointed Harris to the Commission on the Status of Puerto Rico, largely because of her expertise in constitutional law.

On May 19, 1965, Johnson again recognized Harris' increasing leadership abilities, selecting her to replace William R. Rivkin as ambassador to Luxemburg, an appointment that won easy Senate confirmation. Patricia Harris was the nation's first black woman to serve as an ambassador. "I feel deeply proud and grateful the President chose me to knock down this barrier," she told the press, "but also a little sad about being 'the first Negro woman' because it implies we were not considered before." In assuming her ambassadorship, Harris resigned positions in many organizations concerned with civil liberties, welfare, and other community problems, especially in the Washington, D.C., area. She was able, however, to retain her position on the Commission on the Status of Puerto Rico.

During the early 1970s, Harris returned to private life, resuming her career as a law school professor. After the election of Jimmy Carter, in 1976, she was again chosen for an executive leadership position, this time at the Cabinet level. Carter nominated her as his secretary of Housing and Urban Development (HUD), based on her long record of involvement with urban issues and problems.

Ironically, it was at this time that Harris had to defend herself against suggestions that she was out of touch with the mainstream of black America, for which she was now seen as a spokesperson in government circles. *The New York Times* reported that at hearings before the Senate Banking, Housing and Urban Affairs Committee in 1977 she "bristled at the suggestion by Senator William Proxmire that she might not be able to defend the interests of the poor. 'I am one of them,' she said passionately. 'You do not seem to understand who I am. I am a black woman, the daughter of a dining-car worker. I am a black woman who could not buy a house eight years ago in parts of the District of Columbia.'" Confirmed as secretary of Housing and Urban Development, she served in that post until she was appointed secretary of Health, Education, and Welfare. When this department became the Department of Health and Human Services in a governmental reorganization, Harris became its first secretary.

Patricia Roberts Harris was known as a blunt executive, with no fear of confronting either her subordinates or superiors in the administration. Stuart E. Eizenstat, who served as Carter's domestic policy advisor, noted that "Mrs. Harris typically got what she wanted in bureaucratic battles in the Carter Administration." Jimmy Carter, said Eizenstat, could not turn her down.

Returning to the private sphere after Carter's defeat in 1980, Harris ran for mayor of the District of Columbia two years later. "I looked at the nation's capital and saw that it was not living up to its potential," she told a *Washington Post* interviewer. "Seventy percent of us here are black. This is seen as a black town. But it's not working well." In a bitter campaign that divided black groups in the city, Harris was defeated by Marion S. Barry, Jr. She was viewed as the candidate of middle-class blacks and whites, while Barry, a civil-rights activist, came to be seen as the candidate of lower-income blacks. Harris concluded her career as a full-time professor of law at the George Washington National Law Center from 1983 to 1985.

> She was a fine lady, and a fine Cabinet Officer, sensitive to the needs of others and an able administrator.
>
> **—Jimmy Carter**

Patricia Harris, like other black women of her generation, entered professional realms previously barred to women of color. She used her political commitments and legal education as preparation for governmental service under two Democratic presidents. In addition to her distinguished service as a government executive and professor of law, Harris was a lifelong, ardent Democrat who had seconded the presidential nomination of Lyndon Johnson at the 1964 Democratic National Convention. She also served in 1964 as an elector for the District of Columbia in Washington's first participation in a national election in the 20th century. She held a variety of Democratic Party positions, including temporary chair of the credentials committee in 1972. Her professionalism earned her the respect of blacks and whites alike, although she did not become involved in the turbulence within the civil-rights movement of her time. Her proficiency in the posts for which she was chosen made it easier for later presidential administrations to select other non-white executives. Patricia Roberts Harris died of cancer on March 23, 1985, not long after the death of her husband.

SOURCES:

New York Post. November 29, 1963.

New York Post Magazine. June 6, 1965.

The New York Times. March 24, 1985.

Washington Post. March 31, 1964.

Jacqueline DeLaat,
McCoy Professor of Political Science,
Marietta College, Marietta, Ohio

Harris, Phoebe (1755–1786)

British coiner who was one of the last persons in England executed by hanging and burning at the stake.
Born in 1755; died in 1786 (some sources cite 1788).

Coining, at the time considered a serious crime by the British government, involved defacing coins of the realm by melting them down and selling them as gold or silver for profit. Phoebe Harris was a coiner for most of her short life. Caught and sentenced to death in 1786, she became almost as well known for her execution as for her crimes. In what was described as "a barbaric event" (albeit not an uncommon one for women), Harris was first hanged, then burned in front of a throng of 20,000 curious spectators. Harris' execution was among the last of its kind in England. One other woman named **Margaret Sullivan** was similarly hanged and burned two years after Harris. The combination of hanging and burning at the stake was repealed as a form of capital punishment in the 1790s. Hanging, of course, continued.

Harrison, Anna Symmes

(1775–1864)

American first lady and wife of William Henry Harrison, ninth U.S. president, who was the only first lady not to assume any of her duties due to her husband's death one month after his inauguration. *Born Anna Symmes on July 25, 1775, in Morristown, New Jersey; died on February 25, 1864, in North Bend, Ohio; second daughter of John Cleves (sometime chief judge of the New Jersey Supreme Court) and his first wife Anna (Tuthill) Symmes; attended Clinton Academy in East Hampton, New York, and Miss Graham's School in New York City; married William Henry Harrison, on November 25, 1795, in North Bend, Ohio; children: six sons, four daughters (her son John Scott Harrison was the only child to outlive her and was the father of Benjamin Harrison, the 23rd president of the United States).*

At age 65, Anna Harrison wanted nothing more than to share a quiet retirement with her husband. Instead, following the Whig "log cabin and hard cider" campaign of 1840, William Henry Harrison ("Old Tippecanoe") defeated Martin Van Buren to become the ninth president of the United States. A month after delivering what was reported to be an 8,555-word inaugural address in the pouring rain, William Harrison was dead of pneumonia. Anna, who had been forbidden to accompany her husband to Washington because of her own serious illness, also missed his elaborate state funeral.

Anna Symmes Harrison

Born in 1775 at the start of the Revolutionary War, and motherless at age four, Anna Symmes was taken to Long Island, New York, by her father to live with her maternal grandmother in genteel society. Well educated for her day, she attended Clinton Academy in East Hampton and a prestigious boarding school in New York City. At 19, she left her fashionable surroundings to join her father on land he had taken up in the frontier settlement of North Bend, on the Ohio River. There Anna met William Henry Harrison, a young army officer stationed at nearby Fort Washington. Immediately smitten with each other, the couple embarked on a whirlwind courtship. Against her father's wishes, they were wed in November 1795, eloping while Judge Symmes was away on a business trip. Only after William established himself as a military leader did he win his father-in-law's approval, and his famous defeat of the Indians at Tippecanoe during the War of 1812 gained him more than just his famous nickname.

Throughout most of her husband's career as a soldier, delegate to Congress, minister to Columbia, and governor of the Indiana Territory, Anna remained in the background, living an "unguarded" life in the wilderness. With spirit and determination, she managed homes in North Bend and Vincennes, Indiana. When tutors were unavailable for her ten children, she taught them herself and encouraged other children of the settlement to attend her home school. An avid reader and student of religious history, Anna also provided her family with spiritual instruction. One of her few respites from frontier life was a six-month social whirl in Philadelphia with her husband, soon after his election to Congress.

After William's landslide victory of 1840, while Anna continued her recuperation from influenza, a number of proud and enthusiastic relatives accompanied the president-elect to Washington. His daughter-in-law ***Jane Irwin Harrison**, widow of his namesake son, served as hostess for the single month William Harrison resided in the White House.

Remaining in North Bend, Anna lived 22 years after her husband's death. Congress awarded her the earliest pension ever paid to a first lady—William's first year presidential salary of $25,000. She also received free postage privileges for the rest of her life. She lived alone until her house burned down in 1855. Moving in with her son John Scott Harrison, she supervised the education of her grandson, Benjamin Harrison, who became the 23rd president of the United States. Anna Harrison died at age 89 and was buried next to her husband in her beloved North Bend.

SOURCES:

Healy, Diana Dixon. *America's First Ladies: Private Lives of the Presidential Wives*. NY: Atheneum, 1988.

Klapthor, Margaret Brown. *The First Ladies*. Washington, DC: The White House Historical Association, 1979.

Melick, Arden David. *Wives of the Presidents*. Maplewood, NJ: Hammond, 1977.

Paletta, LuAnn. *The World Almanac of First Ladies*. NY: World Almanac, 1990.

COLLECTIONS:

James Albert Green-William Henry Harrison Collection, Cincinnati Historical Society.

Harrison, Beatrice (1892–1965)

Britain's premier cellist in the 1920s and 1930s who was world renowned as "The Lady of the Nightingales." *Born in Roorkee, India, on December 9, 1892; died in Smallfield, Surrey, England, on March 10, 1965; daughter of Colonel John Harrison (an officer in the Royal Engineers) and Annie Harrison (a singer); sister of May Harrison (1891–1959), a violinist, Margaret Harrison, a pianist, and Monica Harrison.*

First female cellist to play in Carnegie Hall; first woman and first cellist ever to win the Mendelssohn Medal (1907).

Beatrice Harrison liked wandering in the woods on the grounds of Foyle Riding, her country home in Oxted, Surrey, and giving open-air concerts to an audience of none with her cello. One day to her amazement, a nightingale sang while she played, creating a beautiful duet. Harrison persuaded the British Broadcasting Company to bring recording equipment to Oxted in May 1924 to capture this performance. It was the first time a broadcast of outdoor bird-song had ever been recorded, and she received thousands of letters from throughout the world. During the nightingale season, visitors journeyed to Foyle Riding to hear the birds sing. The Harrisons built a music room and often had guests to listen to the birds until dawn. John Gielgud, ***Peggy Ashcroft**, Paul Robeson, and Princess ***Victoria** (1868–1935) were among the many guests.

Born into a conventional family with a military background, Beatrice Harrison was the second of four daughters. When she was quite young, the family moved back to England from India where her father had served in the Anglo-Indian army. At 18 months, Beatrice was taken to a regimental band concert where she first heard the sound of a cello. Though she was heard to exclaim, "Baba wants 'tello,'" gratification was delayed until she was nine. The young Harrison made such great progress that by age 11 she had entered the Royal College of Music where she studied under W.E. Whitehouse. Throughout her life Harrison loved to work, spending hours a day practicing. In 1907, she went to the Continent and was the first woman to win the Mendelssohn Medal. She began to concertize with her sister, ***May Harrison**, and the girls caused a sensation when they revived a seldom-heard Brahms Double Concerto. Beatrice made her American debut in 1913 and repeated her success. Many composers wrote music for her. Frederick Delius wrote the Cello Sonata, the Double Concerto, the Cello Concerto, and the *Caprice and Elegy.* John Ireland wrote a Sonata for her as well.

Some rank Beatrice Harrison's finest achievement as her performance with Sir Edward Elgar in 1919. When ***Guilhermina Suggia**, the famous cellist, asked for too much money to play for the recording, Harrison was asked to play in her place. She responded with her soul, transforming a work to which few had previously paid much attention. Elgar began to ask her to play whenever the work was performed. In 1928, the Elgar Cello Concerto was re-recorded and this work alone established Harrison's reputation in the musical world.

Beatrice Harrison played often at London's popular Promenade Concerts and continued to play throughout the Second World War. Her last performance was on television in 1958, playing a cello solo Roger Quilter had written for her. Harrison's public was always devoted to her and to the liquid notes which came from her cello.

SOURCES:

Cleveland-Peck, Patricia. "The Lady of the Nightingales," in *The Strad.* Vol. 103, no. 1232. December 1992, pp. 1174–1177.

Webber, Julian Lloyd. "A Pioneering Spirit of her Age," in *The Strad.* Vol. 103, no. 1232. December 1992, p. 1172.

John Haag,
Associate Professor, University of Georgia, Athens, Georgia

Harrison, Mrs. Burton (1843–1920).

See Harrison, Constance Cary.

Harrison, Caroline Scott (1832–1892)

American first lady (1889–1892) who was the wife of the 23rd U.S. president, Benjamin Harrison. *Name variations: Carrie. Born Caroline Lavinia Scott on October 10, 1832, in Oxford, Ohio; died on October 25, 1892, in Washington, D.C.; third daughter and third of five children of Mary Potts (Neal) Scott and John Witherspoon Scott (a Presbyterian minister, founder and president of Oxford Seminary, professor at Miami University in Ohio); attended Oxford Seminary; married Benjamin Harrison, on October 20, 1853, in New York, New York; children: Russell Harrison (1854–1936, was a member of the Indiana House and Senate);* ***Mary Scott Harrison*** *(1858–1930, later Mrs J. Robert McKee); another daughter died at birth (1861).*

Caroline ("Carrie") Scott first captured Benjamin Harrison's attention when she was a young student at Oxford Female Institute, a school her father had founded in Oxford, Ohio. Benjamin transferred his law studies to nearby Miami University so he could be near his "charming and loveable" Carrie. They were married in 1853, while Benjamin was still a student, and made their first home in North Bend. In March 1854, they moved to Indianapolis, living in a boarding house while Benjamin eked out a living as a court crier. A move to their first small house was occasioned by the birth of a son that same year. Daughter Mary was born in 1858. Despite Caroline's frugal housekeeping, Benjamin often had to borrow money from a friend just to meet household expenses. About the time his law firm was beginning to show a profit, the Civil War intruded.

Caroline Scott Harrison

While Benjamin distinguished himself in the military, Caroline stayed in Indianapolis, raising their two children alone. An accomplished watercolor artist who painted china patterns, she busied herself with classes in china painting at the First Presbyterian Church. She taught Sunday school and joined the missionary society. Her outgoing charm and creative talent won her many friends and would later become a great asset to her husband's career.

Returning from the war a brigadier general, Benjamin set about once again to build a law practice from the ground up. He launched his political career with an unsuccessful run for governor on the Republican ticket but was elected to the Senate in 1881. Caroline became one of Washington's most popular hostesses, possessing just enough down-home charm to balance her husband's somewhat cold and forbidding personality. Although Caroline was supportive of her husband's career in the Senate, she objected to his run for the presidency, fearing that he would die in office like his grandfather William Henry Harrison. Nonetheless, Benjamin accepted a nomination and won the election of 1889.

When Benjamin took office, a huge brood followed him into the White House. In addition to the children and their families, Caroline's father and widowed niece lived with them. With only five bedrooms and one bath in the living quarters, Caroline faced a logistical challenge. In an effort to "see the family of the President provided for properly," she submitted several different plans to Congress for expansion of the executive mansion, but they were all turned down. Unthwarted, she undertook instead an extensive top to bottom renovation. Armed with a meager budget, she supervised all the work, even joining the bucket brigade from time to time. She established order in the kitchen and sorted and identified the variety of china from past administrations, providing the basis for the White House china collection. She had a conservatory built so that plants from the White House—especially her beloved orchids—could be used for receptions. She also began the tradition of setting up a Christmas tree in the Oval Room, where it was decorated by family and staff alike.

Caroline lent her progressive views and support to a number of local charities. She helped raise funds for the Johns Hopkins University medical school, on condition that they admit women. She served as the first president general of the National Society of the Daughters of the American Revolution, founded in 1890, when the Sons of the American Revolution would not allow women to join.

Caroline Harrison became ill during the last year of her husband's term, probably with tuberculosis. She died in the White House in October 1892, at age 60. After her death, Benjamin had no desire to run for reelection. Three years later, he married his wife's niece, ***Mary Scott Dimmick (Harrison)**. His children, all older than the bride, were shocked by the union. He died in 1901, leaving his second wife with a young daughter, **Elizabeth Harrison** (1897–1955), who later established the Benjamin Harrison Memorial Home in Indianapolis, Indiana.

SOURCES:

Klapthor, Margaret Brown. *The First Ladies.* Washington, DC: The White House Historical Association, 1979.

McConnell, Jane and Burt. *Our First Ladies: From Martha Washington to Lady Bird Johnson.* NY: Thomas Y. Crowell, 1964.

Melick, Arden David. *Wives of the Presidents.* Maplewood, NJ: Hammond, 1977.

Paletta, LuAnn. *The World Almanac of First Ladies.* NY: World Almanac, 1990.

Barbara Morgan,
Melrose, Massachusetts

Harrison, Constance Cary
(1843–1920)

American author and social leader. *Born on April 25, 1843, in Lexington, Kentucky; died on November 21, 1920, in Washington, D.C.; daughter of Archibald and Monimia (Fairfax) Cary (daughter of the 9th lord of Fairfax); married Burton Harrison, in 1867 (died 1904); children: sons, Francis Burton, Fairfax, and Archibald.*

Constance Cary Harrison was born in 1843 in Lexington, Kentucky, the daughter of Archibald and **Monimia Fairfax Cary**. Her family was a blend of English nobility and American patriotism. Constance's father was descended from Thomas Jefferson and had spent his early life on a plantation in Virginia. Her mother's father, Thomas, was descended from the ninth lord of Fairfax. The Cary family never achieved the affluence of their ancestors, but Archibald instilled a strong sense of family tradition in his daughter. After Constance's birth, Archibald moved the family to Vaucluse, Monimia's father's estate near Arlington, Virginia.

The family soon moved to Martinsburg, Virginia, then eventually settled in Cumberland, Maryland. Constance began her education at Miss Jane Kenah's day school there, studying Latin. When she was 11, her father died of typhoid fever and her mother returned to Vaucluse where they lived until the outbreak of the Civil War. Constance continued her education with a French governess and later attended the boarding school of M. Hubert Lefebre in Richmond.

Although the family opposed slavery, their sympathies lay with the South, and Constance's mother worked as a nurse at the Culpeper Court House and Camp Winder near Richmond. When her brother joined the Confederate forces, Constance went to Richmond to live with an aunt and uncle. During this time, she and her cousins, **Hetty** and **Jennie Cary** of Baltimore, entered into Richmond society. The three girls were immediately popular, and Constance became known for her wit and amateur theatrics. The cousins did their part in supporting the Confederate cause by nursing soldiers in military hospitals and making Confederate flags.

While in Richmond, Constance published her first book, *Blockade Correspondence,* a fictional account of letters between "Secessia" in Baltimore and "Refugitta" in Richmond. She also met her future husband, Burton Harrison, private secretary to declared president of the Confederate states Jefferson Davis. Burton was captured along with Davis and held prisoner by Union forces at Fort Delaware. In 1865, Constance and her mother went to Washington to secure Burton's release. The couple's reunion was brief as Constance had arranged to study voice for a year at the Paris Conservatoire in France, but the two wed upon her return to the United States near the end of 1867. They settled in New York City, and Burton set up a law practice.

Harrison kept busy by taking an active part in local theater, serving as a visitor at Bellevue Hospital, and managing the board of the Nursery and Child's Hospital. She resumed her literary career, publishing the short story "A Little Centennial Lady" in *Scribner's Monthly* in 1876. Richard Watson Gilder, editor of *Scribner's*, encouraged her to write about the Old South and published a series on "Battles and Leaders of the Civil War" to which she contributed several articles.

During the next 20 years, Harrison published several novels, magazine stories and historical sketches. For the most part her novels dealt with Southern life, including *Flower de Hundred: The Story of a Virginia Plantation* (1890), *Belhaven Tales* (1892), and *A Daughter of the South, and Shorter Stories* (1892). She did not, however, write only about the South. One of her better-known books, *The Anglomaniacs* (1890), applied gentle satire to New York society, and *Good Americans* (1898) satirized Americans in Europe.

Constance Cary Harrison was versatile, showing an interest in various subjects. Her sharp wit is demonstrated in her etiquette book, *The Well-Bred Girl in Society* (1898), which is a commentary on social attitudes more than a manual on proper behavior. She expressed an interest in decorative home art with *Woman's Handiwork in Modern Homes* (1891), and she translated *Short Comedies for Amateur Players* (1896) from French. She also penned a book on Virginia history and wrote *Externals of Modern New York* (1896), a supplement to ***Martha J.R. Lamb**'s *History of the City of New York*. Her memoirs, *Recollections Grave and Gay*, were published in 1911.

Harrison's husband died in 1904, and she moved to Washington, D.C., to be near her two surviving sons. She died in Washington on November 21, 1920, and was buried beside her husband at Ivy Hill Cemetery in Alexandria, Virginia.

SOURCES:

Edgerly, Lois Stiles. *Give Her This Day.* Gardiner, ME: Tilbury House, 1990.

James, Edward T., ed. *Notable American Women, 1607–1950.* Cambridge, MA: The Belknap Press of Harvard University Press, 1971.

Judith C. Reveal,
freelance writer, Greensboro, Maryland

Harrison, Elizabeth (1849–1927)

American educational reformer, author, and lecturer. *Born on September 1, 1849, in Athens, Kentucky; died on October 31, 1927, in San Antonio, Texas; daughter of Isaac Webb and Elizabeth Thompson (Bullock) Harrison; studied with Halsey Ives, director of the St. Louis Art Museum (1882); studied with Susan E. Blow; studied with Maria Eraus-Boelté; studied abroad with Henrietta Breyman Schrader in Berlin and Baroness von Marenholtz-Bülow in Dresden.*

Elizabeth Harrison was born in 1849 in Athens, Kentucky, one of five children raised in an intellectually stimulating environment where reading was a cherished pastime. When she was seven, the family moved to Davenport, Iowa, where Elizabeth and her sisters enjoyed staging plays of Biblical stories and other classics for the neighborhood children. She excelled in Davenport's public schools—graduating first in her class—although science was the only subject of real interest to her.

On a visit to Chicago, Harrison's interests broadened to include the fledgling kindergarten movement. She soon enrolled in ***Alice Harvey Whiting Putnam**'s training classes for kindergarten teachers and graduated in 1880. After further training in Davenport, in New York City, and with ***Susan E. Blow** in St. Louis, she settled in Chicago and established her career there. Together with Putnam, she founded the Chicago Kindergarten Club to provide teachers with a means to improve their teaching skills and to advance the kindergarten cause. Mothers were invited to join in discussion groups about education, and soon Harrison was lecturing throughout the area. Many of the elite families of the time participated in her discussions and she was able to persuade a group of them to underwrite a course of literary lectures conducted by Denton J. Snider, a philosopher, educator and critic.

In 1887, Harrison's training program became institutionalized as the Chicago Kindergarten Training School. She then studied abroad with **Henrietta Breyman Schrader** in Berlin and **Baroness von Marenholtz-Bülow** in Dresden. Under their influence, she changed the name of her school to the Chicago Kindergarten College and changed the curriculum to a three-year course. The school underwent several more name changes, including the National Kindergarten College (1912) and the National Kindergarten and Elementary College (1917). In 1930, after Harrison's death, it would become the National College of Education. Harrison, encouraged by the favorable public response to her programs, held national conferences for mothers in 1894, 1895, and 1896. These conferences paved the way for ***Alice McLellan Birney**'s National Congress of Mothers, which later became the National Congress of Parents and Teachers. The Chicago Kindergarten Club and the Chicago Kindergarten College sponsored a lecture series of eminent scholars and educators, conducted from 1887 to 1894, under the name Chicago Literary Schools.

Elizabeth Harrison set high standards for her students, requiring a high school education or its equivalent for entry. Her three-year course of study included the humanities, sciences, social sciences, the arts, and kindergarten subjects. Until this time, average training schools accepted women with an eighth-grade education and provided only six months of study. Harrison's high standards made it difficult for the college to compete with other schools for students, and she often supported her school with earnings from lectures and book royalties. Despite financial difficulties, the school became a model for the highest standards of kindergarten education.

Harrison suffered frequent bouts of ill health but maintained a busy calendar of lecture tours, traveling throughout the nation addressing groups such as the International Kindergarten Union and the National Education Association. Her lecture series, published in 1890 as *A Study of Child Nature*, enjoyed more than 50 reprints.

In 1913, Harrison visited with Dr. ***Maria Montessori**, observing her Casa dei Bambini in Rome. After this visit she wrote a report for the U.S. Bureau of Education, *Montessori and the Kindergarten*. Her writings were influential in her area of expertise and included *A Vision of Dante* (1891), *In Storyland* (1895), *Two Children of the Foot Hills* (1900), *Some Silent Teachers* (1903), *Misunderstood Children* (1908), *Offero, the Giant* (1912), *When Children Err* (1916) and *The Unseen Side of Child Life* (1922).

Between her lecture schedule, her responsibilities as president of the college, her committee work and the stress of keeping the school financially sound, Harrison's health worsened. She had a heart attack in 1920, resigned her presidency and retired from teaching. Elizabeth Harrison died in San Antonio, Texas on October 31, 1927 and was buried in Oakdale Cemetery in Davenport, Iowa.

SOURCES:

James, Edward T., ed. *Notable American Women, 1607–1950*. Cambridge, MA: The Belknap Press of Harvard University Press, 1971.

McHenry, Robert, ed. *Famous American Women*. NY: Dover, 1983.

Judith C. Reveal,
freelance writer, Greensboro, Maryland

Harrison, Hazel (1883–1969)

African-American concert pianist who was the first fully American-trained performer to appear with a European orchestra. *Born Hazel Lucille Harrison on May 12, 1883, in La Porte, Indiana; died on April 28, 1969, in Washington, D.C.; daughter of Hiram and Olive Jane (Woods) Harrison; married Walter Bainter Anderson, on September 1, 1919 (divorced late 1920s); married Allen Moton, in 1950s (divorced).*

Hazel Harrison was born in LaPorte, Indiana, in 1883, and grew up an only child in a musical environment. Her father played piano at the First Presbyterian Church and was the director and a soloist for the church choir. Hazel displayed exceptional musical talent early in her life when she began piano lessons at the age of four. She was encouraged in her endeavors by her father and Richard Pellow, an English organist at the First Presbyterian Church who was also her first teacher.

By the time she was eight, Harrison was supplementing the family income by playing at local dance parties. At one such affair, she came to the attention of German musician Victor Heinze who became her teacher for many years. He proved to be instrumental in her development as a musician; under his tutelage, she acquired an amazing keyboard technique, a lyrical quality to her performance, and a large repertory of music. When Heinze moved to Chicago, Harrison commuted between La Porte and Chicago to remain under his guidance. Many of his patrons considered her his most gifted student.

In 1902, Harrison graduated from La Porte High School and continued her studies for a career on the concert stage. During this time, she also continued entertaining at dance parties as well as teaching the children of many of La Porte's upper-class families. Harrison's professional career got off to an auspicious start. On October 22, 1904, she performed as a soloist with the Berlin Philharmonic Orchestra, under the direction of August Scharrer. It was the first appearance with a European orchestra by an American performer who had not studied outside the United States, and she impressed German critics.

When Harrison returned to America, she resumed her teaching and touring schedule in La Porte. The critical acclaim she received, after a recital at Kimball Hall in Chicago in 1910, resulted in the financial support needed for a return trip to Germany for additional study. In 1911, she began lessons in Berlin with Hugo van Dalan who arranged for an audition with Italian pianist and composer Ferruccio Busoni. Upon hearing her, Busoni was so impressed with her style that he agreed to oversee her training even though he had previously decided against taking new students.

Harrison developed a close bond with Busoni and his family. He encouraged her to visit museums and art galleries and to expand her knowledge of the arts. She studied German philosophy and literature and at the same time worked with Busoni's assistant, Egon Petri, a Dutch pianist. With the outbreak of World War I, Harrison returned to America, moving to Chicago.

On September 1, 1919, Harrison married Walter Bainter Anderson, but the marriage failed; they were divorced in the late 1920s. During this period, Harrison's fame grew as she criss-crossed America on recital tours. The Depression years of the 1930s were difficult, however, and Harrison was forced to increase her teaching hours in order to make a living.

Harrison championed contemporary European, German, Russian and Polish composers, and frequently included works by black composers as well as variations of Strauss waltzes and Bach organ works in her recitals. For her strong yet sensitive performances, she continued to receive praise and played at such locations as Town Hall and Aeolian Hall in New York City, Jordan Hall in Boston, and Kimball Hall in Chicago. She was applauded for her performances by such well-established critics as Glenn Dillard Gunn, music reviewer for the Washington (D.C.) *Times-Herald,* and yet, despite the immense praise, she was denied access to many of the mainstream concert halls in America because of her race. Although lauded by the black press as a premier black pianist and the greatest pianist of all time, widespread recognition by white Americans eluded her.

Thus Harrison's performances were restricted to specialized audiences and special occasions. She performed with the Minneapolis Symphony under Eugene Ormandy in 1932 in a concert at Tuskegee (Ala.) Institute and, in 1949, she appeared with the Hollywood Bowl Symphony under the direction of Izeler Solomon during a convention of the National Association of Negro Musicians. A 1922 review, filled with praise for her talents, ended on a somber note: "[I]t seems too bad that the fact that she is a Negress may limit her future plans."

As a piano teacher, Harrison developed many talented young musicians. In November of 1931, she joined the School of Music at Tuskegee Institute and remained there until 1937 when she joined Howard University in Washington, D.C., as the head of its piano faculty. She taught at Alabama State College in Montgomery, at Jackson College in Mississippi, and in 1945 established the Olive J. Harrison Piano Scholarship fund at Howard University in honor of her mother. The scholarship was funded by the proceeds from her recitals as well as her students' recitals.

Hazel Harrison gave recitals for war relief during the 1940s and 1950s and supported various causes, including civil uprisings in the Soviet Union, Spain, and Latin America. She took leave from Howard University from 1947 to 1950 to tour America and in 1952 toured the western provinces of Canada. For a brief time during the 1950s, Harrison was married to Allen Moton, but this union also ended in divorce. In 1955, she resigned from Howard. She died in a nursing home on April 28, 1969.

SOURCES:

James, Edward T., ed. *Notable American Women, 1607–1950.* Cambridge, MA: The Belknap Press of Harvard University Press, 1971.

Smith, Jessie Carney, ed. *Notable Black American Women.* Detroit, MI: Gale Research, 1992.

Judith C. Reveal,
freelance writer, Greensboro, Maryland

Harrison, Jane Ellen (1850–1928)

English classical scholar. *Born in Yorkshire, England, in 1850; died in 1928; attended Cheltenham College; graduate of Newnham College, Cambridge, 1874–79 (received second class in classical tripos, 1879); never married; no children.*

Known for her innovative use of archaeology in the interpretation of Greek religion, scholar Jane Harrison was the recipient of numerous academic awards. She was educated at Newnham College and later studied archaeology in London and in Greece. While a lecturer in classical archaeology at Newnham College (1880–98), she served as vice president of the Hellenic Society (1889–96). Harrison wrote numerous books on her chosen field, including *Myths of the Odyssey in Art and Literature* (1882), *The Mythology and Monuments of Ancient Greece* (1890), *Introductory Studies in Greek Art* (1895), *Prolegomena to the Study of Greek Religion* (1903), *Themis* (1912), *Ancient Art and Ritual* (1913), and *Epilogomena to the Study of Greek Religion* (1921). In later life, she took up the study of Russian with her friend **Hope Mirrlees**. The two women collaborated on three books on Russian language and literature, including *The Book of the Bear* (1927), a series of translations.

Harrison, Jane Irwin (1804–1846)

Served briefly as White House hostess. *Born Jane Findlay Irwin in 1804; died in 1846; daughter of Archibald Irwin and Mary (Ramsey) Irwin; daughter-in-law of Anna Symmes Harrison (1775–1864) and William Henry Harrison (president of the United States); married William Henry Harrison, Jr., in 1824; children: two sons.*

Jane Irwin Harrison was born in 1804. One of her sisters married John Scott Harrison and was the mother of Benjamin Harrison, the 23rd president of the United States. Jane married William Henry Harrison, Jr., son of ***Anna Symmes Harrison** and William Henry Harrison, in 1824. Jane's husband, a lawyer, died in 1838, leaving Jane a widow with two sons. The eldest later married the daughter of a John Kennedy of Ireland.

Jane Harrison accompanied her father-in-law William Henry Harrison to Washington when her mother-in-law was forbidden to travel because of illness. She and her aunt and namesake, **Jane Findlay,** were just beginning to set up the White House when Harrison died. They had done no formal entertaining, but did attend the inaugural ball. They accompanied the president's body back to North Bend, Ohio, where Jane died five years later.

Harrison, Joan (c. 1908–1994)

British movie producer, screenwriter, and scenarist who worked for Alfred Hitchcock for several years.

Born Joan Mary Harrison in Guildford, Surrey, England, on June 20, 1908; died on August 14, 1994, in London, England; daughter of Walter and Maelia (Muir) Harrison.

Joan Mary Harrison was born in Guildford, Surrey, England, on June 20, 1908, the daughter of Walter Harrison, a newspaper publisher, and **Maelia Muir Harrison**. Her father's success in publishing placed the family in moderately well-to-do society, and Harrison received a solid education in a private school in Kent. She studied literature, philosophy, languages, and political economy in preparation for taking her proper place in English society. With a year at the Sorbonne and a B.A. from St. Hugh's College at Oxford, Harrison had hoped for a position at one of her father's newspapers. Her parents objected to the idea, feeling this career was inappropriate for a young lady of her standing and urging her to marry and settle down. Harrison had other ideas and after several months of staying at home, she left to make her way in London.

For the next several years Harrison worked at a variety of jobs including copywriter at the London Press Exchange, freelancer for magazines, and secretary to several writers. In 1933, she had a stroke of luck when she interviewed for a secretarial position with movie director, Alfred Hitchcock. Later in her life, she admitted she was not a very good secretary, but she proved her worth, moving quickly from secretary to script reader.

Harrison experienced a turning point in her career in 1937 when she collaborated on the screen adaptation of *The Girl Was Young*. Her hard work paid off in 1939 when she received her first screen credit for work on the adaptation of ***Daphne du Maurier**'s *Jamaica Inn*. In the spring of 1939, Harrison accompanied Hitchcock to Hollywood as an important member of his staff. During her time with Hitchcock, Harrison worked on du Maurier's *Rebecca* (1940), followed by *Foreign Correspondent* (1940), a film for which she wrote her first full script, *Suspicion* (1941), and *Saboteur* (1942). Harrison gleaned valuable experience from Hitchcock which she would draw on in the future.

A knowledgeable woman, aggressive and firm, Harrison was ready to move her career forward by 1941. She left Hitchcock to concentrate on screenwriting and for the next two years experienced a series of disappointments. Her first effort, a film originally designed for Charles Boyer, met with various setbacks and never materialized; her adaptation of *The Sun Is My Undoing* (1941) was badly handled during its transference to the screen and only vaguely resembled her work. Just as she was considering leaving freelance work, she encountered a mystery novel *The Phantom Lady* and was invited to write the script. At a time when mysteries and detective novels were the domain of men, this was a rare opportunity. Although initially reluctant because of her recent bad experiences, she presented Universal Studios with her ideas for the film and stood firm. The studio was impressed by her resolve and offered her the role of associate producer, a rare offer for a woman, which she quickly accepted.

Joan Harrison took her role as associate producer at Universal seriously. She worked closely with her directors and maintained contact with every department that had any responsibility for the film's production. She showed foresight, common sense, and a good sense of organization, taking each step of production in its proper order. She spent an unprecedented $60,000 on Franchot Tone, her star, "on the theory that unusual casting brings a different flavor to [the] picture." She then went for simplicity and naturalness in costumes and makeup. *The Phantom Lady* received mixed reviews. In praise of the film, critics wrote of Harrison's handling of emotions below the surface and her clever use of lighting and silence to build suspense. Others found the film tedious, with odd and disturbing effects.

Nevertheless, Harrison continued to move her career forward. She worked as associate producer on *Dark Waters*, a melodrama starring *__Merle Oberon__ originally published in the *Saturday Evening Post* and adapted by Harrison and **Marian Cockrell**. The movie received praise from *The New York Times* as a "killer diller of a thriller."

Throughout her long and successful career, Harrison worked on many pictures, including *Shadow of a Doubt, Ride the Pink Horse* (1947), and *Circle of Danger* (1951). Most of her work was on mysteries and dark thrillers, where she applied the lessons learned during her days with Hitchcock. An attractive woman, she was frequently asked why she remained behind the camera rather than in front. She responded that she was not an actress, that her job was "to make cops and robbers more exciting than *__Dorothy Lamour__."

SOURCES:

The Day [New London, CT]. August 25, 1994.

Rothe, Anna, ed. *Current Biography 1944*. NY: H.W. Wilson, 1944.

Judith C. Reveal,
freelance writer, Greensboro, Maryland

Harrison, Marguerite (1879–1967)

American journalist, adventurer and spy. *Born Marguerite Elton Baker in October 1879, in Baltimore, Maryland; died on July 16, 1967; eldest of two daughters of Bernard Nadal Baker (the founder of Atlantic Transport Lines); attended St. Timothy's School for Girls, in Catonsville, Maryland; attended Radcliffe College for one year; married Thomas Bullitt Harrison, in 1901 (died 1915); married Arthur Middleton Blake (an actor), in 1926 (died 1949); children: one son, Thomas Bullitt Harrison II ("Tommy").*

Had Marguerite Harrison's husband not died and left her alone with a child to support, she might have lived out her life as a comfortable Baltimore matron. Instead, she became one of the earliest correspondents in the United States and an American spy.

Born into wealth and esteemed lineage, Marguerite Elton Baker was the daughter of the founder of Baltimore's lucrative Atlantic Transport Lines. She and her younger sister, **Elizabeth Baker (Ritchie)**, grew up in luxury and privilege, though Harrison later recalled her early years as stifled and lonely. Alienated from her mother whom she felt had not welcomed her birth, she also felt estranged from her sister who was her opposite in temperament. She later wrote that she felt closest to her father, and "loved him with a passionate devotion that amounted to adoration."

After five unhappy years at the exclusive St. Timothy's School where she excelled in languages, she was sent off to Radcliffe for a year, ostensibly to further her education but in reality to prepare for a good marriage. On her own for the first time, Harrison rebelled by immediately becoming engaged to her landlady's son. The affair was nipped in the bud by her mother, who immediately took her out of college and sent her off to Italy. No sooner had she returned, however, then she attached herself to Thomas Bullitt Harrison, the charming stepson of Dr. Joseph S. Ames, who later became the president of Johns Hopkins University. Despite her mother's misgivings about the match, the couple had a wedding that Harrison described as "one of the most splendid ever seen in Baltimore." In March 1902, just nine months after her marriage, Harrison gave birth to her son Tommy and settled into blissful family life.

With the untimely death of her husband in 1915, Harrison was left penniless, with a young son to support, and an incurred debt of nearly $70,000. Initially, she converted her large home into a boarding house; when that failed to provide enough income, she applied for a job at the *Baltimore Sun*. Having no experience in journalism, but armed with a letter of introduction from her brother-in-law, Harrison was hired as assistant society editor. A quick study, she was soon producing such quality work that she was promoted to music and drama critic. In addition, she also produced the column "Overheard in the Wings," a weekly feature of interviews with visiting artists. She was soon earning $30 a week, which was augmented by an additional $25 yearly, earned through an appointment to the State Board of Motion Picture Censors.

In 1917, when the United States entered World War I, Harrison was assigned to cover the role of women in the war effort. By 1918, despite 14-hour days that left her little social life or time with her son, she was growing restless. With the war now raging in Europe, she was particularly curious about conditions in Germany, where she had traveled as a child. With all paths to Europe pretty much closed, especially to a woman, Harrison chose an unusual means of fulfilling her goal: she became a spy. Applying to General Marlborough Churchill, the chief of the army's Military Intelligence Division (MID), Harrison presented him with a letter from her stepfather-in-law who happened to be a friend of the general's. Accepted on the basis of her intelligence, her fluency in German and French, and a promise of discretion, she was hired at a salary of $250 a month. Before she could start, however, an armistice was declared; it appeared that her career as a spy was over. The MID, however, sent her to Europe to report political and economic matters of possible interest to the U.S. delegation at the upcoming peace conference. Traveling under the cover of a correspondent on special assignment to the *Baltimore Sun*, Harrison sailed for France in December 1918, en route to Germany.

In addition to being one of the earliest correspondents in the United States, she was the first English-speaking woman reporter to reach Berlin after the armistice. Arriving in the city after an arduous journey, Harrison set out to acquaint herself with every aspect of political and social life that might be of interest to the MID, often preparing her reports late at night after a full day of continuous activities. She also regularly filed stories for the *Baltimore Sun*. A British journalist, S.K. Ratcliffe, recalled Harrison in her double role as spy and journalist during the Berlin days. "Marguerite Harrison possessed all the qualifications, as her journalist colleagues and enemies were alike ready to admit. She was brilliantly attractive in appearance, and assured in manner; she had a steely intelligence, and she was everywhere at home. Language had few difficulties for her. In public speech she was swift and pointed."

The signing of the Versailles peace treaty in June 1919 ended Harrison's work in Berlin, and she returned to her job at the *Sun*. But civilian life now bored her. Newly intrigued by the Bolshevik attempt to transform the formerly imperialist society in Russia, Harrison consulted her former MID employer, General Churchill, about operating in Russia as a secret agent. He eagerly welcomed her back, and in November 1919 (with a warning about "considerable risks and many hardships"), she sailed for England with orders to enter Russia and report on conditions in Moscow and other key cities. Carrying credentials from the *Sun,* she was assigned as a temporary Moscow correspondent by the London bureau of the Associated Press. Then, after placing her son in a school in Lausanne, Switzerland, Harrison embarked on the difficult journey to Moscow, which included a six-week delay in Warsaw and a dangerous and prolonged passage through Minsk, the Polish front lines, and an outpost of the Russian front.

Upon her arrival in Moscow, the commissioner of foreign affairs initially allowed Harrison only two weeks in the city, during which time she mastered the language, held interviews, attended meetings, and talked with a variety of people. Her attachment to the Russians was instant and when she was given permission to remain an additional month, she redoubled her attempts to learn as much as she could about social, artistic, and intellectual life in Russia. Her articles for the *Sun* were written late at night and scrutinized by the Foreign Office before they were telegraphed to the United States. Harrison was unaware of a leak in the MID and was taken completely by surprise when she was arrested by the Russian police one night while walking home after filing a story. Brought before the authorities and accused of spying, she was presented with evidence that the Russians not only knew of her present assignment, but had information about her covert work in Germany. Harrison faced serious consequences, but was unexpectedly offered her liberty if she agreed to become a counterspy. After agonizing over her options, she agreed. "In that moment, I renounced everything that hitherto made up my existence," she later wrote. "It was finished—and I

Marguerite Harrison

felt as if I had already died and been born into a new nightmare world."

Released, Harrison attempted to placate her captors with bland reports, while smuggling information to U.S. military officials that she had been caught. Although MID officials were optimistic about her ability "to extricate herself," she lived under constant surveillance in Moscow and the certainty that she was pretty much doomed. On October 24, 1920, her worst fears were realized, and she was hauled off to Lubianka, part of the vast Soviet penal system that Russian writer Aleksandr Solzhenitsyn later called "Gulag Archipelago." The first American woman ever held in a Bolshevik prison, Harrison spent ten harrowing months in deplorable conditions. Her incarceration began with a four-month period of solitary confinement, during which time she sustained herself through a method of self-hypnosis. "I learned to detach myself utterly from the world which seemed irretrievably lost and to find a new world of my own, bounded physically by four walls, but spiritually limitless."

Removed from isolation, Harrison spent the next six months in a small room which variously held 7 to 14 women. Many of the women contracted typhus and syphilis from the unsanitary conditions, one filthy toilet for 125 prisoners, and the continually attacking vermin. Harrison eventually succumbed to tuberculosis and was removed to Novinsky, a prison hospital which she described as "terrestrial paradise," when compared to Lubianka. Certain she would die there, she was unexpectedly freed through the intervention of the American Relief Administration which offered food for famine-ravaged Russia in exchange for the release of prisoners, including Harrison.

Weak and exhausted from her ordeal, Harrison returned to Baltimore and a joyous reunion with her son. Severing her ties with the MID, she devoted her time to lecturing and writing *Marooned in Moscow,* a recounting of her Russian experiences. By the spring of 1922, shortly after completing the book, she was on the move again, this time to write a series of articles about the Far East.

Aboard ship during the first leg of what turned out to be an around-the-world journey, she completed a second book of memoirs, *Unfinished Tales from a Russian Prison*. After visiting Tokyo, Kyoto, Korea, Manchuria, and China, Harrison ventured to Chita, the capital of southeastern Siberia, eager to set foot again on Russian soil despite her ordeal. Unfortunately, shortly before her arrival, that Far Eastern Republic was taken over by the Soviets, and although she held a valid passport, she was again arrested, charged with espionage, and ordered to Moscow. "The iron self-control to which I had schooled myself almost gave way," she remembered later. Once again finding herself in Lubianka, she was also once again given an ultimatum. She would be freed if she became a defector, living with her son in Russia at government expense, and acting as an informant. Refusing, she endured another ten weeks in prison, then was scheduled for trial for espionage and high treason. At the brink of complete despair, however, she was once again rescued by an officer of the American Relief Administration who threatened cessation of food relief unless she was freed.

Returning home in March 1923, Harrison settled into the Hotel Schuyler in Manhattan with her son, who was now 21. She kept busy on the lecture circuit and began another book, *Red Bear or Yellow Dragon*, published in 1924. By the spring of 1925, however, she was once again overcome by wanderlust. A fortuitous meeting with Colonel Merian Cooper, whom she had met during her first visit to Russia and who was now involved in making travel films, led to her next adventure: the production of a new kind of travel film. Forming a partnership, they invited cinematographer Ernest Beaumont Schoedsack to join them on a project to document the migration of the Bakhtiari of Persia, some 1,500 miles away. They departed "with nothing in the world but a camera, fifty thousand feet of precious film and our ten thousand dollars," Harrison wrote later. The result of this incredible journey with the Bakhtiari, during which Harrison endured a dangerous trek across the formidable Zardeh Kub in the Zaros Mountains of Persia, as well as a debilitating bout with malaria, was the documentary *Grass*, a watershed film which can still be viewed at various libraries. It was shown privately at the Plaza Hotel in March 1925 and had its public debut at the Criterion Theater where it played for four months. Although reviewed favorably, critics hardly knew what to make of the movie, having nothing like it for comparison. Harrison, however, was disappointed in the effort, stating that as a record of a natural drama, it should have been treated in a more natural manner. "I wanted to tell the story of the migration simply and straightforwardly without overstatement or exaggeration," she wrote, "but I was over-ruled by Merian and Shorty, and the scenario writer from the editorial staff of Famous Players. . . . Their titles were melodramatic, artificial, and of the theater. They put impossible speeches into the mouths of the Bakhtiari tribesmen ['Br-r-r, this water's cold!'], whose language was as primitive as their lives."

In early 1925, Harrison and three other women explorers, ***Blair Niles, Gertrude Mathews Selby,** and **Gertrude Emerson,** formed the Society of Woman Geographers, an organization for women who had "blazed new trials in geography, ethnology, natural history, and kindred sciences." Originally established to dignify the professional image of female writers, journalists, and explorers who resented being treated like dilettantes, the organization blossomed to include some of the most distinguished women of the 20th century. Harrison considered the founding of this society as well as her part in establishing the Children's Hospital School in Baltimore, the most important accomplishments of her life.

At age 47, after reputedly leaving a trail of broken hearts in her wake, Harrison married an attractive English actor by the name of Arthur Middleton Blake. Claiming she was tired of "wandering the world alone," she settled down to lecturing and writing articles and books. In 1928, she published what is considered her best work, *Asia Reborn*, a political and economic analysis of the new movements in the Far East. Her autobiography, *There's Always Tomorrow*, came out in 1935, as did her translation of Edward Stucken's *The Dissolute Years: A Pageant of Stuart England*.

Following her husband's death in 1949, Harrison returned to Baltimore, residing with her son and his second wife. She continued to travel despite her age, making a journey to South America when she was 78. Subsequently, she visited Africa and Australia, and in her 80s flew to Berlin. Harrison remained in good health to the end of her life and died of a stroke on July 16, 1967, at 88. In accordance with her wishes, her son Tommy scattered her ashes in the Atlantic. "Mother loved the ocean," he said, "and I thought there was an appropriate symbolism that her last remains should have gone out on the ebb tide to be swept restlessly on and on across the face of the earth by the tides of the ocean."

SOURCES:

Olds, Elizabeth Fagg. *Women of the Four Winds: The Adventures of Four of America's First Women Explorers*. Boston, MA: Houghton Mifflin, 1985.

Barbara Morgan,
Melrose, Massachusetts

Harrison, Mary Scott Dimmick

(1858–1948)

Second wife of Benjamin Harrison, 23rd president of the U.S. *Name variations: Mary Scott Lord; Mary Scott Dimmick; Mary Lord Dimmick; Mary Lord Harrison; Mary Dimmick Harrison. Born Mary Scott Lord on April 30, 1858, in Honesdale, Pennsylvania; died on January 5, 1948, in New York, New York; daughter of Russell Farnham (chief engineer, and later general manager, of the Delaware and Hudson Canal Company) and* **Elizabeth (Mayhew) Scott** *(sister of Caroline Scott Harrison); married Walter Erskine Dimmick, on October 22, 1881 (died 1882); married her uncle Benjamin Harrison (U.S. president), on April 6, 1896, in New York, New York; children: (second marriage)* **Elizabeth Harrison** *(1897–1955, who became a successful lawyer and married James Blaine Walker, Jr., grandnephew of James G. Blaine, Harrison's secretary of state).*

Mary Scott's first husband, Walter Dimmick, died just three months after their marriage, leaving Mary a widow at age 24. She returned to her mother's home in Washington. When her mother died, her aunt ***Caroline Scott Harrison** invited her to live in the White House and serve as her social secretary. Three years after Caroline's death, when she was 37, Mary married her uncle, ex-president Benjamin Harrison, then 62. Benjamin's children, her cousins, disapproved of the union and did not attend the ceremony. (Benjamin and Caroline's daughter was also named **Mary Scott Harrison** and was also born in 1858.) In 1897, Mary gave birth to a daughter, Elizabeth.

Mary was widowed again at the age of 43. During World War I, she served as chair of the

Mary Scott Dimmick Harrison

New York City division of the War Camp Community Service and was active in Republican Party affairs. She died in 1948 and is buried in the Harrison family plot in Indianapolis, Indiana.

Harrison, May (1891–1959)

English violinist known for her recordings of Delius as well as for her concerts. *Born in Roorkee, India, in March 1891; died in South Nutfield, Surrey, England, on June 8, 1959; daughter of Colonel John Harrison (an officer in the Royal Engineers) and Annie Harrison (a singer); sister of Beatrice Harrison (1892–1965), the cellist, Margaret Harrison, and Monica Harrison; studied at the Royal College of Music and in St. Petersburg.*

May Harrison's mother **Annie Harrison** studied singing with Sir George Henschel and Gustave Garcia but gave up hopes of a career after her marriage to John Harrison. A colonel in the Royal Engineers, John was posted to India where May was born in 1891. John loved India; Annie hated it. Though she had taken her piano, Annie missed the rich musical life she had known in England; so the family returned shortly after May's birth.

May Harrison

Both parents encouraged their four daughters' musical development, and all four were extremely talented. John gave up his career in the War Office to devote himself to their musical careers, and Annie did the same. ***Beatrice Harrison** and May became concert string players while **Margaret Harrison** was a concert pianist. As an infant, May played "God Save the Queen" on a rubber band stretched from her teeth. She sang in tune before she could walk; her pitch was perfect. By three, she was playing the piano and at five the violin. At age ten, May beat out 3,000 competitors of all ages and both sexes to win the Gold Medal of the Associated Board's Senior Department. She was also awarded a scholarship to the Royal College of Music.

Harrison studied with Leopold Auer (1845–1930), founder of the Russian school of violin playing. She also studied with Spain's Enrique Fernandez Arbos and the Spanish-American Sergei Achille Rivarde. In 1904, she made her London debut with Sir Henry Wood conducting at St. James' Hall. This performance led to many private concerts and recitals in Spain as well as two appearances before the Spanish royal family. That same year, three Harrison sisters were at the Royal College of Music. In 1908, May and her older sister Beatrice went to Frankfurt where they learned German at a local school and attended concerts or the opera. From there, they went to Berlin where they were joined by the entire Harrison family. In the winter, May and her mother went to St. Petersburg to study with Auer for three months. While there, her face was badly burned by a faulty stove, but she played in concert nonetheless to rave reviews. Her Berlin debut was in 1909. In 1911, Harrison was in London where she played the Brahms' Double Concerto with Beatrice. The two were soon touring throughout European capitals. In St. Petersburg, Harrison appeared in a concert conducted by Glazunov, a good composer but poor conductor, especially when he had been drinking, and he drank a great deal. Under the influence, Glazunov had to be tapped on the arm to begin, then proceeded to conduct all movements at the same tempo. Nonetheless, May had the thrill of playing Glazunov's Concerto under the composer's baton and lived to tell about it.

Harrison was often a soloist at London's popular Promenade Concerts. Very much at home in the upper echelons, she performed everywhere and spent many weekends at country houses where she often met the best conductors and composers. Princess *Victoria (1868–1935) was a great admirer which guaranteed that the diminutive violinist was on the guest list for major royal occasions. While her sister frequently appeared in the United States, May played mainly in Great Britain. From 1935 to 1947, she taught at the Royal College of Music.

Among musicians, she was highly regarded because of her marvelous playing and professional manner. It had taken her only two weeks to learn the Elgar Concerto in 1919. When Delius wrote his Double Concerto, the Harrison sisters advised him during its composition. May so impressed the composer in 1920 that he asked her to record it. Sir Arnold Bax's Third Sonata in 1930 was dedicated to her as he also admired her technique.

After World War II, Harrison's career declined, and she performed less and less, but every recorded note is fortunately available on compact disc. She excelled in the Late Romantic music of Delius and Bax but lived in an age when orchestras played quietly, so some find her playing "delicate." May Harrison began her career when women were routinely excluded from symphony orchestras. Despite the fact that she worked in an area dominated by males, she was extremely successful on the concert stage. Her career helped doom the stigma of gender which had dominated the musical world for centuries.

SOURCES:

Potter, Tully. "May Harrison," in *The Strad.* Vol. 101, no. 1204. August 1990, pp. 628–630.

Sadie, Stanley, ed. *New Grove Dictionary of Music and Musicians.* 20 vols. NY: Macmillan, 1980.

John Haag, Associate Professor,
University of Georgia, Athens, Georgia

Harry, Myriam (1869–1958)

Palestinian-born French author who was a significant literary figure in pre-1914 Paris and was awarded the first Prix Fémina. *Name variations: Mme. Perrault-Harry. Born Maria Rosette Shapira in the Old City of Jerusalem, then part of the Ottoman Empire, in April 1869; died in Neuilly-sur-Seine, France, March 10, 1958; daughter of Moses Wilhelm Shapira and Rosette Jockel Shapira; had sister, Augusta Louisa Wilhelmina Shapira; married Emile Alfred Paul Perrault.*

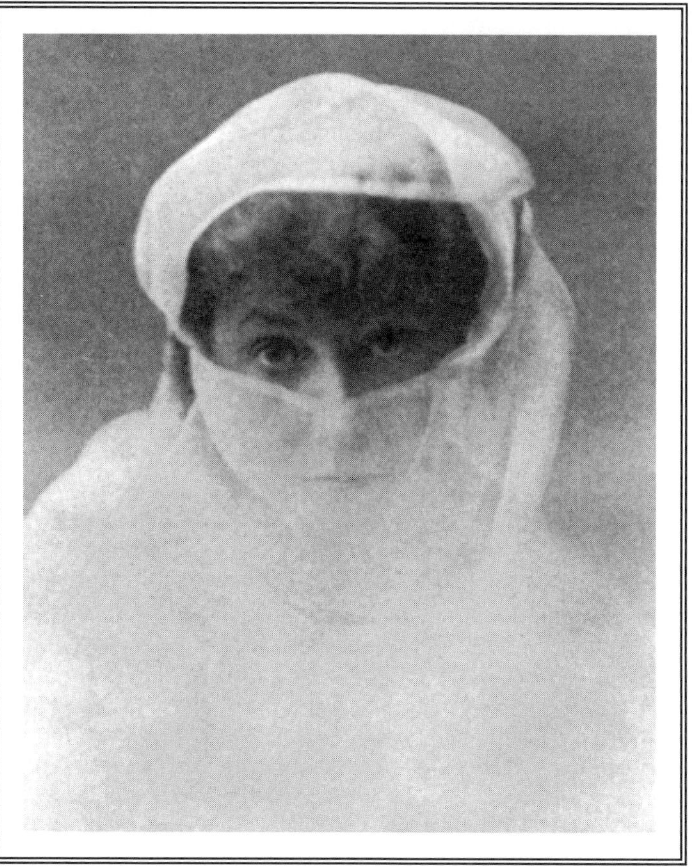

Myriam Harry

Some authors' lives have been just as colorful as their books. This is certainly the case of the French author who called herself Myriam Harry. The first decades of her long life can only be described as highly unconventional. She was born in the Old City of Jerusalem, then part of the Ottoman Empire, in April 1869 (she always stated her date of birth to be February 21, 1875) and was baptized with the name Maria Rosette Shapira in the Anglican Christ Church of Jerusalem on May 2 of that year. She grew up in a venerable whitewashed Saracen house and thrived in the nooks, crannies, and alleyways of the Old City of Jerusalem. Her parents, who had been living there for a number of years, were both from unconventional backgrounds. Her father Moses Wilhelm Shapira had been born a Jew in Russia but had converted to Anglicanism and made his living as a bookseller and antiquarian. Maria's mother **Rosette Jockel Shapira** was a German, a Lutheran deaconess to be precise, who found the Middle East too exotic at times, dreaming at Christmastime of the snow-covered fields and fir trees of her native Hesse. The languages Maria learned from her parents were English and German; from the streets, she picked up Arabic and occasionally Hebrew phrases, and, from one of her family's Arab servants, she learned a few words of imperfect French. Maria's lifelong love of travel and adventure doubtless began in these early years, when she journeyed with her father into the exotic provinces of Syria and Arabia.

One day in 1883, Moses Wilhelm Shapira came across an ancient artifact he believed to be the original manuscript of the Hebrew Pentateuch. After a complex series of contacts and negotiations, the British Museum was prepared to purchase the document at a substantial fee, but at this juncture an eminent French archaeologist, M. Clermont-Ganneau, came up with proof that Shapira's "Pentateuch" was in fact not genuine. His reputation shattered in the sensational "Shapira Affair," Maria's father committed suicide on March 9, 1884. After the tragedy, Rosette Shapira returned to Germany with Maria and her older sister, Augusta. In Germany, where she attended a boarding school for three years, Maria's already marked interest in literature and writing became even more pronounced. Within a short time, some of her short stories began to appear in print, and before long she was being published in major magazines and newspapers, including the distinguished *Berliner Tageblatt.* At this point, Maria Shapira was culturally more German than anything else, although it was clear that her unique background made it much easier for her to experience the world from a cosmopolitan perspective.

Feeling restless in Germany, Maria decided to study French literature in Paris. The visit was a revelation, and the young woman who felt herself artistically and emotionally secure in the English and German languages now fell profoundly in love with the French language and its rich literary tradition. For several years, she was able to publish nothing, literally finding herself in an unformed state between languages, moving rapidly away from her familiarity with German but not yet fully comfortable with French. Soon, however, she was convinced that she had achieved total mastery of the French style and began to write in that language. Once settled in France, she began to travel, visiting much of Europe as well as Egypt, Ceylon (modern-day Sri Lanka), parts of China, and several French colonies and protectorates including Indo-China (modern-day Vietnam) and Tunisia.

In 1899, Maria Shapira announced her debut to the French literary world by appearing in print under the name she would henceforth use, Myriam Harry. In that year, she published *Passage de Bedouins,* followed in rapid succession by a series of novels set in French Indo-China. All of these works received good reviews, but it was not until 1904, when she published *La Conquête de Jérusalem,* that Harry's writings began to be regarded seriously by the leading Paris critics. The book became a literary sensation, and as a result she was awarded the first-ever Prix Fémina (1904), created by 22 members of the editorial staff of the journal *Vie heureuse* because women were unlikely to win the prestigious Goncourt Prize. (In 1905, despite an all-woman jury, the Goncourt was awarded to Romain Rolland for his novel *Jean Cristophe.*)

All of Myriam Harry's novels (she published at least 35 in the course of her career) were escapist works for a bourgeois reading public for whom travel meant travel in Europe, not the Near East or Asia, places that were too distant and too dangerous to visit. As **Marie Louise Fontaine** enthused in 1913, *The Conquest of Jerusalem* places its readers in an ancient and mysterious city "peopled with strange beings, some Biblical and peaceful, others wild-eyed and enfevered."

Myriam Harry's depiction of Jerusalem and the Middle East is part of a Western perspective on non-Western peoples now often explained in terms of the notion of Orientalism. As defined by the noted scholar Edward Said, Orientalism was constructed by Western scholars not so much to understand and learn from non-Western cultures and peoples as to denigrate, control, and dominate them in a world dominated by imperialist and racist assumptions. Although Myriam Harry was neither a scholar nor in any way a member of a conspiracy to control the non-European world, her work nevertheless falls into the general category of Orientalism and its stereotypical view of non-Europeans as the Other.

In her 1901 novel *Petites épouses* (*Little Brides*), set in French Indo-China, she describes as inevitable the physically degenerate state of a half-breed child, with its thin, waxy white body, round ivory head, and blue eyes that its French father cannot bear to look at. The father, Alain, at first worries about what will happen to his son after he departs for France, and for a time seriously considers taking the boy with him, or perhaps even remaining in the colony. Will the boy, with "his expatriate eyes and his white soul . . . be able to acclimatise among his yellow relatives and the black water-buffaloes?" Soon, however, Alain notices that his son is in fact much more "a native" than he is European, paying no attention to the European toys he brings him, preferring instead to watch his young maternal uncles as they torture butterflies, even encouraging them to continue. At this crucial point in her novel, Harry presents Alain as pondering deeply "the prodigies of atavism which had already transmitted to this brain—his very own son's!—the Asian sense of artifice and cruelty."

The exoticism so central to Myriam Harry's novels made her popular with French audiences for several decades, but by the 1930s both her subject matter and her florid prose style had largely fallen out of favor with large sectors of the literate public. Her books, which had once fascinated readers by conjuring up apparently endless pageants of exotic peoples and scenes of alien cultures, now seemed stale and dated. Harry could neither change her approach to literature nor did she wish to retire, so she continued to publish books to smaller audiences and less enthusiastic critics. Starting in the 1920s and until the end of her long life, she was as much a celebrity as she was a distinguished citizen of the republic of letters. Year after year, she would appear at sessions of the Prix Fémina jury dressed in flowing Bedouin robes, a colorful turban on her head. Having authored a highly romanticized biography of ***Cleopatra VII**, she soon claimed to be an authority on the long-departed ruler of the Nile, claiming on several occasions that Cleopatra's mummy had in fact been buried in a courtyard within the walls of the French National Library. Myriam Harry remained to the end of her days a strong-willed, eccentric, and incorrigibly Romantic woman. She died, out of step with a world that had less time for her kind of exotic fantasy, in Neuilly-sur-Seine, on March 10, 1958.

SOURCES:

Abitol, Michel, and Guy Dugas, eds. *Israël: Rêve d'une terre nouvelle.* Paris: Omnibus, 1998.

Allegro, John Marco. *The Shapira Affair.* Garden City, NY: Doubleday, 1965.

Apter, Emily. "Acting Out Orientalism: Sapphic Theatricality in Turn-of-the-Century Paris," in *L'Esprit Créateur.* Vol. 34, no. 2. Summer 1994, pp. 102–116.

Caroz, Yaël. "Relire l'oeuvre de Myriam Harry: La Petite Fille de Jerusalem," in David Mendelson and Michaël Elial, eds., *l'intersiecle 2: écrits français d'Israël de 1880 a nos jours.* Paris: Lettres Modernes-Minard, 1989, pp. 39–47.

"Cleopatra Said to Be Buried in Paris 'Neath French Library's Chestnut Trees," in *The New York Times.* December 16, 1934, section IV, p. 2.

"Enver Bey's Gold-Shod Horses," in *The Literary Digest.* Vol. 52, no. 26. June 24, 1916, pp. 1874, 1876.

Fontaine, Marie Louise. "Some French Women Writers of Today," in *The Bookman.* Vol. 37, no. 7. March 1913, pp. 32–41.

Harry, Myriam. *The Conquest of Jerusalem: A Tale of To-Day.* Boston, MA: H.B. Turner, 1906.

———. *The Little Daughter of Jerusalem.* With an Introduction by Jules Lemaitre. Translated by Phoebe Allen. NY: E.P. Dutton, 1919.

———. *Siona à Paris.* Paris: A. Fayard & Cie., 1919.

———. *Siona chez les barbares.* Paris: A. Fayard & Cie., 1918.

———. *A Springtide in Palestine.* Boston, MA: Houghton Mifflin, 1924.

Lefévre, Fréderic. *Une heure avec . . . Myriam Harry.* [VI. série]. Paris: Flammarion, 1933.

Mailloux, Auguste. *Myriam Harry.* Paris: M. Mendel, 1920.

Mansoor, Menahem. "The Case of Shapira's Dead Sea (Deuteronomy) Scroll of 1883," in *Transactions of the Wisconsin Academy of Sciences.* Vol. 47, 1959, pp. 183–225.

"Mummy of Cleopatra in Paris, Says Writer; Believes Napoleon Brought It From Egypt," in *The New York Times.* July 30, 1926, p. 19.

Pierrot, Roger. "Myriam Harry et Jerusalem," in *Études art et litterature Université de Jerusalem/Hebrew University Studies in Literature and the Arts.* Vol. 18, 1991, pp. 49–57.

Said, Edward. *Orientalism: Western Conceptions of the Orient.* Rev. ed. NY: Penguin Books, 1995.

Shapiro, Sraya. "In Search of a Lingua Franca," in *Jerusalem Post.* February 1, 1990.

Silberman, Neil Asher. *Digging for God and Country: Exploration, Archeology, and the Secret Struggle for the Holy Land, 1799–1917.* NY: Alfred A. Knopf, 1982.

"Some Successful French Women Authors," in *American Review of Reviews.* Vol. 47, no. 5. May 1913, pp. 613–615.

Yee, Jennifer. "Neither Flesh nor Fowl: 'Métissage' in fin-de-siecle French Colonial Fiction," in *L'Ésprit Créateur.* Vol. 38, no. 1. Spring 1998, pp. 46–56.

John Haag,
Associate Professor of History,
University of Georgia, Athens, Georgia

Hart, Alice (fl. late-19th c.)

British-born social activist who, with husband Ernest Hart, established the Donegal Famine Fund and the Donegal Industrial Fund. *Flourished in the late 19th century.*

In a visit to Donegal, Ireland, in 1883, England's Alice Hart and her doctor-husband Ernest Hart established the Donegal Famine Fund to assist those suffering from the meager harvests that had afflicted the area. Alice sought to revive the cottage industries in the region to ease the economic distress and, in 1883, started the Donegal Industrial Fund. After rousing some interest through a display of woven tweeds from Donegal at the Health Exhibition in London, Hart opened a shop in London to sell Donegal products and experimented with various dyes made from indigenous wild plants. Subsequently, some hosiery made in Donegal and colored with these dyes won the medal of the Sanitary Institute of Great Britain for "innocuous vegetable dying."

Hart also encouraged Irish women to keep alive a technique which came to be known as

"Kells Embroidery," the designs of which, done on linen with dyed threads made of flax, were taken from early Irish manuscripts. The "Kells Embroidery" won a gold medal at the Inventions Exhibition held in London in 1885. The following year, Hart moved to a larger shop which became known as Donegal House. She also had a hand in bringing specialized teachers to Donegal to help revive wood-carving and carpentry. The work was exhibited in Edinburgh, Liverpool, Paris, Dublin, Chicago, and Olympia. Unfortunately, the project, successful at the time, did not continue after the Harts retired in 1896.

Hart, Doris (1925—)

American tennis player who was a one-time champion at Wimbledon and two-time U.S. Open champion. *Born Doris J. Hart in June 1925 in St. Louis, Missouri.*

Won the Australian singles title (1949); won the French Open singles title (1950 and 1952); won the French Open doubles championship with P.C. Todd (1948), and with Shirley Fry (1950, 1951, 1952, 1953); won the singles championship at Wimbledon (1951); won the U.S. Open (1954, 1955); won the U.S. Open doubles championships with Shirley Fry (1951, 1954); won the U.S. Open mixed doubles with Frank Sedgman (1951, 1952), and with Vic Seixas (1953, 1954, 1955); won the Italian singles (1951, 1953); won the South African singles and doubles (1952).

Doris Hart was placed on the tennis courts at age six, to counter an attack of what was thought to be polio (later diagnosed as osteomyelitis) which had permanently damaged her right knee. Hart went on to become one of the more graceful players in women's tennis and one of its best servers, winning all three major championships. The early knee damage caused her to shuffle more than run as she crisscrossed the court. "Her drop shots were especially cunning," wrote ***Billie Jean King**. "She reasoned that if she could not run as fast as her opponents, she would make them do most of the running."

From 1944 to 1955, Hart was in the semifinals or finals of every U.S. championship. Her Wimbledon record includes doubles wins with **Pat Canning Todd** in 1947, as well as with ***Shirley Fry** in 1951, 1952, and 1953, and mixed-doubles championships with partners Frank Sedgman and Vic Seixas from 1951 to 1955. Her singles title in 1951 made Hart a Wimbledon triple event champion. Until then, only three women had managed the same feat: ***Suzanne Lenglen**, ***Alice Marble**, and ***Louise Brough**. Hart beat her good friend and doubles-partner Shirley Fry in that 1951 singles final without losing a set. As Fry rushed to the net to congratulate Hart, she graciously offered to replay the match. Hart, who did not take her up on it, turned professional in 1955.

SOURCES:

King, Billie Jean. *We Have Come a Long Way, Baby.* NY: McGraw-Hill, 1988.

Hart, Judith (1924—)

British politician who was minister of overseas development. *Name variations: Lady Hart. Born Constance Mary Judith Ridehalgh in Burnley, Lancashire, England, in 1924; attended the London School of Economics; married Dr. Anthony Hart, in 1946; children: two sons.*

Judith Hart, born in Lancashire, England, in 1924, was a member of the Labour Party and active in politics for most of her life. Hart became a member of Parliament in 1959, elected by the Scottish constituency of Lanark. From 1964 to 1971, she held a number of ministerial posts, including joint parliamentary under-secretary of state at the Scottish Office (1964–66), minister of state for Commonwealth Affairs (1966–67), minister of social security (1967), and paymaster-general (1968).

Hart's greatest contribution, however, was as minister of overseas development, a post she held from 1969 to 1970, 1974 to 1975, and 1977 to 1979. She was particularly outspoken about the United Kingdom's moral responsibility to third world countries, a subject she also explored in *Aid and Liberation: A Socialist Study of Aid Policies* (1973). Trained as a sociologist, Hart had a well-informed grasp of the problems in third-world development. She had nearly finished a restructuring of British aid policy to offer rural development in villages and priority to the poorest countries in 1979, but this seemed to conflict with the agenda of Britain's Foreign and Commonwealth Office. She was also opposed to membership in the European Economic Community (EEC) and for that Prime Minister Harold Wilson asked Hart to transfer to the ministry of transport so that he might incorporate her ministry with the Foreign and Commonwealth Office. With that, she resigned. Starting in 1969, Hart also served as a member of the Labour Party National Executive, and chaired the industrial policy sub-committee and the finance and economic sub-committee. Married in 1946 to Dr. Anthony Hart, she has two sons.

Hart, Lady (b. 1924).

See Hart, Judith.

Hart, Nancy (c. 1735–1830)

Legendary hero of the American Revolution. *Name variations: Aunt Nancy. Born Ann Morgan in either Pennsylvania or North Carolina, around 1735; died near Henderson, Kentucky, in 1830; daughter of Thomas Morgan and Rebecca (Alexander) Morgan; married Benjamin Hart; children: Morgan, John, Thomas, Lemuel, Mark, Sukey (Sally), Benjamin, and Keziah.*

Facts surrounding the birth and lineage of Revolutionary hero Nancy Hart are sketchy at best. She was born Ann Morgan (but was known as Nancy throughout her life), in either Pennsylvania or North Carolina, around 1735, although there is no documentation to support that date. It is often stated that she was a first cousin to Daniel Boone (whose mother was **Sarah Morgan Boone**) and that General Daniel Morgan was a cousin of both Nancy and Daniel, but there is no evidence to support those claims either. Although no date is given for Nancy's marriage to Benjamin Hart, the couple is known to have lived in South Carolina for a short time before moving to Wilkes County, Georgia, around 1771. It was there that Nancy, who was reputedly six feet tall, solidly built, and could handle a rifle as well as anyone, made her reputation as a stalwart defender of the Whig cause during the fierce fighting in the Georgia colony during the Revolution. Although many women and children of patriot families left the region during what came to be called the "War of Extermination," Nancy Hart, or Aunt Nancy as she came to be called, stayed on to fight against the Tories.

Stories abound about her exploits, the most famous of which centers on her capture of a band of Tories. As the tale goes, five or six Tories arrived at her cabin and demanded that she cook them dinner. Hart put a turkey on to roast and plied the men with whiskey while her daughter slipped away to warn neighbors. When the Tories sat down to eat, she grabbed one of their rifles from the corner, shot one of them dead, wounded another, and held the rest at bay until the Whigs took them away to be hanged. Other narratives tell of Hart's exploits as a spy for Georgia's patriot forces. In one, she was said to have crossed the Savannah River on a raft of logs tied with grapevines in order to bring back information from enemy camps.

After the war, the Harts moved to Brunswick, Georgia, where Benjamin died. Nancy later moved to Clarke County, Georgia, and then Kentucky, where she died in 1830. Her Revolutionary exploits were first published in a newspaper story which appeared in 1825, on the occasion of General Lafayette's visit to the United States. In 1848, ***Elizabeth Ellet** included the popular story about the hanging of the Tories in her book *Women of the American Revolution.* Further stories about Nancy Hart appeared in George White's *Historical Collections of Georgia* (1854) and Joel Chandler Harris' *Stories of Georgia* (1896), and ***Margaret Mitchell** wrote a piece on her for the *Atlanta Journal.* A Georgia county was named for Hart in 1853, and, in 1856, the county seat was named Hartwell in her honor.

SOURCES:

James, Edward T., ed. *Notable American Women, 1607–1950.* Cambridge, MA: The Belknap Press of Harvard University Press, 1971.

McHenry, Robert, ed. *Famous American Women.* NY: Dover, 1983.

Barbara Morgan,
Melrose, Massachusetts

Hart, Nancy (c. 1846–1902)

Confederate spy. *Possibly born in 1846, probably in Virginia; died in 1902; married Joshua Douglas (a soldier turned farmer), around 1862.*

Many of the unsung heroes of the Civil War were women and some were in the dangerous business of spying, among them Nancy Hart. She was born around 1846 and raised in the western part of Virginia, where there were no plantations and few slaves, but her parents were nevertheless Southern sympathizers. Hart was still a teenager when her brother-in-law was killed in battle, prompting her to leave home and join a group of pro-Southern guerrillas dubbed the Moccasin Rangers. A sharpshooter and an excellent equestrian, Hart had no difficulty keeping pace with the men on raids, but she also capitalized on soci-

Nancy Hart (c. 1846–1902)

ety's "weaker sex" attitudes when necessary. Captured during one raid and taken to a Union camp, she lulled her captors into thinking she was harmless. They let her go, but not before she had committed to memory vital information about troop strength and battle strategy which she then shared with her compatriots.

Following the death of their leader in 1962, the Moccasin Rangers disbanded, and Hart married a fellow soldier, Joshua Douglas. When her husband enlisted in the Confederate army and went off to fight, Hart took to the mountains where she began spying on the Union troops. After a year under cover, she was caught, arrested, and taken to the Union-occupied town of Summersville. Once again, she charmed her guard, convincing him to let her hold his gun. With the weapon in her possession, she shot him through the heart, then mounted the Union commander's horse and rode off, leaving her pursuers in the dust. She returned a week later accompanied by 200 Confederate horse soldiers who swept the town clean of Union troops.

Pearl Hart

Following the war, Hart and her husband retired to the mountains and took up farming. She died in 1902 and was buried in a mountain crag marked by stones. Years later, when her granddaughter tried to locate the grave, it was gone, replaced by a beacon tower. There is at least one extant photograph of Hart, housed in the West Virginia State Archives. It was taken during one of her imprisonments, supposedly at the request of a smitten Union soldier who wanted a keepsake. Hart had initially refused to pose, claiming she did not have the proper clothes, but the determined soldier outfitted her with a borrowed dress and a chapeau fashioned from a Union soldier's hat done up with feathers and ribbons. Despite the finery, Hart appears grim-faced.

SOURCES:

Coleman, Penny. *Spies*. Betterway Books, 1992.

Barbara Morgan,
Melrose, Massachusetts

Hart, Pearl (c. 1875–c. 1924)

Canadian-born stagecoach robber. *Born in Ontario, Canada, around 1875; died in Kansas City, Missouri, around 1924; married a man named Hart.*

Oddly distinguished as the last person to rob a stagecoach in America, Pearl Hart was either a female desperado or a misguided angel of mercy, depending on the source. Born in Ontario, Canada, around 1875, she eloped in the early 1890s with a man by the name of Hart, whom she subsequently left behind in 1893. For several years, she roamed the Southwest and may have married a second time. She later took up with an unsuccessful mining prospector called Joe Boot.

It may have been Boot who talked Hart into robbing one of the last stagecoaches still operating in the Arizona desert, although in one version of the story, it was an urgent message that her mother was ill and needed money that prompted Hart to resort to crime. Whatever the case, in 1897 Hart and Boot held up the stagecoach outside of Globe, Arizona, netting a total of $431 from the four men aboard, whom they allowed to escape. Quickly apprehended by the local sheriff and identified by their victims, the thieves were carted off to jail, where Hart became something of a celebrity. She declared that it was unfair for her to be indicted, tried, convicted, or sentenced under a law that she, as a woman, had no hand in making. The jury, evidently agreeing, acquitted her while sentencing Boot to 30 years. The outraged judge, however, called for a retrial, and Hart was eventually found guilty.

Pearl Hart served two years of her five-year sentence at the Yuma Territorial Prison, receiving a pardon by the governor in 1902, due to "lack of accommodations for women prisoners." She then went to live in Kansas City with her sister who wrote a play about the incident, *The Arizona Bandit*. Some say Hart toured as its star. Others claim that the play was never produced, and that Hart spent the final days of her life running a Kansas City cigar store. She died around 1924.

Hartel, Lis (1921—)

Danish equestrian who, though paralyzed, became a two-time Olympic silver medalist in individual dressage. *Name variations: Lis Hartel-Holst; Liz Hartel. Born in Denmark on March 14, 1921; married with children.*

Won the Olympic silver medal for individual dressage on Jubille at Helsinki (1952) and Melbourne (1956).

Lis Hartel was 23, pregnant, and one of Denmark's leading dressage riders when she was stricken with polio in 1944. Though almost completely paralyzed, she was determined to continue her career and began a long, painful rehabilitation while still pregnant, first relearning how to lift her arms, then concentrating on her thigh muscles. After giving birth to a healthy daughter, Hartel persevered, regaining enough use of her legs to walk haltingly with crutches. Then she began riding again. Her initial outing with a horse left her so exhausted, however, that it took two more weeks for her to regain enough strength to try once more. In 1947, she entered the Scandinavian Riding championship, finishing second. When the 1952 Olympics were scheduled for Helsinki, Lis Hartel had no trouble making Denmark's dressage team.

The 1952 Olympic Games were momentous not only for Hartel, but for women equestrians throughout the world. Dressage (a non-jumping event in which horse and rider perform a series of gaits and maneuvers) had become part of the equestrian competition at the 1912 Stockholm Games, but for the next 40 years was open only to male commissioned military officers. As of 1952, men and women competed against each other and together.

Although Hartel remained paralyzed below the knees and had to be assisted both on and off her horse, she put in an amazing performance at the 1952 Olympics, coming in second behind gold-medal winner Henri St. Cyr of Sweden. During the emotional awards ceremony, St. Cyr stepped down from his first-place position on the platform to assist Hartel off her horse and

Lis Hartel

onto the podium for the medal presentation. Four years later, in 1956, Hartel won a second silver medal in the Helsinki Olympic competition which was held in Stockholm. St. Cyr, winning another gold, once again helped Hartel to her place of honor.

Hartigan, Grace (1922—)

American abstract-expressionist painter who rose to prominence in the 1950s. *Born in Newark, New Jersey, on March 28, 1922; the eldest of four children of Matthew Hartigan (a certified public accountant) and Grace (Orvis) Hartigan; attended Milburn, New Jersey, schools, 1929–40; studied privately with Isaac Lane Muse, New York, 1942–46; married Robert Jachens, on May 10, 1941 (divorced 1947); married Harry Jackson (an artist), in March 1949 (annulled 1950); married Robert Keene (a gallery owner), in 1958 (divorced 1960); married Dr. Winston H. Price (an epidemiologist), on December 24, 1960 (died 1981); children: (first marriage) one son, Jeffrey.*

Selected works: Secuda Esa Bruja *(1949);* Months and Moons *(1950);* The King Is Dead *(1950, Edward Tyler Nahem Fine Arts, New York);* Kindergarten Chats *(1950, private collection);* Knight, Death, and the Devil *(1952, private collection);* The Tribute Money *(1952);* River Bathers *(1953, Museum of Modern Art, New York);* The Persian Jacket *(1952, Museum of Modern Art, New York);* Orange #4 *(*The Changing Dialectics of Our World, *1952–53, Gallery K, Washington, D.C.);* Orange #6 *(*The Light Only Reaches Halfway, *1952–53, Gallery K, Washington, D.C.);* Grand Street Brides *(1954, Whitney Museum of American Art, New York);* Masquerade *(1954, Art Institute of Chicago);* Giftwares *(1955, Neuberger Museum, State University of New York at Purchase);* City Life *(1956, National Trust for Historic Preservation, Nelson A. Rockefeller collection);* The Vendor *(1956, Oklahoma Art Center, Oklahoma City);* Montauk Highway *(1957, private collection);* Billboard *(1957, Minneapolis Institute of Arts);* New England October *(1957, Albright-Knox Art Gallery, Buffalo, New York);* Dublin *(1958–59, private collection);* Sweden *(1959, Whitney Museum of American Art, New York);* The Fourth *(1959);* August Harvest *(1959, Baltimore Museum of Art);* No Man Is an Island *(1959–63, Israel Museum, Jerusalem).*

Dido *(1960, Marion Koogler McNay Art Museum, San Antonio, Texas);* Pallas Athens—Fire *(1961, private collection);* Phoenix *(1962, private collection);* William of Orange *(1962, Baltimore Museum of Art);* Lily Pond *(1962, private collection);* The The #1 *[sic] (1962, State of New York, Governor Nelson A. Rockefeller Empire State Plaza Art Collection, Albany);* Marilyn *(1962, private collection);* The Hunted *(1963, private collection);* Human Fragment *(1963, Walker Art Center, Minneapolis);* Mistral *(1964, private collection);* Mountain Woman *(1964, Arthur M. Huntington Art Gallery, University of Texas at Austin);* Barbie *(1964, Signet Bank, Baltimore);* Skin Deep *(1965, private collection);* Frank O'Hara, 1926–1966 *(1966, National Museum of American Art, Smithsonian Institution, Washington, D.C.);* Reisterstown Mall *(1965, private collection);* Modern Cycle *(1967, National Museum of American Art, Smithsonian Institution, Washington, D.C.);* Fire and Water *(1969);* The Anatomy of Calvert Street *(1969);* When the Raven Was White *(1969, Albright-Knox Art Gallery, Buffalo, New York).*

Saint George and the Dragon *(1970, Old Saint Paul's Church, Baltimore);* Year of the Cicada *(1970);* Dragons and Other Animals *(1970, private collection);* Beware of Gifts *(1971, Watkins Collection, American University, Washington, D.C.);* Another Birthday *(1971, Museum of Fine Arts, Boston);* Summer to Fall *(1971–72);* Black Velvet *(1972, Flint Institute of Arts, Flint, Michigan);* Autumn Shop Window *(1972, Baltimore Museum of Art);* Purple Passion *(1973);* Coloring Book of Ancient Egypt *(1973);* Blood and Wine *(1975);* Testament *(1975);* Bread Sculpture *(1977);* I Remember Lascaux *(1978, private collection);* Twilight of the Gods *(1978, private collection).*

Lexington Market *(1980, Federal Reserve Bank, Baltimore);* Constance *(1981, private collection);* Eastern Avenue Florist *(1982, private collection);* Saint Martin *(1983);* Joséphine *(1983, private collection);* Theodora *(1983, Solomon R. Guggenheim Museum, New York);* Renaissance Woman *(1984, private collection);* Saint George *(1985, Birmingham Museum of Art, Birmingham, Alabama);* Lady Gathering Pomegranates *(1985, private collection);* Renaissance Card Game *(1985, private collection);* Crowning of the Poet *(1985, C. Grimaldis Gallery, Baltimore);* Bacchus *(1985, private collection);* Spanish Vendor *(1985, private collection);* Visions of Heaven and Hell *(1985);* Malibu *(1986, private collection);* Tarzana *(1987);* Madonna Inn *(1987);* Casino *(1987);* Society Wedding *(1988, private collection);* The Hunt *(1988, private collection);* Chicago *(1988, Kouros Gallery, New York);* West Broadway *(1989, Grimaldis Gallery, Baltimore).*

A disciple of Jackson Pollock and Willem de Kooning, Grace Hartigan emerged from the New York School of abstract expressionists to become the most visible woman painter in the United States during the late 1950s. She was the single woman represented in the Museum of Modern Art's exhibition, "Twelve Americans" (1956), and in its international touring show, "The New American Painting (1958–59)." Her works were purchased by the Museum of Modern Art, the Metropolitan Museum of Art, and the Whitney. Although Hartigan's popularity waned with the Minimalism and Pop art movements of the 1960s and 1970s, she was discovered once again with the arrival of the "new figurative" and new expressionist painting of the 1980s. Through five decades, the artist continued to evolve, moving alternately between abstraction and figuration, drawing subject matter from both past and present and synthesizing it through her own rich and varied life experiences.

Grace Hartigan was born in Newark, New Jersey, in 1922, the eldest of four children of an Irish-English family. Her early years were spent in a two-family house in the industrial city of Bayonne. A free-spirited, difficult child, Hartigan was alienated from her mother, but had a close bond with her father whom she later credited with unleashing her creativity and her independence. "My father was the one who told me I could do anything I wanted to do," she later wrote. As a youngster, her maternal needs were met by her grandmother, who told her stories and sang old English and Welsh ballads. At the age of five, Hartigan suffered a yearlong bout with pneumonia, after which the family moved to Milburn, New Jersey, hoping that the country air might improve their daughter's health. She flourished in the more open environment which also seemed to unleash her rich fantasy life. At Milburn High School, Hartigan became interested in literature, debate, and drama, everything except the visual arts. At age 17, fresh out of high school, she married Robert Jachens, "the boy next door." After seeing the movie *Call of the Wild*, the couple decided to set out for Alaska. "We traveled as far as Los Angeles," Hartigan later recalled. "We were pregnant, we were broke, and World War II began. A triple calamity."

Fortunately, Hartigan's young husband was sensitive to her creative impulses and urged her to take art classes at night. Having had little practical experience, Hartigan was frustrated at first but persevered, drawing whenever she could throughout her pregnancy and after her son Jeffrey was born. When her husband was conscripted into the armed services, Hartigan returned East with her son and enrolled in a night course in mechanical drafting at the Newark College of Engineering. She then took a job as a mechanical draftswoman in an airplane factory and spent evenings creating watercolor still-lifes. Her first experience with contemporary painting came when a co-worker showed her a book on Henri Matisse. It made a lasting impression. Unsuccessful in attempts to duplicate Matisse's style on her own, she began art lessons with Isaac Lane Muse, an avant-garde teacher in Newark. In 1945, she moved to New York with Muse and rented a house on 19th Street and 7th Avenue. Working to support the household, she commuted daily to a drafting job in White Plains. "Slowly, I realized the terrible unfairness of it all," she said later. (By the end of the war, Hartigan and her husband had gone their separate ways. They would divorce in 1947, and, because Hartigan was certain that her penniless, bohemian lifestyle was not good for her son, Jeffrey would grow up with his father in California.)

In January 1948, Hartigan attended the first exhibition of Jackson Pollock's controversial large-scale drip paintings, an event that changed her life. "I was mesmerized and fascinated," she recalled, "but I can't say that I liked the paintings initially." Upon returning home, she fought with Muse who did not appreciate Pollock or abstract painting. Soon after, she left him and established her own small studio. After contemplating Pollock's paintings for several months, Hartigan and another young painter, Harry Jackson, hitchhiked to Long Island to visit Pollock and his wife, artist ***Lee Krasner**. Hartigan spent a week immersed in Pollock's paintings and came away with a renewed dedication. "I knew the paintings and the person who painted them were one-and-the-same," she said. "Painting was not an activity but a total life. And you would do anything to keep painting, even if you starved. You were the paintings and the paintings were you."

Through Pollock, Hartigan met Willem de Kooning, whose influence was more intellectual, less visceral, than Pollock's, though his message about commitment was the same. De Kooning, whom Hartigan viewed as "a great classicist," advised her to study the masters and to discover her own subject matter. "De Kooning provided a model for Hartigan of freely expressive but masterly painting technique," writes Robert Mattison in his book *Grace Hartigan: A Painter's World*.

In March 1949, Hartigan married Harry Jackson (the marriage was annulled in 1950) and spent a year with him in San Miguel de Allende, Mexico. With Jackson's money from the GI Bill, the couple rented a villa and painted full-time. Some of Hartigan's earliest preserved works date from this period, and reflect the themes of witchcraft and folklore she found in Mexican folk art.

Representative is *Secuda Esa Bruja* (The witch is flying), a painting that resembles the late Surrealist works of Mark Rothko, whom Hartigan had met while living with Muse.

Returning to New York, Hartigan began to paint large abstract canvases and to associate with other artists of the New York School, including **Helen Frankenthaler**, ***Joan Mitchell**, and Franz Kline. She also befriended poet Frank O'Hara, with whom she collaborated in 1952, creating a series of poem-paintings based on his work, *Oranges*. In the spring of 1950, art critics Clement Greenberg and Meyer Schapiro had included Hartigan's *Secuda Esa Bruja* in their landmark exhibition "New Talent," held at the Kootz Gallery. Following "New Talent," Hartigan had her first solo exhibition at the Tibor de Nagy Gallery, which later became the leading showcase for the younger New York School artists. The exhibition featured ten of her works, including the large canvases *The King Is Dead*, *King of the Hill*, and *Months and Moons*, described by **Charlotte Rubinstein** in *American Women Artists* as "energetic swaths of dripping housepaint and collage." Though reviews were sympathetic, the exhibition was not well attended, and the one painting that sold was returned the following day. Public apathy as well as perpetual poverty were constants for Hartigan, who, until the late 1950s, often had to stop painting for a month or so and take a job to pay for paint and canvases.

In 1952, around the time of a second solo exhibition at Tibor de Nagy, Hartigan became dissatisfied, declaring herself "fed up with everything I am doing." Feeling a need to learn the secrets of the past and incorporate them into her work, she temporarily gave up abstraction and spent a year doing free studies of the masters, including Dürer, de Zurbarán, Rubens, Matisse, Velasquez, and Goya. This foray temporarily alienated her from painters like Pollock, Kline, and Rothko, who viewed her as a defector. However, according to Mattison, it provided Hartigan with "important compositional lessons about space, tactility, form, structure, and light." Her search for personal style and subject matter continued, as did her rise as an artist of note. During her third solo exhibition in March 1953, Alfred H. Barr, Jr., purchased *The Persian Jacket* (1952) for the Museum of Modern Art. It was her first painting to be acquired by a major museum, an occasion that marked her arrival as an important American artist of the "advanced tendency."

Hartigan's largest and most complex painting of the 1950s was *Grand Street Brides* (1954), a work inspired by the rows of bridal shops on nearby Grand Street. "I passed by a store window jammed full of mannequins in cheap white lace bridal gowns with a seated figure in a bilious violet maid of honor dress," Hartigan recalled. "It would make a marvelous group picture, a kind of modern court scene." In preparation and as reference for the work, Hartigan purchased a wedding gown and collected a group of photographs of store windows, taken by Walter Silver, which she tacked to her painting wall. "As the mannequins and store windows were in themselves distanced from life, the photographs provided another degree of removal," writes Mattison. "Thus Hartigan was allowed a wide latitude in the reinvention of imagery and structure." (This method of gathering, assimilating and synthesizing images continued to be used by the artist, with slight variations, throughout her career.) In this work, Hartigan also utilized a new painting technique that involved scraping and rubbing down through the layers of paint, "as if," says Mattison, "she were digging down to the essence of personality."

During the late 1950s, Hartigan produced some of her best-known works, including *Shop Window* (1955), *City Life* (part of the "Twelve Americans" exhibit in 1956 and purchased by Nelson Rockefeller), and *Billboard* (1957), as well as several works from her first trip to Europe in 1958, including *Dublin* (1958–59) and *Sweden* (1959). By the end of the decade, the artist was something of a celebrity. She was the subject of a *Life* magazine photographic essay, "Women Artists in Ascendance" (1957), while a *Newsweek* article contained her photo by Cecil Beaton. Hartigan began to find public acclaim distracting. "I must close my door so I can be alone again," she wrote in her notebook. "I must have time to think and paint without constant interruption."

In the winter of 1958, Hartigan married art dealer Robert Keene and, in the summer of 1959, purchased a permanent residence on Long Island, where her husband owned a gallery. That summer was a prolific one for Hartigan, despite mounting friction with Keene. She completed 17 oil paintings, among them *The Fourth*, a large work which embodies the spirit of Independence Day, with vibrant splashes of red, white, and blue exploding at the top of the painting like fireworks.

Hartigan's life changed dramatically in 1960 when she divorced Keene, married epidemiologist Dr. Winston Price (noted for his work on developing a vaccine for encephalitis), and moved to his home in Baltimore, Maryland.

Hartigan had met Price in 1959, when he purchased one of her paintings, and they fell in love immediately. (Both divorced their respective spouses so they could marry.) Hartigan wrote to a friend after the wedding: "All that this letter could possibly be is a song of my love; the first time I have ever loved so deeply or committed myself so completely. This is the man of my life. There is no doubt about it."

Price's emotional and intellectual support had a tremendous impact on Hartigan's work, which became more sensual, brighter in color, and more transparent in painting style. The paintings *No Man Is an Island* (1959–60), *Phoenix* (1962), *William of Orange* (1962), and *Lily Pond* (1962) are all reflective of Hartigan's new-found security and happiness. During this period, she also invented the watercolor collage, called "second expression," in which she used luminescent washes in combination with overlays of torn paper. In 1962, Hartigan turned from what Mattison refers to as "a lyrical state" to undertake a personal and psychological study of ***Marilyn Monroe**, a haunting abstraction that she simply called *Marilyn* (1962). Inspired by a collection of photographs and Monroe's comment, "Fame may go by—and, so long I've had you," the painting reflects the tragedy of Marilyn's inability to cope with the crushing responsibilities of her fame. It also encompasses Hartigan's feelings about the decline of her own celebrity after 1960.

The tense and fearful mood of *Marilyn* persisted in Hartigan's subsequent paintings, *The Hunted* (1963), *Human Fragment* (1963), and *Mistral* (1964), all of which embodied the artist's reaction to a world exploding in crisis—the civil-rights movement, the Vietnam War, and the assassination of John F. Kennedy. "The world was ill at ease," she recalled. "Socially and morally as well as culturally, America suddenly seemed a frightening and foreign place." Other paintings of the period are indicative of Hartigan's continuing search for images. A series of works—*Barbie* (1964), *Skin Deep* (1965), and *Beauty Mask* (1965)—were inspired by dolls.

Hartigan was sometimes playful and irreverent in her themes. In *Reisterstown Mall* (1965), she explores the shopping mall as a cultural phenomenon. A humorous painting, *Modern Cycle* (1967), had its genesis in Hartigan's teaching, which also began during this period. To counteract her loneliness and isolation from the New York artistic community, she began instructing graduate students from Maryland Institute. (The classes later evolved into the Hoffberger School of Painting, where Hartigan served as director.) Hartigan's first few students were interested in motorcycles as well as art, so Hartigan indulged them with her own "cycle." Inspired by a poster of Marlon Brando and ads cut from the motorcycle magazine *Modern Cycle*, the painting is a playful ode to machine worship.

During the 1970s, Hartigan endured a series of crises: the loss of her father, the illness of her husband, a bout with alcoholism, a painful hip-joint problem, and a suicide attempt. Amid her personal upheavals, painting became a lifeline. Mattison finds her works in this period new and complex in structure. They are comprised of "split images, obsessively crowded surfaces, hidden and submerged colors—all revealing attempts to order a fragmented world vision. . . . These paintings are some of the most difficult works in Hartigan's career to interpret, yet they are also among the most rewarding." Hartigan's art was also increasingly out of step with the popular styles of Minimalism, Color Field, hard-edge painting, and superrealism. She was so far ahead of her time that when the Museum of Fine Arts in Boston received her painting *Another Birthday* (1971) through a donation, they locked it away in storage until 1984.

> Without the "rage for order" how can there be art?
>
> —**Grace Hartigan**

Perhaps most deeply troubling to Hartigan throughout the 1970s was her husband's illness, which was the result of his experiments with live encephalitis vaccine. Beginning with bouts of severe depression, Price suffered a slow mental and physical decline until his eventual death in 1981. In a two-year period preceding 1978, Hartigan actually believed that her husband might recover. He had told her that he was working on important new experiments and that he was about to receive an inheritance. In truth, however, he was delusional, growing worse, and spending their savings. In 1978, the truth about his illness and their disintegrating financial situation came crashing in on Hartigan, who painted what she believed to be her last work, *I Remember Lascaux* (1978), and then attempted suicide by combining sleeping pills and alcohol. Discovered by her husband, Hartigan was taken to the hospital and revived, but the painting, *I Remember Lascaux,* serves as a lasting reminder of this painful episode. Ironically, it is one her calmest works, executed in muted tones and depicting a group of wild beasts organized around a beautiful gazelle at the center. The reference to the Lascaux caves in Southern France harkened back to her 1958 trip to Europe when she was among the last tourist parties to view the caves before they were closed to the public in 1963. "In her recollection of the caves Hartigan transformed the animals," explains Mattison. "Whereas the creatures depicted in Lascaux are characterized by their animation . . . Hartigan's animals are at rest. The mood in her work is restrained, quiet, and contemplative in a way that the paintings on the cave walls are not."

After her husband's death in 1981, Hartigan suffered a deep depression and succumbed to an increasing dependence on alcohol that had begun during the difficult '70s. In 1982, she entered Johns Hopkins Medical Center, where she underwent treatment and subsequently joined Alcoholics Anonymous. Hartigan's recovery was followed by a vigorous return to life and to her art. *Eastern Avenue Florist*, her first painting after leaving the hospital, is referred to by Mattison as her "resurrection painting," executed in a thin wash that "glows like stained glass and seems about to dissolve before the viewer's eyes." Coinciding with Hartigan's personal renewal came renewed public interest. Exhibitions of her work appeared more frequently, including solo shows at the Baltimore Museum of Art (1980), the Fort Wayne (Indiana) Museum of Art (1981), and American University, Washington, D.C. (1987). Hartigan was also included in two important surveys of painting of the 1950s, organized by the Newport Harbor Art Museum, Newport Harbor Beach, California: *Action/Precision: The New Direction in New York, 1955–60* (1984) and *The Figurative Fifties: New York Figurative Expressionism* (1988).

Many of Hartigan's later works harken back to the figurative painting of the 1950s and utilize a variety of tools, from Japanese brushes to wool mitts, to sticks, and even, on occasion, to her own hands and feet. Her subjects included a watercolor series "Saints and Martyrs" (inspired by the illustrations of 12th-century Catalan frescoes), a "Great Queens and Empresses" series (***Joséphine**, ***Elizabeth I**, ***Theodora**), and a group of Renaissance paintings (*Renaissance Woman*, *Lady Gathering Pomegranates*, *Renaissance Card Game*, *Crowning of the Poet*, *Bacchus*, and *Visions of Heaven and Hell*).

In the late 1980s, Hartigan made another foray into Modernism with her "American Places" series, a group of ten large canvases begun in 1986. One of these, *Malibu*, a seven-foot square oil painting inspired by a trip to California the previous year, is Pollockesque. Hartigan took the finished painting from the wall, placed it on the floor, and poured paint over the images. Compelled to be closer to it, she then walked onto it, pushing the paint around with her hands and feet. Working in this manner, she said, brought back to mind Pollock's statement: "When I am in my painting. . . I see what I have been about." Mattison calls the painting "elemental" and "somewhat mad." He further describes it as "the very essence of sand, sea, sun, and bodies—a breakthrough painting of this period." Other California-inspired paintings in the group include *Tarzana* (1987) and *Madonna Inn* (1987). The "Places" series also includes the later works: *Casino* (1987) is an expressionistic work inspired by the compulsive gambling that Hartigan observed in Atlantic City; *Chicago* (1988) includes images of some of her favorite performers; and *West Broadway* brings the artist full circle to the city of her artistic birth.

In 1989, as he finished his biography on Grace Hartigan, Robert Mattison set to wondering what he might find when he next visited her, for it seemed clear to him that as long as life engaged her, Hartigan would continue to evolve as an artist. "Somehow, in painting I try to make some logic out of the world that has been given to me in chaos," the artist once said. "I have a very pretentious idea that I want to make life, I want to make sense out of it. The fact that I am doomed to failure—that doesn't deter me in the least."

SOURCES:

Baigell, Matthew. *Dictionary of American Art*. NY: Harper & Row, 1979.

Mattison, Robert Saltonstall. *Grace Hartigan: A Painter's World*. NY: Hudson Hills Press, 1990.

Moritz, Charles, ed. *Current Biography*. NY: H.W. Wilson, 1962.

Naylor, Colin, ed. *Contemporary Artists*. Chicago, IL: St. James Press, 1989.

Rubinstein, Charlotte Streifer. *American Women Artists*. Boston, MA: G.K. Hall, 1982.

Barbara Morgan,
Melrose, Massachusetts

Hartwig, Julia (1921—)

Polish poet, essayist and translator who emerged as a powerful literary voice in the late 1960s. *Born in Lublin, Poland, on August 14, 1921; married Artur Adam Miedzyrzecki (a writer and critic, b. 1922).*

Julia Hartwig, born in Lublin in 1921, grew up between two world wars in a politically and economically unstable Poland, surrounded by a culture in which literature played a key role in defining the national spirit. Hartwig survived the terrors of World War II, during which she was a student in one of Warsaw's "flying" (i.e., underground and illegal) universities which was affiliated with the resistance movement. The immediate postwar years in Poland were scarcely easier to live through, and Hartwig and the overwhelming majority of the population suffered from both physical privations and the arbitrary repressiveness of a Stalinist regime subservient to the Soviet Union. At the same time, she worked to perfect her craft as a writer, observing, reading, and taking risks by publishing in a literary environment that was hypercritical and unsettled. As a student at the University of Warsaw, she studied Polish philology and philosophy. Also active in writers' organizations, she joined the Polish Writers' Union in 1945.

In 1967, Hartwig published her first collection of poems, *Wolne rece* (Unconstrained Hands). This volume was followed by several more works which culminated in both a selection of poems published in 1981 from various phases of her writing career and a poetry anthology published two years later. Although only a small selection of her verse has appeared in English translation (1991), non-Polish critics consider Hartwig to be a major contemporary poet in Poland, worthy of comparison to ***Wislawa Szymborska**, the Nobel Prize laureate. Hartwig came to full artistic maturity in late middle age, and her major book of the 1980s, the 1987 verse collection *Obcowanie* (Relations), was viewed by critics as a significant artistic and spiritual breakthrough.

Rochelle Stone, writing in *World Literature Today,* notes that Hartwig describes the most fundamental aspects of life and living in her poetry through "calm, simple and concise language." A philosophically grounded writer who is also alert to mundane realities, she has written of daily existence in works like "What does one hear in the kitchen?" and "Portrait I, II, III" (of a cow). Hartwig's poems have been characterized as "paintings in words, saturated with color, filled with light and space," and she has been noted for an ability to portray emotional states without using symbol or allegory.

Julia Hartwig and her husband, writer and critic Artur Adam Miedzyrzecki, have both been active in organized literary life in Poland since the end of the Stalinist regime in 1956. Starting in that year, she became an active member of the Polish PEN Club, greeting foreign literary visitors and promoting international cultural exchanges. Her travel to France resulted in a number of books and articles on French writers, including Gerard de Nerval, Max Jacob, and Guillaume Apollinaire. A visit to the United States resulted in *Dzienik Amerykanski* (American Journal), a book published in 1980. With the demise of Communism in Poland in 1989, Hartwig became a leading personality of a reborn Polish Writers' Association and, in 1990, was an active member of the election committee of Tadeusz Mazowiecki. In November 1993, concerned about Poland's difficulty in achieving a balanced perspective about the Holocaust that had taken place on its soil, she maintained that books would continue to serve as important tools for remembering "the period of extermination, about which everyone would like to forget but about which no one is allowed to forget." A major poet, Julia Hartwig enjoys universal respect as one of Poland's most renowned literary artists.

SOURCES:

Baranczak, Stanislaw, and Clare Cavanagh, eds. *Polish Poetry of the Last Two Decades of Communist Rule: Spoiling the Cannibals' Fun.* Evanston, IL: Northwestern University Press, 1991.

Hartwig, Julia. *Apollinaire.* Translated by Jean-Yves Erhel. Paris: Mercure de France, 1972.

"Promotional Evening of Books Related to Holocaust Held in Warsaw," in *PAP News Wire.* November 16, 1993.

Pynsent, Robert, and S.I. Kanikova, eds. *Reader's Encyclopedia of Eastern European Literature.* NY: HarperCollins, 1993.

Stone, Rochelle. Review of *Chwila postoju* (Cracow: Wydawnictwo Literackie, 1981), in *World Literature Today.* Vol. 56, no. 4, 1982, p. 720.

John Haag,
Associate Professor of History,
University of Georgia, Athens, Georgia

Haruko (1850–1914)

Empress of Japan. *Name variations: Princess Haru; Princess Haruko; Shōken Kōtaigō; Empress Dowager Shōken; Meiji empress. Born Ichijō Haruko on May 28, 1850; died of Bright's disease at the Numadzu Palace on April 9, 1914; third daughter of Prince Ichijō Tadaka (a Kuge or noble attached to the imperial court and a member of the house of Fujiwara); married Mutsuhito (1852–1912, son of Emperor Komei), emperor of Japan (r. 1867–1912), on February 9, 1869 (died, July 29, 1912); children: none, but she adopted the son of a secondary wife of Mutsuhito, Yoshihito Haru-no-miya (1879–1926, who, as Emperor Taisho, reigned as emperor of Japan, r. 1912–1926), and also adopted four daughters.*

Princess Haruko was the third daughter of Prince Ichijō Tadaka, a noble attached to the imperial court and a member of the house of Fujiwara. At the time of her birth in 1850, the

Japanese were forbidden to leave their country, and foreigners were not allowed to enter. In 1869, Haruko married Mutsuhito, two years after he had succeeded his father as emperor of Japan, and four months after his coronation. Mutsuhito encouraged, and became the symbol for, the dramatic transformation of Japan from a feudal closed society into one of the great powers of the modern world. Empress Haruko, a beautiful and elegant woman, was as "advanced and intuitive in meeting the new order of things as Mutsuhito himself," writes Japanese historian Douglas Sladen. She did not have shaven eyebrows and blackened teeth like her predecessors and often wore Western dress at court occasions. Haruko appeared in public, loved art and literature, wrote poetry, and was a generous patron of female education, the Red Cross Society, and other philanthropic enterprises. By her example, she raised the status of women in Japan. Soon after her husband's death on July 29, 1912, Haruko became ill. She died 20 months later.

Ethel Browne Harvey

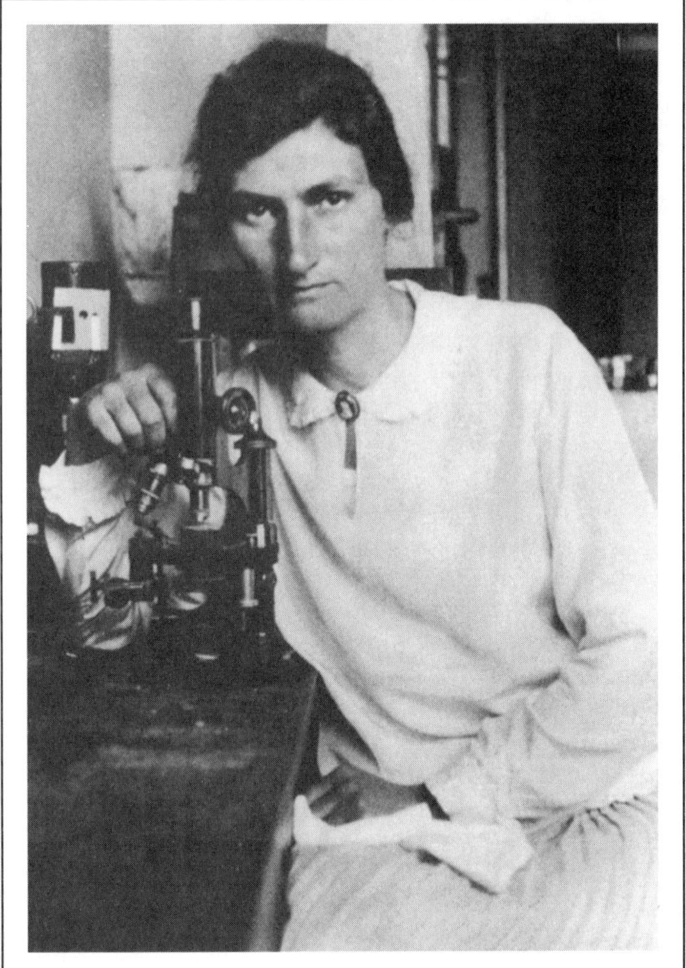

SOURCES:

Sladen, Douglas. *Queer Things about Japan.* London: Kegan Paul, 1913.

Harvey, Ethel Browne (1885–1965)

American cell biologist and embryologist recognized for her work on cell division in the eggs of sea urchins. *Name variations: Ethel Browne. Born Ethel Browne in Baltimore, Maryland, in 1885; died in Falmouth, Massachusetts, in 1965; the youngest of two sons and three daughters of Bennet Bernard Browne (a physician) and Jennie (Nicholson) Browne; attended Bryn Mawr Preparatory School; Woman's College of Baltimore (later renamed Goucher College), A.B.; Columbia University, A.M., 1907, Ph.D., 1913; married Edmund Newton Harvey (a biology professor), in 1916; children: Edmund Newton Harvey, Jr. (b. 1916); Richard Bennet Harvey (b. 1922).*

Destined to become a pioneering scientist recognized for her work on cell division in the eggs of sea urchins, Ethel Browne Harvey was born in Baltimore, Maryland, in 1885, and raised in a progressive family that championed professional careers for women. She was the daughter of **Jennie Nicholson Browne** and Bennet Browne, a successful Baltimore obstetrician-gynecologist and a professor of gynecology at the Woman's Medical College of Baltimore. Both of her sisters, **Mary Nicholson Browne** and **Jennie Browne**, became physicians. Ethel was educated at Bryn Mawr School and the Woman's College of Baltimore and, in 1906, entered Columbia University for doctoral study in cell biology, supporting herself by teaching high school science and math and by working as a lab assistant. In 1909, while still a predoctoral fellow, she published a paper entitled "The Production of New Hydranths in Hydra by the Insertion of Small Grafts," a culmination of her experiments in inducing the formation of new hydra (a freshwater polyp) in the body column of another hydra through a process of grafting. The hydra experiment, though groundbreaking, went unnoticed, and Ethel received her Ph.D. in 1913, writing her thesis on male germ cells of the aquatic carnivorous insect genus *Notonecta.*

In 1916, Ethel married Edmund Newton Harvey, a Princeton biology professor, and started a family. Giving birth to a son in 1916 and another in 1922, she placed them in the care of nurses and governesses so she could continue her work. She conducted research in the United States and abroad, working in laboratories as far away as Japan. Aside from a three-year post at

New York University as an instructor in biology (1928–31), she spent most of her career at Princeton, where she received neither title nor compensation, and was forced to share laboratory space. During summers, she worked out of an office shared with her husband at the Woods Hole Marine Biology Laboratory on Cape Cod.

During her career, Harvey published over 100 papers, the best-known of which is "Parthenogenetic Merogony of Cleavage without Nuclei in *Arbacia punctulata*," a complex treatise published in *Biological Bulletin* (1936), documenting her experiments with cell division in sea urchin eggs. Although it was believed at the time that the cell nucleus was generally the part of a cell that "directed" cell division and embryo development, Harvey discovered that the nuclei could be removed from the cells, yet continue to divide. Further, when placed in a solution of concentrated sea water, the nuclei-free cells would live up to a month. Based on these finding, Harvey further hypothesized that cell division might be controlled by parts of the cell other than the nucleus. Her discoveries gained public recognition in late 1937, with articles on her findings appearing in the popular journals *Time, Life,* and *Newsweek.*

Ethel Harvey worked well into her 70s, and in her later years earned many honors for her scientific contributions. She was made a trustee of the Woods Hole Laboratory and was elected a fellow of the American Association for the Advancement of Science and the New York Academy of Science. Ethel Harvey died in 1965, after suffering an acute attack of appendicitis.

SOURCES:

Bailey, Brooke. *The Remarkable Lives of 100 Women Healers & Scientists.* Holbrook, MA: Bob Adams, 1994.

Sicherman, Barbara, and Carol Hurd Green, ed. *Notable American Women: The Modern Period.* Cambridge, MA: The Belknap Press of Harvard University Press, 1980.

COLLECTIONS:

Ethel Harvey's papers are at the Maine Biological Laboratory Library in Woods Hole, Massachusetts.

Barbara Morgan,
Melrose, Massachusetts

Harvey, Lilian (1906–1968)

British-born German motion-picture actress who was Germany's most popular film star in the early 1930s.

Born Lilian Muriel Helen Pape on January 19, 1906, in Muswell-Hill, England; died in Cap d'Antibes, France, on July 27, 1968; daughter of Walter Bruno Pape; married Valeur Larsen, in 1953.

In a poll of its readers conducted by the German movie journal *Licht-Bild-Bühne* a few weeks before Adolf Hitler became German chancellor in January 1933, the female film actress chosen as the number one star was neither ***Marlene Dietrich** nor ***Greta Garbo**, but British-born Lilian Harvey. The trilingual Harvey starred in French, British, and American films, as well as German ones, and for some years was Germany's closest equivalent to an international star. She was born Lilian Muriel Pape in a suburb of London in 1906. The daughter of a German father and British mother, Lilian was eight when her family moved to Germany. Within months, World War I began, and the country was thrown into turmoil, but her parents were able to remove her from danger by sending her to Switzerland where she attended school in Solothurn. At war's end, Lilian returned to Berlin. There, she studied dance with a noted teacher, **Mary Zimmermann**, and by age 16 had joined a Viennese dance company. Lilian toured the major cities of Germany as well as Budapest, Prague, and Vienna. There, she caught the eye of film director Richard Eichberg, who cast her in her debut film, *Der Fluch* (*The Curse*), in 1925. The film's success led to 11 more leading roles in Vienna for Lilian Harvey—her film name—over the next several years.

By 1926, when she appeared opposite Willy Fritsch (1901–1973) in the filmed operetta *Die keusche Susanne* (*Chaste Susanne*), Harvey had become famous in German-speaking Central Europe. But it was with the appearance of talkies in the late 1920s that she was rapidly able to assert herself as an international screen star. Completely trilingual, she made French- and English-language versions of her films after she had completed her German original. In 1932, the readers of the French magazine *Pour Vous* voted her the most popular non-French actress. Thus it was scarcely a surprise to international audiences when she co-starred with Charles Boyer and Laurence Olivier in the respective French and British versions of an originally German film. With her doll-like features and her ability to sing and dance, she was invariably cast as the flirtatious but basically virtuous girl next door, the kind of young woman whom millions of middle-class mothers regarded as the ideal daughter-in-law.

In 1930, Harvey became a superstar by appearing in *Liebeswalzer* (*Waltz of Love*), once again courted by Willy Fritsch (in all, she would make 14 films with Fritsch), who serenaded her with "Du bist das süsseste Mädel der Welt" ("You are the sweetest girl in the world"). In the British version of this international hit, filmed the same year, she appeared opposite John Batten. Offering pure escapism to a troubled world, *Liebeswalzer* was a worldwide hit in the first full year of world economic depression, taking people's minds off their woes for an hour or two. Even in Japan, audiences packed theaters in Tokyo and elsewhere to hear, "You are the sweetest geisha in the world." Lilian Harvey possessed the indefinable qualities of a major star even though London's *Times* noted in 1974 that her "appeal (and perhaps this is its potency) is elusive of definition. She danced moderately, sang rather plaintively, acted to the best of her small strength. Her face was rather bony and angular, so that she could look quite old and plain if she were not sympathetically lit."

The year 1930 brought an even greater hit for Harvey when she appeared in *Die drei von der Tankstelle* (*The Three from the Filling Station*). This escapist operetta, which was also released in a French version, once again paired Harvey and Fritsch as the innocent lovebirds. The story reflects the rapidly advancing Depression by telling the tale of three penniless young people whose lives are sustained on hope for a better future. In 1931, Harvey and Fritsch starred in *Der Kongress tanzt* (*The Congress Dances*), a film operetta set in Vienna in 1815 at the time of the Congress of Vienna. Instead of investigating the complexities of international diplomacy, the film focuses on Harvey as a modest little glove-maker dazzled by Tsar Alexander I of Russia. She delighted her audiences by singing the waltz tune "Das gibt's nur einmal, das kommt nie wieder" ("This only happens once in a lifetime, and never again") as her carriage slowly made its way through the narrow streets of Old Vienna.

As Germany's most popular film actress, Harvey almost inevitably was beckoned by Hollywood. Between 1933 and 1935, she starred in four Hollywood films, receiving mostly positive reviews, though the films themselves were of less than stellar quality. By 1935, when she appeared in *Let's Live Tonight,* she had decided that it would be prudent to return to Europe. Besides the rather mediocre screenplays of her American films, she doubtless took notice of the stiff competition in Hollywood which included several blondes who were at least as attractive and talented, stars such as ***Jean Harlow**, ***Carole Lombard**, and ***Ginger Rogers**. After making the film *Invitation to the Waltz* in England in 1935, Harvey returned to Germany that same year.

Much had happened in Germany during Harvey's two-year absence. The Nazi dictatorship which now controlled the country boasted that it would exist for the next thousand years. Many of Harvey's colleagues in the German motion-picture industry, including Erich Pommer and Wilhelm Thiele, who had produced and directed several of her most successful films, had fled the country because they were Jewish. The entire intellectual and artistic life of Germany was now in the hands of Minister of Propaganda and Public Enlightenment Joseph Goebbels. Many in Germany felt vindicated when Harvey "returned home" from a "racially polluted" Hollywood. Harvey, who had little knowledge of or interest in political matters, discovered that far fewer musicals were now being made, and while many films appeared on the surface to be devoid of political content that was not often the case.

In the first film made after her return, *Schwarze Rosen* (*Black Roses*), a number of attractive musical selections were interspersed with an anti-Communist tale of the Finnish struggle against the oppressions of both Tsarist and Bolshevik Russia. Many of the film's viewers yearned for the days when a Lilian Harvey film meant music and dancing, and were delighted with her 1936 film *Glückskinder* (*Lucky Kids*), a frothy concoction directed by her real-life lover, Hungarian-born Paul Martin. This comedy, in which Harvey is once more paired with Fritsch, is set in New York City, and its mood is zanily escapist, seeming to prove that Goebbels kept his word when he noted in May 1933 that "one mustn't deal in ideology [*Gesinnung*] from dawn to dusk." Much of the film was plagiarized from Hollywood (including plot segments from *It Happened One Night*), but it pleased the film critics, including the Nazi Party's chief organ, the *Völkischer Beobachter,* which reported in September 1936 that "One hasn't been so amused in the Gloria-Palast for ages." The Berlin correspondent of the American entertainment journal *Variety* reported positively on the UFA Studios' "first serious attempt to go Broadway. . . . The film looks to be a smash." In his *Ministry of Illusion: Nazi Cinema and Its Afterlife,* Eric Rentschler has characterized *Glückskinder* as a mass entertainment commodity made in Nazi Germany that "replicated a Hollywood film in a Babelsberg studio set, imitating a generic pleasure made in a foreign dream factory, in effect creating the illusion of an already illusory world, raising artifice to a higher power by frankly admitting its own derivation and desire."

By 1937, when Harvey starred in the film **Fanny Elssler,* her youthful beauty had started to fade, but she was determined to sparkle in a

lavish production that presented a highly romanticized version of early 19th-century Central European history. In this fairy-tale version of the life of Vienna's reigning ballerina superstar, Elssler is assigned by Prince Metternich to keep an eye on Napoleon's son, the Duke of Reichstadt, with whom she falls in love. After the failure of his political schemes, the duke dies, and Fanny goes on to a fabled stage career. *Fanny Elssler* was by far the most lavish of Harvey's film vehicles, boasting six beautifully choreographed and opulently staged production numbers, with a *corps de ballet* of almost 150 dancers. Another 1937 film, *Sieben Ohrfeigen* (*Seven Slaps*), continues the successful formula of Harvey and Fritsch, with pleasant songs and dances, a light-as-air plot, and a "they-lived-happily-ever-after" ending.

In her 1938 film *Capriccio,* Harvey retains some of her traditional "fairy-like" persona while taking on a *Hosenrolle,* a pants role. Harvey's cross-dressing performance allows her to include what Antje Ascheid has described as "an astoundingly liberal array of parodic references." Although *Capriccio* was released in the fifth year of the Nazi dictatorship, the outfits worn by its lead actress link this film to the liberal-minded Weimar Republic, when it was common to see women wearing men's clothing. Besides revealing many touches of Hollywood style, *Capriccio* also exploited for comedic effect several allusions to lesbian themes (in one scene, critically appraising the "girls" in a bordello, she chooses them all).

After shooting a 1938 film in Italy, *Castelli in aria* (*Castles in the Air*), which was poorly received, Harvey returned to Germany in 1939 to make what would turn out to be her last film in Nazi Germany. In *Frau am Steuer* (*Woman at the Wheel*), she is once again partnered with Fritsch, but this time the dream couple no longer displays a tenderly romantic relationship. In a socially reactionary and misogynistic Nazi German version of the Hollywood comedy of remarriage, Fritsch and Harvey are involved in a fierce power struggle that ends in defeat. Realizing that the film's script called for her to play an unsympathetic role, one that in fact heralded her demise as a romantic heroine, Harvey at first resisted performing in *Frau am Steuer.* But after her employer, the powerful UFA Studios, threatened a penalty of 1.5 million reichsmarks if she did not honor her contract, she felt she had little choice but to proceed. In this film, Harvey found herself transformed against her will into a strident career woman humbled and "made small" by Willy Fritsch, now decreed by German fascist ideology to be her naturally dominant partner.

Lilian Harvey went to Paris on the eve of World War II, hoping to rekindle her career. She had long been a star in France, a country where the eminent composer Charles Koechlin (1867–1950) composed two albums of piano music in her honor and named a movement of his Seven Stars Symphony for her. In order to finance two films, *Sérénade* and *Miquette* (both released in 1940 and not successful), she went into debt by selling her jewels and her lavish castle in Tetélen, Hungary.

When Germany conquered France in June 1940, Harvey fled to Spain and then to South America. Eventually she appeared in Los Angeles, believing that she could resume her film career there. But she received no offers and eventually accepted a job as a nurse. Fortunately, her old friend Noël Coward heard about her plight and offered her a leading role in his comedy *Blithe Spirit,* which enabled her to appear on stage for several months. In 1951, six years after the war, Harvey returned to Germany, but the aging star was unable to make a comeback. Willy Fritsch and others, including female film stars like ***Zarah Leander** and ***Kristina Söderbaum,** were able to reignite their careers after 1945. But Lilian Harvey was not so lucky. Considered a has-been, she began to live in a world of denial, and a brief marriage in 1953 to Danish impresario Valeur Larsen failed after little more than a year.

In 1960, the Berlin Film Festival gave a tribute to the stars of the old UFA Studios. Convinced she was still a star, Harvey insisted that she would attend the event only if contemporary stars like ***Maria Schell** and ***Romy Schneider** also attended, to avoid creating the impression that her career was in the past. Although the new stars did not appear, Harvey attended nevertheless, and the magazine *Stern* reproduced a photo of an aging Harvey, swirling around in a ballerina gown from her 1937 UFA film *Fanny Elssler.* The image recalled ***Gloria Swanson** in the role of Norma Desmond in the 1950 classic *Sunset Boulevard.* Retiring to the French Riviera, Harvey returned a final time to Germany in the 1960s for appearances in small theater productions. She died at her villa, "Asmodée," at Cap d'Antibes, France, on July 27, 1968, having been affectionately cared for during her last days by an old friend, the famed dancer Serge Lifar.

SOURCES:

Ascheid, Antje. "Nazi Stardom and the 'Modern Girl': The Case of Lilian Harvey," in *New German Critique.* No. 74. Spring–Summer, 1998, pp. 57–89.

Belach, Helga, ed. *Wir tanzen um die Welt: Deutsche Revuefilme 1933–1945.* Munich and Vienna: Hanser Verlag, 1979.

Borgelt, Hans. *Das süsseste Mädel der Welt: Die Lilian-Harvey-Story.* Munich: Heyne Verlag, 1976.

Cziffra, Geza von. *Es war eine rauschende Ballnacht: Eine Sittengeschichte des deutschen Films.* Frankfurt am Main: Ullstein Verlag, 1987.

Habich, Christiane, ed. *Lilian Harvey.* Berlin: Haude & Spener Verlag, 1990.

"The Harvey Girl," in *The Times [London].* July 16, 1974, p. 7.

Harvey, Lilian. "Wiedergeburt des romantischen Films," in *Tages-Post* [Linz, Austria]. June 13, 1932.

Kreimeier, Klaus. *The Ufa Story: A History of Germany's Greatest Film Company 1918–1945.* NY: Hill and Wang, 1996.

Rentschler, Eric. *The Ministry of Illusion: Nazi Cinema and Its Afterlife.* Cambridge, MA: Harvard University Press, 1996.

Romani, Cinzia. *Tainted Goddesses: Female Film Stars of the Third Reich.* Translated by Robert Connolly. NY: Sarpedon, 1992.

Traudisch, Dora. *Mutterschaft mit Zuckerguss?: Frauenfeindliche Propaganda im NS-Spielfilm.* Pfaffenweiler: Centaurus Verlag, 1993.

Witte, Karsten. "The Indivisible Legacy of Nazi Cinema," in *New German Critique.* No. 74. Spring–Summer, 1998, pp. 23–30.

———. "Too Beautiful to Be True: Lilian Harvey," in *New German Critique.* No. 74. Spring–Summer, 1998, pp. 37–39.

Wulf, Josef. *Theater und Film im Dritten Reich: Eine Dokumentation.* Frankfurt am Main: Ullstein Verlag, 1989.

RELATED MEDIA:

Koechlin, Charles. *L'album de Lilian: deuxieme serie, Op. 149.* Paris: M. Eschig, 1986.

———. *L'album de Lilian: premiere série, Op. 139* (*oeuvre posthume*). Paris: M. Eschig, 1985.

———. *The Seven Stars Symphony, Op. 132.* [La Voix de Son Maitre LP ASD 1731391].

John Haag,
Associate Professor of History,
University of Georgia, Athens, Georgia

Hasbrouck, Lydia Sayer

(1827–1910)

American editor and reformer who was the first American woman to hold elected office. *Born Lydia Sayer on December 20, 1827, in Warwick, New York; died on August 24, 1910, in Middletown, New York; daughter of Benjamin and Rebecca (Forshee) Sayer; attended*

Elmira High School and Central College; married John Whitbeck Hasbrouck, July 1856; children: Daisy (1857–1859); Sayer (b. 1860); Burt (b. 1862).

Lydia Sayer, born on December 20, 1827, in Warwick, New York, was the fifth of eight children of a prosperous farmer and distiller of apple brandy and a descendent of Thomas Sayre, an original settler of Southampton, Long Island. From early childhood, she displayed a fierce independence that would characterize the remainder of her life. For example, she started wearing knee-length skirts and pantaloons, then popularly known as "Bloomers," in 1849, eschewing the cumbersome and uncomfortable traditional dress of the times. But what began as an issue of comfort soon flared into a larger issue of women's rights when she was refused admittance to Seward Seminary in Florida, New York, because of her unconventional outfits.

In 1856, the editor and publisher of the Middletown *Whig Press*, John Whitbeck Hasbrouck, invited her to participate in a lecture tour about dress reform and soon established a feminist periodical, *Sibyl*, for her. She became its editor. The first edition appeared on July 1, 1856, and on July 27, Sayer and Hasbrouck were married. (Hasbrouck and her husband would have three children, Daisy, Sayer and Burt. Daisy would die in 1859 at the age of two.) Published biweekly until 1861, *Sibyl* then became a monthly periodical. It was considered, more than anything else, a dress-reform organ, providing information on the National Dress Reform Association, of which Hasbrouck served as president from 1863 to 1864. The goal of *Sibyl* was to emphasize the superiority of reform clothing over the normal dress of the day. Under her direction, the periodical was extremely personal, and included information on her family's health, the state of the agricultural endeavors at the family farm, and in-depth editorials on "hygeopathy," which advocated a lifestyle of good eating, exercise, fresh air and frequent baths.

Hasbrouck championed medical training for women, increased educational opportunities, and women's suffrage. When she refused to pay taxes on the grounds that she was not allowed to vote, Hasbrouck found herself in the midst of a tax struggle. A tax collector managed to steal a Bloomer outfit from her home and advertised it for sale to cover the taxes. When an editorial in *Sibyl* denounced him as a "vulgar sneak," he was apparently shamed into dropping the issue. Hasbrouck, however, continued to fight against unfair taxation. In 1863, she declined to pay a road tax and had to work for several days on a highway repair project.

As time progressed, *Sibyl* lost momentum, and the final issue appeared in June of 1864. Hasbrouck continued to help her husband edit his newspaper until 1868 when it was sold. The couple worked in reform journalism for a brief time with a periodical entitled the *Liberal Sentinel*. In 1880, New York enacted a law permitting women to vote for and hold school offices and Hasbrouck was elected to the Middletown board of education, becoming the first American woman to hold an elected office. By the mid-1880s, she was working in real estate and played a prominent role in establishing a block of stores and offices in downtown Middletown. On August 24, 1910, Hasbrouck died in Middletown of paresis and was buried in Warwick.

SOURCES:

James, Edward T., ed. *Notable American Women, 1607–1950*. Cambridge, MA: The Belknap Press of Harvard University Press, 1971.

McHenry, Robert, ed. *Famous American Women*. NY: Dover, 1983.

Judith C. Reveal,
freelance writer, Greensboro, Maryland

Hashepsowe (c. 1515–1468 BCE).

See Hatshepsut.

Haskil, Clara (1895–1960)

Rumanian pianist known for her recordings with some of the 20th century's best instrumentalists. *Born in Bucharest, Rumania, on January 7, 1895; died in Brussels, Belgium, on December 7, 1960; studied in Vienna with Ernst von Dohnanyi; studied at the Paris Conservatory with Alfred Cortot; studied in Berlin with Ferruccio Busoni.*

A child prodigy, pianist Clara Haskil made her debut in Bucharest at the age of nine, and then went on to study in Vienna and at the Paris Conservatory, where, at 14, she won the *premier prix*. During her concert career, which began in 1910, she played with a number of renowned artists, including violinist Georges Enesco, pianist Théophile Ysaÿe, and cellist Pablo Casals, and also soloed with major symphony orchestras throughout Europe and America. Haskil was known as a superb chamber-music performer. Though she was limited in power by her small stature and also plagued by a muscular deficiency which forced her to schedule her concerts around periods of remission, her pianism has been said to have radiated humanity and in-

Clara Haskil

telligence, and her profound musicianship and determined spirit more than compensated for her physical limitations. Haskil made a number of recordings that are still regarded by many to be highly authoritative readings, particularly of key works of Beethoven, Chopin, Mozart, and Schubert. Considered particularly fine are those she made with Belgian violinist Arthur Grumiaux. The pianist died in an accident in Brussels in 1960. A piano competition is held annually in her memory in Geneva, Switzerland.

Haslam, Anna (1829–1922)

Irish feminist who campaigned on many women's issues and founded the first women's suffrage society in Dublin (1876). *Born Anna Maria Fisher in Youghal, County Cork, Ireland, in April 1829; died in November 1922; daughter of Abraham Fisher (a corn miller) and Jane (Moore) Fisher; educated at Newtown School, Waterford, and the Quaker School, Ackworth, Yorkshire; married Thomas Haslam, in 1854 (died 1917); no children.*

Was a founder member of the Irish Society for the Training and Employment of Educated Women (1861); campaigned for the repeal of the Contagious Diseases Acts (1869–86); was a founder member of the Association of Schoolmistresses and Other Ladies Interested in Irish Education (1882); founded the Dublin Women's Suffrage Association, later the Irish Women's Suffrage and Local Government Association (1876), of which she was secretary (1876–1913) and life-president (1913–22).

The general election of November 1918, the first in which women in Great Britain and Ireland were entitled to vote, found Ireland in a state of political conflict and even suffragists divided on a number of issues. Nevertheless, on Election Day, all differences were forgotten. As the suffrage paper, *Irish Citizen*, noted:

> The League was represented with its banners and colours at joint demonstrations organised by the various suffrage and women's organisations for Mrs Haslam, the veteran Irish suffrage leader. She recorded her vote in the midst of an admiring feminine throng

to cheer her, was presented with a bouquet in suffrage colours for the occasion. . . . It speaks well for the broadmindedness of the new women voters that the women of all parties joined heartily to honour Mrs Haslam and suffrage.

It was the fitting culmination of a career spanning well over half a century, which had been dedicated to the betterment of women's condition. Born in 1829 into a middle-class Quaker family in Youghal, the young Anna Maria Fisher became aware at an early age of her responsibility towards her fellow citizens. Her parents were involved in a variety of reforming and philanthropic causes, and Anna took part in relief efforts during the Great Famine of 1845–49. As Friends, the Fishers placed a high value on education for both girls and boys, and Anna went first to the Quaker Newtown School, and then to the Quaker School at Ackworth in Yorkshire.

In 1853, she met Thomas Haslam, a fellow Irish Quaker, whom she married in the following year. The couple settled in Dublin, where Anna ran a stationer's shop and quickly became involved in a number of organizations campaigning for improved educational and employment opportunities for women. Thomas was as committed a feminist as his wife, and the support which he provided was essential to her activities. As she admitted late in life, she "could never have undertaken what she did in later years if it were not for his sympathy and help."

By the 1870s, Anna Haslam was a leading figure not only in efforts to improve female access to education and employment, but also in campaigns to achieve property rights for married women, and for the repeal of the Contagious Diseases Acts, which provided for the compulsory medical examination of any woman suspected of prostitution. As Haslam remarked wryly of this particular battle, "When it began, I remember one old friend saying, it was such an obviously just demand, that . . . it could not be possible that such things should endure more than a few months. It took us eighteen years."

Underlying the various injustices to which women were subject was their lack of a political voice. The first female suffrage petition submitted to the House of Commons in 1866 had 1,499 signatories, including 15 Irishwomen, among them Anna Haslam. In 1870, the first public suffrage meeting was held in Dublin, followed over the next few years by others throughout the country, and in February 1876 Haslam established the Dublin Women's Suffrage Association (DWSA), the first permanent suffrage society in Ireland, and only the third in the British Isles.

Over the next 20 years, the DWSA devoted itself to a policy of education and persuasion. Meetings were organized, signatures were collected for a series of parliamentary petitions, suffrage literature was distributed, and letters were sent to members of Parliament and to newspapers to solicit support for suffrage bills coming before Parliament. Initially the DWSA's growth was slow: in 1896, it had only 44 members. In that year, however, the movement gained its first victory, when women were permitted to stand for election as poor law guardians. In 1898, women achieved the local government franchise on the same terms as men, a move which Haslam hailed as "the most signal political revolution that has taken place in the history of Irishwomen."

The parliamentary vote, however, remained elusive. A number of younger members of Haslam's association (now renamed the Irish Women's Suffrage and Local Government Association, IWSLGA) were impatient with the slow progress made so far and, in 1908, broke away to form the militant Irish Women's Franchise League. Haslam, while disapproving of violence, nevertheless retained her links with the dissidents, and while her own association maintained its constitutional stance, she recognized that the militants could sometimes achieve what more peaceful means could not.

Although she resigned as secretary of the IWSLGA in 1913, Haslam continued to be active in the suffrage movement and on other women's issues. Her husband Thomas died in 1917, but she survived to witness the 1918 Representation of the People Act which offered limited female suffrage, and to vote in the General Election of that year. Before her death in 1922, at age 93, Haslam was conscious that the victory to which she had contributed so much was only the beginning of women's struggle for equality, but she was confident, too, that it was absolutely vital to any further advance. As she had told the International Suffrage Congress in 1908, "our parliamentary enfranchisement is only the first step . . . but it is the first, and the *most indispensable* to the realisation of the rest."

SOURCES:

Cullen, Mary, "Anna Maria Haslam," in *Women, Power and Consciousness in 19th-century Ireland.* Edited by Mary Cullen and Maria Luddy. Dublin: Attic Press, 1995, pp 161–196.

Cullen Owens, Rosemary. *Smashing Times.* Dublin: Attic Press, 1984.

Rosemary Raughter,
freelance writer in women's history, Dublin, Ireland

Haslett, Caroline (1895–1957)

British engineer and founder of the Women's Engineering Society. *Name variations: Dame Caroline Haslett. Born Caroline Haslett on August 17, 1895, in Sussex, England; died on January 4, 1957; the eldest daughter of Robert Haslett (a railroad engineer) and Caroline Sarah (Holmes) Haslett; attended Haywards Heath High School, Sussex; never married; no children.*

Caroline Haslett, a leader in opening the engineering industry to British women, was born in Sussex, England, in 1895, and raised in a modest though progressive home in Sussex. She left high school at the outbreak of World War I to take a clerical post in a boiler company, and while there decided to become an engineer. Requesting a transfer from the office to the plant, Haslett worked for the next five years to qualify first as a general, then as an electrical, engineer.

In 1919, Haslett became the secretary of the newly formed Women's Engineering Society, founded to encourage the "establishment of highly trained women in engineering." In addition to persuading employers that women had the aptitude to train for light engineering work, Haslett assured engineering institutions that much was to be gained by allowing women to join their ranks. She also founded and edited the society's journal *The Woman Engineer*. In 1924, when the society founded the Electrical Association for Women, Haslett became its director and editor of its organ *Electrical Age*. In addition to working to expand educational opportunities for women in the field, Haslett increased her efforts to educate housewives in the advantages of electrical devices, and to encourage manufacturers to produce products for the home. By 1956, when Haslett left her post, the Electrical Association had grown from a one-room office to an organization with 90 branches and over 10,000 members.

Caroline Haslett

During World War II, Haslett advised the British Ministry of Labor on women's training for industry. "She tramped through factories all over the country," reported ***Margaret Culkin Banning** in *Independent Woman*, "talking to employers about their reaction to women in their plants, analyzing part-time work, putting up a fight for actual equal pay for equal work." Haslett also championed the admission of women to factory training programs on an equal basis with men, and the continued recruitment of women in the field even after the war. In a visit to the United States in 1941, she spent two months in New York studying the participation of American women in industry. She visited America again in 1944, under the auspices of the British Federation of Business and Profession Women, for which she served as president for several years. Among the ideas she took back to England for postwar use were "shelves that do not bump the head, less noisy vacuum cleaners and thermostats, more effective uses of plastics, glass, and nylon, and the Tennessee Valley Authority," which she called "the greatest piece of social engineering in the world." In 1945, she visited Sweden and Finland, where she again spoke out about the necessity of women doing their share in the postwar world.

Haslett, described by **Helen Worden** in the *New York World Telegram* as "tall and capable, with frank eyes and a friendly manner," served on the British Electrical Authority, a board formed to manage the nationalized electrical industry, as well as other government bodies. She was a member of the governing boards of several educational institutions, held membership in numerous engineering organizations, and was created a Dame of the British Empire (DBE) in 1947.

SOURCES:

Rothe, Anna, ed. *Current Biography*. NY: H.W. Wilson, 1950.

Barbara Morgan,
Melrose, Massachusetts

Hassall, Joan (1906–1988)

British wood engraver and first woman elected Master of the Art Workers' Guild. *Born in London, England, on March 3, 1906; died on March 6, 1988, in England; daughter of John Hassall (an artist and art* *school proprietor) and Constance (Brooke-Webb) Hassall; sister of Christopher Hassall (1912–1963, a noted biographer, poet, playwright, and librettist); attended Froebel Educational Institute; studied art at the Royal Academy (1927–33), and London County Council School of Photo-Engraving and Lithography, 1931; never married; no children.*

Selected illustrations: Francis Brett Young, Portrait of a Village *(Heinemann, 1937); Richard Church,* Calling for a Spade *(Dent, 1939);* ***Elizabeth Gaskell,*** Cranford *(Harrap, 1940); Robert Louis Stevenson,* A Child's Garden of Verses *(Hopetoun Press, 1946);* ***Mary Webb,*** Fifty-One Poems *(Cape, 1946); Anthony Trollope,* Christmas Day at Kirkby Cottage *(Sampson, Low, 1947);* ***Mary Russell Mitford,*** Our Village *(Harrap, c. 1947); Anthony Trollope,* Parson's Daughter, and Other Stories *(Cassell, 1949); S. Sitwell,* Theatrical Figures in Porcelain *(Curtain Press, 1949); Christopher Vernon Hassall,* Notes on Verse Drama *(Curtain Press, c. 1950); Anthony Trollope,* Mary Gresley, and Other Stories *(Folio, 1951); Iona Opie and Peter Opie,* Oxford Nursery Rhyme Book *(Oxford University Press, 1955);* ***Jane Austen,*** Pride and Prejudice *(Folio, 1957); Richard Church,* Small Moments *(Hutchinson, 1957); Jane Austen,* Sense and Sensibility *(Folio, 1958); Jane Austen,* Mansfield Park *(Folio, 1959); Jane Austen,* Northanger Abbey *(Folio, 1960); Jane Austen,* Persuasion *(Folio, 1961); Jane Austen,* Emma *(Folio, 1962); Robert Burns,* The Poems of Robert Burns *(Oxford University Press, 1965); Jane Austen,* The Folio Jane Austen *(Folio, 1975).*

Work appears in numerous institutions, including British Museum, Victoria and Albert Museum, National Gallery of Canada, and National Gallery of Victoria (Melbourne).

Although Joan Hassall was the daughter of John Hassall, an artist known as the "Poster King" of London advertising agencies, she was encouraged by her father to pursue teaching, a less bohemian career, and spent several years preparing for the classroom before she discovered that it simply was not for her. In 1927, she took a position as a secretary at the London School of Art, where her father was the principal. Before long she too was bitten by the art bug and left her job to begin her studies. In 1931, while she was attending the Royal Academy of Art, a friend told her about a class in wood engraving being offered in the city. (Wood engraving is a relief printing technique in which the engraver cuts into the surface of a block of wood, leaving the design or picture in relief. A print is then made by applying ink to the block and pressing paper over it to create an impression.) Hassall, who had never heard of wood engraving but did not want to disappoint her friend, reluctantly enrolled in the class. When the instructor showed the class a stunning engraving he had created, Hassall experienced something of an epiphany. "As I looked at his block, a feeling of absolute certainty, more like remembering, came to me that I too could engrave like that," she later said.

Hassall's career was launched with the aid of her brother, who upon having a book of poetry accepted for publication, suggested that his sister might provide an engraving for the title page. The publisher (Heinemann), agreed and paid Hassall a commission of £5. The assignment took her three months to complete, but Heinemann liked her work so much that they commissioned a book from Francis Brett Young in order to use more of her engravings. The resulting book, *Portrait of a Village* (1937), containing Hassall's exquisite engravings of the Worcestershire countryside, became one of her best-known works, and she was in much demand as an illustrator. Despite an often overwhelming workload, Hassall never sacrificed quality, often taking the time to recut a block if it did not please her.

Over the course of her career, Hassall produced over 1,000 engravings, which were published in books, magazines, calendars, greeting cards, and bookplates. They included pastoral scenes of the Yorkshire Dales where she loved to visit (and eventually lived), as well as animals, and even occasional portraits. (One of the few examples of her portraiture is a likeness of Peter and ***Iona Opie**, compilers of the *Oxford Nursery Rhyme Book*; Hassall is seated with them.) In 1948, Hassall became the first woman to design a British postage stamp, for which she created portraits of King George VI and Queen ***Elizabeth (Bowes-Lyon)**. She was also the first woman admitted to the Art Workers' Guild, founded by William Morris. Around 1977, Hassall was forced to give up her work because of failing eyesight. She retired to her beloved Yorkshire Dales, where she remained active as a church organist for many years. A modest woman, quick to credit others before herself, she was awarded the OBE (Order of the British Empire) in 1987.

SOURCES:

Faiers, Philip. "Joan Hassall." *This England*, Winter 1987.

SUGGESTED READING:

The Wood Engravings of Joan Hassall. NY: Oxford University Press, 1960.

Hasse, Faustina (c. 1700–1781).

See Bordoni, Faustina.

Hasso, Signe (1910—)

Swedish actress. *Born Signe Larsson on August 15, 1910, in Stockholm, Sweden.*

Selected films: House of Silence *(Sweden, 1933);* Witches' Night *(Sw., 1937);* Career *(Sw., 1938);* Geld fällt vom Himmel *(Ger./Sw., 1938);* Us Two *(Sw., 1939);* Steel *(Sw., 1940);* Journey for Margaret *(U.S., 1942);* Assignment in Brittany *(U.S., 1943);* Heaven Can Wait *(U.S., 1943);* The Story of Dr. Wassell *(U.S., 1944);* The Seventh Cross *(U.S., 1944);* Dangerous Partners *(U.S., 1945);* Johnny Angel *(U.S., 1945);* The House on 92nd Street *(U.S., 1945);* Strange Triangle *(U.S., 1946);* A Scandal in Paris *(U.S., 1946);* Where There's Life *(U.S., 1947);* To the Ends of the Earth *(U.S., 1948);* A Double Life *(U.S., 1948);* This Can't Happen Here/High Tension *(Sw., 1950);* Outside the Wall *(1950);* Crisis *(1950);* Maria Johanna *(Sw., 1953);* Taxi 13 *(Ger./Sw., 1954);* The True and the False *(U.S., 1955);* Picture Mommy Dead *(U.S., 1966);* The Black Bird *(U.S., 1975);* I Never Promised You a Rose Garden *(U.S., 1977).*

A stage actress while still in her teens, Swedish actress Signe Hasso made the transition to starring roles in films during the 1930s. Discovered by Hollywood in 1942, she appeared in American movies throughout the next decade, most often playing strong-willed women. Notable among her American films are *The House on 92nd Street* (1945), a spy drama made in documentary style with William Eythe and Lloyd Nolan, and *To the Ends of the Earth* (1948), a well-crafted thriller with Dick Powell. Her later career included stage, screen, and television appearances in the United States and Europe. She also wrote the lyrics for several Swedish songs.

Hastings, Agnes (fl. 1340s).

See Mortimer, Agnes.

Hastings, Anne (b. 1355).

See Manny, Anne.

Hastings, Anne (c. 1487–?)

Countess of Derby. *Born around 1487; daughter of Edward Hastings of Hungerford, Lord Hastings; married Thomas Stanley, 2nd earl of Derby, in 1507; children: Edward Stanley, 3rd earl of Derby (1509–1572, who married Dorothy Howard);* ****Margaret Stanley.***

Hastings, Anne (d. after 1506)

Countess of Shrewsbury. *Died after 1506; interred at St. Peter's, Sheffield; daughter of* ****Catherine Neville*** *(fl. 1460) and William Hastings, 1st Lord Hastings; married George Talbot, 4th earl of Shrewsbury, before June 27, 1481; children: Henry Talbot; Francis Talbot, 5th earl of Shrewsbury (b. 1500).*

Hastings, Elizabeth (1682–1739)

British philanthropist. *Name variations: Lady Elizabeth Hastings. Born in 1682; died in 1739; daughter of Theophilus Hastings, 7th earl of Huntingdon (1650–1701, lord-lieutenant of Leicester and Derby).*

A noted philanthropist, the beautiful Lady Elizabeth Hastings was the daughter of Theophilus Hastings, 7th earl of Huntingdon, who was imprisoned for attempting to seize Plymouth for King James II in 1688 and on suspicion of treason in 1692. Elizabeth founded scholarships at The Queen's College, Oxford, and supported charities at Ledsham and in Isle of Man. A friend of William Law, author of *Serious Call,* Elizabeth was likened to ***Aspasia** in the *Tatler* by Richard Steele and William Congreve.

Hastings, Flora (1806–1839)

English aristocrat involved in a well-publicized scandal in the court of a young Queen Victoria. *Name variations: Lady Flora Hastings; Lady Flora Elizabeth Hastings. Born Flora Elizabeth Rawdon Hastings in 1806; died in 1839; daughter of Francis Rawdon Hastings (1754–1826), 1st marquis of Hastings (a soldier and diplomat); never married.*

Lady Flora Hastings, born in 1806, was the daughter of Francis Rawdon Hastings, a soldier and diplomat who, among many accomplishments, fought at Bunker Hill and was governor-general of Bengal. By the time she was 30, Flora was still unmarried and serving as lady of the bedchamber to ***Victoria of Coburg**, duchess of Kent, mother of Princess Victoria (later Queen ***Victoria** of England). Unfortunately for Flora, the younger Victoria despised her mother. When she ascended the throne in 1837, Victoria maintained close ties with her prime minister, Lord Melbourne, and was easily swayed by his influence. Melbourne also had an antipathy for Victoria of Coburg; he and his queen also disliked Sir John Conroy.

Thus, the queen was incensed when it was rumored that Flora Hastings and John Conroy were conducting an affair, and allegedly even traveled from London to Scotland in the same carriage, a great taboo at the time. Victoria was so furious that she chronicled the tale in her journal.

When Flora Hastings began to increase in girth, there were whispers that she was carrying Conroy's child. Melbourne sought to keep this quiet to avoid discrediting Victoria's court. In an attempt to bring down Conroy, it was ordered that Hastings should be examined by a physician. When she was found not to be pregnant, her brother called for a public apology from the court, but Melbourne—working to keep the queen's reputation free of taint—refused to admit error. The Hastings family then took the matter to the newspapers, and the resulting stories caused a public outcry against Victoria and her court. It was one of the lowest periods in Victoria's reign, and there were rumors that even the unmarried queen and her prime minister were romantically involved. As for the hapless Flora Hastings, the physical examination that proved she was not carrying a child did not manage to detect a deadly cancerous growth. Her distended midsection had been the result of an abdominal tumor, and she died in 1839, age 33, not long after the press-fueled public furor. She was a writer of poetry, and a collection of her work was published two years after her death.

SOURCES:

Auchincloss, Louis. *Persons of Consequence*. NY: Random House, 1979.

Carol Brennan,
Grosse Pointe, Michigan

Hastings, Selina (1707–1791)

English religious leader and founder of a sect of Calvinistic Methodists known as the Countess of Huntingdon's Connexion. *Name variations: Countess of Huntingdon; Selina Hastings Huntingdon; Selina Huntington; Selina Shirley. Born Selina Shirley on August 24, 1707, at Stanton Harold in Leicestershire, England; died on June 17, 1791, in London; daughter of Washington Shirley, 2nd earl of Ferrers, and Lady Mary Shirley (Lady Ferrers); married Theophilus Hastings, 9th earl of Huntingdon, on June 3, 1728; children: seven, including Francis (b. 1729); George (b. 1730);* ***Elizabeth Hastings*** *(b. 1731); Ferdinando (b. 1732); Selina Hastings (b. 1737); Henry (b. 1739).*

The English countess Selina Hastings is best known as the founder of a Methodist college. Raised primarily in Leicestershire, England, and on her family's Irish estates, Selina was one of three children of Washington Shirley, 2nd earl of

Selina Hastings

Ferrers, and Lady **Mary Shirley**, known as Lady Ferrers. When Selina was young, her parents separated, and Lady Ferrers left her children with their father and moved to Paris. This event, which Selina perceived as her mother's abandonment of the family, led Selina to develop a lifelong enmity for her mother and a deep devotion to her father. In 1728, Selina married Theophilus Hastings, earl of Huntingdon, a wealthy aristocrat 11 years her senior. It was a happy union, and Selina was deeply devoted to her husband, with whom she had seven children. The countess' married life was typical of the leisured life of an 18th-century English noblewoman, showing little of the remarkable activity and religious zeal which characterized her later years.

In 1738, Selina underwent a profound spiritual conversion to Methodism. Her experience was the result of the preaching of her Methodist sister-in-law and a period of long illness which it was feared she would not survive. The next year, she joined John Wesley's Methodist society in Fetter Lane, London, the message of which—an emotional faith in God and an emphasis on individual morality—was beginning to gain in popularity across England. Selina's wealth, her previously hidden talent for widescale organization, and her dedication to her new faith led to her emergence as a major figure in the Wesleyan movement.

With the death of her husband Theophilus in 1746, Selina devoted herself wholeheartedly to an evangelical life. Her existence became a cycle of endless short crises of faith and periods of extreme ill health (documented in her copious correspondence), followed by renewed faith and activism. She concentrated her efforts on converting the upper classes to Methodism, employing her wealth and social position as a peeress to gain the support of the elite. Selina appointed Methodist clerics as chaplains in the towns she held as countess, and with her own funds established over 60 chapels, forming a religious network called "The Countess of Huntingdon's Connexion." She led missionary trips across England, although she never preached herself and was outspoken in her belief that women should not preach. In 1768, she founded Trevecca House, a college for training preachers in Brecknockshire, Wales. Among other Methodist preachers Selina supported George Whitefield, who won converts with his emotional sermons in England and North America. She gave Whitefield a scarf as her chaplain in 1748, and as such he preached in her London house on Park Street to audiences that included Walpole, Chesterfield, and Bolingbroke. In Selina's chapel at Bath, there was a curtained recess known as "Nicodemus's corner" where some bishops sat incognito to hear Whitefield. Selina also tried unsuccessfully to reconcile the Methodist factions of Whitefield and Wesley after the two leaders split over issues of doctrine.

In 1779, the Church of England refused to allow her Methodist ministers to continue in their offices in her towns. Selina always considered herself part of the established Church of England, although the Church disagreed, and so was greatly disappointed by this ruling. In order to evade the injunction, she was compelled to take shelter under the Toleration Act. This forced her to register her chapels as dissenting places of worship and had the effect of severing several eminent and useful members from the Connexion, including William Romaine (1714–1795) and Henry Venn (1725–1797). The countess was also disappointed in her efforts to convert her three surviving children, none of whom followed their mother's faith.

Selina Hastings remained active until her final illness in 1791. After her death at age 83, her college was relocated to Hertfordshire and then Cambridge. Many of her chapels are still in operation under Methodist congregations.

SOURCES:

Schlenther, Boyd S. *Queen of the Methodists.* Durham, England: Durham Academic Press, 1997.

Wright, Helen. *Lady Huntington and Her Circle.* NY: American Tract Society, 1853.

SUGGESTED READING:

The Coronet and the Cross, or Memorials of Selina, Countess of Huntingdon, 1857.

The Life of the Countess of Huntingdon. 2 vols. London, 1844.

Stevens, Abel. *The Women of Methodism; Its Three Foundresses, Susanna Wesley, the Countess of Huntingdon, and Barbara Heck; With Sketches of Their Female Associates and Successors in the Early History of the Denomination.* NY: Carlton & Porter, 1866.

Tytler, Sarah. *The Countess of Huntingdon and her Circle,* 1907.

Laura York,
Riverside, California

Hatasu (c. 1515–1468 BCE).

See Hatshepsut.

Hatchepsout, Hatchepsu, or Hatchepsut (c. 1515–1468 BCE).

See Hatshepsut.

Hatcher, Orie Latham (1868–1946)

American pioneer in vocational guidance. *Born on December 10, 1868, in Petersburg, Virginia; died on April 1, 1946, in Richmond, Virginia; daughter of William Eldridge and Oranie Virginia (Snead) Hatcher; graduated from Vassar College, A.B., 1888; graduated from University of Chicago, Ph.D. in English literature, 1903.*

Orie Latham Hatcher was born in 1868 in Petersburg, into an old Virginia family with a distinguished lineage. Her father, William Eldridge Hatcher, was a descendent of a member of the Virginia House of Burgesses and participant in Bacon's Rebellion of 1676, and was a prominent man in his own right as pastor and founder of Fork Union Military Academy in Virginia. He also served as president of the board of trustees of Richmond College (later the University of Richmond). Her mother, **Oranie Snead Hatcher**, wrote books and pamphlets on primarily religious topics and served as a trustee of Hartshorn College for Negro girls. In the Hatcher family, Orie was the third child and second daughter.

Hatcher graduated at 15 from the Richmond Female Institute in 1884 and remained at the Institute as a teacher for one year before entering Vassar College in 1885. She returned to the Institute after graduation and was instrumental in its transformation into the Woman's College of Richmond in 1894. At this time, Hatcher was named a professor of history, English language and literature.

In 1903, she received her Ph.D. in English literature from the University of Chicago and joined the Bryn Mawr College faculty as a reader in English. In 1910, she became chair of the college's department of comparative literature, and from 1912 she was an associate professor of comparative and English literature. In this capacity, Hatcher contributed much to literary scholarship, including the books *John Fletcher: A Study in Dramatic Method* (1905) and *Book for Shakespeare Plays and Pageants* (1916).

However, Hatcher turned from teaching and scholarship in order to pursue her interest in fostering educational opportunities for women. She resigned from Bryn Mawr in 1915 so she could assume the presidency of the Virginia Bureau of Vocations for Women, an organization she helped found. The bureau originally concentrated on opening up vocational and educational opportunities for Southern women on an individual level and, to those ends, was influential in founding the Richmond School of Social Work and Public Health in 1917 and gaining admission for women to the Medical College of Virginia in 1920. That same year, the bureau became the Southern Woman's Educational Alliance. Hatcher's concern for women's education led her to publish *Occupations for Women* (1927), *Rural Girls in the City for Work* (1930) and *A Mountain School: A Study Made by the Southern Woman's Educational Alliance and Konnarock Training School* (1930).

Hatcher's research soon encompassed an awareness of the problems of young rural men, and in 1930 she published *Guiding Rural Boys and Girls* (later *Child Development and Guidance in Rural Schools* written with ***Ruth Strang** [1943]). It soon became apparent that the Alliance would have to expand again to embrace this new focus, and in 1937 it became the Alliance for Guidance of Rural Youth. Hatcher was active in establishing chapters of the Alliance in New York City and Chicago and displayed endless energy in fund-raising activities.

Orie Latham Hatcher died of bronchial pneumonia on April 1, 1946, in Richmond, Virginia. She was buried in the family plot at Hollywood Cemetery in Richmond.

SOURCES:

James, Edward T., ed. *Notable American Women, 1607–1950*. Cambridge, MA: The Belknap Press of Harvard University Press, 1971.

McHenry, Robert, ed. *Famous American Women*. NY: Dover, 1983.

Judith C. Reveal,
freelance writer, Greensboro, Maryland

Hathaway, Anne (1556–1623)

English wife of William Shakespeare. *Name variations: Anne Shakespeare. Born in Shottery, near Stratford, in 1556 (some sources cite 1557); died in 1623; daughter of Richard Hathaway (a farmer) and his first wife (name unknown); married William Shakespeare, in 1582; children:* ***Susanna Shakespeare*** *(b. 1583); (twins)* ***Judith Shakespeare*** *and Hamnet Shakespeare (b. 1585).*

Anne Hathaway was born in Shottery, a small hamlet inside the parish of Stratford, in 1556, the eldest daughter of Richard Hathaway, a landowner, and his first wife. A year before Anne married, her father died and left her a marriage portion in his will. Anne's brother Bartholomew, the eldest son, was left with most of the land and a request that he be "a comfort unto his brethren and sister."

Anne Hathaway was 26 and pregnant when she married 18-year-old William Shakespeare. ***Marchette Chute** in *Shakespeare of London* suggests that Hathaway, from a solidly respectable background, was likely neither trapped by her pregnancy into demanding marriage nor a seductress of a young man, but rather that she and William had a pre-contract which freed Hathaway to conduct herself as a married woman before the actual marriage ceremony. Elizabethan church law took a pre-contract, which was almost as binding as the ceremony, in earnest; refusal to marry after a pre-contract was grounds for excommunication. On the marriage license, issued on November 27, 1582, Hathaway's name is spelled "Whateley" due to a clerical error. Although it is not known what church the marriage took place in, it is known that it was somewhere in Worcester diocese and that it was not in the parish church of the Holy Trinity in Stratford.

It is likely that William and Anne followed the custom in Stratford that saw the eldest son bringing his bride back to his father's home. The middle house on John Shakespeare's property had a wing at the back with a private entryway, back parlor and kitchen, as well as its own stairway to the second floor, which made it well suited for an additional family. In 1583, Anne and William's first child, a daughter, was born, probably in this middle house; on Trinity Sunday of that year, she was christened Susanna. The choice of her daughter's name, which was one favored by the Puritans, as well as factors in Hathaway's family background, has led to speculation that Hathaway might have been brought up as a Puritan. From this theory, Chute finds a possible explanation for the apparent estrangement between Anne and William that was to ensue a few years after their marriage. Unlike many people at the time who expressed casual contempt for the acting profession, the Puritans attacked actors for being a threat to salvation. Writes Chute:

> The language of some of these tracts is almost unbelievable in its violence. When Shakespeare was twenty-three a book was published in London which described actors as "fiends that are crept into the world by stealth," "sent from their great captain Satan (under whose banner they bear arms) to deceive the world, to lead tht [sic] people with enticing shows to the Devil." The author also describes them as apes, hell hounds, vipers, minotaurs, painted sepulcres [*sic*], dogs and of course caterpillars, and his book is most suitably entitled *A Mirror of Monsters.*

Two years after the birth of Susanna, Hathaway gave birth to twins, christened on February 2, 1585, and named Hamnet and Judith, in all likelihood after the Shakespeares' friends Hamnet and Judith Sadler of High Street. Chute cites the break between Anne and William as probably occurring three or four years after their marriage and relates it to his decision to seek a career on the stage. He headed for London about this time, as did young men all over England. The year he entered the acting profession is unknown, but by 1592 he was an established, successful actor, a fact which points to his having entered this arduous and highly competitive field several years earlier. Chute also remarks that had the household situation been stable it is most likely that Anne would have followed him there once he was settled, which she did not. For nearly 20 years, William lived in hired lodgings in London.

Hamnet died at age 11, two months before Shakespeare's father John was awarded a grant of arms. It is said that given the dynastic ambition of the day and Shakespeare's conduct in his worldly affairs, the death of the only son must have been a hard blow. The welfare of his wife and two daughters is said to have become his primary family preoccupation, and he purchased New Place in 1597 for them. Located a few minutes' walk from his parents' house, this was an imposing mansion on which he spent freely for improvements to the house and garden.

Anne's eldest daughter Susanna married in 1607, to Dr. John Hall, a respected physician, and the first grandchild, Elizabeth, was born in 1608. Anne Hathaway outlived her husband William, who died on April 23, 1616. She died in 1623.

SOURCES:

Chute, Marchette. *Shakespeare of London.* Great Britain: Four Square Press, 1962.

Hathaway, Sibyl (1884–1974)

Dame of Sark who from 1927 to 1974 held feudal dominion over Sark, the fourth largest of the Channel Islands. *Born Sibyl Mary Collings on the Channel Island of Guernsey, England, on January 13, 1884; died at her home on Sark, on July 14, 1974; daughter of William Frederick Collings and Sophia Wallace Collings; had one sister; married Dudley John Beaumont (died); married Robert Woodward Hathaway, in 1929 (died); children: four sons and three daughters.*

As the 22nd individual to succeed to the seigniory of a tiny island in the English Channel, Dame Sibyl Hathaway stood firmly on her traditional feudal rights, keeping her domain intact during a five-year Nazi occupation and taking measures to keep the 20th century at bay, inspired by the notion that "What was good enough for William the Conqueror is good enough for us."

Approximately two square miles (c. 1,200 acres) in area and with a resident population of under 600, the island of Sark lies 7 miles from the island of Guernsey and 22 miles off the coast of France, which is visible on a clear day. Sark—part of the Channel Islands which were once part of the Duchy of Normandy and which by the 13th century became the only part of Britain's Norman possessions to remain loyal to the English Crown—stands 300 feet above sea level and is surrounded by 42 miles of rugged cliffs. The island boasts a varied scenery of banked and hedged fields, wooded valleys, and cliffs covered with wildflowers. Automobiles are not permitted on Sark (the only motorized transport allowed are tractors), so transportation is by horse and carriage, bicycle or on foot. The principal industry is tourism but the island is also extensively farmed, and fishing is a major activity.

Although the island had been inhabited during much of the Middle Ages, raiders drove off the population except for pirates and French privateers. In 1565, however, the premier seigneur of Jersey, Helier de Carteret, requested and received from Queen ***Elizabeth I** the grant of Sark as an adjunct to his own fief in Jersey. With the feudal system thus initiated, the seigneur was required to maintain at least 40 men for the defense of the island. To muster these men, he divided Sark into 40 landholdings and, for a modest annual *rente* of chickens, wheat and barley, gave the land in perpetuity to 40 families. To guarantee political representation, he created a parliament, known as Chief Pleas, from the heads of the 40 families. Sark continues to this day to be governed through Chief Pleas, making its own laws and raising its own taxes. Law is upheld on Sark by two unpaid constables elected annually by Chief Pleas. The administration of justice is carried out by a court comprised of the seneschal (magistrate), prévôt (sheriff), and greffier (clerk to the court), all of whom are appointed by the seigneur.

Sark was ruled by the founding de Carteret family until the 18th century; they were succeeded by the Le Pelleys, who went bankrupt in the early 1850s when a vein of silver found on the island ran out. The Le Pelleys were forced to sell out to a new seigneur, Reverend William Thomas Collings. In 1882, William Thomas was succeeded by his son William Frederick Collings. The new seigneur—over six feet tall and sporting a splendid mustache—was a fearless sailor, cliff climber and crack shot who enjoyed the respect of the Sarkese population. He was also more than a mite eccentric, often drinking to excess, and because of his wild and sometimes terrifying antics he soon became a legend throughout the Channel Islands. On one occasion, he became so inebriated that he somehow turned up in Guernsey at dawn, clad only in a woman's petticoat. Sibyl Mary Hathaway was his daughter.

William Frederick Collings, ignoring his daughter's gender and the fact that one of her legs was shorter than the other, taught her to sail, shoot, and climb cliffs. When she dared to disagree with him, Sibyl had to dodge a book thrown in her direction as well as such epithets as "You are a damned Virago." On one occasion, he punished what he deemed to be an act of rebellion in the following manner: "Father came into my room about midnight, dragged me out of bed and downstairs in my nightgown and, without saying a word, opened the front door and threw me out of the house."

In 1899, Sibyl met Dudley John Beaumont when he visited the island and painted her portrait. Two years later, after a fierce argument with her father, she fled to England and married Beaumont in London. The couple went on to have seven children, four sons and three daughters. Sibyl's interest in her children was often minimal; she said she found them boring, preferring instead to be involved in amateur theatricals. Her husband died during the influenza epidemic of 1918. At this time, recently widowed and in financial difficulties, Sibyl explained her plight to her father who responded with: "I brought you up to be independent and I refuse to allow you to come to me for help."

Soon after the war, she took a job with the British Army of the Rhine in the occupied zone of Germany. There she learned German, a skill which would turn out to be valuable for Sark two decades later. In June 1927, Sibyl's father died, and she succeeded him, taking the title of Dame of Sark. After a number of years of investigating the possibilities of marriage, she almost married a man who was later convicted of bigamy and fraud, but fortunately the engagement was broken off. In 1929, she married American-born Robert Woodward Hathaway, son of a Wall Street banker. According to Sark law, her marriage turned Robert into the seigneur of Sark. But force of personality proved more powerful than law, and from the start of their marriage (Robert Hathaway died in December 1954) it was evident that Sibyl would continue to rule Sark. At meetings of the Chief Pleas, Sibyl—unofficially still the Dame of Sark—sat next to her husband, prompting his every action and continuing (although quite illegally) to give voice to her own opinions.

In 1940, the fall of France to a victorious Nazi Germany made it clear that the Channel Islands—Guernsey, Jersey, Alderney, and Sark—all within shelling range of the coast, could not be defended. The British government declared the islands to be an "open" territory and offered to evacuate all who wished to leave. Dame Sibyl warned the Sark population of the hardships ahead, but, although a few of the Britishers on the island chose to leave, the entire native-born population remained. The German forces arrived on the island on July 3, 1940, and they were met by the seneschal who accompanied them to the seigneurie, the Dame's house, where the Dame's maid announced them as if they were normal guests. After Dame Sibyl had seen to it that the orders of occupation were publicized, she invited the German occupation officials, Major Lanz and his aide Dr. Maass, to lunch with her. After lunch, they signed her visitors' book before departing. They, and their counterparts in the other Channel Islands, were the first invaders to set foot on British soil in nearly one thousand years.

In August 1940, German Commandant Major Lanz announced that he hoped Germany's occupation of the Channel Islands would "be a model to the world." By 1945, the Channel Islands were supporting 37,000 German troops and had become heavily armed. In the final years of the war, food became scarce, clothing and shoes had to be patched, and soap was virtually nonexistent. Two unsuccessful British commando raids on Sark made both Germans and the native population nervous. Cordial relations existed between the Dame of Sark and a number of German officers even though her own husband had been deported to a prison camp in Germany, where he was held for more than two and a half years. Heiner Magsam, commandant of Sark from 1943 to 1945, met with the Dame on a weekly basis, and their amicable discussions usually ended with a spot of tea and a game of bridge.

On the other Channel Islands, German rule, while clearly less brutal than in other parts of Nazi-occupied Europe, was still ultimately a case of the "iron fist in a velvet glove." Although most Jews had been evacuated in 1940, a handful of foreign-born Jewish refugees from Nazism remained, and several of them would lose their lives in death camps. A number of individuals lost their lives because of various offenses, including listening to the BBC. On the island of Alderney, between 1,000 and 1,250 Slavic and French North African slave laborers lost their lives under the most inhumane of conditions. On Sark, however, a number of factors made life under the occupation regime relatively humane. The Dame of Sark's powerful personality (and her knowledge of the German language) doubtless played a role in carving out as good a diplomatic situation for her domain as was possible.

Sark was the most fortunate of the Channel Islands because it had no town population to support (the island has no village as such) and never had to undergo the construction of vast concrete fortifications or the importation of German construction battalions or Soviet prisoners of war and other slave laborers. A German garrison of about 275 men was a genuine burden on a population numbering 470, and by the last year of the war hunger had become a real issue with starvation not far behind. In January 1945, a Red Cross ship brought food parcels for the islanders. Near starvation, the German troops began to appear at doors to beg for food. Although they faced severe punishment if caught, the Germans began stealing vegetables, pigs, chickens, and even cats and dogs to eat. Maintaining discipline, however, the Germans never took the islanders' Red Cross food parcels.

Although hostilities in Europe had ended several days earlier, Sark was not liberated until May 10, 1945, when three British officers arrived on the island and asked the Dame if she would mind being left in charge of the 275 German troops on her land until British troops could be spared. She remained in command until May 17, ordering the Germans to "clean up the mess you've made these past five years," insisting that they remove 13,000 land mines before their departure.

Sibyl Hathaway regained her full legal status as Dame of Sark in December 1954 when her husband died. For the next two decades, she continued to rule her small domain in a queenly and convincing fashion. She also continued to show how skillful she was in dealing with the media in press, radio and television interviews which invariably emphasized the unique aspects of life on Sark. On one such occasion, she summed up her many decades of rule: "If I am a dictator, I'm certainly a benevolent one. I prefer to regard myself as head of one big happy family with the Queen, whom we still regard as the Duke of Normandy, as my overlord." Aspects of the Dame's family life had been far less than ideal, and by the time she died on Sark on July 14, 1974, she had outlived five of her children, several of whom had succumbed to alcoholism and personal problems. Dame Sibyl passed her authority over the island to her grandson, aeronautical engineer Michael Beaumont.

During his May 1995 visit to Sark, Charles, prince of Wales, paid tribute to the Dame's success in keeping the 20th century at bay when he stated, "What you have here is utterly timeless. Don't ever let anyone tell you you're old-fashioned. Fashions change. This kind of approach is perfectly relevant whatever century you live in."

SOURCES:

Bunting, Madeleine. *The Model Occupation: The Channel Islands under German Rule, 1940–1945.* London: HarperCollins, 1995.

"The Dame and Status Quo," in *Sunday Times* [London]. January 13, 1974, p. 24.

"The Dame of Sark," in *The Times* [London]. July 15, 1974, p. 14.

"Diehards of Sark keep Women in their Place," in *The Times* [London]. June 20, 1973, p. 4.

Douglas-Home, William. *The Dame of Sark: A Play.* NY: French, 1976.

Ewen, A.H., and Allan R. de Carteret. *The Fief of Sark.* Guernsey: Guernsey Press, 1969.

"A Feudal Survival," in *The Times* [London]. September 2, 1912, p. 6.

Foote, Timothy. "How to Keep the 20th Century Mostly at Bay," in *Smithsonian.* Vol. 17, no. 2. May 1986, pp. 92–98, 100, 102, 104–105, 170.
Hardman, Robert. "Prince Won Over By Timeless Sark," in *Daily Telegraph.* May 11, 1995, p. 20.
Hathaway, Dame Sibyl Collings. *Dame of Sark: An Autobiography.* NY: Coward-McCann, 1962.
———. *Maid of Sark.* NY: Appleton-Century, 1939.
Hawkes, Ken. *Sark.* Guernsey: Guernsey Press, 1983.
Lempriere, Raoul. *History of the Channel Islands.* London: Robert Hale, 1974.
Owen, Willa. "Ruling a Paradise of the Past," in *The Times* [London]. January 12, 1974, p. 12.
Parkinson, C. Northcote. *A Law Unto Themselves: Twelve Portraits.* Boston: Houghton Mifflin, 1966.
Peake, Mervyn. *Mr. Pye.* Woodstock, NY: Overlook Press, 1984.
"Sark May Give Married Women More Freedom," in *The Times* [London]. October 4, 1973, p. 2.
"Sibyl Hathaway: Dame of Sark, 90, Ruler of Channel Island, Dead," in *The New York Times Biographical Edition.* July 1974, p. 965.
Stoney, Barbara. "Hathaway, Dame Sibyl Mary," in C.S. Nicholls, ed., *The Dictionary of National Biography: Missing Persons.* Oxford: Oxford University Press, 1993, p. 294.
———. *Sibyl, Dame of Sark: A Biography.* London: Hodder and Stoughton, 1978.
Tremayne, Julia. *War on Sark: The Secret Letters of Julia Tremayne.* Exeter, England: Webb & Bower, 1981.

John Haag,
Associate Professor of History,
University of Georgia, Athens, Georgia

Hatheburg (fl. 906)

Saxon princess. *Flourished around 906; daughter of Erwin of Saxony; became first wife of Henry I the Fowler (c. 876–936), Holy Roman emperor (r. 919–936), in 906; children: Thangmar (d. July 28, 938). Henry's second wife was ****Matilda of Saxony*** *(c. 892–968).*

Hathumoda (d. 874)

First abbess of Gandersheim. *Name variations: Hathumonda. Died on November 29, 874; daughter of ****Oda*** *(806–913) and Liudolf (c. 806–866), count of Saxony; sister of ****Gerberga*** *(d. 896).*

Hatice (fl. 1500–1536)

Sister of Suleiman. *Name variations: Hatice Sultana. Born in Trebizond, a Black Sea caravan city in Asia Minor (present-day Turkey); daughter of Selim I the Grim (r. 1512–1520) and Hafsa Hatun (d. 1534); sister of Suleiman or Suleyman I, Ottoman sultan (r. 1520–1566); sister-in-law of ****Roxelana.***

Hatice Sultana was born in Trebizond, a Black Sea caravan city in Asia Minor, the daughter of Selim I the Grim and ***Hafsa Hatun.** She was the sister of Suleiman I, the great Ottoman sultan. It is thought that Hatice married Ibrahim Pasha, Suleiman's grand vizier (prime minister), in May 1524; Ibrahim was executed by Hatice's brother in 1536.

Hatshepsout (c. 1515–1468 BCE).

See Hatshepsut.

Hatshepsut (c. 1515–1468 BCE)

Female pharaoh of Egypt's 18th Dynasty who served as regent for a designated heir, later ousted him from power, then reigned for 20 more years in an era that saw significant political, cultural and economic achievements. *Name variations: Hatasu; Hatchepsout; Hatchepsut; Hatshepset; Hatshepsout; Hashepsowe; throne name was Ma-Ka-Re or Makare. Born around 1515 BCE; died around 1468 BCE; eldest daughter and only surviving child of Thutmose I and Queen Ahmose; married half-brother Thutmose II; children: daughter Neferure; possibly a second daughter; (stepson) Thutmose III.*

Hatshepsut, whose throne name was Ma-Ka-Re, was born around 1515 BCE probably in the great palace, founded by her father Thutmose I, at Egypt's capital city of Memphis, located at the apex of the Nile Delta, southwest of modern Cairo. Her father—a military leader of common ancestry married to a royal princess, **Ahmose**—succeeded his heirless brother-in-law Amenhotep I on the throne. Thutmose I had two sons and two daughters with Queen Ahmose, but the sons predeceased him, which led Thutmose to promote his son by a secondary wife as his heir, because the kingship of Egypt was, by tradition and religious myth, a male prerogative. His eldest daughter Hatshepsut was thus forced to marry her half-brother Thutmose II; brother-sister marriages were frequent among Egyptian royalty as a means of keeping the throne within the ruling family. Only one child, a daughter, is known to have been born to Hatshepsut and Thutmose II. However, a concubine had borne Thutmose II a son, and this youth, also named Thutmose (III), was designated as his father's heir before Thutmose II died about 1490 BCE after a reign of at least four and possibly as many as twelve years. This left Hatshepsut to rule the country, because her husband's designated heir was too young to assume the kingship. Hatshepsut should have been in her 20s, at least, by this time. During its long history, many of

Egypt's queens acted as regent for minors, but only five women are known to have assumed the kingship. Hatshepsut was one of these five.

Among the greatest female figures known from the ancient world, Hatshepsut has left us many monuments, making her one of the best-documented personalities from ancient Egypt's 3,000-year history. The monuments emphasize her public image and divine status, however, and tell us little about her as a human being.

The strong-willed daughter of a great warrior king, Hatshepsut no doubt felt that her credentials to rule her country were far stronger than those of the son of her husband's concubine. Already as a young girl, she could reflect on the distinguished line of her mother's family, who had rid Egypt of a humiliating and century-long foreign domination by the Hyksos. Among her female ancestors were several formidable women who were honored, not only by their sons and husbands, but by the nation as well, for the roles they played in the liberation of their country from this hated domination. Her grandmother ◂ **Ahmose-Nefertari** had become a goddess whose cult was popular among common people for centuries. Judging from the education she provided her own daughter, Hatshepsut must have been trained to read the difficult hieroglyphic script and memorize the revered aphorisms of the sages of yore, which were part of the usual school curriculum available to promising young men of the time. Her leadership qualities, self-confidence, and ambition would not have allowed her contentment in the arranged marriage to Thutmose II, who was the son of a non-royal mother and could not boast of such a distinguished royal lineage, but his early death offered her an opportunity that she could not resist.

Women of the royal household were not secluded but were involved in temple, court, and national activities. Thus it was quite acceptable, in Egyptian tradition, for a senior royal female to rule on behalf of an infant prince. By doing this, they avoided a dynastic crisis and kept power in the hands of the ruling family. Hatshepsut's distinguished grandmother Ahmose-Nefertari had done this successfully for her son Amenhotep I. It was quite another thing for a woman to claim all the titles and powers of kingship itself, however.

Hatshepsut must have plotted her claim to kingship for some time, as the pair of great obelisks which she contributed to Karnak temple to celebrate her assumption of supreme power, in only the second year of the supposed joint rule with the child Thutmose, were ordered early in her career, while she still was known as Great Royal Wife and depicted as the God's Wife of Amun. The product of seven-months' labor at the Aswan quarry, these monolithic shafts of stone, each 185 feet long, required for their transport downstream exceptional barges over 300 feet long towed by 27 ships, manned by 864 rowers. Once at Karnak temple (home of Amun-Re, the King of the Gods), the obelisks were sheathed with gold and erected at the eastern entrance of the great

▸ **Ahmose-Nefertari** (c. 1570–1535 BCE)

Queen of Egypt at the start of the New Kingdom, her husband being the first king of the illustrious 18th Dynasty, who, upon widowhood, ruled the land as regent for her under-aged son. *Name variations: Ahmose-Nofretari; Ahmes-Nefertary. Ruled with her mother Ahhotep around 1570 to 1546* BCE*; daughter of *****Ahhotep****; married her brother Ahmose I; children:* ***Ahmose*** *(the mother of Hatshepsut), and Amenhotep I.*

Ahmose-Nefertari was an Egyptian queen and wife of Ahmose I who founded the 18th Dynasty (1567–1320 BCE). Since she was often portrayed posthumously with black skin, her parentage is debated. After ridding the country of foreign overlords, Ahmose I died young, leaving Ahmose-Nefertari to rule the country as regent for her son Amenhotep I. She bore the title Female Chieftain of Upper and Lower Egypt. Ahmose-Nefertari is credited with restoring temples and official cults throughout the land after decades of neglect by the Hyksos dynasty. She also founded a college of Divine Votaresses at the Karnak temple where she was herself a high priestess, holding the title of God's Wife of Amun. When she died, she was placed in a coffin 12 feet long and fitted with a lofty plumed crown which may indicate it was kept upright for some time to facilitate viewing by her subjects. Because her husband founded the dynasty which brought Egypt to the pinnacle of world power, Ahmose-Nefertari may well have been regarded as the mother of her country. She was deified after death, and her cult was popular among the common people, particularly in Upper Egypt, for at least four centuries.

Barbara S. Lesko,
Department of Egyptology, Brown University, Providence, Rhode Island

Hatshepsut

surrounding wall of the temple. The engineer in charge of the entire operation was a commoner named Senenmut, who apparently had served Hatshepsut as a steward during Thutmose II's reign. His successful completion of this difficult mission won him the admiration and confidence of his sovereign to the extent that she promoted him to many high positions in her realm and gave him the tutelage of her daughter and designated heir, Princess **Neferure**, and possibly also the oversight of the young Thutmose III.

Problems with reconstructing Hatshepsut's personal life are many due to the uncertain chronology of events and the silence of the monuments. For example, Senenmut is depicted in ten statues holding Neferure portrayed as an infant. Yet if the princess was the daughter of Thutmose II, she should have been older than three years by the time Senenmut was assigned to her education. The artistic canon of the Egyptians tended to depict minors as much smaller than adults, and thus such portrayals were not truly accurate. No one has suggested that Neferure was not the child of Thutmose II, but both ancient and modern observers have commented upon the close relationship between Hatshepsut and the courtier who rose from humble origins to hold 20 important positions under the female pharaoh. It has also been observed that a number of important men in her court remained bachelors, as did Senenmut.

> I was foretold for an eternity as 'she will become a conqueror.'
>
> **—Hatshepsut**

Some historians of the past have denounced Hatshepsut as both a cruel and unreasonable woman, while others have decided she was talented and charming as well as a pacifist. Hatshepsut's personal daring and courage is, however, clearly documented. Because of her father's wars, which terrorized Nubia and penetrated western Asia further than the pharaohs had ever gone, Hatshepsut inherited a large and stable realm and seldom had to contend with uprisings. Nonetheless, three eyewitness accounts place the queen with her troops on a campaign south into the Land of Kush (northern Sudan), control of which was essential for economic reasons, it being a prime source of gold and other luxury products. There is a reference to her armies' protecting Egypt's eastern flank as well. Thus her foreign policy was not one of benign neglect. Rather she attempted to preserve her father's empire. Her artists portrayed Hatshepsut as a lion trampling Egypt's enemies and the more than 100 sphinxes (recumbent lion statues with Hatshepsut's head) created for just one of her temples emphasized her invincible pharaonic power.

She did not eye the outside world as entirely hostile, however, and sought the products of foreign lands through peaceful trading expeditions. International trade was well established throughout the eastern Mediterranean at this time, and Egypt ruled the Red Sea and its routes to equatorial regions. In her fifth year of reign, she sent a mining expedition to Sinai in search of turquoise. In her ninth year of reign, Hatshepsut's navy sailed to Eritrea, then known as Punt, on the east coast of Africa and the southern end of the Red Sea, from which it brought back myrrh trees, piles of frankincense, and other African products like ebony wood, gold, and ivory. Her claims to foreign victories, her trading expeditions, and the transport of the obelisks were recorded on the walls of Hatshepsut's magnificent terraced temple built for the funerary cult of her father and herself on the western bank of Thebes (modern Luxor), erected in a natural amphitheater against a curtain of towering limestone cliffs. The site is known today as Deir el Bahri. This innovative temple on three levels was spectacularly decorated with detailed painted wall scenes commemorating major events of Hatshepsut's life and was outfitted with hundreds of colossal images of the queen in various guises—Osiride statues and sphinxes, male and female images. Groves of incense trees and reflection pools created a parklike setting in front of it on the arid plain. Senenmut, her steward, is credited with the innovative design of the funerary temple.

While this was his most spectacular production, Senenmut was in charge of all the numerous building projects in the region of the religious capital. Nearby on the West Bank, a temple to Amun-Re was erected at Medinet Habu and to the south, in Senenmut's own home town of Armant, was built a temple to its patron god Montu. On the East Bank in the great religious center of Thebes itself, Hatshepsut contributed several rooms and central shrines to Karnak temple, including the now dismantled Red Chapel of which some 300 inscribed blocks survive. The eastern sanctuary of Amun-Re was cut from a single huge block of alabaster. Stations for the sacred bark along the processional ways to the temple were built, and she inaugurated the southern axis of approach between this major temple and the area sacred to Amun's consort, the goddess Mut, and thus was responsible for the 8th pyloned gateway at Karnak. Mut was known as the Lady of the Crowns and often was portrayed wearing the great double red-and-white crown of Egypt—for the Two Lands of Upper and Lower Egypt—just as Hatshepsut herself would have. Rock cut shrines were hewn to the north near Beni Hasan (Speos Artemidos); in Nubia, Elephantine and Kom Ombo, Gebel es Silsileh and Faras, Qasr Ibrim and Semna-Kumma all received her attention.

Just as significant as the number of her buildings is the fact that her reign introduced innovations in architecture and in art, particularly in the naturalistic style of royal portraiture in sculpture, the detailed, lively, and expansive wall scenes of the temples, and in the design of royal sarcophagi. The female pharaoh also proclaims in one inscription that she spent much effort throughout the land repairing older temples which had fallen into a dilapidated state. Hatshepsut no doubt wanted the priesthood solidly behind her, as they made up a large proportion of the educated elite of her country, but she would also have needed the approval of the great gods themselves, and thus she built and equipped temples throughout the kingdom, using the gold of Nubia and the bountiful harvests of Egypt (collected as royal-tax revenues) to employ the labor of a large proportion of the peasantry during the long and idle months of the annual Nile inundation. Hatshepsut made the rounds of her country escorted by troops, heralds, fan bearers, and grooms with hunting leopards and a traveling throne which was carried on a portable platform. The remains of a chair bearing her name, inlaid with ivory and fitted with gold, is now in the British Museum.

Women of ancient Egypt were full legal personalities and many led active lives outside the home, laboring in temple and palace workshops, for instance, and some are found in palace and temple administration as well. Numerous women belonged to temple cultic phylae, and it is believed that the presence of a woman on the throne opened up more positions of leadership in the cults for the elite women of her realm, as there is a noticeable increase in the portrayal of priestesses at this time.

The king of Egypt was regarded as the living incarnation of the god Horus, son of the deities Osiris and Isis, and also as the son of the sungod Re. Hatshepsut's inscriptions often employ masculine titles as well, mixed with feminine pronouns. Thus Hatshepsut was truly flying in the face of age old tradition by proclaiming herself the "Daughter of Re" and the "Female Horus." On religious monuments, she frequently had herself portrayed as being crowned by Amun-Re, the king of the gods, and also in texts claimed that her own father, Thutmose I, had publicly proclaimed her as his heir. On the walls of her temple at Deir el Bahri, Hatshepsut's divine lineage is emphasized: showing her father, in the guise of Amun-Re, cohabiting with her mother, Queen Ahmose, and explaining that the queen was impregnated by the god. Once the queen gave birth, her daughter is shown being nursed by goddesses.

It is doubtful that Thutmose I truly intended his daughter to be his heir when he had sired a son who, indeed, did succeed him. However, political support for her unconventional rule came from former officials of her father, such as Ineni who had been his chief advisor, as well as new men of talent who were promoted by Hatshepsut herself. Whether she and her father had been truly close is impossible to say, but she certainly used their blood relationship for all it was worth and went to great lengths to demonstrate her love for him.

Even though she defied tradition by her claim of what was supposed to be only a male-held office, no one apparently dared to dissuade the fully royal scion of a preceding pharaoh. The circumstances that precipitated her move toward greater power were unusual, but later ages remembered her as a co-regent with the younger Thutmose III. Hatshepsut never disposed of this young stepson, who, while he began life as a temple acolyte, was later put in charge of the army and still did not make a move against Hatshepsut while she lived. Being younger than she, he could obviously see that his opportunity to rule would come eventually, and were it not for later actions taken against her memory on his behalf long after her demise, one would think that the royal family got along together fairly well.

Princess Neferure, the sole daughter who inherited her mother's supreme religious role as God's Wife in the Amun cult, seems to have played the ceremonial role of "queen" in this regime, and may well have been intended originally to follow her mother as ruler in a true and innovative matriarchy. She is often shown alone on monuments and bore the queenly title of Mistress of the Two Lands, and that of Regent of the South and North. There is no evidence that she married Thutmose III. However, Neferure seems to have died as a young woman, probably still in her teens, and Hatshepsut then had to bow to political necessity and accept the inevitability of a Thutmoside succession. The universal belief in the divinity of pharaoh had probably protected Hatshepsut from an organized revolt, but also the spectacular feats of her career, Egypt's secure borders, prosperity, wonderful buildings and awe-inspiring monuments would have silenced the doubters and demonstrated that the gods still loved Egypt even if it was ruled unconventionally by a woman. By her 16th year (counting from the time she succeeded her husband), Hatshepsut was ready to celebrate a royal jubilee with the ages old *sed* festival of kingly renewal. To mark the occasion, she again stressed her early enjoyment of her father's support by erecting another pair of obelisks inside the hall he had built at Karnak temple. However, these were but 90-feet tall and were covered with a gold alloy only at their tips which extended above the roof line of the temple to reflect the sun's rays.

Often Hatshepsut, as female pharaoh, was portrayed with the same kingly costume as a male ruler, including the false beard that kings donned for special occasions. Statues will show her with the cloth *nemes* headdress and short kilt of archaic times, used in portraits of male kings. Her body is then shown naked to the waist, just as male kings would have appeared. Wall reliefs do not emphasize a female figure and often give her the helmet-shaped Blue Crown popular with Empire period kings. Only a few of Hatshepsut's statues portray her in feminine dress. Yet she tells us she was attractive and her delicate face with its arched eyebrows and dimpled chin is easily recognized and probably authentically portrayed by her sculptors. Thus it is the artistic canon of traditional ways of presenting a pharaoh that has influenced much of her portrayals. There is no reason to believe Hatshepsut did not wear clothing appropriate for females.

Although Hatshepsut had a tomb created for her, high in the cliffs south of Deir el Bahri when she was Thutmose II's queen, once she became a full-fledged king she desired her final resting place to be in the secluded valley inaugurated by her father as a royal necropolis. Eventually the Valley of the Kings on the West Bank opposite Thebes would hold 62 tombs, all of the Empire period. Of these, Hatshepsut's (KV20) would be one of the longest, descending some 214 meters (700 feet). Presumably planned on the same axis as her temple so as to penetrate and end up with the burial crypt beneath her great mortuary temple on the other side of the cliffs from the necropolis, the rock proved too friable and the excavators changed course, curving the corridors and bringing the succession of steps and galleries around in a half circle. Her father's reign had seen, not only the first tomb in the Valley of the Kings, but also the first documented use of inscribed chapters of the royal book of the Netherworld, the spells of the *Amduat.* The walls of Hatshepsut's tomb were also provided with slabs of stone upon which such texts were inscribed, to ensure her safe progress through an eternity of traveling with the sun god. Howard Carter excavated her tomb in 1903 and two sarcophagi were found in it, as the daughter wanted her illustrious father buried with her, just as she provided for his funerary cult in her grand mortuary temple.

This temple's construction and design were taken over by Senenmut from her regnal year seven. In this same year, he began an immense tomb with a portico for himself prominently placed high in the necropolis of nobles nearby, on a hill now known as Sheikh Abd el Gurna. However, Senenmut decided to have more than one tomb and his hubris led him to cut one within the sacred precinct of his sovereign's mortuary temple. He also had his image placed behind open door leafs of shrines within the temple whose construction he oversaw. At some point, these transgressions were discovered and firmly countermanded. The name and titles of the royal steward were hacked from his tomb, but those of Hatshepsut were not, leaving little else as explanation other than that she was the one who retaliated against his presumption. With this episode came his fall from grace, around year 16, although at least three of Senenmut's statues bear the name of Thutmose III, which suggests he may have lived on into the next reign, even if he had lost his official positions, or at any rate Senenmut may have been remembered with honor by Thutmose III himself.

The betrayal by Senenmut was the second blow endured by the female pharaoh, as surely the early death of her daughter was of the severest disappointment to her. With Neferure's demise, Hatshepsut began to allow more prominence to Thutmose III in ceremonies and in temple wall scenes, and their rule became a true coregency, an arrangement resorted to by many Egyptian kings before and after. Hatshepsut died during their 22nd regnal year, probably of natural causes, but no details have survived. Many years after she died, Thutmose III replaced his stepmother's names on her monuments with those of his father and erased most of the images and ordered the statues of the female pharaoh to be destroyed.

However, Hatshepsut's reign was not forgotten. Her temple at Deir el Bahri remained in use as the most important focal point for annual religious celebrations on the West Bank for centuries to come. Women named their daughters after her for generations, and a thousand years later the presence of a female on the throne of the pharaohs, who reigned nearly 22 years, was still recounted by historians, even though Hatshepsut was ignored on some monumental king lists in temples of the 18th and 19th dynasties, probably because they deemed her only a regent for the man whose military exploits made him Egypt's most illustrious ruler. However, Hatshepsut had managed her realm successfully and handed over to Thutmose a country so stable and prosperous that he was able immediately to launch an aggressive foreign policy involving 17 war campaigns that took him out of the country for many years. Politically, Thutmose III would prove to be a worthy successor of his stepmother and her line of warrior kings, as he aggressively expanded and organized the Egyptian empire to the furthest extent it ever enjoyed, making Egypt the most powerful kingdom in the world during the second half of the second millennium BCE. Hatshepsut's reputation has also stood the test of time; she is known as one of the greatest of the pharaohs of ancient Egypt.

SOURCES:

Callender, V.G. "Ancient and Modern Perceptions of Female sovereignty in Pharaonic Egypt," in *Shadow.* Vol. 9, 1992, pp. 49–66.

———. "Female Officials in Ancient Egypt and Egyptian Historians," in *Stereotypes of Women in Power: Historical Perspectives and Revisionist Views.* Edited by B. Garlick, S. Dixon, and P. Allen. NY: Greenwood Press, 1992.

Dorman, P.F. *The Monuments of Senenmut.* London: Kegan Paul International, 1988.

Gardiner, A.H. "Davies's copy of the great Speos Artemidos Inscription," in *Journal of Egyptian Archaeology.* Vol. 32, 1946, pp. 43–56 and double plate.

———. *Egypt of the Pharaohs.* Oxford: Oxford University Press, 1961, pp. 177–198.

Habachi, L. *The Obelisks of Egypt: Skyscrapers of the Past.* NY: Scribner, 1977.

———. "Two Graffiti at Sehel from the Reign of Queen Hatshepsut," in *Journal of Near Eastern Studies.* Vol. 16, 1957, pp. 88–104.

Hayes, Wm. C. "Varia from the Time of Hatshepsut," in *Mitteilungen des Deutschen Archäologischen Instituts, Kairo.* Vol. 15, 1957, pp. 78–82.

Karkowski, J. "Notes on the Beautiful Feast of the Valley as represented in Hatshepsut's Temple at Deir el Bahari," in *50 Years of Polish Excavations in Egypt and the Near East.* Warsaw: Centre d'Archéologie Mediterranéenne de l'Académie Polonaise des Sciences, 1992, pp. 155–166.

Lacau, P., and H. Chevrier. *Une chapelle d'Hatshepsout a Karnak.* Vol. I. Cairo: Le Service des Antiquités de l'Égypte, 1977.

Lesko, B.S. "The Senenmut Problem," in *Journal of the American Research Center in Egypt.* Vol. 6, 1967, pp. 113–118.

Naville, E. *The Temple of Deir el Bahari.* 7 vols. London: Egypt Exploration Fund, 1894–1908.

Nims, C.F. "The Date of the Dishonoring of Hatshepsut," in *Zeitschrift für aegyptische Sprache und Altertumskunde.* Vol. 93, 1966, pp. 97–100.

Ratie, S. *La reine Hatchepsout: Sources et problemes.* Leiden: E.J. Brill, 1979.

Redford, D.B. *History and Chronology of the Eighteenth Dynasty of Egypt: Seven studies.* Toronto: University of Toronto Press, 1967, pp. 58–87.

Seipel, W. "Hatschepsut I," in *Lexikon der Ägyptologie.* Vol. II, Wiesbaden: Otto Harrassowitz, 1977, pp. 1045–1051.

Wysocki, S. "The Temple of Queen Hatshepsut at Deir el Bahari: its original form," in *Mitteilungen des Deutschen Archäologischen Instituts, Kairo.* Vol. 42, 1986, pp. 213–228.

Yoyotte, J. "La date supposée du couronnement d'Hatchepsout," in *Kemi.* Vol. 18, 1968, pp. 85–91.

SUGGESTED READING:

Desroches Noblecourt, Ch. *La femme au temps des Pharaons.* Paris: Éditions Stock, 1993, pp. 124–162.

Frank, G. "Pharaoh Hatshepsut: History's First Liberated Woman," in *Field Museum of Natural History Bulletin.* September, 1974, pp. 3–13.

Hayes, Wm. C. "Egypt: Internal Affairs from Tuthmosis I to the Death of Amenophis III." Chapter IX in Edwards, I.E.S., Gadd, C.J. and Hammond, N.G. eds. *Cambridge Ancient History* II. 1–2: History of the Middle East. 3rd ed. Cambridge: Cambridge University Press, 1973, pp. 313–332.

Lesko, B. *The Remarkable Women of Ancient Egypt.* 3rd ed. Providence: B.C. Scribe Publications, 1996.

———. "Women's Monumental Mark on Ancient Egypt," in *Biblical Archaeologist.* Vol. 54, no. 1, 1991, pp. 4–15.

Robins, G. *Women in Ancient Egypt.* Cambridge: Harvard University Press, 1993.

Roehrig, C. "Hatshepsut and the Metropolitan Museum of Art," in *KMT: A Modern Journal of Ancient Egypt.* Spring 1990, pp. 28–33.

Teeter, E. "The Wearer of the Royal Uraeus: Hatshepsut," in *KMT: A Modern Journal of Ancient Egypt.* Spring 1990, pp. 4–13, 56–57.

Tefnin, R. *La Statuaire d'Hatshepsout.* Monumenta Aegyptiaca IV, Bruxelles: Fondation Égyptologique Reine Élisabeth, 1979.

Tyldesley, Joyce. *Hatchepsut: The Female Pharaoh.* NY: Viking, 1996.

COLLECTIONS:

The largest assemblage of Hatshepsut's statuary, from her temple at Deir el Bahri, is in the Metropolitan Museum of Art in New York.

Barbara S. Lesko,
Administrative Research Assistant, Department of Egyptology,
Brown University, Providence, Rhode Island

Hatzimichali, Angeliki (1895–1956)

Greek writer and folklorist. Born in Greece, in 1895; died in 1956; daughter of a professor of Greek literature.

The daughter of a professor of Greek literature, Angeliki Hatzimichali devoted her life to the study and preservation of traditional Greek culture, both Byzantine and modern folk. Living much of her life among the peasants in the countryside, Hatzimichali painstakingly observed and recorded daily life, customs, and handicraft techniques. She was instrumental in the establishment of professional schools for the preservation of traditional crafts as well as workshops where immigrant women from Asia Minor could also practice their native crafts. Hatzimichali's writings on folk arts and crafts were widely published in folk-art journals in Greece and abroad, and in 1921, she organized the first exhibit of folk art in Greece.

Hatzler, Clara (fl. 1452)

German scribe. *Flourished in 1452 in Augsburg, Germany.*

Little is known about Clara Hatzler, except that she was a successful German clerk, or scribe. She was not affiliated with a convent, as most women scribes were, but practiced professionally to support herself in the growing town of Augsburg. Scribes were employed for all types of copying jobs, and had to be quick, skilled calligraphers. Hatzler started her own very profitable studio in 1452 and remained in business for 24 years.

Laura York,
Riverside, California

Hauck, Amalia Mignon (1851–1929).

See Hauk, Minnie.

Haucke, Countess von (1825–1895).

See Hauke, Julie von.

Haughery, Margaret Gaffney (1813–1882)

Irish-born American philanthropist and businesswoman who was known as the "Bread Woman of New Orleans." *Born Margaret Gaffney near Killeshandra, County Cavan, Ireland, in 1813; died in New Orleans, Louisiana, on February 9, 1882; second daughter and the fifth of six children of William Gaffney (a tenant farmer) and Margaret (O'Rourke) Gaffney; married Charles Haughery, on October 10, 1835 (died 1836); children: one daughter, Frances, who died in infancy.*

Born in Ireland to tenant farmers in 1813, Margaret Haughery emigrated to Baltimore with her mother and father in 1818. After the death of both parents in the yellow fever epidemic of 1822, Haughery was cared for by a neighbor who could not afford to educate her. Unable to read or write, she worked as a domestic servant for several years before her marriage to Charles Haughery, in 1835. The couple moved to New Orleans, where a year later Haughery gave birth to a daughter, Frances. Both Charles and the baby suffered ill health, and, before another year had passed, Haughery had lost both her husband and child. She worked briefly as a laundress in the city's elegant St. Charles hotel, then assisted the Sisters of Charity at the Poydras Orphan Asylum, where she also lived.

With her earnings from the hotel laundry, Haughery purchased a pair of cows to start a dairy. By 1840, although she distributed much of her milk to the city's poor, she owned 30 to 40 cows and was delivering milk to some of the city's most fashionable neighborhoods. Her prosperity enabled her to help the Sisters of Charity finance a new orphanage, the New Orleans Female Orphan Asylum, which opened in 1840. Over the years, Haughery helped establish and maintain 11 such institutions, among them St. Vincent's, an orphanage for infants in which she took particular pride. Haughery's charity was as boundless as her energy. She nursed victims of frequent yellow fever outbreaks and assisted families stranded by the recurrent flooding of the Mississippi.

In 1858, Haughery was overtaken by another entrepreneurial urge. Receiving a small bakery as payment for a debt, she gave up the dairy to concentrate her efforts on expanding the new business, which eventually employed 40 workers. She moved the operation to a better part of town and purchased the newest steam-operated equipment. She also came up with the idea of packaged crackers, an innovation that turned the bakery into the largest export business in New Orleans. Success did not alter Haughery's charitable nature, however. From her office, she dispensed advice, sympathy, and, when necessary, money to those in need. During the Civil War, she organized sewing and knitting groups and conducted "free markets" two or three times a week. She gave special attention to helping sick soldiers from both the North and South. After the war, as her business continued to expand, she directed her efforts to the elderly, particularly the Home for the Aged run by the Little Sisters of the Poor.

At the height of her success, Haughery continued to live modestly. She dressed in black, as was the custom for widows at the time, wearing one of two dresses she owned, one for weekdays and another for Sundays. She conducted her philanthropy with such humility that much of her good work went unnoticed during her lifetime. Often, she requested secrecy from the recipients of her generosity, and she never kept records of her gifts. After her death from cancer in 1882, her will, signed with a simple X, divided her estate of nearly half a million dollars among various Catholic, Protestant, and Jewish institutions. In 1884, a statue of Haughery, purchased with public funds and inscribed simply "Margaret," was unveiled in a New Orleans park bearing her name.

SOURCES:

Bird, Caroline. *Enterprising Women.* NY: W.W. Norton, 1976.

James, Edward T., ed. *Notable American Women, 1607–1950.* Cambridge, MA: The Belknap Press of Harvard University Press, 1971.

McHenry, Robert, ed. *Famous American Women.* NY: Dover, 1983.

Barbara Morgan,
Melrose, Massachusetts

Hauk, Minnie (1851–1929)

American dramatic soprano, the first international opera superstar to emerge from the U.S., who was particularly celebrated for her Carmen. *Name variations: Minnie Hauck. Born Amalia Mignon Hauck in New York City, on November 16, 1851; died at Villa Tribschen, Switzerland, on February 6, 1929; daughter of James Hauck; married Baron Ernst von Hesse-Wartegg.*

The first full-fledged, internationally acclaimed operatic prima donna to be produced by the United States, Minnie Hauk was born Amalia Mignon Hauck (she later chose to drop the *c*) in New York City during 1851. She was the only child of a German-born father, a carpenter who had fled Germany after the failure of the 1848 revolution, and his American wife. The Hauck family moved to Providence, Rhode Island, where at the age of five, Minnie attended her first theatrical performance while seated on her mother's lap. She later reminisced about this experience, recalling that after returning home she did not even look at her dolls, "sitting in a row near my bed. I had seen at the theatre much larger, much finer ones." Stagestruck, the young girl became obsessed by ***Jenny Lind**, "the Swedish Nightingale." She owned many pictures of the singer, read a biography of Lind "at least once a week," and named her dogs and cats Jenny.

In the late 1850s, the Hauck family moved again, this time to the frontier town of Sumner City, north of Kansas City and situated on the Missouri River. With her father working as a boatbuilder and her mother running a boarding house, Minnie was often on her own. She took advantage of her freedom to stroll across the prairies, often winding up in a nearby Native American camp. As she recalled, "The Indians would call me their 'Prairie flower'; they would give me fruit, carry me in their arms, and take me for a ride on their little ponies. Their children would show me how to string a bow and shoot an arrow, would dance or have a sham battle or a pony race for my amusement, and, towards evening, they would accompany me a good distance on my homeward way." Alarmed by their wandering daughter, the Haucks sent her off to a girl's seminary in nearby Leavenworth. Here, her irrepressible spirits quickly got her expelled.

After a fierce flood on the Missouri River virtually destroyed Sumner City, the Haucks again decided to move on. James Hauck built a boat, loaded it with his small family and all their worldly possessions, and they set sail for New Orleans where life would be easier. Just south of St. Louis, however, their houseboat was rammed by a steamboat and demolished. As Minnie and her parents floated in the water, clutching debris from their vessel, they watched everything they owned sink into the mighty Mississippi. The steamboat's captain rescued the shaken family and took them free of charge to their destination. By the time the Haucks arrived in New Orleans, the Civil War had begun, the city found itself blockaded, and economic life was at a virtual standstill. Soon, however, Minnie's parents were able to find employment and a modest lifestyle was enjoyed by the family. Minnie attended the Belleville School and took singing lessons from a European basso, Gregorio Curto.

Minnie Hauk

Before long, she was facing an audience, singing in the city's grand opera house at a charity concert to raise money for wounded soldiers.

Convinced of her talent, Minnie's parents again relocated. In late 1862, with the Civil War still raging, they sailed from New Orleans to the Florida Keys, and from there to New York City. In Manhattan, Minnie soon became a musical sensation, regularly singing in the homes of the social elite, including Naval Commodore Ritchie, August and **Caroline Perry Belmont**, and racetrack entrepreneur Leonard Jerome, father of ***Jennie Jerome (Churchill)**. After a brief but intensive course of study with Achille Errani, who had gained fame as a teacher of a number of successful American sopranos, Minnie made her operatic debut, singing in *La Sonnambula* at the Brooklyn Academy of Music on October 13, 1866. A month later, she made her Manhattan debut at the Winter Garden, singing the role of Prascovia in Giacomo Meyerbeer's *L'Étoile du Nord*. *The New York Times*' assessment of her performance was highly enthusiastic, noting that she was "an artist who in time will rank among the foremost. Her power is quite equal to her brilliancy, and experience will beyond a doubt develop in her an artist quite equal, if not superior, to any we have yet heard."

Youthful and supremely confident, Minnie Hauk quickly emerged as a prima donna, adding major roles to her repertoire at a dizzying pace. The only component left to secure her career was a trip to Europe, and funds for this undertaking were provided by the music publisher Gustav Schirmer, whose confidence in Hauk's talents was repaid quite literally with interest soon after her first engagements on the Continent. Traveling with her mother—who would serve as Hauk's best friend, constant companion and closest adviser—the young soprano's first stop was London. Although no engagements materialized in the British capital, Hauk attended the opera, made a number of important connections, and carefully studied the singing techniques of several of the city's reigning singing stars including ***Adelina Patti** and ***Christine Nilsson**. In Paris, however, she secured an engagement in the role of Amina in *La Sonnambula*. Hauk became the instant darling of the French public not only because of her vocal and dramatic talents, but also because her colorful American frontier background provided great copy for the local newspapers, which described her in fantastic terms as a half-civilized ***Pocahontas** figure who in the wilds of the New World was accustomed to riding a mustang bareback.

Within months of her Paris debut, Hauk was singing in the major opera houses of London, The Hague, and Russia. In Russia, she appeared in both Moscow and St. Petersburg's imperial opera houses, and it was during these Russian engagements that she began to earn a reputation for displaying a fiery stage temperament. A simmering artistic jealousy between Hauk and ***Désirée Artôt**, then one of the leading sopranos on the Russian operatic scene, came to a head during a performance of *Don Giovanni*. Artôt's husband, Mariano Padilla, jerked Hauk's hand at the end of their duet in Act I. Convinced that Padilla was intentionally trying to cause her to break a high note, Hauk slapped him in the face. The audience, entranced by the events, gave both singers such an ovation that the entire duet had to be repeated.

Hauk's Russian successes made her an internationally recognized singing sensation. For the next decade, she would sing mostly in Vienna and Berlin, making her Viennese debut in May 1870. She quickly mastered the German language both to meet the requirements of daily living and because the non-German operatic repertory was customarily sung in German. At the time of her first appearance in Vienna in the role of Marguerite in Gounod's *Faust*, Hauk had not yet completely mastered the complexities of German. A slip-up she made in performance served to endear her to Vienna's music enthusiasts: responding to Faust, she told him she intended to go home *ungekleidet* (undressed) instead of the correct word, *unbegleitet* (unaccompanied). The sophisticated Viennese audience was delighted by the imperfect German of the American girl from the Wild West, and she became an immediate star. She enjoyed a comparable success at the Berlin Opera, where she starred in, among other popular operas of the day, Goetz's *Taming of the Shrew*.

Despite her late and rather sketchy vocal training, Minnie Hauk was a quick study and mastered not only the German language, adding dozens of roles to her repertory in a brief period, but also learned roles in exotic languages. In Budapest, for example, she sang the role of Maria in Ferenc Erkel's *Hunyadi László* in the original Magyar, even though she never learned a sentence of conversational Hungarian and learned the words, as she would later note, "like a parrot." Now a world-class artist, Hauk met many of the composers of operas she starred in including Richard Wagner whom she met after a Budapest performance of *Der fliegende Holländer*. On that occasion, she told him that she always made an effort to "act in accordance with the symphonic indications of the orchestra." A grateful Wagner replied, "That is right, that is right! Thank goodness! Here is an artist who knows how to act and sing according to my intentions."

Always willing to sing in contemporary operas that were fresh to the ear and even controversial, Hauk was glad for the opportunity to sing in Bizet's *Carmen.* In May 1878, when that opera was only three years old, she sang in the starring role at the Théâtre de la Monnaie in Brussels. Her performance was a huge hit, at least in part because in order to totally master her role she had immersed herself in the French language, read the Prosper Mérimée short story the opera was based on, and took dancing lessons from the Monnaie's ballet master. On June 22, 1879, Hauk performed *Carmen* in London, singing it in Italian, the operatic language favored by British audiences of the day. Here, too, it was an immense success. Although she married the wealthy Austrian journalist and globetrotter Baron Ernst von Hesse-Wartegg in 1881, Hauk had no intentions of abandoning her immensely successful singing career, which by the 1880s had made her name as well-known in the United States as it had become in Europe during the previous decade. She toured constantly in the United States and Canada, and was invited by President Chester A. Arthur to perform at the White House.

Fearing that her success as Carmen might doom her to being seen as a one-role artist, Hauk was constantly searching for, and mastering, new roles, which included Hector Berlioz' rarely performed *La Damnation de Faust.* Among other novelties, Hauk introduced Massenet's *Manon* to the United States in December 1885. She sang at New York's Metropolitan Opera during the 1890–91 season, and her appearance in *Carmen* on April 2, 1891, marked her final New York performance. As a last hurrah for her fans, she founded the Minnie Hauk Grand Opera Company in mid-1891 to make an American tour. During this tour in Chicago on September 30, 1891, she appeared in Mascagni's sensational new opera *Cavalleria Rusticana,* in what was one of its earliest American performances. With the death of her mother in 1896, Minnie Hauk retired from the hectic but stimulating life of an operatic prima donna. She and her husband retired to their Swiss villa outside of Lucerne, the same Tribschen that Richard Wagner had occupied at the time he composed his masterpieces *Die Meistersinger von Nürnberg* and the mighty Ring cycle of music dramas. Here, she and her husband lived an idyllic existence until World War I destroyed their Austrian investments. After her husband died in 1918, Hauk became virtually destitute, a situation she attempted to remedy by dictating her memoirs, even though she was enfeebled and blind. Fortunately, operatic star ***Geraldine Farrar** and the Music Lovers Foundation raised sufficient funds to make Hauk's final years financially comfortable. Minnie Hauk died at Villa Tribschen on February 6, 1929.

SOURCES:

Davis, Peter G. *The American Opera Singer: The Lives and Adventures of America's Great Singers in Opera and Concert, from 1825 to the Present.* Garden City, NY: Doubleday, 1997.

———. "Ball of Fire: The Sizzling Life and Times of Minnie Hauk, America's First International Opera Superstar," in *Opera News.* Vol. 61, no. 13. March 22, 1997, pp. 14–19, 27.

"Hauk, Minnie," in Dumas Malone, ed. *Dictionary of American Biography.* Vol. 8. NY: Scribner, 1932, pp. 399–400.

Hauk, Minnie. *Memories of a Singer.* Reprint ed. NY: Arno Press, 1977.

John Haag,
Associate Professor, University of Georgia, Athens, Georgia

Hauke, Julie von (1825–1895)

Countess of Hauke. *Name variations: Countess von Haucke. Born Julie Theresa in Poland in 1825; died in 1895; daughter of Maurice von Hauke and* ***Sophia Lafontaine****; became morganatic wife of Alexander of Hesse-Darmstadt, in October 1851 (died 1888); grandmother of Louis Mountbatten, earl Mountbatten of Burma; children:* ****Mary of Battenberg*** *(1852–1923); Louis of Battenberg, 1st marquess of Milford Haven (1854–1921, who married* ****Victoria of Hesse-Darmstadt****); Alexander I, prince of Bulgaria (1857–1893); Henry of Battenberg (1858–1896, who married* ****Beatrice****, daughter of Queen* ****Victoria****); Francis of Battenberg (1861–1924).*

Hautval, Adelaide (1906–1988)

French physician who, as an Auschwitz prisoner, refused to participate in medical experiments on Jewish prisoners. *Name variations: Haidi Hautval. Born in Hohwald im Elsass, Germany (now Le Hohwald, Alsace, France), on January 1, 1906; died on October 17, 1988; daughter of a Protestant pastor.*

Israel's Yad Vashem recognized her as a "Righteous Among the Nations" (April 1965).

Adelaide Hautval was born in 1906 into the family of a Protestant pastor in Alsace when that province was part of the German Reich. Known to her friends as Haidi, she received a medical degree in psychiatry from the University of Strasbourg and then returned in 1938 to her village of Le Hohwald to help in the management of a home for handicapped children. She had found employment in a clinic in southwestern France when Nazi Germany defeated and occupied France in mid-1940. In April 1942, after receiving word that her mother was mortally ill, she requested travel permits to visit her. Refused, Hautval decided to travel without authorization. She was detained at the demarcation line between the German-occupied region and the "free" area of France controlled by the collaborationist regime in Vichy. While waiting for a train on the station platform at Bourges, she witnessed German mistreatment of a Jewish family. Speaking to them in their own language, she told the Germans to leave the Jews in peace. When one of the tormentors asked her, "But don't you see they're only Jews," she retorted, "So what? They are people like any others, leave them alone." With this, the infuriated Nazis had enough of Hautval's "insolence" and took her to the local jail.

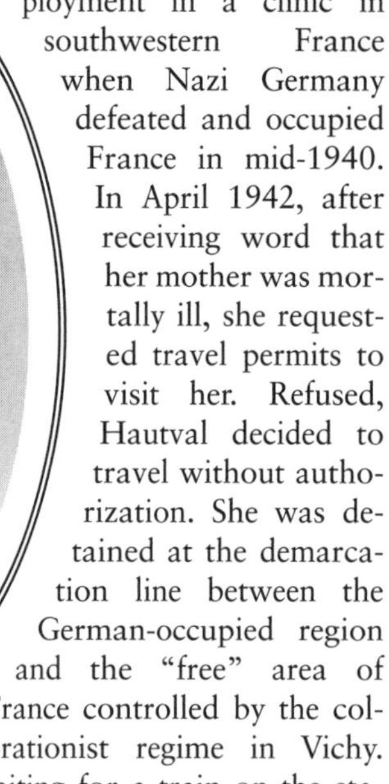

Adelaide Hautval

Soon after she was locked in her cell, a Jewish woman joined her as a fellow prisoner. When she noticed that the woman was wearing a yellow Star of David marked "Juif," Hautval improvised a paper star to wear herself, soon complaining to her Gestapo jailers that there was no valid reason for French Jews to be treated in such a demeaning fashion. Hautval made a detailed listing of the degrading laws imposed on Jews, including their being barred from travel on the Metro and having to ride in the rear compartments of the railroads. Gestapo officials, outraged by her bold defense of Jewish human rights, presented Hautval with one last chance to regain her freedom, offering to release her on condition that she retract her attacks on their anti-Semitic policies and persecutions. Her response remained defiant: "But why should I say anything different? The Jews are people like any others." Having run out of patience, one of the Gestapo officials in attendance snapped at Hautval, "Since you wish to defend them, you will share their fate."

For nine months, Hautval was moved to several collection camps for French Jews slated for deportation to the dreaded East. At Pithiviers, Beaune la Rolande, and finally Romainville, she experienced fear, hunger, and cold along with hundreds of her fellow prisoners, virtually all of whom were Jewish. Because of Hautval's refusal to change her attitudes, the Gestapo compelled her to stitch a Star of David on her coat along with a cloth band marked "A friend of the Jews."

In the bitterly cold month of January 1943, Hautval was deported to Auschwitz as one of a trainload of 230 French women political prisoners (mostly non-Jewish Communists). After a hellish three days, with a view of an electrified fence stretching to the horizon, Hautval and her half-starved group defiantly sang the "Marseillaise" as they were marched in fog to their barracks in the women's quarters at Auschwitz-Birkenau (Auschwitz II). Soon, all of Hautval's group were tattooed, her own designated number being 31802. Inhumane living conditions quickly took their toll; within three months of their arrival, 160 of the 230 French prisoners had died. Although still alive, Hautval had lost much weight and began to suffer from spreading ulcers on her legs.

At this point, one of Auschwitz's Nazi doctors, Dr. Eduard Wirths, asked Hautval if she wished to practice gynecology. She thought the request was odd, given the fact that the officials were aware that her medical specialty was psychiatry. Suspicious, she asked Wirths precisely what kind of medical activities he would expect her to be involved in. His refusal to provide an answer deepened her concerns, but she accepted the "invitation," knowing she was now playing an extremely dangerous game with her captors. Hautval was convinced that if she managed to survive Auschwitz, whatever details of Nazi criminality she might witness would prove to be of significance when the time came to bring Hitlerism to the bar of world justice. She would be able to offer specific testimony against physicians who ignored the humane ideals embodied in the Hippocratic Oath they had once sworn to uphold.

Soon after her conversation with Wirths, Hautval was transferred along with ten Jewish women to Block 10, one of the most notorious blocks in the main Auschwitz camp. A crudely constructed two-story building, it held about 100 Jewish women mostly from France and Greece. Soon it became clear to Hautval that Block 10 contained individuals earmarked for medical experiments. In time, Block 10 would become abysmally crowded, somehow housing between 400 and 500 women, many of them in poor health and all slated to be victims of inhumane experimentation. From the start of her incarceration in Block 10, Hautval took great risks in saving as many lives as possible. On one occasion, after a convoy of women suffering from typhus arrived from Birkenau, she was able to hide them on the Block's top floor, treating them as best she could and saving a number of lives. Had the camp officials discovered the existence of the group, all would have been sent en masse to the gas chambers. Hautval was certain at this point that neither she nor any of her comrades would survive Auschwitz, but she did all she could to uphold essential standards of human decency. She told a fellow prisoner, "None of us are going to get out of this alive, but so long as we are here we must behave like human beings."

Hautval was informed by Eduard Wirths and his brother Helmut Wirths, a Nazi stormtrooper who described himself as a gynecologist, that the goal of their experiments was to discover a cure for cancer of the uterus. After examining a number of women suffering from pre-cancerous uterine growths, Hautval became suspicious of the high incidence of the disease in the small group of women available and informed Eduard she could not continue to carry out examinations. Eduard ordered her to report to Professor Carl Clauberg, who was carrying out sterilization experiments by injecting caustic fluids into women's uteruses, which invariably caused atrocious pain. Asked by Helmut what her views on sterilization were, Hautval responded that she was "absolutely opposed." Surprised by her answer, Helmut argued that a psychiatrist like herself should be sympathetic toward a procedure aimed at race preservation; she replied that the process was highly debatable and subject to abuses. Helmut was incredulous and tried to reason with her. After all, he said, all the patients are "only Jews." Hautval shot back, "We have no right to dispose of the life and destiny of others." The medical staff refrained from assigning her to Clauberg's group.

The group headed by Carl Clauberg included other doctors (including Josef Mengele, Horst Schumann, and a Polish physician, Wladyslaw Dering) who experimented on hundreds of Jewish and Polish women, as well as women of other nationalities, either by exposing them to high dosages of X-rays, or by surgically removing their ovaries. The goal of this "scientific research" was to perfect a means to one day, after the victory of Nazi Germany, carry out on a worldwide scale the sterilization of all half- and quarter-Jews who remained alive. Hautval quickly discovered evidence of these plans in considerable detail.

On one occasion, Hautval gave in to the intense pressure of the Nazi medical experimenters. She was called on to anesthetize two young Greek Jewish girls, both still in their teens, whose cervixes were to be removed in the interest of experimentation. The surgeon in this instance was Dr. Maximilian Samuel, a distinguished German-Jewish gynecologist who had been awarded the Iron Cross in World War I and was strongly nationalistic. Possibly for these reasons, when he arrived at Auschwitz he was temporarily spared from the gas chambers even though he was in his 60s and in declining health. Samuel was described by Hautval as a broken man "overwhelmed by fear and a desire to please the authorities." Ultimately, he failed in his attempts to save the life of his young daughter by offering to collaborate in Nazi medical experiments (his wife had been gassed upon his family's arrival at Auschwitz), and he was shot when younger Jewish doctor-inmates arrived at the camp. After this experience with the two young girls, Hautval refused to work for Samuel, and because of this he denounced her to Eduard Wirths.

When Wirths confronted her and demanded to know if she had in fact refused to participate in the "experiment" by not giving anesthetic to the next group of women, Hautval admitted that Samuel's accusation was correct. Wirths asked why; she answered that it was contrary to principles she held as a physician. "Can't you see that these people are different from you?" asked Wirths. "Dr. Wirths," replied Hautval, "there are a great many other people who are different from me, starting with you." Though Hautval feared the worst sort of retribution after this encounter, she was only transferred back to the nearby Birkenau camp. There, she practiced medicine as best she could, saving lives, until she was transferred in August 1944 to the infamous Ravensbrück women's concentration camp. Despite ongoing hardships, Hautval survived Ravensbrück and was liberated in April 1945. After her health was restored, she returned to her medical practice in France and wrote her memoirs, though they were not then published.

Adelaide Hautval survived to present damning testimony against the Nazi doctors at Nuremberg after the war. She appeared again as a witness in the dramatic libel trial that took place in London in April and May of 1964. One of the Auschwitz physicians, the Polish-born Dr.

Wladyslaw Dering, sued Leon Uris, author of the novel *Exodus,* for libel because he had been mentioned as one of the Nazi staff who carried out the infamous medical experiments in Auschwitz. After weeks of detailed, ghastly testimony, one of the most memorable episodes of the trial took place with the testimony presented by Hautval. Her story made it clear that unlike Dering, who argued that it would have been futile and suicidal to refuse to obey orders in the world of Auschwitz, she had rejected the SS commands to participate in the sterilization of women and still survived. In his summation to the jury, Justice Frederick Horace Lawton described Adelaide Hautval, who had refused to obey orders from Nazi doctors on four separate occasions, as being "a most distinguished person . . . one of the most impressive and courageous women who had ever given evidence in the courts of this country."

A year after the trial, in which Dering was awarded derisory damages of one half-penny, Hautval was invited to Israel to receive the award of the Medal of the Righteous. On that day, April 17, 1965, her response was modest, first noting that only God, not mere mortals like herself, deserved such an honor. "What I did," she said, "was perfectly natural, logical and derived from a moral obligation." Noted Leon Uris: "If we had had more friends like Dr. Hautval, there could never have been a Nazi era." Hautval revised her memoirs in 1987. Though they were published in 1991 as *Médecine et crimes contre l'Humanité*, she did not live to see that day, having terminated her own life on October 17, 1988.

Following her death, the story of Haidi Hautval and her refusal to become an accomplice in an infamous chapter in the history of medicine has continued to provide a powerful instance of *Zivilcourage* in the face of evil. French and German sympathizers have met in her home village of Le Hohwald to commemorate her acts of courage at Auschwitz and the other camps she survived. In October 1998, on the tenth anniversary of her death, a large gathering carried out a "March Against Our Forgetting" from Le Hohwald to the nearby memorial site of the former Struthof Nazi concentration camp. In November 1991, Le Hohwald had honored its most distinguished native daughter with a memorial fountain inscribed with one of Hautval's aphorisms: "Think and behave like the clear waters of your nature." She received an additional honor when the street facing the medical clinics of the University of Strasbourg was renamed. Strasbourg mayor **Catherine Trautmann** noted in her dedicatory address that the individual whom the street had previously commemorated, French Nobel Prize-winner Alexis Carrel, no longer deserved such a distinction, having been exposed as a champion of euthanasia and as a scientist whose definition of a desirable eugenics policy included the gassing of individuals "of poor quality." In July 1993, Adelaide Hautval's name replaced his.

SOURCES:

"Adelaide Hautval—Andenken an eine Gerechte; Solidaritätsmarsch zur Erinnerung an Haidi Hautval," in *Antifaschistische Nachrichten.* No. 20, 1998.

Breur-Hibma, Aat. *Een verborgen herinnering.* Amsterdam: Tiebosch, 1983.

Bross, Ester. "Französisch-deutsches Jugendtreffen im Jahr der Menschenrechte: Das Vermächtnis von Dr. Haidi Hautval," in *AntifaNachrichten* [VVN-BdA Baden-Württemberg]. No. 3. July 1998.

"Die Carrel-Strasse in Strassburg mit neuem Namen," in *Neue Zürcher Zeitung.* July 9, 1993, p. 11.

Dunin-Wasowicz, Krzysztof. *Resistance in the Nazi Concentration Camps 1933–1945.* Warsaw: PWN—Polish Scientific Publishers, 1982.

Fogelman, Eva. *Conscience & Courage: Rescuers of Jews during the Holocaust.* NY: Anchor Books, 1994.

Gutman, Yisrael and Michael Berenbaum, eds. *Anatomy of the Auschwitz Death Camp.* Bloomington: Indiana University Press, 1994.

Hautval, Adelaide. *Médecine et crimes contre l'Humanité.* Le Mejan, Arles: Actes Sud, 1991.

Hill, Mavis M. and L. Norman Williams. *Auschwitz in England: A Record of a Libel Action.* NY: Stein and Day, 1965.

Langbein, Hermann. *Against All Hope: Resistance in the Nazi Concentration Camps 1938–1945.* Translated by Harry Zohn. NY: Paragon House, 1994.

Lifton, Robert Jay. *The Nazi Doctors: Medical Killing and the Psychology of Genocide.* NY: Basic Books, 1986.

Miller, Neil. "Who Were the Rescuers?," in *World: The Journal of the Unitarian Universalist Association.* Vol. 10, no. 3. May–June 1996, pp. 24–27.

Paldiel, Mordecai. *The Path of the Righteous: Gentile Rescuers of Jews During the Holocaust.* Hoboken, NJ: KTAV Publishing House, Inc./The Jewish Foundation for Christian Rescuers/ADL, 1993.

Shelley, Lore, ed. *Auschwitz—The Nazi Civilization: Twenty-Three Women Prisoners' Accounts.* Lanham, MD: University Press of America, 1992.

Silver, Eric. *The Book of the Just: The Unsung Heroes Who Rescued Jews from Hitler.* NY: Grove Press, 1992.

Wieviorka, Michel. "Nouveaux témoignages sur les camps nazis," in *La Quinzaine littéraire.* No. 575. April 1–15, 1991, pp. 22–23.

John Haag,
Associate Professor of History,
University of Georgia, Athens, Georgia

Havel, Olga (1933–1996)

First lady of the Czech Republic. *Name variations: Olga Havlova. Born Olga Splíchalová in Prague, Czechoslovakia, in 1933; died in Prague on January*

27, 1996; married Václav Havel (a playwright and president of the Czech Republic), in 1964.

The beloved first lady of the Czech Republic and a remarkable woman in her own right, Olga Havel had humble beginnings. Born in a working-class district in Prague in 1933, Olga was six when her parents divorced, and as a teenager she helped raise her eldest sister's five children. She was employed at a shoe factory before meeting Václav Havel, the intellectual son of a millionaire, in the mid-1950s. They were as different in appearance as in background, he short and stocky, she tall, slim, and elegant. After a long courtship, which Václav celebrated in a poem, they were married in 1964. She subsequently supported her husband throughout his early career as a writer and resident playwright at the Theatre on the Balustrade, where she also worked. After the Soviet invasion of 1968, she saw him through his 20-year rise from a leader in the dissident movement to his ultimate position as president of the country. She was of particular strength to her husband during the years of his imprisonment, which he documented in letters, later published worldwide as *Letters to Olga*.

As first lady, a role she was anything but eager to assume, Havel proved invaluable in providing advice based on her deep understanding of the so-called "ordinary" people. She also established her own areas of interest, founding and heading up the Committee of Good Will, which in 1992 merged with the newly formed Olga Havel Foundation to carry out work with the mentally and physically handicapped as well as those afflicted with chronic illnesses. The foundation also spearheaded a campaign to prevent the spread of AIDS and initiated several projects aimed at disadvantaged children. Even after being diagnosed with cancer, Havel continued to pursue her charitable work. In 1995, she was nominated by the Czech Republic as the European woman of the year. Upon her death in January 1996, tens of thousands stood in line at the Castle in Prague for a chance to pay their respects to her.

SOURCES:

Ash, Timothy Garton. "On Olga Havel (1933–1996)," in *The New York Review of Books*. March 21, 1996.

Havemeyer, Mrs. Henry O. (1855–1929).

See Cassatt, Mary for sidebar on Louisine Havemeyer.

Havemeyer, Louisine (1855–1929).

See Cassatt, Mary for sidebar.

Olga Havel

Haver, June (1926—)

American film actress of post-World War II musicals. *Born June Stovenour in Rock Island, Illinois, on June 10, 1926; middle of three daughters of Fred and Marie Stovenour; attended high school in Hollywood, California; married Jimmy Zito (a musician), in March 1947 (divorced 1949); married Fred MacMurray (an actor), on June 28, 1954; children: (with MacMurray) adopted twin girls, Katie and Laurie, in 1956.*

Filmography: Swing's the Thing *(short, 1942);* Trumpet Serenade *(short, 1942);* The Gang's All Here *(1943);* Home in Indiana *(1944);* Irish Eyes Are Smiling *(1944);* Where Do We Go from Here? *(1945);* The Dolly Sisters *(1945);* Three Little Girls in Blue *(1946);* Wake Up and Dream *(1946);* I Wonder Who's Kissing Her Now? *(1947);* Scudda-Hoo! Scudda-Hay! *(1948);* Oh, You Beautiful Doll! *(1949);* Look for the Silver Lining *(1949);* The Daughter of Rosie O'Grady *(1950);* I'll Get By *(1950);* Love Nest *(1951);* The Girl Next Door *(1953).*

In a career that lasted only a decade, June Haver made her mark in the Technicolor musicals of the 1940s, before she was waylaid in her career, first by a religious calling and then by marriage.

Haver was a musically gifted child who, at age eight, won the Cincinnati Conservatory of Music's Post Music Contest and played the piano as one-time guest artist with the Cincinnati Symphony Orchestra. As a teenager, she sang with several bands and made two musical film shorts before signing a contract with Twentieth Century-Fox. In 1943, she debuted with another newcomer, *__Jeanne Crain__, in *The Gang's All Here*, a Technicolor musical starring *__Alice Faye__ and *__Carmen Miranda__. Haver later became a protégé of staff producer George Jessel, who jump-started her career by casting her with *__Betty Grable__ in *The Dolly Sisters* (1945), a film about the turn-of-the-century show-business sisters, **Jenny** and **Rosie Dolly**. Although Fox head Darryl F. Zanuck tapped Haver as an eventual replacement for Grable, it never came to pass.

Haver went on to top billing in *Three Little Girls in Blue* (1946), with *__Vivian Blaine__ and *__Vera-Ellen__. The story of three sisters hunting for rich husbands in 1902 Atlantic City was a remake of *Three Blind Mice* (1938) and *Moon Over Miami* (1941). It would reappear yet again in 1953 as *How to Marry a Millionaire*. Haver then sang her way through a series of musicals that caught the fancy of the public but never impressed the critics. Notable were *Oh, You Beautiful Doll!* (1949), a salute to turn-of-the-century composer Fred Fisher, and *Look for the Silver Lining* (1949), in which she played Ziegfeld star *__Marilyn Miller__.

Around 1950, Haver began to lose interest in her movie career and, in February 1952, announced that she planned to become a nun. "I know what I want to do," she told the press. "But what I want must also be what God wants. May His will be done." She entered the Sisters of Charity convent in Leavenworth, Kansas, but left after a few months, reportedly due to ill health. Her first public performance after her confinement was in a "Lux Radio Theatre" adaptation of *Trouble Along the Way* in 1954. Soon after, she abandoned her career again to marry actor Fred MacMurray, a widower. (Haver had been married briefly to trumpeter Jimmy Zito.) The couple adopted twin girls in 1956, and a year later Haver told an interviewer. "I had ten good years in the movies. I'm here now. I do the marketing and worry about the laundry. . . . I'm a mother. I'm needed."

SOURCES:

Parish, James Robert. *The Fox Girls*. NY: Arlington House, 1974.

June Haver with Mark Stevens, in I Wonder Who's Kissing Her Now.

———, and Michael R. Pitts. *Hollywood Songsters.* Garland, 1991.

Barbara Morgan,
Melrose, Massachusetts

Havergal, Frances Ridley (1836–1879)

English-born hymn writer and author of religious poems, tracts, and children's books. *Born at Astley, Worcestershire, England, on December 14, 1836; died, age 42, at Caswell Bay, Swansea, South Wales, on June 3, 1879; youngest of six children of Reverend William Henry Havergal (writer of sacred music and rector of Astley, Worcestershire) and Jane (Head) Havergal; sister of* ***Maria Vernon Graham Havergal*** *(who wrote* Frances R. Havergal: The Last Week, *1879, and edited Frances'* Memorials *in 1880,* Poetical Works, *1884, and* Letters, *1885), and* ***Jane Havergal Crane*** *(who edited Maria's autobiography in 1887 and published a biography of their father in 1882); educated by her mother and elder sister Jane; studied for a year in Düsseldorf, Germany.*

Selected poetry: The Ministry of Song *(1870);* Under the Surface *(1874);* Loyal Responses *(1878);* Life Chords *(1880);* Life Echoes *(1883);* Poetical Works *(1884);* Coming to the King *(1886).*

Children's books: A Little Worker for Christ *(1872);* Little Pillows: or, Good Night Thoughts *(1874);* Morning Bells: or, Waking Thoughts *(1874).*

Born in Astley, Worcestershire, England, in 1836, the daughter of a minister, Frances Havergal inherited her father's musical talent as well as his Christian faith. It was said that she prayed three times a day, and studied Greek and Hebrew so that she could better understand the Bible. Havergal wrote the well-known hymn "I Gave My Life for Thee" at the age of 18, after which she endured a period of illness which required her to abandon her work for nine years. Upon her father's death in 1890, she prepared *The Ministry of Song* for the press, claiming that her inspiration was from God. "I never seem to write even a verse by myself," she once said, "and feel like a little child writing what is dictated."

Havergal's poetry has been criticized as scattered and repetitive, but some of her hymns have been called excellent. The best of them, including "True-Hearted, Whole-Hearted," "O Savior, Precious Savior," "I Gave My Life for Thee," and "Tell It Out Among the Heathen," have stood time's ultimate test.

SUGGESTED READING:

Darlow, T.H. *Havergal: A Saint of God,* 1927.

Haviland, Laura S. (1808–1898)

Canadian-born abolitionist and welfare worker. *Born Laura Smith on December 20, 1808, in Ontario, Canada; died on April 20, 1898, in Grand Rapids, Michigan; daughter of Daniel and Sene (Blancher) Smith; attended public school in Canada and the Union Free School in Lockport, New York; married Charles Haviland, Jr., on November 3, 1825; children: Harvey S. Haviland; Daniel S. Haviland;* ***Esther M. Haviland; Anna C. Haviland;*** *Joseph Haviland;* ***Laura Jane Haviland; Almira Ann Haviland; Lavina Haviland.***

Laura Smith was born in Kitley Township, Leeds County, Ontario, Canada, on December 20, 1808, the eldest of eight children of Quaker parents. Smith found the Quaker faith of her parents to be too rigid, and leaned more toward frontier revivalism which emphasized humanitarianism. She married Charles Haviland, Jr., on November 3, 1825. A young Quaker, Charles shared his wife's religious and humanitarian convictions. In September of 1829, they moved to a Quaker settlement in Raisin Township, Lenawee County, in Michigan territory, where they joined ***Elizabeth Margaret Chandler**—another Quaker sympathetic with their beliefs—and formed the first antislavery society in Michigan. After objections from other Quakers regarding their abolitionist activities, they withdrew from the Society of Friends.

In 1837, Haviland and her husband opened a small school at their farm, for orphans and indigent county charges. Two years later, it became the River Raisin Institute, a preparatory school that did not discriminate on the basis of race or sex. It frequently served as a haven for fugitive slaves and received support from Michigan abolitionists.

By 1844, Haviland had become a minister in the Wesleyan Methodist Church. The following year, an erysipelas epidemic took the lives of her husband, both of her parents, one sister and her youngest child. After this tragedy, she placed the River Raisin Institute in the care of trustees and turned to antislavery activities. Haviland devoted the next 20 years to welfare work among African-Americans, including riding the Underground Railroad, giving speeches, and teaching in black schools. During the Civil War, she visited and worked in hospitals and prison camps, aided refugee slaves in religious instruction, and helped with the care of black children.

In 1864, Haviland traveled widely through the South as a paid agent of the Michigan Freedmen's Aid Commission. She remained with the

Laura S. Haviland

Freedmen after the war, moving to Kansas in 1879 to work with African-Americans who flocked to the state. During the war, the River Raisin Institute underwent several changes, finally being converted to an orphans' home under the direction of the Freedmen. The home closed, but, as a result of its work, the state of Michigan investigated the need for such homes, contributing to the founding of the State Public School for Dependent and Neglected Children. Haviland led a successful movement to found a State Industrial School for wayward girls.

In later life, Haviland put her energies toward the temperance crusade and the women's suffrage movement. In 1872, she returned to the Quaker faith. Laura S. Haviland died of apoplexy at 81, on April 20, 1898, in Grand Rapids, Michigan, and was buried in the Friends Cemetery near Adrian.

SOURCES:

James, Edward T., ed. *Notable American Women, 1607–1950*. Cambridge, MA: The Belknap Press of Harvard University Press, 1971.

Judith C. Reveal,
freelance writer, Greensboro, Maryland

Havilland, Olivia de (b. 1916).

See de Havilland, Olivia.

Havlova, Olga (1933–1996).

See Havel, Olga.

Havoc, June (b. 1916).

See Lee, Gypsy Rose for sidebar.

Hawaii, princess of.

See Nahienaena (c. 1815–1836).
See Kamamalu, Victoria (1838–1866).
See Kaiulani (1875–1899).

Hawaii, queen of.

See Kamamalu (c. 1803–1824).
See Kinau (c. 1805–1839).
See Kalama (c. 1820–1870).
See Kapiolani (1834-1899).
See Emma (1836–1885).
See Liliuokalani (1838–1917).

Hawaii, queen-regent of.

See Kaahumanu (1777–1832).

Hawarden, Clementina (1822–1865)

English photographer of posed figure studies. *Name variations: Lady Clementina Hawarden. Pronunciation: HAY-ward-en. Born Clementina Elphinstone Fleeming (pronounced "Fleming") at Cumbernauld House, near Glasgow, Scotland, in 1822; died in South Kensington, London, England, in 1865; daughter of Admiral Charles Elphinstone Fleeming and Catalina Paulina (Alessandro) Fleeming; married Cornwallis Maude, later 4th viscount Hawarden and 1st earl de Montalt, in 1845; children: ten (seven daughters and one son survived infancy).*

Part of a group of aristocratic British women who began to practice photography during the 1850s, Lady Clementina Hawarden distinguished herself by moving beyond the role of family chronicler to that of experimental artist.

The daughter of the Honorable Charles Fleeming and his Spanish wife **Catalina Alessandro Fleeming**, Hawarden married the future fourth viscount Hawarden in 1845, and during the next 20 years gave birth to ten children, eight of whom lived beyond infancy. She did not take up photography until 1857, after her husband's inheritance increased the family income. Working from her townhouse in London, and occasionally from the family's Irish estate in Dundrum, Hawarden had only eight productive years before her untimely death of pneumonia in 1865. Using her children as subjects (primarily her three eldest daughters), she explored the medium in new ways, writes Val Williams in *The Other Observers*. "Rather than seeking to convey solidity and unity, she made significant experiments with posing and with surface, creating a picture of a secret world of echoing interiors, mysterious draped windows and dramatic figures." Williams further points out that Hawarden's use of mirrors and fabric backgrounds strongly influenced such later photographers as ***Barbara Ker-Seymour** and **Helen Muspratt**. Hawarden was among the first amateur women photographers to be recognized by the Photographic Society of London, where she won awards for her work and was elected for membership in 1863.

After her death, Hawarden fell into obscurity until 1939, when her family gave 775 of her collected prints to the Victoria and Albert Museum. Her work became part of the exhibition *From Today Painting is Dead*, mounted by the museum in 1972. Subsequently, in 1991, a solo exhibition of Hawarden's photographs was held at the J. Paul Getty Museum in Malibu, California.

SOURCES:

Rosenblum, Naomi. *A History of Women Photographers*. NY: Abbeville Press, 1994.

Williams, Val. *The Other Observers*. London: Virago Press, 1991.

Barbara Morgan,
Melrose, Massachusetts

Hawes, Harriet Boyd (1871–1945)

American archaeologist. *Name variations: Harriet Boyd. Born Harriet Ann Boyd in Boston, Massachusetts, on October 11, 1871; died in Washington D.C., on March 31, 1945; graduated from Prospect Hill School in Greenfield, Massachusetts, 1888, and Smith College, 1892; studied at the American School of Classical Studies in Athens, Greece, 1896; awarded M.A. from Smith, 1901; married Charles H. Hawes (a British anthropologist), in March 1906.*

While instructing in Greek archaeology, epigraphy, and modern Greek at Smith College, Harriet Boyd Hawes used her many leaves of absence to investigate Greece and Crete. In 1896, still in her 20s, she had been awarded a scholarship to study at the American School of Classical Studies in Athens, Greece. Though she was encouraged, because of her gender, to use her knowledge as an academic librarian, Hawes begged to be allowed to assist in field work. When her request was denied, the spirited Hawes took what was left of her stipend and set off on her own expedition to the island of Crete. "Riding on muleback in Victorian attire," wrote a biographer for the Archaeological Institute of America, "accompanied by the faithful Aristides, a native of northern Greece with his mother as chaperon, she was apparently perfectly unconscious of doing anything unusual or courageous." While in Kavousi, Hawes discovered some Iron Age tombs (1900). At Gournia, she was the first to discover and excavate a Minoan town from the Early Bronze Age (1901, 1903, 1904), and the first woman to direct a major field project, bringing her worldwide attention. From 1920 to 1936, Hawes lectured on pre-Christian art at Wellesley College.

Hawise.

Variant of Hadwig or Hedwig.

Hawise (d. after 1135)

Countess of Penthievre. *Died after 1135; married Stephen, count of Penthievre, before 1100 (died 1136); children: Alan III the Black, 1st earl of Richmond (d. 1146).*

Hawise of Brittany (d. 1072)

Duchess of Brittany. *Died in 1072; daughter of Alan III, duke of Brittany, and* ****Bertha of Chartres*** *(d. 1084); married Hoel, duke of Brittany; children: Alan IV, duke of Brittany.*

Hawise of Normandy (d. 1034)

Duchess of Brittany. *Name variations: sometimes mentioned as Hedwig or Hadwisa. Died on February 21, 1034; daughter of Richard I the Fearless (d. 996), duke of Normandy (r. 942–996), and* ****Gunnor of Denmark*** *(d. 1031); married Geoffrei or Geoffrey I (d. 1008), duke of Brittany (r. 992–1008), around 997; children: Alain or Alan III, also known as Alan V (d. 1040), duke of Brittany (r. 1008–1040); Odo de Porhoet, count of Penthievre (d. 1079);* ***Adela of Rennes*** *(d. 1067, abbess of St. Georges Rennes).*

Hawise of Salisbury

Countess of Dreux. *Name variations: Hawise de Salisbury. Married Rotrou the Great, count of Perche; married Robert (c. 1123–1188), count of Dreux.*

Hawkes, Jacquetta (1910–1996)

British archaeologist and writer who was one of the foremost popularizers of archaeology. *Born Jacquetta Hopkins in Cambridge, England, on August 5, 1910; died on March 18, 1996; daughter of Sir Frederick Hopkins (a Nobel prizewinner); educated at Newnham College, University of Cambridge, and subsequently took part in many archaeological excavations between 1931 and 1940, in Britain, Ireland, France, and Palestine; married Christopher Hawkes (died 1992, an archaeologist), in 1933 (divorced 1953); married J.B. Priestley (the novelist, broadcaster, and playwright), in 1953 (died 1984); children: (first marriage) one son.*

During World War II, Jacquetta Hawkes worked for the British government at the Ministry of Education. She was principal and secretary of the United Nations' National Commission for UNESCO (1943–49); vice-president of the Council for British Archaeology (1949–52); adviser to the Festival of Britain (1951); governor of the British Film Institute (1950–55); and a member of the Central Committee of UNESCO (1966–79). She was awarded an OBE in 1952.

Hawkes' many publications include *The Archaeology of Jersey* (1939); *Prehistoric Britain* (1944), written with her first husband Christopher Hawkes; *Early Britain* (1945); *A Land* (1951); *The World of the Past* (1963); *Atlas of Ancient Archaeology* (1975); and the *Shell Guide to British Archaeology* (1986). Paul G. Bahn, her collaborator on the *Shell Guide,* found his first stay at Kissing Tree, the house near Stratford she shared with her second husband, novelist J.B. Priestley, daunting, as he tried to converse with "these formidable intellects" over dinner. "I remember asking Jacquetta, in my ignorance, if she had ever done much work on the Palaeolithic period, and she replied that she had not, 'although I did find the Tabun skull' (one of the most famous Neanderthal skulls). After dinner I sat between them, watching television in the massive study, with its floor-to-ceiling books, grand piano and enormous desks—their two favourite shows were 'Call My Bluff' and 'One Man and his

Dog.'" Though Hawkes appeared to be aloof and formal, Bahn found her "shy, and very gracious, kind and generous."

Jacquetta Hawkes also wrote poetry and plays and a biography of Sir Mortimer Wheeler. With Priestley, she co-authored *Journey Down a Rainbow* (1955), a memoir of their travels in New Mexico and Texas.

SOURCES:

Bahn, Paul G. "Obituary," in *British Archaeology.* No. 14, May 1996.

Elizabeth Rokkan,
translator, formerly Associate Professor,
Department of English, University of Bergen, Norway

Hawkins, Paula Fickes (1927—)

U.S. Republican Senator (January 1, 1981–January 3, 1987). *Born Paula Fickes on January 24, 1927, in Salt Lake City, Utah; daughter of Paul B. Fickes (navy chief warrant officer) and Leoan (Staley) Fickes; graduated from high school in Logan, Utah; attended Utah State University; married Walter Eugene Hawkins, on September 5, 1947; children: Ginean Hawkins; Kevin Brent Hawkins; Kelley Ann Hawkins.*

Paula F. Hawkins

The daughter of a navy chief warrant officer, Paula Fickes Hawkins was born in Salt Lake City, Utah, in 1927 and spent her early years living in a variety of locales dictated by her father's postings. She graduated from high school in Logan, Utah, then attended Utah State University, where she later took a job as a secretary. Following her marriage to Walter Hawkins, she moved to Atlanta, then in 1955 relocated again to central Florida.

During the 1960s, Hawkins served as a Republican Party volunteer, organizing the successful House campaign of Edward Gurney in 1966 and serving as a Florida co-chair for Richard Nixon's presidential campaigns in 1968 and 1972. In 1972, she mounted her own successful campaign for public office, winning statewide election to the Florida Public Service Commission. She served two terms with the commission, gaining a reputation as a consumer's-rights advocate and battling rate-hikes of the public utilities. In 1979, she left the commission to become vice president for consumer affairs for Air Florida.

Having sought election as U.S. senator in 1974, and as lieutenant governor in 1976, Hawkins ran for the Senate again in 1980. Failing to win a majority in the primary, she gained the nomination in a runoff, then narrowly defeated William Gunter in the general election. During her Senate tenure, Hawkins served on the Committee on Agriculture, Nutrition, and Forestry and the Committee on Labor and Human Resources. She also served on various Congressional committees, including the Joint Economic Committee (97th Congress), the Committee on Banking, Housing, and Urban Affairs (98th Congress), and the Special Committee on Aging (99th Congress).

During her second year in the Senate, Hawkins initiated an investigation into the problem of missing children, a cause that would dominate her remaining years in office. One result of the study was the Missing Children's Act of 1982, through which a central information center for missing children was established. Hawkins also sponsored legislation to provide guidelines to prevent abuse in day-care centers and other institutions, drawing attention to the issues by revealing her own abuse as a child.

When the Democrats regained control of the Senate in 1986, Hawkins lost her seat to Florida governor Bob Graham. She then settled in Winter Park, Florida.

SOURCES:

Office of the Historian. *Women in Congress 1917–1990.* Commission of the Bicentenary of the U.S. House of Representatives, 1991.

Hawley, Florence (1906–1991).
See Ellis, Florence Hawley.

Hawthorne, Rose (1851–1926).
See Lathrop, Rose Hawthorne.

Hawthorne, Sophia Peabody (1809–1871)

American, one of the famous Peabody sisters, who edited her husband Nathaniel Hawthorne's notebooks for publication after his death. *Born Sophia Amelia Peabody in Salem, Massachusetts, on September 21, 1809; died in London, England, of typhoid pneumonia in February 1871; daughter of Nathaniel Peabody (a dentist) and Elizabeth Palmer Peabody (1778–1853, a teacher and writer); sister of Elizabeth Palmer Peabody (1804–1894) and Mary Peabody Mann (1806–1887, wife of Horace Mann); married Nathaniel Hawthorne (the novelist), in July 1842 (died 1864); children: Julian Hawthorne (b. 1846);* ***Una Hawthorne*** *(b. 1844); Rose Hawthorne Lathrop (1851–1926).*

Born in 1809, Sophia Peabody was the youngest of three extraordinary daughters of Nathaniel Peabody, a dentist and homeopath from Salem and Boston, and **Elizabeth Palmer Peabody** (1778–1853), a teacher and writer. Her sisters were ***Elizabeth Palmer Peabody** (1804–1894) and ***Mary Peabody Mann** (1806–1887). Sophia passed most of her youth as an invalid, suffering from piercing headaches which childhood surgery did nothing to alleviate. Spending most of her time alone in her room, Sophia, who remained cheerful and docile in the face of her adversities, studied art and languages diligently, learning to read Plato in Greek and the Old Testament in Hebrew. For a while during the early 1830s, she supported herself as a painter, doing portraits or copying masterpieces, but a severe illness forced her to break off this work and take a long convalescent trip to Cuba in 1834 with her sister Mary. Sophia enjoyed the heat: "When it is ninety-eight degrees, then I am comfortable."

The author Nathaniel Hawthorne was first friendly with Sophia's gregarious older sister Elizabeth, who admired his writings. But after he met Sophia in 1838, the two quickly fell in love and secretly became engaged. The Peabodys knew many of the leading figures of Boston literary society, including Bronson Alcott and Ralph Waldo Emerson, and, before meeting Hawthorne, Sophia had written of Emerson: "I think Mr. Emerson is the greatest man that ever lived. . . . He is indeed a 'Supernal Vision.'" Though Sophia and Nathaniel remained engaged, they separated for four years while he worked in the Boston custom house and saved his money; both had resolved to wait until her health improved before marrying. Their long separation gave rise to an eloquent and now famous series of love letters from both sides.

In 1842, Sophia married Nathaniel, whom she described as "the angel of the Apocalypse, so powerful and gentle," and they went to live at the Old Manse in Concord, taking great joy in each other's company. For the first year of their marriage, they even kept a joint diary. After a miscarriage, Sophia gave birth twice in Concord, first to Una (1844) then to Julian (1846).

Nathaniel hated the idea that his "angel" should do any housework and, when they were too poor to afford a servant, he did the cooking and kitchen work. Finally, he bowed to financial necessity and went back to work as a customs inspector, this time in Salem. While there, and with her urging, he finished his novel, *The Scarlet Letter.* On first reading, Sophia was so upset by its ending that she developed a severe headache and went to bed in tears. Hawthorne, though concerned, saw this reaction as a good omen for the book's success. Indeed, the work relieved some of their financial worries, and they moved to Lenox in the Berkshires, where their daughter ***Rose Hawthorne (Lathrop)** was born in 1851. Herman Melville, who lived nearby, claimed that Sophia Hawthorne was one of the few readers ever to fully appreciate his masterpiece *Moby Dick*.

The Hawthornes prospered in the 1850s, first in Liverpool and later in London, Paris, Florence, and Rome. In Italy in the late 1850s, they befriended Robert and ***Elizabeth Barrett Browning** and joined them at spiritualist seances, which Sophia entered into eagerly while Nathaniel remained suspicious. Sophia continued to suffer in cold climates and took cures in Portugal and Italy, where the family spent much of 1858 and 1859. They were back in America at the onset of the Civil War.

When Nathaniel Hawthorne died in 1864, the heartbroken Sophia edited his notebooks for publication, but made extensive cuts, excluding intimate details about their personal lives, strong language, and references to Nathaniel's many aversions. She took her fami-

Sophia Peabody Hawthorne

ly back to Europe after the Civil War and died of pneumonia in London, just before Rose Hawthorne's 1871 wedding.

SUGGESTED READING:

Tharp, Louise Hall. *The Peabody Sisters of Salem.* Boston, MA: Little, Brown, 1950.

Hay, Elzey (1840–1931).

See Andrews, Eliza Frances.

Hay, Lucy (1599–1660)

Countess of Carlisle. *Born in 1599; died in 1660; daughter of Henry Percy, 9th earl of Northumberland; married James Hay, 1st earl of Carlisle, in 1617.*

Born in 1599, Lucy Hay, countess of Carlisle, went on to establish strong political ties. She exercised influence over Queen ***Henrietta Maria** (sister of Louis XIII of France and wife of Charles I), was an intimate of Thomas Wentworth (earl of Stafford) and John Pym, and acted as an intermediary between Scottish and English leaders during the English Civil War. The countess was imprisoned in the Tower of London from 1649 to 1650 and died ten years later. Distinguished by her great beauty and wit, Lucy Hay inspired a number of English poets, including Thomas Carew, John Suckling, Robert Herrick, Edmund Waller, and William D'Avenant.

Hay, Mary Garrett (1857–1928)

American suffragist and temperance reformer. *Born on August 29, 1857, in Charlestown, Indiana; died on August 29, 1928, in New Rochelle, New York; daughter of Andrew Jennings Hay and Rebecca H. (Garrett) Hay; lived with Carrie Chapman Catt.*

On August 29, 1857, Mary Garrett Hay was born into a prominent family in Charlestown, Indiana, the eldest of four daughters and a son of Andrew Jennings Hay and **Rebecca H. Hay**. Mary was especially close to her father, a physician active in politics. She first tasted the political world by joining him at meetings and entertaining his Republican friends at their home.

Mary Hay briefly attended Western College for Women in Oxford, Ohio, from 1873 to 1874, but chose to return home and involve herself in the two causes near to her heart: prohibition and women's suffrage. She joined the Woman's Christian Temperance Union (WCTU) and became the secretary-treasurer for her local branch. She also worked as treasurer of the Indiana state WCTU for seven years and by 1885 found herself in charge of one of the smaller departments of the national organization.

At about the same time, Hay joined the local woman suffrage movement and soon advanced to a state office. She formed a close association with ***Carrie Chapman Catt** who was organizing Western women to campaign in their home states for suffrage amendments. In 1895, Hay assisted Catt with the formation of the Organization Committee of the National American Woman Suffrage Association and was soon recognized as Catt's right-hand woman. That same year, Hay moved to New York City to help with organizing the committee's offices. The following year, Hay organized California's suffragists at all levels during the California referendum campaign.

In 1899, Hay and Catt traveled 13,000 miles, visiting 20 states to organize women's groups. In 1900, Hay resigned from the Organization Committee but continued to work in an unofficial capacity with Catt. In 1905, after the death of Catt's husband, the two women moved in together, and Hay became active in club work in New York City. During the campaigns of 1915 and 1917, she directed the city's suffrage movement, lobbying for a state constitutional amendment. The first campaign failed, but, as a result of her strong work with the women's trade union movement, the second campaign achieved victory.

Her success in New York City led to Hay's transfer to Washington D.C. to help direct federal amendment work among Congressional Republicans. A dedicated Republican, she had been a delegate to the 1918 New York Republican convention. Her influence with women voters had helped her secure the post of chair of the convention's strategic platform committee—an unprecedented appointment for a woman—and she obtained a plank that endorsed the federal suffrage amendment. Once the women's suffrage amendment passed in Congress in June 1919, Hay threw her energies into campaigning for its ratification in state legislatures.

Nationally, Hay had been one of the original appointees to the Republican Women's National Executive Committee in 1918, and in 1919 she had become its chair. However, Hay's vigorous campaigning against the reelection bid of Republican Senator James W. Wadsworth, Jr.—a bitter anti-suffragist—strained her relations with other committee leaders, and she resigned in 1920. Despite accusations of disloyalty to her party, Hay continued to fight for Wadsworth's defeat and realized her goal when he lost to the Harding ticket that November. Hay had also assumed the chair of the newly formed New York City League of Women Voters in 1918, but once again her strained relationship with other league leaders forced her resignation in 1923.

Having realized her dream of women's suffrage with the ratification of the 19th amendment, Hay returned to the cause of prohibition in her later years. She served as chair of the Women's Committee for Law Enforcement in the fight to enforce prohibition. While waiting for the arrival of guests to her 71st birthday party, Mary Garrett Hay died of a cerebral hemorrhage in New Rochelle in the home she shared with Catt. She was buried in Woodlawn Cemetery, New York.

SOURCES:

James, Edward T., ed. *Notable American Women, 1607–1950*. Cambridge, MA: The Belknap Press of Harvard University Press, 1971.

Judith C. Reveal,
freelance writer, Greensboro, Maryland

Hay, Timothy (1910–1952).

See Brown, Margaret Wise.

Hay**a**, Maria Eugenia (1944–1991).

See Marucha.

Hayashi Fumiko (1903–1951)

First woman fiction writer in modern Japan who enjoyed both popular success and critical recognition during a 20-year career which produced 278 books.

Pronunciation: HAH-yah-SHE FOO-me-KOE. Born in Yamaguchi Prefecture, Japan, in 1903; died in 1951; fourth illegitimate child of Hayashi Kiku (mother) and Miyata Asataro (father), both of whom were itinerant peddlers; graduated from Onomichi Higher Girls' School in Hiroshima Prefecture, Japan; married Tezuka Ryokubin (a painter), in 1926.

Hayashi Fumiko lived in and wrote about the margins of Japanese life. Because her mother and stepfather were peddlers, she was frequently uprooted and attended seven different primary schools, with many long-term absences. She worked her way through high school, as a maid and as a factory worker on a night shift. After graduation, she went to Tokyo, where she supported herself in a number of odd jobs, working as a clerk, waitress, salesperson, and bath-house attendant. She also suffered from a series of ill-advised romances. From these experiences, Hayashi gained great insight into the lives of the poor and social outcasts who rarely were depicted in Japanese literature. She wrote in her first book, *Vagabond's Song,* published in 1930: "Women are tossed about like flags in a breeze, I think as I wait in this long line. These women around me wouldn't be here if their circumstances were better. It is their need for work that binds them. Unemployment is an assault, your life becomes confused like that of an unchaste woman." Immediately, her work met with both popular success and critical acclaim.

Beginning in the 1930s, Hayashi traveled extensively throughout Asia and Europe. Her masterpiece novel, *Ukigumo* (*The Floating Cloud,* 1950), was based on her travels to Southeast Asia during the war years and is the story of a young woman and man who have been spiritually devastated by the war. A writer of poetry, short stories, and novels, Hayashi died in 1951, at the peak of her career. Her funeral was attended by a vast number of mourners, not only the intellectuals of publishing circles, but also ordinary women in aprons, carrying shopping bags.

SOURCES:

Tanaka Yukiko. *To Live and to Write: Selections by Japanese Women Writers, 1913–1938.* Seattle, WA: The Seal Press, 1987.

SUGGESTED READING:

Lippit, Noriko Mizuta, and Kyoko Iriye Selden, eds. *Japanese Women Writers: Twentieth Century Short Fiction.* Armonk, NY: M.E. Sharpe, 1991.

Haydée, Marcia (1939—)

Brazilian dancer and director. *Name variations: Marcia Haydee. Born Marcia Pereira da Silva in Niteroi, Brazil, in 1939; studied with Yvonne Gama e Silva, Yucco Lindberg, and Vaslav Veltchek, as well as the Sadler's Wells Ballet (1954–55).*

One of the greatest ballerinas of her day, Marcia Haydée made her professional debut with the Ballet Madeleine Rosay in Quitandinha, Petropolis, in 1953; that same year, she danced with the Rio de Janeiro Teatro Municipal. In 1957, she joined the Grand Ballet of Marquis de Cuevas, soon becoming a soloist. Four years later, in 1961, she moved to the Stuttgart Opera Ballet. There, under the direction of John Cranko, Haydée created roles in *Romeo and Juliet* (1962), *Onegin* (1965), *Carmen* (1971), and *Initials R.B.M.E.* (1972). She was appointed artistic director of the Stuttgart Ballet in 1976 and set about expanding the repertoire. Under Haydée, renowned choreographers, such as Maurice Béjart and William Forsythe, created new works. Moreover, she fostered a new generation of talented dancers. Haydée retired from the Stuttgart in 1996, after 35 years.

Hayden, Mary (1862–1942)

Irish historian, senator, and campaigner for women's educational rights. *Born Mary Teresa Hayden in Dublin, Ireland, on May 19, 1862; died in Dublin on July 12, 1942; daughter of Thomas Hayden and Mary Anne (Ryan) Hayden; educated at Alexandra College, Dublin and Royal University of Ireland; awarded B.A. (1st class honors) in 1885, and M.A. (1st class honors) in 1887; never married.*

Mary Hayden was born in Dublin, Ireland, on May 19, 1862, the only daughter of **Mary Anne Hayden** and Dr. Thomas Hayden, a distinguished Dublin doctor who was professor of anatomy at the Catholic University (founded by Cardinal John Henry Newman). Her father was a major influence in her life and his early death in 1881 dealt a considerable blow. Hayden graduated with honors in 1885 from the Royal University of Ireland (RUI) and was awarded a master's degree in modern languages in 1887. During the 1880s and 1890s, she was engaged to be married but her fiancé died after a lingering illness. She traveled extensively, visiting India, Egypt, America and, especially, Greece, to which she took parties of friends and students. Fluent in modern Greek, she also learned Hindustani and Sanskrit.

In 1888, Hayden was the first to sign **Margaret Tierney Downes**' protest, *The Case of the Catholic Lady Students of the R.U.I. Stated,* which complained of the "curt and supercilious" attitude of the Royal University senate on the women's position. But little was achieved and in 1895, when Hayden was elected to a senior fellowship in History and English at the Royal University, she was forced to accept a demotion to junior fellowship because, as a woman, she could not deliver senior fellowship lectures at University College Dublin (UCD). The Royal University was only an examining body; students studied either at home or at special colleges, the most important of which was the Jesuit-run University College Dublin which had on its staff many of the examining Fellows of the Royal University. It was a major grievance of women students that they were refused admission to the Fellows' lectures at UCD.

In 1902, Hayden made a forceful presentation to the Royal Commission on university education which subsequently recommended that women should attend lectures, pass exams and obtain degrees on the same basis as men. Hayden was against separate women's colleges. In the same year, she was elected vice-president of the newly formed Association of Women Graduates. When the National University of Ireland was established in 1908, she was the first woman member of its senate, and three years later she was appointed Professor of Modern Irish History at UCD, now a constituent college of the new university, a post she held until 1938. "All her life," her friend Professor **Mary Macken** wrote after her death, "she preached and practiced a gospel of work for her sex—no less a work than full cooperation in all the business of living. That and nothing less, she held, was the right of every human being." Hayden considered it her duty to explode the fallacious arguments being deployed against women's rights.

Hayden was active in the cause of women's suffrage and was also involved in the Irish language movement through which she met Patrick Pearse. She became one of Pearse's closest friends, and they often went on holiday together. In 1910, she joined the board of governors of Pearse's school for boys, St. Enda's, but, to Pearse's annoyance, showed little interest in the girls' school, St. Ita's. Hayden wrote later that Pearse tended to idealize both women and children, and when Pearse told her that he would not marry and intended to dedicate himself to St. Enda's, she replied that "there is a part of human nature that asks for human relationships and human sympathies." Pearse's increasingly deep involvement in nationalist politics disturbed Hayden, and they saw less of each other after 1914. Macken noted that evolution rather than revolution was Hayden's watchword and that she loathed violence. In 1916, Pearse was one of the leaders of the Easter rebellion against British rule in Ireland and was executed. Hayden wrote that he was "heart and soul in a cause which, deeply as I sympathise with everything done for Ireland, I could not in conscience help."

In 1921, in the middle of the Irish war of independence, she published, with George A. Moonan, *A Short History of the Irish People from the Earliest Times to 1920.* In the preface, the authors declared that they wrote "from a frankly national standpoint" but their anti-British tone attracted criticism. Over the next 40 years, it became the most widely used school and college text in Irish history and went through several editions. In the view of *Irish Historical Studies*, the leading historical journal in Ireland, although it "combined a vigorous style with a high degree of objectivity . . . in subsequent editions, [Hayden's] strong personal feelings on more recent events somewhat obtruded into her narrative." An influential lecturer to generations of students at UCD, Hayden demonstrated her wide knowledge of history, literature and languages. She had, as Macken observed, a "penetrating gift of analysis and a remarkable clearness of observation allied to an interesting and forthright method of presentation."

Hayden continued to interest herself in women's causes, notably the appointment of women jurors (women were rarely appointed to Irish juries until the 1960s) and women police officers. She did voluntary police work in Dublin and became involved in the alleviation of child poverty. She also set up the St. Joan Club in Dublin for poor families and many of her coworkers were women staff and students from UCD. Weeks before her death, Hayden delivered her last historical lecture, on charity children in 18th-century Dublin.

SOURCES:

Hayden, Mary. "My Recollections of Padraig Pearse" in Mary Brigid Pearse, *The Home Life of Patrick Pearse*, 1934; new ed. Dublin: Mercier Press, 1979.

Macken, Mary M. "In Memoriam: Mary T. Hayden," in *Studies* [Dublin]. Vol. 31. September 1942.

Obituary of Mary Hayden in *Irish Historical Studies* [Dublin]. Vol. 3, no. 12, 1943.

Deirdre McMahon,
lecturer in History at Mary Immaculate College,
University of Limerick, Limerick, Ireland

Hayden, Melissa (1923—)

Canadian-born ballerina. *Born Mildred Herman on April 25, 1923, in Toronto, Canada; daughter of Jacob and Kate Herman; attended Lansdowne Street* *elementary school; studied ballet with Boris Volkoff, Toronto, and Anatole Vilzak and Ludmila Shollar, New York; married Donald Hugh Coleman, Jr., in February 1954; children: one son, Stuart.*

Canadian-born ballerina Melissa Hayden was working as a bookkeeper and part-time secretary and attending dance classes at night when Anatole Chujoy, editor of *The Dance Encyclopedia*, saw her in a ballet class and encouraged her to become a professional dancer. Following his suggestion, Hayden went to New York in 1945 and almost immediately found a job as a member of the Radio City Music Hall *corps de ballet*. Continuing her studies with Anatole Vilzak and **Ludmila Shollar,** Hayden was next influenced by choreographer Michael Kidd, who saw her dance and recommended her to ***Lucia Chase**, director of the Ballet Theatre (later American Ballet Theatre). Chase put Hayden in the company's *corps de ballet*, but the young dancer rose swiftly to the rank of soloist. After two and a half years, Hayden left the company for an engagement with the Ballet ***Alicia Alonso**, on tour in South America. She returned in 1950 to join George Balanchine's New York City Ballet, where, aside from a brief return to the American Ballet Theatre, and various guest appearances with the Chicago Opera Ballet, she spent the length of her career.

Her debut with the New York City Ballet, in *The Duel* in February 1950, was highly praised. The role of the Saracen girl, wrote dance critic John Martin in *The New York Times* (February 25, 1950), "is danced magnificently by Melissa Hayden, who brings a tremendous dramatic strength onto the stage with her, as well as a technique that is lithe, powerful and supremely controlled. It is no less than an inspired performance." A month later, Hayden distinguished herself again as Profane Love in the premiere of Frederick Ashton's *Illuminations*. On December 4, on the occasion of her appearance in the Jerome Robbins' ballet, *The Age of Anxiety*, Martin wrote: "There is a mature, dramatic grasp of the role. . . . Here is truly danced emotion. There is no question that Miss Hayden dominates the work."

Hayden went on to perform in numerous ballets, including Bolender's *The Miraculous Mandarin* (1951), Robbins' *The Pied Piper* (1951), Balanchine's *Caracole* (1952), and Robbins' *The Cage* (1952). In 1952, she appeared in Charlie Chaplin's film *Limelight*, doubling for **Claire Bloom** in the dance sequence *Death of a Harlequin*, which Hayden performed with André Eglevsky. That year, she also appeared on television, dancing again with Eglevsky on the "***Kate Smith** Show." It marked one of the earliest performances of classical ballet on the new medium.

Melissa Hayden

From April 1953 to May 1954, Hayden rejoined the American Ballet Theatre, during which time she also married. She then retired to have a baby, returning to the New York City Ballet in February 1955. During the next decade, she made acclaimed appearances in Balanchine's *Ivesiana* (1955), Bolender's *Still Point* (1956), and in the premiere of Balanchine's *Divertimento No. 15* (1956). She also danced in *Agon* (1957), *Stars and Stripes* (1958), *A Midsummer Night's Dream* (1962), and *In the Night* (1970) and frequently guest starred with other ballet companies, including the National Ballet of Canada, the Royal Ballet of London, and the Cullberg Ballet of Stockholm. In 1962, she received the Albert Einstein Award for Woman of Achievement of the Year.

Melissa Hayden retired in 1973, at which time she was awarded New York City's Handel

Medallion. She performed for the last time at Wolf Trap Farm, Virginia, in September 1973, in *Cortège hongroise*, a ballet created especially for her. In retirement, Hayden served as artist-in-residence at Skidmore College, and in 1974 opened a dance school in Saratoga, New York. She became artistic director of the Pacific Northwest Dance (Seattle) in 1976. Her biography, *Melissa Hayden—Off Stage and On*, was published in 1963.

SOURCES:

Candee, Marjorie Dent, ed. *Current Biography.* NY: H.W. Wilson, 1955.

McHenry, Robert, ed. *Famous American Women.* NY: Dover, 1983.

Barbara Morgan,
Melrose, Massachusetts

Hayden, Sophia (1868–1953)

American architect. *Born in Santiago, Chile, on October 17, 1868; died of pneumonia at a convalescent home on February 3, 1953; one of two daughters and three sons of Dr. George Henry Hayden (a New England dentist) and his Spanish wife (name unknown); graduated from West Roxbury (Massachusetts) High School; graduated with honors from Massachusetts Institute of Technology, 1890; married William Blackstone Bennett (an artist), by 1900 (died 1913); children: (stepdaughter)* ***Jennie Bennett*** *(b. 1890).*

The first woman to graduate from the four-year course in architecture at the Massachusetts Institute of Technology, Sophia Hayden was also the first prizewinner in the contest to design the Woman's Building of the World's Columbian Exposition in 1893.

Sophia Hayden

Born in 1868 in Santiago, Chile, Hayden was one of five children of an American dentist and his Spanish wife. From age six, she lived with her grandparents in Jamaica Plain, Massachusetts. In 1866, following her graduation from high school, she entered the Massachusetts Institute of Technology to study architecture. The talented, determined Hayden was the first woman to complete the rigorous four-year course, graduating with honors. Her senior thesis was a design for a Fine Arts Museum of classic design. Hayden heard about the competition for the Woman's Building from friends in Chicago, as well as from her fellow student ***Lois Howe**, who had completed a special two-year course in architecture at MIT. The two women decided to enter. On March 25, 1891, while teaching mechanical drawing at the Eliot School in Jamaica Plain, Hayden received word that she had won the $1,000 first prize. Her friend Lois Howe had come in second, winning $500.

For the next two years, Hayden traveled back and forth to Chicago, preparing working drawings for the building. The demands of the project, which often included placating the demanding Board of Lady Managers, took their physical and mental toll on Hayden. Following the informal dedication of the Woman's Building in October 1892, she suffered a nervous breakdown and was unable to attend the fair which opened in May 1893.

Hayden never practiced architecture as she had planned. In 1894, she designed a Memorial Building for the Women's Clubs of America, but it was never constructed. She later married artist William Bennett, and her name slipped into obscurity. When she died in 1953, her obituary did not even note her accomplishment.

SOURCES:

Torre, Susan, ed. *Women in American Architecture.* NY: Whitney Library of Design, 1977.

Haydock, Mary (1777–1855).

See Catchpole, Margaret for sidebar on Mary Reibey.

Haydon, Julie (1910–1994)

American actress who created the part of Laura in **The Glass Menagerie.** *Born Donella Lightfoot Donaldson on June 10, 1910, in Oak Park, Illinois; died of abdominal cancer on December 24, 1994, in La Crosse, Wisconsin; daughter of Orren Madison (an editor and publisher) and Ella Marguerite (Horton)*

Donaldson (a musician and music critic); attended Gordon School for Girls, Hollywood, California; married George Jean Nathan (a drama critic) on June 19, 1955 (died, April 8, 1958); no children.

In a career dominated by a handful of memorable stage roles, Julie Haydon is perhaps best remembered for her sensitive portrayal of the vulnerable Laura, whose life is focused on her collection of glass figurines, in Tennessee Williams' autobiographical drama *The Glass Menagerie* (1945). A "memory play," *The Glass Menagerie* revolutionized the American theater with its expressionistic staging.

Haydon was born in 1910 in Oak Park, Illinois, but grew up in Hollywood, where before launching her acting career, she worked as a sketcher for a costume designer. Her stage debut was as the maid in a West Coast production of *Mrs. Bumpstead-Leigh* (1929), and during the 1930s, she played minor roles in the movies. (Haydon also dubbed the screaming for ***Fay Wray** in 1933's *King Kong*.) She made her New York stage debut as Hope Blake in *Bright Star* (1935). Before playing Laura in the world premiere of Williams' play, Haydon distinguished herself as yet another maid in *Shadow and Substance* (1938), and as Kitty Duval, the thoughtful streetwalker, in William Saroyan's Pulitzer Prize-winning play, *The Time of Your Life* (1939).

In 1955, Haydon married drama critic George Jean Nathan, who was 28 years her senior. After his death in 1958, she toured, performing readings from his works. During the 1960s and 1970s, Haydon toured again in *The Glass Menagerie*, this time as Amanda (the mother), originally played by ***Laurette Taylor**. Julie Haydon died of abdominal cancer on December 24, 1994.

Haye, Nicolaa de la (1160–1218).

See Siege Warfare and Women.

Hayes, Catherine (1690–1726)

English murderer who was burned alive at the stake. *Born Catherine Hall near Birmingham, England, in 1690; burned at the stake at Tyburn in 1726; married John Hayes (a carpenter and merchant), in 1713.*

Born near Birmingham, England, in 1690, Catherine Hall ran away from home at age 15; an army officer quartered at Great Ombersley in Worcestershire spotted her as she walked the road and enticed her into camp with gold pieces. Willingly, it is said, she offered her services to other officers for money, but they soon grew tired of her and drove her from the camp. According to one biographer, for the next few years she "ran about the country like a distracted creature," reputedly working as a domestic servant and possibly as a prostitute.

She was then employed by a farmer named Hayes in Warwickshire, against the instincts of his wife. Now 23, Catherine was soon involved in an affair with the son of the household, 21-year-old John Hayes, a carpenter, and in 1713 they were secretly married. Though initially opposed, John's father offered the couple a cottage on the farm and a generous allowance. For the next six years, Catherine chafed under the pastoral life, taking lovers to dispel her boredom. She finally convinced her husband to move to London in 1719. There, John Hayes prospered as a coal merchant and money lender with offices on Tyburn Road. Catherine complained that he was miserly and continued to ask him for money. John responded by beating her and withholding funds. By early 1725, the two despised each other.

Then Thomas Billings, a young tailor, appeared at the Hayes' door, seeking lodging. Catherine, who claimed he was a relative, convinced her husband to rent him a room. (It was later rumored that Billings was Catherine's illegitimate son and that the arrival was prearranged.) Billings and Catherine were quickly caught up in an affair. When John left town, the two allegedly threw parties and spent freely.

Catherine Hayes (1690–1726)

When John returned, he beat Catherine to such a degree that she was bedridden for the better part of a week.

Thomas Wood, a friend of John and Catherine's from Warwickshire, was also granted lodging. He too became involved with Catherine. Eventually, she convinced Wood and Billings to help kill her violent husband, offering them part of John's fortune.

On March 1, 1725, Wood and Billings challenged John Hayes to a drinking match. While they drank beer, Hayes drank six pints of wine and collapsed on his bed in a stupor. Ere long, Billings sunk a coal hatchet into the back of John's head, but the blow only fractured his skull. A **Mrs. Springate**, who lived upstairs, heard John Hayes shriek and appeared at the door to inquire about the noise. Catherine assured her nothing was amiss, saying only that "her husband was going away on a trip and was preparing to leave." Meanwhile, Billings and Wood continued attacking John Hayes with the hatchet. Blood was everywhere.

Her co-conspirators would later maintain that it was Catherine Hayes who convinced them that the only way to dispose of the body beyond recognition was to cut off the head and throw it in the river. But when Billings and Wood reached Horseferry Wharf with bucket in hand, a watchman came toward them, and they panicked, hurling the contents of the bucket into the Thames. Unfortunately for the murderers, it was low tide, and the head was quickly discovered where it had landed in the mud. Hours later, parish officers cleaned up the head and had it impaled on a pike at St. Margaret's churchyard in Westminster in hopes that the hapless victim might be identified. Unaware, Billings and Wood returned home, hacked up the remains, placed them in a trunk, and tossed the trunk into a pond in Marylebone Fields. Woods, totally distraught, left for the country. Billings remained with Catherine.

Consequently, a man named Robinson thought he recognized the head atop the pike at St. Margaret's churchyard as that of John Hayes and went to inform Catherine. She dismissed his suggestion with: "My husband is in good health." Then a man named Longmore arrived to suggest a resemblance to John. Catherine turned him away also, saying her husband was out of town on business. Then a man named Ashby, a business associate of John's, quizzed Catherine as to his whereabouts, grew suspicious, and went to the authorities. Ashby identified the head as belonging to John Hayes.

A justice of the peace, who arrived at the home of Catherine Hayes to make inquiries, found her in bed with Billings. Catherine, Billings, and Mrs. Springate, who was then thought to be involved, were arrested and charged with murder. When Wood was arrested in the country and brought to London, he broke down and confessed, detailing the events, placing all the blame on Catherine Hayes.

The case created a sensation, and Catherine Hayes became the subject of many pamphlets and broadsheets. All were tried, except for Springate, and condemned to death. Wood died in prison of fever, and Billings was hanged in irons. On May 9, 1726, Catherine Hayes was taken by cart to a square in Tyburn. Though she was supposed to be strangled before being burned, someone lit the fire too soon, and the executioner, burning his hands, released her neck before death. Logs of wood were hurled into the fire at the screaming Hayes in an unsuccessful attempt to knock her out before she was burned alive.

SOURCES:

Crimes and Punishment. Vol. 6. BPC Publishing, 1974.

Nash, Jay Robert. *Look for the Woman.* NY: M. Evans, 1981.

Hayes, Catherine (1825–1861)

Irish soprano. *Name variations: Mrs. Bushnell. Born at 4 Patrick Street, Limerick, Ireland, on October 29, 1825; died at Sydenham, Kent, England, on August 11, 1861; daughter of poor parents; married William Avery Bushnell (a former electioneering agent who became her manager), in 1856 (died 1858).*

Soprano Catherine Hayes was born in Limerick, Ireland, in 1825, to poor parents and acquired the patronage of a Bishop Knox who paid for her to study in Dublin under Antonio Sapio. After a series of successful public concerts, Hayes furthered her training in Paris and in Milan, where she was a student of Felici Ronconi. Hayes made a triumphant debut at Milan's La Scala in 1845, then successfully toured in Vienna and Venice. In 1849, she made her first appearance at London's Covent Garden, performing in *Linda di Chamouni.* In New York, in 1851, she met an electioneering agent, William Bushnell, whom she contracted as manager of an American tour. Her success was such that one California concertgoer paid $1,000 to hear her sing. She then made an extensive world tour, singing in South America, India, Polynesia, and Australia. In 1856, she returned to England, where she married Bushnell. Unfortunately, he fell ill and died in 1858, at age 35. Hayes remained in London, enjoying popularity as a ballad singer until her own premature death on August 11, 1861, at the age of 36.

Hayes, Evelyn (1874–1945).

See Bethell, Mary Ursula.

Hayes, Helen (1900–1993)

American actress known as the first lady of the American stage. *Born Helen Hayes Brown on October 10, 1900, in Washington, D.C.; died on March 17, 1993, in Nyack, New York; daughter of Catherine (Hayes) Brown and Francis Van Arnum Brown; received a Catholic school education, graduating from Washington's Sacred Heart Academy, 1917; married Charles MacArthur (a playwright), in 1928 (died 1956); children:* **Mary MacArthur** *(1930–1949); (adopted) James MacArthur (an actor).*

Made her Broadway debut at age nine (1909); was recognized as one of America's finest actresses with her performance in Dear Brutus *(1918); began working in Hollywood films (1930s), winning an Oscar for her first film before returning triumphantly to Broadway for what is considered her finest role in* Victoria Regina *(1935); maintained an active and much-honored career in legitimate theater, films and, later, television until her retirement from the stage (1971) with two Tony Awards to her credit; continued to work sporadically in films and television for the next 20 years, winning a second Oscar and being awarded the National Medal of the Arts by President Ronald Reagan (1988), as well as publishing six volumes of memoirs and co-writing a novel.*

Filmography: Jean and the Calico Doll *(1910);* The Weavers of Life *(1917);* Babs *(1920);* The Sin of Madelon Claudet *(1931);* Arrowsmith *(1931);* A Farewell to Arms *(1932);* The Son-Daughter *(1932);* The White Sister *(1933);* Another Language *(1933);* Night Flight *(1933); (unbilled cameo)* Crime Without Passion *(1934);* What Every Woman Knows *(1934);* Vanessa: Her Love Story *(1935); (cameo)* Stage Door Canteen *(1943);* My Son John *(1952); (cameo)* Main Street to Broadway *(1953);* Anastasia *(1956); (unbilled cameo)* Third Man on the Mountain *(1959);* Airport *(1970);* Herbie Rides Again *(1974);* One of Our Dinosaurs Is Missing *(1975);* Candleshoe *(1978).*

One afternoon in 1968, in a dingy rehearsal hall in New York's Greenwich Village, the assembled cast of the struggling Phoenix Repertory Company waited nervously for the final member of their group to appear. They were about to begin rehearsals for a revival of *You Can't Take It With You.* Assistant director Jack O'Brien thought it improper to begin the day's work before the tardy cast member arrived, even though her role—as the Grand Duchess Olga Katrina—was a small one, and she would only be on stage for a few minutes in the last act. Finally, recalled O'Brien 25 years later, Helen Hayes, who had adopted the Phoenix Theater and supported it financially and by appearing in its productions, arrived "stuttering, fumbling, all insecurity and apology." She delivered a nearly flawless, word-perfect run-through of her scene, then turned to O'Brien and relieved the tension by inquiring earnestly, "Will that do, do you think?" It was entirely in keeping with the reputation of the five-foot, blue-eyed, gray-haired woman who had been dubbed the "first lady of the American theater" when she was only in her 30s and whose career at her death had spanned the most vigorous period of creativity and innovation in American dramatic art. "She looked like someone's misplaced aunt," recalled one U.S. Army official who saw her on a State Department tour of South Korea in the mid-1960s, and Hayes was well aware how important the image was to her. "I always thought the secret of my success," she once observed, "is that I'm like somebody down the street who lives in the neighborhood."

Her childhood in Washington, D.C., could hardly have resulted in any other life but the theater. Although her father Francis Brown, a traveling dealer for a meat-packing plant, extolled the pleasures of a quiet home life and liked nothing better than to take his daughter to see the old Washington Senators play a game of baseball on his days off, Helen's mother was of a different persuasion. **Catherine Hayes Brown**, whom everyone called "Brownie," was a vivacious, extroverted woman of Irish descent with pretensions to a theatrical career—perhaps inherited from her father, who had been known for his stirring recitations of Shakespeare induced after sufficient refreshment in local watering holes; or perhaps from one of her father's cousins known as "the swan of Erin," who after emigrating from Ireland during the Great Famine had gained some notoriety entertaining goldrushers in 1849 California with her impassioned warbling. Undaunted by the birth of her daughter Helen on October 10, 1900, Brownie took to the road with touring companies nearly as often as her husband did for his meat-packing bosses. It was Brownie's mother Ann—Helen's beloved "Graddy Hayes"—who entertained her granddaughter with stories and, when money was to be had, plays and silent films. "Graddy would act out a film we'd just seen," Hayes once remembered, "regaling the family with her mimicry—a talent she passed on to my mother and probably to me." But it was Brownie who first suspected that the Hayes theatrical blood coursed in her daughter's veins, when four-year-old Helen refused to leave the old National Theater after mother and daughter had seen a performance of Franz Lehar's operetta, *The Merry Widow.* Helen, who insisted that the actors come back on stage and start from the beginning, had to be bodily carried out of the place. "I didn't want to leave the theater," Hayes told an audience at the very same theater 80 years later, "and I guess I never really have."

Helen's first known public performance came just a year later, at age five, when she appeared as Peaseblossom in a production of *A Midsummer Night's Dream* at Washington's Holy Cross Academy, where Brownie, a devout Catholic, had placed her in an effort to shield Helen from a smallpox epidemic then ravaging Washington. Anticipating the care and attention she would give to Helen's career in years to come, Brownie detected a certain lack of poise in the girl's stage manner and packed her off to Miss Minnie Hawke's dance academy, in whose 1907 "May Ball" recital Hayes was expected to perform an Irish jig but ran sobbing from the stage instead. The next year's recital, however, found a more confident Helen singing the lament of a Dutch girl stranded at the Zuyder Zee by her fickle lover; and in the 1909 show, given at the Belasco Theater, across Lafayette Square from the White House, she brought down the house with her imitation of a famous music-hall performer of the day. To Brownie's satisfaction, no less than three Washington newspapers devoted space to Hayes' appearance, describing her as "most clever" and "perfectly delightful." In the audience at one afternoon's performance was actor and theatrical manager Lew Fields, who told Brownie to bring Helen to him in New York when she felt the child was ready. Fields' specialty was musical comedy, not suited to Brownie's higher-brow tastes, but she took Fields' interest as a sign that her instincts about Helen had been right.

Brownie next found Helen work with the Columbia Players, the repertory company of Washington's Columbia Theater. On May 24, 1909, serious theater audiences got their first look at Helen Hayes Brown in her professional debut as a young Prince Charles in the costume drama *A Royal Family,* in which she was acclaimed as "another star, and already a warm favorite" by the press. Hayes would appear in nearly a dozen productions with the Columbia Players over the next several years, being tutored by mail by the Sisters of the Sacred Heart in Washington (from which she would graduate in 1917) when she was on the road. While Helen was still with the Columbia Players, Brownie tried to arrange an audition for her with Charles Frohman, then the most respected producer of quality drama on Broadway, but Frohman had no interest in child actors and declined to see the girl.

Although she considered it second-best, Brownie took Lew Fields up on his offer. Fields was so impressed with Hayes' talent that he had a number written especially for her and inserted in his upcoming production of Victor Herbert's musical, *Old Dutch,* in which Hayes made her Broadway debut on November 22, 1909, as "The Little Mime." It was also her first appearance as Helen Hayes, since Fields discovered that "Helen Hayes Brown" was too long to fit on his marquee. Hayes was paid $50 a week, nearly as much as her father's weekly earnings, and fell in love once and for all with the theater. "The actors and crew were my playmates," she once remembered, "and the backstage area was my special, magical playground." She appeared in several more Fields productions between 1909 and 1912, in addition to her work with the Columbia Players back in Washington between New York bookings. In later life, Hayes traced her ability to learn a part quickly from her days in repertory, which often required her to learn a new role every week. But it was to her mother that Hayes always gave credit for the working habits that would bring her such success.

Although Brownie took care never to interfere openly with the guidance and direction Hayes received during rehearsals, she spent hours coaching her daughter privately—reading Helen's parts aloud to help her memorize them, indicating line readings and appropriate gestures, and teaching Hayes the rudiments of character development. Brownie laid the groundwork for Hayes' later method of sketching out a role in broad strokes and then paring it down to the essentials. "Always leave them wanting more," was her advice, warning Hayes against the overacting and mannered gestures then so common on the stage and encouraging her daughter to take her inspiration from the movements and speech of ordinary people. Helen also learned from her mother what she later proclaimed as the first rule for any stage actor—never to let the audience know if anything goes wrong. The unruffled calm for which she would

Helen Hayes

later become famous among her peers was evident early on, during a performance of *Little Lord Fauntleroy* for the Columbia Players in 1911. Hayes, in the title role, was required in an early scene to remove from a breast pocket a red bandanna—a crucial prop which appears to great effect later in the play—and hand it to the actor playing her grandfather. Discovering at the critical moment that the bandanna was missing, Hayes merely adlibbed, "Well, I must have left it in my room!," then left her fellow actor to fend for himself alone on stage while she ran into the wings and retrieved the bandanna from a waiting prop man.

While working in New York for Fields, Hayes began joining the stream of legitimate stage actors who publicly disdained the new, plebeian form of entertainment provided by silent films, but quietly slipped across the Hudson River to New Jersey's Vitagraph Studios to act anonymously for extra money in hastily produced shorts. Helen and Brownie were horrified when her first film, 1910's *Jean and the Calico Doll,* opened at a theater across the street from one in which Hayes was then appearing in a Fields musical. Even worse, the movie house's marquee mentioned her by name—a tribute to her drawing power as a child star but viewed as an insult by Brownie, who forced the movie house to remove the offending words. Hayes' relations with the film industry would hardly improve during her lengthy career.

In 1917, Hayes appeared in her first drama, *The Prodigal Husband,* staged by Charles Frohman, in which she played opposite John Drew. The show toured the country after its Broadway run, Hayes' first whistlestop tour of the nation that would take her to heart as its favorite actress. Her fame was further assured by her tour with George Tyler's production of *Pollyanna,* during which, Hayes later claimed, she brought an audience of hardened Montana cowhands to tears with her second act speech as the play's relentlessly optimistic "glad girl." Tyler, who rivaled Frohman as the show world's most prolific impresario and who had guided the American careers of ***Eleonora Duse** and ***Sarah Bernhardt**, was Hayes' most important mentor after Brownie. He took care to choose her clothes, her friends, her roles, even her reading material, ruling her life and her career (which were by now the same thing) with an iron hand. It was Tyler who encouraged her to study the techniques of the greatest actors of the day, so that Hayes came to view the theater not only as a livelihood but as a classroom. She remembered watching ***Laurette Taylor**'s performance for five consecutive nights when Taylor was appearing in another of Tyler's Broadway dramas; going backstage to meet ***Ethel Barrymore** for advice and suggestions, which was the start of a lifelong friendship with that remarkable woman; and watching 20 consecutive performances by a popular comedienne of the day to learn that successful comedy is never spontaneously produced but is born of painstaking attention to detail.

In 1918, George Tyler gave Hayes the two roles that brought her professional respect and critical acceptance. The first was as Margaret Schofield in his production of *Penrod,* which Booth Tarkington had adapted for the stage from his popular novel of adolescent romance. It was the first of several Tarkington works in which Hayes would appear in the next ten years. "She is endowed with dainty, girlish exuberance," burbled one critic, "and is vivacious and altogether winsome." Next, Tyler cast her in his 1918 production of *Dear Brutus,* J.M. Barrie's inventive and poignant reworking of *A Midsummer Night's Dream.* Although her character appeared only in the second act and she played opposite the formidable talents of William Gillette, Hayes' work as the wistful, fantasy-inspired daughter of Gillette's bohemian artist captured the hearts of audiences and reviewers alike. Even the usually acerbic ***Dorothy Parker** wasn't immune, telling her *Vanity Fair* readers that "Hers is one of those roles that could be overdone without a struggle, yet she never once skips over into the kittenish, never once grows too exuberantly sweet—and when you think how easily she could have ruined the whole thing, her work seems little short of marvelous." Hayes had obviously taken Brownie's advice to heart.

Now Broadway's favorite ingenue, Helen Hayes sailed into the "roaring '20s" with all flags flying and became the toast of the town for several "flapper girl" roles, portraying that peculiar form of womanhood marked by sequined skirts and tasseled blouses, the Charleston and a teasing, coy sexuality. She was as quick a study with this new genre as she had been playing young boys and quivering, adolescent girls, and had soon mastered the gestures, facial expressions, and programmed responses the form demanded. She toured with just such a character in a Tyler play called *On the Hiring Line,* playing opposite Alfred Lunt; in an Atlantic City showcase called *The Golden Age*; and on Broadway in Tyler's *Clarence*—all during 1919 and 1920. Late in 1920, Tyler cast her in *Babs,* based on a collection of short stories by popular author ***Mary Roberts Rinehart**. Trying to design his marquee, Tyler first attempted:

BABS
BY
EDWARD CHILDS CARPENTER
FROM THE BOOK BY
MARY ROBERTS RINEHART

Discovering this lengthy statement would never fit, Tyler finally settled on:

HELEN HAYES
IN
BABS

Brownie, who had rarely interfered directly in the management of her daughter's career, pleaded with Tyler to come up with something else and relieve Hayes from the pressure of top billing, knowing better than anyone that her daughter wasn't ready for such scrutiny. But Tyler insisted, putting up the marquee outside the old Park Theater on Columbus Circle as planned. As Brownie had predicted, Hayes was stung by the first negative reviews of her 11 years on the stage. Critics who had earlier praised Hayes' spontaneity and naturalism now complained that her work was strained, stiff, too mannered; and even Hayes realized that her performances were growing even more so each time the curtain went up.

Desperate to salvage her work, Hayes threw herself into a round of voice and technique classes (even resorting to a chart which specified which facial expression accompanied which emotion), along with boxing, fencing, and interpretive dance. The strain to replace the instinctive acting of her youth with a more mature style based on solid technical training was considerable, with Hayes still working on developing her character long after the other actors in the cast had "set" their performances—a habit she maintained for the rest of her life. When the actor playing Hayes' father died of a heart attack, Tyler decided not to recast the part and closed *Babs* early. Realizing that Hayes needed a break from the stage, Tyler withdrew her from the cast of his next production, Eugene O'Neill's *The Straw,* and accompanied Hayes and Brownie on a long, leisurely tour of Europe at his own expense during the summer of 1921.

Adding to Hayes' turmoil during *Babs*' run was the actors' strike which had gripped Broadway in 1919 and showed no sign of weakening. Prompted by the virtually complete control exercised over them by producers like Frohman, Abe Erlanger, and Tyler himself, actors were calling for unionization and basic rights—demands which would eventually lead to the formation of Actors' Equity. The producers' response was to close any show which contained actors known to sympathize with such demands and blacklist them from further work. Tyler warned Hayes that any agitation on her part would end their relationship, and Hayes dutifully remained a member of The Fidelity League of actors, loyal to their producers, throughout the run of *Babs* and during her work in *The Wren,* in which she appeared opposite Leslie Howard on her return from Europe. But in 1924, Hayes informed Tyler she was joining Actors' Equity. True to his word, Tyler severed their relationship.

Years later, Hayes marked this event as the beginning of her life as a serious actress, and the first time she felt responsible for her own career. Now freed from the ingenue roles imposed on her by Tyler, Hayes appeared to good reviews in a production of Oliver Goldsmith's *She Stoops to Conquer* staged by that venerable actors' club, The Players (to which she was admitted as the first female member nearly 45 years later). There followed roles in summer stock and repertory, and a return to a post-strike, newly invigorated Broadway in a J.M. Barrie premiere, *What Every Woman Knows,* in 1926. The following year, she opened in the romantic drama, *Coquette,* produced by Jed Harris, known as much for his mercurial temperament as for his creative genius. *Coquette* ran for more than a year, during which Hayes met the man who would become the great romance of her life.

Harris took her to a party one night in Greenwich Village, that headquarters of 1920's bohemianism and intellectual acrobatics. The rebellious, free-wheeling atmosphere was a completely new experience for a young girl with a Catholic school education still living with her mother. At a loss in the sea of witty conversation and clever comment, Hayes retired to the sidelines to wait it out until a handsome young man strolled to her side, held out his hand, and inquired if she would care for some peanuts. As he poured them into her waiting palm, Charles MacArthur gazed into Hayes' eyes and murmured, "I wish they were emeralds."

"He was the most beautiful, the most amusing, most amazing and dazzling man I had ever met," Hayes said many years later. "He brought me out of the shadows and helped me grow both as an actress and as a woman." MacArthur, a journalist and *bon vivant* who would soon make his mark as a playwright, had recently separated from his first wife and was a member in good standing of the Algonquin Round Table, along with the likes of Dorothy Parker, Robert Benchley, and Alexander Woollcott. The unlikely romance between the conservative Irish Catholic girl and the urbane, wisecracking journalist began slowly and took its time maturing. Brownie declared MacArthur would only bring Hayes heartbreak, and MacArthur's fellow Round Tablers complained that Hayes was much too polite and proper for MacArthur. But MacArthur admitted to being as smitten with Hayes as she was with him, although he told Hayes he felt dishonorable marrying her as long as she made more money than he did. The answer to MacArthur's dilemma was his sparkling satirical comedy *The Front Page*, written with partner Ben Hecht and produced by none other than Jed Harris, who thoughtfully closed *Coquette* on *The Front Page*'s opening night, allowing Hayes to attend. Too nervous to stay in the theater during the performance, MacArthur and Hecht paced outside on a fire escape while Hayes ran out to them after each act to report on the audience's reaction, obvious to anyone within earshot of the theater. The laughter was raucous and enthusiastic, making Helen's breathless report of "It's a hit!" after the second act superfluous. MacArthur proposed to Hayes there and then. After a brief ceremony in a civil court on 42nd Street on August 17, 1928, MacArthur promised her, "You may never be rich, but you'll never be bored."

Very few ladies are perhaps as foolhardy as I am. I'm the girl who can't say no.

—Helen Hayes, at age 87

The first year of their marriage had to be conducted long-distance, for Jed Harris had decided to send *Coquette* out on tour. MacArthur was forced to catch up with Hayes for weekend visits until July of 1929, when the tour reached Los Angeles and Hayes announced she was pregnant. Harris closed the show and refused to pay severance to his actors on the grounds that Hayes' pregnancy was an "act of God," leading to much pointed witticism in the show-business press. The daughter born to Hayes and Charlie on February 15, 1930, was dubbed "the act of God baby," although the proud parents preferred to call her Mary. The couple set up house in a two-story apartment in midtown Manhattan, allowing a nanny to tend to Mary upstairs free from the disturbances of Helen and Charlie's late-night, show-business schedule. Hayes was now appearing in *Mr. Gilhooley*, one of her few Broadway roles as a thoroughly bad character. Brownie predicted that audiences wouldn't accept her in such a role and, as usual, was proved right when the show closed to poor reviews.

Meanwhile, Charlie and Ben Hecht had been receiving increasingly lucrative offers from Hollywood, which had been much impressed by the success of *The Front Page* and which was eager to produce a film version. Hayes reluctantly left her beloved theater behind, moving with MacArthur to California and signing a contract with MGM. Hayes was the first to admit that she wasn't cut out to be a glamorous screen star. When Louis Mayer suggested she appear at a studio publicity function in a slinky, white silk gown, telling her, "It will be very revealing," Hayes retorted by pointing out that that was precisely the problem. "I just wasn't combustible," she wrote years later. "I didn't have Crawford's bone structure or Garbo's mystery. I wasn't sexy like Harlow or naughty like [Marion] Davies. There were so many things I didn't have, or wasn't, that it seemed best for me to quit there and then."

Opposite page

Helen Hayes as Queen Victoria in the Broadway production of Victoria Regina, *1935.*

Mayer was eventually forced to adopt her point of view, deciding that if he couldn't promote Hayes as a sex symbol, he'd emphasize her prestige value as The Great Actress and use her for dramatic roles drawn from novels and the stage. In 1931, the same year that United Artists released MacArthur and Hecht's film version of *The Front Page* to great acclaim, Hayes appeared in her first film for a major studio. In MGM's *The Sin of Madelon Claudet,* based on a weepy, melodramatic play by Edward Knoblock, Hayes played a mother who sacrifices her virtue to save her daughter. It very nearly wasn't released at all after preview audiences responded negatively and Louis B. Mayer pulled the film from its release schedule. The film was salvaged by Mayer's head of production at the time, Irving Thalberg, who turned to MacArthur and Hecht to write a new ending and additional scenes. The new version was released to great acclaim and won Hayes the Oscar for Best Actress in 1932—the first time the award was offered for a specific performance rather than cumulative work. It may have been another sign of Hayes' disaffection with Hollywood that she immediately misplaced the revered golden statue, discovering it two days later in the trunk of her car. Over the next three years, Hayes played opposite some of Hollywood's most desirable leading men in a number of MGM's "serious" films—Gary Cooper in *A Farewell to Arms*, Clark Gable and John Barrymore in *The White Sister,* and Robert Montgomery in *Another Language*.

In between their acting and writing assignments, Hayes and MacArthur fled back to their beloved New York and used their Hollywood earnings to buy a 19-room Victorian house overlooking the Hudson River in Nyack, some miles north of the city. MacArthur admitted that they'd probably paid too much for it and named it "Pretty Penny." Over the years, it became a magnet for show-business luminaries and would remain Hayes' home for the rest of her long life. Its attractions became more and more alluring the longer Hayes worked in California, for while her subsequent films were respectfully received, she chafed under the rigid rules of filmmaking. "It was hard to adjust to those endless takes followed by endless waits," she once said. "Only a short part of each day was spent acting; the rest was a game of patience." MacArthur, too, became increasingly cynical about his studio bosses and their demand for commercial success at the expense of creative freedom. Although he would continue to write for the screen intermittently and Hayes would return to films from time to time, the couple decided in 1933 that they had had enough of Hollywood and moved back to New York. It was a fortuitous decision for Hayes, for her two greatest stage roles were waiting.

Hayes came into her own as a tragic actress and made a triumphant return to the Broadway stage in the role of ***Mary Stuart, Queen of Scots**, in Maxwell Anderson's *Mary, Queen of Scotland,* which opened in 1933. There was some surprise at the casting of a five-foot tall woman to play one of the tallest queens in English history, especially since the actress playing **Elizabeth I** stood at five-foot-six. Four-inch lifts inserted in Hayes' shoes helped; her technique took care of the rest. "I *think* myself tall," she told an inquiring admirer. Two years later, on December 26, 1935, Hayes created what is widely considered to be her masterpiece—her performance as Queen ***Victoria** in Laurence Housman's *Victoria Regina,* in which she aged each night during the play's two-year run from the prim 20-year-old royal princess to the dour octogenarian of the English throne. Audiences were fascinated with the challenges presented by the aging process, especially the convincing puffiness of the old queen's face. Hayes revealed that she at first tried a suggestion from Charles Laughton and stuffed half of an apple in each cheek which, although flavorful, slowly dissolved over the course of the play's final act. She finally settled on thick cotton pads soaked in antiseptic. Hayes later said that she based her Victoria on Graddy Hayes, who had seen the real Victoria pass by in her wedding procession with Albert through London in 1840, and who had imitated many of Victoria's gestures and mannerisms for her granddaughter. Her performance won Hayes the Drama League's Medal of Honor and the first of many invitations to the White House. "She transmuted a rather dull, prosy woman into an overpowering presence," remembered theater critic Brooks Atkinson 40 years after Hayes' Victoria. "She made a living person out of a myth. She made the theater larger than life." Hayes would play Victoria more than a thousand times between 1935 and 1939, taking the show on tour after its Broadway run to 43 cities and an estimated total audience of some two million. During this regal tour, Hayes and MacArthur adopted a second child, James. Their two children often appeared in small roles in plays starring their mother, with

Mary being marked early on as a talented actress and James MacArthur becoming known to millions 40 years later as Danno on the TV series "Hawaii Five-O."

It was during her reign as Victoria that Hayes—now and forevermore respectfully referred to as "Miss Hayes"—came to realize how much she had missed a live audience during her discouraging days in Hollywood. "I need that contact with the audience to guide me and tell me where I'm going off track and how to get back on it," she once wrote. "They talk to me, in absolute silence or in their laughter or restless movements. I am not mistaken in my impression of how I read them." She gauged the success of any performance by such audience dynamics, and always said that her finest appearance as Victoria came, not on Broadway, but on a rainy night in Columbus, Ohio, when the mutual feedback between audience and actor reached a peak of intimacy.

Further triumphs lay ahead: 1943's *Harriet,* based on an incident in the life of ***Harriet Beecher Stowe**; 1947's *Happy Birthday*, which won Hayes her first Tony Award (it was, in fact, the first year the Tonys were offered); and 1950's *The Wisteria Trees*, which was her difficult return to the stage after the death of her daughter Mary from polio in 1949. "The very worst thing that can happen is to bury your young," she said. Further tragedies awaited. Brownie passed away in 1953, at age 72, to Hayes' great sorrow; and in 1956, MacArthur died of kidney disease at age 60. He had never recovered from Mary's death and had sought comfort for his despondency in alcohol, although Hayes would always deny he had been an alcoholic. "He was the perfect husband in every way," Hayes said, recalling that, true to his word, life with him had never been boring. She especially remembered the handful of emeralds Charlie had sent her from Burma, where he had been stationed during World War II. "I wish they were peanuts," he had written.

Hayes refused all offers of work for some time after MacArthur's death, spending her days tending her roses at Pretty Penny and giving no interviews. Her return to public life came, not on the stage, but on screen, as the imperious Grand Duchess in Anatole Litvak's 1956 *Anastasia*, opposite ***Ingrid Bergman**. She was never idle from then on, winning her second Tony for 1958's *Time Remembered*, playing opposite Richard Burton, whom she pointedly warned about building a career on what she called "shenanigans." Also that year, the old Fulton Theater on 45th Street was renamed the Helen Hayes Theater in her honor. She became active in social causes, especially adopting the desegregation of the National Theater in Washington, in which she had appeared as a young girl, and speaking out for programs designed to help the elderly. Now in her 60s, Hayes also traveled abroad on cultural tours for the State Department (which brought her to South Korea), formed the Helen Hayes Repertory Company in New York, toured with a one-woman show in which she played several wives of American presidents, and bought a second home in Cuernevaca, Mexico, where she spent several weeks during the winters. She ventured into television, appearing with her son James on an episode of "Hawaii Five-O" and with ***Mildred Natwick** in a mystery series, "The Snoop Sisters." In 1971, Hayes won her second Oscar as Best Supporting Actress for her work as the wily Ada Quonset in *Airport*. Outside of a minor problem with low blood pressure and increasingly troublesome allergies, Hayes continued to enjoy the remarkable good health and vitality that had supported her since her touring days as a child. "If you rest, you rust," she said. Nonetheless, she announced her formal retirement from the stage in 1971, citing bronchial asthma brought on by "theater dust" as the reason. Her last stage performance was in O'Neill's *Long Day's Journey into Night*, given in her hometown of Washington. Six years later, what would be her last film, 1977's *Candleshoe,* was released.

In 1982, New York's theater world was outraged at the razing of the Helen Hayes Theater to make way for a sprawling hotel complex in Times Square, although Hayes chose not to join the protests against its demolition. "Look at it this way," she told an interviewer. "It's gratifying that I outlived all that stone and mortar." She managed to rescue a chandelier and a few of the old theater's red plush seats before the building came crashing down. Not long after, the Little Theater, which Hayes remembered opening in 1912 when she was appearing as a girl in Lew Fields' productions, became the "new" Helen Hayes Theater. Perhaps as further compensation, the U.S. Mint issued a commemorative gold coin in 1984 bearing her likeness. In 1987, Hayes collaborated on a murder mystery with writer Thomas Chastain, *Where the Truth Lies,* in which the evil deed takes place during the Academy Awards. She admitted gleefully that the book provided a way for her to vent some of her long-held distrust of Hollywood, announcing during a press tour for the novel that she had declined to attend that year's Academy Awards banquet. "I don't know whether I'd dare," she said. Hayes added to her collection of awards and honors in 1988 by traveling to the White House to receive the National Medal of the Arts from Ronald Reagan. Always a staunch Republican, she delivered the seconding speech for George Bush at that year's GOP convention.

In 1990, she published the last and most frank of her six memoirs. While the previous five had been essentially collections of anecdotes and memories of theater life, *My Life in Three Acts* took much of the modern stage to task for abandoning what Hayes saw as its traditional role of elevation and education. She criticized contemporary playwrights for emphasizing the world's evils rather than the power of human dignity, and advocated a return to works which celebrate lives "lived quietly and gracefully and decently." She warned actors not to confuse the stature that comes from quality work with the more short-lived stardom born of controversy. "Celebrity," she wrote, "has always struck me as a dubious and transitory claim to achievement in our society." And she emphasized her commitment to helping change attitudes toward the elderly. "People ought to be told well in advance what may happen to them as they age," she pointed out. "If they don't like what they hear, then they should agitate for improved conditions." She confessed that, at 90, she had only recently given up swimming five laps a day in the pool at Pretty Penny and had substituted a long walk each day—especially enjoyable to her, she said, in the rain. By now, she lived mostly on the ground floor of the old "gothic steamboat," having closed off the rest of the place to most visitors.

On St. Patrick's Day, 1993, the last of the great ladies of the 20th-century American stage died quietly in her sleep. Helen Hayes had given 80 years of dedicated service to the stage, her gifts being some of the legitimate theater's most memorable performances, all the while maintaining a reputation for self-deprecating modesty. "I don't seem to have learned anything through my whole life but my *own* life," Hayes once wrote. "A lot of people don't even get to learn that, do they?"

SOURCES:

Atkinson, Brooks. *Broadway*. NY: Macmillan, 1970.

Hayes, Helen, with Katherine Hatch. *My Life in Three Acts*. NY: Harcourt, Brace, Jovanovich, 1990.

Johnson, Jill. "Transformation: A Memory of Helen Hayes," in *American Heritage*. Vol. 44, no. 6. October 1993.

Murphy, Don, and Stephen Moore. *Helen Hayes: A Bio-Bibliography*. Westport, CT: Greenwood Press, 1993.

O'Brien, Jack. "Helen Hayes: 1900–1993" (obituary), in *American Theater*. Vol. 10, no. 5–6. May–June 1993.

Shapiro, Harriet. "Where the Truth Lies" (book review), in *People Weekly*. Vol. 29, no. 11. March 21, 1988.

Norman Powers,
writer-director, Chelsea Lane Productions, New York

Hayes, Lucy Webb (1831–1889)

American first lady (1877–1881), wife of the 19th president Rutherford B. Hayes, who is remembered primarily for her pro-temperance stand. *Born Lucy Ware Webb on August 28, 1831, in Chillicothe, Ohio; died on June 25, 1889; the youngest of three children and only daughter of Dr. James Webb and Maria (Cook) Webb; graduated with high honors from Ohio Wesleyan Female College in 1852; married Rutherford Birchard Hayes (later president of U.S.), on December 30, 1852, in Cincinnati, Ohio; children: Birchard Austin Hayes (1853–1926); Webb Cook Hayes (1856–1935, who became the first presidential son to win the Congressional Medal of Honor, for his heroism during the Spanish-American War, and established the Hayes Presidential Center in Fremont, Ohio); Rutherford Platt Hayes (1858–1927); Frances, known as* ***Fanny Hayes*** *(1867–1950); Scott Russell Hayes (1871–1923); and three who died in infancy.*

At the inauguration of Rutherford B. Hayes in 1877, speculation about the new first lady went beyond her severe hair style, lack of make-up, and plain—though elegant—clothing, to questions of character and intent. Would her early interest in reform benefit the emerging women's movement? Would she exert special influence in the White House beyond that of her predecessors? For many, Lucy Ware Webb Hayes ushered in the era of the "new woman." No other first lady before her had finished college. For some, she was a great disappointment. Others understood the limitations imposed on her as a political wife.

Lucy Hayes graduated with high honors from Wesleyan Female College in Cincinnati, Ohio. As a student, she was a member of the debate team and wrote her commencement essay on "The Influence of Christianity on National Prosperity." She met Rutherford Hayes, a rising young attorney, during a summer vacation. They married in a quiet ceremony in December 1852, and settled in Cincinnati, where Rutherford's law practice grew along with their family. The couple had eight children—seven sons (three of whom died in infancy) and one daughter—in the course of 20 years.

Lucy Webb Hayes

The early years brought the couple in contact with the city's art and literary set, and it is said that Lucy was friends with Ralph Waldo Emerson. During this time, the burgeoning feminist movement caught the attention of Rutherford's sister **Fanny Hayes**, who took her sister-in-law along to a number of famous speeches on women's rights. Lucy Hayes was so moved by ***Lucy Stone**'s lecture on improving women's wages that, in a letter to her husband, she defended "violent methods to achieve change."

When Rutherford put his law practice on hold to support the Union cause in the Civil War, Lucy followed when family demands allowed. She endeared herself to her husband's regiment, tending the wounded, sewing uniforms, and writing letters. The men referred to her as "Mother Lucy" and would present her with an inscribed silver platter on her 25th wedding anniversary, which was celebrated in the White House.

After the war, Rutherford reluctantly entered politics as a member of Congress, and his new career progressed steadily. Lucy sometimes left her children with relatives so she could join him in Washington. A staunch abolitionist, she sat in the gallery to watch the Congressional debates on Reconstruction. When her husband was elected governor of Ohio, she traveled throughout the state visiting prisons and mental hospitals, and collecting contributions for a home for children displaced by the war. During his 1876 presidential campaign, she was lauded for her ability to talk intelligently about politics and was compared favorably to ***Sarah Polk**. Rutherford Hayes was elected president by a slim margin over Samuel J. Tilden as the nation celebrated the 100th anniversary of the signing of the Declaration of Independence. The race was so close that a commission had to decide the winner.

The temperance issue seemed to overshadow everything else in the Hayes administration. Although it was a way of life for the first family, the ban on alcohol in the White House was not easily downplayed. It captured the attention of press mills across the country, as did Lucy's early morning prayer meetings and Sunday evening hymn sings. Although Washington society may have found the Hayes administration dull, temperance was a popular issue of the day, and "Lemonade Lucy," as the first lady was dubbed, won as many friends as critics. She never officially joined the Women's Christian Temperance Union (WCTU), possibly due to their reputation for militancy, or maybe because she had slightly more tolerance for the opposition than did her husband.

Lucy's early support of equality for women evidently did not extend to suffrage, and her silence on that front angered leaders in the movement. It is said that when ***Susan B. Anthony** and ***Elizabeth Cady Stanton** came to the White House to discuss issues with the president, Lucy's only participation was a house tour after the meeting. Despite her popularity and the countless requests made of her to promote women's issues, Lucy opted for a less controversial role. She began what is now an annual Easter Egg Roll on the White House lawn, and aligned herself with social issues such as Native American welfare, veterans' benefits, and rehabilitation of the defeated South. She also kept an ornate scrapbook detailing official White House functions, including seating arrangements and menus. The book, now on display at the Hayes Presidential Center in Fremont, Ohio, was borrowed and duplicated during the Reagan administration.

Rutherford Hayes stuck to an earlier resolution to serve only one term as president, and he and Lucy returned to Ohio in 1881. During the subsequent Garfield administration, a portrait of Lucy Hayes commissioned by the WCTU was presented in a White House ceremony, with high praise of the former first lady. The Illinois Chapter also gave her six gilt-edged volumes containing autographs and tributes to her pro-temperance stand from celebrities throughout the nation.

In later years, Lucy continued to devote time to bettering prison conditions and aiding veterans of the Civil War. She also served as president of the Woman's Home Missionary Society of the Methodist Episcopal Church, formed to work for poor and destitute women in the United States. Lucy Hayes died suddenly in 1889, of a massive stroke, and was buried in Oakland Cemetery in Fremont, Ohio. Her husband died in 1893 and was buried beside her.

SOURCES:

Boller, Paul F., Jr. *Presidential Wives*. NY: Oxford University Press, 1988.

Caroli, Betty Boyd. *First Ladies*. NY: Oxford University Press, 1987.

McConnell, Jane and Burt. *Our First Ladies: From Martha Washington to Lady Bird Johnson*. NY: Thomas Y. Crowell, 1964.

Paletta, LuAnn. *The World Almanac of First Ladies*. NY: World Almanac, 1990.

Barbara Morgan,
Melrose, Massachusetts

Hayes, Mary (1754–1832).

See joint entry entitled Two Mollies for Mary Hays Ludwig McCauley.

Hayes, Nevada (1885–1941)

Duchess of Oporto. *Born Nevada Stoody on October 21, 1885, in Ohio; died on January 11, 1941; married Lee Agnew; married William Henry Chapman; married Philip van Volkenburgh; married Alfonso (1865–1920), duke of Oporto, on September 26, 1917.*

Hayles, Alice (d. after 1326)

Countess of Norfolk. *Name variations: Alice Italys. Died after May 8, 1326; daughter of Roger Hayles;*

married Thomas of Brotherton, earl of Norfolk (son of King Edward I and ***Margaret of France*** *[1282–1318]), around 1316; children: Edward Plantagenet (c. 1319–c. 1332);* ***Margaret, duchess of Norfolk*** *(c. 1320–1400);* ***Alice Plantagenet*** *(d. 1351).*

Hayne, Julia Dean (1830–1868).

See Dean, Julia.

Haynes, Elizabeth Ross (1883–1953)

African-American social worker, sociologist, author. *Born Elizabeth Ross on July 30, 1883, in Lowndes County, Alabama; died on October 26, 1953, in New York City; daughter of Henry and Mary (Carnes) Ross; Fisk University, A.B., 1903; Columbia University, A.M. in sociology, 1923; married George Edmund Haynes, on December 14, 1910; children: one son, George Edmund Haynes, Jr. (b. July 17, 1912).*

Elizabeth Ross Haynes was born on July 30, 1883, in Mount Willing, Lowndes County, Alabama, of former slaves Henry and **Mary Carnes Ross.** Her father had served in the Union Army during the Civil War and had used his pay to purchase land in Alabama. Through hard work, he eventually converted his property into a 1,500-acre plantation. Elizabeth was an intelligent child, and her parents made sure she received the best possible education. She was class valedictorian at State Normal School in Montgomery and won a scholarship to Fisk University, where she earned an A.B. in 1903. Between 1905 and 1907, she spent her summers attending graduate school at the University of Chicago.

Elizabeth Ross' long-standing association with the Young Women's Christian Association (YWCA) began when she became the organization's first black national secretary in 1908. In this role, she worked largely among African-American college students and traveled extensively to provide a detailed account of student life. Although Ross resigned from this position in order to marry George Edmund Haynes in 1910, her work with the YWCA was far from over. She continued to volunteer after the marriage and the birth of her only child, George Jr., in 1912.

George Haynes was a sociologist and later a founder of the National Urban League. Like Elizabeth, he yearned to make a difference for African-American workers and, to this end, accepted the position of director of Negro economics in the Department of Labor in 1912. Elizabeth followed her husband to the Department of Labor, volunteering in what would later be known as the Women's Bureau, and serving in the U.S. Employment Service as a domestic service secretary. The experiences she gleaned from volunteering gave her keen insight into the plight of black female workers who were almost invariably relegated to the worst jobs because of their race and gender. In 1922, she published a watershed study on black women and employment entitled "Two Million Negro Women at Work," which was her master's thesis at Columbia University. In it, she reported on the deplorable working conditions and poor quality of life African-American female laborers endured.

Not content to just report on the problems of black women in labor, Haynes fought to alleviate them. Along with several prominent African-American women, including ***Mary Church Terrell** and **Elizabeth Carter**, she petitioned the International Congress of Working Women to offer programs of relevance to black women in 1919. One of their hopes was realized when the Council for Interracial Cooperation (CIC) organized in Atlanta in 1920. In 1924, Haynes became the first black woman elected to the national board of the YWCA. The organization was still highly segregated, and she had to fight for leadership opportunities. She remained in this post until 1934 when George moved the family to Harlem.

Elizabeth again worked side-by-side with her husband when he became secretary of the Commission on Race Relations for the Federated Council of the Churches of Christ in America. She was active in interracial work for the council. In November of 1935, she was elected as co-leader of New York's 21st Assembly District. In this role, she energetically tackled numerous concerns, including unemployment, assistance to the elderly, soldiers' and widows' pensions, delinquency and legislation. By 1936, she was a member of the Colored Division of the National Democratic Speakers Bureau.

In 1937, Governor Herbert H. Lehman appointed Haynes to the New York State Temporary Commission on the Condition of the Urban Colored Population, the only woman to receive such an appointment. She worked diligently to upgrade schools and library services in Harlem and focused attention on integrating nursing and social work staffs in city hospitals. She was active on Mayor Fiorello La Guardia's City Planning Commission as well as the National Advisory Committee on Women's Participation in the 1939 New York World's Fair, and the Harlem

Better Schools Committee. During and after World War II, Haynes actively supported the Emergency Committee to Save the Jewish People of Europe.

Elizabeth Ross Haynes' deep and abiding belief in the importance of black history led her to write *Unsung Heroes* (1921) which recounts the lives and achievements of various African-Americans. In 1952, she published *The Black Boy of Atlanta* (1952), a biography of R.R. Wright. She died in New York Medical Center in New York City on October 26, 1953.

SOURCES:

Sicherman, Barbara, and Carol Hurd Green, eds. *Notable American Women: The Modern Period.* Cambridge, MA: The Belknap Press of Harvard University Press, 1980.

Smith, Jessie Carney, ed. *Notable Black American Women.* Detroit, MI: Gale Research, 1992.

Judith C. Reveal,
freelance writer, Greensboro, Maryland

Haynes, Margery (fl. 15th c.)

English businesswoman. *Flourished in the 15th century in Wiltshire, England.*

Margery Haynes is representative of the ingenuity and resourcefulness of many medieval townswomen who became businesswomen when they were widowed and could live independent lives. A widow and entrepreneur of Wiltshire, England, Haynes capitalized on the property she inherited when her husband died. Childless, she was left with three grain mills and had to support herself. Margery had probably assisted with the family business while her husband was alive, and now took over as manager of the mills. She expanded the business, reinvesting wisely and eventually building a small shop with her profits.

Laura York,
Riverside, California

Haynie, Sandra B. (1943—)

American woman golfer who won the LPGA championship and the U.S. Women's Open in the same season. *Born Sandra Jane Haynie on June 4, 1943, in Fort Worth, Texas; daughter of Jim Haynie, also a golfer.*

Entered first golf tournament at age 11 (1954), and in less than a year played first pro tourney; captured first of five consecutive Austin City Women's golf titles (1956); turned professional golfer (1961); struck by car while in South Africa but escaped serious injuries (1972); earned place on Golf Magazine*'s All-America team (1974); elected to Ladies Professional Golf Association's Hall of Fame (1977) and Texas Golf Hall of Fame (November 1984); competed in the Sprint Titleholders Senior Challenge (1993–97), placing second (1997).*

Won the Texas State Publinx (1957 and 1958); won the Texas Amateur (1958 and 1959); won the Austin Civitan Open and Cosmopolitan Open (1962); won the Phoenix Thunderbird Open (1963); won the Baton Rouge Open and Las Cruces Open (1964); won the Cosmopolitan Open and the LPGA championship (1965); won the Buckeye Savings Invitational, the Glass City Classic, the Alamo Open, and the Pensacola Invitational (1966); won the Amarillo Open and the Mickey Wright Invitational (1967); won the Pacific Open (1968); won the St. Louis Invitational, the Supertest Open, and the Shreveport Kiwanis Invitational (1969); won the Raleigh Invitational and the Shreveport Kiwanis Invitational (1970); won the Burdines Invitational, the Dallas Civitan Open, the San Antonio Alamo Open, and the Lem Immke Buick Open (1971); won the National Jewish Hospital Open, the Quality First Classic, and the Lincoln-Mercury Open (1972); won the Orange Blossom Classic, the Lincoln-Mercury Open, the Charity Golf Classic (1973); won the Lawson's Open, the George Washington Classic, the National Jewish Hospital Open, the Charity Golf Classic, the LPGA championship, and the U.S. Women's Open (1974); won the Naples-Lely Classic, the Charity Golf Classic, Jacksonville Open, and the Ft. Myers Classic (1975); won the Henredon Classic (1981); won the Rochester International and the Peter Jackson Classic (1982).

Sandra Haynie

Born on June 4, 1943, in Fort Worth, Texas, the daughter of golfer Jim Haynie, Sandra Haynie was soon putting on the green. Often accompanying her father to courses at country clubs, she practiced her game under his strict tutelage. By the time she was 11, she had entered her initial tournament, the Women's West Texas and, though she did not win, played her first pro tourney, the Texas Open, within a year. Another two years passed, and she succeeded in capturing the first of five consecutive Austin City Women's titles. At age 14, she won the first of two Texas Women's Publinx trophies and the next year opened a three-year reign as Texas women's amateur champion.

In 1961, Haynie turned pro and hit the LPGA tour. A year later, she began an amazing string of golf victories; she won at least one major championship every year from 1962 to 1975. She had four victories in 1964, four in 1971 and 1975, and three in 1969, 1972, and 1973. In 1965, she won her first LPGA championship.

But 1974 was the year of Haynie. Adding her name to that of ***Mickey Wright**, she became the second woman to win the LPGA and the USGA Women's Open in the same season. (This elite group would later include **Se Ri Pak** and **Meg Mallon**.) Haynie also finished as runner-up twice and was among the top ten in fifteen tourneys. Her six victories tied her with ***JoAnne Carner** for the most wins on the women's 1974 tour. With her 1974 earnings, Haynie was the second highest moneymaker in women's golf at that time, second only to ***Kathy Whitworth**. Haynie would be ranked second on the LPGA-season money list on five separate occasions, including 1982, and surpass the $1 million mark in career earnings. All this success earned her a place on *Golf Magazine's* 1974 All-America team.

In 1975, Haynie had the lowest per round scoring average, an even 72, and would tie her career low of 64 at the 1982 Henredon Classic. But due to injuries and business interests, she slowed down in 1977, rejoining the LPGA Tour full-time in 1981. Once again injuries forced her out of competition in 1985, when she underwent knee surgery as well as electrode treatment to deaden the sensitivity in her lower back. Haynie's last full season was in 1989. Though her earnings reached $50,000 that year, her best finish was a tie for 12th at the Sara Lee Classic. Sandra Haynie became an influential figure in the development of women's golf in America, having served on the LPGA Executive Committee. She was elected to the LPGA Hall of Fame in 1977.

Jo Anne Meginnes,
freelance writer, Brookfield, Vermont

Hays, Mary (1754–1832).

See joint entry entitled Two Mollies for Mary Hays Ludwig McCauley.

Hays, Mary (1760–1843)

English novelist and feminist. *Name variations: (pseudonym) Eusebia. Born in Southwark, London, England, in 1760; died in London, England, in 1843; never married; no children.*

Works: Letters and Essays, Moral and Miscellaneous *(1793);* Memoirs of Emma Courtney *(1796);* An Appeal to the Men of Great Britain in Behalf of Women *(1798);* The Victim of Prejudice *(1799);* Female Biography *(six volumes, 1803);* The Brothers; or Consequences *(1815);* Family Annals; or The Sisters *(1817).*

Feminist writer Mary Hays was a member of what was referred to at the time as a Dissenting family. Growing up with her widowed mother and two sisters, she attended lectures at the Dissenting Academy in Hackney and, in 1792, gained some notoriety with her defense of public worship entitled *Cursory Remarks*. Published under the pseudonym Eusebia, it was in answer to an attack on Gilbert Wakefield, one of the teachers at the Academy. The work brought her to the attention of some of the eminent radicals of the day, including ***Mary Wollstonecraft**, who became her friend and mentor. (Hays helped nurse Wollstonecraft through her final illness and, after Wollstonecraft's death, wrote several moving tributes to her.) Wollstonecraft exercised influenced over Hays' subsequent writings, particularly her *Letters and Essays, Moral and Miscellaneous* (1793), in which Hays argues against tyranny in religion and marriage. The later *Appeal to the Men of Great Britain in Behalf of Women* (1798), published anonymously and advocating greater freedom for women, was also attributed to Hays.

Hays' novels were also feminist in nature. In the first, *Memoirs of Emma Courtney* (1796), the independent heroine, against the advice of a confidant, declares her passion for her beloved and offers to live with him without benefit of clergy, a plot twist that brought Hays some unexpected notoriety. An illegitimate orphan is the heroine of her second novel, *The Victim of Prejudice* (1799), in which Hays decries sexual inequality. She was also the author of *Female Biography* (1803), a six-volume work on historically significant women, and two collections of what might be called morality tales, *The Brothers; or Consequences* (1815), and *Family Annals; or The Sisters* (1817).

Mary Hays never married; an early love affair was discouraged by her mother and father. She settled in London in 1824 and died there at that age of 83.

Hayward, Susan (c. 1917–1975)

***American actress who, after four Academy Award nominations, finally won an Oscar for her performance in* I Want to Live!** *Born Edythe Marrener in Brooklyn, New York, on June 30, 1917 (also seen as 1918 and 1919); died in Los Angeles, California, on March 14, 1975; second daughter and third child of Walter (a transit worker) and Ellen (Pearson) Marrener; attended Girls' Commercial High School, Brooklyn; married Jeffrey (Jess) Thomas Barker (an actor), on July 23, 1944 (divorced 1956); married Eaton Chalkley (lawyer and businessman), on February 8, 1957 (died 1966); children: (first marriage) twin sons, Timothy and Gregory (b. 1955).*

Filmography: Hollywood Hotel *(1937);* The Sisters *(1938);* Comet Over Broadway *(1938);* Girls on Probation *(1938);* Our Leading Citizen *(1939);* Beau Geste *(1939);* $1,000 a Touchdown *(1939);* Adam Had Four Sons *(1941);* Sis Hopkins *(1941);* Among the Living *(1941);* Reap the Wild Wind *(1942);* The Forest Rangers *(1942);* I Married a Witch *(1942);* Star Spangled Rhythm *(1942);* The Parade of 1943 *(1943);* Young and Willing *(1943);* Jack London *(1943);* The Fighting Seabees *(1944);* The Hairy Ape *(1944);* And Now Tomorrow *(1944);* Deadline at Dawn *(1946);* Canyon Passage *(1946);* Smash-Up: The Story of a Woman *(1947);* They Won't Believe Me *(1947);* The Last Moment *(1947);* Tap Roots *(1948);* The Saxon Charm *(1948);* Tulsa *(1949);* House of Strangers *(1949);* My Foolish Heart *(1950);* I'd Climb the Highest Mountain *(1951);* Rawhide *(1951);* I Can Get It for You Wholesale *(1951);* David and Bathsheba *(1951);* With a Song in My Heart *(1952);* The Snows of Kilimanjaro *(1952);* The Lusty Men *(1952);* The President's Lady *(1953);* White Witch Doctor *(1953);* Demetrius and the Gladiators *(1954);* Garden of Evil *(1954);* Untamed *(1955);* Soldier of Fortune *(1955);* I'll Cry Tomorrow *(1956);* The Conqueror *(1956);* Top Secret Affair *(1957);* I Want to Live! *(1958);* Woman Obsessed *(1959);* Thunder in the Sun *(1959);* The Marriage-Go-Round *(1961);* Ada *(1961);* Back Street *(1961);* I Thank a Fool *(1962);* Stolen Hours *(1963);* Where Love Has Gone *(1964);* The Honey Pot *(1967);* Valley of the Dolls *(1967);* The Revengers *(1972).*

Born in the Flatbush section of Brooklyn, New York, screen actress Susan Hayward grew up in the shadow of poverty. At age six, while crossing the street, she was struck by a car and suffered multiple injuries that left her with a slight but permanent limp (which later evolved into her trademark "rolling" gait). She attended Girls' Commercial High School where she studied stenography and made regular appearances in school plays. After graduating in 1935, she worked in a handkerchief factory making cloth designs. When she had saved enough money, she quit her job and enrolled in the Feagin School of Dramatic Arts at Rockefeller Center. Because of her beautiful red hair, green eyes, and porcelain complexion, Hayward was a natural for the new color magazine ads and soon landed a modeling job with the Walter Thornton Agency. In 1937, when director George Cukor saw an advertising spread featuring Hayward in the *Saturday Evening Post*, he persuaded producer David Selznick to test her for the coveted role of Scarlett O'Hara for his film *Gone With the Wind*. With stars in her eyes, Hayward left for Hollywood, accompanied by her sister **Florence Marrener**. Selznick, however, was unimpressed with her test and told her to go home and take some acting lessons.

Ignoring Selznick's advice, Hayward stayed in Hollywood. With some further assistance from Cukor, who put her in touch with a Hollywood agent, she eventually landed a contract with Warner Bros. But the studio only used her for color publicity photos and as an extra, then dropped her. After some acting lessons and a concentrated effort to lose her Brooklyn accent, she signed a $200-a-week contract with Paramount and made her first "A" movie, *Beau Geste* (1939), with Gary Cooper and Ray Milland. For the next seven years, she struggled through an apprenticeship of minor roles at Paramount and on "loan out" assignments. Hayward vigorously campaigned for better roles, and her less than demure approach did not endear her to the studio bosses. Of the 16 movies she made during her early career, only three—*Adam Had Four Sons* (1941), *Reap the Wild Wind* (1942), and *The Hairy Ape* (1944)—are noteworthy.

Beginning in 1945, Hayward made a series of pictures with independent producer Walter Wanger, including *The Lost Moment* (1947) and *Smash-Up: The Story of a Woman* (1947), in which she played an alcoholic wife struggling to get her life in order. *Variety* called the picture Hayward's "biggest break to date," and it was the first to showcase her talent in what would become her trademark role as the feisty woman who triumphs over adversity. For her work in

Smash-Up, Hayward received the first of her five Academy Award nominations. She later credited Wanger for the launch of her career.

Hayward received a second Academy Award nomination for *My Foolish Heart* (1950), a war story in which she played a college girl who falls in love with a callous young man (Dana Andrews), who is subsequently killed in battle. *Newsweek* called it "Hayward's picture," and fan-magazine polls confirmed a surge in her popularity. Her three subsequent Oscar nominations were all for roles in films based on actual women: *With a Song in My Heart* (1952) recounts the life of singer ***Jane Froman**, *I'll Cry Tomorrow* (1956) recalls the downfall of singer ***Lillian Roth**, and *I Want to Live!* (1958) details the life of ***Barbara Graham**, the first woman to be sent to the gas chamber in California.

The role of Jane Froman, the popular singer of the 1940s whose legs were severely injured in a plane crash during the war, not only advanced Hayward's career, but did much to repair her reputation as difficult and cold on the set. She threw herself into preparation, taking dancing lessons and spending hours studying Froman's singing style and movements, incorporating minute nuances. (Froman recorded 30 songs for Hayward to mime in the film.) Those who worked on the film found Hayward to be both competent and likable. Her co-star Rory Calhoun, who also co-starred with the actress on *I'd Climb the Highest Mountain* (1951), thought her the most professional woman he had ever worked with. The film was a huge success and established Hayward as a top box-office draw. In addition to the Academy Award nomination, the Foreign Press named Hayward and John Wayne the most popular stars in the world.

Hayward actively campaigned for the lead in *I'll Cry Tomorrow* after reading Lillian Roth's autobiography, tracing her long struggle with alcoholism. Hayward won the role over a dozen other top stars, but it came at a price. The actress was then suffering through a difficult period in her own life. Her first marriage to actor Jess Barker (which produced twin boys in 1955), was publicly unraveling; she was also mourning the death of several friends and resolving some ongoing issues with her mother and sister. Throwing herself into the emotional role of the tormented singer, Hayward delivered astounding performances by day but seemed unable to step out of character at night. She became increasingly distraught and depressed, and one night, while studying her scene for the following day, she overdosed on prescription sleeping pills combined with alcohol. Rushed to the hospital near death, she made a quick recovery and returned to complete the filming. Upon release, the movie surpassed all of MGM's expectations. Hayward's performance was cited as her finest to date, and she easily received her fourth Academy Award nomination as Best Actress. Her loss to ***Anna Magnani** was a crushing blow that Hayward attributed to the scandal of her divorce and to Hollywood's general dislike of her.

Although her role as Barbara Graham in *I Want to Live!* was as grueling as that of Lillian Roth in *I'll Cry Tomorrow*, Hayward's life had stabilized. She had settled into a happy second marriage with Southern lawyer-businessman Eaton Chalkley, and it was Chalkley who helped her make the transition each day from Graham to Hayward. The film was another *tour de force* for Hayward who was at the peak of her skills. The wrenching final scene, where Graham is executed in the gas chamber, was so masterfully acted that people on the set felt as though they had actually witnessed someone die. When the film was released, the execution scenes (Graham was taken to the gas chamber to die on three separate occasions before she was finally executed), caused great controversy, and were either partially cut or, in some parts of the world, banned entirely. The reviews were overwhelmingly positive, for Hayward and the film. Bosley Crowther of *The New York Times*, never before a fan of Hayward's, called her performance "vivid" and "shattering." ***Eleanor Roosevelt** publicly praised the film, and *Life* magazine devoted an article to it. Academy Award night held no disappointment for Hayward, who finally won her Oscar and, along with it, the elusive approval of her peers.

During the 1960s, Hayward was cast in a series of tearjerkers and, by 1964, had pretty much called it quits. For several years, her husband had suffered recurring bouts of hepatitis; he died in 1966, at age 57. The loss was devastating to the actress who disappeared from the Hollywood scene for a year, returning in 1967 to play an aging Broadway singer, Helen Lawson, in the movie version of ***Jacqueline Susann**'s *Valley of the Dolls*. In 1968, Hayward signed on to play Auntie Mame in a Las Vegas production of the musical *Mame*, undergoing a grueling regimen in order to prepare herself for the demanding song-and-dance numbers. As it turned out, her Mame was unconventional but highly effective, writes Robert C. Jennings, "glutted with

Susan Hayward

Susan Hayward's own very special brand of sexiness and suffering."

Susan Hayward's last film role was a cameo in a low-budget western called *The Revengers* (1972). That same year, the actress was diagnosed with brain cancer which she fought valiantly for several years. In 1974, during a seemingly miraculous period of remission, Hayward appeared live on television to present the Best Actress award at the Oscar ceremonies, a remarkable feat which she called a "miracle of faith." The actress died on March 17, 1975.

SOURCES:

Candee, Marjorie Dent, ed. *Current Biography 1953.* NY: H.W. Wilson, 1953.

LaGuardia, Robert, and Gene Arceri. *Red: The Tempestuous Life of Susan Hayward.* NY: Macmillan, 1985.

SUGGESTED READING:

Linet, Beverly. *Susan Hayward: Portrait of a Survivor.* NY: Atheneum, 1980.

Barbara Morgan,
Melrose, Massachusetts

Haywood, Eliza (c. 1693–1756)

English novelist and playwright. *Born Eliza Fowler in London, England, around 1693; died on February 25, 1756; daughter of a London tradesman named Fowler; married Reverend Valentine Haywood, in 1717 (separated 1721); children: two.*

It is written that Eliza Haywood lived a reckless youth. At age 21, in 1714, she surfaced on the stage as an actress in Dublin, then moved on to London. Three years later, she entered into an unhappy marriage with the Reverend Valentine Haywood. In 1721, she revised a play, *The Fair Captive,* by a Captain Hurst for Lincoln's Inn Fields. Her first original play was *A Wife to be Lett* which opened at the Drury Lane in 1723; she also collaborated on an adaptation of Henry Fielding's *Tom Thumb.* But like ***Mary de la Rivière Manley**, Haywood left her mark by writing nearly 40 sensational and sizable novels, many based on social scandals of the day. Her first, *Love in Excess, or the Fatal Enquiry* (1719–1720), met with substantial commercial success; that same year, she published *Letters from a Lady of Quality to a Chevalier* (1720), by subscription. Haywood's *British Recluse* came out in 1722, followed by *The Injur'd Husband* (1722) and *Eovaai* (1736).

After Haywood's husband abandoned her and her two small children in 1721, her literary enemies had circulated slanderous stories about her, possibly founded on her works rather than her personal history. In her *Memoirs, of a certain Island adjacent to Utopia, written by a celebrated author of that country. Now translated into English* (1725), Haywood appended a key in which the characters were explained by initials to denote living persons. The actual names to these initials are supplied in the copy at the British Museum. *The Secret History of the Present Intrigues of the Court of Caramania* (1727) also implicated real-life individuals. Alexander Pope satirized Haywood in *The Dunciad,* which was made obvious by a note alluding to the:

> profligate licentiousness of those shameless scribblers (for the most part of that sex which ought least to be capable of such malice or impudence) who in libellous Memoirs and Novels reveal the faults or misfortunes of both sexes, to the ruin of public fame, or disturbance of private happiness.

Jonathan Swift wrote to ***Henrietta Howard**, countess of Suffolk (1688–1767): "Mrs Haywood I have heard of as a stupid, infamous, scribbling woman, but have not seen any of her productions." Haywood responded, attacking Swift in her *The Female Dunciad* (1729); she also went after Samuel Richardson, mocking his *Pamela* with her *Anti-Pamela, or Feign'd Innocence Detected* (1740). Eliza Haywood continued to be a prolific writer of novels until her death on February 25, 1756. Her later works are characterized by severe propriety, though an anonymous story of *The Fortunate Foundlings* (1744), claiming to be an account of the children of Lord Charles Manners, is generally ascribed to her. In later life, she was the editor for *The Female Spectator* (1744–1746), contributed to *The Tea Table,* and had moved into the realm of domestic realism with *Miss Betty Thoughtless* (1751) and *The History of Tommy and Jenny Jessamy* (1753). A collected edition of her novels, plays and poems appeared in 1724, and her *Secret Histories, Novels and Poems* in 1725.

SUGGESTED READING:

Whicher, G.F. *The Life and Romances of Eliza Haywood* (1915).

Hayworth, Rita (1918–1987)

American actress whose beauty and charisma epitomized Hollywood glamour in the 1940s and 1950s. *Name variations: Rita Cansino. Name pronunciation: HAY-worth. Born Margarita Carmen Cansino on October 17, 1918, in New York City; stricken with Alzheimer's disease in 1981, lived under care of her second daughter Princess Yasmin Aga Khan until her death on May 14, 1987, in New York City; daughter of Eduardo Cansino and Volga (Haworth) Cansino; attended high school up to ninth grade in Los Angeles; married Edward C. Judson, in 1936 (divorced 1942); married Orson Welles, on September 7, 1943 (divorced); married Ali Shah Khan, in 1949 (divorced 1953); married Dick Haymes, in 1953 (divorced 1955); married James Hill, on February 2, 1958 (divorced 1961); children: (with Welles)* ***Rebecca Welles;*** *(with Ali Shah Khan)* ***Yasmin Aga Khan.***

Rita Hayworth

Filmography: (as Rita Cansino) Under the Pampas Moon *(1935); (as Rita Cansino)* Dante's Inferno, *1935; (as Cansino)* Charlie Chan in Egypt *(1935); (as Cansino)* Paddy O'Day *(1935); (as Cansino)* Human Cargo *(1935); (as Cansino)* Meet Nero Wolfe *(1935); (as Cansino)* Rebellion *(1936); (as Cansino)* Trouble in Texas *(1937); (as Cansino)* Old Louisiana *(1937); (as Cansino)* Hit the Saddle *(1937);* Girls Can Play *(1937);* The Game That Kills *(1937);* Criminals of the Air *(1937);* Paid to Dance *(1937);* The Shadow *(1937);* Who Killed Gail Preston? *(1938);* There's Always a Woman *(1938);* Convicted *(1938);* Juvenile

Court *(1938);* Homicide Bureau *(1939);* The Renegade Ranger *(1939);* The Lone Wolf *(1939);* Spy Hunt *(1939);* Only Angels Have Wings *(1939);* Special Inspector *(1939);* Music in My Heart *(1940);* Blondie on a Budget *(1940);* Susan and God *(1940);* The Lady in Question *(1940);* Angels Over Broadway *(1940);* The Strawberry Blonde *(1941);* You'll Never Get Rich *(1941);* Affectionately Yours *(1942);* Blood and Sand *(1942);* My Gal Sal *(1942);* Tales of Manhattan *(1942);* You Were Never Lovelier *(1942);* Cover Girl *(1944);* Tonight and Every Night *(1945);* Gilda *(1946);* Down to Earth *(1947);* The Lady from Shanghai *(1948);* The Loves of Carmen *(1948);* Affair in Trinidad *(1952);* Salome *(1953);* Miss Sadie Thompson *(1953);* Fire Down Below *(1957);* Pal Joey *(1957);* Separate Tables *(1958);* They Came to Cordura *(1959);* The Story on Page One *(1960); (also producer)* The Happy Thieves *(1962);* Circus World *(1964);* The Money Trap *(1966);* The Poppy Is Also a Flower *(1966);* L'Avventuriére *(*The Rover, *Italian, 1967);* I Bastardi *(*Sons of Satan, *It., 1969);* Sur la Route de Salina *(*The Road to Salina, *Fr.-It., 1970);* The Naked Zoo *(*The Grove, *1971);* The Wrath of God *(1972).*

As one of the most enduring of Hollywood legends, Rita Hayworth offers a fascinating example of the sacrifices that were necessary to appeal to mainstream American audiences during and immediately after World War II. Hayworth the "Love Goddess," as she came to be called, may well be the best representative of a self-constructed star in the 20th century, whose persona was elevated and enslaved by publicity and the power of mass communications.

Eduardo Cansino, Rita's father, was descended from a family of Spanish dancers with a tradition that goes back to the middle of the 19th century. Eduardo's father, Antonio Cansino, made his debut at an early age in Seville and rapidly gained enough popularity to sustain himself with the money he made by dancing. He had 11 children, taught all of them to dance, and even used some of them in a dancing troupe. The Cansinos, led by Antonio, went on tour in and outside Spain. Unfortunately, two of the children died during one of the tours, and Antonio decided to abandon his dancing career and dedicate himself to teaching. Rita Hayworth's grandfather had started a trend in the Cansino family that would not die, however, for two of his children, Eduardo and **Elisa**, continued dancing. The young Cansinos traveled to the United States to present their act in 1913. A hit in New York, they were hired by Martin Beck and decided to stay in the States.

The "dancing Cansinos" became a household name on the New York scene, building enough of a reputation to be invited to appear in the Broadway musical *Follow Me* as guest artists. During this engagement, Eduardo met **Volga Haworth**, a young woman from Washington, D.C., who had run away from her parents—both English actors—to pursue an artistic career in Manhattan and was soon hired for the *Ziegfeld Follies*. Following her marriage to Eduardo, Volga joined the Cansinos in their dancing tours, became pregnant at the beginning of 1918, and gave birth to Margarita Carmen Cansino on October 17, in Brooklyn, New York.

The beginning of Rita Hayworth's life marked the end of her mother's career. Volga went from aspiring actress to full-time mother, while Eduardo and Elisa reached the peak of their collaboration, appearing before New York's finest audiences. As **Barbara Leaming** writes in *If This Was Happiness*, "in the first years of Margarita's life . . . Volga routinely handled all her husband's practical business so that he could devote himself fully to his art." Volga had two more children: Eduardo (born October 13, 1919) and Vernon (born May 21, 1922).

When young Hayworth showed a proclivity for dance, Eduardo wasted no time in linking his daughter's talent to the Cansino family tradition and enrolled her in dancing lessons. Eduardo was not keen on giving his children a formal education, however, so it took Volga several confrontations to convince Eduardo to register their daughter in school at the age of six. The stability that the young Cansinos enjoyed during these first years lasted until Eduardo decided that his future lay in film, the medium that was then becoming popular, and that they had to leave New York to pursue his dream. In 1927, he split with his sister Elisa and moved his family West, settling in Los Angeles. Though Eduardo never enjoyed the film career that he dreamed of, he and his family managed to live from his art. He set up a dance school and required Hayworth to attend dance lessons after school every day. Leaming writes that "Eduardo had singled her out as the only one in the family who shared his artistic talent, but as a consequence he placed a great burden of responsibility on her that her two brothers happily escaped." It was clear to everyone in the Cansino household that Rita would continue dancing and, hopefully, succeed in a way that her talented father never could. It was also clear that her dancing would be the point of departure for her career; thus, dancing became the focus of her training. Everything else was secondary.

It soon occurred to Eduardo, as he observed his daughter dancing and growing, that the youngster might afford him the opportunity to revive the "dancing Cansinos" and establish himself as a dancer on the West Coast. Thus, during Hayworth's years of elementary education at Carthay School and her first year at Hamilton High School in Los Angeles, she was forced to focus more on the training sessions than on her school work. As a consequence, Hayworth's education suffered. The young girl made her stage debut in a school play when she was 11 and her professional debut, in 1932, at the Carthay Circle Theater in Los Angeles.

Hayworth stopped attending school while in ninth grade when the Cansinos moved once again, this time across the U.S.-Mexico border. Father and daughter were engaged first for 18 months at the Foreign Club in Tijuana and then in Agua Caliente, Mexico. During their stay, 13-year-old Rita, who looked enough of a grown-up to pass as Eduardo's wife and dance-partner, could not leave the house. When it came to his daughter, Eduardo was extremely domineering, and it is suspected that his restrictions might have stemmed from incestuous motives. Hayworth would later tell Orson Welles that during this period her father had repeatedly engaged in sexual relations with her.

Eduardo's initial attempts to have his daughter cast in movies yielded little or no result. Eventually, however, she received an offer from Winfield R. Sheehan, who worked for Fox Film Corporation, to dance and play a supporting role in *Dante's Inferno,* starring Spencer Tracy. Eduardo was asked to choreograph his daughter's dance sequence. If *Dante's Inferno* was a big-budget failure, it was not a failure for Hayworth, as she received a yearlong contract to work for Fox when she finished shooting the film. It was 1939.

Now billed Rita Cansino, because studio publicists felt the name "Margarita" was too long, she was slow to loosen up before the camera; most of what she knew about performing involved dancing. Determined to improve, she signed up for acting lessons. She then appeared in *Under the Pampas Moon* as an Argentine dancer and in *Charlie Chan in Egypt* as an Egyptian dancer. At age 16, Hayworth was already learning her craft, capitalizing on the ethnic ambiguity of her looks, and fighting her shyness.

Eduardo's daughter did not receive an offer from Fox to continue appearing in their movies when her yearlong contract ended, and the news threw the Cansinos into financial turmoil. To sustain her relatives, Hayworth spent several months playing minor roles that required dancing—usually as either "Latin" or "Indian"—though she had no offers for a steady job. A year after her dismissal from Fox, Rita signed a seven-year contract with Columbia Pictures, added a "y" to her mother's maiden name to become Rita Hayworth, and made her first movie with them, *Girls Can Play.* In 1937, after finishing the filming of *The Game That Kills,* she escaped her father's house to marry Eddie Judson, an erstwhile car dealer and businessman who acted as her agent.

Under Judson's influence and her desire to become more marketable star material, Hayworth cut her hair, used electrolysis to raise her forehead, and underwent private coaching in both acting and singing. This process of body and facial transformations took eight months and resulted in the almost-mythical Rita Hayworth the world remembers best. The change in appearance proved effective and the new Rita was cast to play the adulterous wife in Howard W. Hawks' *Only Angels Have Wings* (1939) with Cary Grant and ***Jean Arthur** and produced by Columbia. Other important films followed: *The Strawberry Blonde* (1941), for Warner Bros., and *Blood and Sand* (1941), for Fox. By 1941, Rita Hayworth's star was on the rise.

> Sometimes when I find myself getting impatient, I just remember the times I cried my eyes out because nobody wanted to take my picture at the Trocadero.
>
> **—Rita Hayworth**

"The knowledge that she had been in large part *created* would remain a source of immense anxiety," writes Leaming. "Did she really have any acting talent, or was it all a publicist's hype?" The year 1941 marked the beginning of the myth of Rita Hayworth and the end of the private life of Margarita Cansino. On August 11, *Life* magazine published a photo of a negligee-clad Hayworth that many American soldiers carried with them during World War II after the Japanese attacked Pearl Harbor. The famous picture has, since the time of its publication, become ingrained in the minds of many Americans and elevated Hayworth to the status of "cultural icon," "the Love Goddess," according to *Life*.

It was obvious to Columbia that Hayworth was one of its best assets and that pairing her up with the king of American dance, Fred Astaire, in *You'll Never Get Rich*, would bring in more revenue and increase renown for its star. The film

was an immediate hit and established her as a "glamour girl who can dance" in the view of the public and as a hard worker in the view of those filming with her in the studio, including Astaire. The two dancers collaborated a second and last time for the movie, *You Were Never Lovelier*. Hayworth went on to work with Gene Kelly in *Cover Girl* (1944), and Glenn Ford in *Gilda* (1946), one of the films for which she is best remembered for her impromptu striptease with elbow-length gloves while singing "Put the Blame on Mame." Though there were other blockbuster movies released that year, "none were as provocative as *Gilda* where Hayworth jiggles in and out of one strapless evening gown after another, her long neck and elongated torso, her long, hefty legs twisting and turning snakelike to heart-thumping music," write Jay Nash and Stanley Ross. "Critics remained indifferent to the film but returning GIs flocked with their wives and sweethearts to see Columbia's sex goddess." Though Hayworth was a reigning pinup star with soldiers pre-*Gilda,* the movie made her more so. Her likeness and her name was painted upon the test A-bomb dropped on Bikini Atoll. Hayworth appeared in a less well-received movie in 1947, *Down to Earth*, a copy of which remains in a 20th-century time capsule for the perusal of generations in the forthcoming millennia.

Lady from Shanghai (1948) emerged out of Hayworth's professional collaboration with her second husband, Orson Welles, who co-starred and directed the film. A masterpiece of the film noir genre, *Lady from Shanghai*'s most famous setting features Hayworth standing in a hall of mirrors. The scene is a cinematic marvel both because of Hayworth's sophisticated, mature acting, and because of Welles' mastery of direction and his memorable use of mirror images. After *Lady from Shanghai*, Hayworth made one more movie, *The Loves of Carmen* (1948), and then retired temporarily from the movie business when she became the bride of Prince Aly Khan, whose father Aga Khan III, was Imam (or pope) to 15 million Asian and African Ismaili Muslims; the family claimed direct descent from ***Fatimah**, daughter of the Prophet Muhammed.

Hayworth's marriage to Aly Khan, like all of her previous marriages, piqued the interest of the American public and kept the press hunting for stories. By 1952, the year she made *An Affair in Trinidad*, Hayworth had been married three times and had two daughters: Rebecca with Welles and Yasmin with Khan. Rita made two movies in 1953, *Salome* and *Miss Sadie Thompson*, divorced Aga Khan, and then abandoned the big screen again, this time to marry singer

Dick Haymes. She returned to the movies in 1957 to film *Fire Down Below* for Columbia and then shoot a film version of *Pal Joey*, a musical by Rodgers and Hart.

Notwithstanding the many difficulties in her personal life, Rita Hayworth was known to be consistently professional until her fourth marriage, her beauty, her success, and her health all started to decline. In 1959, when she gave what is arguably her best performance in *They Came to Cordura*, critics remarked on her age and the impending loss of the beauty that had made her famous.

By the end of 1961, the year Hayworth divorced her fifth husband, her behavior was being influenced by Alzheimer's disease, but the disorder that was starting to affect her everyday life had yet to be diagnosed. Like her mother Volga Haworth, Hayworth was also an alcoholic. The combination of the two problems made life difficult for the people surrounding her, especially her young daughters who lived through her fits of anger and moodiness. The deterioration of her brain also affected Hayworth's professional life: it became extremely difficult for her to memorize her lines and thus keep up the standards she had upheld for so long. She continued to make films until 1971 and even had offers to appear on stage, which she rejected. By the time she shot *The Wrath of God* in 1971, Hayworth was unable to remember more than a line at a time. She attempted to make another movie in 1972, but her memory had been so severely damaged by then that she forgot to return to the set. Hayworth continued to make public appearances, however, and even went on a disastrous tour of South America, specifically Argentina and Brazil. Photographs taken at this time illustrate the sad final metamorphosis that she underwent. Despite efforts made by her agent to keep the press at bay, her physical deterioration became fodder for the international media. Pathetic images filled the tabloids, while writers compared the glorious Hayworth of the 1940s to this disintegrating, incoherent woman.

By 1976, unable to care for herself, Hayworth was admitted to Hoag Memorial Hospital in Newport Beach, California, where her problem was diagnosed as alcoholism. She stayed at the hospital until her daughter Yasmin took her back to the East Coast, set her up in an apartment, and oversaw her care. Hayworth was forced to abstain from drinking, and Yasmin consulted with several doctors, one of whom, in 1980, stopped assuming that the problem was alcohol and actually examined Hayworth's brain before making his diagnosis. Nineteen years after the first symptoms had presented themselves in a noticeable fashion, Hayworth's problem was finally understood to be the then little-known disease, Alzheimer's.

Princess Yasmin Aga Khan became her mother's legal conservator in 1981 and moved Rita to a New York City apartment near her own, overlooking Central Park. By this time, Hayworth was so far gone that she was unable to recognize even family members. The only thing that could move her was music. "Whenever music was played for her," writes Leaming, "her shoulders and feet might briefly come alive in her chair." Rita Hayworth died in her New York apartment on May 14, 1987.

SOURCES:

García-Johnson, Ronie-Richele. "Rita Hayworth," in *Notable Hispanic American Women*. Detroit, MI: Gale Research, 1993.

Leaming, Barbara. *If This Was Happiness: A Biography of Rita Hayworth*. NY: Viking, 1989.

"Rita Hayworth," in *Current Biography 1960*. NY: H.W. Wilson, 1960.

SUGGESTED READING:

Hill, James. *Rita Hayworth: A Memoir.* London: Robson, 1983.

Kobal, John. *Rita Hayworth: The Time, the Place, and the Woman*. NY: Norton, 1978.

Morella, Joe. *Rita: The life of Rita Hayworth*. NY: Delacorte Press, c. 1983.

Peary, Gerald. *Rita Hayworth*. NY: Pyramid, 1976.

Ringgold, Gene. *The Films of Rita Hayworth: The Legend and Career of a Love Goddess*. Secaucus, NJ: Citadel Press, 1974.

Carlos U. Decena,
Ph.D. candidate in American Studies, New York University

Hazard, Caroline (1856–1945)

American author and educator who was the fifth president of Wellesley College. *Born on June 10, 1856, in Peace Dale, Rhode Island; died on March 19, 1945, in Santa Barbara, California; the second of five children and first of three daughters of Rowland Hazard (the superintendent and later owner and manager of the Peace Dale Woolen Mills) and Margaret Anna (Rood) Hazard; educated by governesses and tutors; attended Miss Mary A. Shaw's School, Providence, Rhode Island, and private study abroad; never married; no children.*

Awards, honors: University of Michigan, A.M. (1899), Brown University, honorary Litt.D. (1899), Tufts College, LL.D. (1905), Wellesley College, LL.D. (1925); Mills College, Litt.D. (1931).

Selected works: Life of J.L. Diman *(1886); (editor)* Works of R.G. Hazard *(4 vols., 1889);* Thomas Hazard, Son of Robert *(1893); (poetry)* Narragansett

Opposite page

Rita Hayworth in Gilda.

Ballads *(1894);* The Narragansett Friends' Meeting *(1899);* Some Ideals in the Education of Women *(1900); (poetry)* A Scallop Shell of Quiet *(1907);* A Brief Pilgrimage in the Holy Land *(1909);* The College Year *(1910); (poetry)* The Yosemite and Other Verse *(1917);* Anchors of Tradition *(1924); (editor)* ***Esther Bernon Carpenter's*** South County Studies *(1924);* From College Gates *(1925);* Songs in the Sun *(1927); (editor)* John Saffin: His Book, 1664–1707 *(1928);* A Precious Heritage *(1929); (poetry)* The Homing *(1929); (editor)* Nailer Tom's Diary *(1930); (poetry)* Schards and Scarabs *(1931); (poetry)* The Golden State *(1939). Author of a bi-weekly column in the* Providence Evening Bulletin.

Born in 1856, Caroline Hazard grew up in Peace Dale, Rhode Island, where her father was the superintendent, and later the owner and manager, of the prosperous Peace Dale Woolen Mills, a family enterprise founded by his grandfather. The five Hazard children enjoyed a cultured environment that included religion and literature along with music and the arts. Caroline's formal education consisted of tutoring and attendance at a private school in Providence, followed by the customary European tour. As a young woman, she remained at home, devoting much of her time to writing poetry; she published her first volume, *Narragansett Ballads*, in 1894. She also pursued an early interest in the history of Rhode Island and its forebears, producing a number of volumes of local history, eventually becoming an authority on the subject. Along with writing and research, Hazard was active in charity work, particularly on behalf of the children of workers in her father's mills.

Through the years, Hazard apparently gained a reputation in educational and philanthropic circles. In 1899, when **Julia Josephine Irvine** resigned as president of Wellesley College, a school for women in Wellesley, Massachusetts, Hazard was recommended to the position by her friend ***Alice Freeman Palmer**. Since several of the college's trustees knew her, she was promptly elected the fifth president of the institution. Humbly accepting the position, the 45-year-old Hazard, who had neither a college degree nor administrative experience, promptly discovered that the 24-year-old college was deeply in debt, the result of the necessary but costly addition of elective studies instituted by her predecessor.

As the trustees had obviously known, Hazard had the right background and skills to bring the college back into solvency. Confident, energetic, with excellent writing and speaking skills, she also had access to the moneyed set in New York and New England. Making a large contribution to the college herself, as a gesture of good will, Hazard embarked on a development campaign. Over the next 11 years, she raised enough money for five dormitories, five academic buildings, a library, a gymnasium, an observatory, a botany building, a music hall, and several residence halls. During her tenure, enrollment doubled, four academic departments were added, and the number of full professorships increased, along with salaries and opportunities for sabbaticals. She also stabilized the budget and raised a million dollars in endowment funds.

Hazard also sought to enhance the quality of the Wellesley experience by encouraging the addition of courses and activities that she felt rounded out the standard academic offerings. A lover of music, she was influential in the creation of a choir and a solid music department. Her belief in health education gave rise to a graduate department of hygiene and physical education, and her strong Christian faith and commitment to social causes resulted in the addition of social work as an extracurricular activity. In facilitating change, however, Hazard was careful to consider the suggestions of her colleagues and always deferred to the faculty on academic matters. As a result, the spirit of the college community rose in direct proportion to the institution's material gains.

Poor health forced Hazard to resign from the college in 1910, and she spent the remaining years of her life in more leisurely pursuits. She wintered in the mild climate of Santa Barbara, California, where she painted, wrote, and contributed to the cultural and civic life of the city. She continued to publish poetry and essays until well into her 70s. Caroline Hazard died on March 19, 1945, at age 89.

SOURCES:

James, Edward T., ed. *Notable American Women.* Cambridge, MA: The Belknap Press of Harvard University Press, 1971.

Barbara Morgan,
Melrose, Massachusetts

Hazen, Elizabeth Lee and Rachel Fuller Brown

American scientists who discovered and patented nystatin, the first highly active antifungal agent to be found safe and effective for use in humans, and assigned all royalties to the Brown-Hazen Fund to expand research and experimentation in biology.

Rachel Fuller Brown (1898–1980). *Born Rachel Fuller Brown on November 23, 1898, in Springfield,*

Massachusetts; died on January 14, 1980, in St. Peter's Hospital, Albany, New York; daughter of George Hamilton Brown (a real estate and insurance agent) and Annie (Fuller) Brown; attended public elementary school, St. Louis, Missouri, and later grades at Central High, Springfield, Massachusetts; received A.B. in chemistry and history from Mount Holyoke, 1920, and, subsequently, an M.S. and Ph.D from the University of Chicago; lived with Dorothy Wakerley; never married; no children.

Awards: Squibb Award in Chemotherapy (1955); elected fellow of the New York Academy of Science (1957); honorary Doctor of Science from Hobart and William Smith Colleges in Geneva, New York (1969); Rhoda Benham Award of Medical Mycology Society of the Americas (1972); honorary Doctor of Science from Mount Holyoke (1972); Chemical Pioneer Award (1975).

Following work at the University of Chicago, became a chemist at the Division of Laboratories and Research in Albany, New York; developed simple tests for standardizing antisera used in treatment of pneumonia, vaccines and purification of antigens (1926–48); improved precipitation tests used to diagnose syphilis; paired with mycologist, Elizabeth Lee Hazen, to find antifungal agents (1948); with Hazen, discovered nystatin (1950); assigned rights and royalties of nystatin to establish the Brown-Hazen Fund (1951); with Hazen, discovered the antibacterial agents, phalamycin (1953) and capacidin (1959).

Selected publications: Government: The Future Role of Women in Science and the World *(1980); (with E.L. Hazen)* Activation of antifungal extracts of actinomycetes by ultrafiltration through gradocol membranes *(1949); (with A.B. Wadsworth)* A Specific Antigenic Carbohydrate of Type I Pneumococcus *(1931).*

Elizabeth Lee Hazen (1883–1975). *Name variations: Lee. Pronunciation: HAY-zen. Born Elizabeth Lee Hazen on August 24, 1883, in Coahoma County, Mississippi; died on June 24, 1975, at the Mount St. Vincent Hospital, Seattle; daughter of William Edgar Hazen (a cotton farmer) and Maggie (Harper) Hazen, both of whom died before she was three years old; raised by her Uncle Robert (Lep) Hazen and Aunt Laura (Crawford) Hazen; attended local Lula School; received B.S. in science and dressmaking certificate from Mississippi Industrial Institute and College at Columbus (currently the Mississippi University for Women), 1910; attended University of Tennessee and University of Virginia; received M.A. in biology from Columbia University, 1923; Ph.D. in microbiology, 1929; never married; no children.*

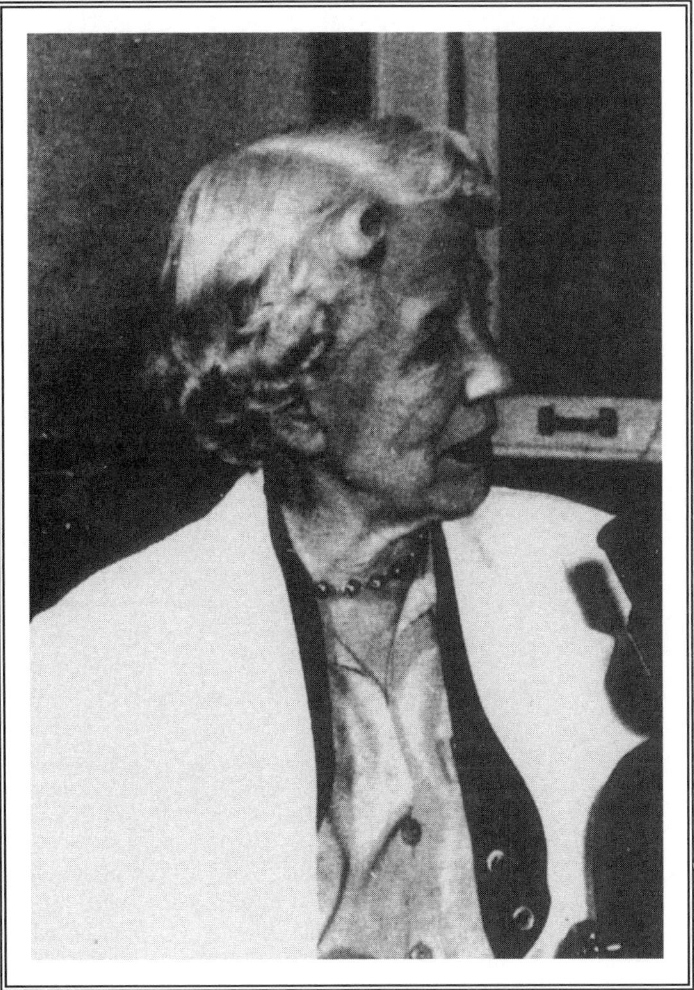

Elizabeth Lee Hazen

Awards: Squibb Award in Chemotherapy (1955); honorary Doctor of Science from Hobart and William Smith Colleges, Geneva, New York (1968); Rhoda Benham Award of Medical Mycology Society of the Americas (1972); Chemical Pioneer Award (1975).

Served as a technician in the Army diagnostic lab at Camp Sheridan, Alabama (1918–19); became assistant director of Clinical and Bacteriology Laboratory of Cook Hospital, Fairmont, West Virginia (1919–23); appointed resident bacteriologist at Presbyterian Hospital (1928); was a member of the teaching staff at College of Physicians and Surgeons, Columbia University (1929); took charge of bacterial diagnosis lab at New York State Department of Health, Division of Laboratories and Research (1931); paired with chemist, Rachel Fuller Brown, to find antifungal agents (1948); with Brown, discovered nystatin (1950); with Brown, applied for patent and assigned rights and royalties of nystatin to establish the Brown-Hazen Fund (1951); with Brown, discovered the antibacterial agent, phalamycin (1953);

with Brown, discovered capacidin, an antifungal agent (1959).

Selected publications: General and Local Immunity to Ricin *(1927);* Unsuccessful Attempts to Cure or Prevent Tuberculosis in Guinea Pigs with Dreyer's Defatted Antigen *(1928); (with A. Schatz)* Distribution of soil microorganisms antagonistic to fungi pathogenic for man *(1948); (with R.F. Brown)* Activation of antifungal extracts of actinomycetes by ultrafiltration through gradocol membranes *(1949); (with Frank Reed)* Laboratory Identification of Pathologic Fungi Simplified *(1955).*

The early part of the 20th century heralded an exciting era of important discoveries in the medical battle against infectious diseases. Alexander Fleming discovered penicillin. A few years later, Selman Waksman provided streptomycin, a broad-spectrum antibiotic that was effective against a wide array of bacterial diseases. But as research scientists began to win the battle against bacteria, another deadly collection of pathogens gained strength, the Mycota or fungi.

As an antibiotic attacks the bacteria in a patient's system, it also cleans the body, including the intestinal tract, of the normal bacteria that inhabit it. As a result, biological competition is reduced and an overgrowth of any other organism present takes place. As the number of available antibiotics increased in the 1930s and 1940s, so did the number of patients with fungi infections. Pathogenic fungi are responsible for a host of diseases ranging from relatively minor ones like ringworm and athlete's foot to coccidioidomycosis, which can become as malignant as cancer and lead to death. Fungi that attack the respiratory system, such as blastomycosis, histoplasmosis and cryptococcosis, mirror influenza in the early stage. If untreated they can cause gross damage. Until the discovery of nystatin (pronounced nye-state-in), by Brown and Hazen, there was no known antifungal drug that could be used to combat these diseases without harming the patient.

Rachel Fuller Brown had already been working as an organic chemist at the New York State Division of Laboratories and Research in Albany for several years when Elizabeth Lee Hazen was hired in 1931 to take charge of the division's bacterial diagnosis lab in Manhattan. Brown worked extensively with polysaccharides (carbohydrates) to develop simple tests that standardized the antisera used to treat pneumonia. During this time, she was also responsible for developing a simple screening procedure for identifying the presence of syphilis in blood samples. Later, working with a staff scientist analyzing soil microorganisms with antibacterial qualities, Brown became adept at isolating the specific substance in the microorganism having antibacterial properties. This skill was to prove invaluable during her work with Hazen.

Elizabeth Lee Hazen was a gifted scientific investigator and, while working at Columbia University during the 1920s, she solved quite a few mysteries. An outbreak of anthrax, a disease usually associated with cattle and horses, was traced by Hazen to the animal bristles being used in a New York brush factory. She was also responsible for pinpointing unexpected sources of tularemia (rabbit fever), an infectious disease of rodents that can be transmitted to humans through insect bites or by handling the flesh of infected animals. One of Hazen's most important early discoveries, however, was the first reported case of Clostridium botulinum, Type E, which she traced back to canned fish from Germany and Labrador.

The Division of Laboratories and Research had no mycologist on their staff when Hazen was hired. Her strong background in bacteriology and her innovative research abilities made her the perfect candidate to become one. Working with **Rhoda Benham**, a recognized authority on pathogenic fungi, Hazen learned mycology. She began an extensive collection of systemic fungi found in soil samples she either dug herself or had given to her by fellow researchers. Hazen's original objective had been to develop standard methods of examination for disease-causing fungi, and her collection of cultures was the first step in providing comparative data. In 1944, she returned to Columbia University to formally study mycology.

During the course of testing soil for various microorganisms, Hazen found some samples that contained streptomycetes with strong antifungal activity. Now all she needed was a chemist to isolate the active material. Gilbert Dalldorf, director of the division, believed that Rachel Brown's skill in isolating active principles would help Hazen, so he arranged for Hazen to meet with Brown in her Albany laboratory. For the many years of their collaboration, Hazen and Brown would continue to work 150 miles away from each other, Hazen in New York City and Brown in Albany.

Hazen concentrated her research investigations on two pathogenic fungi: *Cryptococcus neoformans,* the cause of a chronic disease that affects the lungs, skin, and the central nervous system, and *Candida albicans* (candidiasis), a commonly occurring fungi that can become lethal in patients receiving large doses of strong antibiotics. After gathering soil samples, Hazen would mix some of each with sterile saline and seed them on a nutrient base until any actinomycetes—the microorganisms most frequently having antifungal properties—grew to the stage where they could be seen and identified. The cultures that were the most promising were placed on another nutrient base growing test fungi. Their action against the fungi were then observed.

Brown's job was to find the active properties of those cultures that most strongly affected the growth of the test fungi, separate them from the mass, and refine them so that they could be further tested. In 1948, Brown identified two properties that showed great promise: Fraction N, which turned out to be very toxic to humans, and Fraction AN. Further tests showed that Fraction AN was effective against both *Cryptococcus neoformans* and *Candida albicans,* as well as 14 other fungi. Many more long months of tests and research were required until, in 1950, Brown and Hazen were able to report that the toxicity level of Fraction AN in guinea pigs, rats, and mice was very low. It still had not been tested in humans, but nystatin, as it eventually came to be called, appeared to be the antibiotic they were looking for. They reported their discovery to the National Academy of Sciences in October 1950. Nystatin would become one of the most effective agents against *Candida* and *Aspergillus* infections in the mouth, skin, vagina, and intestinal tract.

The Brown-Hazen method of producing nystatin was expensive, too expensive for commercial production. In addition, the Division of Laboratories and Research had no patent policy. The division recommended that Brown and Hazen turn to The Research Corporation—a nonprofit establishment with expertise in patenting and licensing inventions for colleges, universities, and research institutions. Under the terms of The Research Corporation's policy, Brown and Hazen were required to give all rights to their invention to the corporation, which would use any financial gains for philanthropic purposes.

The final agreement with the corporation stated that half of all royalties would go to the corporation for use in its own philanthropic activities. The other half, some $6.7 million over the next 20 years, was designated to be used to support the Brown-Hazen Fund, from which distributions would be made to "non-profit scientific and educational institutions and societies for the advancement and extension of technical and scientific investigation, research, and experimentation in the field of biologic and related sciences." In the early years, the Fund supported both fledgling and seasoned researchers. It especially encouraged grant applications from women working in the sciences. In later years, it was expanded to provide funds for biology departments to encourage undergraduates, and for several years it was the single largest source of nonfederal funding for research and training in medical mycology.

At the time The Research Corporation took on the handling of the patenting process for Brown and Hazen, only 1% of all patents in the U.S. had been awarded to women. The organization also found an inexpensive way to produce nystatin using peanut meal. E.R. Squibb & Sons, a pharmaceutical house already known for its interest in antibiotics, contacted the researchers, and a license agreement was signed that gave Squibb exclusive rights for five years to manufacture and sell nystatin.

> The time is already past when an occasional woman scientist, such as Mme. Curie, was grudgingly recognized for her pioneering contributions to chemistry and physics.
>
> **—Rachel Fuller Brown**

In 1954, Federal Drug Agency (FDA) approval was given for sale of Mycostatin (Squibb's name for nystatin) in oral dosage form. It was recommended for the treatment of intestinal candidiasis, a condition that occurred often in patients receiving intensive or long-term courses of antibiotics. Nystatin was subsequently sublicensed to most of the other major drug companies.

In 1966, when the Arno river flooded in Florence, another use was found for nystatin. Because it had no effect on any of the pigments used in paint, nystatin was used on salvaged works of art to retard the growth of fungus. Four years later, it was also used successfully to fight Dutch elm disease.

Although a total of $13.4 million in royalties were paid to The Research Corporation between 1955 and 1976, the only money either Brown or Hazen ever saw from the discovery was a $5,000 honorarium in 1955. It was presented with The Squibb Award in Chemotherapy for "conspicuous accomplishment in the advancement of chemotherapy through their discovery and evaluation of nystatin." Neither woman permitted the discovery of nystatin to make any significant change in her life. Both continued to work in their respective fields, discovering several more antibacterial agents for fungi. Both remained single but were committed to strong family and religious ties, as well as close friendships. Hazen, who continued to work as the head of Mycology at the Division of Laboratories and Research until she retired in 1958, kept her personal and professional life separate, refusing to talk about work when visiting friends or relatives. Personal time for this small, delicate, meticulous woman meant the theater, canasta, dabbling in the stock market or encouraging young relatives to enter college.

Brown, who remained at the division until her retirement in 1968, maintained a lifelong friendship with **Dorothy Wakerley**. They met while both were involved with St. Peter's Episcopal Church. Brown, a handsome and energetic woman, taught Sunday school for 40 years at St. Peter's and was the first woman to be elected to the vestry of the church. Over the years, Rachel Brown and Dorothy Wakerley "adopted" many Chinese visitors who came to the division to study. As the years passed, the Chinese visitors sent their daughters and sons, nieces and nephews, to live with Rachel and Dorothy while they attended U.S. colleges.

The crowning achievement for Rachel Brown and Elizabeth Hazen came in 1975 at a meeting of the American Institute for Chemists in Boston when they were presented with the Chemical Pioneer Award. This was most unusual for two reasons. First, the institute had to change its bylaws to recognize Hazen, who was not a chemist. Second, it was the first time the award had been given to women.

In addition to funding the work of researchers, between 1960 and 1969 ten grants totaling $355,000 were made from the Brown-Hazen Fund for upgrading biology departments in liberal arts colleges. The 1968 grant to Pacific-Lutheran University helped fund a cooperative effort of two departments: biology and chemistry. It marked the beginning of molecular and cellular biology at an institution that had previously only offered classical biology.

Both Brown and Hazen actively encouraged women to enter the sciences and personally campaigned to get women to apply for Brown-Hazen grants. Brown was continually frustrated in not finding many women interested in science, with the result that she became instrumental in beginning a summer program that provided practical education in biology at Vassar in 1969 and 1970. Funds for scholarships and fellowships given to Mount Holyoke, named for Brown, and those given to the Mississippi University for Women, in Hazen's name, were restricted to advancing the studies of women in science.

In 1980, five years after Elizabeth Hazen's death, Rachel Brown was a contributor to a special issue of *The Chemist* that focused on women in science. Her closing thoughts are a key to the path both she and Hazen took in their careers. She said that the woman scientist must "recognize her own potentials, believe in herself, and determine to give unstintingly of herself to her chosen career. Only then can she expect to achieve on a par with her male counterparts."

SOURCES:

Baldwin, Richard S. *The Fungus Fighters.* Ithaca, NY: Cornell University Press, 1981.

Haber, Louis. *Women Pioneers in Science.* NY: Harcourt Brace Jovanovich, 1979.

Sicherman, Barbara, and Carol Hurd, eds. *Notable American Women: The Modern Period.* Cambridge, MA: Harvard University Press, 1980.

Yost, Edna. *Women of Modern Science.* NY: Dodd Mead, 1959.

Paula A. Steib,
freelance writer, Kaneohe, Hawaii

Hazlett, Olive C. (1890–1974)

American mathematician. *Born Olive Clio Hazlett in Cincinnati, Ohio, in 1890; died in 1974; attended public schools in Boston, Massachusetts; Radcliffe College, B.A., 1912; University of Chicago, S.M., 1913, Ph.D., 1915.*

Deemed one of the most notable American women in the field of mathematics, Olive C. Hazlett was a pioneering academic in an area dominated by men. Born in Cincinnati, Ohio, in 1890, but moving to Boston at the age of nine, she attended public schools and received her undergraduate degree from Radcliffe in 1912. Hazlett obtained both her S.M. and Ph.D. degrees from the University of Chicago, writing her master's thesis and her doctoral dissertation on linear associative algebras. She began her academic career at Harvard (1915–16) as an ***Alice Freeman Palmer** Fellow of Wellesley College, then, in the fall of 1916, she moved on to teach at Bryn Mawr, After two years, she took a position as assistant professor at Mount Holyoke, where she shifted her attention to modular invariants and covariants.

Olive C. Hazlett

In 1925, wanting more time for research, she accepted a post at the University of Illinois, where she was active in the professional community. From 1923 to 1935, she was a cooperating editor of the *Transactions of the American Mathematical Society* and also served on their council for two years. In 1928, she received a Guggenheim Fellowship which enabled her to study in Italy, Switzerland, and Germany. A prolific writer, Hazlett wrote 17 research papers, the last three of which were published in 1930. She officially retired from the University of Illinois in 1959, after spending 14 years on disability leave.

Hazrat Mahal (c. 1820–1879)

Begum of Oudh and Muslim queen-mother who, in the name of her underage son, led local resistance against the British East India Company during the Indian Mutiny (1857–58). *Name variations: Surname reportedly Iftikarun-nisa; took name Hazrat Mahal, Begum ("honored lady") of Oudh, when raised to the status of King's Wife after the birth of her son. Pronunciation: HAZ-rat mah-HALL. Born around 1820 in Faizabad, Oudh (or Oudhad), India (modern-day Awadh); died in 1879 while in exile in Nepal; married Wajid Ali Shah (king of Oudh, deposed by the British* *for incompetence in 1857); children: son Mohd Ramzan Ali Bahadur Birgis Qadr (b. around 1845 and crowned king of Oudh in July 1857).*

Born into a poor family in the provincial town of Faizabad, Oudh, India (c. 1820); trained as a dancing girl; entered the harem of Wajid Ali Shah some time before 1845; gave birth to her son Birgis Qadr, possibly after a liaison with Mammu Khan (c. 1845); led resistance in Oudh after the arrest of her husband (1857–59); driven into exile in Nepal and died there (1879).

"The Indian Mutiny, or the Sepoy War as the Victorians often called it, was one of the decisive events of British imperial history, which set a seal upon the manner and purpose of the Empire," writes James Morris. The Mutiny united Hindu and Muslim in ways that had never happened before and would never happen again, and had a great impact upon the manner in which the British controlled their empire in general and India in particular. Instead of being ruled by agents of the British East India Company, the country became a crown property ruled directly by ***Victoria**, the queen of England. One of the chief movers of the rebellion was the *de facto* regent of the state of Oudh, the Queen-Mother Hazrat Mahal. Acting in the name of her son Birgis Qadr, Hazrat Mahal rallied the resistance in Oudh and led several attacks against the British forces before she was decisively defeated in 1859. She was driven into exile in Nepal by the British and died there in 1879 without ever surrendering. Hazrat Mahal was the last free leader of the Mutiny.

No one knows exactly where Hazrat Mahal came from, or even who her parents were. She was apparently born in the city of Faizabad, the daughter of a poor but respectable citizen. According to tradition, she was very beautiful and, perhaps because of this, trained as a dancing girl. She caught the eye of the king Wajid Ali Shah, "who not only took her into his harem but, when she gave birth to a son, raised her to the rank of one of his wives, under the title Hazrat Mahal," notes P.J.O. Taylor. But the king was probably deceived. According to Taylor, all the evidence indicates that the true father of her son was her companion and fellow commander Mammu Khan. "He was her lover when she was a dancing girl, and in fact he never left her, despite her marriage.... He certainly stayed with her after her husband's banishment to Calcutta, and they raised their son to the throne at the earliest opportunity."

The British were partly responsible for the decline in authority of the Mughal emperors: they encouraged local rulers to break away from the central government in exchange for trading concessions. Oudh, writes Rudrangshu Mukherjee, "was one of the biggest of these successor states. Founded in 1722 by an Iranian adventurer entitled Saadat Khan who refused the imperial order transferring him to Malwa, it was among the first regional powers to become independent of Delhi." Oudh maintained its independence through a careful balance of diplomacy between the Mughal emperor in Delhi and the British representatives in India. By the time Wajid Ali Shah became its ruler, about one hundred years after its founding, the state was well established. As the British East India Company won governmental powers for itself, local governments gained and lost autonomy. By the 1850s, the Mughal emperor in Delhi, Bahadur Shah Zafar, had become largely a powerless figurehead. Indians, both Hindu and Muslim, resented the British company's power. By the time the company annexed Oudh in 1856, the natives were ready to resist the British with force.

There were two major factors that led to the outbreak of the Indian Mutiny. Native Hindi and Muslim Indians believed that the English wanted to destroy their traditional religious practices. Rumors spread among native troops that the new ammunition cartridges provided to them were greased with a mixture of pig and beef fat—violating the religious taboos of both Hindus and Muslims. The British excuse for annexing Oudh was that corruption ran rampant in the court of Wajid Ali Shah. Wajid's government traditionally farmed out the right to collect taxes to a variety of important men in the state, who paid a large fee for the privilege. These tax collectors realized a profit from their investment by squeezing extra money from the taxpayers and by skimming off a part of the money due to the government. Often bribes were paid to government officials to prevent investigations or inquiries. So widespread was this practice that it penetrated even the court of Wajid Ali Shah and touched the king himself.

Disgusted with the king's administration and his inability to repay his debts, the British East India Company's court of directors instructed Lord Dalhousie, the governor-general, to begin the process of expansion. Lieutenant General Sir James Outram, the British representative or Resident in Oudh's capital city of Lucknow, was given a new treaty for the king to sign. "Both the Queen Mother and the King's brother pleaded against annexation, to no avail, with the Regent," explains Taylor. "The King himself, recognizing the *fait accompli,* then sorrowfully took off his turban and placing it in the Resident's hands, said, 'Treaties are necessary between equals only.' Now that his title, rank and position were gone, it was not for him to sign a Treaty. Thus the kingdom of [Oudh] passed into British hands at 9 a.m. on 7 February 1856." On March 13, Wajid Ali Shah traveled to exile in Calcutta, leaving his young heir Birgis Qadr, his 71 other children, and his 60 concubines and wives, including the Begum Hazrat Mahal, in charge in Lucknow.

It is not clear exactly what happened in Oudh between the departure of the king and the outbreak of the Mutiny in Delhi 14 months later. The British left a quarrelsome and intolerant representative, C. Coverley Jackson, in charge. Jackson, the officiating chief commissioner stationed in Lucknow to negotiate the transfer of power from Wajid Ali Shah to the East India Company, was not the best man for the job. "When he was not quarreling with his chief assistant," writes Taylor, "he spent most of his energies in devising petty insults and annoyances for the dethroned royal family of Oudh." Jackson was replaced in March of 1857 by Sir Henry Lawrence, a much more charismatic man, but by that time Hazrat Mahal and her son had been totally alienated from the British.

The Mutiny that broke out in Delhi on May 11, 1857, quickly spread to other territories in northwest India. On May 31, Lawrence reported in a letter to the lieutenant-governor of India in Agra that he had chased a band of mutineers seven miles out of Lucknow, taking 30 prisoners. By June 9, he reported to the commander-in-chief that communications with the town of Cawnpore (modern Kanpur) had been cut. On June 13, he explained to the commissioner at Benaras that he had lost all communications with the outside world, and that the town was effectively besieged. Lawrence made an attempt to break out of Lucknow on June 30, but he was driven back at the town of Chinhut. He was forced to take shelter with 600 Europeans and a few loyal Indians in the Residency, the 37-acre compound where the British kept their headquarters.

What exactly Hazrat Mahal and her son Birgis Qadr were doing during this period is uncertain. At some point, she managed to convince Wajid Ali Shah's other wives and concubines to support her son Birgis Qadr as king, even though Wajid Ali Shah himself was still alive. She then persuaded the Mughal emperor Bahadur Shah Zafar to name Birgis Qadr as acting regent for Oudh. Hazrat Mahal began undoing some of the corruption of her husband's administration, confiscating the property of crooked officials. For example, she discovered that Ali Nucky Khan, former chief officer of Wajid Ali Shah, had hidden a great deal of money in his house, which she used to pay her troops. Hazrat Mahal also united both Hindus and Muslims under her son's administration, largely by recruiting Jai Lal Singh, a respected Hindu leader, to her side. "With the Hindu infantry sepoys," writes Taylor, "Rajah Jai Lal Singh had the most influence; they took little persuading that he was the best military leader available, and that they should support the crowning of Hazrat Mahal's son, Birgis Qadr, as King of [Oudh]. The boy was only twelve years old: it was assumed, though not explicitly, that Hazrat Mahal should rule in his name. She did, and from that moment she had great power."

Although Hazrat Mahal's forces greatly outnumbered those of the Europeans in the Residence, she proved unable to take the compound. This was partly because of disagreement among her commanders and the presence of Indians within the compound—half the defending force were natives—but it was also because of the Residence's strong defenses. The Residents had built their home solidly and encircled the compound with strong, easily fortifiable walls. Hazrat Mahal's officers surrounded the enclosure with snipers and kept up a constant artillery bombardment. Sir Henry Lawrence was one of the first British casualties; he died on June 2, hit by artillery fire from the Indian guns pounding the Residence. The besiegers also practiced mining—driving tunnels under the walls and exploding bombs in them in hopes of collapsing the masonry above. "It was not until September 23, after 90 days of siege," writes Morris, "that the defenders heard gunfire on the other side of the city, and two days later there burst into the compound a column of Highlanders, ragged, unshaven, kilted and furiously warlike, under the joint command of two remarkable generals, Henry Havelock and James Outram."

The arrival of Havelock and Outram and their men did not change the status of the besieged occupants of the Residence. There were only about 1,000 soldiers in the relieving force, and Hazrat Mahal's troops quickly tightened the siege again. Finally, on November 17, General Colin Campbell forced his way into Lucknow and began evacuating the Residence, leaving Hazrat Mahal in uncontested control of her capital city. Campbell, however, left a strong British force under James Outram at the Alambagh—the "world-garden," the chief home of the former Queen-Mother of Oudh—about three miles south of Lucknow. In late November or early December, Hazrat Mahal summoned a Durbar, or high council, demanding that her commanders attack the Alambagh and drive the British away.

There is some evidence that Hazrat Mahal was losing control over her army commanders. The British offered favorable terms and clemency for soldiers who had mutinied, provided that they had not killed any British citizens. Several important *talukdars,* the landowners of Oudh, showed signs of making peace separately with the British. "Great things were promised from the all-powerful Delhi and my heart used to be gladdened by the communications I received from that city," said Hazrat Mahal, as she addressed her commanders:

> but now the King has been dispossessed and his army scattered; the English have bought over the Sikhs and the rajas, and have established their government West East and South, and communications have been cut off; the [Sahib, ruler of Cawnpore] has been vanquished; and Lucknow is endangered; what now is to be done? The whole army is in Lucknow, but it is without courage. Why does it not attack the Alambagh? Is it waiting for the English to be reinforced and Lucknow to be surrounded? How much longer am I to pay the sepoys for doing nothing? Answer now, and if fight you won't, I shall negotiate with the English to spare my life.

The commanders reportedly replied, "Fear not, we shall fight, for if we do not we shall be hanged one by one; we have this fear before our eyes." Writes Taylor, "There is almost an echo of Queen Elizabeth addressing her troops at Tilbury" in Hazrat Mahal's demand for action. "She displays the same courage, but her message is full of reproach instead of encouragement."

In accordance with Hazrat Mahal's wishes, the Indian troops made six separate assaults on the Alambagh between December 22, 1857, and February 25, 1858. Although they mustered up to 30,000 soldiers, the Indians never managed to break Outram's defenses. Even the presence of the Maulvi of Faizabad, a renowned Muslim religious leader, failed to shift the balance. Finally, on March 16, 1858, the British marched into Lucknow and recaptured the city, and Hazrat Mahal and the Maulvi retreated with the remnants of their army. Hazrat Mahal sought help from Jung Bahadur, the maharajah of Nepal, but he had been helping the British and refused to assist her. In June of 1858, Hazrat Mahal, the Maulvi, and a force of 18,000 men were attacked by General Sir Hope Grant and were driven into the north of the country.

As the months "dragged on," writes Taylor, "the rebel army was still formidable and had not been decisively defeated or dispersed. There was hope. Hazrat Mahal's writ still ran in much of the old Kingdom of [Oudh], and she proved to be a talented administrator. Even the British admitted that had she been the ruler instead of her husband there would have been scant excuse for the annexation." It was not until the first of November of 1858 that the British brought their most powerful weapon into play. Queen Victoria announced in a proclamation that the British East India Company's government in India was dissolved, and from that time the country would be ruled directly by the British government under the queen.

Hazrat Mahal responded to the queen's proposal with a proclamation of her own, issuing the following statement, critical of British attitudes, in the name of her son Birgis Qadr:

> In the Proclamation it is written, that the Christian religion is true, but no other creed will suffer oppression, and that the laws will be observed towards all. What has the administration of justice to do with the truth or falsehood of a religion? That religion is true which acknowledges one God, and knows no other. Where there are three Gods in a religion, neither Mussulmans nor Hindoos—nay, not even Jews, Sun-worshippers, or Fire-worshippers can believe it true. To eat pigs and drink wine, to bite greased cartridges, and to mix pig fat with flour and sweetmeats, to destroy Hindoo and Mussulman temples on pretence of making roads, to build churches, to send clergymen into the streets and alleys to preach the Christian religion, to institute English schools and to pay people a monthly stipend for learning the English sciences, while the places of worship of Hindoos and Mussulmans are to this day entirely neglected; with all this, how can the people believe that religion will not be interfered with? The rebellion began with religion, and for it, millions of men have been killed. Let not our subjects be deceived; thousands were deprived of their religion in the North-West, and thousands were hanged rather than abandon their religion.

She continued with an analysis of the political situation of Oudh under the British:

> In the Proclamation it is written that all contracts and agreements entered into by the Company will be accepted by the Queen. Let the people carefully observe this artifice. The Company has seized on the whole of Hindoostan and if this arrangement be accepted, what is then new in it. . . . [R]ecently, in defiance of treaties and oaths, and notwithstanding that they owed us millions of Rupees, without reason, and on the pretence of the

> misgovernment and discontent of our people, they took our country and property worth millions of Rupees. If our people were discontented with our Royal predecessor, Wajid Ally Shah, how come they are content with us? And no ruler ever experienced such loyalty and devotion of life and goods as we have done? What then is wanting that they do not restore our country?
>
> Further it is written in the Proclamation that they want no increase of territory but yet they cannot refrain from annexation. If the Queen has assumed the government why does Her Majesty not restore our country to us when our people wish it?

Despite the points that Hazrat Mahal made in her response, she continued to lose adherents. By December of 1858, General Campbell had her forces in retreat around the town of Bareitch in northern Oudh. Hazrat Mahal received an offer to spare her life, grant her asylum, and receive a pension in exchange for her surrender. "She was tempted," writes Taylor, "and might have accepted; we shall never know for certain; her chiefs got wind of the possibility, struck camp and fled, taking her and her son as virtual hostages." By the time she was able to approach the British again, the offer had been withdrawn, partially because of rumors that she had been involved in the deaths of British citizens.

Most historians agree that Hazrat Mahal was not responsible for mass murders of British civilians the way some of her colleagues were. She went on record protesting the killing of 200 British women and children at Cawnpore on July 15, 1857—known as the "Bibigarh massacre." But there is some evidence that she revenged herself on certain Europeans who had hurt her. She was accused of having Coverley Jackson's niece, **Georgina Jackson**, and nephew, Sir Mountstuart Jackson, killed. The two young people, along with their sister, **Anna Madeline Jackson**, sought refuge with the Rani of Dhouraira after the outbreak of the mutiny. The rani protected them at first, but later was compelled to send them to Hazrat Mahal in Lucknow. Anna Madeline survived and wrote an account of her escape. Witnesses later testified that a telegraph operator named Deverine was killed by mutineers. His head was cut off, writes Taylor, and "was sent to the [Hazrat Mahal]'s private apartments, that she might feast her eyes on the sight, and . . . the bearer of the trophy was rewarded with a *killat.*" Historians speculate that rumors such as these played an important part in Hazrat Mahal's refusal to surrender.

She was still at large in January of 1859, but her cause was becoming more and more hopeless. By the end of that year, she was left with only 1,500 adherents, most of them without guns, ammunition, or food. Eventually she and her son found shelter with the maharajah of Nepal, Jung Bahadur. "The months passed, the years passed, and Hazrat Mahal refused to surrender," Taylor explains. "The *Times* in London briefly chronicled her history. At the end of 1858 it was saying 'Like all the women who have turned up in the insurrection she has shown more sense and nerve than all her generals together.'" Hazrat Mahal died in exile in 1879.

SOURCES:

Bhatnagar, G.D. *The Annexation of Oude.* Vol. 3. Uttaara Bharati: [n.p.], 1956.

———. *Awadh under Wajid Ali Shah.* Varanasi: Bharatiya Vidya Prakashan, 1968.

Jafri, Rais Ahmad. *Hazrat Mahal.* Lahore: Sheikh Ghulam Ali, 1969 (written in Urdu).

Lawrence, Henry Montgomery. *Letters of Sir Henry Montgomery Lawrence: Selections from the Correspondence of Sir Henry Montgomery Lawrence (1806–1857) during the Siege of Lucknow from March to July, 1857.* Edited by Sheo Bahadur Singh. New Delhi: Sagar Publications, 1978.

Llewellyn-Jones, Rosie. *A Fatal Friendship: The Nawabs, the British and the City of Lucknow.* Delhi: Oxford University Press, 1985.

Morris, James. *Heaven's Command: An Imperial Progress.* NY: Harcourt Brace Jovanovich, 1973.

Mukherjee, Rudrangshu. *Awadh in Revolt 1857–58: A Study of Popular Resistance.* Delhi: Oxford University Press, 1984.

Pemble, John. *The Raj, the Indian Mutiny, and the Kingdom of Oudh.* 1st American ed. Cranbury, NJ: Fairleigh Dickinson University Press, 1976.

Stokes, Eric. *The Peasant Armed: The Indian Revolt of 1857.* Edited by C.A. Bayly. Oxford: Clarendon Press, 1986.

Taylor, P.J.O. *A Feeling of Quiet Power: The Siege of Lucknow 1857.* Delhi: HarperCollins, 1994.

———. *A Star Shall Fall: India, 1857.* Delhi: HarperCollins, 1993.

———, general ed. *A Companion to the "Indian Mutiny" of 1857.* Delhi: Oxford University Press, 1996.

SUGGESTED READING:

Hibbert, Christopher. *The Great Mutiny: India, 1857.* NY: Viking Penguin, 1978.

Kenneth R. Shepherd,
Adjunct Instructor in History,
Henry Ford Community College, Dearborn, Michigan

H.D. (1886–1961).

See Doolittle, Hilda.

Head, Bessie (1937–1986)

Internationally recognized South African author who lived as an exile in Botswana for 15 years before being granted citizenship there. *Pronunciation: HED. Born Bessie Amelia Emery on July 6, 1937, in Pieter-*

maritzburg, South Africa; died in Botswana of hepatitis on April 17, 1986; daughter of Bessie Amelia "Toby" Birch (a mother classified white) and an unknown father (classified black under apartheid legislation); classified as "coloured"; raised by foster-parents Nellie and George Heathcote and in orphanages; affected by the death of her foster father and biological mother at the age of seven; educated at Umbilo Road High School; trained as a primary teacher; married Harold Head (a journalist), on September 1, 1961 (separated in her early 20s and later divorced); children: one son, Howard Head.

Taught primary school in South Africa and Botswana for three years; worked as journalist at Drum Publications in Johannesburg for two years; fled to Botswana (1964) and joined a refugee community at Bamangwato Development Farm; granted Botswanan citizenship (1979); worked as writer and unpaid agricultural worker in Botswana; published her first novel, When Rain Clouds Gather *(1969);* The Collector of Treasures and Other Botswana Village Tales *nominated for the Jock Campbell Award for literature by new or unregarded talent from Africa or the Caribbean (1978); altogether published six full-length works, about 25 short stories, and one poem; a number of her unpublished stories and letters have appeared posthumously, including one long work of fiction,* The Cardinals.

Selected writings: (novel) When Rain Clouds Gather *(1969); (novel)* Maru *(1971); (novel)* A Question of Power *(1973); (short stories)* The Collector of Treasures and Other Botswana Village Tales *(1977); (historical chronicle)* Serowe: Village of the Rain Wind *(1981); (historical chronicle)* A Bewitched Crossroad: An African Saga *(1984); contributor to periodicals, such as the London* Times, New African, New Statesman *and* Transition*; posthumous publications include (short stories)* Tales of Tenderness and Power *(1990); (autobiography)* A Woman Alone *(1993);* A Gesture of Belonging: Letters from Bessie Head, 1965–1979 *(1991); (novel)* The Cardinals *(1993).*

Occupying the southern tip of the African continent, South Africa is a country of vast natural resources and tremendous wealth. Most of its wealth, however, belongs to its over 5 million white citizens, while the majority of its 35 million nonwhite citizens live in poverty. Over the course of three centuries, racist concepts became the basis of South African society. In the 20th century, the word *apartheid* (Afrikaans for "apartness") came to dominate race relations, as Africans ("coloureds") and Indians were forced to live in separate, undesirable areas away from whites. In the decades before and after World War II, racist attitudes and practices were written into discriminatory and restrictive legislation. For example, the Population Registration Act authorized the government to classify all South Africans according to race, and the Group Areas Act provided for residential separation. In *The Long Walk to Freedom,* Nelson Mandela writes: "The often haphazard segregation of the past three hundred years was to be consolidated into a monolithic system that was diabolical in its detail, inescapable in its reach, and overwhelming in its power." Bessie Head was born during the consolidation of this system, and her life was molded by it.

Bessie Head was named after her mother, **Bessie Amelia Birch**. Bessie Birch, nicknamed Toby, was the daughter of South African immigrants from England who settled in Harrismith in the Orange Free State in 1892. Toby was born there two years later, in 1894. The Birch family, which included seven children, relocated to Johannesburg in the early 20th century, and Toby's father Walter Birch built a lucrative business as a painting and redecorating contractor. In 1915, Toby Birch married Ira Garfield Emery, an Australian who had emigrated to South Africa during his teen years. The couple settled in a suburb of Johannesburg and had two sons, Stanley and Ronald. In December 1919, however, the young family was shattered by the death of their eldest son Stanley, who was crossing the road in front of the house when he was killed by a speeding car. Toby never recovered from her child's violent death; her mind and her marriage were ultimately destroyed by the event. Ira Emery blamed his wife for the death of their son, and the couple divorced in 1929.

Even so, Toby continued to refer to Ira Emery as her husband, and her mental state deteriorated rapidly in the early 1930s. On August 26, 1933, precariously unstable, she was committed to the Pretoria Mental Hospital. She was discharged for a six-month leave of absence in 1935, was readmitted later that year, and then discharged again in 1936. After her release, Toby lived with her sisters and mother **Alice Birch** in Durban. In April 1937, her sister realized that Toby was pregnant. Although some sources maintain that the father was a black stablehand who worked for the Birch family, according to **Gillian Stead Eilersen**, this is unlikely. There is no record of the father's identity or knowledge of the circumstances surrounding Bessie Head's conception.

Bessie Amelia Emery was born at Fort Napier Mental Institution in Pietermaritzburg in July 1937. Unaware of her parentage, the hospital gave her in adoption to a white family, but her prospective parents soon returned the child because they said she looked "strange." She was then given to a "coloured" couple, George and **Nellie Heathcote**, who, as foster parents, received a monthly payment of £3 for the child's care. Although the Heathcotes were quite poor, they made a home for Bessie and her stepsister, **Rhona**, and raised them in the Roman Catholic faith. Alice Birch, Bessie's grandmother, evidently visited several times during those first years. Unfortunately, when Bessie Head was six years old, George Heathcote died. Around the same time, on September 13, 1943, Bessie's biological mother, who had remained at Fort Napier Mental Hospital, also died. The causes of death were given as "lung abscess" and "dementia praecox," an obsolete term for schizophrenia. Bessie Head remained with Nellie Heathcote until she was 13, at which time economic conditions in the home deteriorated, and she was sent by welfare authorities to St. Monica's Home, an Anglican mission school for coloured girls.

When Bessie arrived at St. Monica's, she was ignorant of the events surrounding her birth. She

Bessie Head

believed that Nellie Heathcote was her biological mother and later described herself as "fanatically attached" to the only mother she had ever known. When Bessie insisted on going home to see her mother for the holidays, the principal of the St. Monica's, Louie Farmer, coldly informed her that she would not be going home because Nellie Heathcote was not her mother. This event, and other negative encounters with Farmer, caused Head to distrust missionaries and Christianity in general. Despite this, she loved and admired a subsequent principal, **Margaret Cadmore.** Head would name the main protagonist of her second novel, *Maru,* after the woman. While at St. Monica's, Bessie continued to write and visit her foster mother, and their relationship improved as Bessie grew older and became successful in her studies. In fact, Nellie was so proud of Bessie's success that in 1953 she paid for her Junior Certificate examination, a public examination taken by all pupils at age 16 in Natal.

Her vision included whites and blacks, men and women. What she feared was the misuse of power, what she strove towards was human goodness and love. The idea of the basic goodness and decency of the ordinary person never left her.

—Gillian Stead Eilersen, 1989

Bessie Head was an excellent student in most subjects and quickly read all the books in St. Monica's library. She was sent from St. Monica's to Umbilo High School, where in 1955, she earned a Natal Teachers' Senior Certificate; she was appointed to the teaching staff of Clairwood Coloured School in Durban in January 1956. Head did not enjoy teaching, however, and resigned her position in June 1958. She moved to Cape Town where she secured a position as a reporter with the *Golden City Post,* a weekly tabloid owned by Drum Publications that specialized in sensational stories. After a month on the job, Bessie had not received any pay; in desperation, she wrote Margaret Cadmore, who responded with the remainder of Bessie's inheritance, £20, money that had been left from her mother's estate.

In April 1959, Head moved from Cape Town to work for the *Golden City Post* in Johannesburg. There she wrote a column for teenagers, consisting of a newsletter entitled "Dear Gang" and an advice column called "Hiya Teenagers." She wrote her first long work of fiction while in Johannesburg, but this initial novel, *The Cardinals,* was not published until her death. Head undoubtedly drew upon her experiences as a reporter to produce many of the disturbing and powerful scenes in this story. While the tabloid newspaper for which she worked could not afford to offend the South African government by attacking apartheid itself, it encouraged its reporters, including Bessie, its only woman reporter, to crusade on minor matters of race discrimination.

During this period, Head became an African nationalist, a supporter of the Pan-Africanist Congress (PAC) and its leader, Robert Mangaliso Sobukwe. In 1960, the Congress sponsored a Positive Action Campaign, a passive resistance crusade against the Pass Law, which required any African man or woman to produce a pass upon demand by the police or any white person. Crowds thronged at police stations in the black suburbs of major cities and demanded to be arrested. Robert Sobukwe and his followers, including Bessie Head, gathered outside the police station at Soweto. At first, the police refused to arrest anyone for abrogating the Pass Law but later decided to arrest Sobukwe and the PAC leaders on the much more serious charge of "incitement." Head had gone home by the time the police made their charge and thus escaped arrest. She was, however, arrested at a later date, scooped up in one of the many raids. She later wrote that she became the state's witness as the result of violent treatment. This event, along with others, plunged her into deep depression, and she attempted suicide. She was hospitalized and, after her release, returned to Cape Town.

Still too depressed to work, she resigned from her job and, for the next year, wrote her own newspaper, *The Citizen,* selling it on the streets and in hotel lobbies. During that time, she met Harold Head, a freelance journalist who was also a political activist and an opponent of white supremacy. After a courtship of only a few weeks, the two were married on September 1, 1961, and sought quarters in a rooming house in the "Coloured" ghetto of Cape Town. In addition to her work as a journalist, Bessie wrote poetry and stories; her one published poem and six of her stories appeared in *The New African,* the journal of the South African Liberal Party. Because the journal was anti-colonial and somewhat militant, it was closely watched by the Security Police who confiscated two issues and then charged the editors of the journal under the Obscene Publications Act. In 1963, the Heads, with their baby Howard, moved to Port Elizabeth, where Harold became the first black reporter on the *Evening Post,* a progressive daily newspaper.

The South African government declared a State of Emergency following the 1960 Sharpesville massacre, a nonviolent demonstration that turned into a bloodbath as police fired into a crowd of unarmed PAC members demonstrating against the Pass Law. After the emergency was over, the government proceeded to suppress a number of political activist groups, including the South African Liberal Party. Many were arrested, and many more went into exile to avoid prison. When the Heads, who were mutually unhappy in their marriage, were targeted for prison, they decided to leave the country and go their separate ways. They would eventually divorce.

In 1964, Harold escaped to London. Bessie took their son and went to the British Protectorate of Bechuanaland, now the Republic of Botswana. She had been given a one-way exit permit. This move enabled her to begin a teaching assignment at the Tshekedi Memorial School in the village of Serowe. Friends in London and South Africa, such as Randolph Vigne, Kenneth McKenzie, **Myra Blumberg**, Paddy Kitchen, and Robin Farquharson, sent Bessie and her son monetary and moral support to enable them to survive in the somewhat hostile and rather desolate area in which they made their home. In a letter of October 27, 1965, Bessie related that the principal of the school in which she taught had made sexual advances toward her. She wrote that there was little chance she would survive the year, that the authorities did not want her there, and that the people of her village were hostile towards her, mostly because she was different and because she had flouted authority. She wanted to leave Botswana because she felt that her life was threatened. She expressed hope that Amnesty International or the United Nations might help her relocate. Over the next few years, she wrote of possibly emigrating to India, Israel, Britain, the United States, or Kenya, among other countries.

On December 28, 1965, Head was informed by letter that she had been blacklisted by the Main School Committee in Serowe "for having deserted your post." After the loss of her teaching position, she worked for several months as an "odd job man" on a remote farm, and then had an even briefer stint as a typist for a road construction company near Palapye. Head wanted to study agricultural courses because she believed she could contribute to the development of agriculture in Botswana. She also sent out numerous applications for scholarships and grants and began assembling her short stories for possible publication as a book. Most of her fund-raising efforts were futile, though she did see her stories published in various journals. After publication of "The Woman from America" in the *New Statesmen,* publishers in London and the United States began to give more serious attention to her work.

From 1965 to 1968, Head lived in Francistown, a refugee community in Botswana. Desperately poor, she often gave her food to her son Howard so that he might not go hungry. She made and sold guava jelly and, for years, wrote at night by candlelight because she had no electricity. Despite such hardships, she was determined to make a success of her writing career. She became an inveterate letter writer and added to her following of friends and supporters, both in Africa and abroad. In December 1966, the publishing firm of Simon and Schuster sent Head £80 to buy writing materials. She had already begun what was originally thought to be her first novel, a work published as *When Rain Clouds Gather*. She wrote about the agricultural and political problems faced by the people of Botswana as viewed by two men, one a political refugee from South Africa, the other a Cambridge-educated immigrant from Britain. *When Rain Clouds Gather* was a success, though Head regretted that Simon and Schuster had designated it as a book for teenagers.

In 1968, she withdrew her son from the Francistown school. Howard had been assaulted by a group of older students for asserting that he was a Motswanan. He was not a "superior" Motswanan, they roughly informed him, but only "coloured." In January 1969, Bessie Head decided to transfer back to Serowe and place Howard in Swaneng, the progressive and academically excellent school established by Pat van Rensburg. Although the people of Serowe continued to malign her, Head became more secure in Botswana and began to speak of her parentage, her belief in God, and the precarious hold she felt she had on life. She began construction on a two-room brick house with the money she had received from her novel. She named her cottage Rain Clouds and formalized the name by sending to England for a name plate. After her house was completed, she turned her attention once more to agriculture. She established a seedling nursery on the land adjacent to her house and invited the women of Serowe to participate in a communal agricultural project.

Head produced her second novel, *Maru,* a short, intensely personal book of 30,000 words, in 1969. At the time, she proclaimed it her masterpiece, writing that it "glories friendship between a man and a man and friendship between a woman and a woman." In 1971, she suffered a breakdown and was confined to Lobatse Mental Hospital for three months. Although her doctor declared her "completely cured," she continued to suffer from her terrors and obsessions. Both *Rain Clouds* and *Maru* received critical acclaim when they were published, but Head's third novel, *A Question of Power*, got mixed reviews. The novel, however, sold very well and was on the short list for the Booker Prize in 1974. *A Question of Power,* a novel which juxtaposes and explores both the nature of goodness and the nature of evil, is a book written from the inside out, a book whose protagonist faces the misery and terror of never knowing the identity of her parents. *A Question of Power,* her most complex and ambitious undertaking, is now considered Head's greatest work.

In 1977, she published her first collection of short stories: *The Collector of Treasures and Other Botswana Village Tales.* Head later said that the stories came from interviews she conducted while gathering information for a history of Serowe. In 1977, she left Botswana for the first time since her arrival. She was invited to attend an international writing program at the University of Iowa in Iowa City for the fall semester. Before returning to Botswana, she spent a day in London with her friend, Randolph Vigne, then visited Germany and Denmark. After publishing three novels of a clearly autobiographical nature, Head began a semi-documentary account of the history of her village. *Serowe: Village of the Rain Wind* was published in 1981. Head shaped the book around interviews with people of all age groups and occupations, reproducing a cross-section of the lives and the culture of the village. In the last book issued in her lifetime, *A Bewitched Crossroad*, published in 1984, Bessie Head examines the African tribal wars of the early 19th century and interprets the history of Africa from a black, not a white, perspective. All her books were linked and helped explicate the previous characters and plots.

The energy and power contained in Bessie Head's writing come from the conflicts in her life: from the issues of identity in her tragic childhood to the image of herself as the paradigm of the African woman struggling against entrenched cultural mores. She wrote out of the vision of a better world for black people, but her crusade for gender and social justice included whites and blacks, men and women. She especially concerned herself with the victimization of women in Africa and created situations where women could be seen as equal partners in relationships. Her writing also conveys courage and humor, the courage of a "woman alone," and the humor brought forth from a woman with backbone and tenaciousness.

Bessie Head was 49 years old and working on her autobiography when she died in Serowe, Botswana, in 1986. She had also continued to correspond with friends, agents, publishers, and literary contacts throughout the world, leaving behind an enormous collection of letters. She saved carbon copies of the letters she wrote and kept letters received in classified order. One collection, *A Gesture of Belonging: Letters from Bessie Head 1965–1979,* was published by her longtime friend and editor, Randolph Vigne. Vigne's collection provides an invaluable source for those who wish to know about Bessie Head. The Khama III Memorial Museum in Serowe, set up and maintained by the government of Denmark, has become a repository for her papers.

In 1993, two of Bessie Head's works were published posthumously. *The Cardinals,* written between 1962 and 1963, explores the sexual taboos of South African society. Her first work of long fiction reflects the anger that Head felt both toward the Immorality Act, the law that forbade sexual contact between different races, and toward her own birth and upbringing in the country that invented apartheid. *A Woman Alone* contains her unfinished autobiography and previously unpublished essays. More of Head's letters will undoubtedly be published, and the critical analysis of her life and work continues.

SOURCES:

Barnett, Ursula A. *A Vision of Order: A Study of Black South African Literature in English.* Amherst, MA: University of Massachusetts Press, 1983.

Eilersen, Gillian Stead. *Bessie Head: Thunder Behind Her Ears.* Portsmouth, NH: Heinemann, 1996.

Head, Bessie. *The Cardinals: With Meditations and Short Stories.* Ed. by M.J. Daymond. Portsmouth, NH: Heinemann, 1993.

——. *Tales of Tenderness and Power.* Intro. by Gillian Stead Eilersen, Portsmouth, NH: Heinemann, 1990.

Heywood, Christopher, ed. *Aspects of South African Literature.* London: Heinemann, 1976.

Ola, Virginia Uzoma. *The Life and Works of Bessie Head.* Queenstown: Edwin Mellen Press, 1994.

Vigne, Randolph. *A Gesture of Belonging: Letters from Bessie Head, 1965–1979.* Portsmouth, NH: Heinemann, 1990.

SUGGESTED READING:

Abrahams, Cecil, ed. *The Tragic Life: Bessie Head and Literature in Southern Africa.* Lawrenceville, NJ: Africa World Press, 1994.

Head, Bessie. *A Woman Alone.* Portsmith, NH: Heinemann, 1993.

Yvonne Johnson,
Assistant Professor of History,
Central Missouri State University, Warrensburg, Missouri

Head, Edith (1897–1981)

Last great costume designer under contract to a major Hollywood studio, who greatly influenced fashion trends during her 58-year career in the movies and won a record 8 Academy Awards while being nominated for 35. *Name variations: Edith Spare. Born Edith Claire Posener in San Bernardino, California, on October 28, 1897, according to county records (although Head claimed birthplace as Searchlight, Nevada, and early years in Mexico); died at Good Samaritan Hospital on October 24, 1981, several days before her 84th birthday, attributed to myelofibrosis myeloid, a rare disease of the bone marrow, or myeloid metaplasia, a progressive blood disease; daughter of Max Posener and Anna (Levy) Posener; following parents' divorce, adopted stepfather's surname, Spare, and grew up in desert mining town of Searchlight, Nevada; graduated from Redding, California, elementary school, 1911; graduated with honors in French from University of California at Berkeley; earned master's degree in Romance languages at Stanford University; studied art at Otis Art Institute and Chouinard School of Art, both Los Angeles; married Charles Head, in early 1920s (divorced 1938); married Bill (Wiard Boppo) Ihnen, on September 8, 1940 (died 1979).*

Moved to Los Angeles at age 12 to an apartment at the YWCA (1909); taught Spanish at the Bishop School in La Jolla, then French at the Hollywood School for Girls; hired as sketch artist at Paramount (1923); became assistant designer (1929), then chief designer (1938); when contract was not renewed after a corporate merger, moved to Universal Studios (1967); also worked on films at other studios, including MGM, Warner Bros., Columbia and Fox; designed uniforms for Pan Am World Airways and the United Nations tour guides; served as fashion editor of Holiday *magazine; made many radio and television appearances; lectured on dress to women's clubs and traveled the U.S. and abroad with her Hollywood costume fashion show.*

Selected publications: (with Jane Kesner Ardmore) The Dress Doctor *(Little, Brown, 1959); (with Joe Hyams)* How to Dress for Success *(Random House, 1967); (with Paddy Calistro)* Edith Head's Hollywood *(E.P. Dutton, 1983).*

Won Academy Awards for costume design in black-and-white and color film (sometimes with associates as indicated): (with Gile Steele) The Heiress *(b&w, 1949); (with Charles LeMaire)* All About Eve *(b&w, 1950); (with Dorothy Jeakins,* ****Elois Jenssen****, Gile Steele, Gwen Wakeling)* Samson & Delilah *(color, 1950);* A Place in the Sun *(b&w, 1951);* Roman Holiday *(b&w, 1953);* Sabrina *(b&w, 1954); (with Edward Stevenson)* The Facts of Life *(b&w, 1960);* The Sting *(color, 1973).*

Academy Award nominations for costume design in black-and-white and color film include: The Emperor Waltz *(color, 1948);* Carrie *(b&w, 1952); (with Dorothy Jeakins, Miles White)* The Greatest Show on Earth *(color, 1955);* The Rose Tattoo *(b&w, 1955);* To Catch a Thief *(color, 1955);* The Proud and the Profane *(b&w, 1956); (with Ralph Jester, John Jensen, Dorothy Jeakins, Arnold Friberg)* The Ten Commandments *(color, 1956); (with Hubert de Givenchy)* Funny Face *(color, 1957); (with Ralph Jester, John Jensen)* The Buccaneer *(color, 1958);* Career *(b&w, 1959);* The Five Pennies *(color, 1959);* Pepe *(color, 1960);* Pocketful of Miracles *(color, 1961);* The Man Who Shot Liberty Valance *(b&w, 1962);* My Geisha *(color, 1962);* Love with the Proper Stranger *(b&w, 1963);* A New Kind of Love *(color, 1963);* Wives and Lovers *(b&w, 1963);* A House Is Not a Home *(b&w, 1964); (with Moss Mabry)* What a Way to Go *(color, 1964);* The Slender Thread *(b&w, 1965); (with Bill Thomas)* Inside Daisy Clover *(color, 1965);* The Oscar *(color, 1966);* Sweet Charity *(color, 1969);* Airport *(1970);* The Man Who Would Be King *(color, 1975).*

Edith Head was a Hollywood institution. For 58 years, she generated costumes for legendary film stars in a wide variety of roles. Those same costumes then influenced fashions. Though Edith Head grew up, along with the American film industry, in California, her beginnings were far from glamorous. Born in 1897 in San Bernardino, Head thought of her childhood as "boring and unimportant." She was the daughter of Max Posener and **Anna Levy Posener** but was secretive about her maiden name, Edith Claire Posener, and claimed that she had lived in Mexico during her early years. (Head had an abiding interest in things Mexican, as reflected in the Spanish-style hacienda that served as her residence for most of her Hollywood career.) After her parents divorced, she moved with her mother and mining-engineer stepfather to a mining town, Searchlight, in the Nevada desert. Back in Los Angeles at age 12, she lived in an apartment at the YWCA, the reason for her lifelong interest in gymnastics. In college, she adopted the dark glasses that became her trademark: "I think they became a protective coloration from the beginning, so effective that I never had any sense of being part of the campus at all; I was a spectator." Head rarely smiled because of some bad teeth that were finally fixed after many years in Hollywood. "I always wanted to look like Shirley Temple," she recalled, "but the mirror told me I was a zero with thick glasses and straight hair. It was years before I had any confidence and learned to smile." Her hairstyle evolved from that of a short bob with bangs (*à la* silent-film star ***Louise Brooks**) to her signature bangs and bun later in life. At 5'1", Head dressed simply, in neutral colors.

Her degrees in French and Spanish from the University of California at Berkeley and Stanford led to a job in 1923 teaching French at the exclusive Hollywood School for Girls, where filmmaker Cecil B. De Mille's daughters, **Cecilia De Mille** and ***Katherine De Mille**, were among her students. In the early years of the film industry, each studio churned out movies at a rate of 50 to 60 a year. When Head worked at the Hollywood School and Cecil B. De Mille was filming his spectaculars, school would close so that teachers and students could watch the filming at the Famous Players-Lasky studio (later Paramount) at Sunset and Vine. Edith Head was intrigued.

She also taught art classes and studied at night at the Otis Art Institute, later transferring to Chouinard. She specialized in seascapes. While at Chouinard, she met and married Charles Head, the brother of another art student, but it was an unhappy marriage. A salesman for the Super Refined Metals Company, Charles traveled often and drank heavily. Edith, a staunch Catholic, would try to maintain her marriage but socialized without her husband; few of her friends and colleagues knew him. They would divorce in 1938. In 1940, she would marry her second husband, good friend Bill Ihnen, an Academy Award-winning art director.

By the mid-1920s, Hollywood was a movie center, and the men who ran it had often started their careers in some aspect of the garment business; image was intrinsic to the cinema. The influence of film costumes on fashion seems to have been inevitable. Costume designers became recognized, emerging from anonymity as major contributors to the look of period films. Fan magazines launched in the '20s, as well as fashion magazines like *Vogue* and *Harper's Bazaar,* perpetuated the cult of celebrity, provided outlets for film publicity, and printed fashion articles for their readership. But in the beginning California had few fashion sources to support the burgeoning film industry—actors often used their personal wardrobes in early films and shooting schedules allowed no time for shopping or dressmakers—so the studios had to supply special costumes for epics, period films, musicals and Westerns. By the 1930s and the start of talking pictures, major studios would house wardrobe departments that operated like small factories, employing up to 200 workers—cutters, fitters, tailors, staff beaders, furriers, milliners, armorers, jewelers, and researchers. Studios would produce hundreds of costumes to project an actor's role. Costumes would be routinely photographed to see how they would appear on camera; the results would be used for publicity. Costumes would be elegant and smart, and the numerous fashion ideas they generated would be adopted by the public, everything from ***Greta Garbo**'s beret to ***Claudette Colbert**'s hem length. Styles adapted from the movies would be manufactured and merchandised widely; thus Hollywood would make fashion. Given the backdrop of the Depression, Hollywood glamour would seem even more desirable to millions of moviegoers.

In 1923, Head answered an ad for a sketch artist at Paramount, then Hollywood's most important studio, to work on a De Mille picture, *The Golden Bed.* Her colleagues at art school, who had dared her to seek the job, had all chipped in drawings for her portfolio. The subterfuge was needed; Head was ill-trained for sketching the human body. Because art from so many sources reflected a range of styles, Howard Greer, the studio's chief designer, was impressed by Head's apparent versatility and hired her. (In the '20s, most major studio costume departments were run by men.) Her ruse was discovered the first day on the job, but, instead of firing her, Greer pumped her for ideas for the movie. She offered some, he liked them, and he and assistant designer Travis Banton trained her to enlarge and colorize costume designers' original small drawings, called *croquis.* Greer also allowed her to watch him drape the garments. "It was like watching the drawings come to life," she recalled. As a beginner, Head, though shy, willingly accepted every assignment. She rolled and painted fabric, handed pins to the seamstress, and, as part of the fitting-room team, watched or took notes as the designers, head fitters, and wardrobe women worked on a costume.

Head, told to create a candy-ball sequence for *The Golden Bed*, featured actors with peppermint stick fingernails, lollipop beards, and chocolate necklaces for her first design challenge. She forgot, however, that camera lights were hot, and candy melted. The embarrassing incident almost ended Head's fledgling career, but De Mille's designer ***Claire West** salvaged the work, and critics called the sequence "colorful."

In the 1920s, MGM's motto—and Hollywood's—was "Make it big. Do it right. Give it class." "Sex, sets, and costumes" was the formula for De Mille's riveting spectacles shot at Paramount. Historical accuracy was not an issue; exaggeration had commercial value. "I want clothes that will make people gasp when they see them," De Mille directed the wardrobe department. "Don't design anything anybody could possibly buy in a store." Hollywood costumes were made to be photographed, not worn; some were so tight, they could only be worn standing up, or were made in several versions to accommodate sitting. Unlike retail fashion, they fit the technical needs of the film, complemented the story, and interpreted the characters. In those days, Head would recall, a "designer was as important as a star. When you said Garbo, you thought of Adrian; when you said Dietrich, you said Banton. The magic of an Adrian or Banton dress was part of the selling of a picture. Sets, costumes, and makeup just aren't considered the art forms they used to be."

In 1929, when Greer resigned because of problems with alcohol, Banton was promoted chief designer, and Head became Banton's assistant. "He was a god there," said Head. "Nobody

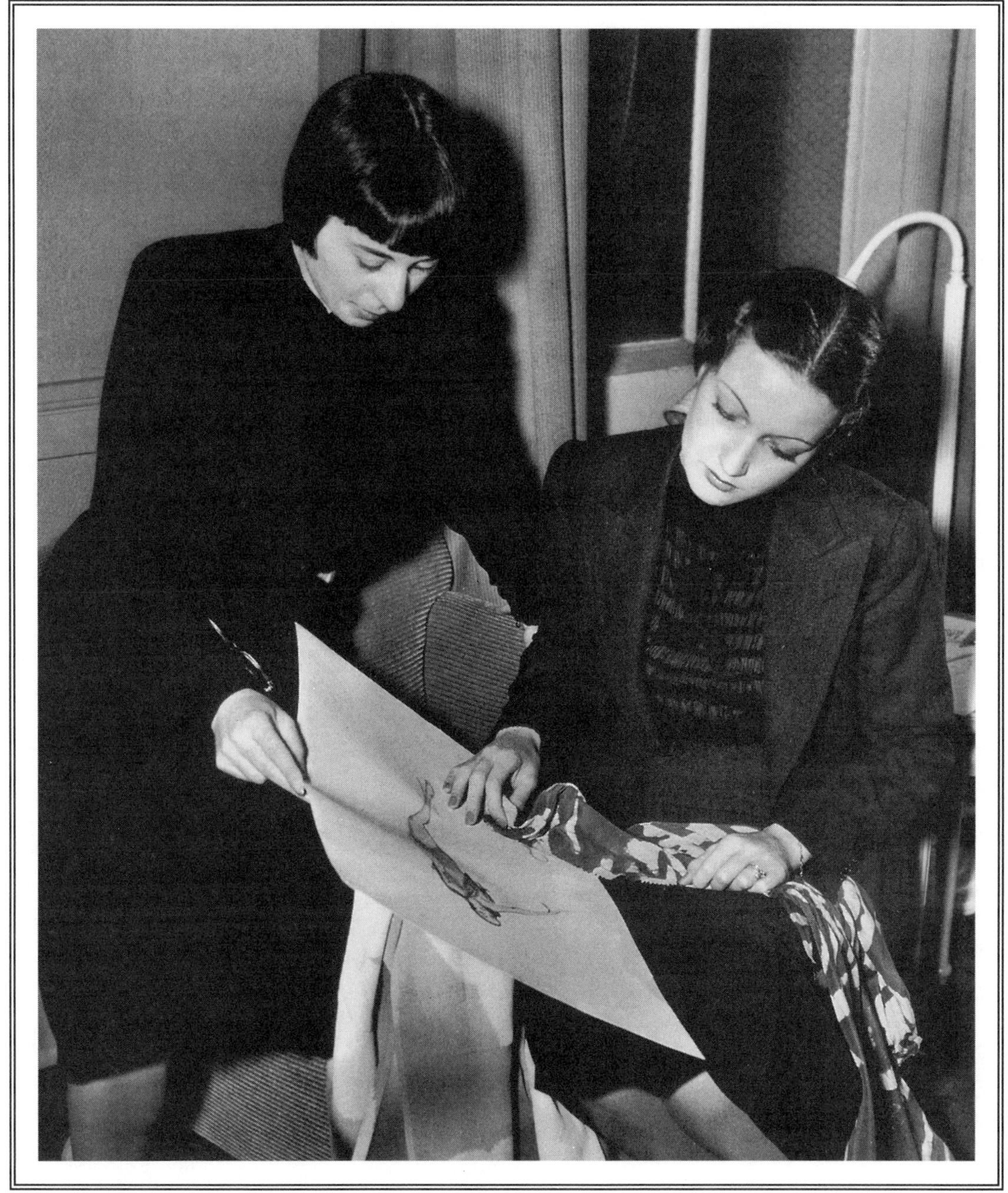

Edith Head (left) with Dorothy Lamour.

dared oppose him about anything, including budgets." Banton was known for his glamorous designs, especially for film icon *Marlene Dietrich. "He was a marvelous designer," Edith recalled. He helped her develop her potential as a designer, gradually assigning her to stars he did not have the time or inclination to handle. One such was *Clara Bow, the "It" girl, who projected a sexy image on-screen. Offscreen, Bow had no fashion sense and insisted on wearing high heels and ankle socks with every outfit, even bathing suits and gowns. Head also soothed the ego of Latin beauty *Lupe Velez, who was put out for being passed off to a mere assistant designer, by speaking Spanish with her to gain trust.

I make people into what they are not—ten years older or younger, fatter or thinner, more handsome or more ridiculous, glamorous or sexy or horrible. The camera never lies, after all, so my work is really an exercise in camouflage.

—Edith Head

On *She Done Him Wrong* (1933), Head's first important film and her first on-screen credit, she began a successful working relationship with *Mae West, an actress who infuriated the censors with her bawdy dialogue. Her voluptuous figure and huge hats were hallmarks of her personal style. "Edith is the only designer who can dress Mae West as Mae West," said West, "tight enough to show I'm a woman, but loose enough to show I'm a lady." Head consulted with Mae West extensively, because the star knew what worked for her and preferred gowns with "a little *insinuendo* about them." Edith emphasized Mae's height, using chevrons and other optical illusions on her costumes. Financially, *She Done Him Wrong* helped Paramount out of a sticky financial situation and helped launch Edith Head's career.

Technicolor was first used in 1934 and presented new challenges to designers who were accustomed to working in black and white and using costumes in odd color combinations to photograph in the proper shades of gray. Colors appeared unnatural in early films, and designers and art directors worked with Technicolor consultants, including *Natalie Kalmus, to correct erratic hues. Clothing had to be dyed just the right shade for a desired effect.

Like his predecessor Howard Greer, Travis Banton also had a problem with alcohol, and in 1938 he left the studio to work in private couture. Edith Head was named chief designer of Paramount, the first woman with sole responsibility for a major studio's costume department. She would remain there for 29 years. When Head took over, Paramount was by then the least glamorous of the studios, specializing in B pictures, which had sustained the studios after the Depression. The work schedule was hectic. "You could just make it if you worked every day until midnight and weekends. In some ways it was easier than today," she said in later years, "because we knew way in advance what pictures we were going to do and who would be in them." She also knew the tastes of actresses under studio contract, and B-picture directors were not so involved with costumes as directors of major motion pictures.

Head's name appeared on numerous films, and she considered these challenges great training. "I was never going to be the world's greatest costume designer," she said, "but there was no reason I could not be the smartest. . . . I have always said that I am a better politician than I am a designer. I know who to please." Her discussions with new clients encompassed their likes and dislikes, and she took them into consideration as she designed costumes to satisfy the film's requirements. "When you talk with an actress, it's a little like a doctor diagnosing a patient. . . . You have to make the stars feel like you are designing *with* them," she advised. "When I've designed a square neckline and a star wants it round, I don't argue with her." The director's perspective was also important to Head; she discussed everything with the director first and showed several sketches after these discussions. Some had definitive ideas about characterization through costuming; others left it up to her. Over the years, she cooperated with producers, directors, cinematographers, sound recorders, choreographers, actors, and art directors. Some suggest that this attitude contributed to her Oscar count—all those professionals vote for the Academy Awards.

In 1941's *The Lady Eve,* Edith Head's talent for camouflage transformed *Barbara Stanwyck into a fashion trendsetter and paved the way for her glamour roles. It also made Head famous after 18 years of hard work. *The Lady Eve* required Head to transform Stanwyck from a gambler to an aristocrat. For the gambler, she dressed Stanwyck in contrasting black and white or solid black or white. As the British noblewoman, Stanwyck wore luxurious fabrics in subtle colors. Using a belt that was wider in back and narrower in front, Head raised Stanwyck's waistline and disguised a low derriere. The Latin flavor of her gowns influenced world fashion, and the studio gave her costumes full publicity. Head created both on- and off-screen wardrobes for Stanwyck, and for the next seven years she was written into Stanwyck's contracts and loaned out to other studios to do the actress' costume design.

Wartime meant shortages to the film industry. The L-85 government directive limited the amount of fabric used in garments—no pleats, ruffles, cuffs, long jackets or other extras were allowed. This situation spurred Head's creativity and won her acclaim. For *The Road to Morocco* (1942), she substituted sheer cotton for silk and painted kidskin gold to simulate gold metallic trim. The *Road* comedies of the '40s, featuring Bob Hope, Bing Crosby, and ***Dorothy Lamour**, enabled Head to experiment with exotic styles to reflect film locations. (This was not the first time she had designed for Lamour. Head's sarong for the actress in *Jungle Princess* would forever be associated with the Lamour image. Sewn into her sarong, Lamour was given matching underwear to satisfy the censors.) Head also supported the war effort with her fashion updates to women: "All designers are turning to cotton. Silk is out of style for 1942. . . . Double-duty clothes will cut down on budgets. Coats with zip-in, changeable linings and suits with reversible jackets are the fashion news."

***Ginger Rogers** presented design challenges to Head. In *The Major and the Minor* (1942), Rogers had to metamorphize from a 31-year-old to a 12-year-old in full view of the camera. Wrote Head:

> Ginger appeared first in a simple belted blouse that could be quickly unbelted into a low-slung middy blouse, a knee-length plaid skirt that could be hiked up above her knees easily, stockings that could be crumpled down to look like anklets, and a wide-brimmed hat that looked extremely *ingenue* with two blond pigtails hanging out.

Head also designed the most expensive gown in Hollywood history for Rogers—a mink overskirt lined with sequins and worn over a matching sequined bodysuit in a dream sequence in *Lady in the Dark* (1944). But costume budgets fell after World War II, and the star system and extravagant treatment began to break down. Between 1942 and 1946, Head sensed changes in her field: "I felt that in the future, clothes would get more and more comfortable, and I tried to employ that theory in the film. Once people began to wear easy clothes, I knew it would be impossible to get them into restrictive garments again."

Head regarded her 1949 film *The Heiress*, based on Henry James' *Washington Square*, as "possibly the most perfect picture I have ever done." "Every dress was perfect," said ***Olivia de Havilland**, the star of the film. "Just putting them on, I became these women and I knew right where they were in the story. Edith even came to New York with me before *The Heiress* and we studied the underwear at the Brooklyn Museum so it would be absolutely authentic." The clothes reflected both the Victorian era with its crinolines and the Edwardian era with its bustles. Edith and director William Wyler discussed the costumes' role in story development. As an unfashionable spinster, the heiress Catherine Sloper is dressed simply (to communicate her insecurity, Head designed clothing of luxurious fabrics but without the right fit—there were gaps and wrinkles); when she meets a lover, her costumes are overdone (too much ribbon and lace to reflect unsophisticated taste); when the lover deserts the heiress, her costumes become dark and tailored; and when she executes her plan of revenge against her returning lover, the costumes are beautiful, self-confident and exciting. Even though the movie was filmed in black and white, Head asked de Havilland her preference in color of the gown she wears at the end of the film, when she extracts her revenge. The actress chose a soft mauve, a period color signifying vulnerability and femininity which photographed as a soft, misty white. *The Heiress* won an Academy Award for Best Costumes that year.

In 1948, the Academy of Motion Picture Arts and Sciences established an award for Best Costume in two categories—color films and black and white. (In 1967, they were merged as one.) The Oscars originally were designed to award costumes that moved the story along. By the end of her career, Head had received 8 Oscars, the most awarded to any designer, and a record number of 35 nominations. Costume designer Bob Mackie, who worked as a sketch artist for Head during the '60s, called her "the ultimate survivor. She was an executive very much ahead of her time. She knew how to delegate. She knew how to get the best out of everyone. I really admired her." According to Mackie, "By the time she edited the sketches, everything looked like Edith Head designed it. That's what was important. *That* was a big part of her talent." Costume consultant Robert L. Green noted, "She was the greatest diplomat in Hollywood. She was willing to make compromises. *That's* why she has so many Oscars." Other designers and colleagues viewed her differently. Her biographer Paddy Calistro writes that some of her colleagues from the 1950s—fitters, sketch artists, and seamstresses—maintained that, if

Head thought it necessary, she would claim others' work and ideas as her own.

Head was aware that her public image would help her to maintain her position at the studio. Although extremely nervous at the beginning, she made monthly appearances on Art Linkletter's radio show, "House Party," offering fashion advice and tidbits about the stars. (At her request, he would critique her performance, teaching her how to be more conversational and less timid). Later when Linkletter moved to television, she went with him as his most popular guest, doing instant makeovers of audience members. Head tirelessly promoted Hollywood as the world's fashion center, gave fashion advice to *Photoplay* readers who sent her full-length photographs of themselves, and received her own fan mail from women wondering how they could adapt on-screen looks for the office. Beginning in the early 1950s, with **June Van Dyke**, Head staged Hollywood fashion shows around the country and abroad, complete with models resembling the original stars who wore the dresses. Vogue Patterns sold some of her designs, which would become a major source of income in the 1970s and a way to maintain her visibility.

By the early 1950s, movies were competing with television, causing the reemergence of epics. C.B. De Mille offered the public a "Bible story with sex appeal" in *Samson and Delilah* (1949). Head disliked working with the "egotistical, tactless" De Mille who had no respect for historical accuracy. The censors provided more obstacles: though it was acceptable to show Victor Mature's navel, it was not acceptable to unveil ***Hedy Lamarr**'s. (Designers tried to get around the censors by stuffing pearls in women's navels.) De Mille demanded 20 to 30 sketches per costume—the average picture required three to four—and kept copies of accepted sketches to ensure that the final product was what he had approved. For a scene featuring ***Delilah** on her throne just before Samson pulls down the walls of the temple, De Mille demanded a costume with feathers; the rest was up to Head. On De Mille's ranch, her staff collected almost 2,000 peacock feathers during molting season which were subsequently sewn and glued onto a cape for Lamarr (the cape is currently on display at the De Mille estate in Los Angeles). The film garnered incredible publicity, including a fashion show featuring the cape and Seventh Avenue's version of Delilah gowns. The lack of costume authenticity bothered Head, but she won an Oscar for the extravaganza.

Opposite page

Edith Head (right) with Susan Clark.

For *Sunset Boulevard* (1950), silent-film star ***Gloria Swanson** returned to the screen. Her character, Norma Desmond, bore a resemblance to Swanson as a movie star past her prime, but Norma was also on the verge of madness. Swanson, who had designed and manufactured clothes herself, asked to work with Edith Head. "It became a project where I actually designed *with* the star instead of *for* her, because she was recreating a past that she knew and I didn't," said Head. The resulting costumes were contemporary but reminiscent of the silent-film era. The black-and-white film showcased clothes with discordant notes, such as a black velvet afternoon suit trimmed in ermine fur. Edith used tulle, brocade, taffeta, leopard-printed crepe, and fur trim. The resulting clothes, bizarre and dreamlike, were for an actress lost in her own inner world. "I tried to make her look as if she was always impersonating someone," said Head.

All About Eve (1950) also reflected the passing of an era, but this time in the New York theater. ***Bette Davis**, as middle-aged actress Margo Channing, is pushed aside by a younger actress, Eve Harrington (***Anne Baxter**), who is scheming her way to the top. Davis' costumes echoed ***Tallulah Bankhead**'s style, the supposed prototype for the Channing character, especially the off-the-shoulder dress in the famous cocktail-party scene that was similar to one Bankhead wore in a Broadway play. The design came by accident. The movie dress was mistakenly made with an enlarged bodice and neckline. With no time to spare before shooting the scene, Davis pushed the neckline off her shoulders, and Head secured it with some stitches. Head said of Davis, "When she puts on something, you don't think it's a costume designed for her. You say, 'It belongs to Bette Davis.'" The film earned another Oscar for Edith Head.

Roman Holiday (1953), the story of a princess who wants to escape her role, gave Head the opportunity to work with ***Audrey Hepburn**, a young actress with a slight figure and classic beauty. Head claimed that Hepburn had a better understanding of fashion than any star except Marlene Dietrich. But *Sabrina* (1954), which also starred Hepburn, created a controversy that would raise questions about Head's work on the film long after her death. This Cinderella story concerns the daughter of a chauffeur who falls in love with the son of her father's rich employers, goes to Paris, and returns as a sophisticate. Head saw the film as a perfect opportunity to be creative—"three wonderful stars and my leading lady looking like a Paris mannequin." However, director Billy Wilder wanted Hepburn to buy Paris originals from French designer Hubert de Givenchy for the film. Head was outraged at the news that she would only be designing Hepburn's clothing as the not very fashionable chauffeur's daughter before her transformation in Paris. Hepburn, who preferred Givenchy's classic, sleek style, showed Head the courturier's notebook of suggested sketches and the wardrobe she bought from him. The hit costume of the movie was a black cocktail dress with a boat neckline and tiny black bows at the shoulders; manufacturers made thousands of copies of the dress with the *Sabrina* neckline. Head never acknowledged that the design was actually created by Givenchy. Publicity was geared toward emphasizing the French fashion angle, and the film opened in Paris during the couture shows. "Do You Look Like Sabrina?" contests and other promotions added to the excitement. When the film, which was nominated for a number of Academy Awards, only won the 1955 costume award, Edith Head accepted it without a word of acknowledgment then or ever for Givenchy's work. The dress became part of her touring costume collection.

"Edith always thought she designed everything in town," observed **Irene Heymann**, Wilder's agent. "She was notorious for never giving an assistant credit, even if she hadn't done a thing." And Warren Harris, Audrey Hepburn's biographer, wrote that it was Head's clout as chief designer at Paramount that blocked Givenchy's share in the Oscar. He also observed that her habit of taking credit for other people's work was the reason for her many Oscars and her unpopularity among peers. Harris also notes, however, that Edith Head was entitled to take credit for film costumes herself, according to her contract as chief of Paramount's design department.

Head regarded her clothes as "middle of the road in terms of current fashion trends" and attributed her longevity in the business to this position; she believed in moderate design to avoid dating movies. She translated the popular New Look of French couturier Christian Dior—small waists and full skirts—into a timeless look. Her restraint made her look like a fashion forecaster in *A Place in the Sun* (1951). ***Elizabeth Taylor** plays a beautiful, spoiled heiress who entices Montgomery Clift away from his pregnant and plain girlfriend, ***Shelley Winters**. In the 1950s, designers were creating a younger look, and teenager Elizabeth Taylor was a popular role model. The fashion blockbuster from the film was Taylor's debut gown. Timeless white violets were the focal point; they adorned the bodice and were sprinkled over the full tulle skirt which covered a pastel underskirt. The strapless gown highlighted Taylor's beautiful face; because of

the full bodice, her small waist was made to look smaller. Sandy Schier, costume historian, recalled, "You could go to any party that year and see at least ten women wearing that same dress." Head was as famous as the stars she dressed. She made a personal appearance in *Lucy Gallant* (1955), narrating a long fashion show segment which featured "Paris originals" actually designed by Head.

In the 1950s, Head began work with director Alfred Hitchcock; she would eventually design for 11 of his films. Hitchcock told her, "It's really very simple, Edith. Keep the colors quiet unless we need some dramatic impact," and Head agreed. In *To Catch a Thief* (1955), he saved the strong color for the climax, when ***Grace Kelly** wore a gold lamé balloon-skirted ballgown and matching gold wig, both festooned with gold birds. Other dresses were designed as a background for a jewelry close-up shot. In *Rear Window* (1954), Head made Kelly look like a piece of untouchable china; her sophistication contrasted with James Stewart's scruffy photographer. "He spoke a designer's language," Head said of Hitchcock, "even though he didn't know the first thing about clothes."

By the early 1960s, the studio designer was history; the studio shopper who hunted in stores for clothes that would meet the designer's request was common. Fewer films made it difficult for Paramount to justify Edith Head's salary. When the company merged with Gulf and Western in 1967, her contract was not renewed. Without a tribute from her 44-year employer, she moved quietly to Universal as its resident costume designer. She designed only 34 movies during her eight years there; she had designed 34 movies in 1941 alone.

At Universal, after a string of mediocre movies, Head lobbied for something better. She basically dressed *Butch Cassidy and the Sundance Kid* (1969), with Robert Redford and Paul Newman, from Universal and Western Costume's stock wardrobe. Her second film with the two stars, *The Sting* (1973), exerted a strong influence on men's clothes—chalk-stripe suits, newsboy caps, and broad lapels; Head could not recall a previous male cast having so much influence on fashion. She made Redford's character look more naive by adding a wide-patterned tie and newsboy cap. Head found men much easier to dress than women. "It took only an hour to dress the world's two handsomest men," she said of Newman and Redford. The movie won her another Oscar. Although Head always claimed *The Sting* and its "perfectly accurate wardrobe" as one of her "greatest achievements," there were some rumors, according to Calistro, regarding the lack of credit for Vincent Dee and Peter Saldutti of the Universal men's wardrobe department for their contributions to the film.

After purchasing Casa Ladera in 1949 on more than five acres in Beverly Hills, Edith Head and her husband Bill Ihnen used the Spanish-style hacienda as a retreat from their Hollywood lives. At home, she wore "the kind of eye-popping housecoats I love, and colorful Mexican blouses and skirts." After 40 years of marriage, Bill Ihnen died in 1979, age 91. "It was always very important to me to be taken care of," said Head, "but Bill's greatest contribution to our marriage was his strength of character and his ability to accept my career. There were not many men like him in 1940." Even though her own health was failing, she continued her hectic work pace. Head claimed to have worked on 1,131 films throughout her career (the *Edith Head's Hollywood* filmography lists over 750 documented by research), but many records of her work are gone. As Paramount's chief of design, she took an interest in or expressed an opinion about all the studio's films. Edith Head died several days before her 84th birthday in 1981.

SOURCES:

Chierchetti, David. *Hollywood Costume Design.* NY: Harmony Books, 1976.

Collins, Amy Fine. "When Hubert Met Audrey," in *Vanity Fair.* December 1995, pp. 278–296.

Harris, Warren G. *Audrey Hepburn: A Biography.* Simon and Schuster, 1994. pp. 90–91, 102–105, 129, 137.

Head, Edith, and Paddy Calistro. *Edith Head's Hollywood.* NY: E.P. Dutton, 1983.

LaVine, W. Robert. *In a Glamorous Fashion; The Fabulous Years of Hollywood Costume Design.* NY: Scribner, 1980.

Leese, Elizabeth. *Costume Design in the Movies.* NY: Frederick Ungar, 1976.

Maeder, Edward. *Hollywood and History: Costume Design in Film.* NY: Thames and Hudson, 1987.

McConathy, Dale, with Diana Vreeland. *Hollywood Costume: Glamour, Glitter, Romance.* NY: Abrams, 1976 (based on Metropolitan Museum of Art Costume Institute's 1974 exhibit, "Romantic and Glamorous Hollywood").

Stein, Mike. *Hollywood Speaks: An Oral History.* NY: Putnam, 1974. Edith Head interview, pp. 247–258.

RELATED MEDIA:

"Edith Head: An American Film Institute Seminar on Her Work" (microfilm, pt. 1, no. 78), Beverly Hills, CA: AFI Seminars (1977).

"The Hollywood Fashion Machine" (60 mins.), aired on American Movie Classics (AMC) cable television.

Lucy Gallant (1955; color; 173 mins.), starring Charlton Heston, ***Jane Wyman**, ***Thelma Ritter**, ***Claire Trevor** (Head makes an appearance as a commentator for a fashion show featuring Paris fashions, which were actually her own designs).

The Oscar (1966; color; 109 mins.), starring Stephen Boyd, **Elke Sommer**, ***Eleanor Parker**, Milton Berle, Joseph Cotten, **Jill St. John**, Ernest Borgnine, **Edie Adams**, Tony Bennett (a tinsel view of Hollywood and those competing for Academy Awards, featuring many guest stars, including Head).

Laurie Norris,
freelance writer, New York City

Heap, Jane (1887–1964).

See Anderson, Margaret for sidebar.

Hearn, Mary Anne or Marianne (1834–1909).

See Farningham, Marianne.

Hearst, Catherine Campbell (1917–1998)

American philanthropist, socialite, and mother of prominent kidnap victim Patty Hearst. *Born Catherine Wood Campbell on July 5, 1917, in Kentucky; died on December 30, 1998, in Los Angeles, California; graduated from Washington Seminary, 1930s; married Randolph Hearst, son of publishing magnate William Randolph Hearst, in 1938 (divorced); children—five daughters: Catherine Hearst; Virginia Hearst; Anne Hearst; Victoria Hearst; Patricia Campbell Hearst (b. 1954).*

A child of privilege, Catherine Campbell Hearst was born on July 5, 1917, in Kentucky, but raised in Atlanta, Georgia. She attended Sacred Heart School in Atlanta and graduated from Washington Seminary in the 1930s. In 1938, after moving to San Francisco, she married Randolph Hearst, son of publishing magnate William Randolph Hearst, president of the *San Francisco Examiner* and chair of the Hearst Corporation.

Catherine Hearst lived the life of a socialite and philanthropist, organizing events on behalf of several charities. She was a member of the Junior League, served as director of the San Mateo Society for Crippled Children and Adults, and was a trustee for Crystal Springs School for Girls. She was also an amateur artist and exhibited her works in several private exhibitions.

A conservative Republican, Hearst was appointed to a two-year replacement term on the University of California board of regents in 1956, where she remained for 20 years. During the 1960s, she and the other regents faced a multitude of battles on campus including those over the limits of free speech and the university's role in military research. She supported restrictions forbidding Communists to speak on campus and was an advocate for the removal of radical activist ***Angela Davis** from a teaching position at the school.

Hearst's world shattered on February 4, 1974, when an obscure left-wing terrorist group, the Symbionese Liberation Army, kidnapped her daughter, ***Patricia Campbell Hearst**. The group, intending to embarrass capitalists like Hearst, threatened to kill Patty unless her parents donated $2 million worth of food to the poor in California. Though the family contributed the food, the group did not release Patty. Throughout the months of the ordeal, Catherine Hearst had to wait helplessly as her daughter became increasingly brainwashed by the group, began to identify herself with her captors, and denounced her parents as "pigs" of wealth. When police arrested Patty Hearst after her participation in a bank robbery, Catherine used her network of influential friends to petition for her release. President Jimmy Carter commuted her daughter's sentence after Patty had served 22 months of her seven-year term. Catherine Hearst died at the age of 81 at the UCLA Medical Center following a stroke.

SOURCES:

The Day [New London]. January 1, 1999.

Judith C. Reveal,
freelance writer, Greensboro, Maryland

Hearst, Millicent (1882–1974).

See Davies, Marion for sidebar.

Hearst, Patricia Campbell (1954—)

American kidnap victim turned bank robber. *Name variations: Patty Hearst; Tania. Born Patricia Campbell Hearst in 1954, in San Francisco, California; daughter of Randolph Apperson Hearst and Catherine (Campbell) Hearst (1917–1998); attended Santa Catalina boarding school; graduated from Crystal Springs School for Girls; attended Menlo Junior College; attended University of California at Berkeley; married Bernard Shaw, in 1979; children: daughter.*

Born in San Francisco, California, in 1954, into the wealthy and well-known Hearst family, Patricia Campbell Hearst led a pampered life as a child. Her father Randolph Apperson Hearst was chair of the board of the Hearst Corporation and the son of publishing magnate William Randolph Hearst. Her mother ***Catherine Campbell Hearst** was a genteel Southern woman from Atlanta. The middle of five daughters, Patty was encouraged by her parents in athletics and displayed talents at tennis, swimming and horseback riding. She enjoyed deep-sea fishing and duck hunting with her father who taught her how to use a rifle, and she became proficient at skeet shooting.

Hearst's high school years began at Santa Catalina School, a boarding school in Monterey, south of San Francisco, run by Dominican nuns. She was not an outstanding student and in her junior year (1970), she enrolled at Crystal Springs School for Girls. While there, she fell in love with a young teacher, Steve Weed, and they began a lengthy affair. Upon graduation from high school, Hearst attended Menlo Junior College but had no career plans. When Weed won a fellowship and teaching grant to the University of California at Berkeley, she followed him and enrolled at there. They became engaged in December of 1973.

In February of 1974, the life Patty Hearst had known came to an end. The Symbionese Liberation Army (SLA), an obscure terrorist group consisting of three men and three women, broke into her apartment and kidnapped Hearst, while Steve Weed looked on helplessly. The group's goals were confused and methods ill-planned from the beginning. Hearst was kept in a closet and brainwashed for two months while her captors demanded a ransom of $2 million in food to be distributed to the poor. By April of 1974, Hearst had pledged her allegiance to the SLA, calling herself "Tania" and referring to her father as a "corporate liar." The nation was spellbound by her situation, debating the question of whether she was a willing SLA accomplice or a victim of the group.

That April, Hearst participated in a robbery of the Hibernia Bank in San Francisco as a member of the SLA. She remained with the terrorists until 1975, eluding the authorities at every turn. As the pressure intensified, the small group became paranoid and anxious, moving quickly from place to place to avoid detection. Hearst was finally captured on September 18, 1975, in an apartment in San Francisco. After a lengthy trial, she received a sentence of seven years in a California prison for armed robbery.

Despite the wealth and power of the Hearst family and the efforts of well-known defense attorney, F. Lee Bailey, all attempts to overturn her conviction were unsuccessful. However, President Jimmy Carter commuted her sentence in February of 1979 after she had served less than 23 months. Hearst married her former bodyguard, Bernard Shaw, two months after her release. In 1996, in collaboration with **Cordelia France Biddle**, Patricia Hearst published her first novel, *Murder at San Simeon*. She has also appeared in several movies directed by John Waters, including *Cry-Baby* and *Pecker*.

SOURCES:

Hearst, Patricia Campbell, with Alvin Moscow. *Every Secret Thing*. NY: Doubleday, 1982.

Judith C. Reveal,
freelance writer, Greensboro, Maryland

Hearst, Phoebe A. (1842–1919)

American philanthropist. *Born Phebe Apperson (her given name was spelled Phebe until later years) in Franklin County, Missouri, on December 3, 1842; died of influenza at her home, La Hacienda del Pozo de Verona, near Pleasanton, 30 miles east of San Francisco, California, on April 13, 1919; interred at Cypress Lawn Cemetery in Daly City; eldest of three children of Randolph Walker Apperson and Drucilla (Whitmire) Apperson; married George F. Hearst (U.S. senator from California), on June 15, 1861 (died 1891); children: William Randolph Hearst (b. 1863).*

Phoebe Apperson Hearst, who worked for a time as a teacher, married U.S. Senator George F. Hearst of California in 1861, and was the mother of newspaper magnate William Randolph Hearst. Phoebe was active in charitable and philanthropic enterprises and gave extensively, especially to educational institutions. In San Francisco, she established kindergarten classes for children of the poor, as well as a manual training school, and organized a number of working girls' clubs.

At both Lead, South Dakota, and Anaconda, Montana, Phoebe Hearst built and, at first, maintained public libraries, and in Washington, D.C., she built the National Cathedral (Episcopal) School for Girls. She was also a major contributor to the restoration of Mount Vernon. From the early 1890s on, she turned her attention to the University of California at Berkeley, where she erected and equipped the mining building as a memorial to her husband who died on February 28, 1891. She was also responsible for Hearst Hall, an athletic center for women students. Phoebe Hearst became a regent at the university on July 28, 1897.

Her charities were widespread, and hundreds of needy individuals and institutions were in receipt of her bounty at the Christmas season. She also contributed greatly to the causes of archaeology and anthropology, financing expeditions to Italy, Mexico, Russia, and Egypt. Her last years were spent at Pleasanton, California, near San Francisco. During her life, she distributed about $20 million to charity, philanthropies, education and public works.

Hearst, Mrs. William Randolph
(1882–1974).

See Davies, Marion for sidebar on Millicent Hearst.

Heath, Sophia (1896–1936)

American aviator and sports administrator. *Born in 1896; died in 1936.*

Sophia Heath conquered incredible odds to pursue a career in aviation, and she also helped pave the way for women in the Olympics. In 1919, overcoming the International Commission for Air Navigation's ban on women, Heath qualified in all the medical and aptitude tests to become the first female airline pilot hired by the Royal Dutch Airline. In addition to her flying duties, Heath devoted herself to improving air safety and reliability. During her career, she was the first woman to fly solo from South Africa to England, and also set a record by taking off and landing at 50 different airfields (and 17 "likely landing fields") in England in a single day, with only six refuelings.

In sports, Heath founded the Women's Amateur Athletic Association in 1922. It was largely through her efforts that in 1928, the Olympic Committee finally allowed women athletes to participate in Olympic events. Heath suffered serious injury in a plane crash and died in 1936.

Hebard, Grace Raymond
(1861–1936)

American educator, author, and suffragist. *Born Grace Raymond Hebard on July 2, 1861, in Clinton, Iowa; died on October 11, 1936, in Laramie, Wyoming; daughter of Reverend George Diah Alonzo Hebard and Margaret E. Dominick (Marven) Hebard; State University of Iowa, B.S., 1882, M.A., 1885; earned a doctorate at Illinois Wesleyan University, 1893.*

Born July 2, 1861, in Clinton, Iowa, Grace Raymond Hebard was the third of Reverend George Hebard and **Margaret E. Dominick Hebard**'s four children. Her father died when she was young, and Grace was educated at home by her mother.

Hebard formed her suffragist opinions during her early college years at the State University of Iowa when her enrollment in traditionally male courses met with prejudice. In 1882, she received a B.S. in civil engineering and after graduation worked as a draftswoman in the land office of the U.S. surveyor general at Cheyenne, Wyoming, the only woman on a staff of 40. Hebard remained there for nine years, while also furthering her studies. She received her master of arts degree from Iowa State (1885) and eight years later earned her doctorate from Illinois Wesleyan University through a correspondence course.

Appointed a trustee of the University of Wyoming at Laramie in 1891, Hebard also became secretary of the board of the four-year-old institution, but her first impressions of the school were bleak: "There were no trees, no fences, no grass, no bushes. North of the [only] building there was still a buffalo wallow, and to the east nothing but sagebrush." She soon became involved with administrative details, including directing policy, hiring and firing faculty, and supervising the physical plant. Her determination to see the university soundly established caused some to accuse her of usurping power from the president of the board. In 1903, she left the board of trustees but remained its secretary until 1908.

Hebard turned from administration to teaching when she became the associate professor of political economy at the University of Wyoming in 1906. By the end of her career, she was head of the department. For 25 years, from 1894 to 1919, she also served as university librarian.

Grace Hebard's achievements extended beyond her myriad roles at the university. In 1898, she became the first woman admitted to the Wyoming bar, although she never practiced law. In 1914, she was admitted to practice before the Supreme Court of Wyoming. For a time, she was the Wyoming state tennis champion, both singles and doubles; she was also the state golf champion. She supported numerous causes, including child-labor reform, woman suffrage, and immigration restriction, and was a leader at the Cheyenne women's convention of 1889. With an intense interest in the history of the American West, particularly Wyoming, Hebard wrote seven books; the most significant were *The Bozeman Trail* (1922), *Washakie* (1930), and *Sacajawea* (1933). Although popular when written, over the years her writings have suffered under scrutiny and are often considered more folklore than history. Hebard spent many summers doing research among the Shoshoni Indians and championed the movement to preserve and identify the historic trails in Wyoming. She was adopted into the Shoshoni tribe and named "the good woman, the woman with one tongue."

Hebard retired in 1931 and died in 1936 at the age of 75 in Laramie, Wyoming. She was buried in Green Hill Cemetery. Her extensive library and manuscript collection were bequeathed to the University of Wyoming library.

SOURCES:

Edgerly, Lois Stiles. *Give Her This Day.* Gardiner, ME: Tilbury House, 1990.

James, Edward T., ed. *Notable American Women, 1607–1950.* Cambridge, MA: The Belknap Press of Harvard University Press, 1971.

Judith C. Reveal, freelance writer, Greensboro, Maryland

Hébert, Anne (1916—)

Noted French-Canadian poet and prose writer who has been praised for her psychological insight as well as her expression of the growing discontent of Quebec's French-speaking population under English rule. *Name variations: Anne Hebert. Pronunciation: Hay-BARE. Born on August 1, 1916, at Sainte-Catherine-de-Fossambault in the Province of Quebec, Canada; daughter of Maurice Hébert (a writer and government official) and Marguerite Marie Taché; attended Collège Notre-Dame-de Bellevue and Collège Mérici in Quebec.*

Published first poems and stories (1939); endured death of her cousin, Hector de Saint-Denys Garneau (1943); began work as script writer for Canadian National Film Board (1953); began residence in Paris (1954); published first novel (1958); elected to Royal Society of Canada (1960); settled permanently in Paris (1965); received Molson Prize (1967); received honorary doctorate from the University of Toronto (1969); received Prix des Libraires de France *for her novel* Kamouraska *(1970); film version of* Kamouraska *appeared (1973); won* Académie française *prize for novel* Les Enfants du sabbat *(1976); received* Prix Fémina *(1982).*

Major works (poetry): Les Songes en équilibre *(*Dreams in Equilibrium, *1942);* Le Tombeau des rois *(*The Tomb of Kings, *1953);* Poèmes *(1960);* Le Jour n'a d'égal que la nuit *(*Day Has No Equal but Night, *1992).*

Major works (novels, stories, and plays): Le Torrent *(*The Torrent, *1950);* Les Chambres de bois *(*The Silent Rooms, *1958);* Le Temps sauvage *(*Season of Innocence, *1963);* Kamouraska *(1970);* Les Enfants du sabbat *(*Children of the Black Sabbath, *1975);* Héloïse *(1980);* Les Fous de bassan *(*In the Shadow of the Wind, *1982);* L'Enfant chargé de songes *(*The Child Burdened with Dreams, *1992).*

Anne Hébert, whose literary career has taken place in both Canada and France, is one of French-Canada's most distinguished writers. Her work, which often presents characters in situations of acute despair, and which shows only some of them able to escape to lead lives of freedom, has been interpreted by some critics as concerned principally with universal human dilemmas. But others have seen a substantial degree of social commentary and political awareness in her writing. Hébert first appeared on the French-Canadian literary scene as a poet whose works expressed human emotions in the face of death on a profound level. Her volume of poems, *Le Tombeau des Rois,* published in 1953, is broadly considered to be her crowning achievement as a writer of verse.

In addition to her work as a poet, Hébert has also written six novels. Her early prose works dealt at first gingerly, then more specifically, with a critique of French-Canadian society, notably the prevailing attitudes among the upper-middle class in her native Quebec. When she relocated to France in the mid-1950s, her reputation as a prose writer soared. Two of Hébert's novels, both of them written in France, won leading literary prizes and established her as a prose writer of note. Hébert's use of main characters who are females trapped by their upbringing and their role in a society dominated by males has led some critics to identify her as a prose writer with what Maurice Gagnon calls "fundamental feminist preoccupations." Much of her work deals directly or, more frequently obliquely, with what critic Murray Sachs has called "the victimization of women by certain facets of patriarchal Quebec society."

The French-Canadian literary world into which Hébert had entered by the 1940s was in the midst of great change. A literary tradition that had revered religious faith and moral preaching faded, and traditional concerns that included the promotion of national identity and the glorification of a rural lifestyle were increasingly challenged. In 1944, the first Quebec novel placed entirely in an urban setting, Roger Lemelin's *Au pied de la pente douce* (*The Town Below*), appeared. There was a new sense of realism that concentrated on describing the increasingly urbanized society now taking shape. In Gagnon's words, with Quebec's partial transformation into an industrial society, "the balance was to shift away from the idealized rural novel of clerico-nationalist aims to the urban novel." Moreover, questions of human psychology increasingly interested some of the region's authors.

Anne Hébert was born in the village of Sainte-Catherine-de-Fossambault, Quebec, on August 1, 1916. Her birthplace was the family's summer home located approximately 25 miles northwest of Quebec City, the capital of the province of Quebec. The daughter of Maurice Hébert and **Marguerite Marie Taché**, Anne Hébert belonged to a distinguished French-Canadian family whose earlier members included the architect who designed the province's Parliament building. Her father was a government official who also developed a reputation as both a writer and a literary critic. While still a young child, she followed his work by listening to the programs that he was writing for Canadian radio. Although Hébert has been famous for her reticence in discussing her private life, she has made it known that her father was a key influence in her decision to become a writer.

Childhood illness restricted Hébert to a reclusive existence in Quebec City and Sainte-Catherine-de-Fossambault, and the future poet and novelist received only the conventional, superficial formal education typical for an upper-class girl of her era in French-speaking Canada. Nonetheless, she read extensively, with her father serving as the guide to her program of self-study. After examining some of his daughter's early works, the elder Hébert declared firmly that she had the talent to become a professional author.

A second figure who played a major role in shaping her work was her cousin, Hector de Saint-Denys Garneau. Along with other young friends, Anne and Hector put on theatrical productions in the village where their family had its summer home. It was Hector, himself a poet who published a notable volume of his work in 1937, who encouraged Anne to write her first set of poems, *Les Songes en équilibre*. This work was marked by short lines, free verse, and an effort to recapture a vision of the world through the eyes of a young child. **Lorraine Weir**, in *Canadian Writers, 1920–1959*, has noted how this early work reflects a religious innocence that was still a fundamental part of "a conservative Catholic girlhood." Delbert Russell, another prominent student of Hébert's work, has found that this initial publication reflected both the in-

Anne Hébert

fluence of Hector in its stress on childhood innocence as well as that of the noted French poet Verlaine in its poetic techniques. He also noted that such lasting themes in Hébert's work as the importance of death, the link between dream and reality, and the role of the artist in the world, made their first appearance here.

In addition to her initial set of poems, Hébert also produced several plays and short stories. An early short story, *La Maison de l'esplanade* (*The House on the Esplanade*), published in 1943, was in Russell's words, "a mordant criticism of the artificiality and emptiness of the life of the *haute bourgeoisie* of Quebec." Living in a half-deserted mansion, its main character is an aged woman who passes each day of her life in a rigid and sterile routine. Hébert's critical view of the society in which she had grown up was to form a significant theme in her future writing.

Through her exploration of the classic themes of guilt, evil, violence, . . . she has created a fully unified oeuvre which is both brilliantly executed and profound in its understanding of the psychology of pain and entrapment.

—**Lorraine Weir**

Le Torrent stands as Hébert's most significant early work of prose. Published in an abridged version in 1947, then presented in its entirety three years later, it was a collection of short stories written over the previous decade. The title work in the volume is the account of a tormented young man who believes he has committed matricide, and then, years later, finds himself driven by guilt to take his own life. This tale has been praised for its acute psychological insight, but some critics have found in it as well a critique of the harsh Jansenist variety of Catholicism prominent in Quebec life. In this view, the hero François has been warped from childhood by his mother's effort to inculcate in him the Jansenist call to renounce the real world and to sink into a life of self-denial. The social implications of Hébert's theme help account for the fact that the story was initially published only in a censored version. When it appeared in its full form in 1950, it had to be published at Hébert's expense, and it faced a harsh critical response. As Weir has put it, many in Hébert's audience apparently felt that such stories "were altogether too revealing of a side of Quebec life that should be kept hidden."

In contrast, the collection of poems in Hébert's second volume of verse, *Le Tombeau des rois,* received enormous acclaim when the book appeared in 1953. In Russell's words, it is "now regarded as an undisputed masterpiece." In both her homeland and France, critics lauded the combination of feeling, imagery, and precise language Hébert put into these 27 poems. The verses focus on the theme of death and the emotional reactions produced by facing this human reality, and the symbolism the poet employed included a bird, jewels, water, bones, and light. Hébert evidently found herself drawn to examining the end of a human's existence by the loss of two beloved individuals. Her cousin, Hector de Saint-Denys Garneau, died of a longstanding heart ailment in October 1943 at the age of 32. In 1952, her younger sister **Marie Hébert**, then only 30, also passed away.

In 1953, Hébert took a job with Canada's National Film Board. In this capacity, she spent most of her time writing commentaries to accompany educational films. Within a year, she received an offer of financial support from the Royal Society of Canada. She accepted and used the funds to relocate to Paris where she was able to devote herself full-time to her writing. She continued to maintain a home in Quebec until 1965, but thereafter returned only for visits. Despite her increasing absence from her home country, her achievements as a Canadian writer brought her election, in June 1960, to the Royal Society of Canada. Much of her prose continued to focus on French-speaking Canada, but she now viewed that society from the perspective of a sojourner in a foreign country.

Hébert's first novel, *Les Chambres de bois,* appeared in 1958. Its cycle of short, loosely connected chapters drew on her skills as a poet. As Gagnon notes, she was now exploring "a multifaceted dreamlike world of anguish and evil" like the one in her verse. The book tells the story of a newly married Parisian couple. The husband Michel has remained erotically tied to his sister. Catherine, the wife and the book's heroine, breaks away from this claustrophobic and unhealthy world to reclaim her freedom. *Les Chambres de bois* concentrates on the growing awareness within Catherine's mind, and it shows how she becomes more and more conscious of the meaning of the sensations she experiences. Nonetheless, Gagnon saw this intensely personal story as linked to political currents. He noted that frequently in the novels by Quebec authors a principal character's psychology "coincides with the historical themes of possession and dispossession of land and country under Anglophone authority." Thus, as French-Canada was growing increasingly uncomfortable with English domination, so too "Catherine/Quebec no longer accepts her lot as a passive plaything of an authoritarian ruler." Russell discounted such a view, claiming that the work "pays more attention to the interior world of the small group of characters than to their social environment."

The novel was followed in short order by a new collection of poems, *Mystère de la parole* (*Mystery of the Verb*), in 1960. Departing from the terse style of *Le Tombeau des rois,* in which the author employed brief lines and irregular rhythms, this work of seven years later employed new techniques. Delbert Russell noted the similarity between Hébert's "long, stanza-like verses" and verses found in the Bible. In contrast to the overpowering sense of alienation found in *Le Tombeau des rois,* this later work, critics felt, discards such pessimism and offers a celebration and new acceptance of life.

Despite Hébert's physical distance from her homeland, she remained concerned about French Canadians' immersion in religious ritual and their unwillingness to attempt a profound examination of their links to the harsh physical reality around them. Her play *Le Temps sauvage,* first performed in 1966 in Quebec City, shows a tormented family whose children struggle for independence from a domineering mother, Agnès Joncas. In the end, Agnès sees her children escape their claustrophobic home environment on a mountainside north of Montreal. Weir interpreted the play's meaning in personal terms to show that even this most domineering mother "is powerless to prevent the incursions of chaos" inserted into her tiny family circle by the outside world. Thus, with "her dream of perfect motherhood shattered, Agnès is left with her own corrosive bitterness." But other critics have put the play into a different, more politicized context. Writing in *The Oxford Companion to Canadian Theatre,* **Renate Benson** described the climax to the plot as "analogous to Quebec's liberation from a repressive past."

Hébert expressed her growing interest in the history of her homeland in both essay and novel form. Her essay, entitled "Quebec," appeared in the Montreal newspaper *La Presse* in 1967. Described by Russell as "a prose poem which recounts the Quebec experience from a historical and human point of view," it consists largely of the names of locales and individuals who appear throughout the history of Quebec, the center of French-speaking Canada.

After four years of work, in 1970 Hébert completed a major historical novel, *Kamouraska,* considered by many critics to be her most masterful work of prose. It was a fictionalized account of a famous murder and subsequent murder trial in Quebec City at the close of the 1830s. The heroine, Elizabeth, arranges the murder of her tyrannical husband; she is then tried but acquitted for the crime. The course of events is seen through Elizabeth's mind and recollections. Hébert portrays Elizabeth as a woman reared in an oppressive moral code that she subsequently breaks but cannot escape. As Gagnon put it, Elizabeth "cannot but remain imprisoned in the irreducible contradictions brought about by a set social, moral, and religious education." Unfortunately for her, she dwells in "a society that condemns more than it condones and does so on absolute religious terms incompatible with human needs and failings." According to Sachs, the novel combines a variety of potent elements: "the colonial mentality in nineteenth-century Quebec, . . . class, sex, and economic differences, . . . the proper role of tradition, morality, and the Church in the life of the individual." The novel was made into a highly regarded film in 1973. It served to introduce Hébert to an English-language audience, and much of her work was now translated into English for the first time.

Hébert presented a more optimistic picture of an individual caught in an oppressive religious system in her subsequent novel *Les Enfants du sabbat.* Published in 1975 and set in the Quebec countryside during the Depression, this shows Sister Julie, a young novice in a religious order, who successfully escapes to freedom. Writes Gagnon, the heroine rejects "a comportment tainted by feelings of prison and death." Instead, she chooses "authenticity and autonomy." This novel presents the most direct attack so far in Hébert's writing on the role of the Catholic Church in Quebec society. It features a picture of a convent community marked by sexual repression, hallucinations, and a search for hidden sorcerers. As Russell described it, the book "effectively presents and condemns a religious climate in Quebec which was finally to come to an end during . . . the 1950s and 1960s." He has also noted how, in both *Kamouraska* and *Les Enfants du sabbat*, "the physical substance of recaptured times and places is added to the intensity of feeling found in her best poetry."

Hébert's next novel, *Héloïse*, was set entirely in Paris. Like *Les Chambre de bois*, this work shows a young married couple starting their life together in an apartment. This time, however, Hébert offers neither of her main characters an escape. The book ends with both of them in the midst of dead animals and plants, a preview of the fate that hangs over their heads.

In 1982, Hébert's fifth novel, *Les Fous de basson* was placed back in the familiar setting of Quebec. Unlike her previous writing, which had examined the lives of French-Canadians, the book dealt with the Protestant Anglophones of Canada. In a series of separate segments told from different points of view, her characters recall the death of two citizens of the small village of Griffin Creek in the summer of 1936. It is a profoundly pessimistic work in which the characters, in Gagnon's words, live in a "sense of helplessness and hopelessness."

In 1992, Hébert presented her latest works of both prose and poetry. Her novel, *L'Enfant chargé de songes,* presents a male protagonist, living in Paris just after World War II and recalling his Quebec childhood. Her volume of poetry, *Le Jour n'a d'égal que la nuit,* was her first since 1960. It contained 49 poems, written between 1961 and 1989.

Since the late 1950s, Hébert has been an honored writer in both her native country as well as France. In addition to the numerous literary prizes she has won in Paris, such as the Prix des libraires de France in 1971 for *Kamouraska* and the Prix Fémina in 1982 for *Les Fous de Bassan*, she has received a host of awards in Canada as well as doctorates from three Canadian universities: the University of Toronto in 1969, the University of Quebec at Montreal in 1979, and McGill University in 1980.

Evaluations of Hébert's work necessarily involve balancing a consideration of her achievements as a writer and an assessment of her role in reflecting and commenting on the society that produced her. Critics like Albert LeGrand have described her work as a product of the Quebec psyche. But Delbert Russell has presented the more widely accepted view in noting that she will "be remembered not primarily as a Quebec poet, but as a poet." For Weir as well, Hébert's achievement has been to create "a complex and tightly unified system which transcends particularized settings," one which explores "the profoundest forces at work in human life."

SOURCES:

Benson, Eugene, and L.W. Conolly, eds. *The Oxford Companion to the Canadian Theatre.* Toronto: Oxford University Press, 1989.

Gagnon, Maurice. *The French Novel of Quebec.* Boston, MA: Twayne, 1986.

Lewis, Paula Gilbert, ed. *Traditionalism, Nationalism, and Feminism: The Women Writers of Quebec.* Westport, CT: Greenwood Press, 1985.

Mitchell, Constantina Thalia, and Paul Raymond Cote. *Shaping the Novel: Textual Interplay in the Fiction of Malraux, Hébert, and Modiano.* Providence, RI: Berghahn Books, 1996.

Moritz, Albert and Theresa. *The Oxford Illustrated Literary Guide to Canada.* Toronto: Oxford University Press, 1987.

New, William H., ed. *Canadian Writers, 1920–1959.* First Series. Detroit, MI: Gale Research, 1988.

Russell, Delbert W. *Anne Hébert.* Boston, MA: Twayne, 1983.

Toye, William, ed. *Oxford Companion to Canadian Literature.* Toronto: Oxford University Press, 1983.

SUGGESTED READING:

Green, Mary Jean. "Witch and the Princess: the Feminine Fantastick in the Fiction of Anne Hébert," in *American Review of Canadian Studies.* Vol. 15, no. 2, 1985, pp. 137–46.

Story, Norah. *The Oxford Companion to Canadian History and Literature.* Toronto: Oxford University Press, 1967.

Neil M. Heyman,
Professor of History,
San Diego State University, San Diego, California

Heck, Barbara Ruckle (1734–1804)

German religious pioneer who, with Philip Embury, organized the first Methodist society in New York City, now regarded as the beginning of the Wesleyan movement in the U.S. *Born Barbara Ruckle in 1734 at Ruckle Hill in Balligarane, Ireland; died on August 17, 1804, near Augusta, Canada; daughter of Sebastian Ruckle; married Paul Heck, in 1760 (died 1792 or 1795); children: two daughters and three sons.*

Emigrated to America with husband and others from a German Methodist colony in County Limerick, Ireland, settling in New York City (1760); with husband and other members of the community, moved upriver to farmland near Salem in Washington County, New York (1770); for political reasons, moved with family to Montreal (1774); when husband received a grant of land for his military service in Maitland, near August in Upper Canada, she and family moved and remained there for the rest of their lives (1785).

The members of Barbara Heck's small German-speaking community in Ireland were the descendants of late 17th-century immigrants to Ireland from the Palatinate on the Rhine. These Palatinate Germans were missionized by John Wesley on his visit to Ireland in 1747. Members of this community, including Heck, emigrated to the American colonies together in 1760, although it was not until six years after their arrival that the group began to establish Methodism in America. Also in 1760, Barbara married Paul Heck with whom she would have five children.

Discouraged by the community's lack of belief, in 1766 Barbara Heck encouraged Philip Embury, who had been an itinerant Methodist preacher in Ireland, to begin preaching once again to their community. The congregation grew from a small one in Embury's house, to one large enough to fill space in the Rigging Loft in William Street in New York, and eventually into a strong community with the resources to build their own Wesley Chapel. Members of the British Army stationed in New York were active in this community, contributing heavily, and on October 30, 1768, the first official Methodist Chapel in America was opened on John Street in the heart of New York's financial district and was named the Wesley Chapel. The John Street Methodist Chapel still stands on the site on which the Wesley Chapel was built, and a plaque dedicated to Barbara Heck and Philip Embury in the church reads: "Their works do follow them."

Due to political beliefs, in 1774 Heck moved with her family to Montreal, where her husband enlisted as a volunteer in the British Army. Heck spent the majority of the war years in Montreal and Quebec and repeated her activities on behalf of Methodism. In 1786, following the family's move to land provided by the British government for war services near Augusta, Heck encouraged the construction of a Wesleyan chapel, and brought the style of Methodist prayer to this area. This is believed to be the first Methodist chapel in Canada and was led by Samuel Embury, Philip Embury's son. Heck's husband Paul died in 1792, or 1795, and Barbara continued her devotion and leadership in this Methodist community as a lay leader until her death in 1804. She is buried beside her husband in the Old Blue Churchyard of the Wesley Chapel in Maitland, Canada.

SOURCES:

Caddell, G. Lincoln. *Barbara Heck: Pioneer Methodist.* Cleveland, OH: Pathway Press, 1961.

Withrow, William Henry. *Barbara Heck: A Tale of Early Methodism.* Toronto: William Briggs, 1895.

SUGGESTED READING:

Stevens, Abel. *The Women of Methodism; Its Three Foundresses, Susanna Wesley, the Countess of Huntingdon, and Barbara Heck; With Sketches of Their Female Associates and Successors in the Early History of the Denomination.* NY: Carlton & Porter, 1866.

COLLECTIONS:

Some artifacts and papers relating to Barbara Heck, including her Bible, are housed at Victorian University, Toronto.

Amanda Carson Banks,
Vanderbilt Divinity School, Nashville, Tennessee

Heckler, Margaret M. (1931—)

American politician and Republican Congressional representative from Massachusetts (1967–1983). *Name variations: Mrs. John M. Heckler. Born Margaret Mary O'Shaughnessy on June 21, 1931, in Flushing, New York; daughter of John O'Shaughnessy and Bridget (McKeown) O'Shaughnessy; Albertus Magnus College, B.A., 1953; postgraduate work at the University of Leiden (Holland), 1953; Boston College Law School, LL.B., 1956; married John M. Heckler, on August 29, 1952; children: Belinda West Heckler; Alison Anne Heckler; John M. Heckler.*

Barbara Ruckle Heck

Margaret N. Heckler was born in Flushing, New York, on June 21, 1931. She earned a bachelor of arts from Albertus Magnus College in 1953 and did postgraduate work at the University of Leiden in the Netherlands. Heckler continued her education at Boston College Law School, where she edited the college's law review while earning her degree, and was admitted to the Massachusetts bar in 1956. She began her political career in 1962 when she won a seat on the Massachusetts Governor's Council to which she was reelected in 1964. She was a member of the Republican town committee of Wellesley, Massachusetts, from 1958 until 1966, when she decided to run for a seat in the House of Representatives.

On September 16, 1966, Heckler challenged incumbent Joseph W. Martin for the Republican nomination to the House. She faced the daunting task of halting one of the legendary political careers in Massachusetts politics. Martin had been a Congressional representative since 1925 and had served as House Republican leader for 16 years. In her campaign, Heckler used the same argument against the 81-year-old Martin that he had used when he originally ousted the 83-year-old incumbent: that the district needed a more vigorous individual in Washington. She won the Republican nomination and was victorious in the general election over Democratic candidate Patrick H. Harrington, Jr.

Heckler devoted much of her energy to veterans' affairs and became the second-ranking Republican member of the Veterans' Affairs Committee. As an advocate of childcare, Heckler was critical of President Richard Nixon's 1971 veto of a comprehensive child-development program. She was tireless in her work for the Equal Rights Amendment (ERA) and co-sponsored a 1977 joint resolution to extend the deadline for its ratification. She also drafted the Equal Credit Opportunity Act of 1974 and worked with New York Representative *****Elizabeth Holtzman** to organize the Congressional Caucus for Women's Issues in 1977. Heckler opposed the use of federal funds for abortions and endorsed tax credits for parents with children in private, non-profit schools.

Margaret M. Heckler

In 1982, when the electoral map underwent redistricting, Heckler's Tenth District was removed, and she found herself competing with the Fourth District's Representative Barney Frank. Although she lost the race, she was nominated by President Ronald Reagan as secretary of the Department of Health and Human Services on January 12, 1983, and won confirmation by the Senate on March 3 of that year. In this role, Heckler established new guidelines for the Social Security disability program and campaigned to increase federal funding for research and care for patients with Alzheimer's disease and AIDS.

In 1985, she was named ambassador to Ireland and remained in that position until October of 1989. Following this appointment, Heckler returned to Wellesley.

SOURCES:

Office of the Historian. *Women in Congress, 1917–1990.* Commission on the Bicentenary of the U.S. House of Representatives, 1991.

Judith C. Reveal,
freelance writer, Greensboro, Maryland

Hector, Annie French (1825–1902)

Irish-born novelist. *Name variations: Mrs. Hector; (pseudonym) Mrs. Alexander. Born Annie French in Dublin, Ireland, on June 23, 1825; died in London, England, on July 10, 1902; interred at Kensal Green cemetery; educated by governesses; married Alexander Hector (a merchant), in 1858 (died 1875).*

Novelist Annie Hector French was born in Dublin in 1825; when she was 19, her family moved to England. Married at age 33 to Alexander Hector, a wealthy merchant, she was widowed 17 years later, at age 50. She then turned to writing novels, producing over 40 titles, including the extremely successful *The Wooing O't* (1873), as well as *Ralph Wilton's Weird* (1875), *Her Dearest Foe* (1876), *The Frères* (1882), *At Bay* (1885), *Mona's Choice* (1887), and the semi-autobiographical *Kitty Costello* (1902).

Hedvig (d. 1436)

Countess of Oldenburg. *Name variations: Hedwig; Hedwig von Holstein. Died in 1436; daughter of Gerhard VI, duke of Holstein (r. 1386–1404), and* ***Elizabeth of Brunswick****; married Balthasar, prince of Mecklenburg, in 1417 (died 1421); married Didrik also known as Diedrich or Dietrich (c. 1390–1440), count of Oldenburg, in 1423; children: (second marriage) Christian I (1426–1481), king of Denmark, Norway* *and Sweden (r. 1448–1481). Dietrich first married* ***Adelheid von Delmenhorst****, around 1401.*

Hedvigis (1374–1399).

See Jadwiga.

Hedwig (d. 903)

Duchess of Saxony. *Name variations: Hedwige. Died on December 24, 903; daughter of Henry (d. 886), margrave of Mark (some sources claim that Hedwig was the daughter of* ****Oda of Bavaria*** *and Arnulf of Carinthia, king of Germany, but dates do not correspond); married Otto (c. 836–912), duke of Saxony, around 869; children: Liudolf; Thangmar (d. 938); Henry I the Fowler (c. 876–936), Holy Roman emperor (r. 919–936); Oda (who married Zwentibold, king of Lorraine).*

Hedwig (c. 915–965)

Duchess of France, countess of Paris, and duchess of Burgundy. *Name variations: Hadwig, Hedwige, or Avoie. Born in the duchy of Saxony around 915 (some sources cite 922); died on March 10, 965, in Aix-la-Chapelle (Aachen); daughter of Henry I the Fowler (c. 876–936), king of Germany, Holy Roman emperor (r. 919–936), and* ****Matilda of Saxony*** *(c. 892–968); sister of Otto I the Great (912–973), king of Germany (r. 936–973), Holy Roman emperor (r. 962–973); married Hugh the Great also known as Hugh the White (c. 895–956), count of Paris and duke of Burgundy, in 938; children: Beatrice (b. 938, who married Frederick, count of Bar); Hugh Capet (939–996), duke of France (r. 956–996), king of France (r. 987–996, first of the Capetian kings, who married* ****Adelaide of Poitou****); ****Emma of Paris*** *(d. 968), duchess of Normandy; Odo or Otto (b. around 945), duke of Burgundy; Otto Henry the Great (b. around 948), duke of Burgundy; Herbert, bishop of Auxerre. Hugh the Great's first wife was* ****Edhild*** *(d. 946).*

Hedwig (1374–1399).

See Jadwiga.

Hedwig, Saint (1174–1243).

See Hedwig of Silesia.

Hedwig of Denmark (1581–1641)

Electress of Saxony. *Born on August 5, 1581; died on November 26, 1641; daughter of Frederick II (1534–1588), king of Denmark and Norway (r. 1559–1588), and* ****Sophia of Mecklenburg*** *(1557–1631); sister of* ****Anne of Denmark*** *(1574–1619); married Christian II (1583–1611), elector of Saxony (r. 1591–1611), on September 12, 1602.*

Hedwig of Eberhard (930–992)

Countess of Ardennes. *Born in Germany in 930; died in 992; married Siegfried of Luxemburg (c. 922–998), count of Ardenne (r. 963–998), around 950; children: possibly Henry I of Luxemburg (d. 1026); Frederick I of Luxemburg (born around 965), count of Salm or Solm;* ****Cunigunde*** *(d. 1040?, who married Henry II, Holy Roman emperor). Henry I was possibly a son from a previous marriage of Siegfried's.*

Hedwig of Habsburg (d. 1286)

Margravine of Brandenburg. *Birth date unknown; died before October 27, 1286; daughter of* ****Anna of Hohenberg*** *(c. 1230–1281) and Rudolph or Rudolf I of Habsburg (1218–1291), king of Germany (r. 1273), Holy Roman emperor (r. 1273–1291); married Otto, margrave of Brandenburg.*

Hedwig of Holstein (d. 1325)

Queen of Sweden. *Name variations: Hedwig von Holstein. Died around 1325; daughter of Gerhard I, count of Holstein, and* ***Elizabeth of Mecklenburg****; married Magnus I Ladulas, king of Sweden (r. 1275–1290), on November 11, 1276; children: Eric; Berger, king of Sweden (r. 1290–1318); Erik, duke of Sudermannland; Richiza Magnusdottir (abbess of St. Klara);* ****Ingeborg*** *(d. 1319); Valdemar or Waldemar, duke of Finland.*

Hedwig of Holstein-Gottorp (1636–1715)

Queen of Sweden. *Name variations: Hedvig. Born Hedwig Eleanor on October 23, 1636; died on November 24, 1715; married Karl X also known as Charles X Gustavus (1622–1660), king of Sweden (r. 1654–1660), on October 24, 1654; children: Charles XI (1655–1697), king of Sweden (r. 1660–1697).*

Hedwig of Oldenburg (1759–1818).

See Charlotte of Oldenburg.

Hedwig of Poland (1513–1573)

Electress of Brandenburg. *Name variations: Jadwiga. Born on March 25, 1513; died on February 7, 1573; daughter of* ****Barbara Zapolya*** *and Sigismund I, king* *of Poland (r. 1506–1548); became second wife of Joachim II (1505–1571), elector of Brandenburg (r. 1535–1571), on September 1, 1535. Joachim's first wife was *Magdalene of Saxony (1507–1534).*

Hedwig of Silesia (1174–1243)

Duchess of Silesia, German noble, and saint. *Name variations: Saint Hedwig; Jadwiga of Silesia. Pronunciation: Hate-vik. Born in Andrechs castle, Bavaria, in 1174; died in Silesia in 1243; daughter of Count Berthold III of Andrechs (marquis of Meran, count of Tirol, and duke of Carinthia and Istria) and Agnes of Dedo (daughter of the count of Rotletchs); sister of Agnes of Meran (queen of France for five years) and Gertrude of Andrechs-Meran (queen of Hungary); aunt of Elizabeth of Hungary (1207–1231); married Duke Henry I of Silesia also known as Henry the Bearded, duke of Cracow (r. 1228–1229, 1232–1238), in 1186 (died 1238); children: Henry II the Pious, duke of Cracow (r. 1238–1241); Conrad; Boleslas; Agnes; Sophia; and Gertrude.*

Duchess Hedwig of Silesia, a German noble, was renowned as a holy woman. Born to Count Berthold III of Andrechs, marquis of Meran, and **Agnes of Dedo**, she had two sisters: the eldest, ***Agnes of Meran**, was queen of France; the second, ***Gertrude of Andrechs-Meran**, was queen of Hungary and mother of Saint ***Elizabeth of Hungary** (1207–1231). Hedwig spent her early years at the convent of Franken. At 13, she married Duke Henry I of Silesia and would eventually have a large family. Always a deeply pious woman (probably due in part to her years at the convent), Hedwig was distressed at her husband's refusal to become a Christian and worked for years to convert him to the faith, eventually succeeding. Her children were also raised as Christians, and the entire family was soon noted for its devotion and generosity to charitable causes.

Hedwig used her substantial resources to establish numerous hospitals, especially for lepers. She herself worked in the hospitals, as did most of her children. Hedwig also founded and endowed many monasteries and convents, of which the most famous is the Cistercian convent at Treibnitz, near Breslau. When her husband died in March 1238, she retired to the convent at Treibnitz, where she lived her remaining years in great austerity, although she did not become a nun. Her reputation for piety grew until it included allegations of miracles of healing she had performed, and she was said to be so blessed that she could bring the dead back to life. Hedwig was 69 when she died; over two decades later, she was canonized (1266 or 1267) and became the patron saint of Silesia. Her feast day is celebrated on October 17. (*See also entry on Elizabeth of Hungary.*)

SOURCES:

Anderson, Bonnie S., and Judith P. Zinsser. *A History of Their Own*. Vol. I. NY: Harper & Row, 1988.

Echols, Anne, and Marty Williams. *An Annotated Index of Medieval Women*. NY: Markus Wiener, 1992.

Laura York,
Riverside, California

Hedwig Sophia (1681–1708)

Princess of Sweden and duchess of Holstein-Gottorp. *Name variations: Hedwig Sophie of Sweden; Hedwig von Simmern. Born on June 26, 1681; died on December 22, 1708; daughter of *Ulrica Eleanora of Denmark (1656–1693) and Charles XI (1655–1697), king of Sweden (r. 1660–1697); married Frederick IV (1671–1702), duke of Holstein-Gottorp (r. 1695–1702), on June 12, 1698; children: Charles Frederick (1700–1739), duke of Holstein-Gottorp (r. 1702–1739, who married *Anne Petrovna [1708–1728], daughter of Peter the Great and *Catherine I of Russia).*

Hedwig Wittelsbach (fl. late 1600s)

Daughter of the Elector Palatine. *Name variations: Hedwig Elizabeth Amelia of Pfalz-Neuburg. Flourished in the late 1600s; born Hedwig Elizabeth; daughter of Philip William, Elector Palatine, and possibly *Elizabeth Amalia of Hesse (1635–1709) or, more likely, *Anna Constancia (1619–1651); married James Sobieski (son of John III Sobieski and Marie Casimir); children: five, including *Clementina Sobieski (1702–1735).*

Hedwige.

Variant of Hedwig and Jadwiga.

Heemstra, Ella van (1900–1984).

See Hepburn, Audrey for sidebar.

Heenan, Frances "Peaches" (b. 1911).

See Kuhn, Irene Corbally for sidebar.

Heer, Anna (1863–1918)

Swiss physician who played a decisive role in founding Switzerland's first professional nursing school. *Born in Olten, Switzerland, on March 22, 1863; died in Zurich, Switzerland, on December 19, 1918.*

Born in 1863 into comfortable bourgeois circumstances, Anna Heer grew up in a Switzerland known during the late 19th century for its progressive attitude towards women's higher education. In 1864, the University of Zurich entered the first woman, a Russian, on the register of its medical faculty. By the 1870s, growing numbers of both Swiss and foreign-born women were studying at Zurich's renowned medical school. Anna Heer initially strove for a career as an artist and only slowly came to see medicine as her life's calling. Once the decision was made, however, she pursued her goal with tenacity and was awarded her medical degree by the University of Zurich in 1888. Heer began practicing medicine as one of Switzerland's first woman physicians, and it became clear to her that the quality of nurses varied dramatically; some were both knowledgeable and conscientious, while an alarming number displayed neither of these virtues. Since the comfort and even the lives of patients were potentially at stake, Heer concluded that nursing needed to be raised to the status of a true profession. In 1896, she began working with two other Swiss women physicians, **Ida Schneider** and ***Marie Vögtlin,** to create a professional nursing school in Zurich. Despite both professional and financial obstacles, in 1901 the Swiss Nurse's School opened its doors in Zurich. By maintaining high professional standards, this training academy, which included an attached women's hospital, became a model for other, similar institutions throughout Switzerland and soon gained an international reputation.

Of diminutive stature, Heer was affectionately called *die Kleine* (the little lady) by many of her professional colleagues. She was, however, a giant in the history of Swiss women's professional advancement. Anna Heer died in Zurich on December 19, 1918. Switzerland has honored her in many ways, including naming a street in Zurich after her and depicting her on a special charity postage stamp issued on June 1, 1963.

SOURCES:

Baumann Kurer, Sylvia. *Die Gründung der Schweizerischen Pflegerinnenschule mit Frauenspital in Zürich 1901 und ihre Chefärztin Anna Heer (1863–1918).* Zurich: Juris Verlag, 1991.

"Dr. med. Anna Heer," in *Biographisches Lexikon verstorbener Schweizer: In Memoriam.* Zurich and Basel: Schweizerische Industrie-Bibliothek, 1950, Vol. 3, pp. 108–109.

Hildebrandt, Irma. *Die Frauenzimmer kommen: 16 Zürcher Porträts.* 2nd rev. ed. Munich: Eugen Diederichs Verlag, 1997.

Marks, Geoffrey, and William K. Beatty. *Women in White.* NY: Scribner, 1972.

Segesser, Anna von. *Dr. med. Anna Heer, 1863–1918, Mitgründerin und erste Chefärztin der Schweizerischen Pflegerinnenschule in Zürich.* Zurich: Schulthess Verlag, 1948.

Swiss postage stamp honoring Anna Heer, issued on June 1, 1963.

John Haag, Associate Professor, University of Georgia, Athens, Georgia

Hegamin, Lucille (1894–1970)

African-American jazz singer. *Born Lucille Nelson in Macon, Georgia, on November 29, 1894; died in New York City on March 1, 1970; married William "Bill" Hegamin (a pianist), in 1914 (divorced 1923).*

Born in Macon, Georgia, in 1894, Lucille Nelson first sang in the church choir and local theaters before leaving home at 15 to tour with the Leonard Harper Revue. A few years later, she found herself stranded in Peoria, Illinois, and made her way to Chicago where she performed in various clubs with sidemen Tony Jackson, Jelly Roll Morton, and pianist Bill Hegamin; she married Hegamin around 1914. Lucille moved West with her own band and made an extended appearance in Seattle, Washington. In late 1919, she returned to New York to sing lead and record with the Blue Flame Syncopators, a group that included Charlie Irvis. In 1921, she soloed at The Shuffle Inn and fronted her own Dixie Daisies. From 1926 to 1927, she sang with the Sunnyland Cottonpickers, accompanied by pianist Cyril J. Fullerton. During the 1920s, Hegamin appeared in several Broadway shows, earning the sobriquet "The Cameo Girl." She also worked with George "Doc" Hyder's Southernaires, before going into semi-retirement. After brief appearances in 1933 and 1934 at the

Paradise in Atlantic City, Hegamin became a registered nurse in 1938. During the 1960s, she reappeared at charity events and made one more recording in 1962. Lucille Hegamin's most renowned recordings include "Everybody's Blues" (1920), "Some Early Morning" (1923), and "Number 12"; the latter was featured on her album *Basket of Blues* (1962).

Hegan, Alice (1870–1942).

See Rice, Alice Hegan.

Heggtveit, Anne (1939—)

First Canadian skier to win an Olympic medal. *Name variations: Anne Heggtveit-Hamilton. Born on January 11, 1939; grew up in Ottawa; daughter of Dr. Halvor Heggtveit (who qualified for Canada's 1932 Olympic ski team but did not compete); married.*

Won the combined title at the Aalberg-Kandahar (1959); won an Olympic gold medal in the slalom (1960).

On skis by age two, Anne Heggtveit trained under Canada's skiing champion Ernie McCulloch. She then went on to train under Pepi Salvenmoser. Heggtveit came to international attention when, at age 15, she won the 1954 Holmenkollen Giant Slalom event in Norway, the youngest winner in the event's 50-year history. In 1956, she missed the Olympic games at Cortina because of a broken leg that was slow to mend, and in early 1960 someone accidentally stabbed her leg with a snow shovel at a European meet, forcing another layoff. But Heggtveit, now an Ottawa secretary, was ready by the time Squaw Valley held the 1960 Olympics, during which she roomed with ***Nancy Greene**. Heggtveit finished a distant 12th in the first two races, the downhill and the giant slalom. On her first run of the slalom, however, she finished in 54.0, two seconds ahead of **Marianne Jahn** from Austria. On the second run, Jahn fell, clearing the way for Heggveit's gold medal after a safe, sure run. Heggveit was the first Canadian to win an Olympic gold medal in skiing. **Betsy Snite** of the U.S. placed 2nd, followed by **Barbara Henneberger** of Germany. Soon after, Heggtveit retired from skiing to raise a family.

SOURCES:

Batten, Jack. *Champions: Great Figures in Canadian Sport.* Toronto: New Press, 1971.

Opposite page

Johanne Luise Heiberg

Heiberg, Johanne Luise (1812–1890)

***Danish writer, director, actress, and brilliant comedian who achieved prominence as a tragedian toward the end of her career in Schiller's* Maria Stuart *and Shakespeare's* Macbeth.** *Born Johanne Luise Pätges in Copenhagen, Denmark, in the winter of 1812; died in 1890; daughter of Christian Pätges and Henriette Hartvig Pätges (both of German descent); her father was Catholic, her mother of Jewish heritage; married Johan Ludvig Heiberg (a writer and critic), in 1831; no children.*

Started her training at the ballet school of the Danish Royal Theater and continued her career there as an actress; from age 14 until retirement (1864), performed lead roles in plays written for her by prominent Danish playwrights of the time as well as in dramas by Molière, Scribe, Calderon, and Sheridan; after husband's death (1831), adopted three motherless girls from West Indies; rejoined the Danish Royal Theater as its primary director (1867–74); spent the remainder of her life writing her memoirs.

Selected writings: (light comedy) En Söndag paa Amager *(*A Sunday in the Country, *1848); (light comedy)* Abekatten *(*The Monkey, *1849);* Et Liv Gjenoplivet i Erindringen *(*A Life Re-lived in Memory, *published in three editions with significant omissions and reinstatements); (ed. by A.D. Jörgensen)* Et Liv Gjenoplivet i Erindringen, I–II *(1891–92); (ed. by Aage Friis)* Et liv gjenoplivet i erindringen, I–IV *(1944); (ed. by Niels Birger Wamberg)* Et liv gjenoplivet i erindringen, I–IV *(1973-74).*

The eighth of nine children, Johanne Luise Pätges was born during the Copenhagen winter of 1812 in a room so spare, destitute, and devoid of heat that icicles formed under the bed where her mother **Henriette Pätges** lay. The Pätgeses' wine shop had been destroyed during the English bombardment of the city in 1807, and with that had gone their economic resources. To provide food for the table, the Pätgeses ran boarding houses with varying success until finally they lost everything. At that point, Henriette declared herself head of the household and started selling German specialties, an enterprise which met with astounding success. Temporarily at least, money became a secondary worry; the primary obstacle to family contentment was Christian Pätges who resorted to excessive drinking in an effort to shore up the dignity he had lost with his wife usurping the role of breadwinner.

In this environment of poverty and increasingly violent parental brawls, Johanne Luise grew up as a painfully shy little girl, quiet to the point of being mute. Yet, she radiated a promise of unusual abilities which forced people to pay attention. From the time she was five, she was given dancing lessons by one of her mother's boarders; at eight, she started training at the ballet school of the Danish Royal Theater. Johanne tolerated the swishing cane of the ballet master because she loved dancing, but disparaging remarks directed at her old-fashioned, long outgrown clothes stung like nettles. The dark and melancholy disposition which would plague her throughout her life was relieved only in the soaring of the dance, precursor to the brilliance and lightness with which she would play the lead in lyrical romantic comedies.

Johanne Luise cried tears of rage and protestation when on one occasion she and her younger sister were made to dance on their father's billiard table to entertain his customers. She was saved, however, by the intervention of one of them, Johan Gebhard Harboe, who not only put an end to such performances but brought books, pens, and papers to the Pätges house. Fascinated by Johanne and moved by her projected anxiety, he took it upon himself to teach her and her little sister to read and write. Their parents could do neither, but they permitted Harboe's interference and perhaps encouraged the attention he lavished on their daughter, who was 13 years his junior. Harboe walked Johanne Luise back and forth to the theater, gave her presents, and on the whole tried to become indispensable. She readily acknowledged his role as savior from the squalor of her childhood, but she grew up to find his physical presence increasingly burdensome and his implicit demands an iron harness ready to descend on her when she was old enough to wear it.

Her discomfort and sense of guilt, increased by rumors about her engagement to Harboe, became so acute that the manager of the Royal Theater arranged for her to stay with the Wexschalls, a violinist and his actress wife. Their hospitable home was a lively and vital center for artists who came and went on a daily basis. With them, the "born old" Johanne Luise experienced being young for the first time, "as if given wings for both body and soul." For one full year, she enjoyed the admiration and attention of everyone. Men flocked around her, attracted by her elfish ways of invitation and withdrawal, and her singular beauty. Pictures show a very dark young girl with blue-grey eyes, and her contemporaries describe her hands and feet as small and expressive. Her walk was especially enchanting. "When she entered a room," wrote one admirer, "we had a feeling she descended to us, not by a staircase, but from the airy realms of imagination where she was queen." Her holiday year ended as it had to—in the name of convention

and for the sake of reputation—with an engagement. A young actor, Christopher Hvid, proposed, and before she could say either yes or no, he had declared the matter settled to someone entering the room. More a matter of timing than inclination, this accidental yet inevitable engagement should not be seen as a contradiction to Johanne Luise Pätges' belief at the time that of all miseries, "none is greater than marriage."

She had stood firm on that conviction the previous year, in 1828, when Johan Ludvig Heiberg had proposed for the first time. He had seen her three years earlier as the ingenue in a dialogue between young sweethearts and had gone backstage to inquire about "the little girl." She was 14, then; he, professor at the University of Kiel, drama critic and writer, was 35 years old. He had borne her refusal gracefully, continuing to treat her in a kind and courtly manner and letting her understand that in him she would always have a loyal and faithful friend. But he never let her go. She was not only his beloved but his muse. He wrote one play after another for her, and she performed her parts to perfection, apparently unaware that the roles she played and the words she spoke were his declaration of love.

We humans could accomplish nothing without absorbing ourselves in the accomplishment; and we do that at the risk of losing ourselves; resolving that dichotomy is our most difficult task.

—Johanne Luise Heiberg

Johan Ludvig was less than pleased when Johanne Luise moved in with the young and lively Wexschalls, and her engagement he considered a considerable—although temporary—setback. By then, he had secured a position as dramatist and translator of plays at the Royal Theater and with his mother, **Thomasine Gyllembourg-Ehrensvärd**, he had moved into an apartment in Copenhagen. Though her identity was kept secret, Gyllembourg was an author in her own right. At age 53, after the loss of her second husband, Carl Frederik Gyllembourg-Ehrensvärd, she had published her first story, "The Polonius Family." Twenty-three stories followed, all focusing on domestic issues and everyday life. Influenced by English novels such as Samuel Richardson's *Pamela,* Gyllembourg wrote about women and the conflicts of love. She held progressive views of women's position in society which she demonstrated by placing her female characters in conflicting roles and showing their attempts at liberation within the paternalistic order of things. Men, too, she argued, were confined by existing cultural mores and patterns; women, therefore, should seek their independence within, rather than outside, those walls.

Gyllembourg lived in conformity with her literary prescriptions although that had not always been the case. At 16, she had married her 31-year-old teacher, Peter Andreas Heiberg, with whom she had fancied herself in love. Marriage had proved a disillusionment, and to compensate for her mistake she had turned her love and attention to her son, a precocious and intelligent child. With that focus of affection, she might have remained in the marriage had she not fallen in love. But she did, "as inevitably as the chrysalis turns into a butterfly," in the words of her future daughter-in-law, and she demanded a divorce when her husband went into political exile, a bold and unusual request for her time. P.A. Heiberg consented, but on condition that their son not be permitted to live with his mother. Thus, absence had added to incipient symbiosis when she moved in with her son Johan Ludvig after Carl Gyllembourg's premature death in 1815.

At the time of Johan Ludvig's first proposal in 1828, Johanne Luise had become an established guest in their home. In the company of Thomasine Gyllembourg, she lost her usual reticence and spoke freely and at length. Those visits continued, and she felt increasingly included in the circle of well-educated, artistic people who were their friends. Not surprisingly, she turned to Gyllembourg in April 1830, "red-eyed and despondent," when the Wexschalls' divorce left her homeless. The older woman took her in for life, first as a boarder then as her daughter-in-law. She saw in Johanne a creature who "united the warmth and loveliness of youth with the sense and seriousness of later years." She also recognized the unexpected and uncustomary depth of her son's commitment to her, and she found a way to help Johanne Luise speak the words that would put an end to her meaningless engagement to Christopher Hvid. Johan Ludvig, who at this time had acquired his own apartment, became a daily guest in his mother's house, and soon his visits and his witty, learned conversation became the high point of their days.

Other prominent men who proposed marriage to the rising star did so on condition she leave the theater; as an actress, she would compromise their position in society. Johan Ludvig Heiberg and Thomasine Gyllembourg took the

Gyllembourg-Ehrensvärd, Thomasine

(1773–1856)

***Danish author and baroness.** Name variations: Baroness or Countess Thomasine Gyllembourg. Pronunciation: Gullem-BORG AY-rens-verd. Born Thomasine Christine Buntzen on November 9, 1773, in Copenhagen, Denmark; died in Copenhagen on July 2, 1856; married Peter Andreas Heiberg (a writer), in 1789 (divorced 1800); married Swedish baron Karl or Carl Frederik Gyllembourg-Ehrensvärd, in December 1801 (died 1815); children: (first marriage) Johan Ludvig Heiberg (a writer).*

Thomasine Gyllembourg was one of Denmark's first great women writers and one of its first realists, but she initially attracted notice because of her great beauty. Before age 17, she married the famous writer Peter Andreas Heiberg. In the following year, she gave birth to her son, Johan Ludvig Heiberg, who would become an acclaimed poet and critic. In 1800, after her husband was exiled for liberalism, she obtained a divorce. In December 1801, she married the Swedish baron Carl F. Ehrensvärd. Ehrensvärd, who had taken refuge in Denmark and adopted the name Gyllembourg, was also a political fugitive: he had been implicated in the assassination of Sweden's Gustavus III. Carl died in 1815.

In 1822, Thomasine followed her son to Kiel, where he was appointed professor, and in 1825 she returned with him to Copenhagen. When her son married the legendary actress ***Johanne Luise Heiberg** in 1831, Thomasine lived with them as part of an intense *menage à trois.*

In 1827, she had first appeared as an author by publishing her novel *Familien Polonius (The Polonius Family)* in her son's newspaper *Flyvende Post.* The following year, the journal had published *The Magic Ring,* which was immediately succeeded by *En Hverdags historie (Everyday History).* The popularity of this anonymous work was so widespread that the author would write under the name "The Author of *Everyday History*" until the end of her life. Thomasine published three volumes of *Old and New Novels* (1833–34), *New Stories* (1835–36), *Montanus the Younger* (1839), *Ricida* (1839), *One in All* (1840), *Near and Far* (1841), *A Correspondence* (1843), *The Cross Ways* (1844), and *Two Generations* (1845).

From 1849 to 1851, Thomasine was immersed in bringing out a library edition of her collected works in 12 volumes. Her literary identity remained a secret, even from her closest friends, until the day she died in her son's house in Copenhagen on July 2, 1856. At the turn of the century, her style was considered by critics as clear, sparkling, and witty, and she was favorably compared to ***Elizabeth Gaskell.**

SUGGESTED READING:

Heiberg, Johanne Luise. *Et Liv Gjenoplivet i Erindringen* (*A Life Re-lived in Memory*), published in three editions.

Heiberg, Peter Andreas. *Heiberg og Thomasine Gyllembourg* (in Danish), 1882.

opposite view: to demand that Johanne Luise Pätges turn her back on the stage would be as cruel as cutting out the tongue of a nightingale. So Johan Ludvig gradually won her over by asking nothing more than she was willing to give, and his mother promoted his suit by making the young actress feel grateful for her protection. Together, they enclosed her in a circle of three that would remain unbroken even after the two elder members had passed away.

Johanne Luise Pätges and Johan Ludvig Heiberg married in 1831 without letting anyone know beforehand. They celebrated their honeymoon in a village outside Copenhagen while Thomasine was busily at work decorating and arranging the home the three of them would share. She directed the carpenters and the painters and bought sheets and other linen. Divorced and widowed, she had lost her home twice and would let nothing interfere with her plans for future happiness with her son and daughter-in-law. Johan Ludvig wanted to set up his own household but renounced the idea when his mother let him understand that their living together was a matter of life and death for her. His wife was too grateful and too young to offer an opinion contrary to that of her mother-in-law.

At the theater, Johanne Luise Heiberg's star was in steady ascension. Her husband continued to write plays for her, appealing to the lighthearted, girlish part of her nature that he loved. She reached perfection not only in his satirical comedies but in the romantic plays Denmark's other leading dramatists produced in her honor, as well as in the French conversation pieces for which she had been trained in Madame Gyllembourg's drawing room. Those plays released her playfulness, her elfin grace, and charismatic manner. She was showered with flowers, gifts, and anonymous letters. Her dress and hair became fashion statements, and her picture appeared on handkerchiefs and perfume bottles.

Wherever she went, people crowded around her, fascinated by her radiance. A few nights before her 30th birthday, the students of Copenhagen honored her with a torchlight procession; her audience disengaged the horses from her coach and pulled it through the streets themselves. On that occasion, they paid tribute to an actress who had brilliantly emerged from the comedies of her earlier repertoire to roles of complex and intriguing individuals, roles for women that had begun to appear in the plays of the early 1840s.

Johanne Luise Heiberg's first appearance in a part that explored and demanded her entire being was afforded her by the playwright Henrik Hertz, who had spent a summer with the Heibergs and Thomasine Gyllembourg and had fallen deeply in love with Johanne Luise. In the process, he had come to understand that her magnetism, her enduring sweetness, had a darker side, which she experienced as desperate loneliness and a need for physical contact. From childhood on, Heiberg had felt ashamed of her mother's Jewish heritage. She considered it sinful and strange and had striven to be a good Christian and a light-hearted Dane. Hertz, himself a Jew, had intuited the conflict. He recognized that her success, based on artistic brilliance and domestic perfection, was achieved by a transformation of opposing forces, an insight Heiberg shares in her memoirs when she describes herself as a child. "Whoever saw me in the world of performance would consider me a happy and playful child, and yet, I believe the partly unconscious interest I awakened in the audience was due to the backdrop of melancholy." Heiberg was well acquainted with her emotional range that went from sensitive aesthetic refinement to coarse sensuality. As a child, she had learned to harness her forces in the cause of survival. As an adult, under the guidance of her husband, she had become civilized; but from time to time, she reckoned with the demons within, the filter through which she released her tragic roles and achieved her artistic stature. As one of her critics put it, "Only through the demonic has Mrs. Heiberg been great."

Johan Ludvig's civilizing influence on the barely literate young girl he married may be considered in the image of Pygmalion forming and shaping his Galatea. He taught her philosophy, religion, and aesthetics, and under his guidance she became the hostess of the most cultured, most refined home in Copenhagen where artists of all kinds, politicians, theologians, and philosophers would gather for food and conversation. Yet this diet which fed the artist so richly may be said to have starved the woman who suffered the lack of physical intimacy and children. Johan Ludvig did not miss them. An aesthete to the core and by nature transitory in his affections, he would continue to feed his fancy by the presence of young girls. The actress in his wife had responded to his demands and played the parts he had written for her with incomparable grace and lightness. Perhaps to accommodate her wider range, he added a moonlight dimension in his most famous play *The Elf Hill,* but he never came to understand the deeply melancholic aspects of her being. He thought them a woman's hypersensitivity, an aberration which reason could control; therefore, he ignored them and encouraged her to suppress them, which she did at her peril.

Instead of children, Johanne Luise Heiberg had her mother-in-law whom she loved and whose opinions she shared in the main. If either encountered matters that disturbed, the other was always available with open ears and loving sympathy. It was the little things that wedged them apart. "Never in my life have I seen such a combination of big and little as it existed in her," wrote Heiberg in her memoirs. "She who could grasp the greatest concepts in religion, art, and poetry would be equally concerned about the smallest domestic things. . . . What I thought the most unimportant thing in the world she would find exceedingly important, and thus we two very different creatures found it difficult to pull together. When I went at a trot, she chose a footpace, when I broke into a gallop, she would at best go at a trot. That caused perpetual jerks which tired me and tired her, so none of us was really comfortable in our closeness with one another—because we were too close."

Heiberg's ability to sublimate her sufferings into art did not fail her when in the course of the 1840s she fell in love with her leading man, Michael Wiehe. She "discovered" him among the young aspiring actors at the theater, and together they became the romantic lovers of the century—on stage, for all to see. When after more than a decade of joint performances, Wiehe left the theater in the wake of a friend who had been fired, she was deeply hurt and "unspeakably sad," because "the actor with whom my artistic work was so closely fused [would] no longer perform his art by my side. . . . Few people, perhaps no one, has caused me greater suffering than he. And yet I think no one was dearer to his heart than I. Where I am concerned, there were years during which I attached myself to him with a fervor I thought inextinguishable. It was an illusion. He poured a mountain of ice on my heart and I tore his picture from it."

But it was her husband that had done the firing. Michael Wiehe's walk-out took place in 1855, six years after Johan Ludvig had been made manager of the Danish Royal Theater. The promotion had come too late in his career. Twenty-five years earlier, he had been a revolutionary, bringing the age of sentimentality to an end with his light satirical comedies and his incisive critiques. His sure critical taste, based on years of literary studies, and his sharp, precise and elegant phrasing had gradually set the standards for literary achievement. He knew what was good, and that certainty prevented his acknowledgment of the changing times. By mid-century, he was considered a reactionary. The new revolutionaries, among them the leading actor Frederik Ludvig Hoedt and, to a lesser extent, Michael Wiehe, argued for more realism and naturalism in the performance of roles. They rejected the romantic soaring, the Tristan approach to a Romeo, and demanded presentations which were anchored in reality. When Johan Ludvig fired Hoedt in 1855, Wiehe went with him.

Johan Ludvig's stance put his wife in a difficult position. Twelve years earlier, in 1833, she had been the ringleader of a group of women, leading actresses at the Royal Theater, who demanded decent dressing rooms with sofas, chests of drawers with keys, and full-length mirrors, as well as respect on a par with that accorded their male colleagues. As the wife of the chief administrator and the leading actress, she was in the middle of the warring parties. Understandably, this ideological strife and attendant politics, the tension between the old and the new, and the loss of Michael Wiehe led to a physical breakdown. Heiberg had worked hard for many years, sometimes playing four different major roles in the course of seven nights, and always demanding the utmost from her performance. She was of the conviction that an actor frequently knows the character she portrays better than the dramatist who created it. Her task, then, was to present the character so the audience could see exactly what the writer intended, a feat which depended for its success on sublime concentration.

In the summers of 1854 and 1855, she spent time at two German spas, Marienbad and Franzenbad, seeking a cure for stomach and side pains. Her letters home show her longing for her husband, who at 60 no longer connects with her. "There is in your everyday relationships something cold," she writes, "no matter how amiable they are. Your kind thoughts rarely find expression in words. . . . You rarely feel the need to caress those you love." Johan Ludvig did not hear her cry for help, nor did her doctor. One admonished her against giving in to melancholia, the other diagnosed her as suffering from nervous tension and recommended she take the baths.

To put her mind to rest and let go of the oppressive thoughts which pursued her everywhere, she started writing her memoirs during the winter of 1855. She intended to focus on memories of her childhood, youth, marriage, and career and describe the development she had undergone:

> I will write openly, honestly, and truthfully about events and people in my life and about the development I have gradually undergone in encounters with people who have crossed my way. . . . My writings must be candid, open, forthright and truthful; after all, the recollections of a lifetime are not a story, a novel or a play.

Initially, she had little thought of anyone reading her outpourings, and she allowed herself a certain nostalgia in the descriptions of bygone times. The early sections of her memoirs seem less problematic and considerably brighter than the later years from which her writings were to serve as a means of escape. The frequently moralizing tone is especially prevalent in the third volume which depicts the actors who had opposed Johan Ludvig Heiberg as vain and capricious. She poses the "vulgar" public, the "childish" actors led by the "tactless" Hoedt under the banner of the "coarsest naturalism" and the "liberal" press in opposition to the cultured, truth-loving Johan Ludvig. Johan Ludvig "represented to my mind the fine, educated man *vis a vis* coarse and foolish arrogance, defamation and vile assailment." Heiberg wrote her memoirs between 1855 and 1890, and the gradual metamorphosis from being a story of her life to becoming a monument to her husband and his "unappreciated" work shows her never-failing sense of duty to the man who had shaped her and cultural life in Denmark for three decades.

Thomasine Gyllembourg's long life came to an end in 1856; she was 83 years old. That same summer, Johan Ludvig tended his resignation from the theater, and his wife asked for a leave of absence. Four years later, in August 1860, Johan Ludvig passed away with her hand in his. Johanne Luise Heiberg remained with the theater as an actress until 1864 and returned as a director of plays from 1867 to 1874. By then, she had adopted three little girls from the West Indies and built a house for the four of them at the outskirts of Copenhagen. There she had a room with a lock where only she could go. And there she completed the memoirs which in three different editions have invited readers to see and not see the truth of the Heibergs' public and private lives.

SOURCES:

Dalager, Stig, and Anne-Marie Mai. *Danske Kvindelige Forfattere* (in Danish). Copenhagen: Gyldendal, 1982.

Forssberger, Annalisa. *Johanne Luise Heiberg* (in Danish). Copenhagen: Nordisk Forlag, 1973.

Johanne Luise Heibergs tanker ved et slambad (in Danish). Edited by Niels Birger Wamberg. Copenhagen: Jorgen Fiskes Forlag, 1986.

Wamberg, Bodil. *Johanne Luise Heiberg* (in Danish). Copenhagen: G.E.C. Gad, 1989.

Inga Wiehl,
Yakima Valley Community College, Yakima, Washington

Heiden, Beth (1959—)

American speed skater. *Name variations: Beth Heiden Reid. Born in 1959 in West Allis, Wisconsin; sister of Olympic speed skater Eric Heiden; attended University of Vermont, early 1980s; married.*

Set the national record in the mile for high school girls (1975); won the World championship in speed skating in Den Haag, Netherlands (1979); won the World championship in bicycling in Sallanches, France (1980); won the bronze medal in 3,000-meter speed skating at the Olympic Games in Lake Placid, New York (1980); won the NCAA Cross Country Ski championship in Bozeman, Montana (1983).

Beth Heiden

Beth Heiden was born in West Allis, Wisconsin, in 1959 and grew up experiencing the harsh Wisconsin winters that are so ideal for skaters. The petite Beth originally pursued figure skating, but was soon attracted to her brother Eric Heiden's sport of choice: speed skating. What she lacked in size Beth made up for in grit, overcoming her physical limitations with concentration, discipline, and determination. "There was many a time when Beth wanted to hit the ice," her brother recalled, "and I'd say, 'Aw, let's forget it today.' But her tenacity would get the better of me—and that's what made the difference between success and failure."

The Heiden siblings began training with Olympic gold-medal speed skater ***Dianne Holum** (winner of the 1500-meter race in 1972). Holum designed a program of bicycling, weightlifting, duck-walking, and many hours of skating for the duo which took its toll on the less-muscular Beth. Neither injury nor setback, however, could defeat Beth's drive, and in 1979 she outskated larger, stronger women to win a World championship.

As the 1980 Olympics approached, Beth and Eric encountered high expectations for their performances. Eric amply fulfilled American dreams of gold medals—winning five of them—while Beth finished a disappointing third in the 3,000-meter race to take the bronze. Whereas her World championship had been won on the basis of her overall performance in four events, medals are awarded separately in the Olympics for each event; although Beth, skating with an injured ankle, had the best overall performance at the Games, she could not capture the gold medal America had been hoping for. Her treatment at the hands of the press added to the disappointment of her loss, as reporters chided her for not keeping up with her brother.

Heiden then moved on to new challenges. Having bicycled extensively as part of her cross-training for speed skating, she took it up as a sport, winning a World championship in bicycle racing in 1980. She began cross-country skiing on a whim while working on a physics degree at the University of Vermont and won the NCAA championship in the 7.5-kilometer event in 1983. Beth Heiden assisted in the development of numerous extensive cross-country facilities in Michigan's upper peninsula.

SOURCES:

Connors, Martin, Diane L. Dupuis, and Brad Morgan. *The Olympic Factbook*. Detroit, MI: Visible Ink, 1992.

Johnson, Anne Janette. *Great Women in Sports*. Detroit, MI: Visible Ink, 1998.

Judith C. Reveal,
freelance writer, Greensboro, Maryland

Height, Dorothy (1912—)

American organization official who worked on behalf of civil and women's rights. *Born Dorothy Irene Height in Richmond, Virginia, on March 24, 1912; daughter of James Edward (a building contractor) and Fannie (Burroughs) Height; graduated from Rankin High School, Rankin, Pennsylvania; New York University, B.A. and M.A.; attended New York School of Social Work; never married; no children.*

Distinguished for her untiring work as a champion of civil and women's rights, Dorothy Irene Height served over three decades as president of the National Council of Negro Women (NCNW), which, founded by ***Mary McLeod Bethune** in 1935, had as its mission "to unite middle- and upper-class black women in humanitarian causes and social action programs." Trained as a social worker, Height spent most of her professional career with the Young Women's Christian Association (YWCA), where she rose to the post of associate director of leadership training services and director of the Office for Racial Justice.

Raised in the small mining town of Rankin, Pennsylvania, where her family moved in 1916, Height spent much of her early life in church. "My mother, who was a nurse, did a lot of work through the church missionary society," she told **Maria Eckman** of the New York *Post* (April 18, 1972). "I sort of followed her around and got into the idea of organizing clubs." Height was an exemplary student all through school; in high school, she was a prize debater and, at 5'9½", a center on the basketball team. Upon graduation, she applied to Barnard College but was turned away; the school had already reached its self-determined limit with two black students. Height ended up at New York University, graduating in 1933, with a master's degree in educational psychology. She spent her early career as a caseworker in the New York City Department of Welfare and took courses at the New York School of Social Work in order to strengthen her background.

In 1937, Height began working with the YWCA, where she steadily rose through the executive ranks, becoming director of the Emma Ransom House in New York City, and then assuming the executive directorship of the ***Phillis Wheatley** YWCA in Washington, D.C. There, she also joined the Delta Sigma Theta Sorority, working on a national project aimed at increasing job opportunities for black women. Height became president of the sorority in 1944, and during her nine-year tenure expanded the organization's focus to include the relationship between black women in America and in Third World countries. Height also assisted in the formation of an international chapter of the sorority and, on the home front, helped organize bookmobiles and a series of nationally broadcast town meetings.

Dorothy Height

In 1957, after stepping down as head of Delta Sigma Theta, Height became president of the National Council of Negro Women, where she became a driving force in a variety of economic, political, and social issues affecting black women. Under her leadership, the organization sponsored training sessions, conferences, and career meetings for young people and focused attention on problems of educational inequity and teen-age pregnancy. During the civil-rights movement of the 1960s, the NCNW held voter registration drives in the South and voter education drives in the North. In conjunction with the Student Nonviolent Coordinating Committee (SNCC), they also raised funds to aid students who postponed college to participate in the struggle.

In the 1980s, the organization was involved of the revival of black family life through the recognition of historical, traditional, and cultural values. In 1986, Height founded the "Black Family Reunion Celebration," intended to counter negative images of black life depicted in the media. The *Wall Street Journal* praised the celebrations as possibly "the best thing that ever happened to the black underclass." Height has led the council in numerous other projects, including the publication *Black Woman's Voice* and the establishment of the Women's Center for Education and Career Advancement, an information center for minority women in nontraditional jobs. She was also largely responsible for the erection of the Bethune Memorial statue, the first monument of an African-American ever erected in a public park in Washington, D.C.

Height, who never married, lived for many years in a Harlem apartment, where she loved to cook both soul food and unusual foreign dishes. Her other interests include reading, music, and singing coloratura in vocal groups. She has been the recipient of numerous awards and honors, including the John F. Kennedy Memorial Award of the National Council of Jewish Women, the Elks Lovejoy award, and the 1966 Ernest O. Melby Award of the Alumni Association of New York University's School of Education. In 1994, she received the Presidential Medal of Freedom, the nation's greatest civil honor.

On September 15, 1998, **Hillary Clinton**, ***Oprah Winfrey**, ***Maya Angelou**, and **Jessye Norman**, among others, gathered at the Grand Hyatt Washington to pay tribute to Height who was given less than her share of recognition as a leader at the center of the struggle. "She was there every step of the way," said John Lewis, but "the leadership of the civil rights movement was very chauvinistic." Height was unconcerned: "If you worry about who is going to get credit, you don't get much work done."

SOURCES:

Moritz, Charles, ed. *Current Biography 1972*. NY: H.W. Wilson, 1972.

Smith, Jessie Carney, ed. *Notable Black American Women*. Detroit, MI: Gale Research, 1992.

"Unsung Heroine," in *People Weekly*. October 19, 1998, p. 107.

Barbara Morgan,
Melrose, Massachusetts

Heilbron, Rose (1914—)

English lawyer. *Name variations: Dame Rose Heilbron. Born in England in 1914; attended Belvedere School, Liverpool; graduated from Liverpool University, 1935; received LL.M. from Gray's Inn, 1937; married Dr. Nathaniel Burstein, in 1945; children: one daughter.*

An honor graduate of Liverpool University, Dame Rose Heilbron studied law on scholarship at Gray's Inn, receiving her LL.M. in 1937. She was called to the bar in 1939, and her legal career advanced rapidly. A Queen's Counsel, she was appointed recorder of Burnley on December 5, 1956, a post she held until 1974. In 1974, she was appointed second High Court Judge (after ***Elizabeth Lane**), on the Northern Circuit in the Family Division. She advanced to Presiding Judge of the Northern Circuit in 1979. Heilbron was married to Dr. Nathaniel Burstein in 1937. She was made DBE in 1974 and served as chair of the Home Secretary's Advisory Group on Rape in 1975.

Heilly, Anne d'.

See Étampes, Anne de Pisseleu d'Heilly, Duchesse d' (1508–c. 1580).

Heim-Vögtlin, Marie (1845–1916).

See Vögtlin, Marie.

Heinecke, Iraida (c. 1895–1990).

See Odoevtseva, Irina.

Heinel, Anna (1753–1808)

German ballerina. *Born in Bayreuth, Germany, on October 4, 1753; died in 1808; married Gaëtan Vestris (a dancer and choreographer), around 1792; children: son Adolphe-Apoline-Marie-Angiolo Vestris (b. May 1791); (stepchild) Auguste Vestris.*

Ballerina Anna Heinel, renowned for introducing the *pirouette à la seconde* (multiple pirouette), was dubbed by the French *La Belle Statue*. She was born in Bayreuth, Germany, in 1753 and began dancing, at age 14, at the highly respected opera house in Stuttgart. Shortly thereafter, in 1768, she debuted at the Paris Opéra in *danse noble,* impressing critics with her tall, stately figure and, of course, her dazzling pirouette. Heinel had affairs with the Prince de Conti and Comte de Laraguais (the husband of ***Sophie Arnould**).

Heinel became extremely popular at the Opéra, even eclipsing the renowned dancer and choreographer Gaëtan Vestris, who was reputedly so jealous that he used his position as ballet master to discredit her. When he tried to hide her in minor roles, the public hissed Vestris and sided with Heinel. Even so, the backstage mood was so unpleasant that she asked for a leave of absence.

Heinel finally took refuge in England, where she contracted at the King's Opera House in 1771. She returned to Paris in 1776 and appeared as Roxane in *Apelles et Campaspe*, which was staged by Jean Georges Noverre as his first offering in Paris. Over the next few years, Heinel's ongoing feud with Gaëtan Vestris apparently dissolved, and the two fell in love. An astonished public learned that Heinel had taken up with her former nemesis, and both had applied to the directors for permission to retire to pursue family life. Vestris was then 53, Heinel 29. They were eventually married in time to welcome their son in May 1791.

SOURCES:

Migel, Parmenia. *The Ballerinas: From the Court of Louis XIV to Pavlova*. NY: Macmillan, 1972.

Heink, Ernestine Schumann- (1861–1936).

See Schumann-Heink, Ernestine.

Heiss-Jenkins, Carol (1940—)

American figure skater who won more international titles than any North American woman skater. *Name variations: Carol Heiss. Born Carol Elizabeth Heiss in New York City on January 20, 1940; first child of Marie (Gademann) Heiss (a textile designer) and Edward Heiss (a baker); both parents were from Germany; sister of skater* ***Nancy Heiss****; attended New York University; married Hayes Alan Jenkins (a figure-skating champion), in 1960.*

Carol Heiss-Jenkins was born in New York City in 1940, the daughter of **Marie Gademann Heiss**, a textile designer, and Edward Heiss, a baker. Her love of figure skating came innocently enough with a pair of roller skates, given to her when she was four. Seeing her obvious talent, her parents decided to put her on ice skates, and she began to practice at the Brooklyn Ice Palace where she made her first amateur appearance at age six. At eight, Heiss started lessons with Pierre Brunet and **Andrée Joly**, world pair champions, and practiced five to eight hours a day for the next few years. Because the financial demands of competitive figure skating are high, Heiss' parents, who were German immigrants working to establish themselves in a new country, scrimped so that their daughter could continue skating. In 1951, Heiss won the National Novice title; the following year, she took the National Junior championship. In 1953, as the youngest member of the U.S. team competing for the World championship in Davos, Switzerland, the 13-year-old finished fourth.

Heiss was well on her way to establishing her preeminence in the skating world when she had a serious accident in 1954. During practice, she collided with her sister whose skate severed the tendon on Heiss' left leg. For several months, the injury took Carol off the ice, but by 1955 she had sufficiently recovered to place second behind ***Tenley Albright**, five years her senior, in the 1955 World Ladies Singles championship in Vienna. For two years, from 1953 to 1955, Albright would be her major competitor, placing first in every event while Heiss consistently placed second. In 1956, when Heiss journeyed to Cortina, Italy, as the youngest girl to skate for the United States in the Winter Olympics, she had promised her terminally ill mother she would win the gold medal. But the narrow margin of victory handed Albright the gold (169.6 points) over Heiss' silver (168.1) and sparked rumors of conflict between the two girls. True or not, the stories added to the drama when, two weeks later, Heiss met Albright again at the World championship in Garmisch-Partenkirchen, West Germany. Finally, Heiss outscored her opponent with 5.9s from all nine judges. At 16, she had won her first World title. "The tears she had never shed," reported *Life*, "when time and again she lost to her perennial rival, Tenley Albright, finally slid down Carol Heiss's cheeks."

Not long after this triumph, her mother died of cancer (October 1956), and Heiss greatly missed her chief supporter. But she went on to win four straight U.S. National Ladies Singles titles (1957 to 1960), four consecutive World titles (1956 to 1959), and two North American crowns (1958 and 1959). It surprised no one that she was the favorite at the 1960 Squaw Valley Olympics, where her graceful performance easily earned her the women's figure skating title and the Olympic gold medal. Her "magnificent exhibition in the free skating stirred a capacity crowd of 8,500 to tears and cheers," claimed the official U.S. Olympic Committee (USOC) report. "Clad in crimson costume, embellished with spangles and a tiara in her blonde hair, she bedazzled the judges, her opposition, and the spectators with her sheer artistry."

That same year, Heiss married Hayes Alan Jenkins, also a figure-skating champion, and retired to devote her efforts to teaching and coaching. (One of her students was **Tania Kwiatkowski**, national silver medalist in 1996.) Many American champions like *__Peggy Fleming__ and *__Dorothy Hamill__ would follow in Carol Heiss' footsteps, but none would win as many competitions. Her domination of women's figure skating during the last half of the 1950s helped establish the popularity of the sport among millions of Americans.

SOURCES:

Hollander, Phyllis. *100 Greatest Women in Sports*. NY: Grosset & Dunlap, 1976.

Moritz, Charles. *Current Biography, 1959*. NY: H.W. Wilson, 1960.

The Olympic Story. Danbury, CT: Grolier, 1979.

Parker, Robert. *Carol Heiss: Olympic Queen*. Garden City, NY: Doubleday, 1961.

Woolum, Janet. *Outstanding Women Athletes: Who They Are and How They Influenced Sports in America*. Phoenix, AZ: Oryx Press, 1992.

RELATED MEDIA:

Heiss gamely played the part of Snow White in the 1961 movie *Snow White and the Three Stooges*, starring the inevitable Larry, Moe, and Curly.

Karin L. Haag,
freelance writer, Athens, Georgia

Heiter, Amalie (1794–1870).

See Amalie of Saxony.

Helaria (fl. 6th c.)

Deaconess of the early Frankish church. *Flourished in the 6th century in France; daughter of Remy, bishop of Rheims; never married; no children.*

Helaria belonged to a small group of ordained women of France in the early Middle Ages. Her father Remy's influential position as bishop of Rheims (he was eventually canonized) may have affected the Frankish Church's decision to consecrate Helaria as a deaconess after she was widowed. She was a highly educated woman whose upbringing taught her to dedicate her life to serving God. In the 6th century, numerous women like Helaria were consecrated. The office of deaconess proved highly problematic for the early Christian church; a woman in such a position, who was always a widow, was granted the spiritual authority to act as a priest, was allowed to administer the sacraments, and was permitted to travel and preach as a cleric.

Laura York,
Riverside, California

Helburn, Theresa (1887–1959)

American theatrical producer, director, and playwright, who served as co-director of the Theatre Guild in New York. *Name variations: Terry Helburn. Born on January 12, 1887, in New York City; died on August 18, 1959, in Weston, Connecticut; younger child and only daughter of Julius Helburn (a businessman) and Hannah (Peyser) Helburn; graduated from the Winsor School, Boston, Massachusetts, 1903; Bryn Mawr College, B.A., 1908; attended the Sorbonne, Paris, France, 1913; married John Baker Opdycke (a high school English teacher and author), in 1919 (died 1956); no children.*

Under the co-direction of Theresa Helburn and Lawrence Langner, the Theatre Guild was one of the most successful ventures of America's little theater movement, which flourished during the second decade of the 20th century. During her 30-year association with the Guild, Helburn was a leading force in the development of the American theater, helping to bring to attention numerous playwrights, actors, and designers.

Helburn was born in New York City in 1887 on West 46th Street, which later became the heart of the theater district. As a child, she was educated at home, where her mother **Hannah Peyser Helburn** ran an experimental primary school. Theresa, known as Terry, attended her first play, at age nine, and was captivated. "I entered a world that was unlike anything I have ever imagined, but that I recognized at once as my own," she later recalled. "The theater was not a dream, or a goal—it was home."

When the family moved to Boston in 1900, Helburn entered the exclusive Winsor School, graduating in 1903. At Bryn Mawr College, which offered no drama courses at the time, she wrote her sophomore thesis on the plays of Arthur Wing Pinero, obtaining her source material from the Philadelphia Library. She also produced, directed, and acted in all of the college plays, often driving herself to the point of exhaustion. After graduating with numerous honors, she enrolled in George Pierce Baker's playwriting class (English 47) at Radcliffe.

Following a modest social debut in 1910, she moved to New York and immersed herself in writing, achieving some success publishing her verses and short stories. She was active in the Poetry Society of America and also joined a weekly play-reading group, where she met Lawrence Langner, a Welsh patent attorney with a passion for theater. The group, which included Lee Simonson, a theater designer, and Philip Moeller, a director, later established the Washington Square Players, an amateur group dedicated to producing plays of artistic worth.

In 1913, fresh from a year in Paris, Helburn was invited to act in the Players' first production, a play by Langner entitled *Licensed*. Two weeks into rehearsal, however, Helburn's family, who disapproved of her acting, discovered the play was about birth control and yanked her from the cast. (Ironically, Helburn appeared on stage many years later in another Langner play, *Suzanna and the Elders*, which dealt with the subject of free love and multiple marriages.)

Having no intention of giving up the theater, Helburn took up her playwriting in earnest, finishing her first drama, *Enter the Hero*, in 1916. Accepted by the Washington Square Players for production, it went into rehearsal with poet ***Edna St. Vincent Millay** in a major role. Unfortunately, Millay was not much of an actress, and the play was ultimately abandoned. Several of Helburn's subsequent plays, including *Prince Prigio*, *Crops and Croppers,* and *Denbigh*, were produced without much success, although down through the years they have resurfaced as community theater productions.

Helburn rounded out her theater apprenticeship by serving as a drama critic for *The Nation* during 1918, the same year that Langner reorganized the Washington Square Players as a subscription-based repertory company called the Theatre Guild. (The name harkened back to the medieval trade guilds, known for their cooperative organization and pride in craft.) The Guild included original members of the Washington Square Players, Moeller, and Simonson, as well as newcomers actress ***Helen Westley**, banker Maurice Wertheim, and artist Rollo Peters. Helburn was recruited as a playreader for the fledgling group, but during a managerial crisis in 1919, she stepped in as executive secretary. That year, she also married John Baker Opdycke, an English teacher, who went on to author some 20 books on prose style and advertising technique.

The Theatre Guild's early mission was to produce plays of substance and quality, and it also served as a protest against the commercially minded producers that dominated the Broadway scene. During the first season, the group presented two plays, the first of which, *Bonds of Inter-*

Theatre Guild Board of Managers, including Theresa Helburn (seated center), with Helen Westley to her left.

est by Jacinto Benavente, was produced on a shoestring and lasted only a few weeks. Opening night was disastrous. Due to budgetary constraints, the leading lady's dress had been fashioned out of oil cloth which was painted gold to simulate a more luxurious fabric. "The actress stood up to make an exit," said Helburn, "and her chair came up with her. When Dudley Digges, who was playing opposite her, gently plucked the chair away from the dress—it left a great white patch." The Guild's second production, *John Ferguson* by St. John Ervine, proved to be an artistic and financial success, providing a much-needed transfusion to the operating budget and establishing the Guild as one of New York's viable new art theaters. Helburn, who had impressed board members with her innate business sense and her quick grasp of theater management and production, was promoted to executive director. With the new title came a membership on the Guild's board, and an equal voice in the selection and casting of new plays.

By the end of its first decade, the Theatre Guild had built its own playhouse in the Broadway district and boasted 25,000 patrons. Between 1926 and 1928, it produced 14 successful new productions, an unprecedented number. Much of the early success can be directly attributed to Helburn. It was through her insistence that Alfred Lunt and ***Lynn Fontanne** were cast together in *The Guardsman* (1924), which established them as the most distinguished acting team in America. Helburn also fought against the censorship of Eugene O'Neill's *Strange Interlude* (1928) and was instrumental in producing the plays of S.N. Behrman and Philip Barry.

In 1934, reacting to dissension on the board, Helburn took a leave of absence to work in films. For a year, she was a producer for Columbia Pictures, but she missed the theater and returned to New York in 1935, to take up once more with the Guild. While in California, however, Helburn, with the help of seven major film companies, had organized the Bureau of New Plays, which held several national competitions for new playwrights and then sponsored seminars for the winners. When she returned to New York, the seminars were transferred to the New School for Social Research, under her directorship.

In the late 1930s, after a succession of failures brought growing economic and managerial concerns, the Guild reorganized, replacing the six-member board with Helburn and Langner as co-directors, and bending the mission to embrace more commercial offerings. Helburn's role expanded considerably to include not only play selection, but all aspects of production. Still, much of her managerial effort was devoted to working with playwrights in developing scripts, and she often rankled some of the writers in her role as "play doctor." Several major playwrights, including Maxwell Anderson, Sidney Howard, Elmer Rice, and Robert E. Sherwood, became so disgruntled that they left the Guild to form the Playwrights Company. More often than not, however, Helburn's instincts were on the mark. In 1943, when the Guild was once again on the brink of bankruptcy, she had the idea to turn the play *Green Grow the Lilacs* by Lynn Riggs into a musical, and she brought together Richard Rodgers and Oscar Hammerstein II to write it. The resulting production, *Oklahoma!*, with its tightly integrated music, story, setting, and dance (choreographed by ***Agnes de Mille**), not only saved the Guild but changed musical comedy forever. Two years later, Helburn once again enlisted Rodgers and Hammerstein to rework Ferenc Molnar's play *Lilliom* which they turned into the musical *Carousel* (1945), another smash hit for the Guild.

Opposite page

Anna Held

An elfin woman, snub-nosed and crinkly-eyed, Helburn was described by Lawrence Langner as having nerves "like whipcord," and will-power "like steel." Richard Rodgers thought her "the quietest and most imperturbable woman I've ever known," but added that during her later years she turned into something of a character. Helburn and her husband, who died in 1956, maintained an apartment in New York City, and spent weekends in their Connecticut country home called Terrytop, "Terry" being Helburn's nickname. She remained active in the Theatre Guild until 1953, when her health began to fail. She died of a heart attack on August 18, 1959, at her Connecticut home. Helburn's memoir, *A Wayward Quest* (1960), was completed after her death by her assistant **Elinore Denniston.**

SOURCES:

Current Biography. NY: H.W. Wilson, 1944.

Rodgers, Richard. "A Remembrance of Terry," in *Critics Choice.* Vol. 3, no. 3. November 1969.

Sicherman, Barbara, and Carol Hurd Green, eds. *Notable American Women: The Modern Period.* Cambridge, MA: The Belknap Press of Harvard University Press, 1980.

Wilmeth, Don B., and Tice L. Miller, eds. *Cambridge Guide to American Theatre.* MA: Cambridge University Press, 1993.

SUGGESTED READING:

Eaton, W.P. *The Theatre Guild: The First Ten Years.* New York, 1920.

Nadel, Norman. *A Pictorial History of the Theatre Guild.* Crown, 1969.

Waldau, R. *Vintage Years of the Theatre Guild, 1928–1939*. Cleveland, OH, 1972.

Barbara Morgan,
Melrose, Massachusetts

Held, Anna (c. 1865–1918)

Polish-born musical entertainer who became an American theatrical legend. *Born in Warsaw, Poland, on March 18, around 1865; died in New York City on August 12, 1918; daughter of Maurice (a glove-maker) and Yvonne (Pierre) Held; married Maximo Carrera (a tobacco planter), in 1894 (divorced around 1896); married Florenz Ziegfeld (theatrical producer), in 1897 (divorced 1913); children: (first marriage) one daughter, Liane.*

The facts surrounding Anna Held's early life have been obscured by the extravagant publicity that made her a legend of the American theater. Her memoirs, published years after her death, only add to the confusion. She was born in Warsaw, Poland, on March 18, around 1865, to French parents, Maurice (sometimes seen as Shimmle) and Yvonne (sometimes seen as Hélène) Held. According to her memoirs, she was the last of 11 children; the others died young. She also wrote that her mother was a devout Catholic who raised her in that faith, although other sources suggest that Held was Jewish. Around 1871, the family moved to Paris, which Held later claimed as her birthplace. When she was 12, her father was taken ill, and Held went to work as a seamstress to help the family's dwindling finances.

After her father's death in 1855, Held and her mother went to London to seek lost relatives. Finding none, they barely scraped by until Held joined Jacob Adler's Yiddish Theatre. Held was with Adler for five years, until the company disbanded. She then found her niche as a music-hall comedian. Capitalizing on her considerable endowments, which included a laced 18-inch waist and large expressive brown eyes, she cultivated a "naughty" French stage persona that quickly made her one of the most popular stars in Europe. In 1894, shortly after her successful Paris debut, Held was secretly married to Maximo Carrera, a wealthy South American tobacco planter 20 years her senior.

During a London engagement in 1895, Held came to the attention of the young American theater impresario Florenz Ziegfeld, who, after seeing her perform, wangled an introduction to the star by sending a diamond bracelet and a basket of rare orchids to her dressing room. It

took Ziegfeld one hour to convince Held to sign a contract with him and come to America. Before departing for her new life, however, she gave birth to her only child, Liane, whom she sent off to Paris with a nurse; she also separated from her husband. Carrera, according to ***Billie Burke**, Ziegfeld's second wife, was a reasonable man who recognized that he was too old for Held and, though it broke his heart, let her go with "the lucky American." Held and Carrera would divorce a year later. Around the time of her arrival in the United States, Held took up residence with Ziegfeld, and in 1897 or 1898, the two were married in what was apparently a common-law ceremony.

Held made her American debut at New York's Herald Square Theater in September 1896, in a Ziegfeld revival of the farce *A Parlor Match*, in which she charmed audiences with a song that became something of a trademark, "Won't You Come and Play Wiz Me?" Most critics found her delightful, although some thought her Parisian mannerisms a little too suggestive. Coinciding with Held's debut, Ziegfeld launched a publicity blitz about his new star that fascinated an eager public. It was written that she bathed daily in gallons of milk, and that she chased a runaway horse on her bicycle to rescue a former Brooklyn magistrate. In her autobiography *With a Feather on My Nose*, Billie Burke recounts how Ziegfeld contrived a well-publicized bet with movie director Julius Steger, in which Steger wagered he could kiss Held 200 times without losing his vigor. "The contest ended at one hundred and fifty-two kisses, Anna pale with exhaustion and Steger wobbly—or so the story goes."

Held subsequently starred in a series of light musical farces, including *The French Maid* (1898), *Papa's Wife* (1899), in which she also toured, *The Little Duchess* (1901), *Mlle. Napoleon* (1903), and *Higgledy-Piggledy* (1904), the first show that Ziegfeld produced with Joseph Weber after Weber's separation from Lew Fields. (The collaboration between Ziegfeld and Weber was short-lived due to artistic differences.) In *Parisian Model* (1906), Held created a sensation with the Gus Edwards' song, "I Just Can't Make My Eyes Behave."

According to Burke, Held was the first to suggest the *Follies*, those dazzling productions celebrating the comely side of American womanhood that drove Ziegfeld's career for the next 20 years. *Follies of 1907*, the first outing, was a triumph for Held. The show presented her in a series of extravagant costumes, displayed one after another, in front of a chorus in flesh-colored tights. As a result, American women rushed out to buy Anna Held corsets, cosmetics, and cigars. Unfortunately, Held would not benefit from subsequent *Follies*. In 1908, after the musical *Miss Innocence*, she left for Paris, claiming that Ziegfeld was never home and, when he was, never talked to her. "He was exhibiting that 'withdrawn' quality which later became so familiar to me," wrote Burke, "and which I finally understood." In 1912, Held began divorce proceedings, believing that Ziegfeld would never permit it, "but he did permit it," Burke said, "and it broke her heart."

Held continued to perform in America and abroad and, in 1915, made her only movie, *Madame la Présidente*. But, according to Burke, her final years were unhappy. "In spite of her enormous acclaim as a wicked French actress who performed naughtily on the stage, Anna was a *hausfrau*. She was frugal, domestic, and maternal." In November 1916, Held opened in the musical *Follow Me*. While touring with the show in Milwaukee in January 1918, she was stricken with what was diagnosed variously as myeloma and pernicious anemia. (Some reports say that her illness was the result of years of tight corseting causing pinching of her internal organs.) She recovered sufficiently to return to New York, where she died the following August at the age of 45. At the end, Flo Ziegfeld did not forget Held, asking his wife Billie Burke to send her some things to help her through her illness. "I did," writes Burke. "I was glad to. I sent fresh eggs, baby broilers, fresh vegetables and butter . . . daily, and my own doctor. But it was too late."

SOURCES:

Burke, Billie, with Cameron Shipp. *With a Feather on My Nose*. NY: Appleton-Century-Crofts, 1949.

James, Edward T., ed. *Notable American Women 1607–1950*. Cambridge, MA: The Belknap Press of Harvard University Press, 1971.

Wilmeth, Don B., and Tice L. Miller, eds. *Cambridge Guide to American Theatre*. MA: Cambridge University Press, 1993.

Barbara Morgan,
Melrose, Massachusetts

Heldman, Gladys (1922—)

American sports magazine editor who was a major force behind women's tennis. *Born Gladys Medalie on May 13, 1922, in New York City; daughter of George Z. and Carrie (Waplan) Medalie; graduated from Stanford, B.A., 1942; University of California at Berkeley, M.A., 1943; married Julius D. Heldman (a tennis player), on June 15, 1942; children: Carrie Medalie Heldman; Julie Medalie Heldman (b. 1945).*

Gladys Heldman began playing tennis after her second child, tennis-player ***Julie Heldman**, was born. As an amateur tennis player from 1945 to 1954, Gladys ranked #2 in the southwest and #1 in Texas. She also played doubles with ***Althea Gibson** from 1953 to 1954 and won a berth on the Wimbledon team. Her tennis career ended on a Wimbledon backcourt in the first round; Heldman did not take a single set. "It's all right, I still love you," shouted her tennis-player husband from a bleacher seat. "Only not as much."

Fortunately for world tennis, and especially women's tennis, Heldman stayed with the game but in a different capacity. In 1953, she launched, published, and began to edit *World Tennis* magazine; by the mid-1960s, *World Tennis* would have a circulation of 43,000 and would be the most successful tennis magazine in the world. With Pancho Gonzales, she also wrote *The Book of Tennis*. Heldman underwrote the U.S. Lawn Tennis Association's 1959 National Indoor championship when the USLTA considered its cancellation because of continued losses. That year, she put the event into the profit column. It was also Heldman who paid to recruit foreign talent for the U.S. Open at Forest Hills.

In 1970, though tennis was becoming more and more popular, the disparity of prize money between the men and women players was widening. The reason was simple; men ran, owned, and promoted the tournaments, and they had very convincing arguments woven into a strangulated syllogism: (1) men's games were longer; (2) men could beat women; (3) therefore, few people would come to watch women play. "If we women were seemingly powerless in the first years of open tennis," wrote ***Billie Jean King**, "we were blessed with an important ally in Gladys Medalie Heldman, a forward-thinking woman who had always believed that women could work and have careers if they wanted them." Heldman made it a habit of documenting the inequities in her magazine. For example, when the prize money for the women's singles event was less than the prize money for the men's doubles winner in the 1970 Australian Open, Heldman raised cain.

Then, in 1971, Jack Kramer began promoting a tournament and was offering prize money on a ratio of 12 to 1 in favor of the men. Heldman approached Kramer and begged him to change the ratio but was unsuccessful. She decided that the only way for women to be treated decently at a tournament was to hold their own. It would be held in Houston . . . as an alternative to Kramer's. Though the USLTA was up in arms and threatened women who chose Houston with suspension, the women held firm. Meanwhile, Gladys Heldman was speaking with her friend Joe Cullman of Philip Morris for sponsorship money. A sympathetic Cullman offered her prize money and the use of the name Virginia Slims; Heldman personally added about $100,000. Nine players signed one-dollar contracts with Heldman and began their September 1970 tour (**Valerie Ziegenfuss**, Billie Jean King, **Nancy Richey**, **Peaches Bartkowicz**, ***Rosie Casals**, **Kristy Pigeon**, **Judy Dalton**, **Kerry Melville**, and Julie Heldman). The tour quickly grew with the addition of ***Françoise Durr**, **Ann Jones**, and **Betty Stove** from the Netherlands.

"From her forum, Gladys made enemies," wrote King, "hundreds of them. She edited every word in her magazine, and every month she and her staff blasted the governing officials of tennis for their archaic and self-serving rules. The male hierarchy disliked her intensely; they wanted tennis to stay the same, and Gladys represented change."

Heldman, Julie (1945—)

American tennis champion. *Born Julie Medalie Heldman in Berkeley, California on December 8, 1945; daughter of Gladys (Medalie) Heldman (b. 1922, a publisher and tennis player) and Julius Heldman (a tennis player who also worked on the Manhattan Project); graduated Stanford University, 1966; married Bernard Weiss (a businessman), in 1978.*

Won the Italian Open, the Maccabiah Games, and played #1 for the U.S. in the Wightman Cup competition (1969); a graduate of UCLA Law School, became an attorney after retiring from professional tennis (1975); became a television commentator and was the first woman to give commentary on a men's tennis tournament (1976).

Julie Heldman's parents both played tennis so it was natural for her to take up the game as a young girl. Her father Julius Heldman won the National Junior championship in 1936 and her mother Gladys was a champion at Texas State in the early 1950s. In 1953, ***Gladys Heldman** founded *World Tennis* magazine. In 1954, Julie Heldman was sent to Hoxie Tennis Camp in Hamtramck, Michigan, America's first tennis campsite. For seven summers, she would attend Hoxie. In 1958, Heldman won the Canadian Junior championship and, in 1960, the U.S. National. Graduating from high school at 16, Heldman entered Stanford which had no women's tennis team at the time. In 1963, like her father, she won the National Junior tournament title. In 1966, she swept all five of her matches in the Federation Cup tournament, a five-nation event held in Turin, Italy.

Graduating from Stanford in 1966 with a degree in history, Heldman left tennis and went to live in a commune in Woodside, California. When this quickly got old, she began playing competitively again. In 1969, she won the Italian Open, as well as singles, doubles, and mixed doubles in the Maccabiah Games. At that time, Heldman was ranked #2 in the United States and #5 in the world. Injury in 1970 forced Heldman off the court for a time, and in 1972 she underwent surgery for torn cartilage in her knee. Training with **Angela Buxton** and Jimmy Jones, Heldman overcame her injuries and had a better year in 1974, but a shoulder injury in 1975 terminated her professional tennis career. Heldman began writing articles for *World Tennis* and worked as a television commentator. She was the first woman to comment on a men's tennis tournament, the Avis Challenge Cup in Hawaii in 1976. Heldman entered University of California at Los Angeles (UCLA) law school in 1978, the year she married, and joined a law firm in 1982.

SOURCES:

Robertson, Max, ed. *The Encyclopedia of Tennis*. London: George Allen & Unwin, 1974.

Slater, Robert. *Great Jews in Sports*. Middle Village, NY: Jonathan David, 1983.

Karin Loewen Haag,
freelance writer, Athens, Georgia

Heldy, Fanny (1888–1973)

Belgian soprano. *Born Marguerite Virginia Emma Clementine Deceuninck on February 29, 1888, in Ath, near Liège, Belgium; died on December 13, 1973, in Passy, France; studied at Liège Conservatory.*

Debuted at the Théatre de la Monnaie in Brussels (1910); debuted at the Opéra-Comique in Paris (1917); appeared at the Teatro alla Scala and Covent Garden (1926).

For 20 years, from 1917 until 1937, Fanny Heldy was the acknowledged star of the Opéra-Comique and the Paris Opéra. A scholarship founded in her name continues to be awarded to promising young singers. Some did not find Heldy a serious soprano and claimed that she was more interested in her racehorses than in her performances. This criticism seems unfair in light of her staying power as a star. Her voice, wrote one critic, was "never hard," but her intense presentation "would infallibly make for hardness in a less skillful artist." However, it is still felt that a hardness in the ringing quality and a tone too bright for comfort can be detected in recordings Heldy made. This hardness, however, emerges in her later recordings while the earlier ones have a freshness and charm which established Heldy as a perennial favorite in France.

John Haag,
Athens, Georgia

Helen.

Variant of Yelena.

Helen (fl. 1100s)

Queen of Sweden. *Flourished in the 1100s; married Inge I the Elder, king of Sweden (r. 1080–1110, 1112–1125); children:* ***Katerina Ingesdottir*** *(who married Bjorn, prince of Denmark); ****Christina of Sweden*** *(d. 1122); ****Margaret Frithpoll*** *(d. 1130); Rognvald of Sweden. Inge I was also married to* ***Maer.***

Helen (fl. 1275)

Countess of Mar. *Flourished around 1275; became countess of Mar in 1291; more than likely a daughter of Llywelyn the Great (b. 1173), prince of Wales; married Malcolm (MacDuff), earl of Fife (r. 1228–1266); married Donald, 6th (some say 10th) earl of Mar (died around 1292); children: (first marriage) Colbran, earl of Fife; (second marriage) Gratney or Gartnait, 7th earl of Mar (d. before September 1305);* ***Margaret of Mar*** *(who married John of Strathbogie, earl of Atholl); ****Isabella of Mar*** *(d. 1296).*

Helen (b. 1950)

Rumanian princess. *Name variations: Princess Helen; Helen Hohenzollern; Helen Medforth-Mills. Born on November 15, 1950, in Lausanne, Switzerland; daughter of Michael, king of Rumania, and ****Anne of Bourbon-Parma*** *(b. 1923); married Robin Medforth-Mills, on July 20, 1983; children: Nicholas (b. 1985).*

Helen Asen of Bulgaria (d. 1255?)

Nicaean empress. *Name variations: Helena. Died around 1255; daughter of Asen II also known as Ivan Asen II, ruler of Bulgaria (r. 1218–1241); married Theodore II Lascaris, Nicaean emperor (r. 1254–1258); children: ****Irene Lascaris*** *(d. around 1270, who married Constantine Tich, tsar of Bulgaria); ****Maria*** *(who married Nicephorus I of Epirus); John IV Lascaris, Nicaean emperor (b. 1251, r. 1258–1261).*

A Bulgarian princess, daughter of King Ivan Asen II, Helen Asen was brought to the Nicaean court as a child where she grew up as Theodore II Lascaris' intended bride. She had at least two daughters and one son before her early demise.

Helen of Denmark (d. 1233)

Duchess of Brunswick-Luneburg. *Died on November 22, 1233; daughter of ****Sophie of Russia*** *(c. 1140–1198) and Valdemar also known as Waldemar I the Great (1131–1182), king of Denmark (r. 1157–1182); married William of Winchester (1184–1213), duke of Brunswick-Luneburg, in July 1202; children: Otto I Puer also known as Otto the Child (1204–1252), duke of Brunswick-Luneburg (r. 1235–1252).*

Helen of Gnesen (d. 1299).

See Yolanda of Gnesen.

Helen of Greece (1896–1982).

See Lupescu, Elena for sidebar.

Helen of Hungary (fl. mid-1000s)

Queen of Croatia. *Born around 1040; daughter of ****Richesa of Poland*** *(fl. 1030–1040) and Bela I, king of Hungary (r. 1060–1063); sister of St. Ladislas I (1040–1095), king of Hungary (r. 1077–1095) and Geza I, king of Hungary (r. 1074–1077); married Zwoinimir, king of Croatia.*

Helen of Nassau (1831–1888)

Duchess of Waldeck and Pyrmont. *Name variations: Helene or Hélène Henrietta von Nassau. Born Helen Wilhelmina Henrietta Pauline Marianne on August 12, 1831; died on October 27, 1888; daughter of William (b. 1792), duke of Nassau, and ****Pauline of Wurttemberg*** *(1810–1856); married George II Victor, prince of Waldeck and Pyrmont, on September 26, 1853; children:* ***Sophie Nicoline*** *(1854–1869);* ***Pauline Emma*** *(1855–1925, who married Alexis, 4th prince of Bentheim and Steinfurt); ****Maria of Waldeck*** *(1857–1882); ****Emma of Waldeck*** *(1858–1898, queen and regent of the Netherlands); ****Helen of Waldeck and Pyrmont*** *(1861–1922); Frederick, prince of Waldeck and Pyrmont (1865–1946); Elizabeth (b. 1873, who married Alexander, prince of Erbach-Schönberg).*

Helen of Rumania (1896–1982).

See Lupescu, Elena for sidebar on Helen of Greece.

Helen of Schleswig-Holstein (1888–1962)

Princess of Schleswig-Holstein-Sonderburg-Glücksburg. *Name variations: Helene of Schleswig-Holstein. Born on June 1, 1888; died in 1962; daughter of Frederick Ferdinand (1855–1934), duke of Schleswig-Holstein (r. 1885–1934), and ****Caroline Matilda of Schleswig-Holstein*** *(1860–1932); married Harald (son of ****Louise of Sweden*** *and Frederick VIII, king of Denmark); children:* ***Feodora Caroline-Mathilde*** *(1910–1975, who married Prince Christian Nicholas of Schaumburg-Lippe); ****Caroline Matilda of Denmark*** *(1912—);* ***Alexandrine-Louise*** *(1914–1962, who married Luitpold Alfred, count of Castell-Castell); Gorm Christian (b. 1919); Oluf (b. 1923), count of Rosenburg.*

Helen of Waldeck and Pyrmont (1861–1922)

Duchess of Albany. *Born Helene Friederike Auguste, princess of the small German principality of Waldeck-Pyrmont, in Arolsen, Hesse, Germany, on February 17, 1861; died in Hinterris, Tyrol, Austria, on September 1, 1922; daughter of George Victor, prince of Waldeck*

Helen of Waldeck and Pyrmont (1861–1922)

*and Pyrmont, and *Helen of Nassau (1831–1888); sister of *Emma of Waldeck (1858–1898, queen and regent of the Netherlands); married Leopold Saxe-Coburg (1853–1884), duke of Albany, in 1882; children: *Alice of Athlone (1883–1981); Charles Edward Saxe-Coburg, 2nd duke of Albany (1884–1954).*

Helen of Waldeck and Pyrmont (1899–1948)

Grand duchess of Oldenburg. *Name variations: Princess Helene or Hélène Bathildis Charlotte zu Waldeck. Born Helen Bathildis Charlotte Mary Fredericka on December 22, 1899; died on February 18, 1948; daughter of Frederick, prince of Waldeck and Pyrmont (1865–1946), and* ****Bathildis of Schaumburg-Lippe*** *(1873–1962); married Nicholas (b. 1897), grand duke of Oldenburg, on October 26, 1921; children: Anton (b. 1923);* ***Rixa Elizabeth*** *(1924–1939, who died after she fell from a horse); Peter (b. 1926);* ***Eilika of Oldenburg*** *(b. 1928); Egilmar (b. 1934); Frederick Augustus (b. 1936), duke of Oldenburg;* ***Altburg Elizabeth*** *(b. 1938); Hans-Frederick (b. 1940) and Huno-Frederick (b. 1940). Two years after the 1948 death of Helen of Waldeck and Pyrmont, Grand Duke Nicholas married* ***Anne-Marie von Schutzbar.***

Helen Paleologina (c. 1415–1458)

Queen of Cyprus. *Name variations: Helen Paleologa; Helen Palaeologa. Born in Greece around 1415; died in April 1458 at a Dominican monastery and was interred there; daughter of Theodore II Paleologus, despot of Morea and duke of Sparta; married John II, the Lusignan king of Cyprus (r. 1432–1458), in 1442; children: Cleopatra (died in infancy); Charlotte of Lusignan (1442–1487). John II was first married to Medea; he also had an illegitimate son, James II the Bastard, king of Cyprus (r. 1460–1473), with Marietta.*

Helen Paleologina was the daughter of Theodore II Paleologus, despot of Morea and duke of Sparta. Theodore was also the second son of the Byzantine emperor, Manuel II, whose position in relation to the Turks was extremely tenuous. Morea under Theodore's rule was Byzantium's most flourishing province: his court at Mistra harbored many intellectuals and artists, and was one of the last bastions of Byzantine culture. Thus, Helen as a child was steeped in the ancient glories of a failing civilization—a fact which would influence her adult life. In 1442, Helen married John II, the Lusignan king of Cyprus. (John's first wife, ***Medea,** died in 1440, after only a few months of marriage.)

A brief review of Cyprus' history is pertinent. In 1191, King Richard I of England (on Crusade) seized Cyprus from its rebellious Byzantine governor, Isaac Comnenus. In need of money, Richard tried to sell Cyprus to the Knights Templars, but when they could not come up with the agreed sum, he reclaimed the island and resold it to Guy of Lusignan, the dispossessed king of Jerusalem. Under Guy, Cyprus became a haven for the Franks whom the Muslims were driving from Palestine as they reclaimed lands lost to the Christians during the First Crusade. Thus supplied with a manpower base familiar with the social institutions of Western Europe, Guy built a feudal state of some power. The Lusignan dynasty enjoyed its heyday during the first three-quarters of the 14th century: for Cyprus, a period of peace and prosperity. Prosperity, however, attracted the attention of Venice and Genoa, intense rivals in the maritime trade of the eastern Mediterranean. In addition, as a remote Christian outpost, Cyprus also attracted the attentions of the Turks and Egypt, themselves by no means friendly, though both were Islamic powers. Thus, Cyprus became the epicenter of intense trade and of religious conflicts which adversely affected its prosperity. Cyprus' decline was especially precipitous after the Genoese seized Famagusta (1372), a rich emporium and a gateway for Christians to the east. In 1426, an Egyptian raid overran most of Cyprus, imperiling what the Lusignans still held of the island.

Into this hornet's nest came Helen Paleologina in 1442. She was an energetic woman with a political and cultural agenda. Extremely hostile to the Latin religious rite and to the Westerness which then dominated what had for so long been a Byzantine possession, Helen determined to re-Hellenize her adopted home. Helping her to realize this dream was her foster-brother, Thomas of Morea, who came to be much hated by Cyprus' latinized ruling establishment. Although she met much opposition, Helen became a force to be reckoned with for at least two reasons beyond the intensity of her personality. First, if Cyprus was to remain in Christian hands, it needed all the help it could get from Christian allies. Given the various rivalries which undermined the West's willingness to unify in Cyprus' interest, John II had to maintain good relations with Morea, however endangered that Byzantine province was. And second, there was John himself. When Helen came to Cyprus, she quickly took the measure of her husband and found him less interested in ruling than he should have been. As a result, she sought recognition as John's regent, even though he was both an adult and of sound mind. Ostensibly as a result of his "health," John supported her request, and Helen won her regency. As John gave himself over to self-indulgence, Helen took over the rule of Cyprus. She became a champion of Greek Orthodoxy and was intent upon releasing Cyprus' Greeks from the subjection which the various Western interests had imposed upon them since the time of Guy Lusignan. As such, she alienated the existing power structure of her kingdom to such a degree that she was presented in the worst light by our primarily Western sources. Regardless, she effectively dominated the politics of the island for 16 years, and John clearly came to fear opposing any of her policies.

With John, Helen had two daughters: Cleopatra, who died in infancy, and ***Charlotte of Lusignan**, who was her mother's hope for the future. Probably before Charlotte was born, however, John fathered a bastard son, James II, with a mistress named ***Marietta** from the Greek city of Patras (in either 1440 or 1441). James posed a real threat to Helen's ambitions, since she never produced a legitimate male heir for her husband. In addition to the political menace posed by James to Helen's line and her Hellenic ambitions, Helen seems to have been extremely jealous of Marietta—at least that would explain the fact that, at some point, to mar her rival's beauty, Helen literally bit off Marietta's nose. Henceforth, the unfortunate Marietta was commonly referred to as "Crop-nosed" and the rivalry of Helen's and Marietta's progeny intensified.

Helen Paleologina's attempt to foster the advance of Greek Orthodoxy on Cyprus was opposed by Pope Pius II in Rome, a detail which proved an obstacle in the winning of the military support Cyprus needed to maintain its freedom from Muslim control. This, and the fact that her policy of Hellenization alienated so much of the Latin establishment of Cyprus, spelled doom for the Christian control of the island. Helen's opposition rallied around James, whom John, despite his fear of Helen, favored over Charlotte as his political heir. (This despite the fact that James was impetuous in the extreme: for instance, angered by a political maneuver, James murdered Thomas of Morea, Helen's foster-brother and ally. Even though she was livid, James did not suffer any lasting punishment for his blatant crime.) In an attempt to secure Cyprus for her line, Helen sought an appropriate husband for Charlotte. Helen's preference was John of Portugal (the grandson of the king of Portugal), though her advisors suggested that he was a poor choice. In fact, Helen's advisors were correct, because after John married Charlotte (1456), he became a vocal opponent of Helen's Hellenic policy. Whether or not Helen was behind it, after raising this opposition, John died. Helen was suspected of treachery.

Charlotte's second marriage was negotiated by her father, over the objections of Helen. John chose Louis of Savoy, count of Geneva, who happened to be Charlotte's first cousin. Although marriage between cousins was permissible in the West, among the Orthodox, such marriages were anathema. Helen's disapproval, however, went for naught, because she died in April of 1458 at a Dominican monastery (where she was also buried) before this marriage was consummated. John II died three months later, and Charlotte married Louis within a year of her parents' deaths. Charlotte's only child with Louis was to be a still-born son. Louis also proved to be less than a match for James II: the latter was recognized as Cyprus' king in 1460. James' was a moot victory, however, for in 1489 the Lusignan dynasty gave way on Cyprus to the Venetian Republic (which laid claim to the island after James' death through his Venetian wife ***Caterina Cornaro**), and Venice ruled the island for 82 years. Thereafter, it fell to the Ottoman Empire.

William Greenwalt,
Associate Professor of Classical History,
Santa Clara University, Santa Clara, California

Helena.

Variant of Elena; (French) Heléna, Hélène; (German) Helene; (Italian) Elena, Eleonora and Leonora.

Helena (fl. after 333 BCE)

Ancient Greek painter who painted a famous picture of the battle of Issus. *Name variations: Helen or Helene. Flourished after 333 BCE; daughter of an otherwise unknown Timon from Egypt.*

Helena is the only name of a female painter of antiquity not mentioned by Pliny the Elder in his catalogue of women artists in the *Natural History.* For all of the scant information we possess on her career, we must look to a single sentence in the *Myriobiblion,* the encyclopedic work of a 9th-century patriarch of Constantinople named Photius. There he tells us that her father was a certain Timon, "from Egypt." Given the thoroughly Greek names of father and daughter, we can assume that they were either inhabitants of one of the Hellenistic Greek cities of the region, or Hellenized natives. We are further told by Photius that Helena "painted in her own times the battle of Issus." This battle was fought near the modern Turkish town of Iskenderun on the Gulf of Alexandretta in 333 BCE between the Greek forces of Alexander the Great and Darius III, Great King of the Persians. It resulted in the defeat of the latter, and marked the imminent fall of the Achaemenid Persian Empire and the beginning of Alexander's eastward sweep through to Northern India. It is not surprising, then, that the battle was a popular subject for contemporary and subsequent artists, and the names of several others who composed on the theme are mentioned in our classical sources.

Of Helena's famous painting, Photius tells us that the Roman emperor Vespasian (r. 69–79 CE) "relocated it in the Temple of Peace," northeast of the Roman Forum at the center of the city. Since Vespasian himself dedicated this temple in 75, and it was used to house the spoils of his eastern campaigns in Egypt and especially Jerusalem, we may surmise that Helena's already antique painting had been kept in the east previous to its appropriation by the triumphant emperor. Our information about Helena's "Issus" makes it very tempting to identify it with a well-known Pompeian mosaic on the subject, which is almost certainly a copy of a Hellenistic Greek painting. In truth, she has no more claim to the picture than any of the other ancient painters who are said to have painted on the theme. Many scholars, in fact, think it most probable that a certain Philoxenus of Eretria provided the model. In any case, this splendid mosaic, which captures a dramatic moment in the battle as Alexander watches Darius reach out towards a dying Persian noble, all against a backdrop of clashing cavalry and bristling lances, illustrates very well a major achievement of Hellenistic composition and technique, and helps us to envision in some sense the artistic milieu in which Helena worked.

SOURCES AND SUGGESTED READING:

Allgemeines Lexikon der Bildender Künstler von der Antike bis zur Gegenwart. Edited by Ulrich Thieme and Felix Becker. S.v. "Helene." Leipzig: W. Engelmann, 1908–50.

Enciclopedia dell'Arte Antica Classica e Orientiale. S.v. "Helene." Rome: Instituto della Enciclopedia Italiana, 1958–66.

Photius, Patriarch of Constantinople. *Opera Omnia.* Vol. 3. Edited by J.-P. Migne. Paris: Garnier Fratres, 1900, p. 619 [149.B].

RELATED MEDIA:

Good reproductions of the Pompeian mosaic of the battle of Issus are available in many works on Greek and Roman art; two easily accessible books with good color reproductions and brief discussions of the mosaic are John Boardman's *The Oxford History of Classical Art* (Oxford: Oxford University Press, 1993) and H.W. Jansen's *History of Art* (5th ed. revised and expanded by Anthony F. Jansen. NY: Harry N. Abrams, 1995).

Peter H. O'Brien,
Boston University, Boston, Massachusetts

Helena (c. 255–329)

Roman empress and mother of Constantine the Great who made a famous pilgrimage through the Holy Land in search of relics and the sites associated with the life of Jesus, thereby helping to set a trend in religious piety which would help to define the Middle Ages. *Pronunciation: HEL-in-a. Name variations: Saint Helena; Helena of Constantinople. Born around 255, of lowly origins, probably in northwestern Asia Minor; died around 329; buried in Rome, where her remains were long sought out by fellow Christians pilgrims; became consort, or possibly wife, of Constantius I Chlorus (Western Roman emperor with Galerius, r. 305–306), probably in the 270s (died 306); children: Flavius Valerius Aurelius Constantinus Magnus, known as Constantine I the Great (c. 285–337), Roman emperor (r. 306–337).*

Rose to the top of Roman imperial society when she became the companion of Constantius I Chlorus (probably in the 270s); had son Constantine (c. 285) but was dismissed by the father of her child when he married the daughter of one of the two Roman senior emperors in order to assure his (and Constantine's) political future; when Constantius called Constantine to the West (306), she followed in his train, to be established in the German city of Trier; became a devout Christian and may have influenced Constantine increasingly towards Christianity (which he was the first to legalize); when Constantine defeated several rivals to control the Western Empire (312), she seems to have left Trier for Rome, where she probably remained until 326, acting as her son's liaison in the West and dispensing imperial largesse; probably called East (326) to play some role in the tragedy which saw Constantine first (unjustly) execute his oldest son for treason, and then his wife; named by her son an Augusta (324), was thereafter without peer in her son's life until she died; to atone for the family murders and to help overcome the contemporary tendency for the Church to disintegrate into different theological factions, made a famous pilgrimage to the Holy Land, where she again dispensed largesse in the name of her son, built churches, and perhaps sought religious relics (this early excursus helped to establish the Medieval passion for pilgrimage, especially to the Holy Land).

Helena was born around 255 CE into what appears to have been a family of inn or barkeepers, but her birthplace is not known for certain. Long rumored to have been a native of Britain, though no historical source says so, she was more probably from northwestern Asia Minor, both because her interest in Christianity seems to have predated that of her famous son and perhaps, even more significantly, because a city rechristened "Helenopolis," apparently in her honor, lay on the Anatolian shore of the Hellespont.

Other than the fact that she was of lowly status and had to work for a living before her association with Constantius I Chlorus, one of the most important political figures of the late 3rd century CE, we know nothing of Helena's youth. Some of her near contemporaries believed her to have been of Jewish heritage, but this is by no means certain. How she even came to meet the man who would rescue her from obscurity is unknown. Nonetheless, it is probable that Helena met Constantius through her job, for he traveled much in the imperial service and frequented numerous inns and taverns while doing so. Helena was almost certainly a remarkable as well as resourceful woman, for *something* brought this lowly waitress to the attention of a highly ranked imperial magistrate and kept her at his side for an extended period within a circle which was acutely status conscious. Whether Constantius actually married Helena, however, is another question. To have been the consort of such a lofty figure would not have brought shame to a woman of Helena's origin. The best evidence that Helena remained a consort dates from the year 292, when Constantius—with little ado and no scandal—put Helena aside in favor of an expedient marriage to a woman named ⊱ **Theodora**—who was quite a political catch, being the stepdaughter of Maximian, the senior emperor (Augustus) of the Roman West.

Helena's and Constantius' time together, probably at least a decade, bore much fruit in the person of their son, Constantine, born at Naissus on the lower Danubian frontier (c. 285). This future emperor, to be known as Constantine I the Great, would alter the course of Western history. In contrast to Helena, Theodora had six children—none even remotely as noteworthy. Following Helena's separation from Constantius, when Constantine was about seven, we hear little of her until the political emergence of her son, but it is probable that she continued to live at Constantine's side. This posed no embarrassment for Constantius, for he was seldom in the same vicinity as Helena, and in 293 he assumed the office of junior emperor (Caesar) of the West, with responsibilities in Britain and along the Rhine. This promotion came as part of the newly constituted "Tetrarchy" or "rule of four emperors"—two senior and two junior, one each in both the East and West. Although his father traveled west, the young Constantine remained in Nicomedia, in northern Anatolia, at the court of Diocletian, the Augustus of the East, in part as a hostage to ensure his father's loyal behavior.

Although Helena would attain a personal fame thanks to her devotion to Christianity, it is not known for certain whether she had converted to the faith as early as the 290s. If she was a Christian at the time, she almost certainly kept quiet about the fact, for Diocletian—an enthusiastic supporter of traditional Roman religion—was no friend to Christians. In fact in 303, incited by Galerius, the Caesar of the East, Diocletian inaugurated the era of the "Great Persecution" of Christians, which lasted eight years and only ended when it became painfully obvious to all concerned that force was not going to eradicate the Church. However, it is not impossible that Helena could have been a "quiet" Christian at Diocletian's court, for others there had Christian sympathies during this period. Although not provable, all indications suggest that Helena was at least leaning towards Christianity during the period of Constantine's youth. Later developments further suggest that she reared her son to sympathize with Christianity even as it remained a technically illegal religion.

Despite their probable different approaches to religiosity, Constantine served Diocletian loyally and well in the East, both at court and as a soldier, until both Diocletian and Maximian abdicated their positions as senior emperors in 305. It should be noted that Maximian did so reluctantly, but Diocletian insisted that both step down to allow for a smooth transition of power. His own youth having been beset by bitter imperial rivalries, Diocletian wished to establish the precedent whereby aging emperors would retire so as to permit their younger imperial colleagues to ascend to the status of "Augustus." Hence, in 305 Constantius and Galerius were jointly promoted.

⊰ **Theodora (fl. 290s).** *See Constantia (c. 293–?) for sidebar.*

In early 306, Constantius (the new Augustus of the West) requested of Galerius (the new Augustus of the East) that Constantine be allowed to assume a post in Britain at his side—a request which Galerius unwillingly granted in an attempt to sustain a precarious harmony between East and West. (This peaceful, if tense, transition of power involving four emperors was unprecedented in Roman history and transpired amid much intrigue as the new players jockeyed for relative influence.) With approval granted, Constantine quickly joined his father and briefly fought at his side in southern Scotland before Constantius died suddenly and unexpectedly at York in northern England. When Constantine traveled west, Helena accompanied him but probably advanced no further than the city of Trier on the Moselle River in modern Germany, which had served as Constantius' well-fortified seat for some time. There, Helena appears in the frescoes of the city's cathedral, testifying to the local Christian community's special devotion to her—a devotion which seems to have been engendered by personal acquaintance. His mother safely established in a well-protected fortress, Constantine continued on to Britain and war. How long Helena remained in Trier is unknown, but it is most likely that she stayed there to be joined by her son when he returned to the Continent.

Constantius' sudden death precipitated a turbulent period in the history of the Roman Empire, for the shaky peace which had linked Constantius and Galerius eroded quickly after Constantius' army, now leaderless, hailed Constantine an "Augustus." This ad hoc elevation upset the delicate balance which the Tetrarchy had attempted to maintain. It angered not only Galerius, but also Severus and Maximin Daia, the two Caesars who had been promoted to their positions as junior emperors at the same time that Constantius and Galerius had been advanced to the senior posts. Open civil war was temporarily averted by Galerius granting Constantine the rank of "Caesar," but the notion of a balanced "Tetrarchy" began to erode. Moreover, this concession to Constantine prompted Maxentius, the previously overlooked son of Maximian (the ex-Augustus of the West) to claim the status of Caesar for himself. The situation rapidly deteriorated as the egos of too many ambitious men threw the empire into war. The upstarts Constantine and Maximian arranged an alliance of convenience and fortified their agreement through the political marriage of Constantine to Maxentius' sister, ➧ **Fausta**. (Thus, Constantine's first legitimate wife was the sister of his stepmother Theodora.) A regional division of spoils was arranged at the time of this marriage, with Constantine claiming the Rhineland as his base and Maxentius, Italy. Constantine and Maxentius initially remained allies despite the many intrigues that followed (including an attempt by Maximian to "un-retire" and seize the advantage his son Maxentius had gained after defeating first Severus, and then Galerius, in Italy). However, after the aging Maximian's attempt to reestablish himself failed (a failure which led to his suicide in 310), and, after Galerius died in 311, the new opportunities generated by a clearing of the political landscape sparked a war for the West between Constantine and Maxentius: a war which Constantine won in 312.

During this conflict, Constantine's open affiliation with Christianity began. To start, Constantine issued the famous "Edict of Milan," which legalized Christianity. (Contrary to popular perception, this edict did not end the Great Persecution—that had already occurred in 311, when a dying Galerius lifted the purges. However, Galerius did not take the next step and legalize Christianity.) Although Constantine long continued to respect the ancient Roman religious tradition (there remained among his subjects many pagans) and although he never outlawed paganism, by the second decade of the 4th century he had begun to lavish increasing attention and greater largesse upon the Church, apparently convinced that the power of the Christian God had played a critical role in his victory over Maxentius.

By 313, a temporary calm descended upon a Roman Empire divided into two halves. This was so because, while Constantine was consolidating his Western base, a newcomer Licinius, who began his rise under Galerius and was the husband of Constantine's half-sister ***Constancia** (c. 293–?), struck down Maximin Daia in the eastern portion of the empire. Then began a nervous period as the two ambitious and leery survivors began to spar with an eye to the future elimination of the other. Although half-hearted attempts were made to secure peace between Constantine and Licinius, these had no chance of success. Both Augusti had but one aim—to re-unite the empire under one emperor. A new phase of civil war opened in 314 with Constantine the aggressor in Thrace. Thereafter, Constantine, the greatest general of his time, maintained the pressure on his eastern rival. The loser of several major battles, Licinius abdicated and was summarily executed in 324. After 18 years of civil war, the pauses in which were filled with campaigns against barbarians, Constantine stood as the empire's sole imperial master. Nevertheless, foreign affairs, personal tragedies, and religious squabbles combined to undermine whatever notions Constantine might have had about a peaceful reign. However, the very problems which beset Constantine during his period of absolute dominance led him to turn increasingly to Helena as a potent public and private ally.

This is not to say that Helena had not been a valuable ally previously, for she had. It is probable that while Constantine was battling Licinius, Helena remained in Rome where she continued to represent Constantine's interests which appear to have been identical with her own. There she seems to have dispensed various forms of expected imperial largesse, such as restoring public baths and undertaking new building projects—including the construction of Christian churches. Her own palace would be turned into a church after her death. It is not known how long she remained in Rome, but she certainly was fondly remembered there and throughout the West, and a number of inscriptions suggest that her stay in the West was an extended one—perhaps lasting until 326, when Constantine returned to the old imperial capital to celebrate his *vicennalia* (the 20th anniversary of his reign).

But to appreciate fully Helena's importance, we must recognize the empire's situation at the time of, and immediately after, the Edict of Milan. When Constantine legalized Christianity, the vast majority of Christians lived in the East, where his pagan rival, Licinius (himself once intimately associated with the Great Persecution), reigned. The practical impact of the Edict in lands controlled by Constantine was minimal as of 312, but by legalizing Christianity as a showdown with Licinius loomed, Constantine not only wanted to acknowledge his debt to the Christian God, but also to create a kind of fifth column of loyal allies in the land of his opponent. What Christian would fight against the first emperor to legitimize Christianity? The tactic was so successful that, when open war developed, Licinius could not count on the support of a significant number of his subjects. Although the Christians were still a minority in the East even at this late date, they were a united and motivated block, whose unity Constantine desperately wished to maintain for political as well as religious reasons.

But, immediately after the legalization of Christianity, the solidarity of the Church began to unravel. An illicit sect and once persecuted, Christianity had long been unified primarily by its opposition to the pagan empire. Of course, Christians believed in the resurrection of Christ as their name attests, but, beyond a few core beliefs, there were numerous differences of opinion as to exactly what must be accepted as part of the essential faith. To add to the problem, in the early 4th century there was no accepted head of the entire Church: the Roman papacy was yet to emerge as a See with extensive influence, and no bishop anywhere could claim to speak authoritatively for all on behalf of orthodox doctrine. As

Fausta (d. 324)

Byzantine and Roman empress. *Name variations: Flavia. Born Flavia Maxima Fausta; died in 324 (some sources cite 326); daughter of Maximian, senior emperor (Augustus) of the Roman West (r. 285/286–305), and* ****Eutropia****; sister of Maxentius and* ****Theodora*** *(fl. 290s); married Flavius Valerius Aurelius Constantinus Magnus, known as Constantine I the Great (285-337), Roman emperor (r. 306–337, the first Christian emperor of the Roman Empire, who founded Constantinople), in 307; children: Constantine II (b. 317); Constantius II (b. 323), Roman emperor (r. 337–361); Constans (b. 324);* ****Constantina*** *(c. 321–c. 354);* ***Helena*** *(c. 320–?, who married Julian, Byzantine emperor).*

In 308, the Roman Empire obeyed six masters: Galerius, Licinius, and Maximin Daia in the East; as well as Maximian, Maxentius, and Constantine I the Great in the West (the father, brother, and husband, respectively, of Fausta). In 307, the union of the Western Augusti had been cemented by the marriage of Constantine to Fausta, daughter of Maximian, at the same occasion when Maximian and his son Maxentius acknowledged Constantine as Augustus. Before long Maximian was forced by disagreements to flee from his son Maxentius and to take refuge with Constantine. Once more Maximian abdicated the throne, but while Constantine was on campaign Maximian began plotting with his son to overthrow him. Constantine discovered the rebellion and pursued Maximian to Marseilles where he besieged the town. The inhabitants gave up Maximian, and Constantine quelled the rebellion. Despite his status as Fausta's father, Maximian was put to death in 309. Constantine's authority was now secure in Britain, Gaul, and the recently acquired Spain.

Fausta's brother Maxentius, however, was gathering a large force in Italy with which to invade Gaul. But Constantine, with a large veteran army and many German auxiliaries, secured the loyalty of more of his subjects by ordering a stop to the persecutions of the Christians in his dominions. He then crossed the Alps into Italy, inflicting defeats on Maxentius' forces at Turin and Verona. On October 28, 312, at a battle fought outside Rome, Maxentius was finally defeated, his forces routed, and he himself drowned in the Tiber as he was driven off the Milvian Bridge—six years from the day that his rebellion had brought him to power. Constantine, now emperor of the entire West, added Italy and Africa to his holdings, and entered Rome. But in 324, personal upheaval marred imperial peace. Constantine's wife Fausta was accused of high treason, arrested, and put to death. (Another source maintains that Fausta was charged with adultery because of a liaison with a palace official.) She was either boiled in oil or died from suffocation in an overheated bath.

long as Christians were unified by their hatred of the empire and its devotion to the pagan gods, the diversity within the Christian Church hardly mattered, for all Christians could rally around their opposition to the way things stood. However, as soon as a friendly emperor embraced the Church, and even began to delegate certain imperial duties to bishops, it could no longer stand united by its antagonism to imperial society.

In the first decade of its legalization, two major heresies—that is, positions held by significant minorities within the Church—were denounced by the majority. These were sparked by priests named Donatus and Arius, neither of whom believed himself to be anything but devout and "orthodox." In lieu of any other extant authority, Constantine stepped in to enforce the will of the majority, with the result that both movements came to be persecuted by their Christian brethren. The punitive actions taken by Constantine to enforce "truth" created rifts in the Church, sent the Donatists and Arians underground and/or beyond the empire, and, was much resented by those who saw little difference between the persecutions of pagan and "Christian" emperors. Constantine did all he could to prevent the splintering of the Church, including hosting the famous Council of Nicaea in 325, but no power could overcome the differences in doctrinal opinion held by his contemporaries. Nevertheless, Constantine attempted to maintain the unity of the Church both for reasons of conscience and because Christians were among his most rabid supporters in the wars against Licinius, not completed until 324.

Another problem which beset Constantine was more mysterious in nature, probably involved Helena in the intrigue, and ended somewhat gruesomely. Constantine had sons by two different women, ⚘▸ **Minervina** and Fausta. Minervina was probably a consort (being to Constantine what Helena had been to Constantius), and although she gave birth to his first-born son, Crispus, around 305, she was either dead or dismissed before Constantine's marriage to Fausta. Fausta, married to kindle Constantine's imperial ambitions, produced three sons and two daughters: Constantine II (b. 317), Constantius II (b. 323), Constans (b. 324), ***Constantina** (c. 321–c. 354), and ⚘▸ **Helena** (who married the Byzantine emperor Julian).

Although Crispus' lineage through his mother was not as lofty as that of his half-brothers, Constantine nevertheless entrusted him with important commands, among them one at Trier, and elevated him to the rank of Caesar at about the time he reached puberty. Crispus had proved himself a worthy heir to his father's military talent, but his very success threatened the dynastic interests of Fausta, whose three sons were far younger than Crispus and unable as yet to establish themselves in their father's service. Crispus' achievements undoubtedly troubled Fausta and certainly were on her mind when she brought charges of treason against him in 326. Constantine came to believe these charges and had Crispus executed. This was not the end of the affair, however, for not long after Crispus' death, Constantine, convinced that Fausta had borne false witness against Crispus and feeling exceedingly guilty over his role in the execution of his first-born son, had Fausta executed in a harrowing way—she was boiled in oil.

What plots and counterplots lay behind these two executions are irretrievable, since the whole affair was hushed up as much as possible. However, certain rumors spread which suggested that the ease with which Fausta originally convinced Constantine as to Crispus' guilt, and Constantine's brutal treatment of Fausta later, may have had something to do with accusations of an attempted rape, or seduction, of Fausta by Crispus. Incestuous sexual attraction may have played some part in the affair, but if so, it is not clear whether Crispus was attracted to Fausta, or vice versa. If the latter, than a rejection of Fausta by Crispus may have lain behind her first strike. Regardless, sex and marriage were never far from politics in the 4th century, so that the whole lurid episode undoubtedly had a taint of treason somewhere—but by whom and for what purpose is lost in the mists of time.

And what of Helena at this time? As the grandmother of Crispus, Constantine II, Constantius II, and Constans, she had no dynastic interest one way or the other in the rivalries between the half-brothers. In addition, Helena's probably extended absence from Constantine's presence—it is likely that she came East with him only shortly before or after the death of Crispus—undoubtedly meant that she was not completely familiar with the intrigue of the eastern court. However, both Helena and Fausta had jointly been elevated to the status of "Augusta" (empress) in 324. Their elevation to this exalted status is confirmed numismatically, for their portraits appear on some of the obverses of Constantine's coins along with their new titles. Such honors were reserved for those whose imperial standing was being broadcast for all to respect.

An Augusta was an influential presence at court, and the fact that Constantine named both his mother and his wife to this status implies that he equally valued their advice and political acumen. Yet, built into their joint elevation was a natural rivalry for Constantine's ear, so that it is likely that both queens maneuvered to surpass the other when it came to influencing Constantine, that is, once Helena had been reunited with her son. With this reunion, Fausta undoubtedly took offense that, even though she had produced three sons for her husband, he nevertheless denied her an unparalleled position at court by looking with equal favor to mother and wife. For her part, Helena may have been jealous that Fausta could come between her and Constantine emotionally. Regardless, although Helena probably had no foreknowledge of the intrigues leading to Crispus' fall, she did come to denounce Fausta's role in the affair—a denunciation which led to Fausta's destruction. Perhaps coming to have a familiarity with the ins and outs of the women's quarters at Constantine's court gave Helena access to damaging information originally unavailable to her son. Notwithstanding, Helena's attacks quickly turned Constantine against Fausta, and his revenge was brutal. Whether or not the fate of Fausta was welcomed by Helena, from the time of Fausta's execution until her own death some three years later, the mother of Constantine was without feminine peer in the Roman Empire. In addition, during this period she acted as her son's agent in a policy intended both to purify Constantine's dynasty and to rally all Christians around common interests. Helena became a pilgrim.

Helena may not have made the first Christian pilgrimage to the Holy Land, but her well-publicized visit in part to consecrate sites associated with the "historical" Jesus helped to launch a movement which may have crested in the Middle Ages, but which remains intact to the present time. Her trip began soon after the deaths of Crispus and Fausta and must on one level be understood as a pilgrimage undertaken to expiate her son's guilt in the gruesome affair. On another level, moreover, it appears that her visit to the Holy Land was also intended to heal the wounds which had splintered the Christian community of her time. By focusing much of her attention on retracing the steps of the living Jesus, it seems clear that through her, Constantine intended to reestablish the common ground which linked all Christians. On this plane too, the emperor seems to have been seeking repentance, for the theological arguments which had led to the definition of distinct heresies had caused Constantine, in the name of orthodoxy, to punish (sometimes with death) many heretics who remained convinced

Minervina (fl. 290–307)

Roman consort. *Flourished around 290 to 307; consort, possibly first wife, of Constantine I the Great, Roman emperor (r. 306–337); children: Crispus (b. around 305); possibly* ****Constantina*** *(c. 321–c. 354).*

Minervina was either dead or dismissed before Constantine's marriage to ***Fausta** (d. 324), in 307.

Helena (c. 320–?)

Byzantine and Roman empress. *Born around 320; daughter of Constantius also known as Constantine I the Great, Roman emperor (r. 306–337), and* ****Fausta*** *(d. 324); granddaughter of* ****Helena*** *(c. 255–329); married Julian, Roman emperor and Byzantine emperor (r. 361–363).*

that they were as good Christians as anyone else. Although her publicized journey did not reunify either the Church or her own family for very long, as a result of it, Helena attained a widespread popularity among Christians of all hues. She became so revered that in the eastern calendar of saints, she shared a Holy Day (May 21) with her son. Her veneration became so pronounced that at least one subsequent empress (***Pulcheria**, c. 398–453) would name herself a "new Helena," and in the 6th century Justinian would name a whole province after her.

How did she come to be so revered? Although it is difficult to differentiate myth from fact in regards to her pilgrimage, a few things can be confidently asserted. First, Helena did not travel as a humble penitent but as the "Augusta," dispensing generous largesse upon towns, soldiers, and especially upon Christian projects. In addition, she measured out imperial mercy by releasing prisoners, restoring exiles, endowing the poor, and establishing relief funds. In order to carry out her mission, Helena had complete access to the imperial treasury, and it is clear that she was meant to maintain the highest possible profile. In short, she was to be, on Constantine's behalf, a "doer of good deeds."

Nevertheless, posterity came to remember this imperial progress most for the building it stimulated at holy places associated with Jesus' life. At least three important churches—at Golgotha, Bethlehem, and the Mount of Olives—were begun, or at least proceeded, under her direction. Each of these was subsequently adorned in her memory by Constantine. Somewhat more tenuous is Helena's association with the contemporary excavation of Jesus' tomb and the discovery of the "True Cross." Whether or not she had a role in "archaeological" discoveries of a Christian nature, Helena later came to be associated with them, if for no other reason than that her visit stimulated in many an active interest in the physical topography of Jesus' life. Although contemporary evidence is lacking, by the end of the 4th century Helena was reputed to have gone to the Holy Land primarily to seek out the True Cross, to have discovered it (it being identified by an inscription referring to "Jesus, King of the Jews" and the miracles thereafter attributed to it), and to have sent it, along with the nails which had pierced Jesus' flesh, to Constantine at his new capital in Constantinople. Thus, whether or not Helena actively sought such relics, many soon came to think that she did, and, spurred by her example, a passion for religious relics spread like wildfire.

Where and exactly when Helena died is unknown, but it seems that she died about 329, perhaps while still in the Holy Land. Where to bury her for the most political effect undoubtedly cost Constantine emotionally, for it is clear that he always remained close to his mother. Nevertheless, she died before Constantinople had become firmly established in everyone's mind as the new center of the Roman world—even though the emperor had taken up residence there and was undertaking a lavish building program of his own. Thus, to inter her in a city with which she had so little association, which was so far from the geographical heart of the empire, and which had yet to assert its superiority over Rome as the empire's emotional capital, seemed inappropriate. In Constantine's mind, the only possible choice of burial sites was Rome itself, where Helena had already constructed a mausoleum for their family, even if few of its members would subsequently be buried there. Although he would not dwell near the place of her burial, Constantine made evidence of his maternal piety by having Helena buried in the sarcophagus elaborately decorated with symbols of victory, symbolic of both worldly success and salvation, he had intended for himself. Always the political animal as well as a devoted son, Constantine intended Helena's burial place to reflect the military success, made possible through his and Helena's devotion to the Christian God, which had won him an empire and seen his mother, a one-time waitress, esteemed throughout the Roman world as an Augusta.

SOURCES:

Eusebius. *The Life of the Blessed Emperor Constantine*, esp. 3.42–3.47, in *A Select Library of Nicene and Post Nicene Fathers of the Christian Church*. Ser. 2, vol. 1. Edited by P. Schaff and H. Wace. New York, 1890 (reprinted 1952).

SUGGESTED READING:

Grant, Michael. *Constantine the Great*. NY: Scribner, 1993.

Hunt, E.D. *Holy Land Pilgrimage in the Later Roman Empire*. London: Oxford University Press, 1982.

W.S. Greenwalt,
Associate Professor of Classical History,
Santa Clara University, Santa Clara, California

Helena (c. 320–?).

See Helena (c. 255–329) for sidebar.

Helena (1846–1923).

See Victoria for sidebar.

Helena Cantacuzene (fl. 1340s)

Byzantine empress. *Flourished in the 1340s; daughter of ****Irene Asen*** *and John VI Cantacuzene, emperor of Nicaea (r. 1347–1354); married John V Paleologus (d. 1391), emperor of Nicaea (r. 1341–1347, 1355–1391); children: Andronicus IV Paleologus (d. 1385), emperor of Nicaea (r. 1376–1379); Manuel II Paleologus, emperor of Nicaea (r. 1391–1425); Theodore I, despot of Morea.*

Helena Dragas (fl. 1400)

Byzantine empress. *Name variations: Dragases. Born in Serbia; flourished in 1400; married Manuel II Paleologus, emperor of Nicaea (r. 1391–1425); children: John VIII Paleologus (1391–1448), emperor of Nicaea (r. 1425–1448); Theodore II; Andronicus; Constantine XI Paleologus, emperor of Nicaea (r. 1448–1453); Demetrius; Thomas.*

Helena Lekapena (c. 920–961)

Byzantine empress. *Name variations: Helen Lecapena or Lecapenus. Born around 920 in Constantinople; died on September 19, 961 (some sources cite 960); daughter of Romanos I Lekapenos also known as Romanus I Lecapenus (r. 919–944, who reigned as co-emperor with Constantine VII), and ****Theodora*** *(fl. early 900s); sister of Theophylaktos, patriarch of Constantinople; married Constantine VII Porphyrogenitus (c. 906–959), Byzantine emperor (r. 913–959), on April 27, 919; children: Romanos or Romanus II, Byzantine emperor (r. 959–963); and five daughters, including Agatha and ****Theodora*** *(late 900s, who married John I Tzimiskes, emperor of Byzantium [r. 969–976]).*

After Romanus I married off his young daughter Helena to the 13-year-old Constantine

(VII Porphyrogenitus), he had himself proclaimed senior co-emperor (919); the joint reign lasted 25 years. In 944, during a short-lived coup, two of Helena's brothers whisked their father off to an island of exile; Constantine then had them join their father in the pleasures of gardening. All five daughters born of the marriage of Helena and Constantine shared in their father's intellectual pursuits and served as secretaries in the compilation of some of his books. Their only son, however, was a wild boy with none of his father's scholarly tendencies. By the time he ascended the throne as Romanus II, he had married the head-strong *Theophano (c. 940–?). The 18-year-old Theophano's first official act was to banish Helena from court and have her five daughters sent to distant convents; Helena died in sorrow some months later.

Helena of Alypia or Alypius (fl. 980s).

See Zoë Porphyrogenita for sidebar.

Helena of Constantinople (c. 255–329).

See Helena.

Helena of Epirus (fl. 1250s)

Queen of Sicily. *Flourished in the 1250s; second wife of Manfred, king of Naples and Sicily (r. 1258–1266, illegitimate son of Frederick II, Holy Roman emperor [r. 1215–1250]). Manfred's first wife was ***Beatrice of Savoy**.*

Helena of Italy (1873–1952).

See Elena of Montenegro.

Helena of Montenegro (1873–1952).

See Elena of Montenegro.

Helena of Russia (1882–1957)

Grand duchess of the imperial court in St. Petersburg. *Name variations: Helen, Helene, Hélène Romanov, Helen Vladimirovna. Born Helen Vladimirovna on January 17, 1882; died on March 13, 1957; daughter of ***Maria of Mecklenburg-Schwerin** (1854–1920) and Grand Duke Vladimir Alexandrovitch (son of Alexander II, tsar of Russia); married Prince Nicholas (Oldenburg) of Greece (uncle of England's Prince Philip), on August 29, 1902; children: ***Olga Oldenburg** (1903–1981); ***Elizabeth Oldenburg** (1904–1955); ***Marina of Greece** (1906–1968).*

Helena of Saxe-Coburg (1846–1923).

See Victoria for sidebar on Helena.

Helena of Russia

Helena of Serbia (fl. 1100s)

Queen of Hungary. *Flourished in the 1100s; married Bela II, king of Hungary (r. 1131–1141); children: ***Jolanta** (who married Boleslas of Kalisz); Geza II (1130–1161), king of Hungary (r. 1141–1161); Ladislas II, king of Hungary (r. 1162); Stephen IV, king of Hungary (r. 1162–1163).*

Helena Pavlovna (1784–1803)

Russian princess. *Name variations: Helene or Hélène Romanov. Born on December 24, 1784; died on September 24, 1803; daughter of ***Sophia Dorothea of Wurttemberg** (1759–1828) and Paul I (1754–1801), tsar of Russia (r. 1796–1801); sister of ***Anna Pavlovna** (1795–1865), ***Marie Pavlovna** (1786–1859), and ***Catherine of Russia** (1788–1819); became first wife of Frederick Louis (1778–1819), duke of Mecklenburg-Schwerin, on October 23, 1799; children: Paul Frederick, grand duke of Mecklenburg-Schwerin (b. 1800). Frederick Louis' second wife was ***Caroline Louise of Saxe-Weimar** (1786–1816).*

Helena Victoria (1870–1948)

Princess of Great Britain. *Born Victoria Louise Sophia Augusta Amelia Helena on May 3, 1870, in Windsor, Berkshire, England; died on March 13, 1948, in London; daughter of *****Helena*** *(1846–1923), duchess of Schleswig-Holstein-Sonderburg-Augustenberg, and Christian of Schleswig-Holstein-Sonderburg-Augustenberg.*

Helene.

Variant of Helena.

Helene (1903–1924)

Duchess of Wurttemberg. *Born on October 30, 1903, in Linz; died on September 8, 1924, in Tubingen; daughter of *****Maria Cristina of Sicily*** *(1877–1947) and Archduke Peter Ferdinand (1874–1948).*

Helene Louise of Mecklenburg-Schwerin (1814–1858)

Duchess of Chartres and Orléans. *Name variations: Hélène Louise of Mecklenburg-Schwerin; Helen of Mecklenburg-Schwerin; Helene Louise Elisabeth d' Orleans. Born on January 24, 1814; died on May 18, 1858; daughter of Frederick Louis, grand duke of Mecklenburg-Schwerin, and *****Caroline Louise of Saxe-Weimar*** *(1786–1816); married Ferdinand Philippe (1810–1842), duke of Chartres and Orléans (r. 1830–1842), on May 30, 1837 (killed in a carriage accident on July 13, 1842); children: Louis Philippe (1838–1894), count of Paris; Robert (1840–1910), duke of Chartres.*

Helene of Bavaria (1834–1890)

Princess of Thurn and Taxis. *Born on April 4, 1834; died on May 16, 1890; daughter of *****Ludovica*** *(1808–1892) and Maximilian Joseph (1808–1888), duke of Bavaria; married Maximilian Anton Lamoral, prince of Thurn and Taxis; children: *****Elizabeth Maria of Thurn and Taxis*** *(1860–1881).*

Helene of Brunswick-Luneburg (d. 1273)

Duchess of Saxony. *Died on September 6, 1273; daughter of *****Matilda of Brandenburg*** *(d. 1261) and Otto I Puer also known as Otto the Child (1204–1252), duke of Brunswick-Luneburg (r. 1235–1252); became second wife of Albrecht also known as Albert I, duke of Saxony (r. 1212–1261), in 1247. Albert I was previously married to* ***Agnes of Thuringia****.*

Helene of Moldavia (d. 1505)

Princess of Moscow. *Died on January 18, 1505; daughter of Stephen III, hospodar of Moldavia; married Ivan the Younger (1456–1490), prince of Moscow (r. 1471–1490), on January 6, 1482; children: Dimitri of Moscow (b. 1485).*

Helene of Moscow (1474–1513)

Queen of Poland. *Born on May 19, 1474 (some sources cite 1476); died on January 24, 1513; daughter of *****Sophia of Byzantium*** *(1448–1503) and Ivan III (1440–1505), grand prince of Moscow (r. 1462–1505); married Alexander (1461–1506), king of Poland (r. 1501–1506), on February 15, 1495.*

Helene of Schleswig-Holstein (1888–1962).

See Helen of Schleswig-Holstein.

Helene of Wurttemberg (1807–1873)

Grand duchess of Russia. *Name variations: Charlotte; Helene von Württemberg. Born on January 9, 1807; died on February 2, 1873; daughter of *****Catherine Charlotte of Hildburghausen*** *(1787–1847) and Paul Charles Frederick (1785–1852), duke of Wurttemberg; married Grand Duke Michael of Russia (1798–1849), on February 20, 1824; children: Marie Michailovna Romanov (1825–1846); *****Elizabeth Romanov*** *(1826–1845); *****Catherine Romanov*** *(1827–1894); Alexandra (1831–1832); Anna (1834–1836).*

Helfman or Helfmann, Guessia (d. 1882).

See Gelfman, Gesia.

Helia de Semur (fl. 1020–1046)

Duchess of Burgundy. *Name variations: Helie de Semur-en-Brionnais. Flourished between 1020 and 1046; daughter of Damas I de Semur-en-Brionnais and Aremburge de Bourgogne; married Robert I (1011–1076), duke of Burgundy (r. 1032–1076), around 1033 (divorced 1046); children: Hugh (b. 1034); Henry (1035–1066), duke of Burgundy; Robert (b. 1040); Simon; *****Constance of Burgundy*** *(1046–c. 1093, who married Alphonso VI, king of*

*Castile & Leon). Robert I was also married to *Ermengarde of Anjou (1018–1076).*

Hellenes, queen of.

See Amalie (1818–1875).
See Olga Constantinovna (1851–1926).
See Sophie of Prussia (1870–1932).
See Elisabeth (1894–1956).
See Manos, Aspasia (1896–1972).
See Fredericka (1917–1981).
See Anne-Marie Oldenburg (b. 1946).

Hellman, Lillian (1905–1984)

Major American playwright, distinguished for her unprecedented success for a woman on Broadway and for her literary career, including screenwriting and memoirs, which spanned nearly 50 years. *Name variations: Lily; Lillian Kober. Pronunciation: HEL-men. Born Lillian Hellman on June 20, 1905, in New Orleans, Louisiana; died at Martha's Vineyard on June 30, 1984; daughter of Max Hellman (a salesman) and Julia (Newhouse) Hellman; attended public school in New Orleans and Public School 6 in New York City; graduated from Wadleigh High School in New York City, 1921; attended New York University for two years; married Arthur Kober (a press agent), in 1925 (divorced 1933); lived with Dashiell Hammett; no children.*

Awards: Drama Critics Circle Award for Watch on the Rhine *(1941) and* Toys in the Attic *(1960); American Academy of Arts and Letters (1962); MacDowell Medal for Contributions to Literature (1976); National Book Award for Arts and Letters for* An Unfinished Woman *(1969); awarded honorary doctorate from Yale University, Columbia University, and Smith College, as well as honorary degrees from various other schools.*

Family moved back and forth between New Orleans and New York City before settling in New York when Hellman was 16; at 19, worked for Liveright Publishing Company as clerk-reader until she married Arthur Kober (1925); moved to Paris and then to Hollywood with husband, landed a job as a script reader for MGM; met Dashiell Hammett (1930); wrote The Children's Hour, *her first hit play (1934); became a screenwriter for MGM but continued theater work, maintaining a residence in New York City; known for her political and social activism, particularly in the 1930s and '40s; supported the anti-fascist cause in Spain by raising money, financing and collaborating on film documentary on the Spanish Civil War; was one of the chief sponsors of the Waldorf Peace Conference (1949); called to testify before the House Un-American Activities Committee (1952) where she made her famous statement and narrowly avoided being cited for contempt for her refusal to "name names"; blacklisted from Hollywood (late 1940s–early 1950s) due to alleged Communist affiliations; after 12 original plays and 3 adaptations, her illustrious career in the theater was over by 1963; collaborated on her final screenplay,* The Chase *(1966); in her 60s, embarked on an even more rewarding literary career with her critically acclaimed memoirs; organized and chaired the Committee for Public Justice (1970s).*

Selected publications—plays: The Children's Hour *(1934, ran for 691 performances);* Days to Come *(1936);* The Little Foxes *(1939);* Watch on the Rhine *(1941);* The Searching Wind *(1944);* Another Part of the Forest *(1946);* Montserrat *(adaptation, 1949);* The Autumn Garden *(1951);* The Lark *(adaptation, 1955);* Toys in the Attic *(1960).*

Screenplays: (co-scripted) The Dark Angel *(United Artists, 1935);* These Three *(based on her play* The Children's Hour, *Goldwyn/U.A., 1936);* Dead End *(U.A., 1937);* The Little Foxes *(RKO, 1941);* The North Star *(also titled* Armored Attack, *RKO, 1943);* The Searching Wind *(Paramount, 1946);* The Chase *(Columbia, 1966).*

Books: An Unfinished Woman *(Boston: Little, Brown, 1969);* Pentimento *(Boston: Little, Brown, 1973);* Scoundrel Time *(Boston: Little, Brown, 1976);* Maybe *(Boston: Little, Brown, 1980).*

Lillian Hellman's image was that of a courageous and highly moralistic woman who stood her ground before the mighty HUAC (House Un-American Activities Committee) in 1952—and won—an uncommon feat, to be sure. But both her image and her stance belie the complexity and contradictions that haunted the renowned American playwright, screenwriter, and memoirist in her later years. She went to her grave with a $2 million lawsuit pending against fellow writer ***Mary McCarthy**, who branded Hellman a liar on national television in 1980. "Every word she writes is a lie," said McCarthy on the "Dick Cavett Show," "including 'and' and 'the'." The lawsuit was dropped following Hellman's death in 1984.

But McCarthy's damning words, aimed mainly at some of the slippery "facts" reported in her memoirs, could not negate Hellman's literary achievements or her justifiable claim to fame. Having produced 12 original plays and 3 adaptations over almost a 30-year span (1934–61), she cut a swath in the American theater unrivaled by most of her contemporaries. Biographer William Wright reminds us that:

> Even before the memoirs, she was honored by as many leading universities as any other playwright; her plays are performed regularly and around the world, and her position as a dramatist is debated periodically in intellectual journals, which is remarkable.

Her successful playwriting contemporaries Clifford Odets, Irwin Shaw, S.N. Behrman, Robert Sherwood, and Phillip Kaufman have not survived as well, critically or commercially. For this reason, Hellman would, understandably, bristle at American critic George Jean Nathan's double-edged compliment: "the best of our women playwrights." A male bastion unaccustomed to accomplished women playwrights, particularly in the 1930s and 1940s, Broadway provided the stage for Hellman's zenith and nemesis. During the playwriting years of her career, she turned to Hollywood screenwriting for easy money, while in her later years she forged an entirely new literary identity. Her four slender memoirs won even greater critical acclaim than her plays, revived her popularity, and secured her stature in American literary history.

Hellman's place of birth and death—New Orleans in the South and Martha's Vineyard in the North—parallel the cultural disparity in her parentage and upbringing. Her father Max Hellman was a German Jew whose family had settled in and around New Orleans where Hellman was born in 1905. Born in Alabama, her Southern aristocratic mother **Julia Newhouse Hellman**—also of Jewish extraction—married beneath her, though it was Max who enjoyed the upper hand in the marriage. Lillian, an only child, was ferried between her father's sisters' New Orleans boarding house and her parents' apartment in Manhattan, the swankier upscale home base of Hellman's maternal relatives. After losing the shoe business in which his in-laws had set him up, Max Hellman made his living as a traveling salesman. In her memoirs, Hellman admits to being taken more with her lively colorful father and his family than with her demure docile mother and their claim to social status and wealth. In fact, while Lillian idealized her father's cousin Bethe and his sisters Jenny and Hannah in the second memoir *Pentimento,* she immortalized her mother's kinsfolk as the greedy evil Hubbards in the plays *The Little Foxes* and *Another Part of the Forest.* Ironically, Hellman herself always enjoyed lavish spending and the fineries of life, while remaining a firm supporter of social justice and the underdog.

An intelligent and precocious child, Lillian read voraciously and kept track of her observations on the interesting people who moved through her aunts' New Orleans boarding house in her writer's journal. Accustomed to having her way with her doting parents, she admittedly used her wrath as a weapon. (See *Pentimento.*) Her anger figured prominently in her life, as the catalyst in her fervor for justice and as the sign of an irascible and difficult personality.

An unexceptional but competent student, Lillian completed high school in Manhattan where her family had finally moved when Hellman was 16. After two years at New York University, she dropped out but managed to get hired as a clerk-reader for the prestigious Liveright Publishing Company, one of the future homes of up-and-coming American writers like William Faulkner and Ernest Hemingway. During this time, she met her husband Arthur Kober, a theatrical press agent and, like Hellman, an aspiring writer. Following their wedding in 1925, she left her job and worked on her fledgling writing career, producing stories that she would later refer to as "lady writer stories." Although she did get published in journals like the *Paris Comet,* which then-husband Arthur Kober edited, the stories did not amount to much, leaving Hellman frustrated and without direction. Apart from small jobs, like reviewing books for the *New York Herald Tribune,* she mostly moved with Kober and his jobs to Paris and then to Hollywood where the burgeoning film industry was importing writing talent from New York in the late 1920s. This move proved to be a crucial turning point in her life and career, for it was in Hollywood that Hellman met her mentor and the love of her life, famed detective fiction writer Dashiell Hammett.

Hellman's marriage to Kober was reportedly pleasant but unfulfilling for the headstrong adventurous Lillian, who was known to go off on her own, gamble for high stakes and engage in "flings." Hellman was not a conventional woman, even by today's more liberal standards. But she met her match in Dashiell Hammett. Given to womanizing, extended drinking bouts, and profligate spending, yet praised by those who knew him for his honesty and integrity, Hammett was a paradox—a most unconventional conventional man. In her memoirs, Hellman spoke extensively of Hammett, characterizing him in *Pentimento* as a "Dostoyevsky sinner-saint."

In 1930, the dashing Hammett cut quite a figure in Hollywood. Admired by men and

Lillian Hellman

adored by women, he had reached the pinnacle of both artistic success and economic potential. The author of *Red Harvest, The Dain Curse,* and *The Maltese Falcon* had everything to win in Hollywood where his talents were being courted for the big screen. He was 36 when he met the 25-year-old Hellman who, apart from working as a low-paid script reader for MGM, was still floundering as a writer.

In *Pentimento,* Hellman recalls her first encounter with the "cool teacher" she felt she so needed. Their 30-odd-year relationship as mentor-protege-lovers must go down in the annals of such famous couplings as Spencer Tracy and *__Katharine Hepburn__, and Jean Paul Sartre and *__Simone de Beauvoir__. While witnesses and biographers dispute the time and location of their first encounter pinpointed by Hellman, none question the extent of Hammett's influence on the neophyte writer. With Hammett firmly affixed in her life, her short "pleasant" marriage ended in a friendly divorce, and Arthur Kober became a devoted and lifelong friend.

Hammett effectively guided Hellman toward the craft of playwriting and functioned as her personal editor. Tough and relentless in his criticism, he enjoyed a privileged hand in her work that Hellman accorded to no other individual at any time in her nearly 50-year professional career. But as her literary star ascended, his waned. Indeed, over time her work superseded his, in terms of productivity, critical importance, and staying power. In the early years of their relationship, he wrote and published *The Thin Man,* featuring the popular Nick and Nora Charles. (Nick, of course, sports many of Hammett's own

Tallulah Bankhead as Regina Hubbard in Lillian Hellman's The Little Foxes.

qualities, while the female villain as well as Nora, played in the movies by ***Myrna Loy**, are loosely fashioned on Hellman.) But apart from some screenplay adaptation and touching up, his comparatively short writing career skidded to a halt as Hellman's steamed ahead.

They sustained a relationship of changing colors over a 30-year period—as lovers, confidantes, friends—sometimes in the same house and sometimes not, sometimes in the same city and sometimes not. But they remained committed companions, despite the innumerable "casual ladies" in Hammett's life and Hellman's intermittent and more serious romantic attachments.

Hammett is credited with suggesting the basis for Hellman's first play. She transformed William Roughead's factual account, "The Great Drumsheugh Case," into an acclaimed drama entitled, *The Children's Hour.* Her first dramatic effort—about two friends and managers of a boarding school destroyed by a child's "lie" accusing them of lesbianism—took Broadway by storm in 1934. In fact, as William Wright points out, the Drama Critics' Circle Award originated because theater critics were dismayed that *The Children's Hour* was not awarded the Pulitzer Prize. Nor was the play's success (one of Hellman's longest-running plays) slowed as a result of being banned from the stages of Boston and Chicago because of its unorthodox topic. *The Children's Hour* also established the long-term relationship between Hellman and Herman Shumlin, a major Broadway director and producer.

The tight well-made structure of the play became vintage Hellman, although this form of dramatic realism was well-established in the work of British writer Arthur Wing Pinero and of Norwegian Henrik Ibsen. But along with the play's commercial and critical success came the charge of "melodrama" that undermined Hellman's dramatic achievement. Her instant and consistent commercial success on Broadway seemed to work against her artistic status. Nonetheless, Hellman's reputation as a writer was cinched, and, lured by MGM, she returned to Hollywood as a highly paid screenwriter for Samuel Goldwyn. She reportedly enjoyed an uncommonly privileged professional and personal association with Goldwyn, head of one of Hollywood's major studios. Eventually, she would establish a home base in New York City, but in the 1930s and 1940s Hellman remained closely connected with Hollywood, which at that time was a hotbed of progressivism.

The decade following the Great Depression saw a heightened awareness of the need for social justice. Many liberal Americans, particularly artists and writers, looked favorably on the egalitarian Marxist theories that inspired the Communist revolution in Russia. With fascism on the rise in Italy, Germany, and Spain, Americans and Russians also shared—for once—a common enemy. As a result, a number of these socially conscious Americans courted Communism as a means of solving domestic problems, like low wages, unemployment, poverty, and disparity between the rich and the poor.

> I cannot and will not cut my conscience to fit this year's fashions.
>
> **—Lillian Hellman**

As a rule, Hellman did not mix politics with art, and she avoided socialistic enterprises like the Federal Theater Project, the Trade Union Theater, and the Group Theater. (These government-subsidized projects were intended to relieve unemployment and encourage new writers in the post-Depression years.) But in her private life and especially during the 1930s and 1940s, Hellman was politically active. This involvement resulted in her being the subject of an ongoing FBI file as well as being blacklisted in Hollywood from the late 1940s into the 1950s. Unlike Hammett, Hellman swore she was not a "card-carrying" Communist, even though others had reported differently. But she shared Hammett's politics of social justice and humanitarianism, cementing the bond between them. Hellman consistently used her energy, influence, and talent to support causes like the moribund Screenwriter's Guild which she helped to revive and to organize. That she was a highly paid screenwriter at the time, unlike her poorly paid colleagues, seemed irrelevant. Hellman was also an active supporter of the Loyalists in Spain in their fight against fascism and General Francisco Franco. She helped to raise money for the refugees and to finance a documentary about wartorn Spain in the hopes of waking up sleepy Americans unmindful of the swelling fascist threat abroad. Hellman's account in *An Unfinished Woman* (1969) of her 1937 visit to Spain during the war is one of the topics on which her veracity is attacked by ***Martha Gellhorn**, a war correspondent and fellow supporter of the Loyalist cause, who was then a lover and later a wife of Ernest Hemingway.

During this same 1937 trip, Hellman made her first trip to Russia, having been honored by an invitation to the Moscow Theater Festival. In 1944, she again visited Russia on a cultural mission and, while there, visited the Russian front and made lasting friends. (Sergei Eisenstein, the great Russian film director, was one.) In the 1960s, she traveled to Russia a third time, and a diary account of these visits is contained in *An Unfinished Woman.* But her amicable relations with Russia and its people would be used as evidence of her un-Americanism in the chilly postwar climate of the late 1940s, when American hatred and fear of Communism reached a fevered pitch.

Hellman bought a piece of property in Connecticut which she named "Hardscrabble Farm" where she and Hammett lived contentedly and productively during a good deal of the '40s. But the HUAC hearings led by Senator Joseph McCarthy were in full swing by the end of the decade, and, with the cooperation of Hollywood's studio heads, the HUAC compiled a lengthy list of names (writers, actors, directors, etc.), resulting in the "blacklist" by which artists were branded as subversives and prevented from getting work. Hellman fell into this category, as did Hammett, who went to jail for six months in 1947 for refusing to cooperate with the committee. During this time, Hellman regretfully sold her farm, said goodbye to her happiest time with Hammett, and prepared herself for her own appearance before the HUAC in 1952. In a letter to the committee, she made her famous statement in which she agreed to talk about herself but not about others, refusing to "bring bad trouble" to old friends. (See Hellman's account in *Scoundrel Time.*) Although she was apparently not the first to take this stance, she was the first to frame her position so eloquently, publicly, and with such moral persuasion: "I cannot and will not cut my conscience to fit this year's fashions." Her letter was mistakenly read aloud in court and made public record, leading to the technicality which prevented the committee from finding Hellman in contempt. Despite her narrow escape, the hearings had exacted their toll on Hellman's life (loss of farm, Hammett's greatly deteriorated health) and career (loss of work and income).

Although she told PBS interviewer **Marilyn Berger** in 1980 she wished she had "told them all to go to hell," in this public moment of her private life Hellman held to the demand for moral rectitude that permeates her dramatic work. In her plays, morality is not an abstract notion but something that must be grasped on an individual basis, as through the lie one tells to another (*The Children's Hour*) or the lie one tells to one's self (*Toys in the Attic, Autumn Garden, The Searching Wind*). Elsewhere Hellman probes the greed and lust for power that would lead individuals to commit blackmail, theft, and even murder (*The Little Foxes, Another Part of the Forest, Watch on the Rhine*). The struggle is always between "good and active evil," as **Edith Issacs** explained in an article in which she praised the dramatist for her "creative skill and technical equipment" in presenting the same theme so variously and effectively. Drama critic Allan Lewis put it this way: "Hellman's dark world of those who triumph for a calculated disregard of moral values is as grim and full of pain as is the most extreme theatre of the absurd. Her dramas . . . are portraits of people and not of abstract symbols." Unlike the social protest drama of her contemporaries, Hellman's moralistic drama has better stood the test of time.

She was also unique in her ability to grow as a writer and try other forms, including editing, adapting, screenwriting and, most important, the autobiographical memoir. By the early 1960s, her playwriting career was over, the HUAC trouble was behind her, and Hammett was dead. Now in her 60s, she began writing her memoirs. She even mined new territory in this traditional genre, by using the skills of the dramatist to provide narrative structure and to enliven the scenes and characters remembered. Her memoirs were enormously successful with audience and critics alike, and novelist **Maureen Howard** tried to capture the charm of Hellman's new and distinctive literary voice in *The New York Times Book Review:* "Memory has become a liberation: as she speaks directly to us her voice, unshared with her characters, has a new freedom. For a mind like Hellman's the imagination is enlarged not limited by the facts of her life."

Hellman's dramatic imagination, which served her art so well in the memoirs, apparently collided with fact. Accusations of untruthfulness followed, particularly after *Julia,* the well-received film adaptation of *Pentimento,* came out in 1976. One of the key issues concerned whether or not Julia was an actual friend of Hellman's as claimed, or a composite based on ***Muriel Gardiner**, the only known American anti-fascist underground fighter. Hellman went to her death denying that and other charges, despite weighty evidence to the contrary. But her final memoir, *Maybe,* entertained the idea of whether or not we can trust memory or even know the "truth," and this may be Hellman's best answer to her accusers. Partially paralyzed and nearly blind, Lillian Hellman continued writing until she died in 1984, at age 79.

SOURCES:

Howard, Maureen. *The New York Times Book Review.* April 25, 1976, p. 2.

Issacs, Edith J.R. "Lillian Hellman: A Playwright on the March" in *Discussions of American Drama.* Ed. by Walter J. Meserve. Boston, MA: D.C. Heath, 1966.

Lewis, Allan. *American Plays and Playwrights of the American Theatre.* NY: Crown, 1970.

Nathan, George Jean. "Playwrights in Petticoats," in *American Mercury.* June 1941, pp. 750–55.

Waites Lamm, Kathleen. "Lillian Hellman: Revisioning from Drama to Memoir." Diss. University of Nebraska-Lincoln, August 1986.

Wright, William. *Lillian Hellman: The Image, The Woman.* NY: Simon and Schuster, 1986.

SUGGESTED READING:

Mellen, Joan. *Hellman and Hammett.* San Francisco, CA: HarperCollins, 1996.

COLLECTIONS:

Papers, letters, manuscripts located at the Lillian Hellman Collection at the University of Texas in Austin.

RELATED MEDIA:

Another Part of the Forest (106 min.), starring Fredric March, ***Florence Eldridge**, and ***Ann Blyth**, 1948.

The Children's Hour (107 min.), produced by United Artists, directed by William Wyler, starring ***Audrey Hepburn, Shirley MacLaine, Fay Bainter**, and ***Miriam Hopkins**, 1962 (titled *The Loudest Whisper* in Great Britain).

Dash and Lilly (television movie about Hammett and Hellman), starring Sam Shepard and **Judy Davis**, A&E Network and Granada Entertainment Production, directed by **Kathy Bates**, premiered on May 31, 1999.

Julia (116 min.), based on *Pentimento,* was filmed by 20th-Century Fox, directed by Fred Zinnemann, with an Academy Award performance by **Vanessa Redgrave**, also starred **Jane Fonda**, ***Cathleen Nesbitt**, with an early credit for **Meryl Streep**, 1977.

The Little Foxes (115 min.), produced by RKO, directed by William Wyler, starred ***Bette Davis** (nominated for an Academy Award), Herbert Marshall, and ***Teresa Wright** and **Patricia Collinge** (both nominated for Best Supporting Actress), screenplay by Hellman, Arthur Kober, ***Dorothy Parker**, and Alan Campbell, 1941.

These Three (93 min.), produced by United Artists, directed by Samuel Goldwyn, starring Miriam Hopkins, ***Merle Oberon**, and ***Bonita Granville**, screenplay by Hellman, 1936.

Toys in the Attic (88 min.), produced by Mirisch-Claude/U.A., directed by George Roy Hill, starring ***Geraldine Page, Yvette Mimieux**, ***Wendy Hiller**, ***Gene Tierney**, and Dean Martin, 1963.

Watch on the Rhine (114 min.), produced by Warner Bros., directed by Herman Shumlin, starring Bette Davis, ***Geraldine Fitzgerald**, Paul Lukas, ***Beulah Bondi, Lucile Watson** (nominated for Best Supporting Actress), screenplay by Hellman and Hammett, 1943.

Kathleen A. Waites Lamm,
Professor of English and Women's Studies at
Nova University, Fort Lauderdale, Florida

Helm, Brigitte (1908–1996)

***German actress who starred in the cult classic* Metropolis.** *Born Eva Gisela Schittenhelm (also seen as Gisele Eve Schittenhelm) in Berlin, Germany, on March 17, 1908 (some sources cite 1906); died in Anscona, Switzerland, on June 11, 1996; married Hugh Kunheim (an industrialist).*

Filmography: Metropolis *(1926);* Am Rande der Welt *(*At the Edge of the World, *1926);* Der Liebe der Jeanne Ney *(*The Loves of Jeanne Ney, *1927);* Alraune *(*Unholy Love, *1928);* L'Argent *(Fr., 1928);* Abwege *(1928);* Crisis *(1928);* Die wunderbare Lüge der Nina Petrowna *(*The Wonderful Lies of Nina Petrovna, *1929);* Manolescu *(1929);* Die singende Stadt *(1930);* The City of Song *(UK version of* Die singende Stadt, *1931);* Gloria *(German and French versions, 1931);* Im Geheimdienst *(1931);* The Blue Danube *(UK, 1932);* Die Herrin von Atlantis *(*L'Atlantide, *1932);* Die Gräfin von Monte Christo *(*The Countess of Monte Cristo, *1932);* Inge und die Millionen *(1933);* Der Läufer von Marathon *(1933);* Spione am Werk *(1933);* Die Insel *(1934);* Gold *(1934);* Ein idealer Gatte *(1935);* Gilgi Eine von Uns *(1937).*

Tall, blonde and beautiful, Brigitte Helm starred in over 35 movies during the Germany film industry's golden age. She was born Eva Gisela Schittenhelm in 1908, the daughter of a Prussian army officer who died when she was an infant. A serious student, Helm acted in school plays while attending boarding school, but the movie industry did not remotely interest her. It was frowned upon by the Prussians as an immoral profession.

Even so, Helm's mother sent her daughter's photograph to ***Thea von Harbou**, the screenwriter and wife of director Fritz Lang, and the 16-year-old Helm was tricked into doing a screen test. As a result, the teenager was given the lead in Lang's expressionistic masterpiece *Metropolis*, an allegory of totalitarianism written by von Harbou, which was shot in 1924–25 and released in 1926. Helm worked every day for 18 months playing the role of Maria, an oppressed, idealistic working girl in a futuristic city who sparks the social conscience of her fellow workers but convinces them to enlist a mediator for their grievances rather than resort to violence. At the urging of the Master of Metropolis, however, Maria is transformed into the "false Maria," a robot in her likeness, by the mad scientist Rotwang. As a *doppelganger* (divided self), she is evil incarnate, fomenting a workers' rebellion as part of the Master's plan so that he might replace them with robots. The ambitious movie is famous for its flying machines and special effects. Helm, who had to hang upside down or stand in water to her waist for hours on end, hated the experience. "After one torturous ordeal," reports *The New York Times News Service,* "when she wondered why a double could not have taken her place during the nine days it took to shoot a scene in which she was encased in a metallic robot shell, her face obscured, Lang haughtily claimed an auteur's creative sensibility." *Metropolis* was Hitler's favorite film, for all the wrong reasons.

With the film's release, Helm became an international star. She appeared in two important early films directed by Austrian-born G.W. Pabst, master of the new realism. *Die Liebe der Jeanne Ney,* concerning love and the Russian Revolution, contains an innovative, two-minute section in which Pabst uses 40 cuts between three separate characters in a heated argument. The other, *Crisis* (1928), is a look into the sexual experience of a woman.

In 1929, the sought after but reluctant Helm turned down Josef von Sternberg's offer to star in the *Blue Angel,* a part that went to ***Marlene Dietrich**. After nine years in front of the camera, appearing in many German films and some British and French, Helm retired from the screen and married. She lived in seclusion for over 30 years before she died in Anscona, Switzerland, in 1996.

Helmer, Bessie Bradwell (1858–1927).

See Bradwell, Myra for sidebar.

Helmrich, Dorothy (1889–1984)

Australian singer and founder of the Arts Council of Australia. *Born Dorothy Jane Adele Hellmrich (later changed to Helmrich), in Woollahra, New South Wales, on July 25, 1889; died in Strathfield, Australia, on September 1, 1984; the youngest of six children of John Hellmrich (an architect) and Esther Isobel (Pepper) Hellmrich; attended Mosman Academy and High School; studied singing at the New South Wales State Conservatorium and at the Royal College of Music, London; never married; no children.*

Born into a musical family, singer Dorothy Helmrich took piano and voice lessons as a child and began her musical career with the Mosman Musical Society. Through a generous benefactor, Lady **Alice Cooper**, Helmrich was able to study at the New South Wales State Conservatorium and later at the Royal College of Music in London. She made her London debut at Wigmore Hall, followed by engagements throughout the provinces as well as radio broadcasts. Through the years, she built an international reputation and toured widely in Britain, Europe, and America. From 1941 to 1974, she also held a teaching post at the Conservatorium.

In 1943, Helmrich founded the Australian Council for the Encouragement of Music and the Arts (CEMA), a group of volunteers whose mission was "to bring art in all forms, to the people." By 1946, it had evolved into the Arts Council of Australia, of which Helmrich served as vice president and later president of the New South Wales division for 20 years. Through her leadership and resourcefulness, the organization expanded to provide art, drama, music, and arts education nationwide, particularly in schools and rural areas. Unable to obtain commonwealth funding, the volunteer group struggled with a restrictive budget until 1967, when it was superseded by the Australian Council for the Arts.

From 1908 on, Helmrich was also a proponent of theosophy, which she called "a philosophical basis for living . . . for which I am extremely grateful." She was a member of the United Lodge of Theosophists in London and the Theosophical Society in Australia. The singer never married. "I was fated to live my life in single blessedness," she said. In recognition of her achievements, Helmrich was awarded an Order of the British Empire (OBE) in 1959. She died at Strathfield in 1984.

Hellmuth, Hermine Hug (1871–1924).

See Hug-Hellmuth, Hermine.

Heloise.

Variant of Lois.

Heloise (c. 1100–1163)

Highly educated French abbess of the 12th century who was the mistress and wife of the medieval philosopher Peter Abelard. *Born around 1100; died on May 16, 1163 (some sources cite 1164); educated at convent of Argenteuil; tutored by Peter Abelard, around 1117, in Paris; married Peter Abelard, around 1118 (died 1142); children: Astrolabe.*

Gave birth to her only child Astrolabe and subsequently married Peter Abelard (c. 1118); became a nun at Argenteuil (1118); installed as abbess of the Paraclete (1129); corresponded with Peter Abelard (early 1130s).

Educated women in the 12th century were so rare as to stand out as an anomaly, but this alone does not account for the widespread fame of Heloise. Her affair with one of the great teachers of her day increased public awareness of her status as an unusually talented woman. This great French abbess attracted the attention of her contemporaries in three periods of her life: as a young girl (when her reputation for learning was known to many 12th-century scholars and clergy), as a young woman (when her passionate affair with the towering intellectual Peter Abelard resulted in love songs immortalizing the relationship), and as a maturing woman (when she went on to become the abbess of her own convent). Heloise's spiritual grace and effective administration of church properties won her the praise of popes and abbots alike.

Though abbesses of medieval convents were certainly important women, Heloise's enduring interest to scholars and the general public stems from her relationship with a charismatic teacher in 12th-century Paris, Peter Abelard. Long after their affair, marriage, and tragic separation, the pair wrote letters to each other which give an unusually valuable window into medieval hearts and minds. In fact, these letters, written in the early 1130s, constitute our most important source of information about the life of Heloise; thus it is important to examine briefly the quality of this source.

The letters number seven in all, and their authenticity has been a subject of enormous concern to scholars. Opinions have ranged from the assertion that Abelard himself wrote *all* of the letters; to the view that a third, later source wrote the collection; to the belief that the letters are actually what they purport to be, a genuine correspondence. Even this latter view, however, is problematic. Some believe that the collection was subject to editing by Heloise, or Abelard, or later church personnel into whose hands the manuscripts fell. Recent scholarship has generally affirmed the view that the correspondence is genuine, though editing by Heloise is a strong possibility.

Little is known of Heloise's childhood. Born around 1100, she may have been the daughter of a minor noble; another possibility proffered by scholars is that she was illegitimate. Direct evidence does not exist, however, to support either position. She was placed under the care of her uncle Fulbert, who was a canon at the cathedral of Notre Dame in Paris, and her early education took place at the convent of Argenteuil, near Paris. Apparently, Heloise made outstanding progress in her pursuit of secular learning at Argenteuil, for by the time she rejoined Fulbert in Paris around 1116 or 1117, she was widely acknowledged as a highly intelligent and learned young woman. Her reputation soon attracted the attention of the man who was to dominate her life, the charismatic teacher of philosophy, Peter Abelard.

Our knowledge of Heloise's early relationship with Abelard comes from the latter's own hand. In his *Historia calamitatum,* purportedly a letter of consolation which Abelard wrote to an unnamed friend around 1130, he admitted that his initial interest in Heloise was less than pure:

> There lived in Paris a maiden named Heloise, the niece of a canon named Fulbert, who from his deep love for her was eager to have her advanced in all literary pursuits possible. She was a lady of no mean appearance while in literary excellence she was the first. . . . I . . . decided she was just the one for me to join in love.

At this time, Heloise was around 17 and Abelard was some 20 years her senior. His pursuit of this young woman was fueled by his enormous ego: "I then enjoyed such renown and was so outstanding for my charms of youth that I feared no repulse by any woman whom I should deign to favor with my love."

Fulbert was anxious for his niece to continue her study of philosophy and classical literature. Although such scholarship would not have led to a career in the modern sense, it was a sign of Fulbert's great affection for Heloise that he enabled her to pursue her scholarly inclinations. Abelard called Fulbert "a very avaricious man," who could not refuse Peter's offer to live with Fulbert in exchange for tutoring Heloise. Indeed, Fulbert encouraged the pair to spend hours together in intellectual collaboration. Very soon, Abelard's goal was achieved:

> What was the result? We were first together in one house and then one in mind. Under the pretext of work we made ourselves entirely free for love and the pursuit of her studies provided the secret privacy which love desired. We opened our books but more words of love than of reason asserted themselves. There was more kissing than teaching; my hands found themselves at her breasts more often than on the book.

As the affair progressed, Abelard composed love songs praising Heloise. These popular songs contributed both to public awareness of the relationship and to the enhancement of Heloise's reputation as an outstandingly literate woman who was worthy of the love of such a great man.

The affair continued for some months. Fulbert finally discovered the pair in bed together and demanded that they stop seeing each other. Still, clandestine meetings were achieved. When Heloise discovered that she was pregnant,

Abelard arranged for her to travel to his sister in Brittany. There, she gave birth to their son, whom she named Astrolabe. Abelard's sister raised the child.

Abelard remained in Paris and, to placate Fulbert, offered to marry Heloise—with the condition that their marriage remain a secret, in order to protect his credibility as a teacher. In 12th-century Paris, teachers normally were unmarried clerics; although, conceivably, a cleric in lower orders could wed without relinquishing his teaching position, it would have been difficult for such a man to be considered credible by his students, as the moral ideals of the day required a celibate clergy. By this standard, marriage was merely a public admission that one was unable to remain chaste.

At a time when nearly the whole world is indifferent and deplorably apathetic towards [secular learning] . . . you have surpassed all women in carrying out your purpose and have gone further than almost every man.

—Letter of Peter the Venerable, abbot of Cluny, to Heloise

The wedding took place in 1117 or 1118, though the bridegroom had found it difficult to persuade Heloise to agree to the marriage. Her objections to the union were made out of concern for Abelard's scholarly status and future prospects: first, she stated that a "secret" marriage would not appease Fulbert in the long run; his pride would ultimately lead him to demand public acknowledgement of the marriage. Second, Heloise objected to the marriage on the grounds that Peter was too great an intellectual treasure to waste on one mere woman. In Abelard's account of Heloise's objections to the idea of marriage, he noted:

> What punishment would the world demand of her if she deprived it of such a shining light? What curses, what loss to the Church, what weeping among philosophers would ensue from our marriage; how disgraceful, how lamentable would it be if I, whom nature had produced for all, should devote myself to a woman and submit to such baseness!

Heloise's objections to the marriage were supported by classical and Christian authorities—a clear indication of the extent of her scholarly learning. For example, in warning Abelard of the myriad obligations a married man has to his household, she noted that Socrates was severely hindered in his pursuit of wisdom by his wife ***Xanthippe**'s perpetual complaints. Overall, Heloise's position was that she loved Abelard far too much to place him under similar constraints. Her arguments appear not only in Abelard's *Historia calamitatum,* but also in her own first letter to Abelard:

> God knows I never sought anything in you except yourself; I wanted simply you, nothing of yours. I looked for no marriage-bond, no marriage portion, and it was not my own pleasures and wishes I sought to gratify, as you well know, but yours. The name of wife may seem more sacred or more binding, but sweeter for me will always be the word mistress, or, if you will permit me, that of concubine or whore.

In short, Heloise's position reflected both a Christian viewpoint grounded in such writers as St. Paul and St. Jerome, as well as a classical viewpoint. She clearly demonstrated her impressive familiarity with secular learning.

Her prediction that Fulbert would not be content with a secret marriage proved all too true. Abelard's visits to his wife were often marred by violent quarrels with her uncle, who wished to make the marriage publicly known despite his initial agreement to abide by Peter's terms of secrecy. To avoid confrontations with Fulbert, Abelard sent Heloise to the convent of Argenteuil. He continued his clandestine visits with her. But Fulbert assumed that Abelard wished to dissolve the marriage by making Heloise a nun. The offended canon hatched a plan to avenge his wounded honor, and he had Abelard castrated. According to Peter, Fulbert's attackers "cut off the organs" by which he had "committed the deed which they deplored."

His castration was a public humiliation, fully described in Abelard's *Historia calamitatum,* which drove husband and wife into cloistered religious life. After recovering from the wounds, he entered the monastery of St. Denis. At Argenteuil, Heloise took the veil which signified her submission to a life of conformity with the monastic rule. The brief, passionate affair between the great scholar Abelard and the most learned young woman in France had been brought to a dramatic end—yet their relationship continued.

Heloise's entry into the convent was not a voluntary choice; she became a nun in deference to the wishes of her beloved husband. "It was not any sense of vocation which brought me as a young girl to accept the austerities of the cloister, but your bidding alone," she wrote in her first letter to him.

Abelard's life as a monk of St. Denis was filled with stress and personal danger: the monks

Heloise

found him overbearing and too zealous in his efforts to reform their religious life. Conflict resulted, and eventually Abelard feared for his personal safety. When his theological views were condemned by a council at Soissons in 1121, he sought refuge in another monastery, St. Ayoul in Provins. Here, he fared no better: his irritating personality caused him to clash with the monks once again, and only his friendship with the prior made his situation tolerable. Finally, by appealing to the French king Louis VI, Abelard received permission to leave St. Ayoul and live a monastic life in solitude. But as he wrote in his *Historia calamitatum:* "When my former students discovered my whereabouts, they began to leave the cities and towns and to flock there to dwell with me in my solitude." His oratory was first called the Holy Trinity, which engendered yet another conflict with church authorities who found it an unsuitable name for a church. Soon the oratory was renamed the Paraclete (the Comforter, i.e., the Holy Spirit); the conflict with church authorities continued, as the latter found it sacrilegious to stress only one element of the Trinity.

Meanwhile, Heloise was quietly living at the convent of Argenteuil. By 1125, she became prioress of her community, but in 1129 she and her nuns were expelled from their convent by the abbot of St. Denis, who claimed the property of Argenteuil for his own monastery. By then, Abelard had abandoned the Paraclete in order to become the abbot of a monastery in Brittany. When word of Heloise's homeless wanderings with her sisters reached him, he granted her the property of the Paraclete. There, with his help, Heloise established her religious community. Abelard noted that Heloise's community prospered despite early hardships and deprivations.

> As a woman is the weaker sex, so her dire need more readily arouses human sympathy and her life of virtue is the more pleasing to God and man. God granted such favor in the eyes of all to my sister who was over the other nuns that bishops loved her as a daughter, the laity as a mother, and all alike admired her spirit of religion.

In 1129, Heloise became the abbess of her community of the Paraclete and remained in this position for the rest of her life.

Abelard, as founder of the convent of the Paraclete, assisted Heloise's community in its earliest days. But his frequent presence there outraged his enemies, who questioned whether his motives were spiritual or carnal: "As a result, gossip engendered by envy arose . . . my calumniators with their usual perverseness . . . [charged] that I was still in the power of a lingering delight in carnal lust and could scarcely endure . . . the absence of my old lover."

Heloise and Abelard's correspondence reflects their activities during the early 1130s. Her first letter to Abelard (1132 or 1133) expressed concern for her beloved's safety, as the monks of St. Gildas were making attempts on his life. She also reproached him for writing a long comforting letter to a friend (the *Historia calamitatum*), yet failing to attend to her own great need for consolation:

> Tell me one thing, if you can. Why, after our entry into religion, which was your decision alone, have I been so neglected and forgotten by you that I have neither a word from you when you are here to give me strength nor the consolation of a letter in absence? . . . While I am denied your presence, give me at least through your words . . . some sweet semblance of yourself.

Abelard's response was a mild apology. He claimed that Heloise's exemplary life was so widely admired that he assumed she had no need of consolation at all. On the contrary, *he* requested *her* prayers.

Heloise's second letter clarified her position to Abelard: "Of all wretched women I am the most wretched, and amongst the unhappy I am the unhappiest." She wanted Abelard to understand unequivocally that her entire life was lived in devotion to him, not God; the compliments of church officials were empty praise. Only Abelard's written communications could satisfy her. In his lengthy response, Abelard criticized Heloise for her "old perpetual complaint against God concerning the manner of our entry into religious life and the cruelty of the act of treachery performed on me." He asked her to be content with the spiritual daughters she was so successfully nurturing and contrasted her success with his own inability to get along with the monks under his care.

Heloise's third and last letter to Abelard acknowledged her acceptance of his command to stop bringing up old wounds:

> I would not want to give you cause for finding me disobedient in anything, so I have set the bridle of your injunction on the words which issue from my unbounded grief.

True to her promise, Heloise never again upbraided Abelard for his insensitivity to her love; she turned her focus on a series of practical questions regarding the lifestyle of women under monastic rule. Abelard obviously felt more comfortable dealing with his wife on this spiritual level, for he wrote two very long letters giving spiritual direction to her community and composed liturgical verses for them as well.

When Abelard died in 1142, his body was taken to the Paraclete for burial. Heloise's great loss elicited a warm letter from Abbot Peter of Cluny, one of the most respected ecclesiastics of his day. He assured Heloise that her beloved husband had experienced a peaceful and holy death at one of Cluny's affiliated monasteries. From Heloise's response to this letter, we know that her son Astrolabe was pursuing an ecclesiastical career, for she asked Abbot Peter to attempt to secure a prebend from the archbishop of Paris for her son.

Heloise lived on for another 21 years. In the death list of the Paraclete, her demise is noted on May 16 of either 1163 or 1164. Her years without Abelard were successful ones. Under her guidance, the Paraclete became one of France's most flourishing religious establishments, and several daughter houses were founded by it. The woman who was praised for her devotion to learning, whose intelligence attracted the leading scholar of Paris, used her extraordinary education to enhance female religious life. Unable to remain Abelard's physical wife, she became his spiritual wife and sister. Heloise was buried in her husband's tomb, and the grave is still visited and honored by many.

SOURCES:

Muckle, J.T., trans. *The Story of Abelard's Adversities: A Translation with notes of the Historia Calamitatum.* Toronto: The Pontifical Institute of Mediaeval Studies, 1964.

Radice, Betty, trans. *The Letters of Abelard and Heloise.* NY: Penguin Books, 1974.

SUGGESTED READING:

Dronke, Peter. *Abelard and Heloise in Medieval Testimonies.* W.P. Ker Lecture no. 26, University of Glasgow Press, 1976.

———. *Women Writers of the Middle Ages.* NY: Cambridge University Press, 1984.

Gilson, Etienne. *Heloise and Abelard.* Ann Arbor, MI: University of Michigan Press, 1960.

Shahar, Shulamith. *The Fourth Estate: A History of Women in the Middle Ages.* London: Routledge, 1983.

Southern, R.W. *Medieval Humanism and Other Studies.* NY: Harper Torchbacks, 1970.

Cathy Jorgensen Itnyre,
Professor of History, Copper Mountain College
(College of the Desert), Joshua Tree, California

Heluidis.

Variant of Helvidis.

Helvidis (fl. 1136)

French physician. *Name variations: Heluidis. Flourished in 1136 in Lille, France.*

Helvidis, who worked as a physician and lay healer, has the distinction of being the first woman doctor of northern Europe who is listed as such in contemporary records. Her name and occupation are found in a listing of benefactors of a small church, built around 1136. Unfortunately, nothing else is known about Helvidis' life or work.

Laura York,
Riverside, California

Helvig.

Variant of Helwig.

Helvig of Denmark (fl. 1350s)

Queen of Denmark. *Name variations: Heilwig Ericsdottir; Helvig of Slesvig or Schleswig. Flourished in the 1350s; died around 1374; daughter of Erik, duke of Schleswig, and* **Adelheid of Holstein***; sister of Valdemar or Waldemar III, duke of Schleswig; married Valdemar IV also known as Waldemar IV Atterdag, king of Denmark (r. 1340–1375), in June 1340; children:* ***Margaret I** (1353–1412), queen of Denmark, Norway, and Sweden;* ***Ingeborg** (1347–1370, who married Henry of Mecklenburg); Christof (1344–1363), duke of Laaland; Margaret (1345–1350); Katherina Valdemarsdottir (b. 1349); Waldemar (b. 1350).*

Helvig of Slesvig (fl. 1350s).

See Helvig of Denmark.

Helwig.

Variant of Helvig.

Helwig of Prague (fl. 14th c.)

Leader of Beguines in Germany. *Flourished in the 14th century in Prague; never married; no children.*

A German member of the Beguine religious order, Helwig of Prague was an acknowledged leader of the sect when it was condemned by Pope John XXII in 1332. The Beguines, an order of women devoted to a simple life of supporting themselves without a particular rule, and not subject to obeying Church officials except the pope himself, came under suspicion as heretics for their contrary views and independent lives. Group leaders like Helwig managed the daily activities of their followers without the approval of priests or bishops. Often, it was the independent spirit and self-sufficient attitudes of Beguine leaders like Helwig that brought condemnation as much as any truly heretical or radical theology. After her group was forcibly disbanded, the rest of Helwig's life becomes obscure.

Laura York,
Riverside, California

Hemans, Felicia D. (1793–1835)

English poet and dramatist. *Name variations: Felicia Browne. Born Felicia Dorothea Browne in Duke Street, Liverpool, England, on September 25, 1793; died at Redesdale, near Dublin, on May 16, 1835; fifth of seven children of George Browne (a merchant* *of Irish extraction) and Felicity (Wagner) Browne (daughter of Austrian and Tuscan consul at Liverpool); educated at home by her mother; married Captain Alfred Hemans, in 1812 (separated 1818); children: five sons.*

The fifth of seven children, Felicia Hemans was born in Liverpool, England, in 1793. She was only seven when her father's business failed, and the family moved to Gwrych, near Abergele, Denbighshire, in Wales. There, the young romantic grew up by the sea, surroundings she would recall with pleasure. Distinguished for her beauty and precocity, Hemans' education in the hands of her mother was thorough, though haphazard. She studied Italian, Spanish, Portuguese, and German, played piano and harp, and devoured books—especially romances, histories, and poetry of all sorts.

In 1808, when Felicia was only 14, a quarto of her *Juvenile Poems* was unwisely published by her adoring parents. After receiving a drubbing in the *Monthly Review,* the young poet took to her bed. In 1812, she tried again, publishing *The Domestic Affections and Other Poems.* She also married Captain Alfred Hemans, an Irish soldier, who had served—along with her brothers—in the 1808–1814 Peninsular War, caused by Napoleon's attempt to annex Spain.

For some time, Hemans lived in Daventry, where Captain Alfred was adjutant of the Northamptonshire militia. Following the birth of a son and the death of her father, she and her husband moved in with her mother at Bronwylfa, near St. Asaph in North Wales, Lancashire. Hemans continued to write. In a three-year span, she published *The Restoration of Works of Art to Italy* (1816), *Modern Greece* (1817), and *Translations from Camoens and other Poets* (1818). But the marriage was not a happy one. After the birth of five sons in six years, Alfred journeyed to Rome, Italy, in 1818, supposedly for his health, and decided to remain. There seems to have been a tacit agreement that they should separate, and they never met again. Though in poor health herself and still living with her mother, Hemans now devoted her time to the education of her children and writing, generating income to add to the family's meager finances.

In 1819, she published *Tales and Historic Scenes in Verse* and *The Meeting of Wallace and Bruce on the Banks of the Carron;* in 1820, she issued *The Sceptic* and *Stanzas to the Memory of the late King.* She won the Royal Society of Literature award for her poem *Dartmoor* in June 1821 and, in the summer of 1823, published the poems, "Sieve of Valencia," "Last Constantine," and "Belshazzar's Feats." On December 12, 1823, her play *Vespers of Palmero* opened at Covent Garden, starring Charles Kemble, but closed after one performance. When the play was performed the following year in Edinburgh, however, ***Joanna Baillie** requested an epilogue written by Sir Walter Scott and read by ***Harriet Siddons**, and the play met with more success. It was the start of a close friendship between Hemans and Walter Scott; Felicia and her boys often stayed at Scott's Abbotsford. In 1824, she started work on *The Forest Sanctuary.*

In spring of 1825, Hemans moved from Bronwylfa to Rhyllon, a house across the river Clwyd, where she celebrated her beautiful surroundings in more poetry. The loss of her beloved mother in January 1827 had a profound effect on Hemans' health; from that time on, she was an acknowledged invalid. In the summer of 1828, the *Records of Woman* was published; that same year, she moved to Wavertree, near Liverpool, for her sons' education, but she was not happy with the provincial Liverpudlians. When Hemans moved to Dublin to live with a brother in 1831, her poetry was becoming more and more religious in tone. She died in Dublin on May 16, 1835, at age 41.

In her lifetime, Hemans' poetry was in great demand, and she received many awards and honors. She was admired by notables, including Lord Jeffrey, Lord Byron, ***Marguerite, Countess of Blessington**, and Christopher North. ***Maria Jewsbury** found her "totally different from any other woman I had ever seen. . . . She did not dazzle, she subdued me. . . . I never saw one so exquisitely feminine. . . . Her birth, her education, the genius with which she was gifted, combined to inspire a passion for the ethereal, the tender, the imaginative, the heroic—in one word, the beautiful."

Though extremely popular in her day, Hemans' poetry is now largely considered to be a compilation of sentimental love lyrics. Scott complained that her work was "too poetical," that it contained "too many flowers" and "too little fruit." Without great originality or power, her poetry was pleasing, and, like Longfellow, some of her lyrics, "The Voice of Spring," "The Better Land," "Casabianca," "The Graves of a Household," "The Treasures of the Deep," and "The Homes of England" were found in many school collections. In later life, Felicia Hemans regretted the haste in her work, but her prolific pen was often propelled by economic necessity.

SUGGESTED READING:

Chorley, H.F. *Memorial of Mrs. Hemans.*

Courtney, J.E. *The Adventurous Thirties.*

Hemans, F. *Works* (an 1839 edition contained an introductory memoir by her sister).

Hemenway, Mary Porter Tileston (1820–1894)

American philanthropist. *Born Mary Porter Tileston in New York City, on December 20, 1820; died in Boston, Massachusetts, on March 6, 1894; eldest of nine children of Thomas Tileston (a shipping merchant) and Mary (Porter) Tileston; attended private schools in New York; married Augustus Hemenway (a merchant), on June 25, 1840 (died 1876); children: five:* ***Charlotte Augusta Hemenway*** *(b. 1841); Alice (1845, died at age two);* ***Amy Hemenway*** *(b. 1848);* ***Edith Hemenway*** *(b. 1851); and Augustus Hemenway (1853).*

One of nine children of **Mary Porter Tileston** and Thomas Tileston, a wealthy New York shipping merchant, Mary Hemenway was educated privately and then busied herself at home until her marriage in 1840 to Augustus Hemenway, a wealthy Boston merchant 15 years her senior. While her husband was away overseeing the expansion of his business interests, Hemenway endured the long separations by tending to the couple's five children. In 1860, Augustus suffered a nervous breakdown and was hospitalized in a sanatorium for 14 years. (He died in 1876.) During that time, Hemenway embarked on her long career in philanthropy.

Hemenway's major concern was the practical education of Boston's public school children, and her manner of philanthropy was to provide seed money and provisions for particular projects until they were well established and could be taken over by public funding. One of her early projects was to supply materials and teachers for sewing classes in a Boston public school, a program that was ultimately taken over by the school system. In 1883 and 1884, she sponsored a summer manual training school for girls, a project that was expanded with her gift of a school kitchen (the first in the United States), as well as money for cooking teachers. In 1887, she established the Boston Normal School of Cookery to train more teachers, and a year later, the program was also taken over by the public schools. In the same manner, she supported physical education, establishing a Normal School of Gymnastics, which was later financed by Wellesley College.

Believing that education was also a key in restoring the South and promoting national unity after the Civil War, in 1871 Hemenway donated funds to establish the Tileston Normal School in Wilmington, North Carolina, for the education of poor whites. She continued to support the institution throughout its 20-year history and also contributed to Tuskegee and Hampton Institutes. In 1880, she purchased land for the construction of the Brambleton School in Norfolk, Virginia. In Boston, she gave $100,000 toward the restoration of the Old South Meeting House, where she later instituted a community program in American history, including a yearly summer lecture series by eminent scholars and the publication of leaflets and supplementary source material. In 1881, she provided money for a yearly essay contest for high school students, who were assigned to write on the subject of American History.

In 1886, after meeting a group of visiting Zuñi Indians, Hemenway commissioned the Hemenway Southwestern Archaeological Expedition to carry out archaeological and ethnological field studies among the Zuñi and Hopi tribes. The expedition, under the direction of Frank Cushing and later of J. Walter Fewkes, was carried out over a seven-year period. Hemenway also underwrote a report of the work, which appeared in five volumes of the *Journal of American Ethnology and Archaeology* (1891–1908).

Mary Hemenway also supported the Unitarian Church and, in 1878, transformed her summer home in Milton, Massachusetts, into a shelter for orphans, the Hillside Home for Boys. The philanthropist died in her Beacon Hill home on March 6, 1894, leaving a trust fund for the continued support of her enterprises.

SOURCES:

James, Edward T., ed. *Notable American Women.* Cambridge, MA: The Belknap Press of Harvard University Press, 1971.

McHenry, Robert, ed. *Famous American Women.* NY: Dover, 1983.

Barbara Morgan,
Melrose, Massachusetts

Hemessen, Caterina van (c. 1528–c. 1587)

Flemish painter. *Born in Antwerp, Belgium, around 1528; died in Spain, around 1587; daughter of Jan van Hemessen (a painter); married Chrétien de Morien (a musician), in 1554; no children.*

One of the first Flemish women artists ever documented, Caterina van Hemessen was the daughter of Jan van Hemessen (1500–1563), a notable artist of the period. Ten paintings, dated between 1548 and 1552, have been attributed to van Hemessen, eight small portraits of women and two religious works probably based on prints. In 1554, the artist married Chrétien de Morien, organist at Antwerp Cathedral, after which she apparently gave up painting. In 1556, the couple joined the court of Queen ***Mary of Hungary** (1505–1558), former regent of the Netherlands, who died two years later, leaving them a generous pension.

It is generally believed that van Hemessen was trained by her father, although in style her work reflects little of his influence. Her religious paintings, among which *Christ and St. *Veronica* (undated), is representative, are restricted and less significant than her portraits, which **Germaine Greer**, in *The Obstacle Race*, describes as kind of expanded miniatures, "typical in their abstracted, introverted expression, limited colour range and restricted lighting of the Flemish portrait tradition as it was to develop." **Ann Harris** and **Linda Nochlin** point out that two van Hemessen portraits—*Self-Portrait* and *Young Woman Playing the Virginals* (a likeness of her older sister), wood panels of equal size and dated 1548—were painted with the two women facing left and right, so they could be hung as a pair. The authors also note that Hemessen, like many of her contemporaries, had difficulty drawing hands. Though van Hemessen gave up painting before she had time to mature, her work adds significantly to the substantiation of the ten or so women artists that were active in Flanders during the mid-16th century.

Eppes, Maria Jefferson. *See Jefferson, Martha for sidebar.*

SOURCES:

Greer, Germaine. *The Obstacle Race*. NY: Farrar, Straus & Giroux, 1979.

Harris, Ann Sutherland, and Linda Nochlin. *Women Artists 1550–1950*. LA County Museum of Art: Knopf, 1976.

Barbara Morgan, Melrose, Massachusetts

Hemings, Sally (1773–1835)

African-American slave who for years was the subject of speculation regarding her relationship with the nation's third president, Thomas Jefferson, now thought to be the father of at least one of her children. *Name variations: Sally Hemmings; Black Sally. Pronunciation: HEM-ings. Born Sally Hemings in 1773, on one of the Virginia plantations belonging to John Wayles; died in 1835 (some sources cite 1836), in Albemarle County, Virginia; daughter of John Wayles (a wealthy planter and slave trader) and his mulatto slave Elizabeth (Betty) Hemings; half-sister of Martha Jefferson; no legal marriage noted; children: Thomas (whose actual existence is questionable but may have been Thomas Woodson [1790–1879]); Edy (b. 1796, died in infancy); Harriett (1795–1797); Beverly (1798–?); Harriett (1801–?); Madison (1805–1877); Eston (1808–1852).*

Arrived at Monticello as an infant (1774), among slaves inherited by her half-sister Martha Jefferson, wife of Thomas Jefferson; lived in Paris as a personal servant to the Jefferson daughters (1787–89), and upon return to Monticello resumed duties as a housemaid; freed by Jefferson's daughter, Martha Jefferson Randolph, not long after Jefferson's death; went to live with her two freed sons, Madison and Eston, for the remainder of her life; DNA tests proved that at least one son, Eston, is of the Jefferson blood-line (1999).

Sally Hemings attracted the singular attention of Thomas Jefferson in 1787, when she accompanied Jefferson's nine-year-old daughter **Maria Jefferson (Eppes)** to Paris as Maria's personal servant. From 1784 to 1789, Jefferson was the American minister to France, and Maria's older sister ***Martha Jefferson (Randolph)** was already abroad with him. That the care of Maria was entrusted to young Sally, who was only 14 at the time, was a surprise to Jefferson. Before going to Europe, Maria and Sally had been staying with Maria's aunt and uncle, Francis and **Elizabeth Eppes**. Jefferson had asked the Eppeses to send "a careful negro woman, Isabel, for instance, if she has had the small pox." Since Isabel was about to give birth, Sally was sent as a substitute.

***Abigail Adams**, wife of the American minister to England, John Adams, was asked by Jefferson to look after Maria and her slave servant during a stopover in England. Abigail was shocked to find that Sally "is quite a child" and informed Jefferson that Captain Ramsay, who had charge of the ship that brought the girls over, thought that Sally "will be of so little service that he had better carry her back with him." Abigail added, however, that Jefferson should be the judge. Sally "seems fond of the child and appears good naturd." It has been speculated that Captain Ramsay himself wanted to make the beautiful young slave a subject of his affections.

Even in Paris, as it would be at Monticello, the Jefferson home in Virginia, Hemings' life is shrouded in mystery. Jefferson never mentioned her in his correspondence during the Paris years. Sally and her uncle, James Hemings, whom Jefferson had assigned to French caterers to learn French cooking, had a good deal of independence. Under French law, they were free, having the same status as whites. Jefferson had Sally vaccinated in Paris, and his records indicate that he purchased fine clothes for her. In 1788, he began paying Sally and James monthly wages, about one-half of what French servants made. During their French stay, it is likely that Sally resided most of the time with Maria and her sister Martha at a convent boarding school and not at Jefferson's own close quarters at the Hôtel de Langeac. For five weeks, Sally lived with **Madam Dupré**, Jefferson's laundress. During these years, Hemings gained sophistication, some knowledge of French, and accompanied Jefferson's daughters on social occasions.

Thomas Jefferson had little privacy in Paris. There were frequent visitors and guests, none of whom mention Hemings, a fact used to refute the charge that beginning in Paris in 1789, Jefferson formed a sexual liaison with the 16-year-old Hemings. According to one theory, Sally, upon becoming pregnant in France, gave Jefferson the ultimatum that she would return to Virginia and resume the status of a slave only if Jefferson agreed to free all her future children when they reached age 21. This Jefferson, indeed, did, whether he had made such a pledge or not. Was Sally Hemings the mistress of Thomas Jefferson? A definitive answer has eluded historians. There are conflicting statements from credible witnesses and circumstantial evidence on both sides of the case. Jefferson remained completely mute on the subject.

Sally Hemings was a quadroon, that is one-fourth African and three-fourths Caucasian. Isaac, one of Jefferson's slaves, said of her that she was "mighty near white . . . very handsome, long straight hair down her back." She was also the half-sister of ***Martha Jefferson**, widow of Bathurst Skelton, who had married Thomas Jefferson in January 1772. Martha was aunt to Sally's children, and, conversely, Sally was aunt to her charges, the Jefferson daughters. Martha Jefferson was the daughter of John Wayles and his third wife **Martha Eppes Wayles**. After the death of Martha Wayles in 1761, John Wayles made Sally's mother **Betty Hemings** his mistress. Betty Hemings, the daughter of an English sea captain and an African slave woman, had six children with Wayles, Sally being the youngest. Upon John Wayles' death in 1773, Martha Jefferson inherited property that included 11,000 acres of land and 135 slaves. (Among them were the Hemings family, of whom six were Martha's half-sisters or brothers.)

Sally Hemings appears to have received no more than the preferential treatment afforded all members of the Hemings family at Monticello. All of Betty Hemings' surviving children became household servants or artisans. The reason for their placement among the elite in the slave hierarchy was owing to the respect that Jefferson had for his wife's half-siblings, especially so after Martha Jefferson died in 1782.

Sally's tasks at Monticello varied. As a housemaid, she could be expected to do cleaning (such as dusting), serve meals, arrange the dining table, run errands, and even do some outside work, such as helping with gardening and cutting shrubbery. Most essentially, as expected of all the women house slaves, she made clothes, which involved weaving, carding, and spinning wool. Thomas Jefferson expected his daughters to learn "the needle and domestic economy," so that they could better supervise the work of the household slaves. Domestic black servants, like Hemings, had better food than the field hands, because they ate leftovers prepared for their master and his family. They also had the better clothes among the slaves, often wearing garments handed down from the white family members. One drawback in Hemings' routine, as with other domestic slaves, was that she was at the Jefferson family's beck and call during all hours of the day and night.

> It is well known that the man *whom it delighteth the people to honor*. . . has kept as his concubine, one of his own slaves. Her name is SALLY. . . . THE AMERICAN VENUS is said to officiate as housekeeper at Monticello.
>
> **—James T. Callender (1902)**

Visitors at Monticello were surprised that the Hemings family could almost pass as white. The Duc de la Rochefoucauld-Liancourt, during a stay at Monticello in 1796, noted that some of Jefferson's slaves "neither in point of color nor features, showed the least trace of their original descent." Thomas Jefferson Randolph, Jefferson's oldest grandson, recalled that on one occasion "a gentleman dining with Mr. Jefferson looked so startled as he raised his eyes from the latter to the servant behind him, that his discovery of the resemblance was so perfectly obvious to all." Even in regard to one of Sally's sons, Randolph also remarked, "the resemblance was so close, that at some distance or in the dusk the slave, dressed in the same way, might have been mistaken for Mr. Jefferson." However, visitors at Monticello reported that Jefferson gave no indication of paternal affection toward those slaves who bore his likeness.

The Jefferson-like resemblance of Sally Hemings' children indicate a kinship between the Hemings and Jefferson families. Although miscegenation was illegal in Virginia, it was prevalent among the gentry and their slaves; no one asked questions as long as the slave did not become a public charge. Jefferson had pledged to his wife upon her deathbed in 1782, that he would not remarry, a promise he kept. Nine months before the birth of each of Hemings' children, he was at the same location as Sally. For Jefferson, however, to acknowledge or be proven the father of slave children would greatly damage his integrity and political career. He himself denounced miscegenation, and he had a reputation for being a kind master. Jefferson could ill afford being revealed as a hypocrite, especially one who debauched slave women under what was considered his "care." Were this the fact, an elaborate cover-up to conceal paternal relationship would compound the discredit. If Jefferson did not father Sally's children, who did? The debate is even more heated with DNA tests which provide conclusive evidence that Sally's progeny had a blood link to at least some member of the Jefferson family.

Sally Hemings was introduced to the public in a sensational article by James T. Callender in the *Richmond Recorder* of September 1, 1802. Callender charged that Jefferson "for many years has kept, as his concubine, one of his own slaves. Her name is SALLY." In the same newspaper, on September 22, Callender predicted that if more Virginians followed Jefferson's example "you would have FOUR HUNDRED THOUSAND MULATTOS in addition to the present swarm." There would likely be a racial civil war. Callender advised that the Democratic-Republican Party (one of the two major political parties of the time), in order to save itself, should ditch Jefferson. Callender, out for revenge for being denied a political appointment by President Jefferson, had already descended to scandal-mongering by accusing Alexander Hamilton and Jefferson of inappropriate sexual conduct (to which both men conceded). Jefferson acknowledged that he had tried to seduce a married woman, Mrs. John Walker (**Elizabeth Walker**). Despite his vindictive journalism, if Callender was truthful regarding other accusations, could he not also be accurate as to a Jefferson-Hemings liaison?

The most intriguing aspect of the Jefferson-Hemings controversy is Callender's claim that living at Monticello, in 1802, was a 12-year-old boy, Tom, Jr., presumably the child that Sally conceived in France in 1789. Though there is no paper trace of a Tom, Jr., biographer **Fawn Brodie** and alleged descendants of Tom contend that the boy disappeared from Monticello as soon as the Callender story broke. Supposedly Jefferson sent Tom to the Goochland plantation of Josiah Woodson, where Tom assumed the Woodson name. An 1820 census lists Tom Woodson as a mulatto who, though a slave, lived as a free man. He married a free black woman and moved first to Greenbrier County, Virginia, and then to Ohio, where he died in 1879. Tom Woodson told his grandchildren that he was Jefferson's son.

The Tom, Jr. story was picked up over succeeding generations by those who had motives to discredit Jefferson. The English novelist, ***Frances Milton Trollope**, after visiting America, wrote a book disparaging American democracy and manners (published in 1832). She suggested that Jefferson was the progenitor of "innumerable generations of slaves." The "hospitable orgies" at Monticello "were incomplete unless the goblets he quaffed were tendered by the trembling hand of his own offspring."

After the Civil War, the revelations of Sally's son, Madison Hemings, played out in a political milieu, particularly with the Republicans. The party which had saved the Union hoped to further malign the Democrats by showing that Jefferson, representative of the Democratic leadership of the past, had made a harlot of a slave woman. Madison, an octoroon (seven-eighths white) who could have passed as white, gained his freedom at age 21 (presumably because of the pledge Jefferson made to Sally in France). He remained in Albemarle County (the same county as Monticello), until his mother died in 1835, and then moved to Pike County, Ohio, living in a black community there. In 1873, S.F. Wetmore, a staunch Republican and holder of patronage jobs of postmaster and federal marshall, published an interview of Madison Hemings in the local paper that Wetmore edited, the *Pike County Republican*. Madison recollected that his mother had told him she had been Jefferson's "concubine" in Paris. Thus, accepting Madison's account, Sally had a child in 1790 who either lived or died or became the person known as Tom Woodson. Although the refined style of the language attributed to Madison does not comport with his meager education, Madison's account as a surviving witness nevertheless has credibility.

Testimonies of Jefferson's slave, Isaac, and an overseer at Monticello (1806–22), Edmund Bacon, made no mention of a slave son of Jeffer-

Thandie Newton as Sally Hemings (with Estelle Eonnet as Polly Jefferson) in the film Jefferson in Paris.

son named Tom. Still, the overall question remains: did any one or several of Sally's children have Thomas Jefferson as a parent? A case has been made that either or both Peter and Samuel Carr, sons of Jefferson's sister, **Martha Jefferson Carr,** and her husband Dabney Carr (died 1773), were responsible for the paternity of some or all of Sally Hemings' children. This theory depends on the dismissal of the assumption that Sally conceived a child (Tom, Jr.) in Paris, since no Carrs were in France at that time. Peter and Samuel Carr, Jefferson's favorite nephews, were brought up at Monticello and later were frequent visitors who lived nearby.

In 1868, Henry Randall, a biographer of Jefferson, reported in a letter to James Parton, also a Jefferson biographer, that in the 1850s Thomas Jefferson Randolph, grandson of Jefferson, had told him that Peter Carr was the father of Sally's children. He maintained that Sally had been the mistress of Peter Carr, and her mother Betty that of Samuel Carr. Randolph, who owned Edgehill plantation next to Monticello, had lived with his mother Martha Jefferson Randolph in Jefferson's home and had managed Jefferson's plantation. Randolph claimed that he had slept within sound of Jefferson's breathing and that he had known of no liaison between Jefferson and Sally Hemings. In 1858, **Ellen Randolph Coolidge**, another of Martha Jefferson Randolph's children, had written that she believed Samuel Carr was the father of Sally Hemings' children. Edmund Bacon, the former overseer at Monticello, in an interview published in 1862, stated that a person (name withheld) other than Jefferson was the father of Sally's daughter, **Harriett Hemings**, born in 1801.

Jefferson either freed Sally's children or allowed them to run away. He gave Harriett $50 and permitted her to take a stagecoach to Philadelphia. **Beverly Hemings** also went to the same city, where both she and Harriet passed as white. Eston Hemings joined Madison in Ohio after their mother's death. Eston, who played the violin, as did Jefferson, and who became a popular band leader, eventually moved to Wisconsin. Strangely, though her children were freed by Jefferson, Sally was not. The probate inventory of Jefferson's estate listed Sally, then 54 years old, as having the slave value of $50. Within two years after Jefferson's death, his daughter and heir, Martha Jefferson Randolph, freed Sally, who lived out the rest of her life with sons Madison and Eston. All three, in the 1830 census, were listed as white. When Sally died in 1835, she was buried not at Monticello but in a cemetery for blacks.

The case for a Jefferson-Hemings sexual relationship has received a substantial boost from the appearance of the immensely popular novels, *Sally Hemings* (1979) and *The President's Daughter* (1994) by **Barbara Chase-Riboud**, the 1995 motion picture *Jefferson in Paris*, and the exhaustively researched psychobiography *Thomas Jefferson: An Intimate History* (1974) by Fawn Brodie. **Annette Gordon-Reed**, in *Thomas Jefferson and Sally Hemings: An American Controversy* (1997), judiciously weighs all the evidence and comes up with an advocacy for the existence of the relationship.

DNA testing may yet settle the controversy over the paternity of several of Sally Hemings' children. Dr. Eugene A. Foster, a retired pathology professor at the University of Virginia, conducted tests to determine if there is a genetic link between the Jefferson and Hemings families. A unique chromosome is present through a male line. Unfortunately Jefferson's only son died in infancy. Only two Jeffersons—Thomas Jefferson and his uncle, Field Jefferson—have known male descendants living today. The male line of Jefferson's brother, Randolph, expired in the 1920s and 1930s. Foster took blood samples from five male descendants of Field Jefferson, and also from male descendants of the Woodson, Carr, and Hemings families, and found a match only between Jefferson family males and the descendants of Eston Hemings, demonstrating indeed a Jefferson-Hemings family line, with Thomas Jefferson the likely candidate to be named as Eston's father.

Madison Hemings' line could not be tested because of his three sons, one vanished and the other two had no children. Tests on descendants of two of Thomas Woodson's sons—Lewis and James—yielded no connection. But there could have been breaks in the Woodson male line, such as certain family members being illegitimate. There are plans to test descendants of yet another Woodson, William. Only a Woodson link would verify definitively Jefferson's paternity of a son by Sally Hemings. (No other Jefferson kin was in France at the time Tom was conceived.)

In 1999, for the first time in 170 years, the Hemings descendants were invited to attend the annual gathering of the Jefferson family's Monticello Association. "I hope this is the beginning of a long relationship," said James Truscott, a white descendant of Jefferson's daughter Maria and vice president of the association. At the same meeting, Truscott's nephew, Lucian Truscott, challenged the members of the association to fully admit the Hemings descendants and allow them to be buried at the family graveyard at Monticello. However, while the reunion day was cordial, filled with handshakes and shared family stories between white and black descendants, the association voted against allowing Hemings' line full membership, with attendant burial rights. A 17-year-old descendant of Sally Hemings remained hopeful. "We're still going to be family regardless of what the Monticello Association does," she said. Thus, the Jefferson-Hemings controversy is still not resolved.

Thomas Jefferson's only direct reference to Sally Hemings is in a 1799 letter mentioning that Sally had given birth; two other letters refer to Sally in the context of measles among slave children. Jefferson seldom mentioned women in his letters, and if he tried to conceal a relationship with Hemings, that would be all the more reason not to refer to her. One might take heart, however, from Madison Hemings' statement that "we were the only children of [Jefferson] by a slave woman." Were this a fact, then Jefferson was possibly faithful to one woman for 37 years—Sally Hemings.

SOURCES:

Adair, Douglas. "The Jefferson Scandals," in *Fame and the Founding Fathers: Essays of Douglas Adair.* Edited by Trevor Colbourn. NY: W.W. Norton, 1974, pp. 160–191.

Brodie, Fawn M. *Thomas Jefferson: An Intimate History.* NY: W.W. Norton, 1974.

Egerton, Douglas K. "Thomas Jefferson and the Hemings Family: A Matter of Blood," in *The Historian.* Vol. 59, 1997, pp. 327–345.

Gordon-Reed, Annette. *Thomas Jefferson and Sally Hemings: An American Controversy.* Charlottesville, VA: University Press of Virginia, 1997 (appendices include a name glossary, the *Memoirs* of both Israel Jefferson and Madison Hemings, and a key letter each from Henry S. Randall and Ellen Randolph Coolidge).

McLaughlin, Jack. *Jefferson and Monticello: The Biography of a Builder.* NY: Henry Holt, 1988.

Murray, Barbara, and Brian Duffy. "Jefferson's Secret Life," in *U.S. News and World Report.* November 9, 1998, pp. 58–63.

Reed, David. "Jefferson and Hemings descendants gather in Va.," in *The Day* [New London, CT]. May 16, 1999.

SUGGESTED READING:

Adams, William H. *The Paris Years of Thomas Jefferson.* New Haven, CT: Yale University Press, 1997.

Bear, James A., Jr., ed. *Jefferson at Monticello: Memoirs of a Monticello Slave as dictated to Charles Campbell by Isaac and Jefferson at Monticello: The Private Life of Thomas Jefferson* by Rev. Hamilton Wilcox Pierson. Charlottesville, VA: University Press of Virginia, 1967.

Chase-Riboud, Barbara. *Sally Hemings.* NY: Viking, 1979.

Duray, Michael. *"With the Hammer of Truth:" James Thompson Callender and America's Early National Heroes.* Charlottesville, VA: University Press of Virginia, 1990.

Miller, John C. *The Wolf by the Ears: Thomas Jefferson and Slavery.* NY: The Free Press, 1977.

Smith, Jessie Carney. *Notable Black American Women.* Detroit, MI: Gale Research, 1993.

RELATED MEDIA:

Jefferson in Paris, starring Nick Nolte (as Thomas Jefferson) and **Thandie Newton** (as Sally Hemings), produced by Ismail Merchant and James Ivory, 1995.

"Thomas Jefferson: a View from the Mountain" (videocassette, 114 min.), Central and Northern Virginia Public Television, Richmond, VA, 1996.

Harry M. Ward,
William Binford Vest Professor of History, Emeritus, University of Richmond, author of *The War for Independence and the Transformation of American Society* (University College of London Press, 1999), and 12 other books on early America

Heminilde.

Variant of Emnilde.

Hemma of Bohemia (c. 930–c. 1005)

Duchess of Bohemia. *Born around 930 in Prague, Czechoslovakia; died around 1005; second wife of Boleslaw also known as Boleslav II the Pious (c. 920–999), duke of Bohemia (r. 972–999); children: possibly Boleslav III, duke of Bohemia; Jaromir Premysl, duke of Bohemia; Ulrich (b. around 966), duke of Bohemia. Boleslav's first wife was possibly* ****Elfgifu*** *(c. 914–?).*

Hempel, Frieda (1885–1955)

German-born American coloratura soprano whose operatic performances, particularly those of Mozart and Strauss, made her one of the leading singers in the world. *Born in Leipzig, Germany, on June 26, 1885; died in West Berlin on October 7, 1955; daughter of Emil Hempel and Augusta (Morler) Hempel; married William B. Kahn (divorced 1926).*

Frieda Hempel was born in Leipzig, Germany, in 1885, and showed exceptional musical talent as a small child. At age 15, she enrolled at the Leipzig Conservatory, specializing in piano, but it soon became clear that she possessed great vocal abilities. In 1902, she moved to Berlin to study voice with **Selma Nicklass-Kempner** at the Stern Conservatory. Hempel made a brilliant debut as Mrs. Ford in Nicolai's *Die lustigen Weiber von Windsor* (*The Merry Wives of Windsor*) at Berlin's Royal Opera House on August 22, 1905. While she was based at the Schwerin Opera House during the next several years, her reputation rapidly spread through Germany. By 1907, she was singing at London's Covent Garden opera, starring in both a Mozart role and in Engelbert Humperdinck's *Hansel und Gretel.* Both critics and audiences were delighted by her purity of tone and stylistic sophistication.

In 1908, Hempel starred in a Berlin revival of Meyerbeer's grand opera, *Les Huguenots*, which was lavishly staged and under the personal supervision of the German Kaiser Wilhelm II. With Hempel at its center, this production was a gala event that transfixed the German capital's social elite and was the talk of much of European royalty for the musical season. Hempel received the coveted title of *Kammersängerin* (Court Singer), a tangible sign of her success in Berlin. In addition to receiving decorations from Kaiser Wilhelm II, the rising young star also was awarded honors by the king of Belgium, the grand duke of Mecklenburg-Schwerin, and the duke of Anhalt.

Having mastered the major classical opera roles, in 1911 Hempel became a significant figure in the advancement of contemporary music when she sang the role of the Marschallin in the Berlin premiere performance of Richard Strauss' new opera, *Der Rosenkavalier.* Strauss, who regarded Hempel as one of the finest interpreters of his works, was in awe of her vocal powers, particularly her high F-sharps.

Hempel became an undisputed international singing star when she made her debut at New York City's Metropolitan Opera House on December 27, 1912, singing the role of Marguerite de Valois (***Margaret of Valois** [1553–1615]) in *Les Huguenots.* Although she had been extremely nervous during her performance, it still prompted enthusiastic reviews, including one from Henry Krehbiehl of the *New York Tribune* who praised Hempel as an artist with a "highly finished style of vocalization, a flexible voice, and good taste." During the next seven seasons, Hempel was one of the Metropolitan Opera's leading sopranos, giving outstanding performances as Rosina in Rossini's *The Barber of Seville*, the Queen of the Night in Mozart's *The Magic Flute*, Olympia in Jacques Offenbach's *The Tales of Hoffmann*, Violeta in Verdi's *La Traviata*, Gilda in Verdi's *Rigoletto*, and the title role in Donizetti's *Lucia di Lammermoor.*

Frieda Hempel

By the end of her career, Hempel had mastered over 70 leading soprano roles, only 17 of which she appeared in during her years at the Metropolitan Opera. With her farewell Met performance on February 10, 1919, she had made 187 appearances with the company, 155 in New York City and 32 while on tour. Her outstanding performances during these years included her portrayal of the Marschallin in the American premiere of *Der Rosenkavalier* on December 9, 1913, and the numerous times she sang opposite Enrico Caruso in Donizetti's *Elisir d'amore* as well as in Verdi's *Un Ballo in Maschera.* Another great triumph for Hempel was her appearance in the title role of the American premiere of Carl Maria von Weber's *Euryanthe*, which was conducted by Arturo Toscanini on December 19, 1914.

Although Hempel left her strongest musical impressions at the Metropolitan Opera, she thrilled audiences not only in her native Germany but in other countries as well. In addition to her successful appearances in Paris, she was immediately regarded as a major vocal artist during her appearances in London in 1914, when she sang in the epoch-making Drury Lane season directed by Sir Thomas Beecham. Her characterization of the Queen of the Night in Mozart's *The Magic Flute* was an unqualified success in London's musical circles. At the time, some music lovers were already acquainted with her 1911 recording of the aria "Der hölle Rache" from this, one of Mozart's greatest and most beloved works.

By 1917, the animosities released by World War I were leaving a profound mark on musical life in America. The U.S. declaration of war on Germany in April of that year quickly led to a massive explosion of hatred for all things German. German books were burned in public, the

German language was driven from school curricula, and staples of German origin were rechristened with patriotic names: sauerkraut became Liberty Cabbage. German music was banned by many orchestras, and German-born artists, including Hempel, found many doors shut. Both she and Austrian-born violin virtuoso Fritz Kreisler were banned from a number of American cities, and many other musicians would never again perform in the United States. Orchestras and even the Metropolitan Opera banished German compositions from their wartime programs as a sign of their patriotic purity, and German-born artists like Hempel became viewed as cultural pariahs in a land that had once hailed their gifts.

Hempel's operatic career ended in 1921 with her having made relatively few recordings (unfortunately she never made recordings of works by either Richard Wagner or Richard Strauss). After a few stage performances with the Chicago Grand Opera Company in San Francisco, she retired from the operatic stage. Now in her 30s, she was not ready, however, to end her singing career.

On October 6, 1920, Hempel had appeared in Carnegie Hall to present an exact duplicate of the concert given in 1850 by the famous ***Jenny Lind** at New York's Castle Garden (Lind's first appearance in the United States). During the 1920s, Hempel gave more than 300 Jenny Lind concerts, clad in a costume similar to that of the fabled Norwegian singer, and charming her sold-out audiences with both her personality and vocal art. She not only performed as Jenny Lind throughout the United States, but made two acclaimed tours of the United Kingdom. While some critics voiced misgivings about this form of performance due to its resemblance to the mass-appeal entertainment style that marked Jenny Lind's career (which had been orchestrated by none other than the showman P.T. Barnum) both the box-office results and Hempel's artistic satisfaction with her efforts outweighed the impact of such criticism. After she finished the Jenny Lind concerts, Hempel concentrated on giving Lieder recitals. For more than three decades, these were appreciated by cognoscenti of the German art song. Critics would long rave about her Lieder performances, as did Richard Aldrich of *The New York Times* in January 1921, when he praised Hempel's voice for its beauty and "its rounded smoothness, its color, [and] its equality through its range." Although her vocal powers were in decline by the late 1930s, much of her musical artistry remained intact, and it was not until 1951 that she gave her last New York recital.

In 1936, Hempel's name made the newspapers for reasons other than music. She initiated a lawsuit against the philanthropist August Heckscher because of his termination in December 1935 of an annual income of $50,000 that he had begun paying her in 1928. In return, she was obligated to give private performances and appear at charitable events. In point of fact, Hempel had divorced her husband William B. Kahn in 1926 in order to become the mistress of the wealthy, and elderly, Heckscher, who soon after this began making annual payments to her. When Heckscher's payments ceased in 1935, and Hempel quickly turned to the courts, the press found the scandal good copy, and it was reported in considerable detail. The matter was finally settled with Hempel being guaranteed an annual income of $15,000 by Heckscher for the remainder of her life. On October 7, 1955, while on a visit to Germany, Frieda Hempel died suddenly in Berlin.

SOURCES:

Hempel, Frieda, with Elizabeth Johnston and William R. Moran. *My Golden Age of Singing*. Portland, OR: Amadeus Press, 1998.

"Jenny Lind Brought Back to Life," in *The Literary Digest*. Vol. 77, no. 8. May 26, 1923, pp. 46, 48.

Reed, P.H., G.T. Keating, and B.F. Stone. "The Recorded Art of Frieda Hempel," in *The Record Collector*. Vol. 10, 1955–56, pp. 53–71.

Vacha, J.E. "When Wagner Was Verboten: The Campaign Against German Music in World War I," in *New York History*. Vol. 64, no. 2. April 1983, pp. 171–188.

John Haag,
Associate Professor, University of Georgia, Athens, Georgia

Henderson, Alice Corbin (1881–1949).

See Monroe, Harriet for sidebar.

Henderson, Annie Heloise Abel (1873–1947).

See Abel, Annie Heloise.

Henie, Sonja (1912–1969)

Norwegian figure skater who won three consecutive gold medals and became a movie box-office attraction surpassed in her day only by Shirley Temple and Clark Gable. *Name variations: Sonia Henje. Born in Oslo, Norway, on April 8, 1912 (some sources erroneously cite 1910); died of leukemia on board an ambulance plane traveling from Paris to Oslo on October 12, 1969; daughter of Selma (Nilsen) Henie and Wilhelm Henie (a fur merchant and former champion cyclist); married Dan Topping, in 1940; married Winthrop Gardner, in 1949; married Niels Onstad, in 1956.*

In addition to three Olympic gold medals (1928, 1932 and 1936), won ten consecutive World titles

(1927–36) and six European championships (1931–36); starred in films (1927–58); along with Niels Onstad, acquired a superb art collection, the major part of which was donated to Norway where it found a home in a new art museum the Ostads erected outside Oslo (1968).

Awards: The Norwegian Government's Medal for Versatility and Achievement in Sport (1931); honorary member of the Navajo Indian Tribe (1937); The Order of St. Olav (1938).

Filmography: Svy Dager for Elisabeth *(Norwegian, 1927);* One in a Million *(1937);* Thin Ice *(1937);* Happy Landing *(1938);* My Lucky Star *(1938);* Second Fiddle *(1939);* Everything Happens at Night *(1939);* Sun Valley Serenade *(1941);* Iceland *(1942);* Wintertime *(1943);* It's a Pleasure *(1945);* The Countess of Monte Cristo *(1948);* Hello London *(*London Calling, *1958).*

The unseasonal blizzard that struck Norway on April 8, 1912, would have had no faster swirls and spins than those executed by Sonja Henie 24 years later at Garmisch-Partenkirchen. Born that day in April, she revolutionized figure skating, making what had been a "stiff and pedantic" set of maneuvers into a ballet on ice, which she performed in short skirts and gray, beige or white boots and stockings.

Sonja Henie began training early. From the age of four, she skied with her parents and older brother Leif in the family hunting lodge at Geilo. Simultaneously, she started her much-loved ballet lessons. Her instructor was Love Krohn, an Oslo ballet master who had been a teacher of the great ***Anna Pavlova**. Henie continued her ballet lessons as she took up skating; gradually the idea of combining the two took hold in her imagination.

Because her parents thought a six-year-old too young for the unforgiving ice, she had to beg for her first pair of skates. When they finally relented, she tagged along after her elder brother, who rarely succeeded in ruses to avoid her, whenever he skated in Oslo's Frogner Park. By the age of seven, she could negotiate the slippery surface on her own. She was an absorbed, wildly enthusiastic skater, forgetting meals as she lost track of time doing her figures and swirls. Her efforts drew the attention of a young woman, Hjordis Olsen, who belonged to Frogner's private club. Olsen had observed the child, who appeared to live on the ice from sunup to sundown, and invited her into the secluded area where club members practiced their spins and jumps. There, Olsen started with simple lessons in school figures which Henie practiced so assiduously that her father Wilhelm Henie, on Olsen's recommendation, entered her in the children's competition held each year. Henie took first prize: a silver paper cutter with a mother-of-pearl handle.

The following year, when she was eight, Sonja won the Junior Class C competition and went from there to the Senior A category, Norway's national championship. To train for that, she was given lessons by Oslo's leading skating instructor, Oscar Holte. She was also put on a schedule—three hours of skating in the morning, two in the afternoon—and a diet regimen that called for her to eat breakfast, lunch, and dinner at regular hours.

In the spring and summer, she continued her ballet lessons. School became a series of tutorings. Henie counted herself extremely fortunate to have been born in a family that could afford private lessons, not only at home but also in the countries where she would go to train and perform. After winning the Norwegian championship, she went with her family to St. Moritz and Chamonix and, in 1924, was entered in the Chamonix Olympic Games just to have the experience of the competition. Though one of the judges gave her top ranking in free skating, she took last place. Old sports reels show her spinning round and round in her coat and hat, a small blonde 11-year-old who would become the most famous figure skater in the world.

At 14, Sonja was entered in the 1927 World championship in Oslo, the youngest contestant ever in that event. Skating before thousands of onlookers, including Norway's King Haakon VII and Queen ***Maud**, she twirled herself to victory and into a decade of travel and international ice rinks. Henie's top ranking stirred some controversy, however, because two of the five judges—the Austrian and the German—gave their first place votes to ***Herma Planck-Szabo**, gold-medal winner of the 1924 Olympic games. Though the three Norwegian judges prevailed, the International Skating Union instituted a rule that only one judge per country be allowed in international meets.

Sonja Henie spoke of three elements in her preparation which were crucial to success. One was anticipation. She worked intensively on all 80 school figures, any of which might be selected for the Olympic test of 1928, her next immediate goal. Secondly, she sought exhibition experience wherever she could find it. Her father Wilhelm, who was also her supportive and promoting manager, would bring a phonograph

Sonja Henie

to the ice where she was practicing, and admirers would line up to watch her performance. Finally, she had a role model which offered unending inspiration: Pavlova, the unsurpassed Russian dancer.

The summer between the World championship and the St. Moritz Olympics, her mother **Selma Henie** took her to London to see the famous ballerina. Pavlova's performance, which according to Henie went "beyond dancing, transcending technique to such an extent that the onlooker was unaware of technique," steeled her determination to make her free-skating program a combination of dancing and skating. She would make her performance a dance, she decided, "with the choreographic form of a ballet solo and the technique of the ice," a radically untraditional approach.

[Being a skater is] having a feeling of . . . speed lifting you off the ice far from all things that can hold you down.

—Sonja Henie

At the 1928 Olympics in St. Moritz, no one debated Sonja Henie's top ranking. It was awarded her by six of the seven judges. Only the American judge voted for **Beatrix Loughran** of the United States, who took third place. With that victory, Henie felt herself stepping into a world of "incessant rivalry . . . exploding jealousies, explosions of temperament, milling acquaintances, and a few firm friendships; a world of trunks and suitcases; fast trains, steamships, hotel suites, parties; music, costumes, spotlights—and all the time the necessity to sleep long hours, eat regularly and rightly, and train constantly." Nor was she spared the experience of mob hysteria. On one occasion, a waiting crowd outside the skating rink surrounded her so closely they nearly squeezed her to death. She was saved by her father forcing himself through a crowd that would not yield to his protestations that he was her father but only to the officials he hailed for help. On her way back to her hotel, the same crowd exerted enough pressure on her car to shatter the glass of the windows.

Occasionally, she marveled at her father's continued support and encouragement as well as his willingness to spend the thousands of dollars needed to keep her going from competition to competition. She marveled equally at her mother's steadfast vigilance in the office of chaperon. Selma Henie, in fact, became her daughter's constant companion and closest counselor. From time to time, Sonja was even amazed at her own unflagging interest in competition, but she never questioned her desire to skate. "Not many people can spend their lives doing what they like to do best. I happen to be one of those few who can," she wrote in her memoirs. "All my life I have wanted to skate, and all my life I have skated." Professional skating was an idea yet to be discovered, so participating in competitions was the only way to stay on top in the "business" of skating.

Opposite page

Sonja Henie

The St. Moritz Olympics were succeeded by the World championships in London. In addition to another first place, Henie took pleasure in learning that the meet had occasioned an increased public interest in figure skating, evidenced by the addition of four new skating rinks in the city of London. She was less thrilled at the thought of the royal *faux pas* she committed there as she responded to Queen ***Mary of Teck**'s questions about skating with the suggestion that the queen take up roller skating. Henie considered that the safer sport.

After Europe, America beckoned. In December of 1929, Henie sailed for New York to give performances in Madison Square Garden before traveling to Canada where she won her fourth World championship title. Reading newspaper reports of her performances, she was intrigued with the predilection of the American press for the "little" things: the number of skates and dresses in her trunk, the length of her skirts, or the shortness rather. European skaters had raised their hemlines, and Sonja followed fashion. She, too, as it turned out, would become attached to "little" things, such as the Roxy motion picture theater in New York which impressed her with its comfortable decor and glamorous atmosphere.

The mature phase of Sonja Henie's skating, she noted, was "clouded by the envy and jealousy of rivals and their supporters." Her first place at the Olympic Games in Lake Placid in 1932 was unrivalled; she was the unanimous choice of the seven judges. That event also saw two Sonja Henie clones, one of whom would be the first reminder of the ever ticking clock. **Megan Taylor** and ***Cecilia Colledge** from Great Britain—both 11 years old—took seventh and eight place.

Rumors began circulating that Henie would be accepting proposals for professional engagements in the States, one of them from a film company. Though her father turned them down because they were not particularly good offers, and the family did not like the idea of professionalism in sports, it did not still the voices. Gossip had also been ignited in Canada when, on their arrival in Montreal, Wilhelm stuck by his decision to decline the invitation to skate in two clubs there. His refusal was complicated by the fact that he had accepted an engagement on his daughter's behalf at the New York Skating Club. His reasoning was that, unlike Montreal, the New York performance followed long enough after the Lake Placid Games to give Sonja a chance to rest. Newspapers, however, made a point of noting that Wilhelm had made such exorbitant demands for expense money that the Canadian clubs would have had to renege on their invitations anyway. In subsequent performances in New York, Paris, and Oslo, Sonja was greeted warmly by the audience, which soothed her mind and spirit, but in the summer following her second Olympic gold medal, she considered retiring for the first time.

Henie ended such considerations after entering an automobile race for amateur drivers in Stockholm. Taking second place, she once again felt the adrenalin rising. With renewed vigor, she therefore made plans for performances in Paris and Milan where she made her debut in the Swan dance, her ice version of Pavlova's solo. The Italians loved it, and Sonja felt that a new career of dancing on ice was opening up to her.

And yet, she was not quite ready to embrace the challenges of that envisioned future. She felt she had one more Olympic medal in her and one more World championship. She consequently exerted the utmost pressure upon herself by announcing that she would retire from competition after the 1936 World championship which would follow one week after the Olympics in Garmisch-Partenkirchen, West Germany. Henie won her gold medal, only 3.6 points ahead of young Cecilia Colledge of Great Britain, who had soared from eighth place four years earlier. A week later, Henie won her tenth straight World championship. Only Ulrich Salchow, who won 11 consecutive World titles from 1901 through 1911, had done better.

After winning 1,473 cups, medals, and trophies, Sonja Henie decided to go professional. In March 1936, she signed a contract with Arthur Wirtz to give four exhibitions in New York and four in Chicago. After that, she would go to Los Angeles. She was convinced that the cinema would be the perfect medium for projecting dancing on ice.

Henie arrived in Hollywood after giving seventeen appearances in nine cities between March 24 and April 15 of 1936. When the Henies learned that the city had an ice rink—"The Polar Ice Palace"—Wilhelm Henie arranged to rent it for several days and planned two exhibitions. Realizing that Hollywood was not "ice con-

scious," they sent out a deluge of invitations and advertised the shows in the newspapers. It was to their great advantage that reporters with the major papers had heard of Sonja Henie's work abroad and wrote helpful promotional pieces. The two performances went beyond anyone's expectations. Hollywood's gliterati came to see Sonja Henie, and many returned on the second night. In the audience was Darryl Zanuck, the man for whom this whole extravaganza had been performed. The Henies had heard of his reputation for welcoming new ideas and possessing the persistence to realize them. But Zanuck was hesitant when he asked her what she wanted in a film and Henie replied, "the title role." She was not interested in a supporting part that would sell a movie on her reputation. After lengthy negotiations, she was offered the lead in *One in a Million.* Her performance put Zanuck's doubts to rest. *Million* was a huge popular success, and nine films would follow.

Living and performing in Hollywood, Henie learned to transform herself from a skating champion to a businesswoman. At first, she had the steady guidance of her father who saw her through the writing of the initial contract as well as the filmmaking. Her mother's presence, from their rising at five o'clock in the morning through the grueling day on the set, offered further comfort and stability in a world that held little of either. But when she lost her father in May of 1937, Henie felt the responsibility for her future falling on her own shoulders. She would miss his "vision, guidance, and encouragement, . . . his tricks of competition and business," but as it turned out, she had inherited a good share of his business acumen. She quickly learned, as she put it, to "make no decision hastily, to judge no man by his front, and to remember that the world never puts a price on you higher than the one you put on yourself."

Film followed film interspersed with tours. Miss Sonja Henie with her Hollywood Ice Revue, which hit the road after her third film *Happy Landing,* was finally dancing on ice, just as she had imagined it: a spectacle of lights, costumes, music and dance-like motions, with numbers ranging from Liszt to the Susi-Q. Finally in 1940, skating to *Les Sylphides,* she felt that ballet had arrived on the ice.

In December 1937, the Navajo Indians made her an honorary member of their tribe, christening her Ashonogo Sonnie Tin-Edil-Goie, "graceful young lady who skates on ice." The following year, January 1938, she was awarded Norway's highest distinction, the Order of St. Olav, the youngest person ever to receive the decoration. The tribute was paid for her "unique contribution as a sportswoman, an artist, an interpreter of the ideals of Norway's youth, and one who has upheld the honor of the flag of Norway."

An ill-considered refusal to aid Norwegian refugees in Canada during the early years of the Second World War incurred their censure, however. Later donations and performances for the troops were mitigating factors, but on the whole the decade of the 1940s proved emotionally challenging. Henie had not only lost her father, the mainstay of her life, her two marriages to Dan Topping and Winthrop Gardner failed. In the mid-1950s, she finally found the happiness and sense of security she sought in her union with Niels Onstad, a distinguished Norwegian shipowner. With his encouragement, she transferred her focus from figure skating to art collecting, a field in which Onstad was a longtime connoisseur. Henie had previously collected old masters, but when her husband introduced her to contemporary painters, she quickly developed an eye for the boldness and balance of abstract art as well. Together they traveled to "keep track of what was going on," as he put it, buying whatever appealed to them. By and by, their collection exceeded their wall space, and they began to contemplate where they might find a "house" for their artists. After careful deliberation about which country most needed a modern art collection—America or Norway—they decided on Norway. At mid-century, modern art was poorly represented in public Norwegian collections, none of which had received private donations. By deeding separate gifts, they therefore established the Sonja Henie-Niels Onstad Foundation. The donations comprised 110 paintings by 20th-century masters as well as means to erect a building that would not only house and show this collection but also encompass activities within the other arts, such as music, theater, dance, film and multimedia. Additional means were allotted for the upkeep and running of the art center, which was opened on August 23, 1968, by King Olav V of Norway. It is Norway's largest museum of international modern art. In October 1969, Henie became ill while in France and died of leukemia on board an ambulance plane traveling from Paris to Oslo.

SOURCES:

The Complete Book of the Olympics. Edited by David Wallechinsky. New York, 1984.

Durant, John. *Highlights of the Olympics.* NY: Hastings House, 1965.

Henie, Sonja. *Wings on My Feet.* NY: Prentice-Hall, 1940.

The Olympic Story. Danbury, CT: Grolier Enterprises, 1983.

RELATED MEDIA:

Sonja Henie: Queen of the Ice (60 min. documentary), aired on PBS, 1995.

COLLECTIONS:

Henie-Onstad Foundation, Oslo, Norway.

Inga Wiehl,
a native of Denmark, teaches English at
Yakima Valley Community College, Yakima, Washington

Henje, Sonja (1912–1969).

See Henie, Sonja.

Henning, Anne (1955—)

American speed skater. *Born on September 6, 1955, in Raleigh, North Carolina; daughter of William Henning (a hospital consultant) and Joanne Henning.*

Won the gold medal in the 500 meters at the World championship in Helsinki, Finland (1971); won the gold medal in the 500 meters at the World Sprint championship in Inzell, Germany (1971); set a new world record in both the 500- and 1000-meter events in Davos, Switzerland (1972); won the gold medal in the 500 meters and the bronze medal in the 1,000 meters at the Olympic Games in Sapporo, Japan (1972).

Prohibited from competition in the local Little League program, Anne Henning set her sights on becoming the fastest woman skater in the world. Fortunately, her hometown of Northbrook, Illinois, boasted an excellent speed-skating program, due mostly to the efforts of Ed Rudolph, who was the park commissioner and a world-class speed-skating coach. (By 1975, Northbrook was known as the "Speed Capital of the World" and had trained twenty-nine national champions, eight world team members, and ten Olympic team members, of which eight were women.) Rudolph first saw Henning skate when she was ten and recognized her talent immediately. "I saw nothing but gold medals dancing before my eyes," he later said.

With her parents' approval, Henning began training with Rudolph and, for the next six years, devoted her life to skating. It was always a struggle, and she often wanted to quit. "For a while I wouldn't go out to practice," she recalled. "Then my parents and Mr. Rudolph sat down with me and let me see how close I was." At age 12, she won the U.S. National championship in both the 500 and 1,000 meters. At 15, after setting speed-skating records in both the women's 500 and 1,000 meters, she began to prepare for the 1972 Winter Olympic Games at Sapporo, Japan.

Henning carried the hopes of the entire skating world with her to Japan, and the pressure was nearly unbearable. She won the gold medal in the 500 meters event, but not without incident. Halfway through her heat, she and her opponent, Canadian **Sylvia Burke**, almost collided while taking a curve. To avoid contact, Henning let Burke pass, losing precious tenths of a second. Although she eventually won the heat, she feared that subsequent competitors might better her time. "I was so upset I wanted to go home right then," she recalled. The judges, however, decided that she had been fouled and let her race again. Knocking four-tenths of a second off her time, she took the gold, although she later learned that her first time of 43.7 would have also put her in first place. Exhausted both physically and mentally from the first event, Henning finished third in the 1,000 meters, winning the bronze medal. (***Dianne Holum**, another Northbrook resident and student of coach Rudolph, won the gold medal in the 1,500-meter event.)

See following page for illustration

With the World Games looming later that winter, Henning decided that she had had enough. "I'd packed a lifetime of energy into six years and I didn't have any more left," she said. Hanging up her skates, Henning entered Carroll College in Waukesha, Wisconsin, to major in art and lead a more normal life. The years she spent training for the Olympics then haunted her. "I have this feeling that I missed a part of my life I'll never be able to recall," she said, at age 19. "Would I do it again? Nope."

SOURCES:

Jordan, Pat. *Broken Patterns.* NY: Dodd, Mead, 1977.

Markel, Robert, and Susan Waggoner. *The Women's Sports Encyclopedia.* NY: Henry Holt, 1997.

Henning-Jensen, Astrid (1914—)

Danish film director and screenwriter. *Born Astrid Smahl on December 10, 1914, in Frederiksberg, Denmark; married Bjarne Henning-Jensen (1908-1995), on August 10, 1938; children: Lars.*

Awards: Catholic Film Office Award, Cannes Festival for Paw *(1960); Best Director, Berlin Film Festival for* Winter Children *(1979).*

Filmography—director or co-director with husband Bjarne Henning-Jensen: SOS Kindtand *(1943);* Nar man kun er ung *(1943);* De danske sydhavsoer *(*Danish Island, *1944);* Flykningar finnar en hamm *(*Fugitives Find Shelter, *1944);* Dansk politi I Sverige *(*The Danish Brigade in Sweden, *1945);* Skibet er ladet med *(1945);* Ditte Menneskebarn *(*Ditte, Child of Man, *1946);* Stemning I April *(*Impressions of April, *1947);* De pokkers unger *(*Those Blasted Kids, *1947);* Denmark Grows Up *(1947);* Kristimus Bergman *(1948);* Palle Allene I Verden *(*Palle, Alone in the

Anne Henning

World, *1949);* Vesterhavsdrenge *(*Boys from the West Coast, *1950);* Kranes konditori *(*Krane's Bakery Shop, *1951);* Ukjent man *(*Unknown Man, *1952);* Better than Cure *(1953);* Solstik *(1953);* Tivoligarden Spiler *(*Tivoli Garden Games, *1954);* Ballettens boern *(*Ballet Girl, *1954);* Kaerlighed pa kredit *(*Love On Credit, *1955);* Hest pa sommerferie *(*Horse on Holiday, *1959);* Paw, Boy of Two Worlds *(1960);* Forraederiet *(1962);* Kviden og soldaten *(1962);* Een blandt mange *(1962);* Den jagede *(1963);* Der er noget I luften *(1964);* Et minde om to mandage *(1964);* Vend dig ikke om *(1964);* De bla undulater *(1965);* Min bedstefar er en stok *(1967);* Nille, Utro *(*Unfaithful, *1968);* Mej och dej *(*Me and You, *1969);* Vinterboern *(*Winterborn, *1978);* Ojeblikket *(1980);* Hodia fra Pjort *(1985);* Barndommens gade *(*Streets of My Childhood, *1986);* Bella min Bella *(*Bella, My Bella, *1995).*

Astrid Smahl began her career as an actor in the Copenhagen theater where she met fellow actor Bjarne Henning-Jensen. The two married in 1938. Within a couple of years, Bjarne began work as a film director for Nordisk Films Kompagni; Astrid was his assistant director. The couple worked on several undistinguished films before making their breakthrough *Ditte Menneskebarn* in 1943 which established them as the most promising co-directorial team in Danish cinema. An adaptation of a five-part novel by Martin Andersen-Nexo, *Ditte Menneskebarn* concerns a girl from the country, born illegitimate, who herself becomes an unwed mother and thus a victim of her social circumstances. Starkly realistic, the film was a turning point for Danish cinema and certainly for the Henning-Jensens whose feature films had been lightweight comedies.

While continuing to make realistic features in the style of *Ditte Menneskebarn,* though none were as successful, the Henning-Jensens collaborated on many documentaries, most notably, *Dansk politi I Sverige* (*The Danish Brigade in Sweden*, 1945), using sophisticated technology. Brilliantly edited, the film reenacts the training of 200 Danish officers who fled the German occupation and is often considered a stylistic forerunner to American director, Errol Morris' controversial film, *The Thin Blue Line,* which also stretched the limits of the documentary. It too was a "reenactment."

Astrid Henning-Jensen, who made her first solo film in 1945, continued to work either alone or in collaboration with her husband until his retirement in 1974. Subsequently, she made a number of documentaries and features in Denmark, Norway, and Geneva, Switzerland, where she worked for UNESCO. In her documentaries, as well as her feature films, Henning-Jensen explores the everyday lives of working-class men and women. Her films often combine dreamlike fantasies conjured by child heroes who must cope with and live in a world filled with the harsh realities of poverty and loss of innocence. *Palle, Alone in the World* (1949) is an example of such a film and is one of the few Henning-Jensen films that found an international audience.

Though Henning-Jensen may not be well-known worldwide, she is celebrated in Denmark, and her career has spanned six decades. Her film *Bella min Bella* (*Bella, My Bella*), released in 1995, the year the director turned 80, earned her the Berlinale Camera at Berlin in 1996. The movie, based on her own experiences and that of a friend, revolves around Bella who is in her late teens and lives with her mother Maj. The two are very close. But when Maj flirts with their male tenant, Bella distances herself from her mother by turning her attention to a young Bosnian refugee in search of asylum. At film's end, Bella discovers that she needs her mother more than ever. In 1996, Henning-Jensen also appeared as herself in the Danish film *Danske piger user alt* (*Danish Girls Show Everything*).

SOURCES:

Foster, Gwendolyn. *Women Film Directors: An International Bio-Critical Dictionary.* Westport, CT: Greenwood Press, 1995.

Kuhn, Annette, and Susannah Radstone, ed. *The Women's Companion to International Film.* Berkeley, CA: University of California Press, 1994.

Lyon, Christopher. *International Dictionary of Films and Filmmakers.* Chicago, IL: St. James, 1984.

Deborah Jones,
Studio City, California

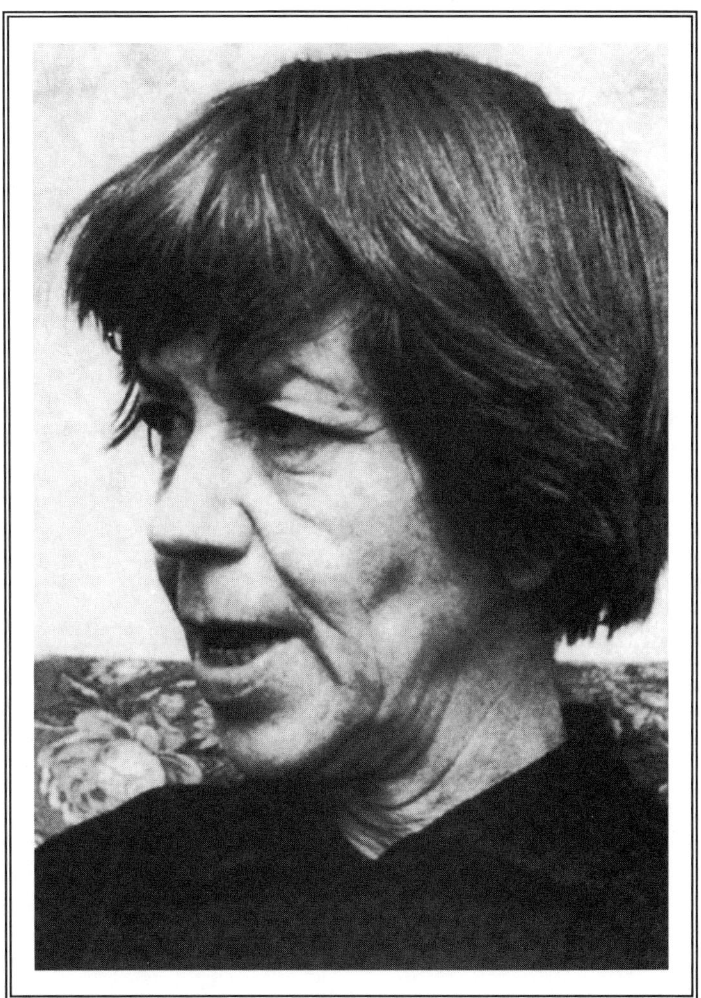

Astrid Henning-Jensen

Hennings, Betty (1850–1939)

Danish actress. *Name variations: Betty Schnell. Born Betty Schnell in 1850; died in 1939; married.*

Betty Schnell, whose married name was Betty Hennings, began her career as a ballet star, dancing leading roles for August Bournonville, a major figure in Danish ballet during the golden age of Romanticism. In 1878, Hennings gave up ballet while still quite young to star as the first Nora in Ibsen's *A Doll's House*, opposite Emil Poulsen (1842–1911). The play opened at the Royal Theatre in Copenhagen on December 21, 1879, and would be performed in Stockholm, Christiania, Helsinki, Munich, and Berlin, all in the following year. Hennings, the first great Ibsen actress, continued working with Poulsen. For many years, they played the principle roles in the world premieres of Ibsen's plays in Copenhagen, with William Bloch producing.

Hennock, Frieda B. (1904–1960)

American lawyer and first woman to serve as a Federal Communications Commissioner, who worked to establish educational television in the United States. *Name variations: Frieda Barkin Hennock Simons. Born on September 27, 1904, in Kovel, Poland; died on June 20, 1960, at George Washington University Hospital, following surgery for a brain tumor; daughter of Boris Hennock (a businessman in banking and real estate) and Sarah (Barkin) Hennock; attended Morris High School, Bronx, New York, graduated 1921; Brooklyn Law School, LL.B, 1924; extension courses at Columbia University, City College of New York, and the New School of Social Research; married William H. Simons, in March 1956; no children.*

Youngest of eight children, emigrated with her family to the U.S. (1910); obtained U.S. citizenship through father's naturalization (1916); worked as law clerk during law school for Thomas & Friedman, for Miller, Boardman & Ruskay, and for John D. Flynn; admitted to state bar in New York, age 22, and entered private practice (1926); joined in law partnership, Silver & Hennock (1927); dissolved firm and resumed private practice (1934); served as assistant counsel to Mortgage Commission of the State of New York (1935–39); was associated with law firm Choate, Mitchell and Ely (1941–48); served as member of the executive committee of the National Health Assembly (1948); served as Federal Communications Commissioner (1948–55); resumed law practice in Washington, D.C. (1955).

Selected publications: "TV 'Conservation'," in The Saturday Review of Literature *(December 9, 1950); "TV—Problem Child or Teacher's Pet?" in* New York State Education *(March 1951); "Educational Opportunities in Television," in* The Commercial and Financial Chronicle *(March 15, 1951); "The Free Air Waves: An Administrative Dilemma," in* Women Lawyers Journal *(Fall 1950); "My Most Rewarding Experience in TV," in* The Journal of the Association for Education by Radio-Television *(April 1954); "Television and Teaching," in* Educational Outlook *(May 1951).*

On June 8, 1953, as dignitaries were gathering for the dedication ceremonies at KUHT-TV, the first educational television station in the United States, engineers at the transmitter site were struggling with a glitch in the television signal that was causing a black band across the middle of the screen. Unless they could remove it, the audience's view of the keynote speaker would show only her hairdo at the top of the screen and her chest at the bottom. With only minutes left before the show was to air, the chief engineer gave the transmitter a healthy kick, and to everyone's surprise, the black band disappeared and KUHT-TV began its inaugural broadcast on time. Moments later, Federal Communications Commissioner Frieda B. Hennock was able to tell the viewing audience, "here in Houston begins the practical realization of the tremendous benefits that television holds out to education. With TV, the walls of the classroom disappear; every set within viewing range of the signal is a potential classroom."

Frieda Barkin Hennock, the woman credited with establishing educational television in the United States, was six years old, and the youngest of eight, when her parents, Boris and **Sarah Hennock**, gathered up their two sons and six daughters to emigrate from Kovel, Poland, to the United States. Boris Hennock found work in New York City's banking and real estate businesses and became a naturalized citizen in 1916, conferring the same citizenship on his minor children, then including Frieda.

As a young girl, Hennock attended New York public schools and showed enough talent playing the piano for her parents to encourage her to consider a career in music. In 1921, after graduation from Morris High School in the Bronx, she received little support for her decision to enter law school, but her parents did not try to stop her; with the drive and determination that would mark her entire life, she enrolled in night

Frieda B. Hennock

classes at Brooklyn Law School. To support her studies, she found work as a law clerk at several firms, including Thomas & Friedman, as well as Miller, Boardman & Ruskay, and John D. Flynn. In 1924, when she earned her LL.B. degree, she was too young to be admitted to the bar.

In 1926, Hennock was admitted to the New York State Bar at age 22, reportedly the youngest woman lawyer to practice in New York City. To set up her private practice, she provided legal services to a real-estate office in exchange for rental space and demonstrated her expertise in criminal law by successfully defending several clients accused of murder and robbery before deciding to limit her practice to civil law. As she told an interviewer, "I'm glad I was a criminal lawyer when I was very young. Knowing these people gave me an adult sense of values."

In 1927, recognizing that clients might accept her more readily if she had a male colleague, Hennock entered into a law partnership agreement with Julius Silver that lasted seven years. One of Silver's clients was Edwin H. Land, the inventor of the Polaroid camera, who had given Silver company stock in exchange for legal work. In 1934, when Hennock's partnership with Silver ended, the Polaroid stock was included in the assets listed in the dissolution agreement. When Silver refused to honor Hennock's eligibility to receive a share of the stock, Hennock filed a court claim and won a cash settlement that would have repercussions many years later.

Each woman undertaking a new and challenging public office must feel that she carries the trust of her sex as well as that of the nation.

—Frieda B. Hennock

From 1935 to 1939, Hennock served as assistant counsel to the Mortgage Commission of the State of New York and taught a course at Brooklyn Law School in 1936. In 1941, she joined Choate, Mitchell and Ely, where she was reportedly the first to be employed as a female lawyer, a Jewish lawyer, and a Democrat, in what was then one of the nation's largest and most distinguished law firms. During these years, she continued to live with her parents, contributing to the support of the household as her father's health began to fail. When a sister divorced and returned home, Hennock helped her regain custody of her two daughters. According to friends, she also helped raise the two nieces and financed their college educations.

As an active member of the Democratic Party, Hennock worked on the election campaigns of Franklin Delano Roosevelt, Mayor William O'Dwyer, and Harry S. Truman. Her skill as a fund raiser for candidates won her recognition and friends within the party, including ***India Edwards**, then associate director of the Democratic National Committee women's division. Edwards was an effective advocate for women's participation in positions of responsibility. As she explained to oral historian Jerry Hess, her strategy was to be ready to recommend a specific candidate when an opening in government occurred. In 1948, when Clifford J. Durr declined to be renamed to another term as Federal Communications commissioner, President Truman was required by law to name a Democrat to fill the position, in order to maintain political balance. Hennock's candidacy had already been suggested for a judgeship in New York, and now Edwards was ready to recommend her to the president for the position at the Federal Communications Commission (FCC). The recommendation found support among many influential persons and groups, and in May 1948 Truman forwarded Hennock's nomination to the Senate.

During confirmation hearings before the Senate Subcommittee on Interstate and Foreign Commerce, questions were raised about Hennock's experience in broadcasting and the common carrier services that the FCC was responsible for regulating. When she freely acknowledged that her only experience with radio was in raising considerable money for the Roosevelt campaign, Senator Owen Brewster responded to her candor by observing that perhaps what was needed at the FCC was just such a breath of fresh air. The full Senate was not so ready to act, however, as a number of members were reluctant to approve a nomination made by a president about to run for reelection and, in the opinion of many, not likely to win. Attempts to bring the appointment to a vote failed until the final day before the Senate adjourned for the year. In the last hours of the session, Senator Wherry succeeded in bringing the nomination to a vote, and Hennock was confirmed.

In 1948, the Federal Communications Commission was deeply involved in crucial decision-making regarding the future of radio and TV broadcasting. Radio broadcasting promised to be vastly improved by the fidelity of FM signals, but broadcasters were hesitant to invest in transmitters when there was no guarantee that listeners would buy the radios that could receive the FM signal. In television, 16 stations were on the air, with additional licenses approved, but interference among them was being reported, and it was clear that the number of very-high frequency (VHF) channels available was inadequate to serve the entire country. Ultra-high frequencies (UHF) could be used for additional channels, but technical disadvantages and lack of home sets to receive them made these less desirable, and the FCC faced a potential repeat of the chaotic conditions experienced in the early days of radio broadcasting. When Hennock arrived at the FCC, a freeze on granting television licenses had been in effect since the previous April, 1948. Tests of competing systems for broadcasting color television signals were meanwhile under way, proposals for pay-television services were being submitted, and other critical issues were under consideration. In the short speech she made at her swearing in, Hennock referred to the responsibility facing the commission in developing policies to regulate "the nation's most important public service industries—radio, telephone, telegraph." She acknowledged that "each woman undertaking a new and challenging public office must feel that she carries the trust of her sex as well as that of the nation," and she pledged to dedicate herself "to this trust and endeavor to discharge it in the interest of all the people."

Soon immersed in the technical aspects of the electronic and telephone industries, Hennock wrote to friends about the long hours she spent studying millivolts, microvolts, contours, and tropospheric propagation. But her concerns went far beyond the technical matters. According to Stanley Neustadt who served as her legal assistant, Hennock "was looking for a good cause, one that she could get behind wholeheartedly," and she was keenly aware of the role radio and television played in the lives of individual listeners. Soon she found her cause in the use of television to educate its audiences.

As Hennock's congressional testimony had indicated, her familiarity with non-commercial radio broadcasting had begun with WNYC, working on public-service campaigns to register voters. In 1949, when she attended the Institute for Education by Radio, a meeting of educational broadcasters held at Ohio State University, she met and talked with many people directly involved in educational programming. Most participants were concentrating their efforts on radio and only a few were experimenting with television.

In 1945, in recognition of the differing needs of educators and commercial broadcasters, FCC policy had set aside 20 FM radio channels for educational use. As discussion of television channel allocations began, there was no organized support for comparable set-asides. The technical nature of TV band-width requirements made fewer television channels available, and commercial television broadcasters, foreseeing a profitable future, were eager to apply for licenses for all available channels, while costs made it difficult for educational broadcasters, with limited funds, to compete. Hennock, recognizing the power and influence of the commercial interests, decided to take a stand. When the FCC's proposed table of television assignments included no channel reservations for education, she first wrote a dissenting opinion, arguing that part of the UHF band should be reserved for non-commercial use; then she set about an ambitious campaign to rally support from educators and civic organizations.

Hearings on the allocation plan were scheduled for the fall of 1950. Hennock began to alert educators to the need to testify, and some responded by forming an ad hoc committee, the Joint Committee on Educational Television (JCET). The FCC chair became an advisor to the group, referring them to legal counsel and technical experts, while she continued to write, phone, and meet with others who could testify about the importance of television for educating both children and adults. She kept up a heavy schedule of public appearances, debating once with an advertising consultant on the question of "who should be responsible for education on television" on the ABC network's "America's Town Meeting of the Air"; she exchanged views with a former president of the National Association of Broadcasters on "Mrs. Roosevelt Meets the Public"; and she wrote articles for a number of publications, including *The Saturday Review of Literature*, *Women Lawyers Journal*, and *Educational Outlook*.

At the opening of the hearings, representatives of civic groups, public-school systems, colleges, universities, and foundations stood ready to testify. When commercial broadcasters argued that non-commercial stations were unnecessary because they were serving the public's educational needs, educators countered with the results of monitoring studies that revealed little variety in programs and few programs that could be considered anything more than superficially educational. Hennock took an active role, supplying monitoring studies and other evidence to establish a case for channel reservations. In March 1951, when the FCC's notice of rule making was published, proposals for reserving television channels for education were included, but the reservations did not appear to be permanent. In response, Hennock produced a separate new opinion, arguing for the permanence of the reservations.

In June 1951, Truman nominated Frieda B. Hennock to fill an opening as federal judge in New York. According to some, this was the appointment that Hennock had long hoped for, but as the senate hearings proceeded she found herself embroiled in controversy. The appointment was applauded by many groups, including the National Association of Women Lawyers, the Women Lawyer's Association of the State of New York, and the New York Women's Bar Association. Her fellow FCC commissioners testified strongly in her support, and many other prominent individuals voiced their approval, before reservations began to arise about the appointment of any woman to the federal bench. The American Bar Association and the New York City Bar Association, both of which had only just begun to admit women, flatly opposed the nomination.

In confirmation hearings before the Senate Committee on the Judiciary, questions then arose about Hennock's lawsuit against Silver, her former law partner, as well as allegations that she had used her personal friendship with a judge to secure business for a law firm she had been associated with, and rumors regarding her moral character. Transcripts of those hearings are incomplete, but those that remain suggest that the charges of ethical or moral impropriety were based on anonymous comments in a letter sent to the committee. Notes that Hennock wrote in preparation for the hearings are in her papers at the Schlesinger Library, Radcliffe. In them, Hennock referred to the charges as "hearsay of a nature which women are defenseless to combat." Witness after witness spoke highly of her qualifications and good character. None could recall any incident damaging to her integrity or reputation, and, in public, Truman continued to support her. But as the hearings dragged on and confirmation grew more doubtful, Hennock finally asked that her name be withdrawn.

Returning to her work at the FCC, Hennock renewed her efforts on behalf of educational television. When the FCC's Sixth Report and Order was issued on April 11, 1952, it included 242 specific channel reservations for non-commercial television. Even though channels had been reserved for non-commercial use, Hennock realized that getting educational stations on the air was crucial in preserving those reservations. Taking her usual hands-on approach, she worked closely with communities, encouraging cooperation between competing interests and providing advice on fund raising and procedural matters. She also encouraged corporations to provide grants to help finance purchases of equipment for the new stations.

When the first educational television station, KUHT-TV in Houston, began broadcasting in June 1953, Hennock's vision had become a reality. By the following July, six more such stations were on the air. Two years later, when her term expired in mid-1955, over 50 non-commercial license applications had been filed and 12 stations were on the air.

That year, when her term at the FCC expired, President Dwight D. Eisenhower chose not to reappoint Hennock. As she later told a subcommittee investigating questions of ethical misconduct in regulatory agencies, she was not surprised. Her outspoken opposition to practices of the commercial networks, her criticism of violence in television programming, her recommendation that broadcasters give free air time to candidates in presidential elections, and her warnings about what she saw as growing monopolies in the industry had made her unpopular with many broadcasters.

Hennock resumed private law practice, joining the firm of Davies, Richberg, Tydings, Beebe & Landa in Washington, D.C. In March 1956, she married William H. Simons, a real-estate broker, and set up a private legal practice. In June 1960, she underwent surgery for a brain tumor; she died on June 20.

In oral history interviews, Stanley Neustadt recalled his former boss as a superb negotiator; she was vivacious, charming, but highly emotional. When Hennock disagreed with her fellow commissioners, she did not hesitate to express her views and add her dissenting opinions to the public record. But as Neustadt has pointed out "on almost every issue on which she took any noticeable position, she was ultimately—sometimes long after she left the Commission—ultimately shown to be right." What is clear about the portrait that emerges from such recollections is that public television in the United States owes its existence in large part to Frieda B. Hennock's energy and commitment to pursue a course she believed would benefit generations to come.

SOURCES:

Congressional Record. June 19, 1948, p. 9169.

"First Woman Member of FCC Makes Impression on Senators with Frankness," in *The Washington Post.* July 6, 1948, p. 2.

"Frieda Hennock," in *Current Biography: Who's News and Why 1948.* NY: H.W. Wilson, 1949.

"Frieda Hennock Simons Dead," in *The New York Times.* June 21, 1960, p. 33.

"Glamour at the Inquiry," in *The New York Times.* April 4, 1958, p. 12.

"Miss Commissioner Hennock," in *The Baltimore Sun.* August 8, 1948, p. A-5.

"Miss Hennock Says Networks Hinder TV," in *The New York Times.* April 4, 1958, p. 1.

Public Television's Roots Oral History Project. The Mass Communications History Center, State Historical Society of Wisconsin, Madison, 1982.

U.S. Senate Committee on the Judiciary hearings on confirmation of the nomination of Frieda B. Hennock. Unpublished U.S. government documents (82) SJ-T.10, T.11, T.12, T.13.

"Woman Nominated as Member of FCC," in *The New York Times.* May 25, 1948.

SUGGESTED READING:

Morgenthau, Henry. "Dona Quixote: The Adventures of Frieda Hennock," in *Television Quarterly.* Vol. XXVI, no. 2, 1992, pp. 61–73.

Powell, John Walker. *Channels of Learning: The Story of Educational Television.* Washington, DC: Public Affairs Press, 1962.

Robertson, Jim. *TeleVisionaries.* Charlotte Harbor, FL: Tabby House Books, 1993.

COLLECTIONS:

Personal papers including correspondence, speeches, published articles, and documents related to her work at the Federal Communications Commission, at the Schlesinger Library, Radcliffe College, Cambridge, Massachusetts.

Official papers related to her tenure at the Federal Communications Commission at the Harry S. Truman Library, Independence, Missouri.

Lucy A. Liggett,
professor of telecommunications and film,
Eastern Michigan University, Ypsilanti, Michigan

Henri, Florence (1895–1982)

American avant-garde photographer. *Born in New York City in 1895; died in Compiègne, France, in 1982; studied music in Paris, Italy, and Berlin; studied art in Berlin; attended Académie Moderne, Paris, 1924; attended the Bauhaus, in Dessau, Germany, 1927; married Karl Anton Koster, in 1924 (divorced 1954); no children.*

Identified with the European avant-garde movement of the 1920s and 1930s, Florence Henri was born in New York City to a French father and German mother. She pursued an early interest in music, studying piano in Paris, Italy and Berlin, then embarked on a brief concert career. Concurrently, she began art studies, first at Kunstakademie, in Berlin, and later in Paris with Ferdinand Leger, as well as Amédée Ozenfant who with Charles Le Corbusier had founded an abstract school of painting known as Purism. Married in 1924, Henri continued her studies at the Bauhaus in Dessau, Germany, where, under the influence of Laszlo Moholy-Nagy and Joseph Albers, she began to explore photography. Some of her early experimental portraits, combining Bauhaus and Purist elements, were published in the Dutch journal *110* in 1928.

In 1929, Henri returned to Paris and opened a studio, where she specialized in portraits and also worked on fashion and advertising projects. That year, she was represented in two important exhibitions: *Photografie der Gegenwart*, in Essen, Germany, and *Film and Foto*, in Stuttgart. A one-woman exhibition of her work was held in Paris in 1930. By 1931, Henri had become well-known for her portraits, which included likenesses of many of the avant-garde artists of her day, including Hans Arp, Wassily Kandinsky, and Alberto Giacometti. Her portraits, as well as her still lifes and abstractions, are characterized by the use of multiple mirrors and geometric objects, such as beams, rods, and steel balls, and are considered precursors of the New-constructivist work of the 1980s.

Florence Henri spent the war years in Paris, where she continued to photograph and paint. She moved to Bellival, France, in 1962, and devoted her later years to abstract painting. Her photographs, paintings, and collages were exhibited throughout the 1970s, including a show at the Museum of Modern Art in New York (1970–72). A major retrospective was held at the San Francisco Museum of Modern Art and then toured in 1990.

Henrich, Christy (1973–1994)

American gymnast. *Born in Independence, Missouri, in 1973; died of bulimia and anorexia nervosa on July 26, 1994; daughter of Paul (a gas station owner) and Sandy Henrich.*

Christy Henrich was one of America's more promising gymnasts of the 1980s. In June 1986, at age 13, she was 5th in all-around at the National Junior championship; she finished 10th in 1988 at the Senior Nationals. But Henrich became a lamented symbol of the Peter Pan principle that in order to win, gymnasts must remain tiny and never grow up. According to an American College of Sports Medicine study undertaken in 1992, 62% of females in sports, such as figure skating and gymnastics, have eating disorders; 3 to 6% end in death.

The average size of a gymnast who wants to compete at the top level has been declining over the years. In 1976, female gymnasts averaged 5'3", 105 lbs. In 1992, the average was 4'9", 88 lbs. The ideal is not necessarily self-induced. Most agree that Henrich's turning point came in March 1988 at a meet in Budapest, Hungary, when a U.S. judge warned her that she was too fat and needed to lose weight to make the Olympic squad. Over the ensuing months, Henrich lost several pounds, bringing her weight down to 90. When she failed to make the 1988 Olympic team by 0.118th of a point, her eating problem escalated; she was forced to retire from sports in January 1991. "My life is a horrifying nightmare," she told a reporter. "It feels like there's a beast inside of me." In 1994, Henrich died of multiple organ failure after her weight plummeted to 47 pounds. Fellow sufferers include gymnasts **Kathy Johnson**, ***Cathy Rigby**, and ***Nadia Comaneci**.

SOURCES:

"Dying for a Medal," in *People Weekly.* August 22, 1994, pp. 36–39.

Henrietta.

Variant of Harriet or Henriette.

Henrietta Adrienne (1792–1864)

Married the ex-king of the Netherlands. *Born Henrietta Adrienne Ludovica Flora in Maastricht in 1792; died on October 26, 1864, in Schloss Rahr, near Aachen; became second wife of William I (1772–1843), king of the Netherlands (r. 1813–1840, abdicated in 1840), on February 17, 1841. William's first wife was* ****Frederica Wilhelmina of Prussia*** *(1774–1837).*

Henrietta Anne (1644–1670)

Duchess of Orléans. *Name variations: Henrietta Stuart; Henrietta of England; Henriette-Anne, Duchesse d'Orleans or Orléans; Henriette of England or Henriette d'Angleterre; (nickname) Minette. Born at Bedford House, Exeter, England, on June 16, 1644; died on June 30, 1670, at St. Cloud Palace, Paris; interred at St. Denis Cathedral; fifth daughter of Charles I, king of England (r. 1625–1649), and Henrietta Maria (1609–1669); married Philip (1640–1701), duke of Orléans (r. 1660–1701, brother of King Louis XIV of France), on March 30 or 31, 1661; children: Marie Louise d'Orleans (1662–1689, who married Charles II of Spain); Philip Charles (1664–1666), duke of Valois; Anne-Marie d'Bourbon-Orleans (1669–1728, who married Victor Amadeus II of Savoy); she also had four miscarriages.*

Henrietta Anne

Henrietta Anne was born on June 16, 1644, in the midst of the English Civil War. Her mother ***Henrietta Maria** was, in fact, in the process of fleeing the country at the time of her birth. Fifteen days after the princess was born, Henrietta Maria placed her in the care of a governess, **Lady Dalkeith** (afterwards countess of Morton), and sailed for France. As the war raged on, Lady Dalkeith was constantly on the move, hoping to keep the child safe from capture. Charles I established a household for the princess and ordered them to stay out of the grasp of Parliamentary forces.

When Charles I surrendered in May of 1646, the Parliament demanded that the princess be handed over to be kept with her siblings at St. James's Palace. Lady Dalkeith, whose orders from the king had been to stay with Henrietta Anne at all costs, instead executed a daring escape from their residence at Oatlands in Surrey. She disguised herself as a valet and dressed Henrietta in a tattered frock and referred to her as "Peter," which she believed was the nearest approximation of the child's own lisping of "princess." After walking to Dover and catching a French merchant ship across the Channel, Lady Dalkeith finally brought Henrietta Anne to her mother in Paris.

Henrietta Maria, overjoyed to see her daughter after an absence of two years, vowed to oversee her upbringing personally and to raise her in the Roman Catholic faith. The little princess quickly became a favorite ornament of the French court, where she impressed onlookers with her talent in dancing, which she inherited from her mother. She remained close by her mother throughout her exile in France, and returned to England with her in 1660, where she became equally popular in the English court of her brother Charles II, recently restored to their father's throne.

Henrietta Anne was married to Philip, first duke of Orléans and brother of Louis XIV, in March of 1661. From the very beginning, the two felt no attraction for each other. Philip, who was greatly enamored with one of Henrietta Anne's ladies-in-waiting, showed his wife little attention. In return, Henrietta Anne, who had grown up as a creature of the court, entertained herself in a whirl of extravagance and began to dabble in court politics. She became known as a patron of the arts, and she underwrote works by Racine, Corneille and Molière.

Henrietta Anne was able to use her family connections to act as a mediator in diplomacy between the English and French courts. Her knowledge of state secrets, often those hidden from Philip, enraged her jealous husband. As she became a close confidante of Louis XIV, she aroused increasing ire in her husband, and they quarrelled publicly. Henrietta Anne traveled to Dover in 1670, where she personally negotiated a treaty between her older brother Charles II and Louis XIV, in which Louis promised Charles a substantial subsidy in return for Charles' promise to work toward the restoration of the Catholic Church and of absolute royal power in England.

Louis XIV was so pleased with her efforts that he showered her with money and gifts, publicly honoring her for her role in the treaty. Philip was furious at this escapade, which had taken place entirely without his knowledge, and he insisted that Henrietta leave Versailles. Henrietta Anne, in tears, insisted upon bathing in the Seine, which she did regularly. On the following afternoon, after drinking a cup of chicory-water, Henrietta began to complain of severe stomach cramps. Terrified that she had been poisoned by her husband, she called in her physicians, who were unable to relieve her, and she died at two o'clock the next morning. A quick post-mortem conducted after her death attributed her end to natural causes, but suspicions of foul play were heard throughout Europe.

On August 21, 1670, Henrietta Anne was buried at St. Denis, near her mother, only one year following Henrietta Maria's death. Her admirers were stunned by her untimely demise and declared that "never was any one so regretted since dying was the fashion." Henrietta Anne left behind two young daughters, ***Marie Louise d'Orleans** and ⚘▸ **Anne-Marie d'Bourbon-Orleans**, the eldest of whom later married Charles II of Spain and the youngest of whom later married Victor Amadeus II of Savoy. Within a year of his wife's death, Philip married her second cousin, ***Charlotte Elizabeth of Bavaria** (1652–1722).

SOURCES:

Barker, Nancy N. "Revolution and the Royal Consort," in *Proceedings of the Consortium on Revolutionary Europe, 1990*. Vol. 20, pp. 136–143.

Haynes, Henrietta. *Henrietta Maria*. NY: Putnam, 1912.

Shimp, Robert E. "A Catholic Marriage for an Anglican Prince," in *Historical Magazine of the Episcopal Church*. Vol. 50, 1981, pp. 3–18.

Smuts, R.M. "The Puritan Followers of Henrietta Maria in the 1630's," in *English Historical Review*. Vol. 366, 1978, pp. 26–45.

⚘▸ **Anne-Marie d'Bourbon-Orleans** (1669–1728)

Queen of Sicily and Sardinia. *Name variations: Ana Maria of Orleans. Born on May 11, 1669; died on August 26, 1728; daughter of* ***Henrietta Anne** *(1644–1670) and Philip Bourbon-Orleans, 1st duke of Orléans; married Victor Amadeus II (1666–1732), duke of Savoy (r. 1675–1713), king of Sicily (r. 1713–1718) and Sardinia (r. 1718–1730), on April 10, 1684; children:* ***Marie Adelaide of Savoy** *(1685–1712), duchess of Burgundy (mother of Louis XV of France);* ***Marie Louise of Savoy** *(c. 1687–1714, first wife of Philip V of Spain); Charles Emmanuel III (1701–1773), king of Sardinia (r. 1730–1773), and duke of Savoy; Vittorio (d. 1715).*

Veevers, Erica. *Images of Love and Religion: Queen Henrietta Maria and Court Entertainments*. Cambridge: Cambridge University Press, 1989.

SUGGESTED READING:

***Marie-Madeleine de La Fayette** (1634–1693) composed the history of her friendship with Henrietta Anne sometime between 1665 and 1670, though *Histoire de Madame Henriette d'Angleterre* was not published until 1720.

Kimberly Estep Spangler,
Assistant Professor of History and Chair of the Division of Religion and Humanities at Friends University, Wichita, Kansas

Henrietta Catherine of Nassau (1637–1708)

Princess of Anhalt-Dessau. *Name variations: Henrietta Catherine Orange-Nassau. Born on January 31, 1637; died on November 4, 1708; daughter of* ***Amelia of Solms** *(1602–1675) and Frederick Henry (b. 1584), prince of Orange (r. 1625–1647); sister of* ***Louisa Henrietta** *(1627–1667), electress of Brandenburg; married John George II, prince of Anhalt-Dessau, on July 9, 1659; children: Leopold I (b. 1676), prince of Anhalt;* ***Amelia of Anhalt-Dessau** *(1666–1726).*

Henriette d'Angleterre (1644–1670).

See Henrietta Anne.

Henrietta Maria (1609–1669)

French-born queen of Charles I, during England's Civil War, who used all her influence to try to aid her husband's cause, and whose eldest son was invited to restore the Stuart dynasty to the English throne as Charles II. *Name variations: Henrietta Marie. Born at the Hôtel de Louvre, in Paris, France, on November 25, 1609; died at Château St. Colombes, near Paris, on*

August 31, 1669; buried in the Church of St. Denis, near Paris; daughter of Henry IV the Great (1553–1610), king of France (r. 1589–1610), and Marie de Medici (c. 1573–1642); sister of Elizabeth Valois (1602–1644, who married Philip IV, king of Spain), Christine of France (1606–1663), and Louis XIII, king of France (r. 1610–1643); married Charles I (1600–1649), king of England (r. 1626–1649), on May 11 (some sources cite June 13), 1625; children: Charles II (b. 1630), king of England (r. 1649–1685); Mary of Orange (1631–1660), princess of Orange; James II (b. 1633), king of England (r. 1685–1688); Elizabeth Stuart (1635–1650); Anne Stuart (1637–1640, died of consumption at age three); Catherine (1639–1639); Henry (1640–1660), duke of Gloucester; Henrietta Anne (1644–1670), duchess of Orléans.

Moved from France to England at the time of her marriage (1625); acted frequently in plays in the English royal court; intrigued with Catholic monarchs and the pope for aid to her husband during the English Civil War (1642–49); lived in exile in France until the accession of her son as Charles II (1660); moved to England (1662); returned to France to the Château at Colombes (1665) and died there (1669).

Henrietta Maria lived in an age of turbulent religious struggles, and she was destined to play an integral part in one of the most famous of these, the English Civil War. She was the daughter of ***Marie de Medici** and Henry IV, who had ended the Wars of Religion in France between the Catholics and the Huguenots. The cost of solidifying the throne of France had been Henry's conversion from the Huguenot faith to Catholicism; to satisfy disgruntled supporters, he granted toleration to Huguenots in France in the Edict of Nantes (1598). But even this measure did not end the religious fanaticism rampant during this period. Within a year of Henrietta Maria's birth, in 1610, Henry IV was assassinated by a fanatical monk. Although Henrietta Maria herself escaped violent death, her husband Charles I did not. Her attempts to help him and support him during the political crisis that led up to the English Civil War only stirred up English resentment and suspicion against them and sealed Charles' fate.

Henrietta grew up with all the pomp and circumstance due a child of the royal household. She had two older sisters: the eldest, ***Elizabeth Valois** (1602–1644), was married to Philip IV of Spain when Henrietta was a small child, and the younger, ***Christine of France** (1606–1663), was married to the prince of Savoy when Henrietta was ten. The eldest of her brothers, Louis, had ascended to the throne as Louis XIII upon their father's death, and a regency for him was led by their mother Marie de Medici and her advisor, Cardinal Richelieu.

By the time Henrietta was 12 years old, negotiations between the English and French courts had commenced for a match between Henrietta and Charles, the eldest son of James I. The marriage treaty was completed in 1625, when Henrietta was only 15. English diplomats at work on the marriage treaty described Henrietta as petite, well-formed, and graceful, with sparkling black eyes and a pleasing personality. Henrietta was excited to hear of her upcoming marriage, although she had only met Charles once before. She remembered him as being tall, good-looking and grave, and she exchanged several formal love-letters with her future husband during the two months that preceded their marriage. When James I died on March 27, only days after the marriage treaty had been negotiated, Charles ascended to the throne of England as Charles I. Impatient for his bride, Charles was unwilling to postpone the wedding for the period of mourning, and the ceremony took place by proxy on May 11, at the Cathedral of Notre Dame in Paris, followed by feasting and fireworks. The bride did not leave Paris to meet her bridegroom in England until June, and she did not set foot in England until June 22; she finally met her new husband on the following day.

Despite the great anticipation that both Henrietta Maria and Charles had over their eventual union, the early period of their marriage was rocky. A large measure of their unhappiness stemmed from public disapproval with Henrietta's religion, which was inflamed by the large number of French Catholic ladies-in-waiting and Catholic priests and advisors who made up her household. Many of the English, including Charles' chief advisor, George Villiers, duke of Buckingham, believed Henrietta's household to be comprised of "popish spies." During the second year of their marriage, Charles broke the agreement of their nuptial contract by sending Henrietta's French household packing, replacing her ladies-in-waiting with English Protestant ones. In the end, Henrietta was only allowed to keep one lady and two priests of her own faith and language.

Once the dispute over her household had been resolved, Henrietta found, to her surprise, that she quickly adapted to accommodate English customs and the needs of her husband. The removal of the French household, coupled with the assassination of the duke of Buckingham in August of 1628, left Henrietta and Charles without their closest confidantes. Eventually, they

Henrietta Maria (1609–1669)

turned to each other. Charles began lavishing more time and gifts on his wife, and Henrietta grew increasingly dependent upon him. By 1630, Charles wrote confidently to his mother-in-law Marie de Medici that "the only dispute that now exists between us is that of conquering each other by affection, both esteeming ourselves victorious in following the will of the other."

In 1629, Henrietta gave birth to her first child, a boy, who died shortly thereafter. She bravely overcame her illness and sadness over the birth, and in May of the following year gave birth to another son, who would ultimately succeed his father as Charles II. Both parents were delighted with Charles, and other children followed closely: ***Mary of Orange** in November 1631, James (later James II), in October 1633, ***Elizabeth Stuart** in December 1635, Anne Stuart in March 1637, Henry (later duke of Gloucester) in July 1640.

Charles continued to lavish money and affection on his wife, and Henrietta's fun-loving and spendthrift personality guaranteed that she took advantage of the £18,000 income she received yearly. Henrietta was not fond of literature, but she delighted in putting on plays and masques for the royal court. The lavish entertainments to which she had been accustomed in France were greeted by shock and disapproval by many of her Puritan English subjects, who considered them frivolous at best and scandalous at worst.

> I was the happiest and most fortunate of Queens. Not only had I every pleasure which my heart could desire, but, above all, I had the love of my husband, who adored me.
>
> **—Henrietta Maria in exile in France**

During the early years of her marriage, Henrietta Maria showed no interest in the political machinations of government. From the beginning of his reign, Charles had been embroiled in political controversy with Parliament, which contained a sizeable Puritan element, and Charles had dismissed them over their attempted impeachment of Buckingham in 1629; he would not call Parliament again until 1640. During this "Eleven Year Tyranny," Charles ruled through ministers who could collect revenues without necessitating the calling of Parliament. As Charles took on an increasingly personal role in the administration of his realm, he began to share many of his concerns with his wife, who had become his confidante. To her credit, Henrietta had grown in her loyalty to the English nation during the first ten years of her marriage. From France, Cardinal Richelieu complained that she had lost her loyalty to her native land when she proved unwilling to advance French interests or support Richelieu's officials in England. But unfortunately for her, most of the English continued to be suspicious of her: the Puritans because she was Roman Catholic, and the English Catholics because she was not committed enough to the cause of Catholicism. Henrietta was always moderate in her religious sensibilities, and she began to seek out advisors for her husband, both Protestant and Catholic, whom she felt would pursue moderate policies as well.

Part of the growing influence which Henrietta Maria held in the 1630s was manifested in the relaxation of the laws against Catholics and Catholic priests in England. Charles allowed priests to live undisturbed in London, and even allowed English Catholics to openly attend mass in the chapels of the queen and the French ambassadors. Many Catholics, including priests who had languished for years in prison, were released by Charles, whose heart was becoming softened to their plight. Unfortunately, the softening of the king's heart had little effect on the hearts of his subjects, most of whom remained deeply suspicious of Catholics in England. The Puritans were still a growing and vocal element in English politics, and, in the absence of Parliamentary meetings, many Puritans began venting their hostility to the king's "pro-Catholic" policies in political pamphlets.

Charles' defense of Henrietta's faith also served to exacerbate public opinion when Charles and his archbishop of Canterbury, William Laud, decided to implement a policy which they called "Thorough"—they hoped to eliminate Puritan influences in the English and Scottish Church, and institute a reformed Anglican liturgy for Scotland. When the new liturgy (which Charles had proudly presented to Henrietta as evidence of the similarity of their beliefs) was first presented at St. Giles Church in Edinburgh on July 23, 1637, a riot against the government ensued, which built to such force that it became a major insurrection. Charles was forced to either withdraw the new liturgy or send troops to put down the rebellion. Never one to forgive rebellion or to countenance his own failures, Charles decided to send troops to force the acceptance of the new liturgy. Overwhelmed by the angry Scots, the king's small force was defeated and forced to withdraw. With the Scots rebels poised at the English border ready to invade, Charles called Parliament into session in April 1640 to ask for £800,000 to put down the rebels. Instead, Parliamentary leaders led by John Pym demanded Puritan reforms in the church and an end to Charles' "abuses" of old feudal tax laws and royal prerogative courts, before they would approve a penny. Charles angrily dismissed Parliament and scraped together extra-Parliamentary money to send a second force to Scotland. Before they arrived, a Scottish Presbyterian army invaded England, where they routed Charles' troops in August 1640 and remained in England, demanding that Charles pay £850 a day to the Scottish army until a settlement was reached.

Having exhausted his own revenues, Charles was again forced to call Parliament. In order to get the money he so desperately needed, Charles had to agree to series of embarrassing Parliamentary acts, including laws forbidding the king from dismissing Parliament without its consent, forbidding the king from raising extra-Parliamentary revenue through taxation, and abolishing the king's prerogative courts. The king's chief councilors, Thomas Wentworth and Archbishop Laud, were arrested, convicted of treason, and sentenced to death. By August 1641, Parliament had overturned the traditional foundations of government and rewritten the political rules to the detriment of royal power. Once begun along the revolutionary path, Parliamentary leaders were loath to stop. In September 1641, Parliament abolished the Anglican Church episcopacy; two months later, it drafted the Grand Remonstrance, cataloguing the king's sins and demanding further reform; in February 1642, Parliament enacted the Militia Bill, without the king's signature, placing all naval and military appointments under Parliamentary inspection.

By the winter of 1641–42, a royal party was forming around the king, comprised of royalists as well as moderates who felt that Pym and Parliament were going too far. Although Charles was reluctant to resort to a show of force, he was encouraged by many, including Henrietta, who urged, "Go, you coward, and pull these rogues out by the ears." By the time Charles arrived to arrest Pym and the leaders of the House of Commons, they had fled. Within months, the dispute had intensified into all-out war, as Parliament declared itself the supreme authority of government, and in response Charles raised his standard at Nottingham on August 22, 1642, to begin the English Civil War.

Throughout these tribulations, Henrietta had stood behind her husband, and had worked to secure for him any monetary aid she could find. When she discovered that she could raise little money among the wives of courtiers, she eventually turned to the papacy. By 1640, she was writing frequently, importuning the pope to give aid, and promising that she could convince Charles to ensure the toleration of English Catholics. During the summer of 1641, Henrietta wrote to her sister Christine of France, "I swear to you that I am almost mad with the sudden changes in my fortunes. From the highest pitch of contentment I am fallen into every kind of misery which affects not only me but others. . . . Imagine what I feel to see the King's power taken from him, the Catholics persecuted, the priests hanged, the persons devoted to us removed and pursued for their lives because they serve the King."

As soon as war became inevitable, Henrietta shook off her self-pity and resolutely set out on a series of quests to help her husband. In February 1642, she journeyed to Holland, ostensibly to deliver her ten-year-old daughter Mary to the court of the Prince of Orange, to whom she had been promised in a recent marriage negotiation. While Henrietta Maria was there, she pawned as many of her jewels as she could to raise money for arms and ammunition. By letter, she encouraged her husband to fight the Parliamentary forces and refuse any offers of compromise. She urged him to take care of their children in England, lest they fall into Parliamentary hands. "Charles, be a King," she repeatedly commanded him. When she finally set sail to return to England in January of the following year, her ship was buffeted by a storm for nine days, in which she lost a ship full of war material she had gathered for Charles. When she finally arrived in England, the village where she was staying was shelled by four Parliamentary ships, and she was forced to flee her lodgings for her life. For two hours, the queen and her entourage laid in a ditch outside the village while shells flew over their heads until the Parliamentary forces gave up. It took five months for her and her band, which included an army of a thousand soldiers from Holland, to catch up to Charles and his army. Their happy reunion in Oxford was marred by the rising violence of the war. In May 1643, Parliament impeached her for high treason and declared that she would no longer be allowed the title queen of England.

Henrietta stayed with Charles in Oxford until April 1644. She traveled to Exeter, where she gave birth to her last child, ***Henrietta Anne**, in June. Although desperately weak and ill after the birth of the baby, Henrietta Maria feared the advancing Parliamentary armies, so within a few days of the baby's birth, she fled to Pendennis and from there put to sea and escaped to France. She was greeted warmly by the residents of Brittany, where she landed. She immediately repeated the quest she had begun in Holland, to secure money, arms, and ammunition to aid her husband's cause. Her continual intriguing with foreign monarchs and aristocrats, and with the pope as well, did as much as anything to harden the hearts of the English people against Charles. When she finally arrived in Paris, she was given an enthusiastic welcome, apartments in the Louvre and the Château of St. Germain-en-Laye. Her health improved, and she was reunited with many old friends who had also fled the violence across the Channel. The French crown, now under the control of Cardinal Mazarin as regent for the boy Louis XIV, gave 300,000 crowns in money and munitions to aid Charles' cause. But this aid fell far short of what Henrietta had hoped to accomplish, and she was forced to write to Charles in 1645, "I have not found the means of engaging France as forwardly in your interest as I expected."

The king's fortunes continued to deteriorate despite the exertions of his wife. His troops were routed at the Battle of Naseby in June 1645, and the private papers of the king were seized. Nothing could have been more unfortunate for Charles than for his secret correspondence with Henrietta Maria, which illuminated all of her schemes to raise money as well as his own promises to grant toleration to English Catholics in return for aid. The king's cause faltered even further—the letters, which were published in London, proved him to be shiftless and untrustworthy. Less than a year later, on May 5, 1646, Charles surrendered himself to Scottish forces, in the hopes that he would receive more lenient treatment at the hands of the people of the land of his own birth.

When the Scots discovered that Charles refused to give up the Anglican Church to the Scottish Covenant form of Protestantism, they handed him over to the English Parliamentary leaders. Henrietta spent the next two-and-a-half years in growing fear for her husband and her children; only her youngest daughter Henrietta Anne had been smuggled into France to her mother. In 1648, the French government, overstretched due to its own revolutionary troubles, stopped paying Henrietta Maria's stipend. By the winter, Henrietta was so short of cash that she could not even afford a fire for herself and her four-year-old daughter. Desperate to be with her husband during this time of peril, she wrote letters to Parliament asking for safe-conduct to England. The letters were never opened. On January 30, 1649, Charles I, who had been put on trial for high treason, was convicted and beheaded. Henrietta did not receive the news until several days later. She was so crushed that she was paralyzed with grief; for a time, she did not move or speak or weep. Finally, she gave vent to her anguish and disbelief that the English people could have committed such an outrage. "I wonder I did not die of grief," she later recalled.

To the great comfort of Henrietta Maria, her two oldest sons, Charles and James, arrived in Paris soon after their father's death, and she found herself in the position of chief advisor to her son, whom royalists already referred to as "Charles II." Her two other children, Henry, duke of Gloucester, and Elizabeth Stuart, had been allowed to bid farewell to their father before he was led to the scaffold. Elizabeth never recovered from the shock and died in England soon after. Henry, however, was too young to understand the full import of the events, and in 1653, the Lord Protector, Oliver Cromwell, allowed him to leave England to stay with his sister in Holland. Henrietta insisted that he be brought immediately to Paris, and she was delighted to see her "beautiful little angel" that she had not seen since he was a young child. One of the results of Charles' tragic death was that Henrietta became even more fervent in her Catholic beliefs. The only one of her children whom she was able to raise in the Catholic faith was little Henrietta Anne, but for the remainder of her life Henrietta Maria pressed her other children to convert from the Anglican Church to Catholicism.

The death of Cromwell in 1658 opened the door for a change of fortune for the Stuarts. England, downtrodden and tired from years of civil war, and chafing under the austere directives of the Puritan government, grew tired of the Commonwealth experiment. In secret, a handful of Parliamentary leaders began to carve out a treaty with Charles II, to restore him to the throne of England in return for judicial immunity for themselves. In 1660, Charles II returned to his native land to assume the throne as a limited, but still powerful, monarch.

Although pleased by the accession of her son to his father's throne (she rejoiced in a letter to her sister Christine of France that the family were "vagabonds no more"), Henrietta Maria held on to her grief over her husband's death for the rest of her life. She wore black mourning dress to the end, and often remarked that, were it not for her responsibilities to her youngest daughter, she would enter a convent. In 1651, she used her political connections and influence to found a new convent at Chaillot, where she withdrew for many lengthy retreats over the next several years.

Having failed to convert her older children, she threw herself fully into her schemes to secure a suitable marriage for Henrietta Anne. In 1660, she briefly visited England, but she returned to France in 1661 with the Princess Henrietta Anne, who was married to Philip, the duke of Orléans and brother of King Louis XIV, on March 30. When Henrietta Maria returned to

England in 1662, she moved into her own residence in Somerset House but found herself uncomfortable and ill at ease there. In 1665, she returned to France, from whence she never returned. She retired to her château at Colombes. The stresses of her life began to take their toll, and her health, which had always been delicate, began to fail. Finally, on August 31, 1669, Henrietta Maria took an opiate prescribed by her physicians to help her sleep; she never awoke.

Henrietta Maria was buried with full honors in the Church of St. Denis, the traditional burying place of French kings. Orations to her memory praised her for her dedication to her faith and to her husband. Henrietta Maria has been considered one of the most unfortunate characters in history. But to the end of her life, she was able to acknowledge the tragedies she had experienced in the light of the fact that, for 20 years, she had prospered in a loving relationship with her husband which few queens throughout history have ever enjoyed.

SOURCES:

Barker, Nancy N. "Revolution and the Royal Consort," in *Proceedings of the Consortium on Revolutionary Europe, 1990.* Vol. 20, pp. 136–143.

Haynes, Henrietta. *Henrietta Maria.* NY: Putnam, 1912.

Shimp, Robert E. "A Catholic Marriage for an Anglican Prince," in *Historical Magazine of the Episcopal Church.* Vol. 50, 1981, pp. 3–18.

Smuts, R.M. "The Puritan Followers of Henrietta Maria in the 1630's," in *English Historical Review.* Vol. 366, 1978, pp. 26–45.

Veevers, Erica. *Images of Love and Religion: Queen Henrietta Maria and Court Entertainments.* Cambridge: Cambridge University Press, 1989.

Kimberly Estep Spangler,
Assistant Professor of History and Chair of the Division of Religion and Humanities at Friends University, Wichita, Kansas

Henrietta Maria (1626–1651)

Princess Palatine. *Name variations: Henrietta Mary Simmern. Born on July 17, 1626, at The Hague, Netherlands; died on September 18, 1651, in Fogaras, Hungary; daughter of* ****Elizabeth of Bohemia*** *(1596–1662) and Frederick V, Elector Palatine and titular king of Bohemia; sister of* ****Elizabeth of Bohemia*** *(1618–1680) and* ****Sophia*** *(1630–1714), electress of Hanover; married Sigismund Rakoczy also known as Sigismund Ragotski, prince of Transylvania, or Prince Sigismund of Siebenburgen, on April 4, 1651 (some sources cite June 26).*

Henrietta of Belgium (1870–1948)

Duchess of Vendôme. *Name variations: Henriette of Belgium. Born on November 30, 1870; died in 1948; daughter of* ****Marie of Hohenzollern-Sigmaringen*** *(1845–1912) and Philip (1837–1905), count of Flanders; married Emanuel or Emmanuel of Orleans, duke of Vendôme, on February 12, 1896.*

The daughter of the count of Flanders, Henrietta of Belgium was born in 1870 along with her twin sister Josephine who died the following year. Another sister, ***Josephine of Belgium**, was born in 1872.

Henrietta of Cleves (r. 1564–1601)

Duchess and ruler of Nevers. *Name variations: Henriette de Cleves; Henriette Gonzaga. Reigned from 1564 to 1601; daughter of François or Francis II, duke of Nevers, and* ****Margaret of Vendôme;*** *married Luigi or Louis de Gonzague also known as Ludovico Gonzaga of Mantua (1539–1585), duke of Nevers, count of Rethel; children: Carlo also known as Charles II (1580–1637), duke of Nevers (r. 1601–1637), and at least one daughter.*

Henrietta of Cleves spent a large part of her life foundering in a sea of debt. Her grandfather Francis I and her father Francis II had both served as provincial governors of Champagne and, as such, dissipated much of the family fortune. When Henrietta's father Francis II died in battle in 1562, the family was virtually bankrupt. The job of liquidating the family debts then fell to the guardian of Henrietta's young brother Jacques de Cleves. Before the liquidation process got under way, however, Jacques died, and the family properties and titles passed to Henrietta under an extraordinary permission granted by King Charles IX. (Since there were no further male heirs, the estate might well have gone to someone else.)

Under the terms of the agreement, a marriage was also arranged between Henrietta and Ludovico Gonzaga of Mantua, the prospective heir of some large estates. Although she was now titled as the duchess of Nevers, Henrietta's problems were not yet over. Ludovico had his own debts and his inheritances turned out to be far smaller than those of the family Cleves. Henrietta also had to provide for the dowries of her two sisters, each of whom received land worth £700,000, and dowries totaling another £600,000. In addition, Ludovico was serving as commander of the military and had to borrow money to pay his soldiers. Despite their precarious situation, the Neverses managed to serve as chief creditors of the monarchy during the period of their rule (1564–1601). Henrietta had at least one daughter, and a son Charles II, who became co-governor of Champagne with his father, in 1589, and succeeded as duke when his father died in 1595. Henrietta died in 1601.

Henrietta of Nassau-Weilburg (1780–1857)

Duchess of Wurttemberg. *Name variations: Henriette of Nassau-Weilburg. Born on April 22, 1780 (some sources cite 1770); died on January 2, 1857; daughter of Charles Christian, prince of Nassau-Weilburg, and* ****Caroline of Orange*** *(1743–1787); married Louis Frederick Alexander (1756–1817), duke of Wurttemberg (1806–1817, brother of Frederick I of Wurttemberg), on January 28, 1797; children:* ****Maria of Wurttemberg*** *(1797–1855);* ****Amelia of Wurttemberg*** *(1799–1848);* ****Elizabeth of Wurttemberg*** *(1802–1864);* ****Pauline of Wurttemberg*** *(1800–1873); Alexander of Wurttemburg (1804–1883).*

Henrietta of Savoy (c. 1630–?)

Electress of Bavaria. *Born around 1630; daughter of* ****Christine of France*** *(1606–1663) and Victor Amadeus I (1587–1637), duke of Savoy (r. 1630–1637); married Ferdinand Maria, elector of Bavaria (r. 1651–1679); children: Maximilian II Emmanuel (1662–1726), elector of Bavaria (r. 1679–1726).*

Henriette.

Variant of Henrietta.

Henriette (1727–1752)

French princess. *Name variations: Anne Henriette. Born in 1727; died in 1752; daughter of Louis XV (1710–1774), king of France (r. 1715–1774), and* ****Marie Leczinska*** *(1703–1768); twin sister of* ****Louise Elizabeth****, duchess of Parma (1727–1759).*

Henriette of England (1644–1670).

See Henrietta Anne.

Henriot-Schweitzer, Nicole (1925—)

French pianist, concert artist, and teacher who specialized in the French repertoire. *Born on November 23, 1925, in Paris, France.*

Nicole Henriot-Schweitzer was born in Paris in 1925 and studied there with ***Marguerite Long**, winning a first prize in Long's class in 1938. Her concert tours took her throughout Europe as well as North and South America. Her U.S. debut took place in 1948, with Charles Munch conducting the New York Philharmonic-Symphony Orchestra. Henriot-Schweitzer also made recordings with Munch and the Boston Symphony Orchestra. Specializing in the French repertoire, she taught at the Liége Conservatory from 1970 through 1973 and served on the faculty of the Brussels Conservatory.

John Haag,
Athens, Georgia

Henry, Alice (1857–1943)

Australian American journalist and labor leader. *Born in Richmond, Australia, on March 21, 1857; died in Melbourne, Australia, on February 14, 1943; oldest of two children of Charles Ferguson Henry and Margaret (Walker) Henry; privately educated; never married; no children.*

Wrote for the Melbourne Argus *(1884–1904); emigrated to America (1906), settling in Chicago; was editor of the women's section,* Union Labor Advocate *(1908–11); served as editor of* Life and Labor *(1911–15); served as national WTUL organizer (1918–20); was director of the WTUL education department (1920–22); retired (1928) and returned to Australia (1933).*

Publications: The Trade Union Woman *(1915),* Women and the Labor Movement *(1923), and* Memoirs of Alice Henry *(1944), and numerous articles.*

When Alice Henry came to the United States, early in 1906, she was almost 49 years old and had worked for more than 20 years as a respected journalist and social reformer in her native Australia. She arrived in America, as she would later remember, carrying not much more than the tools of her trade, her "pen and voice." For the next 20 years, Henry put those tools to work for the cause of women's trade unionism. Within a year of her arrival, Henry joined the Women's Trade Union League (WTUL), working out of its national office in Chicago. There, she was an effective speaker for the three primary goals of the WTUL: organization, education and protective legislation for women workers.

Henry was born in 1857 in the Melbourne suburb of Richmond where her parents, both Scottish immigrants who had met on the boat to Australia, had settled. Her childhood was a relatively comfortable one. Although her father briefly tried and failed to establish a dairy farm in the Australian bush, Charles Henry worked most of his life as an accountant, providing a solid middle-class home for his wife, **Margaret Walker Henry**, and their two children, Alice and Alfred. Later in life, Alice Henry would credit her parents with instilling in her a sense that the world could be changed for the better. Coupled with her familiarity and active involvement with social reform in Australia, Alice Henry set foot in America ready to do battle on behalf of working women.

Although she spent her first few months speaking on women's suffrage, by the summer of 1906 Henry turned her attention to women and trade unionism. At the invitation of ***Jane Addams**, Henry stayed at the Chicago settlement, Hull House. There, she met **Margaret Dreier Robins** who was about to become national president of the WTUL. Robins asked Henry to stay in Chicago and act as secretary of the local WTUL office. Henry accepted and within two years was putting her journalistic skills to work for the WTUL as editor of the women's section of the Chicago-based *Union Labor Advocate*. When the WTUL began to publish its own monthly journal, *Life and Labor*, in 1911, Henry took over as editor. During her four years as editor, Henry was assisted by her good friend and fellow Australian, ***Miles Franklin**, a prominent author of such works as *My Brilliant Career* (1901).

Throughout her 20 years with the WTUL, Alice Henry emphasized the benefits of trade unionism for working women. At the same time, she was a staunch advocate of education for those same women. As educational director for the WTUL, Henry established the Bryn Mawr summer school for working women in 1921. She was also a supporter of protective labor legislation for both men and women similar to that passed in Australia before the turn of the century. In America, however, such labor legislation tended to focus on women alone. During the 1910s, Henry was particularly active in the campaign to establish a minimum wage for women.

Alice Henry retired in 1928, returning to Australia for financial and personal reasons in 1933. The last ten years of her life were not easy. The frailty of old age, combined with a sense of being a stranger in the land of her birth, made her final years frequently frustrating. Henry spent those last years dictating her memoirs and corresponding with old friends in America. After a serious fall at age 83, Alice Henry entered a Melbourne nursing home and died there three years later. Using her "pen and voice," she had devoted her life to social reform, especially the cause of working women.

SOURCES:

Kirkby, Diane. *Alice Henry: The Power of Pen and Voice: The Life of an Australian-American Labor Reformer*. NY: Cambridge University Press, 1991.

COLLECTIONS:

Alice Henry Papers, National Library of Australia, Canberra and the Mitchell Library, Sydney.

Kathleen Banks Nutter,
Manuscripts Processor at the Sophia Smith Collection, Smith College, Northampton, Massachusetts

Henry of Battenburg, Princess (1857–1944).

See Victoria for sidebar on Princess Beatrice.

Henrys, Catherine (c. 1805–1855)

Irish-born Australian convict. *Name variations: Jemmy the Rover. Born Catherine Henrys in County Sligo, Ireland, around 1805; died in Melbourne Hospital, in 1855.*

Robins, Margaret Dreier. *See Dreier Sisters.*

Nothing is known about the early life of notorious convict Catherine Henrys, also known as Jemmy the Rover, aside from an obvious bout with smallpox which left her with a pockmarked complexion. Having left her native Ireland for a better life in England, she was living in Derby in 1832, and it is there that she was first brought up on robbery charges. In October 1835, she was convicted of the pickpocket robbery of one Charles Haynes and sentenced to transportation (exile) for life. Henrys was taken along with other female transports to Australia aboard the *Arab,* arriving in Hobart, on the island of Tasmania, on April 25, 1836. She was assigned as a maid to a haberdasher in Hobart Town but was subsequently charged with disorderly conduct and sentenced to six days in prison. Over the next five years, Henrys was assigned to six masters throughout the colony, although her behavior (drunkenness, neglect of duty, use of obscene language) was such that she stayed with some only a matter of weeks. One of her longest tenures was with George Augustus Robinson, the superintendent of an Aboriginal settlement on Flinders Island.

Henrys apparently escaped the authorities in 1841 and enjoyed one year of freedom, during which she lived in the bush and worked as a timber splitter. She was apprehended again in 1842, found guilty of assault and robbery, and sentenced to three years' hard labor. She received a ticket of leave in 1845, only to have it almost immediately revoked because of another infraction. In 1848, she was convicted again for assault and was confined to a female factory.

Within weeks, she escaped, removing the bars of her cell with a spoon and scaling the wall. This arrest-conviction-escape pattern was repeated several times until 1850, when she was granted a conditional pardon and left the island of Tasmania on the *Caroline*. She died in a Melbourne hospital in 1855.

SOURCES:

Radi, Heather, ed. *200 Australian Women*. NSW, Australia: Women's Redress Press, 1988.

Hensel, Fanny Mendelssohn
(1805–1847).

See Mendelssohn-Hensel, Fanny.

Hensel, Luise (1798–1876)

German religious poet. *Born on March 30, 1798, in Linum, Brandenburg, Germany; died in Paderborn on December 18, 1876; sister of Wilhelm Hensel.*

Luise Hensel was born on in 1798 in Linum, Brandenburg, Germany. She was the sister of Wilhelm Hensel, the husband of ***Fanny Mendelssohn-Hensel**. A poet of devotional verse, Luise is best known for her evening hymn, *Müde Bin Ich, Geh' zur Ruh* ("I am weary and go to rest"), considered one of the best pieces of religious verse in the German language. Her poetry was collected into a volume of *Songs*.

Hentz, Caroline Lee (1800–1856)

American author. *Born Caroline Lee Whiting in Lancaster, Massachusetts, on June 1, 1800; died in Marianna, Florida, on February 11, 1856; youngest of eight children of John (a businessman) and Orpah (Danforth) Whiting; married Nicholas Marcellus Hentz (a teacher), on September 30, 1824; children: Marcellus Fabius Hentz (1825–1827); Charles Arnould Hentz (b. 1827);* ***Julia Louisa Hentz*** *(b. 1828); Thaddeus William Hentz (b. 1830).*

Selected works: DeLara; or The Moorish Bride *(a play, 1831);* Constance of Werdenberg, or The Forest League *(a play, 1832);* Lamorah, or The Western Wilds *(a play, 1832);* Lovell's Folly *(1833);* Aunt Patty's Scrap Bag *(1846);* Mob Cap *(1848);* Linda; or, The Young Pilot of the Belle Creole *(1850);* Rena; or, The Snow Bird *(1851);* Eoline; or, Magnolia Vale *(1852);* Marcus Warland; or, The Long Moss Spring *(1852);* Helen and Arthur; or, Miss Thusa's Spinning Wheel *(1853)* Wild Jack; or, The Stolen Child, and Other Stories *(1853);* The Victim of Excitement *(1853);* The Planter's Northern Bride *(1854);* Robert Graham *(1855);* The Banished Son *(1856);* Courtship and Marriage *(1856);* Ernest Linwood *(1856);* The Lost Daughter *(1857);* Love After Marriage *(1857).*

Caroline Hentz was born in 1800 and grew up in Lancaster, Massachusetts, the youngest of eight children of an established New England family. Intelligent and apparently well educated, she wrote poetry from an early age and, in her teens completed a novel. However, it was from the time of her marriage, at the age of 24, that she began the strange odyssey that gave rise to the prolific writing career of her later life.

Hentz, who was by all accounts a beautiful and vivacious woman, could probably have had her pick of husbands. She chose Nicholas Hentz, a brilliant and well-educated French émigré, who spoke three languages, was a skilled engraver and painter, and an entomologist of note. He was also physically frail, given to bouts of depression, and, as later described by his son, "one of the most nervous, jealous, suspicious characters that ever lived." The couple began their married life in North Carolina, where Nicholas taught languages and letters at the new University of North Carolina at Chapel Hill. Over the course of the next ten years, Hentz gave birth to four children (her first son died at age two) and typically moved her household every two years. Despite her husband's ill health and bouts of depression, and her own increasing family responsibilities, Hentz somehow found time to pursue her writing. While living in Covington, Kentucky, where Nicholas ran a school for girls, she finished a play *DeLara; or The Moorish Bride*, a five-act drama set in a Spanish castle during the Moors' conquest of Spain, which won $500 in a competition and was produced at the Tremont Street Theatre, in Boston, and the Arch Street Theatre, in Philadelphia, in 1831. Buoyed by favorable reviews, Hentz wrote two more dramas, *Constance of Werdenberg, or the Forest League*, produced in New York (1832), and *Lamorah, or The Western Wilds*, produced in Cincinnati (1832) and New Orleans (1833). She also had several short stories published in *Western Monthly* and began work on a novel.

In 1832, finding the university restrictive, Nicholas moved the family to Cincinnati, Ohio, where he was employed in a female seminary, and Hentz finished her first novel, *Lovell's Folly*, which was reportedly withdrawn from publication because of "libelous content." During this time, she and her husband were drawn into the local literary circle of Daniel Drake, attended also by the young ***Harriet Beecher Stowe.**

Hentz, with her stunning looks and charming wit, was often the center of attention at these gatherings. Nicholas' jealousy over the attention paid to his wife by another member of the group, and a subsequent incident involving a gun, eventually forced the family to flee Cincinnati. They spent the next 14 years living in a succession of Southern towns (Florence, Tuscaloosa, and Tuskegee, in Alabama, and Columbus, in Georgia), where Nicholas established schools. Hentz held the family together, assisted her husband in teaching, and provided for as many as 20 boarding students. There appeared to be little time for literary pursuits although Hentz achieved some notoriety in 1844, when one of her stories was serialized in the Philadelphia *Saturday Courier*. (It was published as *Aunt Patty's Scrap Bag* in 1846.) Nicholas also wrote and illustrated a collection of scholarly articles on spiders, later collected as *The Spiders of the United States* (1875).

By 1849, Nicholas had succumbed to growing hypochondria and was unable to work. Hentz, out of financial necessity, pursued her writing career full time. Within six years, she published seven collections of short stories, and eight novels, becoming, at age 50, one of the most prolific writers of the period. Though lacking any deep literary qualities, her novels enjoyed immense popularity for 30 years. (Two of her books, *Eoline; or, Magnolia Vale* [1852] and *The Planter's Northern Bride* [1854], were reprinted in the 1970s.) Often referred to as novels of domesticity, Hentz's stories are romantic in nature, populated with beautiful, self-sacrificing women who endure and triumph over tyrannical male figures who are often seriously unstable. *Ernest Linwood, or The Inner Life of the Author*, which was published posthumously in 1856, presented an almost autobiographical account of Hentz's own difficult marriage, even down to the melodramatic account of the incident that forced her family to leave Cincinnati. Setting her stories in the South, Hentz, like other antebellum writers, also helped create and popularize an idealized view of slavery and plantation life. **Lynda W. Brown**, in *American Women Writers*, calls *The Planter's Northern Bride* (1854), written in answer to *Uncle Tom's Cabin*, "a full-blown counter-statement to abolition." Brown also points out that although Hentz traveled in the same literary circles as Harriet Beecher Stowe, they were obviously quite divided on the issue of slavery.

Nicholas' health continued to deteriorate, and in 1854, he went to live with the couple's married daughter in St. Anders, Florida, while Hentz remained with their son in Marianna, Florida, commuting back and forth to care for her husband. On one of her journeys, she contracted pneumonia, which took her life on February 11, 1856.

SOURCES:

James, Edward T., ed. *Notable American Women 1607–1950*. Cambridge, MA: The Belknap Press of Harvard University Press, 1971.

Kelly, Mary. *Private Woman, Public Stage*. Oxford: Oxford University Press, 1984.

Mainiero, Lina, ed. *American Women Writers: From Colonial Times to the Present*. NY: Frederick Ungar, 1980.

Barbara Morgan,
Melrose, Massachusetts

Hepburn, Audrey (1929–1993)

Elegant Dutch actress, nominated for four Best Actress awards, who became an advocate for starving children worldwide. *Born Edda Kathleen van Heemstra Hepburn-Ruston on May 4, 1929, in Brussels, Belgium; died on January 27, 1993, in Tolochenaz, Switzerland; daughter of Baroness Ella van Heemstra and Joseph Victor Anthony Hepburn-Ruston (an English-Irish banker); studied ballet with Marie Rambert and* **Olga Tarassova**; *married Mel Ferrer (an actor), on September 25, 1954 (divorced 1968); married Andrea Mario Dotti (a psychiatrist), on January 18, 1969 (divorced 1983); lived with Robert Wolders; children: (first marriage) Sean Hepburn Ferrer (b. January 17, 1960); (second marriage) Luca (b. February 8, 1970).*

Filmography: (bit) Laughter in Paradise *(British, 1951); (bit)* One Wild Oat *(British, 1951); (bit)* The Lavender Hill Mob *(British, 1951);* Young Wives' Tale *(British, 1951);* Secret People *(British, 1952);* Monte Carlo Baby *(British, 1953);* Roman Holiday *(1953);* Sabrina *(1954);* War and Peace *(1956);* Funny Face *(1957);* Love in the Afternoon *(1957);* Green Mansions *(1959);* The Nun's Story *(1959);* The Unforgiven *(1960);* Breakfast at Tiffany's *(1961);* The Children's Hour *(1962);* Charade *(1963);* Paris When It Sizzles *(1964);* My Fair Lady *(1964);* How to Steal a Million *(1966);* Two for the Road *(1967);* Wait Until Dark *(1967);* Robin and Marian *(1976);* Bloodline *(1979);* They All Laughed *(1981);* Always *(1989).*

Television: played Marie Vetsera opposite Mel Ferrer's Prince Rudolph in "Mayerling" (90-minute special for NBC's "Producer's Showcase"), 1958; appeared with Robert Wagner in television movie "Love Among Thieves" (ABC, 1987).

Awards: American Academy Award and British Film Academy Award for Best Actress in Roman Holiday *(1954); Tony Award for Best Actress in* Ondine *(1954); nominated for an Academy Award for Best Ac-*

tress for Sabrina *(1955),* The Nun's Story *(1959), and* Breakfast at Tiffany's *(1961); New York Critics' Circle Award and British Academy Award for Best Actress in* The Nun's Story *(1959); Cecil B. De Mille Award from the Hollywood Film Producers' Association (1990); British Academy Special Award (1992); Presidential Medal of Freedom (1991); the Jean Hersholt Humanitarian award given posthumously (1993).*

In her early years, Audrey Hepburn was frequently asked to portray ***Anne Frank** in the dramatization of *The Diary of Anne Frank.* Each time, she declined. Then at a charity appearance with the London Symphony Orchestra in 1991, Hepburn read from Anne Frank's diaries. Sheridan Morley was in attendance. "Heart-breakingly fragile," he writes, "looking as though she were made of glass, she stood in front of that huge orchestra and gave a performance of such mesmerizing dramatic intensity that afterwards I was not alone in begging her to return to the stage." Later, Hepburn told Morley: "It is not that I am a very good actress, you know; it is just that my family, too, lived under the German occupation of Holland and I knew so many girls like Anne. . . . That was why I always declined to make the movie; I knew I would have cried too much."

Born Edda Hepburn-Ruston in Brussels, Belgium, on May 4, 1929, Audrey Hepburn was the product of a second marriage for Dutch aristocrat, Baroness **Ella van Heemstra**, who had grown up in The Hague, Netherlands, while spending her summers at the family ancestral castle at Doorn, in Utrecht. Pampered by nannies and maids, Ella's every whim was catered to, except one: she longed to become an actress. Her father, the baron, felt it beneath the van Heemstra name. Instead, to please him, 20-year-old Ella married Jan van Ufford of the House of Orange-Nassau. Five years and two sons later, she'd had enough of his arrogance. On one of Ella's visits to her father, now governor of the Dutch South American country of Suriname, she met the dashing, indulgent commoner Joseph A. Hepburn-Ruston. In 1926, they married and moved to Brussels, where Joseph was managing director of the Belgian branch of the Bank of England.

It was a horrendous mismatch; the Hepburn-Rustons fought continually. The child Audrey stayed in her room with her books, convinced the rows were her fault. "Chocolate was my one true love . . . ," said Hepburn, "I've always said it was either chocolate or my nails in those years. There was a lot of anxiety." The loudest fights were at dinner time. By age six, Hepburn was so miserable that she was clinically depressed and went for days without talking—only a chocolate bar or the ballet barre gave her surcease.

By 1931, Joseph was carousing with a sort of expatriate British bund which included ***Unity Mitford** and ***Diana Mitford** Mosley. Sympathetic to Hitler, in 1935 Joseph moved to London where he marched with Oswald Mosley's fascist group, the Black Shirt Brigade. Ella claimed that their eventual split was caused by the Black Shirts, but there were rumors that he had mismanaged the van Heemstra fortune. When Hepburn begged to visit him, her mother capitulated. "Even at age eleven, I knew Hitler was evil," said Hepburn. "But my father supported him. And I loved my father. I prayed that my father would change his mind, and then maybe the family could get back together. I think for the rest of my life I prayed that my family could get back together." To offset the effects of her parents' 1938 divorce, Hepburn was sent to a London school where she seemed to thrive, began to have friends, and enjoyed her weekly ballet lesson. She had effectively learned how to keep her unhappiness a secret but began to suffer from migraine headaches.

In 1939, when England declared war on Germany, Ella insisted Audrey return to Belgium. Not only was she fearful of a German invasion of Britain, but she knew Joseph's pro-Nazi stance would haunt her daughter while on English soil. Ella took her children to the family estate at Arnhem in Holland, convinced that the Netherlands

Heemstra, Ella van (1900–1984)

Dutch aristocrat who worked in the Resistance. *Born in 1900; died in 1984; third of five daughters of Baron Aarnoud Van Heemstra (burgomeister of Arnhem and a lawyer at the court of Queen ****Wilhelmina***) and Elbrig Van Asbeck (a baroness); married Jan Hendrik Gustaaf Quarles van Ufford of the House of Orange-Nassau (an aristocrat), in 1920; married Joseph Victor Anthony Hepburn-Ruston (an English-Irish banker), in September 1926; children: (first marriage) Alexander and Jan (Ian); (second marriage) ****Audrey Hepburn*** *(1929–1993).*

Ella van Heemstra grew up in a sizeable castle at Doorn in Utrecht, surrounded by a moat. In 1918, her parents sold the estate, now called Huis-Doorn, to Kaiser Wilhelm II as his last refuge when he fled Germany. It is now a museum. One of Ella's sisters was lady-in-waiting for Queen ***Juliana**.

Audrey Hepburn

would remain a neutral country and that Hitler would never violate its sovereignty. Arnhem was 15 miles from the German border.

By spring 1940, those in the Netherlands were bracing for Hitler's assault, and the formerly pampered baroness had become the unofficial leader of the Dutch Resistance in Arnhem. Using a pro-German, aristocratic cover, she spent hours in strategy sessions, creating codes, and throwing informal parties, mixing royalty with commoners, to recruit for her group.

In May of that year, despite the danger, the Sadler's Wells ballet, featuring *Margot Fonteyn, danced in Arnhem. Audrey and her mother were in attendance. Receiving word that Hitler's troops were drawing near, the English dancers nervously abridged their performance, but Ella saw her chance to strengthen the illusion of her pro-German stance. For the benefit of the many Nazi-sympathizers in the audience, Ella, as president of the British-Netherlands Society, stalled the dancer's departure with a long curtain speech, seemingly indifferent to the plight of the British cast, then motioned her daughter to advance with bouquets. As the shy 11-year-old delivered the flowers, Audrey told the artists that she too was a dancer. "It's what I dream about every night." Thirty minutes after the troupe had hastily departed, having abandoned costumes and scenery, German parachutes rained down on Arnhem, and the Hepburn family took to their basement. Said Hepburn:

> I was too exhilarated about meeting Fonteyn to be as frightened as I should. . . . It was almost as if the bombing started and the shooting became constant because I had screwed up my courage and told my idol that I wanted to be a dancer just like she was. . . . Oddly enough, I think my depression began to lift that night. . . . I had discovered a purpose in life. I was to become a dancer.

With the invasion, Queen *Wilhelmina of the Netherlands fled for England, Arnhem became part of the Third Reich, and the Germans commandeered the van Heemstra house, stripping the baroness of all properties and bank accounts. Though the family was allowed to remain in one section of the house, it was primarily a German headquarters. The brutality of the occupation was felt immediately. When he refused to join the Hitler Youth, Audrey's half-brother Alexander was rushed off to a German labor camp. Then Ella's brother was caught blowing up a train and executed, along with five others, in the town square; his son was also shot. Ella cried for hours, recalled Hepburn:

> I had never seen my mother display emotion before, let alone cry. . . . I was so used to seeing my mother in charge, taking care of things, making them right. To see her lose her senses frightened me beyond measure. I made up my mind I would take care of her from then on. And I realized almost intuitively that the best way to do that would be to let her think she was taking care of me, that she had to be strong to make sure I would pull through.

At the Arnhem School of Music, Jewish teachers were dismissed, German language was required, and everything Dutch was eradicated. Fearing for her daughter's life (there was a Jewish ancestor on the genealogical chart), the baroness pulled Audrey out of the school. Meanwhile, food supplies for civilians were becoming dangerously low, the people of Arnhem were starving.

On the surface, Hepburn accepted Nazi rule; secretly, she helped raise funds for the Resistance. After 70 Dutch children, some of them her friends, were sent to prison for acts of sabotage, she heightened her efforts. The amiable little girl with nothing in her stomach skipped about town with coded messages in her socks, forged signatures on identity cards, and, because of her knowledge of English, greeted English parachutists or downed pilots in the Arnhem woods. At one point, Hepburn found herself standing between an advancing German soldier and a British paratrooper who was hiding behind a rock. "I knew I must appear carefree," she said. Bending down, Hepburn picked some wild flowers and pretended to be startled by the German's arrival; then she handed the flowers to him with a shy smile and received a pat on the head before he walked away. A few minutes later, she was entering town and winking at a streetsweeper, in effect telling him there would be a flyer to hide in his home. The skipping, the whistling, the lightheartedness was all an act. Subsisting on lettuce and an occasional potato, Hepburn lived in a continual state of apprehension:

> On a fairly regular basis . . . I would see families being taken away . . . . They would be loaded onto wooden train cars, thrown in there sometimes with such force you could hear the bones break. There was very little air to breathe. You could hear people gasping. The sound of that was so frightening, I would begin to gasp, too. I developed asthma soon after. . . . Everyone seemed to try so hard to maintain dignity. But the spouses were often separated at the station. Of all the tragedies, this one struck me the hardest: that people who loved one another, families, could be pulled apart when they needed each other most.

Then, in 1944, the Germans began rounding up Dutch women for slave labor, and Hepburn was almost caught in the net. While out walking, she had happened upon friends and acquaintances being put into trucks at gunpoint. One of the girls was wearing a red scarf.

> I used to see that scarf next to her books all the time when she was studying. It was a comforting, familiar sight. Now I saw her being pushed with the butt of a rifle into a truck. A woman with a limp, whom the Nazis did not take, was trying to pull back this girl. I presumed it was her mother. In

> those few seconds, I wished the girl would give her mother the scarf. I did not want that red square of pretty material to wind up a ripped and soiled rag in a labor camp. Tears came to my eyes. If I think about it now, I was grieving for the loss of this girl, this human life. But that was too much for me to acknowledge at the time. I just wanted the scarf to be safe and sound.

Moments later, there was a rifle in the small of Hepburn's back, and she was hustled to the boarding area. She watched, terrified, as the Nazis went off to gather more women. Then, for an instant, the only guard became distracted while rolling a cigarette, and she bolted. Fleeing round a corner, she ducked into an alley and raced down the steps into an abandoned cellar. For nearly a month, Hepburn remained there in hiding with the rats. When she finally dared leave for home, she had contracted hepatitis and was suffering from jaundice. "Save for a few tulip bulbs and dirty rainwater," writes **Diana Maychick**, "she had done without [food] for a month. In her mind, she didn't need it. For the rest of her life, in times of great stress [she] would just stop eating."

In September 1944, with the Allies pushing across France and Belgium, the battle for the bridge at Arnhem began. During the conflict, the subject of Richard Attenborough's film *A Bridge Too Far,* 10,000 British soldiers parachuted into a three-square-mile area, unaware that two SS German Panzer armored divisions had moved into the region; 8,000 parachuters would be killed. To escape the bombardment, Audrey and her family sat hunched in the basement with 40 others, subsisting on bug-infested flour from which they concocted a sort of gruel, helplessly listening to the screams of British soldiers shot while still floating in the air. Eventually, they took in six injured airmen who landed nearby. On September 23, the Germans ordered the evacuation of the city: 90,000 citizens were forced to evacuate Arnhem, including the Hepburn-Rustons, 3,000 died on the road. In the battle, the town was sacked; only about 200 houses still stood when the fighting ended. The van Heemstra estate had been demolished by a bomb while they were away.

In April 1945, the Allies liberated what was left of Arnhem. The Germans surrendered on May 5, one day after Hepburn's 16th birthday, and her brother Alexander walked home from Germany. For Hepburn, the war was far from over:

> I could never get rid of this war. I had to live with it. . . . So I used what I witnessed to form a philosophy of life. It's simple. . . . [N]othing is more important than empathy for another human being's suffering. Nothing. Not a career, not wealth, not intelligence, certainly not status. We have to feel for one another if we're going to survive with dignity.

With no assets, the family moved to Amsterdam where the baroness found work as a cook and housekeeper with living accommodations in a basement apartment. Two years later, 18-year-old Hepburn, who had continued her ballet lessons with **Sonia Gaskell**, convinced her mother to accompany her to London. She wanted to study with ***Marie Rambert**.

Arriving with ten dollars between them, Ella took a job while Audrey trained, did odd jobs for Rambert, and changed her name from Edda Hepburn-Ruston to Audrey Hepburn to "give herself a boost." But the 5'7" Hepburn stood out on stage and found it hard to blend in with the troupe. Just as she was becoming aware that her dream might be impossible, she was hired as a chorus girl in a West End production of the musical *High Button Shoes.* The casting agent had noted after her audition: "Lousy dancer, great verve."

> What set her apart . . . was her ability to live . . . with her emotional disabilities. . . . She herself would have held this to be her good fortune rather than something to admire.
>
> —Robyn Karney

When Hepburn danced in two nightclub revues, audiences began to notice the tall, skinny kid in the back row. She started to model, did a walk-on for a film, and was offered a seven-year contract by Associated British Pictures; mother and daughter finally had enough to eat. There followed a few more years of walk-ons until Hepburn landed a bit part in *The Lavender Hill Mob* with Alec Guinness. On his recommendation others took note, and Hepburn was cast as a sister to **Valentina Cortesa** in *The Secret People,* a movie about the Resistance. At first, Audrey had difficulty facing the emotions of certain scenes reminiscent of life in Arnhem. Sent to a corner to concentrate and dredge up the memories, she proved an apt pupil, and the movie established her as a serious actress.

While Hepburn was shooting a small part in Monte Carlo, ***Colette** visited the set and ecstatically turned to her husband, proclaiming, "Voilà. There's our Gigi." For two years, adapter ***Anita Loos** had been searching for a leading lady for Colette's novella which was headed for Broadway. Convinced she did not have the technique to sustain her acting on stage, Hepburn tried to talk Colette out of it. The more she protested, the more she was wanted. The resulting publicity of the casting of an unknown for Broadway brought other offers, including a screen test for the movie *Roman Holiday.* Hepburn sailed for New York, gaining 15 pounds on the 18-day voyage, the result of chocolates. It was the first time she had ventured forth without her mother.

The problems started immediately. In rehearsal, she could not project her voice, and the producer joked about her weight. Hepburn stopped eating, losing 20 pounds, along with her energy and self-confidence. With the help of castmate ***Cathleen Nesbitt** who was giving her diction lessons on the side, Hepburn finally regained control, and, when *Gigi* opened on November 24, 1951, she was a New York sensation. The second week, the marquee was transposed from "*Gigi* with Audrey Hepburn" to "Audrey Hepburn in *Gigi.*" "Oh, dear," said Hepburn. "And I've still got to learn how to act."

For the role of the princess who wanted to be a commoner in the movie *Roman Holiday,* Paramount was eager to sign her to a seven-year contract, but Hepburn would not agree to the long-term condition. Said ***Edith Head**, the film's designer: "What I liked best about her is that she calculated all her business decisions, but made it look as if she didn't have a clue." Advice generally came from her mother. The baroness was the center of her life, writes Maychick, with more influence than any of Hepburn's future husbands. Hepburn would remain close to her mother, living with her or talking to her on the phone daily, until Ella's death in 1984.

Roman Holiday, which also starred Gregory Peck, would be a huge success. When director William Wyler saw the rushes, he claimed he had:

> that rare gut feeling that I was witnessing something very special indeed. She was a princess. . . . But she was also every eager young girl who has ever come to Rome for the first time, and she reacted with so natural and spontaneous an eagerness that I, crusty veteran that I was, felt tears in my eyes watching her. . . . I knew that very soon the entire world would fall in love with her, as all of us on the picture did.

The studio was just as ecstatic. Before *Roman Holiday* was even released, Hepburn was cast for *Sabrina,* in which she conspired with designer Givenchy to permanently set her style: classic, sleek, simple—the minimal look.

While shooting *Sabrina,* Audrey fell hard for co-star William Holden, who was married with two children. When she learned that he had had what was then an irreversible vasectomy, Hepburn, who longed for children, cut short the romance, though she remained the love of Holden's life. On the rebound, Hepburn turned to the twice-married actor-director Mel Ferrer; during the courtship, the two co-starred on Broadway in Jean Giraudoux's *Ondine* in which Hepburn played a water sprite. Unfortunately, Hepburn had a tendency to hand over her power in a relationship, and Ferrer took it gladly, making all decisions, including those concerning costumes. Director Alfred Lunt was irritated by his meddling and rehearsals were tense. Hepburn lost 10 pounds before opening in New York on February 19, 1954. On March 25, she accepted an Academy Award for Best Actress for *Roman Holiday.* Three days later, she won a Tony Award for Best Actress in *Ondine.* Only one other actress, ***Shirley Booth**, had taken both awards in the same year.

But Hepburn was uncomfortable with her lavish success and felt only the "responsibility to live up to it." She was on the verge of a nervous breakdown. Ferrer's domination, along with her mother's dislike of Ferrer, had combined to cause Hepburn to stop eating once again. She even found broth difficult to ingest, and she was now suffering from the effects of malnutrition. In late summer, she had to abandon *Ondine* and seek doctor-ordered bed rest in Switzerland (the doctors also ordered that neither Ferrer nor the baroness accompany her). The fresh air had its effect, and she slowly began to eat.

Ferrer arrived, proposed, and the baroness reluctantly flew to Switzerland for the autumn 1954 wedding. But something was still wrong. Hepburn hated leaving the house and her eating was once again problematic. Nominated for another Academy Award for *Sabrina* (***Grace Kelly** would receive the Oscar for *The Country Girl*), Hepburn abhorred the fact that she was getting all the attention and let it be known that she would not work without her husband. Soon, however, she was blissfully pregnant. She wanted "lots of babies."

Carlo Ponti was willing to hire Ferrer if Hepburn would take the part of Natasha in Leo Tolstoy's *War and Peace.* Hepburn agreed, but, in March 1955, she miscarried. Distracted by the loss of her child, she only went through the motions during the filming. "Too much peace, not enough war," complained one film critic, and the movie did not do well. Preferring something light for her next feature, she chose *Funny Face*. Though thrilled to be dancing with Fred Astaire, Hepburn also had to sing and fight her insecurities. By production's end, she had dropped another 17 pounds.

Following *Love in the Afternoon* with Gary Cooper, Hepburn took a year off before the 1958 filming of *The Nun's Story,* a semi-autobiographical account of the life of ➸ **Marie-Louise Habets,** written by ***Kathryn Hulme.** (Hepburn and Habets would become good friends.) Directed by Fred Zinnemann, the movie was "the most substantial film of her career" writes Robyn Karney. The stellar cast included ***Peggy Ashcroft,** ***Edith Evans,** Peter Finch, as well as ***Colleen Dewhurst** who was then little known outside theater circles. Though Hepburn feared working in the Belgian Congo because of her fragile health, "there was no ego," said Zinnemann, "no asking for favours; there was the greatest consideration for her co-workers." It was the "real humility" of Hepburn, he noted, who brought the same aspect to her character in the film. In the movie, Sister Luke is torn between her medical avocation and her vocation. "Most of my roles were depictions of women who knew exactly what they wanted and went out and got it," said Hepburn. "Well, that wasn't me. I was always more like Sister Luke, always a little unsure." In 1959, the movie was nominated for eight Academy Awards, including Best Actress, but that award went to ***Simone Signoret** for *Room at the Top*.

A year or two earlier, Hepburn and Ferrer had worked together on a disappointing television production of "Mayerling" in which Hepburn starred as ***Marie Vetsera.** In a second effort to resurrect her husband's flagging career, Hepburn played Rima, the jungle girl, opposite Anthony Perkins, in *Green Mansions*. The movie, directed by Ferrer, was another major failure.

Once again pregnant, Hepburn thought it better to work than fret, so she undertook the filming of *The Unforgiven* for John Huston and found herself on location in Durango, a remote area of Mexico, surrounded by baked earth and dust winds. It was an unfortunate decision. She was thrown from a horse that bucked under the lights, causing four broken vertebrae, two sprained ankles, a sprained wrist, and torn muscles in her lower back. After being nursed for 20 days in Los Angeles by friend Habets, Hepburn climbed back on the horse and resumed filming in a back brace, but eventually she miscarried her second child. "I blamed God. I blamed myself. I blamed John Huston. . . . I felt like hell. I looked like hell. And I didn't care." Deep in depression, she turned down one movie after another, smoked two to three packs of cigarettes a day, and refused to eat. Her mother came and went to no avail. Seven months later, in early summer 1959, Hepburn was pregnant once more and took to her bed. Sean Hepburn Ferrer was born on January 17, 1960. His mother was 30 years old.

The following year, she appeared in Truman Capote's *Breakfast at Tiffany's,* playing party waif Holly Golightly and singing "Moon River," written especially for her by Henry Mancini. Though some thought she was miscast, she also took her fourth Oscar nomination. (***Sophia Loren** was the winner for *Two Women*.) Next came ***Lillian Hellman**'s *The Children's Hour* with **Shirley MacLaine**; the story concerned two women teachers accused by a child of being lovers. During the filming, Hepburn was tailed by a stalker and her beloved dog Famous was killed by a car on Wilshire Boulevard. Then reviews of the film were lukewarm, almost hostile. Hepburn returned home to Burgenstock, Switzerland, and rarely went out. With her marriage failing, she eagerly accepted a part in *Paris When It Sizzles* with William Holden, but the filming was a disaster. By then, Holden was an alcoholic, arriving on the set drunk, and Hepburn felt more insecure than ever.

➸ Habets, Marie-Louise (1905–1986)

***Ex-nun whose life was the basis for* The Nun's Story.** *Name variations: Marie Habets. Born in the Netherlands on January 14, 1905; died in May 1986 in Kapaa, Kauai, Hawaii; lived with Kathryn Hulme (1900–1981), a writer.*

Marie-Louise Habets met ***Kathryn Hulme** while nursing at a UN refugee camp in Germany following the war. Hulme was the director of relocation camps in Bavaria. As the two became close friends, Habets told Hulme of her 17 years in the Congo as a nun and her subsequent defection from the convent to work for the Belgian Resistance. Hulme than wrote *The Nun's Story,* using the fictitious name Gabrielle Van Der Mal (Sister Luke). Habets also formed a strong bond with ***Audrey Hepburn** as they worked together on the movie adaptation. Eventually, Habets would nurse Hepburn back to health after her fall from a horse while shooting *The Unforgiven*.

Following their work with World War II Displaced Persons, Habets and her companion Hulme moved to the United States, lived in Connecticut, then southern California, then finally in Kapaa, on the Hawaiian island of Kauai. Hulme died there in 1981; Habets died there five years later, in 1986.

From the movie Two for the Road, *starring Albert Finney and Audrey Hepburn.*

Hepburn was ecstatic when she learned she had the part of Eliza Doolittle in *My Fair Lady.* She assumed she would do her own singing as she had before, and no one said otherwise. Thus, throughout the summer of 1963, she worked 14-hour days to prepare for the film, much of it to improve her voice. The powers that be knew from the start that **Marni Nixon** would dub her voice, but they did not tell Hepburn. When she found out from underlings, it was the lie that bothered her the most. For the first time in her career, she was prickly on the set.

There were other problems. Furious that **Julie Andrews**, who had created the part on Broadway, had been shut out, *My Fair Lady* creator Alan Jay Lerner gave Hepburn the cold shoulder. Said her co-star Rex Harrison: "Audrey also had to weather a great deal of adverse publicity about how much she was being paid, for most of the press had sided with Julie. . . . Audrey is a very sensitive person, and could not fail to feel all this." The media, usually the first to throw bouquets in its love affair with Hepburn, played up Andrews' winning of an Academy Award that year for *Mary Poppins*. The columnists seemed particularly gleeful that Hepburn was not even nominated, though *My Fair Lady* received 12 nominations. She was also panned for lip-synching the vocals. It was another bad year.

Intent on saving her marriage for the sake of her son, Hepburn found an 18th-century farmhouse, La Paisible (The Peaceful), above Lake Geneva in the tiny village of Tolochenaz-sur-Morges, an easy distance from Lausanne. In the winter of 1966, she was pregnant again but miscarried a week after Christmas. Ironically, her next film, *Two for the Road,* was about the death of a 12-year marriage. On the set, Hepburn seemed to let her hair down and shared a close friendship, some say more, with co-star Albert Finney. Her marriage did not survive the disappointment of another miscarriage in August 1967, and the couple separated that September. Once again, Hepburn stopped eating. Once again, she was down to 94 pounds and refused to go out. "Her cheekbones were so pointy," said her close friend actress **Capucine**, "I was afraid if I kissed her they would hurt."

On January 18, 1969, Hepburn married Andrea Mario Dotti, a Neapolitan psychiatrist nine years her junior with an aristocratic background. At first, the couple lived in Rome. Soon pregnant, the 40-year-old Hepburn returned alone in April to Tolochenaz to rest in bed for the next six months. On February 8, 1970, she gave birth to another boy, Luca. Shortly after the wedding, rumors of her new husband's philandering had begun to reach her. Even so, she luxuriated in being a homebody, turning down movie after movie, year after year. It was her friend David Niven who convinced her that if she wanted to stop her husband from straying she should stop being the devoted housewife and go back to work. After nine years away from the screen, she filmed *Robin and Marian.*

Though she did not divorce Dotti until 1982, they had separated much earlier. Meanwhile, Hepburn had met Robert Wolders, who was recovering from the death of his wife ***Merle Oberon**. In 1981, Wolders, who had also grown up in Holland during the war, moved into Tolochenaz and never left. Hepburn began to appear more in public, on his arm.

At home, Hepburn, who had a passion for animals and flowers, spent her days in her garden surrounded by white roses. Though she had no interest in returning to films, she felt purposeless. "I wanted to do something worthwhile. I feel funny . . . phrasing it that way: 'worthwhile.' But I wanted to give back a little of my good fortune—share the wealth, so to speak." Though frail and concerned that her health would not permit her to travel to remote areas, she became involved with the United Nations Children's Fund (UNICEF). For five years, she worked with UNICEF, "travelling in conditions that were often physically as well as emotionally painful for her" writes Karney, publicizing the plight of starving children, walking through the slums of Bangladesh, Guatemala, Honduras, Mexico, Venezuela, Ecuador, the Sudan, Ethiopia, El Salvador, and Vietnam. "She insisted on seeing the worst of the worst," said a UNICEF official who accompanied her. "Lost to the film industry," writes Karney, "she had transcended its ephemeral fame to become an international figure of wider substance."

Convinced she had become famous to use that fame for the good of the children, she became ambassador-at-large in 1988 while Wolders set up schedules and connections. "In the beginning," said Hepburn, "I knew my role was 'the lure.' Starvation in third-world countries was not hot copy." It was Hepburn who first brought the television cameras into Somalia. While there, she began to experience stomach pain. Diagnosed with metastasized colon cancer in November 1992, Audrey Hepburn died two months later on January 20, 1993, with her two sons and Wolders by her side and Dotti and Ferrer in close attendance. She was 63. On the day of her funeral, an exquisite display of flowers arrived from all corners of the globe. Among the profusion was a small bouquet which read, "From all the world's children."

SOURCES:

Karney, Robyn. *A Star Danced: The Life of Audrey Hepburn.* London: Bloomsbury, 1993.

Maychick, Diana. *Audrey Hepburn: An Intimate Portrait.* NY: Birch Lane Press, 1993.

SUGGESTED READING:

Harris, Warren G. *Audrey Hepburn.* 1994.

RELATED MEDIA:

"Gardens of the World," (180 mins.) six-part PBS series, a guided tour with Hepburn of over 60 of the world's best gardens, including Versailles, Mount Vernon, Tintinhull, and Monet's gardens at Giverny.

Hepburn, Edith (1883–1947).

See Wickham, Anna.

Hepburn, Katharine (1907—)

American theater, film, and television actor who excelled in both comic and dramatic roles and won an unprecedented four Academy Awards. *Pronunciation: HEP-burn. Born Katharine Houghton Hepburn on May 12, 1907, in Hartford, Connecticut; daughter of Dr. Thomas Norval Hepburn (a surgeon) and Katharine Martha (Houghton) Hepburn (a suffragist and pioneer for women's rights); graduated Bryn Mawr College in Bryn Mawr, Pennsylvania, B.A., 1928; married Ludlow Ogden Smith, on December 12, 1928 (divorced 1934); no children.*

Made her professional Broadway debut (1928); made her screen debut in A Bill of Divorcement *(1932); won her first Academy Award for Best Actress for* Morning Glory *(1934); met Spencer Tracy (1941), sharing a personal and professional relationship with him that spanned 27 years and included making nine films together; awarded two consecutive Oscars, for* Guess Who's Coming to Dinner? *(1968) and* The Lion in Winter *(1969); made a much celebrated return to the stage to star in* Coco, *her first and only musical (1969); made her television debut (1973); received an Emmy Award for Best Actress in* Love Among the Ruins *(1975); awarded her fourth and last Oscar for* On Golden Pond *(1982); during a professional career that spanned almost seven decades, performed in 43 films, 33 stage plays, and seven television movies.*

Theater roles include: Antiope in The Warrior's Husband *(1932); Tracy Lord in* The Philadelphia Story *(1939); The Lady in* The Millionairess *(1952); Coco Chanel in the musical* Coco *(1969); Mrs. Basil in* A Matter of Gravity *(1976); and Margaret Mary Elderdice in* The West Side Waltz *(1981).*

Filmography: A Bill of Divorcement *(1932); Eve Lovelace in* Morning Glory *(1933);* Christopher Strong *(1933); Jo in* Little Women *(1933);* Spitfire *(1934);* The Little Minister *(1934);* Break of Hearts *(1935);* Alice Adams *(1935);* Sylvia Scarlett *(1936);* Mary of Scotland *(1936);* A Woman Rebels *(1936);* Quality Street *(1937);* Stage Door *(1937);* Bringing Up Baby *(1938);* Holiday *(1938); Tracy Lord in* The Philadelphia Story *(1940);* Woman of the Year *(1942);* Keeper of the Flame *(1942);* Stage Door Canteen *(1943);* Dragon Seed *(1944);* Without Love *(1945);* Undercurrent *(1946);* The Sea of Grass *(1947);* Song of Love *(1947);* State of the Union *(1948);* Adam's Rib *(1949); Rose Sayer in* The African Queen *(1951);* Pat and Mike *(1952);* Summertime *(1955); Lizzie Curry in* The Rainmaker *(1956);* The Iron Petticoat *(1956);* Desk Set *(1957); Mrs. Venable in* Suddenly Last Summer *(1959); Mary Tyrone in* Long Day's Journey into Night *(1962); Christina Drayton in* Guess Who's Coming to Dinner? *(1967); Eleanor of Aquitaine in* The Lion in Winter *(1968);* The Madwoman of Chaillot *(1969); Hecuba in* The Trojan Women *(1971);* A Delicate Balance *(1973); Eula Goodnight in* Rooster Cogburn *(1975);* Olly Olly Oxen Free *(1978); Ethel Thayer in* On Golden Pond *(1981);* The Ultimate Solution of Grace Quigley *(1984); Aunt Ginny in* Love Affair *(1994).*

Television roles include: Amanda Wingfield in "The Glass Menagerie" (1973); Jessica Medlicott in "Love Among the Ruins" (1975); Miss Moffat in "The Corn Is Green" (1979); "Mrs. Delafield Wants to Marry" (1986); Victoria in "The Man Upstairs" (1992); Miss Cornelia in "One Christmas" (1994).

Every theatregoer in New York was talking about it. That fresh, young starlet Katharine Hepburn, their newest toast of the town, was returning to Broadway to star in *The Lake*. After a rather checkered early career, Hepburn had no sooner caught the Broadway public's attention as Antiope in *The Warrior's Husband* than she headed West to make her mark in the movies. And indeed she did. In less than two years, she made four films, including *Morning Glory* (which would win her an Academy Award for Best Actress) and *Little Women*. It was December 26, 1933, just a few months after her Hollywood triumph, and Katharine Hepburn was riding high. A New York newspaper reported that *The Lake* had sold out its first four weeks before the show even opened. In attendance at the Martin Beck Theater on opening night were such celebrities as Noel Coward, George S. Kaufman, ***Amelia Earhart**, and ***Dorothy Parker**—as well as the entire Hepburn family. The lights finally dimmed and came up again on Stella Surrege, the young society woman whose husband had drowned on the very day of their recent wedding. And there she was, Katharine Hepburn as the tragic Stella, speaking her first lines on stage: "The calla lilies are in bloom again. Such a strange flower. I carried them on my wedding day. And now I place them here, in memory of someone who is dead."

The Lake could have—should have—been a smash hit for this rising star, but instead it was a disaster. Dorothy Parker's now famous critique in the *Journal-American* complained, "She ran

Katharine Hepburn

the gamut of emotion from A to B." Hepburn wrote her own critique of that performance in her autobiography *Me*: "My cue came. I walked on. And I walked through the whole opening night. It was perfectly awful. Like an automaton. . . . I just went on and on and on. I hadn't died. I was there. Fully conscious of having given a totally nothing performance." What went wrong? Hepburn claimed that constant sparring with director Jed Harris during rehearsals had made her lose her confidence. On opening night, she responded by losing control of her pitch and her timing, speaking faster and faster as her voice went higher and higher. After only 55 New York performances, *The Lake* closed, but not before Hepburn had made a concerted effort to improve her voice, relaxation, and concentration. And she did improve during the play's short run, although not enough to combat how history would record that opening-night disaster. For most American actors seeking stardom, such a flop would have been devastating to a young career. But not so for Katharine Hepburn.

Katharine Hepburn has enjoyed one of the longest stage and screen careers of the 20th century, due not only to her talent but perhaps even more so to her extraordinary strength of character. She once called herself, in comical understatement, "feisty." She was born a Connecticut Yankee to parents who instilled the values of bravery, integrity, and the belief in equal rights for men and women. "Mother and Dad," as she calls them, were trailblazers who taught their daughter to live up to her potential. Her father Dr. Thomas Hepburn was a surgeon who founded the New England Social Hygiene Association, which was devoted to educating the public about venereal disease. Her mother **Katharine Houghton Hepburn**, for whom she was named, headed the Connecticut Woman Suffrage Association and also championed the cause of birth control. Kate Hepburn grew up in the kind of household where tea was served every day promptly at five and the plays of Shakespeare and Shaw were read aloud. No wonder she proclaimed in *Me,* "What luck to be born out of love and to live in an atmosphere of warmth and interest."

There's been a motto in my family for as long as I can remember. My parents lived by it and so do I. . . . "Listen to the song of life."

—Katharine Hepburn

The second oldest of six children, "Kathy," or "Kath" to her family, grew up in Hartford and happily spent her youth wallowing in sports—tennis, golf, and especially swimming. (She gave herself the nickname "Jimmy" and liked to wear her hair short.) When she was five-and-a-half, her father bought the family a summer home at Fenwick, a small community on the Connecticut coast, and for her entire life Hepburn spent every summer she could there. In addition to sports, amateur theatricals were her favorite summer pastime. Hepburn remembers performing *Beauty and the Beast* on her best friend's front porch—her friend played Beauty and she played the Beast. She also had a miniature stage that she made herself out of a wooden box. Kate made scenery and actor figures and the stories to go with them, performing for her siblings. Dr. Hepburn took the children to the movies every Saturday night, and on special occasions they saw touring productions at the local theater. Kate and her older brother Tom even visited their Aunt **Mary Towle** in New York City, who took them to see plays.

It was in so many ways an idyllic childhood, until tragedy struck when Kate was 14. Her older brother Tom, whom she adored, died. Kate discovered him hanging from a rafter in the attic of Mary Towle's house. The family never knew whether it was an accident or intentional. The incident certainly changed Kate forever. She did not go back to school the following fall, but instead finished her high-school years at home with private tutors. When she enrolled at Bryn Mawr at the age of 16, Hepburn was a shy young woman who kept to herself. But by her sophomore year, she had made a circle of friends and the acting bug had bitten. She performed in several plays at Bryn Mawr, including the May Day production during her senior year of John Lyly's *The Woman in the Moon.* By graduation day 1928, Katharine Hepburn knew she wanted to be an actor.

The very next day after her graduation, Hepburn arrived in Baltimore to see Edwin Knopf, a young producer who ran the Auditorium Theater Players. He had promised her a role as one of four ladies-in-waiting in *The Czarina.* Indeed, Katharine Hepburn's professional theater debut was as a walk-on, a nameless, non-speaking role. After another small part as a flapper in *The Cradle Snatchers,* Hepburn moved to New York, for Knopf had offered her a supporting role in the Broadway-bound *The Big Pond.* In addition to rehearsals, Hepburn started taking lessons from **Frances Robinson-Duff**, one of New York's most respected voice coaches. Robinson-Duff tried diligently to train her new pupil to use her diaphragm rather than speaking from her throat, but the headstrong young Hepburn just could not get it. Her high-pitched nasal voice that became one of her trademarks would also cause her many problems. Just nine days before *The Big Pond* was scheduled to open its pre-Broadway tryout in Great Neck, New York, the leading lady quit and Hepburn replaced her. Frantic to learn her lines and make the transition in time, Hepburn claimed she was terrified, and that terror took over. Her performance was so poor that she was fired; Robinson-Duff had the unhappy task of telling her so the next day.

Everything about those early days in New York was not grim, however. She met **Laura**

Harding, another student of Robinson-Duff, and they became lifelong friends. Miraculously, Arthur Hopkins, a highly respected producer of the Theater Guild, had seen her in Great Neck and saw a spark of talent beneath Hepburn's botched performance. He offered her a small part as a schoolgirl in *These Days,* and Hepburn made her Broadway debut on November 12, 1928. Although *These Days* closed after a disappointing eight performances, Hepburn had other things on her mind. During her senior year at Bryn Mawr, she had met Ludlow Ogden Smith, a Philadelphia socialite who didn't much care for a career of his own and believed wholeheartedly in her acting ability. Luddy was the perfect partner for Kate: his devotion allowed her to be totally consumed in her career—and herself. In *Me,* Hepburn recalled, "I was just full of the joy of life and opportunity and a wild desire to be absolutely fascinating." Exactly a month after her New York debut, Kate and Luddy were married at her parents' home in West Hartford. They rented a small walk-up apartment in Manhattan, and Hepburn continued to pound on producers' doors.

For the next two years, Hepburn's stage career was a combination of near-hits and many misses. She kept getting cast, and she also kept getting fired. She seemed to fight with everyone, because she was a perfectionist and because she had her own ideas about how a role should be played. She also developed a reputation for being rude, bossy, and odd. (There was plenty of gossip concerning her predilection for wearing slacks.) But behind all of her bravura and strange habits, there was an indefatigable energy, a drive in her desire to succeed that could not be squelched. Success finally came with a role that seemed perfectly suited to her athletic physique and forceful personality. It was the Amazon queen, Antiope, in a farce called *The Warrior's Husband.* Hepburn's first entrance called for her to come bounding on stage down a high stairway, throw down a fake stag that she carried on her shoulders, and wrestle with her leading man. The New York critics applauded and even Hollywood took notice. The agent Leland Hayward invited her to take a screen test. Meanwhile, in Los Angeles, film director George Cukor and producer David O. Selznick were searching for a young woman to star opposite the legendary John Barrymore as his daughter. When Cukor saw the screen test, he knew he had found her. Hepburn signed a contract with RKO Pictures, and in July 1932 she boarded a train with friend Laura Harding headed for Hollywood.

Hepburn's screen debut as Sydney Fairfield in *A Bill of Divorcement* marked the beginning of a film career that has never faltered. Her first moments on screen found her once again bounding down a staircase—faintly reminiscent of her *Warrior's Husband* stage entrance, but there the comparison ends. Here, dressed in a stunning white evening gown, she glided down the stairs as if her feet never touched the ground and into the arms of her handsome beau. In every close-up, her face had a radiance that inspired George Cukor to say she was "made for the screen." Neither was Hepburn shy in front of the camera; in fact, she seemed to demand its attention. Her high-powered energy translated into an intensity on the screen that demanded the audience's attention, too. When *A Bill of Divorcement* premiered in New York in the fall of 1932, the critics hailed Hepburn's star quality. Cukor also recognized her potential, and, although they had many confrontations during the film's shooting, he admired her gumption. Cukor and Hepburn became lifelong friends and comrades, making ten films together during the course of their lengthy careers.

Four films followed in quick succession, and the variety of roles was a testament to the breadth of Hepburn's talent. In ***Dorothy Arzner**'s *Christopher Strong,* Hepburn played an adventurous "aviatrix" in love with a married man. In *Morning Glory,* a naive girl from a small town in New England comes to New York to conquer the stage. The story line may have parodied Hepburn's own life, but the mesmerizing performance was still all Hepburn. The stage-struck Eva Lovelace finally brought Hepburn her yearned-for celebrity. With the receipt of her first Academy Award in 1934 for *Morning Glory,* Katharine Hepburn was indeed a star. She followed with *Little Women,* in which she played the charming but spunky Jo March, and *Spitfire,* a drama about a mountain girl who is shunned by her community. The lukewarm reception for *Spitfire* could not dampen the enthusiasm of Hepburn fans.

Hepburn had insisted that her contract with RKO promised her the right to return to the stage in between films. Fortunately, after *The Lake* disaster she quickly returned to the less hostile atmosphere of Hollywood. Screen roles dominated the remainder of the 1930s for Hepburn, although at this time she believed the theater to be a much higher art form than film. Her next seven movies followed a rather rocky road. Besides a few flops, she won her second Oscar nomination for playing the title role in *Alice Adams,* about a working-class girl trying to climb up the social ladder. In *Sylvia Scarlett,* she played a boy so convincingly that audiences left the theater in droves during the scene when she kissed another woman. In 1937, a box-office personality poll ranked Hepburn in 70th place—a scary position, regardless of the huge salary RKO paid her. Then she brought a theater script about a group of would-be actresses to RKO. In *Stage Door,* which had been a hit on Broadway the previous year, Hepburn finally found her vehicle, playing a young society girl desperate to succeed. A critic for *Life* magazine noted that she showed the potential to be "the screen's greatest actress." (The movie's charm also included many fine performances by such up-and-coming starlets as ***Ginger Rogers**, ***Lucille Ball**, and ***Eve Arden**.) Hepburn then teamed with Cary Grant for two more comedies, *Bringing up Baby* and *Holiday,* winning acclaim from virtually all the critics. It seemed that the roller-coaster ride of successes and failures was finally over. Following *Bringing up Baby,* the ever-independent Hepburn—who had actively participated in all of her contract negotiations—bought out the rest of her RKO contract. In the spring of 1938, she went home to Connecticut to rest and contemplate her future as a free agent.

That summer Philip Barry, a friend and the author of *Holiday,* brought her a draft of his new work, *The Philadelphia Story*. Clearly inspired by Hepburn and her own family, this sophisticated comedy was filled with romance and witty dialogue. And it was a *play,* a chance for Hepburn to return to her first love, the stage. After two months of tryouts, it opened on Broadway, March 28, 1939, making theatrical history and linking forever the names of Katharine Hepburn and Tracy Lord, the play's central character. It ran in New York for 415 performances, and she repeated her triumph on film a year later (she owned the film rights), starring with Cary Grant and James Stewart. The comments of *The New York Times* reviewer Brooks Atkinson echoed the accolades she received from both film and theater critics: "[S]he plays with grace, jauntiness, and warmth . . . like one who is liberated from self-consciousness and taking a pleasure in acting that the audience can share." The role of Tracy Lord garnered for Hepburn a third Oscar nomination and prompted her, many years later, to remark, "I gave her life. She gave me back my career."

With her "career" now firmly intact, Hepburn was, unknowingly, on the brink of a new one, for the decade of the 1940s was to be dominated—onscreen and off—by an actor named Spencer Tracy. Several years before, in 1934, her marriage to Luddy Smith had ended quietly and amicably in divorce. The marriage had been more accurately a friendship rather than a romance—proven by the fact that they remained close friends for life. By the early '30s, Hepburn was more consumed with her career than any personal commitment. She had many "beaux," as she called them, before she met Spencer Tracy, including her agent Leland Hayward and the billionaire Howard Hughes. But when she met Tracy in 1941, as they starred together in *Woman of the Year,* she met her match. As Hepburn herself divulged in the documentary *All About Me*: "It was the first of nine films that we did together. And it was the beginning of a 27-year—what shall I call it? Relationship. Madness. Happiness. Love affair. It was everything. And it made me understand for the first time what it really meant to be in love. I always say Spencer grew me up beyond my potential." Although Tracy remained married, his partnership with Hepburn lasted until his death in 1967. The Hollywood press silently respected this liaison between two of its greatest stars, and, for the almost three decades of their relationship, Tracy and Hepburn remained discreet, never attending public functions together. They were both intensely private people who shunned the limelight. Even after Tracy's death, Hepburn refused to talk publicly about him until after the death of his wife **Louise Tracy** in 1983.

Woman of the Year, a comedy about the unlikely romance between an international-affairs columnist (Hepburn) and a sportswriter (Tracy) working on the same newspaper, was an even bigger success than *The Philadelphia Story,* cherished by critics and audiences alike, and earning Hepburn her fourth Oscar nomination. Many commented about what electricity Tracy and Hepburn generated together—and, indeed, it was genuine. Of the ten films Hepburn would make between 1942 and 1950, six of them would be with Tracy. No longer "owned" by the studio, Hepburn had begun looking for her own properties so that she could have more production control (a practice she continued throughout her career). It was she who brought the *Woman of the Year* script to Louis B. Mayer at Metro, suggesting Spencer Tracy as her costar. Following its success and the intensification of her romance with Tracy, Hepburn began searching for quality scripts they could star in together. In *A Remarkable Woman,* biographer **Anne Edwards** compares their careers during this period, pointing out Tracy's status as an independent film star. While Hepburn completed ten films between 1942 and 1950, Tracy made 14 and most of those he made without her were ample hits—proving his position in "the pantheon of film actors." The four films Hepburn made without him were not very successful, and even when they did perform together, all of the scripts after *Woman of the Year* favored Tracy's role over hers. Hepburn didn't seem to care. During this era, she clearly deferred to Tracy, both privately and professionally. And the critics duly observed the effects of their relationship on Hepburn as an actor. Her performances matured as did she. Referring to *Keeper of the Flame,* which followed *Woman of the Year,* Hepburn said that the part of Christine was a "woman," while all her previous roles had been "girls."

Although the Tracy-Hepburn films of the 1940s were not always applauded unanimously by the critics, their audience appeal rarely faltered. Certainly Tracy and Hepburn were one of Hollywood's most popular pairs, and their final film of the decade, *Adam's Rib,* proved it. For the first time since *Woman of the Year,* they each played strong characters who equally shared the spotlight. This sharp-tongued comedy about a husband and wife who are also lawyers—he for the prosecution and she for the defense—showed off their excellent comedic timing and their talent for repartee. Hepburn would have liked nothing more than to follow *Adam's Rib* with another vehicle for them both. But it would be another three years before that happened. In the meantime, she continued to seek scripts that would stretch her in new directions.

In the summer of 1949, Katharine Hepburn was 42 years old. It was more difficult to find scripts for mature women; she was no longer right for the glamour roles like Tracy Lord. But as the decade of the 1950s began, Hepburn was secure in her stardom and her belief in her own talent. She decided to return to Broadway and, for the first time in her professional career, tackle Shakespeare. As Rosalind in *As You Like It,* she played a respectable 180 performances, as well as an extensive road tour. Then she accepted the role of Rose Sayer in *The African Queen* and embarked on one of the greatest adventures of her career. Directed by John Huston and also starring Humphrey Bogart, *The African Queen* involved the unlikely romance between a prim English missionary and a socially outcast river-

From the movie African Queen, *starring Humphrey Bogart and Katharine Hepburn.*

boat pilot. They filmed on location in the Congo, and the horror stories of invasions by wasps, ants, and the like—as well as bouts with malaria and dysentery—made for great publicity. Hepburn published her own memoir of the filming, *The Making of "The African Queen,"* in 1987. Despite all the on-location hardships, the film captured both Hepburn and Bogart giving one of their finest performances. The evolution of their quirky romance made for a movie that was adventurous, tender, funny, and deeply moving. Hepburn had proven once and for all the depth of her versatility as an actor. There would be no more accusations that Hepburn could only play Hepburn. And she had her fifth Oscar nomination to prove it.

The African Queen also ushered in a decade filled with a diversity of roles that Hepburn tackled with finesse. She would do two more films with Tracy during the decade: *Pat and Mike* (1952) and *Desk Set* (1957). ***Ruth Gordon** and Garson Kanin, the same writing team that had created *Adam's Rib,* brought their friend Hepburn a new script when she returned from Africa about a woman training to be a professional athlete and her sports promoter-manager. Hepburn called *Pat and Mike* their best film together. She followed its success with another acting challenge, perhaps even greater than that of Rose Sayer in *The African Queen.* George Bernard Shaw's play *The Millionairess* centered around a character who was domineering, arrogant, and mean. The 15-year-old script had not been well received initially, and its success relied on one thing: a smashing performance by its leading lady. Hepburn's London debut was no less than smashing. The critic for the London *Times* wrote that Hepburn performed Epifania "with such a furious, raw-boned, strident vitality that it sweeps away likes and dislikes and presents the creature as a force of nature." She repeated this "furious" performance for a successful limited run in New York.

Her next project returned her to film, this time portraying a lonely spinster looking for love. *Summertime,* filmed entirely on location in Venice, featured as her costar Rossano Brazzi, an Italian actor at the height of his fame as a romantic leading man. Hepburn created magic with Brazzi as she had with Bogart, and the Academy of Motion Picture Arts and Sciences rewarded her again with her sixth Oscar nomination. Continuing to seek out different acting opportunities, Hepburn then joined members of London's Old Vic theater company on a tour of Australia. For six months in 1955, she performed in a trio of Shakespearean plays, *The Taming of the Shrew* (Katherine), *Measure for Measure* (Isabella), and *The Merchant of Venice* (Portia). In the fall, she launched into the film version of *The Rainmaker* with Burt Lancaster, in which she played a Southwestern farmer's daughter charmed by a con man who wants to seduce her. A seventh Oscar nomination acknowledged Hepburn's subtle performance.

Opposite page

Katharine Hepburn with Spencer Tracy.

In 1956, Tracy and Hepburn teamed up once again to make their eighth film together. Unfortunately *The Desk Set* had a rather slim story that required nothing new from either of them. *The New York Times* critic wrote, "[T]hey lope through this trifling charade like a couple of old timers, who enjoy reminiscing with simple routines." Almost immediately, Hepburn returned to the challenge of the stage, joining the American Shakespeare Festival for two productions: *The Merchant of Venice* (Portia) and *Much Ado About Nothing* (Beatrice). Hepburn won her eighth Oscar nomination for her last film of the decade, Tennessee Williams' drama *Suddenly, Last Summer.* As the eccentric Violet Venable, Hepburn played a role for the first time in her career that supported another star, ***Elizabeth Taylor**, as her niece, Catherine Holly. For the next few years, Hepburn took a hiatus from acting, spending more of her time with the ailing Spencer Tracy than she did making movies.

Then in his early 60s, Spencer Tracy was not in the best of health. Years of too much alcohol had taken their toll on his liver and kidneys. He had difficulty breathing, and he was a fitful sleeper. Apparently more concerned about Tracy's career than her own, Hepburn cared for him as a wife would, cooking their meals and cleaning his small guest house on the grounds of George Cukor's estate—the same house they had lived in for years (she also rented a house nearby). They entertained small groups of friends at home—never in public. She accompanied him on location during the filming of *Inherit the Wind* and *Judgment at Nuremberg,* to name a few, sitting in a corner of the set with her knitting and shrewdly observing every take.

Only one role during those six years was alluring enough to invade her private life with Tracy: Mary Tyrone in Eugene O'Neill's *Long Day's Journey into Night.* Though she and the producer wanted Tracy to play Mary's husband, James Tyrone, Tracy refused but encouraged her to take the part anyway. One of the richest female characters created in the 20th century, Mary Tyrone is a genuinely tragic figure. She is at once noble and pathetic, having endured a marriage she didn't deserve and having struggled valiantly against her addiction to morphine. Hepburn tackled this extraordinary character with only three weeks of rehearsal. The entire film was shot in 27 days. It was also shot on a remarkably small budget, with Hepburn accepting a fraction of her normal salary. Clearly, she did it for the challenge, and she was rewarded unanimous praise. Biographer Anne Edwards called the performance Hepburn's "greatest professional achievement." She received her ninth Oscar nomination and won the 1962 Cannes Film Festival Best Actress Award.

If *Long Day's Journey* represented her greatest professional achievement as an actor, surely *Guess Who's Coming to Dinner?* was her greatest personal one. Shot in 1967, it was the last film Tracy and Hepburn made together. During the first half of the 1960s, Tracy's battle with emphysema was constant. Thanks in part to Hepburn's care, his condition improved enough in 1966 for director Stanley Kramer to approach them with a new script. Progressive for its time, *Guess Who's Coming to Dinner?* is the story of an interracial couple who confront their parents with their desire to get married. Hepburn and Tracy played the young woman's liberal parents who ultimately accept their decision. Tracy's health was so fragile during the spring of 1967 that the shooting schedule was arranged around him. Nevertheless, he rallied, and the challenge of doing the film seemed to bolster his energy. One of the film's final scenes, in which Tracy's character professes his love for his wife while her eyes well with tears, is extraordinarily moving—both in the fictional context of the film and in its real-life context. Although critics lambasted the movie for its fairy-tale, idealistic treatment of the interracial issue, at the box office it was an overwhelming success. Tracy would never know about the controversy—or that Hepburn won her second Oscar. He collapsed in his kitchen, only 15 days after filming was completed, and died.

Katharine Hepburn, always the pragmatist, threw herself back into her work. In the years following Spencer Tracy's death, she achieved some of her greatest triumphs and continued her lifelong practice of seeking out new artistic challenges. In 1968, she won her second consecutive Oscar for the role of ***Eleanor of Aquitaine** in *The Lion in Winter,* creating a superb performance in which she matched wits and wills with Peter O'Toole as King Henry II. In 1969, she returned to the Broadway stage to star in the title role of her first-ever musical, *Coco,* based on the life of fashion designer ***Coco Chanel**. In 1970, for the first time in her distinguished career, she

tackled Greek tragedy, performing Hecuba in a film version of Euripides' *The Trojan Women.* The 1970s also included Hepburn's first foray into television, in which she starred in four made-for-television movies between 1973 and 1979. These included her Emmy-winning performance opposite Sir Laurence Olivier in *Love Among the Ruins* and her irresistible portrayal of Miss Moffat in *The Corn Is Green.* Perhaps Hepburn's greatest personal pleasure of the decade was her experience costarring with the inimitable John Wayne in *Rooster Cogburn* (released in 1975). Although they had never met, these two stars became fast friends, and their on-screen chemistry was cherished by both critics and audiences.

Hepburn had shared the screen with many of Hollywood's most beloved leading men—Barrymore, Fairbanks, Grant, Tracy, Bogart, Lancaster, and, finally, Wayne. In 1980, there was only one actor left of her stature with whom she had not yet performed: Henry Fonda. The perfect vehicle brought them together. *On Golden Pond* is the story of an aging couple coping with the decline of the husband's health. They come to their summer cottage in Maine, probably for the last time, and are visited by their daughter (played by Fonda's real-life daughter, **Jane**), who hopes to make peace with her father before he dies. Despite the fact that she had dislocated her shoulder just a few months before filming began, Hepburn joined the Fondas and crew on location in New Hampshire in July 1980. On the first day of filming, she gave a rumpled cloth hat to Fonda, which she claimed was "Spencer's favorite." He wore it throughout the film, a symbol of their mutual friendship and respect. In his biography, Fonda described his leading lady: "Hepburn is a presence wherever she is. In a room, she is the only one in it. In a big area, she doesn't do anything to dominate, she just does and is." Their admiration and affection for each other translated to the screen, creating two heart-wrenching performances that were both honored with Oscars at the 1982 Academy Awards.

A tragic automobile accident in December of 1982 hampered Hepburn's independence. She was driving the icy streets of Fenwick, Connecticut, when the car skidded and slammed into a telephone pole. Hepburn's right foot was broken in several places and almost severed from her leg. After surgery, months and months of living in casts and therapy followed, and she spent most of the 1980s living relatively reclusively. Apparently, Hepburn grew impatient with retirement in the early 1990s and returned to the screen for a flurry of projects, each time proclaiming that this one would be her last. Her cameo appearance as Warren Beatty's aunt in *Love Affair* (1994) was the high point of the film. Three made-for-television movies were highlighted by "One Christmas" (1994), based on Truman Capote's short story. Hepburn played the crotchety but charming Aunt Cornelia, a New Orleans society matron who befriends a young boy named Buddy. She tells him, "I've always lived my life exactly as I wanted. I wouldn't change a single thing. No regrets." The authenticity of those lines makes them perhaps her most poignant ones ever captured on film.

"I've been around so long that people treat me as some sort of oracle. Or grandmother of the world, maybe," Hepburn mused in *All About Me.* Certainly her durability—her career as an actor of stage, screen, and television spanned nearly seven decades—was an accomplishment in itself. But the fiber of her character and the remarkable richness of her performances distinguished her as one of the most recognized and revered women of the 20th century. For millions of people the world over, she is known simply as "Kate." During the seven decades of her career, thousands of words, both spoken and written, attempted to describe the essence of Katharine Hepburn. She was called bull-headed, self-assured, vain, modest, imperious, imperial, effervescent, magisterial, willful, dignified, intellectual, glamourous, haughty, graceful, gangly, fearless, refined, indomitable. People criticized her independence and stubbornness but respected her dedication to family, friends, and her strong work ethic. Katharine Hepburn's work represents the finest art that acting can be. It also represents the best of the American character. In a 1984 interview, she proclaimed, "There are no rules, except to know yourself." Perhaps the one descriptor encompassing all those that have tried to capture her is *authentic.* She lived her life as she chose, proving her own philosophy: "I think that just being alive is a tremendous opportunity. It's what you do with it that matters."

SOURCES:

Edwards, Anne. *A Remarkable Woman: A Biography of Katharine Hepburn.* NY: William Morrow, 1985.

Hepburn, Katharine. *Me: Stories of My Life.* NY: Knopf, 1991.

SUGGESTED READING:

Carey, Gary. *Katharine Hepburn: A Hollywood Yankee.* St. Martin's Press, 1983.

Dickens, Homer. *The Films of Katharine Hepburn.* Citadel Press, 1971.

Hepburn, Katharine. *The Making of "The African Queen" or How I Went to Africa with Bogart, Bacall and Huston and Almost Lost My Life.* NY: Knopf, 1987.

Higham, Charles. *Kate: The Life of Katharine Hepburn.* NY: W.W. Norton, 1975.

Kanin, Garson. *Tracy and Hepburn.* NY: Viking Press, 1971.

Leaming, Barbara. *Katharine Hepburn.* Crown, 1995.

Spada, James. *Hepburn: Her Life in Pictures.* NY: Doubleday, 1984.

RELATED MEDIA:

Katharine Hepburn: All About Me, autobiographical documentary film narrated by Hepburn, produced by Turner Pictures, 1992.

COLLECTIONS:

Original test footage, full-length films, original scripts, and memorabilia are housed in the archives of the American Film Institute, the Academy of Motion Picture Arts and Sciences, and the Film Collection at the University of Southern California, all located in Los Angeles.

Theater-related material is housed in the Billy Rose Theater Collection, Lincoln Center Library for the Performing Arts, New York, New York.

N.J. Stanley,
Visiting Assistant Professor of Theater,
Bucknell University, Lewisburg, Pennsylvania

Hepworth, Barbara (1903–1975)

English sculptor, one of the leading artists of the 20th century, who accomplished her greatest works using the tools of abstract, geometric forms. *Name variations: Dame Barbara Hepworth. Born Barbara Hepworth in Wakefield, Yorkshire, on January 10, 1903; died at her studio at St. Ives, Cornwall, of injuries sustained in a fire, on May 20, 1975; daughter of Herbert Raikes Hepworth (a surveyor and civil engineer) and Gertrude Allison (Johnson) Hepworth; attended Wakefield Girls' High School; Leeds School of Art, 1920–21; Royal College of Art, 1921–24; married John Skeaping, on May 13, 1925 (divorced 1933); married Ben Nicholson, in 1932, some sources cite 1936 (divorced 1951); children: (first marriage) Paul (d. 1953); (second marriage) triplets, Simon, Rachel, and Sarah.*

Traveled to Italy (1924); gave first exhibition (1927); had first solo exhibition (1928); joined Abstraction-Creation group in Paris (1933); began to work exclusively with abstract forms (1934); moved to Cornwall (1939); moved to Trewyn studio (1949); represented Britain at Venice Biennale and received commissions for statues at Festival of Britain (1950); death of her son in RAF (1953); designed theatrical set for The Midsummer Marriage *(1955); won grand prize at Sao Paolo competition (1959); United Nations building sculpture unveiled (1964); made Dame Commander of the Order of the British Empire (1965); elected to American Academy of Arts and Letters (1973).*

Major works: Pierced form *(1931);* Two heads *(1932);* Mother and child *(1934);* Forms in echelon *(1938);* Sculpture with color (deep blue and red) *(1940);* Sculpture with color (oval form) pale blue and red *(1943);* Pelagos *(1946);* Head (elegy) *(1952);* Winged figure *(1962);* Single form *(1964);* Squares with two circles *(1967);* The Family of Man *(1970).*

Barbara Hepworth was one of the most important and innovative sculptors of the 20th century. Producing over 600 pieces, she became famous for an abstract style that featured piercing the solid form to create new possibilities of light, air, and shadow. Starting in the early 1930s, she engaged in a friendly rivalry with her fellow sculptor Henry Moore. As it turned out, her work plunged even more deeply into the realm of abstraction than his did. A small and fragile woman, she nevertheless produced most of her works by the physically demanding technique of carving directly from wood or stone. Hepworth explained her work by noting: "It is difficult to describe in words the meaning of forms because it is precisely this emotion which is conveyed by sculpture alone."

The British artistic scene of the early part of the 20th century was relatively conservative. In contrast to the ferment in the visual arts centered in Paris, Britain lagged behind in producing figures of the first rank. In the decades following World War I, however, notable talents such as Henry Moore, Barbara Hepworth, and Ben Nicholson emerged. They absorbed the leading trends of the Parisian art world including cubism and abstract art, implanting modern art in their home country.

Barbara Hepworth was born in Wakefield, Yorkshire, on January 10, 1903, the daughter of Herbert and **Gertrude Hepworth**. A surveyor and civil engineer, Herbert Hepworth rose to prominence in his profession, receiving the honor of becoming a Commander of the British Empire shortly after World War II. But the family lived in modest circumstances during Barbara's childhood. In a notable passage in her autobiography, she attributed her attraction to forms and shapes to the business trips she took with her father through the Yorkshire countryside, "moving physically over the contours of fulnesses and concavities, through hollows and over peaks." She drew from these impressions a sense of unity with the shapes around her: "I, the sculptor, am the landscape. I am the form and I am the hollow, the thrust and the contour." Her family vacation trips took her to locales such as Robin Hood's Bay on the northern coast of Yorkshire where professional painters worked. At school, the talented youngster distinguished herself in drawing and painting. Some of her youthful watercolor sketches that she gave to friends still survive.

Hepworth had the good fortune to encounter sympathetic teachers and school administrators who encouraged her to devote her energies to her interest in art. She wrote of an early encounter—at age seven—with a slide show on Egyptian culture. A decade later, she informed the head mistress (director) of her high school that she wanted to become a sculptor instead of pursuing the more conventional route of going on to a university. The sympathetic woman, **Gertrude McCroben**, moved quickly to help her gain a scholarship to study at the Leeds School of Art. According to most authorities, Hepworth began there in the fall of 1920, although, late in life, she recalled starting her art studies in 1919. Her biographer A.M. Hammacher has suggested that her early interest in mathematics and her encounters with her father's designs for buildings and roads stimulated an interest in abstract design even before she began her formal art studies.

In 1921, she and Henry Moore, a fellow student at Leeds, transferred to the Royal College of Art in London. Neither Leeds nor the Royal College provided an encouraging environment for innovative work in sculpture. Moore was stimulated by encounters with non-European works such as the sculpture of Africa, but it is less certain what precise impulses pushed Hepworth forward. Even the Royal College at this time offered no instruction in direct stone carving. The more conventional approach was to model first in clay, then to transfer the image to stone using a mechanical device. Starting at Leeds, Hepworth apparently learned carving on her own, using her free hours in the evening and her time on vacation.

Upon completing her studies in London, the gifted young artist was rewarded with a traveling fellowship in 1924 and used it to live in Italy. Settling near Florence, she met and married a fellow English sculptor, John Skeaping, on May 13, 1925. Together, they went on to study in Siena and Rome. For Hepworth, the stay in Italy was the moment when she developed her true skill in carving marble. It was an ability she continued to use for decades to come.

The two returned to London in 1926 when Skeaping became ill with ulcers. Desperately poor, Hepworth painted portraits of wealthy members of her father's circle of friends. In addition, Herbert Hepworth kept the struggling couple afloat financially by offering them funds regularly from his own pocket. In reporting to the organization that had granted Hepworth her scholarship, she informed them that she had no completed works to show them. She had studied and assimilated the great works around her, and the products of her time abroad were contained in her head.

Hepworth and her husband held their first exhibition in late 1927, and she put on her first individual show in 1928. Most of the work she displayed consisted of carvings in marble, demonstrating her attraction to that form of sculpture rather than casting in bronze. According to Ronald Alley, her surviving carvings from 1927 and 1928 show an effort to capture the likenesses of her subjects, but in the next years she developed "a more stylized treatment."

Her first son was born in 1929, and the marriage collapsed soon after. Hepworth later noted how "suddenly we were out of orbit." Although Skeaping was a talented sculptor from a family of gifted artists, he took his work far less seriously than his single-minded wife did hers. His infidelity, and possibly hers, brought the marriage down. Having a child did not temper her devotion to work. In her autobiography, Hepworth emphatically expressed her determination to continue her career after motherhood. Despite the joys of family life, she wrote, "the dictates of work are as compelling for a woman as for a man. Not competitively, but as complementary." Thus, she noted, "a woman artist is not deprived by cooking and having children . . . one is in fact nourished by this rich life." One needed only, she added, to work each day, "even only a single half hour."

As early as 1931, she produced a work in pink alabaster originally entitled *Abstraction,* but also known as *Pierced form,* which brought forth elements that were to characterize her later work. "I had felt the most intense pleasure in piercing the stone in order to make an abstract form and space," she noted. Although photographs of this important piece in her artistic evolution exist, the work itself did not survive World War II.

In the early 1930s, she established a close personal and professional relationship with Ben Nicholson. Most authorities indicate that they married sometime in 1932, although Hepworth's biographer **Sally Festing** maintains that Nicholson was unable to get a divorce from his wife and marry Barbara until 1936. If so, the birth of their triplets preceded their formal marital tie. Nicholson was a rising young English painter who shared Hepworth's interest in modernism. Ironically, like her first husband, Nichol-

Barbara Hepworth at the unveiling of her sculpture Single Form *at the United Nations in New York.*

son also came from a family with a number of professional artists.

In 1932, Hepworth and Nicholson traveled together to join the art world of Paris. There they encountered the work of Picasso, Braque, Brancusi, and Mondrian. Imbued with the principles and possibilities of abstract art, they joined the French group Abstraction-Création in 1933. Upon returning home, the pair became an important link between the British art world and international currents in abstract art.

Between 1931 and 1934, Hepworth's sculptures grew increasingly abstract. Nonetheless, the human figure remained recognizable. Within these smooth and wavy forms, one could still make out the shape of a hand or face. Sometimes, as in her important work of 1932 entitled *Two heads,* she took the theme of two linked figures. Throughout her later career, she renewed her interest in creating sculptures with multiple, often linked figures.

From 1934 onward, she worked exclusively in what **Wendy Slatkin** describes as "a totally abstract, geometric vocabulary." A central feature of Hepworth's artistic technique involved creating holes in solid bodies, then painting the internal surfaces. This technique resulted in such striking later works as 1940's *Sculpture with color (deep blue and red).* She dated the definite turn in her work to the period after she and Nicholson had their triplets on October 3, 1934. Nothing in her life had changed except the children's appearance, but "my work seemed to have changed direction." She remarked how her departure from naturalism and her new concern with pure forms "initiated the exploration with which I have been preoccupied continuously since then."

The necessary equilibrium between the material I carve and the form I want to make will always dictate an abstract interpretation in my sculpture.

—Barbara Hepworth

Hepworth's reputation benefitted from her association with Herbert Read. One of Britain's leading art critics and an official at the Victoria and Albert Museum, Read promoted the general cause of modern art and, specifically, the plunge Hepworth was making into abstraction. Nonetheless, Hepworth's artistic progress was darkened by financial difficulties. In the 1930s, she and Nicholson often survived doing such commercial work as textile design. Sometimes they were able to sell one of her sculptures or his paintings. From the time their three children had arrived, money was even more of a concern than ever. Even in the mid-1940s, she could write a friend that the sale of three small paintings "completely saved our life—we were at bottom and could not pay school bills or grocer."

By the mid-1930s, the rising political storm in Europe was leading a number of abstract artists to settle in London. Many of them became her personal friends and formed an impressive artistic circle in Hepworth's neighborhood in the London suburb of Hampstead. But the threat of war on England's shores led many of them to leave for the United States.

In late August 1939, Hepworth and her family themselves left London. They relocated at St. Ives, on the coast of Cornwall. With the outbreak of war a few weeks later, this isolated place became a safe retreat. In time, it became Barbara Hepworth's permanent residence and place of work. During the wartime period, however, her days were filled with caring for the children, running a nursery school, and growing a garden for food. Consistent with her principles, she took time at night to continue her work as an artist. Through the help of friends, she and Nicholson were able to place their children in a local private school.

When Hepworth was able to resume her sculpture in 1943, her work was more than ever dominated by pure geometrical forms. A notable product of this period was her *Sculpture with color (oval form) pale blue and red.* A hollowed out oval with the interior painted pale blue, it has taut red and white strings stretched to form a cone within the oval's cavity.

Hepworth has written eloquently about why she made her career as an abstract sculptor. The sculptor, she has said, must translate what he or she feels about humans and nature into material form. And for her, "there are essential stone shapes and essential wood shapes which are impossible for me to disregard." She found years of living at St. Ives inspired her with its scenery: the sea, the lighthouse, the rock formation, and the tides. But the community also inspired her. She has noted how "people both move differently and stand differently in response to changed surroundings." In her view, people walk differently in response to different environs: from the Piazza San Marco in Venice to the small streets of St. Ives. The shapes around people affect them profoundly.

In the late 1940s, a renewed interest in the human form appeared in her work. For example, she drew nude studio models. But, in an imaginative departure from such conventional subjects, she accepted an invitation to watch a number of surgical operations, then recorded the events in a series of drawings. As an artist, she was intrigued by purposeful arrangement of the surgical team's human forms gathered around the operating table.

Several notable events at the start of the next decade turned her work in new directions. The British Council chose her to represent her country at the Venice Biennale in 1950. Soon afterward, the British government asked her to produce works for the Festival of Britain in 1951. These events helped give her an international reputation and a degree of financial security she had never had before. She now began to receive commissions for massive outdoor statues, although she continued to work on a smaller scale as well. The loss of her son Paul, a flyer in the Royal Air Force killed in Thailand in 1953, impelled her to travel to Greece to get away from her grief. The example of Greek art now began to enter her work. Finally, her longstanding tie to Ben Nicholson ended when they divorced in 1951. She continued to live in Cornwall and to draw inspiration from the Cornish landscape.

A further advance in her work took place in the mid-1950s when she began to cast works in bronze after creating the forms in plaster. Heretofore, she had relied upon the physically more demanding technique of carving directly from wood and stone. She also did stage sets, beginning with a production of *Electra* at the Old Vic. She soon followed with the sets for *The Midsummer Marriage* in 1954.

In her last decades as a productive artist, Hepworth created works of unprecedented size, becoming fascinated with the way in which moonlight or the rising sun would change the aspect of each sculpture. "Forms to lie down in, or forms to climb through" excited her imagination. Working happily in her studio at St. Ives, she filled her garden with massive statues. Raw materials awaited her attention. "I love my blocks of marble," she said, "always piling up in the yard like a flock of sheep."

By the 1960s, Hepworth's works were increasingly evident throughout Britain. *Winged figure* decorated the front of a prominent building in London's Bond Street, and *Squares with two circles* stood outside Churchill College at Cambridge University. Other works stood in prominent places throughout the world. One of her most famous pieces was the spectacular bronze entitled *Single form,* unveiled in New York on June 11, 1964. She produced it as a monument to her personal friend Dag Hammarskjöld, the late director of the United Nations. It was, as she stated at the dedication ceremony, "a symbol that would reflect the nobility of his life."

In a tribute to her recognition within the ranks of 20th-century artists, Hepworth was honored repeatedly in the 1960s. She became a trustee of London's Tate Gallery in 1965, and she had a major retrospective exhibition there in 1968. Three years earlier, she had been elevated to the rank of Dame Commander of the British Empire (CBE) by Queen ***Elizabeth II**, the honor her father had earlier received for achievements as an engineer. Honorary degrees, such as a doctorate in letters from the University of Exeter and the University of Oxford, showed the respect in which she was held in the academic community. In 1968, Cornwall, where she had lived at St. Ives since 1939, recognized her by conferring the title of "Bard of Cornwall." Closer to home, the Borough of St. Ives named her "Honorary Freeman," the highest honor the locality could give. A notable moment of recognition from abroad came in 1973 when she was elected to the American Academy of Arts and Letters. By that time, she was confined to a wheelchair by arthritis, and she received the honor at the American Embassy in London.

The noted sculptor continued her work despite declining health. She filled the garden of her studio at St. Ives with a vast collection of works. She had a reunion with key figures in her life like Henry Moore and the Russian sculptor Naum Gabo in March 1970. On that occasion, the three presented works to the Tate Gallery in London in memory of Sir Herbert Read.

Barbara Hepworth died on May 20, 1975, and it was in her longtime workplace that she spent the last moments of her life. Ill with cancer and disabled from a fractured hip, she was caught in a fire that had broken out in her studio; she had apparently caused the fire by smoking in bed. Her former studio with the attached garden has now been transformed into The Barbara Hepworth Museum.

Most critics find Hepworth's greatest achievements in her smaller works rather than the massive public monuments she produced in her last decades. Nonetheless, her career as a whole has established her as a sculptor of the first rank. "She earned herself twenty-five years of international fame," writes Sally Festing. Her "sculpture inhabits countries throughout the world."

SOURCES:

Barbara Hepworth: The Tate Gallery, 3 April–19 May 1968. Introduction by Ronald Alley. London: Tate Gallery, 1968.

Festing, Sally. *Barbara Hepworth: A Life of Forms.* NY: Viking, 1995.

Gardiner, Margaret. *Barbara Hepworth: A Memoir.* Edinburgh: Salamander Press, 1982.

Hammacher, A. M. *The Sculpture of Barbara Hepworth.* Rev. ed. London: Thames and Hudson, 1987.

Hepworth, Barbara. *Barbara Hepworth: A Pictorial Autobiography.* Rev. ed. London: Tate Gallery, 1985.

Slatkin, Wendy. *Women Artists in History: From Antiquity to the 20th Century*. Englewood Cliffs, NJ: Prentice-Hall, 1985.

SUGGESTED READING:

Berthoud, Roger. *The Life of Henry Moore*. London: Faber and Faber, 1987.

Chadwick, Whitney. *Women, Art, and Society*. London: Thames and Hudson, 1990.

Cheny, Sheldon. *Sculpture of the World: A History*. NY: Viking, 1968.

Lewison, Jeremy. *Ben Nicholson*. NY: Rizzoli, 1991.

Lucie-Smith, Edward. *Sculpture since 1945*. London: Phaidon, 1987.

RELATED MEDIA:

"Barbara Hepworth" (15 min.), directed by John Read, produced by BBC, 1961.

"Barbara Hepworth at the Tate" (15 min.), directed by Bruce Beresford, produced by Arts Council of Great Britain, 1968.

Neil M. Heyman,
Professor of History, San Diego State University,
San Diego, California

Herbelin, Jeanne Mathilde (1820–1904)

French painter of miniatures. *Name variations: Jeanne-Mathilde Herbelin. Born Jeanne Mathilde Habert in Seine-et-Oise, France, on August 24, 1820; died in 1904.*

A French miniature painter, Jeanne Mathilde Herbelin painted the first miniature admitted to the Louvre.

Herbert, Anne (1590–1676).

See Clifford, Anne.

Mary Herbert

Herbert, Katherine (c. 1471–?)

Countess of Pembroke. *Name variations: Katherine or Catherine Plantagenet. Born around 1471; illegitimate daughter of Richard III (1452–1485), king of England (r. 1483–1485); married William Herbert (1455–1491), 2nd earl of Pembroke, in March 1484. William Herbert's first wife was ****Mary Woodville*** *(sister of Queen ****Elizabeth Woodville****).*

Herbert, Lucy (1669–1744)

British devotional writer. *Name variations: Lady Lucy Herbert. Born in 1669; died in 1744; daughter of William Herbert (1617–1696), 1st marquis of Powis, and Lady ****Elizabeth Somerset.***

Lady Lucy Herbert was the prioress of the English convent at Bruges from 1709 to 1744. Her *Devotions,* edited by Reverend John Morris, S.J., were published in 1873. Herbert's father, William Herbert, 3rd baron Powis, was imprisoned in connection with the Popish plot, and his estates in England were confiscated.

Herbert, Magdalene (1561–1627).

See Guiney, Louise Imogen for sidebar on Lady Danvers.

Herbert, Mary (1561–1621)

Countess of Pembroke, English aristocrat and scholar. *Name variations: Mary Sidney. Born Mary Sidney in Worcestershire, England, in 1561; died of smallpox in London, England, on September 25, 1621; third daughter of Sir Henry Sidney (president of The Marches of Wales) and Mary Dudley (d. 1586, daughter of Jane Guildford and John Dudley, duke of Northumberland); sister of poet and diplomat Sir Philip Sidney (1554–1586); aunt of poet ****Mary Wroth;*** *became third wife of Henry Herbert, 2nd earl of Pembroke, in 1577 (died 1601); children: four.*

The sister of English poet, diplomat, and soldier Sir Philip Sidney, Mary Herbert was a respected literary figure in her own right. Born in 1561 in Worcestershire, England, she grew up in Ludlow Castle, where she received an excellent classical education. She was the daughter of Sir Henry Sidney, president of The Marches of Wales, and **Mary Dudley**, daughter of the duke of Northumberland. In 1575, following the deaths of her three sisters, Mary joined the court of Queen ***Elizabeth I** and, in 1577, became the wife of Henry Herbert, 2nd earl of Pembroke; he had also been briefly married to Lady ***Catherine Grey**. Mary Herbert collaborated on many of her brother Philip's writings, most notably his famous *Arcadia* (1560), which she both revised and added to, and a metrical version of the Psalms. After Philip's death in 1586, she devoted herself to editing his works. She also translated Plessis du Mornay's *Discourses of Life and Death* (1593) and Garnier's *Antonie* (1592).

Mary Herbert also took over as patron of her brother's literary circle, which included poets

Samuel Daniel, Nicholas Breton, and Ben Jonson. Upon her husband Henry's death in 1601, she received a small inheritance and moved to London with her son. In 1615, she built Houghton House on land granted to her by James I. Mary Herbert died of smallpox in 1621 and was buried in Salisbury Cathedral.

Herbert, Winifred (1672–1749).

See Maxwell, Winifred.

Herbst, Josephine (1892–1969)

American writer and journalist. *Born on March 5, 1892, in Sioux City, Iowa; died of cancer on January 28, 1969, in New York City; the third of four daughters of William Benton Herbst (a salesman) and Mary (Frey) Herbst; graduated from high school in Sioux City, 1910; bachelor's degree from the University of California at Berkeley, 1918; married John Herrmann (a writer), on September 2, 1926 (divorced 1940); no children.*

Selected works: Nothing is Sacred *(1928);* Money for Love *(1929);* Pity Is Not Enough *(1933);* The Executioner Waits *(1934);* Rope of Gold *(1939);* Satan's Sergeants *(1941);* Somewhere the Tempest Fell *(1947); "Hunter of Doves," in* Bottege Oscure *(1954);* New Green World *(1954); "The Starched Blue Sky of Spain," in* The Noble Savage *(1960); "A Year of Disgrace," in* The Noble Savage *(1961).*

Best known for her sweeping trilogy which traces an American family from the Civil War through the 1930s, Josephine Herbst figures prominently in both the literature and the political radicalism of the 1920s and 1930s. Her work includes seven novels, a biography, journalistic reports, and numerous short stories and essays.

Josephine Herbst was born in 1892, in Sioux City, Iowa, where her father sold farm implements and her mother strongly instilled in her a love of books and a sense of family history. "The family for generations had kept diaries and letters," Herbst later wrote, "and the first inkling I had of the complexity and significance of people in relation to each other and the world came from those documents." Out of necessity, Herbst's college education was interspersed with periods of work and stretched into nine years. She attended three institutions (Morningside College, the University of Iowa, and the University of Washington) before receiving her bachelor's degree from the University of California at Berkeley in 1918.

After graduating, Herbst moved to New York and immersed herself in the more radical literary and political circles in the city. Through friends, she met Maxwell Anderson, then a young socialist journalist and poet, who became her first lover. When she became pregnant, Anderson, who was married at the time and the father of two, insisted that she have an abortion. The experience, coupled with her sister's death from an abortion a few months later, brought her close to a nervous breakdown. In 1922, she left her job as a reader for H.L. Mencken's magazine and moved to Berlin. There, living on her own, she completed her first novel, an autobiographical account of her affair with Anderson (never published).

While in Paris in 1924, Herbst met and fell in love with John Herrmann, a charming expatriate writer with a predisposition for alcohol. The pair returned to America and set up housekeeping in an old Connecticut farmhouse. After marrying in September 1926, they eventually bought another farmhouse in Erwinna, Pennsylvania, where Herbst lived for the rest of her life. Over the next ten years, Herbst experienced her most prolific period, producing five novels, the first of which, *Nothing is Sacred* (1928), was widely acclaimed. With the publication of *Pity Is Not Enough* (1933), the first volume of her trilogy, she was hailed as a major literary figure. Meanwhile, Herrmann, never a serious writer to begin with, was writing less and becoming more and more involved in the political activities of the Communist party. (Herbst never actually joined the party, although she was a leftist sympathizer.) Soon, Herbst's literary reputation surpassed her husband's, driving a wedge between them. Infidelities exacerbated the problem, and, by 1935, the two were living apart, though they would not divorce until 1940.

Herbst's trilogy, which includes *Pity Is Not Enough, The Executioner Waits* (1934), and *Rope of Gold* (1939), tells the story of the Trexler and Wendel families, and, in her own words, "covers not only the decay of capitalistic society but also the upthrust of a new group society." Strongly autobiographical, Herbst used her own ancestors, the Freys, as the basis of the trilogy, and in *Rope of Gold,* she also chronicled the deterioration of her own marriage through the characters of Victoria and Jonathan Chance.

During the political unrest of the 1930s, Herbst was also engaged in journalistic pursuits, and her reports from crisis spots throughout the world were widely published in such diverse newspapers as the *New York Post* and *Nation.*

She reported the effects of Hitler's regime in Germany, covered the farmers' strike in her home state of Iowa in 1932, traveled to Cuba during the general strike of 1935, and wrote about the automobile strike in Flint, Michigan, in 1937. That same year, Herbst spent six months in Spain, reporting on the civil war, and in 1939, she was in South America.

During the 1940s, Herbst went through a period of isolation, living alone in Erwinna, anguishing over the dissolution of her marriage. In June 1942, she was unexpectedly discharged from a wartime job in Washington which only added to her misery. Even the two novels of this period, *Satan's Sergeants* (1941) and *Somewhere the Tempest Fell* (1947), were indifferently received. Gradually, however, Herbst emerged from this dark period. She renewed old friendships and the farmhouse at Erwinna became something of a gathering place for literati, particularly younger writers such as Alfred Kazin, Hilton Kramer, Saul Bellow, and the poet **Jean Garrigue** (with whom, by one account, Herbst had an intimate relationship). From the mid-1950s until her death, Herbst devoted herself to her memoirs and to a volume of interrelated novellas about writers she knew, although neither were completed. Her last published works included *New Green World* (1954), a biographical appreciation of botanists John and William Bartram, and some shorter critical essays. Josephine Herbst died of cancer on January 28, 1969.

SOURCES:

Green, Carol Hurd, and Mary Grimley Mason, eds. *American Women Writers: From Colonial Times to the Present*. NY: Continuum, 1994.

Kunitz, Stanley J., and Howard Haycraft, eds. *20th Century Authors*. NY: H.W. Wilson, 1942.

SUGGESTED READING:

Lange, Elinor. *Josephine Herbst: The Story She Could Never Tell*, 1984.

Rideout, Walter. *The Radical Novel in the United States*, 1966.

Barbara Morgan,
Melrose, Massachusetts

Hereford, countess of.

See Margaret of Huntingdon (c. 1140–1201).
See Maud of Lusignan (d. 1241).
See Bohun, Maud (fl. 1275).
See Joan de Quinci (d. 1283).
See Eleanor of Castile (1241–1290) for sidebar on Elizabeth Plantagenet (1282–1316).
See Bohun, Alianore (d. 1313).
See Fitzalan, Joan (fl. 1325).
See Fitzalan, Joan (d. 1419).

Heremburge (d. 1126).

See Ermentrude.

Hereswitha (d. c. 690).

See Hilda of Whitby for sidebar.

Herford, Beatrice (c. 1868–1952).

See Draper, Ruth for sidebar.

Héricourt, Jenny Poinsard d' (1809–1875)

French philosopher, medical practitioner, Communist, and feminist. *Name variations: Jenny d'Hericourt; Jeanne Marie; Mme Marie; (pseudonyms) Félix Lamb; Jeanne Marie; and Poinsard d'Héricourt. Born Jeanne-Marie-Fabienne Poinsard in Besançon on September 10, 1809; died in January 1875; daughter of Jean-Pierre Poinsard (a clockmaker from Héricourt) and Marguerite-Baptiste-Alexandrine Brenet; had at least one younger sister; educated at home; received Instructrice diploma at age 18; diploma from Medical Homeopathic Institute of Buenos Ayres (Paris); diploma of maitresse sage femme; married Michel-Gabriel-Joseph Marie, in August 1832.*

Selected works: (as Félix Lamb) Le Fils du reprouvé *(1844); Icarian movement songs; articles in* Le Droit des femmes, The Woman's Journal, Solidarité, Revue Philosophique et réligieuse, La Ragione *(1855–57); articles in* The Agitator, *including her autobiography, "La Femme [pseud. Poinsard d'Héricourt] 'Madame Jenny P. D'Héricourt'" (1869);* La Femme affranchie: réponse à M.M. Michelet, P.-J. Proudhon, E. de Girardin, A. Comte, et aux autres novateurs modernes *(1860, abridged English publication in 1864 as* A Woman's Philosophy of Woman or Woman Affranchised*).*

Jeanne-Marie-Fabienne Poinsard was born to French Protestants on September 10, 1809. Her father Jean-Pierre Poinsard was a Lutheran clockmaker from Héricourt, in the ancient region of Franch-Comte, and her mother **Marguerite-Baptiste-Alexandrine Brenet** was of Swiss Calvinist lineage. Jenny was nicknamed "Don Quixote" by her parents, because she rose to the defense of other children and animals. Her father died when she was eight, and Jenny moved to Paris with her mother and younger sister.

The life of Jenny d'Héricourt has been hard to trace because she took her father's birthplace as her surname, and her authorship of some pieces under pseudonyms are disputed. She became a teacher after receiving the diploma Instructrice at the age of 18. Despite her humble beginnings, she became the owner of a school for girls. In 1832, she married Michel-Gabriel-

Joseph Marie, an employee of the Palais Bourbon (Chambres des Députés) in Paris. The marriage was extremely unhappy, but divorce was illegal in France (this problem was among the issues Héricourt would address in her writings). She left him after he tried to murder her in order to marry someone else.

In the 1840s, she became a follower of Étienne Cabet, a French Communist theorist. In Cabet's journal *Le Populaire,* Héricourt published a serialized novel about working-class misery. She was later active in his revolutionary club, the Société fraternalle centrale. Her other contributions to French communism include songs for the Icarian movement, a group of French immigrants who wanted to establish a Communist settlement.

Héricourt became an active feminist in the late 1840s and the 1850s, and she published a great deal. She belonged to several women's clubs, worked for the women's revolutionary press, and signed the published manifesto of the Society for Women's Emancipation. In *Voix des Femmes* (*Women's Voice*), she wrote under the name "Jeanne Marie." She also published two pieces of romantic fiction with moral undertones, one about adultery (according to her autobiography) and one about capital punishment, *Le Fils du reprouvé,* under the pseudonym Félix Lamb, in 1844. As a woman, she could not be admitted to the French Medical Academy, but Héricourt studied physiology and medicine at home and then continued her medical studies at a foreign institute in Paris, the Medical Homeopathic Institute of Buenos Ayres. She was then able to work as a medical practitioner and act as a midwife.

Interested in the philosophical implications of recent scientific discoveries, in the late 1850s she published extensively in the *Revue Philosophique et réligieuse* (*Review of Philosophy and Religion*), including a critique of homeopathic practice, and in the liberal Italian philosophy journal *La Ragione* (*Reason*). Her greatest influence was outside France, particularly in Italy and in Russia, because of her intellectual contacts, M.L. Mikhailov and the Shelgunovs.

She believed and argued that women should have equal rights to men and be equally educated. A heated dispute with Pierre-Joseph Proudhon led her to publish in 1860 *La Femme affranchie: réponse à M.M. Michelet, P.-J. Proudhon, E. de Girardin, A. Comte et aux autres novateurs modernes.* In 1864, an abridged English translation was published as *A Woman's Philosophy of Woman or Woman Affranchised.* In this work, Héricourt addressed the major French male intellectual writers of the 1840s and '50s, taking up theories in philosophy of science and medicine, moral epistemology, and politics. In particular, she argued that women are important to the physical and moral continuation of a nation, against Proudhon's view that women are socially and intellectually inferior to men. She also disputed as unrealistic the ideals of femininity espoused by Auguste Comte and Jules Michelet.

In the mid-1860s, Héricourt moved to the United States, settling in Chicago, where she hoped to set up a medical practice for women. In America, as in France, she became involved in the women's movement, publishing in the feminist press of the 1860s and becoming a facilitator between American and French feminists. She became friends with women's rights advocates ***Mary Livermore** (who published Héricourt's writing, including her autobiography, in her periodical *The Agitator*) and **Kate Newell Poggett** (the founder of a literary club for Chicago women known as the "Fortnightly Club" who introduced Jenny to ***Elizabeth Cady Stanton** and ***Susan B. Anthony**).

Héricourt missed France, however, as she expressed in letters published by her friend Charles Fauvety, and she returned there in 1873. She then became involved in the intellectual circle surrounding the periodical *L'Avenir des femmes* (*Women's Future*). Jenny Poinsard d'Héricourt died suddenly in January 1875 and is buried in a common grave in St. Owen at the edge of Paris.

SOURCES:

Offen, Karen. "A Nineteenth-Century French Feminist Rediscovered: Jenny P. d'Hericourt, 1809–1875," in *Signs.* Vol. 13, 1987.

———. "Jenny P. d'Hericourt," in Katharina Wilson, ed., *Encyclopedia of Continental Women Writers.* NY: Garland, 1991.

Waithe, Mary Ellen, ed. *A History of Women Philosophers.* Boston, MA: Martinus Nijhoff Publications, 1987–1995.

Catherine Hundleby, M.A.
Philosophy, University of Guelph, Guelph, Ontario, Canada

Herleva or Herleve (fl. c. 1010).

See Arlette.

Herlie, Eileen (1919—)

Scottish actress. *Born Eileen O'Herlihy in Glasgow, Scotland, on March 8, 1919; daughter of Patrick O'Herlihy and Isobel (Cowden) O'Herlihy; attended Shawland's Academy, Glasgow; married Philip Barrett* *(a producer), on August 12, 1942 (divorced 1947); married Witold Kuncewicz, in 1950 (divorced 1960).*

Selected theater: made stage debut in Sweet Aloes, *with the Scottish National Players (Lyric Theater, Glasgow, 1938); London debut as Mrs. de Winter in* Rebecca *(Ambassadors' Theater, 1942); Peg in* Peg O' My Heart *(Scala Theater, 1943); toured as Regina in* The Little Foxes *(1944); with Old Vic Company, Liverpool (1945–46); Andromache in* The Trojan Women *(Lyric Theater, Hammersmith, 1945); Mary in* The Time of Your Life *(Lyric Theater, 1946); the Queen in* The Eagle Has Two Heads *(Lyric Theater, 1946, and at the Haymarket Theater, 1947); title role in* Medea *(Edinburgh Festival and the Globe Theater, 1948); Paula in* The Second Mrs. Tanqueray *(Haymarket Theater, 1950); Mrs. Marwood in* The Way of the World *(Lyric Theater, Hammersmith, 1953); Belvidera in* Venice Preserv'd *(Lyric Theater, 1953); Irene Carey in* A Sense of Guilt *(King's Theater, Glasgow, 1953); Mrs. Molloy in* The Matchmaker *(Haymarket Theater, London, 1954); Broadway debut as Mrs. Molloy (Royale Theater, New York, 1955); Emilia Marty in* The Makropoulos Secret *(Phoenix Theater, New York, 1957); Paulina in* The Winter's Tale *and Beatrice in* Much Ado About Nothing *(Shakespeare Festival, Stratford, Ontario, 1958); Ruth Gray in* Epitaph for George Dillon *(John Golden Theater and Henry Miller Theater, New York, 1959); Lily in* Take Me Along *(Shubert Theater, New York, 1959); Elizabeth Hawkes-Bullock in* All American *(Winter Garden Theater, New York, 1962); Stella in* Photo Finish *(Brooks Atkinson Theater, 1963); Gertrude in John Gielgud's production of* Hamlet *(Lunt-Fontanne Theater, 1964); Lady Fitzbuttress in* Halfway Up the Tree *(Brooks Atkinson Theater, 1967); Martha in* Who's Afraid of Virginia Woolf? *and Clare in* Outcry *(Ivanhoe Theater, Chicago, 1971); Countess Matilda Spina in* Emperor Henry IV *(Ethel Barrymore Theater, New York, 1973); Queen Mary in* Crown Matrimonial *(Helen Hayes Theater, New York, 1973, followed by U.S. tour); Essie Sebastian in* The Great Sebastians *(Ivanhoe Theater, Chicago, 1975).*

Eileen Herlie

Films: Hungry Hill *(1946); (as Queen Gertrude)* Hamlet *(1948);* Angel With the Trumpet *(1949);* The Story of Gilbert and Sullivan *(*Gilbert and Sullivan, *1953);* Isn't Life Wonderful? *(1953);* For Better for Worse *(*Cocktails in the Kitchen, *1954);* She Didn't Say No *(1958);* Freud *(US, 1962); (film of Broadway stage production)* Hamlet *(US, 1964); (as Polina)* The Sea Gull *(US/UK, 1968).*

Actress Eileen Herlie was alternately extolled and admonished by critics throughout her career. She was born in Glasgow, Scotland, in 1919, to an Irish father and a Scottish mother, and overcame strong parental opposition to enter the theater. After her debut in *Sweet Aloes* in 1938, she toured with the Rutherglen Repertory Company until her marriage in 1942 to Philip Barrett, who had bought the stage rights to ***Daphne du Maurier**'s *Rebecca*. Herlie toured in the play, portraying the second Mrs. de Winter, and also made her London stage debut in the role. In 1945 and 1946, Herlie was with the Old Vic Company at the Playhouse, in Liverpool, where she was seen in a variety of roles.

It was at the small suburban Lyric Theater, in Hammersmith, in November 1946, that Herlie became an overnight success, dazzling audiences as the Queen in Jean Cocteau's *The Eagle Has Two Heads*. Critic **Hannen Swaffer** paid homage to the actress, calling her performance a rare "achievement," and pointing out that the curtain had barely come down "when Noel Coward was in her dressing room almost too moved to pay tribute to her." The play transferred to the Haymarket in February 1947, drawing further raves from the critics, although not all of them were equally enthralled. **Audrey Williamson**, for example, found Herlie's queen "lacking in depth and flexibility of emotion, yet pictorially she was regal and vivid, with a mask of tragic beauty."

Critics were again divided on Herlie's performance in the title role of *Medea,* which she played first at the Edinburgh Festival in August 1948 and again at the Globe Theater in London the following month. Harold Hobson complained that she played all the fury of the character, but none of the pathos, while the *Times* critic, admitting that the actress was hindered by a poor adaptation of the play, still found her performance lackluster. "Miss Herlie is fettered to the leaden-footed dialogue," he wrote, "yet there are passages in which she might break through it . . . . She remains fettered and we are left wondering if she has yet learned to use her emotional energy, her tragic personality, to awe-inspiring effect." Sidney Carroll, the former dramatic critic for the *Sunday Times,* wrote a letter to that paper rebuking the critics and calling Herlie's performance "a dramatic exhibition of Asiatic revenge and hatred that terrifies while it enthralls, a classic purity of diction, a maturity of technique, a passion and a pathos no other actress could surpass."

In December 1955, Herlie made her Broadway debut as Mrs. Molloy in *The Matchmaker,* a play that ran for 488 performance. Remaining in New York, she portrayed Emilia Marty in *The Makropoulos Secret.* In June 1958, she appeared at the Shakespeare Festival in Stratford, Ontario, playing Paulina in *The Winter's Tale* and Beatrice in *Much Ado About Nothing.* She returned to New York, where her various roles included Ruth Gray in *Epitaph for George Dillon,* Lily in *Take Me Along* (1959), and Elizabeth Hawkes-Bullock in the musical *All American* (1962). In April 1964, she played Gertrude in John Gielgud's acclaimed production of *Hamlet* which also starred Richard Burton. (The production would later be filmed.)

In 1973, Herlie appeared as Queen Mary in *Crown Matrimonial,* a play about the abdication of Edward IV, in which she later toured. In Chicago in October 1975, she played Essie Sebastian in *The Great Sebastians.* The actress also made a number of films, among them *Isn't Life Wonderful?* (1953), *Freud* (1962), and *The Sea Gull* (1968).

Little is written of Herlie's personal life. She divorced Philip Barrett in 1947 and subsequently married Witold Kuncewicz, whom she divorced in 1960.

SOURCES:

Katz, Ephraim. *The Film Encyclopedia.* NY: HarperCollins, 1994.

Morley, Sheridan. *The Great Stage Stars.* London: Angus & Robertson, 1986.

Barbara Morgan,
Melrose, Massachusetts

Herlind of Maasryck (fl. 8th c.)

Nun and artist of Belgium. *Flourished in the 8th century in Maasryck, in the Low Countries.*

Herlind of Maasryck was a famous nun and artist whose life is preserved in a biography written a century after her death. She entered the convent of Maasryck in the Low Countries to obey her devout parents, who wanted to show their love for God by dedicating one of their children to the religious life. She was well-educated by the nuns at Maasryck, and her enthusiastic biographer lists numerous accomplishments at which Herlind excelled. Even given the inclination of medieval biographers toward exaggeration, the skills attributed to this nun are remarkable: she was highly literate and a good singer, copied and illuminated manuscripts in the convent's scriptoria, spun and wove cloth, and embroidered beautifully.

Laura York,
Riverside, California

Hermes, Gertrude (1901–1983)

British wood engraver and sculptor. *Born Gertrude Anna Bertha Hermes in Bromley, Kent, England, on August 18, 1901; died in 1983; daughter of L.A. Hermes; educated privately; attended Belmont School for Girls, Bickley; studied at Beckenham School of Art; studied at Leon Underwood's School of Painting and Sculpture, 1922–26; married Blair Rowlands Hughes-Stanton (an engraver), in 1926 (divorced 1932); children: one son; one daughter.*

A British engraver and sculptor, Gertrude Hermes produced distinctive pieces which over the years have found their way into most of the major collections in Europe and North America. Born in Bromley, Kent, in 1901, Hermes studied at the Beckenham School of Art and the Leon Underwood School of Painting and Sculpture. In 1926, she and her husband, Blair Rowlands Hughes-Stanton, worked as engravers at the Gregynog Press, founded by ***Gwendoline** and ***Margaret Davies** in Central Wales.

Following her divorce in 1932, Hermes moved to London, where she produced a variety of sculptures, prints (linocuts), and decorative pieces, including a mosaic pool floor and stone foundation for the Shakespeare Memorial Theater in Stratford. During the war years, she worked in tank factories and shipyards in the United States and Montreal, producing working drawings. Hermes returned to London in 1945, resuming her work in print-making and sculpture, including bronze portrait heads. She also taught at several London art schools and at the Royal Academy School of Arts. The artist became a fellow of the Royal Society of Painters, Etchers, and Engravers in 1951, and was the recipient of the Jean Masson Davidson Prize for portrait sculpture in 1967. On the occasion of Hermes' 80th birthday in 1981, the Royal Academy held a retrospective exhibition of her work. Hermes was made an OBE in 1982, a year before her death.

Maria Hernández

Hermine of Reuss (1887–1947)

Princess of Reuss. *Born on September 17, 1887, in Greiz, Germany; died on August 7, 1947, in Frankfurt-am-Oder, Germany; daughter of Henry XXII (1846–1902), prince of Reuss, and* ****Ida of Schaumburg-Lippe*** *(1852–1891); married Johann Georg (1873–1920), prince of Schönaich-Carolath, on January 7, 1907; became second wife of Wilhelm II, emperor of Germany (r. 1888–1918), on November 5, 1922; children: (first marriage)* ***Henrietta of Schönaich-Carolath*** *(1918–1972, who married Charles Francis Joseph, prince of Prussia).*

Hermine of Waldeck and Pyrmont (1827–1910)

Princess of Schaumburg-Lippe. *Name variations: Hermine of Waldeck-Pyrmont. Born in 1827; died in 1910; daughter of Prince George II; married Adolphus I Georg, prince of Schaumburg-Lippe, on October 25, 1844; children: eight, including* ****Ida of Schaumburg-Lippe*** *(1852–1891); Adolphus (1859–1916), prince of Schaumburg-Lippe.*

Hernández, Maria (1896–1986)

Chicana civil-rights advocate. *Name variations: Maria Hernandez. Born in Mexico in 1896; died in 1986.*

A prominent figure in Mexican-American history, Maria Hernández devoted her life to the civic, social, and educational concerns of Mexican-Americans. A native of Mexico and a longtime resident of Lytle, Texas, she was a co-founder of the Orden Caballeros of America, a civil-rights organization established in 1929, through which she became a forceful and eloquent voice for the Mexican-American community.

Hernández believed in the power of a solid family unit, and she considered the mother's role pivotal in the formation of her children's character. It was through the mother that the child learned the skills needed to help advance society. "She was quick to point out that whatever Chicanas have achieved in this country has been done through strong family unity and the strength of men and women working together," writes historian **Martha Cotera**. "She encouraged each of us to act politically to raise the public consciousness because this type of effort is owed to the family, the community and the nation."

Hernández did not shrink from the activism she advocated for others, tirelessly protesting against civil inequities and the inferior, segregated education that Mexican-American children were receiving. In 1970, in addition to her personal campaigns, she was instrumental in the formation of the Raza Unida Party, which helped carry forth her goals.

Barbara Morgan,
Melrose, Massachusetts

Herodias (c. 14 BCE–after 40 CE)

Jewish princess who ruled with her husband. *Born around 14 BCE; died after 40 CE; daughter of Aristobulus I and Berenice (c. 35 BCE–?); granddaughter of Herod the Great; married paternal half-uncle Herod Philip I (the son of Herod the Great and his wife Mariamne II), around 4 CE; married half-uncle Herod Antipas (son of Herod the Great and Malthace); children: (first marriage) Salome III (c. 15 CE–?).*

Herodias was born around 14 BCE, the daughter of Aristobulus and ***Berenice**, and the granddaughter of Herod the Great. She first married (around 4 CE) her paternal half-uncle, Herod Philip I (the son of Herod the Great and his wife **Mariamne II**). By Herod Philip I, Herodias gave birth to the famous ***Salome III** (of

Herodias

seven veils fame). Herodias, however, quickly found this union uncongenial and abandoned her first husband. She then married another half-uncle, Herod Antipas (the son of Herod the Great and ***Malthace**), who had divorced his first wife, a daughter of Aretas, king of the Nabateans. (Both of Herodias' unions had been contracted in part to consolidate the political interests of the Herodian family.) Herodias' second husband was the tetrarch of Galilee from 4 BCE until 40 CE, and thus was a Jewish ruler who reigned solely at the discretion of Rome. Why

Herodias contracted this second marriage is unknown for certain, but it is likely that she found Herod Antipas more to her liking largely because he seems to have been malleable under her influence. Both John the Baptist and Jesus were technically Herod Antipas' subjects and largely carried out their ministries under his (and Herodias') jurisdiction. However, the former was especially censorious toward Herodias because he considered her marriage to Herod Antipas both incestuous (since she had been formally married to his half-brother) and illicit (because, in order to marry, both Herodias and Herod Antipas had to divorce their first spouses).

John the Baptist's vocal opposition to her second marriage caused Herodias to hate him, but, though she pressured Herod Antipas to punish him, the latter was long reluctant to do so, fearing John's charisma and following. Nevertheless, a birthday party for Herod Antipas (c. 25 CE) gone awry would be John's undoing. Dancing provocatively for her stepfather, a young but voluptuous Salome III was able to solicit from Herod Antipas a promise to grant any boon she requested. Influenced by her mother, Salome subsequently requested John's head on a platter—a grant Herod Antipas was loathe to give, but which the stubborn Salome continued to demand. As a result, John the Baptist was executed at Machaerus, and Herodias had her revenge upon her detractor. Herod Antipas, present in Jerusalem during the passion of Jesus, also seems to have played a marginal role in the inquisition which led to the latter's death.

Actively involved in the politics of her house and region, Herodias was a major force behind Herod Antipas' reign and rivalries, particularly the rivalry with her brother, Herod Agrippa I. Initially, Herodias urged her husband to help her brother with money and some status in his capital (the city of Tiberias), but soon brother and sister had quarreled, and Herod Agrippa fled to Rome to reacquaint himself with Gaius, better known as the Emperor Caligula. When Caligula came to the Roman throne in 37 CE, he reestablished his friend Herod Agrippa in Palestine (over the territory of Batanaa and Trachonitis, to the east of the Sea of Galilee) with the title of "king"—a title as yet denied Herod Antipas. At Herodias' urging, Herod Antipas went in state to Rome to request his elevation to "royal" status so as to be the "equal" of his brother-in-law. This embassy was a failure—not only did Herod Antipas not obtain his wish, he even experienced disaster when Herod Agrippa turned the tables on him by accusing him of disloyalty to Rome before Caligula; these charges led both to Herod Antipas' exile in Gaul and to his realm being turned over to Herod Agrippa to augment the territory already under the latter's rule (40 CE). Thus beaten at the political game by her own brother, Herodias joined her husband in exile, there to die at an unknown date.

William Greenwalt,
Associate Professor of Classical History,
Santa Clara University, Santa Clara, California

Heron, Matilda (1830–1877)

Irish-American actress. *Born Matilda Agnes Heron in Londonderry, Ireland, on December 1, 1830; died at home in New York City on March 7, 1877; interred in Greenwood Cemetery, Brooklyn; third daughter and youngest of five children of John Heron (an Irish farmholder) and Mary (Laughlin) Heron; secretly married Henry Herbert Byrne (a San Francisco lawyer), in June 1854 (separated one month later); married Robert Stoepel (an orchestra leader and composer), on December 24, 1857 (separated 1869); children: (second marriage) Hélène Stoepel (known by her stage name,* ***Bijou Heron****).*

Matilda Heron was born in Londonderry, Ireland, in 1830; 12 years later, she emigrated to America with her parents and settled in Philadelphia. In 1852, she appeared at the Bowery Theater, New York, as Lady Macbeth, Juliet, Parthenia and in other parts, and her success was immediate. In 1885, for the first time, she played Camille, based on the life of ***Alphonsine Plessis**. It was a role with which Heron's name was often identified, and one which was to become the principal feature of her repertory. "Matilda Heron, as an actress, was at her best in the part of Camille," wrote William Winter. "Other parts she acted; that one she lived. She radiated a force of magnetic emotion which it was impossible to resist. She loved the storm and revelled in the frenzy of a nature at war with itself." But, warned Winter, "That kind of nature, unless curbed by dominant intellect and regulated by strong moral sense, inevitably breaks all the bounds of reason, convention, and a serene life. Matilda Heron's career was gloriously bright for a while, and then dark with trouble and sorrow."

Toward the end of her life, Heron became destitute. A benefit performance for her was held at Niblo's Garden in 1872, in which Edwin Booth, ***Laura Keene**, ***Fanny Janauschek**, and others participated. Matilda Heron died five years later. She was a "magnanimous, great-hearted, loving woman," writes Winter, "and she was one of the most potent elemental forces in the histrionic vocation that have ever been exerted on the American Stage."

Herrad of Hohenberg

(c. 1130–1195)

***German abbess, philosopher, artist, and writer, whose best-known work is* Hortus Deliciarum.** *Name variations: Herrad von Hohenbourg or Hohenburg; Herrad of Landsberg; Herrad von Landsberg; Herrad of Landsburg; Herrade of Landsburg. Born around 1130; died on July 25, 1195, at convent of Hohenburg, Germany; possibly educated at the abbey of Hohenberg, Alsace; never married; no children.*

Little is known of Herrad of Hohenberg's early life. She was born around 1130, entered the convent of Hohenburg as a child, and rose to become its abbess. It is unlikely that she could have achieved that position in such an important abbey without an aristocratic background, but she probably did not belong to the family von Landsberg, a name under which she has been known.

Herrad may have been educated at Hohenberg (previously known as Mt. Ste. Odile) in Alsace by her predecessor as abbess, **Rilinda** (Relinda or Relindis). Herrad continued Rilinda's reform work at the abbey with great success when she took over around 1176. She is famous for her production of the *Hortus Deliciarum* or *Garden of Delights,* the first encyclopedia written for women, a work on which Rilinda probably assisted although it is unsure in what capacity or to what extent. The scholarship in this work indicates that Herrad must have been well-educated, and the library at Hohenberg well-stocked.

The *Hortus Deliciarum* was comprised of writings from earlier philosophers of the Church, particularly Augustine, Anselm, and Boethius, but it also included an unusually extensive body of work by Herrad's contemporaries, such as ***Hildegard of Bingen**, Peter the Lombard, Peter Comestor, and Gauthier de Chatillon. The encyclopedia included over 1,160 pieces of prose and poetry covering philosophy, religion, and history, which would be of general interest to educated women of the time.

Herrad felt it was important to illuminate the *Hortus* heavily, as it was to be used as a sort of Latin reader to educate her novices both about history and philosophy and the language as well, and she wanted all levels of students to benefit from it, even if they could not yet read. She oversaw the development of the *Hortus,* which also included numerous moral lessons, and supplied the text, but it was the nuns of her scriptorium who painted the charming miniatures, all 340. The last page of the book was a sort of group portrait of Herrad and her nuns, not individually distinguishable images but with each woman's name written above her picture.

The work became famous over the centuries, and the author was considered saintly. Much of the original was lost to fire in August 1870 while it was housed in Strasbourg, although much of it has been pieced back together. We learn also of the original content through references to it in other texts. Herrad's *Hortus Deliciarum* remains a subject of interest in regard to the history of philosophy, iconography, and the history of women.

SOURCES:

Buck, Claire, ed. *Bloomsbury Guide to Women's Literature.* NY: Prentice Hall, 1992.

Head, Thomas. "Herrad of Hohenberg," in Katharina Wilson, ed., *Encyclopedia of Continental Women Writers.* NY: Garland, 1991.

Waithe, Mary Ellen, ed. *A History of Women Philosophers.* Boston: Martinus Nijhoff Publications, 1987–1995.

Catherine Hundleby, M.A.
Philosophy, University of Guelph, Guelph, Ontario, Canada

Herrad or Herrade of Landsburg

(c. 1130–1195).

See Herrad of Hohenberg.

Herrick, Christine Terhune

(1859–1944)

American writer who specialized in domestic science. *Born Christine Terhune on June 13, 1859, in Newark, New Jersey; died on December 2, 1944, in Washington, D.C.; eldest daughter and the second of six children (three of whom survived) of Reverend Edward Payson Terhune and Mary Virginia (Hawes) Terhune (1830–1922, a writer); studied privately at home and in Rome and Geneva; married James Frederick Herrick (a newspaper editor), on April 23, 1884 (died 1893); children: Horace and James; and two children who died in infancy.*

Christine Herrick was born in Newark, New Jersey, in 1859. Her mother was the well-known writer ***Mary Virginia Terhune**. Her father was the Reverend Edward Payson Terhune, pastor of the First Reformed Church in Newark, at the time of Herrick's birth, then later of the First Congregational Church in Springfield, Massachusetts. Schooled at home by private tutors, Herrick was a voracious reader, devouring her father's theological books when nothing else was available. The family spent two years abroad beginning in 1876, at which time Herrick studied in Rome and Geneva, and traveled in France and Germany. She taught English literature at a private girls' school in Springfield before her marriage in 1884 to James Frederick Herrick, editor of the *Springfield Republican*. In 1886, the couple moved to New York, where James took a position as the editor of a newspaper in Brooklyn. The couple had four children, two of whom, a boy and a girl, died in early childhood.

Christine Herrick's first article, "The Wastes of the Household," appeared in the maiden issue of *Good Housekeeping* in May 1885 and was followed by contributions to other popular journals, including the *Ladies' Home Journal* and *Harper's Bazaar.* By the time her first book, *Housekeeping Made Easy*, was published in 1888, she already had an impressive following. Between 1888 and 1893, she edited the woman's page of the Baptist *New York Recorder* and published four additional books, expanding her purview to cookery and child-rearing. When her husband died in 1893, Herrick was earning enough to send her two surviving sons to private school and college and finance several trips abroad.

Believing that women should continually expand their horizons, Herrick broadened the subject matter of her articles to include books, plays, sports, and even politics ("Do Women Want the Vote?"). In 1918, she published a diet book, *Lose Weight and Be Well*, using her own experience as the basis for a sensible approach to dieting. *My Boy and I* (1917) was also largely biographical. Herrick also collaborated on a series of cookbooks with her mother: *The Cottage Kitchen* (1895), *The National Cook Book* (1896), and *The Helping Hand Cook Book* (1912). In 1926, she adapted her mother's book, *Common Sense in the Household*, to incorporate the use of fuel and electricity in cooking. The result was *The New Common Sense in the Household*. Herrick's largest project was the editing of the *Consolidated Library of Modern Cooking and Household Recipes*, a five-volume set of cookbooks that was published in 1904.

Along with her writing career, Herrick supported a number of community and national organizations. She was active in Sorosis, a pioneering New York women's club, and was a member of the National Society of the Colonial Dames of America. Between 1908 and 1912, she was the comanager of the Chamber Recital Company. In the late 1920s, Herrick retired to Washington, D.C., to be near her son Horace. She died there in 1944, following a fall in which she fractured her leg.

SOURCES:

James, Edward T., ed. *Notable American Women*. Cambridge, MA: The Belknap Press of Harvard University Press, 1971.

Barbara Morgan,
Melrose, Massachusetts

Herrick, Elinore Morehouse (1895–1964)

American labor-relations specialist. *Born in New York on June 15, 1895; died in North Carolina in 1964; daughter of Daniel W. (a Unitarian minister) and Martha Adelaide (Bird) Morehouse (a teacher and educational administrator); attended the MacDuffie School and Technical High School, both in Springfield, Massachusetts; attended Barnard College, 1913–15; Antioch College, Yellow Springs, Ohio, B.A., 1929; married H. Terhune Herrick (a chemical engineer and son of* ****Christine Herrick,*** in 1916 (divorced 1921); children: two sons, Snowden Terhune (1919), and Horace Terhune, Jr. (1920).

A specialist on labor-management relations, and head of the New York office of the National Labor Relations Board for seven years during the Depression, Elinore Herrick obtained her expertise through personal experience on both the labor and management side of the table.

The daughter of a Unitarian minister and an educator, Herrick was born in 1895 in New York but attended school in Springfield, Massachusetts, where the family moved when she was a child. She entered Barnard College in 1913, earning her tuition by working as a cub reporter on a New York newspaper. She left college after two years, married in 1916, and, after three miscarriages, gave birth to two sons.

When her marriage ended in 1921, Herrick found herself with two children to support and no skills, so she embarked on a series of factory jobs, including a position in a shoe-blacking plant and another in a paper-box factory. Eventually, she moved to Buffalo to work at Du Pont's new rayon plant, where, within a year, she had been promoted from pieceworker to production manager. This was due, in part, to several labor-saving and safety devices she had invented after being injured by a defective machine. In 1923, when Du Pont opened a factory near Nashville, Tennessee, Herrick was named production manager and, as such, was responsible for training and supervising 1,800 workers. Although she quickly brought production in the new facility up to the level of established plants, Du Pont made it clear that there would be no promotions. In

1927, feeling dead-ended, Herrick left to further pursue her education.

While attending Antioch College in Yellow Springs, Ohio, Herrick ran a boarding house and worked as an administrative assistant to the president of the college. Often making up 16 beds before leaving in the morning, she received a degree in economics in two years and returned to New York, where she went to work as executive secretary of the New York Consumers League. While there, she campaigned for passage of the New York State minimum wage law and also oversaw studies of the canning, candy, and laundry industries. The studies, aimed at improving conditions for workers, resulted in two publications, *Women in Canneries* (1932) and *Cut Rate Wages* (1933).

In 1933, with the formation of the National Recovery Act, Herrick was tapped to join the labor-relations staff, a position that led to her appointment as the only woman to head a regional office of the National Labor Relations Board, accountable for enforcing the Wagner Act in the eastern New York, northern New Jersey, and Connecticut areas. The $7,000 annual salary the position carried was almost unheard of for a woman during the Depression, but Herrick earned every penny. During the seven years she occupied the post, she administered 6,000 labor cases involving over one million workers. While her decisions often drew criticism from both management and labor, she also received high marks for her impartiality. Herrick, who made no apologies for her sympathy with labor, told **Beulah Amidon** of *Survey Graphic*: "Labor has had the thin end for years. The purpose of the Wagner Act, as I understood it, is to give labor a chance. My job is to protect the rights of labor under the law. But it is my duty to be objective in analysis, to come to my decision not on the basis of my sympathies but of the evidence."

During the war, Herrick resigned from the National Labor Relations Board to become director of personnel and labor relations for the Todd Shipyards, which employed over 140,000 workers in ten port cities. Her challenge began with overseeing the hiring and training of women to replace the men who had been drafted into the armed services. Now approaching 50, Herrick often put in 16-to-18-hour days to oversee three shifts of workers that operated seven days a week.

At the end of the war in 1945, Herrick became head of the personnel department of the New York *Herald Tribune,* with occasional editorial assignments. She used her columns to defend democratic procedures and individual rights. In one of her early editorials, "Reforms That Unions Must Have," Herrick urged labor unions to eliminate objectionable practices and constitutional provisions that discriminated on racial and gender basis. In another column, Herrick defended State Department employees who had been dismissed under loyalty requirements: "When the Government discharges people for security reasons, it must let the accused know the charges and have a real opportunity to answer."

In addition to her editorials for the *Herald Tribune,* Herrick contributed articles to *New Republic, Nation, Independent Woman,* and *The New York Times Magazine,* among other periodicals. Outside of employment responsibilities, she served the labor panel of the American Arbitration Association and the arbitration panel of the New York State Board of Mediation. She was also an organizer and director of the American Labor Party's campaign for reelection of President Franklin Roosevelt in 1936.

Herrick, who was once described as "a good mother, cook, executive, mechanic, mediator, dressmaker, philosopher, and scrapper," relaxed by playing the piano and puttering in her garden. Plump and decidedly unglamourous, she was an open, friendly woman with a well-documented sense of humor. Once, as she viewed a photograph of herself taken at a Todd ship launching just as champagne splattered all over her, she remarked, "Is this the face that launched a thousand ships?" Elinore Morehouse Herrick retired in 1954, due to ill health, and died in 1964 in North Carolina.

SOURCES:

Rothe, Anna, ed. *Current Biography.* NY: H.W. Wilson, 1947.

Barbara Morgan,
Melrose, Massachusetts

Herrick, Genevieve Forbes

(1894–1962)

American newspaper reporter. *Name variations: Mrs. John Origen Herrick. Born in Chicago, Illinois, on May 21, 1894; died in New Mexico in 1962; daughter of Frank G. Forbes and Carolyn D. (Gee) Forbes; attended Lake View High School; Northwestern, B.A., 1916; University of Chicago, M.A., 1917; married John Origen Herrick, on September 6, 1924; no children.*

Like many early female newspaper reporters, Genevieve Herrick started out as a schoolteacher. She joined the *Chicago Tribune* in 1918 and first gained national recognition in 1921, with a story about immigrant women, which she wrote while traveling incognito in steerage. Her later testimony before Congress led to an investigation of the practices of immigration officials on Ellis Island.

Despite her excellent education and background, Herrick spent most of the 1920s covering the crime beat. One of her biggest coups was an interview with the notorious mobster Al Capone. She met her husband, a fellow reporter, when they were both covering the Leopold-Loeb trial in 1924. Continuing to work after her marriage, Herrick was assigned to Washington during the Depression and participated in *__Eleanor Roosevelt__'s famous women-only press conferences. However, the strongly anti-Roosevelt *Tribune* did not appreciate Herrick's admiration of the New Deal Democrats, and she was forced to resign in 1934. Injuries suffered in an accident the following year prevented her from finding a comparable job, although she continued to write for other newspapers throughout the 1930s. During World War II, Herrick provided publicity for several government agencies and eventually became head of the magazine and book division of the Office of War Information. She and her husband John Origen Herrick retired to New Mexico in 1951, and she died there in 1962.

Herring, Geilles.

See joint entry on Somerville and Ross.

Herrmann, Liselotte (1909–1938)

German anti-Nazi activist and the first mother in Nazi Germany to be executed for her political beliefs.

Name variations: Lilo Herrmann. Born in Berlin, Germany, on June 23, 1909; convicted of espionage and high treason in 1937 and executed in Berlin on June 20, 1938; daughter of Richard Herrmann and Elise Fänger Herrmann; never married; children: son, Walter (b. May 15, 1934).

Celebrated in the German Democratic Republic (GDR, East Germany) as a national hero in the struggle against fascism, Liselotte Herrmann had many streets and schools named after her before the collapse of the GDR in 1989–90. In the Federal Republic (West Germany), on the other hand, her life and death were known to only a few scholars and leftist activists who disagreed with the official view that Germans who fought Nazism because of a belief in Marxism and Communism were not "genuine" members of the German resistance, but rather traitors motivated by a fanatical willingness to serve the interests of Moscow. Two generations after Herrmann's execution, bitter controversy over those Germans who resisted Hitler as Communists continues to rage in a now-united Germany. Many Germans still believe that such resisters were little more than agents of an equally vile dictator, Joseph Stalin. In the midst of an argument based on stereotypes of what motivated these resisters to risk their lives, the story of Liselotte Herrmann provides a human face to Germany's Communist resistance.

She was born in Berlin in 1909, five years before World War I, into a family that was financially secure and intellectually liberal. Her father Richard was a successful architect; as a result, the Herrmann family remained largely unaffected by the social and economic turmoil that made life bleak for many millions of Germans during and after the war. Lilo, as Liselotte was known, began her studies in 1915 at one of Berlin's respected private lyceums, that of Dr. Böhm in the Invalidenstrasse. Between 1922 and 1927, the Herrmanns lived in Siegen, then in Frankfurt am Main and returned to Berlin in 1927; there Lilo continued her education at the prestigious Viktoria-Luise-Schule in the upscale Wilmersdorf section of the German capital.

In 1929, Herrmann was awarded her *Abitur,* the school-leaving certificate that qualified her to enroll at one of Germany's universities. By this time, she had already formed strong views on the many problems facing both her country and the world. Although quiet and reserved, she could speak candidly and was described in the student newspaper of the Viktoria-Luise-Schule in the following fashion: "Liselotte is honest and upright, and tells the truth to all, no matter who it might be." She showed aptitude in several fields, had a deep love of nature, and displayed artistic insight, particularly in her sketches and drawings. The year she completed her secondary education (1929) marked the end of a period of prosperity that had in fact never reached the lives of many Germans. Four years of sacrifice during World War I and a devastating monetary inflation in the early 1920s had wiped out the savings of Germany's solid *Mittelstand,* a middle class that made virtues of hard work and thrift. Embittered, many of these men and women were attracted to radical political movements, including a newly formed Nazi Party led by Adolf Hitler.

Although Lilo's parents moved to Stuttgart in the summer of 1929, she chose to remain in Berlin. Having decided to study chemistry at the university, she worked for some months at a chemical factory as a laboratory assistant.

Throughout 1929, the political situation in Berlin and indeed in much of Germany took a decided turn for the worse. Bloody May Day demonstrations in Berlin in the spring of that year were a barometer of bitterness among many industrial workers toward a society which they believed was shortchanging them and their children. Disturbed by a society on the brink of social collapse, Herrmann turned to the ideology of Marxism and the political movement of Communism, as did many intellectuals during this period. While still a student, she had written a term paper on Marxism. After graduation, her interest in Marxist theory, as well as the apparently dramatic social advances taking place in the Soviet Union, caught her attention. A more concrete indication of her growing belief in Marxism came when she joined one of the Berlin branches of the League of German Socialist Students.

Starting with the winter semester of 1929–30, Herrmann began her studies in chemistry at the Stuttgart Institute of Technology (TH Stuttgart) and soon resumed her political activities, becoming an active member of the Red Student Group at the TH. She also joined the local branch of the Communist Youth Organization (CYO). Among the local Communist activists whom she met during the next few years was the author Friedrich Wolf, who enjoyed a reputation for his revolutionary plays and defense of women's right to have legal abortions. Years after Herrmann's execution, Wolf would write movingly about her strong social conscience and love of children.

At the end of 1931, after completing four semesters at the TH Stuttgart, Herrmann transferred her field of study from chemistry to biology and moved to the University of Berlin, where she found sufficient time from her studies to engage in almost daily political activities. By the end of 1931, she had joined the Communist Party of Germany (KPD), which had a numerically small but enthusiastic group at the university. With most of its faculty hostile to democracy and in many cases even sympathizing with the growing Nazi movement, the University of Berlin presented an inhospitable terrain for revolutionary-minded Marxist students like Herrmann. She was particularly disturbed by Berlin's Nazi students' use of violence against the university's Jewish students and faculty members. Disregarding threats to her physical safety, she took the initiative on several occasions to attempt to protect these increasingly endangered members of an academic community in decay.

The Nazi takeover of Germany, which began with Hitler's appointment as chancellor of Germany on January 30, 1933, rapidly made a dramatic impact on the nation's higher education. A "reform" law in April gave the green light for a drastic purge of both Jewish and "un-German" (i.e., democratic and leftist) students and faculty. In May 1933, Nazi students and their allies publicly burned books they deemed to be subversive of the new national spirit. At the University of Berlin—the intellectual heart and soul of a city which the Nazis would always despise because so many of its citizens were "Reds" or Jews or both—a thoroughgoing racial and ideological purge took place. In July 1933, 111 students of the University of Berlin, including Herrmann, were expelled. The immediate pretext for Herrmann's expulsion was that she had signed a petition attacking the evils of fascism and war. Then, and for the remainder of her brief life, Herrmann viewed fascism as the incarnation of inhumanity. Even before they took over the German Reich, radical elements within the Nazi Party held non-Jews like Herrmann in greater disdain than Jews, expecting "Aryan" men and women to instinctively welcome the dawn of a glorious new era for Germany, the Third Reich.

German Democratic Republic postage stamp honoring Liselotte Herrmann, issued on September 7, 1960.

After her expulsion, Herrmann remained in Berlin working in an increasingly dangerous underground environment. She assumed a false name and stayed active as a member of the German capital's illegal Communist youth cadre. Herrmann earned her living by caring for infants and gave birth on May 15, 1934, to a son she named Walter. Because of the dangers and uncertainties of the underground activities she was engaged in, Herrmann never married the child's father and would not divulge his name. He may have been one of her closest collaborators in the resistance movement, Walter Ehlen. Arrested in August 1936, Ehlen was sentenced to 15 years' hard labor at the notorious Mauthausen concentration camp, where he was killed on May 4, 1945, only one day before the camp's liberation.

By September 1934, the Gestapo and other arms of the Nazi state had infiltrated many of the resistance cells in Berlin, and Herrmann left an increasingly perilous situation in the German capital. Arriving in Stuttgart with her infant son, she moved in with her parents. Soon she found work as a secretary in her father's engineering firm. Herrmann also continued her illegal political activities and, by the end of 1934, had established contacts with Stuttgart's small but active underground Communist movement. In January 1935, she met the political head of the illegal KPD in the province of Württemberg, the pattern-maker Stefan Lovasz (1901–1938), with whom she saw eye to eye on virtually all issues of strategy and tactics. Her responsibilities within the underground KPD organization included gathering information on the morale of workers in Stuttgart's major industrial enterprises, including the Bosch and Daimler factories. She also functioned as secretary of the central KPD organization and was responsible for maintaining contact with allied Communist cells in Switzerland. Part of Herrmann's broad mandate was to discover any and all information on secret German rearmament plans. In this sensitive area, the discoveries made by the young locksmith Artur Görlitz (1907–1938) were of crucial importance. Employed at the Dornier industrial facility, Görlitz was able to find incriminating evidence of major restructuring in his factory from peacetime production to an armaments agenda.

More evidence of Nazi secret rearmament came from Josef Steidle (1908–1938), who worked in the boat division of the Bosch factory. Another member of Herrmann's organization, Eugen Beck, discovered plans for a secret German Army munitions facility to be built in the area of Scheuen near Celle. The final member of Herrmann's resistance circle was the salesman Alfred Grözinger (1904–1959), whose espionage work was of lesser significance to the group. Although, when smuggled out of Germany, the information was published as exposés in the still-free nations, a complacent world was not sufficiently alarmed to take serious measures against the Third Reich.

Betrayed by an agent who had penetrated the KPD organization, Herrmann was arrested in her parents' home early in the morning of December 7, 1935. A search by the Gestapo discovered several highly incriminating documents, including a copy of the plan for the Scheuen munitions plant, numerous papers of the illegal KPD organization, and banned Marxist literature. Incarcerated for the next 19 months in Stuttgart's police jail on the Büchsenstrasse, Herrmann was subjected to various forms of physical, emotional and psychological torture and appeared before the investigating judge on crutches. On one occasion, her captors placed her small son in the next cell and had him ask her when she was coming home. On another occasion, she was warned that Walter would be placed in the home of a dedicated Nazi family if she did not provide information on her comrades. For the dreaded interrogation sessions, she was taken from her cell to Stuttgart Gestapo headquarters, known to locals as the "Hotel Silber" on the Dorotheenstrasse, where despite physical and mental torture she never revealed the desired information concerning the membership and nature of underground KPD cells in Württemberg. She informed her interrogators on March 31, 1936, "I simply do not wish to make any further statements." After this and similar remarks, she was written off by her captors and the word *Unverbesserliche* (no change can be expected) entered into her file.

The trial of Liselotte Herrmann, Stefan Lovasz, Josef Steidle, Artur Görlitz, and Alfred Grözinger began at Stuttgart's People's Court on June 8, 1937. All defendants were accused of having engaged in "preparations for high treason," a charge that in Nazi Germany almost always resulted in a sentence of death. The first hours of the trial were open to the public but the afternoon session and all of the remaining deliberations of the Nazi court were held in closed session, the ostensible reason being that some of the testimony would be "injurious to the security of the state." Although 27 witnesses had been invited to present testimony, only 14 of these actually appeared during the trial. The outcome did not surprise the defendants. Announced on the morning of June 12, 1937, the verdict was one of guilty for all five. Alfred Grözinger was sentenced to 12 years' hard labor. The other four, including Herrmann, received the death sentence. These four were taken to Berlin, and

Herrmann was the first to be incarcerated, at the Berlin women's prison on the Barnimstrasse. In the spring of 1938, a few weeks before her execution, Herrmann was moved to the Berlin-Plötzensee penitentiary. During her last year, she wrote letters to her parents which invariably mentioned her son with tenderness. One letter simply stated, "It is very difficult to leave and also to say good-bye to a child, knowing that Germany will be destroyed by war."

Throughout the time of her incarceration, major protests were raised in many European countries against carrying out her death sentence. The fact that she was not only a woman but the mother of a young child was noted in virtually all of the protests, which took place in the United Kingdom, France, Belgium, Czechoslovakia, Switzerland, Norway, Sweden, and several other nations. The Nazi regime remained sensitive regarding its propaganda image abroad, and in a Gestapo report of March 2, 1938, to the Reich Minister of Justice it was noted that in the case of Liselotte Herrmann "for months the protest letters have accumulated to the point that they have turned into virtual mountains."

The worldwide protests were to no avail. After a final authorization from Hitler, the sentence against Lilo Herrmann and her colleagues was carried out by decapitation at Berlin's Plötzensee penitentiary on June 20, 1938. Although a considerable number of women had already been executed on political charges in Nazi Germany by this time—current research indicates the number to be about 15, with many more losing their lives under unexplained circumstances—none of them had been mothers. (The first woman to be executed for political reasons was **Emma Thieme** in August 1933, followed by **Christina Liess** that September.) The objections at Herrmann's death were numerous and impassioned. In a "protest against the murder of a German mother" which appeared in the July 3, 1938, issue of the German exile newspaper *Deutsche Volkszeitung* in Prague, the signers included the renowned authors Heinrich Mann and Lion Feuchtwanger. Even some loyal Nazi women were distressed by the execution of a young mother. One wrote, "Was it really necessary to kill a German mother because of her opinions? With 99 percent of the *Volk* solidly on Hitler's side, why did someone choose to make her baby motherless?" In the United Kingdom, several aristocratic women sent a joint protest telegram to Adolf Hitler, with copies to the British press, noting that such a bloody deed had endangered the chances of the two nations ever achieving a political detente.

In addition to the streets and schools named in her honor in the former German Democratic Republic, major works of art, including a musical melodrama by noted composer Paul Dessau and a biographical poem by Friedrich Wolf, were created. Herrmann remains for many a powerful cultural icon of that area's historical distinctness, with her name continuing to mark streets and child-care centers in Berlin, Chemnitz, Erfurt, Greifswald, Teltow, Weimar, and other towns and cities. Her legacy of courage and sacrifice, however, remains controversial to many Germans. While some regard her as a genuine hero of the struggle against the evils of Nazism, others continue to see her as an agent of an alien ideology which competed with but was by no means superior to fascism.

SOURCES:

Altmann, Peter, et al. *Der deutsche antifaschistische Widerstand 1933–1945 in Bildern und Dokumenten.* Frankfurt am Main: Röderberg-Verlag, 1975.

Behr, Alfred. "Ein schwäbischer Streit der Historiker um ein Denkmal: Ende einer DDR-Legende über Lilo Herrmann," in *Frankfurter Allgemeine Zeitung.* February 4, 1993, p. 4.

Bohn, Willi. *Stuttgart Geheim! Widerstand und Verfolgung, 1933–1945.* 3rd ed. Frankfurt am Main: Röderberg-Verlag, 1978.

Burghardt, Max. *Briefe, die nie geschrieben wurden: Lilo Herrmann zum Gedächtnis.* 2nd ed. Berlin: Verlag Neues Leben, 1968.

———, et al. *So kannten wir Dich, Lilo Herrmann, eine deutsche Frau und Mutter.* Berlin: Verlag Neues Leben, 1954.

Clemens, Ditte. *Schweigen über Lilo: Die Geschichte der Liselotte Herrmann.* Ravensburg: Verlag Otto Maier, 1993.

"Der Proteststurm gegen die Ermordung Lilo Herrmanns," in *Rundschau über Politik, Wirtschaft und Arbeiterbewegung.* Vol. 7, no. 35. July 7, 1938, p. 1191.

Lilo Herrmann: Eine Stuttgarter Widerstandskämpferin. Stuttgart: Vereinigung der Verfolgten des Naziregimes—Bund der Antifaschisten, Landesverband Baden—Württemberg, 1993.

Weber, Ernst. "Eine deutsche Mutter hingerichtet!," in *Rundschau über Politik, Wirtschaft und Arbeiterbewegung.* Vol. 7, no. 33. June 23, 1938, pp. 1115–1116.

Wolf, Friedrich. *Lilo Herrmann, die Studentin von Stuttgart: Ein biographisches Poem.* Berlin: Aufbau-Verlag, 1963.

Zorn, Monika. *Hitlers zweimal getötete Opfer: Westdeutsche Endlösung des Antifaschismus auf dem Gebiet der DDR.* Freiburg im Breisgau: Ahriman-Verlag, 1994.

RELATED MEDIA:

Dessau, Paul. *Lilo Herrmann: Ein Melodram für eine Sprechstimme, sechs Soloinstrumente und gemischten Chor nach dem gleichnamigen biographischen Poem von Friedrich Wolf.* [Berlin Classics CD 0090702, Music in the GDR, Vol. 2: Vocal Music, 1995].

John Haag,
Associate Professor, University of Georgia, Athens, Georgia

Hersch, Jeanne (1910—)

Swiss philosopher. Name variations: Jeanne Hersche. Born in Geneva, Switzerland, on July 13, 1910; attended primary and secondary school in Geneva; granted degree in literary history from the University of Geneva, 1931; University of Basel, Ph.D., 1946.

Taught at École Internationale in Geneva (1933–55); received the Montaigne Prize; was professor of philosophy, University of Geneva (1956–77); served as director of the Department of Philosophy, UNESCO, Paris (1966–68); was Swiss representative on the executive council of UNESCO (1970–72); was president of the Karl Jaspers Foundation in Basel; served as guest scholar for the Karl Jaspers Lectures, University of Oldenburg, c. 1995.

Selected works: Entretiens Sur le Temps: sons la direction de Jeanne Hersch et René Poirier *(*Conversations on Time: Under the Direction of Jeanne Hersch and René Poirier, *1967);* Le Droit d'être un Homme *(*Birthright of Man, *1968);* Problemes Actuels de la Liberté *(*Contemporary Problems of Freedom, *1976);* Karl Jaspers *(1979);* Die Voraussetz ungen der Freiheit in den Medien: Analysen und Vorschläge *(*Prerequisites for Freedom of the Press: Analysis and Suggestions, *1982);* Die Hoffnung Mensch zu Sein *(*The Hope of Being Human*);* Das Philosophische Staunen *(*Philosophical Amazement*);* Schwierige Freiheit: Gerspräche mit Jeanne Hersch *(*Difficult Freedom: Conversations with Jeanne Hersch*).*

Jeanne Hersch was born in Geneva, Switzerland, in 1910. Her education included undergraduate work at the Sorbonne in Paris, in Heidelberg, Freiburg, and Geneva, culminating in a degree in literary history from the University of Geneva in 1931. For 22 years, she taught at the École Internationale in Geneva. Hersch traveled to Chile (1935–36) and Thailand (1938–39), then completed her doctoral studies at the University of Basel in 1946. She received a post-doctoral teaching qualification and lectured privately for the next ten years, then worked as a professor of philosophy at the University of Geneva from 1956 to 1977. During her academic career, she was a visiting professor at Pennsylvania State University (1959) and at Hunter College, New York University (1961–62), and was extremely active in UNESCO.

As a disciple of the philosopher Karl Jaspers, Hersch has been concerned with how human existence relates to truth. Also influenced by Immanuel Kant and his recognition that we must accept ourselves as subjective knowers, she sees a consciousness of history as helpful to this acceptance. Her political philosophy emphasizes the importance of freedom, advocating a socialism tempered with democracy.

SOURCES:

Kersey, Ethel M. *Women Philosophers: a Bio-critical Source Book.* NY: Greenwood Press, 1989.

Rodden, Warwick J. "Jeanne Hersche," in Katharina Wilson, ed., *Encyclopedia of Continental Women Writers.* NY: Garland, 1991.

Catherine Hundleby, M.A.
Philosophy, University of Guelph, Guelph, Ontario, Canada

Herschel, Caroline (1750–1848)

German-born astronomer who assisted her brother, Sir William Herschel, in the discovery of the planet Uranus, was the first woman to discover a comet, and is credited with identifying eight comets and some 2,500 nebulae. *Name variations: Lina. Pronunciation: HER-shel. Born Caroline Lucretia Herschel on March 16, 1750, in Gartengemeinde, Hanover, Germany; died on January 9, 1848, in Hanover; daughter of Isaac (a musician) and Anna Ilse Herschel; sister of Sir William Herschel and aunt of Sir John Herschel, both famous astronomers; tutored by her father; no formal education; never married; no children.*

Awards: gold medal of the Royal Astronomical Society (1828); honorary member of the Royal Astronomical Society (1835); honorary member of the Royal Irish Academy (1838); gold medal of science from the king of Prussia (1846).

Moved from Hanover to Bath, England, to live with brother William (August 1772); had singing career in England (1773–82); served as assistant to William in astronomy (1782–1822); discovered her first comet (August 1, 1786); completed Index of stars in "British Catalogue" (1798); completed list of errata with 561 omitted stars, published by the Royal Society (1798); retired to Hanover (1822–48).

Caroline Herschel was a pioneer in the field of astronomy. She was the first woman to discover a comet, and by the end of her life she had been credited with the discovery of seven more. She also identified and catalogued some 2,500 nebulae. She was the key assistant to her brother Sir William Herschel and was instrumental in his discovery of the planet Uranus in 1782. Although she received limited recognition for her work during her old age, for the most part her contributions have been overshadowed by those of her brother and his equally famous son, Sir John Herschel.

Born in Hanover, Germany, on March 16, 1750, Caroline Lucretia Herschel was the youngest of eight children; she had four brothers and three sisters. Her father Isaac Herschel was an ex-soldier who had fought in the War of Austrian Succession with George II (king of England and elector of Hanover). Wounded during the war, Isaac later supported his family by giving music lessons. He taught Caroline to read and to write and gave her violin lessons. Caroline's mother **Anna Ilse Herschel**, however, showed little patience for academic pursuits. She insisted that Caroline take part in the day-to-day running of the Herschel household, teaching her sewing and knitting. Caroline was set to work darning her brother's stockings; she was so little that the stockings reached the floor while she stood finishing the toe.

Herschel's early memories of her family were less than happy. She received harsh treatment from all of her brothers except William, 11 years her elder, who showed great affection for his little sister. Of her family members, William and her father Isaac were the only two whom she regarded with fondness. When her father died in March 1767, Caroline was heartbroken. She agonized over her future, reflecting in her journal that the only marketable skills she had were in housework. But her plain looks and lack of a dowry narrowed her chances of matrimony considerably. Constant toil in the Herschel household made it impossible for her to acquire any formal education. So, at 17, Caroline began taking secret lessons in embroidery, hair-braiding, and dressmaking from a consumptive girl who lived across the street, in hopes that one day she could secure a position as a governess in some family "where the want of a knowledge of French would be no objection."

In 1772, Herschel's dim prospects brightened when her brother William, who had settled in England to work as a concert director, invited her to join him in order to train for a career in singing. Flabbergasted by the offer, Caroline expressed grave doubts that she could suddenly be transformed from a domestic drudge into a prima donna. She was determined, nevertheless, to seize the opportunity to make a better life for herself and began exercising her voice. She practiced by mimicking the solo parts of violin concertos with a gag between her teeth, ignoring the sneers of her disbelieving relatives. When Caroline's mother balked at releasing such a useful household servant, William agreed to give Anna monetary compensation with which she could hire a housekeeper in her daughter's place.

Finally, filled with trepidation and doubt that she had made the right decision in venturing to another country and abandoning all that was familiar, Caroline left Hanover for England in August of 1772. After an uncomfortable journey with William across the English Channel, she recalled being "thrown like balls by two sailors" onto English soil. They finally arrived in Bath "almost annihilated." Caroline immediately began intensive training in English, arithmetic, and singing. In return for her room, board and lessons, she took over household duties for her brothers William and Alexander and responsibility for shopping and accounts-keeping. Household duties were shared with her brother's housekeeper, a temperamental Welsh woman whose brusque manner often wreaked havoc on Caroline's fragile nerves.

Caroline Herschel

Herschel gradually became accustomed to a more cosmopolitan existence in England, although she was continually appalled by the expense of clothing and equipage. She described the great majority of society women whom she met as "very little better than idiots." While working strenuously at her singing and deportment lessons, she concentrated especially on removing the last vestiges of her German accent from her English pronunciation. Within only a few months, she began singing soprano parts at small parties in Bath. In the winter of 1772, she sang the lead in concerts conducted by William in Bath and Bristol and was so successful that she received an offer to appear in a music festival in Birmingham. She refused, expressing her resolution to sing only with her brother.

Before making her formal debut, Herschel studied under a dancing mistress responsible for drilling her "for a gentlewoman." With her debut in 1773, she was soon hailed as "an ornament to the stage." She began to hope that she had finally found a way in which to make an independent life. An invaluable asset to her brother William, Herschel arranged rehearsals and copied scores, while working indefatigably to maintain the household.

But no sooner had her musical star begun to rise than her hopes for a successful singing career were dashed. By the mid-1770s, more of William's attention had turned away from music, toward astronomy. Over 50 years later, Caroline Herschel would recall: "I have been thoroughly annoyed and hindered in my endeavours at perfecting myself in any branch of knowledge by which I could hope to gain a creditable livelihood." Her utter devotion to William, however, prevented her from voicing her disappointment, and she set out to assist her brother in his new obsession with grinding telescope mirrors for astronomical observations. Although she and William still performed until 1782, William gradually gave up music to spend his time perfecting his new pursuit.

The art of mirror grinding was a demanding one, requiring long hours of patient labor to produce a mirror free from distortions. William worked tirelessly polishing his mirrors, while Herschel read aloud to him from *Don Quixote* and *The Arabian Nights* and fed him his meals "by putting victuals by bits into his mouth." As William learned to master this new craft, Herschel learned with him and eventually became proficient at copying scientific papers, interpreting tables, and performing complex mathematical calculations involving trigonometry, logarithms, and conversions from sidereal (time measured by the diurnal motion of stars) into solar time (a sidereal day is about four minutes shorter than a solar day, with hours, minutes, and seconds all proportionally shorter). She humbly stated, "I became in time as useful a member of the workshop as a boy might to his master in the first year of his apprenticeship," and lamented that her memory was like "sand, in which everything could be inscribed with ease but as easily effaced." She admitted to always carrying a copy of the multiplication tables in her dress pocket; but, nevertheless, her calculations were unfailingly accurate.

With his sister's help, William discovered the planet Uranus in 1782, and from then on he devoted himself exclusively to astronomical observation. They moved from Bath to Datchet, where they inhabited a "dilapidated gazebo" with damp walls and falling plaster. Beginning in 1782, Herschel was allowed to use a small telescope to make her own observations. In late 1783, her efforts were rewarded with the discovery of two nebulae (clouds of interstellar gas and dust), one in Andromeda and the other in Cetus. These discoveries created in her a real and abiding enthusiasm for her new profession.

In December 1783, William began constructing a 20-foot telescope, while his sister carried instruments, kept time and made measurements, regardless of exhaustion, cold or hunger. She often stayed awake all night for days on end, without complaint, merely remarking, "I had the comfort to see that my brother was satisfied with my endeavours to assist him." Once, when she was running through the snow, she fell over a large hook, which tore such a deep wound in her leg that the doctor declared it would entitle a soldier to six weeks' convalescence. Herschel cursorily dressed the wound and stayed at home for a few nights, expressing relief in her journal that the cloudy weather ensured that William "was no loser through the accident."

As she discovered increasing numbers of nebulae, eventually 2,500 in all, she became more and more devoted to arranging catalogues to aid William's observations. She also wrote out his papers to send to the Royal Astronomical Society and kept track of all his discoveries and calculations. During the summer months, she assisted him in relentless mirror grinding and so excelled in this craft that William eventually let her finish one herself. In her brother's absence, she never tired of sweeping the skies for comets, squeezing her own observations in between her regular duties of maintaining the larger telescopes for William, and keeping track of his observations.

During one of William's absences, on August 1, 1786, Herschel spotted a round, hazy object which she took to be a comet. Her observations during the next 24 hours confirmed this discovery. Over the following 11 years, she discovered a total of eight comets. She was the first woman to achieve this, and as such she gained immediate renown. As proud as she was of her comets, however, Herschel always belittled her own achievements in favor of her brother. She was described by contemporaries as "very little, very gentle, very modest, very ingenuous" and "by no means prepossessing, but an excellent, kindhearted creature." In recognition of her discovery, King George III officially appointed her as her brother's assistant and awarded her a salary of £50 per year. She was thrilled to receive "the first money I ever in all my lifetime thought myself to be at liberty to spend to my own liking."

William married the following year, and although Herschel expressed deep regret that she "had to give up the place of his housekeeper" and move into her own lodgings, she eventually became devoted to her sister-in-law. She continued to come to William's observatory each night to assist in his observations. In 1796, she began compiling an index to the stars listed in the "British Catalogue" and added a list of errata with 561 omitted stars. The Royal Astronomical Society financed the publication of her useful compilations in 1798.

Her friendship with **Madame Beckendorff**, an old friend from Hanover who became one of Queen ***Charlotte of Mecklenburg-Strelitz**'s ladies-in-waiting, brought the Herschels into a close friendship with the royal family. The queen and princesses were especially charmed by Herschel's company, and they required her attendance on so many occasions that they became something of an inconvenience. Her popularity with the royal family put her in direct contact with dignitaries and scientists from around the world.

In 1809, Herschel's brother Dietrich, "ruined in health, spirit and fortune," arrived in England, and, as she recalled, "according to the old Hanoverian custom, I was the only one from whom all domestic comforts were expected." He stayed with her for over four years, and she gave a small glimpse at the hardship his arrival brought to her life with her later reflection, "I hope I acquitted myself to everybody's satisfaction. . . . [T]he time I bestowed on Dietrich was taken entirely from my sleep, or what is generally allowed for meals, which were mostly taken running, or sometimes forgotten entirely. But why think of it now?"

By 1817, Caroline Herschel was increasingly absorbed with concern over William's health. By the following year, he was evidently aware that his end was near, and he charged his sister with the task of sorting through every shelf and drawer of his study and making a list of their contents. William became a veritable invalid, but Herschel never ceased her devoted ministrations, noting in her journal with hope when he "walked with a firmer step than usual" and with sorrow when he was "unwell" and "low in spirits."

One month before William died in 1822, Herschel surrendered her entire property worth £500 to her brother Dietrich and announced her intention to retire to Hanover. She was then 73 and did not expect to live much longer. No one was more surprised than she when she survived another quarter of a century, and she soon lived to regret her impetuous decision. "From the moment I set foot on German ground," she recalled, "I found I was alone." Herschel had lived in England for 50 years, and she complained at "not finding Hanover or anyone in it, like what I left when the best of brothers took me with him to England in August, 1772."

Determined to stick to her promise, she remained in Hanover, leading a "solitary and useless life." She most regretted being unable to continue her work, remarking in a letter to her nephew John, himself an astronomer, that "at the heavens there is no getting, for the high roofs of the opposite houses." While in her new home, however, she completed a work which proved to be of immeasurable assistance to her nephew. She created a catalogue, arranged into zones, of all of William's nebulae and clusters, which her nephew Sir John Herschel would use as the foundation of his "General Catalogue" published in 1864. Using her Index, Sir John recalled, "I learned fully to appreciate the skill, diligence and accuracy which that indefatigable lady brought to bear on a task which only the most boundless devotion could have induced her to undertake, and enabled her to accomplish." For her work, Herschel received the gold medal of the Royal Astronomical Society in 1828. In 1835, she was made an honorary member of the Royal Astronomical Society, and three years later she was admitted into the Royal Irish Academy. This recognition was somewhat discomfiting to her. "I cannot help crying out loud to myself, every now and then, What is that for?" she wrote in her journal, and, later, "I think it is almost mocking me to look upon me as a Member of the Academy; I that have lived these eighteen years without finding so much as a single comet."

In her retirement, she indulged her old love of music and attended concerts and plays with such regularity that her absence generated public concern. She also entertained scientists and learned men, all of whom paid her a visit if ever in Hanover. Nevertheless, she regretted her "idle life" and "painful solitude," noting that "the few, few stars I can get at out of my window only cause me vexation, for to look for the small ones on the globe my eyes will not serve me any longer." One of her few consolations was in following the career of her nephew. When she heard of his upcoming trip to the Cape of Good Hope, she exclaimed, "If I were thirty or forty years younger, and could go too!" and she called his successful journey into the southern hemisphere "like a drop of oil supplying my expiring lamp." But she still thought of her brother William and exclaimed, "I fall into a reverie on what my dear nephew's father would have felt if such letters could have been directed to him, and cannot suppress my wish that *his* life instead of *mine* had been spared until this present moment."

As Herschel reached her 90s, she focused increasingly on the past. She wrote to her nephew in 1842: "all my bones ache so that I can hardly crawl," and she spent her time writing books of "Recollections" of Sir William Herschel's life. At age 92, she embarked upon a history of the Herschels which she was prevented from finishing by physical decline. For her 96th birthday, she received the gold medal of science from the king of Prussia. Caroline Herschel died peacefully on January 9, 1848. By her request, she was buried with a lock of "her revered brother's hair, and an old almanac used by her father."

In 1840, the seven-foot reflecting telescope with which Herschel made most of her discoveries was given to the Royal Astronomical Society. Some 40 years later, in 1889, Minor planet No. 281 was named "Lucretia" in her honor. Her "Journals," "Recollections" and correspondence are the only detailed materials available which chronicle her own and William's careers.

Throughout her life, Caroline Herschel remained a woman of iron will and boundless energy, whose sole desire seemed to be in helping others. In an age when women scientists were virtually unheard of, she was a dauntless pioneer in the field of astronomy. Yet, she downplayed her own achievements, remarking, "I did nothing for my brother but what a well-trained puppy-dog would have done; that is to say, I did what he commanded me." She wrote once to Sir John: "My only reason for saying so much of myself is to show with what miserable assistance your father made shift to obtain the means of exploring the heavens." It was this indomitable woman, however, whose work provided the foundation for the contribution of the Herschels to the field of astronomy.

SOURCES:

Clerke, Agnes Mary. *The Herschels and Modern Astronomy*. NY: Macmillan, 1895.

Herschel, John F. *Herschel At the Cape: Diaries and Correspondence of Sir John Herschel, 1834–1838*. Evans, David, et al., eds. Austin, TX: University of Texas Press, 1969.

Herschel, Mrs. John. *Mrs. John Herschel's Memoir and Correspondence of Caroline Herschel*. London, 1876.

Kimberly Estep Spangler,
Assistant Professor of History and Chair of the Division of Religion and Humanities at Friends University, Wichita, Kansas

Hersende of Champagne (fl. 12th c.)

French abbess and healer. *Name variations: Hersende of Fontevrault. Flourished in the early 12th century in southern France.*

Hersende of Champagne was a religious founder from a noble family of southern France. Like numerous other women of her station, she became a supporter of the religious reformer Robert d'Arbrissel. Robert preached many changes; chief among them was to build religious establishments with a convent and monastery together, with authority for both given to an abbess. Robert argued that a woman should oversee both houses because women's nurturing role as mothers made them most fit to be given responsibility for the welfare of others. This idea, and others along the same radical lines, made Robert very popular among upper-class, strong-willed women like Hersende. In response, Hersende planned several such double monasteries, with monks answering to an abbess, and endowed them with her own money. She became abbess at the large monastery of Fontevrault, and also acted as a healer.

Laura York,
Riverside, California

Hersende of Fontevrault (fl. 12th c.).

See Hersende of Champagne.

Hersende of France (fl. 1250)

French doctor and royal surgeon to Louis IX and Margaret of Provence. *Flourished in 1250 in Paris; married Jacques, apothecary to the king, around 1250.*

Hersende of France was one of the most notable of medieval women doctors. Details of her youth and family connections are obscure, but it is clear that she rose to renown in northern France for her great healing abilities and thorough knowledge of medicine as well as midwifery. She was given the honor of being chosen royal surgeon by King Louis IX (Saint Louis) and his queen, ***Margaret of Provence** (1221–1295). While serving in this position, Hersende met and married the king's apothecary, Jacques. When Louis and Margaret left France to lead the Eighth Crusade to Palestine in 1248, Hersende accompanied them.

She was Louis' principal physician and also acted as Margaret's midwife, attending the birth of a prince in 1250. The same year, still in Palestine, the royal doctor was granted a daily pension which she would collect for the rest of her life. Soon after, Hersende left the king and returned to France for unspecified reasons; perhaps she had tired of the dangerous lifestyle of crusading armies. She continued her work in medicine in Paris for some years.

Laura York,
Riverside, California

Hertford, countess of.

See Fitzrobert, Amicia (d. 1225).
Marshall, Isabel (1200–1240).
See Lacey, Maud (fl. 1230–1250).
See Matilda de Burgh (d. 1315).
See Grey, Catherine (c. 1540–1568).
See Seymour, Frances (1669–1754).

Hertford, duchess of.

See Joan of Acre (1272–1307).

Hertford, marquise of.

See Fitzroy, Isabel (1726–1782).

Hertha of Ysenburg and Budingen (1883–1972)

Princess of Schleswig-Holstein-Sonderburg-Glucksburg. *Born on December 27, 1883; died on May 30, 1972; daughter of Bruno, 3rd prince of Ysenburg and Budingen; married Albert, prince of Schleswig-Holstein-Sonderburg-Glucksburg, on September 15, 1920; children:* ****Ortrud of Schleswig-Holstein-Sonderburg-Glucksburg*** *(b. 1925).*

Heruswith (d. c. 690).

See Hilda of Whitby for sidebar on Hereswitha.

Hervé, Geneviève (c. 1622–1675).

See Bejart, Madeleine and Armande for sidebar on Geneviève Bejart.

Hervey, Mary (1700–1768)

Baroness of Ickworth. *Name variations: Mary Lepel or Lepell; Lady Mary Hervey. Born Mary Lepel or Lepell in 1700; died in 1768; daughter of Brigadier-General Lepel or Lepell; married John Hervey, Baron Hervey of Ickworth, in 1720.*

Born in 1700, Mary Lepel married Lord John Hervey, baron of Ickworth, in 1720. As Lady Mary Hervey, she was known for her beauty and lauded in the writings of Alexander Pope, John Gay, Philip Stanhope, 4th earl of Chesterfield, and Voltaire. Her correspondence to Reverend Edmund Morris, which took place between 1742 and 1768, was published in 1821; other correspondence was published in the letters of ***Henrietta Howard**, countess of Suffolk (1824). Lady Hervey's epitaph was written by Horace Walpole.

Hervorden, abbess of.

See Elizabeth of Bohemia (1618–1680).

Herz, Henriette (1764–1847)

German writer and Berlin society leader. *Name variations: Henrietta Herz. Born Henriette de Lemos in 1764; died in 1847; married Markus or Marcus Herz (1747–1803, a Jewish physician and philosopher); studied many languages.*

Born into an Orthodox Jewish family in 1764, Henriette Herz was a childhood friend of the writer, ***Dorothea Mendelssohn**. At 13, Henriette married Marcus Herz, a German physician and philosopher, who provided her education. She went on to become a well-known woman of culture and beauty. As a famous Jewish leader in Berlin society, Herz was the center of a brilliant salon for the greatest intellectuals of her day. Her memoirs and letters were published in 1984 under the title *Henriette Herz in Erinnerungen, Briefen und Zeugnissen* (Henriette Herz: Memoirs, Letters and Testimonies). Herz converted to Christianity in 1817.

Herzeleide (1918–1989)

Princess of Prussia. *Born Herzeleide Ina Marie Sophie Hohenzollern on December 25, 1918, in Bristow, Mecklenburg; died on March 22, 1989, in Munich, Germany; daughter of* ****Ina Maria of Bassewitz-Levitzow*** *(1888–1973) and Karl Heinrich, count von Bassewitz-Levetzow; married Charles Peter Francis Andrew, prince Biron von Curland, on August 16, 1938, in Potsdam; children:* ***Victoria Benigna Ina Marie****, princess von Curland (b. 1939); Ernest-John Charles Oscar, prince von Curland (b. 1940); Michael Charles Augustus, prince von Curland (b. 1944).*

Hess, Myra (1890–1965)

English musical prodigy and concert pianist who organized the daily concerts at the National Gallery for six-and-a-half years during World War II. *Name variations: Dame Myra Hess. Born Julia Myra Hess on February 25, 1890, in London, England; died in London on November 25, 1965; daughter of Frederick Solomon (a textile merchant) and Lizzie (Jacobs) Hess; attended Royal Academy of Music from age 13; never married; no children.*

Started music lessons at age five (1895); won Ada Lewis scholarship at the Royal Academy of Music (1903); made official debut (1907); had first major success with a performance of the Schumann piano concerto in Amsterdam (1912); gave American recital in New York City (1922); made first recordings for Columbia USA, including her famous arrangement of J.S. Bach's "Jesu, Joy of Man's Desiring," (1928); awarded the rank of Commander, Order of the British Empire (OBE) by King George V, the first instrumentalist to have received this distinction (1936); founded and organized daily chamber music concerts in wartime London at National Gallery with assistance of Sir Kenneth Clark (October 1, 1940); received rank of Dame Commander, Order of the British Empire (CBE) from King George VI (1941); received gold medal of the Royal Philharmonic Society, the second woman pianist to be granted the honor (1942); appeared in the 1,000th concert of the National Gallery series (1943); appointed Commander of the Order of Orange-Nassau by Queen Wilhelmina of the Netherlands (1943); gave last of National Gallery concerts (April 10, 1946); resumed career with successful annual tours in the United Kingdom, Europe and the U.S. (1950–60); gave last public concert, Royal Festival Hall, London (October 31, 1961).

In the fall of 1940, Germany's Adolf Hitler launched an ongoing bombing attack on England that became known as the Battle of Britain. Besieged and alone, the people of England, particularly London, carried on, and despite Hitler's predictions, they never became demoralized. One reason that has been given is the symbolic value found in a series of daily concerts held for six-and-a-half years every Monday through Friday, under the glass dome of London's National Gallery. Gathered under the gallery dome, sometimes amid bomb fragments and shards of glass, audiences listened to performers play some of the world's greatest music, rising up as if in answer to the war being rained down on them nightly from overhead. Organized by the renowned British pianist Myra Hess, these daily events became an inspiration to the people of the British Isles in their time of greatest crisis.

Born in London on February 25, 1890, Julia Myra Hess was the fourth child of Frederick Solomon Hess, a textile merchant, and **Lizzie Jacobs Hess**, who had grown up in the family of a well-to-do north-London shopkeeper and money lender. Myra's paternal grandfather, Samuel Hess, was an Alsatian Jew, from the region often in dispute between Germany and France, which he left for the more cosmopolitan London early in the 19th century. Samuel became a successful textile entrepreneur, married the English-born **Alice Cantor**, and built a stylish home in Islington, where the couple raised three sons and four daughters. Frederick, the oldest son, became a partner in his father's business, manufacturing most of the many accoutrements—buttons, insignia, straps, braid, embroidery—for British military uniforms, the London Police, and the distinctively uniformed beefeater guards of the London Tower, as well as richly embroidered ecclesiastical vestments and altar cloths.

Frederick and Lizzie Hess lived in a comfortable home at 86 Alexandra Road, where they had four children. **Irene**, John, and Herbert all preceded the youngest, who was named "Julia" for a paternal aunt who died; at age three, she began to be called Myra. After her birth, the family moved to 78 Boundary Road, in Hampstead, a larger house on a tree-lined street, surrounded with gardens. A nursery on the ground floor opened to the outside, where Myra's father and brothers cultivated vegetables and berries and raised chickens. The family nanny, a **Mrs. Bland**, took the children for daily walks sometimes as far as Hampstead Heath, where Myra was charmed by the sound of singing birds. Mrs. Bland believed in cold baths, plain food, and everyday clothes, and toys and treats were few, but the children's life had pleasures. The children were often taken to dinner and the theater in the West End, a source of keen delight for Myra.

The Hess family was proudly Jewish. Pork and ham were excluded from the table and the Sabbath was strictly observed. Family members were forbidden to ride, drive, or be driven anywhere on that day, and, after Myra's father and brothers attended synagogue on Friday night, the entire family sat down for the Sabbath-eve dinner, an event she recalled with pleasure throughout her life.

Like all her siblings, Myra was given musical instruction. The Misses Reason taught all four children, and Myra began cello lessons at age five. Finding the cello unwieldy, she abandoned it after a few months for the piano, an upright instrument that stood in the nursery. The other children soon grew tired of the lessons, but Myra continued to excel, and was still only seven when **Florence Reason** told Lizzie Hess that she had taught the child all she knew. Shortly thereafter, Myra underwent aptitude testing at Trinity College. Required to play scales, arpeggios, and selected pieces from a prescribed list, to sight read, and answer questions about theory and music history, she became the youngest child ever to receive a Trinity College certificate.

Myra's next teachers were Julian Pascal and Orlando Morgan, who taught her theory and piano at the Guildhall school. Both were composers and later dedicated works to her. Myra was ten, in 1900, when the family went to Brussels because her brother Herbert suffered asthma attacks during the cold English winters. Aware that her youngest child was a prodigy, Lizzie Hess protected the little girl and saw that her music lessons continued in Brussels through the winter months. Back in England, the Hess family loved the theater and attended performances frequently, as Frederick Hess was one of the founders of the Playgoers' Club. Summers were idyllic, spent on the Isle of Wight, hunting blackberries, swimming, digging for clams, exploring

Myra Hess

tidal basins, playing tennis, and building sand castles. Sabbaths in the Hess household were often musical events. The parents invited Myra's fellow music students to join them on Friday after dinner for an evening of entertainment. Young musicians and composers brought their instruments and performed their latest works in gatherings that were part of the happy times Myra recalled often in later life.

In 1902, Myra won the Steinway medal and scholarship. The following year, at age 13, she won the **Ada Lewis** scholarship to attend the Royal Academy of Music, chartered in 1823, and the oldest institution in Great Britain devoted to musical education. Her friend ***Irene Scharrer** had won the Lewis scholarship at age 12, and the two studied there together under Tobias Matthay, whom Myra always referred to as her "only piano teacher." Described as "two very small eternally giggling girls," Myra and Irene were sometimes sent out into the hall when their good humor became too irrepressible, and while waiting for their lessons they would sometimes indulge in musical highjinks together on two grand pianos. At the end of the day, when they took separate buses home, Myra would walk Irene to her bus stop at Oxford Circus, but because they were engrossed in conversation, Irene would then accompany Myra back to her bus stop at the foot of Baker Street. Sometimes it would take three or four trips between bus stops before they reluctantly took leave of each other.

By the end of World War II, she was one of the major pianists; by war's end Hess became to the public more than a pianist—she was a heroine.

—David Dubal

Myra's serious study of the piano began at the Royal Academy. Exposed to Scharrer's fluent technique and powers of memory, she felt compelled to work harder. Of Professor Matthay, she later said, "I thought I was an accomplished pianist. But then I became a pupil of Tobias Matthay and discovered that I was just beginning to learn about music." The diminutive Hess had small hands and feet, and reaching an octave of piano keys remained difficult for her throughout her life. She often described herself as a short rider trying to mount a very tall horse without stirrups.

Matthay had a global perspective on music and often told his pupils, "We cannot snatch at the fine jewels of beauty; we must serve the community and seek the truth first." But he also taught Hess to enjoy music. Her progress was rapid if not spectacular, but she suffered from the common affliction of "stage nerves," and public performances went less well. Matthay provided support by being present at almost every performance, and his kindly reminder, "Enjoy the music," remained in her memory as long as she performed. Myra also became a close friend of Tobias' wife, **Jessie Matthay**, whose talent was reciting verse. Hess was frequently in the couple's home and referred to them as her "Uncle Tobias" and "Aunt Jessie."

In 1906, wearing the academy's regulation white dress with a red sash drawn over one shoulder, Hess soloed in Queen's Hall, with the Matthays sitting proudly in the audience. That same year, she won the prestigious Walter MacFarren gold medal for pianoforte. An academy faculty member later summed up those years, saying, "Myra Hess was, of course, our greatest star at the Royal Academy."

On November 14, 1907, Hess made her official professional debut in Queen's Hall. Following the usual custom of renting the hall and engaging a conductor and musicians at her own expense, she was able to enlist the services of the New Symphony Orchestra and its young conductor, Thomas Beecham. The Hess family fortunes had fallen considerably, and Myra's father considered the venture foolish, so financing the event was no easy task. Also, Beecham did not approve of women musicians and was sometimes inconsiderate. Nevertheless, funding was secured, and the program featured a picture of Hess as a stunning beauty of 17 in a pastel gown. The notices for her performance of Mozart, Beethoven, Chopin, and Saint-Saëns were favorable on the whole, and better than Beecham's for his conducting. While one critic claimed, "A new star has arisen in the musical world, whose light should shine brilliantly for many years to come," Hess' later assessment of that evening was more down to earth: "It was a great success, but it did not lead to immediate or numerous paying engagements."

On December 12, Hess gave a performance in Birmingham. The following month, on January 25, 1908, she gave a solo recital in London's Aeolian Hall. For this event, she decided to charge popular prices, with no seat costing more than six shillings, and on February 22, she played the Aeolian again, with a mostly Beethoven program. Concerts were costly, however, and Hess turned to teaching to support herself, while also accepting every opportunity to play, including entertaining in private homes. Music clubs, local philharmonics and concert societies throughout Britain provided opportunities to perform, and on September 2, 1908, she appeared in one of London's popular Promenade Concerts, as the soloist with Sir Henry Wood in a performance of Liszt's E Flat Concerto. Still her opportunities for a successful career remained uncertain, and Hess became depressed. She had been preparing for another Promenade Concert, when she set out on a lengthy walk along London's Hampstead Heath, carrying a sharp pocket knife, planning to lacerate her fingers so badly that she would not be able to perform the next day, if ever again. In the course of the walk, she was able to recognize such an act as a cowardly escape from her current difficulties and returned home able to continue, a moment she looked upon later as a turning point, after which she never considered giving up her goal of a concert career.

In 1912, Hess enjoyed a major success with her performance of the Schumann piano concerto in Amsterdam, with the Concertgebouw orchestra conducted by Willem Mengelberg. But in 1914, the outbreak of World War I soon put an end to concert performances, and Hess taught until the war was over, in 1918. On January 17, 1922, she made a highly successful New York debut, and her growing popularity led to annual tours of the U.S. after 1923. In 1928, she made a recording for Columbia, playing her signature piece, "Jesu, Joy of Man's Desiring." During that decade, she also joined the London String Quartet for chamber music performances at the annual Bradford Chamber Music Festival. By the 1930s, she was an established star when she formed a successful partnership for performing sonatas with the Hungarian violinist ***Jelly d'Aranyi**. In 1936, King George V awarded Hess with the rank of Commander, Order of the British Empire (OBE), the first instrumentalist to be so honored.

In the late 1930s, while war clouds gathered over Europe, Hess continued to record and perform in concert. In 1939, five weeks before the Nazi takeover of Austria, she played a recital in Vienna. Shortly after Hitler's declaration of war in September, Hess was back in England, spending the weekend with her old teacher, Tobias Matthay, when the idea came to her to institute some sort of concert series. After a discussion with Matthay, who had always encouraged his pupils to serve their communities, and with **Denise Lassimonne**, she approached Sir Kenneth Clark, director of the National Gallery, about performing there, since the gallery's art works had all been put into storage. An announcement soon appeared that chamber music would be performed on weekdays, Monday through Friday, at 1 PM, in the National Gallery for the admission price of one shilling. Any profits would go to the Musicians Benevolent Fund, a group hard hit by the cessation of concerts caused by the war.

On October 10, 1939, as Hess prepared for the first concert, concerned that no one might come, a line began to form, stretching around the corner into Trafalgar Square, long before 1 PM. Roughly a thousand people showed up that day. A few weeks later, the popularity of the concerts was strongly confirmed when **Lady Gater** suggested that a canteen be set up to provide the audiences with lunch sandwiches, and soon there was even more money going into the Musicians Benevolent Fund.

Expenses for the series were kept to a minimum. There was a flat fee for performing, paid to novices as well as to seasoned performers; Hess herself collected nothing. Her goal for the series was to present the complete repertory of chamber music and to provide opportunities for new performers to play alongside established ones. Concerts were planned a month in advance and weekly programs were printed, though they became smaller and smaller as the war effort brought a paper shortage. Audiences were between 250–1,750 daily. Like London's famous burlesque show at the Windmill Theater, the National Gallery Concerts could boast that they were never closed down.

But the war intruded. As bombing over London intensified, the concerts were moved from the National Gallery's glass-roofed dome downstairs to the shelter room. During the winter of 1940–41, as the Germans carried out their nightly air raids, performers and audience members found it necessary to pick their way through the city's smoldering buildings and shattered streets to attend. Inside the National Gallery, the shelter room was unheated and the cold was intense, while large pools of water collected on the stone floor. While the audience sat listening wrapped in rugs and coats, the musicians played with fingers turned blue with cold. On October 15, 1940, Hess was informed that a time bomb had fallen on the gallery and the building must be evacuated immediately. Half an hour later, the audience had been moved to the library of nearby South Africa House and sat listening to the music while the search for the bomb in the gallery went on. On another occasion, a portion of the gallery had been hit, and a time bomb was found buried in the wreckage, requiring that everyone be moved hurriedly to a distant part of the building. Once a bomb went off during a Beethoven String Quartet, but miraculously, despite a terrific explosion, no one was hurt.

While the concerts continued, Hess herself played 146 times and performed with an enormous number of chamber groups. Mastering new works, she found time to learn a dozen Mozart concertos, and although the music might sound shaky in practice sessions, in performance she would rise to the occasion, playing as though she had known the piece all her life. Rather than memorizing the pieces, she began during this time to play from the score. Apologetic at first, she gradually felt free to rely on the sheet music whenever needed. When the bombing subsided, the concerts were moved back to the dome, where they remained until the summer of 1944, when flying bombs began to appear and a return to the shelter room became necessary. On the fifth anniversary of the concert series, a commemorative booklet giving its history was issued, and, as the war drew to an end, more and more performers arriving from abroad were joyously welcomed at the event.

In 1941, while the war still raged, Myra Hess was knighted for her war contribution, awarded the title of Dame Commander, Order of the British Empire (CBE) by King George VI. In 1946, with the war ended, and the nation in recovery, the future of the concerts came under debate. Dame Myra hoped that they might continue but wanted to retire from directing them. Finally it was decided that the series—after 1,698 concerts, involving 238 pianists, 236 string players, 64 wind players, 157 singers, 24 string quartets, 56 other ensembles, 13 orchestras, 15 choirs, and 24 conductors—would end. By April 10, 1946, when the final concert was held, three-quarters of a million people from all walks of life, including ordinary music lovers and those who had never listened before to a live classical concert, as well as England's queen and her daughters, Princess ***Elizabeth (II)** and Princess ***Margaret Rose**, had been part of the concert audiences.

Past her mid-50s, Hess had continued to grow as a performer and was free now to return to her concert career. Recognized as genuine hero as well as a great artist, she was joyously welcomed in the U.S. and throughout Europe. Apart from holding the title of Dame, she had also received the gold medal of the Royal Philharmonic Society in 1942, only the second woman pianist to receive this tribute, and she had been honored by the Netherlands' equivalent of her British title, appointed Commander of the Order of Orange-Nassau by Queen ***Wilhelmina** in 1943. Hess continued to tour throughout the 1950s, but by then illnesses were beginning to take their toll, and she played with increasing difficulty. Her last public appearance was at the Royal Festival Hall on October 31, 1961.

A bleak period followed, as retirement did not suit Dame Myra well. With her hands crippled by arthritis, she could no longer play or teach. Death came finally on November 25, 1965, in London, to the woman revered as a musician and a true war hero, who provided the concerts that became such an important symbol for all of Britain, during its "finest hour."

SOURCES:

Amis, John. "Dame Myra Hess Remembered," in *The Musical Times*. Vol. 131, no. 1764. February 1990, p. 85.

Clark, Kenneth. *The Other Half: A Self-Portrait*. London: John Murray, 1977, pp. 27–30.

Ferguson, Howard. "Myra Hess," in *The Dictionary of National Biography 1961-1970*. Oxford: Oxford University Press, 1981, pp. 508–510.

Hess, Myra. "Britain," in *Musical America*. Vol. 64, no. 3. February 10, 1944, pp. 9, 30.

Lassimonne, Denise, comp., and Howard Ferguson, ed. *Myra Hess, by Her Friends*. London: Hamish Hamilton, 1966.

McKenna, Marian C. *Myra Hess: A Portrait*. London: Hamish Hamilton, 1976.

Myers, Rollo H. "Music since 1939" in Arnold H. Haskell, et al., *Since 1939*. London: Readers Union, 1948, pp. 97–144.

John Haag,
Associate Professor, University of Georgia, Athens, Georgia

Hesse, electress of.

See Wilhelmine (1747–1820).

Hesse, Eva (1936–1970)

German-American sculptor, often associated with the Minimalist movement, who is known for her abstract sculptures. *Born in Hamburg, Germany, on January 11, 1936; died of a brain tumor in New York City on May 29, 1970; the younger of two daughters of Wilhelm Hesse (a lawyer) and Ruth (Marcus) Hesse; attended public schools in New York; graduated from the School of Industrial Arts, 1952; studied at the Pratt Institute, New York, 1952–53; the Art Students League, New York, 1953; Cooper Union, New York, 1954–57; received BFA degree from Yale University, 1959; married Tom Doyle (an artist), on November 21, 1961 (separated 1966); no children.*

The short life of German-born sculptor Eva Hesse was marked by adversity, beginning with her early childhood in Nazi Germany, and including her parents' divorce, her mother's suicide, and her own failed marriage. However, between 1964 and 1970, the year of her death, Hesse created a body of work that stands as a monument to her enormous talent and artistic ingenuity. In an article about the artist for *Ms.* magazine, written on the occasion of a memorial exhibition of her work at the Guggenheim Museum, **Kasha Linville Gula** points out that Hesse's works are not easy to explain, either in content or execution. "They are so unusual," she writes, "that some art critics have retreated into an exegesis of her personal life through their inability to deal with her sculpture, in the hope one would explain away the other."

Born in Hamburg, Germany, in 1936, Hesse was three when her family fled the Nazi regime and settled in Washington Heights, New York. Her father Wilhelm, a criminal lawyer, took up a new career selling insurance. He subsequently divorced his wife and remarried, after which Hesse went to live with him and her stepmother. Hesse's mother Ruth, who had lapsed into a serious depression, committed suicide in 1946. Eva attended public school and received her high school diploma from the School of Industrial Arts in 1952. She then attended Pratt Institute and the Art Students League before enrolling in Cooper Union, where she remained for three years. After spending a summer at the Yale-Norfolk art school on scholarship, she entered the Yale School of Art and Architecture, where she studied painting with Rico Lebrun, Bernard Chait, and Joseph Albers. Receiving her B.F.A. in 1959, Hesse returned to New York determined to succeed as an artist but lacking direction. During this period, she produced unexceptional drawings, although some were included in group exhibitions.

In 1961, Hesse married abstract sculptor Tom Doyle and immediately found herself locked in a struggle to keep her artistic identity from becoming lost in that of her husband's. For the next four years, languishing in Doyle's shadow, she made little artistic progress, although in March 1963 she did have her first one-woman show at the Allan Stone Gallery. In 1964, when Doyle received a commission to work in Germany for two years, Hesse had mixed feelings about returning to the country from which her family had been forced to flee, but she reluctantly went along. It was an unhappy time, during which she confronted her deteriorating marriage and her perceived lack of professional accomplishment. Working in a small section of an abandoned weaving factory which served as their temporary studio, Hesse began to create abstract collages and reliefs, using old cord she found in the factory.

Returning to New York in 1965, the year that marked the end of her marriage, Hesse began to refine her technique into the organically curving abstract sculptures for which she became known. After moving through a geometrical period which focused on serial order, grids, and spheres, she began to create her more imposing pieces. "Taking memory, sexuality, self-awareness, intuition, and humor as her inspiration," explains H.H. Arnason in *History of Modern Art,* "she allowed forms to emerge from the interaction of the process inherent in her materials—latex, rubber, fiberglass, rope, cloth—with such natural forces as gravitational pull. Thus her pieces stretch from ceiling to floor, suspend from pole to pole, sag and nod toward the floor, or tilt against the wall." Writes Kasha Gula: "Hesse made sculpture after 1967 that has a power akin to the visceral impact religious art had for the faithful during the height of Christianity, or that primitive art has for its peoples."

In 1968, Hesse had a one-woman sculpture show at the Fischback Gallery; in 1969, the Museum of Modern Art purchased her work, *Repetition Nineteen.* At the height of her success, she underwent the first of three operations for a brain tumor that was later diagnosed as malignant. During the last year of her life, despite operations, chemotherapy, and debilitating pain, Hesse worked with renewed intensity, often directing constructions from a wheelchair. Until the end of her life, she fought to evolve freely, without even the restraint of her own prescribed style or method. "There isn't a rule," she said in a interview shortly before her death. "I don't want to keep any rules. That's why my art might be so good, because I have no fear." The artist died in a New York hospital on May 29, 1970.

SOURCES:

Arnason, H.H. *History of Modern Art.* 3rd ed. Revised and updated by Daniel Wheeler. Englewood Cliffs, NJ: Prentice-Hall, 1986.

Bailey, Brooke. *The Remarkable Lives of 100 Women Artists.* Holbrook, MA: Bob Adams, 1994.

Gula, Kasha Linville. "Eva Hesse: No Explanation," in *Ms.* April 1973, pp. 39–42.

Heller, Nancy G. *Women Artists.* NY: Abbeville Press, 1987.

Naylor, Colin, ed. *Contemporary Artists.* Chicago and London: St. James Press, 1989.

Sicherman, Barbara, and Carol Hurd Green, eds. *Notable American Women: The Modern Period.* Cambridge, MA: The Belknap Press of Harvard University Press, 1980.

Barbara Morgan,
Melrose, Massachusetts

Hesse, grand duchess of.

See Elizabeth Hohenzollern (1815–1885).

Hesse, landgravine of.

See Sophia of Thuringia (1224–1284).
See Anna of Saxony (1420–1462).
See Jolanthe of Lorraine (d. 1500).
See Christine of Saxony (1505–1549).
See Mafalda of Hesse (1902–1944).

Hesse, princess of.

See Mary of Hesse-Cassel (1723–1772).
See Christine of Hesse-Cassel (b. 1933).

Hesse-Bukowska, Barbara (1930—)

Polish pianist, widely known for her performances of contemporary Polish composers. *Born in Lodz, Poland, on June 1, 1930.*

Barbara Hesse-Bukowska studied at the Warsaw Conservatory with **Margherita Trombini-Kazuro** and won second prize at the Chopin Competition in 1949. In 1953, she received the Chopin prize at the Long-Thibaud Competition. Her tours have taken her throughout Europe as well as India and Japan. In 1973, she began teaching at the Warsaw Academy of Music. Hesse-Bukowska was applauded for her Chopin interpretations and has recorded for both Polish and American recording firms. She is also known for her performances of contemporary Polish composers, whose works she championed.

John Haag,
Athens, Georgia

Hesse-Cassel, duchess of.

See Louise of Denmark (1750–1831).

Hesse-Cassel, landgravine of.

See Charlotte of Hesse (1627–1687).
See Louise Dorothea of Brandenburg (1680–1705).
See Mary of Hesse-Cassel (1723–1772).
See Caroline of Nassau-Usingen (1762–1823).
See Charlotte Oldenburg (1789–1864).
See Alexandra Nikolaevna (1825–1844).
See Margaret Beatrice (1872–1954).

Kerstin Hesselgren

Hesse-Darmstadt, grand duchess of.

See Marie of Hesse-Darmstadt for sidebar on Wilhelmine of Baden (1788–1836).
See Princess Matilda (1813–1862).
See Alexandra Feodorovna for sidebar on Alice Maud Mary (1843–1878).
See Eleanor of Solms-Hohensolms-Lich (1871–1937).
See Victoria Melita of Saxe-Coburg (1876–1936).

Hesse-Darmstadt, landgravine of.

See Magdalene of Brandenburg (1582–1616).
See Caroline of Birkenfeld-Zweibrucken (1721–1774).

Hesse-Darmstadt, princess of.

See Victoria of Hesse-Darmstadt (1863–1950).
See Ella (1864–1918).
See Alexandra Feodorovna (1872–1918).

Hesse-Homburg, landgravine of.

See Caroline of Hesse-Darmstadt (1746–1821).
See Elizabeth (1770–1840).

Hesselgren, Kerstin (1872–1962)

Swedish social worker and champion of women's rights who was the first woman member of the Swedish Parliament. *Born in Sweden on April 1, 1872; died on August 19, 1962; attended Cassel Women Teachers Training College and Bedford College, London.*

Sometimes called the "***Jane Addams** of Sweden," Kerstin Hesselgren devoted much of her life to the social betterment of her native country. As a child, Hesselgren dreamed of becoming a doctor, but ill health forced her to train as a district nurse instead. She later took up the study of home economics and taught domestic science for several years during her early career. In 1906, she was appointed inspector of housing in Stockholm (the first woman ever to hold this position) and, during World War I, functioned as a councilor of the government food commission. Hesselgren, a liberal, became the first woman member of the Swedish Parliament in 1921 and served until 1934. She served again from 1936 to 1944. From 1926 to 1929, she chaired an international society, the Human Relations in Industry.

Beginning in 1937, Hesselgren was one of four experts on a League of Nations committee on the Legal Status of Women. The committee, which included American ***Dorothy Kenyon**, oversaw a three-year investigation which embraced three legal divisions: public law which looked into women's right to vote, to hold office, to obtain an education, and to practice a profession; private law which studied women's rights in marriage, right to separate names, right to earnings, right to make contracts, as well as relationships between parents and children; and criminal law which examined how women's criminal responsibilities differ from that of men.

Hesselgren received many honors for her work, including a medal from the Swedish Government. Well known in America, she was also honored at a luncheon in New York in July 1938, held in conjunction with the tercentenary (300th anniversary) of the founding of New Sweden. Recognizing Hesselgren's more than 20 years of service on behalf of women, ***Eleanor Roosevelt** introduced her as a "woman who has participated so richly in the life of her times that it would be impossible to do justice to all her activities without staying here all afternoon." Kerstin Hesselgren died on August 19, 1962.

SOURCES:

Moritz, Charles, ed. *Current Biography.* NY: H.W. Wilson, 1962.

Rothe, Anna, ed. *Current Biography.* NY: H.W. Wilson, 1941.

Barbara Morgan,
Melrose, Massachusetts

Hester.

Variant of Esther.

Hetepheres I (fl. c. 2630 BCE)

Egyptian queen, "God's Daughter of his body, Mother of the King of Upper and Lower Egypt." *Flourished around 2630 BCE; daughter of Huni, the last king of the Third Dynasty; married King Snefru, who was probably her brother; children: Cheops (Greek) also known as Khufu, an Egyptian king.*

Egyptian queen Hetepheres I, who flourished around 2630 BCE, was the eldest daughter of King Huni, the last king of the Third Dynasty. She was also the wife (and probably sister) of King Snefru who is responsible for no less than three pyramids built at Dahshur and Meidum. Snefru's long reign began the Fourth Dynasty, and their son Khufu followed him on the throne when he was already a mature man. As mother of the mighty Khufu, Hetepheres would have been highly honored in life and was provided, by her son, with a spectacular suite of furniture, covered in gold, for her tomb, which was found at Giza by Harvard archaeologist George Andrew Reisner in 1925. The cult of this queen was maintained for generations after her death.

Barbara S. Lesko,
Department of Egyptology, Brown University,
Providence, Rhode Island

Hetha (fl. 10th c.)

Queen of Zealand and Danish sea captain. *Flourished in the 10th century in Scandinavia.*

In the 10th century, Hetha fought for the Danes as a naval commander at the Battle of Bravalla, and eventually she became queen of Zealand. The facts of her life are uncertain; but she was reported to be a competent leader. The Battle of Bravalla, a fierce fight between Danish and Swedish forces, involved at least 12 tribal Scandinavian states and resulted in the deaths of thousands of warriors. Hetha led her crew into the battle which was taking place on the shore, and there she fought ferociously along with two other Danish women captains, **Wisna** and **Webiorg.**

Laura York,
Riverside, California

Hetty.

Variant of Harriet, Harriot, and Henrietta.

Hewins, Caroline Maria (1846–1926)

American librarian. *Born in Roxbury, Massachusetts, on October 10, 1846; died in 1926; attended Girls' High and Normal School, Boston; studied library science at the Athenaeum, Boston; never married; no children.*

Born in Roxbury, Massachusetts, Caroline Hewins was the oldest of nine children in a family that also included a great-grandmother, a grandmother, two aunts, and an uncle. She later credited all the "elderlies" in her life with instilling in her a love of books. By the time she was 15, she boasted an acquaintance with the works of Dickens, Scott, Irving, Thackeray, Longfellow, Tennyson, and Shakespeare. A bright student, Hewins graduated from high school as the youngest in her class and enrolled in Girls' High and Normal School in Boston, to prepare for a teaching career. While doing research work at Boston's Athenaeum, however, she decided to become a librarian instead. In 1875, after training under the famous Dr. William F. Poole, she took a job as the librarian of the Hartford Young Men's Institute, a subscription library with closed shelves "for the Intellectual and moral improvement of the young men of Hartford." (The library became the Hartford Public Library in 1893.) Hewins spent the next 50 years in Hartford, where she not only expanded and improved adult library facilities but established the first children's library in the city.

Perhaps due to the literary pursuits of her own childhood, Hewins was appalled by the reading habits of Hartford's children. "Within the last month one boy has asked for Jack Harkaway Stories," she wrote in the *Hartford Library Association Bulletin* of 1878, "another for bound volumes of the *Police Gazette*. . . . The demand from girls for the *New York Weekly* novels is not small." By 1882, Hewins had compiled a list, *Books for the Young,* and embarked on a series of classroom talks aimed at encouraging children to expand the scope of their reading. In an old house adjacent to the main library building, she set up a children's room where she presided over story hours and established a reading club. She wrote plays and coached the children in performing them. She oversaw parades on the lawn and a number of festival celebrations. Her success was such that, in 1907, a full-time children's librarian was hired.

Hewins' goals, however, were wider in scope. In 1891, she helped to form the Connecticut Library Association, serving as its first secretary and, later, as its president. She was also instrumental in convincing the legislature to create a Public Library Committee, which, commissioned in 1893, helped establish libraries throughout the state. Hewins was also active as a lecturer, a committee member, and a contributor to library journals. In 1900, she spoke to the American Library Association's meeting in Montreal about her pioneering efforts on behalf of children.

Although Hewins had hoped to see a larger children's library in her lifetime, none was forthcoming. However, in 1926, the Hartford Librarians Club established a fund for the Caroline M. Hewins Scholarship for Children's Librarians, which they presented to her at a dinner honoring her golden anniversary at the Hartford Public Library.

SOURCES:

Danton, Emily Miller, ed. *Pioneering Leaders in Librarianship*. American Library Association, 1953.

Barbara Morgan,
Melrose, Massachusetts

Heygendorf, Frau von (1777–1848).

See Jagemann, Karoline.

Heyman, Katherine Ruth (1877–1944)

American pianist who was an early proponent of Scriabin's work which she helped popularize. *Born in Sacramento, California, in 1877; died in Sharon, Connecticut, on September 28, 1944.*

Born in Sacramento, California, in 1877, Katherine Heyman made her successful debut in Boston in 1899. She played a great deal of American music in Europe, and in America was a staunch believer in Scriabin when his work was seldom heard there. From 1905 to 1915, she toured America and Europe with ***Ernestine Schumann-Heink**, ***Marcella Sembrich** and other noted singers. In 1928 in Paris, Heyman founded an organization advocating the cause of modern music. Of a 1934 recital, Paul Rosenfeld wrote: "Miss Heyman again disclosed the fineness of Scriabin's art and the depth of the experience transmitted by it." She was interested in contemporary American music and performed it not only in the United States but in Europe as well. She also composed and wrote on musical topics.

SUGGESTED READING:

McHenry, Izetta May. "Katherine Heyman," in *Billboard*. April 2, 1921, pg 24.

COLLECTIONS:

Some of Heyman's correspondence can be found in the Library of Congress, Music Division, and some music manuscripts are located at the New York Public Library, Music Division.

John Haag,
Athens, Georgia

Heymann, Lida and Anita Augspurg

Two major leaders of the German women's movement, during the first 30 years of the 20th century, who combined their feminism with pacifism, insisting that the nations of Europe would be spared future wars only when women had the right to vote.

Anita Augspurg (1857–1943). *Name variations: Augsburg. Pronunciation: OWGS-purk. Born Anita Johanna Theodora Sophie Augspurg on September 22, 1857, in Verden an der Aller, Germany; died on December 20, 1943, in Zurich, Switzerland; daughter of Augustine (Langenbeck) Augspurg (from a ministerial and medical family) and Wilhelm Augspurg (a lawyer); attended private schools and college work at the Universities of Berlin and Zurich; granted law degree from the University of Zurich; never married; no children; lived with Lida Heymann.*

First wanted to become a teacher; studied drama at the University of Berlin and acted at theaters in Meiningen, Riga, and Altenburg, Germany (1881–85); studied jurisprudence at the University of Zurich (1893–97); edited the Journal for Female Suffrage *(1907–12); opened highly successful photographic studio in Munich (1900).*

Lida Heymann (1867–1943). *Pronunciation: HAY-man. Born Lida Gustava Heymann on March 15, 1867,* *in Hamburg, Germany; died on July 31, 1943, in Zurich, Switzerland; daughter of Gustav Christian Heymann (a merchant and investor) and Adele von Hennig; educated through governesses, tutors, and exclusive private schools; spent one semester at the University of Berlin and five semesters at the University of Munich; never married; no children; lived with Anita Augspurg.*

Gained multimillion dollar inheritance (1896); founded a progressive kindergarten, a club for single women, and an association of women office workers, and participated in the German abolitionist movement at Munich (1896–98); met Augspurg at a women's meeting in Berlin (1896).

Augspurg and Heymann were among 13 cofounders of the German Union for Women's Suffrage (1902); they participated in the German Women's Suffrage League (1907); worked in the International Women's Suffrage Alliance (1904–09); attended a women's meeting at The Hague which established the Women's International League for Peace and Freedom (1915); Heymann went into hiding after being exiled from Bavaria for her criticisms of the German government and German war policy (1916); Heymann became vice president of the Women's International League for Peace and Freedom (1919); they edited the journal Woman in the State *(1918–33); moved to Zurich (1933).*

Anita Augspurg (left) and Lida Heymann.

Selected publications: Augspurg, Die ethische Seite der Frauenfrage *(Munich: Koumhler, 1893); Heymann,* Frauenstimmrecht und Völkerverständigung *(Leipzig: Verlag Naturwissenschaften, 1919); Heymann, with the assistance of Augspurg,* Erlebtes-Erschautes: Deutsche Frauen kampfen für Freiheit, Recht, and Frieden, 1850–1940 *(edited by Margrit Twellmann, Meisenheiem am Glan: Anton Hain, 1977).*

At the beginning of the 20th century, German women could not become lawyers or judges; could not vote; had their property held only in their husband's name; could attend university classes only if the professor gave special permission; and could not even serve as the head of most girls' schools in their country. The struggle to change such imbalances fell to the German women's movement, which, with its 250,000 members before 1914, was one of the largest in Europe. Two of the most prominent women in the struggle were Anita Augspurg and Lida Heymann, a personal and professional team who rejected both male domination of German society and "men's wars," insisting that women should control their own destiny.

> After the Golden Age of Atlantis had sunk into the past, the dominion of Motherhood, which had prevailed up to this time, was replaced by the dominion of Fatherhood. Man elevated himself to the status of sole authority over the family and state. Woman was exploited and repressed; with her life in danger, she became his instrument and slave. . . . Man portrayed himself as a hero: he was courageous, strong, even loyal to others. Woman, on the other hand, he declared to be fearful, frivolous, disloyal, the weaker sex—and therefore deserving of his domination.
>
> **—Lida Heymann, in *Erlebtes-Erschautes***

Augspurg and Heymann arrived at their feminism in quite different ways. Augspurg, the youngest of five children, was a precocious child who, under the tutelage of an older sister, could read and write by age four. Her father was a jurist. He was interested in politics—he had been jailed for participating in the Revolutions of 1848, which swept across Europe in that year—but he did not discuss politics with his family, and especially not with women. Augspurg remembered her mother as being uneducated but intelligent.

At first, Augspurg wanted to become an artist, but a visit to a Dresden art museum (while she was visiting an older sister who was an artist in that city) convinced her otherwise. She was intrigued by the theater in Dresden, however, and returned home determined to read many dramas and novels. Thinking that she might prepare to become a teacher of physical education, she went to Berlin, where two of her music teachers introduced her to the concerts and theaters of the city. Her interest in the theater was rekindled.

After taking drama lessons in Berlin from 1881 through 1885, Augspurg acted in theaters in Meiningen (where there was a famous court theater), Riga, and at Altenburg. She financed herself with an inheritance from a grandmother. Critics remembered her voice. In a time when microphones and loudspeakers were not available, she spoke in a clear, trained voice which resonated throughout the theater.

Her theater career ended when she met **Sophie Goudstikker**, from a Dutch family which had moved to Germany many years before. Taking up joint residence in Munich, attracted by its artistic and bohemian reputation, they opened a photographic studio which they named "Atelier Elvira." Augspurg handled the business and technical side of the enterprise, and Goudstikker dealt with the customers. The studio was a great success, with even the royal family of Bavaria coming to their studio to be photographed.

Augspurg declared that her work in the studio was part of her own "emancipation process" in which, she said, she had cast off "the last remnants of the conventional life"—among them, the longer hair style worn by most women of the time (both she and Goudstikker wore their hair short). But she noticed that women's achievements were generally regarded as "personal"—of special significance to the woman but not to be recognized as special by society. This realization drove her to become active in the women's movement in the city. She was particularly prominent in a project to build a women's high school in a nearby city, Karlsruhe.

During Augspurg's stay in Munich, feminists were attempting to change the Civil Code of Germany, in order to give equal legal rights to women. Augspurg came to believe that the women's movement could advance only if leading women had legal expertise. In 1893, she began legal studies at Zurich, choosing a Swiss university where professors might be more amenable to women students. Within only four years, she astonished her professors when she pronounced herself ready to take her doctorate examination. Her dissertation concerned the origins of the British Parliament. She was the first German female jurist, although women were not allowed to be practicing lawyers in Germany until the 1920s.

In 1899, Augspurg became editor of a political supplement to a publication of the feminist *Minna Cauer. Returning to Berlin, Augspurg established a household there with one of Germany's first female physicians, **Agnes Hacker**. They enjoyed appearing in public and doing things that were regarded as "unladylike": Hacker and Augspurg frequently rode on horseback in a city park. There, they sometimes met Cauer who, although she was already past her 50th birthday, delighted in riding a bicycle in the park.

In 1896, while attending a women's conference in Berlin, Augspurg met Lida Heymann. Heymann had grown to adulthood in a family of wealth, the result of a fortune her father had made importing coffee and then investing his profits. Her mother was from the old landed aristocracy of Saxony. She recalled little of her mother but "revered" her father, despite his determination to control most aspects of his children's lives. Of the nine children the marriage produced, all four boys died early, leaving five girls.

In this family of wealth and privilege, Heymann was initially educated by governesses and special tutors. At age 14, she and two sisters were sent to an exclusive private school, where Heymann, in her own words, was a "conscientious" student. They were driven to school, and servants often carried their books for them. Like many German feminists of the period, Heymann had become a bit of a religious skeptic, but when she graduated, her father acceded to her mother's wishes and had her go through religious confirmation. Following confirmation, she spent a year at a finishing school run by three Scottish women, who introduced her to the art and theater world of Dresden.

One incident in her youth left a lifelong impression on her. During family preparations for the wedding of one of her sisters, the groom-to-be noted that German laws allowed a man to discipline his wife. When Heymann said that such laws might convince women not to marry, her future brother-in-law responded with a statement that women were inferior to men. It was, Heymann wrote, the first time she had heard such assertions. The event convinced her that the main characteristic of men was arrogance.

Heymann remained in her family until age 28. She taught in a school for the poor and began a sewing school for girls. In 1896, she became financially independent when her father died and left her as an executor of his multimillion dollar estate. Although the judges and bureaucrats of Hamburg resisted the idea of a woman being executor, she won the right to control the estate when she found, in Hamburg city records, a 13th-century case in which a woman had served as an executor.

From 1896 through 1898, she founded organizations which were designed to help women become self-sufficient, sometimes using part of her personal fortune. She established a settlement in one of Hamburg's most exclusive business areas to provide cheap lunches for working women and daycare for their children. Part of the center's activities was to teach boys chores, such as darning socks. She also founded a club for single women, a society of women office workers, a progressive kindergarten, and a reform school where women and men, but particularly the former, might prepare for university studies.

Heymann was past age 35 when she began thinking of the importance of an education for herself. She chose the universities of Berlin and Munich for college study, although she had to confront one of Germany's most famous professors, the economist Lugo Brentano, for permission to audit his course. Brentano insisted that women auditors did not "know anything or understand anything." Heymann's persistent arguments, however, seemed to wear him down; she was allowed to audit the course.

Heymann gained fame, and a certain amount of notoriety, for her work to aid the abolitionist cause in Germany, a movement in which Augspurg was already involved. The abolitionists sought to end the German tradition that each municipality sponsored one or more local bordellos. In her native Hamburg, Heymann drew such attention to the issue that local authorities tried to condemn buildings, where she was scheduled to speak, as fire hazards. She responded by moving her meetings to a nearby town named Altona. Looking back on her life, she wrote that "I was 27 years old before I realized what a bordello was. . . . Women were mistreated, regarded as articles of commerce, exploited, and then stigmatized." Angered by attempts to silence her, she proclaimed in one of her speeches in Hamburg, "These degrading institutions, created by men, deserve only our contempt."

Their activities in the abolitionist cause brought Heymann and Augspurg together. At their first meeting, Augspurg was impressed with Heymann, who was not only ten years younger but who also wore short-cropped hair and dressed in newer "reform" clothing instead of the uncomfortable, heavily corseted styles worn by many women of the time. The two women had much in common. Avid bicyclists, they also opposed vivisection and shared an interest in vegetarianism. While she was a student at Munich, Heymann often spent time at Augspurg's nearby summer residence. They delighted in shocking their fellow citizens with behavior that was considered unconventional for women. Living what one writer has called a "sporty and extravagant lifestyle," they bicycled together, rode on horseback, and drove Heymann's car on journeys throughout Germany without a male escort or "protector."

Yet their colleagues in the feminist movement noticed that their personalities were quite different. Augspurg struck many of her co-workers as having a legalistic mind, and some of them worried that she allowed herself to be too influenced by the outspoken Heymann. But Augspurg was widely admired for her theatrical background, which made her an effective speaker and gave her an understanding of how to stage manage feminist meetings in order to gain maximum attention in the press. Her easy-going manner made her especially effective in dealing with male politicians. Heymann was more confrontational and was sometimes regarded, even by colleagues, as impulsive and contentious. But her courage was never questioned, and a contemporary praised her for "untiring tenaciousness and brave integrity" against strong male opposition in Germany.

What united these two women was a belief that men had proved themselves unqualified to lead European society. They drew this lesson not only from the abolitionist struggle but also from the fact that when German war veterans returned home after World War I, very few expressed regret for the killing they had done. Heymann wrote in her memoirs that "in the most important area of life, the personal life, there is a huge abyss between women and men, and it is unlikely to be bridged." Apparently, she was not joking when she said that if she hit an object when driving her car, she hoped it was a man and not a dog.

When Augspurg and Heymann decided to share a common household, they settled on larger and larger farms, the most famous of which was located in upper Bavaria. The farm reflected their sometimes mischievous humor; in addition to raising a large number of pigs—which popular opinion thought to be too dirty and disgusting a job for women—they cared for two donkeys which they named Tristan and Isolde (after two characters in a Wagnerian opera), cows, fruit trees, and a number of dogs. Their success in running their farming estates brought them a steady stream of male suitors. It also caused them continual amusement that men were attracted to women who excelled at (and made money at) "men's work."

In the major national women's organization in Germany, the Federation of German Women's Associations, Augspurg and Heymann belonged to the so-called "radical wing," in contrast to the more conservative leaders such as ***Helene Lange**. What distinguished them from many German feminists was their optimism that women's political and organizing abilities would overcome obstacles. Active in founding suffrage organizations, they also served as officers in women's organizations and as editors of feminist journals. In 1899, Heymann joined the feminist **Anna Pappritz** in founding the International Abolitionist Federation. Heymann and Augspurg were among the 13 co-founders of the German Union for Women's Suffrage in 1902, with Augspurg saying that its aim was to gain the right to vote for all women. In 1913, both women joined the more aggressive German Women's Suffrage League. Augspurg served as vice president of the League, while Heymann served as vice president of the Union of Progressive Women's Clubs. During the years leading up to World War I, Augspurg was the editor of the *Journal for Parliamentary Affairs and Laws* and the *Journal for Female Suffrage*.

Although their ideas placed them on the political Left in Germany, both women were suspicious of the most leftward party, the Marxist Social Democratic Party (SPD). They believed that although the party argued for gender equality, in practice it was dominated by men who favored equality only in some distant future, when a Marxist revolution would supposedly occur. In 1907, they made their point: when the SPD refused to join in their efforts to organize a drive pressing for the right to vote for German women, they embarrassed party leaders when they mobilized the wives of many SPD officials to speak out.

Among the many political parties in Germany, they tended to support, instead, the various liberal parties, the remnants of the old German Progressive Party. This was particularly true of Augspurg, who thought that the goal of feminism was individual freedom and believed the liberals were most likely to achieve it. The liberal individualism of both women led them to oppose even special laws protecting factory workers. Only during World War I did they change their political allegiance, switching to a splinter group which had seceded from the SPD, the Independent Socialists. Unlike SPD leaders, the Independent Socialists had opposed German participation in World War I and had refused to vote a war budget for the army.

World War I split German feminism. Heymann regarded the war as a "men's war between men's states," while Augspurg said the war was a threat "to our culture and existence." But other leaders in the German women's movement, such as ***Gertrud Bäumer**, disagreed. Bäumer argued that patriotic support for the war effort would bring greater public acceptance of the women's movement when the war was over. Heymann even clashed with Cauer, who believed it was naive to denounce the war. The membership of women's organizations dwindled during the war, possibly because support of the war was seen as a patriotic duty. Heymann said that some suffrage organizations were able to retain only about 10% of their members, and that many of these members stayed only because the organizations were engaged in social welfare work.

In 1915, during the early stages of World War I, they participated in a women's peace congress at The Hague in the Netherlands. The main achievement of the congress was the creation of the Women's International League for Peace and Freedom. Speaking to the congress, Heymann said the League was an important step toward correcting mistakes made by male-controlled governments. "A German woman," she said, "holds out her hand to a French woman, and speaks for the whole German delegation with the hope that we women can build a bridge from Germany to France and from France to Germany, and that in the future we may be able to make good the wrongdoing of men." But later journeys by League members to meet with the heads of major European governments proved fruitless. Not only did the women meet a frosty reception, but governments took steps to make future travel by the women much more difficult. In 1916, the wartime military dictatorship of Germany banned Heymann from public speaking. She went into hiding rather than obey an order for exile from Bavaria.

At war's end, the League met again, and Heymann was named vice president. Referring to the courage which many European feminists had shown in speaking up to their governments during the war, she now added:

> New times call for new actions, and new conditions, new tasks, and perhaps even new principles. . . . We must be prepared. We can triumph if we stand together with the same courage, with the same self-respect and faith in what women have to give to the world, as did the women of 1914.

In the post-World-War-I years, they lived largely off what remained of Heymann's wealth. During the war, many Germans had purchased government bonds which were not honored by the new Weimar government of Germany when the war was over. Heymann had kept her foreign bonds, despite criticism that it was unpatriotic to do so. These bonds financed Heymann's and Augspurg's activities in Germany during the 1920s. Heymann ran unsuccessfully for the National Assembly (the new, democratically elected German legislature) in 1919 as an Independent Social Democrat. Throughout the 1920s, they edited the journal *Woman in the State* (*Die Frau im Staat*).

In January of 1933, Augspurg and Heymann were vacationing in North Africa and Spain when news arrived that Adolf Hitler had been appointed chancellor of Germany. They refused to return to Germany, eventually settling in Zurich. Since their property in Germany had been confiscated by the Nazis, they lived off what money they had on them, plus financial help from friends.

The years in Zurich were difficult for them, as they followed the news of what was happening in Germany. While insisting that it accepted equality of the sexes, the new Nazi government of Germany favored traditional roles for women, as wives and mothers. Leading Nazis insisted that women who participated in politics would become too "aggressive." By the time Augspurg and Heymann died—both in the year 1943—Nazism seemed to be triumphing throughout Europe. France had been conquered; British troops had been driven back to their own island; and Nazi armies had occupied parts of Europe's largest country, the Soviet Union.

As they watched disasters accumulate in Europe, both women kept a certain optimism. Insisting that the major task after the war would be to build a "united Europe and a united World," Heymann added that the slogan of postwar Europe should become "Nothing is impossible." In 1946, after the war was ended and Hitler was defeated and dead, a street in her native Hamburg was named after Lida Heymann. It was the same city where she had fought so bitterly in the abolitionist cause half a century before. She would probably have considered it strong evidence that "Nothing is impossible."

SOURCES:

Evans, Richard J. *Comrades and Sisters: Feminism, Socialism, and Pacifism in Europe, 1870–1945*. Sussex: Wheatsheaf Books, NY: St. Martin's Press, 1987.

———. *The Feminist Movement in Germany, 1894–1933.* Beverly Hills, CA: Sage Publications, 1976.

Gerhard, Ute. *Unerhört: Die Geschichte der deutschen Frauenbewegung.* Reinbeck bei Hamburg: Rowohlt, 1990.

Greven Aschoff, Barbara. *Die bürgerliche Frauenbewegung in Deutschland, 1894–1933.* Göttingen: Vandenhoeck and Ruprecht, 1981.

Hackett, Amy K. "The Politics of Feminism in Wilhelmine Germany, 1894–1933." Ph.D. Dissertation, Columbia University, 1977.

Heymann, Lida, and Anita Augspurg. *Erlebtes-Erschautes: Deutsche Frauen kampfen für Freiheit, Recht, and Frieden, 1850–1940.* Edited by Margrit Twellmann. Meisenheiem am Glan: Anton Hain, 1977.

SUGGESTED READING:

Bussey, Gertrude, and Margaret Tims. *Pioneers for Peace: Women's International League for Peace and Freedom, 1915–1965.* London: WILPF British Section, 1980.

Evans, Richard J. *The Feminists: Women's Emancipation Movements in Europe, America, and Australasia, 1840–1920.* London: Croom Helm, 1977.

Frevert, Ute. *Women in German History: From Bourgeois Emancipation to Sexual Liberation.* Translated by Stuart McKinnon-Evans, with Terry Bond and Barbara Norden. Hamburg: Berg, 1989.

Slaughter, Jane S., and Robert Kern. *European Women on the Left: Socialism, Feminism, and the Problems Faced by Political Women, 1880 to the Present.* Westport, CT: Greenwood Press, 1981.

COLLECTIONS:

The property and papers of both Anita Augspurg and Lida Heymann were confiscated and destroyed by the Nazi government of Germany.

Niles Holt,
Professor of History, Illinois State University, Normal-Bloomington, Illinois

Heyne, Theresa (1764–1829).

See Huber, Therese.

Heyward, Dorothy (1890–1961)

American playwright who, with her husband DuBose Heyward, co-authored the folk dramas* Porgy *(1927) and* Mamba's Daughter *(1939). *Born Dorothy Hartzell Kuhns in Wooster, Ohio, on June 6, 1890; died on November 19, 1961; attended National Cathedral School in Washington, D.C.; studied playwriting with George Pierce Baker at Harvard University; married (Edwin) DuBose Heyward (1885–1940, author and playwright), on September 22, 1923; children: one daughter* ***Jenifer DuBose Heyward.***

Selected plays: Nancy Ann *(1924); (with DuBose Heyward)* Porgy *(1927); (with Moss Hart)* Jonica *(1930); (with Dorothy DeJagers)* Cinderelative *(1930); (with DuBose Heyward)* Mamba's Daughters *(1939); (with Howard Rigsby)* South Pacific *(1943);* Set My People Free *(1948). Selected books:* Love in a Cupboard: A Comedy in One Act *(1926);* Nancy Ann *(1927);* Three-a-Day *(1930); (with Dorothy DeJagers)* Little Girl Blue *(1931);* The Pulitzer Prize Murders *(1932).*

Dorothy and DuBose Heyward are best remembered for the folk play *Porgy,* which was adapted from DuBose's novel *Porgy* (1925) and first produced in 1927. The play later evolved into the legendary opera *Porgy and Bess* (1935), which DuBose wrote with George and Ira Gershwin. Through their plays *Porgy,* and the later *Mamba's Daughters* (1939), the Heywards are also credited with providing the first serious dramas for African-American performers.

Heyward was born Dorothy Hartzell Kuhns in 1890 in Wooster, Ohio, but as a child lived in Washington, D.C., Puerto Rico, and New York. After high school, determined to become a playwright, she entered George Pierce Baker's Workshop 47, at Harvard University. Her first play, *Nancy Ann,* an autobiographical account of a young debutante who escapes a manipulative family by attempting to break into the theater, won the Harvard Prize for 1924. During these early years, Heyward also spent some time as a chorus girl in a traveling show in order to experience backstage life firsthand.

Dorothy first met DuBose in 1921, at an art colony in New Hampshire. A native of Charleston, South Carolina, DuBose made his living in insurance but spent whatever time he could writing. His early short stories and poetry, though of little modern-day interest, reveal his profound talent for depicting African-Americans that inhabited Charleston and the South Carolina Low Country. The couple married in 1923, and Heyward encouraged her young husband to leave the insurance business and write full time. Dubose's novel *Porgy* (1925), a love story about a crippled black man and the fallen woman who transforms his life, was praised for its sensitive, non-patronizing characterizations and became an instant hit. It was Dorothy, however, who saw the dramatic potential in the story and convinced her husband to help rework the novel into a play. They then began a close collaboration, she contributing her knowledge and experience in the theater, and he providing the strong story line and local color.

The play *Porgy,* which the Heywards insisted be cast with black actors instead of the usual white actors in blackface, was an unqualified success, playing in New York for 217 performances before embarking on a successful tour. Interestingly, the later operatic version of the play, *Porgy and Bess* (1935), was not an instant success, running only 124 performances during its first production. A later revival in 1942, which departed from strict operatic structure, substituting spoken language for musical dialogue, enjoyed a longer run. (Producers of this revival did not even list DuBose Heyward among the credits, until Dorothy complained to the Dramatists Guild.) A major production in the early 1950s led to a worldwide tour and a 1977 revival won a Tony Award. The play, though overshadowed by its more famous successor, is still read by drama students as an example of the theatrical experimentation of the 1920s. Writes **Holly Mims Westcott:**

> [T]he depiction of a minority subculture, the serious treatment given its emotions, the use of black performers, the attempt to suggest the Low Country blacks' Gullah dialect, the use of folk music—is not experimentation for the sake of novelty, but experimentation which grows out of the subject matter of the play itself, experimentation of the most valid kind.

In 1930, Dorothy Heyward collaborated with Moss Hart on *Jonica,* and with **Dorothy DeJagers** on *Cinderelative,* both disasters. She teamed up with her husband once more for the play *Mamba's Daughters* (1939), adapted from DuBose's novel of the same name and written for the actress ***Ethel Waters**. The story, concerning three generations of black women, enjoyed moderate success and was the first serious Broadway play to transport an African-American woman to stardom. Waters was set to perform in a musical adaptation of another DuBose novel, *Star Spangled Virgin* (1939), but DuBose died before the collaboration with Arthur Schwartz could get under way.

After her husband's death, Dorothy Heyward attempted two more plays about blacks, but neither was successful. The first, *South Pacific* (1943), about a black man who finds unprejudiced acceptance on a Pacific island during wartime, closed after five performances. (Rodgers and Hammerstein later achieved success with a musical under the same name based on the short stories of James Michener.) The second play, *Set My People Free* (1948), about a Charleston slave, closed after 29 performances.

SOURCES:

Westcott, Holly Mims. "Dorothy Heyward," in *Dictionary of Literary Biography,* Vol. 7. Detroit, MI: Gale Research, 1982.

Wilmeth, Don B., and Tice L. Miller, eds. *Cambridge Guide to American Theatre.* Cambridge, England and NY: Cambridge University Press, 1993.

Barbara Morgan,
Melrose, Massachusetts

Heywood, Eliza (c. 1693–1756).

See Haywood, Eliza.

DuBose and Dorothy Heyward

He Zizhen.

See Jiang Qing for sidebar.

H.H. (1830–1885).

See Jackson, Helen Hunt.

Hickok, Lorena A. (1893–1968)

American journalist. *Born in East Troy, Wisconsin, on March 7, 1893; died in Rhinebeck, New York, on May 1, 1968; eldest of three daughters of Addison J. Hickok (a buttermaker) and Anna (Waite) Hickok; briefly attended Lawrence College, Appleton, Wisconsin, and the University of Minnesota; never married; no children.*

Lorena A. Hickok was born in East Troy, Wisconsin, on March 7, 1893. Surviving an abusive father and a lonely childhood, Lorena Hickok went to work as a housekeeper at the age of 13, following the death of her mother. At 15, she settled in Battle Creek, Michigan, where, with the encouragement of her mother's cousin, "Aunt" **Ella C. Ellis**, and a concerned English teacher, she completed high school. In 1913, after two brief attempts at college, Lorena began her journalistic career at the *Battle Creek*

Evening News. She soon moved on to the *Milwaukee Sentinel*, where she started as a society reporter, but eventually earned a byline writing stories about visiting celebrities. In 1917, she moved to Minneapolis and took a position with the *Minneapolis Tribune*. Mentored by managing editor Thomas J. Dillon, she worked her way up from reporter to Sunday editor to star reporter. She later credited "Old Man" Dillon with teaching her the newspaper business, "how to drink, and how to live."

Lorena A. Hickok

In 1926, Hickok was diagnosed with diabetes and left Minneapolis. After a period of convalescence in San Francisco, she moved to New York, taking a job with the *Daily Mirror*. She was there just a year before transferring to the Associated Press. During the presidential campaign of 1932, she was assigned to cover ***Eleanor Roosevelt**, in whom she found a kindred spirit. By the time of the inauguration in 1933, the two women had become extremely close friends. They made several trips together, and when separated, kept up a lively and loving correspondence. In reporting about the first lady, Hickok, more than any other journalist, presented Eleanor Roosevelt as a caring, powerful friend of the economically depressed. She also advised Roosevelt on how best to publicize the New Deal. By the spring of 1933, however, Hickok realized that her friendship with the first lady impaired the objectivity she needed as a reporter, and she left the Associated Press.

For the next three years, Hickok served as an investigative reporter for the Federal Emergency Relief Administration, traveling around the country evaluating the effectiveness of New Deal programs and reporting on the attitudes and conditions of ordinary citizens mired down by the Depression. Eighty of her reports (in the form of letters to agency director Harry Hopkins) were published posthumously in 1981 as *One Third of a Nation: Lorena Hickok Reports on the Great Depression*. The confidential nature of the letter format offers an exceptionally candid view of the Depression, including a glimpse of the dishonest practices of those who profited during the country's economic crisis.

Beginning in 1937, Hickok spent three years in New York, working as a publicist for the New York World's Fair and spending weekends at her cottage on Long Island. In 1940, she returned to Washington to replace ***Molly Dewson** as executive director of the Women's Division of the Democratic Party. Living in the White House, Hickok saw Eleanor Roosevelt again on a regular basis and also formed friendships with Howard Haycraft and ***Helen Gahagan Douglas**, among others. Hickok's continuing battle with diabetes forced her to leave her job in March 1945, after which she did not seek regular employment, although she did work for the Women's Division of the State Democratic Committee of New York for another five years before failing eyesight forced her to retire. She continued to write, however, producing books on history, and biographies of Franklin D. Roosevelt, Eleanor Roosevelt, ***Helen Keller**, and ***Anne Sullivan Macy**. Her book *Ladies of Courage* (1954), co-authored with Eleanor Roosevelt, also provides a valuable survey of some of the era's prominent women. After Roosevelt's death in 1962, Hickok's own health began to deteriorate rapidly, although she survived her beloved friend by six years, dying on May 1, 1968, following the amputation of a leg.

SOURCES:

Faber, Doris. *The Life of Lorena Hickok*, 1980.

Sicherman, Barbara, and Carol Hurd Green, eds. *Notable American Women: The Modern Period*. Cambridge, MA: The Belknap Press of Harvard University Press, 1980.

COLLECTIONS:

Lorena Hickok's papers are located at the Franklin D. Roosevelt Library, Hyde Park, New York.

Barbara Morgan, Melrose, Massachusetts

Hicks, Helen (1911–1974).

See Berg, Patty for sidebar.

Hicks, Louise Day (1923—)

American politician and U.S. Representative from Massachusetts (January 3, 1971–January 3, 1973). *Born Anna Louise Day on October 16, 1923, in Boston, Massachusetts; graduated from Wheelock Teacher's College, 1938; Boston University School of Education, B.S., 1955; graduated from Boston University School of Law, 1958.*

Although Louise Day Hicks served a term in the U.S. House of Representatives, the notoriety of her political career resulted more from her involvement in local Boston politics during the turbulent years of the civil-rights movement. Hicks was born on October 16, 1923, and grew up in Boston's political milieu as the daughter of a Democratic district court judge. She initially pursued a career as a teacher but switched to the study of law in the mid-1950s. A graduate of Boston University School of Law, Hicks was admitted to the Massachusetts bar in 1959 and formed a partnership with her brother. In 1960, she became counsel for Boston Juvenile Court.

Hicks' first elected office was to the Boston school committee in 1961, where she served most of her two-year term with little controversy. She garnered national attention in 1963, however, when, in opposition to the NAACP and others who hoped to achieve racial integration in the schools, she became a staunch adversary of integration by busing and the leading supporter of "neighborhood schools." Hicks, who had many supporters, won reelection with nearly three-quarters of the vote in 1963. In 1965, as chair of the school committee, Hicks held fast to her position on busing even when faced with a Massachusetts law that deprived local jurisdictions of state funds if they did not implement desegregation plans. A third election to the school committee in 1965 launched her campaign as a mayoral candidate in 1967. Running under the slogan, "You know where I stand," she lost to Kevin White. Undaunted, Hicks continued her political pursuits in 1969 with her election to the Boston City Council.

In 1970, Hicks was elected to fill the seat vacated by John McCormack in the U.S. House of Representatives. Taking her place in the 92nd Congress, she was assigned to the Committee on Education and Labor. As part of this committee, she proposed a system of tax credits for parents of children in private schools and sought a federal ban on busing to achieve desegregation of public schools. Hicks also sat on the Committee on Veterans' Affairs and called for the withdrawal of American troops from Southeast Asia. Although a Democrat, she supported President Richard Nixon on a majority of House votes. While still in the House, Hicks entered the Boston mayoral race for a second time, again losing to incumbent Kevin White. In 1972, after her district had been redrawn, she lost her bid for a second term in the House. Hicks then returned to private law practice and in 1973 again won election to the Boston City Council. She is a past president of the Massachusetts Association of Women lawyers.

Louise Day Hicks

SOURCES:

Office of the Historian. *Women in Congress, 1917–1990.* Commission on the Bicentenary of the U.S. House of Representatives, 1991.

Judith C. Reveal,
freelance writer, Greensboro, Maryland

Hicks, Pamela (b. 1929).

See Mountbatten, Pamela.

Hicks, Peggy Glanville (1912-1990).

See Glanville-Hicks, Peggy.

Hickson, Joan (1906–1998)

British actress. *Born in 1906; died on October 17, 1998, in Colchester, England; studied at the Royal Academy of Dramatic Art, London; married Eric Butler, a physician (died 1967); children: two.*

Known for her television role as ***Agatha Christie**'s septuagenarian detective Miss Marple, British actress Joan Hickson worked on stage, screen, and television for more than half a century before her "overnight" success on the popular BBC television series. "Retirement is fatal," she often said, "Luckily, in my profession you don't have to."

An alumna of the prestigious Royal Academy of Dramatic Art, Hickson made her debut in London's West End in 1928, appearing in *The Tragic Muse,* then spent several years with the Oxford Repertory Company. She won critical acclaim for her role in *A Day in the Death of Joe Egg* (1967), which she reprised in the 1972 movie version. In 1977, she made her Broadway debut in *Bedroom Farce,* which won that year's Tony Award.

Joan Hickson made over 100 films, beginning in 1927 with *Love From a Stranger* and including the "Carry On . . ." comedy series, shown in American art houses. As late as 1992, she appeared in the film *Century,* which was her last acting assignment. She also pioneered in television, appearing in one of the BBC's earliest shows, the mystery *Busman's Honeymoon* in 1947. She was later seen as the receptionist in the dramatic series *The Royalty* and played the housekeeper to the vicar in the 1960s comedy series *Our Man at St. Mark's*. However, it was her performance as the amateur sleuth Miss Marple that captured the attention of worldwide audiences. The series was carried in 30 countries including the United States, where it was broadcast on PBS from 1986 to 1989. Hickson also portrayed Marple in several movies. The actress, who was married to a physician and was the mother of two children, counted among her fans Queen *__Elizabeth II__, who bestowed upon her the Order of the British Empire in 1987.

SOURCES:

"Obituaries," in *The Boston Globe*. October 20, 1998.

"Obituaries," in *The Day* [New London]. October 19, 1998.

Hidalgo, Elvira de (1892–1980)

Spanish soprano. *Born on December 27, 1892, in Aragòn, Spain; died on January 21, 1980, in Milan, Italy; studied with Concetta Bordalba and Melchiorre Vidal.*

Debuted in Naples (1908), Metropolitan Opera (1910), Covent Garden (1924); retired (1932); became a teacher who was best known for her famous pupil, Maria Callas.

Elvira de Hidalgo, the Spanish soprano, is best remembered as the teacher of *__Maria Callas__, though she established a career of her own before becoming a teacher. Born in Spain in 1892, she debuted in Milan and then went on to great success at the Sarah Bernhardt Theater in Paris, the Khedive in Cairo, and finally the Metropolitan Opera. De Hildago's voice had an attractive timbre which reached to a top D. She made a number of recordings which are especially interesting because her style is also reflected in Callas' singing. When de Hidalgo retired in 1932, she went to the Athens Conservatory where she taught Callas, the young American-born singer of Greek parentage, beginning in 1937. The accuracy of embellishments and use of sufficient chest voice characterized de Hidalgo's singing as they also would Callas'.

John Haag,
Athens, Georgia

Hidari Sachiko (1930—)

Japanese actress and filmmaker. *Born in Toyama, Japan, in 1930; married Susumu Hani (b. 1928, a film director); children: daughter Miyo.*

Filmography: Inn at Osaka *(1954);* The Cock Crows Again *(1954);* The Maid's Kid *(1955);* The Crime of Shiro Kamisaka *(1957);* The Insect Woman *(1963);* She and He *(1963);* Bride of the Andes *(1963);* This Madding Crowd *(1964);* The Scarlet Camellia *(1965);* Mishima *(1985);* Sukiyaki *(1995); (as director-producer)* The Far Road *(1977).*

One of the few Japanese women to have worked as an actress, director and producer, Sachiko Hidari is best known in the international film community as one of Japan's leading actresses. Hidari was born in Toyama, Japan, in 1930, and employed briefly as a high school music and gymnastics teacher before she began her acting career in 1952 with an independent film company, Sogo Geijutsu. After working as a bit player in several movies, Hidari's break came with her performances in *An Inn at Osaka* and *The Cock Crows Again.* In 1963, Hidari appeared in two films that garnered her international attention: *She and He* and *The Bride of the Andes.* Both were directed by her husband Susumu Hani.

In 1977, the Japan National Railway Union commissioned Hidari to make *The Far Road.* Hidari produced, directed and starred in the film as Satoko, a working-class wife of a retired railroad worker who grapples with a society that persists in making women second-class citizens. Two years before, Hidari had told **Joan Mellen**: "Ordinary people are the foundation of Japanese life, including the women who support our entire society."

Sachiko Hidari's interest in issues facing women both on and off screen is long-standing. She was an out-spoken advocate of women's rights in the early 1960s, long before others of her generation. "We have to insist sometimes on our voices being heard," she told Mellen. "Japanese women are about one hundred years behind Western women." Though Hidari's career as an actress has extended into the late 20th century, the male-dominated studio system stymied her, as well as Japan's first woman director ***Kinuyo Tanaka** (1907–1977), from pursuing a career behind the camera.

SOURCES:

Kuhn, Annette, and Susannah Radstone, eds. *The Women's Companion to International Film.* Berkeley, CA: University of California Press, 1994.

Mellen, Joan. *Voices of Japanese Cinema.* NY: Liveright, 1975.

Deborah Jones,
Studio City, California

Hideko Fukuda (1865–1927).

See Fukuda Hideko.

Hideko Maehata (b. 1914).

See Maehata Hideko.

Hideko Takamine (b. 1924).

See Takamine Hideko.

Hier, Ethel Glenn (1889–1971)

American composer, pianist, and teacher. *Born in Cincinnati, Ohio, on June 25, 1889; died in Winter Park, Florida, on January 14, 1971.*

Ethel Glenn Hier graduated from the Cincinnati Conservatory in 1911 where she studied composition under Stillman-Kelly and Percy Goetschius and piano under Marcian Thalberg. She then continued her studies at the Institute of Musical Art in New York before going to Europe to study privately with Hugo Kaun in Berlin as well as Gian-Francesco Malipiero in Italy and Ernest Bloch. At that time, European music was greatly influenced by the composers Alban Berg, Egon Wellesz and Arnold Schoenberg of the Vienna School. They, too, would leave a lasting impression on Hier. She wrote many vocal pieces as well as for the piano and orchestra. In 1930–31, she was one of only two women awarded a Guggenheim fellowship.

John Haag,
Athens, Georgia

Higgins, Alice Louise (1870–1920).

See Lothrop, Alice.

Higgins, Marguerite (1920–1966)

American war correspondent and author who, in the 1950s, was the most famous journalist in the world. *Born Marguerite Higgins on September 3, 1920, in Hong Kong; died in Washington, D.C., on January 3, 1966; daughter of Lawrence Daniel Higgins (a businessman) and Marguerite de Godard Higgins (a teacher); graduated University of California, B.S., 1941; Columbia University School of Journalism, M.S.; married Stanley Moore (a philosophy professor), on July 12, 1942 (divorced 1948); married William E. Hall (a lieutenant general, U.S. Army), on October 7, 1952; children: (second marriage) Sharon Lee (died five days after birth), Lawrence O'Higgins, Linda Marguerite.*

Became reporter, New York Herald Tribune *(1942–44), war and foreign correspondent (1944–47), chief, Berlin bureau (1947–50), chief, Tokyo bureau (1950–51), staffer (1951–58), diplomatic correspondent, Washington (1958–63); was a columnist for* Newsday *(1963–65).*

Selected publications: War in Korea: Report of a Woman Combat Correspondent *(Doubleday, 1951);* News is a Singular Thing *(Doubleday, 1955);* Red Plush and Black Bread *(Doubleday, 1955);* Jessie Benton Fremont *(Houghton Mifflin, 1962); (with Peter Lisagor)* Overtime in Heaven: Adventures in the Foreign Service *(Doubleday, 1964);* Our Vietnamese Nightmare *(Harper and Row, 1965).*

Soon after the Korean War broke out, an American infantry regiment stopped a North Korean tank drive just north of Taegu. Suddenly, however, the North Koreans launched a counterstrike, just as a brash female reporter was breakfasting with several officers. In cabling her account of the four-hour battle, Marguerite Higgins wrote: "A coffeepot knocked off the breakfast table by machine-gun fire was the first warning this correspondent and most of the regimental officers had of the attack." She told of hugging the floor to avoid the bullets tearing through the building, after which she remarked, "Medical corpsmen began bringing in the wounded, who were rather numerous. One correspondent learned how to administer blood plasma."

Within three weeks, the 27th's hardbitten colonel, J.H. ("Mike") Michaelis, complained to her newspaper, the *New York Herald Tribune,* that she had left out something important. He supplied it:

> Miss Higgins, completely disregarding her own personal safety, voluntarily assisted by administering blood plasma to the many

> wounded as they were carried into the temporary aid station. This aid station was subject to small arms fire throughout the attack. The Regimental Combat Team considers Miss Higgins' actions on that day as heroic, but even more important is the gratitude felt by members of the command towards the selfless devotion of Miss Higgins in saving the lives of many grievously wounded men.

Marguerite Higgins was born on September 3, 1920, in Hong Kong. Her father Lawrence Daniel Higgins was a businessman who had courted her French-born mother **Marguerite de Godard** while stationed in Paris as an American pilot. At the age of six months, Marguerite was sent to a health resort in Dalat, Vietnam, to recuperate from malaria. When she was five, her family moved to Oakland, California, where her father worked as freight agent for the Pacific Mail Steamship Company.

Growing up in the Higgins household was not easy. Marguerite's volatile father became increasingly alcoholic, while her mother was addicted to fainting spells. Higgins was a scholarship student at Berkeley's prestigious Anna Head's school, where her mother taught French to make ends meet. "Every time my report card showed a B instead of straight As, I risked the loss of the scholarship," she later recalled. In 1937, Higgins entered the University of California. While serving on the student newspaper, the *Daily Californian,* she gained a reputation for cyclonic energy, left-wing politics, a high-living lifestyle, and more than her share of ruthlessness. In 1941, she graduated cum laude with a B.S. degree. That summer, she was a cub reporter for the *Vallejo* (California) *Times-Herald.*

Soon moving to New York City, Higgins arrived—as she later noted—"with one suitcase, a surplus of seven dollars, and a letter of introduction to an uncle and aunt living on Long Island." She enrolled in the Columbia University School of Journalism on a scholarship, where she received her M.S. in 1942. While at Columbia, she was campus reporter for the *New York Herald Tribune,* which she joined as a full-time staff member after graduation. Assignments included the Hartford circus fire, Arabian princes visiting America, female Russian students at Columbia, Chinatown's war effort, Connecticut politics, and a day in the life of the ***Duchess of Windsor**. In her first year as a reporter, Higgins was able to interview such aloof personalities as union leader James Caesar Petrillo and ***Song Meiling** (Madame Chiang Kai-shek).

Tribune historian Richard Kluger describes Higgins as "a pretty but messy sight, fingernails dirty and forehead smudged from handling carbon paper and typewriter ribbons, hair and copy paper flying in all directions." Her aggressiveness, Kluger continues:

> became an office legend, replete with charges that she stepped on those who got in the way, snatched off desirable assignments, arranged to phone in the legwork of others as if it were her own when out on a team assignment, and otherwise comported herself with a competitiveness bordering on the pathological.

By this time, Higgins was becoming a woman of singular beauty. Recalled *Tribune* staffer **Judith Crist** of the 5'8" windblown blonde, "She had a sort of movie-star prettiness, almost like a cross between Betty Grable's and Marilyn Monroe's, with a super figure and those absolutely blue eyes. She looked taller than she was because she was so slender."

On July 12, 1942, Higgins married Harvard philosophy professor Stanley Moore, whom she had met while he was a teaching aide at Berkeley. The couple drifted apart almost immediately, Stanley serving overseas with the Army Air Force, and they were formally divorced in 1948. Marguerite was soon talking quite openly about her frequent infidelities, revealing a pattern of flaunting her many sexual involvements that would last her entire life.

Finding herself blocked in her desire to cover World War II directly, Higgins bypassed her editors and pleaded directly with *Tribune* publisher ***Helen Rogers Reid**. "My main anxiety," Higgins said, "was to get in the war before it ended." In August 1944, she was assigned to the *Herald Tribune*'s London office. Six months later, because of her fluency in French, she was ordered to Paris. By March, she was at the front, covering the Allied invasion of Germany. Working 20 hours a day, she filed up to 3,000 words a night. In that year, she drew more front-page stories than any other reporter.

Accompanying the Seventh Army deep into Austria, Higgins reported Hermann Goering's claim that Adolf Hitler had ordered his execution; the plight of Spanish refugees in the French Forces of the Interior; the discovery of Nazi archives in a vault in Lichtenfels Castle; and execution of French collaborationist Pierre Laval. She provided accounts of the capture of Munich, the American entry into Buchenwald concentration camps, and life at Hitler's lair at Berchtesgaden.

Arriving at Dachau ahead of the American forces, Higgins—together with Peter Furst of the *Stars and Stripes*—had cut across six miles of

Marguerite Higgins

German-held territory to reach the prison compound. Along the way, they passed groups of fully armed Wehrmacht soldiers prepared to surrender. When an SS general surrendered to the two correspondents, German tower guards had Higgins in their sights.

I looked up. There was a watchtower crammed with . . . SS men. They were staring intently at me. Rifles were at the ready, and the machine gun was trained on me. God knows what prompted me other than the instinctive feeling that there was absolutely no point in running. Instead of

> heeding the frantic sergeant, I addressed myself to the SS guards. "Kommen Sie her, bitte. Wir sind Amerikaner." Come here, please. We are Americans.

At this point, 22 SS guards descended from the tower and surrendered to her personally. When the American forces arrived in bulk, the Dachau prisoners were told that they would be quarantined until they were inoculated for typhus. Not only did a major riot break out; in suicidal protest, six camp inmates deliberately threw themselves against the electrically charged fences. Higgins and Furst had to appeal for calm on the camp's loudspeaker. For her story on Dachau, she won the New York Newspaper Women's Club Award for best foreign correspondent of 1945.

Just as the war ended, Higgins formed a passionate if brief attachment to George Reid ("Golden") Millar, correspondent for the *London Daily Express,* whom she called "the most beautiful man I ever met." When the sophisticated Millar sought to have Higgins settle permanently with him in England, she broke off the relationship.

Subsequent Higgins stories included the Nuremberg proceedings, the treason trial of Marshal Philippe Pétain, the Four Power Control Commission in Berlin, and an interview with Czech foreign minister Jan Masaryk in Prague. Driving alone to Warsaw, Higgins saw the brutalities of Soviet rule in both Poland and East Germany. She was arrested once by Poles, once by Russians, and saw her secretary kidnapped by Communist police. The former campus radical was immediately converted to a lifelong abhorrence of Communism.

In 1947, Higgins was promoted to chief of the *Tribune*'s Berlin bureau. To meet the challenge, she put in up to 18 hours a day, often falling asleep at her typewriter from exhaustion. One of her stories, based on an interview with the mayor of Düsseldorf, resulted in emergency American aid for starving Germans. Her beat allowed her to cover the hottest story of 1948, the Berlin blockade. In covering a riot at the Brandenburg Gate, she suffered lacerations of arms and legs and had to be hospitalized. All this time, her competitive streak antagonized fellow correspondents, including powerful *New York Times* bureau chief Drew Middleton.

In April 1950, the *Herald Tribune* made Higgins its Tokyo bureau chief. Although at first angry about what she considered a demotion, her misfortune soon led to the high point of her career: she was able to cover firsthand the initial engagements of the Korean War. On June 27, two days after North Korea attacked South Korea, she made the last American plane into Seoul's Kimpo airfield. Within hours, she was part of the long retreat south, at one point walking 14 miles to the town of Suwan. Although she barely left the front alive, General Douglas MacArthur, UN Commander for Korea, gave her a hitch back to Tokyo and an exclusive interview, one in which he revealed he was requesting fresh American ground troops.

American readers again became used to her front-page bylines. One story, datelined AN ADVANCE COMMAND OUTPOST IN SOUTH KOREA, dealt with the first American soldier to die in the war. It closed with the words:

> The medics brought the dead soldier's body in here, tenderly lifting him from a jeep. The lifeless form was shrouded in a blanket which kept the pelting rain off the blond young face. As medics brought the body in, one young private said bitterly, "What a place to die!"

Lieutenant General Walton H. Walker, Eighth Army commander, soon ordered all female correspondents away from combat zones on the grounds that "there are no facilities at the front." Higgins appealed to Helen Reid, who convinced MacArthur to rescind the order. At a time when women were expected to prefer safer occupations and special treatment, Higgins argued, "I am not working in Korea as a woman. I am there as a war correspondent." MacArthur's cable read: BAN ON WOMEN CORRESPONDENTS IN KOREA HAS BEEN LIFTED. MARGUERITE HIGGINS IS HELD IN HIGHEST PROFESSIONAL ESTEEM BY EVERYONE. Higgins had been equally admiring of the general, writing just before the war broke out that he possessed "the most brilliant and encompassing views of military and world affairs that I've ever encountered. I found him straightforward, charming, and far from pompous."

Higgins always shared the same hardships as the foot-soldiers. She wore the same dirty slacks and shirt for weeks on end, ate rations out of cans, and inhaled more than her share of Korea's brown dust. Once, when injured in a jeep accident, she suffered a slight concussion, but she sneaked out of the hospital that very afternoon so as not to miss a dinner party of the American ambassador. In September 1950, Higgins was supposed to be restricted to covering the Inchon landing from a naval ship. However, the relevant orders were so poorly drafted that she hit the beach with the fifth wave of Marine assault troops. "I walked out of Seoul, and I wanted to walk back in" was her only rationale.

Higgins' desire for scoops aroused the ire of veteran *Tribune* war correspondent Homer Bigart, who sought her removal from the battlefield. Ironically, the competition between Higgins and Bigart resulted in some of the best war coverage ever produced by American journalists. Bigart later paid her a backhanded compliment when he said, "She made me work like hell." Along with five fellow war correspondents, including her archrival Bigart, she won the 1951 Pulitzer Prize for international reporting. Among her 50 other awards was the George Polk Memorial Award of the Overseas Press Club for "courage, integrity and enterprise."

A strong hawk, Higgins advocated use of the atomic bomb once Communist China entered the Korean war. "Korea has shown how weak America was," she wrote. "It was better to find this out in Korea and in June of 1950 than on our shores and possibly too late." Her firsthand account, *War in Korea: The Report of a Woman Combat Correspondent* (1951), portrayed how Soviet-made tanks initially ripped through the ranks of the "whipped and frightened GI's," armed only with bazookas. In this book, she called South Korean president Syngman Rhee "a man of sincere democratic convictions," said that MacArthur's retreat in December 1950 was "one of the greatest strategic withdrawals in history," and claimed that the security of Europe depended upon containment of Communism in Asia.

In October 1952, Higgins married longtime lover William E. Hall, a lieutenant general with a first wife and four children who had directed intelligence during the Berlin airlift. Because of her unconventional personal life, she was the subject of various *romans à clef,* including Toni Howard's *Shriek with Pleasure* (1950) and Edwin Lanham's *The Iron Maiden* (1954). In 1955, Higgins tried her own hand at autobiography with *News Is a Singular Thing.* It was candid about her parents' stormy marriage and her affair with Millar. She did admit that she suffered from "a one-track preoccupied personality [that] can be very wearing and in many ways unattractive." At the same time, she dismissed her first husband in three sentences, never mentioning his name. Much of the book involved warnings about American weakness and a denunciation of U.S. policymakers for not seeking all-out victory in Korea.

Giving birth to several children did not curtail her ceaseless globetrotting. In the course of many trips, Higgins interviewed such leaders as Marshal Tito, Francisco Franco, Jawaharlal Nehru, the shah of Iran, and the king of Siam. In 1954, she became the first American correspondent allowed in the Soviet Union after the death of Joseph Stalin. Covering 13,500 miles in ten weeks, she traveled throughout Siberia without guide, interpreter, or companion. She claimed to have been arrested 16 times, always for taking pictures, but she noted while being held captive that she was always treated correctly and released within several hours. In her narration of her journey, *Red Plush and Black Bread* (1955), she again issued a warning: the current regime, led by Nikita Khrushchev, would pursue its goal of world Communism with far greater intelligence and flexibility than had been displayed under Stalin.

In 1958, Higgins left the Far East to become Washington correspondent for the *Herald Tribune.* She remained at the *Tribune* (which she called her "Holy Mother Church") until the middle of 1963, when the Long Island daily *Newsday* offered her a more attractive salary and generous expense account. Her thrice-weekly column also appeared in 92 other American newspapers.

Higgins traveled to the Congo in 1961, there to interview rebel leader Antoine Gizenga in Stanleyville. The following year, she warned that the Russians were entering Cuba in ominously large numbers. All this time, she was endorsing the increasing American involvement in Vietnam. "Like almost every American in Southeast Asia," Higgins said, "I believe Vietnam to be as much a front line of freedom as Hawaii or San Francisco." The French, she claimed, had not lost the area militarily. Rather, they had cravenly given up at the Geneva conference of 1955.

In 1963, Higgins took one of her many trips there. She traveled throughout the South Vietnamese countryside, interviewing peasants, Buddhist monks, tribal leaders, and American military personnel. As the Buddhist monks that she interviewed denied any persecution at the hands of President Ngo Dinh Diem, she alleged that the self-immolations of Buddhist monks were Communist-inspired. "What did the Buddhists want? Diem's head . . . and not on a silver platter but enveloped in an American flag." Her advocacy of American commitment to Southeast Asia led to another famous feud, this one with *New York Times* correspondent David Halberstam, who found her singularly naive about the South Vietnamese government.

In her book *Our Vietnam Nightmare* (1965), Higgins was particularly critical of "the inglorious role" of the United States in the fall of the Diem regime. To Higgins, Diem was a "misunderstood Mandarin," and Buddhist leader Thich Tri Quang was "Machiavelli with incense." The American bombing of North Vietnam, together with the commitment of U.S. Marines to ground warfare, was the only answer to give to doves like columnist Walter Lippmann and Senator Wayne Morse.

In the autumn of 1965, en route somewhere between Saigon and Karachi, Higgins contracted a rare tropical disease, leishmaniasis, which is incurred from the bite of a sandfly. She was hospitalized at Walter Reed Medical Center in Washington, where despite a raging fever, she continued to produce her column until just before her death on January 3, 1966. Writes her biographer Antoine May, "The decision to bury Marguerite at Arlington National Cemetery seemed appropriate. Not only was she a soldier's soldier and a soldier's wife, but she was also a woman who had often risked death to record the quiet, day-to-day heroism of soldiers." At the top of the editorial page of the *Washington Evening Star* was a drawing of a row of cemetery crosses and a plot of freshly turned earth. The caption read: AND NOW SHE IS WITH HER BOYS AGAIN.

SOURCES:

Higgins, Marguerite. *News is a Singular Thing*. Garden City, NY: Doubleday, 1955.

May, Antoine. *Witness to War: A Biography of Marguerite Higgins*. NY: Beaufort, 1983.

SUGGESTED READING:

Belford, Barbara. *Brilliant Bylines: A Biographical Anthology of Notable Newspaperwomen in America*. NY: Columbia University Press, 1986.

Edwards, Julia. *Women of the World: The Great Foreign Correspondents*. Boston, MA: Houghton Mifflin, 1988.

Elwood-Akers, Virginia. *Women War Correspondents in the Vietnam War, 1961–1975*. Metuchen, NJ: Scarecrow, 1988.

Kluger, Richard. *The Paper: The Life and Death of the New York Herald Tribune*. NY: Knopf, 1986.

COLLECTIONS:

The Marguerite Higgins papers are in the George Arents Research Library, Syracuse University.

Justus D. Doenecke,
Professor of History, New College of the University of South Florida, Sarasota, Florida

Patricia Highsmith

Highsmith, Patricia (1921–1995)

American writer who specialized in psychological crime thrillers. *Name variations: (pseudonym) Claire Morgan. Born in Fort Worth, Texas, on January 19, 1921; died in Locarno, Switzerland, on February 5, 1995; only child of Jay Plangman (a commercial artist) and Mary (Coates) Plangman (a commercial artist); graduated from Julia Richman High School in Manhattan; graduated from Barnard College, New York City, 1942; never married; no children.*

Selected works: Strangers on a Train *(1949); (under pseudonym Claire Morgan)* The Price of Salt *(1952);* The Blunderer *(1954);* The Talented Mr. Ripley *(1955);* Deep Water *(1957); (juvenile with Doris Sanders)* Miranda the Panda Is on the Veranda *(1958);* A Game for the Living *(1958);* This Sweet Sickness *(1960);* The Cry of the Owl *(1962);* The Two Faces of January *(1964);* The Glass Cell *(1964);* The Story-Teller *(1965);* Plotting and Writing Suspense Fiction *(1966);* Those Who Walk Away *(1967);* The Tremor of Forgery *(1969);* The Snail Watcher and Other Stories *(1970);* Eleven *(1970);* Ripley Under Ground *(1971);* A Dog's Ransom *(1972);* Ripley's Game *(1974);* The Animal-Lover's Book of Beastly Murder *(1975);* Little Tales of Misogyny *(1977);* Slowly, Slowly in the Wind *(1979);* The Boy Who Followed Ripley *(1980);* The Black House *(1981);* People Who Knock on the Door *(1982);* Mermaids on the Golf Course and other Stories *(1985);* Found in the Street *(1986);* Tales of Natural and Unnatural Catastrophes *(1987);* Ripley Under Water *(1991).*

The author of some 30 books, most of them in the crime-fiction genre, Patricia Highsmith gained recognition in 1950 with her first novel *Strangers on a Train* (filmed by Alfred Hitchcock in 1951 with a screenplay by Raymond Chandler). She is best remembered, however, for her five-book series centering on Tom Ripley, an opportunistic, amoral gentleman-murderer who made his debut in *The Talented Mr. Ripley* (1955) and whose final escapade, *Ripley Under Water* (1991), was written when the author was

From the movie The Talented Mr. Ripley, *starring Matt Damon and Gwyneth Paltrow, based on the novel by Patricia Highsmith.*

70. Highsmith, a reclusive figure who lived most of her adult life in Europe, won numerous awards for her dark, psychological thrillers which were extremely popular in Europe and attracted a cult following in the United States. The author, however, never took her success too seriously. "It's nothing like James Michener, I'm sure," she once commented.

Highsmith was born in 1921 in Fort Worth, Texas, the only child of commercial artists who separated before she was born. "If your father walked out before you were born and your mother says she tried to abort you by guzzling turpentine, you may grow up with a sour view of humanity," writes Richard Corliss. Reared by her grandparents until age six, Patricia subsequently moved to New York with her mother **Mary Plangman Highsmith** and stepfather, artist Stanley Highsmith. She found solace from a less than happy childhood in books. "I could read like a streak, because my grandmother taught me when I was two," she said later. By the age of eight, Highsmith had read all of the stories of Sherlock Holmes as well as Karl Menninger's *The Human Mind,* a book of case histories about kleptomaniacs, pyromaniacs, serial murderers, and other colorful patients Menninger had treated. "The very fact that it was real made it more interesting and more important than fairy tales. I saw that the people looked outwardly normal, and I realized there could be such people around me."

Highsmith edited her high school newspaper and began writing short stories at age 17. She majored in English at Barnard College and, after graduating in 1942, supported herself for a while writing plots and dialogue for a comic-book publisher. In 1945, she came a step closer to a legitimate writing career with the publication of a short story in *Harper's Bazaar*. With the help of Truman Capote, she joined the Yaddo artists' colony in Saratoga Springs, in upstate New York, where she began her first novel, *Strangers on a Train* (1950), now considered a suspense classic. The story concerns psychopath Charles Bruno, who meets the unhappily married Guy Haines on a train, murders Haines' wife, and then demands that

Haines kill his father as a return favor. This plot line, involving the intersecting of two radically different characters (sometimes good and evil), came to characterize several of Highsmith's later works, including *The Two Faces of January* (1964), Crime Writers of England's novel of the year.

In the first book of the well-known and critically acclaimed Ripley series, *The Talented Mr. Ripley* (1955), Highsmith's charming, cultured, and psychopathic antihero Thomas Ripley, an American traveling in Europe, murders a man and takes on his identity with impunity. Becoming wealthy on the man's inheritance and gaining access to European society, Ripley eventually resumes his own identity. Praised by Anthony Boucher of *The New York Times Book Review* for her "unusual insight into a particular type of criminal," Highsmith won both the Mystery Writers of America Scroll and the Grand Prix de Littérature Policière for the novel, which was also made into a successful film by the French director René Clement in 1961 under the title *Purple Moon*. In 1999, *The Talented Mr. Ripley*, starring Matt Damon, **Gwyneth Paltrow**, **Cate Blanchett**, and **Jude Law**, was released to major acclaim. "Ripley is one of the most interesting characters in postwar fiction," said its director Anthony Minghella. "This sense of a man with his nose pressed up against the window, the sense that there's a better life being led by other people—to me these feelings are familiar and pungent." Another of Highsmith's novels, *The Cry of the Wolf* (1962), was filmed by director Claude Chabrol in 1988.

In addition to her novels, Highsmith authored six volumes of short stories. Written in her detached style, they are as chilling as her longer works. Graham Greene, in a foreword to *The Snail Watcher and Other Stories* (1970), published in England as *Eleven*, notes that Highsmith changed her technique to accommodate the shorter format. "She is after the quick kill rather than the slow encirclement of the reader, and how admirably and with field-craft, she hunts us down."

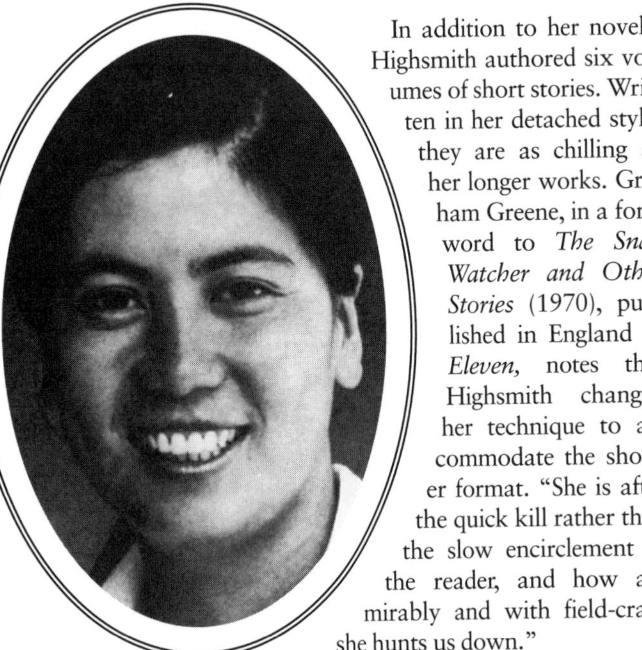

Chako Higuchi

Highsmith lived in Italy, England, and France before settling in a small Swiss village outside of Locarno. Never married, she lived alone with her beloved cat, Charlotte. "I don't like to live with people," she explained. "I don't like to talk all the time and adjust my schedule to others." In addition to writing, Highsmith painted, sculpted, and enjoyed puttering in her carpentry studio. She kept her morning free for business and personal correspondence (including a lively exchange with fellow expatriate Gore Vidal who claimed they shared "the same dim view of America") and worked in the afternoons and early evening, typing out her manuscripts on a manual typewriter that she rescued from the trash. Her stories, she insisted, were never taken from actual crimes or from personal experiences but came to her impulsively. "I do not *ever* think of suspense or unease when I'm writing," she said. "I can't explain where the ideas come from. No, I never try to analyze that, *never*." Patricia Highsmith died in Locarno, on February 5, 1995. In 1998, it was revealed that she had bequeathed her $3-million estate to Yaddo, where she had written *Strangers on a Train*.

SOURCES:

Berch, Bettina. "Patricia Highsmith," in *Belles Lettres*. Summer 1995.

Mainiero, Lina. *American Women Writers*. NY: Frederick Ungar, 1980.

Moritz, Charles. *Current Biography 1991*. NY: H.W. Wilson, 1990.

"Pages," in *People Weekly*. January 11, 1993.

"The Talented Mrs. Highsmith" and "Can Matt Play Ripley's Game?" in *Time*. December 27, 1999, n.p.

RELATED MEDIA:

Strangers on a Train (101 min. film), starring Farley Granger, ***Ruth Roman**, and Robert Walker, screenplay by Raymond Chandler, produced and directed by Alfred Hitchcock, Warner Bros., 1951.

The American Friend (film adapted from *Ripley's Game*), starring Dennis Hopper, directed by Wim Wenders, 1977.

The Cry of the Wolf, filmed by director Claude Chabrol, 1988.

Purple Noon (French film based on *The Talented Mr. Ripley*), starring Alain Delon, directed by René Clement, re-released in U.S., 1996.

The Talented Mr. Ripley (film), starring Matt Damon, Gwyneth Paltrow, Cate Blanchett, Jude Law, Philip Seymour Hoffman, and Jack Davenport, written and directed by Anthony Minghella, Paramount, 1999.

Barbara Morgan,
Melrose, Massachusetts

Higuchi, Chako (1945—)

Japanese golfer. *Born Hisako Matsui Higuchi in Tokyo, Japan, on October 13, 1945.*

Chako Higuchi began playing golf in 1963 and rose quickly to become the top woman player in Japan. She won three Japanese LPGA and Open titles and started competing in America in 1970. In 1973, she played in only eight events in the United States but won more than $10,000. In 1976, she won the Colgate European Open and, in 1977, the LPGA championship. She played less frequently in 1978 and 1979, though she finished close to the top in nearly every tournament she entered.

Higuchi was extremely popular with American galleries due to her petite stature and unorthodox swing that captivated but stymied golf analysts. Though ***Nancy Lopez** questioned her form on the tee in *Women Golfers,* "her steady rhythm and timing" helped her meet the ball at just the right moment. "She doesn't hit a long ball compared to some of us, and often uses a wood for a medium long approach . . . where most would take an iron, but her woods usually fly straight as an arrow and land well placed on the green."

SOURCES:

Lopez, Nancy, with Peter Schwed. *The Education of a Woman Golfer.* NY: Simon and Schuster, 1979.

Hilaria (fl. 304)

German saint. *Flourished in 304; died in Augsburg; possibly the mother of St. Afra.*

Hilaria, who flourished around 304, is possibly the mother of St. ***Afra**. Legend has it that when Afra was martyred during the reign of Diocletian, Hilaria was also martyred at her tomb. Hilaria's feast day is celebrated on August 12.

Hild (614–680).

See Hilda of Whitby.

Hilda, Saint (614–680).

See Hilda of Whitby.

Hilda of Hartlepool (fl. 8th c.)

English abbess. *Flourished in the 8th century at Hartlepool, England.*

Very few discernible facts are available about Hilda of Hartlepool. An English noble, she entered the Benedictine abbey of Hartlepool as a young woman, and eventually rose to be its abbess. Hartlepool was a double monastery where monks and nuns lived communally under the abbess' direction. Hilda continued the tradition of early abbeys as learning centers. She herself had been highly educated in Latin and the classical liberal arts, and saw to it that her monks and nuns were similarly trained. Hartlepool was also a sort of school for children of the Saxon nobility. It is not certain, but the abbey most likely also featured a scriptorium, where manuscripts were copied and illuminated.

Laura York,
Riverside, California

Hilda of Whitby (614–680)

Founding abbess of the noted double monastery of Whitby in the ancient British kingdom of Northumbria, a center of learning where five future English bishops were educated, who was described by the Venerable Bede as "the blaze of light which filled all England with its splendor." *Name variations: Hild; Saint Hilda. Born in 614 in the kingdom of Deira, Northumbria; died at Whitby (Streaneshalch or Streonaeshalch) on November 17, 680; daughter of Hereric (a nephew of Edwin, king of the Northumbria kingdom of Deira), and Berguswida (Breguswith), origin unknown; never married; no children.*

Baptized at York on Easter Sunday (April 2, 627); became abbess at Whitby (657); hosted the Council of Whitby (664); educated five future English bishops; sponsored Caedmon, the illiterate cowherd who first retold the stories of the Bible in Old English verse and became known as the Father of English Poetry; founded monastery of Hackness (680).

On a night in early 7th-century England, a lonely young woman dreamed that she went in search of her absent husband. Although she did not find the man she sought, she did discover a brilliant necklace, hidden in the folds of her gown, which shone so brightly that its light filled the house. This prophetic dream is the earliest story told about Saint Hilda of Whitby. The young dreamer is **Berguswida**, then the pregnant wife of Hereric, a nephew of King Edwin of the Northumbrian kingdom of Deira. Sent to spy for the king in a foreign court, Hereric would be poisoned by his host and die far from home. Hilda, the daughter born after his death, was believed by the chronicler of the dream to be symbolized by the gleaming necklace as one who would one day light all of England.

In 614, the year of Hilda's birth, Northumbria, like most of England, was pagan. Christianity had been introduced by the Romans but had largely vanished with Rome's departing legions, and subsequent Anglo-Saxon invasions had brought the island a Germanic religion with its own idols and temples. Celtic Christianity survived only in the far north of Britain.

It was toward the beginning of the 7th century when Pope Gregory the Great is said to have asked about the handsome, fair-complexioned youths he saw in the slave markets of Rome; told that they were pagan Angles, the pope responded that they had the look of angels. In 596, Gregory concluded that the Angles deserved to receive the good news of Christianity and directed Augustine, a Christian missionary, to travel with a band of 40 monks to their island home to carry out their conversion.

The missionaries were not happy about the assignment. They thought of England as a grim and alien land, peopled with hostile heathens, and could not take consolation in the alluring description yet to be written, some hundred years later, by a scholarly Northumbrian monk known as the Venerable Bede, who was to become the Father of English History. In his *Ecclesiastical History of the English Nation,* the monk would write:

> Britain, an island in the ocean, formerly called Albion . . . excels for grain and trees, and is well adapted for feeding cattle and beasts of burden. It also produces vines in some places, and has plenty of land and water-fowls of several sorts; it is remarkable also for rivers abounding in fish, and plentiful springs. . . . Britain has also many veins of metals, as copper, iron, lead and silver; it has much excellent jet, which is black and sparkling, glittering at the fire, and when heated drives away serpents. . . . The island was formerly embellished with twenty-eight noble cities, besides innumerable castles. . . . And from its lying almost under the North Pole, the nights are light in summer, so that at midnight the beholders are often in doubt whether the evening twilight still continues, or that of the morning is coming on. . . . This island at present, following the number of the books in which the Divine law was written, contains five nations, the English, Britons, Scots, Picts, and Latins, each in its own peculiar dialect cultivating the sublime study of Divine truth.

Augustine would in fact become head of a flourishing English mission with its center at the great church and school of Canterbury. But in the year of Hilda's birth, Northumbria was still dominated by the fierce pagan ruler Ethelfrith. When Hilda was two years old, Edwin succeeded Ethelfrith. Edwin, who was still a pagan and said to be counseled in his youth by a wizard, proved to be a strong ruler who brought peace and union to the small kingdoms of Northumbria. Edwin rode among his people with a standard bearer before him in the old Roman way, brass cups were hung at crossroads where there were springs so that travelers could slake their thirst, and it was said that a woman with her child in her arms could walk in safety across the land.

In time, King Edwin married a Christian princess from Kent, in the south of England. When the young queen ***Ethelberga of Northumbria** came north, she was accompanied by her priest, a Roman missionary who set about trying to Christianize Northumbria. A letter from the pope also urged Ethelberga to bring her husband to the true faith.

The Venerable Bede would write of the questions Edwin addressed to his wise men. Should Northumbrians abandon the religion of their fathers and accept the new God? One advisor replied:

> The present life of man, oh King, is like the swift flight of a sparrow through a room where you sit at supper in winter, beside a hot fire, while rain and snow beat outside. The sparrow, flying in at one door and immediately out another, is safe from the winter storm while he is inside, but after this short space of fair weather, he immediately vanishes out of your sight, into the dark winter from which he came. So this life of man appears for a little while, but we know nothing at all of what went before or what is to follow. If this new religion tells us something more certain, it deserves to be followed.

Accepting this wisdom, Edwin became a Christian. He ordered the construction of a wooden chapel in the old Roman city of York which was his headquarters, and on April 2, Easter Sunday, in the year 627, he was baptized there with members of the royal household, including the teenaged Hilda.

The years of Hilda's young womanhood have gone mysteriously unreported. In 632, King Edwin was killed in battle, and paganism again took hold in the region. As a member of the royal family now out of favor, Hilda may have lived in quiet retreat. Since marriage was typically the only life open to a royal princess, and since the Venerable Bede, who gloried in writing about holy virgins, wrote about Hilda with great admiration but never in those terms, it has been suggested by one modern scholar that she may have accepted a pagan husband. The one certainty is that Hilda remained a Christian.

Around 647, Hilda's life sprang into the full light of history when she was 33 and journeyed south to East Anglia, where her sister **Hereswitha**'s son was king. Hilda had intended to join Hereswitha in a journey to the noted monastery of Chelles in France, to spend the rest of her life in study and devotion. But Hereswitha had already departed across the Channel, and Hilda remained briefly in East Anglia under the protection of her nephew.

While still in East Anglia, she encountered Aidan, a pious counselor to Northumbrian kings and abbot of the austere monastic community of Lindesfarne, off the Northumbrian coast. Aidan was a monk out of the Celtic tradition, who lived an ascetic life, traveling about England on foot, speaking the truth as he saw it to both the mighty and the powerless. Persuaded by the monk's eloquence and no doubt by her own heart, Hilda gave up her dream of a secure and scholarly life and followed his advice that she return to her native Northumbria and begin the challenging task of organizing religious communities among her own people. According to Aidan's instructions, she was first given a small estate, apparently on the banks of the River Wear, where she headed a group of nuns. Next she was called to Hartlepool, originally presided over by Hieu, the first Northumbrian woman to have taken the veil. There Hilda became abbess of a small double monastery, where both men and women lived under her religious rule.

In 657, Hilda's great life work began when her cousin King Oswy granted her ten "hides" of land to found and develop another double monastery, on a promontory where the River Esk flowed into the storm-tossed North Sea. Since the Danish invasions at the end of the 8th century, the site has been known as Whitby, but in Hilda's time it was called Streaneshalch, which has been translated as the Place of the Light, or, according to the Bede, the Bay of the Lighthouse, a name which may have been both symbolic and literal in meaning.

England in the 7th century saw the founding of a number of double monasteries under the rule of powerful abbesses, who were often members of a royal family. The practices within these institutions differed widely. In some, men did the heavy work of farming, raising the barley, oats, wheat, and flax needed to feed and clothe the community, while monks and nuns lived wholly apart. The abbess sometimes lived in seclusion, never speaking directly to a man. At Hilda's monastery, the ruins are too fragmentary to tell us just how the community was arranged, but Bede's writings suggest that considerable openness and freedom existed there. Certainly Hilda could not have remained in seclusion. Men and women called their abbess "Mother" and revered her for her virtue and for her wisdom, a quality much valued in Anglo-Saxon women. All monastery property was communally owned. Small crosses carved of the gleaming black jet dug from the cliffs at Whitby, or taken from the streams nearby, may have been the chief personal possessions of the people in the order.

Hereswitha (d. c. 690)

Saint and queen of East Anglia. *Name variations: Heruswith. Died around 690; daughter of Hereric (a nephew of Edwin, king of the Northumbria kingdom of Deira), and* ***Berguswida*** *(Breguswith), origin unknown; sister of ****Hilda of Whitby****; married St. Ethelbert; married Anna, king of East Anglia; children: one son who was the king of East Anglia; and daughter Ethelburga (d. 665); stepmother of ****Sexburga*** *(d. 699?) and ****Eltheltbrith*** *(630–679).*

With the consent of her second husband, Anna, king of East Anglia, Hereswitha journeyed to France around 646, accompanied by her daughter ***Ethelburga** and her granddaughter **Ercongata**, and took the veil at Chelles. Another queen, St. ***Balthild**, founder of the convent, entered around the same time. Hereswitha's feast day is September 23.

At Whitby, Hilda established a regular rule for all who were in her charge. A town of many buildings was probably contained within its walls, and both monks and nuns spent much of their time studying the holy scriptures in Latin. Devotions were regular and demanding. The first thatched-roof church was soon replaced by a finer stone structure, perhaps like the church still existing at Escomb, County Durham, with altars to St. Peter and St. Gregory. King Edwin's remains are believed to have been brought there for final burial, and there King Oswy would also be laid to rest.

The skill of Whitby masons was much admired in their carved roadway markers and memorial stones. Other talents were also developed there. Throughout Western Europe during the 7th century, patient and talented religious devotees spent their time copying gospels, psalters, complete Bibles and scholarly works onto sheets of vellum they embellished with fine flowing script and illustrations in gold and bright colors. No manuscript from the time of Hilda is known to exist, but Northumbrian manuscripts became noted for their special beauty, and the foundation for their future fame must have been laid in her scriptorium. Men and women shared equally in the access to learning which the scriptorium and the monastery library afforded.

Hilda also established a school where five later bishops were trained, as well as an unknown number of priests. There she taught "justice, piety, chastity and other virtues." No record of her academic curriculum remains, but the excavated book clasps and brass-and-bone styluses used for writing on wax tablets suggest assiduous learning. Latin was certainly taught there; grammar, chant, and dialectic were surely studied, and possibly some rhetoric, astronomy, arithmetic and geometry. ***Elflaed** (d. 714), Hilda's successor as abbess, who was trained from early childhood at Hartlepool and Whitby, wrote a very elaborate Latin, known from a still extant letter. One modern scholar describes Whitby at the middle of the 7th century as "the preeminent center of learning in Anglo-Saxon England." The Venerable Bede called it "the blaze of light which filled all Britain with its splendor."

No woman in the Middle Ages ever held a position comparable with that of Hilda of Whitby.

—**Frank Stenton**

It was at Whitby that the man who was to be called the Father of English Poetry was first identified. According to Bede's story, a cowherd on the monastery grounds, named Caedmon, sat one night drinking and singing with merry companions who followed the custom of passing around a harp which each man used to accompany his own song. But when the harp came to the cowherd, he fled to the stables, too shy to sing.

In the stable, Caedmon dreamed that he was visited by a stranger who commanded him to "Sing the beginning of created beings," whereupon, according to Bede, the cowherd began a verse in praise of God, "the Maker of the Heavenly kingdom," in his native Anglo-Saxon tongue. When Caedmon wakened, he told his overseer about the hymn he had sung so miraculously and remembered. The overseer took him to the abbess, who immediately saw the missionary value in having the gospel translated from Latin into the everyday language and poetic form of the Northumbrian people. Hilda commanded the cowherd to join her monks, learn the gospel stories from them, and translate the works into Anglo-Saxon verse. For many years, much early Christian poetry was attributed to Caedmon, but scholars attribute only nine lines of the surviving original verse to him. Together, however, the abbess and the cowherd began a tradition important to the development of English poetry and to the conversion of the Northumbrians.

In 664, Hilda hosted an occasion crucial to the development of the English church as an institution, when the Council of Whitby was held, attended by her royal cousin, King Oswy, as well as the leading men of the Northumbrian church. The two immediate issues presented for discussion were the tonsure of the clergy and the date for the celebration of Easter, but the larger issue they represented was the question of whether the older Celtic tradition or the Roman tradition introduced by Augustine should dominate the English church. Irish monks wore their hair cut from ear to ear, while the Romans shaved all but a narrow circlet, in memory of Christ's crown of thorns. King Oswy's own household had a lively interest in the question of the Easter date, since Oswy himself had been trained by Irish monks and his queen ***Eanfleda** by missionaries from Rome. As a result, Easter was held twice a year in their domain, resulting in much confusion, if not acrimony, in the royal chapel and possibly in the royal kitchen.

Hilda, trained by her beloved Aidan, favored the Irish position, but Wilfrid, the chief speaker for the opposition, had been trained in Rome and was an eloquent orator, arguing that the old Irish monks had no doubt been holy men but were mistaken in their calculation of the date of the holy day and in other matters. St. Peter, the rock upon which Christ had founded his church, had stood for the Roman way. King Oswy, being a wily politician, listened to all arguments and, at length, declared that when he came to the heavenly gates, it would be St. Peter who held the keys, and the king wanted to be sure that he would be allowed to enter. The king's position proved decisive, and the long Roman rule of the English church was thus assured, with occasional setbacks, not to be ended for 900 years, until the reign of King Henry VIII. Doubtless saddened by the council's decision, Hilda dispatched an anti-Wilfrid delegation to Rome in 679, but she remained abbess at Whitby until her death the following year, on November 17, 680.

For the last seven years of her life, Hilda suffered what Bede called "a great fever" which at last "turned inward." But she remained active in performing her duties and, at the time she was dying, called her people together to admonish them to maintain "ecclesiastical peace." Bede, whose belief in miracles is hard to assess, reported that Hilda's death was marked with visions.

At Harkness, a smaller monastery Hilda had founded early in that year, a pious nun named **Begu** lay asleep, when she heard, according to Bede, "the sound of a bell . . . and opening her eyes, as she thought, she saw the top of the house open, and a strong light pour in from above, looking earnestly upon that light, she saw the soul of the aforesaid servant of God [Hilda] in that same light, attended and conducted to heaven by angels." A nun at Whitby claimed to have had the same vision and called her companions together in prayer for the newly dead.

Hilda was succeeded as abbess by her cousin Oswy's daughter Elflaed, whom she had reared at Hartlepool and Whitby, and by Oswy's widow Eanfleda, with mother and daughter sharing the rule. During their time, a still extant *Life of St. Gregory* was written by a Whitby monk. A life of Hilda herself, though mentioned in old manuscripts, has been lost.

Like Hilda's early years, the fate of her monastery is shrouded in mystery. Almost surely, Whitby shared the devastation inflicted on other great ecclesiastical houses of northern England during the Danish raids at the end of the 8th century. Now a later Norman church, also in ruins, occupies the site. The bones of the saint may have been taken for safekeeping to the famous old abbey at Glastonbury where, according to another colorful legend, the bones of King Arthur and Queen ***Guinevere** were also laid. If so, they would have been part of the devastation wreaked at Glastonbury during King Henry VIII's reign in the 16th century.

Only a few minor miracles have been ascribed to Hilda. She is said to have turned serpents into stones and to have prevented birds from destroying the abbey crops, but no miraculous healings or magic wells, commonly ascribed to saints, have been linked to her. Her actual accomplishment was far more enduring: the protection and furthering of the growth of her church during a crucial, war-torn period of English history. To note, as **Lina Eckenstein** has stated, that "the desire to raise women to sainthood was essentially Anglo-Saxon and was strongest in the time which immediately followed the acceptance of Christianity" does not detract from her contributions.

SOURCES:

Bede, Venerabilis. *Ecclesiastical History of the English Nation*. Reprint. London: J.M. Dent, 1954.

Fell, Christine E. "Hilda, Abbess of Streonaeshalch," in *Hagiography and Medieval Literature—a Symposium*. Edited by H. Bekker-Nielsen. Odense, 1981.

———. *Women in Anglo-Saxon England*. Bloomington: University of Indiana, 1984.

Fisher, D.J.V. *The Anglo-Saxon Age*. London: Longman, 1973.

Owen, Gale R. *Rites and Religions of the Anglo-Saxons*. Devon: David and Charles, 1981.

Rollason, David. *Saints and Relics in Anglo-Saxon England*. Oxford: Basil Blackwell, 1989.

Margery Evernden,
professor emerita of English,
University of Pittsburgh, Pennsylvania, and freelance writer

Hildegard.

Variant of Hildegar or Hildegarde.

Hildegard (c. 802–841)

***Countess of Auvergne.** Born around 802; died in 841; daughter of ***Ermengarde** (c. 778–818) and Louis I the Pious (778–840), king of Aquitaine (r. 781–814), king of France (r. 814–840), and Holy Roman Emperor (r. 814–840); married Gerard (c. 795–841), count of Auvergne; children: Ramnulf I (b. around 820), count of Poitou.*

Hildegard of Bingen (1098–1179)

***Benedictine abbess and visionary who, in her prose, poetry, and musical composition, gave a strong and imageful voice to divine revelation.** Name variations: Saint Hildegard, Hildegarde, or Hildegarda; Hildegard von Bingen; Hildegarde of Rupertsberg. Born in 1098 in Bermersheim near Alzey (Rheinhessen), Germany; died in Rupertsberg near Bingen on September 17, 1179; daughter of noble parents, Hildebert and Mechthild.*

Had first illuminative vision (c. 1101); was offered to God as a tithe (the tenth child of her parents) and placed in the care of the anchorite Jutta at the monastery at Disibodenberg (c. 1106); made monastic profession in the community that had formed around Jutta (c. 1113); at death of Jutta, succeeded her as magistra *of the community (1136); in response to divine command, reluctantly began to record her visions in what would become* Scivias *(1141); Pope Eugenius III (r. 1145–1153) blessed her visionary writing (1147–48); moved community to Rupertsberg (1147–50); established daughter house at Eibingen (c. 1165); Rupertsberg community placed under interdict (1178).*

Selected works: Scivias *(1141–51);* Symphonia armonie celestium revelationum *(1150s);* Lingua ignota *(1150s);* Ordo virtutum *(perf. 1152?);* Liber vitae meritorum *(1158–63),* Physica *(1150s);* Causae et curae *(1150s);* Liber divinorum operum *(1163–70).*

In her remarkable life as a Benedictine nun and abbess, Hildegard of Bingen raised a strong voice of spiritual vision that found an outlet in numerous prose works (visionary, scientific, and hagiographic), public preaching, liturgical poetry, musical composition, and a voluminous correspondence that brought popes and monarchs within her sphere. The breadth of her output, or, as she would more likely have put it, the breadth of what God worked through her, is impressive by any measure, but especially so for a 12th-century woman. Although we generally would place her work in distinct categories—poetry, music, science, visionary prose, etc.—her world view brought them into unity. In her *Scivias,* she writes: "God, who made all things by His will created them so that His name would be known and glorified, showing in them not just the things that are visible and temporal, but also the things that are invisible and eternal." In other words, to her the fullness of creation participates in the praise of God and reveals the immaterial and transcendent in the form of the material and immanent.

Oh humans, look at the human being! For it contains heaven and earth and other creatures in itself, and is one form, and all things hide in it.

—Hildegard of Bingen, ***Causae et curae***

From the age of 15, Hildegard lived as a professed nun, and monasticism offers an important context in which to view both her creative work and her life as a woman. The center of the Benedictine life, in Hildegard's day as in our own, is the *Opus Dei,* the liturgical round of offices (prayer services) sung or recited periodically through the day and night. Relying heavily on the singing of the Latin Psalter (the Biblical book of Psalms), the office required at least rudimentary literacy and musical skill, generally learned by nuns during their novitiate, if not earlier. Hildegard was explicit that her first monastic guardian, the solitary ***Jutta of Sponheim,** was "no scholar" and that her own education was limited. Her *Vita,* rich in autobiographical passages, records that she did not know how to decipher the texts of the Bible (*Vita,* I/1); she states as well that although she composed and sang chant, she "had never studied neums [any of various symbols representing from one to four notes] or any chant notation at all" (*Vita,* I/2). Nevertheless, we can assume that basic liturgical skills were part of her early training. Moreover, the convent traditionally supplied a place wherein women could pursue the liturgical arts and other learning free of the social conventions that would restrict these activities in the secular world. For example, Hildegard's activity as a composer found both a natural outlet and a rich nurture within the conventual liturgy that it would have been denied outside the cloister.

Within the world of the convent, various aspects of Hildegard's womanhood created interesting counterpoints. Presumably the monastic ideal of humility was especially appropriate to medieval "brides of Christ," but, at the same time, monastic formation well equipped some nuns for strong leadership. Hildegard's vigorous homiletics evidences her potent leadership in the world of both high-born, powerful men as well as women. Although as a woman she regularly acknowledged her weakness, this had the effect of authenticating her vision; as **Barbara Newman** suggests in her introduction to *Scivias,* her disclaimers "are meant to persuade readers that, because the author is not 'wise according to worldly standards,' her weakness and foolishness have been empowered by God alone."

It is important to note as well Hildegard's appropriation (along with male writers) of female imagery to describe God. For example, Hildegard represents the dual nature of Jesus, fully divine and fully human, by gender: "Man . . . signifies the divinity of the Son of God and woman his humanity" (*Liber divinum operum*). Strikingly, in the third vision of *Scivias,* the "Omnipotent God, incomprehensible in His majesty and inestimable in His mysteries" appears in the likeness of an egg. Elsewhere, claiming an unsurprising resonance with the visionary evangelist St. John, she compares her "inspired" knowledge to that which John received when he "sucked from the breast of Jesus the most profound revelation" (*Vita,* II/2).

By her own account, Hildegard began seeing illuminative visions in earliest childhood. However, it was not this as much as the fact that she was the tenth child of her parents that led to her being given to God as a tithe, placed in the care of the anchorite (or religious recluse) Jutta at the monastery at Disibodenberg. (Interestingly, infant oblation [the act of making an offering] would be renounced in the 12th century, and Hildegard, in later writings, is critical of the offering of a child without its informed consent.) Jutta's anchorhold would eventually spawn a community of women, professed nuns with Jutta as their *magistra* (abbess); Hildegard took her vows at the age of 15. We have little information concerning the next 20 years or so of her life, although the familiar patterns of the Benedictine day were surely characteristic. Upon the death of Jutta in 1136, Hildegard succeeded her as spiritual leader and *magistra* of the community.

It would not be long before Hildegard would reluctantly accede to the divine command to make her visions public. Although she admitted to "artlessly" speaking of them in her youth, prior to 1141 her visions were generally private, shared only with Jutta and the monk Volmar (a monk of Disibodenberg who would later act as her secretary). However, in 1141, she "heard a voice from Heaven" saying, "Cry out therefore, and write thus"—a command that brought forth *Scivias,* the first volume of her visionary trilogy. (Two other volumes, the *Liber vitae meritorum* and the *Liber divinorum operum* followed in the next decades.) The opening "Declaration" in *Scivias* makes several points clear. It asserts that the book was divinely commanded and that it proceeded from inspired or infused knowledge:

> Heaven was opened and a fiery light of exceeding brilliance came and permeated my whole brain, and inflamed my whole heart and my whole breast, not like a burning but like a warming flame, as the sun warms anything its rays touch. And immediately I knew the meaning of the exposition of the Scriptures.

Another point that emerges is Hildegard's reluctance to begin writing, a reluctance that she embodied in a characteristic sickness that dogged her throughout much of her life and had a way of emerging at particularly important times. That she was so often ill is an odd counterpoint to her longevity as an octogenarian (a person between 80 and 90 years old). Several, including the prolific neurologist-writer Oliver Sacks, have suggested that her visions were a phenomenon of migraine, a "scintillating scotoma."

In an important letter (translated by Peter Dronke) to Guibert of Gembloux written late in her life, Hildegard describes her visionary state, telling him of the illuminative quality of the visions, the wakeful, non-ecstatic way in which she receives them, and the existence of two levels of illumination, one rarer and more mystically affective than the other:

> Since my infancy . . . I have always seen this vision in my soul. . . . And as God wills, in this vision my spirit mounts upwards, into the height of the firmament and into changing air, and dilates itself among different nations. . . . And because I see these things in such a manner, for this reason I also behold them . . . in created things. But I hear them not with my physical ears, nor with my heart's thoughts, nor do I perceive them by bringing any of my five senses to bear—but only in my soul, my physical eyes open, so that I never suffer their failing in loss of consciousness. . . . The brightness that I see . . . I call . . . 'the shadow of the living brightness.' And as sun, moon and stars appear [mirrored] in water, so Scriptures, discourses, virtues, and some works of men take form for me and are reflected radiant in this brightness. . . . And in that same brightness I sometimes . . . see another light, which I call 'the living light,' . . . and for the time I do see it, all sadness and all anguish is taken from me.

The light which characterizes her vision assumes more specific connotations in her writing. To pick one of many examples, in *Scivias,* Jesus is seen as "the sun of justice with the brilliance of burning charity, of such great glory that every creature is illumined by the brightness of His light."

Scivias was completed in 1151 with the assistance of the monk Volmar. Not surprisingly, Volmar's editorial assistance was divinely sanctioned. Hildegard records that in a vision she was instructed that:

> When there is a revelation to you from on high in familiar human form, you shall not describe this in the Latin tongue yourself, for you are not gifted with familiarity in it. Rather, let one who has a skill for polishing language finish it in a form fitting and pleasing to the human ear.

Scivias is a long work in three parts treating the "Creator and Creation," the "Redeemer and Redemption," and the "History of Salvation," the latter concluding with a number of chant texts, the "Symphony of the Blessed," and an allegorical play of vice and virtue, later to be expanded into the *Ordo virtutum.* The breadth of *Scivias* is substantially enriched by the manuscript illuminations that depict and accompany each vision. (The original illuminated manuscript disappeared in World War II, although a modern facsimile made between 1927 and 1933 survives.) A number of the illuminations interestingly feature the mandala-like images of holy circles and wheels. Such images make up an important part of Hildegard's mystical vocabulary, not only in *Scivias,* but also in the poetic texts of her *Symphonia.* There, for instance, Mary addresses Jesus: "O most beloved Son,/ whom I bore in my womb/ by the might of the circling wheel/ of holy divinity." Similarly, virgins are hymned: "O most noble verdure,/ you who are rooted in the sun and who shine in bright serenity/ in a wheel/ that no earthly eminence comprehends."

The decade during which *Scivias* was being completed was an eventful one for Hildegard. It was during this time, for instance, that Pope Eugenius III, while attending a convocation of bishops at Trier (1147–48), became acquainted with Hildegard's visionary writings. With the encouragement of Bernard of Clairvaux, he confirmed and blessed her writing, a confirmation that was all the more valuable given her status as a woman.

Also at this time, Hildegard, guided by a vision, decided to relocate her community to the more austere environment of Rupertsberg near Bingen. The relocation was difficult for a number of reasons. One was that the male monastic community at Disibodenberg was reluctant to lose their celebrated female associate. (The abbot's resistance was ultimately overcome when Hildegard suffered a period of paralysis and "from then on he allowed no further opposition to the divine command, lest he himself incur something worse" [*Vita,* I/2]. Moreover, the move proved unpopular with some within her community as well. Hildegard's nuns, like their *magistra,* were all high-born, and some were reluctant to forgo the comforts to which their birth entitled them. As the *Vita* records, "For just as the children of Israel taxed Moses, so did they; shaking their heads at me and saying: 'What good is this, that wealthy young noblewomen should move from a place in which they lacked nothing to such penury as this?'" (*Vita,* II/2). (The elitism of Hildegard's convent is the subject of an interesting exchange of letters between herself and Tengswich of Andernach.)

In the wake of the move to Rupertsberg, ***Richardis von Stade**, a nun whom Hildegard "deeply cherished," "just as Paul cherished Timothy," left the community to become abbess of Bassum. Hildegard's response to this perceived "defection" was extreme and has elicited interesting comment, including suspicions of "megalomania" and using her "prophetic persona savagely and overbearingly." Hildegard was vigorously certain that Richardis' move was not the will of God; when informed by the archbishop of Mainz that she must relent, Hildegard fierily accused him of simony. And appeals even to the pope proved to no avail. Sadly, Richardis' planned return to Hildegard and the community at Rupertsberg (perhaps for only a temporary visit) never materialized, owing to her premature death. It is a tragic event in a life full of suffering. In the *Vita,* Hildegard prefaces her account of Richardis' leaving with: "Such has been [God's] way in all my affairs since my infancy, to allow me no unruffled joy in this life, by which my mind could become puffed up" (*Vita,* II/2). It was tragic in the pain the relationship occasioned, and tragic that Richardis' death precluded the healing of the rift. But it was also a vivid instance documenting the complexity of Hildegard's temperament.

Despite the fact that the 1150s began traumatically for Hildegard, the decade was an extremely fruitful one; indeed her suffering may well have fed her creativity. Writing of her propensity for illness, her early biographer Theodoric records: "as much as she weakened in her outer self, so did she grow stronger in her inner self, with the spirit of knowledge and fortitude. For as her body wasted away, the warmth of her spirit, marvelous to relate, was kindled" (*Vita,* I/1). Thus, the trials of the relocation of the community and the loss of Richardis may too have "kindled" her spirit. Her two scientific works, *Physica* and the medical *Causae et Curae,* were written in the 1150s, as was the *Lingua ignota,* a collection of words mixing German and Latin to create a private language. Her sung morality play, the *Ordo virtutum,* was likely performed for the 1152 consecration of the monastery church at Rupertsberg. A lengthy allegorical music drama of the virtues, the soul, and the devil, it is by far the earliest extant morality play. Moreover, sung within the context of conventual life, it reminds us of the degree to which female musical activity might aspire. In this case, we can safely presume that all of the sung parts were taken by Hildegard's nuns; the devil's role, significantly a spoken part, was perhaps taken by the monk Volmar.

Hildegard's liturgical chants—sequences, hymns, antiphons, and responsories—were collected probably in the late 1150s in a work entitled *Symphonia armonie celestium revelationum,* with subsequent additions after her death. The poetry of her texts is richly imageful and rhapsodic; the music is constructed of varying formulas sometimes deployed over a strikingly wide vocal range. Not surprisingly, the melodic style of the chants partakes of a sympathetic resonance with the rhapsodic nature of the poetry.

Hildegard's views on music emerge with particular force in correspondence with prelates of the Diocese of Mainz. In 1178, Hildegard's community was placed under an interdict in a dispute regarding the burial of a former excommunicate and were thus denied the singing of the office. Her letter in response is a remarkable reflection on music. Music is seen not only as an incitement to devotion, but a link to the praise of the angels as well. Satan's action is characterized as the removal of the human from out of the celestial harmony (hence his spoken role in the *Ordo*). Moreover, the perfection of bliss in Eden is embodied in the music of Adam's voice. Adam, "still innocent before his fault, had no little kinship with the sounds of the angels' praises. . . . [I]n Adam's voice before he fell there was the sound of every harmony and the sweetness of the whole art of music. And if Adam had remained in the condition in which he was formed, human frailty could never endure the power and the resonance of that voice." Hildegard's letter thus confronts the prelates with a dramatic sense of just what it is of which they have deprived her: the interdict was not just a silencing of liturgical song, but a painful exile from the symphony of creation. The prelates remained unmoved, though the archbishop, in Rome at the time, brought the interdict to a halt.

Hildegard died the following year. Her posthumous reputation was furthered by two vitae. One, begun prior to her death, was by Godfrey, the provost of Disibodenberg, and Theodoric of Echternach Abbey; the second was by Guibert of Gembloux, a member of Hildegard's circle in the last few years of her life. Canonization procedures were begun in both the 13th and 14th centuries, though they were never brought to successful completion. Nevertheless, Hildegard is venerated in the Roman Martyrology on September 17.

SOURCES:

Bent, Ian. "Hildegard of Bingen," in *The New Grove Dictionary of Music and Musicians.* 1980.

Dronke, Peter. *Women Writers of the Middle Ages.* Cambridge: Cambridge University Press, 1984.

Hildegard of Bingen. *Scivias.* Trans. by Mother Columba Hart and Jane Bishop. Preface by Caroline Walker Bynum. Introduction by Barbara J. Newman. Mahwah, NJ: Paulist Press, 1990.

———. *Symphonia.* Trans. and edited by Barbara Newman. Ithaca, NY: Cornell University Press, 1988.

Sacks, Oliver. *The Man Who Mistook His Wife for a Hat.* NY: Harper Perennial, 1990.

Silvas, Anna, trans. "Saint Hildegard of Bingen and the Vita Sanctae Hildegardis [Godfrey and Theodoric]," in *Tjurunga: An Australasian Benedictine Review.* Vol. 29, 1985, pp. 4–25; Vol. 30, 1986, pp. 63–73; Vol. 31, 1986, pp. 32–41; Vol. 32, 1987, pp. 46–59.

Yardley, Anne. "'Ful weel she soong the service dyvyne': The Cloistered Musician in the Middle Ages," in *Women Making Music.* Edited by Jane Bowers and Judith Tick. Urbana, IL: University of Illinois Press, 1986.

SUGGESTED READING:

Dronke, Peter. *Poetic Individuality in the Middle Ages.* Oxford: Clarenden Press, 1970.

Kraft, Kent. "The German Visionary: Hildegard of Bingen," in *Medieval Women Writers.* Edited by Katharina M. Wilson. Athens, GA: University of Georgia Press, 1984.

Lachman, Barbara. *The Journal of Hildegard of Bingen.* NY: Crown, 1993.

Newman, Barbara, ed. *Voice of the Living Light: Hildegard of Bingen and Her World.* CA: University of California, 1998.

Petroff, Elizabeth A. *Medieval Women's Visionary Literature.* Oxford: Oxford University Press, 1986.

Pfau, Marianne Richert. "Hildegard von Bingen's 'Symphonia . . .': An Analysis of Musical Process, Modality, and Text-Music Relations." Ph.D. diss., SUNY Stony Brook, 1990.

Underhill, Evelyn. *Mysticism.* 12 ed. NY: Doubleday, 1990.

Steven Plank,
Professor of Musicology, Oberlin College, Oberlin, Ohio

Hildegard of Burgundy (1050–after 1104)

Duchess of Aquitaine. *Born in 1050; died after 1104; daughter of ****Ermengarde of Anjou*** *(1018–1076) and Robert I (1011–1076), duke of Burgundy (r. 1031–1076); married William VIII (c. 1026–1086), duke of Aquitaine (r. 1058–1086), around 1069; children:* ***Agnes of Aquitaine*** *(d. 1097); William IX the Troubador (b. 1071), duke of Aquitaine.*

Hildegarde, Saint.

See Hildegarde of Swabia (c. 757–783).
See Hildegard of Bingen (1098–1179).

Hildegarde de Beaugency (fl. 1080)

Countess of Anjou. *Flourished around 1080; married Fulk IV the Rude, count of Anjou (r. 1068–1106); children: ****Ermengarde de Gatinais*** *(d. around 1146). Fulk IV was also married to ****Bertrada of Montfort*** *(d. after 1117).*

Hildegarde of Bavaria (c. 840–?)

German princess. *Born around 840; death date unknown; daughter of ****Emma of Bavaria*** *(d. 876) and Louis II the German (804–876), king of the Germans (r. 843–876); first wife of Liutpold, margrave of Bavaria (r. 895–907). Liutpold's second wife was ****Cunigunde of Swabia.***

Hildegarde of Bavaria (1825–1864)

Archduchess of Austria. *Name variations: Hildegarde Wittelsbach. Born on June 10, 1825; died on April 2, 1864; daughter of ****Theresa of Saxony*** *(1792–1854) and Louis I Augustus also known as Ludwig I (1786–1868), king of Bavaria (r. 1825–1848, abdicated); married Albrecht of Austria also known as Albert (1817–1895), archduke of Austria, on May 1, 1844 (d. 1895).*

Hildegarde of Rupertsberg (1098–1179).

See Hildegard of Bingen.

Hildegarde of Swabia (c. 757–783)

Queen of the Franks. *Name variations: Hildigard; Ildegarde; Saint Hildegarde; Hildegarde of Vinzgau. Born around 757 or 758; died on April 30, 783;*

*daughter of Hildebrand, count of Souave; became third wife of Charles I also known as Charlemagne (742–814), king of the Franks (r. 768–814), Holy Roman emperor (r. 800–814), in 771; children: Adelaide (773–774); *Bertha (779–after 823); *Rotrude (c. 778–after 839); *Gisela of Chelles (781–814); Charles (772–811), king of Neustria; Pepin I (773–810), king of Italy (r. 781–810); Louis I the Pious (778–840), king of Aquitaine (r. 781–814), king of France (r. 814–840), and Holy Roman emperor as Louis le Debonaire (r. 814–840); Lothar (778–780).*

Legend has it that Hildegarde of Swabia, third wife of Charlemagne, king of the Franks, was falsely accused of infidelity by a servant named Taland and was subsequently divorced by Charlemagne. She retired to Rome, where she led a life of great piety, devoting herself to tending the sick. There, she met Taland, wandering about, blind, and restored his sight. Overcome by gratitude and stricken by remorse, Taland confessed his lies and led her back to Charlemagne. Charlemagne's other wives were *__Himiltrude__, *__Desiderata__ (d. 773), *__Fastrada__ (d. 794), and *__Luitgarde__ (d. 800).

Hildegarde of Swabia (fl. 1050)

Duchess of Swabia. *Name variations: Hildegarde van Buren or van Büren. Flourished around 1050; daughter of Otto II, duke of Swabia; married Frederick van Büren (d. 1094); children: Frederick I (c. 1050–1105), duke of Swabia; Otto, baron von Strassburg (born around 1050); Ludwig (born around 1055), pfalzgraf of Rhein; Walter; Conrad; Adelheid.*

Hildegarde of Vinzgau (c. 757–783).

See Hildegarde of Swabia.

Hildegund (d. 1188)

German saint. *Died in 1188.*

The German saint, Hildegund, lived as a nun under the name of Brother Joseph in the Cistercian monastery of Schönau, near Heidelberg. Her feast day is April 20.

Hildeletha (fl. 700)

Saint and abbess of Barking. *Name variations: Saint Hildilid. Flourished around 700; born in France.*

Hildeletha succeeded Saint *__Ethelburga__ (d. 676?) as abbess of Barking around 676.

Hill, Abigail (1670–1734).

See Queen Anne for sidebar on Abigail Masham.

Hill, Dorothy Poynton (b. 1915).

See Poynton, Dorothy.

Hill, Ernestine (c. 1899–1972)

Australian novelist and travel writer. *Born in 1899 or 1900 in Rockhampton, Queensland, Australia; died in 1972.*

Born around 1899 in Queensland, Australia, Ernestine Hill would spend most of her life roaming Australia and documenting her travels. She penned a book of verse for adolescents, *Peter Pan Land,* in 1916, many years before her travel writings appeared in print. After her husband's death in 1933, Hill wandered almost continuously, and her first adult publication detailed her five years of travel in the Australian outback, *The Great Australian Loneliness* (1937). In 1947, she published *Flying Doctor Calling,* an account of the establishment of the Australian Inland Mission. The book told of the devotion and grit of John Flynn and others who brought airborne medical care to inland Australia. Hill's book *The Territory,* considered by many to be her best, was published in 1951, by which time Hill had been, in her own words, "twice round Australia by land, clockwise and anti-clockwise . . . three times across it from south to north, many times east and west, and once on the diagonal." Hill's only novel, *My Love Must Wait* (1941), was based on the life of explorer Matthew Flinders and proved to be her most commercial work, selling a remarkable 10,000 copies during wartime austerity.

Ernestine Hill died in 1972, and her final effort, *Kabbarli: A Personal Memoir of* *__Daisy Bates__ (1973), was published posthumously. In this book, she claims responsibility, in large part, for the writing of Daisy Bates' *Passing of the Aborigines* (1938).

SOURCES:

Radi, Heather, ed. *200 Australian Women.* NSW, Australia: Women's Redress Press, 1988.

Wilde, William H., Joy Hooton, and Barry Andrews. *Oxford Companion to Australian Literature.* Melbourne: Oxford, 1985.

Judith C. Reveal,
freelance writer, Greensboro, Maryland

Hill, Grace Livingston (1865–1947)

American author who wrote moral stories that incorporated issues of the day. *Name variations: Grace Livingston Hill-Lutz; (pseudonym) Marcia Macdon-*

ald. Born on April 16, 1865, in Wellsville, New York; died on February 23, 1947, in Swarthmore, Pennsylvania; daughter of Reverend Charles Montgomery and Marcia (Macdonald) Livingston; attended Cincinnati Art School and Elmira College; married Rev. Thomas Franklin Hill, in 1892 (d. 1899); niece of Isabella Alden (1841–1930); married Flavius J. Lutz, 1904 (separated); children (first marriage) ***Margaret Livingston Hill*** *(b. 1893);* ***Ruth Glover Hill*** *(b. 1898).*

Grace Livingston Hill was born on April 16, 1865, the only child of a strict Presbyterian cleric who was descended from an old, distinguished New York family. Deeply religious, Grace had six other Presbyterian ministers in her family in addition to her father. She received her education from both public schools and private tutors, later attending Cincinnati Art School and Elmira College. Her love of writing was inherited from her mother **Marcia Livingston** and her aunt, ***Isabella Alden**, both of whom composed religious literature for children and encouraged her efforts. Grace wrote her first book on her aunt's typewriter at the age of ten. She would later write the preface for Alden's last novel, *An Interrupted Night,* and recall:

> a Christmas long ago when I was just beginning to write scraps of stories myself. . . . [My aunt's] gift to me that year was a thousand sheets of typewriter paper; and in a sweet little note that accompanied it she wished me success and bade me turn those thousand sheets of paper into as many dollars. It was my first real encouragement.

Grace published her first book, *Chautauqua Idyl,* at age 22. This work, about a group of flowers, demonstrated the imagination and simple style which would eventually make her so popular.

In 1892, Grace married Presbyterian minister Thomas Franklin Hill. They moved to Germantown, Pennsylvania, and had two daughters, Margaret and Ruth. Grace wrote little during this time, dedicating herself instead to her family. When her husband died of acute appendicitis in 1899, her obligation to support her daughters drove her to the work she loved, writing. She moved to Swarthmore, Pennsylvania, and wrote a syndicated column entitled "The Christian Endeavor Hour" which appeared in religious papers. She also began to write novels, averaging two to three books per year. By the end of her life, Hill had published a total of 79 books, with sales over three million.

Writing for an intended audience of adolescent females with rural, Protestant backgrounds,

Grace Livingston Hill

Hill adhered to her strong religious upbringing. Her heroines experience various moral challenges before finding love and security founded on firm religious faith. Although her stories followed a formula, she incorporated current issues into her books. For example, *The Red Signal*—a story about a heroine who foils a plot by foreign agents to overthrow the U.S. government—appeared the same year that Americans were in the grips of fear over Communist infiltration in the United States.

Hill married for a second time on October 31, 1904, but her marriage to Flavius J. Lutz was, by all accounts, unhappy and ended in separation. For a period of time during her marriage, she wrote under "Grace Livingston Hill-Lutz" but soon abandoned the name. She also published several books using the pseudonym "Marcia Macdonald," her mother's maiden name.

Taking her position as a role model to young people seriously, Hill traveled around the country to speak to church groups. She also answered a flood of mail from troubled young readers. Among her most popular titles are *The Witness* (1917), *The Enchanted Barn* (1918), *Matched Pearls* (1933), *Beauty for Ashes* (1935), and *April Gold* (1936). Some critics consider *Matched Pearls* to be her best work. In 1918, her collaboration with ***Evangeline Booth** produced a work of nonfiction, *War Romance of the Salvation Army.*

In 1926, Grace Livingston Hill founded a Sunday school mission near Swarthmore, which she continued to support until her death on February 23, 1947, of cancer. She was buried in a family plot in the Johnstown (New York) Cemetery. Hill's staunch morality and disapproval of such modern innovations as movies and jazz reduced her appeal to the post-World War II audience, but her books still sold two decades after her death.

SOURCES:

Edgerly, Lois Stiles. *Give Her This Day.* Gardiner, ME: Tilbury House, 1990.

James, Edward T., ed. *Notable American Women, 1607–1950.* Cambridge, MA: The Belknap Press of Harvard University Press, 1971.

McHenry, Robert, ed. *Famous American Women.* NY: Dover, 1983.

Judith C. Reveal,
freelance writer, Greensboro, Maryland

Hill, Joan (fl. 1460)

English mistress whose son was an emissary for Henry VII. *Mistress of Henry Beaufort (1436–1464), 3rd duke of Somerset (r. 1455–1464); children: Charles Somerset (c. 1460–1526), 1st earl of Worcester (r. 1514–1526).*

Hill, Octavia (1838–1912)

British reformer and social worker who pioneered in housing for the poor and helped found the Commons Preservation Society, a precursor of the National Trust. *Name variations: (nickname) Ockey. Born Octavia Hill on December 3, 1838, at Wisbech near Peterborough, England; died on August 13, 1912, in London, England; third daughter of James Hill (a banker and corn merchant) and Caroline Southwood (Smith) Hill (a teacher); given no formal education; never married; no children.*

Potato famine in Ireland and massive influx of refugees to England (1846); Crimean War (1854–56); Indian Mutiny (1857); introduction of compulsory elementary education in England (1880); Boer War (1899–1902); death of Queen Victoria and accession of Edward VII (1901); outbreak of First World War (1914).

Opposite page

Octavia Hill

Selected writings: Letters to my Fellow-Workers *(1864–1911);* The Importance of Aiding the Poor without Almsgiving *(1872);* Homes of the London Poor *(1875);* Our Common Land and other Short Essays *(1877); contributed various articles to* The Nineteenth Century *(1883–99).*

Octavia Hill was born on December 3, 1838, at Wisbech, a small village located near the then thriving market town of Peterborough, Cambridgeshire, England. Her father James Hill, descended from a long and successful line of country bankers, was an able businessman who consistently impressed his colleagues with his enthusiasm for hard work. Unfortunately, his talents were not enough to prevent him from losing the family bank in the great financial crisis of 1825. James then turned his hand to a variety of business ventures but, in the ongoing climate of economic uncertainty, met with only sporadic success. Despite this, he consistently maintained an active and vigorous interest in a wide assortment of social, cultural, and political issues, such as local government reform, public works, the theater and journalism. Moreover, James sustained a deep concern with the question of children's education and was responsible (during one of his periods of fiscal solvency) for erecting one of the first infants' schools in England.

In 1832, James' first wife died leaving him a widower to raise six young children. Shortly thereafter, he met **Caroline Southwood Smith** whom he hired as the children's governess. Caroline had already established a modest reputation as author of a number of short articles on the principles of children's education. Like James, she was deeply religious and shared many of his social interests and concerns. James and Caroline married in 1835 and, over the course of the next few years, became the parents of five daughters. Octavia was their third.

As a result of the severe economic depression which swept England in 1840, James eventually became completely bankrupt. This development created severe strains on the entire family; James' children from his previous marriage were sent to live with their maternal grandparents while his new wife and daughters were forced to give up their home and seek cheaper lodgings. To make matters worse, James' health began to break down. By 1843, he was no longer physically capable of financially supporting Caroline and the children.

Fortunately at this juncture, Dr. Thomas Southwood Smith, Caroline's father, stepped in and assumed full responsibility for the family by settling them at Finchley then just outside London. Thomas Smith was a well-known public figure, who had gained renown for his work to improve factory conditions and for his connection with the campaign to regulate the employment of children in industry. Later, he fought to bring about wide-ranging sanitary reforms, and his report on this issue formed the principal basis of the first Public Health Act published in Britain in 1848.

Although the Hill children received no formal education, they contrived, with Caroline's assistance, to embrace the rudiments of a range of scholarly subjects. By the age of five, Octavia could read and write fluently and, shortly afterward, was assisting her grandfather by preparing copies of his reports and correspondence on sanitary reform. This early exposure to social questions soon filled her with a deep and genuine sympathy for the plight of working people and their families. She would maintain this concern and compassion for the rest of her life.

In 1851, Caroline was appointed manager of the Ladies Co-operative Guild (an association dedicated to finding employment for, what was termed, "distressed gentlewomen"), and the family moved to a new home in central London. The force behind this enterprise was a man named Vansittart Neale, a leading Christian Socialist. In mid-19th-century England, Christian Socialism was a significant socio-political movement which sought to combine Biblical precepts with, what can now be regarded as, rather mild proposals for socialist reform.

The extreme poverty and misery that stalked the streets of central London came as a great shock to the 13-year-old Octavia. In response, she threw herself into a determined study of the texts published by the Christian Socialist movement in an attempt to understand the origins and causes of this situation. Hill also began to attend some of the movement's many public lectures, and it was at one of these events that she first met Frederick Denison Maurice. Maurice subsequently exerted an important influence on Hill by acting as a kind of intellectual mentor and interpreting, what she later described as, "much that was dark and puzzling in life."

It was Neale, however, who first engaged Hill in practical work among the poor. Not long after they met, he asked her to assume charge of a new toy manufacturing enterprise that he had organized to provide employment for destitute children. Octavia rapidly established herself as an efficient and enthusiastic supervisor in the

day-to-day running of the business. More important, she endeavored to initiate a number of wider beneficial changes in the lives of the 11 children in her charge. She organized regular, nutritious meals, took them on trips to the countryside, and visited each child's home in order to better understand the reality of their social and economic circumstances. It was this latter activity, in particular, which fully revealed to her the extent of the poverty then existing among the working class.

It is on defeats that victories are built.

—Octavia Hill

This enterprise did not prosper for long. By March 1856, it had begun to suffer severe financial difficulties. Though Hill struggled to keep it open for another 15 months, she was forced to supplement her income through other means. Fortunately, her friend Maurice was able to offer her a part-time position as secretary at the Working Men's College, a small educational institute he had recently established. Despite her lack of formal education, Hill was soon given the added responsibility of teaching classes at the institute in basic arithmetic and art (a subject in which she had a lifelong interest). These duties allowed her not only to provide for the immediate needs of her family but, moreover, to satisfy her father's many creditors. Not surprisingly, this considerable responsibility placed an increasingly severe strain on Hill. In April 1857, her health broke down, and it was several months before she fully recovered.

Late in 1862, Octavia and her sisters opened a small school in their new home in Nottingham Place, London. Initially, the school accommodated 14 female pupils who were aged between 12 and 18. None of the co-founders seem to have been particularly concerned about establishing and maintaining a high level of academic excellence. Rather, in Hill's words, their principal aim was to instruct the pupils in "habits of neatness, punctuality, self-reliance and such practical power and forethought as will make them useful in their homes." In this, Hill and her sisters were successful. By 1865, the school was flourishing thanks to the reputation it had established as a training ground for "womanly virtues."

Despite this achievement, Octavia's interests were beginning to turn in new directions. Many of the pupils at Nottingham Place came from poor families, and she was shocked at the miserable conditions of the housing in which they lived. Much of this problem stemmed from landlords who were only interested in receiving their rents on time and who were completely indifferent to the circumstances of their tenants. The tenants responded by making no effort to keep their dwellings in a fit and habitable state. In this situation, it occurred to Hill to become a landlord herself and to institute and encourage new principles of responsibility among her tenants. The most immediate obstacle in the face of this scheme was a lack of money. Fortunately, her friend, the famous art critic John Ruskin, was able to subsidize her project.

In 1865 and 1866, Ruskin purchased a number of properties and turned them over to Hill's direction. The first of these, a row of three houses in the misnamed street of Paradise Place, was typical of further purchases. Each house had six rooms and each room was inhabited by one family. They were in a dreadful condition: the roofs leaked, there was no plaster on the walls, they had no running water, and they lacked any decent sanitary arrangements. Hill immediately set about repairing and cleaning these dwellings, a task she had to repeat many times thanks to the initially hostile reaction of her frequently unemployed and habitually drunk tenants.

From the beginning, she made it quite clear that she was not engaged in an act of charity. Charity, in her opinion, only served to render the poor even more dependent by relying on the goodwill of others. Rather, Hill set out to nurture what she called, the "spiritual growth" of the poor, so that they would eventually come to take responsibility for their own circumstances and a pride in their own achievements. To this end, she insisted on prompt payment of rent (she had no compunction about evicting those who were late) and would only carry out more substantial repairs on condition that wanton damage to the property by the tenants ceased. She insisted on a "perfect strictness" between herself and her tenants that was tempered by a "perfect respectfulness" in their reciprocal duties. Once this was established, however, Hill introduced further improvements that were far in advance of anything offered by any other landlord of the time. She organized an informal bank that encouraged her tenants to save, did what she could to find work for the unemployed, initiated sewing and dressmaking classes (with the help of the pupils from Nottingham Place), and even established a garden and playground to encourage healthy exercise.

Once again, the strain of overwork took its toll on her health, and in October 1867 she left for an extended convalescence in Italy. When she returned 18 months later, Hill was immediately struck by the visible increase in poverty that had been caused by the latest economic slump. The social conditions of the working class were now worse than ever, and she was invited to join the recently formed London Association for the Prevention of Pauperization and Crime (more popularly known as the Charity Organization Society, or COS). Hill's work in Paradise Place was widely admired, and she was asked to take over the management of several properties which the COS had acquired in the London borough of Marylebone. Again in the face of considerable hostility from the sitting tenants (this time because of her policy of withholding free meals and monetary assistance from the incurably indigent), she set about restoring each individual's sense of dignity and self-reliance.

Thanks to many generous donations to the COS, Octavia was allowed to gradually expand her work throughout Marylebone and the surrounding boroughs. At the same time, she initiated a program to train other women in the principles of house management and social work which she had developed. Many of these principles, along with accounts of her current activities and progress of the properties being managed (not to mention frank confessions of her fears and anxieties), were contained in *Letters to my Fellow-Workers,* an annual report prepared by Hill and first published in 1871. Though she was not without her detractors, these *Letters* had a significant impact on public opinion and largely facilitated a further extension of her work to the slums of other major English cities (such as Leeds, Liverpool, and Manchester). They even received notice in parts of Germany and North America.

While Hill's principal interest in these years was centered firmly on the question of housing for the poor, she did not neglect her other main concern, the provision of open spaces. She was elected to the executive committee of the Commons Preservation Society (founded in 1865) which was established to safeguard open lands from industrial and commercial development. In a pamphlet written in 1875, Hill described the aims of the society which was to maintain "places to sit in, places to play in, places to stroll in, and space and place to spend a day in." She worked hard to secure public support for these aims and was happy when she and her co-workers were able to extend their work throughout the United Kingdom. The Commons Preservation Society later formed the basis of the National Trust which continues to seek to preserve the countryside and historic buildings for public enjoyment.

Although she never married, Hill did become briefly engaged in July 1877 to Edward Bond, one of her co-workers in the COS. Bond's mother, however, apparently objected to the proposed union, and in these circumstances Octavia herself called off the engagement. This experience had a negative impact on her health, and, shortly afterwards, her doctor recommended that she take a complete rest. In January 1878, Hill set out for a tour of the Continent with her close friend **Harriot Yorke**. The two companions traveled extensively throughout Europe and only finally returned home in the summer of 1880.

Hill was now widely recognized as one of the country's leading authorities on the housing question. At the end of 1884, the Church of England's Ecclesiastical Commissioners placed a large number of properties under her guidance. These properties, in the London suburbs of Deptford and Southwark, were extremely rundown and were populated by unruly and difficult tenants. Though this was a time of high unemployment and wages were depressed, Hill, as before, rejected the idea of giving charity and sought instead to foster individual well-being and spiritual growth. Her new tenants (particularly in Deptford) were, however, reluctant to adopt her principles and standards. Sensing this change in attitude, Hill wrote that, "the temper of the poor is difficult, the old submissive patience is passing away, and no sense of duty has taken its place." Indeed, she found her experiences in Deptford to be the most difficult and challenging of her entire career. She had more success in Southwark where, in 1888, she managed to open a community center complete with classrooms, entertainment facilities, a library, and a cadet corps for the children.

The last phase of her life was devoted to developing and extending her previous work. She was overwhelmed by volunteers (some of whom came from as far afield as Holland and Sweden) who came to her wishing to learn the principles of house management. Many were turned away, however, as Hill had a strict policy of limiting her trainees to those women that she felt could be trusted to follow her principles to the letter. She had no place for enthusiasts who believed in trying out their own methods of administration. Nevertheless, in response to the repeated calls of the Ecclesiastical Commissioners to take on ever more properties on their behalf, Octavia was forced to gradually expand and enlarge her training program.

By the turn of the century, the type of work pioneered by Hill was beginning to become redundant. More and more local government authorities (especially in the large cities) were taking it upon themselves to build houses for the working class. Octavia was deeply disappointed by this development which she believed undermined the proper relation between landlord and tenant and thwarted any possibility for tenants to attain a position of self-sufficiency and independence. Subsidized housing, of the type proposed by the local authorities, was, in her opinion, little more than disguised charity. It was outside their realm of competence which should properly be confined to providing such things as proper sanitation.

In 1905, Hill was appointed to the Royal Commission on the Poor Law which was established by the British government to investigate reforms to the subsidies then currently paid to the poor. As a member of the commission, she was required to travel around the country collecting evidence from a large number of witnesses. Octavia, then aged 67, found this a tiring and onerous task, but she persevered in what she believed was work of national importance. Shortly after the commission reported early in 1908, she became seriously ill and did not recover for several months. Her last public intervention came in July 1910 in a letter to the London *Times*. There she argued that the tactics of the suffragists (the women's movement demanding the right to vote) was a danger to democracy. Rather, women should recognize that they have "different powers and qualities" from men and that these powers should be used by women in those areas of society (such as house management) where they are most effective.

Around Easter 1912, Hill discovered that the breathlessness from which she had been suffering for some time was due to an incurable lung condition. She then calmly settled her own affairs and ensured that the management of the houses currently in her charge were placed in the hands of trusted colleagues. A few months later, on August 12, she died at home in London. In recognition of her public service, the government offered a funeral at Westminster Abbey, but her family declined the honor. Instead, she was buried at Crockham Hill, a small village outside London where she had spent many happy hours and which had given her, in her own words, "such a delicious sense of space."

SOURCES:

Bell, C. Moberly. *Octavia Hill*. London: Constable, 1942.

Boyd, Nancy. *Three Victorian Women Who Changed their World*. NY: Oxford University Press, 1982.

Hill, Octavia. *Extracts from Octavia Hill's Letters to Fellow-Workers, 1864–1911*. Edited by Elinor Southwood Ouvry. London: The Adelphi Bookshop, 1933.

——. *Homes of the London Poor*. London: Macmillan, 1875.

——. *Life of Octavia Hill as Told in Her Letters*. Edited by C. Edmund Maurice. London: Macmillan, 1913.

——. *Octavia Hill: Early Ideals*. Edited by Emily S. Maurice. London: George Allen and Unwin, 1928.

Hill, William Thomson. *Octavia Hill: Pioneer of the National Trust and Housing Reformer*. London: Hutchinson, 1956.

SUGGESTED READING:

Gauldie, Enid. *Cruel Habitations: A History of Working-Class Housing, 1780–1918*. London: Allen & Unwin, 1974.

Mayhew, Henry. *London Labour and the London Poor*. London: Griffin, Bohn, 1861.

Dave Baxter,
Department of Philosophy,
Wilfrid Laurier University, Waterloo, Ontario, Canada

Hill, Opal S. (1892–1981)

American golfer. *Born on June 2, 1892, in Newport, Nebraska; died in June 1981 in Kansas City, Missouri; grew up in Kansas City, Missouri; married (husband died in 1942).*

In 1914, 22-year-old Opal Hill was diagnosed with a kidney infection and anemia; the doctors gave her three years to live. To offset the illness, mild exercise was prescribed, and Hill eventually took up golf. From 1929 to 1936, she was a consistently formidable golfer, who won the North and South (1928), was selected for the Curtis Cup team (1932, 1934, 1936), and reached the semifinals of the USGA three times and the quarterfinals twice. But the field in those years was unusually strong, with such opponents as ***Glenna Collett Vare**, **Virginia Van Wie**, ***Maureen Orcutt**, and **Charlotte Glutting**. In other tournaments, Hill was far more successful, winning the Western Women's tourney five times, the Trans-Mississippi four times, the Western Open twice, the Missouri Valley twice, and the Missouri State three times. In 1937, she set a world record in women's golf with a blazing 66, then turned pro on October 18, 1938, only the second to do so. Opal Hill was a pioneer in the development of women's professional golf.

Hill, Patty Smith (1868–1946)

American educator and reformer in kindergarten schooling. *Born in Anchorage, Kentucky, on March 27, 1868; died in New York City on May 25, 1946; the third of four daughters and fourth of six children of Will Wallace Hill (a Presbyterian minister and an educator)* *and Martha Jane (Smith) Hill; sister of Mildred J. Hill (1859–1916), a musician; graduated from Louisville Collegiate Institute, 1887; never married; no children.*

Patty Smith Hill was the product of a remarkably progressive upbringing. She was born in 1868 in Anchorage, Kentucky, one of six children of Will Wallace Hill and **Martha Smith Hill**. Her father was a Presbyterian minister who ran his own Bellewood Female Seminary and later became president of the Synodical Female College at Fulton, Missouri. Her mother was privately tutored then followed a full course of study at Centre College, although at the time the school was not open to women. Both parents were deeply interested in developing their children's creative and intellectual abilities and were particularly concerned that their girls be educated in a profession so they would not have to "marry for a home."

Even as a child, Patty Hill planned to work with young children, and after graduating from the private Louisville Collegiate Institute in 1887, she entered a newly opened school for kindergarten teachers in the city. Under the direction of **Anna E. Bryan**, the curriculum offered an experimental approach to early childhood education that challenged the rigid procedures of Friedrich Froebel then in practice. After completing the course in 1889, Hill was put in charge of the demonstration kindergarten. When Bryan resigned in 1893, Hill succeeded her as head of the Louisville Free Kindergarten Association and the Louisville Training School for Kindergarten and Primary Teachers.

Hill continued to keep pace with the new philosophies and techniques in early childhood education, including those of John Dewey as well as Colonel Francis W. Parker, who visited the Louisville Training School in 1891. In 1896, she spent the summer at Clark University, studying with G. Stanley Hall, another pioneer in the field. As Hill became familiar with the newest innovations, she quickly incorporated them into her own work, thus becoming a leader in the burgeoning kindergarten movement. From 1904 to 1905, she participated in a series of lectures at Columbia University Teachers College, along with ***Susan E. Blow**, who defended the conservative Froebelian theories in an alternating series of talks. The presentation, a virtual debate, was so successful that Hill was engaged as a visiting lecturer that fall and, in 1906, was appointed to a full-time faculty position at Teachers College. In 1908, she was elected president of the International Kindergarten Union.

From 1910 on, Hill headed up a new kindergarten department at Columbia, which also ran the experimental Horace Mann Kindergarten. She taught graduate courses for training school teachers and supervisors and was instrumental in formulating new curriculums for the experimental school. Embracing the empirical approach of her colleagues Edward Lee Thorndike and William Heard Kilpatrick, Hill experimented with a more natural, flexible classroom approach, exploiting the child's natural play instincts and making the learning experience realistic and meaningful. In 1923, the experimental work of the Horace Mann Kindergarten was published under Hill's editorship as *A Conduct Curriculum for the Kindergarten and First Grade*. In 1924, as part of her belief in the scientific study of childhood, Hill was instrumental in organizing the Institute of Child Welfare Research at Teachers College, and in 1925 she founded the National Association for Nursery Education.

Of her many achievements, Patty Hill is also credited with the song "Happy Birthday," which she wrote with her sister **Mildred J. Hill** (1859–1916), a musician. The song was originally written as "Good Morning All" for the book *Song Stories for the Kindergarten,* which the sisters published together in 1898. Hill was also the inventor of the large scale Patty Hill blocks, which permitted children to build structures large enough to play in.

Hill, who never married, retired from Teachers College in 1935, after which she established and directed the Hilltop Community Center for underprivileged children. She died in her home at the age of 78. Although Hill left little in the way of writing, her legacy was passed on by her students, who carried her educational reforms to kindergarten classes across the nation.

SOURCES:

James, Edward T., ed. *Notable American Women, 1607–1950*. Cambridge, MA: The Belknap Press of Harvard University Press, 1971.

McHenry, Robert, ed. *Famous American Women*. NY: Dover, 1983.

Barbara Morgan,
Melrose, Massachusetts

Hill, Rosa Minoka (1876–1952).

See Minoka-Hill, Rosa.

Hill, Virginia (1916–1966)

American Mafia associate and drug peddler. *Born Onie Virginia Hill on August 26, 1916, in Lipscomb, Alabama; died on March 24, 1966, in Koppl, Austria, near Salzburg; seventh of ten children of W.M.*

"Mack" Hill (a horse and mule trader and livery-stable operator) and Margaret Hill; attended Roberts Grammar School; possibly married George Rogers/Randell, around 1931 (died); married Ossie Griffin (a college football player), on January 13, 1939 (annulled, June 1939); married Carlos Gonzales Valdez (a rhumba dancer), on January 20, 1940 (divorced); married Hans Hauser (a ski instructor), in March 1950; children: (last marriage) one son, Peter (b. November 20, 1950).

The only woman ever identified as a Mafia associate, Virginia Hill was born into poverty in Lipscomb, Alabama, the seventh of ten children, all of whom suffered abuse at the hands of their alcoholic father. Her seemingly ruthless nature was apparently acquired at a tender age. At 17, armed only with an eighth-grade education, a pretty face, and a willowy figure, Hill left home and headed to Chicago, hoping to land a show-business job at the 1933 World Fair. Instead, she worked as a waitress in a mob-owned restaurant, where she captured the attention of Joe Epstein, who headed up Chicago's gambling concerns for the notorious Al Capone gang. Epstein saw in Hill attributes he could use in his operation, and thus he became her entrée into the mob. Attracted by Epstein's money and his offer of clothes, jewelry, and ready cash, Hill became his willing protégé, receiving her early training in money-laundering scams. As Epstein's "girl," she refined her appearance and mannerisms, though she apparently never lost her distinctively squeaky voice and uncontrollable temper. During her early career, she was employed as a "bag girl," transporting stolen merchandise and cash across state lines. It was a lucrative occupation that enabled her to send some money to her impoverished family back home.

Winning the trust of the gang, Hill was asked to infiltrate the inner circle of the New York family led by Lucky Luciano, which was involved in a cold war against Capone's Chicago gang. She accomplished this assignment through selective liaisons. Initially, she became the mistress of Luciano henchman Joe Adonis, teaming up with him in gambling rackets and money laundering, the same way she had with Epstein, but recording her activities in a secret diary. In the late 1930s, instructed by Adonis, she headed to Los Angeles, where she became involved with the Hollywood elite and enjoyed brief affairs with a string of famous film stars, including Errol Flynn, Victor Mature, and Gene Krupa. In 1940, she entered into a short-lived marriage with Carlos Gonzalez Valdez, a rhumba dancer.

Hill then became involved with the notorious and volatile gangster Bugsy Siegel, another member of the Luciano gang, during her mission to set up narcotics transport from Mexico. Hill developed smuggling routes and reported to Siegel, whom she called her true love. (The two would be portrayed by Warren Beatty and **Annette Bening** in the 1991 film *Bugsy*.) Their covert operations and stormy love affair lasted throughout the 1940s, while Hill lived in a mansion in Beverly Hills, among other residences, dressing in furs, jewels, and designer clothes. The relationship unraveled, however, when Siegel's multimillion-dollar Flamingo Casino in Las Vegas failed, and he was deserted by Hill and the rest of the Luciano mob. On June 10, 1947, after refusing to return money that many mobsters, including Meyer Lansky, had sunk into his unsuccessful enterprise, Siegel was assassinated. Many have speculated that Hill was in on the killing, though she was conveniently in Europe at the time. After Siegel's demise, Hill continued her work for Luciano, transporting money and goods throughout the U.S. and European capitals, including Switzerland, where she regularly deposited syndicate money in Swiss bank accounts.

In 1950, Senator Estes Kefauver, a Democrat from Tennessee, called for a probe into organized crime in America, then spearheaded the committee formed to conduct the hearings, which were televised in 20 cities on the East Coast and in the Midwest. Hill, who was now residing in Spokane, Washington, with her ski instructor-husband Hans Hauser and her newborn son, appeared before the committee on March 15, 1951. Her entrance was described by one reporter as "pure Hollywood pandemonium . . . something like a movie premiere." Dressed in a mink stole and large black hat, Hill screamed obscenities at reporters and shoved her way past them. Once in the courtroom, however, Hill appeared frightened by the bright lights and asked that some be switched off. She appeared nervous during the first few minutes of her questioning but soon resorted to her usual arrogant manner. The testimony concerning Hill's financial affairs and her mob connections yielded very little, however. When asked to tell the committee the story of her life as it pertained to her financial situation and her relationship with any known gangsters, she portrayed herself as a fun-loving party girl who was showered with expensive gifts from a string of admirers. "Well, I worked for a while," she told the committee. "Then the men I was around that gave me things were not gangsters or racketeers or whatever you call these other people. The only time I ever got anything from them was going out and having fun and maybe a few presents." When Kefauver dismissed Hill, the spectators gave her a standing ovation.

Although Hill believed that she had bamboozled the committee and could now break free from her criminal past, she was unaware that the IRS had all it needed to bring a tax-fraud case against her. (It was estimated that she had gone through more than $500,000 without paying taxes.) After receiving $10,000 from Joe Epstein, who had remained her protector, Hill left her husband and baby and went into hiding. She kept the government forces at bay until July 5, 1951, when she was picked up in Denver, Colorado. She was served with a tax lien in the amount of $161,000 for back income taxes for the years 1942 through 1947. Another lien was issued from the Chicago office of the IRS for $48,369 for unpaid taxes for the years 1946 and 1947. Now homeless and unable to elicit help from the mob, Hill adopted a "who cares" attitude, telling a reporter: "I'm fed up with everything. When this is all over, I'm getting out of here to go live with my husband and son." (Her husband Hans and son Peter had left Spokane for Europe.) On August 2 and 3, there was a formal auction of Hill's house and possessions, which raised $41,000 against the unpaid balance of $161,000. With no way to pay up and determined to stay out of jail, Hill fled the country with Joe Epstein.

Reunited with her family, Hill drifted from one European resort to another, receiving money to finance her extravagant lifestyle from several unidentified sources. While the government renewed efforts to indict her, she apparently tried to drown her problems in drink. In May 1954, the Treasury Department pleaded its case against her before a federal grand jury. Ruling in favor of the government, the grand jury issued a warrant for Hill's arrest, and the Treasury Department distributed a "Wanted" poster to major post offices throughout the country. News of the government action soon reached Hill, who was now residing in Klosters, Switzerland. Ostracized by her social circle who found it appalling that a "gangster" resided among them, Hill now succumbed completely to alcohol which took its toll mentally and physically. She became paranoid and on several occasions reportedly attempted suicide by drinking herself into a stupor, then taking barbiturates.

Hill eventually decided to return home, turn herself in, and serve her jail term (as long as it was short and would erase any further debt), and elicited the aid of her lawyer Joe Ross and Clifford Rice, an FBI agent and her one-time neighbor in Spokane. With their help, she arranged to return to the United States, as long as her arrival was known only to the government. When the IRS added a number of impossible conditions to her return, Hill used her secret diary as leverage, but the government was unimpressed and held firm to its demands. Believing that her lawyer was betraying her, Hill fired him and returned to Switzerland to live out what were to be the final months of her life.

Virginia Hill

Separating from Hans Hauser, she moved into a Salzburg hotel with her son Peter, now 15. According to criminal sociologist Dr. **Lorraine Blakeman,** Hill was now on the verge of a complete breakdown. In desperation, she contacted Joe Epstein and Joe Adonis, threatening to reveal the contents of her diary unless they sent money. She also met with Adonis in Naples on March 22, 1966, and the following morning, after supposedly receiving $10,000 in cash from him, was escorted from his house by two "friends" of the mobster. She was found dead two days later, on March 24, 1966, near a brook in Koppl, Austria. Her death was ruled a suicide, and, for the next 25 years, it was believed that she had gorged herself on alcohol and barbiturates, then wandered off to die. **Andy Edmonds**, however, in her 1993 book *Bugsy's Baby: The Secret Life of Mob Queen Virginia Hill,* maintains that Hill did not die by her own hand but was murdered in order to keep her diary from the authorities. To support her theory, Edmonds points to the fact that three days before Hill's death, Joe Epstein received a letter from her with a key to a bank box which contained her diary. Although Epstein knew the letter was from Hill, he made no move to open the box until the day of Hill's death, giving rise to suspicions that he may have had prior knowledge of her fate. Also curious, according to Edmonds, was the existence of a report written prior to Hill's autopsy indicating lateral bruises around her neck, and the fact that the "poison" found in Hill's body was never identified. Finally, Edmonds points out that the "friends" that accompanied Hill from Adonis' were known hit men who probably carried out a preconceived assassination.

SOURCES:

Edmonds, Andy. *Bugsy's Baby: The Secret Life of Mob Queen Virginia Hill.* NY: Birch Lane, 1993.

Barbara Morgan,
Melrose, Massachusetts

Hiller, Wendy (1912—)

***British actress, acclaimed for her portrayal of Mary of Teck in* Crown Matrimonial.** *Name variations: Dame Wendy Hiller. Born Wendy Margaret Hiller on August 15, 1912, in Bramhall, Cheshire, England; only daughter and one of four children of Frank Watkin Hiller (a mill director) and Elizabeth (Stone) Hiller; graduated from the Winceby House School, Bexhill, England; studied acting at Manchester (England) Repertory Theater; married Ronald Gow (a playwright), on February 25, 1937; children: one son; one daughter.*

Selected theater: made her debut as the Maid in The Ware Case *(Manchester Repertory Theater, September 1930); London debut as Sally Hardcastle in* Love on the Dole *(Garrick Theater, January 30, 1935); New York debut in same role (Shubert Theater, February 24, 1936); title role in* Saint Joan *and Eliza Doolittle in* Pygmalion *(Malvern [England] Theater Festival, July 1936); toured as Viola in* Twelfth Night; *Sister Joanna in* The Cradle Song *(Apollo Theater, January 1944); Princess Charlotte in* The First Gentleman *(New Theater, July 1945); Tess in* Tess of the D'Urbervilles *and Portia in* The Merchant of Venice *(Bristol Old Vic Co., 1946); Tess in London production of* Tess of the D'Urbervilles *(New Theater, November 1946); Catherine Sloper in* The Heiress *(Biltmore Theater, New York, September 1947); title role in* Ann Veronica *(Piccadilly Theater, London, May 1949); succeeded Peggy Ashcroft as Catherine Sloper in* The Heiress *(Haymarket Theater, January 1950); Margaret Tollemache in* The Night of the Ball *(New Theater, January 1955); Portia in* Julius Caesar, *Mistress Page in* The Merry Wives of Windsor, *Hermione in* The Winter's Tale, *Emilia in* Othello, *and Helen in* Troilus and Cressida *(Old Vic Company, Old Vic Theater, London, 1955–56); Josie Hogan in* A Moon for the Misbegotten *(Bijou Theater, New York, May 1957); succeeded* ****Celia Johnson*** *as Isobel Cherry in* Flowering Cherry *(Haymarket Theater, London, June 1958); Marie Marescaud in* All in the Family *(Gaiety Theater, Dublin, Ireland, June 1959); Carrie Berniers in* Toys in the Attic *(Piccadilly Theater, November 1960); Tina in* The Aspern Papers *(Playhouse theater, New York, February 1962); Susan Shepherd in* The Wings of the Dove *(Lyric Theater, London, December 1963); Queen Mary in* Crown Matrimonial *(Haymarket, October 1972); Tina in revival of* The Aspern Papers *(Theater Royal, London, 1984).*

Filmography: Lancashire Luck *(1937);* Pygmalion *(1938);* Major Barbara *(1941);* I Know Where I'm Going *(1945);* An Outcast of the Islands *(1951);* Single-handed *(*Sailor of the King, *1951);* Something of Value *(1957);* How to Murder a Rich Uncle *(1957);* Separate Tables *(1958);* Sons and Lovers *(1960);* Toys in the Attic *(1963);* A Man for All Seasons *(1966);* David Copperfield *(1970);* Murder on the Orient Express *(1974);* Voyage of the Damned *(1976);* The Cat and the Canary *(1978);* The Elephant Man *(1980);* Making Love *(1982);* The Lonely Passion of Judith Hearne *(1987).*

Setting her sights on an acting career as a child, Wendy Hiller was encouraged by her mother, who was so enamored of the theater that she named all her children after characters in the plays of Sir James Barrie—René, Michael, John, and, of course, Wendy. Upon finishing her formal education, Hiller joined the Manchester Repertory Company, where she worked her way up from non-salaried apprentice to actor-manager. "For marvelous experience in the theater there's nothing to beat a repertory company," she later said. The company let her go in 1932, telling her she was an inadequate actress, but they called her back shortly thereafter to play Sally Hardcastle in Ronald Gow's adaptation of the novel *Love on the Dole,* because she was the only one they knew who could do a convincing Lancashire accent. In June 1935, after a successful tour, Hiller made her London debut in the

Wendy Hiller

role and was an instant success. She so impressed George Bernard Shaw that he asked her to play *Joan of Arc in his *Saint Joan* and Eliza Doolittle in his *Pygmalion* at the Malvern Festival in 1936. The following year turned out to be a banner one for the actress, who married playwright Gow in February and also launched her film career in *Lancashire Luck,* repeating her role in the movie version of *Love on the Dole.* Her second Hollywood effort, the film version of *Pygmalion* (1938) with Leslie Howard, won her an Academy Award. Although her subsequent movie career was sporadic, Hiller captured another Academy Award in 1958 for her delicate portrayal of the lonely Miss Cooper in *Separate Tables.*

Hiller remains best known for her stage performances, which include appearances in several additional plays by her husband, notably Tess in his adaptation of the Thomas Hardy novel *Tess of the D'Urbervilles* (1946), and the title role in his adaptation of the H.G. Wells' novel *Ann Veronica* (1949). Harold Hobson praised Hiller's Tess as the perfect embodiment of the character. "With rosy cheeks that any intelligent apple would envy," he wrote, "Miss Hiller is physically well suited to Hardy's opulently earthy heroine: temperamentally too: she causes Tess' love for Angel to seem a blessing and benediction, and confounds morality by making murder only a very little thing." Of her portrayal of the title role in *Ann Veronica,* Hobson wrote: "Wendy Hiller reveals Ann's essential tenderness; you can see the femininity beneath the feminism."

Hiller was also memorable as the downtrodden heroine of *The Heiress* (1947), based on the Henry James novel *Washington Square,* and as Josie Hogan in Eugene O'Neill's *A Moon for the Misbegotten* (1937). Of her later roles, the finest was her portrait of Queen ***Mary of Teck** in Royce Ryton's *Crown Matrimonial* (1972), the story of the abdication of Edward VIII. Even critic W. Stephen Gilbert of *Plays and Players,* never a fan of the actress, had nothing but praise. "Wendy Hiller, whom I've found resistible in the past, won me with her firm characterization and her skill with a deadly line—'I've been so lucky with my daughter-in-law . . . so far.' When she entered in her toque as an older Mary, we all gasped. She *was* the woman who waved to me outside Sandringham when I was five."

In 1975, Hiller was made a Dame of the British Empire and also starred as Gunhild Borkman in Ibsen's *John Gabriel Borkman,* a role she repeated in March 1976, with Ralph Richardson and ***Peggy Ashcroft.** In 1974, Hiller appeared in a revival of *Waters of the Moon* and, in 1984, recreated the role of Tina in *The Aspern Papers.*

Throughout her career, Hiller, the mother of two, carefully juggled home and career, admitting that it was difficult to consistently make a success of both. She also remained a quiet, unassuming presence, who quite successfully guarded her private life.

SOURCES:

Hartnoll, Phyllis, and Peter Found, eds. *The Concise Oxford Companion to the Theatre.* Oxford and NY: Oxford University Press, 1983.

McGill, Raymond D., ed. *Notable Names in the Theatre.* Clifton, NJ: James T. White, 1976.

Morley, Sheridan. *The Great Stage Stars.* London: Angus & Robertson, 1986.

Rothe, Anna, ed. *Current Biography 1941.* NY: H.W. Wilson, 1941.

Barbara Morgan,
Melrose, Massachusetts

Hillern, Wilhelmine von (1836–1916).

See Birch-Pfeiffer, Charlotte for sidebar.

Hillesum, Etty (1914–1943)

Dutch intellectual whose diaries, published as* An Interrupted Life, *have become a vademecum for readers around the world. *Name variations: Esther Hillesum. Born Esther Hillesum in Middelburg, Holland, on January 15, 1914; died in Auschwitz on November 30, 1943; daughter of Dr. Louis Hillesum (a teacher of classical languages) and Rebecca (Bernstein) Hillesum (a Russian emigre to the Netherlands after a Russian pogrom); graduated from the municipal gymnasium, 1932; University of Amsterdam, law degree; attended the Faculty of Slavonic Languages; began study of psychology.*

Selected publications: Het Verstoorde leven: Dagboek van Etty Hillesum, 1941–1943 *(De Haan/ Unieboek, 1981, published in America as* An Interrupted Life, *Pantheon, 1983);* Het denkende hart van de barak *(*The Thinking Heart of the Barracks, *De Haan/ Unieboek, 1982, published in America as* Etty Hillesum: Letters from Westerbork, *Pantheon, 1986).*

Etty Hillesum, who was born in Middelburg, Holland, on January 15, 1914, grew up in a house filled with books. After sojourns in Tiel and Winshoten, the family settled in Deventer in 1924, a city east of Holland, where her father was assistant headmaster, then headmaster, of the municipal gymnasium. Dr. Louis Hillesum was a quiet and cerebral scholar; Etty's mother **Rebecca Hillesum,** who had fled Russia during one of the many pogroms in the 1920s, was the polar opposite—passionate, excitable, and chaotic. It was a "tempestuous" house, Hillesum would later recall. She remembered sitting in her father's untidy, impersonal study, "as were all the rooms in all the different houses in which we ever lived," sitting there in a rage and expressing it with her pen. "Red, green, black," she wrote angrily. "Through the leaves of the green tree I see a girl in a bright red dress." Her desire to write was palpable, an outlet that would offer her clarity in the years ahead. But if there was chaos inside, there was peace outside. "There were cornfields I shall never forget," she wrote, "whose beauty nearly brought me to my knees; there were the banks of the IJssel with the colourful parasols and the thatched roofs and the patient horses. And the sun, which I drank in through all my pores."

The Hillesum children were extremely bright: Mischa, who played Beethoven in public by age six, would be considered one of Holland's finest pianists; Jaap, who was a medical student when he discovered new vitamins at age 17, would win entrance to all the academic laboratories; and Etty, who was always ahead of her friends in school, would be the writer. After attending the University of Amsterdam, where she acquired a law degree, she enrolled in the Faculty of Slavonic Languages.

In early 1937, at age 23, Etty Hillesum moved into a third-floor room in a large house at 6 Gabriël Metsustraat, overlooking South Amsterdam's Museum Square with its concert hall on one end and the Rijksmuseum on the other. She had been invited there by Han Wegerif, a 60-year-old widower, to be a sort of housekeeper. It was a communal household that included the nurse **Maria Tuinzing**, the German housekeeper Käthe, the social democrat Bernard, and Hans, Wegerif's son. Hillesum also tutored Russian and began an amicable affair with Wegerif the elder.

Throughout her early 20s, she was often ill and frequently felt the need for two-hour naps. A sometime victim of inflamed kidneys and bladder, Hillesum was also plagued by her hated mood-controlling, tri-weekly periods, for which she took a "monthly pound of aspirins." With her iron will, she was determined to grow independent of her body, to learn to accept her moods, and was especially determined to avoid striking out as she had in her youth. She would later refer to this young Hillesum as the "unhappiest person in the world." She had a craving for knowledge, a longing to write, and a need to give meaning. She yearned for discipline as a writer and counted on her habitual state of unease to propel her.

Then at a party, possibly in January 1941, she met Julius Spier. As a psychochirologist, a person who studies and classifies palm prints, Spier had founded a publishing house; he had also lived in Zurich for analysis training under Carl Gustav Jung, who had encouraged Spier to turn psychology into a fulltime profession. In February, Etty consulted Spier for the first time. After three or four therapy sessions, she became his assistant and would eventually become his lover and "intellectual partner." He was 55, she was 28. But the private lives of these two individuals would soon be controlled by external events.

Etty Hillesum

Throughout the 1930s, Holland had nervously watched the approach of World War II. The Dutch Cabinet had debated the possibility of reaching an understanding with Adolf Hitler, though Queen ***Wilhelmina** had warned her subjects that neutrality might not last forever, since "Hitler has written a book [*Mein Kampf*], and the contents might be of some consequence." When German troops crossed the Dutch frontier in May 1940, and German paratroopers landed near The Hague in an attempt to capture the queen and leaders of Holland's Cabinet, Wilhelmina had evaded them by boarding a British destroyer. The queen would remain in Britain throughout the war, regularly speaking to her occupied country by radio. After her prime minister in exile again mentioned trying to reach an understanding with Hitler, she successfully maneuvered to have him replaced.

Wilhelmina became a symbol for the Dutch underground resistance to Nazi rule. Many citizens in the Netherlands began placing the German occupiers' postage stamps in the upper left-hand corner of the envelope, arguing that the upper right hand corner was reserved for stamps bearing the likeness of Wilhelmina. When German authorities declared in 1940 that Jews would no longer be admitted to the civil service, half of the country's professors signed a letter of protest. More than 80% of university students refused to sign a statement of loyalty to the Nazi regime.

On May 18, 1940, Artur von Seyss-Inquart became Reichs Commissioner for Holland. He had been Hitler's helpmate in the Austrian *anschluss* and deputy to the brutal Hans Frank, governor-general of Poland. Seyss-Inquart promised the Dutch that they would remain sovereign, then tightened his grip. When the Nazis first moved against the Jews in February 1941 and 400 were sent to concentration camps, the Dutch in Amsterdam went on strike. It was the first anti-pogrom strike to break out in European history. After their protest was suppressed, the Dutch took their rebellion underground. Throughout World War II, many concealed and protected Jews.

Etty Hillesum deserves to be counted among the heroes.

—***The New York Times Book Review***

Though Jewish by birth, Etty Hillesum had no strong religious affiliation. In her journals and letters that cover the period of Sunday, March 1941, to September 15, 1943, three of the brutal years of Holland's occupation, Hillesum seems to go from a worldly, pleasure-loving woman suffering from "inner chaos" and "spiritual constipation" to a woman of near mystical intensity and compassion. Through her relationship with Spier, she went from someone who would need to blurt, "I too am religious, you know," to someone who "sometimes actually dropped" to her knees.

She strove for goodness, praying for an inner freedom, clarity, and peace of mind:

> I allow others to formulate what I ought to be formulating for myself. I keep seeking outside confirmation of what is hidden deep inside me, when I know that I can only reach clarity by using my own words. . . . Perhaps my purpose in life is to come to grips with myself . . . with everything that bothers and tortures me. . . . For these problems are not just mine alone. And if at the end of a long life I am able to give some form to the chaos inside me, I may well have fulfilled my own small purpose. Even while I write this down, my unconscious is protesting at such expressions as "purpose" and "mankind" and "solution of problems." I find them pretentious. But then I'm such an ingenuous and dull young woman, still so lacking in courage.

She felt she still needed a "a steady undercurrent," a basic tune. "My ideas hang on me like outsize clothes into which I still have to grow. My mind lags behind my intuition."

Hillesum lived and wrote in a small room often bathed in sunlight. Her one large window, curtains rarely closed, looked out on a sunny veranda, a fading hyacinth, a cherished tree, and the Skating Club. A bookcase near her bed allowed her to reach out with her left hand and grasp Dostoyevsky and Shakespeare and Kierkegaard. On her desk, where she would fill eight blue-lined exercise books, sat a lamp and typewriter, a black telephone, a Moorish statue, a small Bible, Russian grammars and dictionaries, typing paper, carbons, Jung, St. Augustine, three pine cones, and Rilke's *Über Gott,* crushed under *Russian for Businessmen.* In the beginning, she feared deserting her "beloved" desk, her refuge, if she were taken away by the Germans. But eventually she realized that the room would be going with her. "It had become a part of myself," she wrote. "I couldn't have stayed in it all my life anyway . . . so long as I carry it in me I shall always be able to withdraw into it."

On October 24, 1941, new measures to isolate the Dutch Jews were put into effect; many lost their jobs and were forbidden to frequent stores with non-Jews. In April 1942, more measures arrived: Dutch Jews were forced to wear a yellow star, the Star of David, and forbidden to walk on several streets. "In the years to come," she wrote, "children will be taught about ghettos and yellow stars and terror at school and it will make their hair stand on end." These were still "minor vexations," however, "compared with the infinite riches and possibilities we carry within us." But that spring of 1942, when the deportations began, her May 18th entry reads, "The threat grows greater, and terror increases from day to day. I draw prayer round me like a dark protective wall, withdraw inside it as one might into a convent cell and then step outside again."

By June 12, Jews could no longer go to the greengrocers or frequent outside cafes. They had to be off the streets by eight, could not travel by tram anywhere in the city, and would soon have to hand in their bicycles. Even if their work or friends were miles away, walking was the only mode of transportation open to them. "Humiliation always involves two," wrote Hillesum. "The one who does the humiliating, and the one who allows himself to be humiliated. If the second is missing . . . then the humiliation vanishes into thin air."

On June 29, British radio reported that 700,000 Jews had been killed in Germany and its occupied territories in the preceding year, and that all Jews in Holland were being deported through Drenthe Province, across Germany, and into Poland. "What is at stake is our impending destruction and annihilation, we can have no more illusions about that." Hillesum fought despair; her recurrent belief that one is master of one's inner resources grew stronger. "Everything we need is within us," she wrote. While schoolgirl ***Anne Frank** went into hiding with her family just a few miles away, Etty began eating less, preparing her body for less, training herself to go without. She also began preparing her mind to suffer with dignity, to live life from minute to minute and to take "suffering into the bargain."

A good lunch, a basket of cherries, a cup of coffee would give her joy. "As life becomes harder and more threatening, it also becomes richer, because the fewer expectations we have, the more the good things of life become unexpected gifts which we accept with gratitude." One night, as she took the blackout paper off a window at 2 AM while staying with friends, "suddenly there were two stars at the head of the bed. They were not the same stars I see through my window but I felt in touch with them all the same, and suddenly I was quite certain that no matter where I was in the world I would always find stars and be able to flop down on a bed, or on a floor, or anywhere else, and feel absolutely home."

On July 7, 1942, Dutch Jews began to get called up for labor in "work" camps. Etty continued to prepare—for the train, for life in a labor camp. Mentally, she packed and repacked her rucksack. Because of blisters, she fretted about what shoes to take; she wondered if she should pack underwear and food for three days, and whether or not she should take blankets. She would take her small Bible, she thought, and Rilke's *Book of Hours* and *Letters to a Young Poet,* and her two small Russian dictionaries. She would have her hair cut short and throw her lipstick away; she would have a pair of trousers and jacket made out of heavy material and would try to see her parents before she went; she would go to the dentist. The thought of suffering from toothache "out there" was frightening.

The Germans intended to move all Jews to Westerbork, a transit camp near Assen in the northeastern Netherlands, near the German border. Though a concentration camp, it was not an extermination camp; but it was to be the last stop before Auschwitz for more than 100,000 Dutch Jews. Ironically, it had been built by the Dutch in 1939 to house some 1,500 Jews who had fled Germany—political prisoners who had been incarcerated in Buchenwald or Dachau. It was now being used by Hitler's Reich as a holding pen. Instead of the 1,500 it was intended for, the Germans were squeezing in 30,000 to 40,000. Westerbork had its own hierarchy: on top, German supervision; below, Dutch supervision in the form of the Jewish Council.

On July 11, the rumors began—rumors about extermination, about the use of gas. They only served to strengthen Hillesum's inner reserve. "I hope they will send me to a labour camp," she wrote, "so that I can do something for the 16-year-old girls who will also be going. And to reassure the distracted parents who are kept behind." Then the packing of the mental rucksack would begin again. She would take the pure wool sweater that Jopie gave her, the two parts of *The Idiot,* and her small Langenscheidt dictionary. Maybe if she took less food, she could carry more books.

Friends accused her of defeatism. They prodded her to go into hiding, to take an active role in saving herself. "It is not in my nature to tilt against the savage, cold-blooded fanatics who clamour for our destruction," she wrote. "It is not as if I want to fall into the arms of destruction with a resigned smile—far from it. I am only bowing to the inevitable and even as I do so I am sustained by the certain knowledge that ultimately they cannot rob us of anything that matters. But I don't think I would feel happy if I were exempted from what so many others have to suffer."

But her brother Jaap continued the pressure, urging her to take a job with the Jewish Council, which would spare her from internment at Westerbork. Eventually, she did so, despite feelings of having "done something underhand." In retrospect, the Jewish Council was misguided. Goaded into existence by the Nazis, it had been formed to arbitrate between Jews and Germans: the Nazis would hand out edicts and the Council had no choice but to implement them. Since the directives were inevitable, many Council members felt they could at least ease the Jewish burden. Hillesum was not so sure. "Nothing can ever atone for the fact, of course, that one section of the Jewish population is helping to transport the majority out of the country. History will pass judgement in due course."

On July 15, 1942, she began work as a typist in the Council's Cultural Affairs Department.

In that building of stone floors and overcrowded corridors, she was assigned to a small room with 100 voices and typewriters chattering together. Even then, she would steal a few moments to sit in the corner and read Rilke. Though it was a long trek to work on blistered feet, she would trudge a few blocks out of her way to find a flower stall. To her, a red anemone was just as real as all the misery she was encountering.

But Hillesum only lasted two weeks at the office of the Jewish Council; that July, she volunteered to accompany the first Jewish group sent to Westerbork. She was convinced that she could be of more use in the camp as a "social worker" for the Council. On the heath in Drenthe Province, Westerbork was frequently plagued by mud and sandstorms, though one section of the camp, wrote Etty, looked out on "a field of yellow lupins stretching as far as the delousing barracks." Inside its barbed wire, it contained row upon row of wooden barracks, each without electricity, each with three-tiered narrow plank beds left over from the Maginot Line.

"Whenever yet another poor woman broke down at one of our registration tables, or a hungry child started crying, I would go over to them and stand beside them protectively, arms folded across my chest, force a smile for those huddled, shattered scraps of humanity and tell myself, 'Things aren't all bad, they really aren't that bad.'. . . Sometimes I might sit down beside someone, put an arm round a shoulder, say very little and just look into their eyes. . . . And at the end of each day, there was always the feeling: I love people so much." But Hillesum was not quite ready for the constant interaction that internment demands. She castigated herself for wanting isolation. In the dormitory, she would "fling them a piece of myself and run away."

Her diary stops that first month in camp, between July 29 and September 5, 1942. Hillesum had a travel permit for furloughs to Amsterdam occasionally, to bring out letters and return with medicines. On August 14, 1942, during one of these short leaves, she took sick and could not get back for three months. Most of the time she was bedridden, with intestinal hemorrhage or stomach ulcer (the doctors weren't sure). She managed, however, to visit her parents in Deventer and her dear friend Spier, who was seriously ill. On September 15, 1942, the day the Gestapo came to take him to Westerbork, he died.

Though she returned to camp on November 20, 1942, two weeks later she was back in Amsterdam and admitted to the Netherlands Israelite Hospital because of gallstones. She was away from the barracks for another six months. In early June 1943, she returned to camp. By now, she was traveling with one shirt in her rucksack and a very small Bible.

There had been a massive "Jew hunt" throughout the Netherlands that October. Train after train pulled up at Westerbork, threatening to engulf the camp with a tide of humanity. Every Monday, a train pulled in; every Tuesday, a train pulled out. In all, 93 trains would leave Westerbork for Auschwitz, 70 people to a sealed car, bucket in the middle for sanitation, 1,000 men, women, children, and babies to a train. In her notes to friends, the descriptions of the transports had such enormous power that two of her letters were secretly published in book form by the Dutch Resistance in an attempt to ignite the countryside.

> Just now I climbed up on a box lying among the bushes here to count the freight cars at the front for the escorts. The freight cars had been completely sealed, but a plank had been left out here and there, and people put their hands through the gaps and waved as if they were drowning.
>
> The sky is full of birds, the purple lupins stand up so regally and peacefully, two little old women have sat down on the box for a chat, the sun is shining on my face—and right before our eyes, mass murder. The whole thing is simply beyond comprehension.

Call-ups for the Tuesday outgoing transports were issued in the dark of night, just hours before the trains left. If the quota was not filled, more Jews were seized at the last minute. Thus, no one could be sure they would not be on their way to Poland and certain death the following morning.

> After a night in the hospital barracks, I took an early morning walk past the punishment barracks, and prisoners were being moved out. The deportees, mainly men, stood with their packs behind the barbed wire. So many of them looked tough and ready for anything. . . . But the babies, those tiny piercing screams of the babies, dragged from their cots in the middle of the night. . . . The babies were easily the worst.
>
> And then there was that paralysed young girl, who didn't want to take her dinner plate along and found it so hard to die. Or the terrified young boy: he had thought he was safe, that was his mistake, and when he realised he was going to have to go anyway, he panicked and ran off. His fellow Jews had to hunt him down—if they didn't find him, scores of others would be put on the transport in his place. He was caught soon enough, hiding in a tent, but 'notwithstanding' . . . 'notwithstanding', all those others had to go on transport anyway, as a deter-

> rent, they said. And so, many good friends were dragged away by that boy. Fifty victims for one moment of insanity. Or rather: he didn't drag them away—our commandant did. . . . Small bottles of milk are being prepared to take along with the babies, whose pitiful screams punctuate all the frantic activity of the barracks.

Week after week, Hillesum met the trains and saw them off. Then one Monday, on June 21st, as she stood in the rain to greet another incoming train, she was stunned to see her parents and brother Mischa alight from a teeming car. A rare feeling of despair came over her. She wasn't worried about herself, she wrote friends; she had accepted her fate, "but living in fear for your loved ones . . . is something I can't bear."

On Monday, July 5, when Hillesum learned from others that her parents were on the list for the next morning's transport to Auschwitz, she spent most of the day climbing the German chain of command, cajoling those higher and higher up. Though 2,500 evacuees left the next day, she had managed to keep her parents off the list, only to learn they had been put back on for the following week. That afternoon, she fainted twice in the middle of the barracks. She was right, she said; she could handle anything, except for the suffering of her family. "It's best to be on your own. . . . That's very important."

On July 10, she wrote a friend that she could no longer save her parents, that it would be their turn to leave for Poland soon, and her brother Mischa insisted on going with them. Though she felt it was cowardice, she did not want to be on the same train. She couldn't stand the idea of seeing them suffer. "I would like to pack their cases with the best things I can lay my hands on, but I know perfectly well that they will be stripped of everything (about that we have been left in no doubt), so why bother?" She concluded her letter with a casual by-the-way: her identity card had been taken away; she was now an official camp inmate.

In September, a letter arrived at the large house at 6 Gabriël Metsustraat. Addressed to Maria Tuinzing, it was written by a campmate of Etty's named Jopie Vleeschouwer. On September 7, 1943, it said, Etty, her mother, father, and brother Mischa were put on transport, though she "wanted to go through the experience without the pressure of family ties." He watched as she stood on the platform, "talking gaily, smiling, a kind word for everyone she met on the way, full of sparkling humour, perhaps just a touch of sadness, but every inch the Etty you all know so well." Her mother, father, and Mischa were in car #1, she in car #12. Soon after the train had pulled out of Westerbork, Hillesum tossed a postcard out the slotted window of the train. It was found by Dutch farmers outside the camp and mailed for her. It read: "We have left the camp singing."

After three days, the train reached Auschwitz. That day, September 10, 1943, her father and mother were gassed. Mischa would die on March 31, 1944. (Her brother Jaap, who was allowed to remain in Amsterdam much longer because he was a doctor at the Hollandse Schouwburg, was sent to Westerbork in the beginning of 1944. Though he survived the camps, he died returning to Holland.) On November 30, 1943, two months after the death of her parents, the Red Cross reported the death of Etty Hillesum. She was 29.

Hillesum, who had always intended for her diaries and letters to be published, had asked Maria Tuinzing to be their guardian. Through the years, friends had submitted them to publishers, but they had been turned down. Then one day, those eight exercise books, written "in a small hard-to-decipher hand," were given to Jan G. Gaarlandt. In October 1981, 38 years after her death, her diaries were published in the Netherlands as *Het Verstoorde leven: Dagboek van Etty Hillesum, 1941–1943* (later released in America as *An Interrupted Life*). After 14 reprints, 150,000 copies were sold in Holland. "For churches, universities, schools, discussion groups, and thousands of individual readers, the book has become a Vademecum," wrote Gaarlandt. (A vademecum is a handbook or a book carried as a constant companion.) It has been published in Germany, France, Spain, Portugal, Japan, Norway, Finland, Denmark, Sweden, Canada, Italy, England, and the United States. In May 1982, Etty's letters were published as *Het denkende hart van de barak* (*The Thinking Heart of the Barracks*) and published in America as *Etty Hillesum: Letters from Westerbork.*

On April 1, 1942, a prescient Etty Hillesum had written: "All that matters now is the 'deep inner serenity for the sake of creation.' Though whether I shall ever 'create' is something I can't really tell. But I do believe that it is possible to create, even without ever writing a word or painting a picture, by simply moulding one's inner life. And that too is a deed."

SOURCES:

Hillesum, Etty. *An Interrupted Life.* Pantheon 1983.

———. *Etty Hillesum: Letters from Westerbork.* Pantheon, 1986.

COLLECTIONS:

Etty Hillesum Foundation in Amsterdam.

Hilliard, Harriet (1909–1994)

American actress and singer who starred on "Ozzie and Harriet" for 22 years. *Name variations: Harriet Nelson. Born Peggy Lou Snyder in Des Moines, Iowa, on July 18, 1909; died of congestive heart failure in Laguna Beach, California, on October 2, 1994; daughter of Roy Snyder whose stage name was Roy Hilliard (a director of a stock theater company) and Hazel (McNutt) Snyder whose stage name was* ***Hazel Hilliard*** *(an actress); married Oswald George "Ozzie" Nelson, on October 8, 1935 (died of liver cancer in 1975); children: Eric "Rick" (b. May 8, 1940, a rock singer killed in a 1985 plane crash), David (b. October 24, 1936, a producer-director); grandchildren:* ***Tracy Nelson*** *(an actress), and twins Gunnar and Matthew Nelson (popular rock singers who call themselves The Nelsons).*

Filmography: Follow the Fleet *(1936);* New Faces of 1937 *(1937);* The Life of the Party *(1937);* She's My Everything *(1938);* Coconut Grove *(1938);* The Letter *(1940);* Confessions of Boston Blackie *(1941);* Fifty Million Nickels *(1941);* Sweetheart of the Campus *(1941);* Canal Zone *(1942);* Juke Box Jenny *(1942);* Honeymoon Lodge *(1943);* The Falcon

Harriet Hilliard with Ozzie Nelson.

Strikes Back *(1943);* Gals Inc. *(1943);* Take It Big *(1944);* Swingtime Johnny *(1944);* Here Come the Nelsons *(1952). Early work with Ozzie on radio shows of comedians Joe Penner and Red Skelton. "The Adventures of Ozzie and Harriet," CBS radio (1944–49), ABC radio (1949–54), ABC television (October 1952–66).*

Harriet Hilliard gave up a budding career as a bandsinger and movie actress to marry bandleader Ozzie Nelson—or, so she thought. In 1944, "The Adventures of Ozzie and Harriet" bowed on CBS radio on Sunday nights and ran until 1949; then ABC radio aired it from 1949 to 1954. In October 1952, the show began a 14-year run on ABC television. The Nelsons—including sons Ricky and David—became the most popular family in America, with its genial, bumbling dad and its wise-cracking, all-knowing mother, who was generally seen preparing, serving, or cleaning up after meals. Hilliard revealed years later that she did not learn how to cook until after the show's cancellation.

Born Peggy Lou Snyder in Des Moines, Iowa, in 1909, Harriet was the daughter of Roy and Hazel Snyder, theater professionals who used the stage name Hilliard. Since her father was the dramatic director of the Midwest-based North Brothers Stock Company and her mother its "leading lady," Harriet hit the boards early; she had a walk-on, or more accurately, a carry-on role at six months and a speaking role at three years. In summer, she toured with her family in numerous productions, including *The Little Princess* and *Mrs. Wiggs of the Cabbage Patch*. In winter, she attended public schools and St. Agnes Academy in Kansas City, Missouri.

After studying ballet in New York, Hilliard made her Broadway debut at 15 in the ballet line of the Capitol Theater, Eugene Ormandy conducting. Moving into vaudeville as a hoofer on the Orpheum circuit, she appeared with Ken Murray and the *Harry Carroll Revue*. An appearance in the movie short *Musical Justice* led to her new career as a singer for bandleader Ozzie Nelson, followed by "The Adventures of Ozzie and Harriet." When Ozzie, who was writer, director, and producer of their long-running family show, emerged from negotiations with ABC bigwigs, having wangled a 10-year contract, Hilliard looked up from the waiting room couch and said, "What if we get a divorce?"

After years of suffering from emphysema, Harriet Hilliard died on October 2, 1994.

Hillis, Margaret (1921—)

American conductor. *Born on October 1, 1921, in Kokomo, Indiana; daughter of Bernice (Haynes) Hillis and Elwood Hillis; studied at Indiana University; received her Master's in choral conducting, Juilliard School of Music, 1949.*

Was a naval flight instructor for two years during World War II; founded the American Concert Choir and the American Concert Orchestra (1950) which made many international tours for the State Department; conducted the Kenosha Symphony in Wisconsin (1961–68); also conducted the Cleveland Orchestra, Minnesota Orchestra, Akron Orchestra, National Symphony Orchestra, Milwaukee Symphony Orchestra, and Chicago Symphony Orchestra among others.

Margaret Hillis was born in Kokomo, Indiana, in 1921, the daughter of **Bernice Haynes Hillis** and Elwood Hillis. Margaret's earliest memory was of crawling around her grandmother's living room near the pipe organ as an eight-month-old. She would crawl to the grill and keep time by beating the grill work. As a little girl, after listening to a Sousa band, she wanted to conduct an orchestra, not realizing women of that period were not encouraged to conduct male orchestras and bands. In high school, Hillis was as talented at golf as at music and won the Junior State championship. During World War II, she was a naval flight instructor, training for 12 hours a day, 7 days a week. At Juilliard, she studied under Robert Shaw and Julius Herford, receiving her Master's Degree in choral conducting in 1949. For two years, she was Shaw's assistant.

Hillis founded the American Concert Choir and the American Concert Orchestra in 1950. The performing group represented the United States at the Brussels World's Fair, toured extensively for several years, and made numerous broadcasts on all three television networks. By 1977, Hillis was also conducting the Elgin Symphony Orchestra and the Civic Association Orchestra. As conductor of the Chicago Symphony Chorus, she developed one of the finest groups in the world. She also chaired the Department of Choral Activities at Northwestern University.

Margaret Hillis chose choral conducting because orchestral conducting was largely a closed field to women in the 1950s. In later years, she was finally allowed her childhood wish. She took the podium to lead major American musical organizations, including the Chicago, Cleveland, Akron, Minnesota, and Milwaukee symphony orchestras.

John Haag,
Athens, Georgia

Hillman, Bessie (1889–1970)

Russian-born American labor leader who, with her husband Sidney Hillman, founded the Amalgamated Clothing Workers of America, the first union to represent unskilled immigrant workers. *Born Bashe Abramowitz in Russia in 1889; died in 1970; educated at home by tutors; married Sidney Hillman (a labor leader), on May 1, 1916 (died 1946); children: two daughters, Philoine Hillman (b. 1917); Selma Hillman (b. 1921).*

In 1905, at age 15, Bessie Hillman fled her isolated home in Grodno, Russia, to escape the local marriage broker. She arrived in the United States without a skill and without a lesson in English. Settling in Chicago, she took a job as a button-sewer in a sweatshop managed by Hart Schaffner & Marx and went to live in a boardinghouse owned by a family friend. On September 22, 1910, protesting the lowering of her piece rate from 4 cents to 3.75 cents, Hillman put down her needle and led seven women out the door. For her disobedience, she was fired and blacklisted from every shop in Chicago. She sought representation from the president of the United Garment Workers (UGW) but was told that they would have nothing to do with an unskilled immigrant. (The union membership was primarily made up of cutters, who viewed the waves of unskilled immigrants as a threat to their privileges.) Along with many other workers who were denied union help, Hillman went to Hull House, where ***Jane Addams** and ***Ellen Gate Starr**, recognized her as a potential leader and helped her with her English. Within three weeks, Hillman was speaking before a secret meeting of 100 or so Hart Schaffner & Marx workers, urging them to join her and the seven women who had walked out in protest. These workers then returned to their shops to elicit support from some 8,000 tailors who eventually joined in the call for higher wages and a reduction of the work week from 60 hours to 44.

When demands were ignored, strikes spread from company to company, eventually involving 30,000 workers. The walk-out lasted for five months, during which time the strikers faced starvation and police brutality. The UGW did nothing to help, and in the end the workers were forced to return to work. In most companies there were no changes, but at Hart Schaffner & Marx, the strikers, represented by lawyer Clarence Darrow, were permitted to appoint a three-member arbitration committee (the first collective bargaining agreement), of which Hillman was made a member. Over the next several years, Hillman and other strike leaders were successful in laying the groundwork for the formation of the Amalgamated Clothing Workers of America (ACWA), an independent union which was officially named in December 1914. The new union then began organizing clothing workers around the country.

On May 1, 1916, Bessie married Stanley Hillman, co-founder of the union and its first president. The newlyweds went directly from the ceremony to march at the head of the union's annual May Day parade. In the years that followed, for almost a quarter of a century, Hillman and her husband devoted themselves to the union, working out of headquarters at 15 Union Square, in New York City. (After the death of her husband in 1946, Hillman would be voted vice president.) For months at a time, she was on the road, leading campaigns for glove workers in upstate New York or shirt workers in Pennsylvania. The birth of her two daughters, in 1917 and 1921, restricted her activities somewhat, but as soon as the girls were old enough to be left with a housekeeper, she was on the road again. "When I was growing up, I was aware of her being away," recalled her older daughter, **Philoine Hillman**, in 1973, "but I did not feel deprived, because when she came home we were always a part of her activities." Indeed, the Hillman home was a central point in a large Russian community, and it was not unusual for the house to be filled with people. Bessie's younger daughter, **Selma Hillman**, remembered her mother standing on picket lines, or making sensational speeches, but she missed a certain closeness with her. "Mother never discussed her problems with me," she remembered, "which is a shame. If she had been more open, we'd have had something to talk about when she got older and needed companionship."

In her role as union organizer, Hillman took to heart the ACWA slogan, "Touch the worker from cradle to grave," and felt strongly that it was her duty to raise workers' self-esteem along with their wages. She headed up several educational programs, including adult-education courses for union members. She was also sensitive to women's rights and for years was active in the Women's Trade Union League, whose purpose was to give women, who made up a majority of the work force, an equal voice in the union. As a result of her concern for day care, the ACWA instituted a large number of child-care facilities.

Hillman also served on the U.N. Commission on the Status of Women and was on a subcommittee of the President's Commission on the

Status of Women. In an essay, "Gifted Women in the Trade Unions," in the anthology *American Women: The Changing Image* (1961), Hillman wrote: "I have a deep conviction that, given a more important function within the labor movement, women could do much to restore the union image as the indomitable fighter for social justice and enlightenment, an image that has been sadly undermined in recent years."

Bessie Hillman did not give up organizing until the union forced her to retire at age 70 because of her health. She died, five years later, in the middle of an operation for an intestinal tumor.

SOURCES:

Julianelli, Jane. "Bessie Hillman: Up From the Sweatshop," in *Ms.* Vol. 1, no. 11. May 1973.

SUGGESTED READING:

Cassara, Beverly Benner, ed. *American Women: The Changing Image.* Boston, MA: Beacon Press, 1962.

Barbara Morgan,
Melrose, Massachusetts

Hills, Carla (1934—)

American lawyer and public official who was the first woman secretary of the Department of Housing and Urban Development (1975) and the third woman ever to hold a U.S. Cabinet post. *Born Carla Helen Anderson in Los Angeles, California, on January 3, 1934; younger of two children of Carl Anderson (a building supplies executive) and Edith (Hume) Anderson; attended the Marlborough School, Los Angeles, California; graduated cum laude from Stanford University, 1955; Yale University Law School, LL.B., 1958; married Roderick M. Hills (a politician), on September 27, 1958; children: four.*

Born in Los Angeles, California, in 1934, Carla Anderson was headed for a career in law from age 12, when she was inspired by the biography of Alexander Hamilton. She graduated cum laude from Stanford University, where she also captained the tennis team, then worked her way through Yale Law School, receiving her LL.B. in 1958. That same year, Carla married Roderick Maltman Hills, whom she had met while at Stanford. After passing the California Bar in 1959, she worked for two years as an assistant district attorney in Los Angeles.

In 1962, not yet 30, Hills, along with her husband and several other partners, formed the law firm of Munger, Tolles, Hills & Rickershauser. Specializing in antitrust and securities cases, she gained prominence as a trial lawyer. In addition to her work with the firm, Hills served on the advisory board of the California Council on Criminal Justice (1969–71) and on the standing committee on discipline for the U.S. District Court for Central California (1970–73). She was an adjunct professor at the University of California at Los Angeles School of Law (1972), was on the board of councillors of the University of Southern California Law Center (1972–74), and on the Executive Committee on Law and a Free Society of the state bar of California (1973). During this time, Hills also gave birth to four children, adding the responsibilities of motherhood to her already formidable schedule. Then, and later, her children were high priority, particularly when it came to birthdays or school activities. "I might tell the judge I had a conflicting appointment," she told *Business Week* reporter Paul Magnusson in an interview (June 22, 1990). "Fortunately, they never think to ask if the conflict is a birthday party."

Hills left the firm in 1974, when she was appointed assistant attorney general in the civil division of the U.S. Department of Justice. As the highest ranking woman at the Justice Department, Hills oversaw a staff of 250 lawyers in Washington and 94 U.S. attorneys across the country. In February 1975, she was appointed by President Gerald R. Ford as secretary of the Department of Housing and Urban Development. Confirmed despite reservations over her lack of experience in the field, Hills remained in the post until 1977, proving herself to be a tough, no-nonsense administrator. During her tenure at HUD, and for several years afterward, Hills was expected to become the first woman named to the U.S. Supreme Court, although ultimately that honor went to ***Sandra Day O'Connor** in 1981.

In 1978, Hills returned to private law practice, opening Latham, Watkins and Hills, the Washington office of the Los Angeles-based firm of Latham and Watkins. In 1986, she became a co-managing partner of Weil, Gotshal and Manges in Washington, D.C. During this time, Hills' relationship with a Florida developer and the DRC Funding Group, a mortgage lender, came under scrutiny as the result of a Congressional investigation into allegations of corruption at HUD, though she was never implicated in any wrongdoing.

Hills accepted another political appointment in 1988, when she was named U.S. trade representative by president-elect George Bush, the first woman nominee to his Cabinet. At her confirmation hearing, Hills swore to break down unfair barriers to American trade with a crowbar if necessary. Bush presented her with an inscribed crowbar at her swearing-in: "To Carla—I know you'll use this with finesse and strength. George." Over the next four years, Hills, working with a staff of 150, faced numerous challenges, including concluding the Uruguay Round of multilateral trade negotiations, resolving various trade disputes as Europe moved toward integration, and implementing free-trade agreements with Canada and Israel. Her most daunting task by far was to open Japanese markets to American exports. Adhering to a negotiating style that was called at once "conciliatory" and "extremely tough and calculating," Hills was successful in clearing barriers for American manufacturers of supercomputers, semiconductors, telecommunications equipment, and finished-wood products.

In 1993, she left office with the departing Republican administration and, with three of her colleagues from the trade office, established Hills' and Company, a consulting firm representing companies doing business in the global market. Hills' career has included service on the boards of numerous corporations, including IBM, Chevron, Corning Glass Works, and American Airlines. During 1982 and 1983, she was chair of the American Bar Association. She also served as a trustee of Pomona College, the University of Southern California, and the Norton Simon Museum of Art in Pasadena.

SOURCES:

Graham, Judith, ed. *Current Biography 1993.* NY: H.W. Wilson, 1993.

McHenry, Robert, ed. *Famous American Women.* NY: Dover, 1983.

Read, Phyllis J., and Bernard L. Witlieb. *The Book of Women's Firsts.* NY: Random House, 1992.

Barbara Morgan,
Melrose, Massachusetts

Hillyard, Blanche Bingley (b. 1864)

English tennis player. *Name variations: Blanche Bingley; Mrs. George Whiteside Hillyard. Born Blanche Bingley in England in 1864; married Commander George Hillyard, a secretary of the All England (tennis) Club (1907–24).*

Won six singles titles at Wimbledon (as Blanche Bingley, 1886; as Blanche Bingley Hillyard, 1889, 1894, 1897, 1899, 1900).

Born in 1864 and raised in an upper-class English family, Blanche Bingley Hillyard learned to play tennis in her own backyard. Her career at Wimbledon spanned almost 30 years—longer than any other woman in the history of the game. She first competed there in 1884, at age 20; her last game was played there in 1913, at age 49. Though Hillyard did not have much of a backhand, she had nerves of steel.

Her chief rival was ***Charlotte Dod**, whom Blanche managed to beat only once. Hillyard could win the finals at Wimbledon only if Dod was sailing off the coast of Scotland or putting somewhere on the 14th green. In 1889, in a memorable final with Ireland's **Lena Rice**, Hillyard suffered a rare attack of nerves and turned to the umpire. "Mr. Chipp," she said, "What can I do?" "Play better, I should think," he replied. She did—and took her second Wimbledon.

SOURCES:

King, Billie Jean, with Cynthia Starr. *We Have Come a Long Way.* NY: McGraw-Hill, 1988.

Hilo Hattie (1901–1979).

See Nelson, Clara.

Hilsz, Maryse (1903–1946)

French aviator, one of the most admired women flyers, who made a series of spectacular flights to the Far East and Africa in the 1930s and held the women's world altitude record. *Name variations: name often misspelled as Hiltz, Hilz. Born in Levallois-Perret, France, in 1903; died in an airplane accident at Moulin-des-Ponts, on January 31, 1946.*

Was the recipient of the Harmon International Aviation Trophy for women fliers for 1933 (April 21, 1934).

Born in Levallois-Perret, France, in 1903, Maryse Hilsz grew up determined to become a pilot. Because she was excluded from admittance to the French Air Force as a woman, and thus denied years of free flying experience, she had to find a way to finance private flying lessons. To this end, Hilsz became a parachute jumper. Starting in 1922, she appeared at numerous air shows, displaying her courage in the then-novel skill of parachuting. With her earnings, she was able to pay for flying lessons and in 1930 finally obtained her pilot's license. Already enjoying an established reputation for tenacity and coolheadedness under pressure, she inaugurated her flying career with a voyage on the grand scale—a round trip from France to Saigon.

On November 12, 1930, Hilsz departed Villacoublay, France, for Saigon, French Indo-China (modern-day Ho Chi Minh City, Vietnam), in her Morane airplane. After short hops across the eastern Mediterranean, the Middle East and the Persian Gulf region, including stops at Belgrade, Istanbul and Baghdad, she arrived at Karachi, India (now Pakistan) on November 23. Her flight continued with stops at Allahabad and Calcutta until Hilsz arrived safely in Saigon a week later. As the first woman to fly from Paris to Saigon, she was hailed as a hero. Her flight was front-page news in the local press, and she received an invitation to meet the colonial governor. By December 12, Hilsz had embarked on her return flight, retracing her steps across India and the Persian Gulf. In early January, encountering severe weather conditions, she was forced to make an emergency landing in the Greek village of Kakosalessi. She emerged unscathed, but her plane was slightly damaged and had to be transported by train to the nearby Tatoï airport. After her arrival in Athens, Hilsz decided to begin the final leg of her trip by ship, docking with her plane at Marseilles on January 26, 1931. She made the final stage of her journey once again by air, arriving at her final destination of Paris on February 3, 1931.

In early 1932, Hilsz undertook another ambitious flight to the French colony of Madagascar (modern-day Malagasy Republic). She departed from Le Bourget airport on January 31, and her route took her to a number of remote airports in the numerous French-possessed African colonies before she arrived at Tananarive, the capital of Madagascar, on March 31. Her return flight was uneventful, and she was back in France by early June 1932. Later the same year, Hilsz provided the French press with excellent copy (and brought her friends and family to the point of despair) when her plane disappeared in the vast desert of French West Africa. When the Count and Countess Jacques de Sibour went in search of her, they too vanished. A triple tragedy was feared, but, after two weeks' absence, all three returned safely in their own planes.

Determined not to be seen as just a long-distance aviator, Hilsz set altitude records. On August 19, 1932, she topped the existing women's world altitude record of 28,744 feet with 33,456 feet (9,791 meters). But Hilsz was convinced that she could make her mark in further long-distance aviation achievements in which both speed and distance played roles. Piloting a Farman 190 airplane with a 300-horsepower Gnome-Rhône engine, Hilsz departed from Le Bourget field, Paris, on April 1, 1933, with an ultimate destination of Tokyo. Among the more dramatic aspects of this, her second flight to Asia, was her nonstop hop from Karachi across the Indian subcontinent to Dum Dum aerodrome in Calcutta. She arrived safely in Hanoi on April 7, after having spent time in a small Indochinese village rather than at her scheduled stop of Bangkok. By April 15, she was in Seoul, Korea, and arrived in Tokyo the next day. The warm reception Hilsz received there included extensive press coverage, a luncheon invitation from the French ambassador, a visit to a Kabuki theater, and a medal from the Japanese Imperial Aeronautics Association. On April 23, she began her return flight, arriving in Paris on May 14, 1933, to an enthusiastic reception. A representative of the French Air Ministry praised her not only for having covered 40,000 kilometers (25,000 miles), but also for having successfully served France as an ambassador of good will in Asia.

Maryse Hilsz

Hilsz began her second flight to Tokyo on January 26, 1934. Although accompanied by a mechanic, she was the plane's sole pilot and navigator. Her plane, loaned to Hilsz by the French Air Ministry, was an all-metal Breguet with a 650-horsepower Hispano-Suiza engine, a distinct improvement over her previous one. Except for an emergency landing in Tsingtao, China, where the Breguet was forced down by a storm, the flight was uneventful, and Hilsz landed at Tokyo's Haneda airport on March 6, 1934.

After departing from Tokyo on March 21, Hilsz soon encountered serious problems, but she made a safe emergency landing 48 miles east of Seoul, Korea. The rest of the flight back to Europe went smoothly, and she exhibited remarkable stamina on the next-to-last day of her trip by flying one of the longest legs of her voyage, from Syria to Brindisi, Italy, without difficulty. On the day of her arrival, April 28, she flew from Brindisi to Marseilles, where after only a brief interruption she continued on to Paris, landing at Le Bourget field late that afternoon. A large group of officials and personal friends greeted her on the tarmac. With Hilsz's second Paris-to-Tokyo flight, a total of about 18,750 air miles, she beat her earlier round-trip flight record (6 days, 23 hours, 23 minutes) by completing the journey in 5 days, 9 hours, 5 minutes. That April, Hilsz was awarded the Harmon International Aviation Trophy in the women fliers category for the previous year.

Having supplied sufficient evidence that she had mastered the art of long-distance flying, in 1935 Hilsz returned to the challenge of higher altitudes. Flying a Morane-Saulnier 225 pursuit plane powered by a 750-horsepower Gnome-Rhône K.9 engine, on June 17, 1935, she broke the existing women's world altitude record (set by herself in August 1932) with a height of 37,704 feet (11,800 meters). By the end of 1935, however, Hilsz's accomplishment was bested by the Italian aviator Marchesa **Carina Negrone**, who reached a height of 39,510 feet. Hilsz reclaimed the record on June 23, 1936, by flying a Potez aircraft to a height of 46,947 feet (14,310 meters). The Aero Club of France verified her achievement, which not only broke the women's world altitude record but also the altitude record for French male aviators.

The dangers of Hilsz's field of pursuit were made dramatically apparent in two incidents during 1936. On May 23, she and her mechanic were on their way to Stockholm to attend the opening of a new flying field when they were forced to make an emergency landing near Varberg. Although neither suffered significant injuries, Hilsz was hospitalized for several days with deep cuts on her scalp and face. A much more serious episode took place on December 19, when Hilsz survived a freak accident while flying near Marseilles. Attempting to break the women's world speed record, she had reached a speed of over 400 kilometers an hour when she was suddenly tossed from the plane. Amazingly, Hilsz was thrown clear of the machine, and her parachute somehow opened on its own. She made a slow descent, landing in Lake Estence near Istres, while witnesses launched a boat to rescue her. Considering the nature of the incident, she was incredibly lucky, suffering only from shock and several broken ribs.

By December 1937, Hilsz was in the air again, flying to Saigon to break her own records. In a new Caudron-Renault Simoun machine lent her by the French Air Ministry, she landed in Saigon on December 23, 1937, having flown there from Paris in the record time of 3 days, 20 hours, 21 minutes—10 hours and 37 minutes less than the previous record. In early January 1938, while on her return flight from Saigon to Paris, Hilsz again alarmed the French nation. On January 1, while she was flying the Karachi-to-Basra leg of the trip, her plane was reported missing. It was last seen flying over Jask on the Persian Gulf, and many feared the worst. Ground parties began searching for signs of her plane over the Jask-Bushire section of her route; the scheduled Air France plane also looked for signs of life. Ships in the Persian Gulf were alerted. In Paris, a headline in *Le Figaro* reported the complete lack of news from Hilsz for 48 hours as well as searches for her "in the mountains of Iran, on the Persian Gulf, and in the Arabian Desert." Once again, however, Hilsz cheated death, having made a safe emergency landing about 20 miles from Jask on the Gulf of Oman. Severe thunderstorms during the night had stalled her engine, but she was able to bring her plane down with only a minimum of damage. Found by natives, she arrived in Jask tired but safe after a journey of two days by camel and boat.

By the late 1930s, with war on the horizon, the heroic age of lone aviation pioneers like Hilsz was coming to an end. In 1939, Hilsz began serving with the French Air Force in an advisory capacity. After the liberation of France in 1944–45, she was assigned to working in liaison flights and was enthusiastic about the challenges facing postwar aviation, including jet planes. This was not to be. On January 31, 1946, Maryse Hilsz was killed in the crash of a military plane at Moulin-des-Ponts, near Bourg in the Ain département. Three other aviators, all of them male, died with her. On June 10, 1972, Maryse Hilsz was honored by France, along with another French female aviation pioneer, **Helene Boucher** (1908–1934), when she was depicted on a 10 franc airmail stamp.

SOURCES:

"Airwoman Rescued from a Lake," in *The Times* [London]. December 21, 1936, p. 11.

"Aviatrix Sets New Mark," in *The New York Times*. August 20, 1932, p. 2.

Boase, Wendy. *The Sky's the Limit: Women Pioneers in Aviation.* London: Osprey, 1979.
"Depuis pres de 48 heures on est sans nouvelle de Maryse Hilsz," in *Le Figaro* [Paris]. January 4, 1938, p. 1.
"Ends 25,000-Mile Flight," in *The New York Times.* May 15, 1933, p. 7.
"French Airwoman Killed," in *The Times* [London]. February 1, 1946, p. 3.
"French Airwoman's Adventures," in *The Times* [London]. January 6, 1938, p. 11.
"French Aviatrix Flying to Saigon," in *The New York Times.* November 13, 1930, p. 25.
"French Aviatrix Hurt," in *The New York Times.* May 24, 1936, p. 29.
"French Woman Flier Sets Altitude Record," in *The New York Times.* June 18, 1935, p. 10.
"French Woman Flier Thrown from Plane," in *The New York Times.* December 20, 1936, p. 28.
Les grandes Conferences de l'Aviation au Theatre des Ambassadeurs. Paris: Éditions du Comité des Oeuvres Sociales du Ministere de l'Air, 1934.
Lauwick, Hervé. *Heroines of the Sky.* Translated by James Cleugh. London: Frederick Muller, 1960.
May, Charles Paul. *Women in Aeronautics.* NY: Nelson, 1962.
"Miss Hilsz Sets Two Records," in *The New York Times.* June 27, 1936, p. 3.
"Mlle. Hilsz Finishes 18,750-Mile Flight," in *The New York Times.* April 29, 1934, p. 27.
"Post and Settle Win Flying Prizes," in *The New York Times.* April 22, 1934, p. 6.
Reynolds, Siân. "'High Flyers': Women Aviators in Pre-War France," in *History Today.* Vol. 39. April 1989, pp. 36–41.
"Woman Air Pilot Missing," in *The Times* [London]. January 3, 1938, p. 11.
"Woman Flier Killed," in *The New York Times.* February 1, 1946, p. 4.
"Woman's Record Flight to Saigon," in *The Times* [London]. December 24, 1937, p. 11.

John Haag,
Associate Professor, University of Georgia, Athens, Georgia

Hiltrude (fl. 800s)

Frankish princess. *Born between 783 and 794; daughter of *Fastrada (d. 794) and Charles I also known as Charlemagne (742–814), king of the Franks (r. 768–814), Holy Roman emperor (r. 800–814); sister of *Theodrada, abbess of Argenteuil.*

Hiltrude of Liessies (d. late 700s)

Saint. *Died in the late 700s; daughter of a Poitevin noble from Hainaut.*

Resolved to remain a virgin, Hiltrude of Liessies fled her father's house when presented with a suitor and only returned when she learned that the suitor had married her sister. Soon after, the bishop of Cambrai officiated at the ceremony where Hiltrude took the veil; she then lived in a cell attached to the church of Liessies as a recluse until her death.

Himiko (fl. 3rd c.)

Chinese shaman who ruled Japan in the 3rd century and was responsible for opening trade and diplomatic relations with China. *Name variations: Pimiko; Pimiku; Pimiho; Pimisho; Yamato-hime-mikoto; Yametsu-hime. Pronunciation: He-ME-koe. Ruled around 190–247 CE.*

According to ancient Chinese dynastic histories—the oldest written records of Japan—political turmoil in the land of Wa (Japan) culminated in the naming of a woman ruler: "Finally, people agreed to take a woman as their ruler, and called her Himiko. She was adept in the ways of shamanism and could bewitch people." Perhaps still in her teens, Himiko, meaning Sun Daughter (the sun goddess was thought to have created the Japanese islands), was said to have been popular with both the warring chieftains and her subjects because of her abilities in "the way of the demons," a form of shamanism. After having been named ruler around 190 CE, Himiko was sequestered with 1,000 female attendants. Only one male servant was permitted in her midst to serve food and deliver messages. Military guards patrolled her garrisoned palace, permitting no one else to see her.

During Himiko's long rule as queen of Wa, the warrior chieftains and those of the neighboring Korean kingdoms were in conflict. In order to establish ties with the more secure Chinese dynasty, she paid homage to the Chinese emperor and sent him gifts of cloth and slaves. These acts of friendship led to trade and diplomatic relations between China and Japan.

Himiko had a younger brother who was responsible for the day-to-day responsibilities of government. The Chinese dynastic accounts indicate that after she died, around 247, a huge earthen mound was built on her grave site and over 100 female and male servants followed her in death.

SOURCES:

"Gods, Cavemen, and a Mysterious Queen," in *The East.* Vol. II, no. 3, 1965, pp. 11–16.
Yonekura Isamu. "Himiko, Queen of the Wa: Japan Around the Middle of the Third Century," in *The East.* Vol. X, no. 5, 1974, pp. 43–51.

SUGGESTED READING:

Hong, Wontack. *Paekche of Korea and the Origin of Yamato Japan.* Seoul: Kudara International. 1994.

Linda L. Johnson,
Professor of History, Concordia College, Moorhead, Minnesota

Himiltrude (fl. 700s)

Queen of the Franks and wife of Charlemagne. *Name variations: Hamiltrude; Himiltude. Flourished in the 700s; became first wife of Charles I also known as Charlemagne, emperor of the West, king of the Franks (r. 768–814), Holy Roman emperor (r. 800–814), around 768; children: several, including Pepin the Hunchback (c. 769–810).*

A poor Frenchwoman, Himiltrude was the first of Charlemagne's nine wives. Among others, she was followed by ***Hildegarde of Swabia** (c. 757–783), ***Desiderata** (d. 773), ***Fastrada** (d. 794), and ***Luitgarde** (d. 800). Writes L'Epine of Himiltrude in *Croquemitaine,* "Her coronet and her purple robes gave her an air of surpassing majesty."

Himnechildis (r. 662–675)

Queen and regent of Austrasia. *Name variations: Hymnegilde or Hymnégilde; Chimnechild. Reigned as regent from 662 to 675; married Sigibert III (630–656), king of eastern Frankish kingdom of Austrasia (r. 632–656), in 633; children: at least one son, Saint Dagobert II (652–678/79), king of Austrasia (r. 674–678); at least one daughter ****Bilchilde*** *(d. 675).*

Upon the death of her husband Sigibert III, king of Austrasia, in 656, Himnechildis was named co-regent for her nephew Childeric II. Her son Dagobert II had been spirited off to an Irish monastery by Grimoald, mayor of Austrasia, who had tried to install his own son Childebert on the throne but was killed in the process. Before Childeric II was assassinated in 675, Himnechildis, with the help of Vulfoald, the Austrasian mayor, and Wilfred, bishop of York, had Dagobert restored to his proper place on the throne (r. 674–678).

Hind bint 'Utba (d. 610)

Arabian singer, considered a representative of the **jahiliyya** ***period of music.*** *Name variations: Hind Bint'Utba. Birth date unknown; died in 610 CE.*

In the 7th century, in the pre-Islamic period before the advent of Muhammad and his teachings, women enjoyed more liberty. Women artists like Hind bint 'Utba played their instruments at family and tribal festivities, including Muhammad's wedding with ***Khadijah**. In later years, however, women were allowed to perform only in private homes and only if they hid behind a curtain.

In 605, Hind bint 'Utba led women singing war songs and laments for those killed at Badr. A poet and musician, she was considered representative of women performers of the *jahiliyya,* or the days of ignorance, that is a period before harems and confinement. Despite prohibitions, the traditional songs of female musicians survived in the Arabic world. They continue to be much beloved and very popular.

John Haag,
Athens, Georgia

Hind, Cora (b. 1861).

See Coleman, Kit for sidebar.

Hinderas, Natalie (1927–1987)

African-American concert pianist who was one of the first black artists to gain recognition in the field of classical music. *Born Natalie Leota Henderson on June 15, 1927, in Oberlin, Ohio; died of cancer in August 1987 at her home in Philadelphia, Pennsylvania; daughter of Leota Palmer; earned a bachelor degree in music from the Oberlin School of Music, 1945; attended Juilliard School of Music, New York City; attended Philadelphia Conservatory of Music; married Lionel Monagas (a television producer); children: one daughter, Michele.*

A child prodigy, acclaimed concert pianist Natalie Hinderas was born in Oberlin, Ohio, in 1927 into a musical family. Her father was a jazz musician with his own band, and her mother **Leota Palmer** a prominent conservatory teacher. "I grew up with music," she later recalled. "I listened to my mother practice. I still remember her playing Rubinstein's D minor Concerto and Franck's Prelude, Chorale and Fugue." Hinderas received her earliest piano lessons from her mother and, at age eight, was admitted to Oberlin School of Music. In 1945, she became Oberlin's youngest graduate and went on to study with ***Olga Samaroff** at Juilliard. She later studied with Edward Steuermann at the Philadelphia Conservatory of Music.

In 1954, at age 27, Hinderas made her New York debut at Town Hall, playing a program that included Chopin's Ballade in F minor and Mozart's Sonata in F. Despite favorable reviews, Hinderas, an African-American in the white-dominated field of classical music, had trouble getting her career off the ground. She fared better abroad and spent much of the 1950s and

1960s touring in Europe, Asia, and Africa. (Tours in 1959 and 1964 were sponsored by the U.S. Department of State, which appointed her a U.S. cultural ambassador.) During the 1960s, Hinderas also joined the faculty of Temple University in Philadelphia, where she would be professor of music until her death in 1987.

It was not until 1972 that Hinderas finally achieved recognition in the United States, making stunning debuts with the Philadelphia Orchestra and the New York Philharmonic. Her performance of Ravel's Piano Concerto in G, with the Symphony of the New World, was praised in *The New York Times* for its "crisp precision and wonderfully infectious spirit." Hinderas went on to perform with all of the major orchestras in the country and record with leading labels. Best-known among her extensive repertoire were Rachmaninoff's Concerto No. 2 in C Minor, Schumann's Piano Concerto, and *Rhapsody in Blue,* by George Gershwin.

Once established, Hinderas used her stature to bring the work of blacks to attention. Her recording, *Natalie Hinderas plays Music by Black Composers* (1971), was one of the first anthologies of the work of African-Americans. In 1975, through a grant from the National Foundation for the Arts, she commissioned George Walker's Piano Concerto No. 1, which she first performed with the National Symphony Orchestra in 1976, receiving accolades from the *Washington Post* for her "sense of ease and . . . careful attention to the music's dramatic overtones." Hinderas, who was married to television producer Lionel Monagas and the mother of a daughter, **Michele Monagas**, continued to perform until her death of cancer at the age of 60.

SOURCES:

Smith, Jessie Carney, ed. *Notable Black American Women.* Detroit, MI: Gale Research, 1992.

Hindley, Myra (1942—)

British serial killer who, with her boyfriend, was reponsible for the Moor Murders. *Born in July 1942; had liaison with Ian Brady.*

In 1966, not long after a courtroom had heard the taped cries of their victims, Myra Hindley and her boyfriend Ian Brady were convicted of killing two children and a young man. They were sentenced to life in prison. The homicides, dubbed the Moor Murders, were so named because the infamous pair buried their young prey on England's Saddleworth Moor.

Myra Hindley, who was born in July 1942, had grown up in the home of her grandmother and was extremely shy when she first met Brady in January of 1961, while working as a typist at Millwards, a chemical supply firm in Manchester. The two became lovers. Born in 1938, the illegitimate son of a Scottish waitress, Ian Brady had a reputation for torturing other children and animals as a child; he had also become fascinated with Nazism and sado-sexual pornography during a stint in prison. Soon, Hindley was involved in helping him procure children for prurient photographs.

Over the next three years, their crimes became increasingly more sinister. In November 1963, the couple sexually abused and killed 12-year-old John Kilbride; a year later, they murdered 10-year-old **Lesley Ann Downey**. Both bodies were buried in shallow graves on Saddleworth Moor, just outside Manchester. On October 6, 1965, they abducted Edward Evans, a 17-year-old homosexual, and took him to Hindley's grandmother's house. Luring Hindley's brother-

Myra Hindley

in-law David Smith into observing them because they wanted an accomplice, they murdered Evans with an ax and dumped the body in an unused upstairs bedroom. Smith, whom they then released, quickly informed the police who apprehended the pair.

On May 6, 1966, Myra Hindley was convicted for her part in the three murders and sentenced to life imprisonment. When asked why she had gone along with Brady, she replied that she had done it for love. Twenty years later, in 1986, Hindley led authorities to two other graves, that of Keith Bennett, age 12, who had been killed on June 16, 1964, and **Pauline Reade**, age 16, who had died on July 12, 1963. There is speculation that several other children reported missing at the time of the murders may have also been victims of Hindley and Brady.

In *Beyond Belief,* Emlyn Williams wrote a novelized account of the Moor Murders, and Hindley's biography, *Inside the Mind of a Murderess,* attempts to explain her motivations. In 1997, Hindley resurfaced yet again in, of all places, London's Royal Academy, where a giant portrait of the notorious torture-killer was part of a "shock art" exhibit.

In 1999, when polled about the standard policy of releasing prisoners serving life sentences for murder after a certain period of time, 77% of English respondents were against the practice. This figure increased to 83% when it came to the early release of Hindley, who had by then served 31 years at Durham prison. Hindley's lawyers, however, are intent on overturning the 1999 ruling by Home Secretary Jack Straw that, in her case, a life sentence means life. Hindley's minimum sentence, or "tariff" for retribution and deterrence, had been set at 30 years by the Home Office in 1985. It was increased to "whole life" in 1990 by the then Home Secretary David Waddington.

Hinkle, Beatrice M. (1874–1953)

American psychiatrist who was one of the earliest U.S. proponents of Carl Jung. *Born Beatrice M. Van Giesen on October 10, 1874, in San Francisco, California; died on February 28, 1953, in New York City; daughter of B. Frederick Mores Van Giesen and Elizabeth (Benchley) Van Giesen; educated at private schools and with tutors; graduated from Cooper Medical School (later medical department, Stanford University), 1899; married Walter Scott Hinkle (a lawyer), in 1892 (d. February 7, 1899); children: Walter Mills Hinkle;* ***Consuelo Andoga Shepard.***

Beatrice M. Van Giesen was born on October 10, 1874, in San Francisco, California. It was not until after her marriage in 1892, that Beatrice Hinkle entered the Cooper Medical College with hopes of becoming a doctor. Graduating in 1899, the year of her husband's death, she was appointed San Francisco's city physician and as such became the first woman doctor in the United States to hold a public-health position. In 1905, a growing interest in psychotherapy led her to New York, where in 1908, she and Dr. Charles R. Dana established the first psychotherapeutic clinic at Cornell Medical College. Between 1909 and 1915, Hinkle studied in Europe, first with Sigmund Freud in Vienna, and later with Carl Jung, whose theories she later espoused.

Returning to New York in 1915, Hinkle joined the faculties of Cornell Medical College and the New York Post Graduate Medical school, where she became one of the earliest practitioners of Jungian analysis and also made some valuable contributions to the framework of his theories. Her writings included a translation of Jung's *The Psychology of the Unconscious* (1915) and her major work, *The Recreation of the Individual* (1923). She also published a number of articles and a translation of Dirk Coster's *The Living and the Lifeless* (1929).

In her later years, Beatrice Hinkle divided her time between New York City and "Roughlands," a retreat in Washington, Connecticut, where she also ran a small sanitarium. She died on February 28, 1953, in New York City.

Hinkson, Katharine (1861–1931).

See Tynan, Katharine.

Hipparchia (fl. 300s BCE)

Greek philosopher and wife of Crates. *Name variations: Hipparchia the Cynic. Pronunciation: HIP-ark-EE-ah. Born in Maroneia; flourished in the 300s BCE; married Crates, a Cynic philosopher (368–288 BCE).*

Both Hipparchia and her sister **Metrocles** were born in Maroneia in the 4th century BCE. Hipparchia fell in love with the Cynic philosopher Crates (368–288 BCE), who was originally a Theban and a pupil of the Athenian philosopher Diogenes. So intent was Hipparchia upon him that she threatened her parents with suicide unless she was allowed to marry him; she refused to have any other man for her husband. Summoned by her parents, Crates told Hipparchia that he would not have her as his wife unless she agreed to follow his teachings. Hipparchia assented, adopted his manner of dress, and accompanied him everywhere, even to those places and activities which were considered indecent for women. Her sister also became a Cynic.

The Cynics believed that one should live "according to nature" by renouncing wealth and living without possessions. They also defied social conventions by having sex in public, a practice attributed to Crates and Hipparchia. Hipparchia also defied convention by accompanying her husband to public dinners. In one famous incident, she attended a banquet with Crates at the house of Lysimachus. There, she confronted the atheist Theodorus with the following argument: If it is not wrong for Theodorus to do something, then it is not wrong if Hipparchia also does it. Therefore, if Theodorus slaps himself and does no wrong then it is also not wrong if Hipparchia slaps Theodorus. Theodorus, who had no answer for this, tried to embarrass Hipparchia by pulling up her cloak, but she refused to be intimidated and stood her ground. When Theodorus asked if she was the woman who had abandoned her weaving, she replied that, indeed, she was, and that she had made better use of her time by devoting herself to education.

SOURCES:

Hicks, R.D., trans. *Diogenes Laertius: Lives of Eminent Philosophers.* Cambridge, MA: Harvard University Press, 1965.

SUGGESTED READING:

Dudley, D.R. *A History of Cynicism.* 1938.

Dr. John F. Shean,
Visiting Professor, Clarion University of Pennsylvania

Hippisley, E. (fl. 1741–1766)

English actress. *Name variations: Mrs. Fitzmaurice. Flourished from 1741 to 1766; daughter of John Hippisley (d. 1748, an actor and dramatist); sister of* ****Jane Hippisley*** *(d. 1791) and John Hippisley (d. 1767, an actor and author).*

E. Hippisley, the daughter of the well-known comedian John Hippisley, acted under the name Mrs. Fitzmaurice.

Hippisley, Jane (d. 1791)

English actress. *Name variations: Mrs. Green. Died in 1791; daughter of John Hippisley (d. 1748, an actor and dramatist); sister of* ****E. Hippisley*** *and John Hippisley (d. 1767, an actor and author).*

Jane Hippisley played Ophelia opposite David Garrick's Hamlet at Goodman's Fields. She was also the original Mrs. Malaprop in Richard Brinsley Sheridan's *The Rivals.*

Hippius (1869–1945).

See Gippius, Zinaida.

Hippolyta.

Variant of Ippolita.

Hiratsuka Raichō (1886–1971)

Japanese feminist, pacifist, and consumer advocate who was a founder of Seitōsha (Bluestockings) and Shin Fujin Kyokai (New Women's Association). *Name variations: given name, Hiratuska Haruko; Hiratsuka Raichō. Pronunciation: HE-rah-TSU-kah Ray-CHOE. Born in Tokyo, Japan, in 1886; died in Tokyo in 1971; daughter of a government official who had studied constitutional law in Europe; graduated from Japan Women's University in 1906; lived with the painter, Okumura Hiroshi; children: son and daughter.*

Hiratsuka Raichō was born in Tokyo, Japan, in 1886, the daughter of a government official who had studied constitutional law in Europe. During her youth, she was greatly influenced by Western culture, studying English and reading books on Western philosophy. She was also greatly influenced by Zen Buddhism, however, and practiced Zen meditation throughout her life. In 1911, she was a founder of Seitōsha (Bluestockings) and the first editor of its publication, *Seitō.* In it, she wrote eloquently on the history and status of women. She was particularly interested in the role of literature in women's self-fulfillment. In 1919, Hiratsuka was one of the founders of the Shin Fujin Kyokai (New Women's Association), which campaigned for an extension of women's legal rights, higher education, and welfare benefits. In particular, the organization sought repeal of legislation (Peace Preservation Law) which prohibited women from participating in political activity. Hiratsuka retired, for a time, from public activity, but re-emerged in the 1930s when she became active in the organization of consumer unions. After World War II, Hiratsuka was often a participant in women's international peace initiatives. "In the beginning," she wrote, "woman was truly the sun, and a true being. Now woman is the moon. She lives by others, and shines through the light of others. Her countenance is pale, like a patient. We must now restore the sun, which has been hidden from us."

SOURCES:

Andrew, Nancy. "The Seitōsha: An Early Japanese women's Organization, 1911–1916," in *Papers on*

Japan. East Asian Research Center, Harvard University. 1972.

Reich, Pauline C. "Japan's Literary Feminists: The Seitō Group," in *Signs.* Vol. II, 1976, pp. 280–291.

Sievers, Sharon L. *Flowers in Salt: The Beginnings of Feminist Consciousness in Modern Japan.* Stanford: Stanford University Press. 1983.

Linda L. Johnson,
Professor of History, Concordia College, Moorhead, Minnesota

Hirsch, Rachel (1870–1953)

German-Jewish physician, medical researcher, and professor whose major discovery was ignored in her day but found to be scientifically valid almost two generations later and then named the "Rachel Hirsch Effect." *Name variations: Rahel Hirsch. Born in Frankfurt am Main, Germany, on September 15, 1870; died in London, England, on October 6, 1953; daughter of Mendel Hirsch (1833–1900); had eight sisters and two brothers; never married.*

Was the first woman in Prussia to receive the title of Professor of Medicine (1913); fled Germany (1938).

Rachel Hirsch was born into a large Orthodox Jewish family in Frankfurt am Main, in 1870, a time when hopes were high that, with the creation of a new Germany, the age-old discriminations directed against Jews would soon be only memories. In a large, bustling household of 11 children, Rachel carried on a daily battle to assert herself. Learning was highly respected in her family. Her father Mendel Hirsch was first a professor and later principal of both a private high school and a secondary school (Höhere Töchterschule) for the daughters of Frankfurt's Jewish elite. An imposing family tradition of scholarship and piety had been established by Rachel's paternal grandfather Rabbi Samson Raphael Hirsch (1808–1888), who was universally recognized by Germany's Jews as the foremost exponent of Orthodox Judaism at a time when Reform currents were strong within their religious community.

Since women remained barred from receiving university education in Germany until the first years of the 20th century, Rachel Hirsch's medical training began in 1898 at the University of Zurich, in Switzerland, which had pioneered in awarding medical degrees to women beginning in the 1860s. By the time she transferred to the universities of Leipzig and Strassburg (then Germany, now Strasbourg, France), Germany had begun the process of permitting women's access to institutions of higher education. In July 1903, Hirsch was awarded her medical degree by the University of Strassburg. That same year, she accepted an unpaid position in Berlin at Germany's most prestigious medical center, the Charité Hospital.

Berlin in the first decade of the 20th century was the capital of a powerful but often unsettled nation. Domestic class conflicts and the refusal of France and other countries to accept the German Reich as a genuine world power made German political life tense, and the often unstable behavior of Kaiser Wilhelm II only added to this mood. Meanwhile, average Berliners were noted for their sharp tongues and quick wit, and cultural life in the great and bustling metropolis was often exciting. At the Charité Hospital where Hirsch began her medical career with the double burdens of being both female and Jewish, professional standards were high and often unforgiving. A combination of absolute dedication to the profession of medicine and an almost unfailing eye for detail enabled her to gain the respect of most of her almost exclusively male colleagues. Determined to balance her clinical duties with research work, she achieved distinction in both areas.

In 1906, at the start of her medical career, Hirsch published what would turn out to be her single most important scientific paper. Appearing in the prestigious *Zeitschrift für experimentelle Pathologie und Therapie* and entitled "On the Occurrence of Starch Grains in the Blood and in Urine," this research paper gives a clear description of a phenomenon which had not been previously observed scientifically. Hirsch was the first researcher to describe the unchanged passage of orally taken starch grains into the blood vessels through absorption from the intestine. What she had discovered was the mechanism whereby corpuscular elements, after having first passed through the lymphatic vessel system, are then finally eliminated from the blood through the renal capillaries. Rather than initiate further research, Hirsch's findings were regarded as erroneous by most of her medical colleagues, and soon her paper was gathering dust on library shelves. Discouraged, she stopped her investigations in this area of physiological medicine. Not until after her death—some 50 years following her discovery—would another researcher working at Berlin's Charité Hospital, Gerhard Volkheimer, return to Rachel Hirsch's investigations, find them to be scientifically accurate and valid, and publish his results. To honor his predecessor, Volkheimer named the process the "Rachel Hirsch Effect."

In 1908, in recognition of her excellence as a clinician, Rachel Hirsch received an appointment as the director of the polyclinic branch of the Charité Hospital's Second Medical Clinic. This major promotion made her responsible for all ambulatory patients who came to the hospital for diagnosis and/or treatment. Despite the heavy administrative burdens she now held, Hirsch continued to publish scientific papers. She also began to interest herself in those areas where medicine and society intersected. In a monograph she published in 1913 entitled *Körperkultur der Frau* (Woman's Physical Culture), Hirsch provided evidence of strong sympathies for Germany's emerging feminist movement when she asserted with obvious confidence that "the physical and psychic weaknesses of women are not to be regarded as her normal state but rather are the result of bad education and environment. . . . the more women free themselves from their 'general state of weakness,' the more positive will be their prospects for satisfied and useful lives. When this takes place, men can only benefit from such changes. . . . Therefore, men should not hinder the women's movement, but rather they should make efforts to advance, encourage and promote it."

In November 1913, Hirsch became the first woman in Prussia to be granted the title of Professor in the discipline of medicine. Unfortunately, in a number of ways the title of Professor represented considerably less than met the eye, given the fact that it was purely honorific and carried with it neither university teaching duties nor a salary. Only two previous women in Prussia, the zoologist Countess **Marie von Linden** and the bacteriologist **Lydia Rabinowitsch-Kempner**, had been awarded the coveted title of Professor by the time Rachel Hirsch also received it. Not until after World War I, in February 1920, when women were finally granted the right to study for the Habilitation degree (a post-doctoral hurdle qualifying one for university teaching duties), would the women of Germany finally be able to enter fully into the university teaching profession. Even then, serious obstacles of discrimination and economic pressures continued, so that by 1929 only 46 German women in all academic disciplines had earned the Habilitation title, and only two of these had been able to achieve full professorial rank in a German university.

In 1919, for reasons not known, Rachel Hirsch terminated her long association with the Charité Hospital to go into private practice in Berlin. In 1920, her name appeared on what would be her last publication, a "therapeutic handbook of electro- and ray therapy." In the late 1920s, she moved her medical practice to the Kurfürstendamm, one of Berlin's best-known and busiest streets. In early 1933, when the Nazi Party came to power, Hirsch was 62 years old. She moved her medical practice to the Meineckestrasse, in a neighborhood that housed the headquarters of many of Berlin's Jewish organizations. By the late 1930s, it was no longer possible for Jewish physicians to earn a livelihood in Germany, and on October 7, 1938, Hirsch arrived in Great Britain as a penniless refugee. She lived in London with one of her sisters and chose not to continue her medical career. She regarded the necessary qualifying examinations, and the prospect of attempting to start up another medical practice when she was almost 70, beyond her capacities.

Hirsch spent much of her time translating German books into English and worked for a while as a laboratory assistant, a job that was far below her skills and experience. With the outbreak of World War II, she was evacuated from London to a resort town in rural Yorkshire. When she returned to London after the war, Hirsch was in her mid-70s and her health, particularly her mental state, was deteriorating. Subject to mood swings and often depressed, she increasingly lost touch with reality and slipped into a state of paranoia. Eventually she had to be brought to Camberwell House, a home for the mentally ill near London. Forgotten by the medical world and rejected by her German homeland, Rachel Hirsch died in London on October 6, 1953.

SOURCES:

Brinkschulte, Eva. "Professor Dr. Rahel Hirsch (1870–1953)—der erste weibliche Professor der Medizin—vertrieben, verfolgt, vergessen," in Eva Brinkschulte, ed. *Weibliche Ärzte: Die Durchsetzung des Berufsbildes in Deutschland.* 2nd ed. Berlin: Edition Hentrich, 1993, pp. 103–113.

Hirsch, Rahel. *Ein Beitrag zur Lehre von der Glykolyse.* Strassburg: C. Müh & Cie., 1903.

———. *Körperkultur der Frau.* Berlin: Urban & Schwarzenberg Verlag, 1913.

———. *Therapeutisches Taschenbuch der Elektro- und Strahlentherapie.* Berlin: Fischer's medicinische Buchhandlung H. Kornfeld, 1920.

———. *Unfall und innere Medizin.* Berlin: J. Springer Verlag, 1914.

Muntner, S. "The Rachel Hirsch Effect," in *Korot.* Vol. 3, 1964, pp. 337–338.

"Nach der Verdriesslichkeit," in *Frankfurter Allgemeine Zeitung.* June 19, 1996, p. N6.

"Professor Dr. med. Rahel Hirsch," in *Hamburger Israelitisches Familienblatt.* September 25, 1930.

Pross, Christian. *Special Treatment Requested/ Nicht misshandeln: Moabit Hospital Berlin, 1920–1933–1945.* Berlin: Berliner Gesellschaft für Geschichte der Medizin, 1987.

———, and Rolf Winau. *Nicht misshandeln.* Berlin: Edition Hentrich im Verlag Frölich & Kaufmann, 1984.

John Haag,
Associate Professor, University of Georgia, Athens, Georgia

Hitomi Kinue (1908–1931)

Japanese track-and-field champion. *Name variations: Kinuye. Born on January 1, 1908; died on August 2, 1931.*

Won the silver medal in the 800 meters in Amsterdam Olympics (1928).

A world-class athlete before her country even recognized sports for women, Japanese track-and-field champion Kinue Hitomi had a phenomenal career that was cut short by her premature death at age 24. Gifted as a child, particularly in tennis, Hitomi was sent to one of the few physical education schools in Japan. There she trained as an all-around athlete but excelled in sprinting, jumping, and discus. At age 17, she captured a world record in the triple jump, the first of many she would break in 12 different events. After winning two gold medals in the Second World Women's Games in 1926, Hitomi won a silver medal in the 800-meter at the 1928 Olympics in Amsterdam. **Lina Radke** of Germany took the gold medal with a time of 2:16.8; **Inga Gentzel** of Sweden won the bronze. Unfortunately, at the end of the race, a number of women runners fainted, causing the Olympic Committee to ban races of over 200-meters for women until 1960. In the 1930 Women's Games at Prague, Hitomi won two gold medals, one silver, and one bronze, as well as a gold medal as all-around athlete. In 1931, at the height of her career, Hitomi was diagnosed with tuberculosis. She died shortly thereafter.

Hlotechilde or Hluodhild (470–545).

See Clotilda.

Hobart, Henrietta (1688–1767).

See Howard, Henrietta.

Hobbes, John Oliver (1867–1906).

See Craigie, Pearl Mary Teresa.

Hobbs, Lucy (1833–1910).

See Taylor, Lucy Hobbs.

Hobby, Gladys Lounsbury (1910–1993)

American microbiologist who played an important role in making penicillin a mass-produced antibiotic during World War II. *Born Gladys Lounsbury Hobby in New York City on November 19, 1910; died in Kennett Square, Pennsylvania, on July 6, 1993; daughter of Theodore Y. Hobby and Flora Lounsbury Hobby; graduated from Vassar College, 1931; granted M.A., Columbia University, then granted Ph.D. in bacteriology, 1935; never married.*

A native of New York City, Gladys Lounsbury Hobby graduated from Vassar College in the gloomy Depression year of 1931, going on to Columbia University to earn both a Master's degree and a Ph.D. in bacteriology. From 1934 to 1943, she was associated as a research scientist with Presbyterian Hospital and the College of Physicians and Surgeons at Columbia University. During these years, dramatic research findings were opening the possibility of discovering new and effective means of combatting infections that had often resulted in death. The saga of these medical advances had begun in 1928 at St. Mary's Hospital in London, when Alexander Fleming, a bacteriologist, noticed that bacteria adjacent to a mold growing in a petri dish were dead. A stray spore of greenish mold, later identified as *Penicillium notatum,* had found its way onto the dish that Fleming had seeded with a culture of disease-causing *Staphylococcus.* Although Fleming wrote and published several papers describing the antibiotic effect of penicillin *in vitro,* he never attempted to extract penicillin and made no clinical tests.

Throughout the 1930s, research in the area of discovering an effective antibiotic was carried out both in the United Kingdom and the United States. At Oxford University, the team of Howard W. Florey, Ernst Chain, and Norman G. Heatley was able by 1940 to perform the first successful clinical tests of penicillin on animal subjects, after having produced minute amounts of the antibiotic from surface cultures and after developing a reliable method for measuring exact quantities. By August 1940, the Oxford team had published their results in *The Lancet,* prompting an American team at Columbia University consisting of Martin Henry Dawson, Gladys Hobby, and Karl Meyer to push the research one step further. In October 1940, Dawson, working with his team, administered penicillin parenterally (by injection) to patients, though not in sufficient quantity to produce any effects. Soon after this, in February 1941, the Oxford team was able to point to therapeutic results from their administration of penicillin. In October 1942, the New York team led by Dawson used penicillin to effect cures of subacute bacterial endocarditis, a condition that had hitherto been invariably fatal.

In 1944, Gladys Hobby began working for a major pharmaceutical company, Charles Pfizer & Company, as a senior bacteriologist. Here, she carried on significant research that was linked to the large-scale production of penicillin. At Pfizer, Hobby worked closely with John L. Smith, who recognized that the only way to assure the production of sufficient quantities of penicillin was to rely on deep tanks in which a process of submerged fermentation could take place. Before it was certain that this would be the most effective method of producing penicillin, Smith took what would become a winning gamble by assuming that this method would be the only industrial-scale approach to meeting the challenge of making large quantities of the antibiotic available to an eagerly waiting world.

In her 1985 book *Penicillin: Meeting the Challenge,* Gladys Hobby described the immense challenges that scientists, including herself, faced in the late 1930s and early 1940s in transforming Alexander Fleming's observation into an effective and affordable therapeutic agent. Hobby noted that penicillin "was a British discovery—it was discovered in England, first studied in England, first used clinically in England—and it probably was one of Britain's major wartime contributions to society." The British role then became significantly less prominent as teams of American scientists and technicians—and corporate resources, along with generous government funding—sped penicillin on the path to becoming a readily available antibiotic. As Hobby pointed out in her book, "It was American ingenuity, U.S. dollars, and U.S. production acumen that led to penicillin's availability as an effective chemotherapeutic drug." Hobby's book has become a modern classic in medical history.

In 1959, Hobby left the Pfizer laboratory to become scientific director of the Veterans Administration Infectious Disease Research Institute in East Orange, New Jersey. Here she specialized in studying chronic infectious diseases as well as a myriad of related topics including bacteriophages, bacterial variation and enzymes, streptococci, pneumococci, tubercle bacilli, rat-bite fever, experimental tuberculosis, rheumatic diseases, sulfonamides, the chemotherapy of infectious diseases, immunizing agents, and germ-free life. In addition to these subjects, she continued working in several research areas relating to penicillin and other antimicrobial drugs. Until her retirement in 1977, Hobby served as an assistant clinical research professor in public health at Cornell University Medical College. After retiring, she worked as a consultant and freelance science writer. From 1965 to 1980, she served as editor of an internationally recognized monthly journal, *Antimicrobial Agents and Chemotherapy.* Relatively unknown to the public, Hobby, who spent fully one-third of a century working on the development of antibiotics, deserves recognition for playing an important role in both the scientific investigation and the industrial production of one of the great life-saving discoveries of the 20th century—penicillin.

SOURCES:

Cluff, Leighton E. "America's Romance with Medicine and Medical Science," in *Daedalus.* Vol. 115, no. 2. Spring 1986, pp. 137–159.

Hobby, Gladys. *Penicillin: Meeting the Challenge.* New Haven, CT: Yale University Press, 1985.

Neushul, Peter. "Science, Government, and the Mass Production of Penicillin," in *Journal of the History of Medicine and Allied Sciences.* Vol. 48, no. 4. October 1993, pp. 371–395.

Saxon, Wolfgang. "Gladys Hobby, 82, Pioneer in Bringing Penicillin to the Public," in *The New York Times Biographical Service.* July 1993, p. 951.

John Haag,
Associate Professor, University of Georgia, Athens, Georgia

Hobby, Oveta Culp (1905–1995)

First director of the U.S. Women's Army Corps and first secretary of the Department of Health, Education and Welfare, whose influence grew out of politics and newspaper ownership in Texas. *Pronunciation: OH-vet-uh HA-bee. Born Oveta Culp on January 19, 1905, in Killeen, Texas; died in Houston, Texas, on August 16, 1995, after suffering a stroke; daughter of Isaac William Culp (a lawyer and state legislator) and Emma Hoover Culp; attended public schools and Mary Hardin Baylor College; married William Pettus Hobby (former governor of Texas, newspaper publisher), on February 23, 1931; children: William Pettus Hobby, Jr. (b. 1932); Jessica Oveta Hobby (b. 1937).*

Appointed parliamentarian in the Texas House of Representatives (1926–31); was a newspaper columnist and editor for The Houston Post *(1931–41); was chief of Women's Interest Section of the War Department's Bureau of Public Relations (1941); served as director of Women's Auxiliary Army Corps (later WACs) and was first woman to hold rank of colonel (1942–45); served as first secretary of the Department of Health, Education and Welfare and second female Cabinet member in U.S. (1953–55); was sequentially editor, publisher, and chair of the board of* The Houston Post *(1955–83); served as chair of the executive committee of H&C Communications Inc. (since 1983). Awarded many honorary degrees later in life.*

Selected writings: Mr. Chairman: Rules, and Examples in Story Form, of Parliamentary Procedure Written Expressly for Use in Schools and Clubs *(1937);* Around the World in 13 Days with Oveta Culp Hobby *(1947);* Addresses by Oveta Culp Hobby *(1953); also wrote syndicated newspaper column "Mr. Chairman" (1930s).*

After the 1952 election of Dwight D. Eisenhower as U.S. president, Texas-born Oveta Culp Hobby, already well known as former director of the Women's Army Corps, was appointed head of the Federal Security Administration, the agency soon to become the Department of Health, Education and Welfare (HEW). In an interview following her appointment, she noted: "I believe everyone should be chosen on the basis of competence. Most women, I think, would hate to be chosen on the basis of simply being women." The list of her qualifications for this new post were impressive. In 1949, she was on the national advisory council of the American Cancer Society; in 1950, she was on the board of governors of the National Red Cross. She was also a regent for the Texas State Teachers College, a director of the Cleburne National Bank, held various positions with civic organizations, and was writing a book on parliamentary procedure.

Oveta Culp Hobby went on to define herself as "a liberal Republican," or "a middle-of-the-roader; a person who believes in free enterprise but not the freedom to exploit; who sees Government as the tool of the people but not as its master; who realizes that, in a country as large and varied as ours, certain local problems can be handled more intelligently by local governments; but that others, national in nature, need national support and control; who accepts America's position of leadership in the world and the responsibilities that go with it." As a statement of her convictions, it contained the seeds of what would become the worst political difficulties of her career.

Born on January 19, 1905, in the small Texas town of Killeen, Oveta Culp was the daughter of Ike W. Culp, a lawyer and state legislator, and **Emma Hoover Culp**. She was named for a character in a novel her mother liked, reportedly based on an American Indian word for "forget."

Hobby grew up in an atmosphere charged with politics and ambition. As a child, she read the *Congressional Record* aloud to her father, learning the lessons of power early. Her childhood aspirations, however, favored a career as a foreign missionary or actress. She displayed self-confidence from an early age. Before a sixth-grade spelling contest, Oveta advised her teacher to go ahead and inscribe her name in the Bible that would be her prize because she knew she would win. She did.

Oveta's parents were both active in state politics. As a teenager, Oveta would accompany her father to the state capitol at Austin to observe him taking part in the legislative sessions. When William Pettus Hobby ran for governor in 1918, the Culps left Oveta and her sister at home to can peaches while they campaigned, never dreaming that it was Oveta's future husband they were helping put into the highest state office. Up to her elbows in peaches and syrup on a hot summer afternoon, a 13-year-old Oveta had little affection for the candidate.

Oveta attended Mary Hardin Baylor College, in nearby Belton, but left without graduating. She revealed her continued interest in state politics by moving to the capital at Austin to take a job codifying state banking laws, while her mother believed her to be attending law school at the University of Texas. In 1927, she was 22 when Speaker Robert Lee Bobbitt appointed her parliamentarian for the Texas House of Representatives, a job she would hold until 1931. During the 1928 presidential campaign, she served as chair of the Smith-Robinson League of First Voters and executive secretary of the Women's Democratic League of Houston.

In Houston, sharing living space with **Florence Sterling**, sister of Ross Sterling, publisher of the *Houston Post-Dispatch,* Oveta worked as assistant to the Houston City Attorney, John H. Freeman. In 1930, at age 24, she made an unsuccessful attempt at elective office, running to represent Harris County in the state legislature. She participated actively in the Women's Organization for National Prohibition Repeal and campaigned against the governorship of ***Miriam "Ma" Ferguson**, after James "Pa" Ferguson had been impeached.

On February 23, 1931, at her parents' home, Oveta married Will Hobby, ex-governor of Texas and president of the *Houston Post-Dispatch.* She was 26 and his second wife. When Ross Sterling ran for governor that year, Oveta worked on the campaign, undeterred by a broken arm and ankle sustained in a fall from a horse.

Meanwhile, Oveta joined the staff of the *Post-Dispatch* and spent her first six months studying newspaper formats and cleaning out old files. By the end of the year, she had progressed to the position of book editor and become state president of the League of Women Voters. After three years, she was writing editorials for the *Post-Dispatch,* as well as writing a syndicated column about parliamentary procedure. She also wrote a series of articles on various subjects, including one on social welfare, inspired by her appointment to the State Committee for Human Security, an organization for assisting needy blind and dependent children.

In December 1931, J.E. Josey, a Beaumont businessman reportedly acting for Houston banker Jesse Jones, purchased the *Post-Dispatch* from Governor Ross Sterling and announced that Will Hobby would assume the roles of both president and publisher of the newspaper. Will Hobby dropped the *Dispatch,* returning the *Houston Post* to its former name. On January 19, Oveta celebrated her birthday by giving birth to a son, William Pettus Hobby, Jr. The couple called him "Bill" to distinguish him from his father. Oveta continued her private pursuits, collecting Georgian silver and rare books, and taking roles in amateur theatricals put on at The Alley. Not long after Bill's birth, a fire destroyed the Hobby home while Will was away.

Oveta Culp Hobby (on right).

Within Houston's powerful social elite, the Hobbys were part of the "8-F Crowd," a group which met in a suite kept at the Lamar Hotel by the wealthy Brown brothers, George and Henry. Depending on whose interests were served, the Browns were seen either as "master builders" or "puppet masters, who for their own financial gain, pulled the strings of politicians." The Hobbys' purchase of the J.S. Cullinan home in the exclusive neighborhood of Shadyside became an example of the magnitude of the wealth and power controlled by the group. After hiring architect John Staub to renovate the place, Oveta lost interest when the removal of certain walls proved unfeasible. She suggested that it be turned into a meeting place for the nearby Texas Medical Center. Neighbors vigorously objected and obtained a restraining order. Not one to tolerate opposition, Oveta simply had the house demolished and donated the grounds to Rice University.

In 1936, when President **Franklin D. Roosevelt** visited Texas to celebrate the state's centennial, Hobby played host to ***Eleanor Roosevelt** on a yacht trip down the Houston ship channel, then they traveled with *Post* owner Jesse Jones to Dallas for the centennial celebration. When the Hobbys were returning to Houston, their private plane burst into flames, went into a dive, and ended in a crash that left two dead. Afterward, the Hobbys agreed never to fly together again.

In 1937, again on her own birthday, Oveta gave birth to a daughter, **Jessica Oveta Hobby**, named for herself and *Post* owner Jesse Jones. The Hobbys were recognized cultural leaders, helping to found the Houston Symphony Orchestra and generously funding the new University of Houston. Oveta also continued to edit the book page after she was made assistant editor. As her reputation extended beyond Texas, she was appointed to the national advisory committee for women at the New York World's Fair.

In January 1938, the Hobbys traveled to Washington, D.C., where they enjoyed the company of President Roosevelt, Speaker of the House William Bankhead, House Majority Leader Sam Rayburn of Texas, and Texas senators Tom Connally and Morris Sheppard. In March, Oveta was named executive vice-president at the *Post,* which gave her increased responsibility for daily operations. The following year, Jones, who owned the *Houston Chronicle* as well as the *Post,* decided against having a monopoly on the city's newspapers and sold the *Post* to the Hobbys for $5,000, without collateral. The Hobbys improved the paper's physical plant, revamped its appearance, bought a new press, and raised advertising rates. Meanwhile, they had also taken over radio station KPRC, with Oveta as executive director.

In 1941, as America's entry into World War II grew imminent, Oveta Hobby went to Washington to handle business for KPRC. By July, President Roosevelt had enlisted her in the war effort, naming her chief of the Women's Interest Section of the War Department's Bureau of Public Relations. Given the task of "selling" the army to the wives and mothers of soldiers, Hobby left the *Post,* moved to an apartment in Washington, and took up a "commuter marriage" with Will.

In December 1941, the U.S. entered the war, and the country geared up for combat. On May 12, 1942, American women officially joined the nation's armed forces when Congress passed a bill, generated by the War Department and sponsored by Massachusetts Congresswoman ***Edith Nourse Rogers**, creating the Women's Auxiliary Army Corps (WAAC). Given the rank of colonel, Oveta Culp Hobby was chosen corps director; at the request of General George Marshall, she was to plan "the nation's first army of women in uniform."

In 1943, the WAAC became simply the Women's Army Corps (WAC). Between 1943 and 1945, it expanded from a few thousand women assigned to 54 different noncombat jobs to more than 200,000 women doing 239 jobs. These "GI Janes" received pay equal to that of the "GI Joes"—an exceptional situation for women at the time. "A new chapter in American history is being written," said Colonel Hobby. "We are earnestly determined to make the new chapter a serious contribution and not a feminine footnote." As corps director, she left her mark on everything from the WAC uniform to WAC training, choosing the officers' billed cap that became known as the "Hobby hat" and insisting that African-American women officers be integrated into the regular women's officer ranks.

Uprooted to Washington, Oveta maintained her personal lifestyle. Her apartment was furnished with antiques and Chinese hangings; she dressed stylishly for social events, favoring yellow and chartreuse dresses and "absurd headgear." Her children divided their time between Washington and Houston, Jessica lived primarily with Oveta while Bill stayed with his father in Houston. On a typical day, Oveta went to her office before 9, returned home to dine with her daughter at 7:30, and then tackled the work she had brought from the office. One problem remained insoluble:

the WACS had quickly proved so invaluable that Oveta could not find enough women to join the forces to fill the requests from overseas Army commanders. Sophisticated uniforms, moral safeguards, her public exhortation and equal pay were not enough to counter the rising pay women could command in the private sector with so many men overseas. On January 17, 1944, Colonel Hobby was in England inspecting WAC troops. Inspection tours took her everywhere. One shared birthday greeting to her son and daughter came from Algiers. In September 1945, with the war finally over, she was welcomed back to Houston with a celebratory dinner. Speeches in her honor were carried coast-to-coast by NBC. In 1947, she received the Philippine Military Merit Medal for her WAC leadership.

Returning to her work at the *Post,* Hobby also continued her active public life. In 1948, she was a consultant for the Hoover Commission for the Organization of the Executive Branch of the Government, later acting as a board member of the Citizens' Committee for the Hoover Report. In March of that year, she was in Switzerland as a consultant-alternate for the Freedom of Information Conference. In 1949, she was elected president of the Southern Newspaper Publishers Association and would later be chair of its board.

Meanwhile, she lunched with her family every day. If work drew her away from Houston, she conferred daily with Will by telephone; the Hobbys viewed their journalistic properties, which expanded to include television stations, as a public trust, and their own work as public service. In the early 1950s, when 19-year-old Bill joined the army, biographer James A. Clark reports that Hobby said in response: "When you've taught a child to make his own decisions and that he owes a great obligation to his government, you can only respect him for acting accordingly."

In 1943, Oveta had been awarded an honorary law degree from Baylor University; in the 1950s, she received honorary Doctor of Laws, Doctor of Human Letters, Doctor of Humanities, and Doctor of Literature degrees.

By the time she was in her mid-40s, Hobby had a reputation for being "as ambitious as she was charming," tough and shrewd. Like other wealthy Texans, she and Will hated the New Deal legislation implemented during the Roosevelt administration to combat the Great Depression, as well as the Fair Deal legislation proposed by President Harry Truman which expanded Social Security and raised the minimum wage. Equally unpopular was the refusal to support Texas' position on the tidelands by Democratic presidential candidate Adlai Stevenson. (Texas claimed control of a 10.5-mile-wide zone of underwater coastal area based on its previous status as a republic, whereas the federal government sought to limit the state to the three miles of offshore land held by other coastal states.) When the Hobbys came out as leaders of the Democrats-for-Eisenhower, however, regular Texas Republicans were highly disgruntled. Four months before the national conventions, Hobby announced for Ike. She spent much of 1952 in New York City at the Citizens for Eisenhower headquarters, doing "a little of everything," but mostly setting up Democrats-for-Eisenhower campaigns in other states.

With the Eisenhower victory, the press began assessing Hobby's prospects for an appointment in the new administration. When she was named head of the Federal Security Administration—in charge, ironically, of the Social Security Act of 1935—it was with the promise that the position would be raised to Cabinet level. Oveta attended the inauguration with Will, the couple went back to commuter marriage, and shortly the agency became the new Department of Health, Education and Welfare, with Oveta Hobby as its first secretary and the second woman in the U.S. to be a member of a presidential Cabinet.

Almost immediately, however, Secretary Hobby ran into trouble. Her political philosophy of individual initiative and state control ran contrary to the very purposes of her agency. On August 31, 1953, in San Francisco, Hobby opened the 55th annual convention of the American Hospital Association with a speech declaring that middle-class Americans had more problems getting health care than the rich or the poor, but that government should stay out of health care.

What she could not have foreseen was the impact of poliomyelitis, a dread virus which had already crippled or killed an average of 39,000 Americans each year from 1947 to 1951; in 1952, the nation reported 58,000 cases, mostly children. In 1955, the polio vaccine created by Dr. Jonas Salk became available, and Eisenhower declared at Cabinet meetings that "no child must be denied the vaccine for financial reasons." Hobby disagreed. She believed that distribution should be delayed until the states agreed to pick up the tab, or else the public should foot the bill for the vaccine. "By any standards of ability to pay that may be employed," she said, "most families could afford the cost of vaccination for their children." But the three shots required for the inoculation cost an estimated $4.20, at a time when the average per capita income in the U.S. stood at just over $40 per week. Hobby seemed unable to understand why her attitude provoked an ensuing uproar, commenting to a Senate committee, "I think no one could have foreseen the public demand."

In this mid-'50s era, the reactionary "Red Scare" swept the country, targeting Communists and those suspected of communism. Writer Don E. Carleton has surmised that the Hobbys did not believe in the red scare but found it a useful rhetorical tool at the *Post* for restoring conservatives to power; Ike, in fact, credited the Hobbys and the *Post* for his win in Texas. Their public image of "respectable moderation" kept the anti-communist editorials at the *Post* in check. According to Carleton, Hobby felt that the anti-Truman editorials were okay, and she positioned herself as a dedicated Eisenhower Republican and an internationalist but would not be drawn into a more extreme position. In February 1950, she gave the keynote speech to the Alabama Press Association about "irresponsible anticommunism," and she later kept the *Post* from endorsing the slanderous activities of Senator Joseph McCarthy, who accused citizens in all walks of life of subverting American institutions for Soviet purposes.

After joining the Eisenhower administration, Hobby's stance changed when she became the target of just such accusations from a zealous group calling themselves the Minute Women and crusading against what they saw as threats to the "American Way." In July 1953, they fixed their sights on Hobby. They accused her of interfering with a planned visit by Senator McCarthy to the San Jacinto monument in 1954. But "Oveta doesn't brook back-talk," as one observer put it, and an exposé on the Minute Women, authorized by Hobby, appeared in the *Post* in October 1953. This unofficially marked the end of the red scare in Houston.

In August 1955, Hobby resigned her position at HEW, citing her husband's illness. Though many believed the resignation came from her handling of the polio inoculation issue, President Eisenhower praised her as "highly efficient" and as having done "a mighty magnificent job." Back in Houston, Hobby became president and editor of the *Post* while Will moved up to chair the board. In 1956, Oveta again campaigned for Eisenhower but limited her efforts to Texas.

After Will's death in 1964, Oveta assumed control of the newspaper as editor and chair of the board. Throughout the 1960s, she was active on various educational advisory committees and a member of numerous foundation and corporate boards while continuing in public service, most notably as a member of HEW's Vietnam Health Education Task Force. In 1970, she became chair of the board of the Channel Two television company and director of the KPRC radio company. Two years later, she supported her son in his successful bid for the office of lieutenant governor.

In 1978, the Association of the U.S. Army made retired Colonel Hobby the recipient of its highest award, the George Catlett Marshall Medal for Public Service. Designated the "best known American woman military leader during World War II" and the first woman so honored, she accepted the medal at a dinner attended by 3,000 in Washington, D.C. The following year, the Hobby family created H&C Communications Inc., consolidating their newspaper, TV, and radio interests, with Oveta as chair of the board and Bill as president. By 1983, when Bill took over as chair, and Oveta became chair of the executive committee, H&C operations included television stations in Houston, Nashville, Tucson, and Meridian, Mississippi. Still active as she approached 80, Oveta served concurrently on the boards or committees of the Advisory Committee for Economic Development, the University of Texas, the Southern Regional Committee for Marshall Scholarships, the Houston Symphony Society, the Crusade for Freedom, and the Business Committee for the Arts, Inc.

In December 1983, H&C sold the *Houston Post* for $100 million. In September 1984, as part of Women in Texas Week, Oveta was inducted into the Texas Women's Hall of Fame for her contributions to business and finance; that same year, she was named one of the richest people in America by *Forbes* magazine, with a fortune estimated at $800 million. In 1986, she was honored on her birthday by the city of Killeen with a historical marker outside her birthplace, at 319 Young Street. Although she could not attend, her son delivered her personal message during the program at the First Baptist Church, and **Liz Carpenter**, long-time family friend and erstwhile press secretary to ***Lady Bird Johnson**, also spoke.

In 1992, Senator Lloyd Bentsen of Texas requested a belated promotion for the "Little Colonel." Because at the time she served women were not promoted to a rank higher than colonel, he asked that her rank be raised to brigadier general on the retired list on the 50th anniversary of the WACs. However, President George Bush refused to grant the promotion because she was "not eligible for promotion when she left the service as a colonel in 1945."

Oveta Culp Hobby remained active in the affairs of the family business as chair of the Executive Committee of H&C Communications. "She reads everything," said her son, "and she watches CNN and C-SPAN. She knows more about what's going on in the world than we do." After suffering a stroke in April, Oveta Culp Hobby died at home on August 16, 1995.

SOURCES:

Calvert, Robert A., and Arnoldo De Leon. *The History of Texas.* Arlington Heights, IL: Harlan Davidson, 1990.

Carleton, Don. E. *Red Scare!: Right-wing Hysteria, Fifties Fanaticism and Their Legacy in Texas.* Austin, TX: Texas Monthly Press, 1985.

Clark, James A., with Weldon Hart. *The Tactful Texan: A Biography of Governor Will Hobby.* NY: Random House, 1958.

Fuermann, George. *Houston: Land of the Big Rich.* Garden City, NY: Doubleday, 1951.

McAshan, Marie Phelps. *On the Corner of Main and Texas: A Houston Legacy.* Ed. by Mary Jo Bell. Houston, TX: Hutchins House, 1985.

Meyer, Leisa D. "Creating G.I. Jane: The Regulation of Sexuality and Sexual Behavior in the Women's Army Corps during World War II," in *Feminist Studies.* Vol. 18, no. 3. Fall 1992, pp. 581–601.

Stineman, Esther. *American Political Women: Contemporary and Historical Profiles.* Littleton, CO: Libraries Unlimited, 1980.

SUGGESTED READING:

Allen, Ann. "The News Media and the Women's Army Auxiliary Corps: Protagonists for a Cause," in *Military Affairs.* Vol. 50, no. 2. April 1986, pp. 77–83.

Spector, Bert. "The Great Salk Vaccine Mess," in *Antioch Review.* Vol. 38, no. 3, 1980, pp. 291–303.

RELATED MEDIA:

"Colonel Oveta Culp Hobby" (35 min. audiocassette), in *Actual Voices Famous in Texas History.* Limited ed. Latexo, TX: Audio Archives, c. 1985.

COLLECTIONS:

For information on Hobby's WAC days, see the Oveta Culp Hobby papers in the Library of Congress and the War Department General and Special Staffs and Army Staff Records in the National Archives. Information about Hobby's work as Secretary of Health, Education and Welfare is available in the Department of Health, Education and Welfare Records at the National Archives, the Oveta Culp Hobby Papers and Dwight D. Eisenhower as President Papers at the Dwight D. Eisenhower Library, and the Eisenhower Administration Oral History at Columbia University. Correspondence from Hobby can be found in the Margaret Bayne Price Papers at the University of Michigan Bentley Historical Library, the Benjamin Emanuel Youngdahl Papers at the University of Minnesota, the Walter Henry Judd Papers at the Minnesota Historical Society, and the May Thompson Evans Papers at the North Carolina Division of Archives and Library. Articles about Hobby can be found in the Clippings File of the Houston Metropolitan Research Center. All other papers are still in the possession of Oveta Culp Hobby's estate.

Photographs of Oveta Culp Hobby inspecting the WAACs at Fort Meade, Maryland and Bolling Air Force Base, Washington D.C., 1943, in the ***Toni Frissell** Collection at the Library of Congress.

WAAC videotapes in the *Movietone News* films on cassette about World War II, at the Thomas Cooper Library, University of South Carolina, Columbia (over 100 tapes chronicle the WAAC/WAC).

Laura Anne Wimberley, Ph.D.,
Texas A&M University, College Station, Texas

Hobhouse, Emily (1860–1926)

British humanitarian and antiwar activist who tried to help the women and children held in concentration camps by the British during the Boer War in South Africa. *Pronunciation: HOB-house. Born Emily Hobhouse on April 9, 1860, in St. Ive (pronounced Eve), in Cornwall, England; died on June 8, 1926, in London; daughter of Reginald (an Anglican cleric) and Caroline (Trelawny) Hobhouse; educated mainly by governesses; only two terms at a boarding school; never married; no children.*

Lived in St. Ive until 1895; went as a missionary to a mining district in Virginia, Minnesota, where she started a Temperance Society and a Public Reading Room; became engaged; went to Mexico City, Mexico, to purchase a ranch for herself and her fiancé; broke engagement and returned to England (1898); became involved with the South African Conciliation Committee; went to South Africa (1900) to help Boers held in concentration camps; campaigned in England to end the war; developed home industries for women and girls in South Africa after the war; actively opposed the First World War; journeyed behind enemy lines, hoping to develop plans to alleviate the suffering of noncombatants and to find an alternative for POW camps; pursued other humanitarian causes after the war.

Selected publications: The Brunt of the War and Where It Fell *(Methuen, 1902). Translated* Tant Alie of Transvaal *(George Allen and Unwin, 1923). Collected stories and translated* War without Glamour *(Nascionale Pers Beperk, 1927).*

At the close of the 19th century, a war between Great Britain and the two Boer republics in South Africa (the Orange Free State and the Transvaal Republic) began on October 11, 1899. Although the Boers (Dutch farmers who had settled in South Africa in the 17th century) began the attack, they felt Britain had left them no alternative but to fight to maintain their independence. The struggle was overwhelmingly popular in Britain, where the imperialistic spirit of prevailed. However, a small but vocal minority of Britons opposed the conflict and sought an end to the hostilities. Friends and relatives of Emily Hobhouse were in the forefront of this opposition, and she soon became absorbed in the cause as well. She focused her attention upon the plight of women and children who suffered because their homes had been destroyed. Until the end of the war in 1902, she devoted herself to helping these victims of the conflict. As a result, the Boers came to revere Hobhouse as an angel of mercy.

Emily Hobhouse's concern for others developed early in life. The daughter of Reginald Hobhouse, an Anglican cleric, she assisted her father with his responsibilities for the parish of St. Ive in Cornwall, England, especially after her mother's death in 1880. Reverend Hobhouse and **Caroline Trelawny**, had eight children, six of whom survived infancy. Emily, the second youngest, was born in St. Ive on April 9, 1860. She was particularly close to her younger brother, Leonard (born in 1865), although she admitted that she envied him and an older brother, Alfred, for the education they received. The formal education of girls was not considered important during this era, so Emily and her sisters were tutored by governesses. Emily, however, did spend two terms at a boarding school when she was about 15 years old. During her youth, Emily also developed a close attachment to her father's brother, Lord Arthur Hobhouse, and his wife Lady **Mary Hobhouse**, who often cared for their young nieces while Reverend and Mrs. Hobhouse spent time on the French Riviera so he could recuperate from illnesses.

> Emily Hobhouse's hand it was that first was extended to us in our darkest hour and helped us to climb out of the pit.
>
> —**General Jan C. Smuts**

While assisting with the church choir, Emily Hobhouse became interested in a young man, the son of a farmer. Her father quickly squelched what seemed to be a budding romance by indicating that he did not think the fellow's origin was a match for his daughter's social status. The young suitor then departed for America. By 1889, Emily Hobhouse was the only one remaining at home to care for her ailing father. During this time, she assumed most of the non-clerical work of the parish. When her father died in 1895, Hobhouse left St. Ive, uncertain of her future.

Believing that church-related work was all she was suited for, Hobhouse requested a mission assignment from the Anglican Church and received an appointment to the town of Virginia, Minnesota, to work among Cornish miners in the iron-mining camps nearby. She arrived there in August 1895. Although she always kept her church work in the forefront, Hobhouse undertook many social and civic projects as well. Appalled by alcoholism prevalent in the area, she established the Virginia Temperance Union. She also helped set up a Public Reading Room. Romantic interests soon developed, and Hobhouse became engaged to marry John C. Jackson, who operated a general store and had served a term as mayor of Virginia. Not much else is known about Jackson, but he seems to have convinced Hobhouse to purchase land in Mexico. In the fall of 1896, Hobhouse went to Mexico City and bought land for a ranch. Evidently, Jackson also persuaded her to invest money in a speculative scheme which eventually failed. After months of waiting for Jackson to join her there, Hobhouse returned for a visit to England in 1897; but by early 1898, she was again in Mexico awaiting Jackson's arrival and their wedding. Within a few months, however, disappointed evidently by his delays and by her financial losses, Hobhouse broke the engagement and returned to England.

By this time, the British-Boer rivalry in South Africa had reached a serious impasse. Negotiations to resolve conflicting claims and demands had produced no results. For almost a century, the British and the Boers (also known as Afrikaners) confronted each other in South Africa. After the British gained possession of Cape Colony from the Dutch following the Napoleonic Wars, the Boers had trekked to the north and northeast to avoid British rule. They had established two republics, the Orange Free State and the South African Republic (popularly called the Transvaal). A renewed attempt by the British to reassert their sovereignty over the Boers followed the discovery of gold in 1886 in the Transvaal. Miners from European countries rushed into the republic and soon began to demand reform of laws they saw as discriminatory. Since the miners were predominantly from Great Britain, they appealed to the British government to redress their grievances. In late December 1895, a raid led by British subjects from Cape Colony crossed into the Transvaal expecting to aid an uprising by the miners. The uprising never occurred, and the Boers captured the raiders; but from that point on they feared losing their independence. Negotiations during the ensuing years only intensified the anger of the Boers and confirmed their belief that Great Britain planned to annex their republics. Therefore, when the British failed to answer an ultimatum sent by the Transvaal, the Boers invaded Cape Colony on October 11, 1899.

In Great Britain, jingoistic imperialism still swayed the masses. To the majority of citizens, the war was a just one: the Boers had attacked first; they were endangering a part of the empire. However, to outspoken opponents of the conflict the war was unjust. They agreed with the Boers' position that the British themselves had aggravated the assault. Often called "Pro-Boers," these critics protested against the war for various reasons: anti-imperial Liberals opposed it as a land-grab; labor leaders and socialists denounced the expenditures which prevented the funding of welfare programs; pacifists rejected all wars as immoral.

Once back in England, Hobhouse had worked for the Women's Industrial Council in London, but the interests of her friends and relatives in the South African conflict soon caused her to focus her attention upon efforts to stop the war. By November 1899, the South African Conciliation Committee had formed, and Hobhouse became the honorary secretary of its women's branch. She wrote articles urging an end of the conflict; she organized women's protest meetings and spoke at a number of them. At one women's rally, Hobhouse presented a resolution which indicated her strong impulse to help victims of the war. As cited by her biographer, **Ruth Fry**, the resolution stated: "That this meeting desires to express its sympathy with the women of the Transvaal and Orange Free State, and begs them to remember that thousands of English women are filled with profound sorrow at the thought of their sufferings, and with deep regret for the actions of their own Government."

As early as February 1900, the British army had begun burning the farms of Boers who were fighting against them. By the latter part of the year, the press reported more extensive farm-burning operations by the British. These accounts profoundly affected Hobhouse, who later wrote in *The Brunt of the War and Where It Fell,* "A picture of wretchedness lay beneath the bald telegraphic words! That these poor families, bandied from pillar to post, must need protection and organised relief, was certain, and from that moment I determined to go to South Africa in order to help them." With the backing of her aunt, Lady Hobhouse, who received official sanction for a relief committee from Joseph Chamberlain, colonial secretary, and with the aid of other SACC members, Hobhouse created the South African Women and Children Distress Fund. She intended a non-political tone for the relief organization by directing assistance to any homeless war victim, whether Boer or Briton, and by inviting a number of individuals from outside the peace groups to join the Distress Fund staff or to announce support publicly. She hoped to place the agency above the derisive slurs hurled at the antiwar forces. However, because of the prominence of Lord Hobhouse and her brother, Leonard, in the antiwar movement, most Britons saw this as a political attack upon the government.

The second phase of Hobhouse's plan was to demonstrate to those Boers displaced by the war that some people in England were truly sensitive to their sufferings. Hoping also to foster a spirit of reconciliation, Hobhouse sailed for South Africa on December 7, 1900. Using money deposited for her in Cape Town by the Distress Fund, Hobhouse purchased and distributed supplies to those in refugee camps. She found the wretchedness of the refugees appalling. She wrote to Distress Fund committee members to underscore the need for more supplies, and especially for more medical personnel to save the victims—usually children—of measles, typhoid, and heat prostration. Hobhouse tried to work with the military officials to organize reforms within the camps to utilize best the limited supplies of food, fuel, and other necessities. After making headway in a camp, she would organize a committee of Boer women to continue her reforms and then proceed to another site.

These limited gains were soon undermined when the military authorities began interning the entire Boer populations of some districts in an attempt to cope with guerrilla tactics. The old refugee camps, now made to accommodate thousands more, and new centers erected for the overflow, became the hated concentration camps, numbering over 40. As the death rate in these camps mounted, Hobhouse decided to return to England to convince officials to change the system. On May 24, 1901, she was back in Great Britain.

Hobhouse obtained an interview with Secretary of War W. St. John Brodrick, whom she informed about her relief work and the evils of the concentration camps. She came fortified with suggested reforms. A few weeks later, Hobhouse was astounded to learn that, although Brodrick had approved some of her suggestions, he had appointed a Ladies' Commission to investigate the camps and had forbidden her to return to them. Thus thwarted in her attempts to play the non-political, philanthropic role she had intended for herself, Hobhouse enlisted the aid of any who would alert the British public to the disasters of the camp system. Of course, the antiwar factions were eager to use her findings in their attacks upon the government. Her report to the Distress Fund Committee appeared in antiwar publications, and all members of Parliament received excerpts from it. Hobhouse also met with the leader of the opposition, Liberal Party Chair, Henry Campbell-Bannerman, and recounted for him the camp inmates' plight and their rising mortality rates. This led Campbell-Bannerman on June 14, 1901, to condemn the use of the concentration camps as "methods of barbarism." Hobhouse hoped a shocked public would react against the camp system, but prowar newspapers and speakers attacked the accuracy of her accounts and claimed she greatly exaggerated the sufferings and deaths of the inmates. Therefore, during the summer of 1901, she continued to speak at assemblies and to write articles for sympathetic publications. She was determined to enlighten the public and to melt the hearts that remained hardened.

Controversy continued to surround Emily Hobhouse in the latter months of 1901. Denied permission to revisit the camps, she nevertheless sailed for South Africa in October. Partly her journey was a reaction to criticism of her work among Boers only. On this trip, her purpose was to alleviate the suffering of British refugees in Cape Colony left homeless by the war. While her ship was still at sea, Cape Colony was placed under martial law. Upon Hobhouse's arrival, the authorities refused to allow her to disembark and placed her under arrest. They told her to return at once to England. When she refused to obey their orders, she was forcibly placed on another ship for the return voyage.

Despite so many personal disappointments and frustrations in Hobhouse's efforts to instigate drastic reforms in the camp system, some positive results did come from her prodding. The Ladies' Commission sent by Brodrick to investigate camp conditions substantiated most of her findings and more changes occurred. However, had Brodrick and others accepted her reports as accurate and impartial when she first presented them, they could have ordered reforms which might have reduced the deaths from diseases which ravaged the camps. By the end of the conflict in May 1902, the estimates of deaths in the camps alone ranged from 18,000 to 28,000, most of which were children.

Upon the conclusion of the war, Hobhouse wrote *The Brunt of the War and Where It Fell*, which she dedicated to "The Women of South Africa." All royalties from its sale she gave to a fund to help the Boers restore their homes. When leaders of the Boers arrived in England at the end of July 1902 to try to raise money for their devastated homeland, Hobhouse met them and began a friendship with them that lasted for the rest of her life. In May 1903, Hobhouse traveled once again to South Africa, where she attended a general meeting held by the Boers (called the People's Gathering) at Heidelberg. The Boer leaders presented her to the assembly and thanked her for all she had done for the inmates of the camps.

The continued suffering of the Boer people as they struggled to rebuild their farms led Hobhouse to organize fund-raising appeals in Great Britain and at the Cape. In an effort to find ways for the Boers to help themselves, she devised a plan to teach women and girls lace-making and textile-production, which they could do at home. To prepare for this venture, Hobhouse traveled extensively in Europe to study lace-making. When someone pointed out to her that textiles would sell better than lace, she traveled to Ireland to study textile-making. To solicit donations with which to buy spinning wheels and weaving looms, Hobhouse organized the Boer Home Industries Aid Society. In March 1905, she then returned once more to South Africa to set up schools where young women and girls could learn to spin and weave. By 1908, schools which taught both spinning and weaving existed in 12 cities, while those that taught only spinning were located in 14 others. In addition, basket-weaving and leather-working classes soon developed at some of these schools. The colonial governments of the Transvaal and Orange River assumed responsibility for these schools in 1908, at which time Hobhouse returned again to England.

Over the next few years, Hobhouse's health began to fail. She had long suffered from rheumatoid arthritis, and its crippling effects grew worse. In 1913, when the Boers erected a monument at Bloemfontein to honor those who had died in the camps during the war, they invited Emily Hobhouse to unveil it. Hobhouse again traveled to South Africa, eager to participate in the ceremonies. However, when she reached Beaufort West in Cape Colony, her health was such that she could not continue on to Bloemfontein; but the Boers printed and distributed her prepared speech to the vast numbers in attendance. Speakers at the ceremony praised Hobhouse for all she had done for the Boers in the camps and claimed that hers was a name most revered among their people.

At the outbreak of World War I in 1914, Hobhouse again devoted herself to the pursuit of peace. In 1915, she worked for a few months in Amsterdam at the Women's International Bureau. Then, in 1916, her health having improved, she determined somehow to aid noncombatants in Belgium who were affected by the war. Her subsequent actions aroused heated debate at the British Foreign Office, which had in 1915 granted her a visa to Italy, and also in Parliament itself, which questioned whether entering enemy territory was a treasonous act. From Italy, Hobhouse had gone to Switzerland and thence to Belgium, where, under close supervision of a German escort, she toured various cities. In June, she entered Germany itself and had an interview in Berlin with the foreign minister, Gottlieb von Jagow. From this meeting, Hobhouse concluded that Germany was willing to make peace if Britain would make the advances. When she later returned to England, no one took her seriously. Another idea came to Hobhouse during this trip to Germany. She believed it possible for prisoner-of-war camps to be dismantled and the inmates sent to neutral countries until the end of the conflict. This, too, she urged upon her government but with no results. After the conclusion of the war, Hobhouse continued her humanitarian zeal by working for three new relief endeavors: the Swiss Relief Fund for Starving Children, which brought children from war-torn areas of Germany and the former Austrian Empire to rest and recuperate in Switzerland; the Russian Babies' Fund, which Hobhouse chaired, and which sent milk and baby supplies to Russia; and in cooperation with the Save the Children Fund, her own activities to feed hungry children in Leipzig, Germany. When she visited that devastated city in September 1919, she was astounded by the number of malnourished children. After a few months of unrelenting pressure by Hobhouse, city officials finally began a lunch program for about 11,000 children. In gratitude for this work, the German Red Cross honored her, as did the Leipzig city government, which placed a marble bust of Emily Hobhouse in the Rathaus there. Ill health caused her to return home in 1921.

Added to her health problems were financial difficulties. Hobhouse had provided for herself primarily through an inheritance from an aunt, which she had received in 1887. However, in the postwar recession her income from dividends dwindled drastically, and she had to sell many of her possessions. Upon learning of her financial plight, friends and admirers in South Africa collected money as a gift to her for purchase of a house, which she did in Cornwall. However, she later sold that one in 1923 and bought another in London.

During the last few years of her life, Hobhouse's activities were more restricted because of her health. In 1923, she translated and published the personal story of one of her Boer friends, **Alida Badenhorst**, under the title, *Tant Alie of Transvaal: Her Diary, 1880–1902.* She also continued to prepare a collection of stories by Boer women, which she had begun 20 years before, and which was published after her death as *War without Glamour, or Women's Experiences Written by Themselves* in 1927. By 1926, Hobhouse was mostly bedridden and unable to care for herself alone. Arthritis, asthma, angina pectoris, and other ailments took their toll. On June 8, 1926, she died in London. She willed that her body be cremated and her ashes be buried in South Africa. In fulfilling this wish, Boer leaders decided to place her remains in the Bloemfontein monument dedicated to the women and children who had died in the camps, and whom Emily Hobhouse had worked so hard to save.

SOURCES:

Fisher, John. *That Miss Hobhouse.* London: Secker and Warburg, 1971.

Fry, A. Ruth. *Emily Hobhouse.* London: Jonathan Cape, 1929.

SUGGESTED READING:

Koss, Stephen, ed. *The Pro-Boers: The Anatomy of an Antiwar Movement.* Chicago: The University of Chicago Press, 1973.

Patricia A. Ashman,
Professor of History, Central Missouri State University, Warrensburg, Missouri

Hobhouse, Violet (1864–1902)

Irish nationalist. *Born Violet McNeill in County Antrim, Ireland (now Northern Ireland), in 1864; died in 1902.*

A Unionist, Violet Hobhouse toured England speaking out against Home Rule. She was also keen on Irish folklore and culture and was fluent in Irish. Her books included *An Unknown Quantity* (1898) and *Warp and Weft* (1899).

Hobson, Laura Z. (1900–1986)

***Jewish-American writer who advocated tolerance, best known for her novel* Gentleman's Agreement.** *Name variations: (joint pseudonym with Thayer Hobson) Peter Field. Born Laura Kean Zametkin in New York City on June 19, 1900; died on February 28,*

1986; daughter of Adella (Kean) Zametkin and Michael Zametkin (editor of a Yiddish newspaper and labor organizer); Cornell University, A.B.; married Thayer Hobson (a publisher), in 1930 (divorced 1935); children: (with Eric Hodgins of Time *magazine) Christopher Z. Hobson (b. 1941); (adopted) Michael Hobson (b. 1937).*

Selected writings: (with Thayer Hobson under joint pseudonym Peter Field) Outlaws Three *(NY: Morrow, 1933); (with Thayer Hobson as Peter Field)* Dry Gulch Adams *(NY: Morrow, 1934);* A Dog of His Own *(NY: Viking, 1941);* The Trespassers *(NY: Simon & Schuster, 1943);* Gentleman's Agreement *(NY: Simon & Schuster, 1947);* The Other Father *(NY: Simon & Schuster, 1950);* The Celebrity *(NY: Simon & Schuster, 1951);* First Papers *(NY: Random House, 1964);* I'm Going to Have a Baby *(NY: Day, 1967);* The Tenth Month *(NY: Simon & Schuster, 1971);* Consenting Adult *(Garden City, NY: Doubleday, 1975);* Over and Above *(Garden City, NY: Doubleday, 1979);* Untold Millions *(NY: Harper & Row, 1982);* Laura Z: A Life *(NY: Arbor House, 1983).*

Laura Z. Hobson

Laura Z. Hobson was born in New York City in 1900, the daughter of **Adella Kean Zametkin** and Michael Zametkin, a labor organizer and editor of a Yiddish newspaper. After a childhood spent on Long Island, Hobson earned an A.B. at Cornell University and in 1930 married publisher Thayer Hobson but divorced in 1935. Until 1934, Hobson worked as an advertising copywriter. She then worked as consultant and promotion director for such journals as *Time, Life, Fortune, Sports Illustrated,* and *Saturday Review*; spent one year as a reporter for the *New York Evening Post;* had short stories published in *Collier's, Ladies' Home Journal, McCall's,* and *Cosmopolitan*; collaborated with Thayer Hobson on two Westerns written under the joint pseudonym Peter Field (*Outlaws Three,* 1933, and *Dry Gulch Adams,* 1934); and wrote two works of juvenile fiction (*A Dog of His Own,* 1941, and *I'm Going to Have a Baby,* 1967), nine novels for adults, and her autobiography, *Laura Z.* (1983).

Laura Z. Hobson writes of tolerance and challenges her readers to face their unacknowledged prejudices and overcome them. She is particularly sensitive to empty-souled phrases of acceptance which mask a fear of anyone different. Hobson demands that individuals of a minority group have the same rights as individuals in the majority. She most often writes from the point of view of the majority group, creating a protagonist who rises above class, spurred by a sensitivity to the predicaments of others.

"Those who have read Hobson's nine novels already know a great deal about [her]," writes **Sybil Steinberg** in *Publishers Weekly,* "although they may be generally unaware that all were based on episodes from the author's own life." She was a child of socialists (*First Papers,* 1964); an advertising copywriter (*Untold Millions,* 1982); an unwed mother (*The Tenth Month,* 1971); a parent (*The Other Father,* 1950); a critic of the refugee quota system (*The Trespassers,* 1943); a critic of anti-Semitism (*Gentleman's Agreement,* 1947); a sudden celebrity (*The Celebrity,* 1951); the mother of a gay son (*Consenting Adult,* 1975); and a Jew who has questioned her Jewish identity (*Over and Above,* 1979).

Hobson was discouraged by friends from writing *Gentleman's Agreement;* they thought Americans would find it unpalatable. Hobson told her publishers: "I've got an idea for a book that the magazines will never look at, the movies won't touch, and the public won't buy. . . . But I have to do it." *Gentleman's Agreement* was reprinted in *Cosmopolitan,* topped the bestseller list, and was filmed in 1947 by Elia Kazan, with Gregory Peck, *__Dorothy McGuire__, *__Celeste Holm__, and *__Anne Revere__ in the starring roles. That year, Elia Kazan won an Academy Award for Best Director, McGuire was nominated for Best Actress, Celeste Holm won for Best Supporting Actress, and the movie was named the Best Picture of the Year.

In *Gentleman's Agreement,* Philip Green, a Protestant journalist, moves from the West Coast to the East to take a job at *Smith's Weekly,* where he is virtually unknown. For his first assignment, an analysis of American anti-Semitism, he assumes the identity of a Jew. Though Green is aware of the blatant prejudices awash in America, he is not prepared for the more subtle bigotry in his seemingly broad-minded friends. His new love, Kathy, is sympathetic to his assignment but worries about introducing him as a Jew to her establishment family and friends; his future in-laws, who own a cottage in the restricted community of Darien, Connecticut, are terrified over the prospect of selling the cottage to the young couple. In Detroit, Philip's sister fears her husband's job will be in jeopardy if word gets out about her "Jewish" brother. Philip learns that in some cases people are not "consciously antisemitic. . . . They despise it; it's an 'awful thing.' But . . . they help it along and then wonder why it grows." When Philip's son becomes the object of anti-Semitism at school, Philip's anger causes him to reject the "gentleman's agreement" of polite prejudice. "I wrote the book for and about liberals," said Hobson. "I had in mind decent people, who, never having probed their own prejudices, profess disgust for anti-Semitism, castigate the Bilbos and the Rankins, but let it go at that."

Following her divorce, Hobson adopted a son Michael in 1937; she also had a natural son, Christopher, the cherished outcome of a "light and amiable" affair with Eric Hodgins, an editor at *Time* magazine. It is Christopher of whom she writes in *Consenting Adult.*

SOURCES:

Rothe, Anna, ed. *Current Biography.* NY: H.W. Wilson, 1974.

Walden, Daniel, ed. *Dictionary of Literary Biography, Volume 28.* Detroit, MI: Gale Research, 1984.

Hobson, Valerie (1917–1998)

English actress. *Born Valerie Babette Louise Hobson in Larne, County Antrim, Ireland (now Larne District, Northern Ireland), on April 14, 1917; died from a heart attack on November 13, 1998; married Anthony Havelock-Allan (a film producer), in 1939 (divorced 1952); married John Profumo (a politician), in 1954; children: (first marriage) two sons; (second marriage) one son.*

Valerie Hobson

Filmography: Eyes of Fate *(1934);* Two Hearts in Waltz Time *(1934);* Path of Glory *(1934);* Badger's Green *(1934);* Man Who Reclaimed His Head *(1934);* Oh, What a Night *(1935);* Life Returns *(1935);* Chinatown Squad *(1935);* Strange Wives *(1935);* Mystery of Edwin Drood *(1935);* Rendezvous at Midnight *(1935);* Bride of Frankenstein *(1935);* Werewolf of London *(*Unholy Hour, *1935);* The Great Impersonation *(1935);* Tugboat Princess *(1936);* Secret of Stamboul *(*The Spy in White, *1936);* No Escape *(1936);* August Weekend *(*Weekend Madness, *1936);* When Thief Meets Thief *(*Jump for Glory, *1937);* This Man Is News *(1938);* The Drum *(*Drums, *1938);* This Man in Paris *(1939);* The Silent Battle *(*Continental Express, *1939);* Q Planes *(*Clouds over Europe, *1939);* The Spy in Black *(*U-Boat 29, *1939);* Contraband *(*Blackout, *1940);* Atlantic Ferry *(*Sons of the Sea, *1941);* Unpublished Story *(1942);* Sabotage Agent *(*Adventures of Tartu, *1943);* The Years Between *(1946);* Great Expectations *(1946);* Blanche Fury *(1947);* The Small Voice *(*Hideout, *1948);* Train of Events *(1949);* Kind

Hearts and Coronets *(1949);* The Interrupted Journey *(1949);* The Rocking Horse Winner *(1950);* The Voice of Merrill *(*Murder Will Out, *1952);* Passionate Sentry *(*Who Goes There?, *1952);* Meet Me Tonight *(*Tonight at 8:30, *1952);* The Card *(*The Promoter, *1952);* Background *(*Edge of Divorce, *1953);* Monsieur Ripois *(*Knave of Hearts, *1954).*

The daughter of a British army officer, Valerie Hobson was born in Larne, County Antrim, Ireland (now Northern Ireland), in 1917. She attended the Royal Academy of Dramatic Art to study dance but dropped out after an attack of scarlet fever. Instead, she opted for the theater and made her debut on the London stage and screen as a teenager. Hobson was invited to Hollywood in 1934, where she was cast as the leading lady in a number of thriller films, including *The Man Who Reclaimed His Head* (1934), *The Werewolf of London* (1935), and *The Bride of Frankenstein* (1935). After two years, she became disenchanted with her roles and returned to England. She subsequently developed into a leading actress of British films, playing mostly refined, elegant, upper-class women.

Hobson's 1939 marriage to Anthony Havelock-Allan, who produced many of her films, ended in divorce in 1952. She abandoned her acting career in 1954, following her marriage to John Profumo, then a junior minister in the Churchill government. Hobson never wavered in her support of her husband throughout his 1963 sex scandal involving ***Christine Keeler** that brought down Britain's Conservative government and toppled Profumo from office as war minister, once it was revealed that Keeler was also involved with a Soviet military attaché. Hobson turned her attention to mentally handicapped children and lepers.

Höch, Hannah (1889–1978)

German artist, best known for her thought-provoking photomontages from the period of the Weimar Republic. *Name variations: Hannah Hoch. Born Johanne Höch on November 1, 1889, in Gotha, Thuringia, Germany; died in Berlin-Heiligensee on May 31, 1978; daughter of Friedrich Höch and Rosa Sachs Höch; lived with Til Brugman, from 1929 to 1935; married Kurt Matthies.*

In an artistic career that spanned more than six decades, Hannah Höch explored a great range of aesthetic territory, creating bold and often controversial graphics, paintings, collages, photographs, and even puppets. One of the masters of the art of photomontage, she played an important role in the intellectual history of Germany by being the only woman member of the Berlin Dada circle. In the years since her death in 1978, Höch's artistic reputation has grown dramatically. This reevaluation of the importance of her place in the history of modern art was already in evidence during the final years of her life. In November 1977, in his response to a survey by the influential New York journal *ARTnews* as to which artists he considered to be the most underrated, influential art critic Robert Hughes gave Hannah Höch as his first (and only) choice; a similar response came from William S. Lieberman, director of drawings at Manhattan's mecca of modernism, the Museum of Modern Art. By the end of the 20th century, Höch's star had soared as she became recognized as an artist whose work reflected important facets of the modern spirit.

She was born Johanne Höch in 1889 into the comfortable upper-middle-class. Her father Friedrich was director of an insurance company. Her mother Rosa, an amateur painter, introduced Höch to the world of art. As a young girl, Höch followed a long-established custom for young girls of her status, creating books of collages made from magazine cuttings. Such collages were intended to foster a spirit of femininity and domesticity leading to marriage. In 1912, Höch moved from her hometown of Gotha to Berlin and enrolled at the municipal school of applied arts located in the suburb of Charlottenburg. Here, she was trained in various applied arts including calligraphy and embroidery, as well as wallpaper, book, glass, and textile design. Höch's desire to master a number of crafts received further inspiration in 1914 when she traveled to Cologne to visit the important Werkbund exhibition.

In 1915, soon after the onset of World War I, Hannah Höch enrolled at the teaching division of Berlin's highly respected State Museum School, where she studied with the noted graphic artist Emil Orlik. Her strong grounding in crafts can be seen in several needlework designs she published at the time in journals specializing in the preservation of German handicraft traditions. Also in 1915, Höch met and became the constant companion of the artist Raoul Hausmann, through whom she would come in contact with the literary and artistic circle which in 1918 formed Berlin's avant-garde Club Dada. Dada was an innovative artistic and literary movement launched in Zurich in 1916 by a group of young artists, many of them spiritual refugees from a grimly militarized Germany, who were angered and repelled by what they regarded as the pointless slaughter of World War I. Dada accelerated trends already revealed in prewar European intellectual life, including abstract and cubist art, German Expressionism, and the newest trends in French poetry. Embracing nonsense in an irrational world, these artists named their group after a word, *Dada,* which was chosen at random and meant absolutely nothing. The movement was not confined exclusively to Switzerland, quickly spreading to Berlin, Paris, New York and other cities.

Starting in 1916, Hannah Höch worked for a decade on a part-time basis for the Ullstein Verlag, a vast publishing conglomerate. For Ullstein's handicraft division, Höch created needlework patterns and lace tablecloth designs. The job paid her sufficiently to live independently and also allowed enough time for her private artistic pursuits. Of equal importance was the fact that working at Ullstein provided Höch with access to an almost unlimited number of file copies of the company's nearly two dozen mass-circulation newspapers and magazines. These furnished the material for the montages that Höch cut and reassembled. Some of her earliest works of note, dating from 1919, consist of needlework and sewing patterns that she rearranged into eye-catching abstractions.

The unexpected collapse of the imperial German regime in November 1918, after four years of war, shook an already troubled nation to its foundations. Within months of the armistice, Berlin became the site of deadly political struggles which soon culminated in dashed hopes for a socialist transformation. In January 1919, the radical, Bolshevik-inspired Spartacist uprising was suppressed. During this failed attempt at a German Communist revolution, the leaders of the extreme Left, Karl Liebknecht and ***Rosa Luxemburg**, were both assassinated. Berlin's intellectuals, including Höch, were deeply troubled by these events. Although they desired the creation of a new moral, artistic, and political order in Germany, the Dadaists of Berlin were by no means a united group when it came to their political thinking. One group—led by the brothers Wieland Herzfelde and John Heartfield (who had Anglicized his name as a protest against the war), and by George Grosz (who had done the same thing)—was strongly in sympathy with the Bolsheviks and their revolutionary transformation of Russia. In their art works and writings, they attacked a servile militaristic spirit they saw at the heart of Germany's woes.

The other wing of the Berlin Dada movement, of which Hannah Höch was an active member, was led by her lover Raoul Hausmann, "theoretician of contradiction and promoter of direct action." Hausmann advocated a new world order based on radically individualistic anarchy. In this, he was seconded by Johannes Baader, who had previously worked as a mausoleum architect and now reveled in his role of shocking Berlin's bourgeoisie with art flowing from a rich sense of the absurd. Although the ideological differences between the two wings of Berlin Dada were fundamental, the artists remained on friendly terms largely because of the conciliatory and balanced disposition of another leading Dadaist, Richard Huelsenbeck. Höch was in sympathy with the leftist ideals of all Dada members but avoided their often crude forms of social criticism and political propaganda in favor of making points in a more subtle and indirect fashion.

Photomontage was the new and innovative art form through which Höch and several of the other Berlin Dadaists made known their thoughts about the unsatisfactory state of the new Weimar Republic. One of Höch's earliest photomontages, *Cut with the Dada Kitchen Knife through the Last Era of the Weimar Beer-Belly Culture* (1919–20, Nationalgalerie Berlin), is a large work—measuring nearly 45x36 inches—which was exhibited at the First International Dada Fair in 1920. Reflecting the chaos and despair of Germany's immediate postwar years, *Cut with the Dada Kitchen Knife* presents an absurdist panorama of the Weimar Republic's public life. Among other things, the work depicts the forces of political and social reaction, irreverently placing the head of Field Marshal Paul von Hindenburg, the venerable "wooden titan" of World War I fame, on top of a belly dancer's body.

Additional touches in Höch's best-known photomontage include the head of ***Käthe Kollwitz** hovering above the shoulders of a popular child dancer of the period, as well as Höch's own head on a corner of a map depicting those European nations that had recently granted women the right to vote. With its jumbled photographs of artists, political philosophers and leaders, including Karl Marx and Vladimir Lenin, as well as celebrities of the day, such as silent-film star ***Pola Negri**, this photomontage attempted to capture the complex spirit of the chaotic postwar world as it played itself out in Germany's unstable Weimar Republic, which had become the most artistically vibrant nation in Europe.

Although more than one account claims that Hannah Höch and Raoul Hausmann had invented photomontage in 1918 during a vacation to a village on the Baltic when they both noticed photographic portraits affixed to commemorative engravings of soldiers, the technique in fact dates back several generations. In the 1870s, it was a popular pastime to combine photographs with watercolor paintings, and the practice was revived with a new energy in the first decade of the 20th century when cubist painters hit on the idea of mixing mediums. By gluing onto their canvases such odds and ends as wine and cognac bottle labels, words and phrases cut from newspapers, and even actual objects, they gave birth to a new genre of art. During wartime, Dadaist leaders like George Grosz used photomontage to fight censorship, by using, he said, "a mischmasch of advertisements for hernia belts, student song books and dog food, labels from schnapps and wine bottles, and photographs from picture papers, cut up at will in such a way as to say, in pictures, what would have been banned by the censors if we had said it in words."

Hannah Höch did not have to worry about censorship in the intellectually freer Weimar Republic. She thrived in the newly liberalized atmosphere, producing witty and subtle photomontages which commented on the major issues of the day. Her works were innovative in their use of materials gleaned from exhibition catalogues, paper of various colors and textures, typography, fabrics, lace, delicate transparent patterns, the tailors' marks from those patterns, the filet net used as a base for embroidery, as well as the expected fragments from postcards, magazines and newspapers.

At least one critic, Mario Naves, has argued that Höch's most impressive work during the 1920s is not the well-known *Cut with the Dada Kitchen Knife,* but a later work, the 1923 collage *High Finance*. In this, Höch presents the viewer with provocative images including a double-barrel shotgun, aerial views of exhibition halls in the city of Breslau (now Wroclaw, Poland), machine parts, a truck riding over a tire, the banner of Germany's reactionaries, the imperial Reich flag in horizontal stripes of red, white, and red, and last, but by no means least, a portrait of the scientist Sir John Herschel. A satirical commentary on both the world of industrialism and the realm of social power, Höch's *High Finance* has impressed critics from a compositional point of view, with its "dead-on stability and rhythmic counterpoints that would have impressed Mondrian." A work considered "neither novelty nor propaganda," it has been called "an expertly executed work of art and Höch's masterpiece."

By the mid-1920s, Höch had ended her relationship with Raoul Hausmann and the creative energies of Berlin Dada had petered out. She continued to produce works in a variety of mediums and remained open to new ideas, maintaining friendships with many of the most creative personalities of her day, including Kurt Schwitters, Lazlo Moholy-Nagy, **Nelly van Doesburg,** and Hans Arp and ***Sophie Tauber-Arp**. In 1926, Höch entered into an intimate relationship with a Dutch woman, author **Til Brugman** (1888–1956), with whom she lived until 1929 in The Hague, and then until 1935 in Berlin. Höch returned to Germany in 1929 at a time when the relatively stable years of the Weimar Republic were coming to an end with the rise of Adolf Hitler's Nazi movement. Although she had shown little interest in political affairs in recent years, by 1930 Höch was again commenting through her art on the suffering of the German people. In the 1930 collage *Trainer* (Kunsthaus, Zurich), which is completed by a brown (the color of the shirts worn by Hitler's storm troopers, the SA) leather frame, an aggressive masculine pose is combined with fragments of female bodies. Many themes are suggested here, including that of the struggle between the sexes. In the 1931 collage *Strong Men* (Institut für Auslandsbeziehungen, Stuttgart), the Nazi threat is once again depicted as one of aggressively muscle-bound men intent on destruction.

Höch had good reason to look upon the Nazis as foes not only of culture and civilized values, but of her own ability to work freely as a creative artist. Hitler, a frustrated artist who believed himself qualified to judge the creative efforts of others, defined much of contemporary German art as being *entartet* (degenerate), "un-German," and infected with the spirit of *Kulturbolschewismus* (cultural Bolshevism). Even before the Nazis came to power in 1933, Höch was affected by their hatred of all that was innovative and disrespectful of national values and middle-class ideals. In 1932, a planned retrospective of her photomontages scheduled to open at the Dessau Bauhaus was canceled when the local branch of the Nazi Party forced the world-famous art school to close down.

Unlike many other German artists who had been designated "cultural Bolsheviks" by the Nazis, Höch chose to remain in Germany after 1933. Not being Jewish, she did not suffer persecution from the regime's increasingly harsh anti-Semitic racial legislation. Nevertheless, she had to resign herself to marginalization within a new art world dominated by the ideals of National Socialism. Banned from publicly exhibiting her art, she continued work in private, creating collages with materials from inexpensive sources.

Cut with the Dada Knife *by Hannah Höch, 1919.*

Choosing a world of "inner emigration," Höch retreated into private life. Among her few open acts of defiance during this period was her rescue of the papers and art works of the Berlin Dada circle from destruction by the Nazi-controlled Reichskulturkammer (Reich Chamber of Culture). In 1939, she purchased a house in the Berlin suburb of Heiligensee which provided her with both physical rootedness and psychic security. Here, she tended her garden, a lifelong obsession, which provided an aura of calm in an increasingly violent world. The only event of note during these years was Höch's marriage in 1938 to Kurt Matthies, which would end in divorce in 1944.

Condemned by Nazi society, Höch remained highly productive, and her commentaries would prove to be enduring. In a series of works entitled *Pictures in Times of Misery,* she relied, in **Ellen Maurer**'s words, on her own "visionary codes to depict epochal events." Persecution is shown in terms of a chicken with wasted limbs. The violence at the heart of Nazism was suggested in the 1933 collage *Wild Uprising* (Sparkasse Berlin, Berlin), in which a figure springs out of a huge, boorish body, looking resolutely past the work's border. Escape from the suffocating environment of Nazi Germany was hinted at in the 1937 collage *Seven Mile Boots* (Kunsthalle, Hamburg).

After World War II, Höch stayed in Berlin, working in various genres. She continued to grow as an artist, employing a style defined by Maurer as *Stilpluralismus* (pluralism of styles), in which some of the most telling influences are Expressionism, constructivism, *Neue Sachlichkeit* (New Objectivity), and the work of several Symbolist painters, including Odilon Redon. Working with such varied traditions, as well as her own experiences as an artist, Höch remained productive until her last years, producing some works as thought provoking as those of her Dada period.

In many ways a philosophical artist, Hannah Höch created works that asked big questions in an offbeat fashion. Soon after her death in Berlin-Heiligensee, on May 31, 1978, the art world began to see the strong, individualistic views that informed her work as she traveled the same path as 20th-century masters: Max Ernst, Paul Klee, and ***Méret Oppenheim**.

SOURCES:

Ades, Dawn. *Photomontage.* Revised and enlarged ed. London: Thames and Hudson, 1986.

Bergius, Hanne. "The Ambiguous Aesthetic of Dada: Towards a Definition of its Categories," in *Journal of European Studies.* Vol. 9, parts 1–2, nos. 33–34. March–June, 1979, pp. 26–38.

Boswell, Peter W., et al. *The Photomontages of Hannah Höch.* Minneapolis, MN: Walker Art Center, 1996.

Camhi, Leslie. "Piece Work," in *The Village Voice.* Vol. 42, no. 12. March 25, 1997, p. 94.

Carley, Michal Ann. "Meret Oppenheim & Hannah Höch: Laying Groundwork for Art in a New Century," in *Fiberarts: The Magazine of Textiles.* Vol. 24, no. 4. January–February, 1998, pp. 46–51.

Clapp, Jane. *Art Censorship: A Chronology of Proscribed and Prescribed Art.* Metuchen, NJ: Scarecrow Press, 1972.

Dech, Julia, and Ellen Maurer, eds. *Da-da zwischen Reden zu Hannah Höch.* Berlin: Orlanda Frauenverlag, 1991.

Götz, Adriani, ed. *Hannah Höch, 1889–1978: Collages.* London: Institute for Foreign Cultural Relations, 1985.

Hubert, Renee Riese. *Magnifying Mirrors: Women, Surrealism and Partnership.* Lincoln: University of Nebraska Press, 1994.

Jelavich, Peter. *Berlin Cabaret.* Cambridge, MA: Harvard University Press, 1993.

Kallos, Kay Klein. "A Woman's Revolution: The Relationship Between Design and the Avant-Garde in the Work of Hannah Höch, 1912–1922" (Ph.D. dissertation, University of Wisconsin—Madison, 1994).

Lavin, Maud. "Androgyny, Spectatorship, and the Weimar Photomontages of Hannah Höch," in *New German Critique.* No. 51. Fall 1990, pp. 62–86.

———. *Cut With the Kitchen Knife: The Weimar Photomontages of Hannah Höch.* New Haven, CT: Yale University Press, 1993.

Lippard, Lucy R., ed. *Dadas on Art.* Englewood Cliffs, NJ: Prentice-Hall, 1971.

Maurer, Ellen. *Hannah Höch—Jenseits fester Grenzen: Das malerische Werk bis 1945.* Berlin: Gebr. Mann Verlag, 1995.

Meskimmon, Marsha. "Höch, Hannah," in Delia Gaze, ed., *Dictionary of Women Artists.* Volume I. London and Chicago: Fitzroy Dearborn, 1997, pp. 697–701.

Naves, Mario. "A Daughter of Dada: Hannah Höch at MOMA," in *The New Criterion.* Vol. 15. May 1997, pp. 51–54.

Noun, Louise R. *Three Berlin Artists of the Weimar Era: Hannah Höch, Käthe Kollwitz, Jeanne Mammen.* Des Moines: Des Moines Art Center, 1994.

Ohff, Heinz. *Hannah Höch.* Berlin: Gebr. Mann Verlag, 1968.

Ollman, Leah. "The Lives of Hannah Höch," in *Art in America.* Vol. 86, no. 4. April 1998, pp. 100–105.

Owen, Nancy E. "Hannah Höch's Images of Women, 1916–1933" (M.A. thesis, School of the Art Institute of Chicago, 1991).

Roters, Eberhard et al. *Berlin 1910–1933.* NY: Rizzoli, 1982.

Sheppard, Richard. "Dada and Politics," in *Journal of European Politics.* Vol. 9, parts 1–2, nos. 33–34. March–June, 1979, pp. 39–74.

RELATED MEDIA:

"The Female Closet" (videocassette) by Barbara Hammer. NY: Women Make Movies, 1998.

"Hannah Höch" (videocassette) Bonn: Inter Nationes, 1989.

John Haag,
Associate Professor, University of Georgia, Athens, Georgia

Hockaday, Margaret (1907–1992)

American advertiser who launched her own firm.

Name variations: Maggie or Mig; Margaret Hockaday La Farge. Pronunciation: HOCK-a-day. Born Margaret Elizabeth Hockaday on January 8, 1907, in Wichita, Kansas; died in New York City on December 18, 1992, in her Greenwich Village apartment; daughter of Bird Pixlee (Bohart) Hockaday (a publisher's representative) and Isaac Newton Hockaday (ran a hardware store and manufactured paint); attended

Oak Park, Illinois, public schools; graduated Vassar College, 1929; married Reinhardt Bischoff (a German architect), in the late 1940s (divorced mid-1950s); married Louis Bancel La Farge (an architect), in 1962; no children; aunt of artist Susan Hockaday Jones.

Family moved from Kansas to Illinois when she was a child; started career as a copywriter for Marshall Field department store in Chicago; moved to New York and spent two years as fashion editor at Vogue; *moved to* Harper's Bazaar *(1936); worked briefly at J. Walter Thompson; worked for Montgomery Ward (1941); taught social studies at Columbia University's Lincoln School (1942–45); earned master's in education (1947); returned to publishing; became fashion editor for Curtis'* Holiday *travel magazine; opened advertising agency (1949); retired (1970); moved to Nantucket; moved to Pennswood Village in Newtown, Pennsylvania; returned to Manhattan (1989).*

Selected writings: What to Wear Where *(1949);* WAF—A Handbook for Air Force Women *(1954);* The Dunbar Book of Contemporary Furniture *(1956);* The Copywriter's Guide *(Harper & Brothers, 1958, 1959).*

In 1953, Margaret Hockaday, along with her art director and a photographer, transported a Dunbar sofa from New York City to New Milford, Connecticut, then hauled it across a pasture and up a hill, to shoot an advertisement. Never before had Madison Avenue seen so surreal an image: a sofa outside, alone, in the great outdoors. The copy read, "The long green hill of our desire." The unorthodox manner of photographing the sofa, of making advertising an art, broke a century-old tradition that furniture must be photographed in a meticulously arranged room. The concept made headlines and began a trend that became commonplace. Ads in *The New Yorker, The New York Times, House Beautiful* and *House & Garden,* featured Dunbar chairs in trees, on unfinished skyscrapers, in a game of musical chairs, even on the witness stand.

The creative force behind the ads was Margaret Hockaday, a pioneer in the last wave of print advertising. She had a lifelong affair with words, images, packaging, poetry, architecture and design, and her style was described as "calculated whimsy" or "studied conspicuousness." The Dunbar Furniture campaign was such a success that art directors began abandoning their studios for Central Park.

Margaret Hockaday, a perfectionist, was born in Wichita, Kansas, in 1907. She was a descendant of Abraham Lincoln and grew up in a family that believed in education and hard work. Her grandfather was a college professor; her uncle Woody conceived the idea of the yellow line that bisects highways. He shared his idea with President Franklin Delano Roosevelt who instituted it in the early 1930s.

As a child, Margaret lived just outside of Chicago in Oak Park which she later dubbed the "non-chic western suburb." With all the books and magazines in the home—her mother worked as a publisher's representative—she grew up in an atmosphere of print and was fascinated with catalogues and merchandising through the mail. "To me, one of the greatest American inventions is mail order," she said. "Everything is left to the printed catalog page and the imagination of the reader to fill in the reality." While she loved literature, music and design, her early ambition was to become an architect like her brother Lincoln. (She would end up marrying two architects: Reinhardt Bischoff, in the late 1940s, and Louis Bancel La Farge, in 1962.)

Margaret's father, Isaac Newton Hockaday, was an inventive man who had run a large Wichita hardware store and manufactured paint. Following the move to Chicago, he abandoned the family for California, leaving Margaret's mother, **Bird Pixlee Bohart**, to raise Margaret and her brothers, Willard and Lincoln. By some accounts, Bird Bohart was a driven woman who made large demands on her children. Hockaday would later idealize families in her work.

At Vassar College, Margaret majored in English and history. After graduation, she worked as a retailing copywriter at Marshall Field in Chicago. Five years later, she moved to New York to work on the fashion staff of *Vogue* and *Harper's Bazaar.* She also wrote for the Montgomery Ward catalogue. Hockaday remained fascinated with advertising because everything ultimately relied on the customer's imagination. During World War II, however, she felt compelled to take a teaching post at Columbia University's Lincoln School. "I applied advertising techniques to teaching—worked very well," she said. Afterward, she was a fashion editor for *Holiday,* a new venture from Curtis Publishing. While there, she designed and wrote a small book, *What to Wear Where.* The book was later published by Bantam Books.

After WWII, there were increased opportunities for women in advertising agencies. Hockaday started hers in 1949, in a one-chair barber shop on the East Side. She planted red geraniums in the large storefront window and set to work. Her first client was Capezio, Inc., "the dancer's cobbler since 1887." Ad copy ran: "Hail Capezio! With liberty from conformity for all," or "Some people can't—Capezio people can," or "Are you mad enough to wear Capezio stemwear?" The art director was sent to finger-painting school for children and came up with a poster-style ad picturing a strange red, orange and yellow animal called a Polka-Dotta. No shoes were pictured, since Hockaday advertising relied on creating a state of mind.

It was the Dunbar furniture series that first captured attention for Hockaday. In a send up, James Thurber's unicorn in the garden was seen eating roses in a Dunbar bed. And when the Eisenhower-Khrushchev summit conference was making headlines, a Dunbar furniture ad showed photographers, reporters, and military brass waiting near four empty chairs. The copy read:

> They sit at the summit. These four take their place with dignity and command at the top. Each a symbol of design authority in the age of the follower. Each the best of two worlds. The honored skill of the craftsman is powered in technological advance. Dunbar builds a rich and enduring inheritance. Edward Wormly designs it.

The Dunbar Book of Contemporary Furniture, now regarded as a textbook for decorators and architects, started as a catalogue which Hockaday edited and produced for Dunbar. She also authored the WAF handbook on fashion, grooming, and morale at the request of the Air Force.

Hockaday Associates created the "Just wear a smile and a Jantzen" campaign, zeroing in on a model's lips. They also developed a portable package for the bathing suits with the instructions, "Just add water."

Into the staid world of Scotch advertising—which usually emphasized proof, price, flavor, color and age—Hockaday introduced mood and fashion. An attractive young man says to an unseen woman: "As long as you're up, get me a Grant's." The words became such a catchphrase that some women complained. Hockaday then created an ad in which the woman makes the demand and the man does the fetching. "You know if you've arrived in America," said Hockaday, "when millions of people shout your words back to you." Cartoonists often made reference to her ads in their work. A 1963 *New Yorker* cartoon shows a woman reading in bed, a Civil War general nearby. "As long as you're Grant, get me a 7-Up," she says.

Hockaday regarded the hard sell as the easy sell, but the most expensive and desperate. She also avoided advertising by intimidation. She told an interviewer for the February 1959 issue of *Madison Avenue:*

> I don't believe in fear advertising, in advertising that makes people uneasy, uncomfortable, or insecure. I think advertising can be fun, gay, amusing, and still do a good selling job. I agree that our kind of advertising can—in the wrong hands—illustrate the old adage that "Humor does not sell." We have a saying among us—"It's fine but where do you go after the first laugh." We feel we go straight to the point. And a good ad must always make its point in relation to the climate we live in.

Her agency worked on the senses, the attitudes of the consumer, and sales rose.

Hockaday's clients in the \$500,000–\$1,000,000 range, included Adler Co. ("Clean White Sock"), Andrew Arkin ("Arkin Girls" comic strip), French Boot Shop, International Shoe, Royal Worcester Porcelain, Frank Smith Silversmiths, Standard Romper, Health-Tex ("Pecks of Children"), Scarves by Vera, Wayne Knitting Mills, and Belle-Sharmeer. Other clients included the American Cancer Society (the athletes "I Don't Smoke" campaign against cancer, 1960s), Crane stationery ("Complain on Crane's," "Cajole on Crane's," "Gloat on Crane's," etc.), Fuller fabrics ("The Richest Fabric in Town") and Tycora yarn ("Miss Theodora"). For Reed & Barton, the copy warned: "Don't let Daddy give you away till he gives you your sterling." Hockaday also produced television spots, cautioning: "It's like a one-act show—it has to make it in the first minute." Success to Hockaday meant "being on the edge of change and willing to grab it."

Eventually Hockaday's offices were moved to 575 Madison Avenue. Far from office-like, there were walls of windows, poppies, a ceiling-high laurel tree, and a round table for a desk. Her agency had an intimate, creative atmosphere where copywriters were assigned specific accounts, but everyone worked on every problem. "You have to have at least three talents when you're here," she said.

Hockaday was the board chair, Alvin Chereskin, the president, and Joe Giordano, the creative director. For new accounts, she noted:

> We start, obviously, with the product and what we know about the climate—who is buying it, who should be buying it, who is relating to it now. Where does the client want to go with it? More places deeper? Get it upstairs if it's in the basement?
>
> Then we go out and look at it sitting there. How the stores place it, how they sell it. . . . Then we sit down with the copywriters.

Margaret Hockaday

In 1962, Hockaday married Louis Bancel La Farge, an architect and grandson of painter John La Farge. The elegant and debonair La Farge was president of the New York chapter of the American Institute of Architects from 1958 to 1960 and a founding member of the New York City Landmarks Preservation Commission. During World War II, he had served on Dwight D. Eisenhower's general staff as chief of the monuments, fine arts and archives section. After the war, Major La Farge was decorated for supervising the return of art stolen by the Nazis.

Hockaday and her husband lived in a renovated brownstone on East 69th Street in Manhattan. They took long walks in the city, often visiting art galleries on the East Side. She loved to cook and had the opportunity on weekends in New Milford, Connecticut, in their 17th-century restored saltbox farmhouse.

Her friends, who were in the forefront of the fashion and design worlds, included ***Diana Vreeland** of *Vogue* and Hans and ***Florence Schust Knoll** of Knoll Furniture. Hockaday was fascinated with clothes, always dressing with style, wearing the designers of the day, such as ***Bonnie Cashin**. Later, she developed an interest in Japanese aesthetics which included contemporary designers such as Issey Miyake. She loved Matisse and Picasso, traveling with her husband to Europe to see their work, and greatly admired the architects Corbusier and Mies van der Rohe.

In 1970, when her husband retired from his architectural practice, Hockaday retired as well, selling her agency to J. Walter Thompson. The couple moved to Nantucket where, during the ten years they lived there, Hockaday designed her home and gardens. She and her husband also visited the La Farge family property on Tuckernuck Island off the western tip of Nantucket, devoid of cars or electricity.

In 1980, her husband's failing health prompted their move to the Quaker retirement community, Pennswood Village, in Newtown, Pennsylvania. Bancel La Farge died in July of 1989. That September, at age 82, Hockaday moved back to Manhattan. There, though hampered by osteoporosis, she took advantage of the city's films and exhibits, walking or taking the bus. She went gallery hopping in her dramatic straw hats and many-colored scarves. "Mig had the time of her life 'til the end," said her niece, artist **Susan Hockaday Jones**. Margaret Hockaday died in her Greenwich Village apartment on December 18, 1992. One of Hockaday's copywriters once said, "Margaret is a copywriter extraordinaire. She begins a copy block at a point most of us never reach."

SOURCES:

Alden, Robert. "Advertising: Wraith's Plaint Brings Repercussions," in *The New York Times*. October 5, 1960, p. L64.

Applegate, Edd, ed. *The Ad Men and Women: A Biographical Dictionary of Advertising* ("Margaret Hockaday" by R.E. Neuberger-Lucchesi). Greenwood Press, 1994.

Bowen, Croswell. "The New York Woman Advertising Executive," in *Madison Avenue*. February 1959.

"Crane & Co. Stationery Ads Hint at Write-It-Yourself Correspondence," in *Advertising Age*. January 11, 1960.

Flint, Peter B. "L.B. LaFarge, 89, An Architect," *The New York Times*. July 4, 1989.

Hamilton, L.D. "Protest," in *The New Yorker*. October 1, 1960.

Hockaday Jones, Susan. Personal Interview. New York City, 1994.

Howe, Marvine. "Margaret Hockaday is Dead at Age 85; Started Ad Agency," in *The New York Times*. December 22, 1992.

Johnson, Phyliss. "Some People Can't—Hockaday People Can—Create 'Mad,' Informal Ads," in *Advertising Age*. March 11, 1957, pp. 50–51.

Lee, Henry. "Hockaday Associates—Margaret Hockaday," in *Madison Avenue*. December 1963.

McQuade, Walter. "So long as you're up, pour me some nostalgia," in *Architectural Forum*. October 1965, p. 68.

Spielvogel, Carl. "Advertising: Power That Can't Be Skirted," in *The New York Times*. February 22, 1959.

Stebbins, Hal. "Humanizing catalog copy," in *Printers' Ink*. c. 1960.

———. "A Well-timed Tie-in," in *Printers' Ink*. May 20, 1960.

"To Put over a New Idea: Singular Art," in *Printers' Ink*. July 15, 1955.

Ward, Alan. "Visual Directions: Is It Editorial or Is It Advertising?" in *Madison Avenue*. June 1961.

SUGGESTED READING:

"Arkin Startles Fashion Ad Circles with Novel Cartoon Strip Campaign," in *Advertising Age*. September 3, 1956, pp. 27, 79.

"Campaign with Sock," in *Printers' Ink*. May 25, 1962.

"Capezio Extends 'Madness' with Stemwear Push," in *Advertising Age*. December 9, 1957.

Clark, Timothy B. "As Long as Carter's Up He'll Get You a Grant," in *The New York Times*. April 21, 1980, A19.

Duhe, Camille. "Cultivate a Pair of 'Mushroom Eyes,'" in *New York Herald Tribune*. May 26, 1963.

Koehring, Gertrude. "'Twice Slapped' by Woolf, Copy Chief Reports Loyal Following for Both Clients," in *Advertising Age*. June 24, 1957, p. 92.

"New Capezio Ads Hail 'Liberty from Conformity for All,'" in *Advertising Age*. February 27, 1961, p. 1B.

"Offbeat Ad Can't be Beat—If you Dig It: Hockaday," in *Advertising Age*. November 25, 1957.

Russell, Alfred. "Margaret Hockaday Has Got the Creative Touch that Sells," in *New York World Telegram*. April 8, 1963.

Schuyler, Philip N. "When 2+2=5, Then Hockaday is Adding," in *Editor & Publisher*. October 6, 1962, pp. 17, 19.

Tyler, William D. "Creativity May Raise Its Lovely Head," in *Advertising Age*. December 28, 1959, p. 37.

Susan Slosberg,
Adjunct Professor of public relations at Baruch College,
The City University of New York

Hodder, Jessie Donaldson

(1867–1931)

American prison reformer. *Born on March 30, 1867, in Cincinnati, Ohio; died on November 19, 1931, in Framingham, Massachusetts; daughter of William and Mary (Hall) Hodder; entered into common-law mar-*

riage with Alfred LeRoy Hodder (an author and journalist), in 1890 (died 1907); children: Olive (b. 1893); J. Alan (b. 1897).

Little is known about the early life of Jessie Hodder. She was born in Cincinnati, Ohio, in 1867, and, after the death of her mother when she was two, was raised by her grandmother. Moving to New York in 1890, she met Alfred Hodder, then a student of philosopher William James, and entered into a common-law marriage. The couple lived in Germany and Italy (where their daughter Olive was born) until 1893, then they returned to the United States so that Alfred could take a position on the faculty at Bryn Mawr College. After the birth of a son, J. Alan, Alfred sent his wife and children to Switzerland, promising to join them. However, in 1904, he renounced his marriage and wed a fellow Bryn Mawr professor. Shortly thereafter, young Olive died, leaving Hodder in such deep despair that for some time she contemplated suicide. Encouraged by ***Alice Gibbens James**, wife of William James, to return to the United States, Hodder settled in Boston in 1906 and began to reclaim her life.

With a letter of introduction from Alice Gibbens James to ***Elizabeth Glendower Evans**, Hodder secured a job as housemother at the Industrial School for Girls in Lancaster, Massachusetts. A year later, she joined the social service department of Massachusetts General Hospital as a counselor for alcoholics, syphilis victims, and unwed mothers. Her compassionate work with the young girls, whom she counseled to keep their babies rather than give them up for adoption, led to her appointment in 1910 as superintendent of the Massachusetts Prison and Reformatory for Women in Framingham, where ***Ellen Cheney Johnson** had begun a pioneering program of rehabilitation. Expanding on Johnson's work, Hodder turned the reformatory into a model institution. She first convinced the legislature to drop the word *Prison* from the name of the institution and then remodeled the disciplinary wing, unblocking windows to let in the daylight and views of the countryside. Shortening the prisoner's workday by half, she used the extra time for programs of recreation and education. She staffed the institution with trained instructors equipped to teach at various levels, from elementary grades through high school, and offered university extension courses in business, language, and domestic science. Her innovative recreational programs included outdoor activities, as well as music and drama. All the while, Hodder managed to increase production in the institution's established clothing, cattle, and poultry industries. In addition, she arranged for inmates to work outside the institution at regular jobs for which they were paid.

One of Hodder's most valuable contributions was in the study and classification of inmates. Aware of the experiments of ***Katharine Bement Davis** at the New York Reformatory for Women, Hodder recommended that inmates receive medical and psychiatric evaluations and that the mentally ill and uneducable inmates be separated from the reformable population. Beginning in 1912, she appointed a resident social worker and established a research staff that maintained case records and follow-up studies which proved invaluable in later surveys to determine the social causes of delinquency. Although not an original theorist, Hodder succeeded where her predecessors had failed by swaying the legislature to support some of her innovations, and then using the funds allocated to her in a creative manner. A stately woman of great warmth and dignity, she charmed inmates and fellow workers alike. Her maternal instincts were such that she often opened her personal residence to inmates in crisis.

Hodder kept abreast of the newest ideas in penology through outside contacts. The reformatory was frequently visited by European leaders in the field, and Hodder made a tour of European prisons and reformatories in 1921. She was involved with the National Conference of Social Work and the National Prison Association and, in 1925, served as the sole woman delegate to the International Prison Congress in London. Hodder was appointed to the National Crime Commission by President Calvin Coolidge in 1927 and to a committee of the Wickersham Commission on Law Observance and Enforcement by President Herbert Hoover in 1929.

Jessie Hodder died of chronic myocarditis at her home in the reformatory at Framingham in 1931. That same year, criminologists Sheldon and ***Eleanor Glueck** began their renowned study of the Framingham Reformatory and 500 of its women inmates. The work, completed in 1934, cited Jessie Hodder as a leading force in the transformation of the institution into a model facility.

SOURCES:

James, Edward T. ed. *Notable American Women, 1607–1950.* Cambridge, MA: The Belknap Press of Harvard University Press, 1971.

McHenry, Robert, ed. *Famous American Women.* NY: Dover, 1983.

Barbara Morgan,
Melrose, Massachusetts.

Hodges, Faustina Hasse (1822–1895)

English-born American composer and organist. *Born in Malmesbury (some sources cite Bristol), England, on August 7, 1822; arrived in the United States in 1841; died in Philadelphia, Pennsylvania, on February 4, 1895; daughter of Edward Hodges (1796–1867, an English organist, composer and writer who lived in the U.S. from 1838 until the early 1860s).*

Appointed professor of organ, singing and piano at the Troy Female Seminary (1852); composed mostly sentimental ballads before the Civil War and more sophisticated art songs starting in the 1870s.

Although born in England in 1822, Faustina Hodges was a thoroughly American phenomenon. Her father was an organist who did much to elevate New York musical life during the more than two decades he lived in that city. Faustina was able to learn a great deal about the practical, living aspects of music during her many years as a church organist in New York and Philadelphia churches. Her songs, both moving and naive, began to be published in the 1850s, and a number of them, including *Dreams* (1859) and *The Rose-Bush* (1859), clearly deserved to be the popular favorites they were in their day by virtue of the craft that went into writing them. Her hymn tunes and sacred duets were also much praised. An unsophisticated composer, Faustina Hodges' songs reflected the brash, young nation she had chosen as her second homeland.

John Haag,
Athens, Georgia

Hodgkin, Dorothy (1910–1994)

English biochemist, Nobel laureate, and peace activist who is best known for her discovery of the structures of penicillin and vitamin B-12. *Born Dorothy Mary Crowfoot on May 12, 1910, in Cairo, Egypt; died on July 29, 1994, at her home in Shipston-on-Stour, in Warwickshire county in central England, after suffering a stroke; daughter of John Winter (a classics scholar and archaeologist) and Grace Mary (Hood) Crowfoot (a weaver and amateur botanist); graduated from Sir John Lehman School, Beccles, 1928; Somerville College, Oxford, B.A., 1931; Cambridge University, Ph.D., 1936; married Thomas Lionel Hodgkin, on December 16, 1937; children: Luke Hodgkin (b. 1938);* ***Elizabeth Hodgkin*** *(b. 1941); Tobias Hodgkin (b. 1946).*

Honors and awards: fellow, Royal Society (1947); Royal Medalist of the Royal Society (1956); Nobel Prize in chemistry (1964); British Order of Merit (1965); First Freedom of Beccles (1965); Copley Medal, Royal Society (1976); Mikhail Lomonosov Gold Medal, Soviet Academy of Science (1982); Dimitrov Prize (1984); Lenin Plea Prize (1987); numerous honorary doctorates, including Leeds, Manchester, Cambridge, Oxford, York, and Dalhousie universities.

Became fellow of Somerville College, Oxford (1936); discovered crystalline structure of penicillin (1946); appointed university lecturer and demonstrator at Oxford (1946); discovered structure of vitamin B-12 (1954); became university reader at Oxford (1957); served as Wolfson Research Professor of Chemistry, Royal Society (1960–77); discovered structure of insulin (1969); served as president of Pugwash Conference on Science and World Affairs (1975); served as president of International Union of Crystallography (1972–75); served as president of British Association for the Advancement of Science (1977–78); was chancellor of Bristol University (1970–88); was a fellow of Wolfson College, Oxford (1977–82).

Selected writings: Birkbeck, Science, and History *(Birkbeck College, 1970);* Wondering Scientists *(Indian Council for Cultural Relations, 1974);* ****Kathleen Lonsdale:*** A Biographical Memoir *(Royal Society, 1976).*

Thanks to the peripatetic lifestyle of her parents, Dorothy Crowfoot Hodgkin's education was a hodgepodge of private schools, governesses, and private study with her mother and siblings in her early years. In 1923, she was 13 years old when she and her sister Joan left their grandmother's home in England for a six-month stay with their parents in the Sudan, where their father was director of education and antiquities. The Crowfoots had decided a year in that part of the world would be good for the girls, and, while their father worked, their mother concentrated on taking them to museums, galleries, and scientific laboratories in the Sudan and neighboring countries. One visit was to the geological department of the Cairo Wellcome Institute Laboratories, headed by the noted soil chemist Dr. A.F. Joseph, who was a family friend. To amuse the girls, geologists at the laboratory showed them how to collect gold samples by panning the sand from streambeds, and the girls were soon applying the process to the stream in their parents' garden. When Dorothy became curious about a piece of black shiny mineral, she returned with it to the Wellcome Laboratory, where Dr. Joseph helped her to analyze the substance and discover that it was a mixed ore of iron and titanium, called ilmenite. Impressed by Dorothy's interest, Joseph gave her a surveyor's box with reagents for testing mineral samples. Upon her return to England, Dorothy set up a small laboratory in the attic. On her 16th birthday, when she received a children's book on chemistry written by the Nobel Prize-winning physicist William Henry Bragg, which described how X-rays could be used to expose the atoms in crystals, Dorothy knew she had found her life's work.

Born on May 12, 1910, in Cairo, Egypt, Dorothy Crowfoot Hodgkin was the eldest of four daughters of John Winter Crowfoot, who was then an inspector in the Ministry of Education in Cairo, and **Molly Hood Crowfoot**, whose only academic training had been a French finishing school education. Molly Crowfoot became an excellent amateur botanist, however, studying local plants and making drawings for a government survey on the flora of the Sudan during her husband's tenure in the British colony. The couple doted on their children and placed a high value on their education.

In 1914, while the Crowfoots were on vacation in England, the childhood of four-year-old Dorothy, as well as her sisters, was shattered by the outbreak of the World War I. Believing that it was too dangerous for the children to return to the Middle East, the parents left them in the care of a nanny, residing near John's mother's home in Brighton, and returned to his post in the Sudan. In the ensuing four years of war, international travel was restricted by the danger of German submarines, and Dorothy and her sisters only saw their mother once. At the end of the war, Molly spent a year becoming reacquainted with her children, but she spent at least half of every subsequent year residing with her husband at his foreign posts. Dorothy later believed that this early separation helped to make her independent and strengthened her fortitude to face the challenges of her scientific career.

At age 11, Dorothy enrolled at the Sir John Lehman School in Beccles, where the desultory approach to her earlier education left her lagging far behind her peers in several fundamental learning skills, particularly mathematics; then, having caught up in this subject, she discovered that girls in the school were not permitted to study chemistry. Fortunately, the chemistry instructor, who was a woman, decided to make a special exception for Dorothy and another girl to study in her class.

Dorothy graduated from Beccles in 1928, with plans to study chemistry at Oxford University. Once again, however, her educational background stood in her way, since the Oxford entrance examination required a knowledge of both Latin and a second science. Dorothy's mother became her tutor in botany and helped her gain enough understanding of Latin to pass the exam.

Admitted to Oxford, Hodgkin found an academic climate uncongenial to fostering the careers of women in science. During the late 1920s, officials at the university became increasingly worried about what they perceived to be an unhealthy infiltration of women. There was talk of Oxford's rival university at Cambridge being more "virile," because women there numbered only 10%, while 15% of the Oxford students were women. To stem this tide of "feminization," it was decided that women students would be limited to fewer than 800, and their social and educational opportunities would be severely restricted. Women attended classes and studied separate from the men, and were excluded from the Oxford debating club and other prestigious campus organizations. Nevertheless, Hodgkin found friendly scientific instructors at Somerville, the women's college she attended. Its principal was **Margery Fry**, who was especially supportive of Dorothy's scientific ambitions; during vacations, Hodgkin was allowed to

Fry, Margery (1874–1958)

English prison reformer. Born Sara Margery Fry in 1874; died in 1958; attended Roedean and Somerville College, Oxford; never married; no children.

College educated at Oxford, Margery Fry began her career in 1899 as the warden of the women's hostel at Birmingham University, where she remained until 1904. During World War I, she worked in France for the Friends War Victims Relief Committee, after which she became secretary of the Penal Reform League, which was amalgamated in 1921 as the Howard League for Penal Reform. From 1919 to 1926, Fry served as chair of the league, a period also marked by her increasing involvement in the campaign to abolish capital punishment. Appointed a magistrate in 1921, Fry served as the education advisor to Holloway Prison in 1922 and as principal of Somerville College from 1926 to 1931.

Later in her career, Fry became involved in the international aspects of prison improvement, serving as a member of the Colonial Office Advisory Committee on Penal Reform in 1936. She lectured on the subject in China and the United States and frequently participated on the BBC programs "Any Questions?" and "The Brains Trust." Her publications include *The Future Treatment of the Adult Offender* (1944) and *Arms of the Law* (1951).

remain on campus to do research with the college lecturers and demonstrators. One instructor, the well-known chemist E.G.J. Hartley, even lent her the key to his office so she could work there on her own.

Dorothy, who became especially skilled in the use of X-ray crystallography to determine the atomic structure of molecules, studied with the noted chemist H.M. Powell at Oxford and, during one summer, visited the laboratory of Professor Victor Goldschmidt in Heidelberg. By the time of her graduation in 1932, she had an excellent knowledge of inorganic chemistry and X-ray crystallography. Like many other college-educated women, she had difficulty finding a scientific post, until she was recommended by her old friend from Cairo, A.F. Joseph, for a job with John Desmond Bernal, who was then doing pioneer research in X-ray crystallography at Cambridge University.

The job paid only £75 per year, and Hodgkin was forced to borrow £200 from an aunt to meet expenses. But Bernal was among the first to investigate the use of X-ray techniques in the study of biological molecules, particularly proteins, and her work for him exposed her to advanced research in the crystalline structure of biological compounds. Bernal believed that uncovering the molecular structure of a specific biological compound would make its physical properties better understood and lead to its synthesis in the laboratory. Under Bernal's supervision, Hodgkin made some of the earliest X-ray studies of vitamin B-1, Vitamin D, various sex hormones, and other protein molecules.

Bernal was also an excellent scientific role model and firmly committed to equal professional opportunities for women scientists. Because of the many women he hired, crystallography became one of the few branches of chemistry in which significant numbers of women were employed. This congenial laboratory atmosphere was in sharp contrast to the second-class status Dorothy had felt as a student at Oxford.

While still on her fellowship, Hodgkin was offered a teaching position in chemistry at her alma mater, Somerville College. She at first declined, wishing to remain with Bernal, and also perhaps remembering the treatment of women at Oxford. Somerville then offered to extend her fellowship with Bernal for a second year and allow her a third year at Oxford toward completing her doctoral research before she commenced teaching. Since teaching jobs in Britain were scarce at the time, Dorothy reluctantly agreed to Somerville's terms.

Unfortunately, the discrimination she experienced as a teacher at Oxford was similar to what she had faced as a student. According to Dennis Parker Riley, one of her students there, "prewar Oxford was a masculine stronghold and science faculties even more so." Excluded from the mainstream of the university's scientific life, she was denied membership in the chemistry club, which brought together chemists from all the Oxford colleges, excluded from its weekly research meetings. and never invited to present her work before the membership, despite the recognized importance of her research.

Fortunately, the chemistry student organization was more egalitarian. Dorothy was invited to lecture to the group, and her talks were well attended by students as well as some of the same colleagues who excluded her from the chemistry club. Riley found her so impressive that he asked her to be his research advisor, arousing scorn among many male students and members of the faculty. "Here I was," recalled Riley, "a member of a prestigious college choosing to do my fourth year's research in a new borderline subject with a young female who held no university appointment but only a fellowship in a women's college."

Hodgkin also endured inferior research quarters. Her laboratory, located in the basement of the Oxford University Museum, was a dumping ground for old biological specimens and anthropological exhibits, and her equipment was far from adequate. Because Britain was in a severe economic crisis, the chemistry department had only £50 per year to spend on apparatus, and Dorothy's X-ray room was strung with a dangerous collection of electrical wires suggestive of a scene from a horror movie. With the help of Sir Robert Robinson, professor of inorganic chemistry, she obtained a small grant from a British chemical firm for the purchase of some needed equipment, but her research budget remained paltry, and she was seldom able to hire more than one or two students to help in her research.

In the winter of 1934, her woes were compounded by the onset of a chronic illness that was to plague her for the rest of her life. When the joints in her hands became sore and badly inflamed, she was taken by her parents to see a specialist in London who diagnosed severe rheumatoid arthritis. Although the painful disease severely hampered her manual dexterity, Dorothy never allowed it to stop her work.

Continuing the research on biological crystals she had begun under Bernal, Hodgkin wrote her dissertation on the crystalline structure of the

Dorothy Hodgkin

sterols, and focused her research on cholesterol, one of the most difficult substances to analyze. The work was further complicated by the limited capabilities of adding machines then available, so that many of her calculations took months or even years to complete. In 1936, conditions were substantially improved when she was able to purchase a set of Beevers and Lipson strips, which greatly speeded the calculation of X-ray angles.

In 1937, after several years of laboring under difficult conditions, Dorothy completed her doctorate. In the spring of that year, she also met the man who would become her husband. In London to photograph insulin crystals at the Royal Institute, she paid a visit to her old friend from Somerville, Margery Fry, and met Fry's cousin, Thomas L. Hodgkin, the son of the noted historian and provost of Queen's College, Robert H. Hodgkin. Dorothy was attracted to Thomas' sense of humor, the two found they had much in common, and they married in December 1937.

The relationship proved to be more egalitarian than most marriages of the time. According to a friend of Dorothy Hodgkin, **Anne Sayre**, "It was a remarkable marriage because early on Thomas decided she was the more creative of the two and that she was going to have a chance." The couple had three children, and Thomas did the largest share of childcare, usually watching them in the evenings so that Hodgkin could return to work in her lab. Because of Thomas' willing involvement in their childrearing, Hodgkin found it "reasonably easy" to combine motherhood with a career in science, and "had no sense of guilt in continuing with scientific work—it seemed a natural thing to do at that period."

In 1939, the outbreak of another World War led to disruptions throughout Oxford as well as in Dorothy's home life. Young male students were soon joining the armed forces to battle the Axis powers, and when the nearby city of London came under frequent attack from German bombs, Oxford was one of many outlying towns flooded with escaping Londoners. The Hodgkinses joined other local families in taking in these refugees from the blitz, some of whom could pitch in with the housework, adding to the time Hodgkin could spend on her research.

By then, wartime Britain was providing her with a new scientific problem to tackle. Infectious disease, as well as infections from battlefield wounds had become rampant, and soldiers and civilians alike were in desperate need of a newly discovered drug called penicillin, which was known to combat a number of bacterial infections. Discovered in the early 1930s by Britain's Alexander Fleming, the drug was in too-short supply to be of use to many people, and drug companies would remain unable to manufacture it in mass quantities until its molecular structure had been determined. Both British and American authorities, recognizing the drug as vital to the war effort, joined in speeding up the research. (*See Gladys Lounsbury Hobby.*) Hodgkin received a research grant from the Rockefeller Foundation to improve her laboratory, and a state-of-the-art analog computer from IBM to speed up her calculations, and in 1946, four years after she began her work in this area, she cracked the code of the penicillin molecule.

Despite such groundbreaking work, Hodgkin had yet to attain a regular university appointment. It was only when a male colleague at Oxford interceded on her behalf that she was finally made a university lecturer, which paid considerably more than her earlier fellowship post. Oxford was still so slow in promoting her that she did not acquire the position of reader (equivalent in the U.S. to a full professorship) until 1957. Even then, it was another year before she got adequate laboratory facilities.

Because Oxford's ambivalence toward its women scientists continued, most of Hodgkin's accolades came from outside the university. Shortly after the war ended, she was made a fellow of the Royal Society of England, a rare honor for one so young, and even more rare for a woman scientist. In 1956, Hodgkin was made a Royal Medalist of the Royal Society. In 1960, she received an endowed chair at Oxford, funded not by the university but by the Royal Society. Throughout the 1950s and 1960s, Hodgkin received numerous other honors and awards, including a highly coveted place in the American Academy of Arts and Sciences in 1958.

Meanwhile, her study of the crystalline structures of various biological substances continued. Her next major project after penicillin was the vitamin B-12, which was known to prevent and treat pernicious anemia in humans. This work was greatly speeded up through access to relatively powerful computers at the University of California at Los Angeles. In 1957, Hodgkin published the results of her work on B-12, and seven years later, she received the Nobel Prize in chemistry for her work on penicillin and B-12, the first British woman, and the fifth woman, ever to be honored with a Nobel in science. The following year, Hodgkin received the Order of Merit, which had been given to only one other Englishwoman, ***Florence Nightingale**.

After receiving the Nobel, Hodgkin turned to a project that had preoccupied her since her early career at Oxford: the crystalline structure of insulin. Because of its highly complicated structure, and because computer technology had been in its infancy during the early years of her career, the key to the structure of this substance had long eluded her. It was not until 1969, 30 years after she began to explore the problem, that Hodgkin and her staff finally unlocked the secrets of this matter, paving the way for future advances in the understanding and treatment of diabetes, which is caused by low insulin production by the body.

During the 1960s and 1970s, Hodgkin also became increasingly involved in another lifelong passion—the peace movement. Her deep concerns about the issue were inherited largely from her mother, who had lost four brothers killed in World War I; in 1924, she had accompanied her mother to a meeting of the League of Nations in Geneva. In the late 1960s, Hodgkin joined in protests against the war in Vietnam and visited Hanoi and China to demonstrate her desire for a swift end to the conflict. In 1975, she was asked by the noted physicist Rudolf E. Peierls to be president of the Pugwash Conferences on Science and World Affairs, an organization that campaigns for world peace and disarmament. During the late 1980s, Hodgkin encouraged a former student of hers, ***Margaret Thatcher**, to visit the Soviet Union and establish a better rapport with Soviet President Mikhail Gorbachev.

In 1977, Hodgkin retired from scientific life and moved to a home in the Cotswolds north of Oxford. Her husband died of emphysema in 1982. Although wheelchair-bound from arthritis and a broken pelvis, she continued to actively participate in both scientific and peace conferences. In an article for the *Bulletin of the Atomic Scientists,* Hodgkin summed up the relationship between her life in science and in the peace movement: "How to abolish arms and achieve a peaceful world is necessarily our first objective. If some—and preferably all—of the million dollars spent every minute on arms were turned to the abolition of poverty from the world, many causes of conflict would vanish." On July 29, 1994, Dorothy Hodgkin died at her home in Shipston-on-Stour, in Warwickshire county in central England, after suffering a stroke.

SOURCES:

Brasted, Robert C., and Peter Farago. "Interview with Dorothy Crowfoot Hodgkin," in *Journal of Chemical Education.* Vol. 54, April 1977, pp. 214–215.

Dodson, Guy, Jenny P. Glusker, and David Sayre, eds. *Structural Studies on Molecules of Biological Interest, a Volume in Honor of Professor Dorothy Hodgkin.* Oxford: Clarendon Press, 1981.

Hodgkin, Dorothy. "It's Up to Us!" in *The Bulletin of Atomic Scientists.* January 1981, pp. 38–39.

Julian, Maureen M. "Profiles in Chemistry," in *Journal of Chemical Education.* Vol. 59. February 1982, pp. 124–125.

McGrayne, Sharon Bertsch. *Nobel Prize Women in Science.* Secaucus, NJ: Carol Publishing Group, 1993.

Opfel, Olga S. *The Lady Laureates: Women Who Have Won the Nobel Prize.* Metuchen, NJ: Scarecrow Press, 1978.

Shiels, Barbara. *Winners: Women and the Nobel Prize.* Minneapolis, MN: Dillon Press, 1985.

Wolpert, Lewis, and Alison Richards. *A Passion for Science.* Oxford University Press, 1988.

SUGGESTED READING:

Kass-Simon, G., and Patricia Farnes, eds. *Women of Science: Righting the Record.* Bloomington, IN: University of Indiana Press, 1990.

Phillips, Patricia. *The Scientific Lady: A Social History of Women's Scientific Interests.* London: Weidenfield and Nicholson, 1990.

Vare, Ethlie Ann, and Greg Ptacek. *Mothers of Invention.* Morrow Press, 1988.

COLLECTIONS:

Rockefeller Archive Center, Pocantico Hills, NY. Record Group 1.1, Series 401, Box 38, Folders 491 and 487.

Heather Munro Prescott,
Associate Professor of History,
Central Connecticut State University, New Britain, Connecticut

Hodgkins, Frances (1869–1947)

New Zealand painter who worked with landscapes, still lifes, and portraits. *Born in Dunedin, New Zealand, in 1869; died near Dorchester, Dorset, England, in 1947; daughter of Will Hodgkins (an attorney); studied oil painting with G.P. Berti; attended Dunedin Art School; never married; no children.*

Selected works: Flatford Mill *(1930, London, Tate Gallery);* Seated Woman *(1925–30, London, Tate Gallery).*

New Zealand painter Frances Hodgkins studied watercolor technique with her father and oils with Italian painter G.P. Berti. She attended Dunedin Art School, then traveled extensively in Europe, North Africa, and the Middle East, financing her trips by giving piano lessons. In 1907, she settled in Paris, where she became the first woman to teach at the Académie Colarossi. In 1910, she established her own watercolor academy, catering predominantly to women students. From 1912 to 1913, Hodgkins exhibited in New Zealand and Australia, and at the onset of World War I, she moved to England. She exhibited with the London Group in 1928, and that year became a member of the Calico Printers Association and the Manchester Society of Painters. In 1929, she joined the progressive Seven and Five Society. Hodgkins' early works, particularly her watercolor landscapes, are characterized by their soft post-impressionist treatment; her later works (after 1920) reflect the influence of Henri Matisse in their bold colors and stylization.

Hodgson-Burnett, Frances (1849–1924).

See Burnett, Frances Hodgson.

Hodierna (fl. 1100s)

Scottish princess. *Name variations: Hodierna Dunkeld. Flourished in the 1100s; daughter of David I (b. around 1084), king of Scots (r. 1124–1153), and *****Matilda*** *(d. 1130?).*

Hodierna of Jerusalem (c. 1115–after 1162)

Countess and regent of Tripoli. *Name variations: Hodierne. Born around 1115 in the Frankish principality of Jerusalem; died after 1162 in Tripoli; daughter of Baldwin II, count of Edessa, later king of Jerusalem, and Morphia of Melitene; sister of Alice of Jerusalem (b. 1106), Melisande (1105–1160), and Joveta of Jerusalem (1120–?); married Raymond II, count of Tripoli, around 1136; children: Raymond III of Tripoli (b. 1140);* ***Melisande*** *(c. 1143–1161).*

Born around 1115, Hodierna of Jerusalem was the third daughter of the powerful king Baldwin II and his Armenian queen, ***Morphia of Melitene**. She was raised with her three sisters—**Alice of Jerusalem**, ***Melisande**, and ***Joveta of Jerusalem**—in Jerusalem, then the capital city of the Frankish kingdom. The princess Hodierna received an excellent education. Around 1136, she married Raymond II of Tripoli, son and heir of Pons, count of Tripoli. A ruthless, passionate man, Raymond succeeded his father as count when Pons was murdered while fleeing a Muslim army invading Tripoli in 1137.

Alice of Jerusalem. *See Melisande for sidebar.*

During the first years of their marriage, the couple were intensely devoted to one another. Hodierna had two children, a son named after his father, in 1140, and a daughter, named Melisande after her aunt, a few years later. In 1148, Hodierna and her sister, now Queen Melisande of Jerusalem, were the subject of a serious scandal. In that year, the Second Crusade brought thousands of Western European nobles to the Holy Land, hoping to defeat the Muslim forces holding the city of Edessa. Among the crusaders was Alfonso-Jordan, count of Toulouse. Alfonso-Jordan was the son of Raymond of Toulouse, who fought in the First Crusade and made himself count of Tripoli. Hodierna's husband was the grandson of Raymond of Toulouse's bastard son Bertrand; thus in feudal terms, Alfonso-Jordan had a much more legitimate claim to Tripoli than Raymond II of Tripoli.

It was widely believed that Alfonso-Jordan planned to claim Tripoli; thus when he died quite suddenly, many thought he had been poisoned to prevent him from taking Tripoli. The primary suspects for this murder were Hodierna and Melisande. Melisande was suspected of planning the murder at Hodierna's request. Nothing was ever proven, but Hodierna's husband Raymond II was so offended that his wife was being accused of murder that he refused to participate in the crusade at all.

After this time, the relationship between Raymond II and Hodierna deteriorated. The countess had a vivacious, extroverted personality; she was also reputed to be an unchaste wife. After rumors began to spread that Raymond II was not the father of Hodierna's daughter, he sought to keep his wife isolated from his court by secluding her in her own quarters and limiting her contact with others. By 1152, the marriage was in such trouble that Hodierna's sister, Queen Melisande of Jerusalem, came to Tripoli to try to effect a reconciliation. She was somewhat successful, but it was agreed that Hodierna should spend some time in Jerusalem. As the queen and the countess set out on their journey, couriers from Tripoli informed them of the tragic news that Count Raymond II had just been murdered by a band of Assassins, a radical Muslim group.

Hodierna returned to Tripoli, where she assumed the regency in the name of the new count, her son Raymond III, only 12 years old. King Baldwin III of Jerusalem (Melisande's son) assumed the guardianship of Tripoli, however, because it was considered necessary for the country to have a strong male leader to protect it from its Muslim enemies. Hodierna did exert the real authority, though, since Baldwin had to return to Jerusalem soon after becoming guardian. She retained the regency until Raymond III came of age, when she seems to have been content to retire from an active political life.

The sad story of her daughter reveals the importance placed on women's chastity in her time. In 1160, young Melisande was engaged to the widowed Emperor Manuel Comnenus of Byzantium. Her brother Raymond III spent a fortune on her trousseau, and she received costly gifts, befitting a future empress, from her mother and her aunt Melisande. This much-anticipated wedding between the Frankish royalty of the Holy Land and the immensely wealthy Byzantine empire was looked on as one of the most consequential unions of the day. However, Manuel's ambassadors reported to him the old, unsubstantiated rumor about the bride's legitimacy. Despite the fact that there was no proof, Manuel at first hesitated to go forward with the marriage; he probably was carefully weighing the benefits of an alliance with the Frankish East with the risk of marrying a woman whose legitimacy was even remotely questionable. His fears won out, and in 1161 he repudiated the engagement. Young Melisande, humiliated before all of Europe and the East by the emperor's rejection, soon fell ill. She died some months later.

After yielding the government to her son, Countess Hodierna remained in Tripoli until the winter of 1160 when news came that her devoted sister, Queen Melisande, had suffered a stroke. Hodierna hurried to Jerusalem, along with their younger sister Joveta, and remained there nursing Melisande until the queen's death in November 1161. Hodierna returned to Tripoli, where she died sometime after 1162.

SOURCES:

Hamilton, Bernard. "Women in the Crusader States: Queens of Jerusalem" in *Medieval Women.* Edited by Derek Baker. Oxford: Basil Blackwell, 1978.

Prawer, J. *The Latin Kingdom of Jerusalem.* London: Thames and Hudson, 1972.

Laura York,
Riverside, California

Hodierne.

Variant of Hodierna.

Hodson, Henrietta (1841–1910)

English actress. *Name variations: Henrietta Labouchere. Born in 1841; died in 1910; married second husband Henry Labouchere Du Pré (1831–1912, a journalist and politician), in 1868.*

Henrietta Hodson made her theatrical debut in 1858. Four years later, she appeared in Manchester with Sir Henry Irving. A popular comedic actress, Hodson made her London debut in 1866 and joined the Queen's Theatre Company in 1867. The following year, she married Henry Labouchere, later one of the most powerful radicals in the House of Commons, who became sole owner of the Queen's in 1870. Hodson appeared there as Imogen in *Cymbeline* in 1871. In October of that year, Hodson took over the management of the Royalty Theatre where she created the system of the unseen orchestra, revived *Wild Oats,* was praised for her portrayal of ***Peg Woffington**, and introduced ***Lillie Langtry** to the English public. But management of a theater must have had its burdens. In 1877, Hodson issued a pamphlet titled "A Letter from Miss Henrietta Hodson, an actress, to the members of the dramatic profession, being a relation to the persecutions which she has suffered from Mr. William Schwenk Gilbert, a dramatic author." Though Gilbert, the renowned writing partner of Arthur Sullivan, replied with his own pamphlet, Hodson had the last word, with a long letter to the magazine *Era.* Hodson retired to Florence with her husband in 1903.

Hofer, Evelyn

German-born photographer who specialized in portraits, architectural documentation, and book illustrations. *Born in Marburg, Germany; attended Salem School, in southern Germany; studied piano in Madrid, Switzerland, and at the Paris Conservatory of Music; married Humphrey Sutton.*

Photographer Evelyn Hofer, who avoids revealing her date of birth, was born in Marburg, Germany, in the 1920s. As a young girl, she attended a small progressive school in southern Germany and dreamed of becoming a concert pianist. In 1933, one step ahead of the Nazi Party, the Hofers fled Germany for Spain, settling in Madrid. Hofer continued to immerse herself in music and, after studying in Madrid and Switzerland, entered the Paris Conservatory. When she failed a major exam to determine the extent of her talent, she decided on a career in photography and threw herself into this new pursuit with the zeal that had once been reserved for her music. After serving apprenticeships at two commercial photographic studios in Zurich, Switzerland, Hofer moved with her family to Mexico City, where she tried her hand at freelancing. "I encountered so much opposition because I was a woman that I couldn't get assignments," she later recalled. "But I was determined to be a photographer and no amount of Latin parochialism was going to stop me." She finally landed a job at a second-rate magazine, where she worked for four years while expanding her portfolio. When she felt she was ready, she packed up and headed for New York.

Two weeks after her arrival, Hofer met Alexei Brodovich, the progressive fashion designer and art director of *Harper's Bazaar.* He loved her work and hired her on the spot as a fashion photographer. For the next three years, Hofer worked for *Harper's,* learning to work with models, to shoot for mood, and to present a concept and sell an idea through pictures. Although successful in the fashion industry (her work also appeared in *Vogue*), Hofer grew to hate its pretensions and longed to photograph everyday life and people. Her opportunity came when ***Mary McCarthy** asked her to travel to Italy to shoot photographs for *The Stones of*

Florence, a book McCarthy had been commissioned to write. The resulting 1959 publication was an immediate success and propelled Hofer's career. She subsequently collaborated on five more books: *London Perceived, New York Proclaimed, The Evidence of Washington,* and *Dublin: A Portrait* (all with V.S. Pritchett), and *The Presence of Spain* (with James Morris). In addition, her work was seen in some of the nation's top magazines.

During the 1960s, Hofer was a regular photographer for *Life* magazine, and she also created essays for Time-Life Books, *Life* Special Reports series, and *The New York Times Magazine*. The subjects of her photographic essays included Michelangelo, Arthur Rubinstein, life in English prisons, and ghost towns. Known for the brilliant graphic fidelity of her photographs (accomplished with a 4"x5" view-camera), Hofer scorned what she referred to as pretty "postcard" pictures and often spent hours at a location, searching for the one glossy that would tell a story. In 1974, Jim Mencarelli, of the *Grand Rapids Press,* accompanied the photographer as she was shooting background pictures for an article on then Vice President Gerald R. Ford in his hometown of Grand Rapids, Michigan. Hofer visited Ford's old Boy Scout camp on Duck Lake, just north of Muskegon. After spending the day inspecting the half-dozen buildings left standing on the site, she found nothing meaningful to shoot. Just as she was packing up, she wandered past the abandoned dining hall and discovered an old council pit, ringed by tiers of logs, where meetings and initiation ceremonies had been held. "It is perfect," she said. She could envision Ford, standing in the center, facing his group. "He was an Eagle Scout, a leader. Surely, he would've had occasion to address his troop."

Hofer, who at one time lived with her husband Humphrey Sutton in an artist colony on West Street in New York, also painted, spent time at her beloved piano, and loved traveling. Open and friendly, she is fond of discourse, except when working. Then, according to Mencarelli, "she becomes a machine; to some a tyrant, to others a true artist in the singleminded search [for] graphic perfection. When she works, . . . she seems to embody the Zen purity of absolute union between master and subject." Evelyn Hofer had solo exhibitions at the Witkin Gallery in New York in 1977, throughout the 1980s, and as late as 1991. In 1974, the photographer was honored at the Art Institute of Chicago with a solo showing of her work.

SOURCES:

Mencarelli, Jim. "Evelyn Hofer," in *The Grand Rapids [Michigan] Press.* June 30, 1974.

Rosenblum, Naomi. *A History of Women Photographers.* NY: Abbeville Press, 1994.

Barbara Morgan,
Melrose, Massachusetts

Hoffleit, E. Dorrit (1907—)

American astronomer who is best known for* The Bright Star Catalogue, *often defined as "the bible of virtually every stellar astronomer." *Name variations: Dorrit Hoffleit; Ellen Dorrit Hoffleit. Born Ellen Dorrit Hoffleit on March 12, 1907, in Florence, Alabama; daughter of Fred Hoffleit and Kate (Sanio) Hoffleit; Radcliffe College, A.B., 1928, M.A., 1932, Ph.D., 1938; never married; no children.*

Worked as a mathematician, Ballistic Research Lab, Aberdeen Proving Ground (1943–48), then consultant (1948–62); was a lecturer, Wellesley College (1955–56); worked as researcher, Harvard College Observatory (1929–56); was a research associate, Yale University Observatory (1956—); served as director of the Maria Mitchell Observatory, Nantucket, Massachusetts (1957—).

E. Dorrit Hoffleit, whose career spans over 70 years, is one of the most intriguing women in astronomy as well as one of the most visible. Her publication, *The Bright Star Catalogue,* which documents and maps some 9,110 stars visible to the naked eye, has become a bible of sorts to scientists and amateurs alike. Although she retired in 1975, Hoffleit still goes to her Yale office every day at 8:30 AM and rarely leaves before 7 PM. Cataracts now obscure her vision of the stars, but she continues to work, preferring to let nature decide when she should call it quits.

Hoffleit was born in 1907, in Florence, Alabama, and grew up in Cascade, Pennsylvania. Her interest in stars began early, when she saw two stars collide. As a child, she was somewhat overshadowed by her brilliant older brother, who finished high school at 14 and was accepted at Harvard. Despite her slower start, Hoffleit made it into Radcliffe, where she excelled in math and physics. After graduating cum laude in 1928, she accepted a low-paying job as a research assistant at Harvard College Observatory, working under **Henrietta Swope**. At the same time, Hoffleit began work on her master's degree, which she received from Radcliffe-Harvard in 1932.

Hoffleit's work with Swope involved searching Harvard's photographic plates for variable stars and analyzing their light curves. On her own time, however, Hoffleit pioneered a study of the light curves of the meteor trails that had inadvertently been captured on the photographs. Her work caught the attention of the observatory's director Harlow Shapley, who asked her to consider going on for a Ph.D. Hoffleit was reluctant at first, thinking she would be unable to pass the exams, but she was eventually convinced by the associate director, Bart Bok, to accept the challenge when he said emphatically: "If God recommends that you do something, it is your duty to do it." His no-nonsense attitude, she felt, was a turning point. She went on to complete a thesis on the spectroscopic absolute magnitudes of stars and earned her Ph.D. from Radcliffe in 1938, along with a prize for the best original work.

Hoffleit remained at Harvard until the war, when she was called to the Aberdeen Proving Ground's Ballistic Research laboratory in Maryland to work on war-related projects. She remembers that the military had nothing but disdain for female scientists. Despite her doctorate, she received a sub-professional ranking and was paid less for doing the same work as her male colleagues. Her stay there was unpleasant, and she protested. As a result, she was given her due rank and transferred to Washington.

After the war, she returned to Harvard, remaining there until Shapley retired and Donald H. Menzel took over as director of the observatory. Menzel had little use for fundamental research or for Hoffleit's projects, which he deemed obsolete. One of his early directives was the destruction of about a third of Harvard's photographic plate collection, an act that was termed a "slaughter" by some.

In 1956, Hoffleit joined the faculty of Yale, a position that included the directorship of the undergraduate summer program at the ***Maria Mitchell** Observatory in Nantucket, Massachusetts, which was named for America's first female astronomer. To honor Mitchell, who had once remarked, "I believe in women more than I do in astronomy," Hoffleit established a fund to provide summer jobs for female undergraduates

E. Dorrit Hoffleit

doing variable-star research. Over the years, the program flourished, ultimately providing more than 100 young women with a head start in the male-dominated field of astronomy. Hoffleit, who served as mentor, role model, and inspiration to many of the women, views the program as one of the joys of her old age. One of her former students, **Janet Mattei**, is now the director of the American Association of Variable Star Observers. "Where I am today and what I am today, I owe it all to her," said Mattei. "She was such a role model. She influenced my whole life and career."

At Yale, Hoffleit was asked to prepare a third edition of *The Bright Star Catalogue,* which was first published in 1930, then updated in 1940. The third edition, undertaken with part-time assistants, came out in 1964, and a fourth edition, prepared with Carlos Jaschek, was released in 1982; each successive catalogue contained more data than its predecessor.

Hoffleit's retirement years have been as productive as those she spent employed. In 1993, she published a book on the history of astronomy at Yale, and in 1996, with her Yale colleagues William van Altena and John Lee, she completed an 18-year project that culminated in the publication of the fourth edition of *The General Catalogue of Trigonometric Stellar Parallaxes*. The publication, used worldwide by astrophysicists, provides the precise measurements of distances to 8,112 stars. She is currently working on revisions for a fifth edition of *The Bright Star Catalogue*. Hoffleit, who still possesses an almost child-like curiosity, also spends weeks or even months poring over historical or observations records in order to answer some of the numerous requests she receives for miscellaneous information. "I have become as happy and independent as I had been in my youth at Harvard," she says about her retirement.

In May 1998, Hoffleit was inducted into the Connecticut Hall of Fame. On October 20, she was awarded an honorary doctor of science from Central Connecticut State University in New Britain. The citation read:

> It is a basic tenet of stellar astronomy that those stars which burn hottest and brightest and draw the most attention to themselves also burn out the quickest, rapidly becoming nothing more than fading memories. Meanwhile, those unassuming stars which steadily shine in the background, content to diligently produce energy at a more modest pace, continue to influence the universe with their light and heat for many generations to come.

SOURCES:

Greenberg, Brigitte, "Astronomer honored at symposium," in *The Day* [New London, CT]. March 8, 1997.

Hoffliet, Dorrit. "Some Glimpses from my Career," in *Mercury.* January–February 1992.

Levy, David H. "Astronomy's First Lady," in *Sky & Telescope.* Vol. 97, no. 2. February 1999.

SUGGESTED READING:

Shearer, Barbara S. and Benjamin. *Notable Women in the Physical Sciences.* CT: Greenwood Press, 1997.

Hoffman, Claire Giannini (1914—)

American business executive. *Born Claire Giannini in San Francisco, California, in 1914; daughter of Amadeo Peter Giannini (a banker); graduated from Mills College, Oakland, California; married Clifford P. Hoffman (an investment banker).*

The daughter of Amadeo Peter Giannini, the founder of the Bank of America, Claire Hoffman was born in 1914, raised in San Francisco, and attended Mills College in nearby Oakland. After graduating, she became her father's traveling companion and, upon his death in 1949, succeeded him as a director of the bank, the first woman to hold such an office. Hoffman would retain this position for 36 years, resigning only in 1985, after bank leaders sold the bank's headquarters, which she had considered a monument to her father.

In 1962, Hoffman also became the first woman to serve on the board of trustees of the Employees' Profit Sharing Pension Fund of Sears, Roebuck, the largest general merchandise company in the United States; a year later, she became the first woman to serve as director of Sears. Claire Hoffman was also a director of the American International Investment Corporation and a trustee of the Center for International Economic Growth. She served on the board of regents of St. Mary's College of California, and as a trustee of the Rosemary Hall School in Greenwich, Connecticut.

Hoffman, Malvina (1885–1966)

American sculptor of a prolific body of work who is much admired for her classic-style portrait busts and heroic sculpture. *Name variations: Mrs. Samuel Bonaries Grimson. Born Malvina Cornell Hoffman on June 15, 1885, in New York City (Hoffman wrote that the records of her birth were lost and her mother gave her birth date as 1887, but family documents proved the date was 1885); died on July 10, 1966, in New York City; daughter of Richard Hoffman (a noted con-*

cert pianist) and Fidelia Lamson Hoffman; sister of Helen Draper (1871–1951); attended the Chapin School and Brearley School, both New York (1904); during teenage years, attended Women's School of Applied Design and the Art Students League, New York; studied painting with John W. Alexander, modeling with Herbert Adams and George Grey Barnard at the Veltin School, New York, and sculpture with Gutzon Borglum in New York; intermittently between 1910 and 1914, studied in Paris with Auguste Rodin and others; married Samuel Bonaries Grimson, in 1924 (divorced 1936); no children.

Awards: honorable mention for Russian Dancers, *Paris Salon (1910); first prize for* Bacchanal Russe, *Paris Exhibition (1911); honorable mention at Panama-Pacific Exposition, San Francisco (1915); Julia S. Shaw memorial prize for* Bacchanal Russe, *National Academy of Design (1917); George D. Widener gold medal from Pennsylvania Academy of Fine Arts (1920); Helen Foster Barnett prize from the National Academy of Design (1921); Elizabeth N. Watrous gold medal from the National Academy of Design (1924); prize from the Concord Art Association (1925); Joan of Arc gold medal from the National Association of Women Painters and Sculptors (1935); Outstanding Woman of Achievement award from the N.Y. League of Business and Professional Women (1935); award for Eminent Achievement from the American Woman's Association (1937); selected as one of 12 women whose work has contributed most toward human betterment in the last half-century, Career Tours Committee, in cooperation with the N.Y. World's Fair (1939); named Woman of the Year by the American Association of University Women (1957); gold medal for* Mongolian Archer *from the Allied Artists of America (1962); gold medal of honor from the National Sculpture Society (1964). Decorations: Palmes Academiques (France, 1920); Royal Order of St. Sava III (Yugoslavia, 1921); Legion of Honor (France, 1951). Honorary Degrees: Doctor of Literature, Mount Holyoke College (1937); Doctor of Fine Arts, University of Rochester (1937); Doctor of Fine Arts, Northwestern University (1945); Honorary Doctorate, Bates College (1955).*

Selected work in the collections of Metropolitan Museum of Art, American Museum of Natural History, and the Frick Collection, New York; Brooklyn Institute of Arts and Sciences, Brooklyn, New York; Chicago Natural History Museum, Chicago, Illinois; Luxembourg Gardens, Paris, among many other museums and private collections across the world. Some notable works on permanent exhibition: Russian Bacchanale *(bronze group, 1915, Luxembourg Gardens, Paris, stolen by Nazis, 1941);* La Gavotte *(wax, Metropolitan Museum of Art, N.Y., 1915);* The Sacrifice *(stone group, Harvard University War Memorial Chapel, Cambridge, 1920);* 104 Racial Types of the World *(bronze, life-size figures and busts, Chicago Natural History Museum, 1929–33).*

Exhibited extensively in New York, across the country and abroad, beginning in 1910. First exhibit: Grand Central Art Gallery (New York City, 1929), 105 sculptures in 16 different materials along with many life-sized crayon portraits. Major retrospective exhibit: Virginia Museum of Fine Arts, Richmond, Virginia, 1937.

Selected writings: (memoir) Heads and Tales *(NY: Garden City, 1936); (combination autobiography and technical information text)* Sculpture Inside and Out *(NY: W.W. Norton, 1939);* Yesterday is Tomorrow: A Personal History *(NY: Crown, 1965).*

Malvina Hoffman, an internationally recognized sculptor, was born in New York City on June 15, 1885. Her father Richard Hoffman, was a concert pianist, soloist with the New York Philharmonic, and music teacher. A child prodigy in England, he had come to America at age 16, hired by P.T. Barnum as an accompanist for the Swedish soprano ***Jenny Lind** on Lind's first tour of the United States. Malvina's mother **Fidelia Lamson Hoffman**, a member of a socially prominent New York family, was descended from early English colonists. Fidelia's marriage was for many years regarded as a disgrace by the Lamson family.

Malvina's childhood was spent in New York City. Having the actress ***Lillian Russell** as a neighbor provided a "panorama of excitement," recalled Hoffman. "Born and brought up as I was in the lurid atmosphere of Broadway and Forty-third Street, I was nevertheless one of a household which conserved the traditional habits of the Puritanical forefathers and conventional groups of numberless relatives."

Nurtured in a loving family atmosphere where art and music were appreciated and supported, Hoffman was the fourth girl and youngest of six children (the eldest girl died in infancy). She was fascinated by electric batteries, mechanical toys, and horses as a child, and her father encouraged these interests. By devising games that sharpened her powers of observation and developed her memory, he guided her intellectual development. He also defined musical principals of construction, rhythm, balance, and harmony as paradigms for the practice of any art form, instilling in Hoffman a lifelong sense of the artist's vocation.

The Hoffmans summered at Little Boar's Head, Maine, an ongoing experience that Malvina treasured. The town remained an escape for her when social, business, and artistic pressures became too great. In her autobiography, *Yesterday is Tomorrow,* Hoffman depicts the array of experiences for a small child in a "sheltered" family vacation spot, a small child who had the freedom to explore.

She attended two private schools in New York, Chapin then Brearley. While at Brearley, she also took classes at the Women's School of Applied Design and the Art Students League, studying composition, watercolor, and life drawing. A reprimand from a Brearley teacher for her "insubordination" resulted in a visit to the headmaster, James G. Croswell, who soon discovered the cause of Hoffman's short temper: a heavy academic and artistic workload. Recognizing her artistic talent, he asked to see her drawings so that he might keep track of what she was doing, rather than forbid the extra work. Croswell encouraged her to conserve her energy for each task. One summer, when she was ill with fever, the Croswells invited her to their summer home at Deer Island, Maine, to recuperate, binding a lasting friendship. Hoffman did an oil portrait of Croswell the following year which he preferred to the formal portrait the school had commissioned. Later at the Veltin School, she studied painting with John Alexander and sculpture with George Grey Barnard and Herbert Adams.

When Hoffman was 16, the suicide of a family friend resulted in a nervous collapse. This act of desperation shook her to her roots, she wrote, and she became restless and withdrawn. Instinctively, she bought some modeling clay, hoping to work her way out of the mental impasse. "There would seem no other reason why I should have turned to sculpture at that time. There was a consolation in this new struggle in three-dimensional silence that claimed my whole mind and attention." Her first work, a female figure called "Despair," expressed all she knew of grief, and her father encouraged her to have it cast in plaster. He advised her that purging her system of what troubled her would be a release, and if sculpture accomplished this, then the creative effort was a consolation in itself.

Hoffman's next effort was a clay portrait of her father, earning an important critique from Gutzon Borglum, a family friend and mentor, who would execute the Mount Rushmore presidential monument. Borglum encouraged her to submit the plaster cast to the National Academy of Design Exhibition in 1910. That same year, her father died. When Hoffman expressed a desire to carve her father's portrait in marble, another family friend, sculptor Phimister Proctor, taught her the rudiments of carving and offered her the use of his studio in MacDougall Alley while he was away for the summer. Working on the sculpture helped blunt the pain. "Carving became a harbor of safety into which I could steer my thoughts and sense a sort of salvation by self obliteration," Hoffman told **Charlotte Rubinstein**. "It became the deciding factor in my decision to become a sculptor."

After her father's death, Hoffman worked hard to provide an income for her impoverished family. A year later, a windfall in the form of a $1,000 legacy allowed Hoffman to sail with her mother to France. Intent on studying with the great sculptor Auguste Rodin, Hoffman called at his studio five times and was five times refused. In desperation, she informed the concierge that she would stand on the doorstep until she saw the master, as she was bringing regards from one of his patrons. She was finally admitted and caught Rodin's interest by quoting a sonnet by Alfred de Musset that Rodin was trying to recall for a roomful of friends. Examples of her work, along with her persistent efforts and a letter of introduction from Borglum, convinced Rodin of her talent. She studied with him for 16 months, until her money ran out. Once back in New York, Hoffman opened her own studio and also followed Rodin's advice, studying dissection and anatomy under the direction of Dr. George Huntington at the Columbia University College of Physicians and Surgeons. Hoffman resumed her studies with Rodin during the two summers before the outbreak of World War I in 1914. While studying with Rodin and Emanuele Rosales, she also learned bronze casting, chasing and finishing at foundries. It was Rodin who formed Hoffman as an artist.

During her years in Paris, Hoffman was acquainted with author ***Gertrude Stein**, artists Monet, Matisse, and Brancusi, dancer Nijinsky, and was a close friend of dancer ***Anna Pavlova**. Like many other artists of the period, Hoffman was influenced by the Ballet Russe of Sergei Diaghilev. Robert McHenry suggests that Hoffman attempted to capture in her sculpture "that new kind of freedom in the dance" and to convey "its sense of motion and immediacy." Pavlova arranged for Hoffman to make studies backstage and at night, after her performances, would arrive at Hoffman's studio to pose, sometimes with male partners, shouting "Malvinoushka!" as she ran up the stairs. Hoffman's *Russ-*

Malvina Hoffman

ian Dancers won first honorable mention at the Paris Salon in 1911, and *Bacchanale Russe* was awarded the Shaw memorial prize by the National Academy of Design in 1917, both bronze groups portrayed the figures of Pavlova and Mikhail Mordkin. *Bacchanale Russe,* purchased by the French government and placed in the Luxembourg Gardens in Paris, was taken by the Nazis in 1941.

In 1915, Hoffman captured the incredibly slender lightness of Pavlova's movements in *La*

Gavotte, a composition of balanced diagonal lines, playing against the swinging curves of the skirt. Other works based on the dancer were created, including a 26-panel frieze *Bacchanale,* showing the principal movements in Pavlova's wildly erotic *pas de deux*. This project was never exhibited. For Pavlova's birthday, Hoffman threw a masked costume ball for 200 in her Sniffen Court stable-studio. Dancers and mimes in fantastic costumes performed all night in the roped-off alley. At midnight, the gilded doors of a giant icon were opened, revealing Pavlova posed as a Byzantine Madonna, hands folded together in prayer. Hoffman preserved this image in a sculpture she called *Byzantine Madonna.* These sculptures from the Pavlova group launched her career.

With the onset of war, Hoffman returned to New York to work for the Red Cross with her sister, ◂❖ **Helen Draper** (1871–1951). Hoffman also became the American representative of *Appui aux Artistes,* a French war charity benefiting needy artists which she helped found before leaving France. For the U.S. government, she reported on relief work in Greece and the Balkans to Herbert Hoover, who was then chair of the American Relief Committee. After the war, Hoffman continued to aid Yugoslav causes and was for many years chair of the New York Chapter of the United Yugoslav Relief Fund. She directed the work in Yugoslavia at Hoover's child-feeding centers which were founded after the war.

In 1910, Hoffman had received an honorable mention at the Paris Salon for a bust of Samuel Bonaries Grimson. She had formed a deep and close friendship with Grimson, an English violinist and friend of her father. Though the two became engaged, they were separated for some years while each pursued a career. When Grimson was injured by a grenade in WWI and could no longer play violin professionally, both determined to postpone marriage no longer. They were wed in 1924 in New York.

In 1920, Hoffman had been commissioned by **Martha W. Bacon** to create a war memorial to commemorate the deaths of Harvard students killed in World War I. The stone carving, *The Sacrifice* (Harvard University Memorial Chapel, 1922), shows a Madonna-like figure mourning over a fallen crusader, in the manner of a medieval tomb sculpture. Hoffman had entered her heroic phase. In 1924, commissioned by American businessman Irving Bush, she executed a two-figure composition representing Anglo-American friendship, *To the Friendship of English Speaking Peoples* (stone, two heroic figures and altar, London, 1924). Erected on the facade of Bush House in London, the colossal, carved-limestone figures, representing England and America, hold a torch above a Celtic altar in what Rubinstein calls "an archaic neo-Greek relief style." After these 15-foot figures were hoisted into place above the entry of the nine-story office building, Hoffman felt the sun did not hit the work directly. She spent the next five weeks on four boards, 80 feet in the air, deepening the carving to better show the forms. Dramatic photographs show Hoffman at work, far above the street, seated on the shoulder of her gargantuan figures. "She behaved as if she had wings and carried a torch," wrote her close friend, poet ***Marianne Moore**.

In 1926, Hoffman yielded to her restlessness and left New York to find the "islands of the Lotus Eaters" off the coast of Africa. There, she was inspired to create two powerful African heads, *Martinique Woman* and *Senegalese Soldier* (black Belgian marble, Brooklyn Institute of Arts and Sciences, N.Y., 1928). In 1927, approached by a dean of the Harvard Medical School, Hoffman designed the stone monument *The Four Horsemen of the Apocalypse* to be placed in front of the school. With the execution of this piece in mind, she traveled to Yugoslavia to study architectural and equestrian sculpture with Ivan Mestrovic, whose over-life-size portrait she had completed in 1925 (bronze, Brooklyn Institute of Arts and Sciences, N.Y.). Though she returned to finish the Harvard Medical School monument, funding was never secured, and the monument remains only a vision in drawings and studies. Hoffman's first extensive exhibition came in 1929 at the Grand Central Art Gallery in New York City, and included 105 pieces of sculpture in 16 different materials, plus crayon portraits. The exhibit traveled to museums across the country for five years.

❖▸ **Draper, Helen** (1871–1951)

Red Cross worker. *Name variations: Mrs. William K. Draper. Born Helen Hoffman in 1871; died in 1951; daughter of Richard Hoffman (a noted concert pianist) and Fidelia Lamson Hoffman; sister of* ***Malvina Hoffman;*** *married William K. Draper (died 1926).*

During the Spanish-American war, Helen Draper headed the New York chapter of the American Red Cross. By marriage, she was related to solo performer ***Ruth Draper**.

Malvina Hoffman (top) and Anna Pavlova.

The pivotal work that brought Malvina Hoffman international recognition came from a 1929 commission by Chicago's Field Museum of Natural History to be completed for the Chicago World's Fair in 1933. The commission came in the form of a telegram: "HAVE PROPOSITION TO MAKE STOP DO YOU CARE TO CONSIDER IT? STOP RACIAL TYPES TO BE MODELED WHILE TRAVELING AROUND THE WORLD STOP." Hoffman had been singled out from 3,000 artists to receive what was to be the largest sculptural commission ever given to a woman, and possibly the largest ever created by one sculptor anywhere. She convinced the museum officials to give her the entire job, originally planned for three to five artists.

The original commission called for plaster figures, but Hoffman persuaded the committee to cast most of the pieces in bronze. She began the project in Paris, where she had built a house and second studio. At the outset, Hoffman was fortunate to secure models in Paris, because a colonial exposition had brought people from Africa and Asia to the city. She then traveled to Japan, India, Africa, China, Bali and elsewhere on a "head-hunting" expedition. Pneumonia, sunstroke, an infection that nearly took her arm and other ailments felled her periodically, as she and her husband Sam Grimson journeyed by train, steamer, or Chinese junk to remote places. Grimson was her photographer as they moved 27 trunks and sculptural materials around the globe. Returning with models of a series of racial types, Hoffman spent three more years completing the work. The collection, consisting of over 100 heads and figures of men and women from Africa, Asia, Europe, the Pacific Islands and North America, was dedicated on June 6, 1933. Noted the 1940 *Current Biography*: "In the Hall of Man at the Field Museum stood 101 life-size bronze statues, standing as an enduring monument to her perseverance, energy, creative genius." (Sources place the number of pieces in the collection alternately as 104, 105, or 110.) Now most of Hoffman's sculptures for the Hall of Man Exhibit at the Field Museum are in storage, while some copies are in the permanent collections of other museums. Only in old photographs can one glimpse the overall impact made by the original installation of over 100 studies surrounding a central column depicting the so-called white, black and yellow races topped by a central globe. Writes **Myrna Eden**: "Although impressive, the heads and figures in the museum's Hall of Man are more anthropological studies than works of art. Hoffman's attention to detail distinguishes all her work." Notes Rubinstein:

> The commission brought income and publicity, but one may seriously question the impact of the assignment on her life's work. Years of grueling effort, at the peak of the artist's creative period, were devoted to a project that as art historian Linda Nochlin points out "lies somewhere between science and art."

The importance of this work as compared to Hoffman's other efforts is disputed, but the collection remains a focus of her career. It became one of the most popular exhibitions in the world.

To define Hoffman's style, one must look at the complete body of her work. Excited by the Armory Show in New York in 1913, Hoffman wrote:

> The violence of the rejections and cheers disturbed me, and I could not make up my mind how I felt. . . . I was very much aware of the Brancusi head . . . his courage in slashing away all the details . . . but some of the other work in the exhibition seemed false, and I resented any touch of falseness. . . . I thought Classic work had endured, and there must be a reason . . . and even what is "modern" isn't altogether new.

Though she lived through one of the most revolutionary eras in the history of art, she remained true to the classical and realistic while her contemporaries were the innovators. Hoffman's fundamental interest was the personality of the sitter, not in some new formal approach. "I wondered if it might not be some defect in me not to have experimented more," she said. "But I wasn't sufficiently impelled." She rarely took liberties with nature, as is evident in the Hall of Man project. Hoffman's finest works, writes Rubinstein, include the small bronzes and portraits, while the studies of Pavlova convey passion and freedom. *Bill Working* (bronze, Museum of Fine Arts, Springfield, MA, 1923) is a study of her devoted studio caretaker, cleaning the floor, a natural portrait of a close friend. Myrna Eden concurs: "Hoffman's artistry is most fully displayed in her naturalistic portrait busts of friends and acquaintances. An unending interest in people led her beyond the mere recording of physical features to seek the depths of personalities."

At the height of Hoffman's success, she was plagued by an emotionally draining family crisis. Her husband suffered from severe depression, resulting from his war experiences, his injury, and his inability to play the violin. When Grimson's doctors advised a separation, Hoffman was saddened but followed their advice. There was no improvement in his condition, and the doctors recommended in 1934 that their married life come to an end. "I was so stricken by this decision that my life seemed a total shipwreck," Hoffman relates. "In my desolate heart I felt as if there could never be a new dawn. . . . My inner light was blocked out." After an enforced residency in Reno, Nevada, Hoffman was accompanied home by friends. Another close friend, musician Ignace Paderewski, convinced her to write *Heads and Tales*, an account of her travels and work on the Hall of Man project, to divert her from the overwhelming emotional stress that was enveloping her. It was published in 1936, the year of her divorce.

Malvina Hoffman working on a sculpture for Bush House, 90 feet above street level.

With emotional support from friends, Hoffman was able to continue working on her many commissions. For the 1939 New York's World's Fair, she created a cylindrical fountain carved with seven dancers of different nationalities modeled in high relief. Called the *International Dance Fountain* and considered one of the outstanding sculptures at the Fair, it was selected to be one of the permanent pieces to be installed in Flushing Meadows Park after the Fair's close. In reality, to the artist's dismay, it was destroyed when no final plans were established.

Hoffman was continually searching for new avenues to help emerging artists and to hone her own craft. When the studio next door to hers on East 35th Street became available, she purchased it and began a demonstration workshop dedicated to teaching young artists the skills of sculpture, casting, carving, and forge work. During World War II, when Hoffman was again associated with the Red Cross and relief work, the demonstration exhibits were used by the Metropolitan Museum of Art in New York for educational purposes. Hoffman replaced the teaching models in her workshop in 1948.

In the late 1940s and '50s, Hoffman received two important assignments for works in bas-relief. The U.S. Fine Arts Commission engaged her as sculptor in 1948 for a monument to the fallen American soldiers of World War II at Epinal, France, in the Vosges Mountains. Her principal contributions to the American War Memorial Building (marble, Epinal, France, 1948) were two façade panels showing the fighting men. In 1956, she completed a frieze depicting the history of medicine, using an incised, Egyptian-Art Deco style suited to the architecture for the Joslin Diabetes Center in Boston, Massachusetts.

Through her long career until her retirement in 1963, Hoffman modeled such diverse personalities as Wendell L. Willkie (stone bust, Corcoran Gallery of Art, Washington, D.C., 1944), Teilhard de Chardin (1948), and ***Katharine Cornell** (1961). She completed three busts of Ignace Paderewski in 1922–23: *The Statesman* (bronze heroic bust, Steinway Hall, New York), *The Man, The Artist* (bronze head, Metropolitan Museum of Art) and *The Friend.* Relying on her knowledge of anatomy from her early studies at the Columbia University College of Physicians and Surgeons, Hoffman created a series of anatomical models showing human embryological development from conception through birth. The work was commissioned by the Field Museum in Chicago in 1937; the resulting series, reproduced often, was used as a teaching resource in schools worldwide. They are still on display, anonymously, in medical schools throughout the country.

In appearance, Malvina Hoffman was tall and slim; in manner, alert and direct. For posed photographs, she always seemed to have at hand a floppy, velvet beret and a smock, along with the standard mallet and chisel expected of sculptors. If she wasn't daring in her art, she was dauntless in the way she lived. She gave many parties in her East 35th Street studio where she made her home for more than 45 years, parties which were reported in the society columns. Ranging from the birthday ball for Anna Pavlova to a party for merchant marines from the 32 nations at war with Hitler's Germany, Malvina Hoffman made good copy for the tabloid journals of the 1930s, and she seemed to know what would make a story. Her travels around the world, with tales of the peoples she met, kept the journalists busy and the Hall of Man project in the minds of Americans. Her work is in the permanent collections of galleries and museums throughout the world.

Jane Hoge

In 1937, Hoffman had a retrospective exhibit at the Virginia Museum of Fine Arts at Richmond. In 1964, she received the gold medal of honor from the National Sculpture Society. She was made a member of the French Legion of Honor and was awarded honorary degrees by American colleges. As an author, her works include a textbook, *Sculpture, Inside and Out,* and two autobiographies, *Heads and Tales* (1943) and *Yesterday is Tomorrow: A Personal History* (1965). On July 10, 1966, Malvina Hoffman died of a heart attack in her sleep at her studio. She was 81.

SOURCES:

Collins, Jim, and Glenn B. Opitz, ed. *Women Artists in America: 18th Century to the Present.* Poughkeepsie, NY: Apollo, 1980.

Falk, Peter Hastings, ed. *Who Was Who in American Art.* Madison, CT: Soundview Press, 1985.

Hoffman, Malvina. *Heads and Tales.* Garden City, NY: Garden City Publishing, 1943.

———. *Malvina Hoffman* (American Sculpture Series 5). NY: W.W. Norton (under the auspices of the National Sculpture Society, 1948).

———. *Sculpture Inside and Out.* NY: W.W.Norton, 1939.

———. *Yesterday is Tomorrow: A Personal History.* NY: Crown, 1965.

"Malvina Hoffman," in *Current Biography, 1940.* NY: H.W. Wilson, 1941.

McHenry, Robert, ed. *Liberty's Women.* Springfield, MA: G. & C. Merriam, 1980.

The New York Times (obituary). July 11, 1966.

Opitz, Glenn B., ed. *Dictionary of American Sculptors: 18th Century to the Present.* Poughkeepsie, NY: Apollo, 1984.

Rubinstein, Charlotte Streifer. *American Women Artists.* Boston: G.K. Hall, 1982.

———. *American Women Sculptors.* Boston: G.K. Hall, 1990.

Sicherman, Barbara, and Carol Hurd Green, eds. *Notable American Women: The Modern Period.* Cambridge, MA: The Belknap Press of Harvard University Press, 1980.

SUGGESTED READING:

Bouve, Pauline Carrington. "The Two Foremost Women Sculptors in America: Anna Vaughan Hyatt and Malvina Hoffman," in *Art and Archaeology.* June 1928, pp. 74–82.

COLLECTIONS:

Correspondence relating to the National Institute of Arts and Letters are at the American Academy of Arts and Letters, New York City; works are included in the permanent collections of museums, galleries, universities and in cities and parks throughout the world.

Laurie Twist Binder,
Library Media Specialist, City of Buffalo Schools, and freelance graphic artist and illustrator, Lake View, New York

Hoge, Mrs. A.H. (1811–1890).

See Hoge, Jane.

Hoge, Jane (1811–1890)

American reformer who is best known for her work during the Civil War. *Name variations: Mrs. A.H. Hoge. Born Jane Currie Blaikie on July 31, 1811, in Philadelphia, Pennsylvania; died in Chicago, Illinois, on August 26, 1890; daughter of George Dundas (a trader) and Mary (Monroe) Blaikie; graduated from the Young Ladies' College in Philadelphia; married Abraham Holmes Hoge, on June 2, 1831; children: thirteen, eight of whom lived to maturity.*

Moved from Pittsburgh to Chicago (1848); was founder and president of Home for the Friendless (1858); with Mary Livermore, directed Chicago (later Northwestern) Sanitary Commission, 1862–65); was a fund raiser and Board of Trustees member for Evanston College for Ladies (1871–74), when it merged with Northwestern University; headed the Woman's Presbyterian Board of Foreign Missions in the Northwest (1872–85). Publications: The Boys in Blue *(1867).*

Jane Hoge's initial involvement in the Civil War relief effort was an extremely personal one. When two of her sons enlisted, she volunteered as a nurse for son George's regiment which was at Camp Douglas in Chicago. Her final trip to the field in June 1863 was also a private mission, to bring that same son, colonel of his regiment of volunteers, back from Vicksburg because he had sustained a serious head injury.

Although publicity emphasized the motherliness of her dedication to individual soldiers, her work was of much broader importance than that of a nurse. With her friend ***Mary Livermore**, Hoge co-administered the Chicago Sanitary Commission (1862–65), making it a remarkably successful volunteer organization for fund-raising and for collecting and distributing medical supplies and food to northern Civil War soldiers. Mary Livermore praised Hoge for her marked executive ability and appreciated the fact that "her force of character was irresistible, and bore down all opposition." Hoge's version of the war, told in *The Boys in Blue* (1867), is primarily a series of stylized vignettes about individual soldiers, but it does contain a chapter about the Sanitary Fair of 1863, the extremely successful fundraiser organized by the two women, as well as some material written by Mary Livermore (M.A.L.) which does not appear in her own book, *My Story of the War* (1887).

Though Hoge is best known for her Civil War volunteerism, she came to this challenge already experienced as a dedicated benevolent worker. She had helped to found the Chicago Home for the Friendless in 1858, was president of its board, and had been involved on a daily basis in all the practical work of running the Home. After the war, she took up the cause of women's education, helping to raise funds to establish the Evanston College for Ladies (1871) with ***Frances E. Willard** as president. Hoge served on the Board of Trustees until the college made a controversial merger with Northwestern University in 1874. She died in Chicago on August 26, 1890.

SOURCES:

Hoge, Mrs. A.H. [Jane Currie]. *The Boys in Blue.* NY: E.B. Treat, 1867.

James, Edward T., ed. *Notable American Women, 1607–1950.* Cambridge, MA: Belknap Press of Harvard University Press, 1971, pp. 199–201.

Livermore, Mary A. *My Story of the War.* Hartford, CT: A.D. Worthington, 1889.

SUGGESTED READING:

McCarthy, Kathleen D. *Noblesse Oblige: Charity and Cultural Philanthropy in Chicago, 1849–1929.* Chicago, IL: University of Chicago Press, 1982.

COLLECTIONS:

E.B. Washburne Papers and Robert Todd Lincoln Collection, Library of Congress.

Sophie S. Rogers Collection, Genealogical Society of Pennsylvania.

Northwestern University Archives.

Dorsey Phelps,
editorial director of Monthly Review Press, New York City

Hogg, Ima (1882–1975)

***American philanthropist who funded music, education, and the field of mental health.** Born on July 10, 1882, in Mineola, Texas; died in London, England, on August 19, 1975; only daughter and second of four children of James Stephen Hogg (lawyer and governor of Texas) and Sallie (Stinson) Hogg; graduated from Carrington Preparatory School; attended University of Texas (1899–1901); studied piano at the National Conservatory in New York and in Germany; never married; no children.*

Known simply as "Miss Ima" in her home state of Texas, philanthropist Ima Hogg was one of four children of **Sallie Stinson Hogg** and James Stephen Hogg, a political heavyweight and the state's first native-born governor. James, seemingly unaware that he was subjecting his daughter to a lifetime of ridicule, named her after the heroine of a poem, "The Fate of Marvin," written by his brother. The unusual name caused Hogg a lifetime of pain that was sometimes shared by the rest of the family. She later recalled that her older brother Will often came home from school bloodied from schoolyard fights defending her.

Hogg was raised amid the political figures and famous people that frequented the governor's mansion. (She was just nine when she attended her father's inauguration.) It was a privileged, carefree childhood, saddened only by the early death of her mother from tuberculosis. Remaining particularly close to her father and brothers, Hogg attended Carrington Preparatory School and spent much of her free time practicing the piano. She spent two years at the University of Texas, leaving to continue her music studies at the

National Conservatory of Music in New York City, and later in Germany. Meanwhile, her father pursued an interest in the fledgling Texas oil industry. Upon his death in 1906, James Hogg left his children not only a legacy of civic responsibility, but several parcels of real estate in West Columbia bubbling with oil. With the income from her father's estate and her oil profits, Hogg devoted herself to the betterment of Texas.

In 1909, she moved to Houston, where she lived until 1975. In keeping with her interest in music, she undertook a major role in establishing a symphony orchestra in that city. With a group of her friends, she solicited donations, organized the local musicians, and arranged for the first concert, which was held in 1913, at Houston's Majestic Theater. From these early efforts, the Houston symphony rose to become one of the nation's finest orchestras. Throughout her life, Hogg continued to contribute to the symphony, serving as president of the Symphony Society for a number of years and kicking off each season with a gala party in her home. She was influential in bringing world-famous conductors to Houston and, in 1946, donated an extra $100,000 to the annual budget in order to obtain the services of Efrem Kurtz. Called Houston's "Empress of the Symphony" by *Time* magazine, Hogg was honored in 1972 when Artur Rubinstein appeared with the symphony to celebrate her 90th birthday.

Second to Hogg's love of music was her love of antique furniture, which she began seriously collecting in 1920, with the help and encouragement of her brother Will. In 1927, when their combined collection became so extensive that it could not be housed, they commissioned Houston architect John Staub to build Bayou Bend, a house that would provide an adequate backdrop for the collection and also serve as the family home. In 1966, according to a preconceived plan, Hogg gave the mansion and the collection (which included rare Duncan Phyfe and Chippendale furniture, as well as paintings by American artists John Singleton Copley, Charles Willson Peale, and Edward Hicks) to the Houston Museum of Fine Arts for use as a decorative arts museum. "When you love something enough it's easy to give it up in order to see it go on," she said, when asked whether she would miss her home. According to Lee Malone, a director of the museum, the Hogg collection was one of the best in the country, rivaling only that of the Metropolitan Museum's American wing and the Dupont's Winterthur Museum in Delaware.

In conjunction with her love of antiques, Hogg also undertook several important historic restorations, including her parents' first home in Quitman, Texas; the Varner-Hogg plantation near West Columbia, which she donated to Texas in 1958 as a state park; and the historic Winedale Inn in Fayette County, built in 1834, and purchased by Hogg in 1963. After initially thinking she would move the inn to Bayou Bend, Hogg decided to restore it on site. To insure the authenticity of the restoration, she went to New York to study how it should be done, and upon her return took a cottage nearby in order to supervise the work to her perfectionist standards. The completed restoration, authentic down to its square nails and wallpaper designs, was given to the University of Texas in 1965, with an endowment for its support and a plan to make it a center for the study of the ethnic cultures which had migrated to Texas in the early 19th century.

Hogg had two other consuming interests: education and mental health, both of which had also engaged her father. In 1943, at the request of the Citizen's Educational Committee, she ran for a seat on the school board, even though it was against her better judgment. "She was interested in getting a liberal school board," remembered a friend, "in getting visiting teachers and nurses for the schools." Hogg won the election for a six-year term but took a beating for her liberal views and decided not to try for a second term. She never again ran for public office, though she remained committed to the city's young people. She was instrumental in founding the Houston Child Guidance Center, a pioneering institution in child psychiatry, and also supported the children's concerts started by Houston Symphony conductor Ernst Hoffman.

Like her older brother Will, Hogg had strong ties to the University of Texas. When Will died in 1930, he left the bulk of his estate to the university with the stipulation that another family member could determine its use, provided he or she also contributed to the same purpose. In accordance with this provision, and feeling that her brother would approve her decision, Hogg chose to support the field of mental health. In 1940, the Hogg Foundation was established; its mission was to improve quality of life with new approaches to mental health. The Foundation, which was centered at the university, began by sending a group of men and women to small towns and rural areas in the state to lecture on the subject of mental health. (One newspaper referred to them as a "new type of circuit rider.") Through the years, programs shifted to meet changing needs. During the war, efforts were focused on helping resolve the problems of military families and of those working in industry for the

Ima Hogg

first time. In later years, programs were expanded to include community services, the education and training of mental health professionals, publication of books and materials, and contributions to research.

Somewhat shy and overshadowed by her brothers in her youth, Hogg grew more outspoken with age, although her willfulness was always tempered with charm and modesty. Bestowed with numerous honors throughout her life, she was always quick to credit others. When accepting an honorary degree from Southwestern University, she told the audience: "In honoring me you honor many other people, for my fulfillment is due to the work of others." As an old woman, Hogg was a regal presence, quite formal at times, but filled with a zest for living. At a 93rd birthday celebration, she enjoyed hot dogs and chili, washed down with her famous Fishhouse punch. Soon after that birthday, Hogg embarked on a trip to England, although friends cautioned her against traveling so far at her advanced age. "When you're ninety-three, it doesn't matter where you die," she quipped. Ima Hogg was hospitalized in London after a fall from a taxi, and died there of a heart attack on August 19, 1975.

SOURCES:

Crawford, Ann Fears, and Crystal Sasse Ragsdale. *Women in Texas*. Austin, TX: State House Press, 1992.

Iscoe, Louise Kosches. *Ima Hogg: First Lady of Texas.* Austin, TX: Hogg Foundation for Mental Health, 1976.

Sicherman, Barbara, and Carol Hurd Green, eds. *Notable American Women: The Modern Period.* Cambridge, MA: The Belknap Press of Harvard University Press, 1980.

Barbara Morgan,
Melrose, Massachusetts

Hogshead, Nancy (1962—)

American swimmer who won three Olympic gold medals. *Born in Iowa City, Iowa, on April 17, 1962.*

Won a gold medal in the 100-meter freestyle (tying with Carrie Steinseifer), in the 4x100-meter medley relay, and in the 4x100-meter freestyle, and a silver medal in the 200-meter individual medley, in the Los Angeles Olympics (1984).

Nancy Hogshead began swimming competitively in 1976, specializing in the butterfly and individual medley. She soon was placing 2nd and 3rd in many competitions, but it was not until 1977 that she won two gold medals in national competition, both in butterfly, in the 100 yards and 200 meters. In 1978, she won a gold in the 200-yards butterfly. Named to the 1980 Olympic team, Hogshead was in her prime when the American boycott of the Moscow Olympics dashed her hopes for a medal. In 1981 and 1982, she stayed out of competition, deciding that training was simply too grueling.

In 1983, she was named the Comeback Swimmer of the Year after she won a bronze in the 200-yards and 200-meter butterfly. Then, Hogshead began to work on freestyle and at the U.S. Swimming International meet in January 1984, she won bronze medals in the 100- and 200-meter freestyle. She was also high-point scorer. At the indoor nationals that same year, Hogshead took the gold in freestyle.

When the Los Angeles Olympics arrived, the comeback swimmer was ready. Hogshead won a gold medal in the 100-meter freestyle tying with **Carrie Steinseifer** at 55:92, the first time two gold medals were awarded for a dead heat. Teamed with Carrie, **Jenna Johnson**, and **Dara Torres**, Hogshead also won a gold in the 4x100-meter freestyle relay. Swimming with **Theresa Andrews**, ***Tracy Caulkins**, and ***Mary T. Meagher** in the 4x100-meter medley Hogshead picked up her third gold. She then swam behind Caulkins in the 200-meter individual medley to pick up a silver.

Karin Loewen Haag,
Athens, Georgia

Hogue, Micki (b. 1944).

See King, Micki.

Hohenberg, duchess of (1868–1914).

See Chotek, Sophie.

Hohenhausen, Elizabeth (1789–1857)

German poet, dramatist, and novelist. *Name variations: Baroness von Hohenhausen. Born Elizabeth Philippine Amalie von Ochs in Waldau, near Cassel, Germany, on November 4, 1789; died at Frankfort-on-the-Oder, Germany, on December 2, 1857; daughter of General Adam Ludwig von Ochs; married Baron Leopold von Hohenhausen (died 1848).*

In 1817, Baroness Elizabeth Hohenhausen published a book of poetry titled *Flowers of Spring.* She also wrote a historical drama, *John and Cornelius de Witt,* which was well-received. Her recollections were contained in *Nature, Art, and Life.*

Hohenlohe, princess of.

See Anna Maria Theresa (1879–1961).

Hohenlohe-Langenburg, princess of.

See Feodore of Leiningen (1807–1872).
See Adelaide of Hohenlohe-Langenburg (1835–1900).
See Leopoldine (1837–1903).
See Alexandra Saxe-Coburg (1878–1942).

Hōjo Masako (1157–1225)

Japanese regent who significantly strengthened the rule of the Kamakura Shōgunate, the warrior government of medieval Japan, which had been established by her husband Minamoto no Yoritomo. *Name variations: Hojo Masako; popularly known as "the nun-general." Pronunciation: HOE-joe mah-SAH-koe. Born in Izu Province, Japan, in 1157; died in Kamakura, Japan, in 1225; eldest daughter of Hōjo Tokimasa, a warrior; married Minamoto no Yoritomo (1147–1199), shōgun, founder of the Kamakura Shōgunate; children: (sons) Yoriie and Sanetomo; (daughters)* ***Ohime*** *and one other.*

"Hōjo Masako . . . was one of the most powerful and influential women the male-dominated society of pre-modern Japan ever produced," writes Kenneth D. Butler. "Depending on one's viewpoint, she is also either one of the most tragic or one of the most Machiavellian figures in Japanese history." Hōjo Masako significantly strengthened the rule of the Kamakura Shōgunate, the warrior government in which a military general (*shōgun*) governed on behalf of the emperor. Historical chronicles have portrayed her as a treacherous schemer, but her reputation has been rescued by feminist historian **Nagai Michiko**, who has interpreted Masako more positively, in the context of medieval Japanese marriage practices and family customs.

Against the wishes of her father, who wanted to arrange her marriage to another warrior, Masako married her childhood sweetheart, Minamoto no Yoritomo, in 1177. At the time, Yoritomo was bringing warrior groups of Japan under his control. In 1185, he decisively defeated his enemies and established the Kamakura Shōgunate, becoming the first *shōgun.* Masako's relationship with Yoritomo was troubled because of his interest in other women. In one particularly infamous incident, Masako hired goons to destroy the house of one of her rivals. Motivated in part by jealousy, she was nevertheless exercising a socially accepted practice of defending her status as Yoritomo's main wife and protecting her son's right to succession.

After Yoritomo's death in 1199, Masako became a Buddhist nun, but she continued her involvement in politics, choosing a successor to her husband. Masako became regent for her elder son. Eventually with the assistance of her natal family, in the first of many moves which earned her a reputation for treachery, she deposed him for his incompetence. She would subsequently repeat this act with her younger son. Historical chronicles have interpreted these deeds as evidence of her favoring her natal family over her own sons. In reality, she had not been permitted to raise her sons—custom dictated that they be raised by foster families—and they were generally thought to have been unfit for ruling the warrior government. Later, Masako exiled her father when he attempted to conspire against her. She appears to have placed the highest value on maintaining and strengthening the shōgunate government.

In 1221, when the emperor tried to regain the political authority lost to the shōgunate and declared against Masako, she rallied warriors to defeat him (the Jokyu Disturbance). Until her death, four years later, Masako ruled the shōgunate through the Hōjo (her natal family) regents.

SOURCES:

Beard, Mary. *Women as a Force in Japanese History.* Washington DC: Public Affairs Press. 1953.

Benton, Margaret Fukazawa. "Hōjo Masako: The Dowager Shōgun," in *Heroic With Grace: Legendary Women of Japan.* Chieko Irie Mulhern, ed. Armonk, NY: M.E. Sharpe. 1991, pp. 162–207.

Butler, Kenneth B. "Woman of Power Behind the Kamakura Bakufu," in *Great Historical Figures of Japan.* Murakami Hyoe and Thomas J. Harper, eds. Tokyo: Japan Cultural Institute, 1978, pp. 91–101.

Linda L. Johnson,
Professor of History, Concordia College, Moorhead, Minnesota

Hokinson, Helen E. (1893–1949)

American artist known for her cartoons for* The New Yorker *during the 1920s and 1930s. *Born Helen Elna Hokinson on June 29, 1893, in Mendota, Illinois; died on November 1, 1949, in a plane crash near Washington, D.C.; only child of Adolph Hokinson (a salesman) and Mary (Wilcox) Hokinson; graduated from Mendota High School, 1913; attended Chicago Academy of Fine Arts, 1913–18; never married; no children.*

An only child, cartoonist Helen Hokinson was born in 1893 in Mendota, Illinois, then lived in Moline and Des Moines, Iowa, before the family resettled in Mendota in 1905, where her father sold farm machinery. Hokinson's art talent emerged in high school, where she created caricatures of classmates and teachers for the school yearbook. After graduating in 1913, she talked her reluctant parents into sending her to the Chicago Academy of Fine Arts. She studied cartooning and illustrating for five years, living at the Three Arts Club with fellow designer and cartoonist **Alice Harvey** (later Alice Harvey Ramsey) and supplementing her funds by sketching for Chicago's major department stores. In 1920, the two women went to New York to launch their careers.

In Manhattan, Hokinson continued to do freelance fashion work for B. Altman and Lord & Taylor, and also created a short-lived comic strip for the New York *Daily Mirror.* She pursued her art studies at the New York School of Fine and Applied Art under Howard Giles, who introduced her to the principle of "dynamic symmetry," which she later called fundamental to her work. Her interest in fashion slowly waned, and she began to sketch the working people of the city: garbage collectors, snow shovelers, and the like. She also spent several summers in the Adirondacks, painting landscapes.

In 1925, Hokinson sent some of her sketches to Harold Ross, who had just published the first edition of *The New Yorker* magazine. Ross was impressed and printed her first cartoon in the November issue. It showed a bemused clerk translating for a costumer at a perfume counter, "It's *N'Aimez Que Moi,* madam—don't love nobody but me." Soon, her buxom, upper-middle-class women, somewhat out of touch and perpetually bewildered by life's trials, became a regular feature of the magazine. The captions were supplied by the editors of the magazine until 1931, when Hokinson began her collaboration with James Reid Parker, who also became her good friend. Although the cartoons sometimes bordered on cruelty (particularly in the biting satire of Parker's captions), Hokinson's meticulous drawings, with their touchingly out of place wisps of hair and sagging hemlines, imbued the work with such pathos that her caricatures became likeably human.

Described as shy and aloof, Hokinson never became part of the exclusive literary coterie at *The New Yorker,* preferring to spend her time reading English novels, painting watercolors, and producing ceramics. She socialized with a small and select group of friends, often escorted by Parker. Her salary from *The New Yorker,* and occasional work with the *Ladies' Home Journal,* reached $40,000 yearly, almost five times that of the average family income, and allowed Hokinson to enjoy a comfortable lifestyle, including an apartment in New York, summers in Connecticut, and some travel.

In 1931, she published her collected cartoons in *So You're Going to Buy a Book!* A second collection, *My Best Girls,* appeared in 1941, and a third, *When Were You Built?,* in 1948. In her later years, she was also writing a play. Hokinson was en route to speak at the opening of the Community Chest fund drive in Washington, when her plane collided with another over Washington's National Airport. All on board were killed. Hokinson was buried in the Restland Cemetery in her girlhood hometown of Mendota. Three additional collections of her work appeared posthumously.

SOURCES:

Bailey, Brooke. *The Remarkable Lives of 100 Women Artists.* Holbrook, MA: Bob Adams, 1994.

James, Edward T., ed. *Notable American Women, 1607–1950.* Cambridge, MA: The Belknap Press of Harvard University Press, 1971.

SUGGESTED READING:

Sochen, June, ed. *Women's Comic Visions.* Detroit, MI: Wayne State University Press, 1991.

Barbara Morgan,
Melrose, Massachusetts.

Holbrook, Eliza Jane Poitevent
(1849–1896).

See Nicholson, Eliza Jane Poitevent.

Holden, Edith B. (1871–1920)

English illustrator and writer whose Nature Notes, found years after her death, were released as* Country Diary of an Edwardian Lady *and became a literary sensation. *Name variations: Edith Blackwell Smith. Born Edith Blackwell Holden at Holly Green, in Church Road, Moseley, near Birmingham, England, on September 26, 1871; drowned in the Thames on March 15, 1920; fourth child of Arthur Holden (an industrialist) and Emma Wearing Holden; sister of Effie Margaret (b. 1867), Violet Mary (b. 1873), and Evelyn Holden (1877–c. 1969); married Alfred Ernest Smith (a sculptor), on June 1, 1911 (died 1938).*

Selected writings: (illustrator) Margaret Gatty's Daily Bread *(1910); (illus.)* Woodland Whisperings *(1911); (illus.)* Mrs. Strang's Annual for Children *(1914–c. 1925); (illus.)* Animals Around Us *(1912);* The Country Diary of an Edwardian Lady *(1977);* The Nature Notes of an Edwardian Lady *(1989).*

Edith Blackwell Holden, whose middle name was borrowed from her trail-blazing cousin ***Elizabeth Blackwell**, was born near Birmingham, England, on September 26, 1871, the daughter of a Non-Conformist, liberal father. Arthur Holden, whose Unitarian religion and actions tended toward socialism, owned a varnish firm and took good care of his workers. He was also active in his community and on the town council. Edith's mother was **Emma Wearing Holden**, an erstwhile governess, well-educated for her time. Also a Unitarian, Emma had published two slight books for the Society for Promoting Christian Knowledge, *Ursula's Girlhood* and *Beatrice of St. Mawse.* Both parents believed in the supernatural and the possibility of transmitted thought, while Emma dabbled in automatic writing.

Of delicate health, Emma's seven pregnancies left her frail, and she never totally recovered her strength. Even so, she took over the education of her brood—five girls and two boys. The Holdens had a passion for art, poetry, and books. They also enjoyed walks in the countryside and were fairly versed in the birds and local fauna. Emma's greatest love was her garden.

Edith Holden spent her first nine years in a large house called The Elms in the village of Acocks Green, on the outskirts of the industrial city of Birmingham. In 1880, as Birmingham expanded and the area built up, Arthur moved his family to Darley Green, a farming village in Packwood, 15 miles from Birmingham, where they frequently trod the country lanes and revelled in the births of farm animals. While the daughters continued their home tutoring, the sons were packed off to school.

Edith B. Holden

During those periods when Emma took to her bed, the older girls ran the household. When an aunt suggested that one or two of the girls might live with her to lighten Emma's load, the eldest **Effie** volunteered and moved to Bristol. Thirteen-year-old Edith entered the Birmingham School of Art, one of the best provincial art schools in the nation, passing with an Excellent in freehand her first year.

In 1890, when sisters **Evelyn** and **Violet** joined 19-year-old Edith at the School of Art, the family moved once again to a house named Gowan Bank, with its extensive gardens and staff cottage, 300 yards from Kingswood station, to be nearer the railway for the daily 16-mile commute into Birmingham. That year, Edith had her first painting, *A Cosy Quartette,* exhibited in the Royal Birmingham Society of Artists' autumn show. She began to specialize in animal painting, as well as plants.

In August 1891, age 20, Edith was sent to study with animal painter J. Denovan Adam and 25 other students at his Craigmill studio, just outside Stirling, Scotland. Twelve months later, she returned home and began to produce four paintings a year for the Royal Birmingham exhibitions. As many of her paintings reflect, she would visit Scotland six weeks annually and make other ex-

See sidebar on the following page

Holden, Effie M. (b. 1867)

English poet. *Name variations: E.M. Holden; Effie Margaret Heath. Born Effie Margaret Holden in 1867; first child of Arthur Holden (an industrialist) and Emma Wearing Holden; sister of* ****Edith Holden*** *(1871–1920); married Carl Heath (an artist), in 1900.*

In 1891, Effie Holden journeyed to Sweden to study the arts and crafts movement. While there, she met fellow student Carl Heath; they were married in 1900 and became involved with the Humanitarian League, participating in Socialist and Fabian debates. Rather than art, Effie began to be recognized by friends as a writer of poetry; as such, she corresponded and met some of the leading literary figures of her day. By 1905, the 38-year-old Effie had published two books of poetry, including *The Songs of Christine,* which sold out in 1901 and was reprinted in 1903. In all, she published 11 volumes of poetry under the name E.M. Holden. Effie wrote a short book about ***Lucy Stone.**

Holden, Evelyn (1877–c. 1969)

English artist and book illustrator. *Born in 1877; died around 1969; daughter of Arthur Holden (an industrialist) and Emma Wearing Holden; sister of Edith Holden (1871–1920); attended Birmingham Art School; married Frank Matthews, in 1904.*

A successful book illustrator, Evelyn Holden also exhibited with the Royal Birmingham Society of Artists. Her strength was pen and ink, and her watercolors were much bolder than her sister ***Edith Holden's.** In 1904, Evelyn married Frank Matthews and joined him in his commitment to work with crippled children in the slums. Despite being of delicate health since babyhood, Evelyn was over 90 when she died.

Holden, Violet (b. 1873)

English artist and book illustrator. *Born in 1873; daughter of Arthur Holden (an industrialist) and Emma Wearing Holden; sister of Edith Holden (1871–1920); attended Birmingham Art School.*

Violet Holden was also a successful book illustrator. Together with her sister ***Evelyn Holden,** Violet illustrated *The Real Princess,* a fairy story by **Blanche Atkinson,** in 1894. The sisters published their own book of nursery rhymes a year later. In 1904, Violet joined the teaching staff of the Birmingham Art School; she specialized in writing and illumination.

cursions to Dousland in Dartmoor, becoming close with a family who ran the local post office.

The house at Gowan Bank had frequent visitors, especially socialists or spiritualists who had come to speak in Birmingham; the family also held weekly seances, with Emma Holden sometimes acting as medium. Well into adulthood, the younger Holdens and their friends put on theatrical productions in the unused chapel at the side of the garden. One close friend of Edith's, ***Edith Matthison,** later became a professional actress.

In 1897, seeking a smaller house, Arthur Holden moved his entourage once more, this time to Dorridge, a few miles from Kingswood. Daughter **Winnie** had taken over the running of the house, since Emma Holden, now 61, spent most of her time in bed or on the chaise-longue in the drawing room or garden. Emma died of cancer a few months after her daughter Evelyn was married in 1904. The family was soon convinced that Emma was transferring messages to them through Winnie.

At this time, Arthur Holden's extremely successful firm fell on hard times, and there was a split in the family as to how to handle the situation. When a smaller house was unavoidable, Arthur, Winnie, Edith, and Violet returned to Gowan Bank in March 1905. Edith, unsettled by the family feuds, put even more energy into her paintings and began writing her "nature notes" of 1905 and 1906. Traversing lanes and fields on foot and bicycle, happily alone, she went in search of the violet wood or the Wild Canterbury Bell, climbing to the top of craggy hills with paintbox and canvas tucked under her arm. Her notes, abundantly illustrated, had a charming narration:

> May 1st. Very windy, but bright sunshine. Walked to Yelverton and sat on the moor. Watched a handsome little black-headed Stone-chat 'jinkin' thro' the gorse; Follow'd him to another patch of furse and sat down to watch. He scolded terribly and presently the hen-bird came with a beakful of small caterpillars and began to scold too. I moved my station and sat but the hen-bird followed after swallowing her collection of grubs and scolded and chattered at me for half an hour. . . . I kept very quiet and at last had my reward.

The mother bird led her to "a cosy nest hidden away very carefully among the dry grass at the roots of the gorse with five baby stone-chats in it, nearly fledged."

> November 7th. Yesterday I erected a short pole in the garden with a small flat board on top, to serve as a breakfast table for the birds; I strewed it with crumbs and bits of meat; but all day yesterday the birds left it severely alone.

A starling arrived, then two Tom-tits. "After that there was a constant succession of visitors all through the day."

From 1906 to 1909, Holden taught art on Friday afternoons at the Solihull School for Girls, for her friend Miss Burd, the headmistress. "The girls found Edith reserved and reticent about herself," wrote **Ina Taylor**. "She had fairish hair drawn back and usually wore a high-necked blouse and long skirt. She had a very quiet personality and never belittled anyone's efforts, but she demanded high standards from her pupils." Holden continued to exhibit in Birmingham and began to contribute illustrations to the *Animals' Friend* magazine and art work to the Royal Society for the Prevention of Cruelty to Animals.

In 1907, Holden entered *The Rowan Tree* for the Royal Academy summer exhibition in London, where she stayed with her sister Effie. As active members of the Christian Socialist Society, the Fellowship of New Life (which would become the Fabian Society), the Humanitarian League, and the Society for the Abolition of Capital Punishment, Effie and her husband Carl soon broadened Edith's horizons. Holden was fascinated with her sister's lifestyle and, through Effie, made many new friends, including the sculptor Ernest Smith, who was then attending the Royal College of Art.

The situation at home grew worse. As her father's paint-and-varnish business provided an income for all the Holdens, money was in short supply. Edith supplemented her income with her art. Becoming known as an animal illustrator, she began to acquire commissions to illustrate children's books: ***Margaret Gatty**'s *Daily Bread* (1910), *Mrs. Strang's Annual for Children* (1914–c. 1925), *Woodland Whisperings* (1911), and *Animals Around Us* (1912).

In 1911, 40-year-old Edith married Ernest Smith, who was seven years her junior and had been invited to assist the Countess ***Feodora Gleichen**, a gifted sculptor, in her studio in St. James's Palace. Though always welcome there, Edith continued her own career in book illustrating. In 1917, she again exhibited at the Royal Academy.

Not much is known about Edith Holden's nine-year marriage. What *is* known is that on Monday morning, March 15, 1920, while living at 2 Oakley Crescent, Chelsea, she complained of a headache to her husband before he left for work in the St. James's studio. She also told him that she would probably go down to the river to watch the university crews practice that day. When he returned from work, Holden was not there, though the table had been set for dinner. Her body was found by a constable at 6 o'clock on Tuesday morning, lying face down, clutching a bunch of twigs. She had drowned in a backwater of the Thames, near Kew Gardens Walk. An inquest speculated that, while standing on two stumps of wood, Holden had been reaching for a branch of chestnut buds with her umbrella and fallen into the river. There were some who openly wondered about suicide, but many remembered that Edith condemned suicide because of her religious views. She was 48.

Following Edith Holden's death, though her art work has been lost, her Nature Notes for 1906 remained with her husband's family. (Ernest Smith died in 1938.) Eventually, Holden's great-niece, artist **Rowena Stott**, inherited them and, in 1976, took the heavily illustrated diaries to the publishers Webb and Bower. Joining with Michael Joseph, a top London house, Richard Webb and Delian Bower oversaw the publication of *The Country Diary of an Edwardian Lady* on June 13, 1977. The reviews were euphoric, and the book landed on top of the bestseller list the following week. There it stayed for 64 weeks, selling over three million copies in Sweden, Germany, France, America, Holland, Denmark, Norway, Italy, Finland, Japan, Spain, and Portugal. Under the label "The Country Diary Collection," Nigel French Enterprises began to manufacture Holden's designs: 1,000 items, everything from crockery to bed linen, sold in 20 countries. As well, a 12-part television series on Holden's life was produced by Central Independent Television and broadcast in England in spring 1984.

In 1988, there was an amazing discovery. Holden's Nature Notes of 1905—until that time no one was even aware they existed—were found in a dining-room cupboard in Southsea, Hampshire, in the possession of a family completely unrelated to the Holdens. The find was greeted with skepticism until Sotheby's confirmed the authorship. It is thought that the family obtained the manuscript in the 1940s at auction. *Nature Notes of an Edwardian Lady* was published in October 5, 1989, again topping the bestseller list.

SOURCES:

Holden, Edith. *The Nature Notes of an Edwardian Lady.* Devon, England: Webb and Bower, 1989.

Taylor, Ina. *The Edwardian Lady: The Story of Edith Holden.* Devon, England: Webb and Bower, 1980, rev. ed., 1990.

RELATED MEDIA:

The Country Diary of an Edwardian Lady, a 12-part television series, produced by Central Independent Television, starring **Pippa Guard**, broadcast in England, spring 1984.

Holden, Effie M. (b. 1867).

See Holden, Edith for sidebar.

Holden, Evelyn (1877–c. 1969).

See Holden, Edith for sidebar.

Holden, Violet (b. 1873).

See Holden, Edith for sidebar.

Holderness, countess of (1259–1274).

See Isabella de Redvers for sidebar on Avelina de Forz.

Holdsclaw, Chamique (1977—)

African-American basketball player who led Tennessee to three NCAA championships. *Name variations: (nicknames) Meke; the Claw. Born on August 9, 1977 in Astoria, Queens, New York; daughter of William Johnson (an automobile mechanic) and Bonita Holdsclaw (a data-entry worker); graduated from University of Tennessee, 1999, with a major in political science.*

First woman college athlete to win the James E. Sullivan Award; all-time leading scorer and rebounder in Tennessee basketball history; third on NCAA all-time women's basketball scoring list; four-time All-American, two-time ESPY award winner, two-time Associated Press Women's Basketball Player of the Year, and two-time Naismith award winner; named 1999 Rookie of the Year.

Chamique Holdsclaw emerged from a dazzling college basketball career with Tennessee's Lady Volunteers to steal the spotlight as a star player of the Washington Mystics WNBA basketball team. Her unsurpassed accomplishments on the court caused sportswriters to consider her the greatest player to come through the women's college ranks. Holdsclaw's phenomenal skills have invited comparisons to basketball superstar Michael Jordan, whose #23 jersey she shares.

She was born in Astoria, New York, on August 9, 1977, to William Johnson and **Bonita Holdsclaw.** After her parents split when she was 11, Chamique and her younger brother Davon began living with their grandmother, **June Holdsclaw**, a clerk in the medical-records department at the Jamaica Hospital. Two years later, Bonita asked the children to return home, but Chamique said no. "My grandmother gave me so much attention. I was established, going to school and playing basketball, and I didn't want to disrupt it." The rejection drove a permanent wedge in the mother-daughter relationship. "She was upset," said Chamique. "She was very, very upset."

Holdsclaw credits her skill in the game to the skirmishes she enjoyed as a child playing against the neighborhood boys on the playgrounds of the Astoria Houses, a complex which overlooks a section of the East River called Hell Gate, in Queens. She grew up accustomed to winning, having played on championship teams throughout high school. At Christ the King in New York, she led the school to four straight New York state championship titles. From high school, she progressed to the University of Tennessee's Lady Vols basketball team, leading them to three straight NCAA championships. As a political science major, Holdsclaw fought the pressure to leave school early to join the newly formed Women's National Basketball League (WNBA). The 6'2" player was convinced her grandmother would want her to complete her education before turning pro. "What is Chamique doing?," she could hear her say. "She needs to be getting her degree."

In 1998, Holdsclaw was a member of the gold medal-winning team that swept the Women's World Basketball championships in Germany. She averaged 11 points and 5 rebounds per game to assure herself a spot on the 2000 Olympic team. By the time she graduated, Holdsclaw was the most decorated women's basketball player ever: two-time ESPY award winner as the women's college player of the year; four-time All-American; two-time Associated Press Women's Basketball Player of the Year; two-time Naismith award winner; and the first female college player to win the prestigious Sullivan Award as the top amateur athlete. In addition to these accolades, she became the all-time leading scorer and rebounder in Tennessee basketball history.

Holdsclaw was the number-one draft pick when she graduated to the WNBA in 1999, becoming a member of the Washington Mystics team which had experienced a disappointing season the previous year. The young superstar did not disappoint those who believed that she could propel the Mystics out of their slump. She averaged 16.9 points, 7.9 rebounds, and 2.4 assists per game to be named the Rookie of the Year (1999) by an overwhelming majority. She finished the season ranked sixth in scoring and third in rebounding.

Known for her confident presence on the courts, Holdsclaw remains anchored and down-to-earth, characteristics instilled by her grandmother. The combination of her talent and humility made her a favored candidate for lucrative endorsement deals and a ready draw for thousands of fans to the fledgling WNBA franchise. Said Olympian ***Jackie Joyner-Kersee**: "Chamique has changed the face of women's sports. . . . She's brought ordinary people into watching the sport. Now you see men outside the arena holding signs that say, NEED TICKETS."

SOURCES:

Anderson, Kelli. "Star Power," in *Sports Illustrated for Women*. Spring 1999, p. 56.

The Day [New London, CT]. March 10, 1998; July 1, 1999.

Jenkins, Sally. "Eyes on the Prize," in Condé Nast *Sports*. April 1998.

TV Guide. March 13, 1999.

Judith C. Reveal,
freelance writer, Greensboro, Maryland

Holiday, Billie (c. 1915–1959)

African-American jazz and blues singer, one of the great American female vocalists of all time, who was plagued by poverty, racism, and drugs, and whose recordings are considered classics. *Name variations: Lady Day. Born Eleanora Fagan on April 7, 1915(?) in Baltimore, Maryland; died of addiction-related illness on July 17, 1959, in New York; illegitimate daughter of Sarah Fagan and a father variously reported as Clarence Holiday or Frank DeVeazy; educated through fifth grade; married Jimmy Monroe (a jazz trumpeter), on August 25, 1941 (divorced); married Louis McKay, in 1951.*

Educated through fifth grade before moving to New York City and supporting her mother by singing for tips in Harlem night clubs; made her professional debut when she was 20 and remained a respected and popular jazz and blues vocalist with both white and black audiences for the rest of her life, despite drug and alcohol addiction that resulted in several arrests and convictions; published her autobiography, Lady Sings the Blues *(1956).*

Billie Holiday always maintained that the biggest thrill of her life was playing the Royal Albert Hall in London. On that night in 1954, she was astonished at the awed silence that greeted her stage entrance, as if her title "Lady Day" had been bestowed at Buckingham Palace. Equally astounding to her was the careful attention focused on her every lyric, the tumultuous applause that filled the cavernous hall, and the throngs of fans waiting outside with flowers and kisses. It was so unlike anything she had been used to back home in the States, especially during her early career, marked by claustrophobic nightclubs, audiences that talked, drank, and ate through her sets, and whites who would pay good money to hear her but would be horrified at sharing an elevator with her.

She had nearly given up the European tour that brought her to London, unable at first to get a passport because she couldn't produce a birth certificate. Billie never knew her exact birth date but estimated it as April 7, 1915. She was born out of wedlock to **Sarah ("Sadie") Fagan**, who cleaned and kept house for wealthy white families in Baltimore. "It's a wonder my mother didn't end up in the workhouse and me as a foundling," said Holiday:

> But Sadie Fagan loved me from the time I was just a swift kick in the ribs while she scrubbed floors. She went to the hospital and made a deal with the head woman there. She told them she'd scrub floors . . . so she could pay her way and mine. And she did. Mom was thirteen that Wednesday, April 7, 1915, in Baltimore, when I was born.

Billie claimed her father was Clarence Holiday, an itinerant musician who left Sadie soon after their child was born, although work papers filled out by Sadie when she applied for a job in Philadelphia indicate that Billie may actually have been born in that city earlier. At the time, Sadie listed a Philadelphia waiter, Frank DeVeazy, as the father. Whatever the truth, Billie always considered Baltimore her hometown and, throughout her life, never forgot the poverty and squalor of the African-American ghetto called "Pigtown," down by the harbor, near which she and Sadie lived. A few years after her birth, Clarence returned to legalize his union with Sadie. "Mom and Pop were just kids when they got married," Billie remembered. "He was eighteen, she was sixteen, and I was three."

Sadie named her daughter Eleanora, but Billie thought it was "too damn long for anyone to say" and may have taken her name from the one Clarence gave to his roughneck daughter, "Bill." In other accounts, Billie claimed she took the name from a popular silent-film actress of her childhood, ***Billie Dove**. When Sadie found work outside Baltimore, she left Billie in the care of relatives, including a great-grandmother who had been a slave on Charles Fagan's Virginia plantation before the Civil War and who claimed she was one of 16 children Fagan had sired among his workers. From her great-grandmother, Billie heard the family history of discrimination and abuse, no doubt underscored by what was taking place just outside the door. Baltimore in the early 1920s had the largest African-American population of any American city outside of the nation's capital, along with some of the worst discriminatory practices and living conditions of institutionalized racism. Billie Holiday had the misfortune to be born at a time when America's race relations were more troubled than they had ever been since the War Between the States. Lynchings and beatings of blacks remained all too common in the South, and the Federal government would not come to grips with civil rights for another 30 years. Although Holiday was one of the few black women of her generation to enjoy a degree of artistic and economic success, the racial prejudice she experienced as a child followed her into adult life even as her career was being guided and shaped by white men.

By age six, Billie was working "minding babies, running errands, and scrubbing those damn white steps [of brick row houses] all over Baltimore," as she later recalled. One of the businesses for which she ran errands was a brothel around the corner on Pennsylvania Avenue, Baltimore's red-light district. In lieu of cash, Billie was allowed to listen to recordings of ***Bessie Smith** and Louis "Pops" Armstrong on the Victrola in the parlor. She would claim throughout her career that Smith and Armstrong had been the chief influences on her style. "I always wanted Bessie's sound and Pop's feeling," she said.

In 1927, Billie went to join her mother in New York, working for a time alongside Sadie for the white family in whose Long Island home they lived. But after several disputes with the matriarch of the family, who accused Billie of stealing, Sadie sent her daughter to board at what appeared to be a respectable rooming house on Harlem's 114th Street. From her experiences on Pennsylvania Avenue back in Baltimore, Billie knew from the moment she saw the place that it was a well-run, profitable brothel. Barely 14, she was soon earning her keep as a prostitute. When she refused the demands of a particularly important, but threatening, client, she found herself arrested on disorderly conduct charges and sent to a filthy, rat-infested women's prison on Welfare Island in New York's East River. She spent nearly nine months behind bars, although during the last part of her sentence she was allowed to cook for the white prison warden and his family.

On her release, Holiday moved back to Long Island and found a job waitressing, earning extra money by singing for tips at a local Elks Club. But when Sadie was forced to retire from her job because of a stomach ailment, she and Billie moved back to Harlem and took a small apartment on 139th Street, in what had once been America's most lively and prosperous black community. By now, however, the Depression was taking its toll, and the two women were forced to scrape by on the few dollars Billie managed to get from Clarence, who by then had divorced Sadie, remarried, and was playing downtown at Manhattan's Roseland Ballroom with Fletcher Henderson's band.

When the money ran out, Billie trudged up and down Harlem's Seventh Avenue looking for work in any of a multitude of clubs that lined the street, ending up at Pod and Jerry's Log Cabin on 133rd Street. There, she sang "Travelin'" and "Body and Soul," collected $18 in tips, and was offered a full-time job. Starting at the Log Cabin, Holiday went from one club to another, building a following along the way at places like the Yeah Man, the Hotcha, and the Alhambra Grill. Among the growing number of fans was John Henry Hammond, the wealthy white scion of an old New York family and a passionate lover of jazz and the blues, to which he said he was attracted for "its simple honesty and convincing lyrics." In coming years, Hammond would promote the talents of such diverse artists as Benny Goodman and Billie's idol, Bessie Smith.

Hammond was fascinated with Billie Holiday from the first time he heard her sing at Monette's Supper Club. "She sang popular songs in a manner that made them completely her own," he said. "She had an uncanny ear, an excellent memory for lyrics, and she sang with an exquisite sense of phrasing." He was especially intrigued by the fact that Billie would sing the same song at five or six different tables, but never sing it the same way twice. To Billie, it was only natural; otherwise, she said, "It ain't music. It's close-order drill, or exercise, or yodeling, or something, not music."

It was Hammond who arranged for Billie's first recording session in 1933 with Goodman, himself still an unknown. Since the clubs she had been playing were usually in the basements of residential brownstones, Holiday had never used any sort of amplification and was frightened of a microphone; but in a few hours she turned out

Billie Holiday

the first of scores of recordings, "Your Mother's Son-In-Law" and "Riffin' the Scotch," neither of which sold more than a few copies. That same year, however, Prohibition was repealed. The thousands of now-legal bars that sprang up all had those newfangled machines, called jukeboxes, and Hammond quickly realized that black bar owners weren't being serviced by a record industry geared toward whites. Hammond teamed Billie with a pianist he had long admired, Teddy Wilson, and got them a contract for Columbia Records' Brunswick label. Wilson and

Holiday churned out more than 80 jukebox records between 1933 and 1938. As time went on, Wilson added better musicians to back Holiday up, since it was obvious to everyone that a major new talent was in the making. "She could just say 'hello' or 'good morning'," Wilson said, "and it was a musical experience."

It was at one of the Brunswick sessions that Billie first met Lester Young, who played sax for Count Basie's band and who became, in an odd way, the most important man in Billie's life. The two seemed to thoroughly understand each other, musically and emotionally, from the moment they met. "To hear her sing . . . while he was playing a chorus was something to make your toes curl," remembered Max Kaminsky who played trumpet with Basie. "No words; she just scatted along with his tenor sax as though she were another horn." Over the years, Holiday and Lester Young would join forces on some of the most treasured jazz performances ever recorded—numbers such as "This Year's Kisses," "If Dreams Come True," and "I'll Never Be The Same." It was Young who gave Billie her nickname, "Lady Day," while Billie called him "Prez." Young even moved in with Holiday for a time, but in John Hammond's opinion the relationship was never a physical one. "They thought alike and they felt alike," he said many years later. "I don't think there was any sexual relationship there—I think they just understood each other. It was so subtle and so close that I feel embarrassed even *talking* about it."

Has done singing and housecleaning.

—Prison warden's evaluation of inmate Billie Holiday, 1947

While the Brunswick sessions were in full swing, Billie sang for the first time at Harlem's Apollo Theater, appearing with a small jazz combo; she also played a small role in a short film for Paramount, 1935's *Symphony In Black*, which featured Duke Ellington's band and, most important, played her first club date outside Harlem, at Barney Josephson's Café Society Downtown, in Greenwich Village. Josephson, like Hammond, was a political and social liberal and a strong supporter of the NAACP. His clubs (he ran a second Café Society on Manhattan's 58th Street, plus a third club in Harlem) were among the first with integrated audiences, and he delighted in advertising Café Society as "The Wrong Place for the Right People." He had strict rules for his performers, among which was an absolute ban on illegal drugs inside his clubs, forcing Billie to ride around Central Park in a carriage before a performance so she could indulge the marijuana habit she had developed years earlier. It was Josephson who brought Billie a song she was, at first, reluctant to perform, but for which she eventually developed a passionate attachment—a protest song called "Strange Fruit," about the lynchings of blacks in the South. Josephson claimed he had come across the song while traveling in the South, but it is widely believed that Josephson himself wrote it. Its opening verses described a "pastoral scene" with bitter irony:

> Southern trees bear a strange fruit,
> Blood on the leaves and blood at the root.
> Black bodies swaying in the southern breeze,
> Strange fruit hanging from the poplar trees.

Holiday introduced the song one night at Café Society as the last number of her set, with just a soft pinlight focused on her face. Josephson ordered all table service suspended during the number and told Billie to simply walk off when she finished, with no bows or encores. The club remained perfectly silent for moments afterward. Even more profound was the reaction at the Apollo, where Holiday sang "Strange Fruit" before a mostly African-American audience a few nights later. "A moment of oppressively heavy silence followed," remembered Jack Schiffman, the Apollo's manager at the time, "and then a kind of rustling sound I had never heard before. It was the sound of almost two thousand people sighing."

It was an irony of Holiday's life that the very gift for which whites most admired her also created the setting for the racial conflict that would plague her. On tour with Basie's band for eight months in 1938, Billie and the other black members of the orchestra were frequently forced to stay in the homes of admiring African-Americans, since most hotels, including those in the North, had a whites-only policy. In Detroit, where the band played for a chorus line of all-white dancers, audiences complained to the theater management that the musicians were too close to the bare legs of the chorines, who might be "contaminated." Billie was judged to be "too yellow" by many of the managers on the circuit, and she was forced to artificially darken her skin so that no one would mistake her for a "mixed colored," with one white parent. Basie supported Holiday as best he could. "She fitted in so easily," he said. "It was like having another [instrumental] soloist." But the band's financiers weren't as enthusiastic, citing Billie's growing drug and alcohol problems and a "distinctly wrong attitude toward the work" as reasons for letting her go after the tour was completed. There were rumors that Billie, the only woman member of the band, had slept with one or two of her co-workers on the road, and Billie's persistent pattern of showing up late for rehearsals and stage calls was already taking shape. Holiday, on the other hand, claimed that she'd quit the band of her own accord because she wasn't being paid enough.

When Billie migrated to Artie Shaw's band late in 1938, her problems only worsened. Shaw had recognized her talent several years before, when he heard her sing at Monette's in Harlem, and he took a chance on hiring her as the first black singer to appear with a white band. He was forced to hire a second singer, ***Helen Forrest**, after being told by theater owners that Billie couldn't appear unless there was also a white singer. Holiday was not allowed to share the platform where Forrest sat between numbers, and there were understandably rumors of friction between the two women—although years later, Forrest would claim that Billie had been kind to her and encouraged Shaw to use her for more songs. All this, insulting at it was, proved to be the least of Holiday's problems.

The blues, jazz, and rock are considered to be quintessential American music, but the African-American musicians who created this art form often paid a high price for bringing it to white America. For them there were no restrooms, restaurants, or hotels. They were welcome to perform in front of whites as long as they had no personal needs. Holiday was not allowed to sleep in the same hotel or eat in the same dining room with the other band members, usually being sent to the kitchen to take her meals, and complained that she never "ate, slept, or went to the bathroom without having a major NAACP-type production." Wrote Holiday:

> Most of the cats in the band were wonderful to me, but I got so tired of scenes in crummy roadside restaurants over getting served, I used to beg Georgie Auld, Tony Pastor and Chuck Peterson to just let me sit in the bus and rest—and let them bring out something in a sack. Some places they wouldn't even let me eat in the kitchen. Sometimes it was a choice between me eating and the whole band starving. I got tired of having a federal case over breakfast, lunch, and dinner.

When the tour reached the South, a member of the all-white audience stood up after one of Billie's numbers and yelled: "Have the nigger wench sing another song!" Billie mouthed an obscenity at him, pandemonium broke out, and Shaw had to whisk her out of the hall to the safety of the band's bus. But it was back in sophisticated New York that the last straw fell, during a gig at the Lincoln Hotel's Blue Room. Not only was Billie prohibited from entering many of the hotel's public areas, she was not even permitted inside the Blue Room itself except when she was actually singing; when she finished a number, she had to retire to a small room outside the lounge until her next song. Finally, when Southerners staying at the hotel complained of her use of the guest elevators and the management asked her to use the freight elevator instead, Billie quit. By the 1940s, her anger had attached itself to "Strange Fruit"'s grim lyrics. After listening to Billie recite them, poet ***Maya Angelou**'s young son asked Billie what the phrase 'pastoral scene' meant. "It means when the crackers are killing the niggers," Holiday snapped. "That's what they do. That's a goddam pastoral scene."

Despite these indignities, the 1940s saw Billie's career become firmly established, while a degree of security arrived in her personal life with her first marriage, on August 25, 1941, to jazz trumpeter Jimmy Monroe, for whom she had had a long-standing fascination. The two embarked on a tour that took them to Chicago, where Billie sang with Lionel Hampton's band, and then on to Los Angeles, Holiday's first visit to the West Coast. She had accepted an engagement of several weeks at a replica of Barney Josephson's club, called The Café Society, where she was paid $175 a week and was thrilled to meet the film stars who flocked to hear her. Holiday's signature had become a white dress and a white gardenia. But by the end of the gig, Billie and her husband were broke, and friends had to pay her way back to New York while Monroe stayed in California. These same friends noticed that Billie seemed worn out and hazy when she arrived back East, perhaps due to the heroin habit that probably began during her marriage to Monroe, who was a well-known user. The marriage had not been successful, and Billie may have taken up the drug as an attempt to draw closer to her husband.

On her return to New York, Holiday embarked on a series of dates at most of New York's 52nd Street jazz clubs, such as The Onyx, The Famous Door, and The Yacht Club, singing with many of the most respected jazz musicians of the day. In the audience on many of those nights was a rapt Frank Sinatra who, as his own career swept the nation, would frequently list Holiday as his major inspiration. "Billie Holiday was, and still remains, the greatest single musical influence on me," he said years later.

In between her New York shows, Billie—who now had a manager and agent—accepted offers from Chicago, Los Angeles, and San Francisco, and many felt that her personal problems gave added poignancy to her appearances. The marriage to Jimmy Monroe slowly deteriorated until, in 1945, Billie announced she had divorced him and married trumpeter Joe Guy, although there is no evidence that she and Guy actually did marry, and Monroe was still claiming in 1947 that Billie was his wife. The actual date of their divorce is still uncertain.

Also in 1945, Billie learned while on the road that Sadie, the only other constant in her life beside music, had died. Her mother's absence hit Billie particularly hard, leading her to seek comfort even more in drugs. There were repeated arrests and court dates on possession charges, most of which were settled with hefty fines; and several contracts for tours and club dates had to be canceled when Billie either never showed up or arrived late and in no condition to sing.

But it was because of her singing that most people knew Billie, especially after she appeared with her idol, Louis Armstrong, in United Artists' 1946 feature film *New Orleans,* an unsuccessful, muddled tale of the origins of jazz which relegated Holiday and Armstrong to the roles of musically inclined servants to the film's white romantic leads. Although Billie swore never to do a film again, the film's score and her own performance brought her an even wider audience. She gave her first solo performance at New York's Town Hall that same year, but by the time she arrived back in New York from Los Angeles, her affair with Joe Guy had ended and even Billie had begun to realize the toll her drug habit was taking. She checked herself into a Manhattan clinic to rid herself of the addiction; but three weeks after her release, she was arrested in Philadelphia on drug possession charges. This time, fines weren't enough for the court; Billie was sentenced to a year's term at the Federal Women's Reformatory in Alderston, West Virginia.

Strangely, these were to be the most peaceful days of Billie Holiday's life. Although living quarters at the prison were racially segregated, all other activities were carried out in integrated groups, in which no one was any better than anyone else, all tasks were shared in common, and everyone more or less got along. Holiday attended church every Sunday, was free of her drug habit, and modestly refused requests to sing. Her supervisor's report deemed her "generous, quiet, lady-like, [and] matter-of-fact." After serving nine-and-a-half months of her sentence, she was released on parole, returning to New York for a triumphant concert at Carnegie Hall which included six encores. But because of her conviction record, the Police Department refused to issue Billie a "cabaret card," preventing her from singing anywhere that had a liquor license and leaving her with a great deal of free time on her hands. Within a few months, Billie was once again using heroin. "There isn't a soul on this earth," she once said, "who can say for sure that their fight with dope is over, until they're dead."

Opposite page

Billie Holiday

Holiday's career reached its highest plateau under the guidance of producer Norman Granz, whom she had met in Los Angeles. In 1951, Granz added her to the impressive list of artists for his Verve label—a list that included ***Ella Fitzgerald**, Charlie Parker, and Oscar Peterson—and booked her on a round of concerts across the country, followed, in 1954, by her first European tour. Billie played Sweden, Denmark, France, and Switzerland and gave her famous Royal Albert Hall performance. Critic Leonard Feather reported that "Billie was looking and singing better than she has in years. It's a thrill to hear this unique voice back at the pinnacle of its form." *Down Beat* was equally enthusiastic about her second Carnegie Hall concert on her return from Europe, telling its readers that "It was a night when Billie was on top, the best jazz singer alive." In 1956, Holiday published the frank autobiography she had written with journalist friend William Dufty, *Lady Sings the Blues*. She seemed content, even though her second marriage to Louis McKay in 1951 was in trouble, and the two had separated.

In 1957, Holiday filmed a television special on jazz and was reunited with Lester Young, now ill and frail from years of his own alcohol and drug abuse. He and Billie had fought some years earlier and hadn't seen each other since, so the poignancy of their affection was felt even in the control room of the studio when Lester painfully rose to back Billie on a song she had written especially for the show, *Jazz Is*. Nat Hentoff, who co-produced the program, remembered that when it was time for Young's solo, "he blew the sparest, purest blues chorus I have ever heard. Billie, smiling, nodded to the beat, looked into Prez's eyes, and he into hers. She was looking back with the gentlest of regrets at their past."

Close friends were now beginning to notice a marked deterioration in Holiday's voice and talked of the recording sessions for which she was always late and of the quantities of scotch or brandy she had to consume before she could sing. She began to forget lyrics and would stand onstage, silent and staring, for minutes at a time; a second European tour, in 1958, during which she sang badly and was often late getting on stage, was poorly received. In March of 1959, Lester Young died, and Holiday said at his funeral that she thought she'd be the next to go. Said ***Lena Horne**:

> Her life was so tragic and so corrupted by other people—by white people and by her own people. There was no place for her to go, except, finally, into that little private world of dope. She was just too sensitive to survive. And such a gentle person. We never talked much about singing. The thing I remember talking to her about most was her dogs; her animals were really her only trusted friends.

Her last public appearance was on May 25, 1959, at the Phoenix Theater in Greenwich Village. Leonard Feather, who had seen her only a few weeks before, said she appeared to have lost 20 pounds; and after singing just one number, "T'Ain't Nobody's Bizness If I Do," she had to be helped from the stage. Six days later, she collapsed at her apartment in Harlem and was admitted to a hospital as "Eleonora McKay." The diagnosis was cirrhosis of the liver, although she seemed to rally a few days later and even began receiving visitors. But one final indignity awaited. While she was hospitalized, Federal agents raided her apartment, claimed to have found a packet of heroin, and filed charges against her. In July, her condition worsened, and Billie asked for the last rites of the Catholic Church. Two days later, on July 17, 1959, with armed guards stationed outside her hospital room, Billie Holiday died.

From the day of her passing, the tributes to Billie Holiday have never stopped, although the pain she suffered during her short life sometimes overshadows the extraordinary gift it brought to her music. Many of Billie's friends were dismayed by the bleak portrait of her presented in the 1972 film *Lady Sings the Blues*. "The thing I hope kids don't miss, the ones who are discovering Lady," worried Billie's longtime friend ***Hazel Scott**, "is that she took a lot of the tragedy out of her life and made something beautiful out of it. There were many dimensions to her, not just the sad-faced junkie, as so many people picture her." Billie may have had just that concern herself. "The blues to me is like being very sad, very sick, going to church, being very happy," she once said. "It's . . . just according to how I feel. Anything I do, it's part of my life."

SOURCES:

Chilton, John. *Billie's Blues: A Survey of Billie Holiday's Career*. London: Quartet Books, 1975.

Holiday, Billie, with William Dufty. *Lady Sings the Blues.* NY: Doubleday, 1956.

Nicholson, Stuart. *Billie Holiday.* London: Victor Gollancz, 1995.

White, John. *Billie Holiday—Her Life and Times.* NY: Universe Books, 1987.

SUGGESTED READING:

Clarke, Donald. *Wishing on the Moon: The Life and Times of Billie Holiday.* NY: Viking, 1994.

Davis, Angela Y. *Blues Legacies and Black Feminism: Gertrude "Ma" Rainey, Bessie Smith, and Billie Holiday.* NY: Pantheon, 1998.

RELATED MEDIA:

Lady Sings the Blues, directed by Sidney J. Furie, starring *Diana Ross, Paramount Pictures, 1972.

Norman Powers,
writer-producer, Chelsea Lane Productions, New York

Holland, Alianor (c. 1373–1405)

Countess of March. *Name variations: Alianor Mortimer. Born around 1373; died on October 23, 1405; daughter of Thomas Holland, 2nd earl of Kent, and ***Alice Fitzalan** (1352–1416); married Roger Mortimer, 4th earl of March, about October 7, 1388; children: six, including ***Anne Mortimer** (1390–1411); Edmund Mortimer (5th earl of March); Roger Mortimer; and ***Eleanor Mortimer** (c. 1395–1418).*

Holland, Anne (d. 1457).

See Montacute, Anne.

Holland, Anne (d. 1474)

Marquise of Dorset. *Name variations: Anne Grey. Died in 1474; daughter of Henry Holland, 2nd duke of Exeter, and ***Anne Plantagenet** (1439–1476, sister of Edward IV and Richard III); married Thomas Grey, 1st Marquis of Dorset.*

Holland, Anne (fl. 1440–1462)

Countess of Douglas. *Name variations: Anne Douglas, Anne Neville. Flourished 1440 to 1462; died on December 26, 1486; daughter of John Holland (1395–1447), duke of Huntington (r. 1416–1447), and ***Anne Stafford** (c. 1400–1432); married John Neville (great-grandson of 1st earl of Westmoreland), before February 18, 1440; married John Neville (grandson of 1st earl of Westmoreland); married James Douglas, 9th earl of Douglas, after 1461; children: (second marriage) Ralph Neville, 3rd earl of Westmoreland (1456–1499).* The Complete Peerage, *Vol. V, p. 215, makes it clear that Anne Holland is the daughter of Anne Stafford and not ***Anne Montacute** as shown in other sources.*

Holland, Caroline (1723–1774).

See Lennox Sisters.

Holland, Constance (1387–1437)

Countess of Norfolk. *Born in 1387; died in 1437; daughter of ***Elizabeth of Lancaster** (1364–1425) and John Holland (c. 1358–1399), 1st duke of Exeter (r. 1397–1399); married Thomas Mowbray (1387–1405), earl of Norfolk (executed in 1405); married Sir John Grey.*

Holland, countess of.

See Dunkeld, Ada (c. 1145–1206).
See Philippine of Luxemburg (d. 1311).
See Jeanne of Valois (c. 1294–1342).
See Joanna of Brabant (1322–1406).
See Margaret of Holland (d. 1356).
See Maud Plantagenet (1335–1362).
See Margaret of Burgundy (c. 1376–1441).
See Jacqueline of Hainault (1401–1436).

Holland, Dulcie Sybil (1913—)

Australian composer, cellist, pianist, and radio broadcaster who received many awards for her compositions. *Born in Sydney, Australia, on January 5, 1913; studied at the Royal College of Music in London; studied composition with Alfred Hill, piano with Frank Hutchens, and cello under Gladstone Bell at the Sydney Conservatorium; studied privately with Roy Agnew.*

Like many Australians in the music world, Dulcie Holland attended music schools down under before studying further at the Royal College of Music in London. At the Sydney Conservatorium, she studied composition with Alfred Hill, piano with Frank Hutchens, and cello under Gladstone Bell. She also studied privately with Roy Agnew. At the Royal College of Music, where she studied with John Ireland, she won the Blumenthal Scholarship and the Cobbett Prize for chamber composition in 1938. Once she returned to her native country, Holland became an examiner for the Australian music examination board. She also appeared as a concert pianist. In 1965, she won the Warringah and Henry Lawson Festival award. Dulcie Holland received many composition awards from the Australian Broadcasting Company as well as giving many broadcasts on the ABC network. Throughout her career, she composed extensively, writing over a hundred works for orchestra, chamber orchestra, piano, and vocal groups.

John Haag,
Athens, Georgia

Holland, Eleanor (c. 1385–?)

Countess of Salisbury. *Name variations: Eleanor Montacute. Born around 1385; daughter of Thomas Holland, 2nd earl of Kent, and *****Alice Fitzalan****; sister of *****Elizabeth Holland*** *(c. 1383–?), *****Alianor Holland*** *(c. 1373–1405), *****Margaret Holland*** *(1385–1429), and *****Joan Holland*** *(c. 1380–1434); married Thomas Montacute, 4th earl of Salisbury; children: *****Alice Montacute*** *(c. 1406–1463).*

Holland, Elizabeth (1364–1425).

See Elizabeth of Lancaster.

Holland, Elizabeth (c. 1383–?)

English noblewoman. *Name variations: Elizabeth Neville. Born around 1383; daughter of Thomas Holland, 2nd earl of Kent, and *****Alice Fitzalan****; sister of *****Eleanor Holland*** *(c. 1385–?), *****Alianor Holland*** *(c. 1373–1405), *****Margaret Holland*** *(1385–1429), and *****Joan Holland*** *(c. 1380–1434); married John Neville, before 1404; children: Ralph Neville, earl of Westmoreland (c. 1404–1484); John Neville (d. 1461).*

Holland, Joan (fl. 1300s).

See Joanna of Navarre for sidebar.

Holland, Joan (c. 1380–1434)

Duchess of York. *Born around 1380; died on April 12, 1434; daughter of Thomas Holland, 2nd earl of Kent, & Alice Fitzalan (1352–1416); sister of *****Eleanor Holland*** *(c. 1385–?), *****Elizabeth Holland*** *(c. 1383–?), *****Alianor Holland*** *(c. 1373–1405), and *****Margaret Holland*** *(1385–1429); became second wife of Edmund of Langley (c. 1380–1434), duke of York, in 1393.*

Joan Holland, duchess of York, appears in Shakespeare's *Richard II*. She was born around 1380, the daughter of Thomas Holland, 2nd earl of Kent, and ***Alice Fitzalan**, and became the second wife of Edmund of Langley, duke of York, in 1393. Edmund's first wife was ***Isabel of Castile** (1355–1392).

Holland, Lady.

See Lennox Sisters for Caroline Lennox (1723–1774).

See Fox, Elizabeth Vassall (1770–1845).

See Fox, Mary (b. 1817).

Holland, Margaret (1385–1429).

See Beaufort, Joan (c. 1410–1445) for sidebar.

Holland, queen of.

See Hortense de Beauharnais (1783–1837).

Holley, Marietta (1836–1926)

American author and humorist who attempted to expose society's disregard for the rights of women. *Name variations: (pseudonyms) "Jemyma," "Josiah Allen's Wife," and "Samantha Allen." Born in Jefferson County, New York, near Pierrepont Manor, on July 16, 1836; died near Pierrepont Manor, on March 1, 1926; third daughter and youngest of seven children of John Milton and Mary (Taber) Holley; attended local schools until age 14; never married; no children.*

Selected works: My Opinions and Betsy Bobbet's *(1873);* Samantha at the Centennial *(1876);* My Wayward Pardner *(1880);* Miss Richard's Boy *(1882);* Sweet Cicely, or Josiah Allen as a Politician *(1885);* Samantha at Saratoga *(1887);* Miss Jones' Quilting *(1887);* Samantha Among the Brethren *(1890);* Samantha on the Race Problem *(1892);* Tirzah Ann's Summer Trip *(1892);* Samantha at the World's Fair *(1893);* Josiah's Alarm *(1893);* The Widder Doodle's Love Affair *(1893);* Samantha in Europe *(1895);* Round the World with Josiah Allen's Wife *(1899);* The Borrowed Automobile *(1906);* Samantha on Children's Rights *(1909);* Who Was to Blame *(1910);* Josiah Allen on the Woman Question *(1914).*

The youngest of seven children, Marietta Holley was born in 1836 and raised on a farm in Jefferson County, New York; she began writing verses at an early age. Her family's shaky finan-

Marietta Holley

cial situation forced her to leave school at 14, after which she studied, then taught, piano. A few of her early verses were printed in the local newspapers, and, in April 1867, *Peterson's Magazine* printed one of her poems. Four years later, *Peterson's* carried the first of her humorous dialect sketches, "Deacon Slimpsey's Mournful Forebodings," which was signed with the pseudonym, "Josiah Allen's Wife." The sketch also appeared in Holley's first book *My Opinions and Betsy Bobbet's* (1873), which was followed by 20 similar volumes, the last of which, *Josiah Allen on the Woman Question,* appeared in 1914. The books, written in the tradition of Yankee humorists Seba Smith, Benjamin Shillaber, and ***Frances M. Whitcher**, pitted the practical, wifely Samantha Allen, an advocate of woman's rights, against her counterpart, the aging spinster Betsy Bobbet, a sentimentalist and staunch defender of the status quo. The books achieved great popularity, particularly among young girls and women, and sold upwards of two million copies. Holley, who at the height of her career earned a $14,000 advance for *Samantha at the World's Fair* (1893), became something of a reluctant celebrity. Despite her feminist views, and the urgings of ***Frances Willard** and ***Susan B. Anthony**, she shunned organized activities supporting women's rights, temperance, or other reforms. Holley did not stop writing until her 78th year, in 1914. She died at the age of 90 at the family farm near Pierrepont Manor.

SOURCES:

James, Edward T., ed. *Notable American Women, 1607–1950.* Cambridge, MA: The Belknap Press of Harvard University Press, 1971.

McHenry, Robert, ed. *Famous American Women.* NY: Dover, 1983.

Barbara Morgan,
Melrose, Massachusetts

Holley, Mary Austin (1784–1846)

Texas writer and land speculator. *Born Mary Phelps Austin in New Haven, Connecticut, on August 30, 1784; died in New Orleans, Louisiana, on August 2, 1846; the first of two daughters and fourth of eight children of Elijah Austin (a merchant) and Esther (Phelps) Austin; attended local schools; married Horace Holley (a Congregational minister), on January 1, 1805 (died 1827); children:* ***Harriette Williman Holley*** *(b. 1808); Horace Austin Holley (b. 1818).*

Born in New Haven, Connecticut, in 1784, Mary Holly was related on her father's side to Moses Austin and Stephen F. Austin, the founders of Texas. Her father died when she was ten, and Mary was taken in by a well-to-do uncle, Timothy Phelps. On January 1, 1805, she married Horace Holley, a young Congregational minister who had just completed theological studies at Yale University. Horace headed a congregation in Fairfield, Connecticut, and then was called to Boston, where he and Mary eventually succumbed to the more liberal atmosphere of the city and embraced Unitarianism. In 1818, when Horace was offered the presidency of the new Transylvania University, the couple and their two children moved to Lexington, Kentucky. Although Mary hated the lack of culture in what was then the frontier, she endured for nine years, during which time the couple's liberal practices frequently came under fire. In 1827, Horace resigned his post to found a new college in New Orleans. On a return voyage to New England, both he and Mary contracted yellow fever, and although she recovered, Horace died.

Holley was left with little money and took work as a governess in order to support her young son (her married daughter remained in Kentucky). Although she enjoyed her job, her desire to be near her family drew her to Texas, where her brother had reserved land for her on Galveston Bay. In 1831, she made her first visit to the region, gathering material which she turned into *Texas: Observations Historical, Geographical and Descriptive* (1933). The book, the first of its kind in English, not only proved to be a valuable source of information on the politics and social conditions within the State, but was written with such style and wit that it stimulated immigration to the territory.

Holley visited Texas again in 1835, then moved to Lexington, Kentucky, to be near her daughter and to take care of her widowed brother's children. In 1835, at the request of Stephen Austin, Holley prepared *Texas* (1836), an expanded version of her earlier work, designed as an immigrants' guide to promote annexation efforts.

The promotional nature of Holly's writings were, at least in part, motivated by her need for money. It was her hope that with the settlement and annexation of Texas, her land holdings would rise in value, enabling her to pay off debts and achieve some financial security. However, despite return trips to Texas in the late 1930s and early 1840s, she made little profit from her holdings. In 1845, she returned to Louisiana to take another job as governess. Mary Austin Holley died of yellow fever in 1846.

SOURCES:

Edgerly, Lois Stiles. *Give Her This Day.* Gardiner, ME: Tilbury House, 1990.

James, Edward T., ed. *Notable American Women, 1607–1950*. Cambridge, MA: The Belknap Press of Harvard University Press, 1971.

Barbara Morgan,
Melrose, Massachusetts

Holliday, Judy (1921–1965)

American actress typecast as a "dumb blonde" who endowed her roles with heart, intelligence, and an awareness of the characters' predicaments. *Born Judith Tuvim in New York City on June 21, 1921; died of breast cancer on June 7, 1965, at Mount Sinai Hospital in New York City; the only child of Abraham Tuvim (a fund raiser for Jewish and socialist causes) and Helen (Gollomb) Tuvim (a piano teacher); graduated Julia Richman High School in Manhattan, 1938; married David Oppenheim, on January 4, 1948 (divorced 1957); children: Jonathan (b. 1952).*

Awards: Clarence Derwent and Theatre World Award (1945) for her role in Kiss Them for Me*; Academy Award for Best Actress (1950) for* Born Yesterday*; Antoinette Perry Award (1956) for Outstanding Lead in the musical* Bells Are Ringing.

Made film debut in Greenwich Village *(1944); made stage debut in* Kiss Them for Me *(1945); starred in* Born Yesterday *on Broadway (1946–50), with a break to appear in the Spencer Tracy-Katharine Hepburn film* Adam's Rib *(1946); costarred with Broderick Crawford in* Born Yesterday *at Columbia, for which she won an Oscar; blacklisted (early 1950s); made musical comedy debut in* Bells Are Ringing *(1956).*

Filmography: Greenwich Village *(1944);* Something for the Boys *(1944);* Winged Victory *(1944);* Adam's Rib *(1949);* Born Yesterday *(1950);* The Marrying Kind *(1952);* It Should Happen to You *(1954);* Phffft *(1954);* The Solid Gold Cadillac *(1956);* Full of Life *(1957);* Bells Are Ringing *(1960).*

With an IQ of 172, Judy Holliday wanted to be a writer and director, but she had to settle for being an outstanding comedienne. Type cast as the eternal dumb blonde with a heart of gold, she won top honors for her most important roles, proving that her performances were anything but cliché.

She was born Judith Tuvim in New York City on June 21, 1921. Her father Abraham Tuvim was a professional fund raiser who wrote songs on the side; her mother **Helen Gollomb Tuvim** taught piano. The musical gatherings at the family home soon ended with her parents' separation when she was six, so Holliday was raised by her mother in her maternal grandmother's house in Queens, New York. "Mother went to her pupils' homes to teach piano," recalled Holliday, "and she also taught WPA classes at settlement houses. She was gone most of the day. My grandmother took care of the house and did the cooking. Between the two of them, I usually got what I wanted unless it was something we couldn't afford. I never had a bicycle or a Girl Scout uniform, but I never really minded. Somehow the explanation that we just didn't have the money for them seemed quite sensible to me." Though she regularly saw her father, she became extremely protective of her mother; theirs was a warm, friendly relationship.

She attended grade school at P.S. 125 in Queens. While classmates were reading *Nancy Drew and the Mystery in the Old Attic*, she was reading *War and Peace*. Arithmetic, however, left her cold. Overcoming great natural shyness, she took part in dramatics and went so far as to write and act in a Christmas play, even though she was Jewish and her grandparents had fled the tsar's pogroms in Russia. She also edited her school newspaper and won a $50 prize with an essay on "How to Keep the Streets, Parks and Playgrounds of Our City Clean." She then attended Julia Richman, a public high school for girls, graduating first in her class at age 16. Holliday remembered little of those high school years, except that she acted in school plays and had to make up arithmetic in summer school. "I'm afraid I was horribly stuffy about social life," she said. "I guess I was just a natural snob. I got a kick out of being different, and I was eager to improve myself and everyone around me. As a result, I went out mostly with boys who would take me to Broadway shows instead of parties; symphony concerts and recitals instead of dances. I was more interested in writing poetry than passing love notes and in hearing Bach than dancing to Benny Goodman. I must have been obnoxious."

Particularly in the early days of her career, she enjoyed a series of lucky breaks that she was able to maximize because of her talent, drive, and perfectionism. Told she was too young to apply to the Yale Drama School, she took a nonpaying job at Orson Welles' Mercury Theater as an assistant switchboard operator.

While vacationing at a Jewish resort in the Catskill Mountains with her mother, she became friends with Adolph Green who was performing there. Together, they gathered ***Betty Comden**, Alvin Hammer and John Frank, who became "The Revuers," a cabaret group. Back in the city in the fall of 1938, Holliday (the English equivalent of the Hebrew word *Tuvim*) dropped by a cafe called the Village Vanguard and persuaded the manager to let the group give free performances on Sunday nights in return for rehearsal space. Their topical skits, which included honoring the inventor of the shoe horn and ridiculing ***Joan Crawford** fans, were so successful that The Revuers were booked into top clubs like the Rainbow Room. The irony was that while Comden and Green wanted to perform, they were more successful as writers. Holliday, who wanted to write, was more successful as a performer, even though she became physically ill before each appearance. She was terrified of the audience, abhorred the smoke and noise of the nightclubs, and hating having to fight for the attention of drunks. Though she felt trapped and depressed, she enjoyed the company of her fellow artists. She was also bringing in money to augment her mother's income from piano lessons and intent on learning her trade. "The more painful it was," she said, "the more important I thought the experience must be. Hating it, I convinced myself it must be invaluable."

[Judy Holliday] had in common with the great comedians—with Chaplin—that depth of emotion, that unexpectedly touching emotion, that thing which would unexpectedly touch your heart.

—George Cukor

A creature of rapidly changing moods, Holliday was a perfectionist and extremely self-critical. "It wasn't unusual to find her crying between acts because she felt she hadn't done well," said her close friend Betty Comden. "Then, in a matter of minutes, she'd pull herself together and go out and do much better." Her self-imposed demands resulted in an attack of nerves with each new project. Even so, Holliday worked at relaxing everyone else involved.

In 1943, the group (along with Judy's mother Helen) went to Hollywood, rented a small apartment, bought an aging limousine, and set out to find work. Though they soon had a $1,000-a-week booking at the Trocadero, it was Holliday, and Holliday alone, who was offered film work. She turned down all opportunities until Fox agreed (only if she would sign a year's contract) to put her friends in a movie with her. The Revuers ended up on the cutting room floor of the 1944 *Greenwich Village* and, discouraged, broke up. Comden and Green returned to New York while Holliday stayed in Los Angeles with her mother and quickly followed up on her debut with bit parts in *Something for the Boys* and *Winged Victory,* for which she secured a good review. Even so, Fox dropped her option.

Always happiest in New York City, she and her mother returned there in 1945 at the time Comden and Green had their first musical hit, *On the Town.* They persuaded her to try out for the part of a prostitute in *Kiss Them for Me.* Holliday's voice was naturally low, but she worked until she developed a roar that reached the back of the house. For this, her stage debut, she won the Clarence Derwent Award for Best Supporting Actress of 1945.

A year later, when illness forced ***Jean Arthur** to drop out of *Born Yesterday* before it opened in Philadelphia, Holliday was given 72 hours to learn the role of Billie Dawn. Living on coffee and dexadrine in a Philadelphia hotel, she created a part that would endure, causing total strangers to walk up to her for the rest of her life and beg her to repeat her line: "Do me a favor, will ya, Harry? Drop dead." As the slow-witted mistress of an abusive junk dealer who caught on to her lover's crimes and outfoxed him for the good of his victims, she triumphed and won a Tony Award, playing the part on Broadway for almost four years without missing a performance. In 1948, in the middle of her Broadway run, she married the clarinetist David Oppenheim, the head of the classical recording division of Columbia Records.

Harry Cohn wanted her to do the film version of *Born Yesterday* at Columbia, and Holliday agreed on the condition that her contract bind her to no more than one picture a year so that she would have time for her new husband. Cohn rejected Holliday's demand and considered other actresses under contract to him, such as ***Lucille Ball** and ***Rita Hayworth**.

Meanwhile, with the help of Garson Kanin, who wrote *Born Yesterday,* Judy landed a supporting role in the Spencer Tracy-***Katharine Hepburn** film *Adam's Rib,* in which she played Doris Attinger, a jealous housewife who nervously devours candy bars. Kanin, Tracy, Hepburn, and director George Cukor were all pushing Holliday for *Born Yesterday,* and her performance in *Adam's Rib* was outstanding. Cohn had to recognize her screen presence and the fact that Holliday was indeed perfect for the film version of *Born Yesterday,* for which she won the Oscar for Best Actress in 1950.

Returning to New York, Holliday took a two-year hiatus from acting and settled down to the role of wife and the longed-for role of mother. Though she underwent psychoanalysis

Judy Holliday

(which would last four years) to save her marriage, the age old problem of the wife outdoing the husband prevailed, and the marriage faltered. But with the help of those psychiatric sessions and her friend George Cukor, she began to change her attitude toward acting. Cukor showed her that "my so-called desires to write and direct were completely unreal and that acting—really good acting—could be both creative and satisfying. He knocked a lot of nonsense out of me." Psychoanalysis "gave me a far greater understanding of the motivations which underlie action, and it made me look at myself in a much more realistic way."

She went on to do five more film comedies—*The Marrying Kind* (1950), *It Should Happen to You* (1953), *Phffft* (1954), *The Solid Gold Cadillac* (1956), *Full of Life* (1956) and *Bells are Ringing* (1960). To a large extent, she managed to evade the "dumb blonde" stereotype in *The Marrying Kind.* Costarring Aldo Ray, it was a comment on the unrealistic dreams that burden middle-class marriage. In playing Florence Keefer, whose young son drowns in a swimming pool, she displayed her range and sensitivity as an actress, but her performance was over-shadowed by her brush with McCarthyism.

In 1952, Holliday was drawn into the Communist witch hunts of the McCarthy era. Although she was extremely alert in all her dealings, when she testified before the Senate Internal Security sub-committee, she took on the scatter-brained persona of Billie Dawn. Unable to think of anyone she knew to be a Communist, Holliday claimed to have been duped into lending her name to Communist organizations and said that she had hired investigators to find out how she had gotten into such a mess. "I have awakened to a realization that I have been irresponsible and slightly—more than slightly—stupid. When I was solicited, I always said, 'Oh, isn't that too bad. Sure, use my name.'" Her name was listed in a book called *Red Channels,* which cataloged 151 people in the entertainment field (Leonard Bernstein, Arthur Miller, and ***Dorothy Parker** among them) who purportedly had links to Communists. Thus she was blacklisted and effectively banned from appearing on television.

Her success in the 1954 film *It Should Happen to You,* which introduced Jack Lemmon and was directed by Cukor, lifted the cloud. In it, she played Gladys Glover, whose dreams of finding fame in New York falter when she is forced to become a girdle model. She gains some weight and loses her job and decides to advertise herself by renting a billboard on Columbus Avenue. Holliday and Lemmon costarred again in *Phffft* about a tedious lawyer and his wife, a writer of radio soap operas, the following year, but it was

From the movie Born Yesterday, *starring Judy Holliday and Broderick Crawford.*

unsuccessful. Though *The Solid Gold Cadillac,* about a shareholder who battles corrupt executives, earned her solid reviews the next year, she was tired of moviemaking and Hollywood.

In 1956, her old friends Comden and Green gave her the starring role as a ditsy telephone operator in the Broadway musical *Bells Are Ringing*. Holliday drew on her experiences with the Mercury Theater and revealed her talent for vaudeville and impersonation. She also began singing lessons with conductor Herbert Greene. They, too, became close friends. Said Greene: "She understood deeply the nature of her talent, but she was also violently and destructively self-critical, to the point of unreality. Her strongest feelings were negative; she was driven by unfounded fears and feelings of guilt; she had nasty periods of depression, and she doubted her femininity and appeal to men. At the same time, she had enormous insight into other people, intense loyalty and great generosity." Holliday starred in the MGM version of *Bells Are Ringing* four years later.

Bad health and alcoholism plagued her when she was on the brink of expanding into more demanding roles. In 1960, she had the opportunity to play ***Laurette Taylor**, a film and stage star of the '20s whom Constantin Stanislavsky regarded as America's finest actress. In her lifetime, Taylor had been beset by romantic problems and alcoholism, which she conquered before succumbing to a throat ailment. *Laurette* was canceled in New Haven after Holliday herself began having problems with her throat. Audiences in Philadelphia booed her for mumbling her lines. Doctors soon discovered greater problems, and she was operated on for breast cancer. Judy Holliday appeared in one last musical, the unsuccessful *Hot Spot* in 1963, and was writing lyrics to songs by the jazz saxophonist Gerry Mulligan at the time of her death. She died of breast cancer on June 7, 1965, two weeks before her 43rd birthday.

SOURCES:

Carey, Gary. *Judy Holliday: An Intimate Life Story.* Seaview, 1982.

Current Biography. April 1951. NY: H.W. Wilson, 1951.

Holtzman, Will. *Judy Holliday.* NY: Putnam, 1982.

The New York Times (obituary). June 8, 1965.

Shout, John David. "Judy Holliday" in *Notable American Women: A Biographical Dictionary.* Vol. IV. Cambridge, MA: Belknap Press of Harvard University Press, 1980

COLLECTIONS:

Billy Rose Theater Collection, New York Public Library at Lincoln Center.

Kathleen Brady,
author of *Lucille: The Life of Lucille Ball* and of *Ida Tarbell: Portrait of a Muckraker* (University of Pittsburgh Press)

Hollingworth, Leta Stetter

(1886–1939)

***American psychologist, specializing in women, education, and gifted children, who statistically took on erroneous gender assumptions and wrote the highly regarded* Psychology of the Adolescent.** *Born Leta Anna Stetter near Chadron, Nebraska, on May 25, 1886; died in New York, New York, on November 27, 1939; buried in Wyuka Cemetery, Lincoln, Nebraska; daughter of Margaret Elinor (Danley) Stetter and John G. Stetter; attended Valentine High School, Valentine, Nebraska, 1902; granted A.B., University of Nebraska, 1906; A.M., Columbia University, 1913; Ph.D., Columbia University, 1916; married Harry L. Hollingworth, New York, New York, on December 31, 1906.*

Death of her mother (1889); moved to Valentine, Nebraska (1898); moved to New York City (1908); took position with the New York Clearing-House for Mental Defectives (1913); took position with the New York City Civil Service (1914); studied infants at the New York Infirmary for Women and Children (1914); studied effects of menstruation on women (1915); became instructor, Columbia University Teachers College (1916); studied gifted children in association with the New York school board (1920); appointed professor of education, Columbia University (1930); served as research director of the Speyer School (1936); awarded honorary doctorate of law, University of Nebraska (1938).

Selected writings: "Functional periodicity: An experimental study of the mental and motor abilities of women during menstruation," in Teachers College Contributions to Education *(no. 69, 1914); "Variability as related to sex differences in achievement," in* American Journal of Sociology *(no. 19, 1914); "Phi Beta Kappa and woman students," in* School and Society *(no. 4, 1916); "Social devices for impelling women to bear and rear children," in* American Journal of Sociology *(no. 22, 1916); "Differential action upon the sexes of forces which tend to segregate the feeble minded," in* Journal of Abnormal and Social Psychology *(no. 17, 1922).*

Leta Stetter Hollingworth, who was destined to become one of the leading psychologists in the United States, was born May 25, 1886, on a farm near Chadron, Nebraska; her mother **Margaret Stetter** died three years later. Because her father John Stetter, a cowboy, entertainer, and peddler, could not care for her, Hollingworth's maternal grandmother was largely responsible for her upbringing. Like many children born on the prairies, Leta Hollingworth received her early education in a one-room school. She excelled academically and, years later, characterized her education as "excellent in every respect. We had small classes (twelve pupils in all), all nature for a laboratory, and individualized instruction."

In 1898, Hollingworth was reunited with her father in Valentine, Nebraska. At age 15, she graduated from Valentine High School, where she showed promise in creative writing. Psychologist Lewis Terman described one of Hollingworth's early poems as comparing "favorably with the best juvenilia this reviewer had seen." In 1902, she enrolled at the University of Nebraska, where she took classes in literature and creative writing. As well, she was literary editor of the *Daily Nebraskan* and, during her final year, served as associate editor for the *Sombrero,* a student publication.

After graduation, Hollingworth attempted to fashion a literary career, devoting a great deal of time to short-story writing. It was difficult, however, to find a market for her efforts. To earn a living, she taught high school in DeWitt, Nebraska, where she also served as assistant principal. In 1908, she traveled to New York City where, on December 31, she married former university classmate Harry Hollingworth. Her husband was studying under the eminent psychologist James McKeen Cattell at Columbia University. Leta applied for a teaching position in the New York public-school system, only to discover that they did not hire married women. At loose ends, she spent much of her time in the traditional role of housewife. In order to supplement the family income and save money to further his wife's education, Harry began working in the field of applied psychology. He was a consultant to various advertising agencies, an occupation he disliked, but one which entailed considerable financial reward.

Leta enrolled at Columbia University, and in 1913 she was awarded a master's degree in educational psychology. Her research focused on the status of women in American society. Why, she asked, were females regarded as inferior? Was it biology which dictated their status, or was it the discrimination of a male-dominated society? Hollingworth undertook an extensive survey of the literature. Psychologists such as a Cattell, Edward L. Thorndike, and G. Stanley Hall had all published works which asserted that woman were inherently inferior, and yet Hollingworth could find no scientific evidence to support their claims. Thorndike wrote of:

> The patent fact that in the great achievements of the world in science, art, invention, and management, women have been far excelled by men.... In particular, if men differ in intelligence and energy by wider degrees than do women, eminence in and leadership of the world's affairs of whatever sort will inevitably belong oftener to men. They will oftener deserve it.

Thorndike's work, and the work of others like him, was based on that of Charles Darwin. Darwin argued that male intelligence varied more widely than female intelligence. Thus, men were more likely to be either intellectually gifted or defective, while females were inherently less variable, and therefore intellectually mediocre. While the intellectual life of men was dominated by high levels of perception and reasoning, the mental universe of women was filled with emotions and sensory experiences. The emotional nature of women made them suited for domestic tasks and child care. In sum, the variability argument was based on social prejudice, rather than concrete scientific observation.

Such ideas were commonly asserted in the educational, psychological, medical, and sociological literature of the day. A lone voice in the wilderness was the British psychologist Karl Pearson, who in 1897 published research refuting the variability theory. Until Leta Hollingworth's entry into the field, Pearson's work was the only scientific study to challenge conventional wisdom.

In 1913, Hollingworth took a temporary position at what was then known as the New York Clearing-House for Mental Defectives. There she assisted with the mental testing program. In 1914, her skill and expertise led to an offer of permanent employment with the newly created New York City Civil Service. As the first female psychologist hired by the city, she had the opportunity to put the variability argument to the test, while visiting schools, courts of law, and hospitals. Hollingworth discovered that there was a variation in age between men and women who were admitted to mental institutions. She argued that social factors played an important role in the phenomena:

> At present it suffices to point out that the fact that females escape the Clearing-House till beyond the age of thirty years three times as frequently as males, fits very well with the fact that more males than females are brought to the Clearing-House, on the whole. The boy who cannot compete mentally is found out, becomes at an early age the object of concern to relatives, is brought to the Clearing-House, and directed towards an institution. The girl who cannot compete mentally is not so often recognized as definitely defective, since it is not unnatural for her to drop into the isolation of the home,

Leta Stetter Hollingworth

> where she can "take care of" small children, peel potatoes, scrub, etc. . . . Thus they survive outside the institutions.

As Hollingworth noted in a subsequent study: "A girl must be relatively more stupid than a boy in order to be presented for examination and she must be still more stupid, comparatively, to be actually segregated as unfit for social and economic participation."

In 1914, Hollingworth began to use infants as a case study, since she argued they were relatively free from the environmental factors which might account for variability in children and adults. She explained the variation of female and males by the differing social and economic roles which the two sexes played in contemporary society. As she pointed out:

> A woman of natural herculean strength does not wash dishes, cook meals, or rear children much more successfully than a woman of ordinary muscle. But a man of natural herculean strength is free to abandon carpentry or agriculture and become a prizefighter or a blacksmith, thus exercising and enhancing his native equipment.

Hollingworth employed the files of the New York Infirmary for Women and Children to collect her data. Each infant born had its weight, circumference of shoulders, length, and cranial measurements recorded. In a survey of 2,000 infants, she concluded that while male babies were larger than females, there was no inherent variability between the sexes. Her results challenged the variability thesis on a scientific basis.

For several decades menstruation, and the behavioral changes associated with it, were used to characterize women as unstable. Hollingworth planned a study of menstruation for her doctoral dissertation at Columbia University. Her supervisor was Edward L. Thorndike. She tested 23 females and two males for motor skills and mental tasks over a period of three months. Her results revealed that neither motor coordination nor mental ability were impaired by menstruation. Contrary to conventional wisdom, Hollingworth proved that women were neither unreliable or inefficient during menstruation.

In 1916, already the author of one book and numerous scientific articles on the psychology of women, Leta Hollingworth was awarded a Ph.D. from Columbia University. In the same year, she published an article which explored the social control of women in child bearing and rearing. The article was prompted by the commonly held assumption that only abnormal women did not have children, and that normal women found ultimate fulfillment through child care. Hollingworth surveyed the social-control mechanisms imposed by law, medicine, education, and public opinion which underpinned attitudes toward maternity:

> It seems very clear that "the social guardians" have not really believed that maternal instinct is alone a sufficient guaranty of population. They have made use of all possible social devices to insure not only child-bearing, but child-rearing. Belief, law, public opinion, illusion, education, art . . . have all been used to reenforce maternal instinct. We shall never know just how much maternal instinct alone will do for population until all the forces and influences exemplified above have become inoperative. As soon as women become fully conscious of the fact that they have been and are controlled by these devices the latter will become useless, and we shall get a truer measure of maternal feeling.

Through her research, Hollingworth attempted to dispel the myth of the vocational limitations of women. An effort by the Phi Beta Kappa Council to limit female membership led Hollingworth to launch a spirited attack on the proposed policy.

She published her last work on the psychology of women in 1927. In it, she postulated an evolutionary thesis of the development of gender roles. As she wrote:

> The woman question is and always has been simply this: How to reproduce the species and at the same time win satisfaction of the human appetites for food, security, self-assertion, mastery, adventure, play, and so forth. Man satisfies these cravings by competitive attack, both physical and mental upon the environment. As compared with man, woman has always been in a cage, while those satisfactions are outside. The cage has been her cumbersome reproductive system.

Shortly after receiving her Ph.D., Leta Hollingworth accepted a position at Columbia University Teachers College, replacing **Naomi Norsworthy**, who had recently died. Hollingworth's early work on the testing of various aspects of women's psychology led her to study the phenomena of both the challenged and the gifted child, an area of inquiry pioneered by Norsworthy. Over the years, Hollingworth published seventy articles and eight books on the subject.

Her contributions to the field of child psychology and education were many and varied, and constitute her best-known work. While her early research concentrated on intellectually challenged children, by 1920 her work shifted towards gifted children. In particular, Hollingworth was interested in discovering the best way to meet their educational needs. She sought to counter the long held belief that gifted children did not require special programs because of their intellectual precociousness. At Columbia, she created a guidance laboratory to undertake educational and psychological counselling.

In 1920, Hollingworth arranged with the New York School Board for a segregated group of gifted children to be studied over a period of 20 years. She became one of the chief advocates of special classes for the gifted. By 1930, her research had determined that intellectual superiority does not preclude serious maladjustment problems, often caused by the social isolation gifted children experience.

For many years a course on Mental Adjustments and Adolescence had been offered at Columbia. Hollingworth argued that emotions and attitudes played as great a role as poor adjustment in adolescent behavior. In 1928, she published *The Psychology of the Adolescent,* which became a standard text in the field for many years. In 1930, Hollingworth was appointed professor of education at Columbia University.

In 1936, the New York School Board created an experimental school known as P.S. 500, or the Speyer School, with Hollingworth acting as research director. Both gifted and challenged children made up the student body, and innovative teaching methods and subjects were employed to test their effects. Perhaps Hollingworth's most ambitious organizational project was a philanthropic institution known as the Superior Foundation. Its purpose was, in her words, "to achieve a substantial endowment, to be directed toward the discovery, education and conservation as natural resources of the gifted young." As well as those areas mentioned, Leta Hollingworth's research interests varied considerably from the age at which children develop racist attitudes to a physiognomic study of the profiles of gifted and challenged children.

In 1938, she was awarded an honorary doctorate of law by the University of Nebraska. During her visit to Lincoln, Hollingworth made what seemed to her husband a strange request. He recalled that she persuaded him to visit Wyuka Cemetery:

> Where we purchased for ourselves a tiny plot of ground on the eastern slope of a grassy mound. L.S.H., in a mood that was strangely foreign to her up to that time, had become seriously concerned over the provision for our final resting place, and she expressed a desire to make such an arrangement now. The prescient nature of this act was then, by me at least, wholly unsuspected, and I little dreamed that in another eighteen months I would be bringing her there to rest forever in the spot she had chosen.

Leta Hollingworth died of abdominal cancer at the age of 53. At the time of her death, she had many works in progress, as well as plans for future research projects. Some of her research was published posthumously, but the volume of her unfinished work underscores the loss which clinical psychology suffered upon her passing.

Although she had lived more than half her life in New York, Leta Hollingworth's heart never left Nebraska. In a letter to the *Nebraska State Journal* two years before her death, she wrote: "One more thing I would say. Sometime I shall come back to Nebraska for good. I was born there. I was reared there. I was educated there. I shall take the last long sleep there. The East is too alien for the purpose of eternal sleep." After her death, Harry Hollingworth donated $51,000 to create the Leta Stetter Hollingworth Fellowship at Columbia University. The fellowship was to be awarded yearly to a female graduate student who had studied in Nebraska.

Leta Hollingworth was well known in New York feminist circles. She spoke frequently on the topic of women's suffrage and was a member of the Woman's Suffrage Party. As well, Hollingworth participated in suffrage marches and served as an observer at polling stations. Although she considered political reform important, a reform of social attitudes towards women was central to her thinking. A firm advocate of clinical psychology, Leta Hollingworth was instrumental in founding the American Association of Clinical Psychologists. Whatever she undertook, she did so with determination and conviction. As **Stephanie A. Shields** noted: "Pervading each of these areas of interest was a deep sense of personal commitment. Only her closest associates knew that although she had applied for research funds, none were ever granted for the support of her work."

SOURCES:

Benjamin, Lucy T., Jr. "The Pioneering Work of Leta Hollingworth in the Psychology of Women," in *Nebraska History.* Vol. 56. Lincoln, NE: Nebraska State Historical Society, 1975.

***Dorr, Rheta Childe**. *A Woman of Fifty.* NY: Funk and Wagnalls, 1924.

Poffenberger, A.T. "Leta Stetter Hollingworth: 1886–1939," in *The American Journal of Psychology.* Vol. 23. NY: Johnson Reprint, 1940.

Roemelle, Victoria S. "Hollingworth, Leta Anna Stetter," in *Notable American Women: 1607–1950.* Edward T. James, ed. Cambridge, MA: The Belknap Press, 1971.

Rossiter, Margaret W. *Women Scientists in America: Struggles and Strategies to 1940.* Baltimore, MD: Johns Hopkins University Press, 1982.

Shields, Stephanie A. "Ms. Pilgrim's Progress: The Contributions of Leta Stetter Hollingworth to the Psychology of Women," in *American Psychologist.* Vol. 30, no. 8. Washington: American Psychology Association, 1975.

SUGGESTED READING:

Hollingworth, Harry L. *Leta Stetter Hollingworth: A Biography.* Lincoln, NE: University of Nebraska Press, 1943.

Hugh A. Stewart, M.A.,
University of Guelph, Guelph, Ontario, Canada

Hollins, Marion B. (1892–1944)

***American golfer.** Born in East Islip, New York, in 1892; died in Pacific Grove, California, on August 27, 1944.*

Won the Women's Metropolitan (1913, 1919, 1921); won the USGA Women's Amateur (1921).

Dubbed "the golden girl," Marion Hollins grew up around golfers in East Islip, New York, and by the time she was an adult had a sound grasp of the game. After winning the Women's Metropolitan in 1913, she qualified for the finals in the USGA Women's Amateur, but lost to *__Gladys Ravenscroft__ of England. In 1921, she won the event in a surprise upset over **Alexa Stirling**, who had won three years in a row. Hollins was known for her fluid swing and her habit of humming "The Merry Widow Waltz" to keep her rhythm in check. An early feminist, she believed that women should have their own golf courses and was instrumental in building the Women's National Course at Glen Head, Long Island. She also helped plan and promote courses at Cypress Point and Santa Cruz, California. Hollins, who dabbled in horses and promotion schemes, made over $1 million in an oil deal, but lost it all in a depressed real-estate market. She died impoverished in 1944.

Hollister, Gloria (1903–1988).

See Anable, Gloria Hollister.

Holm, Celeste (1919—)

***American actress and singer who won an Academy Award for Best Supporting Actress for her performance in** **Gentleman's Agreement.** Born on April 29, 1919, in New York City; daughter of Theodor Holm (an insurance executive) and Jean (Parke) Holm (an author and artist); attended 14 schools, including Lycée Victor Durée, Paris, France; graduated from the Francis W. Parker High School, Chicago, Illinois, 1934; studied drama at the University of Chicago, 1932–34 (while still in high school); married Ralph Nelson, a director (divorced); married Francis Davies, in January 1940 (divorced); married Wesley Addy, an actor; children: (first marriage) one son.*

Selected stage work: debuted as Roberta Van Renssalaer in The Night of January 16 *(Orwigsburg Summer Theater, Deer Lake, PA, 1936); New York debut as Lady Mary in* Gloriana *(1938); Mary L. in* The Time of Your Life *(Booth Theater, New York, 1939); Ado Annie in* Oklahoma! *(St. James Theater, New York, 1943); Evelina in* Bloomer Girl *(Shubert Theater, New York, 1944); Kate Hardcastle in* She Stoops to Conquer *(New York City Center, 1949); Irene Elliott in* Affairs of State *(Royale Theater, New York, 1950); title role in* Anna Christie *(New York City Center, 1952); temporarily succeeded* ***Gertrude Lawrence** *as Anna in* The King and I *(July 1952); Maggie Palmer in* His and Hers *(48th Street Theater, New York, 1954); Mrs. Price in* Interlock *(ANTA, New York, 1958); Helen Sayre in* Third Best Sport *(Ambassador Theater, 1958); Camilla Jablonski in* Invitation to a March *(Music Box Theater, New York, 1960); title role in* Mame *(tour 1968–69); title role in* Candida *(Great Lakes Shakespeare Festival, 1970);* I Hate Hamlet *(Walter Kerr Theater, New York, 1991).*

Filmography: Three Little Girls in Blue *(1946);* Carnival in Costa Rica *(1947);* Gentleman's Agreement *(1947);* Road House *(1948);* The Snake Pit *(1948);* Chicken Every Sunday *(1949); (off-screen narrator)* A Letter to Three Wives *(1949);* Come to the Stable *(1949);* Everybody Does It *(1949);* Champagne for Caesar *(1950);* All About Eve *(1950);* The Tender Trap *(1955);* High Society *(1956);* Bachelor Flat *(1961);* Doctor, You've Got to Be Kidding! *(1967);* Tom Sawyer *(1973);* Bittersweet Love *(1976);* The Private Files of J. Edgar Hoover *(1978);* Three Men and a Baby *(1987).*

Often referred to as "amazingly versatile," actress Celeste Holm has enjoyed a remarkable career encompassing stage, screen, nightclubs, and television. A talented youngster who entertained her parents' sophisticated friends with imitations from her favorite Broadway shows, Holm seemed destined for the stage. She was educated at 14 different schools in the United States and abroad, and was trained in singing, dancing, and acting. She studied variously with Adolph Bolm of the Ballet Theater, Clytie Hine Mundy of the Covent Garden Opera, and acting coach Benno Schneider, her favorite. Holm made her professional stage debut in a summer-stock production of *The Night of January 16* (1936). She followed that with a bit part in the road company of *Hamlet* and a slightly larger role in the tour of ***Clare Boothe Luce**'s comedy *The Women* (1937). Holm's Broadway debut in the short-lived *Gloriana* (1938) was so inauspicious that biographers often fail to cite it, listing instead her portrayal of Mary L. in William Saroyan's comedy *The Time of Your Life* (1939).

Holm performed capably in a variety of roles before her breakthrough as the lovelorn Ado Annie in Rodgers and Hammerstein's blockbuster musical *Oklahoma!* (1943); her rendition of "I Cain't Say No" was a stand-out. Most critics agreed with Rosco Burton when he noted that Holm "simply tucks the show under her arm and lets the others touch it." Capitalizing on her success while still acting on Broadway, she put together a nightclub act to entertain the after theater crowds at such renowned supper clubs as La Vie Parisienne and the Persian Room at the Plaza Hotel. Cafe society flocked to see her, and the critics were charmed once more. "Her voice is sure. Her timing is exact," wrote a reviewer for *PM*. "Her talent and her intelligence are in perfect control of the situation. She is funny and sweet, and the people stop scraping their chairs around . . . and the room is tense with their listening." During World War II, Holm took her act on the road, performing with the USO for the troops in Europe.

In 1944, Holm had another successful run as the rebellious niece of ***Amelia Jenks Bloomer** in Harold Arlen's *Bloomer Girl* (1944), a Civil War period musical written with her in mind. In July of that year she also launched her film career, signing a long-term contract with Twentieth Century-Fox. She made her screen debut in *Three Little Girls in Blue* (1946) and won an Academy Award as Best Supporting Actress for her third film *Gentleman's Agreement* (1947). Her film career included a wide variety of roles and two subsequent Best Supporting Actress nominations, for *Come to the Stable* (1949) and *All About Eve* (1950).

Holm continued to combine stage and nightclub performances with her film career throughout the 1950s. She made her television debut on the "Chevrolet Show" (CBS, 1949) and appeared in dramatic productions and variety shows through the mid-1970s. Her later stage performances included a nationwide tour with the "Theater in Concert" program (1963, 1964, and 1966) and a national tour in *Mame* (1969), for which she received the ***Sarah Siddons** Award. In the '90s, Holm appeared on Broadway with Nicol Williamson in *I Hate Hamlet* (1991) and in a concert performance of the Rodgers and Hammerstein musical *Allegro* (1994). She was also seen regularly as the grandmother on the television series "Promised Land."

An activist, Holm has been a member of the governing boards of the World Federation of

From the movie Come to the Stable, *starring Elsa Lanchester, Celeste Holm (center), and Loretta Young.*

Mental Health and the National Association for Mental Health. In 1979, she was knighted by King Olav V of Norway. President Ronald Reagan appointed her to the National Council for the Arts in 1982, and the following year she served as chair of the New Jersey Motion Picture and Television Development Commission. Holm has been married four times. With her first husband, director Ralph Nelson, she had her only child, a son. Her fourth husband is actor Wesley Addy.

SOURCES:

Current Biography. NY: H.W. Wilson, 1944.

Katz, Ephraim. *The Film Encyclopedia.* NY: HarperCollins, 1994.

McGill, Raymond D., ed. *Notable Names in the Theater.* Clifton, NJ: James T. White, 1976.

Wilmeth, Don B. and Tice L. Miller, eds. *Cambridge Guide to American Theatre.* NY and London: Cambridge University Press, 1993.

Barbara Morgan,
Melrose, Massachusetts

Holm, Eleanor (1913—)

American swimmer who won 35 U.S. championships but is most remembered for her dismissal from the 1936 Olympics. *Name variations: Eleanor Holm Jarrett. Born Eleanor Grace Holm on December 6, 1913, in Brooklyn, New York; youngest of seven children of Charlotte (Long) and Franklin Holm; married Art Jarrett (a band leader and singer), in 1933 (divorced 1938); married Billy Rose (r.n. William Samuel Rosenberg, an entertainment mogul), in 1939 (divorced 1954); married Tommy Whalen, in 1974 (died 1986).*

Won the National Indoor Junior championships in three different categories; won the Outdoor Junior Medley championship; won the National Women's Indoor championships in five different categories; in all, won 35 U.S. championships; won a gold medal in the 100-meter backstroke in the Los Angeles Olympics (1932).

Eleanor Holm, born the youngest of seven children in Brooklyn, New York, in 1913, always claimed she was a water rat as a child. Her family had a cottage in Long Beach, New York, where they vacationed every summer. Said Holm:

> My mother used to tie water wings on me because I didn't know how to swim. I had no fear of the water, and I used to go way out in the ocean, and a lifeguard had to come out and keep getting me. On the way in he would bawl me out and say, "Don't do that again," but he would also teach me how to swim on the way in. An hour later he'd be out getting me again. . . . I was no dope. I was getting free lessons.

Holm enjoyed watching champion swimmers at the Long Beach Olympic Pool, especially when the Women's Swimming Association (WSA) of New York came there for racing and diving competitions; diver ***Helen Meany** was her idol. Upon joining the WSA, Holm initially became a medley swimmer, but there was one drawback: there were then no Olympic medley competitions. On the advice of her coaches, she concentrated on the backstroke.

From 1927 until 1935, Holm won 35 U.S. championships and set numerous world records. She also captured one or more AAU titles in that period, every year but 1933. In 1928, Holm was selected for the Olympic swim team when she was only 14; she finished 5th in Amsterdam in the 100-meter backstroke. In the 1932 Olympics, she won a gold medal in the 100-meter backstroke in the record time of 1:19.4 and no doubt would have won more medals had her career not been abruptly terminated—for Eleanor Holm is best remembered for being kicked off the Olympic team in 1936 by Avery Brundage, president of the U.S. Olympic Committee (USOC).

In 1933, as a result of her success in the Los Angeles Olympics, the 19-year-old Holm had married popular band leader Art Jarrett, signed a contract with Warner Bros., and immersed herself in Hollywood. Evenings, she sang with her husband's band in nightclubs while continuing to train faithfully by day. Holm won swimming competitions throughout her Hollywood years. In 1936, she boarded the S.S. *Manhattan* along with the entire American Olympic squad, having qualified easily for her berth on the team. "Feeling that a married woman needed less chaperonage than the adolescent girls who made up most of the team," writes Allen Guttmann, Holm "danced, drank [champagne], and ignored reprimands." Though no one accused her of being drunk, Holm was dropped from the team by Brundage and barred from future competition before the ship reached port. The pleas and petitions of over 100 teammates and competitors from other countries fell on deaf ears, and Holm's amateur days were over. "The regulations stated that all team members should continue the same training preparations that we were accustomed to having in the States," said Holm. "That's all I was doing. At home it was my custom to have a glass of wine or champagne every day after a workout."

Brundage, however, had not reckoned on the spirit of the lively swimmer who became the star attraction. Instead of being sent home in ignominy, as Brundage had planned, she became a celebrity reporter; the Associated Press hired her

Opposite page
Eleanor Holm

on the spot. It was Brundage who was punished. Pilloried by the press for overreacting, he had to endure Holm's presence everywhere he went. Night after night, he sulked at parties with Holm in attendance.

> I was everything Avery Brundage hated. I had a few dollars, and athletes were supposed to be poor. I worked in nightclubs, and athletes shouldn't do that. I was married. All of this was against his whole conception of what an athlete should be. It didn't matter to him that I held the world record. . . . It was just that I didn't conform to his image of an athlete. But he rained on my parade for only a very short time. He did make me famous. I would have been just another female backstroke swimmer without Brundage.

Holm was probably right. That summer, the Dutch team cruised past their rivals. **Dina Senff** won the gold in the 100-meter backstroke. ***Rie Mastenbroek** took home the silver in the 100-meter backstroke, the gold in the 100-meter freestyle and the 400-meter freestyle, while her teammate ***Ragnhild Hveger** was a second-place finisher; Hveger would go on to demolish 42 world records between 1936–42.

Hitler used the 1936 Berlin Olympics as a showcase for his fascist government. Even though her political sympathies were not with the Nazis, Holm watched the events from a press box next to Hitler and Goering, and sought Hitler's autograph several times at the request of friends. ***Leni Riefenstahl**, the famous cinematographer, also shot footage of Holm for her documentary of the 1936 games, but it was never used. Stories circulated about Holm's antics in Berlin, but her high profile was simply her way of thumbing her nose at Brundage.

When Eleanor Holm returned to the States, she cashed in on her dismissal from the Olympics, appearing with the Cleveland Aquacade and at the 1939–40 World's Fair, doing swimming stunts for $4,000 a week. Her Aquacade tours were sponsored by Billy Rose, the entertainment mogul. Soon she divorced Jarrett and married Rose. Looking back, Holm said:

> How does one keep her life in perspective given all the bright lights and publicity? . . . I got so used to it, it was just like any everyday event. . . . I never had any problems adjusting because I was never really avid. Working with Arthur's band, doing theater, working in nightclubs, being in the Aquacades, and then marrying Billy Rose, I had all the glamour in the whole world, and I was right in the middle of it.

Following her marriage to Rose, Holm retired from the Aquacade and, for the next 12 years, hosted frequent parties at their lavish estate in Mount Kisco, New York. The marriage seemed idyllic until **Joyce Mathews**, ex-wife of Milton Berle, slashed her wrists in Rose's apartment. Holm promptly retained lawyer Louis Nizer and the three-year "War of the Roses" hit the newspapers. After divorcing Rose in 1954, Holm moved to Miami Beach. She married for a third time in 1974. Well into her 70s, she continued to play tennis and swim.

In 1966, Eleanor Holm was elected to the International Swimming Hall of Fame. In retrospect, her transgression in 1936 seems minor, and many consider her punishment unwarranted. Some maintain it might have had more to do with the perceived limits of her gender than with the limits or rules set by an Olympic Committee.

SOURCES:

Carlson, Lewis H. and John J. Fogarty. *Tales of Gold.* Chicago and NY: Contemporary Books, 1987.

Condon, Robert J. *Great Women Athletes of the 20th Century.* Jefferson, NC: McFarland, 1991.

Greenspan, Bud. *100 Greatest Moments in Olympic History.* Los Angeles, CA: General Publishing Group, 1995.

Guttmann, Allen. *Women's Sports: A History.* NY: Columbia University Press, 1991.

Porter, David L., ed. *Biographical Dictionary of American Sports: Basketball and Other Indoor Sports.* NY: Greenwood Press, 1989.

RELATED MEDIA:

Tarzan's Revenge (70 min. film), starring decathlon champion Glenn Morris and Eleanor Holm, Twentieth Century-Fox, 1938.

Karin L. Haag,
freelance writer, Athens, Georgia

Holm, Hanya (1888–1992)

German-born dancer and teacher, one of the founders of the American Dance Festival, and choreographer for 13 Broadway musicals, including the celebrated* Kiss Me Kate *and* My Fair Lady, *who greatly influenced dancers and choreographers. *Born Johanna Eckert in Worms-am-Rhine, Germany, on March 3, 1888 (some sources erroneously cite 1892 or 1893); died of pneumonia at St. Vincent's Hospital in New York City on November 5, 1992; daughter of Valentin Eckert and Maria (Mörtschel or Moerschel) Eckert; attended Convent of the English Sisters in Mainz; studied piano at the Hoch School in Frankfurt, eurythmics with Dalcroze in Frankfurt and then in Hellerau near Dresden, and modern dance at the Mary Wigman Institute in Dresden; married Reinhold Martin Kuntze (divorced); children: one son, Klaus Holm (a noted specialist in theatrical lighting).*

Awards: The New York Times *Award for* Trend *as best dance composition of the year (1937); New York Drama Critics award for choreography for the musical-comedy* Kiss Me Kate *(1948); Capezio Award; honored by the Federation of Jewish Philanthropies for her contributions to modern dance (1958); honorary degree of Doctor of Fine Arts, Colorado College (1960); Samuel H. Scripps Award (1984); American Dance Festival Award (1984); Astaire Award (1987).*

Joined the Mary Wigman Institute in Dresden (1921); choreographed and directed at Ommen, Netherlands, Euripides' Bacchae *(summer, 1928) and* Plato's Farewell to his Friends *(summer 1929); choreographed* L'Histoire d'un Soldat *(Dresden, 1929); was associate director and co-dancer with Mary Wigman in* Das Totenmal *(Munich, 1930); emigrated to U.S. (1931); opened Mary Wigman School of the Dance in New York City (1932), reopened as the Hanya Holm School of the Dance (1936); choreographed the ballet* Trend, *New York City (December 1937),* Etudes *and* Dance of Introduction, *New York (April 1938),* Dance Sonata, Dance of Work and Play *and* Metropolitan Daily, *New York (February 1939),* Tragic Exodus, *New York (1939),* They Too Are Exiles, *New York (January 1940),* The Golden Fleece, *New York (March 1941),* Parable *and* Suite of Four Dances *(1943),* L'Histoire d'un Soldat, *Aspen Festival (August 1954),* Ozark Suite *in Brooklyn, New York (December 1956).*

Choreographed at the annual Colorado College Summer Sessions, Colorado Springs held each August: From This Earth *(1941),* What So Proudly We Hail *and* Namesake *(1942),* Orestes and the Furies *(1943),* What Dreams May Come *(1944),* The Gardens of Eden *(1945),* Dance for Four and Windows *(1946),* And So Ad Infinitum *(1947),* Xochipili *(1948),* History of a Soldier, Ionization *(1949),* Five Old French Dances *(1945),* Prelude and Quiet City *(1951),* Kindertotenlieder, Concertino da Camera *(1952),* Ritual, Temperament and Behavior *(1953),* Prelude I and II, Presages *(1954),* Desert Drone, Pavane, Sousa March *(1955),* Preludio and Loure *(1956),* Chanson Triste, You Can't Go Home Again, *and* Ozark Suite *(1957),* Music for an Imaginary Ballet *(1961),* Figure of Predestination, Toward the Unknown Region *(1963),* Theatrics *(1964),* Spooks *(August 1967).*

Choreographed for Broadway musicals: (also directed) The Eccentricities of Davey Crockett *(from* Ballet Ballads, *May 1948); (also directed)* The Insect Comedy *(June 1948);* Kiss Me Kate *in New York (December 1948) and in London (March 1951);* The Liar *(May 1950);* Out of This World *(1951);* My Darlin' Aida *(October 1952);* The Golden Apple *(March*

1954); Reuben, Reuben *(Boston, 1955);* My Fair Lady *in New York (March 1955) and in London (April 1958);* Where's Charley?, *London (February 1958);* Christine *(April 1960);* Camelot *(December 1960);* Anya *(November 1965). Choreographed and directed operas* The Ballad of Baby Doe, *Central City, Colorado (July 1956) and* Orpheus and Euridice, *Vancouver, British Columbia (July 1959). Choreographed plays:* E=MC^2, *Columbia University, New York (June 1948);* Blood Wedding *(February 1949). Choreographed for film* The Vagabond King *(1956).*

Hanya Holm was born Johanna Eckert on March 3, 1888, in the historic city of Worms in the old German grand duchy of Hesse. Her father Valentin Eckert was a wine merchant; her mother **Maria Mörtschel Eckert** was a trained chemist, who, though she never practiced professionally, held several patents for her scientific discoveries and was working on a synthetic substitute for cork when she died in 1917. As a child, Hanya was taken to nearby Mainz where she was educated at the Convent of the English Sisters, a private Catholic school known for its progressive methods and low teacher-pupil ratio. There Holm claimed to have developed her love of learning and her appreciation of the interrelationship of all forms of knowledge. Devoted to physical education, she learned to ice skate and was taught to swim in the Rhine. By all accounts, she led a happy childhood in Mainz, where, surrounded by the remains of the past—Roman, medieval, Renaissance and Reformation—the arts intruded into her consciousness at every step. In 1904, at age 16, she began to commute to nearby Frankfurt am Main for piano lessons at the Hoch School and there occasionally took walk-on parts in the productions of the famed director Max Reinhardt, appearing in one of the earliest productions of his opus *The Miracle.*

Although her musical studies were successful, it became clear to Hanya that simply playing music was not enough to satisfy her artistic impulses and that her restless body demanded a more physical approach. Thus, upon her graduation from the convent school (where she subsequently taught for a time), Holm began studying at the institute of the Swiss music theoretician Emile-Jacques Dalcroze. The famous teacher insisted that music be interpreted by physical motion, and he taught his students to move in a rhythmic fashion to the music they played and heard, a technique known as eurythmics. Although she studied at Dalcroze's institute, first at Frankfurt and then at Hellerau near Dresden, Holm remained unsatisfied. In addition, she was experiencing setbacks in her private life for, by 1921, she had met, married, and divorced painter-sculptor Reinhold Martin Kuntze with whom she had a son, Klaus. Even though Holm was now 33 years old, had an infant to care for, and had, as yet, no thoughts of a dance career, she became acquainted in Dresden with the innovative work of ***Mary Wigman**, eventually to be regarded as Germany's greatest dancer, and decided to study with her.

The period following the First World War was difficult for a Germany filled with disillusionment, clouded by defeat, and threatened by almost complete economic collapse. But it was also a period of enormous experimentation and the great age of German expressionism, a movement that sought new modes of expression in painting, theatrical presentation, cinema and dance. Born in Hanover in 1886, Mary Wigman was only two years older than Holm but had begun her career much earlier. Like Hanya, she had studied eurythmics with Dalcroze but had then gone on to study with Rudulf von Laban, inventor of the now indispensable Laban system of dance notation, and had worked as his assistant in Switzerland as early as 1914. Although influenced by the European performances of ***Isadora Duncan**, Wigman was herself a pioneer in modern dance (all too often taken to have been a wholly American creation), adding an emotional quality to the rather mechanical approach of von Laban. Composing works to be performed without music and others for percussion only, she attempted to demonstrate the independence of dance as an art form, while departing entirely from Dalcroze's doctrine that motion must follow music. Her solo *Witch Dance,* in which she made her stage debut in 1914, was anything but beautiful, punctuated by distorted bodily movements and performed in a haunting and disturbingly ugly mask, but it demonstrated the links between the germinating modern dance and the expressionist movement already underway in other branches of the arts in Germany at that time.

Wigman had reached the zenith of her career on stage in 1918, with a performance of her composition *The Seven Dances of Life,* but she was met with strong resistance from the public and the critics, who were too accustomed to the artifices of classical ballet to grasp that what she was doing was equally profound. In 1919, however, she finally experienced success with her solo performances in Zurich and Hamburg, and the following year she founded the Mary Wigman Central Institute in Dresden. Here, she attempted to train dancers in her own choreographic concepts which she called "Absolute Dance," a style placing no reliance on such external elements as music, props, or story line, while she also experimented with new choreographic ideas. Wigman was one of the first choreographers to recognize the importance of the blank spaces between the dancers as a part of the overall composition, soon developing a group of performers notable for their use of space, an aspect of the art that Holm never forgot and used to great effect in her own works. In later years, Hanya Holm often remarked on how fortunate she was to have been able to join the company when Wigman was developing the basic concept of her art, namely that dance was capable of representing and recreating the human drama. Holm's own performances, which she called her "Dance Confessions," were dark with profound emotionalism, and she was determined to make them the choreographic equivalents of the theatrical experimentation going on in Germany.

A creative talent of the first magnitude.

—**John Martin, *The New York Times***

In 1921, however, it was still too early to speak of a "Wigman school." Rather, in the words of Wigman, it was a "club," whose members experimented from one dance to the next, never accepting anything as final. With no teachers (Wigman was self-taught in modern dance), the dancers had to draw from within, and, though the basic concepts were those of Wigman, teacher and pupils learned from one another. Speaking of pupil Holm, Wigman recalled years later:

> On the occasion of one of our improvised dance evenings a short, delicately built girl showed her first study. "Egyptian Dance"—so it said on the program. Certainly it was derivative, there was something assimilated of seen and experienced images about it. And yet behind all this one could see an already sure feeling for style, a sense for clear organic structure and, in spite of the faults of the beginner, the ability to meet the demands on technique and body. The creative will and the ability to shape were well balanced and stood the test. That was Hanya and that was the first artistic impression I received from her.

It was under the guidance of Wigman that Holm became both a dancer and a teacher of dance, and it was in her early years with the Wigman Company that she adopted her professional name: Hanya, a nickname for Johanna, and Holm, meaning "holly," because it alliterated well with Hanya. As Wigman's tours became ever more extended, it was to Holm that she entrusted the care of her increasingly international student body. In her training, Wigman stressed the importance of each dancer seeking to transcend his or her limitations but at the same time taught the necessity of subordinating self to the requirements of group performance. "In the awakening of the group to a communal rhythmic pattern there lies, to some extent, self-denial of individual expression," she said. "But this yielding of ground is not lost. It is absorbed, incorporated, and brought back to life in the totality of the group's creation." It was in this milieu that Holm learned her art and became a distinguished artist in her own right.

Hanya Holm remained with Mary Wigman's Central Institute for ten years, during which time the company grew in size, scope, and reputation, touring various cities in both Germany and Italy. But there was never enough money, the dancers were not paid, and eventually the company had to be dissolved, giving its final performance at the First International Dance Congress held in Essen in 1928. Though the company had folded, the school that had nurtured it continued to thrive, and, on the invitation of Wigman, Holm declined an appointment as dancer-choreographer at a theater in Hanover to remain as chief instructor at the Wigman School, which by now had become a world famous institution with excellent facilities in a villa it had taken over outside Dresden. As her reputation grew, Holm was invited to the open-air theater at Ommen in the Netherlands, two summers in a row, to choreograph and direct Euripides' *Bacchae* (1928) and a new work, *Plato's Farewell to His Friends* (1929). Her first great triumph took place in Dresden, where, in 1929, the pianist Paul Aron arranged to have a performance of Igor Stravinsky's *L'Histoire d'un Soldat* staged, and Holm, now 40, was chosen to dance the role of the princess. Holm's greatest success in this production lay in her bending the art in which she had been trained to the new and extremely irregular and difficult rhythms of the Russian master of modern music. The following year, in Munich, she added additional luster to her reputation when she took part as leader of the women's chorus in the antiwar pageant *Das Totenmal* (The Death Time), a multimedia production based on a poem and score by the Swiss poet Albert Talhoff.

In 1930, Mary Wigman made her first tour of the United States, under the aegis of the impresario Sol Hurok. Back in Dresden, she was visited by Hurok, who encouraged her to open a school to teach the Wigman method in New

Hanya Holm, 1936. Photograph by Imogen Cunningham.

York. It was to her chief instructor that Wigman entrusted this task. On September 25, 1931, in what was to be the great turning point in her life, Hanya Holm arrived in New York, still not certain at 43 in which direction she might best direct her career: to dancing, to teaching, or to choreography. Though respected as a dancer and much esteemed as a choreographer, it was as a teacher that her genius was to manifest itself.

Although it is widely believed that modern dance is an American form that grew out of the pioneering work of Isadora Duncan and *Ruth St. Denis, and although there is no question that the work of Isadora Duncan lies at the root of the modern style, and that almost all of the American pioneers who succeeded her were trained in the school of Denishawn, it is a fact that modern dance as a recognizable genre emerged in Germany a decade before it did in the United States. While *Martha Graham gave her first recital only in 1926, *Helen Tamiris her first concert in 1927, and *Doris Humphrey and Charles Weidman made their New York debut together in 1928, Mary Wigman and her Dresden-based company had already developed a repertoire comprising 16 group dances and 45 solo numbers. Whereas in America the dancers had not yet developed a clear idea of what modern dance should be or in what way it was to be related to indigenous American themes, in Germany a modern dance with clear-cut parameters had already been developed and modern dance was a recognizable style of its own.

After coming to America and meeting the gifted dancers emerging from the limitations imposed by Denishawn but endowed with awesome training, Holm was drawn into intense discussions with Wigman as to what modern dance was all about. Far from being a fanatic on the subject of German dance, Holm relished the stimulation of these encounters, and in her lectures and dance workshops she did all that she could to explain and advocate what she had learned at home, while at the same time rejecting the role of mere observer and throwing herself wholeheartedly into experiencing what was going on in American dance. In explaining the difference between the two modes, Holm wrote:

> The entire orientation of Mary Wigman's dance is toward the establishment of a relationship between man and his universe. It is this philosophical tendency that influences the emotional, spatial and functional aspects of her own dancing and her pedagogical principles. Emotionally, the German dance is basically subjective and the American dance objective in their characteristic manifestations, but I believe that it throws some light on their fundamental emotional departure. The tendency of the American dancer is to observe, portray and comment on her surroundings with an insight into intellectual comprehension and analysis. The German dancer, on the other hand, starts with the actual emotional experience itself and its effect upon the individual. The distinction is one of "being" as contrasted with "doing," of immersing the self in an emotional state as the necessary prelude to creation as contrasted with objective reconstruction of a known situation.

The Mary Wigman School opened in New York City in 1932, in the depths of the Great Depression. The first year, during which Wigman made a visit and the business affairs of the school were handled by Hurok, was a great success. The following year, however, Hurok left to pursue other interests, and Holm was left to manage a struggling institution whose initial novelty had worn off. Rejecting the easy option of returning to Germany, and passing up an offer to teach in the Soviet Union, Holm decided to make her career in America. Immersing herself in the American scene, she mastered English, became an American citizen, traveled extensively, and devoted herself to coming to terms with the American character, so different from that of her students in Europe. She taught at Mills College in California and during summers in Colorado (at Denver, Aspen, and Colorado Springs), and after five years gradually put together a proper company.

In the summer of 1934, four dynamic and determined innovators in dance had met at the avant-garde Bennington College in Bennington, Vermont, for what amounted to a kind of summit conference on the as yet young, experimental and inchoate art of modern dance. Martha Graham, Doris Humphrey, Charles Weidman, and Hanya Holm were all remarkably different dancers; except for Holm, all were American and all had passed through Denishawn, the pioneering if somewhat bizarre and idiosyncratic school of Ruth St. Denis and Ted Shawn. The eventual outgrowth of that summer meeting was the American Dance Festival, which flourished at Bennington until it was later transferred to Durham, North Carolina.

In 1936, Holm was forced to make a difficult decision. Three years before, Adolf Hitler had come to power in Germany and succeeded in imposing a straightjacket over every aspect of German life and art. Given the fact that Wigman had chosen to remain in Germany and had not chosen to separate herself from the views of the Nazis, and with the mood in the U.S. growing increasingly anti-Nazi, it had become impossible to maintain the school under the Wigman name. Holm offered to let Wigman decide whether or not she should remain in New York and continue the school under her own name, or shut it down and return to Germany. Fortunately, Wigman understood the situation and assured Holm that remaining in America and continuing the Wigman School under Hanya's own name would be agreeable to her. Thus, in 1936, the Hanya Holm School of Dance opened in New York. That Holm's decision to settle in America was a wise one was demonstrated when the Nazis shut down the Wigman school in Germany. Wigman was forced to retire in 1942, not reappearing on the German dance scene until after the Second World War ended in 1945.

In changing the name of the school, Holm chose to close the original school in Steinway Hall and move to a new location at 215 West 11th Street in the Greenwich Village section of Manhattan. There the school consisted of a large two-storey room with a good floor surface that provided a dance area of 40 by 45 feet. On the second level was a mezzanine on which were located the business office and faculty lounge, the remainder of the studio on both floors being occupied by dressing rooms and showering facilities. Holm did not limit herself to teaching but also pioneered in the staging of lecture demonstrations at various colleges and what would now be called "workshops," programs in which she stressed movement, relaxation, elasticity, and the handling of space, and which culminated in a dance presented by her and her group. A member of the advisory board of Bennington College (where she taught summer sessions in modern dance from 1934 to 1939), together with Graham, Humphrey, and Charles Weidman, Holm was a founding member of what came to be referred to as the "Bennington Group." This was the most exciting period in the formative history of modern dance, and Bennington College became an electrifying summer mecca for dancers and dance students from all over the country.

After several years of preparation, Holm made her New York debut at age 50 at the Mecca Auditorium (now the New York City Center) on December 29, 1937. She offered *Trend,* an original composition created for the Bennington Festival the previous summer, which depicted a society being destroyed by its own false values. *Trend* established her as a major choreographic force in American dance. With scenery by Arch Lauterer and music by Wallingford Riegger, this 55-minute work was an epic production involving a large company, a sophisticated design, and abstract movements performing on different levels connected by ramps and steps. Reviewing the show, John Martin, dance critic for *The New York Times,* wrote:

> Miss Holm brings to the business of composition a point of view totally different from that of any of our other major choreographers, and opens up a new vista for the production of great dance dramas. "Trend" is far less closely related to "concert" dancing than it is to theater, that heroic type of theater that we are accustomed to call tragedy. It is inevitable in its development, unhurried and driving in its dramatic intensity and makes large demands upon its audience. Though the work falls into sections they are more like scenes in a drama than separate dances, for they grow integrally out of each other. Similarly, the materials from which they are made, are emanations from the emotional situation rather than inventions.

Trend had a theme of social protest found in a number of Holm's dances, which tended to be solemn in tone. On the other hand, her work was not based solely on social criticism. Her choreography could be light-hearted, humorous, and even popular as demonstrated by her later successes with the Broadway musical.

On May 31, 1939, Holm became the first modern dancer to appear on television, a medium so new that it was as yet limited to a small area within New York City. The program, sandwiched in between country singers and a singing guitarist, consisted of an abbreviated version of *Metropolitan Daily* performed on Channel W2XBS. Not until 18 years later would Holm return to television. By that time, the medium had reached maturity. In October of that year, 1957, NBC presented a one-hour ballet based on the story of Pinocchio, with Mickey Rooney in the title role, Alec Wilder as composer, Mata and Hari as dancing marionettes, and Holm as choreographer. Though *The New York Times* review was cool, other critics hailed the production.

In 1941, Holm had established the summer dance program at Colorado College in Colorado Springs, where she continued to teach each season until 1983. She had first gone to Colorado as early as 1933, when she had been invited to teach at the Perry-Mansfield School in Steamboat Springs. When word reached her associates in Colorado that she had formed her own company, she was immediately invited to present her first recitals there. She and her troupe were warmly received everywhere, and from then on Hanya maintained close association with the state and especially with Colorado Springs and its annual festival. For this, she devised some of her most original and memorable dances, including *Dance of Introduction, From This Earth, Metropolitan Daily,* and *What Dreams May Come.*

Bound to New York or touring for much of the year, Holm found her annual eight-week sessions in Colorado Springs to be the ideal environment for renewal. The freedom, the relaxed way of life, the expansiveness of the country, and the majesty of the mountains served to renew her spirits and her creativity, and she continued her working vacations as director of the dance festival until she was 95. She was also instrumental in bringing many of the most highly regarded dancers in America (including, among others, Alwin Nikolais and *__Valerie Bettis__) to the festival, so that for decades the unlikely setting of Colorado Springs became one of the most important centers of dance in the country. Her son Klaus, who used the name Klaus Holm and who had become a noted specialist in theatrical lighting, designed the lighting for several of his mother's productions in Colorado Springs and in New York. The year 1941 had also seen the dissolution of Hanya Holm's dance company, the financial burdens having proved to be more than she could bear. Her summers at Colorado Springs thus became all the more important for it was there that she was able to continue her choreographic work. With the end of her company came the virtual end of her dancing career; except for a few appearances with her students in Colorado, the last in 1948 when she was 60, she ceased to perform in public. Instead, Holm embarked on a completely new phase of her career, the composing of dances for the American musical stage.

Following in the footsteps of *__Agnes de Mille__, another modern dancer and choreographer who achieved her greatest successes on Broadway with her now legendary choreography for *Oklahoma!* (1943), Holm undertook to design the dances for the musicals *The Eccentricities of Davey Crockett* (from *Ballet Ballads*) and *The Insect Comedy* (both 1948). She directed the first and collaborated with José Ferrer on the direction of the second. That same year, she choreographed the now legendary *Kiss Me Kate*. Based on Shakespeare's *The Taming of the Shrew,* this Cole Porter musical dealt with a modern-day comedy duo, formerly married to one another and reunited to perform a musical version of the Shakespearean comedy. This play-within-a-play format required Holm to create dances appropriate for the Renaissance sequences as well as for the modern period, the result being a choreographic extravaganza ranging from the Viennese-style waltz "Wundabar," the soft-shoe number "Brush Up Your Shakespeare," the perky "We Opened in Venice," the raucous "Tom, Dick and Harry" on to the beguine "Were Thine That Special Face." *Kiss Me Kate* was followed almost at once by Holm's second Porter musical, *Out of This World.* Although visually one of the most beautiful productions to open on Broadway and endowed with one of Cole Porter's loveliest songs (the now forgotten "Use Your Imagination"), *Out of This World* suffered from a weak book and from a star, **Charlotte Greenwood**, who, however beloved from her many appearances in films, was not strong enough to carry an entire show. The production was a failure, and Holm's choreography did not receive the plaudits that had become customary.

After choreographing *My Darlin' Aida* (1952), *The Golden Apple* (1954), and the unsuccessful *Reuben, Reuben* (1955), she dazzled Broadway once again with her choreography for *My Fair Lady,* based on George Bernard Shaw's 1914 comedy *Pygmalion.* One of the most successful musicals of the decade, it featured such dances as the rowdy "With a Little Bit o'Luck," the cheery "Get Me to the Church on Time," the clever "The Rain in Spain," and the mischievously satiric "The Ascot Gavotte." She followed this triumph with the dances for a British production of *Where's Charley?* (1957), for the highly successful *Camelot* (1960), and for *Anya* (1965).

As a choreographer for musical comedy, Holm amazed her contemporaries with her ability to submerge the trademarks of her concert dances to develop something equally original for the musical-comedy form. She adapted herself to the American musical genre while at the same time advancing it to another level—doing so, moreover, in old age, when a lesser artist might have become frozen and set in her ways. In addition, Holm supplied choreography for such non-musical productions as *E=MC²* at Columbia University (1949) and Federico Garcia Lorca's *Blood Wedding* for New Stages (1949). She also did the choreography for a single Hollywood film, *The Vagabond King* (Paramount, 1956).

Hanya Holm was a warm, blue-eyed blonde, remembered by her students for her tenacity and drive. She was tiny (5'2"), weighed about 110 pounds, and, with her somewhat squat figure, looked rather ordinary. Certainly she did not look like any of the modern dancers of the day, though there is no doubt that there lay, behind the bland façade, the stuff of genius. Endowed with an inflexible will and a rigid self-discipline, she drove herself without stint and expected her students to do the same. As a teacher, she stressed the basic nature of movement rather than any particular technique. Though her vision broadened from experience and maturity and was expanded by her exposure to American concepts of modern dance, she never changed her basic view of dance as sheer movement within the limits of the body's natural ability. She put emphasis on clarity and precision in movement, the use of the dancing body in space and its relationship to depth, width, and height. In performance, her dancers appeared to be reaching out for some desired yet unobtainable goal, a characterization of Western creative expression whether in philosophical speculation or the creation of dances, dramas, or symphonic music. In the words of her biographer Walter Sorell:

> Most important of all . . . has been Hanya's approach to technique based on her philosophy of setting the dancer free and giving him the tools with which to develop his individual creative ability. At a time when the stress was on the dancer's psychodramatic experience, Hanya kept away from it and taught, above all, the kinetic experience, the logic and understanding of movement per se.

In 1947, nearing 60, Holm realized that she would be unable to organize another company of her own and gave up her studio. Thereafter, she conducted her classes at Michael's Studio on Eighth Avenue (until 1959) and then at the Dance Player's Studio on Sixth Avenue. Eight years later, when the building housing that studio was torn down, Holm accepted the fact that, at nearly 80, her career as a school mistress was at an end. After more than 30 years, the Hanya Holm School of the Dance simply ceased to exist. Nevertheless, Holm continued to take pupils and freelanced at one studio or another—especially at the Nikolais-Louis Dance Theater Lab and the Juilliard School in New York—lecturing and giving master classes deep into her 90s. On June 10, 1984, at age 96, she was presented with the Samuel H. Scripps Award of $25,000 at the opening of the six-week American Dance Festival in Durham, North Carolina. In her last years, Holm became somewhat disenchanted by developments in modern dance, once complaining:

> Technique here in America has become everything today. If I see one more leg extension, I've had it. . . . Form becomes formula. Technique becomes logic. And there is a security in a major leg extension. But it means nothing. The simplest thing is to shun the emotions and emphasize technique. But you become like a nice stove that doesn't give any heat.

Active in many areas of the dance world, Holm pioneered in the use of improvisation, advanced the concept of lecture demonstrations, and was one of the first to support the Dance Notation Bureau, an organization designed to preserve dance in written form through the dance notation system devised by Rudolf von Laban. In 1952, following up similar gifts made by Ted Shawn with Ruth Saint-Denis and by Doris Humphrey with Charles Weidman the year before, she donated her entire collection of dance memorabilia—some 500 photographs, 10 scrapbooks, and 200 programs—to the New York Public Library. There they remain a major component of the library's Dance Collection, one of the most important in the world. Together, these materials document her entire professional life from her days with Wigman in Germany to the height of her career in America, as well as illustrating the career of Wigman and those of such dancers as Bettis and **Eve Gentry**. Hanya Holm died of pneumonia at St. Vincent's Hospital in New York City on November 5, 1992. Although her obituaries gave her age as 99, she was actually 103.

SOURCES:

Chujoy, Anatol and P.W. Manchester. *The Dance Encyclopedia*. New York, 1949, 1967.

The Free Library of Philadelphia, Theater Collection.

Robertson, Allen and Donald Hutera. *The Dance Handbook*. London: 1988, Boston, MA: 1990.

Sorell, Walter. *Hanya Holm: Biography of an Artist*. Middletown, CT: Wesleyan University Press, 1969.

SUGGESTED READING:

Holm, Hanya. "The Dance, the Artist-Teacher, and the Child" in *Progressive Education*, 1935.

———. "Dance on the Campus—Athletics or Art?" in *Dance Magazine*. February 1937.

———. "The German Dance in the American Scene" in *Modern Dance*. Edited by Virginia Stewart, 1935.

———. "Mary Wigman" in *Dance Observer*. November 1935.

———. "The Mary Wigman I Know," in *The Dance Has Many Faces*. Edited by Walter Sorell. New York, 1951 (revised ed. Columbia University, 1966).

———. "*Trend* Grew on Me," in *Magazine of Art*. March 1938.

Kriegman, Sali Anne. *Modern Dance in America*, 1981.

Sorell, Walter, ed. *The Mary Wigman Book*, 1973.

Wigman, Mary. *The Language of the Dance*. English translation, 1966.

Robert H. Hewsen,
Professor of History, Rowan University, Glassboro, New Jersey

Holm, Jeanne (1921—)

American Air Force officer, who was the first woman to achieve the rank of major-general. *Born Jeanne Marjorie Holm in Portland, Oregon, on June 23, 1921; daughter of John E. Holm and Marjorie (Hammond) Holm; graduate of Air Command and Staff College (1952); Lewis and Clark College, B.A. (1957).*

Awards: D.S.M. with oak leaf cluster, Legion of Merit, Human Action medal; received the Distinguished Achievement award from Lewis and Clark College (1968); granted the leadership award from Camp Fire Girls America (1967, 1972); received the Eugene Zuckert Leadership award, Arnold Air Society (1972); named Woman of the Year in Government and Diplomacy, Ladies' Home Journal *(1975), and re-*

ceived the Women's International Center's Living Legacy Award.

Joined Women's Army Auxiliary Corps (1942); commissioned as a second lieutenant (1943); captain of women's training regiment by end of World War II; rejoined service (1948) and transferred to Air Force; became major-general, highest rank achieved by any woman in American armed forces at that time (1973); served as director of women in Air Force (1965–73); retired from service (1975); named special assistant to President Gerald Ford (1976); published Women in the Military: An Unfinished Revolution *(1982).*

Born on June 23, 1921, in Portland, Oregon, the daughter of John E. Holm and **Marjorie Hammond Holm**, Jeanne Holm joined the Women's Army Auxiliary Corps in 1942. One year later, she was commissioned a second lieutenant. By the end of World War II, she was a captain in charge of a women's training regiment. Holm returned to civilian life but rejoined the services in 1948, transferring to the Air Force, and advancing through the years to become a major-general in 1973, the highest rank ever achieved by a woman in the American armed forces at that time.

Her postings included supervising manpower needs at the headquarters of the Allied Air Forces for Southern Europe in Naples (1957–61) and in Washington (1961–65). From 1965 to 1972, she served as director of women in the Air Force. In that role, she implemented enormous advances in career opportunities for women in the service, making changes in assignments and abolishing discriminatory rules. Before she retired in 1975, Holm spent two years as director of the secretariat of Air Force personnel. After retiring, she served as an adviser to the Defense Manpower Commission and also as an advisor to President Gerald Ford (1976–77). She was a member of the Advisory Committee on Women in the Services until 1980.

A strong supporter of women's rights and a member of the National Women's Political Caucus, Holm was the founder and first chair of Women in Government. She is the author of numerous articles on national defense, manpower and personnel and lectured on these subjects as well. Her 1982 book, *Women in the Military: An Unfinished Revolution,* takes a detailed look at what women have accomplished throughout the services, despite the limits that were and still are imposed. Topics covered include the contributions women have made in the military from the Revolutionary War to Vietnam; a discussion of the WAAC bill legislation of 1941; the setup and organization of the WAAC program and problems encountered; changes that have occurred in the military as a result of women; problems encountered by women while serving overseas during World War II; and a hard look at the Women's Armed Services Act (1948), which finally established a permanent place for women in the military. About half of the book is dedicated to the options now open to women in the armed forces, and how, because of the unprecedented expansion of female participation in the military, stunning reversals of many sex discrimination rules and policies have been made, although some barriers still remain.

Jo Anne Meginnes,
freelance writer, Brookfield, Vermont

Holman, Libby (1904–1971)

American actress and singer whose indictment for the murder of her husband, despite her subsequent release, effectively ended her career. *Born Elizabeth Lloyd Holzman (legally changed to Holman two months before the end of World War I) on May 23, 1904, in Cincinnati, Ohio; died on June 23, 1971, in Stamford, Connecticut; middle of three children (two girls and a boy) of Alfred (a stockbroker) and Rachel (Workum) Holzman; graduated from Hughes High School, Cincinnati, 1920; University of Cincinnati, B.A., June 1923; attended Columbia University, New York; married (Zachary) Smith Reynolds (a pilot and adventurer), on September 16, 1931 (died 1932); married Ralph Holmes (an actor), on March 27, 1939 (died 1945); married Louis Schanker (an artist), in late 1960s; children: (first marriage) Christopher Smith "Topper" Reynolds (died in a mountain climbing accident in 1950); (adopted) sons, Timmy and Tony.*

Selected theater: The Sapphire Ring *(1925);* The Garrick Gaieties *(1925);* The Greenwich Village Follies *(1926);* Merry-Go-Round *(1927);* Rainbow *(1928);* Ned Wayburn's Gambols *(1929);* The Little Show *(1929);* Three's a Crowd *(1930);* Revenge with Music *(1934);* You Never Know *(1938);* Mexican Mural *(1942);* Blues, Ballads, and Sin-Songs *(1954).*

"Libby Holman sells the blues like a Gideon salesman to a hotel chain," proclaimed *Variety* following the opening of the Broadway revue *The Little Show* in 1929. "The torch singer par excellence," echoed Walter Winchell, "the best of those female troubadours with voices of smoke and tears, who moan and keen love's labors lost to the rhythm and boom of the Roaring Twenties." Holman was indeed one of

Broadway's brightest stars when a bizarre scandal diverted her promising career and set off a chain reaction of personal tragedies that haunted her for the rest of her life.

Holman was the middle child of a failed Cincinnati stockbroker. Her childhood was dominated by the family's slide into poverty and by her morbid jealousy of her older sister **Marion Holzman**, whom she believed was more beautiful and talented than she. As a child, Libby was precocious, skipping two grades in her first four years of school. In high school and later at the University of Cincinnati, where Marion had matriculated two years earlier, Holman had a stellar academic record but continually pushed the boundaries in dress and behavior. (At the time, bobbing one's hair, wearing make-up, swearing, and flirting were considered major infractions.) She was regularly cast in student productions and also performed at the small Art Theater in downtown Cincinnati, although it was Marion who got the starring roles. Holman graduated from college at the age of 19 (wearing her mortarboard at a cocky angle) and headed for Manhattan to study journalism at Columbia. However, as she told her fellow graduates, her real ambition was "to become a star and to marry a millionaire."

While enrolled in a short-story class, Holman looked for work in the theater. Exotic rather than pretty, she struggled in bit parts for a year before she was cast in Richard Rodgers' and Lorenz Hart's *The Garrick Gaieties,* the first of the small, literate revues that would soon become a popular Broadway alternative. Although her number was eventually cut, and she was relegated to the chorus, the show was a success and led to subsequent roles. Cast as a prostitute in *The Little Show* (1929), Holman sang "Moanin' Low" to her pimp, played by Clifton Webb. The number was a huge audience pleaser, and, from that time on, the song would be associated with her. "The theater had few to match her peculiarities of vocal enchantment," wrote the *Mirror*'s critic about her earthy contralto. "In addition, she possesses striking and colorful adjuncts: a bronzed complexion, luxury of figure, a fine grace and control. . . . She is one of a species so decidedly rare that one speaks her name with unmistakable sanctity. This Holman girl is an artist."

In her next effort, *Three's a Crowd* (1930), Holman stopped the show with her rendition of "Give Me Something to Remember You By" and again with "Body and Soul," which she performed in a long black dress with a plunging neckline. The song was later banned in Boston because of the word "body" in the song title. The New York censors also objected to the line, "My life, a hell you're making," which was eventually replaced with, "My life, a wreck you're making."

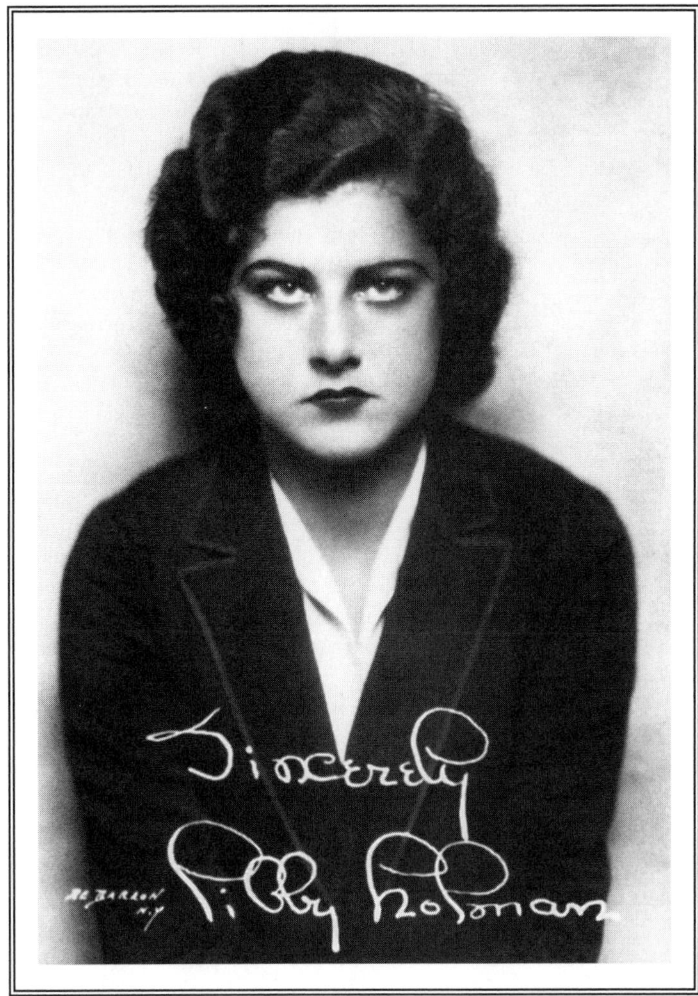

Libby Holman

Now at the height of her popularity, Holman partied nightly with New York's elite and drank more than her share of bootleg whiskey. She was seen on the arms of Manhattan's most eligible men and had numerous love affairs, including an on-again-off-again liaison with **Louisa Carpenter**, an aviator and one of the wealthy Du Pont clan. In 1931, having achieved her goal of stardom, she married her millionaire—Smith Reynolds, the son of tobacco magnate R.J. Reynolds, and heir to a fortune. Smith, a pilot and adventurer of sorts, was known as a strange character, even to his friends. "He was moody, he was wild, he stammered, he was sullen and noncommittal," writes Jon Bradshaw in his biography of Holman, *Dreams That Money Can Buy,* "and he gave a palpable impression of stupidity, although he wasn't stupid."

After a honeymoon in Hong Kong, the couple settled in at the 60-room Reynolds estate in Winston-Salem ("Reynolda"). The marriage was troubled from the start. Smith was possessive and pressured Holman to give up the theater. On one occasion, he reportedly brandished his Mauser, which he claimed to have for protection, and threatened to shoot himself unless she agreed. At first, Holman adored her pampered life, but she eventually grew bored and longed to move back to Manhattan. Smith resisted, grew increasingly moody, and frequently talked of suicide.

In July 1932, following a wild party at Reynolda, Smith was found dead in his bedroom, a bullet wound in his head. After a grand jury ruled out suicide, Holman, now several months' pregnant, was indicted for murder, along with Reynolds' best friend Albert Walker, who came upon the body shortly after Holman. The incident unleashed a frenzy of publicity, including a 27-part series in the New York *Daily Mirror* which, according to Bradshaw's summary, "accused Libby of being haughty and tactless, of wearing mannish attire, of being a heavy drinker and attending mad midnight revels, of being a sensuous sex pirate, a red hot mama, an iceberg of disdain." Holman, however, never went to trial. A month before the court date, the chief prosecutor received a letter from Will Reynolds, Smith's guardian, requesting that he drop the case. Two days later, both Holman and Walker were set free. (In the summer of 1935, MGM released the film *Reckless,* based on the Smith Reynolds tragedy and starring ***Jean Harlow** as Holman.)

Three months after her release, on January 9, 1933, Holman gave birth prematurely to a three-and-a-half-pound boy, whom she named Christopher Smith Reynolds ("Topper"). In the settlement of Smith Reynolds' estate, which took two years to untangle, the infant was awarded $6.25 million, prompting the New York tabloids to dub him the "richest baby in America." Holman received $750,000.

Holman retired to a Rhode Island estate with Louisa Carpenter and her fragile son. In the year that followed, she turned down several chances to return to Broadway, including a request that she join the cast of Cole Porter's *Anything Goes* in the role that ***Ethel Merman** would make famous. Holman was finally urged back to the stage in 1934 by her old friend Howard Dietz, who cast her in *Revenge with Music,* an operetta based on an old Spanish folktale. The musical eked out a short, undistinguished run, and Holman did not return to Broadway again until 1938, in an ill-fated Cole Porter musical called *You Never Know*. Following another four-year hiatus, Holman accepted the part of a peasant woman in *Mexican Mural,* an experimental play that ran for just three weeks. Then the offers dried up. During the 1940s, she enjoyed some success with a nightclub act she performed with African-American singer and guitarist Josh White, featuring a repertoire of early American blues and ballads. (The duo also cut one album, *Blues Till Dawn,* a classic of early American blues.) Later, with pianist Gerald Cook, she toured concert halls and college campuses with a one-woman show, *Blues, Ballads, and Sin-Songs*. The production, which did well in Europe, failed miserably when Holman brought it to Broadway in 1954.

While her career was foundering during the 1930s and 1940s, Holman sought solace with a cadre of friends from the theater and literary world, among them Paul and **Jane Bowles**, Clifton Webb, ***Tallulah Bankhead**, John Latouche, and Tennessee Williams. In 1938, she constructed an enormous house ("Treetops") on a 55-acre site in Stamford, Connecticut, where she lived extravagantly and threw lavish parties. Later, she acquired a town house in Manhattan, so she would have a place to entertain when she was in the city. In the 1940s, she temporarily housed two foster children, then adopted two boys (Timmy and Tony). But eclipsing any positive events in Holman's life were the tragedies, most of them involving the violent deaths of nearly all the men whose lives she touched.

The eerie pattern that began with Smith Reynolds continued with the death of actor Phillips Holmes, with whom Holman had had an affair before marrying his younger brother Ralph Holmes in 1939. Phillips was killed in an air collision aboard a Royal Canadian Air Force plane in 1942, during service in World War II. Holman separated from Ralph Holmes in 1945, after which he committed suicide with sleeping pills. Clifton Webb called Holman "the black angel of death."

Then, in August 1950, Holman's 17-year-old son Christopher died in a mountain-climbing accident in California. His death was "Libby's crucifixion," wrote Bradshaw. "Never again was she to love so yieldingly, so spontaneously. All that remained was remorse and endless recrimination. Her friends agreed that when Libby returned from California, she wasn't Libby anymore." In 1952, after a year in France, Holman established the Christopher Reynolds Foundation, through which she channeled her later work for the environment, civil liberties, race relations, peace, and disarmament. (As of 1985, the foundation had made grants and endowments of $3.5 million, a third of which were awarded in the area of civil rights.)

During much of the 1950s, Holman was involved in an affair with actor Montgomery Clift, whom she first met when they worked together in *Mexican Mural.* "Monty was the abiding obsession of Libby's middle life," writes Bradshaw. "Indeed, he was practically an occupation." The relationship may have been passionate, but it was hardly exclusive, for either of the partners. Clift was bisexual. A talented but troubled man, he nearly lost his life in an automobile crash in 1956. He never fully recovered from the accident, which also altered his appearance and destroyed his acting career. Even with Clift in and out of her life, Holman, still mourning the loss of her son, suffered periods of dark depression and a worsening ulcer condition. Following the failure of her one-woman show, *Blues, Ballads, and Sin-Songs,* in 1954, she attempted suicide by taking an overdose of Seconal, but only succeeded in making herself seriously ill. On New Year's Day, 1956, she underwent surgery to remove a large portion of her stomach. There followed a slow recovery, through which Holman somehow managed to maintain a sense of humor. When a visiting friend asked her if she had finally given up smoking, Holman quipped, "Yes, I have, but every time the doctor puts a thermometer in my mouth, I'm tempted to light it."

In late 1960, at age 56, Holman married Louis Schanker, an abstract expressionist painter whom she had met through a friend. The marriage surprised Holman's friends, who considered Schanker gruff and opportunistic. "Libby wanted to marry someone solid," said her friend Oliver Smith, "and she succeeded in marrying cement." With the marriage came a new house in East Hampton, New York, which Holman bought so Schanker could mingle with the artists who summered there. She threw her usual large bashes for the Hamptons' social set, but friends remarked that she often seemed like a stranger at her own parties. True to most predictions, the marriage barely limped along, giving Holman little joy. She was besieged by yet another series of tragic losses beginning in December 1963, when her sister Marion committed suicide. A year later, her close friend Jack Neustadt, the director of the Christopher Reynolds Foundation, hanged himself. "Libby was distraught, convinced that it was she who inspired her tragedies," writes Bradshaw. "She thought of herself as a kind of medium, a conduit, through which death not only quickened, but radiated to others."

Beginning with a benefit concert in East Hampton in July 1964, Holman embarked on what turned out to be a last burst of activity. She gave additional concerts, made another album (*The Legendary Libby Holman*), and threw another round of lavish parties. But following Montgomery Clift's death in 1966, Holman began to grapple with her own mortality. She became obsessed with Zen, hoping to find peace and dignity, but enlightenment eluded her. Holman spent her final years plagued by ill health and a growing depression that she once described as "bottomless." On the afternoon of June 18, 1971, after a particularly difficult morning, she had lunch by the pool, then simply disappeared. Later, she was found sprawled out on the front seat of her prized Rolls-Royce, barely breathing. She died in the hospital of carbon-monoxide poisoning. Her body was cremated and her ashes scattered at Treetops, in one of the large daffodil beds that adorned the grounds.

In June 1971, some of Holman's friends gathered for a memorial service in New York, among them songwriter Alec Wilder. In a series of somber tributes, those in attendance spoke of her talent, her spirit and energy, and her devotion to the downtrodden and underprivileged. **Yolanda Denise King**, daughter of ***Coretta Scott King** and Martin Luther King, Jr., recalled Holman's donations to her father's work and said she hoped Holman would find her happiness in heaven. As Wilder left the service and made his way down the street, he remembered a remark Holman had once made to him, and started to laugh. "Alec, can you imagine spending an *eternity* in heaven?," she had said. "So *dull,* so *commonplace,* like being detained in some quack's waiting room."

SOURCES:

Bradshaw, Jon. *Dreams That Money Can Buy: The Tragic Life of Libby Holman.* NY: William Morrow, 1985.

Lamparski, Richard. *Whatever Became of . . . ?* 1st and 2nd Series. NY: Crown Publishers, 1967.

Barbara Morgan,
Melrose, Massachusetts

Holmès, Augusta (1847–1903)

French composer of Irish parentage whose* La montagne noire *was one of the few operas written by a woman to be performed in the 19th century. *Name variations: Augusta Holmes; Mary Anne Holmes. Born Augusta Mary Anne Holmès in Paris, France, on December 16, 1847; died in Paris on January 28, 1903; only child of an Irish officer who settled in France (or*

Alfred de Vigny) and a mother of mixed Scottish and Irish origins; mistress of Catulle Mendès; children: (with Catulle Mendès) three daughters.

Augusta Holmès

Augusta Holmès was born in Paris, France, in 1847, the only child of an Irish officer who settled in France and a mother of mixed Scottish and Irish origins. Augusta did not study music until she was 11. Although her parents moved in Parisian artistic circles of the period, her mother discouraged her daughter's musical aspirations. She did, however, encourage Augusta to paint and write poetry. Alfred de Vigny was her godfather and may have been her actual father. When her mother died, Augusta began to study with Henri Lambert, organist of Versailles Cathedral. She took instrumentation from Klosé, and in 1875 César Franck became her teacher. She also corresponded with Franz Liszt who admired her talents. In 1869, Wagner's *Das Rheingold* changed her perception of music, and Wagner would remain a dominant creative influence, though Franck also influenced her greatly. Although a brilliant pianist, she attained distinction entirely through her compositions. In 1875, Holmès wrote the opera *Hèro et Lèandre,* including all her own librettos. This was followed by *Astarté* and *Lancelot du lac* and her four-act lyric opera *La montagne noire* which was produced at the Grand Opera in 1895.

Holmès preferred to write about epic themes on classical or mythological subjects. Her model was the large orchestra and even her songs seem orchestral. She also liked dramatic symphonies and symphonic poems, but her greatest success was with choral works, such as *Les Argonautes* (1881), *Ludus pro patria* (1888), and *Ode triomphale* (1889). Probably best remembered for her songs (she wrote over 130), Holmès' music had great breadth and vitality but was sometimes noisily orchestrated. Describing her work, ***Ethel Smyth** declared that it contained "jewels wrought by one who was evidently not among the giants, but for all that knew how to cut a gem." Holmès was a dominant figure in French musical circles as well as in literary salons. Beautiful and vivacious, she enjoyed the company of poets and musicians. "We were all in love with her," commented Saint-Saëns, who wanted to marry her, while Franck, Wagner, D'Indy, De l'Isle-Adam, and Mallarmé were among her many admirers. A passionate Irish patriot, Augusta Holmès cherished her ancestry and converted to Roman Catholicism shortly before her death at age 56.

John Haag,
Athens, Georgia

Holmes, Julia Archibald
(1838–1887)

American feminist who was the first woman to climb Pike's Peak. *Born Julia Archibald in Nova Scotia, Canada, on February 15, 1838; died in 1887; married James Holmes (an abolitionist), in 1857 (divorced 1870); children: four (two died before reaching adulthood).*

The daughter of staunch abolitionists, Julia Holmes was born in Nova Scotia in 1838. The family first settled in Massachusetts but moved to Kansas in 1848 to assist in the effort to make that territory a free state. Holmes, whose home was a stop on the Underground Railroad, developed into an independent and adventuresome woman and, in 1857, married abolitionist James Holmes. A year later, the couple risked a move further west to New Mexico, an arduous journey that Holmes made mostly by foot while the only other woman in the party chose to travel in a covered wagon.

When the band reached Colorado, Holmes made her historic Pike's Peak climb. Dressed in bloomers, moccasins, and a hat, and carrying a 17-pound pack of supplies on her back, she accompanied her husband and two other men on the trek, while the rest of the group remained in camp. Although it was July, the party encountered several snowstorms on their ascent of over 14,000 feet. On August 5, 1858, from the top of the mountain, Holmes penned a letter to her mother in which she expressed her pride in accomplishing the climb. "Nearly everyone tried to discourage me from attempting it," she wrote, "but I believed that I should succeed; and now here I am. . . . How I sigh for the poet's power of description, so that I might give you some faint idea of the grandeur and beauty."

Holmes and her husband eventually settled in Taos, New Mexico, where she worked as a news correspondent for the *New York Tribune* and gave birth to four children, two of whom did not survive childhood. After divorcing her husband in 1870, Holmes returned East, settling in Washington, D.C. Employed by the federal government, she was one of the first women to be promoted in the civil-service system, advancing to become chief of the division of Spanish Correspondence in the Bureau of Education. She also wrote poetry and worked for the suffrage movement before dying prematurely at age 48.

SOURCES:

Edgerly, Lois Stiles. *Give Her This Day.* Gardiner, ME: Tilbury House, 1990.

Weatherford, Doris. *American Women's History.* NY: Prentice Hall, 1994.

Barbara Morgan,
Melrose, Massachusetts

Holmes, Mary Jane (1825–1907)

American popular novelist. *Born Mary Jane Hawes on April 5, 1825, in Brookfield, Massachusetts; died October 6, 1907, in Brockport, New York; daughter of Preston Hawes and Fanny (Olds) Hawes; married Daniel Holmes, on August 9, 1849.*

Mary Jane Hawes was born on April 5, 1825, in Brookfield, Massachusetts, the fourth daughter and fifth of Preston and **Fanny Hawes**' nine children. She began school at age three and was studying English grammar by age six. Mary Jane was encouraged by both of her parents to seek an education and develop her early interest in writing. At 13, she began teaching in a local school and, at 15, published her first article. She was not, however, the first published author in the family. Her uncle, the Reverend Joel Hawes of the First Congregational Church in Hartford, Connecticut, wrote and published sermons and addresses.

In 1849, at age 23, Mary Jane Hawes married Daniel Holmes, a Yale graduate she had met while working as a teacher. The couple moved to Kentucky where each taught at public schools in and around Versailles. Between 1850 and 1852, they ran the Glen Creek District School. Daniel then decided to study law, and they moved to Brockport, New York, where he was admitted to the bar in 1853. While the couple maintained a permanent residence in Brockport, they also traveled widely to destinations including California, the Far East, Russia, France, and England.

In 1854, Mary Jane Holmes published her first novel, *Tempest and Sunshine; or, Life in Kentucky*. She went on to write nearly 40 novels, approximately one a year between 1855 and 1905. In 1856, she published her best-known work, *Lena Rivers*. After 1859, some of her work was serialized in the *New York Weekly*. She was paid between $4,000 and $6,000 for each installment and retained the right to sell each story for publication as a novel. Holmes distinguished herself less by her subject matter than by her popularity and earnings. Her book sales totaled over two million, and it was said some libraries had to keep up to 20 or 30 copies of each of her works.

Mary Jane Holmes

"I try to avoid the sensational," wrote Holmes, "and never deal in murders, or robberies, or ruined girls; but rather in domestic life as I know it to exist. I mean always to write a good, pure, natural story, such as mothers are willing their daughters should read, and such as will do good instead of harm." Community-minded, Holmes was an active member of the Episcopal Church, formed temperance and literary clubs, established a village reading room in her adopted town of Brockport, and organized soup kitchens during the depression of 1893. Although she had no children of her own, she enjoyed younger people, particularly girls, and organized literary meetings for them in her home. Mary Jane Holmes died of a stroke at age 82 on October 6, 1907. Her work, now considered conventional and sentimental, has been largely ignored in literary histories.

SOURCES:

James, Edward T., ed. *Notable American Women, 1607–1950.* Cambridge, MA: Belknap Press of Harvard University Press, 1971.

McHenry, Robert, ed. *Famous American Women.* NY: Dover, 1983.

Sonya Elaine Schryer,
freelance writer, Lansing, Michigan

Holst, Henriëtte Roland (1869–1952).

See Roland Holst, Henriëtte.

Holst, Imogen (1907–1984)

English pianist, conductor, and teacher who composed orchestral, chamber, and vocal pieces and wrote extensively about her father as well as other composers. *Born Imogen Clare Holst in Richmond, Surrey, England, on April 12, 1907; died at Aldeburgh on March 9, 1984; daughter of Gustav Holst, the renowned composer.*

It has been noted that an unusual number of women composers were born in Britain in the early part of the 20th century. Most of them, including ***Elizabeth Poston**, ***Grace Williams**, ***Elisabeth Lutyens**, ***Elizabeth Maconchy**, and ***Phyllis Tate**, first attended the Royal College of Music. Imogen Holst, one of their contemporaries, attended St. Paul's Girls' School where her father Gustav Holst was music master. Though Gustav was eventually appointed to a position at the Royal College of Music, Imogen was admitted to the school on her own merits, when she won a scholarship in composition in 1927. At the Royal College, women such as Imogen Holst felt they were nurtured by mentors like Gustav Holst and Ralph Vaughan Williams. Once they left the womb of academe, however, all of them struggled for acceptance. Like many women composers, Imogen Holst pursued a variety of interests in order to earn an income. She taught in several schools and wrote extensively about music, including a biography of her father in 1938. She was a member of the Royal Music Association and the Society of Women Musicians, an organization founded in 1911 to deal with the problem of invisibility among women composers and performers. Throughout her career, Holst continued to compose. She became interested in folk music and became known for her arrangements of old tunes. Her highly productive decades-long artistic collaboration with the great British composer Benjamin Britten (1913–1976), and her work at Britten's Aldeburgh Festival, played a crucial role in making his music world-renowned.

John Haag,
Athens, Georgia

Marjorie Sewell Holt

Holstein-Gottorp, duchess of.

See Christine of Hesse (1543–1604).
See Amelia of Denmark (1580–1639).
See Marie Elizabeth of Saxony (1610–1684).
See Frederica Amalie (1649–1704).
See Hedwig Sophia (1681–1708).
See Albertina of Baden-Durlach (1682–1755).
See Elizabeth Petrovna (1709–1762) for sidebar on Anne Petrovna (1708–1728).
See Caroline Matilda for sidebar on Louise Augusta (1771–1843).

Holt, Marjorie Sewell (1920—)

American politician and member of the U.S. House of Representatives, 1973–1987. *Born Marjorie Sewell on September 17, 1920, in Birmingham, Alabama; daughter of Edward Roland Sewell and Alice Juanita (Felts) Sewell; Jacksonville (Florida) University, B.A., 1945; University of Florida College of Law, J.D., 1949; married Duncan McKay Holt, on December 26, 1946; children: Rachel Holt Tschantre; Edward Holt; Victoria Holt Stauffer.*

Selected writings: The Case Against the Reckless Congress *(1976);* Can You Afford This House *(1978).*

Born on September 17, 1920, in Birmingham, Alabama, Marjorie Sewell Holt attended Jacksonville Junior College and received a law degree from the University of Florida in 1949. After practicing law in Florida for 13 years, Holt moved to Maryland, where she was admitted to the bar in 1962 and continued her practice. Between 1963 and 1965, she served as a supervisor of elections in Anne Arundel County. For the following six years, she was clerk of the circuit court in the same county, while strengthening her ties to the Republican Party by working as a campaign organizer and a precinct leader. From 1970 to 1972, Holt was a member of the Maryland Governor's Commission on Law Enforcement and the Administration of Justice, and in 1971–72, she served as legal counsel for the Maryland State Federation of Republican Women. Holt was also a delegate to four Republican National Conventions (1968, 1976, 1980, and 1984).

Marjorie Sewell Holt was elected in 1972 to the 93rd Congress as a Representative of the Fourth District in the State of Maryland, serving through the 99th Congress in 1987. As a Cold-War politician, she concentrated her efforts on matters of national defense and the armed forces, and she consistently advocated increases in defense spending and enhanced benefits for those in the military. She opposed attempts at a nuclear freeze and supported the development of weapons such as the MX missile and the B-1 bomber. Throughout her career in Congress, Holt pushed for reductions in non-military spending, serving two terms on the Budget Committee and in 1978 introducing the now-standard Republican device of the substitute budget proposal. She served on the Committee on Armed Services during each of her 13 years in the House, becoming the ranking Republican on the Subcommittee on Procurement and Military Nuclear Systems in her last term in office. Holt was actively opposed to the busing of schoolchildren to effect racial integration in the nation's public school system; a measure she put forth to outlaw busing by constitutional amendment was approved by the House in 1974.

Holt chose not to run for a seat in the 100th Congress and finished her final term on January 3, 1987. She returned to the practice of law in Maryland, residing in Severna Park. In July of that same year, President Ronald Reagan nominated her to the position of member of the General Advisory Committee on Arms Control and Disarmament.

SOURCES:

Office of the Historian. *Women in Congress, 1917–1990.* Commission on the Bicentenary of the U.S. House of Representatives, 1991.

Sonya Elaine Schryer, freelance writer, Lansing, Michigan

Holt, Winifred (1870–1945)

American sculptor, writer, and philanthropist. *Name variations: Winifred Holt Mather; Mrs. Rufus Graves Mather. Born Winifred Holt in New York City on November 17, 1870; died of hypertensive heart disease in Pittsfield, Massachusetts, on June 14, 1945; interred at Evergreen Cemetery in Morristown, New Jersey; second daughter and fourth of seven children of Henry Holt (the publisher) and Mary Florence (West) Holt; sister of Edith Holt (also a philanthropist); educated in private schools, ending with Brearley School in New York; studied anatomy and sculpture in Florence, Italy, and with Augustus Saint-Gaudens; married Rufus G. Mather (a researcher and lecturer on art), on November 16, 1922; no children.*

Winifred Holt

Selected writings: A Short Life of Henry Fawcett, the Blind Postmaster General of England *(1911);* The Beacon for the Blind *(1914);* The Light Which Cannot Fail *(1922). Also author of numerous papers on the blind.*

Winifred Holt was born in New York City on November 17, 1870, the daughter of publisher Henry Holt and **Mary West Holt**. Her mother died when she was eight. Though Winifred attended private schools and had a fragile constitution, her father intentionally expanded her sphere by having her serve one day a week at the Neighborhood Settlement in the Bowery. In the 1890s, Winifred was waylaid by malaria and advised to travel abroad. While in Florence, Italy, she studied anatomy and sculpture. She later studied with Augustus Saint-Gaudens. Her principal works were portraits, busts, and bas-reliefs, including a sculpture of *Helen Keller.

Winifred Holt is best known, however, as the founder (along with her sister **Edith Holt**) of the New York Association for the Blind. Started in Winifred's home in 1912, the organization soon moved to a rented loft where classes in sewing, typing, stenography, broom making, and other marketable skills were offered. Only one year later, classroom, workshops, and offices were moved to a permanent location and named the Lighthouse. It was dedicated by President William Howard Taft.

In 1915, Holt organized the first Lighthouse for the Blind in France. The following year, she lectured in leading cities of the United States on work for blinded soldiers, and established a number of Lighthouses in France and Italy; eventually, the international Lighthouse movement would spread to over 30 nations. Winifred Holt also created *Searchlight,* the first Braille magazine for children, and was instrumental in mainstreaming blind children into regular public-school classrooms. Her services were honored with various medals, including awards from the National Institute of Social Sciences (1914) and the Chevalier of the French Legion of Honor (1921). In 1922, she published the autobiographical *The Light Which Cannot Fail.*

SUGGESTED READING:

Mather, Winifred Holt. *First Lady of the Lighthouse.* Lighthouse of the New York Association of the Blind, 1952.

Holtby, Winifred (1898–1935)

English journalist, novelist, dramatist, and social reformer who, during the 1920s and early 1930s, campaigned for women's rights and pacifism and was a major orator for the unionization of black workers in South Africa. *Name pronunciation: HOLT-bee. Born Winifred Holtby in Rudstone in Yorkshire, England, on June 23, 1898; died of kidney failure, aged 37, in London, England, on September 25, 1935; buried in her native Rudstone; daughter of Alice (Winn) Holtby (first woman alderman elected by the East Riding County Council) and David Holtby (a farmer); attended Queen Margaret's School, Scarborough; Somerville College, Oxford (1917–21), interrupted during the First World War by her activity in London as a Voluntary Auxiliary Nurse (VAD), 1916–17, and in France as a hostel-forewoman in the Signal Unit of the Women's Auxiliary Army Corps (WAAC), 1918–19; never married; no children.*

Wrote extensively for English newspapers and periodicals; served as director of the feminist periodical Time and Tide *(1926–35); was a public speaker for equal-rights feminism, pacifism, and against imperialist exploitation of native races in South Africa; is best known for her novels, especially* South Riding *(1937) for which she was awarded the James Tait Black Memorial Prize; is celebrated in Vera Brittain's* A Testament of Friendship: The Story of Winifred Holtby *(1940).*

Selected writings: (juvenilia) My Garden and Other Poems *(1911);* Anderby Wold *(1923);* The Crowded Street *(1924);* The Land of Green Ginger *(1927);* Eutychus; or The Future of the Pulpit *(1928);* A New Voter's Guide to Party Programs *(1929);* Poor Caroline *(1931);* Virginia Woolf: A Critical Memoir *(1932);* Mandoa, Mandoa! *(1933);* The Astonishing Island *(1933);* Women and a Changing Civilization *(1934);* Truth Is Not Sober and Other Stories *(1934); (poetry)* The Frozen Earth *(1935);* South Riding *(1936);* Letters to a Friend *(1937); (short stories)* Pavements at Anderby *(1937).*

In April 1932, having already suffered for a year from debilitating headaches and high blood pressure, Winifred Holtby, aged 34, learned from medical authorities that she had only two years before she would succumb to Bright's disease, a form of kidney failure. Holtby kept this diagnosis secret from friends and family residing in England—even from ***Vera Brittain**, her companion since 1919 in a remarkable, mutually creative relationship which is chronicled in Brittain's biography of Holtby, *A Testament of Friendship.* Knowledge of impending death did not frighten Holtby:

> This alone is to be feared—the closed mind, the sleeping imagination, the death of the spirit. The death of the body is to that, I think, a little thing. I do not know whether the spirit survives the death of the body, but I do know that the spirit can be killed while the body lives, and most men walk in the world as skeletons.

During the last year and a half of her life, she attempted, not altogether successfully, to withdraw from her arduous life in London as a speechmaker and journalist to her native Yorkshire seacoast. Holtby sought isolation to write her last novel, *South Riding,* which she completed just three weeks before her death. Published posthumously in 1936, it is universally considered her greatest work. While working on *South Riding,* she continued her responsibilities as a director and manager of the feminist periodical *Time and Tide.*

Holtby's activities in her final two years illustrate her endurance and intellectual commitments. She turned from satirizing imperialism and racism in *Mandoa, Mandoa!* (1933) to an important feminist project. In *Women and a Changing Civilization* (1934), a history of women, Holtby commented on a wide range of topics, including women's right to work; she expressed her recognition that racism and antifeminism spring from the same fear. In keeping with her pacifism, she contributed a chapter to *Challenge to Death,* edited by ***Storm Jameson**, in which Holtby exposed commercial traffic in weapons as one impulse to war. As a champion of civil liberties, she composed an anti-dictator play, *Take Back Your Freedom* (posthumous publication, 1939), which examined and attacked the sort of fascism gaining strength after the First World War in Europe and in England. Winifred Holtby's death in 1935 cut short an already highly productive life; it was generally acknowledged in her obituaries that she was on the verge of even greater contributions as a novelist.

Winifred Holtby was born on June 23, 1898, in Rudstone, a small village on the east Yorkshire coast. She was the second of two children. Her father David Holtby successfully farmed 940 acres; he was from a long line of Yorkshire farmers, suggesting what Brittain was to label a "feudal tradition" as an explanation for Holtby's generosity and characteristic desire to help people. Before marriage at age 40, her mother **Alice Winn Holtby**, also from a Yorkshire farming family, had been a governess.

Holtby's mother was probably the more influential parent in her daughter's life. She encouraged young Winifred's play and poetry writing; she privately published a volume of the 13-year-old Holtby's poems and, three years later, circulated and sold for publication Holtby's letter describing a First World War bombardment at Queen Margaret's School, Scarborough, which she attended from 1909 to 1915. Surprisingly for a woman from provincial Yorkshire whose education was shaped by Victorian and Edwardian values, Alice Holtby insisted that Winifred attend Oxford University's Somerville College. In the 1920s, after moving from Rudstone to Cottingham, a suburb of Hull, Alice was the first woman ever elected to the East Riding County Council and later in the 1930s the first woman alderman. Winifred drew upon her mother's experience for the character of alderwoman Mrs. Beddows in *South Riding.*

Holtby and a number of her women classmates at Somerville College, Oxford, had actively participated in the First World War. During the conflict in 1916 and before going to college, Holtby was a Volunteer Aid Detachment nurse (VAD) for a year in London; she witnessed great physical suffering and death. She attended Somerville for one year, interrupting her education to join the Women's Auxiliary Army Corps (WAAC) in 1918; she was stationed in Hutchennville, France, until after the end of the war. While there, she became close friends with **Jean McWilliams**; Holtby's lifelong correspondence with her would be collected and published posthumously in *Letters to a Friend* (1937). Returning to Oxford University in 1919, Holtby began her friendship with Vera Brittain, three and a half years her senior, who had left Somerville College in 1915 to become a VAD nurse following the death of her fiancé in the war. Both Holtby and Brittain consciously yearned to be writers; they were among a generation of post-suffrage English women who, according to **Carolyn Heilbrun**, "took their own and each other's intellectual ambitions serious-

Winifred Holtby

ly." They shared pacifist and feminist concerns, Holtby becoming conscious of gender discrimination during controversies that erupted around the decision of Oxford University to grant degrees to women in 1921. Holtby and Brittain were among the first women students to take part in the matriculation ceremony which had previously been reserved solely for men. Both took degrees in history.

I want to be about the work in which my real interests lie, the study of inter-race relationships, the writing of novels and so forth. But while the inequality exists, while injustice is done and opportunity denied to the great majority of women, I shall have to be a feminist with the motto Equality First. And I shan't be happy till I get [it].

—Winifred Holtby

After Oxford, Holtby and Brittain moved to London where they shared an apartment and continued the remarkable, supportive, work-oriented relationship they had begun in college. Their friendship, as **Jean E. Kennard** demonstrates in *Vera Brittain & Winifred Holtby: A Working Partnership,* was "the strongest intellectual influence in each other's work." In the 1920s, they both were committed to the principles of peace and cooperation, lecturing for the League of Nations Union. **Dale Spender** notes that, in addition, both were "firm feminists intent on achieving equality for women, and both were concerned with the moral—political and economic—questions of their time." Identifying with ideologies of older feminists who had fought for suffrage, Holtby was an equal-rights advocate who participated in the Six Point Group led by Lady ***Margaret Rhondda**. The group's objectives were to achieve pensions for widows and equal rights of guardianship for married parents, change the law covering assault of children, raise the status of unmarried mothers, and attain equal pay for teachers and equal opportunities for men and women in the Civil Service.

Holtby shared living quarters with Brittain during the remaining years of her life—save for 1925 after Brittain married George Catlin, an English social scientist who taught in the United States at Cornell University. After one year in the States, Brittain returned to live in England, thereafter to be joined by her husband for half of each year. Brittain, Catlin, and Holtby first shared a London apartment, then a house in Glebe Place, Chelsea, where they raised Brittain and Catlin's two children, John Edward and ***Shirley Williams**. Brittain wrote of this unconventional arrangement:

> With its babies, its books, its toys, its friends, and companionship of both G. and Winifred, the household in Glebe Place was the nearest thing to complete happiness that I have ever known or ever hope to know. I believe that Winifred felt the same. Even her last illness, which never destroyed her capacity for enjoyment, did not quench the gaiety of our shared home.

It seems that Holtby had given up on having a family of her own. She and the man she loved—the handsome, debonair Harry Pearson, pal of T.E. Lawrence—sustained an on-and-off relationship throughout her life. Indeed, Pearson proposed marriage to Holtby the day before she died.

Holtby and Brittain worked best when in each other's company. In a letter written during a period of convalescence in Yorkshire during 1934, Holtby would appeal for Brittain's companionship: "When, when, when shall you be able to come? . . . I must get on with my book. You are the only person I know in the world who does not prevent one working."

In January 1926, Holtby traveled to South Africa to visit Jean McWilliams, her WAAC friend who was now headmistress of a girls' school in Pretoria. She arrived in South Africa as a pacifist lecturing for the League of Nations; she left as a speaker for black trade unionism, thoroughly convinced that white prosperity depended unfairly on the subordination of blacks. While in Pretoria, she perceived that if one substituted the noun "women" for the noun "natives" then the "old arguments against women's enfranchisement, women's higher education, and women's entry into skilled employment" coincided with arguments used against blacks. Back in England, through the auspices of Creech Jones, then a trade-union official as well as Labor member of Parliament, Holtby paid from her literary earnings for William Ballinger to travel and live in South Africa, working to advise the black workers' union movement. During the two years before her death, Holtby took pains to find others who would contribute money to support Ballinger's work, which he continued even after the failure of the Industrial and Commercial Workers' Union (ICWU). Because Ballinger's economic survival depended so much on her personal resources, he was one of two people whom she told of her terminal illness.

In 1926, soon after Holtby returned from South Africa, Lady Rhondda asked her to be a director for *Time and Tide,* a weekly periodical initiated when women won the right to vote after the First World War. *Time and Tide* had a distinctly feminist viewpoint, although, in keeping with its equal-rights stance, it also published writing by male intellectuals. Other directors in the mid-'20s included Lady Rhondda, ***Cicely Hamilton**, ***E.M. Delafield**, Professor ***Winifred Cullis**, and ***Rebecca West**. It was to be a magazine run by women, for women, which would keep a sharp eye out for national and international developments as they affected women, and an even sharper eye out for male politicians who professed support for the women's cause but who tended to backslide at the first opportunity.

During the 1920s, Holtby contributed to *Time and Tide*, usually one article, and sometimes as many as four, every week. Dale Spender reports that not all of Holtby's articles are didactic in tone and that some are very amusing. On occasion, Holtby deplored the fact, writes Spender:

> that issues which were to her central—issues such as peace and disarmament, welfare and education for example—were often associated with women, and were marginalized or dismissed. They would not be "minor matters," she argued if women were to have an equal share in the organization of society and its values and priorities. And because she thought it was crucial that these issues should be primary issues of concern in society, she worked for equality.

Holtby's reputation at the end of the 20th century is based mainly on her novels; however, in her own lifetime she was best known as a journalist. Besides writing for *Time and Tide*, she contributed to the *Manchester Guardian*, the *Yorkshire Post*, and the *News Chronicle*, and, influencing an even wider audience, *Good Housekeeping* and *Schoolmistress*.

Her novels are firmly rooted in the realistic tradition, though, as she matured, she also became a political satirist. When at Oxford, the idea for her first novel, *Anderby Wold* (1923), occurred to her while studying economic history where she learned, as Brittain remembers, that new phases drive out the old, "the good of yesterday becoming the evil of to-day, the past making way for the future." She went back to her room after the lecture, and:

> began at once to make notes for the novel I determined to write about it, to instruct myself in the reason for that change which had previously seemed to me unmitigated tragedy. I forced myself to read histories of agriculture, of trade unionism, of Socialism. I tried to see the drama of rural Yorkshire as I knew it, as it had filled my whole horizon until the War destroyed a small and settled world, against the background of historical change and progress, and gradually, reading and thinking, I comforted myself, and invented a story of a young woman.

In *South Riding*, written at the end of her short life, Holtby with infinite compassion pits feudal and chivalric values against her own progressive socialist and feminist ideals. Her woman hero, unmarried, intelligent and competent, is courageous, human, and unable to sacrifice her principles for the sake of a marriage:

> [A]n English Socialist member of Parliament, withdrew in alarm when he found her feminism to be not merely academic but insistent. When he demanded that she should abandon, in his political interests, her profession gained at such considerable public cost and private effort, she offered to be his mistress instead of his wife and found he was even more shocked by this suggestion than by her previous one that she should continue her teaching after marriage. She parted from him with an anguish which amazed her.

Holtby's satires include *Poor Caroline* (1931) in which she lampoons idealistic women activists while presenting a sympathetic depiction of spinsterhood; *Mandoa, Mandoa!* (1933) in which she satirizes the travel industry, Western technology and imperialism in an imagined African country; and *The Astonishing Island* (1933), a dystopian commentary on British customs. As Kennard notes, "Holtby links colonization, racism, and war to British arrogance and false notions of heroism."

Winifred Holtby died in London on September 25, 1935; she was buried on October 2 in Rudstone, Yorkshire. In Holtby's will, she bequeathed her library to St. Margaret's School, Scarborough, and a scholarship to Somerville College, Oxford, in the name of **Dorothy McCalman**, a woman in her 30s whom Holtby had encouraged through a college education. The scholarship, based on the earning of her posthumous publications, was designated for women who had been obliged "as Dot was, to earn a living for several years before going to college." According to Brittain, Holtby's posthumous publications, including royalties from a successful film made of *South Riding*, endowed at least two scholarships by 1940. In June 1937, a library for the use of blacks was founded in Holtby's name in Johannesburg, South Africa.

SOURCES:

Brittain, Vera. *A Testament of Friendship: The Story of Winifred Holtby.* First published 1940 (reprinted, London: Virago Press, 1980).

Catlin, John. *Family Quartet.* London: Hamish Hamilton, 1987.

Heilbrun, Carolyn. Introduction to Vera Brittain's *A Testament of Friendship,* 1940 (reprinted, NY: Wideview Books, 1981).

Holtby, Winifred. *South Riding.* First published 1936 (reprinted, London: Virago Press, 1988).

Kennard, Jean E. *Vera Brittain & Winifred Holtby: A Working Partnership.* Hanover: University Press of New England, 1989.

Spender, Dale. *Time and Tide Wait for No Man.* London: Pandora Press, 1984.

SUGGESTED READING:

Berry, Paul and Alan Bishop, eds. *Testament of a Generation: The Journalism of Vera Brittain and Winifred Holtby.* London: Virago Press, 1985.

Davidson, George. Introduction in *Poor Caroline,* 1931 (reprinted, London: Virago, 1985).

Delmar, Rosalind. Afterword in *A Testament of Friendship,* 1940 (reprinted, London: Virago, 1980).

Hardisty, Claire. Introduction in *The Crowded Street,* 1924 (reprinted, London: Virago, 1981).

Shaw, Marion. Introduction in *Mandoa, Mandoa!,* 1933 (reprinted, London: Virago, 1982).

COLLECTIONS:

Manuscripts and correspondence in the Holtby collection at the Hull Public Library in Yorkshire, England.

RELATED MEDIA:

South Riding (84 minutes), British film, directed by D. Victor Saville, starring Ralph Richardson, **Edna Clements**, **Marie Löhr**, Milton Rosmer, and ***Glynis Johns**, 1938.

"Testament of Friendship," BBC television series (1981), a serial devoted to Vera Brittain's three "testaments," including Testament of Youth and Testament of Experience.

Jill Benton,
author of *Naomi Mitchison: A Biography,* and Professor of English and World Literature at Pitzer College, Claremont, California

Holter, Harriet (1922—)

Norwegian social scientist who was a pioneer of women's studies. *Name variations: Harriet Bog (1945–49), Harriet Gullvåg (1951–56), and Harriet Holter (1958 on). Born Harriet Bog in 1922; married Ingemund Gullvåg; married once more; children: (first marriage) one son.*

Selected writings (as editor or author): (with Willy Martiniussen and Bjørg Grønseth) Hjemmet som arbeidsplass *(The Home as Workplace, Oslo: Universities Press, 1967);* Sex Roles and Social Structure *(Oslo: Universities Press, 1970, 1973); (with E. Dahlström, et al)* Kvinners liv og arbeid *(Women's Lives and Work, Olso: Universities Press, 1974); (with H. Ve Henriksen, et al)* Familien i klassesamfunnet *(Family in a Class Society, Oslo: Pax, 1975);* Kvalitative Metoder *(Qualitative Methods, Olso: Universities Press, 1982);* Patriarchy in a Welfare State *(Olso: Universities Press, 1984); (with M. Saetre and E. Jebsen)* Tvang til seksualitet *(Pressures towards Sexuality, Oslo: Cappelen, 1986); (with others)* På kvinners vis—med kvinners råd *(In the Manner of Women—with Women's Advice, Oslo: NAVF, 1988); (with Acker, et al)* Kvinnors och männs liv och arbete *(Women's and Men's Lives and Work, Stockholm, 1992).*

Harriet Holter was born in East Norway but spent most of her career in Oslo, first at the independent Institute for Social Research, and later at the University of Oslo. She took her first degree, in social economy, at the University of Oslo in 1946, and her doctorate in social psychology at the same institution. Subsequently, she was a professor of social psychology at the University of Oslo from 1972 to 1992. She was also professor emeritus at the Center for Women's Studies, which she had established, as well as a member of the Norwegian Academy of Sciences and of numerous academic committees and commissions, including the Norwegian Research Council. Her later research focused on sexual violence and child abuse.

According to Professor **Karin Widerberg** of Oslo University, Harriet Holter's scholarship has always been wide-ranging, in that she has applied sociological methods to psychological problems, and vice versa, without forgetting the relevance of economics. Her central theme has been the understanding of power and powerlessness in all its aspects. Her intellectual and political breadth make her a significant role model for contemporary and future scholars in women's studies.

Professor Holter's scholarly publications (over 70 in number to date, often in collaboration with her colleagues) include articles and monographs, academic reports and reviews, in Norwegian and international periodicals, besides the full-length works for which she is best known. These are signed Harriet Bog (1945–49), Harriet Gullvåg (1951–56), and Harriet Holter (1958 on).

SOURCES:

Lie, S. Stiver and M.B. Rørslett, eds. *Alma Maters Døtre* (*Alma Mater's Daughters: A Century of Women's Contributions to Higher Education*). Oslo: Pax, 1995.

Elizabeth Rokkan,
translator, formerly Associate Professor, Department of English, University of Bergen, Norway

Holtzman, Elizabeth (1941—)

Member of the U.S. House of Representatives, 1973–1981. *Born on August 11, 1941, in Brooklyn, New York; daughter of Sidney Holtzman and Filia (Ravitz) Holtzman; Radcliffe College, B.A., magna cum laude, 1962; Harvard Law School, J.D., 1965.*

Elizabeth Holtzman was born in Brooklyn, New York, on August 11, 1941. After earning her undergraduate degree from Radcliffe College (1962) and a law degree from Harvard (1965), she began her career in politics as an assistant to New York City Mayor John Lindsay in 1967. Between 1970 and 1972, she served as a Democratic state committeewoman and district leader, in addition to founding the Brooklyn Women's Political Caucus. In 1972, Holtzman challenged 50-year veteran Emanuel Celler for the Democratic nomination to a seat in the U.S. House of Representatives. Running an energetic first campaign with a largely volunteer staff, she focused on constituent needs and her considerable ideological differences with Celler, who had blocked the Equal Rights Amendment and maintained his support for the war in Vietnam. Holtzman won the primary by a narrow margin of approximately 600 votes. She then easily defeated her Republican opponent as well as Celler, who had continued in the general election on the Liberal Party ticket; she was the youngest woman ever elected to Congress.

Holtzman served four consecutive terms in the House of Representatives. In her first term, she distinguished herself during the impeachment hearings of President Richard Nixon with her investigative work as a member of the House Judiciary Committee, and in 1973 she filed suit to end American military involvement in Cambodia. A district court ruled in her favor, but the case was ultimately defeated in the Court of Appeals. Holtzman also gained a seat on the Judiciary Committee during her first term, where she sought to revise immigration laws and contributed to the creation of new rules concerning how evidence is presented in federal courts. When the deadline for the ratification of the Equal Rights Amendment (ERA) neared in 1978, she helped to win an extension. Holtzman also participated in achieving a prohibition against sex discrimination in federal programs. Her efforts to bring Nazi war criminals to justice culminated in the creation of a federal Nazi-fighting unit that expelled hundreds of former Nazis from the United States.

Instead of seeking a fifth term of office in the House of Representatives in 1980, Holtzman ran for a Senate seat. She secured the Democratic nomination but lost in the general election to Republican Alfonse D'Amato. She served as district attorney for Kings County in Brooklyn, New York (1981–90). During her term, she prosecuted cases of rape, battering, incest, and child abuse, among other crimes. In 1989, she was elected comptroller of New York City, a position she held until 1993, when she lost her bid for reelection. In 1992, she made a second unsuccessful bid for the U.S. Senate. After 1994, Holtzman resumed practicing law in Brooklyn.

Elizabeth Holtzman

SOURCES:

Office of the Historian. *Women in Congress, 1917–1990.* Commission on the Bicentenary of the U.S. House of Representatives, 1991.

SUGGESTED READING:

Holtzman, Elizabeth with Cynthia L. Cooper. *Who Said It Would Be Easy?: One Woman's Life in the Political Arena.* Arcade, 1996.

Sonya Elaine Schryer, freelance writer, Lansing, Michigan

Holtzmann, Fanny (c. 1900–1980)

American lawyer. *Born Fanny Ellen Holtzmann in Brooklyn, New York, around 1900; died of cancer on February 7, 1980; one of seven children of Henry Holtzmann (a scholar and tutor) and Theresa Holtzmann; attended P.S. 84, Brooklyn; attended Girls' High School for three years; graduated from a busi-*

ness course at Pernin School, Brooklyn; Fordham Law School, LL.B., 1922; never married; no children.

Considered by some one of America's most brilliant legal strategists, Fanny Holtzmann was not a child of wealth. She was born around 1900 and grew up on Eastern Parkway in the Brownsville section of Brooklyn, New York, a nearly forgotten child in a large Jewish family. A mediocre student who did not finish high school, Holtzmann was inspired by her eldest brother David, the family's first attorney, and was encouraged in her own pursuit of the law by her grandfather "Zaida," to whom she was devoted. Holtzmann received her law degree from Fordham Law School, attending classes at night and working as a clerk in a theatrical law firm during the day. She began her career in New York, and through dedication, creative flair, and a direct approach ("I don't follow precedent, I establish it") made her way into the high echelons of entertainment law, then to England's "castle circuit," and finally into international politics.

Fanny Holtzmann

Holtzmann was thrust into the public eye in 1934 when she successfully represented the Russian royal family in a libel suit against MGM, which involved the misrepresentation of Princess ***Irina** (1895–1970), the niece of Tsar Nicholas II, as the mistress and sponsor of the notorious Rasputin. The trial, which culminated in the largest financial settlement ever resulting from a libel action, brought the film company to its knees and catapulted Holtzmann to fame in England and America. ("***Greta Garbo** of the Bar," she came to be called.) *Good Housekeeping* of London lauded her as "one of the most mentally alert lawyers alive," and American columnist O.O. McIntyre thought her "a satisfactory exemplar of the new freedom of women." Reportedly, she even had something like a fan club in Buckingham Palace. While publishers clamored for her story, Holtzmann declined, preferring to retain her anonymity.

Holtzmann's roster of famous clients included Noel Coward, Clifton Webb, Fred Astaire, George Bernard Shaw, Jacob Epstein, Dwight D. Eisenhower, Louis Bromfield, and Darryl F. Zanuck, but her star client ("in every way," notes friend and biographer Edward O. Berkman) was ***Gertrude Lawrence**, whom she saved from bankruptcy at least once and served as a financial consultant for 20 years. Beyond show business, Holtzmann had early warnings of Hitler's atrocities from her European clients. By soliciting money to ensure that immigrant Jews would not become dependent on public funds, she convinced the U.S. Immigration Service to permit more Jews into the county. Though she saved hundreds, her own relatives died in concentration camps. At the founding session of the United Nations in San Francisco in 1945, Holtzmann was principal U.S. counsel to the Republic of China and assisted China in becoming one of the five countries with veto power. She also used her influence to marshal votes from a number of smaller non-aligned nations for the admission of Israel into the United Nations in 1947.

Holtzmann was described as a small, delicate woman, with fawn-like eyes, and an overriding air of helplessness. "Helpless, indeed!" scoffed playwright Moss Hart, who first met Holtzmann in 1920, when she was instrumental in getting a Broadway hearing for his play *Once in a Lifetime*. "Fanny is about as helpless as the Bethlehem Steel Company and as delicate as 'Jack the Ripper.'" Although Holtzmann's professional life was full, her personal life was quiet. She was notoriously unlucky in love, Berkman writes, perhaps due in part to her success in what was then strictly a man's world. There was an early engagement that was broken and a number of subsequent romances. A later "proposal" to "Fairest Fanny" came from G.B. Shaw, who wrote her, "I have the ideal catch for you. Rich, Famous, and 90. Me." But the domestic life that Holtzmann craved eluded her. According to Berkman, she channeled her "overflowing affection and boundless energy" into her family and a variety of causes, including rescuing British war orphans and stranded Hong Kong refugees, and financing medical research. Other outlets were painting, and later, sculpture, under the tutelage of Jacob Epstein, who was also a client. Through the intervention of Shaw, a series of her paintings was exhibited at London's Leicester Galleries, and her sculptures (mostly heads) were part of a New York Bar Association exhibit.

Around 1974, Holtzmann, who aside from a bout with measles when she was five was never sick, was struck down by a virulent blood disorder that nearly took her life. She was cured by a therapeutic program devised by Dr. Emanuel Revici, whose medical research she had supported since 1953. However, she did not adhere to the regimen of diet and rest and was soon back at work, prompting Revici to call her "a terrible patient." "Fanny had no talent for sickness," concludes Berkman, "her talent was for life." On January 18, 1980, Holtzmann was awarded an honorary doctorate of humane letters from the Hebrew Union College-Jewish Institute of Religion in a bedside ceremony. She died three weeks later, on February 7, of cancer.

SOURCES:

Berkman, Edward O. *The Lady and the Law: The Remarkable Story of Fanny Holtzmann.* Boston, MA: Little, Brown, 1976.

COLLECTIONS:

Fanny E. Holtzmann Papers 1920–1980, American Jewish Archives.

Barbara Morgan,
Melrose, Massachusetts

Holum, Dianne (1951—)

American speedskater. *Born on May 19, 1951, in Chicago, Illinois; married; children: daughter Kirstin Holum (a speedskater).*

Dianne Holum

Selected championships and honors: won a silver medal (three-way tie) in the 500 meters and a bronze medal in the 1,000 meters at the Olympic Games in Grenoble (1968); won a gold medal in the 1,000 meters at the World championships (1971); won a gold medal in the 500 meters at the World championships (1972); won a gold medal in the 1,500 meters and a silver medal in the 3,000 meters at the Olympic Games in Sapporo, Japan (1972).

Born in Chicago, Illinois, in 1951, Dianne Holum was the first American woman to win an Olympic gold medal in speedskating's 1,500-meter event. She trained in Northbrook, Illinois, the "Speedskating Capital of America," under coach Big Ed Rudolph, who also trained championship sprinter ***Anne Henning**. At age 14, Holum became the youngest skater ever to compete in the World championships. At the 1968 Olympic Games in Grenoble, she was involved in a rare three-way tie with Americans **Jennifer Fish** and **Mary Meyers** for the silver medal in the 500 meters (**Ludmila Titova** of the Soviet Union placed first); then Holum went on to capture the bronze in the 1,000 meters. (**Monika Pflug** of Germany won the gold; **Atje Keulen-Deelstra** of Holland took the silver.)

Before the 1972 Olympics in Sapporo, Japan, Holum worked as a waitress for a year to finance a training period in the Netherlands. Her determination was rewarded with an Olympic gold medal in the 1,500 meters, which she won in 2:20.83, breaking the mark of 2:22.40 set by **Kaija Mustonen** of Finland in 1968. (Holland's **Christina Baas-Kaiser** and Atje Keulen-Deelstra placed second and third, respectively.) Holum also walked away with the silver medal in the 3,000-meter event with a time of 4:58.67. Baas-Kaiser won the gold with a time of 4:52.14, an Olympic record.

Holum, who has been credited with revitalizing women's speedskating in America, retired from competition in 1973 to coach. World champion ***Beth Heiden** was her student, as well as Holum's own daughter, **Kirstin Holum**, who at age 16 was America's best speedskating hope for the 1998 Olympics in Nagano, Japan. Kirstin failed to medal in the games, though she set an American record in the Olympic long-track 5,000 meters, completing the course in 7:14.20. In 1996, Dianne Holum was inducted into the Women's Sports Hall of Fame. In 1997, she and **Pat Wentland** were named by the U.S. Speedskating Association and recognized by the U.S. Olympic Committee as National and Developmental Coaches of the Year for their sport.

SOURCES:

Leavy, Jane. "A Rare Pair," in *Sports Illustrated: Women Sport*. Spring 1997, p. 49.

Markel, Robert and Susan Waggoner. *The Women's Sports Encyclopedia*. NY: Henry Holt, 1997.

"Nagano '98," in *The Boston Globe*. February 12, 1998.

Holy Maid of Kent (c. 1506–1534).

See Barton, Elizabeth.

Holy Roman empress.

See Ermengarde (c. 778–818).
See Irmengard (c. 800–851).
See Judith of Bavaria (802–843).
See Engelberga (c. 840–890).
See Matilda of Saxony (c. 892–968).
See Oda of Bavaria (fl. 890s).
See Richilde (d. 894).
See Anna of Byzantium (fl. 901).
See Cunigunde of Swabia (fl. 900s).
See Adelaide of Burgundy (931–999).
See Theophano of Byzantium (c. 955–991).
See Agnes of Poitou (1024–1077).
See Cunigunde (d. 1040?).
See Gisela of Swabia (d. 1043).
See Bertha of Savoy (1051–1087).
See Adelaide of Kiev (c. 1070–1109).
See Richensia of Nordheim (1095–1141).
See Matilda, Empress (1102–1167).
See Beatrice of Upper Burgundy (1145–1184).
See Gertrude of Sulzbach (d. 1146).
See Constance of Sicily (1154–1198).
See Irene Angela of Byzantium (d. 1208).
See Mary of Brabant (c. 1191–c. 1260).
See Beatrice of Swabia (1198–1235).
See Constance of Aragon (d. 1222).
See Yolande of Brienne (1212–1228).
See Isabella of England (1214–1241).
See Anna of Hohenberg (c. 1230–1281).
See Beatrice of Silesia (fl. 1300s).
See Isabella of Aragon (c. 1300–1330).
See Margaret of Brabant (d. 1311).
See Blanche of Valois (c. 1316–?).
See Anna of Schweidnitz (c. 1340–?).
See Margaret of Holland (d. 1356).
See Anna of the Palatinate.
See Anne of Bohemia (1366–1394) for sidebar on Elizabeth of Pomerania (1347–1393).
See Sophia of Bavaria (fl. 1390s–1400s).
See Eleanor of Portugal (1434–1467).
See Sforza, Bianca Maria (1472–1510).
See Isabella of Portugal (1503–1539).
See Anna of Bohemia and Hungary (1503–1547).
See Elisabeth of Habsburg (1554–1592) for sidebar on Marie of Austria (1528–1603).
See Gonzaga, Anna (1585–1618).
See Gonzaga, Eleonora I (1598–1655).

See Maria Anna of Spain (1606–1646).
See Gonzaga, Eleonora II (1628–1686).
See Maria Leopoldine (1632–1649).
See Margaret Theresa of Spain (1651–1673).
See Claudia Felicitas.
See Eleanor of Pfalz-Neuburg (1655–1720).
See Wilhelmina of Brunswick (1673–1742).
See Maria Theresa of Austria for sidebar on Elizabeth Christina of Brunswick-Wolfenbuttel (1691–1750).
See Maria Theresa of Austria (1717–1780).
See Maria Louisa of Spain (1745–1792).
See Maria Teresa of Naples (1772–1807).

Hombelina (1092–1141)

French saint. *Born in Fontaines les Dijon, France, in 1092; died a nun at Jully-les-Nonnains in 1141; daughter of Tescelin Sor (a Dijon knight) and* ***Aleth of Montbard;*** *sister of St. Bernard of Clairvaux (1090–1153). Hombelina's feast day is August 21.*

Home, Cecil (1837–1894).

See Webster, Augusta.

Homer, Louise (1871–1947)

American contralto. *Born Louise Dilworth Beatty in Shadyside, a rural section of Pittsburgh, Pennsylvania, on April 30, 1871; died on May 6, 1947, in Winter Park, Florida; third daughter and fourth of eight children of William Trimble Beatty (a Presbyterian minister) and Sarah Colwell (Fulton) Beatty; studied voice with Fidèle Koenig and acting with Paul Lhérie; married Sidney Homer (a composer), in 1895; children: six, including daughter* ***Louise Homer Stires*** *(1896–1970, who was also an operatic soprano).*

Made debut at Vichy in Donizetti's La Favorita *(June 15, 1898); debuted at Covent Garden (1899); made Metropolitan Opera debut as Amneris in* Aïda *on tour in San Francisco (1900); appeared as a star at the Met for 20 years; gave last performance at the Metropolitan (1929).*

One of the Metropolitan Opera's greatest stars, Louise Homer appeared onstage there for 20 years. She was born in Shadyside, a rural section of Pittsburgh, in 1871, the third daughter and fourth of eight children of William Trimble Beatty, a Presbyterian minister, and **Sarah Fulton Beatty.** Louise studied music in Philadelphia and at the New England Conservatory before marrying her teacher, composer Sidney Homer, in 1895. In 1898, she continued her studies in Paris by taking voice lessons with Fidèle Koenig and acting lessons with Paul Lhérie. Her operatic debut was in Vichy in 1898. She sang at Covent Garden and the Théâtre de la Monnaie in Brussels before returning to the United States and a debut at the Met in 1900. Although first limited to Italian and French opera, Homer quickly branched out, assuming the leading Wagnerian contralto and mezzo-soprano roles. During her tenure, she participated in many historic performances, including the debuts of tenor Enrico Caruso and conductor Arturo Toscanini. When Toscanini revived Gluck's *Orpheus* in 1909, Homer sang the title role. After resigning from the Met in 1919, she appeared with the Chicago Grand Opera, and the San Francisco and Los Angeles operas, before returning to New York for a last performance in 1929. Homer made many recordings with Caruso, Martinelli, and Gigli, among others. A performer of the highest integrity and ability, she was an American star whose career was extremely successful. The composer Samuel Barber was her nephew.

Louise Homer

SUGGESTED READING:

Homer, A. *Louise Homer and the Golden Age of Opera.* New York, 1974.
Homer, Sidney. *My Wife and I.*

John Haag,
Athens, Georgia

Hone, Evie (1894–1955)

Irish artist who became one of the foremost stained-glass designers of the century. *Born Evie Sydney Hone on April 22, 1894 in Dublin, Ireland; died on March 13, 1955, in Dublin; youngest of four daughters of Joseph Hone and Eva (Robinson) Hone; educated at home and in London at Byam Shaw School of Art, Central School of Arts and Crafts and Westminster School of Art; studied in France, 1920–23, with André Lhote and Albert Gleizes; spent two years in an Anglican convent, 1925–27; joined An Túr Gloine (Tower of Glass), 1934; received into the Catholic Church, 1937.*

Awards: honorary doctorate, Trinity College Dublin (1953); honorary member of Royal Hibernian Academy (1955).

Principal works: armorial windows and Pentecost *(Blackrock College Chapel, 1937–41);* My Four Green Fields *(1939);* Saint Brigid *(Loughrea Cathedal, 1942); windows for St. Stanislaus College, Tullabeg, County Offaly (1942); windows for Church of the Immaculate Conception, Kingscourt, County Cavan (1947–48); Eton College Chapel, Berkshire, England (1949–52); St. Michael's Church, Highgate, London (1954).*

Evie Hone was descended from a remarkable family of Flemish artists who settled in Britain and Ireland in the 16th and 17th centuries. One of them, Galyon Hone, completed the windows for King's College in Cambridge. Another of her ancestors was the painter Nathaniel Hone (1718–1784). Nathaniel's two sons, Horace and John Camillus, were also painters.

Evie Hone was born in Dublin in 1894, the daughter of Joseph Hone and **Eva Robinson Hone**; her mother died two days after her birth. At age 12, Evie contracted infantile paralysis which affected one of her hands and also left her lame. She went to Switzerland for treatment, but her disabilities remained, though she did her best to overcome them and bore them without complaint for the rest of her life. In May and June of 1914, Hone visited Assisi, Venice, and Florence and also enrolled at the Byam Shaw School of Art in London. She later moved to the Central School of Arts and Crafts where Bernard Meninsky proved an inspiring teacher. She met fellow Dublin artist ***Mainie Jellett** while she was studying with Walter Sickert at the Westminster Art School in 1917. The two would remain close friends and colleagues and help champion the cause of modernism in Irish art. It was at Meninsky's instigation that she and Jellett went to Paris to study with André Lhote and later Albert Gleizes, both influential teachers of Cubism. Hone and Jellett returned to Dublin in 1923, but over the next decade they managed to spend some time every year in Gleizes' studio at Servières. Gleizes wrote later that the gentle tenacity of Hone and Jellett had terrified him into teaching them, and that they had helped him to clarify the artistic theories which he set out in his influential book *Peinture et ses lois* (1922). Gleizes' non-figurative painting made a rhythmic approach to reality by what he called "translation and rotation." His aims implied a two-fold rejection: rejection of a single perspective and rejection of any necessity for the representation of nature.

Hone could have made a career in France but, like Jellett, chose to return to Ireland where she played a seminal role in disseminating the theories and discoveries of Cubism. Ireland was, initially, stony ground for such an endeavor, and Hone and Jellett met not just with incomprehension but often with derision from Irish art critics and from the Royal Hibernian Academy (RHA), a bastion of conservatism. In 1924, Hone and Jellett held a joint exhibition in which the absence of representational art attracted mystified comment. The few representational works, observed *The Studio,* "when judged by ordinary standards, seemed no better and no worse than the productions of the average uninspired art student in her teens." Despite these put-downs, Hone and Jellett helped to put modernism on a steady footing in Ireland by the Second World War.

In November 1925, Hone gave up painting and entered an Anglican convent, the Community of the Epiphany, in Cornwall. In a letter to Gleizes, she wrote, "I do not feel I have a vocation. It has been very difficult but I feel quite at peace about it and as certain as one can be of anything." Two years later, she returned to France and worked again with Gleizes. She and Jellett were elected to the Abstraction-Creation group and exhibited in Paris at the Salons des Indépendants, Salon des Surindépendants, and the Salon d'Automne.

In the early 1930s, Hone grew tired of the aridity of abstract art and became increasingly interested in stained glass. She studied French Gothic art, visiting Chartres and Le Mans, as well as the more modern work of the French painter Georges Rouault. Dublin had an international reputation in stained glass thanks to An Túr Gloine, the cooperative founded by ***Sarah Purser** and Edward Martyn in 1903. When Hone approached Purser, the latter was at first dismissive but suggested that Hone study with A.E. Child at the Dublin School of Art, which she did. Hone subsequently went to London and sought the advice of the illustrator Arthur Rackham and the stained-glass artist ***Wilhelmina Geddes** in whose kiln Hone made her first panels. She took these to Roland Holst of the Rysakademie in Amsterdam who urged her to continue in stained glass. On her return to Dublin, she joined An Túr Gloine and remained there until Purser's death led to its dissolution in 1943. At An Túr, she had the inestimable benefit of working next to Michael Healy who was a great influence on her work and who, like her, loved the windows at Chartres. Hone received her first commission from Ardcarne Church in Boyle, County Roscommon, and in 1934 she did the windows for St. Naithi's Church in Dundrum, Dublin.

In 1937, Hone was received into the Catholic Church at Blackrock College Chapel in Dublin by its president Dr. John Charles McQuaid, who had commissioned windows for the college chapel from Michael Healy. McQuaid subsequently commissioned work from Hone and, when he became archbishop of Dublin in 1940, was an enthusiastic champion of her work as was the Jesuit priest Father Donal O'Sullivan. In a tribute written after her death, O'Sullivan noted Hone's wide reading—***Julian of Norwich**, Proust, St. John of the Cross, and Max Jacob. O'Sullivan also highlighted the contribution made to Hone's work by her trusted glazier Tommy Kinsella. As art historian **Dorothy Walker** observed, Hone was intimately concerned with specifically Christian subjects, in particular the Gospels, as a consequence of her work in church buildings. In Walker's opinion, Hone may have been influenced in this by the untimely death of Harry Clarke, who was one of the finest stained-glass artists of his generation, "although her style was very different from his, much less theatrical and fantastical, more humble, imbued with compassion and mercy. She greatly simplified the outlines and component parts of her compositions, in contrast to Clarke's extravagant detail, and she preferred broad planes of colour to the jewelled sparkle of Clarke and his mentor Michael Healy."

In 1939, Hone's work received major official recognition when she was commissioned by the Irish government to create stained glass for the Irish Pavilion at the New York World's Fair. She designed the striking *My Four Green Fields* which interpreted the arms of the four Irish provinces in an abstract style. Since the northern province of Ulster had been partitioned in 1920, with six of its nine counties remaining under British control, the title had a potent political message in asserting the Irish government's claim to the six counties of its fourth green field. At the time of Hone's death, *My Four Green Fields* was packed away in crates, but it would later be installed in the more worthy surroundings of Government Buildings in Merrion Street, Dublin.

In the early 1940s, the number of Hone's ecclesiastical commissions increased considerably, though she was as happy working in a small

country church as on a grand project. She did the *Pentecost* window at Blackrock College and created three windows for its sister foundation at Rockwell College in Tipperary. For the Jesuits at Clongowes Wood College, she completed the *Seven Dolours* series begun by Michael Healy (who died in 1941). The Jesuits also commissioned one of her finest creations, the five windows for St. Stanislaus College at Tullabeg in County Offaly which were among her own favorites. Following Sarah Purser's death, An Túr Gloine was dissolved in 1943, and in 1944 Hone established her own studio at Marlay Grange, Rathfarnham, just south of Dublin. Her fellow artist ***Norah McGuinness** noted that the atmosphere there was "unique." Hone was helped by her devoted maid Emmy and guarded by a minute poodle. Her friend, the Dutch artist ***Hilda van Stockum**, did two paintings of her at Marlay which are now in the National Gallery of Ireland. Like Jellett and McGuinness, Hone was a founding member of the Irish Exhibition of Living Art in 1943, but Jellett's early death in 1944 deprived her of a close and supportive friendship.

She leaves a memory of exceptional, serene fortitude and of a tranquil will.

—**C.P. Curran**

After the war, Hone returned to painting and did the Stations of the Cross for the Church of St. Peter and Paul in Athenry, County Galway, in 1946. She did more painting when in 1948 she went on a long visit to Ravenna and central Italy and became particularly interested in the use of mosaic. She also designed Christmas cards for the Cuala Press. However, stained glass remained her chosen medium, and in 1947–48 she created some of her finest work for the University Hall chapel at Hatch Street in Dublin (another Jesuit institution) and for the Church of the Immaculate Conception at Kingscourt, County Cavan. She regarded the *Ascension* window at Kingscourt as one her best pieces of work. The writer and critic C.P. Curran agreed: "I do not think there is in Ireland a lovelier window or one of more original design or of more tender colour or that moves one more by its imaginative beauty."

In 1949, Hone was commissioned by Sir Jasper Ridley and Lord Crawford to replace the great East window at Eton College, near Windsor in England, which had been destroyed during the Blitz. Hone had been recommended by Archbishop McQuaid, and when Ridley and Crawford saw the windows at Tullabeg and Kingscourt they agreed. The huge assignment, which Hone was reluctant to accept, entailed modifications to her studio, and she had to use the gymnasium of a local school to spread out her designs. Some of her detailed studies in paper and glass for the Eton window are considered to be beautiful, moving works of religious art in their own right. Despite its scale (it was one of the largest church windows in the British Isles), the window was executed with some speed. Installed in 1952, it measured 10.4 meters by 8.8 meters, almost a thousand square feet. Hone also designed two side windows. A complex work, containing 18 lights with tracery, it is divided into two great horizontals, with the Crucifixion in the upper window and below it the Last Supper flanked by Melchisidek and Abraham. The entire window is surmounted by tiers of tracery and a wealth of symbolic imagery, most notably the Dove of the Holy Spirit at the apex. Curran felt that the first impression was of flatness but then the color and design began to make themselves felt. He considered her groupings of figures to be outstanding. After Eton, she received other commissions in England of which the most important was St. Michael's Church in Highgate, London.

In 1953, the year she was awarded an honorary doctorate by Trinity College Dublin, Hone continued to work despite ongoing pain and increasing physical infirmity. She died suddenly on March 13, 1955, just as she was entering her parish church in Rathfarnham. Hone left a valuable bequest to the National Gallery of Ireland, including works by Picasso and Gris. Three years after her death there was a memorial exhibition in Dublin, and subsequently in London, of drawings, paintings and stained glass which attracted huge crowds and was one of the rare occasions when major examples of her stained glass could be shown. Two of the St. Stanislaus windows, the *Ascension* from Kingscourt and *My Four Green Fields,* were erected in a specially designed pavilion.

SOURCES:

Arnold, Bruce. *Mainie Jellett and the Modern Movement in Ireland.* New Haven, CT: Yale University Press, 1991.

Fallon, Brian. *Irish Art 1830–1990.* Belfast: Appletree Press, 1994.

Frost, Stella, ed. *A Tribute to Evie Hone and Mainie Jellett.* Dublin: Browne and Nolan, 1957.

Kennedy, S.B. *Irish Art and Modernism 1880–1950.* Belfast and Dublin: Institute of Irish Studies and Hugh Lane Municipal Gallery of Modern Art, 1991.

Snoddy, Theo. *Dictionary of Irish Artists: 20th Century.* Dublin: Wolfhound Press, 1996.

Walker, Dorothy. *Modern Art in Ireland.* Dublin: Lilliput, 1997.

White, James. *Evie Hone: Memorial Exhibition Catalogue.* Dublin, 1958.

Deirdre McMahon,
lecturer in history at Mary Immaculate College,
University of Limerick, Limerick, Ireland

Honecker, Edith (1909–1973).

See Baumann, Edith.

Honecker, Margot (1927—)

East German minister of public education whose 26-year tenure reflected the ideology of the GDR's hard-line Communist regime. *Name variations: Margot Feist. Born Margot Feist in Halle an der Saale, on April 17, 1927; daughter of Gotthard Feist; had one brother; became second wife of Erich Honecker (1912–1994, head of GDR party and state), in 1953; children: daughter,* ***Sonja Honecker Yanez.*** *Erich Honecker's first wife was Edith Baumann (1909–1973); they had a daughter Erika Honecker.*

The breaching of the Berlin Wall in November 1989, and the rapid collapse of the Communist regime of the German Democratic Republic (GDR—East Germany), brought forth a multitude of revelations about the failings and abuses of power of four decades of totalitarianism. Among the most reviled individuals during this time of reckoning were the aging and ill Erich Honecker, former head of both party and state, and his wife. Margot Honecker, who served as GDR minister of public education from 1963 until early November 1989, was known to many East Germans simply as "die Hexe" (the witch).

One of the handful of women to rise to a leadership position in the GDR, Margot Honecker was accused in 1992 of having forced political dissidents to surrender their children for adoption. She was also suspected of having authorized the building of prison-like barracks—called by some "Margot's KZ" (Margot's Concentration Camp)—in which several truant minors had been driven to commit suicide. Whatever their validity, these accusations would never be subjected to the scrutiny of a public trial, because Margot Honecker never returned to Germany to face these or any other charges. In July 1992, she fled Moscow for exile in Chile, finding refuge there with her daughter's family.

Like her husband-to-be Erich, who was born into a working-class family in the industrial Saar region in 1912, Margot was born into a proletarian environment in the industrial city of Halle an der Saale in 1927. Her father Gotthard Feist, an often-unemployed shoemaker, was a militant member of the Communist Party of Germany (KPD). Her mother contributed to the family's modest income by working in a mattress factory. Margot's political education began in her childhood. In 1933, when the Nazis had been in power only a few months, her father was arrested on charges of high treason against the German Reich. With her father in a concentration camp (he would survive seven years' loss of freedom, including several in Buchenwald), the Feist family struggled to survive. Margot's mother worked and scrimped, and spirits were lifted when the illegal Rote Hilfe (Red Aid) organization was able to provide them with much-needed financial support, an indicator of solidarity from the underground cells that still remained active in Halle.

In addition to her father's absence, Margot, her younger brother and her mother endured unannounced and terrifying visits from the Gestapo. While Gestapo agents searched the tiny Feist apartment for evidence of subversive activities, Margot's emotional resources were strengthened by recurrent displays of coolheadedness. On one such occasion, her mother told her unwelcome visitors, "Do not put your dirty boots there," a reference to their attempts to place their muddy boots on her clean kitchen chairs. By placing copies of the Nazi newspaper *Völkischer Beobachter* on her chairs, she ensured that it, and not her furniture, would be soiled. This spirit of defiance was passed on to Margot, who was proud of her parents' hatred of Nazism and was often told by her mother "to be proud of your father. He wanted to do what was right and there is nothing bad in what he did." When one of Margot's teachers, a Nazi, asked his pupils their names and what their fathers did for a living, rather than say her father was a shoemaker she gave the provocative reply: "My name is Feist, and my father is a Communist." A major incident in Margot's youth took place in November 1938 when she was 11. That month, both she and her brother witnessed the savage Kristallnacht pogrom directed against Halle's small Jewish community. The images of broken shop windows and stormtroopers beating Jews who were then dragged blood-soaked through the streets caused her eight-year-old brother to vomit and made a lifelong impression on both of the Feist children.

Gotthard Feist returned to his family from the Buchenwald concentration camp a physical shadow of his former self, but morally unbroken. Entering her teen years, Margot was truly impressed by her father's fearless return to his illegal KPD activities, despite almost constant surveillance by Gestapo and other Nazi secret agents. She was soon the youngest member of her father's cell, taking risks as a "young comrade" even though she was not formally a member of Halle's tiny but active Communist underground. Her responsibilities included acting as a courier, setting up clandestine meetings, and similar high-risk activities. Tension was always high at the Feist apartment with no guarantee that the next knock on the door would not be the Gestapo announcing that her father was again under arrest. In November 1940, Margot's pregnant mother died at age 33 from a botched abortion. During the next months, Margot became the stabilizing element in the family, often following her father into the streets in the middle of the night when he was so distraught with grief that she feared he would commit suicide. She helped her father and brother come to terms with the tragedy while carrying out domestic chores and remaining active in the anti-Nazi resistance.

Bright and personable, Margot was a good student. One of the ironies of her education was that her best teacher was a member of the Nazi Party. Politically naive to an extreme, he was convinced that because the Nazis called themselves National Socialists, and socialism was for him a positive concept, the Nazi state must somehow be a good thing. Despite his beliefs, he had a lasting impact on Margot with his lectures on German art and literature. Among the books which made a strong impression on her were classic writings by Darwin and Tolstoy as well as contemporary authors like Friedrich Wolf whose work had been burned by the Nazi state. Many of the books she read were part of the forbidden "Rote Bücherei" (Red Library) series, but the Gestapo agents who scrutinized them during one of their visits were much too *doof* (stupid) to notice. Faced with the decision of whether or not to continue her education, Margot decided not to enter a teacher-training institute despite her desire to one day be a teacher; she did not feel that she could let herself become part of a profession which would require her to indoctrinate students with a racist and chauvinistic ideology. Instead, she took courses in stenography and typing.

Her father was rearrested, but rather than being sent back to a concentration camp he was made part of a "999" military unit, a penal battalion stationed on the Western front, meant as a guarantee that he would not consider defecting to the advancing Soviet Army. Now without a mother or father, Margot took her brother to live with her grandmother in Silesia. The war was going badly for Nazi Germany and the requirements of "total war" brought 17-year-old Margot into the last-gasp exertions of Hitler's Third Reich. Because of her delicate build and youth, she was not chosen for factory work or even for carrying out the chores of a letter carrier. Instead, she became a telephone operator at the local phone exchange. Margot and her brother survived the final chaotic months of the Nazi state, and both of them arrived on foot back in Halle during October 1945. The Feist apartment had been destroyed in the final weeks of the war, and the siblings had to depend on the solidarity of local anti-Nazis for food and shelter. In time, she received word that her father had survived the war having been captured by the Americans (he would be released from captivity two years later).

As one of the small number of Germans who had resisted Nazism, 18-year-old Margot looked forward to the future. She believed that the only appropriate ideological foundation on which to build peace and justice, both for defeated Germany and the world, was Marxism. At the end of 1945, she joined the KPD. Determined to be more than a passive member of the party, Margot was a co-founder of the Anti-Fascist Youth Committee in Halle, while working at the same time as a typist in the Saxony-Anhalt regional headquarters of the Communist-dominated Free German Trade Unions Federation. In 1946, the KPD merged with the Social Democratic Party in a shotgun marriage of the two major working-class political parties in the Soviet Occupation Zone (SBZ), forming a Communist-controlled entity named the Socialist Unity Party (SED). As a KPD member, Margot automatically became a member of the SED, which claimed to have finally created a united proletarian front that would forever banish the danger of a revival of fascism on German soil.

The factors which had kept Margot from pursuing a teaching career five years earlier were no longer in play. But SED leaders in Halle decided that the ambitious, attractive Margot—a young, energetic and militant Communist with a sterling resistance record—was too great a talent to waste in the classroom. By 1947, when she became a member of the secretariat of the Halle district committee of the Free German Youth (FDJ), it became clear that she was being groomed for rapid advancement as a functionary in the ranks of an emerging German Communist elite. Her area of responsibility was the Young Pioneer youth organization, and for the next several years she quickly moved up within the FDJ leadership ranks.

By the middle of 1948, the division of Germany into an eastern sector, dominated by the Soviet Union, and a western state, sponsored by the United States and its Western allies, appeared all but inevitable. For the Soviet Union, a nation which had suffered grievously in World War II, it was imperative that a stable pro-Soviet political system be created in its occupation zone of Germany. German Communists and sympathizers would play a key role in bringing about such a transformation. Young SED functionaries like Margot enjoyed dizzying upward career mobility as the time neared to create an "independent" German government in the SBZ. This took place in October 1949, when the Soviets permitted a German Democratic Republic (GDR) to be proclaimed as the government of the former SBZ. As the legislating body of this new state, which for more than two decades would be diplomatically recognized only by the Soviet Union and its allies, a Volkskammer (Peoples' Chamber) was created. In late 1949, Margot was elected in a Soviet-style election as a Volkskammer delegate. The same year, she became the director of the entire Young Pioneer organization in the GDR, as well as a member of the FDJ central council. By 1950, when she was elected as a candidate member of the SED Central Committee, the 23-year-old had achieved an extraordinary rise to influence within the world of German Communism.

In the summer of 1949, Margot's public career and private life became inextricably inter-

Margot Honecker

twined when she began a passionate affair with Erich Honecker, a man 15 years her senior and, as co-founder and first chair of the Free German Youth, her boss. Honecker was then married to another FDJ functionary, ***Edith Baumann**, and had a daughter, **Erika Honecker**. Unlike most of the leaders of the GDR and SED, who had spent the years of the Third Reich in exile in the Soviet Union or (in a few instances) Western Europe, Honecker could boast of an enviable anti-fascist pedigree, having been active in the KPD resistance within Nazi Germany until 1935 when he was arrested by the Gestapo. He survived ten years' imprisonment to be liberated in April 1945 from the Brandenburg-Görden penitentiary. He had been active in the prison's resistance organization, somehow surviving the constant terrors of an institution where during his years of incarceration more than 2,000 prisoners were decapitated by an on-site guillotine.

Although Honecker's wife Edith refused to grant him a divorce, he and Margot continued their affair while some SED members gossiped about the relationship. In early 1953, Edith relented, and Erich married Margot as quickly as the divorce papers were finalized. At the time of their marriage, the couple already had a two-year-old daughter named Sonja, who would be their only child. Meanwhile, the GDR found itself mired in crisis. With a government that enjoyed little popularity and was tied to a Stalinist model of politics and economic planning, life in the GDR remained bleak at a time when its West German counterpart, the Federal Republic, was starting to enjoy the first fruits of its economic miracle, the *Wirtschaftswunder*.

By 1953, Erich Honecker was regarded by many as the boy wonder of the GDR, having carved out for himself a position of influence second only to that of paramount leader Walter Ulbricht. There was, however, little to celebrate. In June 1953, the millions of workers in the GDR—which proclaimed itself as "the first workers' and peasants' state on German soil"—went on strike to protest recently increased production quotas as well as higher food prices, setbacks which were only part of a generally dismal (and declining) standard of living. Quickly losing control of the situation, the GDR government had to call on the Soviet military to crush the disturbances, which were more than strikes but never assumed the form of armed rebellion. Working beside her new husband at FDJ headquarters in East Berlin, Margot Honecker heard him chide some of their fellow functionaries for listening to West Berlin's RIAS radio station for the latest news on the spreading chaos. Laughing, she asked, "Where will we get information? The DDR radio is playing operettas!"

Although cautious reforms were put in place in the GDR after the worker rebellion, the SED regime remained essentially hard-line in its policies and ideals. Many of its leaders, including Erich Honecker, had grown up in a world of class-struggle ideological orthodoxy; because of their own traumatic experiences in the anti-Nazi resistance during the era of the Third Reich, they remained convinced that the non-Marxist world was intent on going to war with the Socialist bloc, relying on nuclear weapons and former Nazis to change the geopolitical balance in the heart of Europe.

Before 1953 had ended, Margot Honecker reluctantly heeded the decision of the SED Central Committee, which decreed that she needed to complete her political education at Moscow's Youth University. Months of study and indoctrination in Moscow meant separation not only from her husband but also from her infant daughter. She submerged her personal needs for the greater good of contributing to the victory of Marxism-Leninism on German soil, and as an emerging member of the GDR's ruling class, went to Moscow.

Upon her return in 1954, she began to prepare for a new, more responsible phase of her career. She shifted her emphasis from the FDJ, a mass organization, to the state apparatus and, in 1955, joined the regime as head of the department of teacher training in the Ministry for Public Instruction, a post she would hold until 1958. In August 1958, Honecker became deputy minister of public education and served in this position until November 1963. Reflecting both her own achievements and her husband Erich's growing influence within the SED as well as the government, in 1963 Margot Honecker moved up in the ruling hierarchy of the GDR in two significant steps. In January, she became a full member of the SED Central Committee and that November took charge of GDR educational affairs by being promoted to minister of public education (Ministerin für Volksbildung). Although she would remain a member of the Central Committee until November 1989, she was never selected for membership in the all-powerful SED Politburo—which led some political analysts to suspect that Erich Honecker possibly feared his wife's ambitions and influence.

By this time, the GDR had entered into a new phase of its history. Throughout the 1950s and early 1960s, many hundreds of thousands of East Germans fled the GDR through West

Berlin, with most of them going on to West Germany and its dramatically higher living standards and greater freedoms. The yearly loss of around 300,000 men and women became in time not only a severe blow to GDR prestige but also a matter of the state's economic survival. On August 13, 1961, the Berlin Wall began to be erected so as to prevent any further escape of GDR citizens to the West. Quickly dubbed "the Anti-Fascist Protective Barrier," the Berlin Wall was in many ways an admission of failure as well as a moral obscenity, but it also served to stabilize the GDR economy, and in time the end of the state's loss of skilled people brought about a significant improvement in living standards. Erich Honecker was the architect of the Berlin Wall, and, when its success became clear, his—and Margot's—star continued its inexorable rise to the top of the GDR ruling elite. In 1971, Erich Honecker became the GDR's leading political figure, assuming leadership of the SED and also becoming head of state.

Margot Honecker's 26-year tenure as GDR minister of public education saw significant changes take place in that harshly authoritarian regime's educational system. From the time she began working in the educational realm in 1955 until the late 1960s, it was state policy to favor previously underprivileged children from the industrial working class as well as those of rural and peasant backgrounds. Those who had been born into elite, bourgeois families found it much more difficult in this period to gain admission to institutions of higher education. The policy of state sponsorship of social mobility began to change in the 1960s, when an emphasis was placed on economic growth based on new and advanced technologies. Increasingly, special schools and curricula emerged which emphasized the scientific and technological knowledge individuals possessed, rather than the purity of their proletarian or peasant-class pedigree. By the 1970s and 1980s, it was clear that attempts to radically revise the GDR's class structure had been abandoned. These were replaced by a pragmatism that resulted in the emergence of a new technological-bureaucratic elite, some of whose material privileges were starting to be passed on to the next generation.

Because the Berlin Wall barred both outside influences and the possibility of its citizens abandoning their homes, the GDR regime soon felt itself less threatened by Western influences, and a cautious introduction of intellectual and artistic liberalization followed. In educational affairs, however, many of these reforms remained rhetoric. As a defender of an ideological and political hard line, Margot Honecker viewed educational policy from orthodox Marxist-Leninist perspectives. Under the aegis of her ministry, much effort went into creating new social attitudes and values. The goal of education in the GDR was the creation of what Honecker defined in a 1968 article as a "universally developed socialist personality" (allseitig entwickelte sozialistische Persönlichkeit). Political education came to be seen as not one component of education among many, but as the most important of all. Proceeding from curricular reforms put in place in the late 1960s, GDR educational goals were fully integrated with political-ideological components. This ideology was grounded in a dichotomous concept of a world of friends and foes, and of universal class antagonisms. Writing in an educational journal in 1968, Margot Honecker claimed: "There is no unpolitical subject and there are no unpolitical methods. There are no questions which are ideologically neutral. One cannot teach any subject matter separately from its political implications. What objectively belongs together cannot be artificially separated."

In practice, the Marxist-Leninist ideas and ideals which the educational system under Honecker promoted were more often than not imposed on the school population of the GDR in a blindly authoritarian fashion. An East German dissident of the 1980s, **Freya Klier**, whose book *Lüg Vaterland* (Fatherland of Lies) describes the collapse of educational credibility in the GDR, notes that in that state's schools children and youth were educated in a spirit most closely resembling that of the old Prussian militaristic system. Having been raised in a German society that was based on various forms of discipline and compulsion, Margot Honecker never abandoned her conviction that if it could be defined as being "socialist" in spirit an educational system grounded in a military regimen was in fact a justifiable one.

By the 1980s, glaring contradictions between the rhetoric of state-sponsored ideology and the often shabby reality of the system of "real existing socialism" had become increasingly apparent to GDR citizens, particularly the youth and intellectuals. Margot Honecker, her husband, and the SED ruling class failed to recognize the warning signals that grew with each passing year. In 1988, she declared, "It's nonsense to say we live in a computer age, for all the significance computers and key technology have. We live in an age in which we are still developing and establishing a socialist society, a society in which human beings are the most important factor. We don't want all our children to turn into computer freaks." In the same interview, while arguing that the GDR educational system fostered the growth of "the individual's personality as a whole," she added that while "We don't want our children to be 'obedient' in the Victorian sense. . . . in our society a high level of discipline is necessary."

A flashpoint for the growing alienation between the SED regime and many of its people was the introduction in September 1978 of compulsory military education in all GDR schools for children aged 15 and 16. The brainchild of Margot Honecker, this new policy of educational militarization created an uproar of opposition in the Christian religious community, with both the Lutheran bishop of Berlin and the head of the Roman Catholic community, Cardinal Frings, speaking out strongly against the regime's efforts to get a stronger ideological grip on young people. Increasingly disillusioned by official ideology, GDR youth were profoundly influenced by West German television and radio broadcasts. By the late 1980s, the regime was losing its grip not only on youth but on the population at large.

The reform program initiated in the Soviet Union under the dynamic new leadership of Mikhail Gorbachev contrasted sharply with a GDR that many saw as a Stalinist mausoleum existing on borrowed time and money. Hobbled by bureaucracy, the economy was now burdened by a technology gap with the West estimated at between five and ten years and growing. Only reliance on illegal imports and the copying of West German software programs kept the economy from total collapse. An ecological nightmare had emerged by this time, and, with little or no provision for environmental protection, the health of much of the GDR population was at grave risk and life expectancy had dropped.

By the spring of 1989, when the aging SED ruling class authorized fraudulent regional elections, the GDR regime had lost the support of a great majority of its citizens. An immense network of informers and spies, the Stasi (Ministry of State Security), began to falter in its attempts to control a society based on official lies and a pervasive lack of trust in its own citizens. During the final years of the GDR, hardliners in the regime including Margot Honecker called for inflexible resistance to any and all attempts at reform, including experiments inspired by the changes taking place in Gorbachev's USSR. In a 1987 speech to Young Pioneer leaders in Dresden, she called for a renewed commitment to "socialist patriotism . . . without ifs and buts for the GDR fatherland."

By June 1989, when she addressed the Ninth GDR Pedagogical Congress, Honecker was sounding the alarm bell, warning ominously of those "counter-revolutionaries [who] under the motto of pluralism [are] trying to achieve their nefarious goals." Using rhetoric more appropriate to KPD working-class struggles against the Nazis during the 1930s than to the highly educated citizens of a self-proclaimed advanced socialist state, she announced, "We are now in a period of struggle which needs young people who are willing to fight to strengthen socialism . . . if necessary, with a rifle in their hands."

During the summer of 1989, Erich Honecker became seriously ill. His nation, too, revealed major symptoms of decay, with thousands of GDR citizens fleeing indirectly to the West via Hungary, which had begun a process of major democratization of its politics and society. In October 1989, when the GDR celebrated its 40th anniversary, guest of honor Mikhail Gorbachev warned his host Erich Honecker that little time was left to make major reforms. As anti-regime demonstrations broke out in Leipzig and other cities, and violence was feared, Erich Honecker resigned his party and state posts on October 18, citing health reasons. Sensing that major changes had become inevitable, his wife now called for creating an "open climate," but she chose not to resign her Ministry of Public Education post for 14 more days. She resigned on November 2, 1989, a week before one of the most momentous events of the last decades of the 20th century, the destruction of the Berlin Wall.

The rapid collapse of the SED dictatorship in the last weeks of 1989 led to an eruption of popular fury that resulted in the arrest of Erich Honecker, but it quickly became clear that his health had deteriorated so much that he could not be held in a jail cell. Soon he and Margot, both now homeless, found refuge in the house of the Lutheran pastor of Lobetal, a village near Berlin. Given the widely held belief that their marriage had broken down in the 1960s, and that they were reported to have been divorced in 1970 by the court of Berlin-Lichtenberg, their asylum may have represented the first time they had lived together in over two decades. Charges of treason were raised against Margot's husband in early 1990, and she was accused of having forced political dissidents to surrender their children for adoption, as well as of presiding over that reform school in Torgau known as "Margot's concentration camp" where truant minors were mistreated in dank, dark cells to the point that some committed suicide.

In the spring of 1991, Erich and Margot Honecker fled Germany to find refuge in the Soviet Union, a state and society then in the final stages of dissolution, where they lived at first in a comfortable flat. After the USSR collapsed in December of that year, Erich feared being extradited to Germany by the new Russian government, and both he and Margot sought refuge in the Chilean Embassy in Moscow. The GDR had granted political asylum to a number of Chileans in the 1970s after the overthrow of the Allende government, and the Honeckers' daughter Sonja had married a Chilean, Martinez Yanez, and had moved to Santiago. After spending 232 days as a "guest" in the Chilean embassy, Erich Honecker was handed over to German authorities and flown to Berlin in late July 1992 to stand trial for 49 cases of manslaughter linked to deaths along the Berlin Wall. In Berlin, he was taken to Moabit Prison, where he had been incarcerated by the Nazi regime for a period of time in the 1930s. As his trial began in November 1992, the Berlin newspaper *Sonntagspost* published excerpts from what it said were letters he had received from his wife in Chile, advising him, "Don't beg for forgiveness. You did a lot for peace in Europe. Stand up to your adversaries. Maintain your dignity."

One day after her husband arrived in Berlin for his arraignment, Margot Honecker flew to Chile to be with her daughter. Commenting on her departure from Russia, one of Germany's leading newspapers, the *Frankfurter Allgemeine Zeitung,* noted that many people in the former GDR "would rather see 'the witch Margot' behind bars than Erich Honecker." In the last decades of the GDR, the relatively flamboyant lifestyles of both Honeckers had aroused considerable resentment among citizens. He lived in Wandlitz, a government compound near Berlin where high officials of state and party had access to otherwise unobtainable goods from the West and allowed themselves to be driven around in Volvo automobiles. She, on the other hand, stood out among the members of the GDR cabinet, appearing stylish with her expensive clothes and blue-rinse hair.

In January 1993, Erich Honecker was released from his jail cell in Berlin and permitted to fly to Chile to be with his wife and daughter. United Germany's legal effort to prosecute and convict him ended with his release on grounds of poor health. He was terminally ill with liver cancer at the time he was granted his freedom and died in Chile on May 29, 1994. Although his widow had no desire ever to return to Germany, she retained a hope that the urn with Erich Honecker's ashes might one day be buried in German soil in a "dignified" (*würdig*) manner.

After her husband's death, Margot Honecker remained in Chile with her daughter. Occasionally she was the subject of news stories, including one in November 1994 which reported that she had expressed a wish to spend the remainder of her life in the last hard-line Communist state, North Korea. In September 1996, she lost a five-year legal struggle to regain her two pensions from the German state, one entitled to her as a widow and the other because she had been an "anti-fascist combatant." Basing her claim on the laws of the now-defunct GDR, she was turned down by the social security court which argued that those laws had expressly banned the "export" of pension payments. In April 1997, Honecker celebrated her 70th birthday with her daughter's family in an upper-middle-class suburb of Santiago de Chile. Her life now centered on her grandchildren. Choosing to shun all publicity, she covered herself with a shawl or headscarf when out in public. An acquaintance of hers noted simply, "She does not want to be recognized."

SOURCES:

Andert, Reinhold and Wolfgang Herzberg. *Der Sturz: Erich Honecker im Kreuzverhör.* 4th ed. Berlin and Weimar: Aufbau-Verlag, 1991.

Anweiler, Oskar. "Erziehung, Schule und Ausbildung in der DDR-Gesellschaft unter dem Aspekt des Totalitarismus," in *German Studies Review,* Special Issue: Totalitäre Herrschaft—totalitäres Erbe. Fall 1994, pp. 67–84.

Bentley, Raymond. *Research and Technology in the Former German Democratic Republic.* Boulder, CO: Westview Press, 1992.

"Church Militant versus Militarism," in *The Economist.* September 30, 1978, p. 57.

Dennis, Mike. *Social and Economic Modernization in Eastern Germany from Honecker to Kohl.* London and NY: Pinter Publishers-St. Martin's Press, 1993.

Frey, Gerhard, ed. *Prominente ohne Maske: DDR.* Munich: FZ-Verlag, 1991.

Fulbrook, Mary. *The Two Germanies, 1945–1990: Problems of Interpretation.* Atlantic Highlands, NJ: Humanities Press International, 1992.

Gast, Gabriele. *Die politische Rolle der Frau in der DDR.* Düsseldorf: Bertelsmann Universitätsverlag, 1973.

Gedmin, Jeffrey. *The Hidden Hand: Gorbachev and the Collapse of East Germany.* Washington, DC: The AEI Press, 1992.

Groth, Hendrik. "Hiding from the Press, Margot Honecker Celebrates Her 70th Birthday," in *Deutsche Presse-Agentur.* April 16, 1997.

Hockenos, Paul. "Dark Side of the Wall," in *New Statesman and Society.* Vol. 3, no. 83. January 12, 1990, pp. 16–17.

Honecker, Erich. *Erich Honecker zu dramatischen Ereignissen.* Hamburg: W. Runge Verlag, 1992.

———. *From My Life.* Oxford: Pergamon Press, 1981.

———. *Moabiter Notizen.* 2nd ed. Berlin: Edition Ost, 1994.

Honecker, Margot. "Modern Socialist Education," in *Prisma.* No. 3, 1988, pp. 380–445.

———. *The Social Function of Our Schools.* Berlin: Panorama DDR-Auslandspresseagentur GmbH. DDR, 1978.

———. *Unser sozialistisches Bildungssystem: Wandlungen, Erfolge, neue Horizonte—IX. pädagogischer Kongress der DDR, 13. bis 15. Juni, 1989.* Berlin: Dietz Verlag, 1989.

———. *Zur Bildungspolitik und Pädagogik in der Deutschen Demokratischen Republik: ausgewählte Reden und Schriften.* Edited by Werner Lorenz et al. Berlin: Verlag Volk und Wissen, 1986.

Kalkbrenner, Jorn. *Urteil ohne Prozess: Margot Honecker gegen Ossietzky-Schüler.* Berlin: Dietz Verlag, 1990.

Kinzer, Stephen. "Failing Health and Advanced Age Are Threats to Honecker's Trial," in *The New York Times.* November 18, 1992, p. A6.

Klier, Freya. *Lüg Vaterland: Erziehung in der DDR.* Munich: Kindler-Verlag, 1990.

Lippmann, Heinz. *Honecker.* Cologne: Verlag Wissenschaft und Politik, 1971.

"Margot Honecker Calls for 'Open Climate,'" in *Foreign Broadcast Information Service, Eastern Europe.* October 13, 1989, p. 35.

McCauley, Martin. "Gorbachev, the GDR and Germany," in Gert-Joachim Glaessner and Ian Wallace, eds., *The German Revolution of 1989: Causes and Consequences.* Oxford and Providence, Rhode Island: Berg, 1992, pp. 163–183.

Schmitt, Karl. "Political Education in the German Democratic Republic: Effects and System Relevance," in *International Journal of Political Education.* Vol. 3, no. 1. March 1980, pp. 1–16.

Wyden, Peter. *Wall—The Inside Story of Divided Berlin.* NY: Simon and Schuster, 1989.

John Haag,
Associate Professor, University of Georgia, Athens,
Athens, Georgia

Nan
Wood
Honeyman

Honeyman, Nan Wood (1881–1970)

Member of the United States House of Representatives, 1937–1939. *Born Nan Wood on July 15, 1881, in West Point, New York; died December 10, 1970, in Woodacre, California; married David T. Honeyman, in 1907.*

Nan Wood was born on July 15, 1881, in West Point, New York, where her father worked as adjutant of the U.S. Military Academy. When he resigned in 1883, the family moved to Portland, Oregon, where Nan Wood attended private schools. In 1898, she graduated from St. Helen's Hall and later studied music for three years at the Finch School in New York City. There she began a lifelong friendship with Franklin and ***Eleanor Roosevelt** that in later years developed into a strong working relationship. In 1907, at about the age of 26, Nan Wood married Portland hardware company executive David T. Honeyman.

In 1933, Nan Wood Honeyman began her public life by serving as president of the Oregon State Constitutional Convention that ratified the 21st Amendment, thereby repealing Prohibition. Two years later, she became a member of the Oregon House of Representatives; she also served as a delegate to the Democratic National Conventions of 1936 and 1940. In 1936, Honeyman was elected to represent Oregon's Third District in the U.S. House of Representatives over Republican incumbent William A. Ekwall and an independent candidate.

During her term of office, Honeyman served on the Committee on Indian Affairs, the Committee on Irrigation and Reclamation, and the Committee on Rivers and Harbors. Her close ties to the White House and active support of New Deal policies led some to believe that she would have a fruitful career in Congress. Critics, however, claimed that her promotion of President Roosevelt's political agenda led her to neglect constituent concerns. Honeyman ran unsuccessfully for re-election in 1938, despite support from Secretary of the Interior Harold L. Ickes, and again in 1940; in both elections, she was defeated by Homer D. Angell.

In July 1941, Honeyman was appointed to fill a vacant seat in the state senate, where she served until she resigned in October to take the position of senior representative of the Pacific Coast Office of Price Administration. In May of 1942, Roosevelt appointed her collector of customs for the 29th District in Portland, Oregon, a post she retained until July of 1953. In the mid-1960s, Honeyman moved to Woodacre, California, where she died at the age of 89 on December 10, 1970. She was interred in a family plot at Riverview Cemetery in Portland, Oregon.

SOURCES:

Office of the Historian. *Women in Congress, 1917–1990.* Commission on the Bicentenary of the U.S. House of Representatives, 1991.

Sonya Elaine Schryer,
freelance writer, Lansing, Michigan

Hong, Lady (1735–1850)

Korean queen of the Yi dynasty whose memoir chronicles court life in 18th-century Korea and the tragic demise of her husband. *Born on August 6, 1735, in Kop'yong-dong, Pangsongbang, Korea; died in 1850; daughter and one of three children (two girls and a boy) of Hong Pong-han (the president of the state council) and* ***Lady Yi****; married Crown Prince Sado (1735–1762), on February 23, 1744 (died 1762); children: son Uiso (1750–1752); Chongjo (b. 1752, later king of Korea); daughters, Ch'ongyon (b. 1754) and Ch'ongson (b. 1756).*

In her *Memoirs of a Korean Queen,* written late in life for her son and grandson who became kings, Lady Hong recalled her days as the wife of Crown Prince Sado, who died in 1762 at the hand of his father King Yongjo, the 21st king of the Yi Dynasty. Since the facts surrounding Prince Sado's death were stricken from the royal records, Hong wrote the book to shed light on the dark events that culminated in what came to be known as the Imo Incident, "an affair such as has never been known in ancient times."

Born into a family descended from royalty who had produced several generations of senior government officials, including her father, Lady Hong became the wife of Crown Prince Sado at the age of ten. "I was a mere child when I came to the court," she noted, "and wrote twice a day to my parents." The first ten years of Hong's marriage were uneventful, although her life at court was strictly governed. She gave birth to her first child, Uiso, in 1750, when she was 15 and the crown prince was 17, but the boy died in the spring of 1752. Later that year, Hong gave birth to another son, the royal grandson and future King Chongjo. Two daughters, Princess **Ch'ongyon** and Princess **Ch'ongson**, followed in 1754 and 1756, respectively.

At the time of her marriage, Lady Hong was unaware that Prince Sado had, since the age of ten, suffered from mental illness, a disorder which she would come to believe had been caused by his early estrangement from his father. (The prince had been raised by court servants from infancy.) In the winter of 1752, the illness began to manifest itself more acutely. Sado experienced bouts of hysteria and grew desperately afraid of his father, who was continually critical of his behavior and would not include him in court events. Despite Lady Hong's efforts to comfort her husband, Sado became increasingly more deranged as the years passed, vacillating between suicide attempts and wild parties. During periods of intense rage, he killed a number of court maids and eunuchs, while in his more tranquil moments he appeared quite normal. Lady Hong, sick with worry, thought of ending her own life on several occasions. "It is impossible for me to describe how hard it was to go on living from one day to the next," she wrote. In 1762, shortly after the state wedding of her son Chongjo, heir to the throne, Prince Sado's condition deteriorated to such a degree that his mother, Lady **Sonhui**, believed that the very dynasty was at risk and went before the king to suggest that the prince be killed. "Since the prince's illness has become quite critical and his case is hopeless, it is only proper that you should protect yourself and the royal grandson, in order to keep the kingdom at peace," she told King Yongjo, then begged him to spare the lives of the royal grandson and Lady Hong.

The prince grew increasingly paranoid, as though he knew the fate awaiting him. When the time came, he begged his father to spare his life but was forced to enter a grain box which was then sealed. For days, as Lady Hong languished in bed, contemplating the annihilation of her own life, her husband slowly died. It was only for her son, then 11 years old, that she found the strength to go on. Following the prince's burial on September 10, 1762, Chongjo became crown prince and was taken to live and receive instructions at the Kyonghui Palace, while Hong remained in a separate residence for the period of mourning. The king subsequently presented her with a residence near the palace, Chagyong-jon Mansion, where she lived out the remainder of her life and wrote her memoirs. *Memoirs of a Korean Queen* was edited and translated by **Yang-hi Choe-Wall**, daughter of a Shakespearean scholar and research fellow at the Australian National University. The story was the subject of a highly popular television drama in South Korea in 1985.

SOURCES:

Hong, Lady. *Memoirs of a Korean Queen.* Edited, introduced and translated by Yang-hi Choe-Wall. London and NY: KPI, 1985.

Hong, Qiao (b. 1968).

See Deng Yaping for sidebar on Qiao Hong.

Honner, Maria (1812–1870)

Irish actress. *Born Maria McCarthy in Enniskillen, County Fermanagh, Ireland, in 1812; died in 1870; married Robert William Honner (1809–1852, an actor-manager), in 1836.*

Maria Honner was born Maria McCarthy in Enniskillen, County Fermanagh, Ireland, in 1812. In 1836, she married Robert William Honner, an actor-manager of Sadler's Wells from 1835 to 1840 and the Surrey Theater from 1835 to 1838 and 1842 to 1846. Maria Honner excelled in tragedy; she appeared opposite Edmund Kean and as Julia in *The Hunchback* (1835).

Honor.

Variant of Nora.

Honoria (c. 420–?)

Roman princess. *Name variations: Honoria Augusta; Justa Grata Honoria. Born around 420; daughter of Constantius III, emperor of Rome, and Galla Placidia (c. 390–450); sister of Valentinian III.*

Honoria was born around 420, the daughter of Constantius III, emperor of Rome, and ***Galla Placidia** (c. 390–450). Within a space of two years, Honoria caused two scandals in the Roman palace. The first was her affair with her steward Eugenius; he was executed, she was banished to a convent in Constantinople in 434. When she was finally thought to be safely betrothed, she sent her ring to Attila the Hun, reputedly seeking marriage. Attila used the message as an excuse to invade Italy in 452, while demanding his "marriage portion" of the Roman empire.

Hoo, Anne (c. 1425–1484)

English noblewoman. *Name variations: Anne Boleyn. Born around 1425; died in 1484; daughter of Thomas Hoo, Lord Hoo and Hastings, and ****Elizabeth Wychingham****; married Geoffrey Boleyn (Lord Mayor of London in 1458); children: William Boleyn (c. 1451–1505, grandfather of ****Anne Boleyn****).*

Hood, Lady (1783–1862).

See Stewart-Mackenzie, Maria.

Hoodless, Adelaide (1857–1910)

Canadian welfare reformer. *Born Adelaide Sophia Hunter in Brantford, Ontario, Canada, on February 27, 1857; died in Toronto, Ontario, on February 26, 1910; married John Hoodless (a businessman), in 1881; children: four (perhaps more).*

Adelaide Hoodless' interest in raising the standard of living among rural women in Canada was the result of a family tragedy. She was born Adelaide Sophia Hunter in 1857 and raised on a farm in Brantford, Ontario, one of 12 children. At age 24, she married John Hoodless, moved to Hamilton, and began a family. Following the death of her son from drinking contaminated milk in 1889, Adelaide began a campaign for improved home conditions and education for expectant mothers in nutrition, sanitation, and housekeeping. When she was ignored by authorities, she took matters into her own hands, teaching classes at the Hamilton Young Women's Christian Association (YWCA). After becoming president of Hamilton's YWCA in 1892, she started a school of domestic science.

Unable to secure funding from the Ontario government to continue her work, Hoodless appealed to William Macdonald, a tobacco magnate, who donated money to build the Macdonald Institute, which became part of the Ontario Agricultural Institute at Guelph in 1904. Hoodless continued to teach and lecture on domestic science. One of her talks before the Farmers' Institute at Stoney Creek, in which she suggested the establishment of a similar forum for women, resulted in the formation of the women's department of the Farmers' Institute (later renamed The Women's Institute of Stoney Creek). Established in 1897 as a rural society whose objective was to promote the knowledge of home economics and child care, it served as a model for similar rural societies which began springing up throughout the world. Eventually the societies all affiliated with the Associated Country Women of the World, perhaps the largest non-political women's association ever, with 8 million members in 283 societies in 68 countries. Adelaide Hoodless died on February 26, 1910, while on a fund-raising campaign at St. Margaret's College in Toronto. In 1911, John Hoodless placed the cornerstone on the Hoodless Memorial School at 71 Maplewood Avenue in Hamilton. The elementary school, now known as the Adelaide Hoodless School, celebrated its 75th anniversary in 1986. The Federal Women's Institutes of Canada also honored Hoodless by purchasing her birthplace and transforming it into a historic site in 1967.

Hooker, Evelyn (1907–1996)

American psychologist who conducted early studies on homosexuality. *Born Evelyn Gentry in North Platt, Nebraska, in 1907; died in Santa Monica, California, on November 18, 1996; earned bachelor's and master's degrees from the University of Colorado; Johns Hopkins University, Ph.D., 1932; married twice; second husband Edward Niles Hooker (died 1957); no children.*

A pioneering researcher on homosexuality during the 1950s, psychologist Evelyn Hooker was born in North Platt, Nebraska, in 1907, but spent her childhood in northeastern Colorado. After receiving her undergraduate and master's degrees from the University of Colorado, and her Ph.D. from Johns Hopkins, she joined the faculty at the University of California, Los Angeles, in 1932. Except for a year spent at Bryn Mawr, Hooker remained at UCLA for the next 30 years. It was there, during the 1940s, that she was introduced to the homosexual community at the university.

Hooker's work, financed through a grant from the National Institute of Mental Health (NIMH), was carried out during the 1950s, a period in which homosexuals were either ignored or anathematized by the medical and mental health professions. Writer Christopher Isherwood, who knew Hooker at that time, later recalled: "She never treated us like some strange tribe, so we told her things we never told anyone before."

Hooker's studies included administering three standard personality tests to two groups of 30 men, one heterosexual and another homosexual, who had been matched according to age, I.Q.'s, and educational levels. She then asked a panel of expert clinicians to assess the results without knowing the subjects' sexual orientation. The judges were unable to discern between the two groups on the basis of the test. "The most striking finding of the three judges," wrote Hooker, "was that many of the homosexuals were very well adjusted. In fact, the three judges agreed on two-thirds of the group as being average to superior in adjustment. Not only do all homosexuals not have strong feminine identification, nor are they all somewhat paranoid, but, according to the judges, some may not be characterized by any demonstrable parapsychology." Her findings were delivered to the American Psychological Association in 1956 and published a year later as "The Adjustment of the Male Overt Homosexual" in the *Journal of Projective Techniques.*

As might be expected, Hooker's findings were widely suspect at the time. Many criticized her for recruiting her subjects through "homophile" groups, like the Mattachine Society, believing that the men she tested might be more content with their lives and anxious to prove that they were well adjusted. The study, however, led the American Psychiatric Association to begin to rethink its viewpoint on homosexuality. Seventeen years later, the association removed homosexuality as a psychological disorder from its *Diagnostic and Statistical Manual.* In 1992, 36 years after she had first presented her research, the organization recognized Hooker with an award for distinguished contribution to psychology in the public interest.

In 1967, Evelyn Hooker headed a study group on homosexuality for the National Institute of Mental Health, which recommended a repeal of sodomy laws and better public education about homosexuality. After retiring from UCLA in 1970, she went into private practice and also established the Placek Fund of the American Psychological Foundation, which provides money for research into homosexuality. Hooker was married twice; her second husband, Edward Hooker, died in 1957. Evelyn Hooker died on November 18, 1996, at her home in Santa Monica, California.

SOURCES:

Obituary. *The New York Times.* November 22, 1996.

Barbara Morgan,
Melrose, Massachusetts

Hooker, Isabella Beecher (1822–1907).

See Stowe, Harriet Beecher for sidebar.

Hooper, Ellen Sturgis (1812–1848).

See Adams, Clover for sidebar.

Hooper, Marian "Clover"(1843–1885).

See Adams, Clover.

Hoover, Mrs. Herbert (1874–1944).

See Hoover, Lou Henry.

Hoover, Katherine (1937—)

American composer, flautist, and lecturer who originated the Women's Music Festivals. *Born in Elkins, West Virginia, on December 2, 1937; Manhattan School of Music, M.A.*

Born in Elkins, West Virginia, in 1937, Katherine Hoover studied flute at the Eastman School of Music under Joseph Mariano and then earned a master's degree from the Manhattan School of Music. After additional training in flute with William Kincaid in Philadelphia, she had an active concert career with leading orchestras. Hoover also appeared frequently on television and received a National Endowment composer's grant and an ASCAP award. The Kennedy Center Friedheim Contest named her work *Trio* as one of the ten outstanding compositions of 1978–79. Katherine Hoover taught theory and flute at the Manhattan School of Music. An important figure in the musical world, both as a composer and activist, she originated the concept of a women's musical festival which featured works that had often been overlooked in past centuries as well as in the present. Hoover composed many pieces for orchestra, chamber orchestra, piano, and voice as well as sacred music.

John Haag,
Athens, Georgia

Hoover, Lou Henry (1874–1944)

First lady of the United States from 1929 to 1933, who was identified with the Girl Scouts and the promotion of women's sports. *Born on March 28, 1874, in Waterloo, Iowa; died on January 7, 1944, in New York City; daughter of Florence (Weed) Henry and Charles Delano Henry; degree in geology from Stanford, 1898; married Herbert Hoover, on February 10, 1899; children: Herbert Hoover, Jr. (b. 1903); Allan Henry Hoover (b. 1907).*

Lou Henry Hoover is one of the most neglected and forgotten first ladies of the 20th century. Her contributions to the institution have been overshadowed because of the Great Depression that made her husband's presidency a historical failure and the impact of her successor ***Eleanor Roosevelt**. She was, however, the first wife of a president to give speeches on the radio, and she used her connections with the Girl Scouts to fight the hard times that accompanied the Depression.

Lou Henry was born in 1874, the first child of **Florence Weed Henry** and Charles Delano Henry. Her father, a local banker who had hoped for a son, took his daughter on fishing trips and hikes through the woods near Waterloo, Iowa, and Lou was horseback riding by age six. She was a member of a girls' group in Iowa where at nine or ten she did her first cooking and eating outdoors.

In 1884, Charles decided to move his banking business to California where the climate was better for Florence's asthma. They settled in Whittier, where they lived for the next eight years. At 13, Lou sent a description of her town to *St. Nicholas Magazine* which published her letter in its December 1887 issue.

The Henrys relocated to Monterey in 1892. Lou graduated from the San Jose Normal School in 1893 and worked in her father's bank until the spring of the following year. She would later recall Monterey as a place where she and her father "were always doing things out of doors." During the spring of 1894, she attended a lecture on "The Bones of the Earth" given by Professor John Casper Branner of Stanford University. Branner agreed to let Lou study geology at Stanford. Though her parents warned her that she would be the only woman in the program, she was determined and enrolled in September 1894.

In her geology classes, she met a senior named Herbert Clark Hoover who was her age and had been born in the same part of Iowa. By the end of the school year, they had agreed to write to each other after Herbert's graduation, and there was an understanding that they would spend their future together. Herbert pursued a mining career during the three years that followed, writing Lou from all parts of the world. She graduated in 1898 with a degree in geology, after which Herbert proposed by telegram and asked her to spend their honeymoon in China. They were married on February 10, 1899, in Monterey.

The Hoovers spent their first years of marriage in a Chinese nation experiencing the upheaval of the Boxer Rebellion against foreigners from the West. In 1900, the Boxers besieged the city of Tientsin (Tianjin) where the Hoovers were living. Herbert urged Lou to leave, but she

Lou Henry Hoover

remained and stood guard duty, rode her bicycle through sniper fire, and sought food for the two of them. Possessed with an aptitude for languages since her childhood, Lou learned to read Chinese during their stay and studied the culture extensively.

During the next 15 years, she followed Herbert's mining career around the world, circling the globe with him five times. Meanwhile, they had two sons, Herbert, Jr., born in 1903, and Allan, born in 1907. Lou maintained a home amid the hectic schedule, engaged in philanthropic and volunteer work, and became a member of such organizations as the Society of American Women in London.

In collaboration with her husband, Lou also translated into English a 16th-century textbook on mining, written by Georgius Agricola, *De Re Metallica*. The Latin text was filled with technical mining terms, some of which Agricola had invented, and the translation took the Hoovers five years, during which Lou's Latin skills were crucial to the success of their joint endeavor. The result was a book of nearly 600 pages that brought the work of Agricola to the attention of modern scholars. The Hoovers dedicated the book to their old teacher, Professor Branner, and published it in 1912 at their own expense.

Their lives took an unexpected turn during the summer of 1914 when World War I erupted in Europe. American citizens were trapped in London by the start of hostilities, and Herbert organized relief for his 120,000 stranded fellow citizens through his American Committee. Now president of the Society of American Women in London, Lou coordinated the society's work on behalf of Herbert's Committee, proving herself to be an efficient organizer, fund raiser, and public speaker on behalf of relief activities in England, France, and Belgium. By 1916, she had demonstrated her skills as a leader in working with organized women.

She was recognized during her lifetime as a uniquely intelligent woman, who refused to let official formalities interfere with her deep and friendly interest in people.

—**Ray Lyman Wilbur**

When the United States entered the war in April 1917, the Wilson administration named Herbert head of the Food Administration. Lou became a public force for conserving food supplies and developing recipes that used different grains and cereals. She also organized boarding houses for women who had come to take wartime jobs in Washington, calling her enterprise the Food Administration's Women's Club. In addition, she worked with the American Red Cross to set up a service to escort wounded soldiers from their hospital ships to the trains that would take them to their homes.

After working with the Girl Scouts in Washington for several years during the war, in the postwar years Lou Hoover intensified her commitment to the organization as she explored ways to help children. Hoover concluded that the Girl Scouts (founded in America by ***Juliette Gordon Low** in 1912) were more effective in building character for their members than any other comparable organization for young people. Hoover was soon serving as acting commissioner for the Girl Scouts in Washington, D.C., and she rose steadily in the national organization between 1922 and 1927. She served as national president (between 1922 and 1925) and then chaired the national board of directors of the Girl Scouts (from 1925 to 1928). With a dislike for the more military aspects of Girl Scouting, she encouraged the change from khaki-colored uniforms to a softer green during the 1920s.

Hoover believed that Girl Scouting instilled proper values in the young women who were members. She wanted girls to learn about the outdoors not from the backseat of a car but by experiencing the woods and fields firsthand. The training that Girl Scouts received, she argued, prepared them to be better citizens and homemakers in the future. She expected the Girl Scouts to contribute service to their communities, to set an example of good citizenship, and to be active participants in all the physical activities that Scouting demanded.

Hoover's dedication to athletics and sports for women ran parallel to her commitment to the Girl Scouts. She worried that American women were not getting the proper preparation for the rigors of life, and believed that greater participation in sports could remedy that national problem. To that end, Hoover gave her time to the National Amateur Athletic Federation during the 1920s as a vice president involved with the Women's Division. Hoover cooperated with those educators who did not want women to stress spectator sports or to take part in the Olympic Games. She believed that the focus should be on having as many girls take part in sports as possible rather than on the competition which characterized male athletics. At the same time, she campaigned to broaden the opportunities for women to play sports in areas where most of the resources were devoted to male athletics. Throughout the 1920s and 1930, she gave her own money and time to promote these goals for women athletes.

By 1928, Herbert Hoover, the secretary of commerce, was the Republican candidate for the presidency. His election made Lou Henry Hoover the first lady in March 1929. She had already given radio speeches, and now from the White House and the presidential retreat in Maryland she went on the radio for her favorite causes, including the Girl Scouts. No first lady before her had used the national media in this way. While she did not hold formal press conferences, Hoover often spoke with reporters when she made speeches about the Girl Scouts, a method which proved very effective in getting her messages across to the public.

By not bowing down to the prevalent racial prejudices of the day, Lou Hoover came under attack during her first year in the White House. After the election of 1928, an African-American Congressional representative named Oscar DePriest represented a black district in Chicago, Illinois. Traditionally, the wives of representatives were received at the White House by the first lady. There were warnings to Lou Hoover, particularly from Southerners, that entertaining **Mrs. DePriest** would conflict with the racial segregation that operated in Washington at the time. Though she was careful to make the visit as low-key as possible, Hoover did invite Mrs. DePriest to the White House in June 1929. The episode caused an intense reaction from the press in the South where Hoover's action was depicted as a direct challenge to segregation. The Texas Legislature and several other legislatures in the South passed resolutions denouncing her action as an abuse of her position as first lady. Lou Hoover made no public statements about what had happened; unlike her successor, Eleanor Roosevelt, she did not have the ability to garner press support when she acted on behalf of racial equality.

By the end of 1929, the nation had experienced the Wall Street stock-market crash, and conditions in the economy were worsening. The Hoover presidency endeavored to respond to the onset of the Great Depression, but the next three years were difficult and painful ones for the Hoovers. Growing lines of unemployed, families in poverty, and economic despair across the nation cost them much of the popularity that had swept them into the White House.

Like her husband, Lou Henry Hoover did not believe that the answer to the Depression was to increase the role of the federal government. Instead, she emphasized the volunteer spirit that she saw in the Girl Scouts and her earlier relief work. She believed that the membership of the Girl Scouts—not through a connection with the federal government but by providing a model volunteer force that could support the president's programs—could be a positive element to provide aid to the impoverished and needy in local communities.

Throughout 1931, she made speeches urging charitable groups to rally to the needs of their neighbors and help destitute Americans get through the coming winter. Hoping that the rest of the country would follow the example of the Girl Scouts, Lou Hoover invited the leaders of the national Girl Scout organization to the Hoovers' official retreat in the Rapidan mountains of Maryland (now Camp David) during September 1931. They hammered out a program of volunteer service that was presented to the Girl Scout annual convention the following month as the "Rapidan Plan" to involve 250,000 Girl Scouts in relief work.

The plan was an ambitious undertaking, and the work of the Girl Scouts did some good during the Depression winter of 1932. Hoover had used the influence that a first lady commands on behalf of a generous and caring volunteer endeavor. Unfortunately, the scale of the economic suffering that the Depression caused meant that volunteer campaigns, however well intentioned, could not relieve the misery that the majority of citizens were experiencing. Like the administration of her husband, the Rapidan Plan of Lou Henry Hoover was rejected by the American people in the presidential election of 1932 when Herbert Hoover was defeated overwhelmingly for reelection. The Hoovers left Washington in March 1933 to return to their home in Stanford, California.

In retirement, Hoover kept up an active schedule. She renewed her work with the Girl Scouts and with women's sports, while adding to those commitments the Red Cross, the Community Chest (now the United Way), the Young Women's Christian Association, and several Stanford alumni groups. She founded the Friends of Music in Stanford to support concerts and to bring distinguished artists to the campus.

Because of her natural reserve and dislike of the spotlight, Lou Henry Hoover did not receive acknowledgement for the good she did during her lifetime. Her fame receded during the last ten years of her life amid the popular attention showered on her successor, Eleanor Roosevelt. By the time of her death of a heart attack on January 7, 1944, Lou Hoover was largely forgotten by the public.

After her death, former President Hoover found among her personal papers evidence of numerous acts of private charity that she had performed without asking for credit or notice. In his will, he specified that his wife's personal papers should be closed until 20 years after his own death. He died in 1964, and Lou Henry Hoover's records did not become available until the mid-1980s. With those papers open, biographers and historians are discovering a woman who had an intense commitment to the cause of expanded opportunity for all women and who left an impressive legacy of good works and genuine innovations as first lady of the United States.

SOURCES:

Caroli, Betty. *First Ladies.* Oxford, 1986.

Mayer, Dale C. ed. *Lou Henry Hoover: Essays on a Busy Life.* High Plains, 1993.

Pryor, Helen B. *Lou Henry Hoover: Gallant First Lady.* NY: Dodd, Mead, 1969.

Ryan, Mary C. and Nancy Kegan Smith. *Modern First Ladies: Their Documentary Legacy.* National Archives, 1989.

SUGGESTED READING:

Anthony, Carl Serrazza. *First Ladies: The Saga of the Presidents' Wives and Their Power, 1789–1961.* NY: William Morrow, 1990.

Gutin, Myra G. *The President's Partner: The First Lady in the Twentieth Century.* CT: Greenwood, 1989.

Lewis L. Gould,
Eugene C. Barker Centennial Professor in American History, Emeritus, University of Texas at Austin, Texas

Hope, Eva (1834–1909).

See Farningham, Marianne.

Hope, Laura Lee (c. 1893–1982).

See Adams, Harriet Stratemeyer.

Hopekirk, Helen (1856–1945)

Scottish pianist who, after moving to America, became a champion of the music of Edward MacDowell and a composer of orchestral works as well as Scottish folksongs. *Born in Edinburgh, Scotland, on May 20, 1856; died in Cambridge, Massachusetts, of a cerebral thrombosis on November 19, 1945; interred at Mount Auburn Cemetery; daughter of Adam Hopekirk (a music-shop proprietor) and Helen (Croall) Hopekirk; studied piano with George Lichtenstein; received lessons in harmony, counterpoint, and composition with A.C. Mackenzie; studied with Carl Reinecke and Salomon Jadassohn (composition), Louis Maas (piano) and E.F. Richter (counterpoint) in Leipzig, 1876–78; studied under Theodor Leschetizky in Vienna; studied composition with Karel Navrátil in Vienna; studied composition and orchestration under Richard Mandl in Paris; married William A. Wilson (an Edinburgh merchant and music critic), on August 4, 1882 (died 1926); along with husband, became a U.S. citizen in 1918.*

Helen Hopekirk was born in Edinburgh, Scotland, in 1856. Having begun music studies at age nine, she then studied piano with George Lichtenstein, a Hungarian pianist living in Scotland, and took lessons in harmony, counterpoint, and composition with A.C. Mackenzie. From 1876 to 1878, Hopekirk attended the Leipzig Conservatory; she then studied in Vienna with Theodor Leschetizky. Her early successes took place in Germany, where she made her debut with the Leipzig Gewandhaus Orchestra in November 1878.

Hopekirk championed the music of Edward MacDowell after she and her husband, music critic William A. Wilson, settled in the United States in 1897. In her recitals, she often performed music of the contemporary French school (Debussy and Fauré). She taught for many years at the New England Conservatory of Music in Boston. As a composer, her best-known works were a Concert Piece as well as a Concerto for Piano and Orchestra, performed in 1894 and 1900. She also arranged and edited Scottish folk songs for piano.

SUGGESTED READING:

Hall, Constance Huntington and Helen Ingersoll Hall. *Helen Hopekirk, 1856–1945.* Cambridge, MA: n.p., 1954.

John Haag,
Athens, Georgia

Hopkins, Ellice (1836–1904)

English social reformer who founded the Ladies Associations for the Care of Friendless Girls to tackle the underlying causes of prostitution. *Born Ellice Jane Hopkins in Cambridge, England, in October 1836; died in May 1904; her mother was a talented musician and her father was a distinguished mathematics tutor at Cambridge University.*

Taught in Sunday schools; lectured on Christian morals to working-class men; involved in rescue and reform work; began Ladies Associations for the Care of Friendless Girls (1876); helped pass an amendment to the Industrial Schools Act (1880); founded White Cross Army (1883); helped found the National Vigilance Association (1885); wrote numerous pamphlets on social purity which include "The Visitation of Dens" (1874), "Notes on Penitentiary Work" (1879), "Grave Moral Questions" (1882), "Village Morality" (1882), "How to Start Preventive Work" (1884), "Drawn unto Death" (1884), "God's Little Girl" (1885), "Homely Talk on the New Law for the Protection of Girls" (1886), and "The National Purity Crusade" (1904).

Prostitution caused great concern in Victorian and Edwardian England. Fears that it might infect the respectable world, destroy marriages, the home, the family, and ultimately the nation, led to attempts to regulate it. Considered a social evil, prostitution commanded attention from the church, the state, and feminists, each of which held different perspectives on its cause and offered a range of solutions for its control. Whereas the British government detained suspected prostitutes under the Contagious Diseases Acts, the Church of England incarcerated them in penitentiaries. In these semi-prisons women were compelled to stay for at least two years, had their hair cropped, and wore a special regulatory uniform. Freedom was curtailed, letters inspected, and visits by friends and family limited. In one institution managed by a convent, inmates were taught to bow low before the nuns and to speak only when spoken to.

Ellice Hopkins, an Evangelical feminist, wrote a pamphlet criticizing these penitentiaries as dreary, ugly places in which only the desperate sought refuge:

> How is it, I ask, that Home after Home I go into is so utterly wanting. . . . Unless I had seen it for myself I could not have believed that dreariness and ugliness was such a fine art as we have made it for the benefit of these poor girls. The dingy walls, often of some rhubarb and magnesia hue; the torn book, generally unpinned at one corner, and flapping forlornly in the draft; the spiritual posters in the shape of hideous black and white texts hung up; no bright pictures or pretty illuminated texts . . . these poor girls, shut up with their low memories, low thoughts, low objects, low aims, they want every help.

Prostitutes, she believed, should be offered love and forgiveness, not punishment. Not surprisingly, her ideas were repugnant to many. Just the mention of her name sent quivers into the hearts and minds of many a Victorian gentleman. It was a name that was whispered in hushed tones at dinner tables and spoken with contempt at men's clubs. This small, rather innocuous-looking woman had broken the bounds of propriety expected of well brought up young women. In arguing so forcibly against penitentiaries, Ellice Hopkins ignored some important rules of Victorian England. She spoke out at a time when women were supposed to be silent, and she knew too much about sexual matters. More important, Hopkins challenged the division of women into pure and impure:

> As things are now, men divide us women into two classes: us pure women, for whom nothing is too good, and those others for whom nothing is too bad. But let us prove by our actions that our womanhood is ONE; that a sin against our lost sisters is a sin against us.

Ellice Hopkins was born in Cambridge, England, in October 1836, to gifted parents. Her mother was a talented musician while her father was a distinguished mathematics tutor at Cambridge University. One of five children and the youngest of three girls, Hopkins was the favorite of her father whom she idolized. They were constant companions. He taught her how to think scientifically and objectively and to write in the clearest and simplest language.

Like many young women of her class, Hopkins taught for years in her local Sunday school, but, in her 20s, she instructed a more challenging audience. Hundreds of working-class men, who rarely went to church, were converted to Christianity by Hopkins' vivid religious rhetoric. A gifted speaker, she worked hard to perfect her discourse. Soon audiences were entranced by her hard-hitting, witty lectures. Hopkins continued in this work until her father's death in 1866 when she became inconsolable. Soon after, she became ill, had several operations, stopped preaching, and left Cambridge to live in Brighton, an English seaside resort, to convalesce.

With her health regained, Hopkins experienced a striking shift in her life's work. Walking down one of Brighton's streets, she met a pretty child of 13 or 14 traversing a muddy path with her bare feet. Hopkins took her by the hand, she wrote, and led the girl back home to:

> a common lodging-house and found that her mother, a drunken Irish woman, sold flowers, and left this pretty girl alone with a lot of low men in the lodging-house all day, and with absolutely no employment . . . she was fast going to ruin. The girl was almost naked, and the first step was evidently to clothe her for service. . . . She was literally alive from head to foot with vermin, her tender girlish body was scarred all over with blows, apparently inflicted with a poker, and one of her arms bore the marks of her mother's teeth, where in her drunken fury she had severely bitten her; and her voracious appetite showed she had been half starved.

This incident, recorded by Hopkins in one of her many pamphlets, inspired her to begin her next crusade: the rescue and reform of prostitutes. It was one of the most popular charitable activities of the Victorian age. Middle- and upper-class women like ***Josephine Butler**, and even men like William Gladstone, the prime minister of England, tried to persuade prostitutes to leave the streets to begin a new life. Rescue work was exhilarating, but it could also be dangerous. People often threw rubbish at them: squashy tomatoes, rotten eggs, and even dead fish were common missiles. Rescue workers were also beaten. Undeterred, Hopkins knocked on the doors of brothels to persuade prostitutes working there to repent.

For many years, Hopkins continued in this work despite physical and personal difficulties. Frail, often ill, rather fastidious, highly strung and temperamental, Hopkins seemed an unlikely candidate for such work. Yet her life was devoted to the cause of eliminating prostitution. When it was realized that ex-prostitutes needed somewhere to live, she proposed that pretty and attractive homes be built for women in place of penitentiaries. These homes marked a small subtle shift from a punitive model of reform to a compassionate one, but the problem of prostitution remained.

A fence at the top of the cliff is better than an ambulance at the foot.

—Ellice Hopkins

Prevention, Hopkins argued, was better than cure. In 1876, she founded the Ladies Associations for the Care of Friendless Girls to tackle the underlying causes of prostitution: poor parenting, unemployment, homelessness, and immorality. Ladies Associations were set up in towns and cities across Britain. By 1879, they were established in Birmingham, Bristol, London, Edinburgh, Torquay, Cheltenham, Southampton, Winchester, Bradford, Dundee, and Perth. These chapters set up night shelters to house homeless young women, free registry offices to help women seek work, and training homes for domestic servants. Some set up branches to help single mothers in workhouses to find jobs and persuade reluctant fathers to pay maintenance.

Ellice Hopkins was a complex woman who held a strange mixture of religious and political beliefs. On the one hand, she was a feminist who supported women's suffrage, believed in the unity of women, and criticized the double sexual standard of Victorian Britain. On the other hand, she advocated repressive sexual politics which undermined human rights.

Hopkins believed that young girls who were brought up in immoral surroundings were likely to be sexually abused. In 1880, after years of campaigning, she pressured the government to pass an amendment to the Industrial Schools Act, making it a criminal offense for children under the age of 16 to live with parents who worked in brothels. It gave the police powers to remove these children and place them in Industrial Schools. This act also enabled relatives and "friends" to obtain a search warrant and enter any house suspected of being a brothel. If children were found, they were compulsorily removed, the owner of the house punished, and the mother and father deprived of parental rights. It was called the "Ellice Hopkins Act."

In 1885, a Criminal Law Amendment Act was passed in Britain which raised the age of heterosexual consent to 16, gave police greater powers to close down brothels, and made male homosexuality illegal. In order to help enforce this act, Hopkins, along with people like Josephine Butler, formed the National Vigilance Association (NVA) in the same year. This association dealt with a large variety of subjects connected with the moral well-being of the young. It prosecuted brothel owners and child abusers, tried to prohibit the employment of children on the stage, and attempted to ban obscene literature, photographs, and advertising. As the century progressed, the NVA became repressive and conservative, but Hopkins, unlike Butler, continued to support it. In her effort to improve moral standards, Hopkins distanced herself from the feminist movement she initially espoused.

Hopkins was convinced that men must also change. In 1879, she spoke at a church meeting:

> Would it not be possible to band young men together in some sort of brotherhood, or society, or guild, for the protection of women and children from prostitution and degradation—to give them a more aggressive form of purity, something higher and more vivifying than taking care of their own virtue.

Four years later, Hopkins founded a men's social purity organization, the White Cross Army, to do just that. It was the main work of the last 21 years of her life. The White Cross Army was a working-man's movement which originated at a meeting of 300 miners and clerks organized by the bishop of Durham. Encouraged by their response to her speech, Hopkins traveled miles up and down the country speaking to men about the need for chastity. By 1886, England was dotted over with these associations. Branches were formed in the army, the navy, and in local dioceses. It was a worldwide movement: America, India, Australia, New Zealand, Jamaica, South Africa, China, Canada, Trinidad, Japan and Germany all had branches of the White Cross putting forward the following message:

1. To treat all women with respect, and endeavor to protect them from wrong and degradation;
2. To endeavor to put down all indecent language and coarse jests;
3. To maintain the law of purity as equally binding upon men and women;

4. To endeavor to spread these principles among my companions, and to try and help my younger brothers;
5. To use every possible means to fulfil the command "Keep thyself pure."

It was a repressive policy, but Hopkins hoped that it might keep women safe. Many men disagreed with her moral message. Hopkins often spoke of audiences who were "shouting, singing, crowing like cocks, whistling like parrots, caterwauling like cats and keeping up a continuous uproar" in an attempt to stop her from speaking.

Years of campaign politics and hostile audiences left Hopkins exhausted. In 1888, her health broke down. Excruciatingly painful sciatica combined with inflammation of the eyes made reading, talking, and writing intolerable. For the next 18 months, Hopkins traveled in Italy and Switzerland, leading an invalid life in the fresh mountain air. In August 1903, she suffered from aphasia (losing the ability to speak and listen) and a heart attack from which she never fully recovered. In May 1904, Ellice Hopkins endured a second heart attack which paralyzed her right side. She died that same year.

In a sense, the work of Ellice Hopkins continues. Tucked away in a corner of London, the National Council of Women—a direct descendant of the Ladies Associations—still promotes women's issues. At the end of the 20th century, it was acting as an educational body mainly devoted to women's health: its emphasis was on AIDS.

SOURCES:

Barrett, Rosa M. *Ellice Hopkins: A Memoir.* London: Wells Gardner, 1907.

Bristow, Edward. *Vice and Vigilance.* London: Gill and Macmillan, 1978.

Hopkins, Ellice. *How to Start Preventive Work.* London: Hatchards, 1884.

Prochaska, Frank. *Women and Philanthropy in Nineteenth Century England.* Clarendon Press, 1980.

Paula Bartley,
Senior Lecturer in History, University of Wolverhampton, Dudley, England, author and joint editor of "Women in History" series, Cambridge University Press

Hopkins, Juliet (1818–1890)

Confederate hospital administrator. *Born Juliet Ann Opie on May 7, 1818, in Jefferson County, Virginia; died on March 9, 1890, in Washington, D.C.; daughter of Hierome Lindsay Opie and Margaret (Muse) Opie; attended Miss Ritchie's school, Richmond, Virginia; married Alexander George Gordon (a lieutenant of the U.S. Navy), in May 1837 (died 1849); married Arthur Francis Hopkins (a landowner and president of the Mobile and Ohio Railroad), on November 7, 1854; children: (adopted a niece) Juliet Opie.*

Born in 1818 and raised on a Southern plantation, Juliet Hopkins was 16 when her mother died and she was called home from school to become mistress of a large household which included some 2,000 slaves. She was married at 19 to a Navy lieutenant who died three years later. In November 1854, she married Arthur Francis Hopkins, a landowner, railroad president, and justice of the Alabama supreme court. From that time on, Hopkins made her home in Mobile, Alabama. Although she had no children of her own, she and her second husband adopted a niece, **Juliet Opie**.

During the Civil War, a lack of hospital services made it necessary for individual states and volunteer groups to set up medical facilities for their troops near the battlefields. Hopkins volunteered as superintendent of the Alabama section of the Chimborazo Hospital in Richmond, Virginia. In November 1861, when the Alabama legislature named her husband state hospital agent, Hopkins took over the actual duties of the appointment, administrating the staffing, supplying, and management of field and base hospitals. Recognized as a dynamic manager, Hopkins did everything. She secured buildings for medical facilities, employed and supervised nurses, and worked with doctors to keep the hospitals clean and orderly. She even undertook battlefield rescue missions herself and, at the battle of Seven Pines, suffered a bullet wound in her hip that left her with a limp. The superior conditions and high quality of medical care in her hospitals were recognized throughout the Confederacy, and she was praised by such luminaries as General Joseph E. Johnston. She was also revered by her patients, to whom she was a source of practical assistance and constant encouragement.

In 1863, when the state hospitals were merged into the Confederate Medical Department, Hopkins returned to Alabama. One of her many honors during the war years was the use of her picture on two denominations of Alabama's paper currency. After the war, Hopkins moved to New York City. She died on March 9, 1890, while visiting Washington, D.C., and was buried with military honors in Arlington National Cemetery.

SOURCES:

James, Edward T., ed. *Notable American Women, 1607–1950.* Cambridge, MA: Belknap Press of Harvard University Press, 1971.

McHenry, Robert, ed. *Famous American Women.* NY: Dover, 1983.

Barbara Morgan,
Melrose, Massachusetts

Hopkins, Miriam (1902–1972)

American actress whose performance in* Design for Living *propelled her into the top ranks. *Born Ellen Miriam Hopkins on October 18, 1902, in Bainbridge, Georgia; died of a heart attack in New York City on October 9, 1972; attended Goddard Seminary in Plainfield, Vermont; attended Syracuse University; married four times; married first husband Brandon Peters (an actor), in 1926 (divorced 1931); married third husband Anatole Litvak (a director).*

Selected theater: The Music Box Revue *(1921);* Little Jessie James *(1923);* An American Tragedy *(1926);* Excess Baggage *(1927);* The Camel Through the Needle's Eye *(1929);* Lysistrata *(1930);* Anatol *(1931);* Jezebel *(1933);* The Skin of Our Teeth *(1942);* Look Homeward Angel *(tour, 1960).*

Filmography: Fast and Loose *(1930);* The Smiling Lieutenant *(1931);* Twenty-Four Hours *(1931);* Dr. Jekyll and Mr. Hyde *(1932);* Two Kinds of Women *(1932);* Dancers in the Dark *(1932);* The World and the Flesh *(1932);* Trouble in Paradise *(1932);* The Story of Temple Drake *(1933);* The Stranger's Return *(1933);* Design for Living *(1933);* All of Me *(1934);* She Loves Me Not *(1934);* The Richest Girl in the World *(1934);* Becky Sharp *(1935);* Barbary Coast *(1935);* Splendor *(1935);* These Three *(1936);* Men Are Not Gods *(UK, 1937);* The Woman I Love *(1937);* Woman Chases Man *(1937);* Wise Girl *(1937);* The Old Maid *(1939);* Virginia City *(1940);* Lady With Red Hair *(1940);* A Gentleman After Dark *(1942);* Old Acquaintance *(1943);* The Heiress *(1949);* The Mating Season *(1951);* Outcasts of Poker Flat *(1952);* Carrie *(1952);* The Children's Hour *(1962);* Fanny Hill *(Ger./US, 1964);* The Chase *(1966);* Comeback *(1966, released under the title* Hollywood Horror Home, *1976).*

Miriam Hopkins

Miriam Hopkins was born into a wealthy household in Bainbridge, Georgia, in 1902. She attended the Goddard Seminary in Plainfield, Vermont, and Syracuse University. She then moved to New York to study dance in hopes of becoming a ballerina, but after breaking her ankle settled for a career as a chorus girl. Hopkins made her Broadway debut in *The Music Box Revue* (1921), then successfully switched to drama. Just as Hopkins was making a name for herself on the New York stage, she was lured to Hollywood, where she made an auspicious debut in Paramount's *Fast and Loose* (1930). Subsequent roles in *The Smiling Lieutenant* (1931), *Dr. Jekyll and Mr. Hyde* (1932) and *Design for Living* (1933) established her as a star. A lovely, blue-eyed blonde, Hopkins could play well-bred women or floozies. She turned in a delightfully comic performance in *Trouble in Paradise* (1932) and was considered effectively brittle in the title role in *Becky Sharp* (1935).

Early in her film career, Hopkins was pegged as uncooperative, a problem that seemed to plague her career. In 1939, during a stint with Warner Bros., she was engaged in a feud with ***Bette Davis**, her co-star in *The Old Maid,* and the two clashed again on the set of *Old Acquaintance* (1943). "I don't think there was ever a more difficult female in the world," Davis said later, without a trace of irony. In his memoir, actor Edward G. Robinson called Hopkins "puerile and silly and snobbish, complaining about every line."

When her film career began to wane during the early 1940s, Hopkins returned to the stage, replacing ***Tallulah Bankhead** in *The Skin of Our Teeth* (1942) and then touring in the role. At the request of director William Wyler, she returned to Hollywood in 1949 to play the aunt in *The Heiress.* She worked with Wyler again in two subsequent films, *Carrie* (1952) and *The Children's*

Hour (1962). Her last films were *The Chase* (1966) and *The Comeback,* which was not released until 1976, under the title *Hollywood Horror Home.* The actress, who was married four times, died of a massive heart attack in 1972.

SOURCES:

Blum, Daniel. *A Pictorial History of the American Theatre 1860–1970.* NY: Crown Publishers, 1971.

Bowden, Liz-Anne, ed. *The Oxford Companion to Film.* NY and London: Oxford University Press, 1976.

Katz, Ephraim. *The Film Encyclopedia.* NY: HarperCollins, 1994.

Shipman, David. *The Great Movie Stars: The Golden Years.* Boston, MA: Little Brown, 1995.

Barbara Morgan,
Melrose, Massachusetts

Hopkins, Pauline E. (1859–1930)

African-American writer, editor, and playwright. *Name variations: (pseudonym) Sarah A. Allen. Born in Portland, Maine, in 1859; died in Cambridge, Massachusetts, on August 13, 1930; never married; no children.*

A prolific 19th-century African-American writer, Pauline Hopkins was largely overlooked until four of her novels, including the best-known *Contending Forces,* were reprinted as part of the Schomburg Library's "Nineteenth Century Black Women Writers" series. Not only was Hopkins the author of novels, short stories, and a series of biographical sketches, but she also served as editor of *The Colored American,* the first black magazine established in the 20th century and the main forum for her own work. Hopkins was also an actress and singer of note.

Little is known of Hopkins' early life, aside from her birth in Portland, Maine, in 1859. Her literary career began at age 15, when she won a $10 prize for her essay "The Evils of Intemperance and Their Remedies." **Ann Allen Shockley,** who wrote an article about the writer for *Phylon* in 1972 and was instrumental in bringing her to light, claimed that Hopkins' greatest desire was to become a playwright. Indeed, she emerged in 1879 as the author and leading cast member in a musical drama, *Slaves' Escape: or the Underground Railroad,* which was first performed in Boston on July 5, 1880, by the Hopkins' Colored Troubadors, a group that may have included her mother and stepfather. The troupe played a number of venues in the Boston area. One performance given at Arcanum Hall in Allston, Massachusetts, in 1882, attested to Hopkins' talent as a singer, listing her in the program as "Boston's favorite Colored Soprano."

Hopkins' first novel, *Contending Forces: A Romance Illustrative of Negro Life North and South,* was published in 1900, around the same time that she began her association with *The Colored American.* **Jane Campbell** considers the novel "a fascinating, feminist historical romance" and contends that it "equalled or outranked the novels of Hopkins' male contemporaries—Charles Chesnutt, W.E.B. DuBois, and Sutton Griggs." The novel, her most popular, was followed by *Hagar's Daughter, Winona,* and *Of One Blood,* all of which were serialized within the pages of *The Colored American.* Hopkins also wrote short stories for the magazine, some of which were criticized for their interracial themes. Less controversial was a series of some 21 biographical sketches, including portraits of such prominent African-Americans as William Wells Brown, Frederick Douglass, ***Harriet Tubman,** and Lewis Hayden.

In 1904, suffering a period of ill health, Hopkins left *The Colored American,* although there is evidence that she may have been forced out by new management. From 1904 to 1905, she wrote for another early 20th-century magazine, *Voice of the Negro.* One of her articles focused on the construction of the New York City subway.

In 1905, Hopkins' career began to decline, though she contributed several articles to *New Era Magazine.* She lived in obscurity after 1916 and died on August 13, 1930, at the Cambridge (Massachusetts) Relief Hospital after being badly burned in a house fire.

SOURCES:

Campbell, Jane. "Pauline Hopkins," in *Belles Lettres.* Summer 1992.

Journal of Women's History. Fall 92, p. 190.

Smith, Jessie Carney, ed. *Notable Black American Women.* Detroit, MI: Gale Research, 1992.

Barbara Morgan,
Melrose, Massachusetts

Hopkins, Sarah Winnemucca (c. 1844–1891).

See Winnemucca, Sarah.

Hoppe, Marianne (1911—)

German actress of stage and screen. *Born in Rostock, Germany, on April 26, 1911; attended Königin Luise Academy; studied acting at Deutsches Theater; married Gustav Gründgens (an actor-director), on June 22, 1926 (divorced 1946); children: one son, Benedikt.*

German actress Marianne Hoppe was born in Rostock, Germany, in 1911. She attended business school in Berlin before being accepted at the dramatic arts school of the Deutsches Theater, then under the directorship of Max Reinhardt. In 1928, she made her debut at the Bühne der Jugend, or Young People's Theatre Group, in Berlin. Subsequently, she joined the Deutsches Theater itself, where, due to her slim figure and androgynous face, she often played masculine roles. From 1930 to 1932, she worked in Frankfurt am Main, after which she joined the Kammerspiele in Munich, where for several years she acted under director Otto Falckenberg. She was known for her modern acting style.

In 1933, Hoppe made her screen debut in *Judas von Tirol* (Judas of the Tyrol) and that year also appeared in the patriotic film *Heideschulmeister Uwe Karsten* (Schoolmaster Uwe Karsten). It was the role of Elke in *Der Schimmelreiter* (The Rider of the White Steed), however, that launched her career as one of Germany's leading film actresses. She was best known for her serious parts, notably in the melodramas *Auf Wiedersehen, Franziska!* (1941) and *Romanze in Moll* (Romance in a Minor Key, 1943). Also memorable were her forays into films with a decidedly American flavor, such as *Capriolen* (Caprices, 1938), in which she played a daredevil aviator, and *Kongo-Express* (1939), in which she portrayed Renate Brinkmann, who leaves her alcoholic fiancé to marry an upright German. Hoppe also worked on stage and screen with her husband, actor-director Gustav Gründgens, whom she married in 1936. One of her best film performances was in the role of Effi Briest in *Der Schritt vom Wege* (The False Step, 1939), directed by Gründgens.

Marianne Hoppe

In 1946, following World War II, Hoppe divorced Gründgens and moved to Bavaria with their son, Benedikt. However, her later career included frequent appearances at the Schauspielhaus in Düsseldorf, where Gründgens was director. In 1961, she made her television debut in the long-running detective series "Der Komissar" (The Commissioner). Hoppe was named a permanent member of West Germany's Akademie der Künste in 1965. One of her last memorable stage performances was as the mother in Tankred Dorst's play *Chimborazo* (1975), in Berlin.

SOURCES:

Romani, Cinzia. *Tainted Goddesses: Female Film Stars of the Third Reich*. Translated by Robert Connolly. NY: Sarpedon, 1992.

Barbara Morgan,
Melrose, Massachusetts

Hopper, Grace Murray (1906–1992)

Rear admiral, U.S. Naval Reserve, who pioneered computer technology for military and business applications and was a primary inventor of the standard computer language COBOL. *Born Grace Brewster Murray in New York City on December 9, 1906; died on January 1, 1992, in Arlington, Virginia; daughter of Walter Fletcher Murray (an insurance broker) and Mary Campbell (Van Horne) Murray; Vassar College, B.A. in mathematics and physics, 1928; Yale University, M.A. in mathematics, 1930, Ph.D. in mathematics, 1934; married Vincent Foster Hopper, in 1930 (divorced 1945); no children.*

Became teacher of mathematics at Vassar (1931); enlisted in U.S. Naval Reserve (December 1943); commissioned as a lieutenant (junior grade, June 1944); assigned to the Bureau of Ordnance Computation Project at Harvard University to work on the Mark I Automatic Sequence Controlled Calculator (1944); while working in private industry, developed COBOL computer language (1960); achieved rank of rear admiral (1985); retired from the navy (1986).

Shortly after June 27, 1944, when Lieutenant (junior grade) Grace Murray Hopper received her commission in the U.S. Naval Reserve, she paid a visit to the grave of her great-grandfather, who had been a U.S. admiral, to place a bouquet of flowers beside his headstone and tell him that it was "all right for females to be navy officers." At age 38, Hopper's commission as a member of the Women Accepted for Volunteer Emergency Service (WAVES) had come at the end of a long struggle, begun shortly after the Japanese attack on Pearl Harbor on December 7, 1941, which had propelled the U.S. into full involvement in World War II. For one thing, she was considered over age; for another, as a professor of mathematics at Vassar College, she had what was thought to be a "crucial" civilian occupation. The diminutive Hopper also weighed only 105 pounds, and navy regulations required that WAVES weigh at least 121 pounds and stand 5'6". Professor Hopper got an exemption from the occupational restriction by threatening to resign from Vassar if she was not granted an extended leave of absence; then, showing the typical dedication and drive that marked her life, she maneuvered her way through a succession of waivers until December 1943, when she was finally sworn into the U.S. Naval Reserve. With her country at war, Hopper believed that her active military involvement was "the only thing to do."

Born in New York City on December 9, 1906, Grace Brewster Murray was enraptured by numbers from an early age. An avid reader, musician, and tinkerer, she dismantled an alarm clock at age seven, just to see how it worked. Her attitude toward overcoming all obstacles was largely attributable to her father, Walter Murray, who lost both legs due to hardening of the arteries but refused to succumb to self-pity. At a time when young girls rarely received extensive instruction or support in mathematics and science, Grace was also encouraged by her father to pursue the same educational path as her brother and to acquire job skills that would make her self-sufficient.

At Schoonmakers School in New York City, Grace excelled at athletics, particularly basketball, field hockey, and water polo. In the autumn of 1924, she entered Vassar College, where she was inspired by the convocation speech of Dean **Mildred Thompson** on "The Business of Being a Student." Grace was elected to the Phi Beta Kappa honor society and received a Vassar fellowship which relieved her family of the financial burden of her education. In 1930, she earned a Master of Arts degree in mathematics from Yale University and was inducted into Sigma Xi, the honor society which recognizes outstanding achievement in scientific research.

On June 15, 1930, Grace Murray married Vincent Foster Hopper, a Princeton honors graduate and instructor of English at New York University's School of Commerce, who eventually attained his doctorate in comparative literature from Columbia University. The couple moved to Poughkeepsie, New York, and settled into their separate academic careers. In 1931, Hopper's first teaching position was at her alma mater, at the annual salary of $800, and she would continue to teach mathematics at Vassar until 1943. In 1934, she accomplished the remarkable feat of earning a doctorate in mathematics from Yale, where only two doctorates per year were typically awarded in that field, and rarely to a woman. Before joining the navy, she was awarded another fellowship and taught briefly at Barnard College, the women's college of Columbia.

Hopper separated from her husband in the early 1940s, although the couple did not divorce until 1945. After her admission into the navy, she entered the U.S. Naval Reserve Midshipman's School for Women in Northampton, Massachusetts, early in 1944. Training of women officer candidates differed little from that of men in terms of discipline, drill, navy orientation, physical training, and the detection of enemy ships known as "platform recognition." Once she received her commission, Lieutenant Hopper was ordered to report to the Bureau of Ordnance Computation Project located at the Cruft Laboratory, at Harvard University, to work for Commander Howard Aiken on the new Automatic Sequence Controlled Calculator (ASCC), better known as the Mark I. Taken by the majesty of the 51-foot-long computer, Hopper called it "the prettiest gadget I ever saw." Although she also worked on later-generation computers, the Mark I was to remain her favorite; after it was retired to the Smithsonian Institution, she would go there to visit it.

Under Commander Aiken, Lieutenant Hopper was put to work calculating "coefficients for the interpolation of arc tangents." In the pre-industrial age, when naval battles were generally fought ship-on-ship and at close range, typically only a few hundred yards, the efficiency of naval gunnery had essentially been based on the speed and efficiency of a gun crew in loading and firing. In 20th-century naval warfare, ships became faster and more maneuverable platforms, carrying guns of larger calibre, capable of hurling conical projectiles at targets up to 24 miles away. The iron cannonball of the sailing ship era evolved into the ballistic missile fired off the modern warship, and the problems of controlling the firing became immensely more complicated. For the gun to be correctly elevated and trained on either a stationary shore target or a distant moving ship required the rapid calculation of factors such as wind speed, direction, temperature and density, the speed and course of both the gun-bearing ship and the target, as well as the weight of the shell, bearing, and target range. By World War I, the major naval powers had developed rudimentary analog computers to input data and output gun orders. In World War II, the Mark I represented a great advance in improving the accuracy of firing tables and calculating such problems as the range capabilities of mine-sweeping detection gear towed behind ships and the simulation of shock waves created by an atomic blast.

A ship in port is safe, but that is not what ships are built for.

—Grace Murray Hopper

A joint project of Harvard University and International Business Machines (IBM), the Mark I was built at the IBM laboratory in Endicott, New York, and moved to the Cruft Lab where it was ready for operations by summer 1944. Driven by a four-horsepower motor powering its 800,000 parts, connected by 500 miles of wire, the computer involved 3,300 mechanical relays which were electrically driven, based on input provided by IBM punched key cards. It was the world's first large-scale digital computer, performing three additions per second, which speeded up human calculations by a factor of almost 200. Hopper described it as "man's first attempt to build a machine that would assist the power of his brain rather than the strength of his arm."

By the summer of 1945, the pioneer Mark I was being overtaken by the Mark II, the first large computer capable of multiprocessing, and five times faster than its predecessor. In the era before air-conditioning, when laboratory windows were left open on a hot summer day, the Mark II became the site of a legendary computer event when the machine suddenly stopped, and an investigation revealed a moth had been the cause when it was trapped and killed by an electromagnetic relay, giving birth to the computer term "debugging." The moth's remains have been preserved in the pages of the Mark II daily log book at the museum of the Naval Surface Weapons Center in Dahlgren, Virginia.

Opposite page

Grace Murray Hopper

At Harvard, Hopper's work made her aware of a critical problem limiting the application of computer technology to widespread business and non-scientific use: the necessity of having advanced mathematicians to code, or program, the machines. Solving this problem was to become the driving force of the remainder of her career.

Although she loved teaching, Lt. Hopper had decided by the end of World War II that "computers were more fun," and she declined to return to Vassar. The number of women in the WAVES had reached its peak at 86,000, and she was well past the age limit of 38 for those seeking to transfer into the regular navy, but she was able to remain in the Naval Reserve and continued at the Harvard lab as a civilian employee in the position of research fellow in engineering sciences and applied physics. As a reserve officer, she completed several Naval War College courses which concentrated on tactical problems such as refueling a task force at sea, and others similarly suited to the new computer's capabilities. She worked on the development of the last two computers in the Harvard series, the Mark III and Mark IV. The Mark III, using vacuum tubes and magnetic tapes, increased its speed to 50 times that of the old Mark I, and was in service until 1955; the Mark IV proved three times faster than its immediate predecessor and was not outdated until 1962.

In 1949, Hopper left Harvard to join the pioneering computer firm of Eckert-Mauchly in Philadelphia as senior mathematician, and continued there until her official retirement in 1971. In 1951, when the firm's new Universal Automatic Computer, or UNIVAC I, replaced the punched card with high-speed tape coded to use simple alphabet instructions (A=add, M=multiply, C=clear), the modern computer had come into shape. In 1952, with the development of the Electronic Discrete Variable Automatic Computer, or EDVAC, which implemented the binary system (using only 1 or 0), the same computing ability could occur with a greatly reduced number of vacuum tubes. EDVAC also stored the program for its instructions, and eliminated the need for punched tape or cards to carry the instructions for its sequence of operations, and the modern computer was born.

Still dissatisfied with the "non-user friendly" state of programming, Dr. Hopper became involved in developing a new system. In 1952, she produced her first compiler, called the A-0 System, which translated instructions from mathematical symbols input by an operator into machine code. By allowing the machine to "do the work," this system ended the need for the programmer to write in the complex machine code. In 1952, Hopper wrote a paper on compilers, the first of more than 50 in her career, leading to her promotion to systems engineer, director of automatic programming for Remington Rand, new owners of the company which would later be part of Sperry Corporation and renamed UNYSIS.

As advances in programming continued, Hopper intensified her efforts to create a simple programming language in English which a compiler would translate into machine code. By 1957, her B-0 compiler (B for business), called Flowmatic, had become one of the major programming tools in widespread use, employing simple word commands such as COUNT, DIVIDE, SUBTRACT, REPLACE, and MULTIPLY, but a universal programming language was still needed. Hopper continued to work on the English version.

In 1959, representatives at a joint meeting of members of the military, private business, and government sectors agreed on the shared goal of developing a standard business computer language. Near the end of the following year, Hopper's engineering team was ready to introduce COBOL, or Common Business Oriented Language, which allows simple English key words to program a computer in complex mathematical equations required of previous systems. On December 6, 1960, UNIVAC and RCA introduced their joint version of COBOL, demonstrated on the UNIVAC II and RCA 501 computers. Hopper, using finesse and diplomacy, presented complex engineering problems and solutions to management in simplified, understandable terms that ensured the broadbased support and funding for her future research and development projects, which were often on the cutting edge of technology. Soon COBOL was adopted as the U.S. Defense Department standard and, at the end of the 20th century, continued to be one of the most popular and adaptive business languages available.

In 1966, Hopper had reached the rank of commander in the reserves when she was notified that she must retire due to age. Only seven months after she had done so, in August 1967, she returned to "temporary" active duty, requested to standardize and promote usage of COBOL throughout the navy. Her six-month assignment, soon changed to "indefinite," was to last almost 20 years. In 1973, she reached the rank of captain.

As an adjunct member of the faculties of the University of Pennsylvania and George Washing-

Grace Murray Hopper

ton University, Hopper also continued to teach. Wearing her naval uniform, she presented more than 200 speeches a year, often to audiences of children, firing them with curiosity about science and technology, and challenging them to take risks. Her work earned her the navy's Legion of Merit in 1973, the Meritorious Service Medal in 1980, and the Distinguished Service Medal in 1986. In 1983, she was promoted to commodore, and, in 1985, when she became a rear admiral, the first female admiral in naval history, she advised friends in Philadelphia to keep a sharp eye on her great-grandfather's grave, as he might "rise from the dead."

Civilian honors also came her way in droves. In 1969, she was the first recipient of the Computer Science "Man-of-the-Year" award from the Data Processing Management Association, and in 1971, UNIVAC created the Grace Murray Hopper Award to honor a "significant contribution to computer science." In 1973, she was the first American to become a Distinguished Fellow of the British Computer Society. In 1984, she was inducted into the Engineering and Science Hall of Fame. Overall, she received more than 30 honorary doctorates.

Admiral Hopper's style was not to manage but to lead. Her accomplishments were due to her strong intellect and work ethic, as well as her dogged pursuit of the risky and uncharted track. She was willing to be bold and innovative, and persistence was a trait she constantly stressed, especially to young audiences. As a naval officer, she personified John Paul Jones' admonition that those who do not risk, "cannot win."

Hopper's greatest contribution in the development of programming languages extended beyond military and naval science to the broader worlds of commerce and industry. But as Admiral Hopper, when she accepted the British Computer Society Distinguished Fellowship, despite all her technological achievements, awards and acclaim, she noted, "I have already received the highest award, which is the honor and privilege of serving very proudly in the United States Navy."

SOURCES:

Billings, Charlene W. *Grace Hopper: Navy Admiral and Computer Pioneer*. Hillside, NJ: Enslow Publishers, 1989.

Green, Laura. *Computer Pioneers*. NY: Franklin Watts, 1985.

Rausa, Rosario M. "Grace Murray Hopper," in *Naval History*. Vol 6, no. 3. Fall 1992, p. 58.

Wetzstein, Cheryl and Linda Joyce Forristal. "Grace Murray Hopper," in *The World and I*. August 1987.

Zientara, Marguerite. "Captain Grace M. Hopper and the Genesis of Programming Languages," in *The History of Computing*. Part 11. CW Communications, 1981, p. 51.

SUGGESTED READING:

Brinch Hansen, Per. *Operating Systems Principles*. Englewood Cliffs, NJ: Prentice-Hall, 1973.

Harris, L.S. *Principles of Naval Ordnance and Gunnery*. Pensacola, FL: Naval Publications and Forms Directorate, 1992.

Lysegard, Anna. *Introduction to COBOL*. London: Oxford University Press, 1969.

Padfield, Peter. *Guns at Sea*. London: Evelyn, 1973.

Commander Stanley D.M. Carpenter,
Associate Professor of Strategy at the United States Naval War College, Newport, Rhode Island

Hopper, Hedda and Louella Parsons

Driven, sometimes ruthless, Hollywood rivals whose gossip columns wielded considerable power in the entertainment industry of the 1940s and 1950s.

Hopper, Hedda *(1885–1966). Name variations: Elda Curry; Elda or Ella Furry; Elda Millar. Pronunciation: HED-da HOP-per. Born Elda Furry on May 2, 1885 (she used June 2, 1890), in Hollidaysburg, Pennsylvania; died on February 1, 1966; daughter of David Furry (a butcher) and Margaret (Miller) Furry; studied at the Carter Conservatory of Music, Pittsburgh, around 1903; married William DeWolf Hopper, on May 8, 1913 (divorced 1922); children: William DeWolf Hopper, Jr. (b. January 26, 1915, an actor).*

Selected filmography: Sherlock Holmes *(1922);* The Women *(1939);* Breakfast in Hollywood *(1946);* Sunset Boulevard *(1950);* The Oscar *(1966). Appeared in more than 100 films; hosted radio gossip program (1936).*

Books: From Under My Hat *(1952);* The Whole Truth and Nothing But *(1963); wrote syndicated gossip column (1938–66).*

Parsons, Louella *(1881–1972). Name variations: Louella Oettinger; Louella O. Parsons. Pronunciation: Lu-ELL-ah PAR-suns. Born on August 6, 1881 (she used August 6, 1893), in Freeport, Illinois; died of a stroke, after a lengthy illness, in a Santa Monica, California, rest home, on December 9, 1972; daughter of Joshua Oettinger (a clothing store owner) and Helen (Stine) Oettinger; graduated from Dixon (Illinois) High School, 1901; attended Dixon College and Normal School; married John Dement Parsons, on October 31, 1905 (divorced, date unknown; died 1919); married Jack McCaffrey, around 1915 (divorced, date unknown); married Harry Martin, around 1942 (died 1951); children: (first marriage) Harriet Oettinger Parsons (b. August 23, 1906).*

Films: Hollywood Hotel *(1937);* Without Reservations *(1946);* Starlift *(1951).*

Books: The Gay Illiterate *(1944);* Tell It to Louella *(1961). Wrote one of first U.S. movie columns, for the* Chicago Record-Herald *(1914–18); wrote a movie gossip column for Hearst Publications, syndicated in 400 newspapers (1922–65).*

There are two Hollywoods: the fantasy that exists in the mind of every moviegoer and the harsh realities of the motion-picture industry. Particularly in the first 50 years of film, these worlds had no intersection. The beauty, glamour and goodwill imagined by the audience had nothing in common with the secretive, ruthless business that created these dreams. That is why two aggressive, ambitious gossip columnists, Louella Parsons and Hedda Hopper, yielded so much power. Their newspaper columns, read at their peak by 75 million every day, continually threatened to expose one world to the other.

Louella Parsons seems to have had as many secrets as the tycoons she covered. She claimed to have been born in 1893, but courthouse records in her hometown show her to be 12 years older. Her father, who died when she was not quite nine years old, owned and operated the Star Clothing House in Freeport, Illinois, a town of 15,000. She was the oldest of five children, three of whom died in infancy. The family was Jewish, although Parsons never recognized herself as such and was later to become a deeply devout Catholic convert.

After graduating from Dixon (Illinois) High School, where her new stepfather had moved the family, Louella attended the local college, then taught school and worked as a reporter. It is probably through her newspaper work that she met her first husband, John Parsons. The *Dixon City Directory of 1900* lists him as a reporter for the *Evening Telegraph.* Louella, at the time, was a part-time employee of the *Star.* When they married in 1905 and moved to Burlington, Iowa, she was 24 and he was 32. Their daughter, ***Harriet Parsons,** was born the following year. In later years, Louella claimed that her husband died aboard a transport ship in World War I, which may have been true, but there is strong evidence to suggest that they were divorced before his death. Unhappy in small-town Iowa, she moved to Chicago with her daughter, where she met and married her second husband, Jack McCaffrey, probably in 1915. It is not known how long they were married; once in Hollywood, she never mentioned his name and always called Dr. Harry (Docky) Martin, whom she married in 1931, her second husband.

Hedda Hopper

Parsons combined her romanticism with a practical tenacity. During her years in Chicago, she worked in the syndication department of the *Chicago Tribune* and wrote film scenarios at night for a small movie studio, which later hired her as a story editor. When she suspected, accurately, that she was about to be fired from that job, she wrote a book, *How to Write for the Movies,* that sold well and was serialized. In 1914, she started a gossip column in the Chicago *Record-Herald.* When the paper folded four years later, she moved to New York and took a job with the *Morning Telegraph* and, later, the *American.*

Hedda Hopper took a more circuitous route to her gossip column. Born Elda Furry in 1885 (not 1890 as she later claimed), she was the middle child in a family of nine children, seven of whom survived infancy. Her Quaker parents worked in their butcher shop in Hollidaysburg, Pennsylvania, and had little time to coddle their children. As George Eells writes in his biography, *Hedda and Louella:* "It was not by chance that Elda grew into a woman who found it difficult, if not impossible, to express any kind of tenderness . . . and who gloried in a reputation for bitchiness."

Hopper left school in the eighth grade to become a bill collector for the by-then-defunct butcher shop. Her parents squelched her early theatrical ambitions; in 1903, at age 18, she ran away. She is thought to have attended the Carter Conservatory of Music in Pittsburgh at some point during the next five years. In 1908, she moved to New York, telling everyone she was 18.

It did not take long for Elda Curry, as she had begun to call herself, to get a job as a chorus girl. She first appeared onstage in New York on December 3, 1908, in *The Pied Piper,* where she met her husband, actor DeWolf Hopper, who, at 50, was five years older than her father. She became his fifth wife in 1913. A son, William DeWolf Hopper, Jr., who would be known for his role as private detective Paul Drake on the "Perry Mason" television series, was born two years later. She continued a stage career, with moderate success, and began to get screen roles, four of them in 1917 alone. She had been calling herself Elda Millar but, in 1919, decided another new name might be the career boost she needed. She went to a numerologist who, for $10, recommended "Hedda Hopper." Hopper was apparently pleased, because it was the final name she gave herself. Indeed, it seemed to work. In 1926, Louella Parsons dubbed Hopper "Queen of the Quickies."

Parsons, already well established as a gossip columnist by that time, was dogged by a persistent rumor that she kept her job by blackmailing her boss, William Randolph Hearst, about a murder she had seen him commit aboard his yacht off the California coast in 1924. It was nonsense. She was a dogged reporter who worked longer and harder than her colleagues; Hearst was her career-long supporter because her columns sold newspapers.

In 1926, Hearst sent Parsons to Los Angeles to recuperate from lung problems. She regretted leaving her daughter, who was a Wellesley college student, but she could not resist the chance to become motion-picture editor for Hearst's Universal News Service, where her work would appear not only in the New York *American* but in six other newspapers, including the Los Angeles *Examiner.* Her timing was fortuitous. The era of the silent film was coming to a close and, with it, an industry recession. The advent of "talkies" posed the first serious threat to the legitimate theater and gave Hollywood a much-needed boost. Parsons' personal life, as well as her career, benefitted. In 1931, she married Dr. Martin and finally found a measure of marital happiness.

Hedda Hopper had moved to Hollywood, too, but did not fare as well. After her 1922 divorce, she was the sole support of herself and her son and was working hard to give him the social and educational opportunities she never had. But she lost her savings in the 1929 stock market crash. During the Depression, her film career ended. She had no offers, though her price had dropped from $1,000 per week in 1917 to $1,000 per film in 1935. Hopper resorted to selling real estate and cosmetics and at times was

Louella Parsons

nearly destitute. Then in 1935, at age 50, a friend who admired her vivid speaking style offered her a job writing a weekly Hollywood fashion article for a Washington, D.C., newspaper. As Eells notes: "That a washed-up, middle-aged actress represented a potential challenge to the uncrowned queen of Hollywood was beyond anyone's wildest dreams."

But not for long. By 1938, Hopper was writing a Hollywood column for the Esquire Features Syndicate that was carried by 13 newspapers, one of them the Los Angeles *Times*. With a local outlet, she could no longer be ignored. A year or two later, her style became more caustic, and more successful. As Eells observed: "It is a devastating comment upon our society that not until Hedda resorted to bare-nailed bitchery was she able to put her career into orbit."

Meanwhile, it was said that Louella was beginning to see herself more as a star than a fan. She took some film roles, with disastrous results. In 1939, she suffered three major setbacks:

Hedda scooped her on the James Roosevelt-◀ Betsey Cushing divorce; the *Saturday Evening Post* published a scathing profile of her; and she found out about Clark Gable's marriage to *Carole Lombard no sooner than other members of the press. In her line of work, these were catastrophic events, and she was devastated.

▶ **Betsey Cushing.** *See Cushing Sisters for Betsey Cushing Whitney.*

In comparison, Hopper was getting more readers every day. Her column had been acquired by other syndicates and was carried by 85 metropolitan papers and 5,000 smaller ones. A feud was inevitable. Parsons still had the power of the Hearst organization behind her, but people now had a choice. (Everyone in Hollywood, of course, read both columns.) As Louella said, "She is trying to do in two years what took me thirty." Their public and private sniping continued for two decades, despite a highly publicized but short-lived reconciliation.

In a society where everyone was either on the way up or on the way down, Louella and Hedda shared a determination not to lose footing.

—George Eells

Hedda had always been the more glamorous of the two, with a famous collection of kooky hats, and she was becoming more feared as well. Parsons had always been pro-Hollywood. As Eells writes, "Whether the problem was drug addiction among stars, manslaughter or murder . . . Louella was sympathetic, and the industry welcomed her public relations work." Her staples were births, marriages, and deaths. But Hedda was tougher. Always a Quaker at heart, her columns often were didactic and moralistic. In the 1950s, she was virulently anti-Communist, at a time when a casual mention of someone's name in the wrong context could ruin a career. She had become the self-appointed guardian of Hollywood's moral life, and people hated her for it. All of the things that people had disliked in Louella for so long—her disregard for the facts, her favoritism—seemed suddenly benign.

For Louella, the 1950s were an "Indian summer," writes Eells. CBS ran a favorable, hourlong drama of her life in 1956. She enjoyed a romance with songwriter Jimmy McHugh after her husband died in 1951. But by the early 1960s, her health had badly deteriorated. When her retirement was announced in 1964, at 83, she was already in a nursing home.

Hedda Hopper had outrun her best rival. She had accomplished in old age what she had never quite managed as a young actress: she was at the top. But in 1966, she was 81, five years older than she admitted, and, like Louella, she could never acknowledge her own advancing age and failing health. When she died on February 1, from kidney damage due to medication for pneumonia, it was after only two days in the hospital; she had written her last column just a few days before.

Louella Parsons died in a nursing home in 1972. By that time, Hollywood was a different town: the secretive, dictator-driven studio system that had allowed these two women such puzzling power no longer existed. There would never be anything quite like them again.

SOURCES:

Block, Maxine, ed. *Current Biography 1940.* NY: H.W. Wilson, 1940.

——. *Current Biography 1942.* NY: H.W. Wilson, 1942.

Eells, George. *Hedda and Louella.* NY: Putnam, 1972.

Friedrich, Otto. *City of Nets: A Portrait of Hollywood in the 1940s.* NY: Harper and Row, 1986.

Hopper, Hedda. *From Under My Hat.* NY: Doubleday, 1952.

Parsons, Louella. *Tell It to Louella.* NY: Putnam, 1961.

RELATED MEDIA:

"Malice in Wonderland" (television movie), starring *Elizabeth Taylor and Jane Alexander, 1985.

Elizabeth L. Bland,
reporter, *Time* magazine

Horna, Kati (1912—)

Hungarian-born photographer of the Spanish Civil War. *Born in Hungary of Spanish descent on May 19, 1912; married José Horna (a painter and sculptor), in 1938.*

Kati Horna was born in Hungary on May 19, 1912, of Spanish descent. She studied photography in Hungary and started her photographic career in Paris in 1933. Horna arrived in Spain shortly after the Civil War began in July 1936 and started working for the Propaganda Committee of the anarchist trade union, the Confederación Nacional de Trabajo. From January 1937 until her departure from Spain in 1938, Horna worked as a photographer and graphics editor for leftist journals. Many of these were anarchist publications: *Tierra y Libertad* (*Land and Liberty*), *Tiempos Nuevos* (*New Times*), and *Mujeres Libres* (*Free Women*). Politics and art motivated her photography more than the desire to sell her works, and Horna consequently did not join any of the major photo distribution networks.

Most of her photographic work was lost after the Nationalists overran the Republican zone. Horna herself took only 270 negatives with her when she left for France. With the outbreak of World War II, she went to Veracruz, Mexico, in 1939, which became her home. There, she and her husband José Horna provided a hub for exiled and Mexican surrealists. José, a noted painter and sculptor, made toys in collaboration with *Remedios Varo and his wooden puppets were used in the production of puppet shows written by *Leonora Carrington. Varo stayed with the Hornas when she separated from her husband. In 1979, the Spanish Ministry of Culture purchased Kati Horna's negatives and added them to the National Historical Archives collection on the Civil War. The photographs portray the war's effects on civilians within territory held by the Republic.

SOURCES:

Horna, Kati. *Fotografías de la guerra civil española (1937–1938)*. Salamanca: Ministerio de Cultura, 1992.

Kendall W. Brown,
Provo, Utah

Hornby, Lesley (b. 1946).

See Twiggy.

Horne, Alice Merrill (1868–1948)

American educator, legislator, social and political activist. *Born in Fillmore, Utah, on January 2, 1868; died on October 7, 1948; fourth of fourteen children of Clarence Merrill (a telegraph operator and farmer) and Bathsheba (Smith) Merrill (a thespian); attended Old Rock Schoolhouse in Fillmore; graduated University of Deseret (later the University of Utah), 1887; married George H. Horne (a banker), on February 20, 1890; children: Mary (b. November 26, 1890); Lyman (b. September 20, 1896, who married* ****Myrtle Horne****);* Virginia (b. October 12, 1899); George, Jr. (1902–1903); Zorah (b. June 12, 1905); Albert (b. September 10, 1910).

The fourth of fourteen children of **Clarence Merrill**, a telegraph operator and farmer, and **Bathsheba Smith Merrill**, the daughter of a Territorial Legislature president, Alice Merrill Horne was born on January 2, 1868, in a log cabin in Fillmore, Utah. At age nine, Horne went to live with her grandmother in Salt Lake City, where she completed grade school and enrolled in the University of Deseret (later the University of Utah). There she studied art and literature and launched a Shakespearean Society for the study and performance of Shakespeare's plays before graduating in 1887 with a degree in pedagogy. Her grandmother **Bathsheba Bigler Smith** was well-established in Salt Lake City society; through her, Alice came to know many of the territory's leading artists and politicians (Utah would not become a state until 1896). Alice studied privately with intermountain artists and became involved with arts programs, women's suffrage, and several local charitable organizations.

In 1890, Alice married George H. Horne, a local banker who assisted and encouraged her in her interests outside the home. Together they would have six children, one of whom would die in infancy.

A year after her marriage, Alice Horne was appointed chair of the Utah Liberal Arts Committee for the 1893 World's Columbian Exposition. To demonstrate Utah's developing culture, she published a book of poems written by Utah women poets and illustrated by Utah women artists, and personally delivered the exhibit to Chicago. She went on to visit New York City, Boston, and Washington, D.C., gaining ideas for many of the civic, artistic, and educational programs she would champion in the future. After

Alice Merrill Horne

returning to Utah, Horne resumed teaching, which she continued through most of the ensuing years, and in 1894 began her political career by successfully sponsoring a candidate for election to the Board of Education. The Democratic Party selected her to run for State Representative in 1899; when she won, she became the second woman in Utah to be elected to a state office (21 years before the 19th Amendment would establish women's right to vote).

As a legislator, Horne sponsored a bill to establish an umbrella state agency for the arts. Upon signing the bill into law, the governor, Heber Wells, proclaimed: "This Art Bill assures that Utah is the first state in the Union to provide a state institution for the encouragement of the fine arts." Among her other acts as a legislator were a public health bill and a Fish and Game bill, and as chair of the University Land-Site Bill she placed the University of Utah in its present location on the foothills overlooking Salt Lake City. Alice Horne also proposed a free four-year scholarship bill for teachers, through which over 200 teachers were educated. Then, pregnant with her third child, Horne chose not to run for re-election.

From 1901 to 1916, Horne served on the General Board of the Relief Society (the women's organization of the Church of Jesus Christ of Latter-day Saints), holding workshops, writing lesson programs, and sponsoring a "Clean Milk for Utah" campaign which established rigid inspections and standards for milk sold in the state. This was a personal issue for Horne, who believed the death of her fourth child to have been caused by tainted milk. In 1902 she was an organizer for the Daughters of the Utah Pioneers, writing its constitution and by-laws and serving as secretary and later as president. She was chair of the Peace Committee in 1903, and received commendation for extensive community participation from ***May Wright Sewall**, the national chair. At the 1904 International Congress of Women in Berlin, Germany, Horne represented the National Women's Relief Society and the United States and gave invited addresses on the Utah art movement as well as her experience as a woman in politics.

After resigning from the General Board of the Relief Society, Horne was Salt Lake County chair of the Democratic Party and was active in the Sites Committee which identified areas suitable for monuments to honor pioneers. She wrote *Devotees and Their Shrines: A Handbook of Utah Art* in 1914, and a children's play, *Columbus Westward Ho!* in 1922. In the 1930s, she organized the "Smokeless Fuel Federation" to eliminate the environmental hazard of coal as a home-heating fuel, and was pivotal in organizing the Women's Chamber of Commerce in support of the program. However, one of Horne's most important contributions to her state, and in particular to the intermountain region around Salt Lake City, began with the establishment of her art galleries in 1921. Within ten years, she was able to note that she had sold 474 paintings from more than 40 exhibiting artists for over $49,000. Her salons continued into the late 1940s, promulgating her stated beliefs that "in each home should hang a good picture, no matter how small," and that the best way to learn about art was to "live with it: make it a part of your home and of your experience." Wanting Utah children to have the advantage of original art around them, Horne installed 40 art collections in the state's schools and in Idaho and Wyoming, involving scores of paintings by intermountain artists; she also held art exhibitions throughout Utah.

Alice Horne was one of the first inductees to the Salt Lake City Council of Women's Hall of Fame after its establishment in 1932, and received a Medal of Honor for her civic service from the Academy of Western Culture in 1942. A Heritage Hall at Brigham Young University was named after her in 1954. Replacing paintings in exhibits and working up to the end of her life, she was taken ill at 80 while at an art exhibit and died in the hospital on October 7, 1948.

SOURCES:

Arrington, Harriet Horne. "Alice Merrill Horne, Art Promoter and Early Utah Legislator," in *Utah Historical Quarterly*. Vol. 58. Summer 1990, pp. 261–276.

———, and Leonard J. Arrington, "Alice Merrill Horne, Cultural Entrepreneur," in Mary E. Stovall and Carol Cornwall Madsen, eds., *A Heritage of Faith*. Salt Lake City, UT: Deseret Book Company, 1988, pp. 121–136.

Olpin, Robert S. *Dictionary of Utah Art*. Salt Lake City, UT: Salt Lake Art Center, 1980, pp. 126–128.

Pioneers of Utah Art. Logan, UT: Kaysville Art Club, Educational Printing Service, 1968, pp. vii–viii.

Swanson, Vern G., Robert S. Olpin, William C. Seifrit. *Utah Art*. Springville, UT: Springville Museum of Art and Peregrine Smith Books, 1991.

Widtsoe, Leah T. "The Story of a Gifted Lady," in *Relief Society Magazine*. Vol. 32. March 1945, pp. 150–155.

Harriet Horne Arrington,
women's biographer, Salt Lake City, Utah

Horne, Lena (1917—)

African-American singer and actress whose amazing career spanned over six decades. *Born on June 30, 1917, in Brooklyn, New York; daughter of Edwin and Edna (Scottron) Horne; married Louis Jones, in 1937* *(divorced 1940); married Lennie Hayton, in 1947 (died February 1971); children: (first marriage) Gail Lumet Buckley (b. 1937); Teddy Jones (1940–1971).*

Spent most of childhood on the road with her mother, an actress; dropped out of high school at age 16 to join the chorus line at Harlem's Cotton Club (1933); while gaining recognition on the nightclub circuit, was discovered by Hollywood, though film roles were mainly limited to cameo singing appearances; blacklisted from film and television industry during the McCarthy era (1950s); returned to the screen (1969) in her first non-musical role; worked nearly continuously in films, television, and live concert appearances, winning a Tony Award on Broadway (1982), undertaking a world tour with her one-woman show (1982–83), and receiving the Kennedy Center's Lifetime Achievement Award (1984).

Filmography: The Duke Is Tops *(1938);* Panama Hattie *(1942);* Cabin in the Sky *(1943);* Stormy Weather *(1943);* I Dood It *(1943);* As Thousands Cheer *(1943);* Swing Fever *(1943);* Broadway Rhythm *(1944);* Two Girls and a Sailor *(1944);* Ziegfeld Follies *(1946);* Till the Clouds Roll By *(1946);* Words and Music *(1948);* Duchess of Idaho *(1950);* Meet Me in Las Vegas *(1956);* Death of a Gunfighter *(1969);* The Wiz *(1978).*

Lena Horne marked the beginning of her 77th year, in June of 1994, with a surprising admission. "I really do hate to sing," she told an interviewer, even though that same month marked the latest album release in a recording career spanning 50 years and, little more than ten years before, she had won a Tony, a Grammy, and a Drama Desk award for her record-breaking one-woman show, *Lena Horne: The Lady and Her Music.* But to anyone who had known Horne since her Cotton Club days back in 1930's Harlem, Lena's dissatisfaction with her vocal abilities was nothing new.

A career in show business, in fact, had not seemed at all likely for the daughter born to Teddy and **Edna Horne** in Brooklyn, New York, on June 30, 1917. Both her parents were from solidly respectable middle-class families who had escaped the poverty of the antebellum South by setting down roots in the more prosperous North in the last decade of the 19th century. Edna's parents, the Scottrons, appeared at all the best society affairs staged by Brooklyn's African-American bourgeoisie; while Teddy's parents, Edwin and **Cora Horne**, were equally well-regarded. Cora in particular was known for her passionate attachment to social causes, having been one of the earliest supporters of the National Association for the Advancement of Colored People (NAACP) in its infancy and having made sure her two-year-old granddaughter appeared in the NAACP's official magazine as the organization's youngest member. Although this streak of social activism would surface in Lena many years later, her family's secure position shielded her from the plight of the majority of African-Americans. The Hornes and the Scottrons lived in a world that mirrored that of upper-class American whites, with its opera houses, debutante balls, and high teas. But it was Lena's parents, Edna and Teddy, who would break the mold.

Horne once described her father as a renegade and claimed that the day she was born Teddy was desperately trying to win back the cash earmarked for hospital bills that he had lost at the card table. Teddy had a comfortable desk job with the N.Y. State Department of Labor but ignored his father's pleas to settle down by abandoning Edna and his young daughter in 1920 and moving to Pittsburgh, where he opened the hotel he would manage for the rest of his life. Almost immediately afterward, Edna succumbed to her girlhood dream of being an actress and joined the Lafayette Players, the stock company of Harlem's venerable Lafayette Theater. Lena was left in the care of her Horne grandparents, and Cora made sure to tutor her granddaughter in the nobility of the African-American cause and in the treachery of whites. Lena rarely saw Edna for the next four years, although Teddy paid sporadic visits to Brooklyn to keep an eye on his daughter's upbringing. In 1924, Edna sent a message that she was ill and asked Lena to come and stay with her in Harlem; but as soon as she recovered, Edna went back on the actors' circuit playing tent shows and vaudeville houses throughout the deep South. This time, Lena went with her. In the shanty towns, muddy field camps and urban ghettos on Edna's route, Lena learned for the first time how the majority of American blacks actually lived and the exploitation they suffered at the hands of whites.

By 1928, Lena was back in Brooklyn with her grandparents and was enrolled in the Brooklyn Girls High School, where dramatics and dancing were part of the curriculum. She performed for the first time in public as part of a dance recital staged by the dancing academy which she was also attending on weekends. But with Cora and Edwin Horne's deaths in 1932, Lena's peripatetic childhood found her back with Edna, who had now settled in Harlem and married an ex-officer from the Cuban army, Miguel Rodriguez. With money and steady work in short supply, Edna suggested that an audition could be arranged for Lena at the Cotton Club, which billed its chorus line as "tall, tan, and terrific" and, more important, paid $25 a week.

Now 16, Horne certainly fit the first two qualifications of the Cotton Club's description, for she was leggy and thin with the *café au lait* complexion and Caucasian features which the Cotton Club's white audience found so attractive. (Cora had claimed the Hornes carried Senegalese, Blackfoot Indian, and white blood.) But even Lena admitted her singing and dancing could not be described as "terrific." "I could carry a tune," she once remembered, "but I could hardly have been called a singer. I could dance a little, but I could hardly have been called a dancer. I was tall and skinny and I had very little going for me except a pretty face and long, long hair that framed it rather nicely." It was, indeed, her looks and not her talent that got her the job doing three shows a night wearing little else than three large ostrich feathers. She never went back to school, with Edna keeping the truant officer at bay by claiming that her daughter had simply disappeared.

Despite its location at 142nd Street and Lenox Avenue in the heart of Harlem, the Cotton Club's clientele was strictly white. It was run by the mob in those heady, violent Prohibition days and was no place for an attractive, light-skinned black girl. Edna came to the club every night to fend off, not always successfully, the advances made on her daughter by white patrons. Many years later, Horne would say that it was at the Cotton Club that she learned to hate white men. Even the swaggering bravado of Edna's husband Miguel was little help, with Miguel finding his head stuck down a toilet one night after foolishly suggesting to the Club's management that Horne should be given a raise. Finally, Edna called on her friend, bandleader Noble Sissle, for assistance.

Noble Sissle's Society Orchestra was one of the first all-black bands to be accepted by white audiences, especially after Noble's work on the score of Broadway's first musical with an all-black cast, *Shufflin' Along*. Sissle avoided the innovative and sensual jazz forms of the Harlem bands and provided his audiences with much more genteel dance music; he agreed to audition Lena after advising Edna that her underage daughter's contract with the Cotton Club gave her the right to simply leave work one night and never come back. Soon Lena found herself auditioning for Noble with the song "Dinner For One, Please, James." "When I think that really great singers like ***Ella Fitzgerald** were signing with competing bands like Chick Webb's," Horne remembers, "I don't know why Noble wanted me. All I could do was carry a simple tune simply." But that was all Sissle wanted, for he knew that Lena's exotic beauty would do the rest. It was Sissle who gave Horne her first lessons in sophistication and style. "Remember," he would tell her, "you're a lady, not a whore. Don't let them treat you like one." His advice may have been belied by the discrimination the band experienced on the road, often sleeping in their bus and even, one night in Indiana, in a circus tent when whites-only hotels refused them accommodation.

After a year touring with Sissle, Horne obtained Edna's permission to spend Christmas of 1936 with her father in Pittsburgh. During the visit, Teddy introduced her to a young man of his acquaintance, Louis Jones, a minister's son and recent college graduate then working as a clerk for the county coroner's office. The two were married early in 1937, followed by the birth of a daughter **Gail (Lumet Buckley)** later that same year. Jones had no doubt expected Horne to settle down and raise a family, and even went so far as to forbid her to work, but Lena quickly discovered that being a housewife was not to her taste. Many years later, she would describe her first marriage as the biggest mistake she ever made, its only saving grace being the two children it produced. After a son Teddy was born in 1940, Horne left Jones, put her children in the care of relatives, and auditioned for the man who would do more for her career than anyone else to this point.

Charlie Barnet billed his all-white band as "The Blackest White Band of All." Barnet's idol was Duke Ellington, whose music and style he attempted to emulate, so it was no surprise to anyone when Barnet became one of the first white bandleaders to hire a black female singer. (Artie Shaw had also hired ***Billie Holiday** at about this time.) Barnet's male singer, Bob Carrol, remembers the tall, thin woman with the long hair who showed up one night to sing. "She ran down a few tunes in the basement of the theater and then, without any arrangements, she did the next show—not only did it, but stopped it cold. She was just great!" Horne's experiences with Barnet's band laid the groundwork for her lifelong affection for musicians, black or white. "They didn't seem to care a thing about me except as a singer and a human being," Lena recalls. When Horne was sometimes refused a room in a hotel where the band planned to spend the night on the road, the entire orchestra walked out with her; and Barnet shrugged off

Lena Horne

complaints from, on the one hand, audiences who objected to his hiring a black singer, and, on the other, fans who accused Barnet of fakery because Lena didn't look black enough. Still, Horne was forced to sit out her time between numbers in a convenient restroom rather than remaining on stage, and even Barnet suggested that Lena stay home when the band toured the deep South.

But it was Barnet who taught Horne the emotional phrasing and dramatic overtones that are the trademarks of her style, along with the technical knowledge to carry it off. "I learned more about music from the men I worked with in bands than I learned anywhere else," Horne says. "They taught me discipline and the value of rehearsing and how to train." Barnet's work with her paid off, for during this period Horne released her first album for RCA, *The Birth of the Blues,* and made her first appearance at New York's prestigious Café Society Downtown, then a showcase for new jazz and blues talent. But even with her first flush of success, Horne found it hard to forget her grandmother's warnings about the ways of white people, or the fact that she was a black performer in a mostly white entertainment business. She rarely socialized with any of her white admirers after finishing a show, while at the same time defending herself against the criticisms of other black entertainers who refused to perform for society whites. "Those audiences were getting a singer, not *me,*" she would point out.

A survivor, honey, is exactly what I am.

—Lena Horne

Encouraged by this early success, Horne decided to move to Los Angeles, where she had been told work was more plentiful. Leaving Barnet's band, she opened a solo act at Hollywood's Little Troc club, where she was seen by manager Arthur Freed. Freed candidly admitted that the quality of Lena's voice was not what had attracted him, but rather the way she used it. "When she sings about love," he said, "that's *love* and you've heard all about it." Freed sensed that Horne's combination of singing and acting made her a natural for film work, and his instincts proved right when Louis B. Mayer signed her to a seven-year contract with his MGM studio in 1941. Her father, to whom Lena had remained close, flew out from Pittsburgh to help with the negotiations and make sure his daughter didn't suffer the same fate as many other blacks working in the film business. "I can hire a maid for her," Teddy told studio executives. "Why should she have to act one?" Consequently, the contract guaranteed her a starring role in at least one mainstream, big-budget MGM musical and contained language that protected Lena against the discriminatory practices of white Hollywood. Horne was among the first African-American performers to sign a long-term deal with a major movie studio, but the distinction was not without cost.

Her first screen test was not to the studio's liking because, it was felt, Horne looked too white, while a second test, in which she was slathered in blackface, was downright grotesque. The legendary Max Factor was called in to concoct a solution, which turned out to be what Factor called "Light Egyptian"—a skin coloring that proved so effective that Horne, some years later, lost the role of the mulatto Julie in the 1951 remake of *Showboat* to ***Ava Gardner**. MGM finally found a part for her in a Red Skelton film called *Panama Hattie,* in which Lena sang "Just One of Those Things." Shrewdly, however, the studio made sure that Horne's character had nothing whatever to do with the main storyline of the film, thus allowing her to be cut from the prints when the picture was distributed in the South. The next year, 1943, proved a busy one for Lena, with appearances in *As Thousands Cheer* and, fulfilling the terms of her contract, starring roles in two adaptations of Broadway musicals featuring the top black entertainers of the day, *Cabin in the Sky* and *Stormy Weather,* the film that gave Horne her signature song. Between pictures, Lena joined her Hollywood peers in touring with USO shows at World War II training camps around the country, although she was usually sent out with an all-black troupe which was housed separately from white entertainers. Horne and fighter Joe Louis were the two main attractions for both black and white audiences on such tours, and it was said that the two became lovers during the war years.

As in New York, Horne felt trapped between two worlds. Black actors, who could only find film work as butlers and maids or in so-called "jungle films," resented Horne for the treatment her contract specified. Some even accused her of being a propaganda tool for the NAACP. At the same time, Horne was forced to remove her daughter Gail from a private school after a white teacher refused to punish another child for calling Gail a "nigger." Adding fuel to the fire, Lena had met and fallen in love with a white man, a musician named Lennie Hayton who was composing film scores for MGM during Horne's years at the studio. Their relationship probably began long before the two were married in Paris in 1947, and it is possible that Lena left Hollywood when she did because gossip columnists like ***Louella Parsons** were about to reveal her relationship with Hayton. After their marriage became public, Lena's mother refused to speak to her; Hayton's family similarly rejected the couple, to say nothing of the difficulty a black-Jewish couple experienced in finding hotels which would accept them and neighborhoods in which they could purchase a home. In the Los Angeles neighborhood where Horne and Hayton finally settled, Lennie felt compelled to purchase a shotgun after threats began showing up in the mail.

But to Lena, her love for Hayton made perfect sense. "Given my experience, I don't think I could have married anyone but a musician," she said, "since they had become the only people with whom I could feel I was myself."

It was Lennie Hayton who gave the final polish to Horne's nightclub act, finding her the right material, arranging it himself to suit her unique style, and then booking her in the clubs where she would receive the most exposure. Both Horne and Hayton knew that her natural environment was in an intimate nightclub setting. "It's so physical," Lena said. "It's all body." Her attraction to nightclubs and cabarets was fortunate, for by the early 1950s Lena found herself blacklisted from Hollywood after being labeled as a suspected Communist during the McCarthy hearings.

Starting with her arrival in Los Angeles some ten years earlier, Horne had often spoken for, and worked with, organizations like the Council on African Affairs and the Hollywood Independent Citizens Committee for the Arts, among the many liberal groups the House Un-American Activities Committee considered "communistic." Lena also suffered from her friendship with actor Paul Robeson, an outspoken proponent of African-American dignity and racial tolerance whose acting career in the United States was ruined because of his suspected ties with left-wing groups. Although she was never officially accused of being a Communist, Horne was cited in McCarthy's published mouthpieces, *Red Channels* and *Counterattack*. "Sure those years hurt me financially," she once said, "but they also educated me to a lot of things. I began to grow as a person under the blacklist/redlist. I didn't torture myself because it's never unusual for black people to have a bad time." Like many others who had been named or publicly accused, including Robeson, Horne found refuge in Europe, where Lennie booked her into the Palladium in London and at the same club where ***Josephine Baker** was playing in Paris.

When the couple ventured back to America, Lennie managed to keep Lena's career on track, finding that nightclub and cabaret audiences

were more interested in having a good time than in worrying about who was or was not a Communist. Under Hayton's guidance, contracts were negotiated that allowed Horne privileges then thought unusual for a black performer, such as being allowed to enter and leave a hotel by the front door, call for room service, and use the main elevators rather than the freight elevator. Horne took swift action against any hint of discrimination, suing a restaurant in Chicago for refusing her service and canceling her appearance at a Miami Beach hotel which denied her and her musicians rooms. "Discrimination deteriorates you mentally," she said as, with the rise of the civil-rights movement in the late 1950s and early 1960s, she took a more activist stance against racial prejudice. She joined the Congress of Racial Equality (CORE) and donated the proceeds of her performance at a benefit concert in 1963 to the Southern National Christian Conference (SNCC), both organizations being at the forefront of the struggle for civil rights. She electrified the audience at the benefit by singing the protest song "Now!," which had been especially written for the occasion and which included the lyrics: "We want more than just a promise, Say goodbye to Uncle Thomas."

Playbill *from* Lena Horne: The Lady and Her Music.

Horne's recording of the song sold well, even though many radio stations considered it inflammatory and refused to play it. Later in that tumultuous decade, Lena attended a conference on civil rights arranged by then-Attorney General Robert Kennedy, appeared with Dr. Martin Luther King, Jr., and spoke with Medgar Evers just two days before his assassination in Mississippi. Friends warned Horne that her carefully cultivated public image as the "good negro" was in danger, but her anger became increasingly evident in her public speeches, especially after the murders of Robert Kennedy and Dr. King. "All of us who have been symbols of Negro aspirations for the past couple of decades have minded our manners . . . and nothing has come of it," she said. "My generation has been sold a bill of goods . . . a *cheap* bill of goods." Even after the passage of anti-discrimination legislation and Lyndon Johnson's Great Society programs, Horne still smoldered. "When people say 'Hasn't there been progress?,' I'm forced to say, 'Yes, a little.' But I don't like to settle for a little!"

Despite her friends' warnings, Horne's career only seemed to prosper. One sign was the first movie offer from Hollywood in nearly 20 years, *Death of a Gunfighter,* in 1969. It was her first non-musical role, playing the madam of a brothel in the Old West who falls for the local sheriff, played by Richard Widmark, whom she dubbed "my blue-eyed soul brother." The end of the film, in which Horne's and Widmark's characters marry, mirrored Lena's real-life interracial marriage to Hayton. While shooting the picture, Lena found that Hollywood was a different place from the old red-baiting days, and she began to think that maybe that little bit of progress had been worth something after all. "Now that I admit that I have prejudices and so do [whites], I find myself a little more at ease with people," she said. "I'm not afraid to feel things, even though I'm angry just as much." While keeping up a recording and touring schedule, Horne also appeared in several television specials during the late 1960s and early 1970s, finding comfort in her work when three of the people closest to her died within a year: her father, of whom she said that "everything inside of me that was like him has protected me," then her husband Lennie, and finally her son Teddy, who died of a kidney infection.

In 1978, Horne appeared on Broadway in a revival of the musical *Pal Joey* and found a new, younger audience by playing Glinda, the good witch, in Sidney Lumet's film *The Wiz,* in which she sang the show-stopper "If You Believe." (Lumet was her former son-in-law, having married and divorced Gail some years earlier.) Then, in May of 1981, Horne returned to Broadway with what was to have been a one-month engagement at the Nederlander Theater of a one-woman show, *Lena: The Lady and Her Music.* No one involved with the show, including Horne, was prepared for its phenomenal success, running for 13 months before closing on Lena's 65th birthday, on June 30, 1982. Musicologist Jonathan Schwartz called her performance an "unnarcissistic presentation of self: an adult woman, intensely awake, a performer without facade at full vocal and emotional power." Horne put it more simply. "On the stage," she said, "I'm not lying about anything." Her work won her a special Tony Award, a Drama Desk Award, and a Grammy, spurring Lena to take the show on a world tour in 1982 and 1983.

After taking Broadway by storm, Horne began to give herself more time between appearances and, since the mid-1980s, has performed mainly at benefit concerts or special cabaret appearances. But she continued to record, her later albums being a tribute to the late composer Billy Strayhorn, 1994's *We'll Be Together Again* and 1995's *How Long Has This Been Going On.* But even after a half-century of singing, Lena Horne still saw room for improvement. "The truth is that these days I'd like to sound like Aretha Franklin. But I'm not," she says with a smile. "I'm Lena."

SOURCES:

Buckley, Gail Lumet. *The Hornes: An American Family.* NY: Knopf, 1986.

Dahl, Linda. *Stormy Weather: The Music and Lives of a Century of Jazz Women.* NY: Pantheon, 1984.

Horne, Lena and Richard Schickel. *Lena.* NY: Doubleday, 1965.

Howard, Brett. *Lena.* Los Angeles, CA: Holloway House, 1981.

Moore, Trudy. "Lena Horne Releases New Album," in *Jet.* Vol. 86, no. 7. June 20, 1994.

Schwartz, Jonathan. "Lena," in *Town and Country Monthly.* Vol. 149, no. 5184. September 1995.

Norman Powers,
writer-producer, Chelsea Lane Productions, New York

Horne, Marilyn (1929—)

American mezzo-soprano. *Born Marilyn Bernice Horne in Bradford, Pennsylvania, on January 16, 1929; studied with her father, and with William Vennard, Lotte Lehmann, and* ***Gwengolyn Koldofsky****; attended the University of Southern California; Rutgers University, Mus.D., 1970; Jersey City State College, D.Litt.; attended St. Peter's College; married Henry Lewis (a composer).*

Made debut as Háta in Smetana's The Bartered Bride, *Los Angeles Guild Opera (1954); appeared at the Venice Festival by invitation of Igor Stravinsky (1956); appeared as Marie in Berg's* Wozzeck *at San Francisco Opera (1960), at Covent Garden (1964); made debut at La Scala in* Oedipus Rex *(1969); made debut at the Metropolitan Opera as Adalgisa in Bellini's* Norma *(1970); other roles include Rosina in* Barber of Seville, *Neocle in* The Siege of Corinth, *both La Scala (1969), Isabella in* L'Italiana in Algiere, *title role in* Carmen, *both Metropolitan Opera (1972–73); also appeared with the American Opera Society of New York City for several seasons which included roles in Gluck's* Iphigenie en Tauride *and Rossini's* Semiramide; *appeared with the Vancouver Opera (Adalgisa in* Norma*) and at Philharmonic Hall, New York City; appeared as Italiana at La Scala (1975), as Rosina at Vienna Opera (1978); has recorded for London (often with Joan Sutherland), Columbia, and RCA records; has received several Grammy awards.*

Marilyn Horne

Marilyn Horne was born in Bradford, Pennsylvania, in 1929, but the Horne family moved to

Los Angeles when she was 11. She studied with William Vennard at the University of Southern California and also took part in *Lotte Lehmann's master classes. Horne first came to public attention as the dubbed voice of *Dorothy Dandridge in the 1954 film *Carmen Jones,* the all-black version of Bizet's *Carmen.* That same year, she debuted as Háta in Smetana's *The Bartered Bride* with the Los Angeles Opera. An early association with Igor Stravinsky led to her participation in the Venice Festival in 1956. Horne then spent three years as a member of the Gelsenkirchen company in Europe before appearing as Marie in Berg's *Wozzeck* on October 4, 1960, at the San Francisco Opera. In 1969, Horne appeared at La Scala as Rosina in *Barber of Seville,* and Neocle in *The Siege of Corinth.* She then appeared as Carmen under Bernstein's baton in 1972, a performance which was later recorded.

In what was to become known as the modern bel canto revolution, a dynamic pairing with *Joan Sutherland led to many international concerts. Horne first worked with Sutherland in a concert version of Bellini's *Beatrice di Tenda* at Carnegie Hall in 1961. The two reunited in Rossini's *Semiramide* in Boston in 1965. In 1967, Horne appeared at Covent Garden as Adalgisa to Sutherland's Norma in the Bellini opera; they reprised their roles at the Metropolitan in 1970.

Horne has sung at the White House for Republican and Democratic presidents, and in 1993 sang at Bill Clinton's Inaugural. Her voice has extraordinary range, as concerts which included Rossini arias and Brünnhilde's immolation scene demonstrate. Horne's other great roles include Handel's Rinaldo, Rossini's Isabella and Rosina, Verdi's Amneris, Princess Eboli, and Mistress Quickly, Meyerbeer's Fides, and Gluck's Orfeo. In 1994, Horne launched the Marilyn Horne Foundation which is devoted exclusively to the art of the vocal recital which she termed "an endangered species of the performing arts." In 1995, she was honored at the Kennedy Center for inspiring an "impressive body of new work, ranging from Igor Stravinsky to William Bolcom," and for being "especially instrumental in nourishing and popularizing new American music."

SUGGESTED READING:

Horne, Marilyn. *My Life* (autobiography). London, 1984.

John Haag,
Athens, Georgia

Horne, Myrtle (1892–1969)

Utah nurse. *Name variations: Myrtle Clara; Myrtle Carolyn. Born Myrtle Clara Swainston on March 24, 1892, in Cottonwood, Uintah County, Wyoming; died in Salt Lake City, Utah, of acute myocardial infarction, on December 3, 1969; daughter of Ebenezer James Swainston (a farmer and horticulturist) and Harriet Ann (Hughes) Swainston; attended grade school and high school in Wyoming; graduated L.D.S. Hospital School of Nursing, Salt Lake City, Utah, 1918; married Lyman Merrill Horne, M.D., January 3, 1923; children: Harriet Ann (b. June 22, 1924); twins Carolynn and Marilynn (b. March 29, 1926); Alice Merrill Horne (b. December 20, 1928); twins Robert Hughes and Richard Hughes (b. September 15, 1932); twins Jonathan Hughes and David Hughes (b. October 25, 1935).*

Myrtle Horne received her R.N. degree in June of 1918, just in time to serve during the great influenza pandemic of that year. A trip to Hawaii to visit a friend from nursing school resulted in her appointment as superintendent of the Kapi'olani Hospital in Honolulu, where she worked until 1922 and learned to surf. She continued to work as a nurse after her marriage in 1923 to Lyman Horne, the first trained obstetrician-gynecologist in Utah, and was president of the Utah State Nurses Association from 1927 to 1930. From the early 1930s until 1952, Horne was a lecturer to groups of teenage girls on the topic of "maturation and femininity," much in demand by youth group leaders throughout the Salt Lake City region.

SOURCES:

Andrew, Bishop Richard. *Monument Park II Ward History,* privately published.

Arrington, Leonard J. "The Influenza Epidemic of 1918–19 in Utah," in *Utah Historical Quarterly.* Vol 58, no. 2. Spring 1990.

Ogden Standard Examiner [Ogden, Utah]. Issues from November 2, 1918–December 31, 1918, addressing the flu epidemic.

Swainston family genealogy and manuscript history by Minnie Hinck.

Harriet Horne Arrington,
women's biographer, Salt Lake City, Utah

Horney, Brigitte (1911–1988)

German actress and major film star who also enjoyed a considerable following abroad. *Pronunciation: HORN-eye. Born in Berlin, Germany, on March 29, 1911; died of heart failure after a two year bout with cancer in Hamburg, Germany, on July 27, 1988; daughter of Oscar Horney and Karen (Danielsen) Horney (1885–1952, the prominent psychoanalyst); married Konstantin Irmen-Tschet; married Hanns Swarzenski (curator for the Decorative Arts at the Boston Museum for Fine Arts), c. 1953.*

Brigitte Horney

Selected filmography: Abschied *(*Farewell, *1930);* Ein Mann will nach Deutschland *(*A Man Wants to Reach Germany, *1934);* Liebe, Tod und Teufel *(*Love, Death, and the Devil, *1934);* Savoy-Hotel 217 *(1936);* Befreite Hände *(*Unfettered Hands, *1939);* Feinde *(*Enemies, *1941);* Das Mädchen von Fanö *(*The Girl from Fanö, *1941);* Münchhausen *(*The Adventures of Baron Münchhausen, *1943);* Am Ende der Welt *(*At the End of the World, *1944). Began screen career in 1930 and with some interruptions kept working until the last weeks of her life, starring in a popular West German television se-*

ries, "Das Erbe der Guldenburgs" (Legacy of the Guldenburgs).

Born in Berlin, Germany, in 1911, three years before the start of World War I, Brigitte Horney grew up in a family of social prominence and affluence which valued intellectual and professional achievements. Her father was a physician; her mother was ***Karen Horney** who in later years became one of the leading psychoanalysts in the world. After completing secondary school, Brigitte—nicknamed "Biggy" by her family and friends—began preparing for an acting career. To gain admittance to Berlin's prestigious Academy of Dramatic Arts, one had to perform at the Deutsches Theater in the presence of the world-famous director Max Reinhardt. Not only was Horney admitted, but she was presented with a prize by Reinhardt. In the summer of 1930, she took a screen test at the vast UFA studios in the suburbs of Berlin. Awarded a contract, she appeared that year as a frustrated sales clerk in her first film, *Abschied* (Farewell). Within a few years, both the film's director, Robert Siodmak, and the author of its screenplay, Billy Wilder, would flee a Nazi-ruled Germany.

Impressed by Horney's acting in *Abschied,* UFA's management offered her a one-year contract, but she turned it down, saying she did not feel ready to appear in any more film roles. Instead, she concentrated on gaining acting experience by performing on stage at Berlin's Volksbühne (People's Theater). Not until 1934, by which time Germany had become a Nazi dictatorship, did Horney feel ready to stand in front of a film camera again. By this time, she had gathered a growing number of fans who were entranced by her husky voice, high cheekbones, thick black hair, and dark eyes. The film she starred in, *Ein Mann will nach Deutschland* (A Man Wants to Go to Germany), was laden with Nazi propaganda, telling an improbable tale of a wife's wait for her husband to return to the Third Reich from South America where he had been employed as an engineer. Many moviegoers paid scant attention to the plot, enjoying instead Horney's stunning appearance and her intense, expressive acting style. Some filmgoers detected in her work that indefinable "something" that ***Marlene Dietrich**—who had already decamped for Hollywood—possessed.

Horney made a number of films in the 1930s, virtually all of which proved to be immensely popular with the German public. In *Savoy-Hotel 217* (1936), set in Tsarist Russia on the eve of World War I, she starred in a tragic tale of love and intrigue. Film critics praised her performance, describing her as "the gleaming jewel who lights up the entire film" and as an actress who played her part "with an intensity that at times is almost painful." In a film released during the early months of World War II, Horney again starred in a vehicle that was highly successful with the German public, *Befreite Hände* (Unfettered Hands). This 1939 film, the story of a talented farm girl who finds both artistic maturity and love, received praise from critics as well as the public. In December 1939, the reviewer for the *Münchener Neueste Nachrichten* wrote: "Brigitte Horney's performance alone would make it worth seeing."

Released in January 1941, *Das Mädchen von Fanö* (The Girl from Fanö) had an unusual story and setting, taking place on the Danish isle of Fanö in the storm-swept North Sea. Once again Horney's acting received rave reviews, as did that of her handsome co-star, Joachim Gottschalk. The tragic fate of this film star would never be forgotten by Horney, who greatly respected him both as an artist and as a person. Faced with the impending deportation to the Theresienstadt concentration camp of his son Michael and wife **Meta Gottschalk**, who under German law was considered to be Jewish despite her conversion to Christianity, Joachim pleaded to accompany them. When he was denied, the Gottschalks fed their son a fatal dose of sleeping pills, then committed suicide by turning on the gas in the kitchen stove. News of the Gottschalk family suicide was kept secret from the German public by propaganda chief Joseph Goebbels, but word of the tragedy spread quickly through Berlin's motion-picture community. After initial outbursts of shock and rage, most decided to keep their feelings to themselves in view of the prevalence of Gestapo informers and the fact that the spreading of rumors could easily land one in a concentration camp. Only a handful of Gottschalk's close friends, including Brigitte Horney, **Ruth Hellberg**, as well as Gustav Knuth and his wife **Elisabeth Lennartz**, showed up for the funeral, which took place at the Stahnsdorf cemetery in the outskirts of Berlin. Gestapo agents were ever present in the vicinity of the freshly dug graves. Easily visible behind trees and shrubs, they took photographs of all who attended.

Shot in Agfacolor, Horney's next film *Münchhausen* (1943) was a cinematic extravaganza more resembling a Hollywood film than one produced in Nazi Germany. Almost two years in the making, it was a technical tour de force that included trick photography, elaborate special effects, and shots of Meissen china and gold tableware that had been borrowed from museums. To film a breathtaking regatta, the film crew went to Venice. Horney's performance, in which she portrayed ***Catherine II the Great** of Russia, received the usual rave reviews.

Starting in March 1944, when it was clear that Hitler had lost the war, Horney began work on the aptly titled *Am Ende der Welt* (At the End of the World), which told the story of a landowner's daughter and her dream of opening a cabaret (a plan she drops after realizing that to do so she would have to cut down the woods she loved as a child). Almost daily Allied bombing raids slowed down the production, and by the time the film was in the can, Horney was in poor health. In December 1944, the film was banned by Joseph Goebbels, and a few weeks later, in January 1945, Horney fled to Switzerland.

Her health remained fragile for some time after her arrival in Switzerland, as she struggled with pneumonia, asthma and other problems. In 1946, some news stories reported falsely that she had died in a Swiss sanatorium. In time, her health was restored, and Horney began appearing on the Zurich stage, including starring roles in plays by such contemporary playwrights as Max Frisch and Jean-Paul Sartre. After the war, Horney resumed long-severed contact with her famous mother, who had left Germany in 1932, and whose work was never recognized in the Third Reich where psychoanalysis had been regarded as "a Jewish swindle." By the late 1940s, Horney was living in the United States, and in 1951 she married her second husband, Boston art curator Hanns Swarzenski. After Karen Horney's death in 1952, Brigitte chose to live permanently in the United States and eventually received dual West German-United States citizenship.

By the late 1950s, Horney was returning to West Germany on a regular basis to appear in television dramas, some of which had Cold War political colorations, such as the 1960 anti-Soviet war movie "Nacht fiel über Gotenhafen" (Night Fell on Gotenhafen). Among the more intriguing roles she played was that of Aunt Polly in a 1980 combined German-language version of Mark Twain's *Tom Sawyer* and *Huckleberry Finn*. Determined not to let either her age or failing health keep her from working, during the last years of her life she starred in a highly popular West German television series, "Das Erbe der Guldenburgs" (Legacy of the Guldenburgs), in which she portrayed the matriarch of a German brewing dynasty. Although she was now battling cancer, Brigitte Horney refused to stop acting; she spent her nights at a local hospital and worked in the daytime filming on the Studio Hamburg set of the highly rated series. She died of a heart attack in Hamburg on July 27, 1988.

SOURCES:

"Brigitte Horney," in *Variety.* August 3, 1988.

"Die Gage wird der Tod sein: Ulrich Liebes Dokumentation über Schauspieler als Naziopfer," in *Süddeutsche Zeitung.* October 23, 1992, p. 19.

Franken, Lia, ed. *Ich ging meinen Weg: Frauen erzählen ihr Leben.* 2nd ed. Bern: Scherz Verlag, 1996.

Horney, Brigitte and Gerd Host Heyerdahl. *So oder so ist das Leben.* 4th ed. Bern: Scherz Verlag, 1992.

Paris, Bernard J. *Karen Horney: A Psychoanalyst's Search for Self-Understanding.* New Haven, CT: Yale University Press, 1994.

Romani, Cinzia. *Tainted Goddesses: Female Film Stars of the Third Reich.* Translated by Robert Connolly. NY: Sarpedon Publishers, 1992.

Wistrich, Robert S. *Who's Who in Nazi Germany.* London: Routledge, 1995.

Zentner, Christian and Friedemann Bedürftig, eds. *The Encyclopedia of the Third Reich.* 2 vols. NY: Macmillan, 1991.

John Haag,
Associate Professor, University of Georgia, Athens, Athens, Georgia

Horney, Karen (1885–1952)

German-American psychoanalyst who argued that women's development had to be viewed on its own terms, not seen as a derivative of male development.
Pronunciation: HORN-eye. Name variations: Karen Danielsen. Born Karen Clementine Danielsen on September 15, 1885, in Eilbek, Germany; died on December 4, 1952, in New York; daughter of Berndt Wackels Danielsen (a sea captain) and Clotilde (von Ronzelen) Danielsen; married Oskar Horney (an economist), in 1909 (separated 1920); lived with Gertrude Lederer-Eckardt (a physical therapist); children: Brigitte Horney (1911–1988, an actress); Marianne Horney Lederer Von Eckardt (b. 1913, a psychiatrist); Renate Horney (b. 1915).

Studied medicine at the University of Berlin (1909–13); entered analysis (1911); received medical degree (1913); trained at Lankwitz Sanitarium (1914–18); taught at Berlin Psychoanalytic Institute (1920–32); separated from husband (1920); served as assistant director of Institute for Psychoanalysis in Chicago (1932–34); taught at New York Institute for Psychoanalysis (1934–41); founded American Institute for Psychoanalysis and Association for the Advancement of Psychoanalysis (1941); Karen Horney Clinic founded in New York (1952).

Selected writings: The Neurotic Personality of Our Time *(1927);* New Ways in Psychoanalysis *(1939);* Self-Analysis *(1942);* Our Inner Conflicts

(1945); (editor) Are You Considering Psychoanalysis? *(1946);* Neurosis and Human Growth: The Struggle Toward Self-Realization *(1950); (edited by Harold Kelman)* New Perspectives in Psychoanalysis *(1965); (edited by Kelman)* Feminine Psychology *(1967);* The Adolescent Diaries of Karen Horney *(1980); (edited by Douglas Ingram)* Final Lectures *(1987).*

A theorist and author on psychoanalysis and human psychology, Karen Horney was among the most influential of 20th-century psychologists through her critiques and revisions of Freudian theory. Born in a small village near Hamburg, Germany, in 1885, Karen Clementine Danielsen was the eldest child of an authoritarian Lutheran sea captain and his liberal second wife. It was in some ways a difficult childhood; her parents' marriage was unhappy, and Horney felt that her parents favored her older brother. She attended elementary and secondary school in Hamburg, where her intellect and curiosity made her an excellent student.

Horney's diaries, kept throughout her teen years, provide a unique source for her maturing views and her ultimate rejection of most of her father's values. Having adopted her mother's religious freethinking and tolerant attitudes, Horney resented the strict discipline and conservative religious thinking of her high school; by her late teens, she had become agnostic. Karen was drawn to the sciences and wanted a career where she could help others. As she recorded in her diary, she decided to become a physician around age 12, though she also considered careers in the theater and in teaching. Although her father was opposed on principle to women achieving a higher education, he agreed to let her go to college after she promised not to ask him for financial support.

By the early 1900s, most colleges and universities in Germany had been opened to women. Though there were still few female students, Horney could choose from a number of good medical schools because of her strong preparation. She began her medical education at the University of Freiburg, but as her interests in psychology developed, she transferred to Göttingen and finally to the University of Berlin, the most prestigious of Europe's medical schools. In Berlin, she set up a household with her mother, who had separated from her husband in 1904.

For the most part Horney's early college years were demanding but contented. She worked hard and enjoyed an active social life. In 1909, she fell in love with and married a fellow university student, Oskar Horney, who was studying political science and economics. Horney soon found the demands of being a wife and completing medical school exhausting. Her responsibilities increased with the birth of her first daughter, ***Brigitte Horney**, in 1911. In that year Karen also faced two other deeply emotional events—the unexpected death of her mother **Clotilde**, and the beginning of serious marital problems.

She soon sought psychoanalytic treatment for depression. Her analyst was Karl Abraham, one of Sigmund Freud's followers and the first practicing analyst in Berlin. At that time, Freud's theories of human psychology were revolutionizing the mental health profession in Germany and across Europe. The field of psychoanalysis had only recently emerged as a viable scientific occupation. Since Horney had always been interested in the emotional and psychological causes and manifestations of illness, she felt drawn to the psychoanalytic explanations of the unconscious motivations of behavior. Although she terminated her own psychoanalysis after a year, she had found her calling in psychiatry and became a founding member of the newly formed Berlin Psychoanalytic Society. After completing her medical degree and passing her examinations in 1913, Horney served an internship in the Urban Hospital of Berlin. There, she treated both physically and mentally ill patients, finding the work challenging but rewarding.

The internship was followed by residencies in the Neurology Clinic of Berlin and in a private psychiatrist's practice where she assisted in the treatment of veterans experiencing psychoses following the trauma of war. At the outbreak of the First World War in 1914, Horney began to train in psychiatry at the Berlin-Lankwitz Sanitarium, assisting the professional psychiatrists. She remained there until 1918. Becoming a licensed medical practitioner in Germany required a doctoral thesis in addition to clinical training after college, and Horney completed her thesis on post-traumatic psychosis in 1915. In that year her third and last child, **Renate Horney**, was born; her second child **Marianne** (**H. Von Eckardt**) had been born in 1913.

The problems in her failing marriage and the burden of raising three small children did not deter Horney from her determination to go into practice as a psychoanalyst. This caused considerable tension in the Horney household; as adults, her daughters resented what they perceived as their mother's detachment and the series of governesses who raised and educated them in Karen's absence.

Karen Horney

Following Germany's defeat in World War I, Berlin psychoanalysts saw a dramatic increase in the number of people seeking psychiatric treatment. Horney finally felt ready to go into practice in 1919 and became the first female analyst at the Berlin Psychoanalytic Clinic and Institute. She was one of only a handful of women analysts in Germany but generally found acceptance among her male peers; this acceptance may have been due to the positive reception of her thesis on post-traumatic psychosis by Sigmund Freud himself. She was affiliated with the Berlin Clinic for over a decade, as both an instructor and analyst. Yet while she enjoyed considerable professional success in the early 1920s, her personal life was unhappy, and she re-entered analysis under Dr. Hans Sachs in 1921.

Oskar Horney had prospered as a manager in a Berlin investment firm until the general postwar economic downturn and rapid inflation caused the firm to collapse. Following this and some poor investments of the family money, he was forced to declare bankruptcy in 1923. The sudden end to his career and fortune led to an emotional breakdown in 1924 from which he never fully recovered. The couple lived apart after 1920, formally separated in 1926, and finally divorced in 1937. Horney did not remarry. Although in the 1930s she was involved in numerous love affairs with male colleagues, none of the relationships were serious or lasting.

Fortunately, analysis is not the only way to resolve inner conflicts. Life itself still remains a very effective therapist.

—Karen Horney

In 1922, Horney presented her first paper at the Psychoanalytic Congress in Berlin. Her presentation drew the largest audience at the conference and generated considerable controversy when she strongly criticized the widely accepted theory of penis-envy (that all girls subconsciously wish to have a penis, which affects their emotional development). It was one of the basic tenets of Freudian theory, and, as Freud himself was chairing the Congress, Horney was making a bold and possibly risky statement in presenting her paper. While she did not reject the concept of penis-envy entirely, she did deny Freud's insistence on its primacy in a woman's psychological development. Instead Horney argued that women's development had to be viewed on its own terms, not seen as a derivative of male development. Horney further surprised her audience by suggesting that there was evidence that women's primary role in reproduction caused "womb-envy" in men. She continued to publish articles which further developed her theory of feminine psychology and sexuality through the 1920s. She also came to question Freud's biological determinism in terms of sexual development, and challenged the male-centered view that patterns of women's psychic growth are the products of their physical difference from men. Although modern-day analysts commonly recognize these ideas as valid, most of Horney's colleagues were unwilling to deviate from Freud's views of women's inferiority, and she often found her ideas rejected by other analysts. In 1931, Horney quit the Berlin Psychoanalytic Society by mutual consent with its members, who saw her ideas as revolutionary and unacceptable.

By 1932, Horney's ideas had spread to the emerging psychoanalytic community in the United States, and she was offered the position of assistant director of the Chicago Psychoanalytic Institute. The director of the Institute was a former colleague and friend, Franz Alexander. She accepted and left Berlin with her two younger daughters, hoping to find in the United States a more open professional atmosphere in which she could develop her theories. Horney also hoped to escape the worsening economic crisis in Germany and the growing threat of National Socialism, which attacked psychoanalysis as a "Jewish science." She served in an administrative and teaching role until she passed the American medical exams in 1933, which allowed her to practice psychiatry, and she began to see patients in addition to her other duties. In this period, Horney's modifications to Freudian theory continued to evolve beyond her critique of his views on feminine psychosexual development. Although her work would always remain rooted in Freudian psychology, her publications began to discuss the possible origins of psychological problems in the patient's social and cultural milieu instead of looking for the source of disorders only in childhood development, as Freud did. Again her ideas generated controversy among her peers.

After only two years, Horney left the Chicago Institute to join the faculty of the New York Psychoanalytic Institute. Her decision to leave Chicago was primarily the result of disagreements with the administrative and psychiatric practices of Franz Alexander, who had come to reject Horney's emphasis on the social origins of mental illness. Settling in New York, Horney also accepted a faculty position at the New School for Social Research, and started a flourishing private psychoanalytic practice as well.

Horney's first book was published in 1937. *The Neurotic Personality of Our Time* outlined her theory of the social origins of neuroses. Aimed at a non-professional audience, it offered a strongly worded critique of Freud's emphasis on the role of instinctual drives in child development. Horney believed that socialization, especially treatment by the parents, was more influential than instinct in determining a child's adult personality and behavior. In this book, Horney pioneered the use of supporting evidence from fields outside psychiatry to support psychoanalytic theory; she drew not only on the cases of analysis patients but on anthropological studies which emphasized the role of culture in an individual's life. *The Neurotic Personality of Our Time* presented a significant challenge to traditional Freudianism by suggesting that the processes of psychic growth which Freud had seen as universal to humanity were really variable and culturally determined.

In 1939, Horney published *New Ways in Psychoanalysis,* a collection of essays which continued her critique of Freudianism but focused on new methods and techniques of therapy. At no point in her career, however, did Horney reject Freudian psychology entirely, or consider her work destructive of its principles; indeed she admired Freud immensely and considered herself a follower. Instead, Horney saw herself as refining Freud's ideas, working within a basic Freudian framework but discarding parts of his theories which had proven themselves, in her opinion, to be fruitless or invalid.

Despite the controversy these two books generated, or perhaps because of it, both were widely read by psychologists and students for years after they were issued. However, Horney again faced considerable opposition from her peers, and in 1941 she resigned her position at the New York Psychoanalytic Institute after the disapproving administration curtailed her teaching duties.

Together with fellow analysts Erich Fromm and ***Clara Thompson**, Horney then organized the Association for the Advancement of Psychoanalysis, with an affiliated educational institution, the American Institute for Psychoanalysis, of which Horney would serve as dean. These actions upset the membership of the American Psychoanalytic Association, which voted to expel Horney. In part, this move was a reaction to her unorthodox views. More important, the APA saw the new professional organization as a threat, for in founding a rival association of analysts, Horney was essentially splitting the psychoanalyst community into two camps.

Undaunted by the APA's expulsion, Horney and her supporters launched a new scholarly journal, *The American Journal of Psychoanalysis,* to provide a forum for like-minded psychiatrists to discuss new theories and techniques. In addition to her duties as dean of the institute, she also served as editor of the journal from 1941. The 1940s were characterized by the maturing of Horney's theory of neurosis. In her next three books, *Self-Analysis, Our Inner Conflicts,* and *Neurosis and Human Growth,* Horney also began to develop a model for the individual's growth towards what she called "self-realization," the fulfillment of one's innate potential. Yet again Horney inspired both criticism and admiration from colleagues. Some endorsed her theory of treating the "total self" and the benefits of self-analysis; others saw as unrealistically optimistic Horney's positive view of the potential to overcome neurosis through analysis, which could bring out creative, constructive forces.

During the years of World War II, Horney, now approaching 60, divided her time between New York and her daughter Renate's home in Mexico. This was a period of personal change for Horney, and a period of reconciliation with her grown daughters. As all of her adult life had been devoted to her work, Horney had not developed close relationships with her children. Her priorities appear to have changed after 1940, however; although she remained remarkably active as a teacher, writer, and private analyst, she made efforts to reestablish relationships with her children, especially Marianne, who had followed her into psychiatry. Horney also developed an intimate friendship with **Gertrude Lederer-Eckardt**, a twice-married physical therapist; they met when Marianne Horney married Lederer's son. Lederer and Horney became friends, and by 1942 their relationship had become so close that they decided to live together. The two women bought houses together and traveled frequently, sharing a home until Horney's death. Although some biographers have seen Lederer as merely a secretary to Horney, the length and intimacy of their relationship shows a genuine devotion and emotional connection unlike any of Horney's previous attachments. Lederer was a companion and confidante whom Horney depended on emotionally. Her obvious importance in Horney's life challenges the conclusion of biographers that Horney did not form close emotional attachments to others as an adult.

The later years of the decade were for Horney a period of spiritual, artistic, and philosophical learning. Her search for personal "self-realization" led her to explore painting and the arts as well as the Eastern religions, particularly Zen Buddhism and existentialist philosophy. Although she never practiced any religion, she hoped to derive from Zen philosophy a spiritual dimension to enrich her scientific, psychoanalytic theory. Despite failing health in 1950 and 1951, she continued her internal effort to connect her own spiritual, physical, and psychological selves. In the summer of 1952, she traveled to Japan to study the ideas of Zen Buddhism in more depth, although she confessed that reconciling its complex principles with her own theories proved more difficult than she had expected.

After returning to New York, Horney became critically ill with liver cancer. Despite the care she received from doctors, Gertrude Lederer-Eckardt, and her daughter Brigitte, her health failed rapidly. She died on December 4, 1952, at age 67. Although Horney's intellectual influence waned for a period following her death, many of her theories have now become commonplace in our understanding of human psychology and behavior. The publication in 1967 of her collected essays on women's psychosexual development, *Feminine Psychology,* brought Horney to the attention of the emerging feminist movement in the United States and Europe, and her works have been widely rediscovered in the past several decades. Her *American Journal of Psychoanalysis* is still a leading publication, and her Institute is still in operation as well. The Karen Horney Clinic in New York, founded in 1952, and the International Karen Horney Society also testify to ongoing professional recognition for Horney's originality and insight into the human psyche.

SOURCES:

Quinn, Susan. *A Mind of Her Own: The Life of Karen Horney*. NY: Simon & Schuster, 1987.

Rubins, Jack. *Karen Horney: Gentle Rebel of Psychoanalysis*. NY: Dial Press, 1978.

SUGGESTED READING:

Horney, Karen. *The Adolescent Diaries of Karen Horney*. NY: Basic Books, 1980.

———. *Feminine Psychology.* Edited by Harold Kelman. NY: W.W. Norton, 1967.

Mitchell, Stephen. *Freud and Beyond: A History of Modern Psychoanalytic Thought*. NY: Basic Books, 1995.

COLLECTIONS:

Correspondence of Karen Horney, Rare Book and Manuscript Library, Columbia University, New York.

Papers of Karen Horney, Brill Library, New York Psychoanalytic Institute, New York.

Laura York,
freelance writer in women's history and medieval history,
Riverside, California

Horniman, Annie (1860–1937)

English theater patron and manager who pioneered the modern repertory movement. *Name variations: Miss Horniman; Miss A.E.F. Horniman. Born Annie Elizabeth Fredericka Horniman in Manchester, England, in 1860; died in 1937; daughter of F.J. Horniman (a tea merchant); attended Slade School; never married; no children.*

A major influence in early 20th-century theater in England and Ireland, Annie Horniman was born in 1860, the daughter of a wealthy Manchester tea merchant who had few cultural interests and would not let her attend the theater. Horniman's fascination with drama was sparked by her introduction to poet and playwright William Butler Yeats, whom she met at a gathering of the Order of the Golden Dawn (a congregation of theosophists), in London. She subsequently served as Yeats' secretary for five years, during which time she became impassioned with his plays and determined to make them known. In 1894, she funded a repertory season at London's Avenue Theater (later the Playhouse), which included the first commercial presentation of Yeats' play *The Land of Heart's Desire*. Thereafter, Horniman turned her attention to the Irish National Theater (later the Irish National Dramatic Society), the pet project of Yeats and Lady ***Augusta Gregory**. In 1904, Horniman purchased two adjacent buildings in Dublin, the Mechanics Institute in Abbey Street, a theater built in 1820, and the City Morgue in Marlborough Street, both known as fire hazards. Under the direction of architect Joseph Holloway and technical advisor Willie Fay, they were transformed into the Abbey Theatre which opened on December 27, 1904. Horniman continued to provide an annual subsidy for the theater and often made up for the losses the company incurred on tour.

Annie Horniman, self-described as "a middle-aged, middle-class, suburban, dissenting spinster," was reputedly a stubborn and difficult woman. Tall, thin, and given to costuming herself in heavy robes of tapestry-like material, she was a formidable presence and often interfered in matters beyond her province. By some accounts, Horniman withdrew her subsidy of the Abbey in 1910, when Yeats refused to close the theater during the funeral of Edward VII. In reality, she had already abandoned the Abbey two years earlier for a new theater project, a turn of events that drew venom from Jack Kahane of the Obelisk Press. "I despise Miss Horniman," he wrote, "the ugly bedizened spinster in whose veins ran tea . . . for having begun a fine scheme, set alight a blaze of endeavor, and then wrecked it, doused it for I know not what stupid, spoiled rich woman's whim. Bad cess [luck] to her."

In 1908, Horniman purchased and refurbished the Gaiety Theater, a former music hall in her hometown of Manchester, England, and turned it into England's first repertory theater. Between 1908 and 1917, she produced more than 200 plays, most of which were directed by Lewis Casson (husband of actress ***Sybil Thorndike**, a member of the company). Half of the productions were of new works, including

St. John Ervine's *Jane Clegg,* Stanley Houghton's *Hindle Wakes,* Harold Brighouse's *Hobson's Choice,* and John Mansfield's *The Tragedy of Nan.* Never a financial success, the venture shut down in 1917, after which Horniman apparently found new challenges outside the theater.

Annie Horniman's contribution to the British theater was unique and far-reaching. Her support of George Bernard Shaw was in itself of major significance to the modern stage, and her pioneering work at the Gaiety gave rise to repertory theaters in London and other British cities. (Theater manager ***Lilian Baylis** is said to have modeled the Old Vic after Horniman's Gaiety.) Annie Horniman was awarded the rank of Companion of Honour before her death in 1937.

SOURCES:

Hartnoll, Phyllis and Peter Found, eds. *The Concise Oxford Companion to the Theater.* Oxford and NY: The Oxford University Press, 1993.

Macgowan, Kenneth and William Melnitz. *The Living Stage: A History of the World Theater.* Englewood Cliffs, NJ: Prentice-Hall, 1955.

Rogers, W.G. *Ladies Bountiful.* NY: Harcourt, Brace & World, 1968.

Barbara Morgan,
Melrose, Massachusetts

Horsbrugh, Florence (1889–1969)

British minister of education who was the first woman to serve in the Cabinet of a Conservative government. *Name variations: raised to the peerage in 1959 as Baroness Horsbrugh, P.C., G.B.E. Born Florence Gertrude Horsbrugh in Edinburgh, Scotland, in 1889; died in Edinburgh on December 6, 1969; daughter of Henry Moncrieff Horsbrugh (a chartered accountant) and Mary Harriet Stark (Christie) Horsbrugh; attended Lansdowne House, Edinburgh, and St. Hilda's, Folkestone, Kent; had two sisters; never married.*

Awarded the Commander of the British Empire (CBE, 1929); made a life peer (1959).

Was a Conservative member of Parliament, representing Dundee, the first Conservative from that district in 100 years (1931–45); was parliamentary secretary for the Ministry of Health (1939–45); was parliamentary secretary for the Ministry of Food (1945); appointed minister of education by Winston Churchill (November 2, 1951), becoming the first woman to hold a post of Cabinet rank in a Conservative government; served in that position until 1954.

Florence Horsbrugh, who played an important role in the preparatory stage of creating a national health system for the entire United Kingdom, did much to advance the cause of women. She was born in Edinburgh in 1889, the youngest of three daughters of an accountant, and received a solid education at Lansdowne House, Edinburgh, and St. Hilda's, Folkestone. A conservative and a patriot, Horsbrugh did voluntary service during the last two years of World War I in canteens and national kitchens, work for which she received an MBE in 1920. She was elected to Parliament as a Conservative in 1931, representing Dundee. Her legislative interests included children's welfare issues, and she introduced the private member's bill which in 1939 was passed into law as the Adoption of Children (Regulation) Act of 1939. That same year, she was appointed CBE. Although not an ideological feminist, Horsbrugh worked conscientiously at fulfilling her Parliamentary duties and, in so doing, raised the general status of women in British political life.

In 1936, she was the first British woman serving in the House of Commons to move the address in reply to the King's speech. This took place during the short reign of Edward VIII, and Horsbrugh had to consult the Chief Whip about appropriate dress at a time when male members of Parliament wore court dress and knee breeches, but nobody knew what a woman should wear. According to Horsbrugh, "For a full minute he looked at the floor stunned and speechless, and then said with the utmost gravity—'Evening dress, but *no tiara*'." Other firsts for women achieved by Horsbrugh included being a privy councillor in 1945 and a GBE in 1954. She was one of the first British women delegates to the League of Nations Assembly, serving there in 1933, 1934, and 1935. In 1945, she was a member of the British delegation to the United Nations meeting in San Francisco where that international body's charter was drawn up. In the early 1950s, she was the chief United Kingdom delegate to the seventh session of the general conference of UNESCO in Paris.

On the eve of World War II, Horsbrugh was appointed parliamentary secretary to the Ministry of Health. Once war began, she played an active role in the evacuation of children from London and other large cities to the countryside; she retained this role until 1945, remaining in London throughout the conflict and suffering injuries from a bomb blast during an air raid in 1944. As the war was drawing to a close, she was working on the complex plans for a postwar national health system for the United Kingdom. Although the plan was put into effect by the Labour government after 1945, she made a significant contribution to many of its details. In the caretaker government of June 1945, Horsbrugh was parliamentary secretary to the Ministry of Food, dealing with the countless problems relating to shortages of food supply and transportation issues.

As part of a national rejection of the Conservatives, in 1945 Horsbrugh lost her seat for Dundee. She then became Conservative candidate for Midlothian and Peebles, but was again defeated in the general election of 1950. Pure chance on this occasion brought her back to Parliament. Since the Conservative candidate for the Moss Side division of Manchester had died before polling day, the election there was postponed. Quickly, Horsbrugh was nominated as Conservative candidate and was elected two weeks later in an "extended general" election, winning with a handsome majority. When the Conservatives led by Sir Winston Churchill returned to national power in 1951, she was appointed to the post of minister of education. At first, Horsbrugh was not a member of Prime Minister Churchill's Cabinet, but in 1953 her position was promoted to the status of full member of the Cabinet—making her the first woman to hold a Cabinet post in a Conservative government. Although she had many plans for major improvements in the national educational system, most of these could not be implemented during her period of tenure, which ended with her resignation in October 1954. The large number of children entering schools at the time created unprecedented strains on resources, and with housing a national priority it proved difficult to achieve major educational growth; thus, much of her time in office was a period of consolidation rather than dramatic changes.

Upon her resignation from the government in October 1954, Horsbrugh was created GBE. She did not withdraw from public life, serving as a delegate to the Council of Europe and the Western European Union during the years 1955 through 1960. In 1959, she was made a life peer with the title Baroness Horsbrugh. Often seen in academic circles, she received a number of honorary degrees, including Doctor of Letters from California's Mills College in 1945. The venerable University of Edinburgh awarded Florence Horsbrugh an honorary LL.D. in 1946, and in that same year the Royal College of Surgeons of Edinburgh conferred honorary fellowship of their college on her, making Horsbrugh the first woman to receive such an award in their 440 years of existence. In her obituary, *The Times* of London noted that she "was spirited in controversy and never shrank from the rough and tumble of the party fight. But she was also less severe than she looked; and if her Scots mannerisms were sometimes reminiscent of a very senior school mistress, there was usually a merry twinkle in her eye." A "brilliant and attractive" speaker in Parliament, she was appreciated by those who knew her well for her sense of humor and as a generous friend. Baroness Horsbrugh died at her home in Edinburgh at the age of 80 on December 6, 1969.

SOURCES:

"Baroness Horsbrugh, First Conservative woman Cabinet Minister," in *The Times* [London]. December 8, 1969, p. 10.

Elliot, Katharine. "Horsbrugh, Florence Gertrude," in E.T. Williams and C.S. Nicholls, eds., *The Dictionary of National Biography 1961–1970*. Oxford: Oxford University Press, 1981, pp. 540–541.

"Horsbrugh's gift," in *The Times* [London]. December 8, 1969, p. 8.

John Haag,
Associate Professor, University of Georgia, Athens, Georgia

Horta, Maria Teresa (b. 1937).

See The Three Marias.

Hortense, Queen (1783–1837).

See Hortense de Beauharnais.

Hortense de Beauharnais (1783–1837)

French composer, artist, queen and regent of Holland, and mother of Napoleon III. *Name variations: Hortense, Queen of Holland; Hortense Beauharnais; Hortense Bonaparte; Eugenie Hortense de Beauharnais. Born Eugénie Hortense de Beauharnais in Paris, France, on April 10, 1783; died in Arenenberg, Switzerland, on October 5, 1837; daughter of Alexander (d. 1794), vicomte de Beauharnais, and Empress Josephine (1763–1814, Joséphine Tascher de la Pagerie, later Bonaparte); sister of Eugene de Beauharnais (1781–1824, a viceroy); stepdaughter and sister-in-law of Napoleon I; daughter-in-law of* ****Letizia Bonaparte*** *(1750–1836); married Louis Napoleon (Napoleon's brother who would become king of Holland), in 1802; children—three sons: Charles Napoleon (1802–1807); Napoleon Louis (1804–1831); Louis Napoleon (1808–1873), later Napoleon III, king of France (r. 1852–1870).*

Hortense de Beauharnais was destined to play a role in history if only because Napoleon I was her stepfather. She was born in Paris, France, in 1783, the daughter of Alexander, vicomte de Beauharnais, and Joséphine Tascher de la Pagerie, later Empress ***Josephine.** When Alexander and Josephine separated, Hortense spent her early years on the island of Martinique. After her father's death by guillotine during the bloody Reign of Terror in July 1794, her mother married Napoleon I in 1796. Hortense (age 12) and her brother Eugene de Beauharnais (age 14) were much loved by their stepfather: they returned his affection and would remain loyal to him, even after his fall from power.

In 1802, Empress Josephine arranged the marriage of her 18-year-old daughter to Napoleon's brother Louis Bonaparte, in hopes that Napoleon might accept their children as his heirs. The marriage was doomed from the beginning, with Louis desperately in love with Hortense's cousin Emilie. Louis suffered from a mood disorder as well as crippling arthritis caused by syphilis. He was said to be insanely jealous, often accusing his wife of affairs. When Louis was made king of Holland after French troops conquered that country, she became queen. Hortense and Louis were accepted by the Dutch as the only alternative to being annexed to France.

Far from Paris and locked into a miserable marriage, Hortense initially amused herself with

Hortense de Beauharnais

young officers, including the comte de Flahault who had once been a staff officer of Napoleon. She gave birth to three sons: Charles Napoleon, who died at age four and a half; Napoleon Louis (1804–1831), who would die at age 27; and Louis Napoleon (1808–1873), who would later be known as Napoleon III, king of France (r. 1852–1870). She also branched out into composing and drawing. Her *Partant pour la Syrie* would become the national song of France when Napoleon III reigned, though the composer Drouet claimed falsely that he had written it. Franz Schubert used her *Le bon chevalier* as the basis for his *Variations on a French Song*. Hortense de Beauharnais composed many romantic songs in both French and German.

In 1809, her husband sought, but was not allowed, a divorce by his brother Napoleon and, in the following year, was driven by his domestic misery into exile, abdicating the throne of Holland in favor of his son Napoleon Louis; Hortense was made regent. Her husband spent the rest of his days in Germany and Italy. (Meanwhile, Napoleon, in desperate need of a son and heir, had divorced Josephine in 1809 and married ***Marie Louise of Austria** in 1810.)

The fall from power of Napoleon I, following the defeat at Waterloo in 1815, further disrupted the family. With the empire's end, Hortense and her two sons were issued passports to Switzerland. While they were journeying to a new life, an agent of her husband came to claim the elder son, Napoleon Louis, whose custody he had won; French laws at that time considered only the rights of the father. And, in 1816, the Restoration government passed a law exiling all Bonapartes from France forever.

By 1817, Hortense and her other son, Louis Napoleon, were living in relative seclusion in Thurgau, Switzerland, where she had purchased the Château of Arenenberg. In 1830, Louis Napoleon completed an artillery course with the Swiss army at Thun, and in the following year he and his brother Napoleon Louis associated themselves with an anti-papal rebellion in central Italy. When Napoleon Louis died from a fatal case of measles, Hortense traced Louis Napoleon to a rebel base and transported him out of Italy in a move to protect her sole surviving son. After a brief, quasi-secret and completely illegal stop in France, the mother and son went to England for three months before they secured safe passage back to Switzerland.

Napoleon I's only son died in July 1832, nine years after his father, leaving Louis Napoleon the logical heir to the emperor's legacy. At Strasbourg in October 1836, with a band of fellow conspirators, the young Louis unsuccessfully attempted a coup d'état. He received a lenient punishment; the French authorities placed him on a New York-bound ship, but he returned to Europe the following year to care for his ailing mother. Hortense died of cancer in 1837, after a long illness.

Following her death, when France felt Louis' presence in Switzerland too threatening, he moved voluntarily to England. But Louis-Philippe, the king of France, was deposed in the February 1848 revolution, paving the way for the return of Louis Napoleon to France. He became Emperor Napoleon III in a December 1, 1852, ceremony and made his official imperial entrance to the capital the next day.

SOURCES:

Cohen, Aaron I. *International Encyclopedia of Women Composers*. 2 vols. NY: Books & Music (USA), 1987.

Commire, Anne, ed. *Historic World Leaders*. Detroit, MI: Gale Research, 1993.

Decaux, Alain. *Napoleon's Mother*. London: The Cresset Press, 1962.

Jackson, Guida M. *Women Who Ruled*. ABC-CLIO, 1990.

Seward, Desmond. *Napoleon's Family*. NY: Viking, 1986.

Stirling, Monica. *Madame Letizia: A Portrait of Napoleon's Mother*. NY: Harper & Brothers, 1961.

John Haag,
Athens, Georgia

Hortensia (fl. 1st c. BCE)

***Roman orator.** Flourished in the 1st century BCE; daughter of Quintus Hortensius Hortalus (114–50 BCE), a Roman orator.*

Hortensia was the daughter of the Roman orator Quintus Hortensius Hortalus, known as Hortensius, who, as a leader of the aristocratic party, often clashed with or worked with the orator Cicero. In 42 BCE, Hortensia protested a proposed law that would allow women's possessions to be taxed to fund a civil war. Hortensia argued that women should not be required to fund men's follies when women were not legally involved in the decision making. Though the speech is no longer extant, Roman writer Quintilian noted its importance, and Greek historian Appian issued his own version.

Horton, Ann (1743–1808)

***Duchess of Cumberland and Strathearn.** Name variations: Ann or Anne Luttrell. Born on January 24, 1743 (some sources cite 1742), in St. Marylebone,*

London, England; died on December 28, 1808, in Trieste, Italy; daughter of Simon Luttrell, Lord Irnham, 1st earl of Carhampton, and ***Judith Maria Lawes;*** *married Christopher Horton, on August 4, 1765 (died); married Henry Frederick (1745–1790), duke of Cumberland and Strathearn, on October 2, 1771; children: (first marriage) one son.*

Ann Horton was a widow when she married Henry Frederick, duke of Cumberland, brother to King George III, in 1771. Her father Simon Luttrell, who sat in the Irish House of Lords and British House of Commons, was considered somewhat of a scoundrel. Because of this, the marriage was a joke in higher circles. George III had objected to the impending nuptials because "in any country a prince marrying a subject is looked upon as dishonorable." When Henry Frederick married Ann Horton without the king's consent, George demanded that his brother never mention the marriage and never let Ann Horton take his name publicly. Henry refused. It was announced from the palace that any who paid court to the duke and duchess would not be received by the king and queen. Wrote John Brooke in *George III*: "Ann Horton was a good wife to the Duke of Cumberland. She kept him straight—after his marriage he never looked at another woman—and she did her best to prevent him making a fool of himself in politics. It was not her fault if she failed." Allegedly, Henry had previously been married to ***Olivia Wilmot**, who died in 1774.

SOURCES:

Brooke, John. *George III*. London: Constable, 1972.

Horton, Christiana (c. 1696–c. 1756)

English actress. *Born around 1696; died around 1756.*

Discovered by the actor-manager Barton Booth at Southwark Fair, Christiana Horton first appeared in London at Drury Lane as Melinda in *The Recruiting Officer* in 1714. She would remain there for the next 20 years, followed by 15 years at Covent Garden. At both houses, she was cast in all the leading tragedy and comedy parts. Booth claimed that the actress was the rightful successor of ***Anne Oldfield**. Christiana Horton was the original Mariana in Henry Fielding's *Miser* (1733). She also appeared as Mrs. Millamant in *Way of the World* and as Belinda in *Old Bachelor.*

Horton, Gladys.

See Marvelettes.

Horton, Mildred McAfee
(1900–1994)

Seventh president of Wellesley College who was also director of the U.S. Navy's WAVES during World War II. *Name variations: Mildred McAfee; (nickname) Miss Mac. Born Mildred Helen McAfee in Parkville, Missouri, on May 12, 1900; died in Randolph, New Hampshire, on September 2, 1994; daughter of Dr. Cleland Boyd (a minister) and Harriet (Brown) McAfee; graduate of the Francis W. Parker School, Chicago, Illinois; Vassar College, B.A., 1920; attended Columbia University; University of Chicago, M.A., 1928; married Douglas Horton (a minister and the first world leader of the Congregational Christian Churches), in 1945.*

Served as dean of women and professor of sociology at Centre College, Kentucky (1927–32); served as dean of the college of women at Oberlin (1934–36); chosen president of Wellesley College (1936); appointed director of the women's reserve of the U.S. Naval Reserve (1942), with the rank of lieutenant commander; held the rank of captain (1943–46); resigned as president of Wellesley College (1949) to join husband in church and educational work in New York City; became first female president of the American Board of Commissioners for Foreign Missions of the Congregational Christian Churches (1959).

The daughter of a minister, and descended from a long line of church people and educators, Mildred McAfee was born in Parkville, Missouri, in 1900. She was a graduate of Vassar College and received her master's degree from the University of Chicago in 1928. Horton taught at various schools in the Chicago area and at Tusculum College in Tennessee before her appointment as professor of sociology and dean of women at Centre College in Kentucky, a position she held from 1927 to 1932. For two years beginning in 1932, she served as secretary of the Associate Alumnae of Vassar College, then became dean of women at Oberlin College. In 1936, at age 36, Horton was appointed president of Wellesley, the second youngest president in the history of the college. Horton was selected after an exhaustive 18-month search, during which trustees interviewed some 100 candidates and 1,000 alumnae, looking for a combination of "intellectual honesty, leadership, tolerance, *savoir faire*, sympathetic understanding of youth, vision, and a sense of humor." Upon her appointment, Horton declared herself a staunch conservative. "I haven't attempted any innovations at Oberlin College," she said, "and I don't contemplate any at Wellesley."

In 1942, when President Franklin Roosevelt signed the bill creating the Women's Reserve in the navy, Horton, who had served on the Educational Advisory Committee for the Navy Training Program, was appointed to direct the Women Appointed for Volunteer Emergency Service (WAVES). Given a leave from Wellesley, she became the first female officer in the Naval Reserve and, as such, directed the 82,000 navy women who served as decoders, radio operators, and air-traffic controllers during World War II.

Horton returned to Wellesley in 1946, where she was affectionately known as "Miss Mac," even after her 1945 marriage to Reverend Douglas Horton, a widower of 54 who had served as dean of Harvard Divinity School and was the first world leader of the Congregational Christian Churches. Horton, who left Wellesley in 1949, later became the first female president of the American Board of Commissioners for Foreign Missions of the Congregational Christian Churches (1959).

Mildred McAfee Horton received numerous award and honors during her lifetime, including the Distinguished Service Medal, the American Campaign Medal, and the World War II Victory Medal. In 1969, she was given the University of New Hampshire's Charles Holmes Pettee Medal for her "outstanding service to the state, the nation and the world." Earlier, in 1960, Wellesley College had named a new $1 million dormitory "McAfee Hall." Mildred McAfee Horton died in a New Hampshire nursing home at the age of 94.

SOURCES:

Black, Maxine, ed. *Current Biography 1942*. NY: H.W. Wilson, 1942.

"Milestones," in *Time*. September 12, 1994, p. 37.

"Obituaries," in *The Boston Globe*. September 3, 1994.

Barbara Morgan,
Melrose, Massachusetts

Hosmer, Harriet (1830–1908)

First American woman to achieve an international reputation as a neoclassical sculptor. *Name variations: "Hatty." Born Harriet Goodhue Hosmer on October 9, 1830, in Watertown, Massachusetts, a city on the Charles River in the heart of "literary" New England; died on February 21, 1908, at the home of friends in Watertown; daughter of Hiram Hosmer (a physician), and Sarah (Grant) Hosmer; only one of their four children to survive to adulthood; educated at Mrs. Charles Sedgwick's School for Girls in Lenox, Massachusetts; studied sculpture with Paul Stephenson in Boston; denied admittance to Boston Medical School's anatomy course; moved to St. Louis, studied anatomy at Missouri Medical College.*

Created first major sculpture, Hesper, the Evening Star *(1852); traveled to Rome (November 1852); studied with renowned British sculptor John Gibson; established reputation in Rome (1853) with marble busts of* Daphne *and* Medusa, *followed by the full-length* Oenone *(1855); completed two popular sculptures,* Puck *and* Will o' the Wisp, *followed by the critically acclaimed* Beatrice Cenci *(1857); her seven-foot marble,* Zenobia *(1859) brought international praise; rendered last full-scale sculpture* Queen Isabella *for the World's Columbian Exposition in Chicago (1893).*

Collections—major sculptures: Daphne *(Metropolitan Museum of Art, American Wing, 1853);* Medusa *(Detroit Institute of Art, 1854);* The Clasped Hands of the Brownings *(Schlesinger Library at Harvard, Armstrong-Browning Library, and Baylor University, 1853);* Waking Faun *and* Sleeping Faun *(Forbes Collection, New York, 1854);* Oenone *(St. Louis Mercantile Library, and Steinberg Gallery, Washington College, 1855);* Puck *(National Museum of American Art, Wadsworth Atheneum, Hartford, and Chrysler Museum, Norfolk, 1856);* Will o' the Wisp *(Chrysler Museum, Norfolk, 1856);* Beatrice Cenci *(St. Louis Mercantile Library, 1857);* Tomb of Judith Falconnet *(Max-Planck Institut, Rome, 1857–58);* Zenobia *(Wadsworth Atheneum, Hartford, 1859);* Thomas Hart Benton *(Lafayette Park, St. Louis, 1868).*

As a child, Harriet Hosmer enjoyed a life of remarkable freedom. A family friend was heard to remark that the young Harriet, known then and throughout her life to friends and family as Hatty, was the lamentable product of "too much spoiling." The indulgence of her doting father, a physician in Watertown, Massachusetts, was understandable; before Hatty's fifth birthday, Hiram Hosmer had lost first his wife, then Hatty's two infant brothers, and finally her sister Helen—all to tuberculosis. Dr. Hosmer became convinced that a vigorous, unconstrained outdoor life was indispensable to the health, and perhaps survival, of his remaining child. He furnished young Hatty with a pistol, a horse, a dog, and a small, silver-prowed gondola with velvet seats, and he encouraged her to explore nature. Hatty obliged, spending much of her time out of doors and filling her room with wild creatures she had killed and stuffed.

By all accounts, Hosmer was something of a wild creature herself, and neighborhood families were loath to have their children play with the roughneck whose misdeeds and pranks were legendary in the small community on the banks of the Charles River. Hosmer would later recall (not without some pride), that by the time she reached adolescence she had been expelled from three different schools. In her early years, Hosmer's stubborn individuality and creative energy found an outlet in her secret "studio," a clay pit beneath a riverbank, where she modeled horses, dogs, sheep, women, and men, for hours on end. A playmate later recalled coming across Hatty one day, armed with her ivory-handled pistol, proud of the fact that she had just shot a robin to use as a model for one of her clay sculptures. A crack shot, young Hosmer was known as well for her daredevil stunts on horseback and for her dexterity with bow and arrow. In an era of conformity in which young ladies were expected to spend their time in learning needlework, music, and the art of conversation, Hatty Hosmer was widely—and unfavorably—regarded as "eccentric."

After a pair of particularly outrageous escapades in her 16th year—one in which she was caught uncoupling the passenger cars from a train's engine, and the other in which she inserted a death notice in the local newspapers for a very-much-alive neighbor—Dr. Hosmer made arrangements to send Hatty to Mrs. Charles Sedgwick's School for Girls at Lenox, Massachusetts.

A progressive educator, **Elizabeth Sedgwick** succeeded in intellectually and artistically challenging her young charges; although the ebullient Hatty Hosmer was scarcely subdued, she did settle in and enjoy her years at the school. Hosmer developed a lifelong fondness for Sedgwick, a feeling that was reciprocated. Though Elizabeth Sedgwick pronounced Hatty "the most difficult pupil to manage that I ever saw," she added that she had never seen one "in whom I took so deep an interest and whom I learned to love so well." Hosmer's high spirits were infectious, and her classmates remembered her as "the life of the house."

Among other subjects at Mrs. Sedgwick's, Hatty studied Latin, Greek, French, and hygiene. There too she became acquainted with some of the leading figures of the age. Frequent visitors at "The Hive," the name given to the Sedgwick residence, included Ralph Waldo Emerson, Charles Sumner, Nathaniel Hawthorne, actress ***Fanny Kemble**, and ***Catharine Sedgwick**, the well-known novelist and sister of Charles Sedgwick. It was there too that Hatty formed the friendship with **Cornelia Crow (Carr)** that would prove the most durable and consequential legacy of her years at Mrs. Sedgwick's School.

Harriet Hosmer

Wayland Crow, Cornelia's father, was a wealthy and influential St. Louis businessman who developed a special bond with Hatty Hosmer. He was a self-made man who perhaps saw in her exuberance and ambition a spirit kindred to his own. He would prove a loyal and lifelong benefactor, providing Hosmer with the support and encouragement she often lacked from her own father. Although Hiram Hosmer supported his daughter's ambition to be a sculptor, he was a lonely widower who would have preferred to keep his only child closer to home, a task that would prove impossible.

Leaving Mrs. Sedgwick's in 1849, Hosmer returned to her father's home determined to become a "real" sculptor. Rejecting the acceptable outlets for a woman's artistic inclinations—the genteel art of cameo carving, or the painting of delicate watercolors—Hosmer instead set her sights on carving marble and casting bronze. She envisioned her own monumental works exhibited alongside the ranks of those she had long admired in Boston's Atheneum. In her ambition, she displayed the characteristic indifference to custom that had marked her early years. Her dreams may have been helped along by the Atheneum's acquisition in 1848 of its first sculpture by a woman, a bust of Robert Rantoul done by **Joanna Quiner**, an older woman who lived in nearby Beverly, Massachusetts.

With her father's help, Hosmer began her studies in Boston with Peter Stephenson, an English-born sculptor and highly regarded teacher. Hosmer took to her studies with the same exuberant energy that had characterized her childhood projects, and soon she had completed a portrait bust of a child as well as a wax sculpture of the head of Byron. Stymied by her lack of knowledge of human anatomy, a fundamental field of study for would-be sculptors, Hatty persuaded her father to try to use his influence in the Boston Medical Society to procure her a place in an anatomy class. Dr. Hosmer's inquiries met with shock and disapproval on the part of his colleagues. A disappointed and frustrated Hatty left soon afterwards to visit her friend Cornelia Crow in St. Louis.

Wayland Crow succeeded where Hiram Hosmer had failed; he convinced a friend, Joseph Nash McDowell, director of the Missouri Medical College, to allow Hatty to matriculate in order to study anatomy. This she did, attending every lecture in a plain brown bonnet—intended perhaps to preserve her modesty—that would become her trademark in St. Louis. At the end of her course of study, Hosmer traveled alone down the Mississippi on a steamboat, enjoying a series of hair-raising adventures prior to her return to Watertown. Once back in New England, Hosmer returned to her work. Wielding a four-and-a-half-pound lead sculptor's mallet, she put in ten hours a day in the studio her father had built for her, working on a marble bust of *Hesper, the Evening Star*.

It was while she was working in Watertown and studying in Boston that Hatty met the famous author and abolitionist, ***Lydia Maria Child**. Child brought *Hesper* to the notice of the public, writing lyrically of the grace and charm of the statue. That summer, Hosmer also met the famous actress ***Charlotte Cushman**, who was immediately drawn to the talented young sculptor. Cushman lived in Rome when she was not fulfilling speaking and acting engagements, and she encouraged Hatty to come to Rome to study with the greatest male sculptors of the age. Hatty needed no convincing, but Dr. Hosmer only gradually acceded to Cushman's ambitious plans for his daughter.

In the autumn of 1852, Hatty and her father sailed for Rome. In Hosmer's portmanteau were her diploma in anatomy from the Missouri Medical College and two daguerreotypes of *Hesper*. Arriving in Rome, she and her father were able to gain an audience with John Gibson, widely regarded as England's foremost sculptor. Although Gibson did not customarily take students, after viewing the pictures of *Hesper,* he agreed to take Hatty on. She was elated, writing home to describe the thrill of being assigned to work in the studio where the great sculptor Canova had worked some 50 years before.

The friendship that sprang up between teacher and pupil was deep and lasting. Hosmer worked diligently, doing engravings, books, casts, and copying the masterpieces of classical sculpture. Gibson was pleased with her progress, admiring both her industry and her talent. A visit by the great German sculptor, Christian Rauch, drew praise for her artistic merit, a fact Gibson reported in a letter to Hiram Hosmer.

After Hosmer had been in Rome for six months, she received her first commission; Wayland Crow agreed to purchase her first statue. She began work on *Daphne,* which she described in detail in a letter to him. Altogether absorbed in her art, the young artist wrote her friend Cornelia on April 22, 1853:

> Don't ask me if I was happy before, don't ask me if I am happy now, but ask me if my constant state of mind is felicitous, beatific, and I will reply, "yes." It never entered into my head that anybody could be so content on this earth, as I am here. I wouldn't live anywhere else but Rome. . . . America is a grand and glorious country in some respects, but this is a better place for an artist.

Hatty's exuberance was no doubt enhanced by the pleasure she took in turning over to a team of Italian workers the heavy task of executing the actual final marble statue itself. Whereas in Watertown, she had been exhausted by having to work the marble herself, the custom among neoclassical sculptors in Rome was to produce first a *concetto,* the concept, followed by a rough model, the *bozzetto,* generally a clay model. The studio workers then assisted the sculptor in building a skeleton to support a full-size clay model, the *modello grande.* This became the working model for the final marble statue itself, which was executed by skilled artisans using a series of frames and plumb lines to duplicate exactly the artist's creation.

Outside the studio, Hatty had become part of an expatriate artists' colony that included some of the most eminent figures of the age. Along with sculptors Thomas Crawford, Frederic Leighton, and Randolph Story, Hosmer was soon spending "salon" evenings with Robert and ***Elizabeth Barrett Browning**, Luther Terry,

Fanny Kemble and her sister ***Adelaide Kemble** Sartoris, the novelist William Thackeray, and Charlotte Cushman, who continued to take a lively interest in Hosmer's career.

In 1853, Hosmer completed *Daphne,* its delicately curved lines and neoclassical form demonstrating her increasing mastery of form. This was followed by *Medusa,* in which the subject's snake-like locks were depicted as a sort of tiara. In order to render the snakes more faithfully, Hosmer caught and chloroformed a live snake (later set free). Gibson was very pleased with the *Medusa,* writing to Hatty's father that her ability to portray the roundness of flesh was "unsurpassed." Indeed, Hosmer's *Medusa* was a powerful rendering of a familiar subject—one in which the coldness of marble and the strict adherence to classical form was softened by the warmth and humanity of the facial expression.

Hosmer essayed her first full-length sculpture in 1855, with *Oenone,* the wife deserted by Paris when he fell in love with Helen of Troy. Oenone is depicted sitting on the ground gazing downward, the picture of dejection, the curve of back and arm testifying to Hosmer's increasing skill as a sculptor. While her first subjects had all been women, for her next subject Hosmer turned to Puck, the beloved Shakespearean sprite, perhaps sensing the commercial appeal of a lighter and more playful subject. *Puck,* "a laugh in marble" in the words of one critic, was a great success; Hosmer earned almost $30,000 by selling marble copies. The Prince of Wales purchased a copy of *Puck,* bringing Hosmer no small measure of public attention. *Will o' the Wisp,* a companion piece to *Puck,* was completed soon after, and while not as popular as *Puck,* it nonetheless further enhanced Hosmer's reputation.

On commission from an anonymous friend of Wayland Crow's, Hosmer created **Beatrice Cenci* in 1857, a figure from Italian history that had more recently been the subject of a play by Shelley. In the play, Cenci arranged the murder of her brutal and incestuous father. Hosmer chose to portray Cenci sleeping on her prison couch, awaiting execution. *Beatrice Cenci* proved the most critically successful of all Hosmer's efforts to date. It traveled to England, where it was exhibited at the Royal Academy and treated to an evening illumination, a dramatic show intended to heighten the statue's effect. There the artist Charles Eastlake, president of the academy, declared it "really a beautiful work of art." From London, *Beatrice Cenci* traveled to Boston, where it drew visitors from throughout New England. It went on to triumph in New York and Philadelphia before reaching its final destination, St. Louis.

Hosmer's next work brought her an unusual honor. She was commissioned in 1857 to do a sculpture for the tomb of **Judith Falconnet** in S. Andrea delle Fratte Church in Rome. This was the first Italian tomb sculpture ever done by an American, and one of the few before or since to have been created by a woman. Adjudged an artistic triumph, its completion was a major accomplishment for its diminutive 27-year-old creator.

By 1859, Hosmer had secured enough commissions and learned enough from John Gibson to establish her own studio. It was in that year too that she was honored with membership in the Accademia de' Quiriti, an accomplishment that she hoped would prove "bitter" to those artistic friends who "laughed at the idea of a woman becoming an artist at all."

> [B]ut what a country mine is for women! Here every woman has a chance, if she is bold enough to avail herself of it. . . . I honor every woman who has strength enough to stand up and be laughed at, if necessary. That is a bitter pill we must all swallow in the beginning, but I regard these pills as tonics quite essential.
>
> —**Harriet G. Hosmer, July 29, 1869**

Hosmer's next major project was larger than any work to date. **Zenobia* depicted the legendary Palmyran queen who was brought in chains and paraded through the streets of Rome. Nathaniel Hawthorne described the partially finished clay model at Hosmer's Rome studio, writing afterwards of having "never been more impressed by a piece of modern sculpture." *Zenobia* would be displayed majestically against a Pompeian red background at the London International Exposition of 1862. Subsequently, it went on to be displayed in Boston, New York, and Chicago. In Boston, it attracted over 30,000 viewers and was praised in print by Lydia Maria Child and by poet John Greenleaf Whittier.

Although Hosmer sold *Zenobia* for $15,000 and received a number of orders for copies, its critical reception was mixed. Alternating with high praise were intimations of the beginnings of a move away from the aesthetics of strict neoclassicism. In addition, Hosmer was enraged by public charges that her statues were not her own

Harriet Hosmer at work on her statue of Senator Thomas Hart Benton.

creations, but were the executions of Italian artisans. She returned to Rome determined to file a libel suit against the publications reporting this story. She also published a lengthy article in the December 1864 *Atlantic Monthly* describing the creative process in which she drew a sharp distinction between the artist who conceived and modelled the work in clay and those who simply carried out the artist's commands in marble. Hosmer insisted upon, and received, printed apologies from the journals that had carried the charge that her statues were not her own.

At the Dublin Exhibition in 1865, Hosmer's most recent creation, *The Sleeping Faun,* became one of the most celebrated and admired works, selling on opening day for £1,000, a figure that exceeded the $15,000 she had received for *Zenobia.* Still, the controversy over the originality of her compositions had not died down altogether.

Upon her return to Rome, Hosmer supervised the completion of her new studio. The death of her father in 1862 had left her with an independent income, and the professional success she was enjoying allowed her to build a large and handsome establishment. Flowers and birds filled the interior courtyard, and Hosmer's work studios were large and sunny. In this studio, over the next five years, Hosmer would turn out a steady procession of sought-after works, many of these on commission to her wealthy friends, which now included a number of titled Englishwomen.

In 1868, Hosmer completed a commission for the state of Missouri, a ten-foot statue of Senator Thomas Hart Benton. Cast in bronze in Munich and shipped to St. Louis, its dedication was cause for a city-wide celebration. The public acclaim, though not the last that Hosmer would receive, represented an apogee of sorts. Following the Civil War, neoclassicism had come to be replaced by a new realism. Hosmer was unwilling to adapt to the new aesthetics, and her bids to win commissions for a Lincoln Memorial and for a Freedman's Memorial both met with failure.

From the late 1860s on, Hosmer spent increasing amounts of time away from her studio, often traveling from one country home to another in England and France, visiting her titled and literary friends. She was inadvertently caught up in the civil insurrections that led to fighting in the streets of Rome in 1870, and the subsequent political unrest cast a pall for Hosmer on the lustre of her beloved city. Though she continued to spend part of each year there for some years afterward, and although she was but 40 years old, the period of her greatest productivity as an artist was over.

Hosmer's last important project was a commission from a woman suffragists' organization to do a full-sized *Queen *Isabella I* for the World's Columbian Exposition, held in Chicago in 1893. Among women's groups, Hosmer had achieved legendary status as a pioneer woman artist; in addition, following a meeting in the late 1860s with suffragist ***Phebe Hanaford,** Hosmer had become a more outspoken advocate of women's rights. An internecine squabble in Chicago as to whether Hosmer's statue should be placed in the Women's Pavilion, or whether it should take its place in the wider exhibition of American art, resulted in its location outside the California pavilion—a decision that may have pleased no one. *Queen Isabella* was exhibited in plaster, and funds for a permanent model never materialized.

Unwilling in later years to conform to the new aesthetic norms for sculpture—works she likened to "bronze photographs"—Hosmer turned to mechanical inventions. She tinkered for years with a magnetic perpetual motion machine and tried as well to develop a substance that could be cast as plaster but that had the artistic properties of marble.

Hosmer returned to Watertown in 1900, boarding with the family of a jeweler named Gray. It was while living with the Grays that she developed a fatal respiratory ailment, dying on February 21, 1908. Her old friend Cornelia Crow Carr took charge of Hosmer's estate. Harriet Hosmer died a pauper, but the artistic legacy she left was rich and enduring. Statues by Hosmer—each a monument to her courage and persistence—grace the Metropolitan Museum of Art, the National Gallery of Art, the London Academy, and other venues of distinction.

SOURCES:

Carr, Cornelia, ed. *Harriet Hosmer: Letters and Memories.* NY: Moffat, Yard, 1912.

Sherwood, Dolly. *Harriet Hosmer: American Sculptor; 1830–1908.* Columbia, MO: University of Missouri Press, 1991.

SUGGESTED READING:

Lee, Hannah. *Familiar Sketches of Sculpture and Sculptors.* Vol. 2. Boston: Crosby, Nichols, 1854.

Rubinstein, Charlotte Streifer. *American Women Sculptors: A History of Women Working in Three Dimensions.* Boston, MA: G.K. Hall, 1990.

COLLECTIONS:

Archives of American Art, Smithsonian Institution, Washington; Schlesinger Library at Radcliffe College and Harvard University.

RELATED MEDIA:

Ross, Jane M. *A Woman Bold Enough.* Washington Playwrights Forum, 1995.

A Visit with the Playwright: The Life of Sculptor Harriet Hosmer. Old Hat Productions, Bethesda, Maryland, 1996.

Andrea Moore Kerr, Ph.D.,
author of *Lucy Stone: Speaking Out for Equality* (Rutgers, 1992) and women's historian and independent scholar living in Washington, D.C.

Hossain, Rokeya Sakhawat

(1880–1932)

Bengal Muslim emancipator and educator. *Name variations: Begum Rokeya Sakhawat Hossain. Born*

Rokeya Saber in rural Rangpur (present-day Bangladesh), in 1880; died in 1932; married Sakhawat Hossain (deputy magistrate of Bhagalpur); no children.

Rokeya Sakhawat Hossain was born in 1880 in rural Rangpur (present-day Bangladesh) and raised in the *ashraf* way of life. Observing *purdah* (the practice of secluding women) from the age of five, she was confined to her house and forced to keep hidden from all visitors, including women. In this restrictive environment, Hossain managed to receive an education through the efforts of her eldest brother, Ibrihim Saber, who studied with her in the darkness of night. Hossain was not only bright and curious but hard-working, often studying through the night until morning prayers. Ibrihim was also instrumental in postponing Hossain's date of marriage for as long as possible, and, when the time came, he enthusiastically endorsed Sakhawat Hossain, the educated, Westernized man she eventually wed. Hossain was additionally inspired by her older sister **Karimunnessa Saber**, a determined and resourceful young girl who learned to read and write by eavesdropping on her brothers' tutors. Karimunnessa later married into a liberal, modern family who encouraged her to further her education. She read thousands of books and was a gifted poet. Karimunnessa not only served as a mentor to the young Hossain, but also inspired her to constantly question and to seek her own identity.

The date of Hossain's marriage is unknown, but her husband was the deputy magistrate of Bhagalpur and a man of some power. Educated in England and a frequent visitor to the Continent, Sakhawat championed education for women and encouraged his wife to fulfill her potential. He helped her improve her English and stimulated her intellect with books and new ideas. Later, he assisted her in her own educational causes and, upon his death, left her a large sum of money to spend on schools for Muslim girls.

Relieved of her domestic duties and having no children, Hossain began actively promoting female education by starting a school with a handful of local girls, personally conducting them to school in a specially designed *purdahnasheen* carriage. In 1911, she established the successful Sakhawat Memorial Girls' School in Calcutta. She simultaneously campaigned for the emancipation of *purdahnasheen* women by establishing the Bengal branch of the Anjuman-e-Khawatin Islam, in 1916.

Rokeya Hossain was also a noted writer, producing a novel, several plays, poems, and short stories. Her best-known work, *Sultana's Dream*, was written to impress her husband when he returned from a tour. It was published in the *Indian Ladies Magazine*, in 1905, and continues to be anthologized. Hossain also published regularly in other journals.

SOURCES:

Hossain, Yasmin. "The Education of the Secluded Ones: Begum Rokeya Sakhawat Hossain 1880–1932," in *Canadian Woman Studies*. Vol. 13, no. 13. Fall 1992.

SUGGESTED READING:

Williams, A. Susan, ed. *The Lifted Veil: The Book of Fantastic Literature by Women*. NY: Carroll & Graf, 1992.

Barbara Morgan,
Melrose, Massachusetts

Hotchkiss, Hazel (1886–1974).

See Wightman, Hazel Hotchkiss.

Hotot, Agnes (fl. 14th c.)

***English noblewoman.** Flourished 14th century in England; daughter of the earl of Dudley.*

Agnes Hotot was an English noblewoman who fought a tournament in disguise for the honor of her father, the earl of Dudley. When the earl was too sick to participate in a tournament to settle a dispute against another earl, Agnes went in his place. She easily hid her identity from her opponent with her helmet and armor, and then proceeded to win the tournament—obviously the art of jousting was something Agnes had practiced before that day. Supposedly, she then removed her armor and helmet in front of the conquered man to reveal her gender to him.

Laura York,
Riverside, California

Ho Tzu-chen.

See Jiang Qing for sidebar on He Zizhen.

Houdetot, Sophie, Comtesse d' (1730–1813).

See Épinay, Louise d' for sidebar.

Houghton, Edith (1912—)

***American baseball player and scout for the Philadelphia Phillies.** Born in Philadelphia, Pennsylvania, on February 12, 1912; never married; no children.*

One of ten children, Edith Houghton was born in Philadelphia in 1912 and, by age six, was playing hardball, posing for pictures in a pint-sized uniform. At age eight, she was the mascot of the Philadelphia police baseball teams and, at ten, was playing shortstop for the Philadelphia Bobbies, a team founded by **Mary O'Gara** in 1922 and comprised of young female players from 13 to 20. Houghton, the youngest on the team, had to tighten her cap with a safety pin and punch holes in her belt in order to hold up her billowing uniform. In 1925, she toured Japan with the Bobbies, who were joined at the time by major-league catcher Eddie Ainsmith and pitcher Earl Hamilton. Booked to play 15 games against men's college teams, the first "American Team" was initially a huge attraction in Japan, and Houghton was singled out by the Japanese and English-language press for her extraordinary hitting and fielding. Unfortunately, Houghton's talent could not carry the team, and when they began to lose games the public and press soon tired of them. Reportedly, when their sponsors would not pay for their fare home, they were stranded in Kobe until a sympathetic hotel owner took pity and financed their return journey as far as Seattle.

Once back in Philadelphia, Houghton left the Bobbies and joined other teams, including a stint with the Passaic (NJ) Bloomer Girls whose opponents included the Pennsylvania men's teams. "This Miss played as good a brand of ball as any male player has displayed at Maple Shade this season," wrote one reporter of Houghton's afternoon performance. "In addition to pasting out five hits, including two doubles and a screaming homer, she handled six tries at short in major league fashion." In 1931, Houghton played with the Hollywood Bloomer Girls, who barnstormed through Texas and Oklahoma during the Depression, often playing against minor league teams. As the Bloomer era came to a close in 1933, Houghton tried out and was accepted by the Fisher A.A.'s, a men's semipro team. Playing first base, she received no special treatment from either the pitchers or the fielders. "They sent the ball over the plate to her with just as much speed," wrote a reporter, "and threw them to first base with as much zip as though she had a couple of baseball hams for hands."

By the mid-1930s, baseball opportunities for women had pretty much dried up, and Houghton was forced to play softball, which she initially hated. After mastering the technique of hitting the large, sluggish ball, she played for a few years with the Roverettes in Madison Square Garden. Her career was interrupted by World War II, during which time she joined the WAVES (Women Appointed for Volunteer Emergency Service), working in supplies and accounts. She also joined the department's baseball team, where she hit .800 during a streak.

After the war, Houghton took a job as a glassware buyer for a Philadelphia wholesaler, but she missed baseball. In 1946, she wrote Bob Carpenter, owner of the Philadelphia Phillies, requesting an interview. Letting her scrapbook serve as a resume, Houghton asked for a job as a scout. In an unprecedented move, Carpenter took her on, thus making her the first woman ever hired as a major league scout. During her six-year tenure, she signed approximately 15 players, two of whom made it to Class B ball.

Houghton was called up by the navy to serve during the Korean War; following her stint, she did not return to scouting, finding it too competitive. "The way I feel about scouting," she said, "is if you see somebody who's great, you can bet your buttons ten others are after him, too." She eventually retired to Florida.

SOURCES:

Gregorich, Barbara. *Women at Play: The Story of Women in Baseball.* NY: Harcourt, Brace, 1993.

Barbara Morgan,
Melrose, Massachusetts

Hoult, Norah (1898–1984)

Irish novelist, journalist and short-story writer. *Born on September 20, 1898, in Dublin, Ireland, of Anglo-Irish parentage; died in April 1984.*

Selected works: (short stories) Poor Women *(1928);* Time! Gentleman, Time! *(released in America as* Closing Hour, *1930);* Apartments To Let *(1932);* Youth Can't Be Served *(1933);* Nine Years Is a Long Time *(1935);* Holy Ireland *(1936);* Coming From the Fair *(1937);* Four Women Grow Up *(1939);* Augusta Steps Out, House Under Mars, Smilin' on the Vine *(1941);* Father and Daughter, Husband and Wife, There Were No Windows, Only Fools and Horses Work, *and* Not for Our Sins Alone.

Born in 1898 in Dublin, Ireland, Norah Hoult was educated in England, owing to the death of both her parents when she was quite young. Hoult accepted a position on the editorial staff of the Sheffield *Daily Telegraph,* where she worked for two years. She subsequently worked for Pearson's Magazines, Ltd., in London, wrote book reviews for the Yorkshire *Evening Post,* became active as a free-lance journalist, and wrote fiction. Her first book, a collection of short stories titled *Poor Women,* was well-received. Her work became known for its readability and accurate character portrayals. Hoult's many novels include *Holy Ireland, Father and Daughter, Husband and Wife, There Were No Windows, Only Fools and Horses Work,* and *Not for Our Sins*

Alone. Her "best work has been seriously neglected" wrote one critic.

Houston, Lucy (1858–1936)

English philanthropist whose concerns included the defense of London. *Name variations: Lady Houston; Dame Fanny Houston. Born Fanny Lucy Radmall in 1858 (some sources cite 1857) in Camberwell, southeast of London (at the time of her death, the* Times *placed her birth in St. Margarets, Twickenham); died on December 29, 1936; married Theodore Brinckman (a future baronet), in 1883 (divorced 1895); married George Gordon, 9th Lord Byron, in 1901 (died 1917); married Sir Robert Paterson Houston, in 1924 (died 1926).*

Dame Lucy Houston was born in 1858 and grew up on the fringe of Victorian England; her father was a maker of boxes. Houston always maintained that she began her career at age 11 as an "actress and ballet dancer"; others thought not. By age 16, she was in Paris, being tutored by **Madame de Polès**, a hostess skilled in the art of money—investing, divesting, and acquiring. Back in London in 1883, Houston dabbled with the women's suffrage movement, and, at age 25, married Theodore Brinckman. The union lasted 12 years until their divorce in 1895. In 1901, she married and settled in Hampstead with George, the 9th Lord Byron, also known as "Red-Nose George." Unfortunately, George was not the most disciplined of men.

Lucy Houston

Lucy was becoming increasingly involved in the suffrage movement. It has been written that she bought 615 parrots and taught them all to shriek "Votes for Women!" An eccentric, she also took to carrying a handbag stuffed with £5 notes, reports Alen Jenkins, "because she liked talking to tramps, whom she would reward with money and a little screech of laughter—'Mind you don't spend it all on drink.'" Lucy Houston was made a Dame of the British Empire (DBE) in 1917 for founding a rest home for nurses during World War I.

Following Lord Byron's death that same year, 60-year-old Houston turned her attention to 65-year-old Sir Robert Paterson Houston, a Liverpool shipowner and robber baron. They were eventually married in 1924. Two years later, Sir Robert died, and Lucy Houston was bequeathed four-fifths of his fortune (between £6 and £7 million); she promptly moved to the island of Jersey to avoid income tax. When a few socialist MP's complained that she owed death duties on her husband's estate, she invoked her Jersey location. But she did hand the chancellor of the exchequer a personal gift of £1½ million because she admired him. The chancellor, Winston Churchill, was more than happy to receive the check to be used for the defense of England.

By then Houston's politics had veered to the extreme right: one of her friends was editor of an anti-Semitic review and Benito Mussolini was a personal hero. She set up an information bureau about Socialists and some Labour MPs to show that they were unpatriotic and published the results as *Potted Biographies: A Dictionary of Anti-National Biography.*

Houston offered then Prime Minister Ramsay MacDonald £200,000 to defend London against enemy attacks. When he turned her down because of the strings she had attached, Lucy installed a six-foot high electric sign on her yacht, *Liberty,* which read "TO HELL WITH RAMSAY MACDONALD" as it cruised along the Thames. She bought the weekly *Saturday Review* and made a dramatic changeover. "There was perhaps a hard core of fascist-minded readers who took it seriously," writes Jenkins; "but the great majority of its 60,000 purchasers . . . bought it for uproarious amusement."

After the 1935 election Stanley Baldwin was prime minister and there were long missives to Downing Street from Lucy Houston. She had written Hitler saying, "Join Britain in an alliance and we will crush Russia," and wanted Baldwin's approval for her effort. She demanded he fight socialism, rearm against Germany, and pull out of the League of Nations; she also took on the new head of the Foreign Office, Anthony Eden, who championed the League.

With the threat of war, Houston sent another check for £200,000 to the chancellor of the exchequer, now Neville Chamberlain, to buy fighter planes to defend London. But Britain still believed that bombers would save the nation, not fighter planes. When it came to aviation, however, Lucy Houston was ahead of her time. In 1931, she had financed the struggling Schneider Trophy wherein seaplanes competed over water. It was an important competition which spurred development of new high-speed aircraft. She also financed Lord Clydesdale's flight over Mt. Everest in 1933 to great fanfare. Without Houston's involvement, there might never have been a fighter plane dubbed a Spitfire, and Spitfires would win the Battle of Britain, earning Houston the titles "Fairy Godmother of the RAF" and "The Woman who Won the War." But Lucy Houston did not live to see this. She died on December 29, 1936, leaving all her money to her friend **Juliana Hoare**, aunt of one of Lucy's political targets, Sir Samuel Hoare, first lord of the admiralty; Juliana, however, had predeceased Lucy by ten months. In 1958, on the centenerary of Houston's birth, Lord Tedder, marshal of the RAF, publicly regretted that the white cliffs of Dover lacked a monument to Lucy Houston.

SOURCES:

Jenkins, Alan. *The Rich Rich: The Story of the Big Spenders.* NY: Putnam, 1978.

Houston, Margaret Lea

(1819–1867)

Wife of Sam Houston and first lady of Texas. *Born Margaret Moffette Lea on April 11, 1819, near Marion, Alabama; died in 1867 in Independence, Texas; one of three children of Temple Lea and Nancy (Moffette) Lea; attended Judson Female Institute; became third wife of Sam Houston (1793–1863, soldier, statesman, and hero of San Jacinto who was instrumental in earning Texas its independence and statehood), on May 9, 1840; children: four sons and four daughters; granddaughter:* ***Margaret Bell Houston*** *(d. 1966, an American novelist and poet). Sam Houston's first wife was* ***Eliza Allen;*** *they were married only one year before divorcing; he then married Tiana Rogers, a Cherokee, in 1830.*

Margaret Lea Houston

Described as intelligent, pious, and striking in appearance, Margaret Houston first met her famous husband in 1839 and fell deeply in love despite the disparity in their ages. Sam, at 46, cut a gallant figure indeed, but it may have been his adventurous spirit that appealed even more to Margaret, who at 20 still harbored a romantic nature.

Back in 1824, Sam Houston had served as congressman and governor of his home state of Tennessee and was headed for a distinguished political career when he resigned the office of governor and went to live in Arkansas among the Cherokee Indians. Marrying **Tiana Rogers**, the daughter of a Native American chief, Houston lived among the Cherokees for six years, during which time he represented the tribe in diplomatic and business affairs. In 1825, as trouble brewed on the Texas frontier, Houston left his wife (the marriage, according to tribal custom, was dissolved) to assist the colonists in their fight for independence from Mexico. After leading the Texans in the historic confrontation with Santa Anna's troops at San Jacinto (April 21, 1836), Houston emerged a hero and became president of the newly formed republic of Texas. It was on a trip to Alabama three years later that he met Margaret and immediately proposed.

A year passed before the couple married, during which time they began a loving correspondence that continued during the long separations in their 23-year union. They were wed in May 1840, at Margaret's brother's home in Alabama, after which Margaret made the arduous trip across the Gulf of Mexico to Texas, bringing along her maid and lifetime friend Eliza. After the initial trip, Margaret, who was a poor traveler, made very few journeys away from home, although Sam, who served a second term as president of Texas and later as a U.S. senator and governor of the state, was away more often than not.

Margaret, a devoted wife, was the mother of eight. She oversaw the education and religious training of the children in a variety of Houston homes, varying from the rugged log houses of the early years to the two-story, yellow-brick governor's mansion in Austin. Margaret never concerned herself too much with either managing the household, which was left to Eliza, or the family finances, which were always on the meager side. Her most pressing duty, it would appear, was to convert her husband to the Baptist Church, a task that took some 14 years.

Due to Sam's unpopular political stand against secession, his years as governor were often unpleasant, and after Texas voted to separate from the union in January 1861 he retired from public life. The couple rented a house in Huntsville, where he died on July 26, 1863. Shattered by her loss, Margaret returned to Independence, where she worked with historian William Carey Crane on a compilation of her husband's papers, letter and documents. When the manuscript was complete, however, there was no publisher interested in the frontier hero. Discouraged and bitter, Margaret burned many of the historic documents, and others were later lost or destroyed. What remained were several hundred letters that the couple had exchanged throughout their years together. In 1998, these became the source of a biography, *Star of Destiny: The Private Life of Sam and Margaret Houston,* by **Madge Thornall Roberts**. In 1867, Margaret Houston succumbed to the yellow fever epidemic, dying at age 48.

SOURCES:

Crawford, Ann Fears and Crystal Sasse Ragsdale. *Women in Texas*. Austin, TX: State House Press, 1992.

Publishers Weekly. January 25, 1998.

Hovick, Rose Louise (1914–1970).

See Lee, Gypsy Rose.

How-Martyn, Edith (1875–1954)

English reformer who co-founded the Women's Freedom League and worked in tandem with Margaret Sanger on birth-control issues. *Born Edith How in Cheltenham, England, in 1875; died in a Sydney, Australia, nursing home on February 4, 1954; educated at the North London Collegiate School for Girls; obtained a degree from University College, Aberystwyth; earned a D.Sc. in economics from London University; married Herbert Martyn, in 1899.*

Then a lecturer in mathematics at Westfield College, Edith How-Martyn was an early recruit to the Women's Social and Political Union (WSPU) and was arrested in 1906 for attempting to make a speech in the lobby of the House of Commons, one of the organization's first members to be sent to prison. But How-Martyn was critical of the leadership of the WSPU. In 1907, she helped found the Women's Freedom League (WFL), along with ***Teresa Billington-Greig** and ***Charlotte Despard**, and was its secretary until 1911, when she began heading the political and militant department. Though still militant in their approach, the members of the WFL insisted on non-violent means. How-Martyn urged women to refuse to pay taxes and to boycott the 1911 census.

Following the passage of the first suffrage bill in 1918, known as the Qualification of Women Act, How-Martyn stood unsuccessfully as an Independent Feminist candidate in that year's General Election. She had more success when she stood for the Middlesex County Council and became its first woman member.

How-Martyn also lent her energy to the birth-control movement led by ***Marie Stopes**. She was particularly concerned with working-class women who were given little information on how to control the size of their families. In 1929, How-Martyn founded the Birth Control International Information Centre (BCIIC) with ***Margaret Sanger**; she also wrote *The Birth Control Movement in England* (1931) and accompanied Sanger on her travels through India in 1935–36, which included Sanger's widely publicized meeting with Mohandas Gandhi. The two worked well together for two decades and developed a brisk correspondence and a special friendship with Sanger writing: "You have a way of winning hearts and its really dangerous! . . . I love the notes you send & the interesting report & everything you do just like I like it done. We must have ruled a world together once Edith." In 1939, with war approaching, Edith How-Martyn moved to Australia; back home in England, her secretary **Eileen Palmer** (d. 1992) rescued her correspondence and files when the How-Martyn house was bombed. Following the war, How-Martyn's poor health kept her from returning to Britain; she died in a Sydney nursing home on February 4, 1954.

COLLECTIONS:

Correspondence between Sanger and How-Martyn in the Margaret Sanger Papers Project, New York University.

How-Martyn's letters to Margaret Sanger, Sophia Smith Collection at Smith College.

Howard, Ada Lydia (1829–1907)

American educator. *Name variations: Mrs. A.L. Howard. Born on December 19, 1829, in Temple,*

New Hampshire; died on March 3, 1907, in Brooklyn, New York; attended New Ipswich Academy; graduated from Lowell High School; graduated from Mount Holyoke Seminary (now Mount Holyoke College), 1853; never married; no children.

Ada Howard, who would devoted her life to teaching and educational administration, was born in Temple, New Hampshire, in 1829. She graduated from Mount Holyoke Seminary in 1853. After a period of study under private tutors, she returned to her alma mater in 1858 as a teacher. She then took a teaching post at Western College for Women (now Western College) in Oxford, Ohio, and also served as principal of the women's department at Knox College in Galesburg, Illinois (1866–69). In 1869, she opened her own school, Ivy Hall, in Bridgeton, New Jersey.

Upon the inauguration of Wellesley College in September 1875, Howard was selected by founder and treasurer Henry F. Durant to serve as its first president. In her post, Howard presided over a faculty of approximately 30 women, though her job was limited to executing the policies set by Durant. After Durant's death in October 1881, Howard herself became ill and was forced to retire before she had the opportunity to run the college on her own. The presidency passed to ***Alice Freeman Palmer**. Ada Howard, who spent her final years in Methuen, Massachusetts, and Brooklyn, New York, died on March 3, 1907.

Howard, Agnes (1476–1545).

See Tylney, Agnes.

Howard, Anne (1475–1511)

English princess and duchess of Norfolk. *Name variations: Lady Anne Howard; Lady Anne Plantagenet. Born on November 2, 1475, at Westminster Palace, London, England; died on November 23, 1511 (some sources cite 1513); interred at Framlingham, Suffolk, England; daughter of Edward IV (b. 1442), king of England (r. 1461–1483), and Elizabeth Woodville (1437–1492); became first wife of Thomas Howard (1473–1554), 3rd duke of Norfolk (r. 1524–1554), on February 4, 1494 or 1495; children: two sons and two daughters (all died young).*

Princess Anne Howard was born in 1475, the daughter of ***Elizabeth Woodville** and Edward IV, king of England. She was the first wife

Ada Lydia Howard

of Thomas Howard, 3rd duke of Norfolk. Following her death, Thomas Howard married ***Elizabeth Stafford** (1494–1558), in 1513.

Howard, Anne (d. 1559)

Countess of Oxford. *Name variations: Anne de Vere. Died in 1559 (some sources claim she died before February 22, 1558); interred at Lambeth Parish Church; daughter of Thomas Howard (1443–1524), 2nd duke of Norfolk (r. 1514–1524), and ****Agnes Tylney*** *(1476–1545); married John de Vere, 14th earl of Oxford.*

Howard, Anne (d. 1662).

See Somerset, Anne.

Howard, Caroline.

See Gilman, Caroline Howard (1794–1888).

Howard, Catherine (fl. 1450)

Baroness Berners. *Name variations: Lady Berners; Katherine. Flourished around 1450; daughter of John Howard (1420–1485), 1st duke of Norfolk (r. 1483–1485), and ****Margaret Howard*** *(fl. 1450); married John Bourchier, 1st baron Berners; children: Henry Bourchier, 2nd baron Berners (d. 1471); ****Joan Neville*** *(fl. 1468, who married Henry Neville).*

Howard, Catherine (d. 1452)

English noblewoman. *Name variations: Catherine or Katherine Hungerford; Catherine Molines or Cather-*

ine Moleyns. Died in 1452; daughter of William Hungerford, Lord Moleyns, and ***Margery Hungerford;*** *first wife of John Howard (1420–1485), 1st duke of Norfolk (r. 1483–1485); children: Thomas Howard (1443–1524), 2nd duke of Norfolk (r. 1514–1524); Anne Howard (who married Sir Edmund Gorges); Isabel Howard; Jane Howard; Margaret Howard.*

Howard, Catherine (d. after 1478)

Baroness Abergavenny. *Name variations: Katherine. Died after 1478; daughter of Sir Robert Howard and* ****Margaret Mowbray;*** *became second wife of Edward Neville, baron Abergavenny (r. 1438–1476), on October 15, 1448. Edward's first wife was* ****Elizabeth Beauchamp.***

Howard, Catherine (1520/22–1542).

See Six Wives of Henry VIII.

Howard, Catherine (d. 1548)

English noblewoman. *Died on April 12, 1548; interred on May 11, 1554; daughter of Thomas Howard (1443–1524), 2nd duke of Norfolk (r. 1514–1524), and* ****Agnes Tylney*** *(1476–1545); married Rhys ap Gruffydd FitzUryan; children: Agnes FitzUryan; Griffith ap Rice FitzUryan.*

Howard, Catherine (d. 1596)

English noblewoman. *Name variations: Lady Berkeley. Died in 1596; daughter of Henry Howard (1517–1547), earl of Surrey, and* ****Frances de Vere*** *(d. 1577); married Lord Henry Berkeley, in 1554. Lord Henry's second wife was* ***Jane Stanhope.***

Howard, Catherine (d. 1633).

See Knyvett, Catherine.

Howard, Catherine (d. 1672)

Countess of Salisbury. *Name variations: Catherine Cecil. Died on January 27, 1672; daughter of Thomas Howard (1561–1626), 1st earl of Suffolk (r. 1603–1626), and* ****Catherine Knyvett*** *(d. 1633); married William Cecil, 2nd earl of Salisbury; children:* ***Elizabeth Cecil*** *(d. 1689, who married William Cavendish, 3rd earl of Devonshire);* ***Anne Cecil*** *(who married Algernon Percy, 10th earl of Northumberland).*

Howard, Catherine (d. 1874)

English noblewoman. *Died on January 27, 1874; daughter of Henry Howard (1757–1842), High Sheriff Cumberland, and* ***Catherine Mary Neave*** *(d. 1849); married Honorable Philip Stourton, on July 28, 1829.*

Howard, Dorothy

Countess of Derby. *Daughter of Thomas Howard (1443–1524), 2nd duke of Norfolk (r. 1514–1524), and* ****Agnes Tylney*** *(1476–1545); married Edward Stanley, 3rd earl of Derby, on February 21, 1530; children:* ***Maria Stanley;*** *Henry Stanley, 4th earl of Derby.*

Howard, Elizabeth (c. 1410–1475)

Countess of Oxford. *Name variations: Elizabeth de Vere. Born around 1410; died in 1475 at Stratford Nunnery; interred at Austin Friars Church, London; daughter of John Howard and* ***Joan Walton;*** *married John de Vere, 12th earl of Oxford, in 1425; children: Aubrey de Vere; John de Vere (b. 1442), 13th earl of Oxford; Sir George de Vere.*

Howard, Elizabeth (d. 1497).

See Tylney, Elizabeth.

Howard, Elizabeth (1494–1558)

Duchess of Norfolk. *Born Elizabeth Stafford in 1494; died in 1558; daughter of Edward Stafford, 3rd duke of Buckingham (1478–1521, executed by order of Henry VIII); second wife of Thomas Howard, 4th duke of Norfolk.*

Howard, Elizabeth (d. 1534)

Countess of Sussex. *Name variations: Lady Fitzwalter. Died on September 18, 1534; interred at Boreham; daughter of Thomas Howard (1443–1524), 2nd duke of Norfolk (r. 1514–1524), and* ****Agnes Tylney*** *(1476–1545); married Henry Ratfliffe also known as Henry Radcliffe (c. 1506–1556), 2nd earl of Sussex, and 8th baron Fitzwalter, before May 21, 1524; children: Thomas Radcliffe (b. around 1525), 3rd earl of Sussex; Henry Radcliffe (b. around 1532), 4th earl of Sussex. Following Elizabeth Howard's death, Henry Radcliffe married* ***Anne Calthorp.***

Howard, Elizabeth (?–1538).

See Boleyn, Anne for sidebar.

Howard, Elizabeth (d. 1567).

See Leyburne, Elizabeth.

Howard, Elizabeth (c. 1599–1633).

See Hume, Elizabeth.

Howard, Elizabeth (fl. 1600).

See Knollys, Elizabeth.

Howard, Elizabeth (d. 1704).

See Percy, Elizabeth.

Howard, Elizabeth Ann

(1823–1865)

Countess of Beauregard and mistress of Napoleon III.

Name variations: Miss Howard; Harriet Howard. Born Elizabeth Ann Haryatt in England in 1823; died in 1865; married Charles Trelawney, in May 1854; children: (with a Major Martyn) son Martin (b. 1842).

Born in England in 1823, the beautiful Elizabeth Ann Haryatt was a skilled equestrian and granddaughter of the owner of the Castle Hotel in Brighton. At age 16, she ran off to London with the well-known jockey Jem Mason and changed her name to Harriet Howard to spare her family. Though Mason soon grew tired of Elizabeth, he continued to support her until she was 18, then passed her off to a Major Martyn who treated her handsomely, setting her up in a great house with numerous servants. Howard gave birth to a son by Martyn and presented it for baptism, claiming it was the son of her mother. Even so, Martyn was delighted with the news of the boy and endowed her with even more wealth and estates.

In 1846, when her son was four, Howard attended a party at ***Lady Blessington**'s, where she met 39-year-old Louis Napoleon Bonaparte (soon to be Napoleon III). The 23-year-old Howard fell in love, left the generous Martyn, and opened a modest lodging house on Berkeley Street. The only other lodgers were Louis Napoleon and his conspiring friends, who were determined to set him up as head of France. Howard, dazzled by the name Bonaparte, was convinced that her son would grow up as a Bonaparte prince. She spent her mornings in study, engaging author Alexander Kinglake as tutor. Kinglake fell in love with the energetic, intelligent Howard but his overtures were spurned, and he grew to detest his rival. At the height of Napoleon III's glory, Kinglake would publish his *History of the Invasion of the Crimea*, in which he maintained that Napoleon and his band concocted the Crimean War to deflect criticism of their misdeeds. This viewpoint would become the credo of Red Republicans in France and poison public opinion of the emperor in England.

Louis Napoleon was so impressed with Elizabeth Howard that he entrusted two of his sons, from a liaison with a laundress at Ham, into her care. Goodhearted and generous, Howard was equally impressed with Louis and willingly handed him her jewels and all her liquid assets, including some rich Italian properties.

When Louis Napoleon left England to become president of the Republic of France, Elizabeth Howard accompanied him. She could often be seen riding with him in the Bois, along with the three boys. For awhile, she remained discreet and stayed in the background, but upon realizing that Napoleon preferred her in the shadows, she began to ask for more: an apartment at his residence at the Château of Saint-Cloud and some kind of position at official functions. When Napoleon turned his attentions to Empress ***Eugénie**, Howard wrote a friend: "His Majesty was here last night offering to pay me off; yes, an earldom in my own right, a castle, and a decent French husband into the bargain. . . . The Lord Almighty spent two hours arguing with me. . . . Later he fell asleep on the crimson sofa and snored, while I wept." Howard threatened scandal and was paid off with 150,000 francs. "This sum may actually have been not hush money, but an installment of Napoleon's huge debt" to her, writes **Betty Kelen**. In the meantime, under a ruse, Napoleon asked Howard to undertake a secret mission to England, and she readily agreed. But when she arrived in LeHavre to set sail across the channel, her ship was delayed, and she stayed the night at an inn. The following morning, Howard picked up a copy of *Le Moniteur* and read of Napoleon's engagement to Eugénie. Furious, she ordered a special train and returned to her Paris house in the Rue de Cirque to find it ransacked. Though none of her valuables were missing, all papers detailing her relationship with Louis Napoleon had been taken.

Eventually, Napoleon returned her estates and repaid her $4 million. In September 1852, Elizabeth Howard purchased the Château de Beauregard, near Paris, and was granted the title countess of Beauregard. When Napoleon grew tired of Eugénie, he was back in her arms. Later, Howard grew plump, lost her two adopted sons to their original mother, and, in 1854, married well-to-do Charles Trelawney of England, who spent her money but despised her. When Elizabeth Ann Howard died, writes Kelen, "her will provided a large sum of money to found a refuge in England for young girls who had been seduced away from their homes." Her portrait hangs at Compiègne.

SOURCES:

Kelen, Betty. *The Mistresses: Domestic Scandals of 19th Century Monarchs.* NY: Barnes and Noble, 1966.

Howard, Frances (d. 1577).

See Vere, Frances de.

Howard, Frances (1593–1632)

English murderer and countess of Somerset. *Name variations: Lady Frances Howard; Lady Somerset. Born in England on May 31, 1593 (some sources cite 1590); died in Chiswick, Middlesex, England, on August 23, 1632; interred at Saffron Waldon, Essex, on August 27, 1632; daughter of Thomas Howard (1561–1626), 1st earl of Suffolk (r. 1603–1626), and Catherine Knyvett, countess of Suffolk; sister of* ****Elizabeth Knollys****; married Robert Devereux, 3rd/20th earl of Essex, on January 5, 1605 (annulled in 1613); married Robert Carr (c. 1587–1645), later earl of Somerset, on December 26, 1613; children: Anne Carr (1615–1684, who married William Russell, 1st duke of Bedford, in 1637, and had ten children).*

Frances Howard (1593–1632)

The short life of Lady Frances Howard is dominated by her involvement in a murder plot that was carried out at the court of King James I of England. Howard was born into nobility, the daughter of Thomas Howard, 1st earl of Suffolk, and ***Catherine Knyvett**, the countess of Suffolk. Something of a femme fatale even in her teens, Frances first appeared at court at age 15 and immediately captured the attention of Robert Carr, a page and one of James I's male favorites. Howard, though married at 12 to Robert Devereux, earl of Essex, entered into a love affair with Carr, keeping her husband at bay by dosing his food with "debilitation powders" that rendered him impotent. After two years, she petitioned James for an annulment of her marriage, which the king agreed to grant in order to keep Carr happy. In the meantime, Carr's confidant (and intellectual superior), Sir Thomas Overbury, criticized the annulment and warned Carr that Frances Howard would be his ruination. For his trouble, Overbury was accused of plotting against the Crown and ordered by James I to the Tower of London.

Not content to have her nemesis locked away and under heavy guard, Howard began sending Overbury food rations laced with exotic poisons, such as rose algar, lapis constitis, cantharides, and white arsenic. The meals were delivered by several Tower guards whom Howard had won over. Overbury had a sturdy constitution, however, and took some time to die, finally succumbing on September 15, 1613. Within three days of his demise, Frances Howard received her annulment and a short time later married Carr in a lavish ceremony in Whitehall. As a wedding gift, James I pronounced Robert Carr the earl of Somerset, and Frances was now known as Lady Somerset.

The Somersets had the run of court, and James rewarded them further with gifts of real estate. Frances Howard's privileged life would have continued had not Paul de Lobel, one of the apothecaries involved in the murder plot, made a deathbed confession that detailed the poisoning of Overbury and named all the accomplices, including Howard, Carr, the Tower guards, and the suppliers of the various poisons. Howard's murder trial was successfully delayed by James I until May 24, 1616, when he finally bowed to pressures from court. She was prosecuted by no less than Sir Francis Bacon, who, in deference to the king, treated her with the utmost kindness. During the proceedings, Howard was said to have looked beautiful and wept openly, admitting her guilt. She was convicted and condemned to death, as was her husband in a subsequent trial. Both were later pardoned by the king and banished to cloistered but comfortable lives in the Tower. Their daughter Lady **Anne Carr** was born there on December 9, 1615. The Somersets were released in 1622 and retired to Oxfordshire, where they lived out their life in less than perfect harmony. Frances Howard died in 1632, at age 39, after suffering a prolonged illness. Robert Carr lived until 1645 and was honored at his burial in the Church of St. Paul's, Covent Garden.

SUGGESTED READING:

Lindley, David. *The Trial of Frances Howard: Facts and Fiction in the Court of King James.* Routledge, 1993.

Barbara Morgan,
Melrose, Massachusetts

Howard, Frances (c. 1633–1677).

See Villiers, Frances.

Howard, Harriet (1823–1865).

See Howard, Elizabeth Ann.

Howard, Henrietta (1669–1715).

See Somerset, Henrietta.

Howard, Henrietta (1688–1767)

English patron and mistress of King George II. *Name variations: Countess of Suffolk; Lady Suffolk; Henrietta Hobart. Born Henrietta Hobart in Norfolk, England, in 1688 (some sources cite 1681); died on July 26, 1767, in Marble Hill, Twickenham, Middlesex; daughter of Sir John Hobart and* ***Elizabeth Maynard*** *(d. 1701); married Charles Howard (b. 1675), 9th earl of Suffolk, on March 2, 1705 or 1706 (died 1733); married Honorable George Berkeley, on June 26, 1735 (died 1746); children: (first marriage) Henry Howard (1706–1745), 10th earl of Suffolk.*

Henrietta Howard was one of England's most notable royal mistresses but made her mark as a patron of letters and the arts. The daughter of a minor aristocrat, Henrietta was one of three children orphaned young, after their father died in 1698 and their mother in 1701. Henrietta and her siblings were then taken in by a distant relative, the earl of Suffolk, who provided them with an excellent education and found profitable marriage alliances for his wards. In 1706, Henrietta brought a large dowry to the earl's family when she married his youngest son, Charles Howard. It was an unhappy union. An army captain, Charles was an alcoholic gambler who soon lost his military commission; after the birth of their only child, Henry, in 1706, the couple separated and the marriage was essentially over.

Henrietta and Charles lived in separate households on the Suffolk estates until 1714, when Henrietta secured a position as Lady of the Bedchamber to Princess ***Caroline of Ansbach**, wife of the Prince of Wales, the future George II. Henrietta liked the fast pace and excitement of court life and became friends with the prince and princess. When Prince George was expelled from court for his misbehavior in 1717 by his father, King George I, Henrietta chose to accompany the exiled court on its wanderings across England. Although even she admitted that she was no beauty, Prince George was drawn to Henrietta's charming and lively personality. By 1720, they had become lovers, in a relationship that would last for 13 years. They enjoyed each other's company immensely, and it was common knowledge that Lady Howard spent almost every evening with the prince. She received a large allowance from the prince's treasury. Her influence led the prince to make her family, the Hobarts, the hereditary earls of Buckingham after he came to the throne in 1727.

In 1724, Henrietta began the construction of a magnificent Palladian country house on her lands in Middlesex. Called Marble Hill, the home is still standing, its classical design and decoration evidence of Henrietta's cultured tastes. After its completion, she divided her time between Marble Hill and the new king's court. In 1731, Henrietta became countess of Suffolk when her husband Charles inherited his father's titles. Charles died only two years later, in 1733, the same year that the relationship between Henrietta and the king came to an end.

The following year, she moved permanently to Marble Hill, where she became known as a patron of artists and writers. Among her friends and clients were three of the great English literary figures of the period, John Gay, Alexander Pope, and Jonathan Swift; all wrote verses about the countess and exchanged verses with her. She also exchanged letters on philosophical issues with other aristocrats of her circle. Henrietta was greatly interested in architecture and interior design and spent the years after her retirement from court planning and decorating the rooms of Marble Hill, as her surviving correspondence shows. Her first love as an art collector was porcelain; she also collected sculpture and, to a lesser extent, paintings, and amassed an extensive library.

In 1735, at age 47, Henrietta married the 42-year-old Honorable George Berkeley, son of the earl of Berkeley and a member of Parliament. Her second marriage was much happier than her first, lasting until George Berkeley's death in 1746. Outliving virtually all of her friends and family, the countess continued her literary and artistic patronage activity until her death in 1767.

Henrietta Howard (1688–1767)

SOURCES:

Benjamin, Lewis. *Lady Suffolk and Her Circle*. London: Hutchison, 1924.

Bryant, Julius. *Mrs. Howard: A Woman of Reason*. London: English Heritage, 1988.

Laura York,
Riverside, California

Howard, Isabel (fl. 1500s)

English noblewoman. *Flourished in the 1500s; daughter of Lord Edmund Howard (d. 1513) and* ***Joyce Culpeper****; sister of ****Catherine Howard*** *(1520/22–1542, 5th wife of Henry VIII).*

Howard, Jane (d. 1593)

Countess of Westmoreland. *Name variations: Jane Nevill; Jane Neville. Died in 1593; daughter of Henry Howard (1517–1547), earl of Surrey, and ****Frances de Vere*** *(d. 1577); married Charles Neville, earl of Westmoreland.*

Howard, Joyce (fl. 1500s)

English noblewoman. *Flourished in the 1500s; daughter of Lord Edmund Howard (d. 1513) and* ***Joyce Culpeper****; sister of ****Catherine Howard*** *(1520/22–1542, 5th wife of Henry VIII).*

Howard, Katherine (1520/22–1542).

See Six Wives of Henry VIII for Catherine Howard.

Howard, Mabel (1893–1972)

New Zealand politician. *Born in 1893; died in 1972.*

Born in New Zealand in 1893, Mabel Howard had a long and distinguished political career, which included 26 years in Parliament (1943–69) and was marked by a number of "firsts." Elected secretary of the New Zealand Federated Laborers Union early in her career, she was the first woman ever to hold such a post in the all-male organization. Her appointment as Minister of Health and Child Welfare in 1947 made her the first woman to hold full Cabinet status. She is also credited with crafting and promoting New Zealand's first animal protection act. Howard was known as a determined champion of women's and children's rights and also campaigned for social security, housing provisions, and consumers' rights. Notorious for her colorful speeches, she once shocked her fellow members of Parliament by holding up a pair of women's bloomers to make a point about sizing.

Howard, Margaret (fl. 1400).

See Mowbray, Margaret.

Howard, Margaret (fl. 1450)

Duchess of Norfolk. *Name variations: Margaret Chedworth. Born Margaret Chedworth; daughter of Sir John Chedworth; second wife of John Howard (1420–1485), 1st duke of Norfolk (r. 1483–1485); children: ****Catherine Howard*** *(fl. 1450).*

Howard, Margaret (fl. 1500s)

English noblewoman. *Flourished in the 1500s; daughter of Lord Edmund Howard (d. 1513) and* ***Joyce Culpeper****; sister of ****Catherine Howard*** *(1520/22–1542, 5th wife of Henry VIII).*

Howard, Margaret (d. 1564).

See Audley, Margaret.

Howard, Mary (c. 1519–1557).

See Fitzroy, Mary.

Howard, Mary

English noblewoman. *Daughter of Lord Edmund Howard (d. 1513) and* ***Joyce Culpeper****; sister of ****Catherine Howard*** *(1520/22–1542, 5th wife of Henry VIII).*

Howard, Muriel (d. 1512)

Viscountess L'Isle. *Died in childbirth on December 14, 1512, in Lambeth, England; daughter of Thomas Howard (1443–1524), 2nd duke of Norfolk (r. 1514–1524), and ****Elizabeth Tylney*** *(d. 1497); sister of ****Elizabeth Howard*** *(d. 1538) and aunt of ****Anne Boleyn*** *(1507–1536); married John Grey, 2nd viscount L'Isle or Lisle, also seen as 4th viscount Lisle (died 1512); married Sir Thomas Knyvett, before July 1506; children: (first marriage) ****Elizabeth Grey*** *(1505–1526).*

Howard, Rosalind Frances (1845–1921)

Countess of Carlisle who was a champion of women's rights and temperance reform. *Name variations: Rosalind Stanley. Born Rosalind Frances Stanley in England, in 1845; died on August 12, 1921; daughter of Edward John (1802–1868), 2nd Baron Stanley of Alderley, and Henrietta Maria Dillon (d. 1895); sister of* ***Henrietta Blanche Stanley*** *(d. 1921, who married David Ogilvy); married George Howard (1843–1911), 9th earl of Carlisle, on October 4, 1864; children: Charles James Howard (b. 1867), 10th earl of Carlisle; Hubert George Howard (b. 1871); Lt. Christopher Edward Howard (b. 1873); Lt. Oliver Howard (b. 1875); Geoffrey William Howard (b. 1877); Michael Francis Howard (b. 1880); Mary Henrietta Howard (who married George Gilbert Aimé Murray, a professor of Greek); Cecilia Maude Howard (d. 1947, who married Charles Henry Roberts); Dorothy Georgiana Howard (who married Francis Robert Eden, 6th baron Henley); Elizabeth Dacre Howard (died young); Aurea Fredeswyde Howard (who married Denyss Wace and Major Thomas MacLeod).*

The daughter of **Henrietta Maria Dillon** and Edward John, second Baron Stanley of Alderley, Rosalind Howard was said to have possessed an astute business sense which she put to use on the political front. She served as president of the National British Women's Temperance Association in 1903, as well as the Women's Liberal Federation from 1891 to 1901, and 1906 to 1914. She married George Howard, the ninth earl of Carlisle, in 1864, and had 11 children.

Howe, Julia Ward (1819–1910)

American poet, author, social reformer and women's suffrage leader, best known for writing the Civil War anthem, "The Battle Hymn of the Republic." *Born Julia Ward on May 27, 1819, in New York City; died on October 17, 1910, in Newport, Rhode Island; buried in*

Mt. Auburn Cemetery, Cambridge, Massachusetts; daughter of Samuel Ward (a Wall Street banker) and Julia Rush (Cutler) Ward (a published amateur poet); married Samuel Gridley Howe (Boston educator and reformer who pioneered with the blind, beginning with ***Laura Bridgman*** *), in 1843; children: Julia Rowana Anagnos (1844–1886); Florence Howe (namesake and god-daughter of* ***Florence Nightingale*** *); Henry Marion Howe; Laura E. Richards (1850–1943); Maud Howe Elliott (1854–1948); Samuel Howe (who died of diphtheria in childhood, 1861).*

Published her first book of poems, Passion Flowers, *anonymously (1854); was active as an abolitionist (1850s); founded one of the nation's first woman's clubs (1868); was first president of the New England Woman Suffrage Association; helped create the Woman's International Peace Association (1870s); for 50 years, wrote and lectured on women's suffrage, social reform, literature and liberal Christianity.*

Selected writings: (poetry) Passion Flowers *(1854);* Words for the Hour *(1857);* At Sunset *(1910); (travel literature)* From the Oak to the Olive: A Plain Record of a Pleasant Journey *(1868);* Trip to Cuba *(1860); (social commentary)* Modern Society *(1881);* Is Polite Society Polite? *(1895); (biography)* Memoir of Dr. Samuel Gridley Howe *(1876);* Margaret Fuller *(1883); (autobiography)* Reminiscences *(1899).*

In the fall of 1861, the nation's capital had been turned into an army camp, as Lincoln and his generals prepared to fight the Civil War. Around Washington, D.C., thousands of Union volunteers pitched their tents. Concerned about sanitary conditions in these makeshift military camps, the federal government asked Dr. Samuel Gridley Howe, a well-known educator and reformer from Boston, to investigate health hazards among the new recruits. In November, he arrived, accompanied by his wife Julia Ward Howe.

I returned to bed and fell asleep, saying to myself, I like this better than most things I have written.

—Julia Ward Howe, after writing the "Battle Hymn of the Republic"

Both of the Howes were outspoken opponents of slavery. Samuel was one of the conspirators who had funded John Brown's failed attempt to incite a slave rebellion in Virginia. Julia never knew the full extent of her husband's involvement with Brown and considered the raid to be a "wild and chimerical" scheme. But in the early 1850s, she had helped her husband publish a newspaper supporting the anti-slavery Free Soil Party, and she was friends with Boston's leading abolitionists, including William Lloyd Garrison, ***Elizabeth Palmer Peabody**, Charles Sumner and Theodore Parker. Touring the camps of the Grand Army of the Republic, Julia Howe was sure that theirs was a righteous cause.

At the same time, she also felt a sense of regret and helplessness. She was a poet, not a soldier; a middle-aged woman, not a young man. A voice within told her, "You cannot help anyone; you have nothing to give, and there is nothing for you to do." Yet, in the middle of the night, she was awakened by another voice, her poetic one. "Because of my sincere desire," Howe later recalled, "a word was given me to say, which did strengthen the hearts of those who fought in the field and of those who languished in the prison."

Rising from her bed, she set down the lyrics to "The Battle Hymn of the Republic," the song that would soon become the Union's war anthem. Borrowing the tune from a popular song about John Brown's martyrdom, her hymn gave voice to the spirit of militant righteousness which many Northerners felt about the war. Using Biblical imagery, she transformed a political and military conflict into an apocalyptic struggle with the Southern "serpent," one which heralded the glorious "coming of the Lord."

> In the beauty of the lilies Christ was born across the sea,
> With a glory in his bosom that transfigures you and me;
> As he died to make men holy, let us die to make men free,
> While God is marching on.

For the next half century, Northern audiences honored Howe for her timely contribution to the war effort. Rarely did she appear in public without hearing a rousing rendition of her "Battle Hymn." To this day, Howe is most often remembered as the author of those six stanzas, written in a flash of inspiration. Yet the very brilliance of that accomplishment has tended to obscure her many other achievements, particularly as a champion of women's rights in the late 19th century.

As the daughter of one of New York's wealthiest men, Julia Ward was born in 1819 into a life of privilege. Lacking an education himself, Sam Ward spared no expense for his children. Julia, along with her two sisters and three brothers, enjoyed the best tutors available in the young nation's fastest growing city. Much of her education was standard fare for young ladies being groomed for positions in the upper class; she became fluent in several European languages, began a lifelong interest in verse, and developed her talents as a vocalist, training that would serve her well years later when she turned to public speaking.

Howe also showed, from an early age, an appetite for philosophy and theology, studies which were generally thought too difficult for delicate female minds. On her own, she worked through many volumes of the latest European philosophers and found herself particularly drawn to the moral idealism of Immanuel Kant. To her father's dismay, she showed no interest in the domestic arts of housekeeping, announcing instead that she planned to become a writer.

While Howe was an earnest student, she also relished social life, mingling with other wealthy New York families. She was an attractive young woman, her red hair framing a face that was enlivened by keen intelligence and a ready laugh. She loved to attend the opera and the theater and to be seen at balls and parties where she was courted by many admirers. But Howe's love of fashion and frivolity during her teenage years was checked by her father. Her mother **Julia Rush Ward** had died in childbirth when Julia was only five, leaving Sam Ward as her sole guardian. Sobered by his wife's early

Julia Ward Howe

death, he became a pious orthodox Christian. To Howe, he was a loving father but a stern moral judge. Though he gladly provided his children with anything for their "moral improvement," he disapproved of the excess of the city's social life and tried his best to shield Howe from its corrupting influence.

Sam Ward died in 1839, his health broken by his successful efforts to save his bank during the great national depression of 1837. Not long after, Howe's beloved brother Henry also died. As a young socialite, she had been carefree and always resentful of her father's strict control. But now she adopted his evangelical faith and his serious view of life. As the oldest daughter, she ruled over her sisters much as her father had, earning the nickname "Old Bird."

Julia's enthusiasm for social life and the arts soon recovered, but the intense commitment to moral principle which she adopted after the death of her father lasted for the rest of her life, motivating her to battle evil through a wide range of reform crusades. Perhaps it was this new spirit of moral earnestness which attracted her to Samuel Gridley Howe. On a sightseeing tour of the Perkins School for the Blind in Boston, Julia met the philanthropist who ran that institution. Though he was 18 years her senior, the two began an intense but stormy courtship, a premonition of the kind of marriage that would follow.

When Julia agreed to marry Samuel, she determined that she would sacrifice her own ambitions, her desire to be a writer and her love of the social life of New York. Instead, she would submerge her identity within her husband's, supporting him as he embarked on crusades against slavery and for a variety of educational reforms. This was precisely the kind of self-sacrifice which Samuel expected of his bride. While he was often supportive of single women who dedicated their life to public service, he held fast to the traditional view that married women should stick to domestic duties and play no part in public life.

For Julia, those domestic responsibilities grew heavier each year. Her first child was born a year after her marriage, followed in regular succession by five more. Samuel, embroiled in his causes, was rarely at home, leaving Julia to raise the Howe children on her own. This was particularly difficult because Howe found herself to be "lamentably deficient in household skill and knowledge." She had traded her philosophy books for nursery tales, her lively social life among New York's elite for the colder climate and sterner society of Boston. She had even sacrificed the comforts of the Ward family's wealth. Her father had left her a large inheritance, but Samuel had insisted that, as the head of the household, he should control his wife's assets. Through unwise investments, he squandered the money.

Feeling isolated and overburdened, Julia found solace by returning to her first love, the writing of poetry. The result was *Passion Flowers,* a slender book of verse which she published in 1854. Samuel strongly disapproved of his wife's literary ambitions, particularly since her verse contained veiled references to their troubled relationship and her own unhappiness; perhaps for this reason she published the book anonymously.

Though Howe's poems have not held the interest of literary critics over time, her first book of verse did enjoy the approval of some of Boston's leading writers in her own day, including Ralph Waldo Emerson, who told Julia that he found the book "warm with life." Encouraged by this reception, Howe ignored her husband's complaints and continued to write, producing new volumes of verse and branching out to write plays, magazine articles, and travel books. Again in defiance of her husband's wishes, she began to put her name on her work. Balancing a writing career with her responsibilities as the mother of six, she published steadily through the 1850s. However, she did not enjoy much critical or commercial success and remained little known until 1862, when *Atlantic Monthly* published her "Battle Hymn," a piece which transformed her overnight into a celebrated literary figure.

In that beloved poem, Howe drew on the Biblical imagery which was central to the orthodox faith of her father, invoking the "fiery gospel" of a stern God of righteous wrath. Yet her own religious beliefs had changed over the years. As a young woman, she had accepted her father's view that "all mankind were by nature low, vile, and wicked," but she now concluded that people were essentially good. God, she decided, was not a stern judge who expected blind obedience to his commandments, but a loving Creator who spoke to His creatures through their reason. Howe became what was then known as a "liberal" Christian. In the mid-1860s, again ignoring her husband's objections, she delivered a series of lectures on religious and philosophical topics; in the late 1860s, she felt called to preach that faith in public.

Howe's theological views were quite conventional among liberal Bostonians, but her decision, as a woman, to promote them through public speaking before a mixed crowd of men and women was more radical. And in these lectures she found a new outlet for her ambitions. Aided by a strong and distinctive voice and a commanding presence on stage, she discovered that she was an effective public speaker. Guided by her deep streak of moral idealism, she also concluded that, as a proponent of religious and moral reform, she could make a greater contribution to society than she ever could hope to as a poet. Though she never gave up her literary interests, in the late 1860s she took up a new career as a lecturer, championing a variety of social causes.

The first cause which attracted the author of America's great battle hymn was peace. Watching men destroy each other, first in the American Civil War and then in the Franco-Prussian War in 1870, she became convinced that women around the world should unite to end war. She issued a manifesto for a women's peace movement, organized a Woman's Peace Congress in England in 1872, and helped to found the American Peace Society.

But Howe made a more lasting contribution in the field of women's rights. In the aftermath of the Civil War, the advocates of women's rights were inspired by the political revolution which had produced the 14th and 15th amendments, transforming thousands of black men from slaves into citizens who were promised full legal and political rights by the Constitution. While many women's rights leaders had been in the forefront of the abolition movement, they found this great victory for civil equality incomplete, since it had done nothing to change the second-class status of women, both black and white, in America. In the late 1860s, they determined that their time had also come, and they organized new women's suffrage associations to win the right to vote.

Though Howe had long been a supporter of the principle of women's suffrage, she chose this moment to take an active role in the cause, joining ***Lucy Stone** in the creation of the New England Woman Suffrage Association in 1868. The public had always considered the proponents of women's suffrage to be radical eccentrics. Howe did the cause a valuable service by lending her prestige and her voice. In turn, working side by side with other women, Howe gained a new sense of confidence about her own powers. Until that point, she later recalled, she had always judged herself against a "masculine ideal of character." Now, for the first time, she felt inspired by what she called "the power, the nobility, the intelligence which lie within the range of true womanhood."

In the late 1860s, when disputes over tactics and goals divided the suffrage movement into radical and moderate camps, Howe took a lead role among the moderates, helping to found the American Woman Suffrage Association. Unlike her more radical counterparts, she felt that the women's movement should work with its male allies within the Republican Party, and that victory could be won gradually, on a state-by-state basis, rather than through a single national amendment. Toward that end, she worked tirelessly for the next 40 years, organizing suffrage conventions, speaking at meetings, testifying before legislatures, editing a woman's journal, and writing a book in defense of higher education for women.

Howe also believed that the cause of women's rights could be advanced through the club movement. In the late 19th century, middle-class women began to organize clubs, meeting to discuss social and literary matters, to promote reforms and to provide their members with the chance to develop skills in public speaking and professional development which were unavailable in the male-dominated public sphere. Howe was an enthusiastic advocate of the idea, believing that such organizations could not only develop latent talents among women but could also be used to improve the moral life of all of society. As women became more cultured and more informed through club activities, she believed, they could use their influence as mothers, as wives, as teachers and caregivers, to purify the lives of those around them. Toward that end, she served for decades as president of the New England Women's Club and the Massachusetts Federation of Women's Clubs. As she traveled around the country on speaking engagements, she spread the gospel of the club movement and helped to found the first woman's clubs in several mid-Western and Western states.

Stirred by a keen sense of purpose and supported by a community of other women committed to the cause of women's rights, Howe continued to ignore her husband's disapproval. Samuel, who had long before realized that he could not keep his wife at home, never fully accepted her decision to pursue a public life. Their marital troubles continued until just before his death in 1876, when the two enjoyed a brief but loving reconciliation.

Samuel's death not only left Julia free to devote herself full-time to public life, but also made it a financial necessity. Always a poor manager of money, he left her in straitened economic circumstances. Julia, who lived for another 35 years, provided for herself by giving public readings and lectures. She was treated as an honored guest on podiums around the country. As the moral fervor of the Civil War years faded to distant memory, replaced by the hectic self-interest of the Gilded Age, the aging poet was transformed by her many admirers into a symbol of America's lost patriotism and idealism. One of the greatest tokens of the public's esteem came in 1908, when she became the first woman to be elected to the American Academy of Arts and Letters, her membership sponsored by Samuel Clemens (Mark Twain).

Julia Howe died of pneumonia in 1910, at the age of 92, a decade before her dream of full women's suffrage was finally realized. Struggling in an unsupportive marriage, she had achieved remarkable things, publishing numerous books, founding dozens of women's organizations, and winning prestigious honors. But perhaps the best example of her legacy to future generations of American women was more personal: all four of Julia's daughters followed in their mother's footsteps, pursuing public careers as writers and educators: ◂⚘ **Julia Rowana Anagnos** (1844–1886); **Florence Howe**; ***Maud Howe Elliott** (1854–1948); and ***Laura E. Richards** (1850–1943).

SOURCES:

Boyer, Paul S. "Julia Ward Howe," in *Notable American Women, 1607–1950: A Biographical Dictionary.* Cambridge, MA: Belknap Press, 1971.

Clifford, Deborah Pickman. *Mine Eyes Have Seen the Glory: A Biography of Julia Ward Howe.* Boston, MA: Little, Brown, 1978.

Howe, Julia Ward. *Reminiscences 1819–1899.* Boston, MA: Houghton, Mifflin, 1899.

Richards, Laura E. and Maud Howe Elliott. *Julia Ward Howe, 1819–1910.* 2 vols. Boston, MA: Houghton Mifflin, 1916.

SUGGESTED READING:

Elliott, Maud Howe. *Three Generations.* Boston, MA: Little, Brown, 1923.

⚘▸ **Anagnos, Julia** (1844–1886)

American poet. *Born Julia Rowana Howe in Rome, Italy, in 1844; died in 1886; daughter of Samuel Gridley Howe and* ****Julia Ward Howe*** *(1819–1910); married M. Anagnos (superintendent of the Perkins Institute for the Blind in Boston, Massachusetts), in 1870.*

Julia Anagnos wrote *Stray Chords* (1883) and *Philosophiæ Quæstor.*

SUGGESTED READING:

Elliott, Maud Howe. *Three Generations.* Boston, MA: Little, Brown, 1923.

Ream, Debbie Williams. "Mine Eyes Have Seen the Glory," in *American History Illustrated.* January–February 1993.

Tharp, Louise Hall. *Three Saints and a Sinner: Julia Ward Howe, Louisa, Annie and Sam Ward.* Boston, MA: Little, Brown, 1956.

Ernest Freeberg, Ph.D.
in American History, Emory University, Atlanta, Georgia

Howe, Lois (c. 1864–1964)

American architect. *Born around 1864; died in 1964; graduated from a two-year course in architecture at Massachusetts Institute of Technology, 1890.*

Lois Howe had a long and prolific career in architecture, unlike her fellow MIT graduate ***Sophia Hayden**. Howe was primarily a designer and renovator of private homes, and she served as architect for buildings that are scattered throughout the Boston suburbs of Arlington, Cambridge, Concord, and Wellesley. After graduating from MIT's special two-year course in architecture in 1890, Howe went to work in the offices of Francis Allen and designed her first house in association with Joseph Prince Loud in 1894. A year later, she opened her own office on Clarendon Street in Boston's Back Bay. In 1913, Howe went into partnership with **Eleanor Manning**, another MIT graduate (1905), establishing one of the most successful women's architectural firms in the country. It was in business until 1937.

Lois Howe became well-known for her experiments using plaster as an exterior finishing material, as well as for her interest in architectural history. Her measured drawings of New England-style architecture were published in collaboration with **Constance Fuller** in 1913. Howe became a member of the American Institute of Architects in 1901 and was made a fellow in 1931. She died in 1964, just shy of her 100th birthday.

SOURCES:

Torre, Susan, ed. *Women in American Architecture.* NY: Whitney Library of Design, 1977.

Howe, Maud (1854–1948).

See Elliott, Maud Howe.

Howes, Barbara (1914–1996)

American poet, editor, and author. *Born on May 1, 1914, in New York City; died in Bennington, Vermont, on February 24, 1996; daughter of Osborne Howes and Mildred (Cox) Howes; Bennington College, B.A., 1937; married William Jay Smith (a poet) in 1947 (divorced 1965); children: two sons, Gregory and David.*

Selected works: The Undersea Farmer *(1948);* In the Cold Country: Poems *(1954);* Light and Dark: Poems *(1959); (editor)* 23 Modern Stories *(1961); (editor)* From the Green Antilles: Writings of the Caribbean *(1966);* Looking Up at Leaves *(1966); (editor with G.J. Smith)* The Sea-Green Horse: Short Stories for Young People *(1970);* The Blue Garden *(1972); (editor)* The Eye of the Heart: Stories from Latin America *(1973);* A Private Signal: Poems New and Selected *(1977);* The Road Commissioner and Other Stories *(1988);* Collected Poems, 1940–1990 *(1998).*

At the time of her death in February 1996, poet, author, and editor Barbara Howes was a friend to many in the literary community; she was also an impressive contributor. Referring to poetry as "a way of life, not just an avocation," Howes viewed it as a practice in which "one orders and deepens one's experience, and learns to understand what is happening in oneself and in others."

Barbara Howes was born in Bennington, Vermont, in 1914. She graduated from Bennington College in 1937, after which she briefly worked for the Farmers Union in Mississippi before moving to New York and beginning her literary career. From 1943 to 1947, she was an editor of the literary quarterly *Chimera,* which introduced Americans to writers from abroad. In 1947, she married poet William Jay Smith and moved with him to Oxford, England, where he was a Rhodes Scholar. The couple had two sons and lived in Italy, France, and Haiti before divorcing in 1965. Howes then moved to a farm in Pownal, Vermont, where she resided for the remainder of her life.

In addition to writing poetry, Howes edited two highly regarded anthologies of Latin American writers, and also published several collections of short stories, including one for children, *The Sea-Green Horse.* She drew her inspiration from everyday life. "As it turns out, I seem to write about things I see," she wrote, "my children, my friends, my attachment, our animals, the view from any window, in no special order or arrangement." In her essay in *Poets on Poetry,* Howes expressed her distrust of "the snarling little ego," and her aversion to writers who "give in to violence and spite." Unlike many contemporary poets, her work is restrained and traditional in form. According to **Alberta Turner**, in *American Women Writers,* Howes' most recurring theme is "that unrestricted emotion blinds and imprisons if allowed to dominate either life or art."

Barbara Howes was the recipient of numerous honors and awards, including a Guggenheim fellowship and two nominations for the National Book Award, one of which was announced just a year before her death for her *Collected Poems, 1940–1990.*

SOURCES:

Mainiero, Lina, ed. *American Women Writers: From Colonial Times to the Present.* NY: Frederick Ungar, 1980.

Meek, Jocelyn. "Obituaries," in *The Boston Globe.* February 26, 1996.

COLLECTIONS:

Barbara Howes' papers are housed at the Yale University Library, New Haven, Connecticut.

Barbara Morgan,
Melrose, Massachusetts

Howitt, Mary (1799–1888)

English poet, essayist, translator, and historian. *Born Mary Botham in Coleford, Gloucestershire, England, on March 12, 1799; died in Rome, Italy, on January 30, 1888; daughter of Samuel Botham and Annie (Wood) Botham, both Quakers; married William Howitt (a writer), in 1821; children: five, including Alfred William Howitt (an English explorer and anthropologist in Australia), and Margaret Howitt (a novelist who edited* Mary Howitt: An Autobiography, *[1889]).*

Mary Howitt, who was educated at home and in Quaker schools, wrote poetry from a very early age. During her marriage to fellow Quaker William Howitt (1792–1879), which extended over a period of 58 years, the couple wrote many works in collaboration. After settling in Nottingham, their first shared publication was a collection of poetry, *The Forest Minstrel,* in 1823.

Upon William's retirement as a chemist, the couple moved to West End Cottage, Esher, where Mary Howitt began to write a series of successful children's books. A residency in Heidelberg, where the Howitts lived in 1840, sparked an interest in Scandinavian literature. From 1842 to 1863, she translated the novels of ***Fredrika Bremer** from the Swedish (the first to present Bremer to an English public).

Returning to England in 1843, she and her husband published *Howitt's Journal,* but it was not successful. In their later years, the Howitts drifted away from their Quaker upbringing and became interested in spiritualism. They moved to Italy in 1870, spending their winters in Rome and their summers in Tyrol. Howitt's husband died in 1879, and Mary lived with her daughter **Margaret Howitt** in the Tyrol. Baptized a Roman Catholic in 1882, Mary died in Rome six years later of bronchitis. She was honored by the Literary Academy of Stockholm.

In addition to collaborations with her husband, Mary Howitt wrote many poems, hymns, ballads, and some novels. Her independent publications number 110 distinct works, including *Literature and Romance of Northern Europe* (1852) and *Ruined Abbeys and Castles of Britain* (1862, 1864).

SUGGESTED READING:

Howitt, Mary. *My Own Story* (an autobiography), 1845.

———. *An Autobiography,* 1889.

Howland, Emily (1827–1929)

American educator, reformer, and philanthropist. *Born on November 20, 1827, in Cayuga County, New York; died on June 29, 1929, in Cayuga County, New York; the second of three children and only daughter of Slocum Howland (a merchant) and Hannah (Tallcot) Howland; attended Miss Susanna Marriott's home school, Aurora, New York; attended Poplar Ridge Seminary, Poplar Ridge, New York; never married; no children.*

Born in 1827 in Cayuga County, New York, Emily Howland was raised in a devout Quaker family and educated in local schools. When she was 16, she left school to take over the household chores from her ailing mother. Bored by domesticity, she sought refuge in painting and the study of French, but her frustration remained so acute that she once signed a letter "Emily Howling!" In 1888, recalling her childhood in a letter to a friend, Howland characterized herself as "a little girl who played too little and who thought too much."

Howland finally found a sense of purpose in the antislavery movement. In 1857, she moved to Washington, D.C., to fill in for the ailing ***Myrtilla Miner** as principal of the Washington School for Colored Girls. For two years, she ran the school with one African-American assistant, returning home a changed woman. In 1863, when the signing of the Emancipation Proclamation brought thousands of freed slaves North, she returned to Washington, teaching and providing medical assistance at the various freedmen's camps set up around the city. Early in 1867, when it became apparent that the government would not fulfill its promise to grant land to each freed slave, she persuaded her father to buy 400 acres in Heathville, Virginia, where she began relocating former slave families and established a school. She remained there until August 1867, when she was called home again to care for her mother in her final illness.

After her mother's death, Howland remained in New York, living in the family home at Sherwood for the rest of her life. Her interest in education was now served through philanthropy. In 1882, she financed an enlargement of the local Sherwood Select School, a Quaker institution which she continued to support until it was taken over by the state of New York in 1927. She also continued to fund the Heathville, Virginia, school for over 50 years, until it too was taken over by the state. Her philanthropy extended to an additional 30 educational institutions for blacks in the South. She took a particular interest in Tuskegee Institute, founded by Booker T. Washington, who was a personal friend. Howland was also a champion of the women's rights movement, and was president of her local suffrage society. She was a regular delegate at the conventions of the National American Woman Suffrage Association, and supported temperance and peace movements as well.

Growing somewhat lame and deaf with age, Howland remained vigorous. At age 99, she traveled to Albany to receive an honorary degree from the University of the State of New York, in recognition of her service to education. She died at Sherwood in 1929, having reached the age of 101.

SOURCES:

James, Edward T., ed. *Notable American Women, 1607–1950.* Cambridge, MA: The Belknap Press of Harvard University Press, 1971.

McHenry, Robert, ed. *Famous American Women.* NY: Dover, 1983.

Barbara Morgan,
Melrose, Massachusetts

Hoxha, Nexhmije (1920—)

Albanian politician. *Born in 1920; married Enver Hodja also seen as Enver Hoxha (1908–1985), prime minister of Albania, 1945–1953.*

Nexhmije Hoxha was born in 1920 and married Enver Hoxha who was prime minister of Albania from 1945 until his death in 1985. For many years, Nexhmije held a series of posts alongside her husband in Albania's Communist Party of Labour (PPSh) as well as affiliated organizations. In 1990, she was removed from her posts, this action being attributable to her strong opposition to reform. In 1991, she was expelled from the Party of Labour and arrested on corruption charges. Hoxha was convicted in January of 1993 of the misuse of public funds between 1985 and 1990. She was sentenced to nine years' imprisonment, but her incarceration was later extended to 11 years.

Kim L. Messeri,
freelance writer, Austin, Texas

Hoxie, Vinnie Ream (1847–1914).

See Ream, Vinnie.

Hoya, Katherina von

(d. around 1470)

German composer who compiled the* Wienhausen Liederbuch *which contained many German and Latin songs. *Birth date unknown; died around 1470; was 15th-century abbess of the Cistercian convent of Wienhausen (1420–70).*

Katherina von Hoya was born of a noble German family in the 15th century and like many women of her station entered a convent. For 50 years, she was the abbess of the Cistercian convent of Wienhausen, near Celle, a powerful position in the Middle Ages. Convents and monasteries were centers of learning and culture, providing resources not normally available in the outside world. It is not surprising, therefore, that many women flourished as composers in this setting, especially as they were in charge of their own creativity. Von Hoya is known for the *Wienhausen Liederbuch* which was compiled by at least five nuns. In it, there were 37 Low German, 17 Latin, and six mixed Latin and German songs. One of the best pieces, No. 24, is attributed to Von Hoya and Nos. 13 and 25 are also thought to be her work.

John Haag,
Athens, Georgia

Hoyt, Beatrix (1880–1963)

American golfer. *Born on July 5, 1880, in Westchester County, New York; died on August 14, 1963, in Thomasville, Georgia; daughter of William Sprague Hoyt and Janet Ralston (Chase) Hoyt; sister of Franklin Chase Hoyt, a judge; granddaughter of Salmon P. Chase, chief justice of the U.S. Supreme Court (1864–73).*

The granddaughter of Salmon P. Chase, chief justice of the U.S. Supreme Court and Lincoln's secretary of the treasury, golfer Beatrix Hoyt was only 16 when she made her mark in the burgeoning game of golf, winning the second USGA Women's Amateur ever held. Hoyt, who remained the youngest winner until ***Laura Baugh** in 1971, went on to win the Women's Amateur qualifying medal for five years in a row, and was also the winner of the championship for three consecutive years. Hoyt retired from the game at age 20, after losing to **Margaret Curtis** in the semifinal.

Hroswitha or Hrosvitha (c. 935–1001).

See Hrotsvitha of Gandersheim.

Hrotrud or Hrotrude (c. 778-after 839).

See Irene of Athens for sidebar on Rotrude.

Hrotsvitha of Gandersheim

(c. 935–1001)

German nun, poet, and historian who resided in the monastery in Gandersheim and was the first woman playwright of the West. *Name variations: Hrosvitha; Hroswitha; Hrotsuit; Hrotsuitha; Hrotsvit; Hrotsvith von Gandersheim; Hrotswitha; Roswitha. Pronunciation: Ros-VI-thuh (name derived from the old Saxon word "hrodsuind," meaning strong voice). Born around 935 in Saxony; died in 1001 at Gandersheim monastery; educated at the St. Benedict monastery in Gandersheim; wrote six plays, eight legends, two epic poems, and a historical account of the founding of the monastery at Gandersheim.*

Plays: Gallicanus *(Parts I and II);* Dulcitius; Callimachus; Abraham; Paphnutius; Sapientia. *Eight narrative religious poems concerned with the Nativity of the Virgin, the Ascension, and a series of legends of saints (Gandolph, Pelagius, Theophilus, Basil, Denis, Agnes). Two versified histories:* Carmen de gestis Oddonis, *detailing the deeds of Otto I; and* De primordiis et fundatoribus coenobii Gandersheimensis, *a history of the foundation of Gandersheim monastery.*

The playwright Hrotsvitha stands as the sole figure connecting the rich theatrical tradition of classical Greece and Rome with the medieval religious drama that was staged throughout Europe between c. 1100 and 1600 CE. During the waning years of the Roman Empire, the Catholic Church issued numerous edicts against theatrical activity, and as a result the theater, an institution that relied upon traditional dramatic literature, was non-existent throughout the Dark Ages. In an age when the theater was looked down upon, Hrotsvitha, a representative of the Church, turned to the drama as a means of promoting the Christian ideals of chastity, poverty and obedience, an almost unfathomable endeavor. Hrotsvitha lived during a time in Western civilization when most of the population was illiterate; education in general was not common, and the education of women was extremely rare. By contemporary standards, she has been regarded not only as the first woman playwright but also the first feminist playwright, because she strove to elevate the status of women in her plays from the more typical shrew or courtesan character

Curtis, Margaret. *See Curtis, Harriot and Peggy.*

seen in the plays of the Roman playwright Terence, whom she imitated, to women of dignity, self-resolve and virtue.

Little is known of her life either before or during her days in the monastery at Gandersheim in Saxony, and she has sometimes been confused with another learned abbess, also named Hrotsvitha, of the same convent who is thought to have died at least half a century earlier. One can only make suppositions about the later, famous Hrotsvitha, based on what is known about life in general during the 10th century and life in monasteries. As a result of the early 10th century decline of the Carolingian Empire of Charlemagne, the political and cultural center of the West shifted from France to Saxony with the accession of Henry I the Fowler as Holy Roman emperor in 919. In 936, Otto I the Great, the son of Henry and *Matilda of Saxony (c. 892–968), was crowned king, and in 962 he was crowned emperor of the Holy Roman Empire by Pope John XII. Otto, who learned to write and to speak Latin, surrounded himself with educated, talented scholars; he and his second wife ***Adelaide of Burgundy** (931–999) aimed at elevating the sensibilities of the court by fostering an interest in culture. As testimony to their concern in creating a more "refined" civilization, both Otto I and Adelaide (as well as their son Otto II and his wife ***Theophano of Byzantium**) were responsible for the establishment of many monasteries, which were traditionally the centers of education during the Dark and Middle Ages. Monasteries were established for both men and women as early as the 6th century.

Monastic life for women was particularly desirable for numerous reasons. Women married early, at an average age of 12 years old. Wives were expected to have children, to raise and to educate them, as well as to take care of the house. Abandonment, divorce, and polygamy were rampant, with little or no recourse for the woman; furthermore, marriage was expensive because of the expected dowry. During the 10th century, infanticide was common, particularly with female babies. Even though the women who joined the monasteries were subject to hard work, the monastic life still held a strong appeal, providing an oasis from the traumas of Germanic married life and a safe haven where a woman could live with some sense of security. Of the numerous monasteries established in Saxony, Gandersheim was one of the most important.

Gandersheim was founded by Liudolf, count of Saxony, and his wife ***Oda**, great-grandparents of Otto I. Oda decided that they should found a monastery for women because of a prophetic vision which her mother **Aeda** had of St. John the Baptist. Oda and Liudolf's daughter ***Hathumoda** was installed as the first abbess of the new community which was housed in a church on their land. After journeying to Rome to obtain the blessing of Pope Serius II, Oda and Liudolf acquired relics of saints Anastasius and Innocent, who would be the monastery's patron saints. As they returned to Saxony, a vision of light was seen that was interpreted as a sign for the exact location of the monastery's buildings. For well over a hundred years, the community had the continued support of the descendants of Oda and Liudolf, as well as their heirs, the Ottos. Hathumoda's sisters, ***Gerberga** (d. 896) and ***Christine of Gandersheim**, followed in her footsteps as abbesses. Another ***Gerberga** (r. 959–1001), daughter of ***Judith of Bavaria**, was consecrated abbess in 959.

The prefaces to Hrotsvitha's works provide the only information about her life in Gandersheim, and this information is very limited. In the "Preface to Her Poetical Works," translated by Christopher St. John, she writes:

> I was trained first by our most learned and gentle novice-mistress Rikkarda and others. Later, I owed much to the kind favour and encouragement of a royal personage, Gerberga, under whose abbatial rule I am now living. She, though younger in years than I, was, as might be expected of the niece of an Emperor, far older in learning, and she had the kindness to make me familiar with the works of some of those authors in whose writings she had been instructed by learned men [p. xxxii *The Plays of Roswitha*].

She notes in the "Preface to The Complete Works," "I found all the material . . . in various ancient works by authors of reputation," and given the philosophical discussions on religious thought and mathematics in at least two of her plays she obviously was educated. Hrotsvitha's sources included *Acta Sanctorum, Aprocryphal Gospels, Passionale Passiones, Apostolorum,* and *Vitae patrum.* She wrote in Latin, which was the only language used for literary work in the West. Her familiarity with the literature of at least the Roman writers is evident from her "Preface to Her Plays." She specifically states that there are many Catholics who prefer the works of the pagan writers to that of the Holy Scriptures. In addition, she notes that there are those who are particularly attracted to the works of Terence, a Roman playwright whose female characters were often courtesans and shrews. It is Terence whom she chooses to imitate, in her writing style, but for the purpose of glorifying "the innocent."

Hrotsvitha's manuscript was discovered in the library of the Benedictine monastery of St. Emnmeran, Ratisbon, in 1494 by Conrad Celtes, a well-known Vienna humanist. Celtes edited the manuscript, and it was published, with eight woodcuts by Albrecht Dürer, in Nuremberg (1501). The manuscript consisted of three parts: eight poems about the saints, six plays, and a lengthy poem in honor of the Ottos. This epic, *Carmen de gestis Oddonis,* was completed in 968 and details the deeds of Otto I. Composed at the request of the abbess Gerberga, it was presented by Hrotsvitha to Otto I and his son Otto II. This work, only half of which is extant, adhered closely to materials provided Hrotsvitha by members of the imperial family and is considered a historical authority. Her narrative religious poems were written in leonine hexameters or distichs and were concerned with the Nativity of the Virgin, the Ascension, and a series of legends of saints (Gandolph, Pelagius, Theophilus, Basil, Denis, and ***Agnes**). Hrotsvitha also composed *De primordiis et fundatoribus coenobii Gandersheimensis,* a work of 837 hexameters which narrates the history of her own convent up to the year 919. This foundation history of Gandersheim and the poems about the saints are significant in their attention to religious history; it is Hrotsvitha's six plays, however, that place her in the annals of Western culture.

With the intent of employing the drama as a means of edification, Hrotsvitha used the popularity of hagiography (lives and legends of the saints) to illustrate the preference for martyrdom and hermetic life as the perfect realization of the Christian ideal. In four of her plays—*Gallicanus, Dulcitius, Callimachus* and *Sapientia*—she illustrates the desirability of martyrdom. And in both *Abraham* and *Paphnutius,* she focuses on the need for hermetic life as a means of getting closer to God. These were popular and accepted ideals of the day within the monastic community. Her fundamental concern is the pronouncement of the Christian faith and the enlightenment and instruction of the followers of Christ. Hrotsvitha accomplished her mission by utilizing a very simple writing style; she structured her plays using a series of short scenes, with precise dialogue and little elaboration.

Her first play, *Gallicanus,* is written in two parts. The first part reveals how Constantia's (***Constantina** [c. 321–c. 354]) vow of chastity results in the conversion of the pagan Gallicanus. The story takes us to the days of the Roman emperor Constantine the Great, who has summoned General Gallicanus to court to impress upon him that there is a Scythian rebellion that must be suppressed. Knowing that battling the Scythians will be dangerous, Gallicanus asks for a reward: the hand of Constantine's daughter, Constantia. Constantine presents Gallicanus' proposal to his daughter who, because she has recently converted to Christianity and to a vow of chastity "for the love of my God," finds Gallicanus' offer repugnant. Constantine faces a dilemma; while he respects his daughter's decision to remain a virgin, he is also concerned with the security of his country for which he requires Gallicanus' help. Constantia, sympathizing with her father's predicament, suggests a somewhat unethical solution: her father should assure Gallicanus that Constantia is amenable to his proposal but she also tells her father that they must pray to God to "recall the soul of Gallicanus" to prevent him from attaining his reward of Constantia's hand in marriage. Gallicanus happily leaves for battle.

> Wherefore I, the strong voice of Gandersheim, have not hesitated to imitate in my writings a poet whose works are so widely read, my object being to glorify, within the limits of my poor talent, the laudable chastity of Christian virgins in that self-same form of composition which has been used to describe the shameless acts of licentious women.
>
> **—Hrotsvitha**

In Thrace, Gallicanus' men, realizing that they are outnumbered and that continued fighting would be useless, want to surrender to the enemy. Gallicanus, despairing, does not know what to do. Constantia's spiritual advisor John, who has accompanied Gallicanus, now assures him that, if he vows his allegiance to the one true God and vows to become a Christian, he will be victorious. Gallicanus agrees, and the enemy, miraculously overcome, surrenders to Gallicanus, who proclaims "let us embrace as allies." Gallicanus does not forget his vow to God and is anxious to be baptized, "to spend the rest of my life in the service of God." Returning triumphant, he recounts the events to Constantine and tells him that because of his conversion and baptism, he has given himself to God and no longer wants to wed Constantia. Gallicanus realizes that he can not stay at court, for despite his conversion and his vows his heart still yearns for Constantia. "It is not wise for me to gaze too often on the unmarried girl I love—more than my very soul." Part One concludes with Gallicanus resigning his commission and seeking permission to live with Hilarianius, a holy man.

Part II of *Gallicanus* takes place 25 years later, during the reign of Julian the Apostate. Julian advocates paganism and is opposed to Christians having the freedom "to follow the laws they were given at the time of Emperor Constantine." Vowing to confiscate the property held by Christians, Julian sends his soldiers to Gallicanus' house; but as each soldier attempts to enter the house, he is struck with leprosy. The emperor, furious, demands that Gallicanus abandon Christianity or risk exile. Undaunted by the prospect of exile, Gallicanus goes to Alexandria where, as reported by the soldiers to Julian, he is arrested and killed. The soldiers also report that John and Paul, the elderly advisors to Constantia, have given her property to the poor. John and Paul are summoned; they vow that they will not serve the pagan emperor and are subsequently arrested. Terrentianus, one of Julian's soldiers, tells John and Paul that they are to be given a second opportunity to abandon Christianity for the Roman gods. When they refuse, he murders them. After hiding the bodies, Terrentianus returns home to find his son "struck down by Divine vengeance." His son's dementia terrifies Terrentianus, who repents his actions and is forgiven. At the conclusion of the play, when his son recovers, Terrentianus proclaims his eternal thanks to God.

Gallicanus illustrates the power of belief that was so critical to early Christian doctrine. Constantia, knowing that her faith in God would remedy any situation, felt secure that Gallicanus' carnal interest in her would be abated once he too turned to Christianity. Likewise, Gallicanus' faith gave him the strength to face exile and eventual death. But it is Terrentianus' conversion and the renewed health of his son that bring the concept of faith in Christianity to its climax.

Hrotsvitha's second play, *Dulcitius,* is a comedy which focuses even more specifically on the power of faith and on women. *Dulcitius* takes place during the 4th century CE, during a time of aggressive persecutions of Christians under Diocletian. The sisters Agape, Chione and Irena (*See joint entry on ****Irene, Chionia, and Agape of Thessalonica***) have converted to Christianity, and this prevents them from being part of Roman society. Diocletian summons the women, offering to wed them to the noblest of Roman men if they renounce their Christian faith. When the beautiful young women shun Diocletian's offer, he threatens to punish them for their stubbornness. Irena proclaims that they "yearn for the day we can embrace [punishment]; We long to be torn asunder for the love of Christ." Diocletian calls for Governor Dulcitius, who upon seeing their beauty is immediately overwhelmed with lust. He orders them jailed in the kitchen, so that he can have easy access to them. Dulcitius arrives at the kitchen, but is placed under a spell whereby he mistakes the kitchenware for the young women. The girls, hearing him arrive, hide in the next room; they peer through the cracks of the walls and see him embracing the sooty pots and pans. This comic moment is prolonged in the next scene when Dulcitius, covered with soot, is mistaken by his men for the Devil. Unaware of his own appearance, Dulcitius seeks redress from the emperor but is turned away because there too he is not recognized. It is not until he returns home that the spell is lifted and Dulcitius sees that he has been made a fool. Outraged, he orders the girls stripped of their clothing, so that they too can be humiliated. Miraculously, the clothing cannot be removed. Diocletian then turns to Count Sisinnius to punish the girls for humiliating Dulcitius. Sisinnius orders the two older sisters to be tortured; they are given the opportunity to renounce Christianity for the Roman gods, and they refuse. They are burned at the stake, but their souls miraculously leave their bodies before dying. Sisinnius then turns to the youngest, Irena. When she refuses to abandon Christ, he threatens to take her to a brothel. Irena retorts: "trials bring the crown of Heaven." As the soldier takes her to the brothel, she vows that they will not succeed. Hours later, the soldiers return to Sisinnius and report that en route two well-dressed men met them on the road and told them that Sisinnius had ordered them to take Irena to the mountain top instead. Sisinnius, furious, goes to the mountain but gets hopelessly lost. He finally finds Irena and orders his men to kill her. She taunts him with her wish for eternal glory and martyrdom. The play concludes with the soldiers shooting their arrows at her as she stands with her arms held up toward Heaven.

Callimachus, Hrotsvitha's third play, centers on Callimachus' admitted love for **Drusiana**, Lord Andronicus' wife. His friends try to convince him that Drusiana is a devout Christian and will never be lured into an affair; she does not even sleep with her own husband. Callimachus, not to be dissuaded, confesses his love to Drusiana. When Drusiana is repulsed by his confession, Callimachus threatens to pursue her until she relents. In her despair, Drusiana prays to God. She fears a scandal if she reveals Callimachus' threats. Drusiana prays for death so that she can preserve her chastity and her husband's reputation. Her prayers are answered, and when Andronicus returns home he finds that his wife has died. Andronicus seeks out St. John the Apostle, who tells him that he should shed no tears for Drusiana because she is with God. While Andronicus is away, Callimachus pays a house servant to take him to the family vault to see Drusiana's body. He buries his head in the folds of her gown and vows to have her now that she is dead. As he is about to carry her off, the house servant, who is with him, sees a large snake, is bitten and dies. Callimachus, viewing this in disbelief, believes the snake to be the Devil. He is so terrified that he dies on the spot. Meanwhile, en route to the tomb, Andronicus and St. John see a vision of Jesus who tells them that He wants both Drusiana and Callimachus resurrected, "So that My Name may be glorified in them." When they arrive, they find the dead bodies of Drusiana, Callimachus and Fortunatus, the servant. Realizing Callimachus' intentions, they do not understand why Christ would want to resurrect Callimachus. However, when Callimachus is resurrected, he repents his deeds and asks forgiveness. When Drusiana is resurrected, she asks for Fortunatus' return to life. Callimachus protests, believing that it was Fortunatus' fault that he was in the tomb; but St. John reminds Callimachus that Christianity requires forgiveness for everyone. When Fortunatus is resurrected, he cannot tolerate looking at Drusiana or Callimachus, who are true Christians. Fortunatus would prefer death, and he gets his wish at the conclusion of the play.

In Hrotsvitha's fourth play, *Abraham,* renouncing the world for a hermit's life becomes the means of achieving closeness to God. Abraham, seeking the advice of the hermit Effrem, is concerned about his orphaned niece, Maria; he wants her to marry Christ and live a life of chastity. Maria, who is only eight years old, does not understand all that Effrem and Abraham relate to her, but she does finally agree to renounce the present world. Abraham builds a small cell for her to live out her hermitage; living next to her, he will be able to instruct her on the ways of the Lord. Twenty years pass and Abraham once again visits Effrem. He tells him that a young man disguised as a monk gained access to Maria and seduced her; though she originally repented this sin, she has now reentered the world and become a whore. Abraham tells Effrem that he will break the vows of a hermit to seek out Maria. Disguised as a would-be lover, Abraham finds Maria and, after pretending he wants to stay with her, reveals his true identity; Maria is so overcome that she repents her evil ways and agrees to go back with him. She returns to her windowless cell next to Abraham's hermitage where she lives the rest of her days safe from the Devil's charm.

In *Paphnutius,* Hrotsvitha's fifth play, the hermit Paphnutius is engaged in a philosophical discussion with his disciples who learn that Paphnutius is saddened by the ways of ***Thais**, a courtesan, whose beauty has seduced many men. Determined to find her and convert her to Christianity, he disguises himself as one of her lovers, and after gaining access to her chambers he convinces her that she has sinned. Thais feels such shame and grief that she agrees to obey Paphnutius and to enter a convent where she can live a life of contemplation and repentance. She is given a small cell where she must remain, never to leave it for any reason. At first, the humiliation of staying in one small space is overwhelming and Thais is reluctant, but she is convinced that this is the way to salvation. Three years pass and when Paphnutius returns to Thais' cell he finds a new woman, one who has finally achieved salvation. Thais then dies and joins Christ.

Hrotsvitha's last play, *Sapientia,* returns to the theme of martyrdom, focusing on the Holy Virgins: Faith, Hope and Charity. The play is set in the Roman world of Emperor Hadrian. His advisor, Antiochus, informs Hadrian that Sapientia and her three children have arrived in Rome; though merely women, they should still be viewed as dangerous to the state since they preach sedition: "This woman . . . encourages our people to abandon their ancestral rites and give themselves over to the Christian religion." Hadrian concurs and demands that they be brought to him so that he can persuade them to return to the worship of the Roman gods. He suggests that he will begin by speaking to them in a kindly manner. Antiochus believes this will prove to be a useful strategy: "for the weak and delicate nature of the feminine sex can easily be softened by flattery." Neither Hadrian nor Antiochus realize that Sapientia has instilled in herself and her daughters such a love of Christ that they cannot be dissuaded. Hadrian gives them three days to reconsider. When they do not change their minds, Antiochus encourages Hadrian to kill the young girls to achieve the most painful punishment for the mother. The young girls, however, married to Christ, yearn to be martyrs. Hadrian's sentence is harsh; he has the girls tortured in a most cruel manner. But their love of Christ allows them to accept the torture and keeps them from feeling any pain. The play concludes with the burial of Sapientia's daughters; Sapientia is assisted by other Christian women, some of whom she had converted when she arrived in Rome. Sapientia offers a prayer to God and asks that she too may join Him and her daughters in Heaven.

Hrotsvitha's plays provide a link between the classical and medieval worlds. She used the dramatic format as a tool to educate. Although there is no evidence that her plays were in fact staged at the monastery, it is likely that they were designed to be read aloud or recited by sisters of the convent. From a modern perspective, Hrotsvitha's importance may have less to do with advocating Christianity than with her ability to overcome prejudice toward the theater and her ability to depict women in a noble and enlightening manner.

SOURCES:

Bonfante, Larissa, trans. *The Plays of Hrotswitha of Gandersheim.* Oak Park, IL: Golchazy-Carducci, 1986.

St. John, Christopher, trans. *The Plays of Roswitha.* London, 1932 (reissued by B. Blom, N.Y., 1966).

Wilson, Katharina M., ed. *Hrotsvit of Gandersheim Rara Avis in Saxonia?* Ann Arbor, MI: Marc, 1987.

SUGGESTED READING:

Case, Sue-Ellen. "Re-Viewing Hrotsvit," in *Theater Journal.* Vol. 35, no. 4. December 1983, pp. 533–542.

Nicoll, Allardyce. *Masks, Mimes and Miracles.* New York, 1931 (reprinted, 1963).

Anita DuPratt,
Professor of Theater, California State University, Bakersfield

Hrotswitha (c. 935–1001).

See Hrotsvitha of Gandersheim.

Hsiang Ching-yu or Chin-yu (1895–1928).

See Xiang Jingyü.

Hsiao Fu-jeh (1902–1970).

See Aylward, Gladys.

Hsiao Hung (1911–1942).

See Xiao Hong.

Hubbard, Elizabeth.

See Witchcraft Trials in Salem Village.

Huber, Therese (1764–1829)

German writer of novels and short stories. *Name variations: Theresa Heyne. Born Therese or Theresa Heyne in Göttingen, Germany, in 1764; died in Augsburg in 1829; daughter of Professor D.C.G. Heyne; married Georg Forster (1754–1794), son of naturalist Johann Reinhold Forster; married Ludwig Ferdinand Huber, a Saxon diplomat (died 1804).*

Therese Huber was one of the most prolific writers of late 18th- and early 19th-century Germany. Born in Göttingen in 1764, she grew up in the intellectually stimulating atmosphere of her father Professor D.C.G. Heyne's home. She wrote more than 60 stories, 6 novels, 3,800 letters, and translated several works from French and English into German. She also edited the popular German newspaper, *Morgenblatt für gebildete Stände* (Morning Daily for the Cultured Classes), from 1816 until 1823.

As the drama of the French Revolution unfolded in the year 1789, Therese greeted the events with enthusiasm. Her first husband Georg Forster, who was an ardent supporter of the French Revolution, had to agree to her decision to leave Mainz for Neufchâtel, Switzerland, in 1792 when his and his family's safety was threatened by the Prussian troops advancing to free Mainz from the French army. Georg was the son of the naturalist Johann Reinhold Forster and had accompanied Johann on Captain James Cook's second voyage around the world (1772–75). Following his death in 1794, Therese married Ludwig Ferdinand Huber, a Saxon diplomat who had accompanied her to Switzerland. As their source of income became uncertain in exile, Therese undertook writing so as to contribute financially to the household. Her first literary attempt was the novel *Die Familie Seldorf* (1795–96), with the French Revolution as its central theme. When L.F. Huber died in 1804, Therese was forced to make writing her profession.

Recognized as one of Germany's first professional women writers, Huber also wrote the first novel in world literature that is set in an Australian penal settlement. Called *Adventures on a Journey to New Holland,* the novel was published in 1801, and tells the story of people caught up in the aftermath of the French Revolution, although it is said to give only a vague picture of the Australian colony. The story was continued in a sequel, *The Lonely Deathbed,* published in 1810. In 1966, *Adventures on a Journey to New Holland* and *The Lonely Deathbed,* translated by Rodney Livingstone and edited by Leslie Bodi, were republished in a single volume.

Therese Huber worked at a time when the German bourgeoisie elevated the family to a position of great import. Women in domestic roles were seen as fulfilling their "natural" destiny.

Familial morals of conjugal love, parental affection, discipline and respect were being propagated through literary and philosophical discourses. Huber's writing also seems to participate in strengthening the foundations of a sentimental family. Women within the family, however, wield power, while men remain either absent or are merely mentioned in her stories and novels. Huber also portrays women as strong individuals who assert themselves by refusing to abide by traditional norms. But these women do not carry their dissent to culmination. They usually accept domesticity as their fate and in the end "happily" turn towards household or maternal duties. Though in her own life Therese was the editor of the newspaper *Morgenblatt,* she remained anonymous for years because she did not want to provoke public criticism against her unfeminine occupation. She insisted in her letters that she had always been a good mother to her four children and had always fulfilled her household duties conscientiously.

When Therese Huber died in Augsburg in 1829, her obituary written by Wilhelm von Humboldt correctly described her as one of the most intelligent women of her time, who loved life and had uncomplainingly faced several hardships.

Vibha Bakshi Gokhale,
author of *Walking the Tightrope: A Feminist Reading of Therese Huber's Stories*

Huch, Ricarda (1864–1947)

German poet, novelist, and short story writer who is often considered the outstanding German woman author of the 20th century. *Name variations: (pseudonym) Richard Hugo. Pronunciation: ree-CARD-AH whok. Born Ricarda Octavia Huch on August 18, 1864, in Braunschweig, Germany; died on November 17, 1947, in Frankfurt am Main; daughter of Richard Huch (a merchant) and Emilie Huch; had one brother and one sister; educated by home schooling; grade school in Braunschweig; college preparatory work in Zurich, Switzerland; bachelor and doctor of philosophy degrees from the University of Zurich; married Ermanno Ceconi in Vienna, on July 9, 1898 (divorced 1906); married Richard Huch (a cousin and former husband of her sister, Lilly), in Braunschweig on July 6, 1907 (divorced 1911); children: (first marriage) one daughter,* ***Marietta Ceconi*** *(b. 1899).*

Moved out of family home to Zurich, Switzerland (1887); became first woman to earn a doctorate from the University of Zurich (1891); published her initial book of poetry, Gedichte *(1891); moved to Trieste with her first husband (1898); published novel* From Triumph Street *(*Aus der Triumphgasse, *1902); took up residence in Munich (1907); published a trilogy of German history,* The Great War in Germany *(*Der grosse Krieg in Deutschland, *1912–14); published her best prose work, the psychological detective thriller* The Deruga Trial *(*Der Fall Deruga, *1917); was made an honorary senator of the University of Munich (1924); awarded the Goethe Prize of Frankfurt (1931); elected to membership in the Academy of Prussian Writers (1931); resigned from the Academy (1933); published a three-part* German History *(*Deutsche Geschichte, *1934, 1937, and posthumously in 1949); received an honorary degree from the University of Jena (1947); published an "Open Letter to the German People" (1947).*

Selected works: Gedichte *(1891);* Neue Gedichte *(1907);* Memories of Ludolf Ursleu the Younger *(*Erinnerungen von Ludolf Ursleu dem Jüngeren, *1893);* The Flowering of Romanticism *(*Blütezeit der Romantik, *1899);* The Rise and Fall of Romanticism *(*Ausbreitung und Verfall der Romantik, *1899);* From Triumph Street *(*Aus der Triumphgasse, *1902);* Histories of Garibaldi *(*Die Geschichten von Garibaldi, *1906);* Luther's Faith *(*Luthers Glaube, *1916);* The Deruga Trial *(*Der Fall Deruga, *1917);* The Great War in Germany *(*Der grosse Krieg in Deutschland, *1912–14);* German History *(*Deutsche Geschichte, *3 vols., 1934, 1937, and 1949).*

Although the German writer Ricarda Huch is not well-known outside her native land, the number and variety of her writings has earned her the reputation in Germany as being the leading German literary woman writer of the 20th century. The wide scope of her work—lyric poetry, short stories, philosophic books, and romantic and historical novels—has also given her a place among the significant writers of the 20th century.

The daughter of **Emilie Huch** and Richard Huch, a German merchant, Huch was born in Braunschweig, Germany, in 1864, and grew to adulthood in a family that emphasized literature and music. One brother, Rudolf Huch, also became a novelist. Ricarda was the last of the family's children, however, since her birth was a difficult one, and doctors advised her mother to avoid having more; from that point on, her father slept in his own bedroom.

The family was very job-oriented, and her father, and occasionally her mother, traveled frequently to both Hamburg and Brazil on business. Despite their absences, Huch remembered a close family unit. In an autobiographical sketch, she cited memories of a family "musical band," in which her father, a "fine" tenor, would sing, her mother would play accompaniment on the piano, and the children would join in with triangles or other instruments.

When her father's trips out of the country became more frequent, Huch's mother and the children moved to the house of the maternal grandparents. Some of Huch's most vivid memories were of being with her maternal grandmother, whose "lively spirit" overcame some of the "dreariness and melancholy" that sometimes prevailed in the family.

Huch's grandmother loved art and frequently took the young Huch to museums, where many of the paintings portrayed mythological heroes. Her grandmother also read to her from ancient literature, including the *Metamorphosis* of Ovid. Huch later wrote that such literature, and especially ancient tales of gods and goddesses, fed her love of historical heroes.

Huch was also influenced by a friend of her sister, **Anna Klie**, a frequent visitor to the family. Klie introduced Huch to the stories of the 19th-century poet and writer Gottfried Keller. In time, Huch would come to bear more than a passing resemblance to Keller: like Keller, she would become the author of poems, short stories, and novels which mixed a "realistic" perspective with more than a few touches of Romanticism.

Ricarda Huch is not just the first lady of Germany, as she is so often described, but quite obviously also the first lady of Europe.

—**Thomas Mann, 1924**

Although Huch was given no formal schooling until she was nine years old, she proved to be an eager student. She showed a special fondness for reading history books which depicted popular revolts against tyrannical rulers. Upon graduation from elementary studies, she chose not to enter high school immediately, rejecting the idea that, as a young German woman, she should either marry or enter a high school designed to prepare students for commercial work. Since her parents' travels had left her with an interest in languages, she chose to do private study in Spanish and Portuguese, using the foreign books in her father's library.

One reason why she remained in the family home was to be near her cousin Richard Huch, with whom she had fallen in love. But Richard was married to her sister, **Lilly Huch**. Although he was more than 13 years older, Ricarda later wrote that she had felt "strong empathy" with Richard. She added that Richard had told his wife that he had "warm feelings" for Ricarda. Richard rejected the idea of leaving his wife and children, however, and expressed particular concern about disapproval from family members.

Frustrated with the thwarted romance, Huch decided to leave Germany. She chose a date in late 1886, when her father was away on a business trip, as an appropriate time to move out of the family home in Braunschweig. On New Year's Day, 1887, she moved to Zurich, Switzerland, and made arrangements for private tutoring which would prepare her for admission to the University of Zurich. Although women were denied admission to universities in Germany (and it would be several years before they might even sit in university classes there, and then only with the permission of the professor), Zurich had become the first German-speaking university to admit women students.

After graduating magna cum laude from Zurich, Huch enrolled in the university's Ph.D. program in history. In 1891, at age 27, she became the first German woman to receive an academic doctor of philosophy degree. She chronicled her experiences as a graduate student in Switzerland in the book *Spring in Switzerland* (*Frühling in der Schweiz,* 1938).

Although she returned to Germany for periodic visits, and even worked for a time as a teacher at a girls' school in Braunschweig, Huch chose to keep her residence in Zurich. She supported herself by working as a librarian. While there, she began to experiment with writing poems and made efforts toward writing her first novel. The same year that she received her doctorate, she published her first book of poems, *Gedichte* (1891), followed by *Neue Gedichte* in 1907.

Several of her early lyric poems were romantic poems about Richard; she called them "little items which I play with to amuse myself." While many of Huch's prose writings won high praise from critics who called them "insightful" or "powerful," her lyric poems were generally regarded as being less successful. During the 1920s, however, when a younger generation of German women came of age and gained political rights which had been denied before, Huch's poetry became popular among women readers.

In a career spanning nearly 60 years, Huch produced more than 50 books and an even larger number of articles, some under the pseudonym Richard Hugo. Her first novel, *Memories of Ludolf Ursleu the Younger* (*Erinnerungen* von Ludolf Ursleu dem Jüngeren*), appeared in 1893. Written in lyrical prose, it described the rise and decline of an upper-class German family. It also followed a pattern that would be seen in many of Huch's novels, focusing on major transforming or deciding events in the life of the main character of the novel.

Many of the leading characters in Huch's novels face inward spiritual struggles, as they attempt to establish meaningful contact with other people or to achieve a meaningful understanding of the universe. In some cases, the decisive moments in her novels are presented as a step toward loving and understanding the universe. Her heroes are generally trying to expand beyond the limits of their own personalities and seek active interchange with other personalities. Her main characters seek, above all, self-realization. Huch's interest in the inner world of her characters culminated in the novel which critics generally believe to be her best prose work, the psychological detective thriller *The Deruga Trial* (*Der Fall Deruga,* 1917).

It was no coincidence that there were certain similarities between Huch's writings and the writings of the German Romantics of the early 19th century. An admirer of Romanticism, the young Huch rejected the naturalist writers of her own time, such as the French writer Emile Zola and the German playwright Frank Wedekind. She complained that they had "constructed a universe in which a triumphant spirit is not possible." In contrast, she believed that the German Romantics had embarked on a quest for "inner freedom" and had sought to unite the rational, sensuous, and emotional sides of their personalities.

Huch analyzed the Romantic search for "inner freedom" in two books, *The Flowering of Romanticism* (*Blütezeit der Romantik,* 1899) and *The Rise and Fall of Romanticism* (*Ausbreitung und Verfall der Romantik,* 1899). When, later in her career, she began writing philosophically oriented books, they were replete with Romantically sounding phrases such as "consciousness," "self-consciousness," and "God-consciousness." An example was her *On the Nature of Men: Nature and Intellect* (*Vom Wesen des Menschen: Natur und Geist,* 1914).

In 1897, Huch moved back to Germany for a brief time. Finding her relationship with Richard unimproved, she decided to relocate to Vienna, Austria, where she would be able to use the library of the University of Vienna to do research for future books. While she was staying in a boarding house there, Huch met and married Ermanno Ceconi, an assistant to a Viennese dentist, and nicknamed her husband, who was six years younger, "Manno." The newlyweds moved to his native city of Trieste, Italy, where he opened his own dental practice. A child, Marietta, was born the following year. In Italy, Huch produced one of her more realistic works, *From Triumph Street* (*Aus der Triumphgasse,* 1902). The book, a novel of social criticism, portrayed in stark terms the living conditions in a slum neighborhood in Trieste.

The two divorced in 1906; the next year, she and Richard were married and took up residence in Munich. That marriage would last little more than three years. Because Richard refused to allow Marietta to live with them, the little girl lived with her father in Italy. Only in 1911, after Ricarda and Richard divorced, did Marietta begin to live with her mother in Munich.

Huch's first historical work appeared in the late 1890s, and more than half of all of her subsequent books had a historical connection. Her historical accounts, while carefully researched, are generally referred to as historical novels, because Huch's treatment of the topics was literary rather than historical. She often chose to depict people struggling for freedom—even artistic freedom—as true heroes. In an autobiographical sketch, Huch traced her interest in such topics to her childhood love of Greek heroes who fought, she said, for liberty.

One of her early historical works, the *Histories of Garibaldi* (*Die Geschichten von Garibaldi,* 1906, which appeared in English translation as *Defeat and Victory* in 1928 and 1929), presented the Italians' struggle to unite their country as a popular movement for political freedom. Other books combined religious and historical themes. Although she had earlier seemed to favor atheism in *Fra Celeste* (1899), her Protestant roots were reflected in her favorable treatment of Luther in *Luther's Faith* (*Luthers Glaube,* 1916). She also surprised many readers by insisting that sin is a necessary part of religious experience. Nevertheless, she also produced a novel about a Reformation defender of the Catholic faith, *Wallenstein* (*Wallenstein: Eine Charakterstudie,* 1915). Other notable historical works included *The Risorgimento* (*Das Risorgimento,* 1908); *Michael Bakunin and Anarchism* (*Michael Bakunin und die Anarchie,* 1923); and *Old and New Gods: The Revolution of the Nineteenth Century in Germany* (*Alte und Neue Göttern: Die Revolution des 19. Jahrhunderts in Deutschland,* 1930).

The most admired of her historical works proved to be her trilogy of German history which appeared between 1912 and 1914 as *The Great War in Germany* (*Der grosse Krieg in Deutschland*). It dealt with a broad sweep of the German history, from the Reformation to the decline of the Holy Roman Empire. Huch's favorite section was on the Thirty Years' War, which she described as a period when an arrogant nobility lived in luxury, while most Germans starved. "While the topic of war bores me,"she wrote, "this war has interested me intensely."

During the decade of the 1920s, Huch, now in her 60s, lived in Heidelberg. When German women were granted the right to vote in 1919, she was asked by a group of women to run for the constituent assembly, the body that would write the constitution for the Weimar Republic, Germany's first democracy. Among those urging her to run was a close friend, the German feminist ***Gertrud Bäumer**. The project had to be abandoned when Huch could not secure the support of major party leaders.

Her growing reputation as a writer brought her a variety of awards and other forms of recognition. She was made an honorary senator of the University of Munich in 1924, and she was awarded the Goethe Prize of Frankfurt in 1931. But the recognition that was most meaningful to her came in 1931, when she was elected to membership in the Academy of Prussian Writers. Believing herself not worthy of sitting with celebrated writers such as Thomas Mann, she initially decided not to accept. Mann himself talked her into attending the induction ceremony. Yet her membership in the Academy proved short-lived: when National Socialism gained power in early 1933, a move was made to force the Academy to expel Jewish members. Huch rejected the idea, and she was appalled when pressure was also placed on members to join a newly created Nazi Academy of Writers.

Huch wrote a letter of resignation from the Academy, protesting the expulsion of Jewish writers in these words:

> I think that it is quite understandable that a German should feel German; but what Germanness is, and how one should feel German, is a matter of quite divergent opinions. What the present government holds to be national sentiment is not my Germanness. . . . The centralization, the oppression, the brutal methods, the defamation of anyone who disagrees . . . I hold these things to be both unGerman and unholy.

She ended the letter with the declaration, "I hereby announce my decision to resign from the Academy."

During the 1930s, when Huch lived in Jena as a virtual recluse, she continued to work on her *German History* (*Deutsche Geschichte,* published in three volumes in 1934, 1937, and posthumously in 1949). The Nazi government was not pleased that her books criticized the "bestial drive" of earlier Germans and praised the "qualities of heroism" exhibited by German Jews of the past. Such comments drew condemnation of Huch from the *National Socialist Monthly,* which insisted that "There is no place for . . . this . . . in the Germany of Adolf Hitler."

Emerging from World War II with her reputation enhanced, Huch received new honors: the University of Jena awarded her an honorary degree in 1947, and she was elected president of a Congress of German Writers convened in Berlin.

In the years immediately after World War II, it was common for Germans to carefully peruse newspapers for word of lost relatives. Taking advantage of this development, Huch in 1947 decided to publish in newspapers throughout Germany an "Open Letter to the German People." The "Open Letter" begged readers to send her documents, letters, and diaries connected with Germans, "living and dead," who had resisted Hitler. She declared her intention to write a book about these and other "martyrs" such as the theologian Dietrich Bonhoeffer. The project never reached fruition. On November 17, 1947, Huch died at Frankfurt am Main during a trip to visit her daughter. But Huch's place in German literature had been firmly established. She had become, in the word of one German literary critic, "the greatest German woman author" and "perhaps the greatest German woman of our time."

SOURCES:

Berger, Dorothea. "The Lyric Poetry of Ricarda Huch," in *Books Abroad.* Vol. 26, 1952, pp. 244–247.

Edinger, Dora. "She Also Bore Witness: Ricarda Huch, 1864–1947," in *The American-German Review.* Vol. 14, 1948, pp. 32–33.

Flandreau, Audrey. "Ricarda Huch's Weltanschauung as Expressed in her Philosophical Works and in Her Novels." Ph.D dissertation, University of Chicago, 1948.

———. "A Study of Ricarda Huch's Novellen with Special Reference to Keller," in *The Germanic Review.* Vol. 25, 1950, pp. 26–36.

Hans-Werner, Peter and Silke Köstler, eds. *Ricarda Huch (1864–1947): Studien zu ihrem Leben und Werk.* Braunschweig, Germany: Huch Gesellschaft, 1997.

Huch, Ricarda. "Autobiographische Schriften" (Autobiographical Writings) in her *Gesammelte Werke* (Collected Works), Volume 11. Cologne: Kipenheuer and Wisch, 1974.

Viereck, Stefanie. *So Weit wie die Welt Geht: Ricarda Huch: Geschichte eines Lebens.* Reinbeck bei Hamburg: Rowohlt, 1990.

SUGGESTED READING:

Boeschenstein, Hermann. *The German Novel, 1934–44.* Toronto: University of Toronto Press, 1949.

Gray, Ronald. *The German Tradition in Literature, 1871–1945.* Cambridge: University of Cambridge Press, 1967.

Robertson, John George. *A History of German Literature.* Edinburgh: Blackwood, 1970.

COLLECTIONS:

Correspondence sent to Huch, as well as diaries and manuscripts of many of her writings, are held in the German Literary Archive of the Schiller Nationalmuseum in Marbach am Neckar, Germany. A Ricarda Huch Society, which was founded in 1980 and is headquartered in Braunschweig, Germany, sponsors regular symposia on Huch's life and writings. It also publishes Ricarda Huch yearbooks.

Niles Holt,
Professor of History, Illinois State University, Normal, Illinois

Huck, Winnifred Sprague Mason (1882–1936)

Member of the U.S. House of Representatives (1922–1923), writer and lecturer. *Born Winnifred Sprague Mason on September 14, 1882 in Chicago, Illinois; died on August 24, 1936, in Chicago; daughter of Congressman William E. Mason (a Congressional representative) and Edith Julia (White) Mason; married Robert Wardlow Huck, on June 29, 1904; children: Wallace Huck; Donald White Huck; Edith Carlyle Huck; Robert Wardlow Huck, Jr.*

Winnifred Sprague Mason was born on September 14, 1882, in Chicago, Illinois, the middle of seven children of William and **Edith Mason**. She attended Chicago public schools until 1890, when her father was elected to the House of Representatives and the family moved to Washington, D.C. After finishing high school there, she married steel executive Robert Wardlow Huck, with whom she would have four children.

Winnifred Sprague Mason Huck

Winnifred Huck's father served in the Illinois State legislature and both houses of the U.S. Congress before dying while in office in 1921. Huck sought to replace him and, after an energetic statewide campaign, became the third

woman elected to Congress in the special election of 1922 (two years after the 19th Amendment established women's right to vote). She also sought the Republican Party's nomination to a seat in the 68th Congress, but lost to Henry R. Rathbone. In succeeding her father, Huck began a trend which was to become known as the "widow's succession" due to the fact that 31 of the 68 women elected to Congress between 1918 and 1963 took the seats of relatives who were earlier incumbents.

Huck was active during her five-month tenure. She was elected to the Committee on Woman Suffrage, the Committee on Expenditures in the Department of Commerce, and the Committee on Reform in the Civil Service, and advocated for independence for the Philippines and Cuba and for self-determination for Ireland. She was also active in reforms popular among women's organizations, including an end to child labor and economic and legal equality for women. However, her best-known proposal was Resolution 423, which she introduced on January 16, 1923. In it, she called for a "war plebiscite" whereby the power to declare war on another country would rest solely with the American public by way of a popular vote. She also introduced legislation that would prohibit trade with and economic concessions to nations that did not do similarly. In March of 1923, Huck sought to fill the House seat left by the death of Representative James R. Mann but was defeated in a primary race by former senator Morton D. Hull. Huck later accused Hull of grossly exceeding campaign-spending limits; the House did not investigate the allegation.

After leaving office, Huck joined the National Woman's Party's political council, which encouraged women to seek public office. Huck then became a lecturer and freelance writer. In 1925, she began a particularly ambitious project which she later detailed in writing and syndicated for the Newspaper Enterprise Association. With the assistance of Vic Donahey, the governor of Ohio, Huck took an assumed name and was tried and convicted of a petty theft in the state of Ohio. She was sent to the women's prison in Marysville, spending a month there before being pardoned and then working her way to New York under her assumed identity by laboring as a house cleaner, factory worker, and hotel chambermaid. In the articles she wrote about this experience, Huck emphasized the humanity of the women inmates and the willingness of employers to hire an ex-convict. Huck went on to work as a staff writer for the *Chicago Evening Post* from 1928 to 1929.

Winnifred Huck died on August 24, 1936, in Presbyterian Hospital in Chicago after surgery for idiopathic ulcerative colitis. She was 53, and was survived by her husband and their four children.

SOURCES:

James, Edward T., ed. *Notable American Women, 1607–1950.* Cambridge, MA: The Belknap Press of Harvard University Press, 1971.

Office of the Historian. *Women in Congress, 1917–1990.* Commission on the Bicentenary of the U.S. House of Representatives, 1991.

Sonya Elaine Schryer,
freelance writer, Lansing, Michigan

Huda Shaarawi (1879–1947).

See Shaarawi, Huda; see also Egyptian Feminism.

Hu Die (1908–1989)

Chinese movie star who won the Best Actress award at the Asian Film Festival in 1960 and a Special Achievement award at the Taiwan Golden Horse Film Festival in 1986. *Name variations: Hu Tieh; Hu Baojuan; Butterfly Wu; Miss Butterfly; Pan Baojuan. Pronunciation: Hu TiEh. Born Hu Baojuan in 1908 (some sources cite 1907 but 1908 is documented), in Shanghai, China; died in Vancouver, Canada, on April 23, 1989; daughter of Hu Shaogong (a railroad inspector); attended Zhonghua Film School, 1924; married Eugene Penn (Pan Yousheng), a Shanghai manufacturer, in 1936 (died 1958); children: son Jiarong; daughter Jiali.*

Made first silent film, Changong *(War Achievement, 1925); made first sound film,* Genu hongmudan *(Singing Peony, 1931); visited Europe (1935); moved from Hong Kong to Chongqing (1943–44); lived in Hong Kong (1948); won Best Actress award for her role in* Houmen *(Back Door, 1960); retired (1966); moved to Taiwan (1967); moved to Vancouver (1975); won a Special Achievement award at the Taiwan Golden Horse Film Festival (1986); published her memoirs (1986).*

Had leading role in about 70 films: Qiushan yuan *(Autumn Fan's Sorrow, 1926);* Bai she zhuan *(Legend of the White Snake, 1927);* Baiyun ta *(White Pagoda, 1927);* Genu hongmudan *(Singing Peony, 1931);* Kuang lu *(Torrents, 1933);* Zimui hua *(Two Sisters, 1935);* Yongyuan di weixiao *(Smile Forever, 1937);* Jianguo zhilu *(The Way of a Nation, 1944);* Jinshou tiantang *(Beautiful Paradise, 1949);* Houmen *(Back Door, 1959);* Kuer liulangji *(Adventure of a Poor Orphan, 1963);* Mingyue jishi yuan *(When Will the Moon be Round Again?, 1966).*

Before the 1920s, there was pervasive discrimination against women entertainers in traditional China. The emergence of film marked a gradual change in attitudes toward female performers, when some distinguished actresses enjoyed an unprecedented popularity. Acting became an art, and the profession received respect. One of the early "stars" was Hu Die, whose achievements in many ways encouraged other women to pursue careers in the performing arts.

At the time of Hu Die's birth in Shanghai in 1908, China was on the threshold of a transformation. Soon the 1911 Revolution brought down the decadent Manchu regime, while the May Fourth movement initiated a social and cultural revolution in 1919. As the political order fell into disintegration, Shanghai, the largest treaty port under Western protection, became an international commercial center. Matched only by Tokyo as the most prosperous city in the Orient, Shanghai was the capital of fashion, where the latest styles from Paris and new films from America were on display. To the younger generation, it was a city of excitement, a city of new opportunities and new ideas. Many successful careers began in this cosmopolitan setting.

Hu Die was born Hu Baojuan, the only child of Hu Shaogong, a Cantonese who worked as a railway inspector in northern China. Because of her father's employment, she spent a large part of her childhood in Tianjin, Beijing, and other northern cities. In 1924, the family finally settled down in Shanghai, and, at 16, she was ready to start a career. An advertisement in a local newspaper recruiting potential actresses for training caught her attention. Under the name Hu Die, a homophonous term for "butterfly," she wrote to the Chinese film company and was invited to study in the Zhonghua Film School for nine months. She made her screen debut in *Changong* (War Achievement), and a star was born.

In 1926, Hu Die was assigned a leading role in the film *Qiushan yuan* (Autumn Fan's Sorrow). That same year, she switched to another company and made several films, including *Fuqi zhi mimi* (A Husband and Wife's Secret) and *Bai she zhuan* (Legend of the White Snake). Afterward, she joined the Star Motion Picture Company. Under the able management of Zhang Shichuan, this company continued to expand, and its growth was due in part to the popularity of her films.

In a few years, Hu Die was a celebrity in the Chinese film world, and one of its most highly paid actresses. Her movies were highly acclaimed by critics. Many writers attribute her success to beauty and talent, but she was also a dedicated worker who brought a higher level of sophistication to her performances. Though most of her films were based on simple themes—historical plays or family issues—her mastery of the art won audience and critical applause.

Hu Die's career spanned two different periods in the history of motion pictures—from silent films to sound. In 1931, she was one of the first actresses who played in a sound film in China. She reached the pinnacle of her career in 1935 when her picture *Zimui hua* (Two Sisters) brought her the accolade, "Movie Queen of China."

In February 1935, Hu Die was chosen to represent China at an international film congress in Moscow, organized by the Soviets. She then visited Western Europe. The following year, she married Eugene Penn (Pan Yousheng), a Shanghai manufacturer. His company later specialized in the making of enamelware with a butterfly trademark, and Hu Die helped promote the product.

The couple left for the British colony of Hong Kong after the outbreak of the Second Sino-Japanese War in 1937. When Japan occupied the colony in December 1941, Japanese authorities put Hu Die under close watch and tried to persuade her to make propaganda films. She demurred and succeeded in escaping. She and Penn fled to Chongqing, Sichuan, where they stayed until the end of the war. In this period, she appeared in one film, *Jianguo zhilu* (The Way of a Nation).

After the war, Hu Die and her husband returned to Shanghai. On the eve of the Communist takeover, they relocated to Hong Kong where Penn ran his own manufacturing company. Between 1948 and 1958, Hu Die worked side by side with her husband, promoting his business. When Penn died in 1958, Hu Die returned to the screen. Two years later, she won the Best Actress award at the Asian Film Festival for her role in *Houmen* (Back Door). She played supporting roles in a few more films before her retirement in 1966. Hu Die moved to Taiwan in 1967 and remained there for eight years. After her children settled in Canada, she moved to Vancouver to live with them.

Hu Die's memoirs were published in 1986. That same year, she was presented with a Special Achievement award at the Taiwan Golden Horse Film Festival, but her health was failing, and she could not make the trip. Hu Die suffered a stroke and died in 1989, at age 81. The story of her success has become legend, inspiring a generation of young girls to seek careers in the film world.

SOURCES:

Feng, Li. *Yinhou Hu Die* (Hu Die the Movie Queen). Beijing: Zhongguo wenlian, 1997.

Hu Die. *Hu Die huiyilu* (Memoirs of Hu Die). Beijing: Xinhua chubanshe, 1987.

Zheng, Renjia. "Hu Die," in *Chuan-chi wen-hsueh, Taiwan (Zhuanji wenxue)*. Vol. LIV, no. 6. June 1989, pp. 146–150.

SUGGESTED READING:

"Hu Tieh." *Biographical Dictionary of Republican China*. Edited by Howard L. Boorman and Richard C. Howard. NY: Columbia University Press, 1968. Vol. II, pp. 154–155.

Henry Y.S. Chan,
Associate Professor of History, Moorhead State University,
Moorhead, Minnesota

Hudson, Martha (1939—)

African-American track star who won a gold medal in the 4x100-meter relay in the 1960 Rome Olympics. *Name variations: (nickname) Peewee Hudson. Born in Eastman, Georgia, on March 21, 1939; oldest of three children of a truck driver and a housewife; attended Tennessee State University, becoming a member of the famous Tigerbelles.*

In 1960, at 4'10", Martha "Peewee" Hudson was the shortest athlete to participate in Olympic competition. Though many doubted her ability to succeed in athletics, she would prove them wrong time and again. In her mind, Hudson was 6' tall. She was born and grew up in Eastman, Georgia, tucked away in the piney woods. On the playground, she often raced against the boys, generally besting them. When she entered Twin City High School, she took up basketball, and her prowess as a guard soon got her elected team captain. Hudson circled the track as well. When the coach from Tennessee State University saw her run in the Tuskegee Relays, he recognized a superior athlete and offered her a scholarship. After graduating as salutatorian of her class in 1957, Hudson attended Tennessee State.

At the time, the university's Tigerbelles had only recently become a name to be reckoned with in the track world. Their fame began in 1955 when Tennessee replaced Tuskegee as national champion at the national outdoor AAU meet in Ponca City, Oklahoma. ***Mae Faggs,** ***Wilma Rudolph,** and ***Wyomia Tyus** were Tigerbelles, a team which would produce some of America's finest runners over the years. When Hudson first arrived on campus, Mae Faggs dubbed her "Peewee," and the nickname stuck. "My big ambition was to beat Mae just once," said Hudson, "but I never did." Even so, the petite runner soon became well known for her abilities. On a basketball as well as track scholarship, she succeeded in both sports. It was on the track, however, that she established her reputation. In 1959, she earned a position on the AAU All-American women's track and field team. She won the indoor 100-yards the same year.

When the 1960 Olympics were held in Rome, four Tigerbelles comprised the U.S. 4x100-meter team—Martha Hudson, ***Lucinda Williams,** ***Barbara Jones,** and Wilma Rudolph. They were running against the fastest women from the Soviet Union, Panama, Australia, and Poland. With Hudson running the first leg, the Tigerbelles took the gold with a time of 44.5, in part because Hudson's short legs (everyone in the race was at least six inches taller) covered 30 feet every second. As Hudson later cracked, "I doubt if ever so much depended on so little."

After graduating from Tennessee State in 1962, Hudson moved to Thomaston, Georgia, where she became an elementary schoolteacher, coached girls' track and basketball, and still shot baskets.

SOURCES:

Davis, Michael D. *Black American Women in Olympic Track and Field*. Jefferson, NC: McFarland, 1992.

Page, James A. *Black Olympian Medalists*. Englewood, CO: Libraries Unlimited, 1991.

Wallechinsky, David. *The Complete Book of the Olympics*. NY: Viking, 1988.

Karin Loewen Haag,
Athens, Georgia

Hudson, Rochelle (1916–1972)

American actress. *Born Rochelle Elizabeth Hudson in Oklahoma City, Oklahoma, on March 6, 1916; died of liver ailment in Palm Desert, California, on January 17, 1972; interred at Montecito Memorial Park; only child of Ollie Lee Hudson (head of the State Employment Bureau in Oklahoma) and Mae (Goddard) Hudson; married Harold Thompson, a story editor and naval reserve officer, in 1939 (divorced 1947); married Richard Hyler (a* Los Angeles Times *sports writer), in 1948 (divorced 1950); married Charles Brust, a Kansas businessman (divorced); married Robert Mindell, a hotel executive, in 1963 (divorced around 1971).*

Selected filmography: Laugh and Get Rich *(1931);* Everything's Rosie *(1931);* The Public Defender *(1931);* Fanny Foley Herself *(1931);* Are These Our Children? *(1931);* Girl Crazy *(1932);* Hell's Highway *(1932);* The Savage Girl *(1932);* She Done Him Wrong *(1933);* Wild Boys of the Road *(1933);* Love Is Dangerous *(1933);* Doctor Bull *(1933);* Mr. Skitch *(1933);* Judge Priest *(1934);* Imitation of Life *(1934);* The Mighty Barnum *(1934);* Life Begins at 40 *(1935);* Les Miserables *(1935);* Curly Top *(1935);* Way Down East *(1935);* Show Them No Mercy *(1935);* The Music Goes 'Round *(1936);* The Country Beyond *(1936);* Poppy Reunion *(1936);* Woman Wise *(1937);* That I May Live *(1937);* She Had to Eat *(1937);* Born Reckless *(1937);* Rascals *(1938);* Mr. Moto Takes a Chance *(1938);* Storm Over Bengal *(1938);* Pride of the Navy *(1939);* Missing Daughters *(1939);* Convicted Woman *(1940);* Men Without Souls *(1940);* Island of Doomed Men *(1940);* Babies for Sale *(1940);* Meet Boston Blackie *(1941);* The Officer and the Lady *(1941);* Rubber Racketeers *(1942);* Queen of Broadway *(1943);* Bush Pilot *(1947);* Devil's Cargo *(1948);* Rebel Without a Cause *(1955);* Strait-Jacket *(1964);* The Night Walker *(1965);* Dr. Terror's Gallery of Horrors *(*The Blood Suckers *or* Return from the Past, *1967).*

Rochelle Hudson was born in Oklahoma City in 1916 and began dancing lessons at the age of three. By age six, she was reciting verse at school pageants. In 1927, her father Ollie Hudson, a direct descendant of explorer Henry Hudson, suffered a nervous breakdown; the prescription was a move to sunny California.

When the family arrived in Van Nuys in 1928, Rochelle began studying with Ernest Belcher, father of dancer **Marge Champion**. Before long, however, her parents separated, and her father moved to Kansas where he ran a cattle ranch. Rochelle remained with her mother **Mae Hudson**, who was pushing her daughter toward a film career. She moved the household to Hollywood to be closer to the studios.

Thirteen-year-old Rochelle was initially signed by Fox, which, thinking she might develop into another ***Janet Gaynor**, provided her with singing lessons but little else. Six months later, when Fox dropped her option, she signed with RKO and made her first film appearance in *Laugh and Get Rich* (1931), a comedy starring ***Edna May Oliver**. Hudson's first lead role was in *Are These Our Children?* (1931) opposite

Rochelle Hudson

Eric Linden, and cinema exhibitors named her Wampas Baby Star of 1931. But RKO was fearful that the public would not accept a 15-year-old in romantic leads, so they did the unusual: they moved her date of birth back two years, and the publicity department claimed she was born in 1914. Even so, they continued to cast her in small roles, and Hudson began to freelance at her contract's end.

She made three movies at Fox with Will Rogers, *Doctor Bull, Mr. Skitch,* and *Judge Priest.* She was then loaned to Warner Bros. for *Harold Teen,* opposite Hal LeRoy. Earning the title "champion loaner-outer," she then went to Universal to play the daughter of ***Claudette Colbert** in *Imitation of Life.* At Fox, Hudson made *The Mighty Barnum* and played Cosette in *Les Miserables* to Fredric March's Jean Valjean. She then played ***Shirley Temple (Black)**'s older sister in *Curly Top* and sang "The Simple Things in Life."

In 1935, when Darryl F. Zanuck took control of Twentieth Century-Fox, Hudson was retained as a contractee, and her first assignment was to replace Gaynor as Anna Moore in the remake of *Way Down East.* After a few successes, she was loaned to Paramount to play W.C. Fields' daughter in *Poppy.* But Hudson was growing up and becoming too candid in interviews; Zanuck began to favor new contractee **Loretta Young.** Hudson was consigned mostly to B movies during the 1930s and 1940s. Her final role for Fox was as an "aviatrix" in Peter Lorre's *Mr. Moto Takes a Chance,* released in 1938. Though she signed with Columbia in 1939, the B movies kept on coming. Hudson was never comfortable with Hollywood's image of her. "They kept me sweet and innocent for years," she said later. "When I finally convinced them I was no longer a teenager I was immediately cast as a chippy, which I remained until I quit."

In 1939, she married story editor Harold Thompson, then a naval reserve officer. During World War II, from 1942 to 1945, Thompson and Hudson worked for Naval Intelligence, making "fishing" trips to Mexico and other Central American countries to engage in espionage. Sent to observe German activity in those areas, the Thompsons located a large cache of high-test aviation gas hidden by German agents in Baja, California. Following the war, the couple moved to Canada, living in Vancouver, until their divorce in 1947. She married sports writer Richard Hyler the following year.

As her film roles began to dry up, Hudson appeared on stage in *Burlesque* (1948) with Bert Lahr, was seen in the television series "Racket Squad" (1951), and was a regular on "That's My Boy," during the 1954–55 season. Of her last films, *Rebel Without a Cause* (1955), with James Dean and ***Natalie Wood,** and *Strait-Jacket* (1964), with ***Joan Crawford,** are the most notable.

In 1956, Hudson moved from Hollywood to Arizona where she ran a 10,000-acre ranch. She then moved to Tulsa and worked for a petroleum company, instructing executives in communication. She married twice more, and divorced twice more. In 1967, Hudson finally settled in Palm Desert, California, where she ran her own successful real estate firm until her death in 1972.

SOURCES:

Katz, Ephraim. *The Film Encyclopedia.* NY: HarperCollins, 1994.

Lamparski, Richard. *Whatever Became of . . . ?.* 3rd series. NY: Crown, 1990.

Roberts, Barrie. "Rochelle Hudson: Square Peg in a Round Hole," in *Classic Images.* No. 272. February 1998.

Huerta, Dolores (1930—)

American Chicana labor organizer, co-founder with Cesar Chávez of the United Farm Workers of America, and a major personality in the world of American unionism. *Born in Dawson, New Mexico, on April 10, 1930; daughter of Juan Fernández and Alicia Chávez Fernández; had two brothers; married Ralph Head (divorced); married Ventura Huerta (divorced); companion, Richard Chávez; children: eleven.*

Although her name translates literally to "Sorrow in the Orchards," Dolores Huerta grew up in circumstances considerably better than those of the migrant farmworkers whose cause she would later champion. She was born in the mining town of Dawson, New Mexico, in 1930. Her father was a miner who in time became a union leader and member of the state legislature where he worked for better labor laws. After her parents divorced when she was five, Dolores and her two brothers were taken by their mother to Stockton, California. While her mother worked two shifts, by night in a cannery, by day as a waitress, the children were raised by their maternal grandfather, Herculana Chávez. Dolores' mother went on to manage and eventually buy a hotel whose Japanese-American owners were interned soon after Pearl Harbor, and she later started a successful restaurant. Although the family now moved into the middle class, they did not forget the hard times they left behind. On many occasions, the hotel hosted down-on-their-luck relatives or virtually penniless farmworkers. During these early years, Dolores learned about charity and solidarity: "We were taught that you didn't receive anything for a favor. We grew up with the mentality of helping people." Her mother's involvement in a cannery strike in 1938, as well as a strike of asparagus workers that shook Stockton in the 1940s, provided an example for Dolores which taught that helping one's neighbors was morally right and which demonstrated the power of workers' solidarity to bring about significant social improvement.

Dolores learned from her mother that women should be treated the same as men, a concept exemplified in her own family where her two brothers received no special favors. In the 1990s, she recalled, "We all shared equally in the household tasks. I never had to cook for my brothers or do their chores like many traditional Mexican families." After taking dance lessons in a WPA program, she dreamed of becoming a professional dancer (in her adult life, dance would prove to be one of her few leisure activities). After graduation from high school, however, she married classmate Ralph Head and soon after gave birth to two daughters. While her mother took care of her children, Dolores attended college, received her teaching credentials, and began teaching in a local elementary school. She soon became frustrated trying to meet the basic material needs of her students, most of whom came to class hungry and without shoes. In a 1995 interview, she recalled a growing belief in the early 1950s that she "could do more by organizing farmworkers than by trying to teach their hungry children."

In 1955, she met Fred Ross, an organizer for the Community Service Organization (CSO), a Mexican-American self-help association based in Los Angeles. Ross had come to Stockton to establish a local CSO chapter, and Dolores Huerta—her new name after she divorced her first husband to marry Ventura Huerta—was at first suspicious of his beliefs and motives. At the time, she was living a middle-class lifestyle and working in a record store, though her mother wanted her to go to law school. Huerta, then a registered Republican, went so far as to check out Ross' non-radical credentials with the local FBI office. She soon became a CSO activist as a founding member of the organization in Stockton, dedicating her time to such projects as voter registration. By the end of the 1950s, Huerta had become a prominent CSO member and was working as a lobbyist for the organization in the state capital, Sacramento. Among the legislation that she successfully supported was a law that required businesses to provide legal immigrants with pensions.

While working for the CSO, Huerta also became an active member of the Agricultural Workers Association (AWA), a northern California group committed to improved labor conditions. At this time, California's mostly Hispanic migrant farmworkers existed in horrid conditions. Working stoop-backed in the searing sun, they picked grapes, tomatoes, and other crops until they were on the brink of collapse, and during the cold nights they often slept in shacks barely fit for animals. The men, women, and children who brought food to the nation's tables received wages so low that every basket might bring a pitiful 50, or in some instances even 20, cents. Some employers deducted from a worker's pay for the water they consumed while working in the fields. Since most of their workers were Mexicans or Mexican-Americans who knew little or no English, some employers swindled their laborers out of significant amounts of their pay with impunity.

Soon after joining the AWA, Huerta met César Chávez, who had also been active for many years in the CSO. A shy, quiet man who

Dolores Huerta

was dedicated to the cause of improving the lives of California's migrant farmworkers, Chávez at first found it difficult to communicate with a woman whose personality differed so completely from his own. Soon, however, they found that they had much in common. Although Chávez had become the CSO general director, in 1962 that group's general assembly rejected his idea of organizing a union for California's farmworkers. From a coldly objective viewpoint, a major organizing effort in the California farm fields was at best a quixotic effort. Even their friends and supporters believed that Chávez and Huerta had lost touch with reality, given the fact that the farmworkers were virtually penniless, powerless immigrants, most of whom did not vote and had no previous experience in labor struggles.

In 1962, Chávez and Huerta co-founded the National Farm Workers Association (NFWA), with Huerta appointed one of the organization's vice presidents. At the time, her personal life was in crisis; she was divorcing her second husband and was locked in a court fight for custody of their five children. Ventura Huerta, who held traditional views of a woman's role, disapproved of his wife's activism and was convinced that as a result she had neglected their children. While attempting to cope with her personal problems, Dolores spent virtually every waking moment organizing the struggling NFWA. She raised her family on her subsistence wages, and her children went to school with holes in their shoe soles. Years later, she noted that living this way served as a reminder of what farmworker families "go through every day of their lives."

In 1965, with about 1,200 members, the NFWA joined an AFL-CIO affiliated union in a major strike against California grape growers in the Delano area of the San Joaquin valley (the strike eventually extended to the Coachella valley in Southern California). In 1966, this organization and the NFWA merged to form the United Farm Workers Organizing Committee (UFWOC), which also affiliated itself with the AFL-CIO. During the grape pickers' *huelga* (strike), which lasted from 1965 to 1970, Huerta was arrested numerous times. J. Edgar Hoover's FBI placed Huerta and Chávez under surveillance, convinced that they were under communist influence (both union leaders were committed to an ideology of nonviolence based on the teachings of Mohandas Gandhi and Martin Luther King, Jr.). In time, the grape strike sparked national media attention, receiving support and encouragement from other unions and from national political leaders including Robert F. Kennedy. By 1967, even though she had previously never even read a union contract, Huerta had become the chief negotiator of UFWOC and successfully hammered out several contracts with wine-grape growers. These agreements brought revolutionary improvements to the grape pickers, including job security, health-care benefits, and significant protection from the toxic pesticides which were starting to be linked to higher rates of cancer in workers and birth defects in their families.

Opposite page

Dolores Huerta

Although some grape growers signed contracts with the union, others dug in their heels and resisted all attempts to negotiate. Using scabs, and counting on the support of local officials, the growers were able to use harsh and violent measures against the strikers. In the face of this situation, the UFWOC called for a national boycott of one of the most stubbornly anti-union growers, which soon escalated into a national boycott of all California table grapes. In 1968, during what was clearly a critical time for the survival of the union's efforts, Huerta was sent to New York City to coordinate the national boycott. Her energy and enthusiasm proved infectious, and the grape boycott became one of the most successful boycotts in U.S. history. Sales of grapes dropped dramatically in supermarkets across the nation. In time, several growers caved, a response which became a mass phenomenon in July 1970 when 26 growers from the Delano area capitulated. Negotiated by Huerta, the contracts brought many hitherto unimagined economic and social benefits for grape workers.

In Huerta's relationship with Chávez, for whom she had immense respect, debates over tactics often led to passionate arguments that sometimes ended with Huerta quitting or Chávez firing her. Quickly, however, their partnership would be renewed in order to bring more victories for the union. "Don't ever stop fighting with me," Chávez once told her. Indeed, she never did. In later years, Huerta would state with a sense of accomplishment that she, Chávez and the thousands of farmworkers who supported the union had "brought to the world, the United States anyway, the whole idea of boycotting as a nonviolent tactic. I think we showed the world that nonviolence can work to make social change." In a decade filled with bloodshed and fear of nuclear annihilation, this peacefully achieved social change was for many a beacon of hope for a better and less violent future global society.

Seen in retrospect, the early 1970s became the high-water mark for the union which Chávez and Huerta had created. While membership expanded dramatically to about 80,000, the union received a charter in 1972 from the AFL-CIO as an independent affiliate and was now known officially as the United Farm Workers (UFW) of America, AFL-CIO. Not surprisingly, business interests did not remain passive during these years, crafting increasingly sophisticated strategies to either negate union contracts or negotiate new ones more favorable to their bottom lines. In 1975, the California legislature passed the Agricultural Labor Relations Act (ALRA), guaranteeing for the first time the rights of farmworkers in that state to organize and hold elections on the issue of union representation; the law also required growers to bargain in good faith for contracts if workers did in fact vote in favor of a union. Soon after this, a special board was created by the legislature to oversee successful implementation of the ALRA. On paper, these moves looked beneficial to the union, but in practice enforcement of the law was significantly undermined by conservative Republican governors who appointed board members not in sympathy with agricultural labor. Steady erosion of union membership took place over two decades, and by the time César Chávez died in 1993, UFW membership had dwindled to a discouraging 22,000.

A new vigor and optimistic spirit could be seen in the UFW in the mid-1990s under the leadership of new president Arturo Rodriguez. Union membership began to rise, and morale improved. As the organization's secretary-treasurer, Dolores Huerta reported that by mid-1997 the UFW had won 15 consecutive secret-ballot elections and signed 16 new contracts with wine-grape and other growers. That same year, the union inaugurated a campaign to organize the workers in California's strawberry fields. Besides meeting the continuing demands of her UFW leadership role, Huerta has worked tirelessly as an activist, appearing at rallies from coast to coast and serving on the boards of numerous organizations including the California Labor Federation, the Fund for the Feminist Majority, and the National Farm Workers Service Center. She has also served as vice president of the Coalition of Labor Union Women.

In 1988, Huerta had participated in a San Francisco demonstration against Vice President George Bush and was beaten by a baton-wielding police officer. She was taken to an emergency room in grave condition suffering from loss of blood due to a ruptured spleen and three broken ribs. Huerta sued, and in an out-of-court settlement she received a substantial sum from the city of San Francisco. More important to her

than the financial component was the city's agreement as part of the settlement to change police crowd-control practices regarding the use of batons and to eliminate the presence of SWAT teams at demonstrations.

Dolores Huerta gave birth to 11 children, the last when she was 46 (by 1997, she could boast of 14 grandchildren and 2 great-grandchildren). After her second divorce, she began living with César's brother, Richard Chávez, with whom she had her last four children. Due to her union commitments, he did not see her for weeks at a time. Often she was so busy with her union activities that she "changed diapers between organizing meetings and nursed babies during breaks in negotiations." There were times when her children lived with friends and union supporters, ate donated food, and had to cope with frequent moves and their mother's imprisonment or absence on trips. When her children showed anger or disappointment over her many absences from home, Huerta would tell them, "Your sacrifice helps 100 farmworker kids." Looking back on these family sacrifices, Huerta's daughter Juanita, a high school teacher and aspiring writer, remarked, "You couldn't argue with that. We saw the conditions with our own eyes." Never interested in acquiring wealth, Huerta sacrificed the material things, "which don't amount to much anyway," she said. Since the UFW constitution forbade paying wages to officials, the union paid Huerta's rent, and she and her family lived on food stamps. A small clothing allowance, often supplemented by donations, resulted in "very exotic wardrobes" for herself and other union leaders.

In her 60s, Huerta did not slow down. In 1998, her daughter Maria Elena noted that Huerta was "like the Tasmanian Devil. Like a whirling dervish. Like a hummingbird." In the late 1990s, she continued to appear at rallies, board meetings, seminars and interfaith prayer breakfasts, crossing the country twice during a typical week. Her passion for fair treatment not only for farmworkers, but for all people, remained the basic motivation of her public life. In the final phase of her career, Huerta remained convinced that "Non-violence is a very strong spiritual force. We have to have a faith that has power and that works. I have seen this. This is why this movement has worked. People that practice non-violence are stronger in many ways. It even changes those people that are themselves oppressing and committing violent acts. I have seen it change people."

SOURCES:

Ferris, Susan and Richard Sandoval. *The Fight in the Fields: César Chávez and the Farmworkers Movement.* NY: Harcourt Brace, 1997.

Garcia, Richard A. "Dolores Huerta: Woman, Organizer, and Symbol," in *California History.* Vol. 72, no. 1. Spring 1993, pp. 56–71.

Gollner, Philipp M. "Thousands Attend Services To Say Goodbye to Chavez," in *The New York Times.* April 30, 1993, p. A11.

Gutiérrez, David G. "Significant to Whom?: Mexican Americans and the History of the American West," in *Western Historical Quarterly.* Vol. 24, no. 4. November 1993, pp. 519–539.

Huerta, Dolores. "Reflections on the UFW Experience," in *The Center Magazine.* Vol. 18, no. 4. July–August 1985, pp. 2–8.

Lopez, Lalo. "Si se puede," in *Hispanic.* Vol. 9, no. 8. August 1996, pp. 141–144.

Loya, Gloria Ines. "Considering the Sources/Fuentes for a Hispanic Feminist Theology," in *Theology Today.* Vol. 54, no. 4. January 1998, pp. 491–498.

Martinez, Rubén. "Labor of Love," in *Hope Magazine.* No. 16. September–October 1998, pp. 36–41.

Rose, Margaret. "From the Fields to the Picket Line: Huelga Women and the Boycott, 1965–1975," in *Labor History.* Vol. 31, no. 3. Summer 1990, pp. 271–293.

———. "Traditional and Nontraditional Patterns of Female Activism in the United Farm Workers of America, 1962 to 1980," in *Frontiers.* Vol. 11, no. 1, 1990, pp. 26–32.

Rose, Margaret Eleanor. "Women in the United Farm Workers: A Study of Chicana and Mexicana Participation in a Labor Union, 1950 to 1980" (Ph.D. dissertation, University of California, Los Angeles, 1988).

Ruiz, Vicki L. *From Out of the Shadows: Mexican Women in Twentieth-Century America.* NY: Oxford University Press, 1998.

Wenner, Hilda E. and Elizabeth Freilicher. *Here's to the Women: 100 Songs for and about American Women.* Syracuse, NY: Syracuse University Press, 1987.

John Haag,
Associate Professor, University of Georgia, Athens, Georgia

Hug-Hellmuth, Hermine

(1871–1924)

Austrian who was the world's first practicing child psychoanalyst. *Born Hermine Hug von Hugenstein in Vienna, Austria, on August 31, 1871; attended University of Vienna; murdered in Vienna on September 8–9, 1924; daughter of Hugo Ritter Hug von Hugenstein; had sister Antonie; never married.*

The dramatic nature of Hermine Hug-Hellmuth's death—murder at the hands of her nephew—has tended to obscure the important role she played in the early years of psychoanalysis. Born Hermine Hug von Hugenstein in 1871 into an aristocratic family in Vienna, she decided on a teaching career, as did her older sister **Antonie Hug**. While Antonie became a professor at the private Halberstam Girls' Secondary School, Hermine began teaching in the Vienna public schools, first in the elementary grades and eventually in grades six through eight. During these years, pressure was growing to open up higher education for women at not only the prestigious University of Vienna, but throughout the universities and technical institutes of the multinational Habsburg Empire. In 1897, Hermine passed her *Matura* examinations and became one of the first Austrian women to enroll at the University of Vienna.

While teaching full-time, she took courses and attended seminars, earning a doctoral degree in 1909 with a dissertation that examined the physical and chemical properties of radioactive substances. She became, however, more interested in the recesses of the human mind than in the natural sciences. After retiring from teaching in 1901 with a small teachers' pension and some private means, she became an independent scholar in psychoanalysis, an area that had become a part of contemporary Viennese intellectual life. Introduced to the discipline by Dr. Isidor Sadger, a nerve specialist and psychoanalyst, she devoured the growing literature on this subject. In 1912, the year that she published the first of her many psychoanalytic papers, she changed her surname from the aristocratic Hug von Hugenstein to the more democratic and contemporary-sounding Hug-Hellmuth. In 1913, she was admitted to the inner sanctum of the psychoanalytic movement, the Vienna Psychoanalytic Society, a clear sign that the society's acknowledged master, Sigmund Freud, had read her papers and approved of their content. Hug-Hellmuth was both one of the very small number of women admitted and one of the few gentiles in a field whose practitioners were almost entirely of Jewish background.

Within a few years of entering the world of psychoanalysis, Hermine Hug-Hellmuth enjoyed the full respect of her fellow psychoanalysts as the new disciple's foremost expert in child analysis and education. She published learned papers in virtually all contemporary academic journals and was often invited to lecture on her work, including before the Vienna Women's Cultural Association, the Adult Education Academy of Vienna's Urania, and the Sixth International Psychoanalytic Congress at The Hague in 1920. The paper she presented at the international congress, "On the Technique of Child Analysis" continues to be regarded as a seminal work in the field, and it is generally considered to have been a major influence on the theories later developed by ***Melanie Klein**. In a letter to a professional colleague, Sigmund Freud personally applauded the work Hug-Hellmuth had done with his grandson Ernst: "Strict upbringing by an intelligent mother enlightened by Hug-Hellmuth has done him a great deal of good."

Although much of her work was quickly looked up to as providing profound and lasting insights into the minds of children, her book *Tagebuch eines halbwüchsigen Mädchens* (The Diary of a Young Girl) created a firestorm of controversy upon its publication in 1919. This work purported to be Hug-Hellmuth's edited version of the detailed diary of a young Austrian upper-middle-class girl which dated to the early years of the 20th century. Highly praised by ***Lou Andreas-Salomé**, Stefan Zweig, and other leading intellectuals of the day, the diary received the all-important imprimatur of Sigmund Freud. In a 1915 letter to Hug-Hellmuth, which was later used as a preface for the book, Freud described the diary as "a little gem" that he believed would "arouse the greatest interest in educators and psychologists . . . [because it provided a] clear and truthful view of the mental impulses that characterize the development of a girl . . . during the years before puberty."

Freud's words of praise could not save *The Diary of a Young Girl* from being skeptically received by some readers, both within and outside the psychoanalytic community, who doubted the work's authenticity. Alfred Adler and members of his dissident circle of analysts strongly suspected the work was a fake, most likely concocted by Hug-Hellmuth on the basis of her own analytical experiences. In succeeding editions of the diary, Hug-Hellmuth did indeed admit that she was its editor, and hoped to stop criticism of the work by providing some information on the author whose name she still chose to keep anonymous. This did little to calm the waters, and several prestigious psychologists of the day, particularly Cyril Burt and ***Charlotte Bühler**, entered the fray by charging that the emotions described in the diary simply did not reflect the appropriate developmental stages of the girl who was said to be its author. Determined to discover the truth, Bühler carried on a vigorous campaign to get Hug-Hellmuth to admit that she had written all or at least major parts of the diary. Hug-Hellmuth, however, would never make such an admission.

Recent research by French scholars **Dominique Soubrenie**, Jacques Le Rider and **Yvette Tourné** has presented compelling arguments for ascribing authorship of the diary to Hermine Hug-Hellmuth. Although the work is more than likely not an authentic "diary of a young girl," it continues to provide strong insights into the mind of an adolescent girl and remains a significant document of the pioneering period of Viennese psychoanalysis. ***Helene Deutsch** summed up the controversy succinctly: "Dr. Hug-Hellmuth had both psychological insight and literary talent. . . . [T]he book is so true psychologically that it has become a gem of psychoanalytic literature."

The final years of Hug-Hellmuth's life were troubled not only by the controversy that raged over *The Diary of a Young Girl,* but also because of growing problems in her personal life. Most of all, she was concerned about the emotional stability of her nephew Rudolph Otto Hug, known to friends and family as Rolf. Born in 1906, Rolf was the illegitimate son of Hermine's sister Antonie. After his mother died in 1915, young Rolf was placed in various foster homes, and he became a troubled, wayward young man. While still a child, he was intensively analyzed by his aunt Hermine and became an important research subject for her psychoanalytical work. In Hug-Hellmuth's first book, *Aus dem Seelenleben des Kindes* (On the Spiritual and Mental Life of the Child), which was published in 1913, Rolf emerged as the major personality, with the author concluding that his external actions were based on abnormal sexual motives and tendencies.

By the end of World War I, young Rolf was living with his aunt. Soon, however, the relationship deteriorated dramatically with many quarrels between the two, and Rolf attempted suicide. He was furious at his aunt for many reasons, including his belief that she never saw him as more than a guinea pig for her work. Embittered and alienated, Rolf was placed in an institution in 1922 after he had been involved in a large number of violent encounters and arrested for theft several times. Unable to settle down either in school or work, he was chronically in need of funds which he often sought from his aunt. Finally, she told him he would no longer be permitted to enter her home.

On the night of September 8–9, 1924, Rolf entered his aunt's home, doubtless intending to steal some money. Hermine Hug-Hellmuth woke up unexpectedly and to end her screams Rolf strangled her. He was quickly arrested in possession of money and a watch, and, when he was unable to explain when and where he had acquired these, quickly confessed to having killed his aunt. The event became a feeding frenzy of sensationalism in the Viennese press which described Rolf as a "delinquent," "black sheep" and "good-for-nothing." Implying that the psychoanalyst had somehow recklessly created the conditions that led to her own murder, Rudolf von Urbantschitsch wrote in Vienna's leading newspaper, the *Neue Freie Presse,* that it was "particularly difficult to talk about what happened to her because it was precisely her nephew who condemned her to a premature and eternal silence—the very same nephew who had frequently been featured in her books, and whose impulses were well known from an early age." Hug-Hellmuth's achievements quickly faded into oblivion because of the dramatic nature of her death, which fascinated both journalists and well-established authors. A fictionalized version of the troubled relationship between Hug-Hellmuth and her nephew appeared soon after in Arthur Schnitzler's novel *Therese: Chronik eines Fraunlebens* (Therese: Chronicle of a Woman's Life).

At his trial, Rolf's former tutor Dr. Isidor Sadger provided much negative testimony against the young man, who was sentenced to 12 years of solitary confinement. To remind him of his heinous crime, the terms of Rolf's sentence stipulated that every year on September 8, the anniversary of his crime, he would be required to spend the entire day in total darkness. After five years' imprisonment, Rolf was released. He immediately demanded of Paul Federn, a leading psychoanalyst and close collaborator of Sigmund Freud, that the Vienna Psychoanalytical Society provide him with money to compensate for the fact that his life had been ruined by his aunt's use of him as an experiment for her research. Rather than provide funds to Rolf, Federn gave him the name and address of Helene Deutsch. Deutsch, who was not consulted in the matter, became concerned for her own safety when Rolf began following her. Finally, a private detective was hired to provide her with security.

As the world's first practicing child psychoanalyst, Hermine Hug-Hellmuth developed a technique of observing children at play which preceded the research later carried out by Helene Deutsch, ***Anna Freud**, and Melanie Klein. Klein developed Hug-Hellmuth's use of play into a play therapy which eventually became a therapeutic vehicle intended to replace free association. It remains to be seen whether or not Hug-Hellmuth's achievements will be given the same life and serious study as her sudden and dramatic death.

SOURCES:

Appignanesi, Lisa and John Forrester. *Freud's Women.* NY: Basic Books, 1993.

Brinkgreve, Christien, Annet Mooij, and Adeline Van Waning. "Hermine Hug-Hellmuth and Sabina Spielrein: Suppressed Pioneers of Psychoanalysis?," in *International Journal of Psychoanalysis*. Vol. 71, no. 2, 1990, pp. 301–307.

Drell, Martin J. "Hermine Hug-Hellmuth, A Pioneer in Child Analysis," in *Bulletin of the Menninger Clinic*. Vol. 46, no. 1. March 1982, pp. 139–150.

Gardner, Sheldon and Gwendolyn Stevens. *Red Vienna and the Golden Age of Psychology, 1918–1938*. NY: Praeger, 1992.

Graf-Nold, Angela. *Der Fall Hermine Hug-Hellmuth: Eine Geschichte der frühen Kinder-Psychoanalyse*. Munich: Verlag Internationale Psychoanalyse, 1988.

Houzel, Didier. *Depressions*. Paris: Bayard editions, 1993.

Hug-Hellmuth, Hermine. *Essais Psychanalytiques: Destin et écrits d'une pionniere de la psychanalyse des enfants*. Translated and edited by Dominique Soubrenie. Paris: Payot, 1991.

———, ed. *A Young Girl's Diary*. Translated by Eden and Cedar Paul. NY: Thomas Seltzer, 1921.

MacLean, George. "A Brief Story About Dr. Hermine Hug-Hellmuth," in *Canadian Journal of Psychiatry*. Vol. 31, no. 6. August 1986, pp. 586–589.

———. "Hermine Hug-Hellmuth: A Neglected Pioneer in Child Psychoanalysis," in *Journal of the American Academy of Child Psychiatry*. Vol. 25, no. 4. July 1986, pp. 579–580.

———, and Ulrich Rappen. *Hermine Hug-Hellmuth: Her Life and Work*. NY: Routledge, 1991.

Müller-Kuppers, Manfred. "Über die Anfänge der Kinderanalyse," in *Praxis der Kinderpsychologie und Kinderpsychiatrie*. Vol. 41, no. 6. July–August 1992, pp. 200–206.

Roazen, Paul. *Freud and His Followers*. NY: Alfred A. Knopf, 1971.

Schnitzler, Arthur. *Therese: Chronik eines Frauenlebens*. Frankfurt am Main: Fischer Tachenbuch Verlag, 1981.

Stephan, Inge. *Die Gründerinnen der Psychoanalyse: Eine Entmythologisierung Sigmund Freuds in zwölf Frauenporträts*. Stuttgart: Kreuz Verlag, 1992.

John Haag,
Associate Professor, University of Georgia, Athens, Georgia

Hughes, Russell Meriwether (b. 1898).

See La Meri.

Hughes, Ruth (1918–1980).

See Aarons, Ruth Hughes.

Hughes, Sarah T. (1896–1985)

U.S. and Texas jurist, state legislator, and feminist who handed down the decision in* Roe *v.* Wade, *based on the right to privacy. *Born Sarah Tilghman in Baltimore, Maryland, on August 2, 1896; died on April 23, 1985, in Dallas, Texas; daughter of James Cooke Tilghman and Elizabeth (Haughton) Tilghman, who kept a boarding house; graduated from Baltimore Grammar School, 1910, and Western High School, 1913; Goucher College, B.S. in Biology, 1917; George Washington University, LL.B, 1922; married George E. Hughes, on March 13, 1922 (died, June 1, 1964); no children.*

Married and moved to Dallas (1922); admitted to bar, Washington, D.C., and Dallas (1922); joined Priest, Herndon, & Ledbetter law firm (1923); elected to Texas House of Representatives (1930, 1932, 1934); appointed to the 14th District Court of Texas (1935); elected (1936); reelected (1940, 1944, 1948, 1952, 1956, 1960); admitted to practice before U.S. Supreme Court (1937); lost congressional primary election (1946); elected national president, Business and Professional Women's Clubs (1950); nominated for U.S. vice president at Democratic National Convention (1952); lost primary race for Texas Supreme Court (1958); appointed Federal district judge (1961); became senior judge (1979); effectively retired (1982).

Sarah T. Hughes was a small, redheaded woman who was once described as "the nearest thing to jet propulsion on two feet." She was slightly over five feet tall and weighed about 100 pounds, but she had a big impact on American law. Best known for being the first and only woman to swear in a president of the United States, Lyndon B. Johnson, she was more important as a women's rights advocate and precedent-setting jurist.

Born in Baltimore on August 2, 1896, Sarah T. Hughes came from an old Maryland family that had settled in the colony in 1660. One of her ancestors, Tench Tilghman, was aide-de-camp to General George Washington. Another, a late 19th-century relative, was U.S. Marshal Bill Tilghman, who served in the Oklahoma Territory. As a child, Sarah worked in the family boarding house and attended grammar school and high school in Baltimore. She graduated at 16, ranking second in her class.

Sarah next attended Goucher College, also in Baltimore, on a four-year scholarship and earned an A.B. (*Artium Baccalaureus*) in biology. While there, she played on the school's basketball and field-hockey teams, was an officer of the athletic association, and worked on the weekly newspaper and monthly magazine. She was also president of the sophomore class, belonged to the Delta Gamma sorority, held office in the YWCA, and worked as a playground instructor during the summers.

Following graduation, the future judge taught physics, chemistry, zoology, and general science at Salem Academy and College in Winston-Salem, North Carolina. She left after two years to join the Washington, D.C., police department and enroll in the George Washington University Law School. Hughes was one of few women on the force and as such handled cases dealing primarily with women and juveniles. She later said that her time as a policewoman proved useful to her as a judge, because she experienced firsthand problems similar to those she later confronted on the bench.

While attending George Washington University, she met George E. Hughes, a fellow student from Palestine, Texas, a small town southeast of Dallas. On March 13, 1922, they married and, after graduating, moved to Dallas. Both were admitted to the Texas bar in 1922. Sarah Hughes joined the firm of Priest, Herndon & Ledbetter in 1923, and George worked briefly for the U.S. Veterans Administration. He later entered private practice but in 1928 returned to the V.A., remaining until retirement in 1962. He died two years later.

As one of four female lawyers in Dallas, Hughes faced blatant sexual discrimination. She quickly addressed the issue by pointing out that "only lunatics, criminals, the feebleminded—and women—are excluded from juries." After she helped change the law in 1953, she told Texas women: "You'll make good jurors. You won't fall for a pretty witness." In her early years with Priest, Herndon & Ledbetter, Hughes handled only minor cases, mostly involving women. She became a critic of the Dallas school district, which in the 1920s did not allow married women to teach.

Hughes' encounter with school-district politics convinced her that she should seek public office. Filing as a Democrat for the state legislature, she spoke or appeared at rallies almost nightly during the months leading up to the election and canvassed "car barns, factories, fire houses, police stations," and "every office building" in downtown Dallas asking for votes. Her victory in 1931 was followed by reelection in 1933 and 1935.

During the three terms she served in the Texas house of representatives, Hughes was a useful member of the legislature. One of the first women elected to that body, in her second term Texas journalists voted her the "Most Valuable Member of the House." Among legislation she influenced were several West Texas land bills, which would have allowed the leasing or sale of part of the state's public school lands to oil interests at prices far below market value. Her action not only blocked the sale at unreasonably low prices, she made certain that when land was sold the state retained mineral rights to it.

Her bill to levy a state income tax was the only one ever passed by the Texas house, and she was proud of the accomplishment. Nevertheless, the state senate would not consider it. Hughes earned the gratitude of Dallas civic leaders by getting the state to finance construction of the Hall of State and to hold a multimillion dollar celebration of Texas' centennial at Fair Park in Dallas. She was humorously dubbed "The Joan of Arc of the Texas Centennial."

Other important legislation Hughes influenced included a law establishing the Trinity River Navigation District and a slum clearance corporation law, both of which accomplished little in the Great Depression years. She also sponsored and helped pass a law requiring children under 15 to attend school, a law establishing "parent homes" for children, which had a board to oversee their operation, bills regulating the hours of labor and minimum wages for women, and a new divorce law. The latter, considered a model to be used by other states, provided that men would pay alimony to their wives while divorce proceedings were pending, but after a final decree was granted payment would stop. Child support was required until the offspring reached their majority.

Active in politics, Hughes supported James V. Allred for governor in 1934 and backed his candidate for speaker of the house in 1935. For these reasons, when Dallas' 14th District Court judgeship became vacant in 1935, Governor Allred appointed her to it. Opposition by the city's state senator, Claude Westerfield, almost blocked her appointment, but Westerfield unadvisedly issued the public statement: "Mrs. Hughes ought to be home washing dishes." Mrs. George Hughes immediately invited journalists to her home and, sporting an apron, stepped up to the kitchen sink to have her portrait taken. This rallied Texas women to her cause, and her good relations with the Dallas business community and bar provided additional help. When the state senate voted on the judiciary committee recommendation, she was confirmed, 24 to 6.

In 1936, Hughes beat back a serious challenge to her continued service on the 14th District bench. She was thereafter reelected every four years—on six occasions—until appointed to the Federal judiciary in 1961. As one of Dallas' several district judges, she controlled the dockets of the Domestic Relations Court and Juvenile Court. Over the years, she campaigned successfully for adequate detention facilities for juvenile offenders and was especially interested in separating young delinquents from hardened criminals. As regards divorce, she believed that every effort at reconciliation should be exhausted before granting a final decree, a position that caused her to be described as "a hard sell." She later explained that her attitude had thwarted many unnecessary separations.

While serving as a district judge, Hughes ran for other offices. In 1946, she was defeated by J. Frank Wilson in a primary election run-off for Congress. Her liberal platform alienated many. She supported pro-labor legislation, expanded power for the United Nations, and conscription of women into the U.S. military. In addition to being active in the Dallas United Nations' association, she was on the executive committee of the U.N. Educational, Scientific, and Cultural Organization (UNESCO) and was a member of the United World Federation. Her 1958 race for the Texas supreme court was even more futile than the one for Congress. She contested a sitting, conservative justice, Joe Greenhill, and lost decisively. She could not overcome her reputation as one of the state's leading liberals.

Sarah T. Hughes

President Harry S. Truman offered Hughes an appointment to the Federal Trade Commission (FTC) in 1950. She had been supported by *India Edwards, vice chair of the Democratic national committee, who was disappointed when Hughes refused. The judge claimed she was not interested in FTC business, did not want to work with Federal bureaucrats, and was unwilling to accept the appointment because it was for only a three-year term.

As a member of many local business and civic groups, Hughes was particularly active in the Business & Professional Women's Club. She was president of the Dallas B&PW in 1937 and was chosen president of the Texas club two years later. She ran unopposed for the presidency of the national organization in 1950 and became first vice president of the International Business & Professional Women's Clubs in 1956. While heading the national group, Hughes received a token nomination for the vice presidency of the United States at the Democratic national convention. The N.Y. state federation had sponsored the idea of nominating women at both the Democrat and Republican conventions. Having made arrangements with Congressional representative Sam Rayburn, who chaired the Democratic gathering, Hughes had her name withdrawn before any voting took place. She commented that her candidacy had been "to encourage women to run for office."

[S]he worked harder than anyone around her to prove she was top notch—and she was.

—Judge Robert Porter

Active in all presidential elections since 1928, her role as co-chair of the 1960 Kennedy-Johnson campaign in Dallas played a part in her appointment to the Federal bench. After the election, she asked a longtime friend, U.S. Senator Ralph Yarborough (D-Texas), to nominate her for the U.S. district judgeship that opened in the Northern District of Texas. Because Senator Yarborough and Lyndon B. Johnson were dividing Texas' senatorial patronage at the time, the recommendation was cleared with the vice president.

Her appointment seemed assured since President John F. Kennedy accepted Yarborough's recommendation. However, the American Bar Association (ABA), which routinely commented on such matters, objected, citing her age. Judge Hughes was 65 years old. Consequently, Attorney General Robert F. Kennedy, who was handling the matter, was prepared to withdraw the nomination. At the time, the younger Kennedy was seeking support from Speaker of the House Sam Rayburn of Bonham, Texas, for a piece of legislation pending in Congress. When Kennedy went to "Mr. Sam's" office to request the Speaker's aid, Rayburn told him, "That bill will pass as soon as Sarah Hughes becomes a Federal judge."

At confirmation hearings before the Senate Judiciary Committee, both Senator Yarborough and Vice President Johnson spoke on her behalf, saying that the ABA had made a grave mistake in stressing her age over her ability. "I have never known a more competent and humane public servant," said Johnson. "I am confident she will make one of the great judges of our time." Added Hughes, "The A.B.A. apparently feels that if a person is over 65, they're senile. If I ever become senile, I hope I can recognize this and get out." The appointment became effective on October 16, 1961. She was the second woman appointed to a Federal district judgeship and the first in Texas.

During her tenure as a U.S. district judge, Hughes was involved with many important cases. By her own estimation the most significant nationally was the abortion decision in *Roe* v. *Wade,* 1971. Her most satisfying was that concerning the Dallas County jail, *Taylor* v. *Sterrett,* 1972. Other decisions, also cited frequently by courts or lawyers preparing cases, include *Buchanin* v. *Batchelor,* 1970, concerning sodomy; *Schultz* v. *Brookhaven,* 1969, and *Reynolds* v. *Wise,* 1974, regarding sex discrimination in the payment of wages; and *Hawkins* v. *Coleman,* 1974, concerning racial discrimination. She also heard the civil action, *Securities and Exchange Commission* v. *National Bankers Life Insurance Company,* 1971, which exposed one of the most infamous cases of bribery in Texas history, the "Sharpstown Scandal." It led to the political demise of a governor, lieutenant governor, and speaker of the Texas house of representatives. Several leading business and civic officials were also found guilty of fraud and deception.

In both the *Roe* and *Buchanin* cases, Judge Hughes, as part of a three-member panel, wrote the decisions. In her concise manner of "getting to the point," she stressed the "right of privacy" as understood in the 9th and 14th Amendments to the U.S. Constitution as established by the Supreme Court in *Griswold* v. *Connecticut,* 1964. In *Buchanin,* a Texas sodomy law that applied to married couples was ruled unconstitutional. Although her judgment was later reversed by the Supreme Court, the decision continued to be cited in sodomy cases thereafter.

The *Roe* case has had continuous repercussions. What Judge Hughes affirmed, and the

Supreme Court later upheld, in part, was that the decision to have an abortion is a private determination between a woman and her physician; that the state has no "compelling interest" to interfere unless it is requiring that abortions be performed by competent persons in adequate facilities; and that the state might forbid abortion when the fetus reached a "quickening" condition—a term better defined by the Supreme Court which determined fetus viability by dividing pregnancy into "trimesters."

Judge Hughes specifically declared the Texas anti-abortion law unconstitutional on the grounds that it was vague, overly broad, and violated the 9th Amendment as applied through the 14th Amendment. When asked later if she had a personal opinion before hearing the case, she answered, "I see no reason for any law." The decision as to whether to have an abortion "is between a woman and her doctor, and I wish people would stop talking about it."

In the case concerning the Dallas County jail (*Sterrett*), Hughes ruled that sanitary conditions should be maintained in feeding prisoners and more room should be provided inmates in cells and in the hospital ward. She also mandated better recreational and rehabilitation programs. Ultimately, she required Dallas County to build a new, $56 million jail. Her decision became a precedent for judges concerned with jails and incarceration of criminals throughout the country.

Hughes believed in swift justice in criminal cases and felt that the law should deter crime and rehabilitate criminals. She defended herself against charges of coddling criminals and causing disrespect for the law with her light sentences by noting that police and community leaders were more responsible than judges for increased crime rates. She maintained that they needed to make changes to attack crime at its roots.

Long a crusader for equal rights for women, Hughes belonged to Women for Change, the National Political Women's Caucus, the National Organization for Women (NOW), and Women's Equity Action League (WEAL). In *Brookhaven Hospital* and in *Reynolds,* Hughes held that if women did the same work as men they should receive similar pay. In each case, the latter involving the national civil service, she ruled that job titles did not of themselves constitute dissimilar work and regardless of classification there should be equal pay for equal work. In the *Hawkins* case, while reinstating a black student who had been expelled from the Dallas school system, Hughes introduced into law the idea of "institutional racism." She had borrowed the concept from a former Dallas superintendent of schools and later admitted that she was not sure what it meant but was certain that it existed.

In 1961, Sarah T. Hughes came to national attention. Following one of the great tragedies of recent American history, the assassination of John F. Kennedy in Dallas on November 22, 1963, she swore in Lyndon Baines Johnson as the 36th president of the United States. She said afterward that she liked to believe that President Johnson chose her for the honor because of their friendship, but that she knew that his feelings toward the other Federal judges in Dallas made her the most acceptable choice. One was a Republican and the other, a Democrat, had ruled against Johnson in an earlier case.

Although Judge Hughes continued on the bench after she took senior status, she increasingly spent more time at home and traveling. She toured Europe on several occasions. She also remained active in a myriad of civic, political, and social organizations and was frequently awarded honors by their local and national bodies. Hughes became ill several years before her death on April 23, 1985. She was interred at the Hillcrest Mausoleum and Memorial Park in Dallas.

Judge Hughes had said early in life that she wanted to make a difference for women; she wanted to get them involved actively in politics, business, and all other avenues of American life. When she became a Federal judge, even though a judge should refrain from politics, she commented that she did not intend to stop battling for women's rights "because I don't think that's politics." She never quit fighting, and because of her, with greater frequency day-by-day, American women are being recognized not for their gender but for their ability.

SOURCES:

Crawford, Ann Fears and Crystal Sasse Ragsdale. *Women in Texas: Their Lives, Their Experiences, Their Accomplishments*. Burnet, TX: Eakin Press, 1982.

Deaton, Charles. *The Year They Threw the Rascals Out.* Austin, TX: Skoal Creek Publishers, 1973.

Federal Supplement. 1969, 1970, 1971, 1974.

Garrow, David J. *Liberty & Sexuality: The Right to Privacy and the Making of Roe* v. *Wade*. NY: Macmillan, 1994.

"Interview with Sarah T. Hughes by Fred Gant, January 15, February 7, February 28, March 21, April 11, May 16, May 27, 1969," North Texas State University Oral History Collection, no. 27, Denton.

"Interview with Sarah T. Hughes by Ronald Marcello, August 23, 1979," North Texas State University Oral History Collection, no. 489, Denton.

La Forte, Robert S. and Richard Himmel, "Sarah T. Hughes, John F. Kennedy and the Johnson Inaugural, 1963," in *East Texas Historical Journal.* Vol XXVII, no. 2, 1989, pp. 34–41.

Riddlesperger, James Warren, Jr., "Sarah T. Hughes: Biography of a Federal District Judge." Master's thesis, North Texas State University, 1980.

"Sarah Tilghman Hughes," in *Current Biography 1950.* NY: H.W. Wilson, pp. 267–269.

COLLECTIONS:

Sarah T. Hughes Papers, Archives, Willis Library, University of North Texas, Denton.

SUGGESTED READING:

Allread, Opal H. "Sarah T. Hughes: A Case Study in Judicial Decision-Making." Ph.D. dissertation, University of Oklahoma, 1987.

Lasher, Patricia. *Texas Women: Interviews and Images.* Austin, TX: Skoal Creek Publishers, 1980.

Weddington, Sarah. *A Question of Choice.* NY: Putnam, 1992.

———, et al. *Texas Women in Politics.* Austin: Foundation for Women's Resources, 1977.

Robert S. La Forte,
Professor of History, University of North Texas, Denton, Texas

Hugo, Adèle (1830–1915)

***Daughter of Victor Hugo who was the subject of the film* The Story of Adele H.** *Name variations: Adele Hugo. Born Adèle Hugo in Paris, France, on July 27, 1830; died in France in 1915; second daughter and youngest child of Victor and Adèle (Foucher) Hugo (1806–1868); sister of Léopold II (b. 1823, who died as an infant), Léopoldine Hugo (1824–1843), Charles Hugo (b. 1826), and François-Victor Hugo (b. 1927).*

The tragic story of Adèle Hugo, youngest daughter of **Adèle Foucher Hugo** and the celebrated French novelist and dramatist Victor Hugo, was the subject of the haunting François Truffaut film *The Story of Adele H* (1975). Starring **Isabelle Adjani,** the movie was based on the book *Le Journal d'Adele Hugo,* by **Frances V. Guille,** who discovered Adèle Hugo's coded diaries in 1955. (An earlier account of Adèle's story was also part of a book by Paul Chenay, a nephew of Mme Hugo, published in 1890.) The movie picks up Adèle's life in 1862 and traces her obsession with an English lieutenant by the name of Albert Pinson.

Truffaut's film, for which Isabelle Adjani was nominated for Best Actress by Hollywood's Motion Picture Academy, indulged his passion for movies based on true stories. He once wrote: "I had been fascinated by the creative process of using real-life events as the basis for a fiction story that would not distort the authenticity of the source material." In the film, he introduces another love interest for Adèle in the form of a well-meaning Canadian book clerk, who supplies her with the reams of paper for her journal and letters and also recognizes her as the daughter of Victor Hugo. However, when he presents her with a copy of Hugo's latest work *Les Miserables,* it only increases her mental distress. She is determined to distance herself from her father because she feels she will only be a disappointment, unable to fill the void left by the death of her sister. Truffaut was granted permission for the film project from the estate of Victor Hugo only after he promised that the writer would not be physically represented on the screen.

Much of what has been written about Adèle is found in various biographies of Victor Hugo and also focuses on the dramatic events of her love affair. She is described as a musically gifted but somewhat sullen child, who spent hours absorbed at the piano. She also lived in the shadow of her older sister **Léopoldine Hugo,** who drowned with her husband in a boating accident shortly after her marriage in 1843, at age 19, leaving her parents inconsolable. During the lengthy confinement of the family's exile at Hauteville House at Guernsey beginning in 1856, Adèle's depression deepened. In a letter to her husband, Mme Hugo expressed growing concern over her daughter's condition. "In the well-nigh cloistral conditions of our present existence, she is forced in upon herself. She thinks a great deal, and her ideas—often erroneous, since nothing flows in from the outside to modify them—become like burning lava."

The passion of Adèle's life at this time was Lieutenant Pinson, whom she met in Jersey and became obsessed with, at one point even telling her father that she was engaged. (Victor, a fierce nationalist, was hardly pleased at the thought of a foreign son-in-law.) During Christmas 1861, after much prodding by Mme Hugo, Pinson was invited to the Hugo home, at which time he and Adèle evidently agreed to part. The separation threw Adèle into a deep despair and fueled her obsession. Taking advantage of her mother's absence in Paris during the summer of 1863, she followed Pinson to his garrison assignment in Halifax, Nova Scotia, hoping to rekindle his affections. She wrote home that she had married Pinson, when in truth the young soldier had no interest in Adèle and had, by some accounts, married another. Leading an isolated life in Halifax, Adèle became more and more delusional as she stalked Pinson each day outside his barracks. She finally wrote home telling her family that Pinson had deserted her, after which her father sent her a monthly allowance. Although Adèle acknowledged receiving the money, she sent word that she did not want her relatives to look for her. She eventually followed Pinson to the island of Barbados, without notifying anyone of her whereabouts. There, alone, with no money, she lapsed

From the movie The Story of Adele H., *starring Isabelle Adjani, based on the life of Adèle Hugo.*

into a further state of mental and physical deterioration. According to André Maurois, it was not until February 1872 that she was identified and brought back to France by **Céline Alvarez Baà**, a black woman of some influence in the colony. Maurois claims that Adèle spent her remaining years at Saint-Mandé, an asylum, where she lived in a bewildered yet contented state, playing her piano and enjoying occasional outings to the Horticultural Gardens and the Bon-Marché. Maurois adds that the poverty of her experience in Barbados caused her "to conceal, like a dog, everything that was given to her."

In a differing account by Matthew Josephson, Adèle's brother François-Victor fetched her home from Nova Scotia in 1864. "After a time she was quietly sent to an asylum in France," he writes, "where she lingered in an obscurity of life and reason for more than fifty years, until her death in 1915."

SOURCES:

Josephson, Matthew. *Victor Hugo: A Realistic Biography of the Great Romantic.* NY: Doubleday, Doran, 1942.

Maurois, André. *Olympio: The Life of Victor Hugo.* NY: Harper & Brothers, 1956.

Nash, Jay Robert and Stanley Ralph Ross. *The Motion Picture Guide.* Vol. VII. Chicago: Cinebooks, 1985.

Barbara Morgan,
Melrose, Massachusetts

Huldah

Biblical prophet consulted regarding the recovery of the lost Book of the Law. *Name variations: Hulda. The wife of Shallum (Josiah's wardrobe keeper).*

One of only three women in the Bible who are called prophets or prophetesses (the other two being ***Miriam the Prophet** and ***Deborah**), Huldah lived in the part of Jerusalem known as the Mishneh (the college), thought by some to be located between the inner and outer wall of the city. Held in high esteem, she was consulted by Josiah when the lost Book of the Law was found in the temple. Huldah prophesied the destruction of Jerusalem but added that it would not occur before the death of Josiah.

Hull, Josephine (1886–1957)

***American character actress who won an Academy Award for her performance in* Harvey.** *Name variations: Josephine Sherwood. Born Josephine Sherwood in Newtonville, Massachusetts, on January 3, 1886; died on March 12, 1957; daughter of William Henry (an importer) and Mary (Tewksbury) Sherwood (a board of education executive); attended schools in Newtonville; graduated from Radcliffe College; married Shelley Vaughn Hull (an actor), in 1910 (died 1919).*

Selected theater: portrayed Penelope Vanderhof Sycamore in You Can't Take It With You *(Booth Theater, New York, December 1936); Abby Brewster in* Arsenic and Old Lace *(Fulton Theater, New York, April 1940); Vita Simmons in* Harvey *(Forty-eighth Street Theater, New York, 1944); Laura Partridge in* The Solid Gold Cadillac *(Belasco Theater, New York, 1954).*

Filmography: After Tomorrow *(1932);* Careless Lady *(1932);* Arsenic and Old Lace *(1944);* Harvey *(1950);* The Lady From Texas *(1951).*

An endearing actress known for her portrayals of eccentric old ladies, Josephine Hull was born in 1886, grew up in Newtonville, Massachusetts, and attended Radcliffe College, where she sang in the glee club and acted in school plays. After completing her education, she joined the Castle Square Stock Company in Boston, making her stage debut under the name of Sherwood in 1905. The young actress then toured with George Ober's company in *What Happened to Jones?* and *Why Smith Left Home*. Other early tours included roles in *The Law and the Man, Way Down East, Paid in Full,* and *The Bridge.*

In 1910, Josephine married Shelley Hull, a well-known actor, and retired from the stage. After her husband's untimely death in 1919, she returned to the theater as a director for ***Jessie Bonstelle**'s stock company in Detroit, Michigan. "I had decided I was through with acting," she said later, "but you know what a stock company is. I found myself filling in each week." After a year in Detroit, Hull returned to New York to become the director of Equity Players but, more often than not, found herself back on stage. Hull directed a performance of *Roger Bloomer* in 1923, and that same year attracted attention in the role of Mrs. Hicks in *Neighbors*. She also scored a hit as Mrs. Frazier in George Kelly's Pulitzer prize-winning play *Craig's Wife* (1926).

Over the next ten or so years, Hull appeared in so many unsuccessful plays that she considered giving up acting and going into writing. A turning point for the actress was the role of Penelope Vanderhof Sycamore ("Penny"), the spacey author-sculptor in the 1937 Pulitzer Prize-winning comedy *You Can't Take It With You* by Moss Hart and George S. Kaufman. That play, which enjoyed a 103-week run, was closely followed by *Arsenic and Old Lace* (1941), the Lindsay and Crouse comedy in which Hull and actress **Effie Shannon** played two elderly sisters who poison their lonely boarders with arsenic-laced elderberry wine. During the play's run of 1,444 performances, Hull was given a leave of absence in order to recreate her role in the movie version which starred Cary Grant.

Hull scored a theatrical hat-trick with yet a third comic triumph in ***Mary Coyle Chase**'s *Harvey,* a fantasy about a lovable dipsomaniac who befriends an invisible seven-foot rabbit. The play began a four-year run on Broadway in November 1944, with Frank Fay as the delusional Elwood and Hull as his distraught sister Veta Simmons. *Variety* hailed her performance as a "masterpiece," and *The New York Times* commented: "Flighty and wide-eyed, Miss Hull is a perfect foil for Mr. Fay's casual ease." In 1947, Fay was replaced by James Stewart, who also played Elwood in the 1951 movie. Hull was also cast in the film and won an Academy Award as Best Supporting Actress.

Josephine Hull was often singled out for her superior performances in otherwise lackluster plays; such was the case with the comedy *Minnie and Mr. Williams* (1948), in which she played a Welsh minister's wife opposite Eddie Dowling. *The New York Times* critic Brooks Atkinson, who called the play "thin and artless," nonetheless adored Hull. "Puffing and flouncing cheerfully around the stage," he wrote, "she plays it with an extraordinary lightness—humorous and motherly, impish and beneficent." Hull was also the only bright note in her next three vehicles: *The Golden State,* which ran for only 25 performances in 1951, *Kin Hubbard,* which tried out in Westport, Connecticut, in the summer of 1951, and *Whistler's Grandmother,* in 1952. "What Mrs. Hull needs," a reviewer from *The New York Times* suggested, "is a playwright half as sublime as she is."

In the meantime, Hull also made numerous television appearances, making the most of her eccentric old-woman persona. "I'm very happy that I'm frankly a character woman, when I see what the camera does to so many faces on the screen," she said. In 1954, however, Hull had

From the movie Arsenic and Old Lace, *starring Jean Adair, Josephine Hull (center), and Cary Grant.*

another successful turn on Broadway as the dowdy Laura Partridge, the stockholder whose questions bring a corporate giant to its knees in *The Solid Gold Cadillac.* Hailed as "an occasion of great rejoicing . . . a howling hit," by William Hawkins (*World Telegram),* the play was a perfect vehicle for the actress, but sadly her last. Josephine Hull, called "everybody's favorite actress," died in 1957.

SOURCES:

Bordman, Gerald. *The Oxford Companion to American Theater.* New York and Oxford: Oxford University Press, 1984.

Bronner, Edwin J. *The Encyclopedia of the American Theater 1900–1975.* San Diego, CA: A.S. Barnes, 1980.

Candee, Marjorie Dent, ed. *Current Biography.* NY: H.W. Wilson, 1953.

Wilmeth, Don B. and Tice L. Miller. *Cambridge Guide to American Theater.* Cambridge, and NY: Cambridge University Press, 1993.

SUGGESTED READING:

Carson, William G. B. *Dear Josephine.* Norman, OK, 1963.

Barbara Morgan,
Melrose, Massachusetts

Hull, Peggy (1889–1967)

Foreign war correspondent who was the first woman to be accredited by the U.S. War Department to cover a war zone. *Born Henrietta Eleanor Goodnough on December 30, 1889, near Bennington, Kansas; died in 1967 in Carmel Valley, California; married George Hull (a reporter), around 1910 (divorced 1914); married John Kinley (a British captain), in 1921 (separated 1925, divorced 1932); married Harvey Deuell (a newspaper editor), around 1932 (died 1939).*

Peggy Hull made history during World War I as the first woman correspondent accredited by the U.S. War Department to cover a war zone. Her colorful life and career included a friendship with pioneering radio commentator *__Irene Corbally Kuhn__, who noted Hull had a "will of iron"; she was "a woman all men loved and no woman ever disliked."

Born on a farm near Bennington, Kansas, in 1889, Peggy Hull began her career as a typesetter for the *Junction City* (Kansas) *Sentinel.* At

21, she married George Hull, a handsome young reporter with a drinking problem. The couple moved to Hawaii, where George worked as a reporter for the *Honolulu Star* and Hull was a feature writer and women's page editor for the *Pacific Commercial Advertiser*. Four years into the marriage, on the day her tipsy husband tried to climb a flagpole naked, Hull left him. Returning to the mainland, she took a job with the *Cleveland Plain Dealer,* writing advertising copy.

In 1916, the Ohio National Guard was mobilized and sent to El Paso, Texas, to join General John Pershing's expedition in Mexico to capture Pancho Villa. Hull requested permission to travel with the Guard. When her editor turned her down, she promptly quit her job and moved to Texas where she worked first for the *El Paso Herald,* then the *El Paso Morning Times*. Hull never made it to the front, but she was allowed to accompany the troops on a grueling two-week training march from El Paso to Las Cruces, New Mexico. During the trek, she slept on the ground like the men and at one point was caught in a sandstorm and separated from the troops. Although Pershing never captured Pancho Villa, the expedition helped prepare the American troops for entry into World War I and served as Hull's training ground as well.

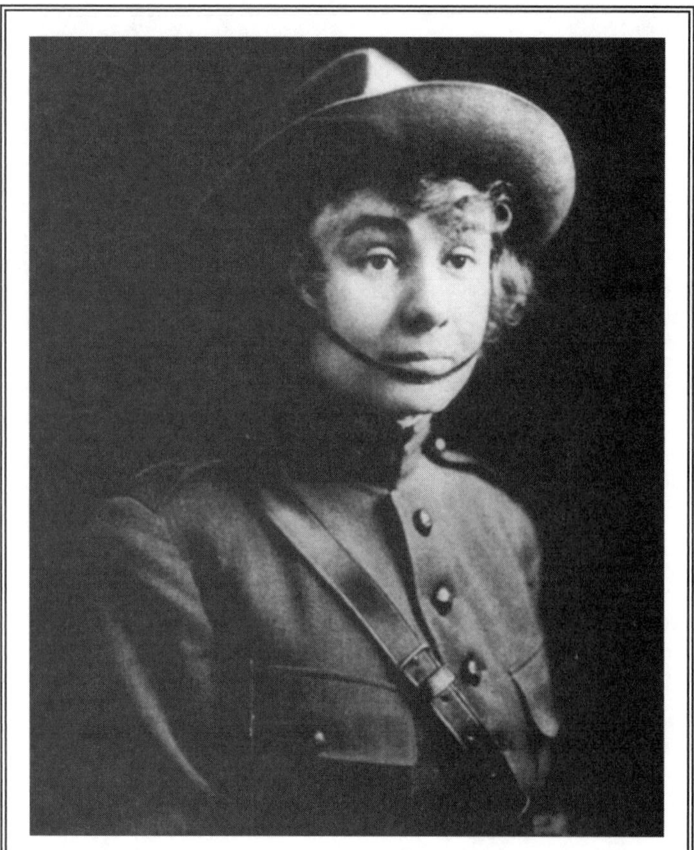

Peggy Hull

With America's involvement in the war, Hull resolved to pay her own way to France with only a promise from the *El Paso Times* to use her articles. Wearing a uniform of her own design, featuring a Sam Browne belt and short skirt, she charmed a State Department official into issuing a passport and bribed a French consular officer to obtain a visa. Once in France, she was side-tracked with an attack of appendicitis, after which she contacted the Paris office of the *Chicago Tribune*. She was able to travel to Le Valdahon through the efforts of Robert R. McCormick, its publisher, and Joseph B. Pierson, manager of the Paris edition, where she convinced the commanding generals to let her stay, even though her newspaper could not afford to have her accredited. While lodging in a barracks with women working for the YMCA canteen, she wrote personally of the war and signed her articles simply "Peggy." Her stories, which appeared in both the Paris and Chicago edition of the *Tribune,* were well-received but caused resentment among the male reporters, who felt that she was receiving preferential treatment.

In December 1917, Hull's mother was taken ill, and Peggy returned to the United States, although she was still determined to go back to Paris to cover the war legitimately. While nursing her mother, however, she became intrigued by plans for an American military expedition to Siberia to guard the Trans-Siberian Railroad, which was delivering supplies to the White Army. Interested more in this new mission than in returning to France, Hull set out to find a newspaper that would sponsor her for accreditation. After 50 rejections, she obtained endorsement of the Newspaper Enterprise Association, the Scripps-Howard press service headquartered in Cleveland. With the further endorsement of General Peyton C. March, whom she had met on the Pershing expedition, Hull boarded a Russian steamer for Siberia on September 1918. Landing in Vladivostok around the time of the Armistice, she began a 9-month, 1,000-mile inspection tour of the Siberian Railroad and reported on the suffering of the masses of refugees trying to escape both the Red and White armies. "Siberia is on the threshold of its blackest period," she wrote. "Twice a victim, first to monarchy and then to anarchy—its people will die by the thousands. They are freezing to death now." **Julia Edwards,** in *Women of the World,* points out that historians later dismissed the American expedition to Siberia as a "foolish venture," but Hull's stories provide one of the few firsthand accounts of what happened there. She left Siberia in July 1919, and after a stop in Shanghai where C.V. Lee, publisher of the *Shanghai Gazette,* offered her a job, she returned to the United States.

Hull went on to Paris in 1920, where she was well received by the very press corps that had treated her so poorly during the war. It was there that she met and befriended Irene Corbally, the 21-year-old correspondent for the *Tribune* who later won fame as Irene Corbally Kuhn. In 1921, when Hull left Paris to accept a job in Shanghai, Corbally, as a lark, joined her at the last minute. In a stopover in Singapore, Hull met a young British captain, John Kinley, who became her second husband. While Hull enjoyed a whirlwind courtship and a hasty marriage, Corbally went on to Shanghai, where she took a job with the *China Press*.

After an extended three-year honeymoon aboard Kinley's ship the *Nile,* Hull finally made it to Shanghai and her job at the *Shanghai Gazette*. After a year, however, her marriage deteriorated, and she returned to the United States only to discover that she had lost her American citizenship by marrying a foreigner. Not until 1932, after a successful campaign to change the law, was she able to divorce Kinley. In the interim, while free-lancing in New York, she fell in love with Harvey Deuell, the managing editor of the *New York Daily News*. In January 1932, while she was in Shanghai divorcing Kinley to marry Deuell, the Japanese attacked, and Deuell cabled her to cover the story for the *Daily News*.

Hull's third marriage ended with Deuell's death in 1939, just weeks before the start of World War II. Once again, she faced difficulty in obtaining accreditation, although ironically it finally came through from the North American Newspaper Alliance and the *Cleveland Plain Dealer,* the newspaper that had refused to send her to the Mexican border in 1917. However, it was not until November 1943 that she received permission from Lieutenant General Robert C. Richardson Jr., a commander general in the Central Pacific, to cover the war in his area. So, at age 53, Hull traveled with the fighting forces to the Pacific Islands, documenting the experiences of the GIs in articles that were likened to those of Ernie Pyle, who died in the Pacific. After the war, Peggy Hull retired to Carmel Valley, California, where she died in 1967.

SOURCES:

Edwards, Julia. *Women of the World: The Great Foreign Correspondents*. Boston, MA: Houghton Mifflin, 1988.

Barbara Morgan,
Melrose, Massachusetts

Hulme, Kathryn (1900–1981)

***American author who wrote* The Nun's Story.** *Born on January 6, 1900, in San Francisco, California; died on August 25, 1981, in Lihue, Hawaii; daughter of Edwin Page and Julia Frances (Cavarly) Hulme; attended the University of California, 1918–21; attended Columbia University, 1922; attended Hunter College (now Hunter College of the City University of New York), 1923; never married; lived with Marie-Louise Habets (1905–1986); no children.*

Selected works: How's the Road *(privately printed, 1928);* Arab Interlude *(1930); (novel)* Desert Night *(1932); (fictional autobiography)* We Lived as Children *(1938); (nonfiction)* The Wild Place *(1953); (fictionalized biography)* The Nun's Story *(1956); (fiction)* Annie's Captain *(1961); (autobiography)* Undiscovered Country: A Spiritual Adventure *(1966);* Look a Lion in the Eye *(1974).*

Kathryn Hulme is best remembered for her book *The Nun's Story*, the biography of her companion ➻ **Marie-Louise Habets** (characterized as Gabrielle Van der Mal, or Sister Luke, in the book), a former nun and nurse she met while working overseas following World War II. Habets served in a mental hospital in Belgium and in a Congo bush hospital before seeking release from her vows to fight with the underground Resistance against the Nazis. Hulme's book sold 700,000 copies and in 1959 was adapted into a major film starring ***Audrey Hepburn.**

Habets, Marie-Louise. *See Hepburn, Audrey for sidebar.*

Hulme was born in San Francisco, California, in 1900. She attended the University of California, Columbia University, and Hunter College before taking her first job as a reporter for the *Daily Californian.* She lived as an expatriate in Paris during the 1930s but returned to the United States at the outbreak of the war, taking a job as a welder in the Kaiser Shipyards. From 1945 to 1947, she served as a deputy director of the United Nations Relief and Rehabilitation Administration (UNRRA) in a U.S. Occupied Zone in Germany, where she met Habets, and then helped organize and served as deputy director of Wildflecken, a camp for displaced Poles in Bavaria. In 1951, she and Habets moved back to the United States, living in Connecticut, Southern California, and, finally, on the Island of Kauai, in Hawaii.

A keen observer of the world around her, Hulme wrote mostly from her own experiences. Her later works are marked by a deep spirituality, the result of her relationship with the mystic-philosopher Gurdjieff, who also influenced such

Leblanc, Georgette. *See Anderson, Margaret Carolyn for sidebar.*

writers as *Janet Flanner, *Solita Solano, *Djuna Barnes, *Jane Heap, *Margaret Carolyn Anderson, and Georgette Leblanc. Hulme's experience with Gurdjieff is detailed in *Undiscovered Countries: A Spiritual Adventure* (1966), which is set in Paris during the 1930s. She credited him with teaching her to "unroll the reels and look at the shadows of forgotten selves buried in the unconscious memory," or, more simply put, "how to believe." This self-knowledge, according to **Linda Ludwig** in *American Women Writers*, accounts for the poignancy of the fictional autobiography *We Lived as Children* (1938). "The self—or selves—that is evoked is androgynous by nature, a wise child—as children tend to be before life dulls them—devastated by an elusive father." Hulme's father also appears in a later work, *Annie's Captain* (1961), a fictionalized account of her parents' marriage.

Travel provided the basis of two of Hulme's books, *Arab Interlude* (1930), a collection of North African sketches, and *Look a Lion in the Eye* (1974), a later work about a safari through East Africa, which is also characterized by Hulme's more "conscious" state. *The Wild Place*, based on Hulme's work with displaced persons following the war, won the *Atlantic Monthly*'s first prize for nonfiction in 1953. *The Nun's Story* also garnered numerous awards, including the Commonwealth Club of California Gold Medal, the National Council of Women of the United States Book Award, and The Brotherhood Award of the National Conference of Christians and Jews. The author died in Hawaii, on August 25, 1981.

SOURCES:

Contemporary Authors. Vol. 104. Detroit, MI: Gale Research.

Mainiero, Lina, ed. *American Women Writers: From Colonial Times to the Present.* NY: Frederick Ungar, 1980.

Hülshoff, Annette von Droste (1797–1848).

See Droste-Hülshoff, Annette von.

Hume, Elizabeth (c. 1599–1633)

Countess of Suffolk. *Name variations: Elizabeth Howard. Born around 1599; died on August 19, 1633, at Greenwich Park Tower; interred at Walden, Essex, on September 25, 1633; daughter of George Hume, earl of Dunbar, and* ***Elizabeth Gordon****; married Theophilus Howard (1584–1640), 2nd earl of Suffolk (r. 1626–1640), also known as 2nd Lord Howard of Walden, in March 1612; children: James Howard (b. 1619), 3rd earl of Suffolk; Honorable Thomas Howard; George Howard (b. 1625), 4th earl of Suffolk; Henry Howard (b. 1627), 5th earl of Suffolk; ****Frances Villiers*** *(c. 1633–1677); Katherine Howard (d. 1650, who married George Stuart, Seigneur d'Aubigny and James Livingston, 1st earl of Newburgh); Elizabeth Howard; Margaret Howard (who married Roger Boyle, 1st earl of Orrery); Anne Howard (who married Thomas Walsingham).*

Hume, Grizel (1665–1746).

See Baillie, Grizel.

Humilitas of Faenza (1226–1310)

Saint and abbess of Italy. *Name variations: Humility; Rosana; Umilita; Umilta. Born in 1226 in Italy; died in 1310 in Faenza; married Hugolotto.*

Born in 1226, Humilitas was a Italian religious founder and saint. Even as a child, she felt drawn to a religious life, although she married young. Both Humilitas and her husband felt called to dedicate their lives to serving God, and they separated after only a few years to pursue their vocations. Humilitas lived as a recluse for several years but eventually emerged as the head of a Benedictine convent at Faenza. Among her other deeds, Humilitas founded the Order of Vallumbrosian Sisters, a religious establishment over which she presided. After her death, the popular abbess' life was preserved in a painting which depicts scenes from her days at the Vallumbrosian convent. Humilitas is portrayed in each scene holding or reading from a book, a symbol of her great classical and contemporary learning and the teaching functions she took on as abbess. Humilitas was declared a saint some years after her death. Her feast day is May 22.

Laura York,
Riverside, California

Humility (1226–1310).

See Humilitas of Faenza.

Humishuma (c. 1882–1936).

See Mourning Dove.

Hummel, Berta (1909–1946)

German illustrator and Roman Catholic nun whose drawings of children became the models for Hummel figurines. *Name variations: Sister Maria Innocentia. Born in Massing, Lower Bavaria, Germany, on May 21, 1909; died on November 6, 1946, in Convent Siessen bei Saulgau, Württemberg, Germany; daugh-*

ter of Adolf Hummel and Viktoria (Anglsperger) Hummel.

Completed art studies (1931); entered a convent, where she drew pictures of children that were sold to the public, first as greeting cards, then as figurines produced by the W. Goebel porcelain factory, the sales of which provided major financial support for her convent; captured in porcelain, Hummel's images of childhood innocence continue to be much beloved throughout the world and many of the figurines have become rare and expensive collectors' items.

Millions of collectors throughout the world cherish the charming Hummel figurines, while others dismiss them as dust-catching kitsch. In some instances, the statues fetch thousands of dollars at auction. The artist responsible for the original images was a shy, reserved South German named Berta Hummel. She was born in 1909 into a large family in the small Bavarian village of Massing, located 20 miles north of Oberammergau, a location known for its breathtaking scenery, guarded by the Alps and skirting the Rott River. Hummel grew up in a secure, supportive atmosphere. Her father Adolf Hummel was a prosperous businessman who ran the family dry goods store, but in his younger years he had dreamed of becoming an artist. The third of six children, Hummel showed an interest in drawing in her earliest years. Her mother **Viktoria Hummel** recalled that even as a young girl Berta used vast amounts of waste paper from the family store for her drawings, and also spent much time designing and sewing costumes for her dolls, which she then presented in shows to entertain her two sisters.

Berta suffered emotionally in her youth, at least in part because of her father's absence during World War I. She began to settle down, however, by age 12, when she was enrolled in a finishing school at Simbach where her artistic talents were encouraged. It became obvious to her family by her fourth year at Simbach that Berta's interests would always be dominated by her need to create art. Her mother recalled that she "would bring her work home when she came for a weekend or a holiday. She was painting still lifes, nature scenes, and of course continuing her little sketches on postcards. My husband began noticing refinement in her style, a self-confidence that let him know Berta really wanted to fulfill his ambition by becoming the family artist."

After graduating from Simbach in 1926, Hummel continued her education at Munich's Academy of Applied Arts. Here, she refined her skills. One of her art teachers recalled that she worked harder than most students, showing "great joy and enthusiasm for all things beautiful." At the academy, Berta struck up a friendship with two Franciscan nuns from the Convent of Siessen. By the time she graduated in 1931, Hummel had decided to enter the convent. At Siessen during her period as a novitiate nun, her talent was both recognized and encouraged. Despite signs of fragile health, she worked with her characteristic intensity, inspired not only by the daily framework of prayer and shared responsibilities that marked convent life, but also moved by the meadows of rural Württemberg that she could see each day from her window in the ancient cloister.

By 1934, a Stuttgart publishing firm had released the *Hummel-Buch,* a small volume of verse illustrated with Hummel's sketches of children, depicting their innocence with simplicity and charm. The book had barely been published when Hummel found herself in a situation that would transform her life and that of her drawings. The proprietor of the Goebel porcelain factory in Oeslau, Thuringia, contacted her, asking permission to reproduce her sketches as porcelain figurines. The situation at the factory was dire; it faced closure and subsequent unemployment for its skilled workers. Hummel agreed to let her art serve as inspiration. Insisting on the highest standards, she asked that artisans from the Goebel factory come to Siessen to consult with her on all production details. When they first appeared on the market in 1935, the Hummel figurines were a hit with a German public that was now under the Nazi dictatorship. The small figurines, sentimental and naive, evoked a peaceful world of innocence and contentment that had vanished.

In 1935, Hummel returned to Munich to continue her art studies, but within a year her health deteriorated, and she was compelled to return to the convent. At Siessen, she divided her time between religious obligations and the creation of a large number of sketches of children as well as ecclesiastical subjects that became holy pictures and tapestries. When her health permitted travel, she would visit the Goebel factory at Oeslau to oversee production of the now world-famous Hummel figures. At that time, a small figurine took 4-to-6 hours to paint and a large one, 8-to-12 hours; in all, 80-to-100 hours of labor were required to manufacture one of the more elaborate Hummels.

In 1937, Hummel took her final vows, leaving behind her former name to become Sister

Maria Innocentia of the Third Order of Saint Francis. Even though the substantial income derived from the sales of postcards and figurines based on her art played a major role in keeping the Siessen convent financially solvent, the fame of her drawings had not changed her, and she sought anonymity. Once while traveling on a train, a woman seated opposite Hummel was deeply absorbed in the *Hummel-Buch.* Noticing Berta's habit, she asked if she were possibly from the same community as Sister Maria Innocentia. "Yes, I am from the same community," replied Sister Maria Innocentia.

At the end of 1940, local Nazi officials invaded the Siessen Motherhouse, having already confiscated other schools in which the 800 nuns of the community taught and worked. Within ten days, the buildings had to be vacated to make room for ethnic German refugees from Rumania. Siessen's superior, Mother **Augustina**, had to dismiss her nuns, including Hummel who returned to Massing to live with her family. Only 40 nuns remained at Siessen during the war years, confined to one wing of the building. By the autumn of 1944, Hummel's years of respiratory problems had turned into a serious attack of pleurisy complicated by a lung infection. This serious setback to her already fragile health confined her to five months in a sanitorium in Isny, Württemberg.

The defeat of Nazi Germany in the spring of 1945 brought French occupation troops to Siessen; they restored the property of the Franciscan nuns to their order. By this time, however, the privations of the war years had permanently weakened Hummel's health. It was now obvious that she was suffering from tuberculosis, and she was taken to a sanitorium in Wangen. When her health did not improve, she was returned to Siessen in September 1946 to end her life within the religious community. Although rapidly weakening and in pain, she lay on a *chaise longue,* racing to complete her last sketches which she named her "Last Gift" to her fellow nuns and the world. These 15 sketches are as freshly innocent as all of the others she produced in previous years. Noting that Hummel was failing rapidly, the nuns sent for her mother. As the Angelus was ringing at high noon on November 6, 1946, Sister Maria Innocentia's spirit departed from her exhausted body.

Berta Hummel's work endures throughout the world. The Goebel porcelain factory continued to produce figurines (and later, plates) based on her sketches in the difficult postwar years in Germany. In 1977, the Goebel Collectors Club was formed to bring together the thousands of enthusiastic collectors of Hummel figurines and plates; the name of the club was changed in 1989 to the M.I. Hummel Club, and by 1994 it could boast of more than 250,000 registered collectors in the United States alone. Worldwide, it is estimated that there are at least four million serious Hummel collectors.

As collectibles, some of the rarer Hummel figurines are remarkably valuable. A 1948 "Merry Christmas" Hummel plate, a prototype, was estimated at $20,000 in 1989, while a "Silent Night" figurine with a black child could fetch $9,000 to $20,000 at auction, depending on the issue number. In the 1980s, some collectors were willing to pay $5,000 for "Stormy Weather," which shows two children huddled under an umbrella, if the little boy was lacking a tie. And the little boy in "Auf Wiedersehen" is much more valuable ($2,000 instead of only $200) if he is depicted waving his hand. After World War II, the earlier version was interpreted by some as showing a Hitler salute. The Goebel factory produced a new version in which the child waves a handkerchief. Hummel figurines with crown marks on the bottom, which were produced only from 1935 through 1949, are much more valuable than the later versions.

In October 1993, the world's only Hummel Museum opened its doors not in Germany, as might be expected, but in New Braunfels, Texas. The guiding spirit in the creation of this museum was German-born **Sieglinde Schoen Smith**, who posed for Hummel as an 18-month-old child in 1942 and is known in collector circles as "the living Hummel." Settling in the United States after World War II, Smith felt that Hummel's legacy deserved a museum setting. She contacted Swiss businessman Jacques Nauer, whose family owns the original Hummel sketches. After considering such sites as New York City and the Epcot Center in Florida, Nauer decided that a former savings and loan building in New Braunfels, a town originally settled by German immigrants, would be the most appropriate location. There are many Hummel originals on display at the museum, along with artifacts from Hummel's Siessen studio and classroom, including her work light, tables, and easel, as well as her German-language edition of *Tom Sawyer.*

Asked why she believed Berta Hummel's drawings and figurines continue to be beloved by millions, Smith responded that she believed Sister Maria Innocentia "worked at a time when there wasn't much love in the world. For a long

time I couldn't figure out what it is that makes her art so popular. Then I realized that what she drew is everybody's memories."

SOURCES:

Commire, Anne, ed. *Something about the Author.* Vol. 43, 1986, pp. 137–141.

Dunn, Betty. "Sister Hummel's Cherubic Legacy," in *Houston Chronicle.* May 15, 1994, p. 4.

"Figuring the Worth of your Figurines," in *Business Week.* No. 2677. March 2, 1981, pp. 135–136.

Flaig, Eleanore. "The Hummel Story," in *The Catholic World.* Vol. 177. May 1953, pp. 128–133.

Fucini, Joseph J., and Suzy Fucini, *Entrepeneurs: The Men and Women behind Famous Brand Names and How They Made It.* Boston: G.K. Hall, 1985.

Hummel, Berta. *The Hummel: Drawings by Berta Hummel with Light Verse.* (Translation of *Hui, die Hummel!*) Munich: Verlag Ars Sacra, 1972.

Hummel Museum, New Braunfels, Texas.

Luckey, Carl F. *Luckey's Hummel Figurines & Plates: Identification and Value Guide.* 11th ed. Iola, WI: Krause, 1997.

Malsam, Margaret. "Happiness is a Hummel," in *Antiques & Collecting/Hobbies.* Vol. 98, no. 7. September 1993, pp. 24–26.

Miller, Robert L., et al. *The M.I. Hummel Album.* NY: Portfolio Press, 1992.

———, and Eric Ehrmann. *Hummel: The Complete Collector's Guide and Illustrated Reference.* Huntington, NY: Portfolio Press, 1979.

Seemann, Margarete and Berta Hummel. *The Hummel-Book.* Translated by Lola Ch. Eytel. 16th ed. Stuttgart: Emil Fink Verlag, 1972.

Stoddard, Maynard Good. "The Beloved 'Children' of M.I. Hummel," in *Saturday Evening Post.* Vol. 254. January–February, 1982, pp. 78–81.

———. "The Immortal Art of Sister Maria Innocentia," in *Saturday Evening Post.* Vol. 262. January–February, 1990, pp. 62–65.

Thomas, Les. "A Hummel Beginning," in *Southern Living.* Vol. 28, no. 10. October 1993, pp. 34–35.

Wiegand, Gonsalva, Sister. *Sketch Me, Berta Hummel! Biography of Sister Maria Innocentia (Berta Hummel).* St. Meinrad, Indiana: Grail Publications, [1951].

Wilson, Craig. "Happiness is a Hummel," in *USA Today.* July 24, 1989, p. 1D.

John Haag,
Associate Professor, University of Georgia, Athens, Georgia

Hummert, Anne (c. 1905–1996)

American writer who, with husband Frank, created the first daytime soap opera. *Born around 1905; died on July 5, 1996, in New York City; graduated magna cum laude from Goucher College, Baltimore, Maryland, 1925; married a journalist (divorced); married Frank Hummert, in 1934 (died 1966): children: (first marriage) one son.*

Anne and Frank Hummert were the creators of the first daytime soap opera "Just Plain Bill," which premiered on radio in 1933 and immediately caught the imagination of radio listeners throughout the nation. The afternoon soaps quickly became a national trend which continued with the advent of television and has only recently fallen victim to a diminished afternoon audience and the popularity of the talk show. During the 1930s and 1940s, however, the Hummerts were churning out a total of 18 popular daytime serials, 90 15-minute episodes a week.

Anne Hummert was born in New York City around 1905, graduated from Goucher College in 1925, and began her career as a reporter, taking a job with the precursor of the International Herald Tribune in Paris. Within a year, she had married and divorced a colleague and was back in the United States with an infant son to support. She settled in Chicago, employed as an assistant to Frank Hummert, a copywriter and partner in the Blackett, Sample & Hummert Agency. They were married in 1934. At that time, commercial radio was in its infancy and programming was limited to the evening hours when listeners were free to gather around the radio. While advertisers were dimly aware that housewives were home all day and were the major purchasers for the family, the Hummerts grasped the opportunity at hand, providing an afternoon drama so compelling that women and afternoon stay-at-homes tuned in. Within months after the introduction of "Just Plain Bill," the saga of a barber in the small town of Hartville who had married above himself, the airwaves were flooded with copycat programs, including several new offerings from the Hummerts. Advertisers, eager to peddle their wares to a captive audience, were lining up in droves to sponsor the new shows.

The Hummerts lived and wrote together for 32 years, until Frank Hummert's death in 1966. Anne, a millionaire several times over, survived another 30 years, healthy and vigorous almost to the end. She died in her New York apartment on July 5, 1996, at the age of 91.

SOURCES:

Thomas, Robert McG., Jr. "Obituaries," in *The [New London] Day.* July 21, 1996.

Humphrey, Doris (1895–1958)

American pioneer in the performance, teaching and choreography of modern dance, known for articulating the meaning of dance and the process of choreography. *Born Doris Batcheller Humphrey on October 17, 1895, in Oak Park, Illinois; died on December 29, 1958, in New York City, of cancer; daughter of Horace Buckingham Humphrey (a journalist and hotel manager) and Julia Ellen (Wells) Humphrey (a musician); completed high school; married Charles F. Woodford, on June 10, 1932; children: Charles Humphrey Woodford (b. July 8, 1933).*

Began dancing at age eight; trained and performed with Denishawn (1917–27); with Charles Weidman, co-founded the Humphrey-Weidman Group (1927); gave first independent concert in New York (1928); helped found the short-lived Dance

Repertory Theater (1930–31); received Choreographic Award of the year from Dance Magazine *(1937); with Weidman, founded the Studio Theater (1940); offered first dance composition class (1945); was artistic director of José Limon dance company (1945–50); granted Guggenheim fellowship (1948); was official director of the Dance Center at the 92nd St. YMHA (1952); received Capezio Award (1954); was artistic director of the Juilliard Dance Theater (1954); wrote* The Art of Making Dances, *published posthumously (NY: Rinehart, 1959).*

Selected choreography: "Soaring" (1920); "Water Study" (1928); "Life of the Bee" (1929); "Salutations to the Depths" (1930); "The Shakers" (1931); "New Dance" (1935); "Theater Piece" (1936); "With My Red Fires" (1936); "Passacaglia and Fugue in C Minor" (1938); "Decade" (1941); "Partita in G Major" (1943); "Lament for Ignacio Sanchez Mejias" (1946); "Day on Earth" (1947); "Night Spell" (1952); "Ritmo Jondo" (1953); "Ruins and Visions" (1955); "Brandenburg Concerto No. 4 in G Major" (1958).

If ***Martha Graham** was the mystical "artiste" of modern dance, Doris Humphrey was its unremitting technician and engineer. Humphrey invented the new American art form of modern dance, along with Graham. Devoted to abstraction in movement and choreography, she gave the form an intellectual underpinning, developing a theory of dance, a technique of movement, and a process of choreography. She also performed, started and directed her own company, choreographed prodigiously, and authored a book about her art form; most important, she talked about and taught the art of choreography. Although she was generally overshadowed in her career by the genius of Graham, and has often been forgotten and overlooked since, her influence spanned the whole of the early modern dance world and indelibly shaped its formation.

Born in 1895 in Oak Park, Illinois, Doris Humphrey came from pioneer Yankee stock, claiming to be a tenth-generation American on both sides of her family. She spent her childhood in the Midwest, where her father Horace B. Humphrey was first a journalist and then a manager of the Palace Hotel in Chicago. Her mother **Julia Wells Humphrey** was a graduate of Mt. Holyoke College for women and the Boston Conservatory of Music, and the couple raised their daughter in the hotel. Julia Humphrey began her daughter's training in the arts with dance lessons at the Parker School when Doris was eight. The lessons were primarily in ballet, and often with European masters who happened to be traveling through Chicago. Following graduation from high school, Doris herself taught ballroom and interpretive dancing in her hometown of Oak Park.

Humphrey's life took a sharp turn when she came into contact with Denishawn, the company and school devised by ***Ruth St. Denis** and Ted Shawn. Precursors of modern dance, these two performers created theatrical spectacles, usually based on Oriental themes, recreating movements borrowed from cultures around the world, particularly India, Japan, and Siam (present-day Thailand). St. Denis also concentrated on what were known as music visualizations, which she described in a 1924 *Denishawn Magazine* as "the scientific translation into bodily action of the rhythmic, melodic, and harmonic structure of a musical composition."

In 1917, Humphrey was 22 when she went to Los Angeles to train at the Denishawn School, and she stayed with the group for the next ten years. She began to choreograph in the Denishawn style, creating a popular solo in 1920 entitled "Soaring" which used a huge scarf that bil-

Doris Humphrey

lowed like a wave. By the time she traveled with the company to Asia on their two-year tour from 1925 to 1927, she was known as a close protege of St. Denis, and she formed other crucial relationships with company members that were to last throughout her life: Charles Weidman became her dance and choreographic partner, and **Pauline Lawrence** became their accompanist, manager, and indefatigable champion.

Humphrey, Weidman, and Lawrence set out in 1927 to form a new company, after personal and professional squabbles created a rift between St. Denis and Shawn. The Humphrey-Weidman Group included both men and women, a unique feature in the female-dominated world of modern dance. Humphrey and Weidman also began to move beyond the Asian-inspired movement and choreography of Denishawn to investigations of movement based on abstract aesthetic principles as well as contemporary American issues. Humphrey and Weidman were like other artists and intellectuals of the late 1920s and 1930s in their concerns about the problems and injustices of their society and hopes for a better world. They were eager to create a dance form characteristic of the *modern* age—confrontational, relevant, and weighty.

Humphrey's "Life of the Bee" (1929) pursued this vision. Adapting the movements described in Maurice Maeterlinck's 1901 study of bees, she was able to explore the subjects of evolution, work, and hierarchial human relations through dance. As she described in a program note: "the workers dance and beat their wings around the cradle of the adolescent princess . . . [and] the pitiless duty of the hive decrees the sacrifice of the individual at last to the immortality of the republic."

Formalistic concerns were what truly captured Humphrey's interest, however: how to coordinate a group, relate movement to music, and work aesthetic principles into the human body. Although she demonstrated social concern over issues such as workers' rights, she never became politically engaged to the degree of ***Helen Tamiris** or other dancers of her era. For Humphrey, the individual and the ideals of art remained sacrosanct. Biographer **Selma Jeanne Cohen** relates that Humphrey's husband once reflected on her lack of interest in politics by saying "that his wife would have given a concert under the auspices of Satan himself—as long as he put up the production money and did not interfere with artistic decisions."

While Humphrey's sources of inspiration were often literary, Nietzschean philosophy formed the basis of her understanding of dance. In the Apollonian-Dionysian dialectic, Apollo represented stability and stolidity, and Dionysus was the anarchic impulse, opposing elements in which Humphrey found her metaphor for the "fall and recovery" of the human body moving through space. For her, the most poignant moment of movement lay between the struggle to resist gravity and the euphoria of suspension in giving into it, and the Humphrey-Weidman technique and choreography contained many falls, arcs, swoops, and rebounds. Balance and unbalance were to battle onstage throughout Humphrey's career.

By the early 1930s, the Humphrey-Weidman Group was recognized as a leading force in modern dance when it joined Graham and Tamiris in forming the short-lived Dance Repertory Theater for concerts in 1930–31. The group was also invited to teach and choreograph at the Bennington Summer School of Dance throughout the 1930s. In the dance world, where everyone struggled to survive financially, teaching was a means to choreograph and perform, and the group scraped together an existence devoted to performing when and where they could.

Humphrey rarely took very good care of herself, relying on Pauline Lawrence to provide the type of maternal nurturing she needed. In the summer of 1931, depressed by a recent knee injury, she went off alone on a cruise to the West Indies to give herself a much-needed rest. This uncharacteristic move changed her life when she met Charles Woodford, an English naval officer, who became her husband the following June. In July 1933, their son Charles Humphrey Woodford was born. Despite the couple's constant separations because of his time at sea and her devotion to her career and touring, the marriage probably gave both what they preferred. They carried on an unflagging correspondence, providing each other unceasing support and encouragement.

Meanwhile, Humphrey continued to focus most of her energy on dance. In the mid-1930s, she created a number of masterpieces that solidified her position as the consummate choreographer of modern dance. Her crowning achievement was a triumvirate of works celebrating human relationships. According to Humphrey's notes, "New Dance (1935)" presented the world as it should be. It was a dance in three sections—the first for women, the second for men, and the third for men and women together—which celebrated the possible harmony of relationships. "Theater Piece" (1936) depicted the present world as "a grim business of survival by competition," while "With My Red Fires" (1936) was an exposé on love. Although the three were never performed in one night, nor given critical attention as the connected pieces of a whole, each dance received individual success. It was Humphrey's vision of them as a trilogy, however, that bespoke her larger artistic purposes. In her endless investigation of the social interactions of humans, the individual remained the defining element, although she did not spend time creating solos or constructing group dances to show the individual in conflict with a larger group. Her focus was on the many ways that people relate to one another. Logically enough, her greatest success was achieved in group choreography, when she was given the Choreographic Award of *Dance Magazine* in 1937 for her work "To the Dance."

Constant, difficult touring consumed the years from 1936 to 1940, with the tours providing a paltry income but a way to get the works before the public. Home base remained New York City, where Humphrey kept a communal apartment with Weidman, Lawrence, her son, her husband when on leave, as well as occasional visitors. The arrangement helped to provide care for her son, to whom Humphrey never gave her full attention. Humphrey also served on the Dance Theater Project of the Federal Works Progress Administration (WPA) for a short stint in 1936 and continued to go to Bennington in the summer and then to Mills College in California, when the summer program moved there in 1939. She and Weidman also gave classes at their studio. In 1940, they devised a Studio Theater, a brilliant concept not fully realized until it took off in the loft performances of the 1960s and 1970s. Within the studio space they used for classes and rehearsals, they created a small theater of 150 seats for the performance of their own works and rental to other dancers, gaining independence from the grandiose expenses and time restrictions of commercial theaters.

Almost always sold out, the Studio Theater helped to sustain the Humphrey-Weidman Group. But by the early 1940s, the personal and professional relations between Humphrey and Weidman began to crumble, and in September 1941 Humphrey took an apartment on her own for herself and her son. Weidman began choreographing many more Broadway and variety shows, and the two rarely collaborated after that time. Humphrey also began to suffer physically, with pain in her left leg and hip. In May 1944, she performed for the last time.

The years after World War II proved particularly difficult for Humphrey, as her role switched from performer to teacher and choreographer and she was forced to reconcile herself to not being able to dance. From the early 1940s to the end of her life, arthritis caused her to walk with a limp. With her collaboration with Weidman essentially ended, she now looked to her student and protege, José Limon, to inspire her.

Returning from military service in World War II, Limon found the Humphrey-Weidman Group in dissolution and decided to form his own company, with Humphrey as its artistic director. Humphrey choreographed some of her best works for Limon's dancers and also served as mentor for his own choreography. During the late 1940s, the Limon Company dominated the new summer school for modern dance at Connecticut College, then became a huge success in its European tour of 1950. Humphrey, teaching and choreographing at this time without being able to demonstrate, now became particularly interested in teaching dance composition. In 1945, she taught her first composition class at the 92nd St. YMHA, and despite her physical frailty she continued with resolute determination, becoming official director of the Dance Center at the 92nd St. YMHA in 1952. Named the artistic director of the Juilliard Dance Theater in 1954, she won the Capezio Award that same year for outstanding contributions to dance.

> To be master of one's body: to find a perfect union between the inner thought and the outer form—to draw from this a radiance and power that makes of life a more glorious and vital experience—this is to dance.
>
> —Doris Humphrey

Doris Humphrey devoted her remaining years to the Limon Company. But as Limon gradually gained a reputation independent of her, she realized that she had given up much of her own recognition to further his. In 1957, she broke with her former student after their European tour, during which she felt painfully forgotten. The following year, she finally turned to completing the book that been on her mind for some time, for which she had been awarded a Guggenheim fellowship to pursue ten years earlier. By the fall of 1958, she was suffering from inoperable stomach cancer, but she managed to complete *The Art of Making Dances* just before her death on December 29, 1958. The book was published posthumously in 1959 and remains an incomparable guide to modern dance.

SOURCES:

Humphrey, Doris. *Doris Humphrey: An Artist First*. Edited and completed by Selma Jeanne Cohen. Middletown, CT: Wesleyan University Press, 1966, 1972.

Muriel Humphrey

Lloyd, Margaret. *The Borzoi Book of Modern Dance.* NY: Knopf, 1949.

Siegel, Marcia. *Days on Earth: The Dance of Doris Humphrey.* New Haven, CT: Yale University Press, 1987.

SUGGESTED READING:

Jowitt, Deborah. *Time and the Dancing Image.* Berkeley, CA: University of California Press, 1988.

McDonagh, Don. *The Complete Guide to Modern Dance.* Garden City, NY: Doubleday, 1976.

RELATED MEDIA:

"Doris Humphrey Celebration," concert commemorating 50th Anniversary of the Doris Humphrey company and school; produced by Dance Notation Bureau, New York, 1978.

"Trailblazers of Modern Dance," WNET-NY's Great Performances: Dance in America Series, 1977.

COLLECTIONS:

Extensive correspondence, manuscripts, notations of dances, programs, scrapbooks, and photographs at the Dance Collection, Performing Arts Library at Lincoln Center, New York Public Library.

Julia L. Foulkes,
former Rockefeller Foundation Postdoctoral Fellow at the Center for Black Music Research, Columbia College, Chicago, Illinois

Humphrey, Muriel (1912–1998)

United States senator. *Name variations: Muriel Humphrey Brown. Born Muriel Fay Buck on February 20, 1912, in Huron, South Dakota; died on September 20, 1998, in Minneapolis, Minnesota; daughter of Andrew E. Buck and Jessie May Buck; educated at Huron College; married Hubert Horatio Humphrey (former vice president and U.S. senator) in 1936 (died 1977); remarried; children: (first marriage)* ***Nancy Humphrey****; Hubert H. Humphrey, 3rd; Robert Andrew Humphrey; Douglas Sannes Humphrey.*

Born Muriel Fay Buck on February 20, 1912, in Huron, South Dakota, Muriel Humphrey was known more for her many years as a politician's wife than for her brief career as a senator. Muriel Buck met Hubert Humphrey while attending Huron College in the 1930s. After they were married, Muriel worked at a utility company as a bookkeeper to support the couple while Hubert finished college. While he was a graduate student at Louisiana State University, she continued to help with family finances by making sandwiches which her husband sold to other students for ten cents each.

The Humphreys' political life began in 1943 when Hubert, a Democrat, ran for mayor of Minneapolis. Humphrey was active in her husband's campaign at a time when few politicians' wives were, and continued to assist him throughout a career that included presidential and senatorial campaigns. She stepped into the forefront of politics on January 25, 1978, when Minnesota Governor Rudy Perpich appointed her to fill the Senate seat left empty by her husband's death until a special election could be held.

On February 6, Muriel Humphrey took the oath of office and became the only woman in the 100-member Senate. Humphrey's reception in the legislative body was cool; save for a few Democrats, the other senators virtually ignored her. Despite this, Humphrey was active during her nine months in the Senate. She served on the Committee on Foreign Relations and the Committee on Governmental Operations and helped to pass legislation that dealt with women's issues, including providing child-care and flexible work schedules for working mothers, lowering female unemployment, and extending the ratification deadline for the Equal Rights Amendment (ERA). She was asked by President Jimmy Carter to chair the Women's Advisory Panel after the forced exit of ***Bella Abzug**, which she declined.

Humphrey supported President Carter on his sale of jet fighter planes to Egypt, Israel and Saudi Arabia, voted in favor of the Panama Canal neutrality pact, and sponsored an amendment to the Civil Service Reform Act of 1978 that offered job security to federal employees exposing fraud or waste. She also sponsored an amendment to the Department of Education Organization Act (which changed the name of the Department of Health, Education, and Welfare to the Department of Health and Human Services).

On November 7, after the special election that elected David Durenburger to Humphrey's seat, Muriel Humphrey retired to Minnesota where she later remarried and used the name Muriel Humphrey Brown. Humphrey was active in work dealing with mental retardation, a condition with which her eldest granddaughter had been born. She also participated in the Minnesota State Fair, winning prizes for her needlepoint. Muriel Humphrey Brown died of natural causes at the age of 86 at Abbott Northwestern Memorial Hospital on September 20, 1998. In her obituary, Walter Mondale was quoted as saying about the Humphreys, "Together they helped change this country to a better, fairer, more decent society."

SOURCES:

Charlton, Linda. "The Newest Senator from Minnesota," in *The New York Times Biographical Service*. January 1978.

Feldman, Trude B. "Muriel Humphrey: Senator or Not, She Continues as a Force," in *Ladies' Home Journal*. October 1978.

Obituary. *The [New London] Day*. September 22, 1998.

Office of the Historian. *Women in Congress, 1917–1990*. Commission on the Bicentenary of the U.S. House of Representatives, 1991.

Karina L. Kerr, M.A.,
Ypsilanti, Michigan

Hungary, duchess of.

See Sarolta (fl. 900s).

Hungary, queen of.

See Gisela of Bavaria (c. 975–1033).
See Anastasia of Russia (c. 1023-after 1074).
See Richesa of Poland (fl. 1030–1040).
See Synadene of Byzantium (c. 1050–?).
See Adelaide of Rheinfelden (c. 1065–?).
See Helena of Serbia (fl. 1100s).
See Preslava of Russia (fl. 1100).
See Euphrosyne of Kiev (fl. 1130–1180).
See Euphemia of Kiev (d. 1139).
See Anne of Chatillon-Antioche (c. 1155–c. 1185).
See Margaret of France (1158–1198).
See Gertrude of Andrechs-Meran (c. 1185–1213).
See Yolande of Courtenay (fl. 1200s).
See Elizabeth of Sicily (fl. 1200s).
See Salome of Hungary (1201–c. 1270).
See Maria Lascaris (fl. 1234–1242).
See Elizabeth of Kumania (c. 1242–?).
See Este, Beatrice d' (d. 1245).
See Agnes of Austria (1281–1364).
See Elizabeth of Poland (1305–1380).
See Jadwiga for sidebar on Elizabeth of Bosnia (c. 1345–1387).
See Maria of Hungary (1371–1395).
See Barbara of Cilli (fl. 1390–1410).
See Elizabeth of Luxemburg (1409–1442).
See Madeleine of France (1443–1486).
See Beatrice of Naples (1457–1508).
See Foix, Anne de (fl. 1480–1500).
See Mary of Hungary (1505–1558).
See Isabella of Poland (1519–1559).
See Zita of Parma (1892–1989).

Hungerford, Agnes (d. 1524)

English noblewoman. *Name variations: Lady Agnes Hungerford. Executed in 1524; married John Cotell; second wife of Sir Edward Hungerford (died 1522).*

Lady Agnes Hungerford was executed for the murder of her first husband, John Cotell.

Hungerford, Catherine (d. 1452).

See Howard, Catherine.

Hunt, Harriot Kezia (1805–1875)

Alternative healer, sometimes called the first woman doctor in the U.S., who sought to expand the legitimacy of women in male-dominated professions and traced mental and physical illness in women to limitations imposed on their lives. *Born Harriot Kezia Hunt on November 9, 1805, in Boston, Massachusetts; died in Boston of Bright's disease on January 2, 1875; daughter of Joab Hunt (a ship's joiner) and Kezia (Wentworth) Hunt; attended private schools and studied alternative medicine for two years; never married; no children.*

Opened a school in her home (1827); began two-year study of alternative medicine (1833); opened practice of alternative medicine (1835); organized the Ladies Physiological Society in Charlestown, Massachusetts (1843); turned to the Swedenborgian religion (1843); applied to Harvard Medical School and denied entry (1847); attended the first National Women's Rights Conference (1850); reapplied to Harvard and admitted (1850); was the first woman to make public protest in Massachusetts against "taxa-

tion without representation" (1852); received honorary M.D. from the Female Medical College of Philadelphia (1853); hosted the founding meeting of the New England Women's Club (1868). Publications: Glances and Glimpses or Fifty Years Social, Including Twenty Years Professional Life *(1856).*

On November 9, 1871, Dr. **Mary Stafford Blake**, a young admirer of Dr. Harriot Kezia Hunt, arrived in Boston to pay tribute to the physician, humanist, and reformer for "all she had done for women," on the occasion of Dr. Hunt's 66th birthday. The two sat by a small open fire that revealed Hunt's perfect teeth and reflected on her silvery grey hair, wrote Blake, which "looked silken and was swept back and fastened in a French twist." Seated in a large armchair, Hunt proudly remarked, "All you see left of me is natural; I have never had time to put on modern gear."

That week was sacred to her for its family memories, Hunt told Blake, including the birthday anniversaries of both her mother and father, and their wedding anniversary. In a family that had always been everything to her, all that now remained were the sons of her beloved sister, **Sarah Augusta Hunt**. For years, Hunt's perseverance had helped to prepare the way for women to enter the medical profession in male centers of learning, and had inspired women toward self-determination in their physical and mental lives. Step by step, she had fought a courageous battle against the cultural marginalization of women within marriage and community, and their exclusion from male-dominated institutions, actions that still stand as a model for women who wish to control their own lives.

Born in Boston in 1805, Harriot Kezia Hunt was the first of two daughters born to Joab and **Kezia Wentworth Hunt** after 14 years of marriage. The parents were of old New England stock. Kezia Hunt was an opinionated woman, described by her daughter as having a "strong love for politics—even more than my father," and a capacity for helping others that was extended to a large circle of relatives. Harriot's father made his living as a ship's joiner, or carpenter, and later as a shipping industry investor, and was a "bright, glad, witty man, without a shade of vulgarity." His adventurous sea stories, culled from the sea captains that were his companions, provided Hunt with her first childhood visions of the world outside of Boston.

In 1808, when Hunt was three, her sister Sarah was born, and the two grew up in what Hunt describes as a "happy—cheerful—joyous" home. According to Hunt, the years her parents had spent without children had allowed them "a season for improvement. . . . No mental dyspepsia marred their blessing." They were avid readers, discussed their ideas freely, and were never bored with each other in their marriage. In adulthood, Hunt idealized the marriage and her mother's role; her mother's intellectual life led Hunt to advocate behaviors for wives and mothers that were the antithesis of married women's ideals of her time. Ironically, Hunt's mother had fulfilled the traditional role as "mother," not the ideals that Hunt proffered.

From 1820 to 1860, the expectations for female behavior were so rigid that historian **Barbara Welter** later coined the phrase the "Cult of True Womanhood" to explain the attitudes of the period. The trend, which reached its height during Hunt's lifetime, maintained that the sphere of a woman's influence was limited to the home, and the four qualities embodied in the idealized "true" or "good" woman were purity, piety, submissiveness, and domesticity. In contrast, what Hunt came to recommend for women within marriage was self-fulfillment rather than self-abnegation, while continuing to believe that their obligation as mothers was to provide their children with a nurturing environment as the salient ingredient for their full development. Since she never married or had children, Hunt never actually lived by the tenets she upheld.

Early in life, Hunt developed a love of books and learning that overrode her interest in domestic chores. As she wrote, "I was not a useful child in many of those domestic arts which tend to make others happy." Her first schooling consisted of lessons from her mother in their small waterfront home at the foot of Hanover Street. Later, she attended private schools. At home, she was encouraged to read widely, discuss what she had read, and be frank, which helped to cultivate her lasting conviction that the value of education for women was in offering a real and tangible pathway to self-fulfillment through work. Hunt's adolescent years were filled with study, dances, and family associations. Her exuberance for life and a distaste for any fossilized ideas may have been the impetus for her nickname, "Zion." She later recalled the invocation of an aunt, who would say, "Zion, lift up thy voice; be not afraid!"

At age 22, with the encouragement of her parents, Hunt began a school upstairs in the family home. Although she loved teaching, she never felt it to be her true vocation, and the pleasures of that year were overshadowed by the death of her father in November 1827.

The turning point in Hunt's life came when her sister became severely ill. The family doctor who treated Sarah was a "regular" physician who followed the current beliefs of traditional, or allopathic medicine. Medical practice at the time was based primarily upon the then-popular belief that all people had a finite amount of "vital force" which had to be kept in balance, and that illnesses in women generally stemmed from problems of the uterus. To restore the proper balance in the body of an ill person, an allopathic physician would purge it of "putrid matter" by bleeding the patient, through cupping or the application of leeches, to the point of fainting. Other techniques included blistering or the ingesting of turpentine and mercury. In treatment for what seems to have been tuberculosis, Sarah endured "blisters and mercurials . . . leeches, calomel, and prussic acid—four drops three times a day." As Hunt wryly noted, "I marvelled—all this agony—all these remedies—and no benefit!"

After more than 100 professional calls over almost a year, the sisters deduced from scouring medical texts that Sarah's case was not understood, and they resolved to resort to "a quack." In an era devoid of strict licensing and regulations, about 20% of those recognized as practicing medicine were alternative healers, who also sought to cure their patients through a balancing of the vital force. Their methods were generally based on less drastic treatments, however, involving small amounts of drugs, medicinal herbs, and water, which were categorized under the practices of homeopathy, botanics, and water curists. The principles of alternative medicinal practices often overlapped, but what they had in common was a requirement of self-sacrifice in their followers, dependent upon a change in the patient's lifestyle that often conflicted with cultural norms. The water-curists, for example, advocated a vegetarian diet, exercise, and loose clothing such as bloomers, as well as cold water therapies instead of dramatic cathartics.

The Hunt sisters' firsthand experience with alternative medicine began with a Mr. and Mrs. Mott, an English couple new to Boston who described themselves as physicians, but were alternative healers. Although Hunt never revealed the exact teachings of the Motts, many of her beliefs proffered throughout her career were closest to the water cures. In Sarah's case, she was diagnosed as consumptive, and recovered completely after treatment involving a combination of alfalfa and cold-water therapy.

Inspired by her sister's recovery, Hunt closed her school in 1833 and moved with her mother and sister into the household of the Motts, where she underwent two years of training. In 1835, along with her sister, she set up a practice. In recognition of their mother's political astuteness, the sisters followed her advice not to include midwifery in their practice, to avoid any conflict with regular physicians who could perceive them as insinuating themselves into general family care; traditional female midwives were already under attack by male physicians.

The first patients seen by the Hunts were mostly women and children who turned to them as a last resort, after their cases had been abandoned as hopeless by allopathic physicians. Concentrating on female physiology, the sisters took a new tack, stressing diet, bathing, exercise, rest, and sanitation. One of Hunt's first recommendations to patients was to throw away their medicine, start a journal, and use the lives of their mothers as inspiration; for some women, she even prescribed dancing. Although barred from hospital practice because they were not schooled through a medical institution, the Hunt sisters began to demonstrate a success that attracted patients from the "highly cultivated, the delicate, and the sensible." And the more patients that Hunt saw, particularly among women of the upper- and upper-middle class, the more she viewed their illnesses as stemming from unhappy lives. Believing in the liberating power of education, she was enraged that girls tended to be educated "for nothing but marriage," with a view "to their future sale for wealth, social position, a home, or any other terms on which a dependent, and ambitious—a weak and silly woman, may be obtained." Over the years, Hunt's interest in the connections of the internal life of women to mental illness increasingly informed her work.

In 1840, Sarah's medical work ended with her marriage, but Harriot continued to build up her practice. She also took on a more public role as an advocate of health education, the financial independence of women, and social reform. In 1843, recognizing how often the spread of disease was rooted in ignorance of the human physique, she organized the Ladies Physiological Society in Charlestown, Massachusetts, to counsel women to be less dependent on physicians. At a time when the delivery of a lecture by a woman was a daring act in itself, she taught women about their own bodies, with a sense of conviction that was so strong, she said, "it seemed a holy thought." Encouraged to discover members of the group reporting medical bills cut by half when they followed her prescriptions for healthy living, Hunt also became convinced by "the earnest looks—the friendly greetings and farewells—the religious element that kindled there," that women priests were needed as well as physicians.

Hunt's sister gave birth in 1843 to a frail baby girl named Harriot Augusta in honor of her aunt, a child Hunt described as "spiritualized to me from her birth." Children's health took on a new importance for the healer, who felt that her love for the child "opened new avenues of love for others. This was her mission for me." Three boys would also be born to Sarah, but Hunt idolized only her little "Sunbeam," while calling upon mothers to oversee the diet, air, exercise, sleep, and bathing of themselves and their children. She declared, "Mothers! never leave your children to the care of servants, foreign or native!"

In 1845, Hunt's beloved niece died. In her bereavement, Hunt was "saddened, afflicted, and disappointed" and questioned her views of religion which up to this point had provided her little comfort. That year, she turned to Swedenborgian religion and said soon after that now, "my patients were my family; and a new purpose to labor more effectively for women, seized my soul. My profession seemed hallowed to me. My love for my sister had become stronger. She was now my all. But she was a wife and mother, and I must be wedded to humanity." As much as she preached mutuality and service to others she remained independent. Sarah had suggested many times that she join Sarah's family, but Hunt continued to live separately and pursue her practice.

In 1847, following the death of her mother who had been her lifelong friend and companion, "Hours of loneliness were often spent in my solitary home and I might have sunk below the blow had not the angel of mercy visited me, and inspired me with the thought of endeavoring to enlighten my sisters on the 'laws of life.'" That year, Hunt applied to Harvard Medical School and found her application denied as "inexpedient." Furious at what she called this "safe and non-committal" rejection, she said that the day would come when "wondering eyes will stare at the semi-barbarism of the middle of the 19th century."

Refused training as her outlet against loneliness, Hunt turned to travel for the first time. In 1848, she made her first visit to an alternative community at the Shaker village at Shirley, Massachusetts. Witnessing such communities, in which women's roles were negotiated or otherwise equalized with men's, reconfirmed her conviction that social reform was the remedy for women's inferior social status. Toward this end, she began to offer free public lectures in physiology and hygiene in 1848, but the effort resulted eventually in a combination of fever, exhaustion and depression until she was forced to take a rest. Following her own prescription of rest, fresh air, and "the free use of water internally and externally," she slowly recovered, with time to reflect on illness as a benefit, as "it draws around us such tender, sweet, and holy spirits."

In 1850, Hunt attended the first National Women's Rights Conference, held in Massachusetts, and found herself among a number of like-minded women, including ***Lucretia Mott**, ***Paulina Wright Davis**, ***Lucy Stone**, and ***Antoinette Brown Blackwell.** "Think what were my reflections when I retired that night," she wrote. "There was a resurrection for women—I rejoiced in my inmost soul, and rose the next morning buoyant as a child."

Invigorated by the event, Hunt again applied to Harvard Medical School, and on December 5th, 1850, she was admitted by the dean of the Medical Faculty, Oliver Wendell Holmes. Unfortunately, she was too ill at the time to take advantage of the opportunity. Her failure to attend gave rise to rumors that appeared in the Boston *Evening Transcript,* which reported that the men of Harvard's senior class were already upset over the admittance of three blacks and had petitioned protesting her entry. Hunt never attended lectures at Harvard and never publicly addressed the issue of this episode, but one cannot help but wonder if the negative public attitude toward her assertiveness kept her away. In any event, the publicity that surrounded her acceptance at the school contributed to her being awarded, three years later, with the honorary degree of Doctor of Medicine from the Female Medical College of Philadelphia.

In her autobiography, *Glances and Glimpses,* Hunt testifies to her devotion to female patients and social change. Yet the book is underscored by a sense of intense loneliness. She describes herself as "having a strong spice of romance in my nature," as a schoolgirl. "I formed many love attachments with the school-girls, entered into correspondence with them, sometimes anonymous." In her day, same-sex attachments and relationships were encouraged for young women. But unlike some of her friends, Hunt's same-sex loves were never supplanted by marriage. Throughout her life, her primary relationships were all with women, and as an adult her frustration with men, especially professionals, was voiced in ways that verged on loathing. She critiqued fathers and husbands and attacked men in politics, medicine, and law, arguing that "Men keep women ignorant, frivolous, and helpless." She was unable to reconcile the chasm between her idealized view of marital union based on her parents' marriage and the "monotonous half-life" of the women she observed daily. She lamented the ways that the exhaustive duties of motherhood caused women to cease interior growth and relinquish reading, discussion, and thought.

In her later years, Hunt argued eloquently for women's higher education, and she actively encouraged women to enter the professions of law, medicine, religion, and police work. In 1868, she hosted the founding meeting of the New England Women's Club, and her activities were followed regularly in the newspapers, while her consulting practice continued late into her life.

According to Blake, shortly before the community-wide celebration of Hunt's 66th birthday, the union between Hunt's medical service and her patients was publicly and privately sanctified, in a service observing the anniversary of her wedded devotion to her profession. A ring was placed upon the doctor's finger, and 1,500 friends, including three generations of patients, were present to offer congratulations. "Oh, I have been so happy in my work," Hunt told them; "every moment occupied, how I long to whisper it in the ear of every listless woman, 'do something, if you would be happy.'" At the later birthday celebration, Hunt rejoiced further in the affection of her patients and friends.

Three years later, Dr. Harriot Kezia Hunt died in Boston. Often called the first woman to practice medicine in the United States, she penetrated previously male-dominated institutions, particularly medicine, and was an ardent advocate of women's education. Equally important was her contribution to the cultural debate on the rights and roles of women within marriage. Her lectures to increase medical self-knowledge of women and their inner lives raised the self-esteem and quality of life for thousands who heard her, making her a model for independent and self-reliant women then as now.

SOURCES:

Blake, Mary Stafford. *The Woman's Journal.* Vol. 3, no. 47. November 23, 1872.

Boston Morning Journal (obit). January 5, 1875.

Hunt, Harriot K. *Glances and Glimpses or Fifty Years Social, Including Twenty Years Professional Life.* Boston: John P. Jewett, 1856.

James, Edward T., Janet Wilson James, and Paul S. Boyer, eds. *Notable American Women, 1607-1950: a Biographical Dictionary.* Vol. 2. Cambridge, MA: The Belknap Press of Harvard University Press, 1971.

Leavitt, Judith Walzer, ed. *Women and Health in America.* Madison, WI: University of Wisconsin Press, 1984.

Levin, Carole. "Harriot Hunt: An Affirmative, Healing Woman," in *Women: A Journal of Liberation.* Vol. 7. no 3, 1981, pp. 40–41.

SUGGESTED READING:

Gevitz, Norman, ed. *Other Healers: Unorthodox Medicine in America.* Baltimore, MD: John Hopkins University Press, 1988.

Wood, Ann Douglas. "'The Fashionable Diseases': Women's Complaints and Their Treatment in Nineteenth Century America," in *Clio's Consciousness Raised.* Edited by Mary S. Hartman and Lois W. Banner.

Roberta A. Hobson,
graduate student in history at San Diego State University and author of "Judith McDaniel, Writer and Activist; Seeking Herself," in *Contemporary Lesbian Writers of the United States,* 1993

Hunt, Helen Fiske (1830–1885).

See Jackson, Helen Hunt.

Hunt, Marsha (1917—)

American actress. *Born Marcia Virginia Hunt on October 17, 1917, in Chicago, Illinois; attended P.S. 9 and the Horace Mann School, in New York; studied acting at the Theodora Irvine School of Dramatics; married Jerry Hopper (editor, then director), in 1938 (divorced 1943); married Robert Presnell (a screenwriter), in 1946.*

Filmography: The Virginia Judge *(1935);* Hollywood Boulevard *(1936);* Gentle Julia *(1936);* The Accusing Finger *(1936);* Desert Gold *(1936);* College Holiday *(1936);* Easy to Take *(1936);* Easy Living *(1937);* Annapolis Salute *(1937);* Born to the West *(1937);* Come on Leathernecks *(1938);* These Glamour Girls *(1939);* The Star Reporter *(1939);* Irene *(1940);* Pride and Prejudice *(1940);* I'll Wait for You *(1941);* The Trial of Mary Dugan *(1941);* The Penalty *(1941);* Blossoms in the Dust *(1941);* Unholy Partners *(1941);* Joe Smith—American *(1942);* Kid Glove Killer *(1942);* Panama Hattie *(1942);* Seven Sweethearts *(1942);* The Human Comedy *(1943);* Thousands Cheer *(1943);* Cry Havoc *(1943);* Lost Angel *(1944);* None Shall Escape *(1944);* Music for Millions *(1944);* The Valley of Decision *(1945);* A Letter for Evie *(1946);* Smash-Up *(1947);* Carnegie Hall *(1947);* Raw Deal *(1948);* Take One False Step *(1949);* Mary Ryan—Detective *(1950);* Actors and Sin *(1952);* The

Happy Time *(1952);* No Place to Hide *(1956);* Bombers B-52 *(1957);* Blue Denim *(1959);* The Plunderers *(1960);* Johnny Got His Gun *(1971); (cameo)* Rich and Famous *(1981).*

Born in Chicago, Illinois, in 1917, and raised in Manhattan, Marsha Hunt attended the **Theodora Irvine** School of Dramatics, paying for acting lessons by modeling for John Robert Powers. She broke into movies in the 1930s, working first for Paramount, where she was offered nothing but sweet, simpering roles which she hated. "Ingenues were a writer's device," she said. "Something the hero met, won, lost, and had to win back." Hunt left Paramount after three years and free-lanced for six months before signing with MGM. There she made a name for herself playing leads in B pictures and supporting roles in major productions, including *Pride and Prejudice* (1940), *Blossoms in the Dust* (1941), *The Human Comedy* (1943), *Cry Havoc* (1943), *The Valley of Decision* (1945), and *Smash-up* (1947).

Hunt was one of many victims of the casting wars surrounding *Gone With the Wind.* Told by David O. Selznick that she had the role of Melanie, she was devastated to read in the papers the next day that the part had gone to ***Olivia de Havilland.** Her career suffered a far more serious setback in the 1950s, when her second husband, screenwriter Robert Presnell, was accused of sympathizing with the Hollywood Ten, a group who refused to testify at the House Un-American Activities Committee (HUAC) hearings. "I was a political innocent. I was never a communist," said Hunt. "When I replaced [Franchot Tone] on the Screen Actors Guild board of directors, I went every Monday night and sat with the very conservative board. They were all mesmerized by this communist issue. I was baffled. I thought why are we so deeply interested in the communist party? If it's such a menace to our society and film industry, why don't we let our government . . . outlaw it, and we can get back to our business here, helping actors and tending to the issues and concerns of SAG. *They* decided I must be [a communist]." Then a group of writers and directors were called up before the HUAC; any who refused to explain their political beliefs were cited for contempt of Congress and sentenced to one year in prison. Hunt and her husband joined in an industry movement to protest the committee's methods and chartered a plane for Washington; fellow protesters included Humphrey Bogart, **Lauren Bacall**, ***Jane Wyatt**, Danny Kaye, Paul Henried, and **Gloria de Haven.** As a result, Hunt was blacklisted by the studios; she could no longer find work in film, radio, or television. Instead, she returned to the stage, appearing as Judith Anderson on Broadway in *The Devil's Disciple* and Hannie in *Borned in Texas* (both in 1950). She also replaced ***Celeste Holm** in *Affairs of State* and would continue to work in theater for years. In 1997, she appeared in *On Golden Pond.*

Marsha Hunt

Hunt returned to Hollywood for a few films at the end of the decade and appeared on numerous television programs, including "Marcus Welby, M.D." Since the 1950s, however, most of her time has been devoted to charitable causes, including cerebral palsy and various United Nations agencies. In Los Angeles, she founded The Valley Mayors Fund for the Homeless and served as its president for six years.

SOURCES:

Bangley, Jimmy. "Marsha Hunt: Hollywood's Youngest Character Actress," in *Classic Images.* April 1997.

Katz, Ephraim. *The Film Encyclopedia.* NY: HarperCollins, 1994.

Lamparski, Richard. *Whatever Became of . . . ?* 4th Series. NY: Crown, 1973.

Barbara Morgan,
Melrose, Massachusetts

Hunt, Violet (1866–1942)

British novelist and biographer. *Born Isobel Violet Hunt in 1866 in Durham, England; died on January 16, 1942, in London, England; daughter of Alfred William Hunt (pre-Raphaelite painter) and Margaret Raine Hunt (novelist, sometimes used pseudonym Averil Beaumont); educated at Notting Hill High School (one* *of the first girls' high schools) and South Kensington Art School; married (not legally) Ford Madox Hueffer (later known as Ford Madox Ford), in 1911.*

Wrote sexually frank novels, such as Unkissed, Unkind *(1897) and* The White Rose of Weary Leaf *(1908, considered her best); wrote collections of short stories, such as* Tales of the Uneasy *(1911) and* The Tiger Skin *(1924); wrote a biography of Elizabeth Siddal entitled* The Wife of Rossetti *(1932).*

Violet Hunt was born in Durham, England, in 1866, the daughter of painter Alfred William Hunt and novelist **Margaret Raine Hunt**. She grew up surrounded by pre-Raphaelite artists and writers, including Oscar Wilde, John Ruskin, ***Elizabeth Siddal**, and the Rossettis, and attended Notting Hill High School with the daughters of William Morris and Edward Burne-Jones. ***Christina Rossetti** was the first person to whom Hunt showed her poetry. Alfred Hunt had wanted Violet to be a painter and encouraged her in that study from an early age. Although she attended South Kensington Art School and continued to paint until the age of 28, she followed her mother's path and instead became a writer. She also followed her mother's example of working for women's suffrage, organizing the Women Writers' Suffrage League and supporting ***Radclyffe Hall** as she fought to keep *The Well of Loneliness* from being banned.

Although Hunt never legally married, she lived with Ford Madox Hueffer (another child of the pre-Raphaelite circle who would later be known as Ford Madox Ford) for nearly ten years. They met in 1908 when he was the founding editor of the *English Review,* a publication that had among its contributors Thomas Hardy, Joseph Conrad, H.G. Wells, and W.B. Yeats. Hunt also contributed a short story to the publication. Hueffer was already married, and his wife would not grant him a divorce. However, many referred to Hunt as "Mrs. Hueffer," including a newspaper (because of the incident, Hueffer's wife sued the paper and won). As well, Hunt's entry in *Who's Who* noted "married 1911." The scandalous affair alienated many of Hunt's friends and family. By 1918, Hunt and Hueffer had parted ways. When Hunt wrote an autobiography in 1926 about her life with Hueffer entitled *The Flurried Years* (published in America as *I Have This to Say*), she reopened many of the wounds the affair had caused.

Hunt's writings reflected her personality, which has been called that of a "typical New Woman." She was intelligent, independent, and progressive, and her novels emphasized sexual relationships, neurotic heroines, and unblushing portrayals of prostitution, adultery, and promiscuity. Much of her work—including *The Celebrity at Home* (1904) and *The Celebrity's Daughter* (1913)—drew on autobiographical details, and provide an intimate glimpse into the literary society of which she was so much a part. During the height of her career, Hunt lived in London and knew numerous celebrities of the day. Besides the *English Review,* Hunt also wrote for *Black and White* and had a weekly column in the *Pall Mall Gazette*. She was also well-known as a host, and her friends included Wells, Ezra Pound, ***Rebecca West**, Wyndham Lewis, Conrad, Henry James, W.H. Hudson, and D.H. and ***Frieda Lawrence**. During her career, Hunt wrote 17 novels, and her work was admired by Lawrence, West, ***May Sinclair**, and James (although James preferred her short stories). Unlike those of many of her friends, however, Hunt's books are not much read today. Her other principal works include: *The Maiden's Progress* (1894), *A Hard Woman* (1895), *The Human Interest* (1899), *Affairs of the Heart* (1900), *Sooner or Later* (1904), *The Cat* (1905), *The Wife of Altamont* (1910), *The Doll* (1911), *The Desirable Alien* (with Heuffer, 1913), *Their Lives* (1916), *The Last Ditch* (1918), *Their Hearts* (1921), and *More Tales of the Uneasy* (1925).

As Hunt grew older, she became less active in writing and society, instead opting to remain at home with her Persian cats. Suffering from an advanced case of syphilis and living in virtual solitude, Hunt died on January 16, 1942, at South Lodge, her London home.

SUGGESTED READING:

Belford, Barbara. *Violet.* NY: Simon and Schuster.

Hardwick, Joan. *An Immodest Violet: The Life of Violet Hunt.* London: Andre Deutsch, 1993.

Karina L. Kerr, M.A.,
Ypsilanti, Michigan

Hunter, Alberta (1895–1984)

American blues singer who bridged the gap between classic blues and cabaret pop, recorded extensively during her long career performing well into her 80s, and traveled throughout the world expanding jazz from an American to an international phenomenon.

Name variations: Alberta Prime; Josephine Beatty. Born in Memphis, Tennessee, on April 1, 1895; died on October 17, 1984 in New York City; daughter of Charles E. Hunter (a sleeping car porter) and Laura (Peterson) Hunter; married Willard Saxby Townsend, on January 27, 1919 (divorced 1923).

Alberta Hunter was a popular blues performer for over 40 years and, during World War II, traveled with the USO to China, Burma, India, Korea, and Europe. At age 62, with her star fading, she became a nurse; at age 82, forced to retire from nursing, she relaunched her singing career. Before long, she was singing at the White House.

Alberta Hunter was born in Memphis, Tennessee, in 1895, the second daughter of Charles E. Hunter, a sleeping car porter, and **Laura Peterson Hunter**. Alberta's father abandoned the family by the time she was five. To support her daughters, Laura took a job as a maid for two white women, known as the sporting ladies, who ran a bordello; she also moonlighted at the Memphis Steam Laundry. Laura Hunter was prudish about her daughters' upbringing, however, and Alberta and her sister La Tosca learned very little about their mother's employers—except for grammar. "I'd say, 'Those ladies is so funny,'" said Alberta. "And my mother would say, 'Not *is*. Ladies are more than one. So those ladies *are*.' And you know where my mother got it from? The sporting ladies."

Alberta Hunter

Around 1906 or 1907, Laura married Theodore Beatty. Alberta hated him, and he despised Alberta. "He hated my intestines because I'd hit him when he'd hit my mother," she said. She also claimed that other men on the periphery of her life sexually abused her. In the long run, Hunter did not know who walked out on whom, her mother or her stepfather, but as Hunter said, "There was some leaving done."

In July 1911, at age 16, with the help of an unsuspecting teacher, Hunter ran away from home to Chicago. Her first appearances as a singer were in flop joints and seedy saloons, but she gradually worked her way up. Jazz flourished in New Orleans, Memphis, New York, and Chicago in the 1920s where a variety of clubs provided work for black artists. In 1921, after success in Chicago, Hunter went to New York to launch her recording career. Her first songs appeared on the Black Swan label, but in 1922 she contracted with Paramount where she did some of her finest work.

In 1919, Hunter had married a soldier, Willard Saxby Townsend, to dispel rumors that she was a lesbian, but she never slept with her husband and divorced him in 1923. She never married again. Because of the prevailing attitudes towards homosexuality, Hunter tried to hide her predilection for women. One of her most enduring relationships was with **Lottie Tyler**, niece of the black comedian Bert Williams.

Hunter wrote many of the songs she sang, such as "Down Hearted Blues" which was a bigger hit for ***Bessie Smith** than it was for her. By the late 1920s, her performances had helped define classic blues. She sang "Your Jelly Roll is Good," "Sugar," "Beale Street Blues," and "Take that Thing Away." In 1927, she left New York for London and the Continent. At home, she played the Cotton Club in Harlem with Louis Armstrong and the Teddy Hill Band. She continued to record on the Biltmore label as Alberta Prime, on the Gennett label as Josephine Beatty, and on Okeh, Victor, and Columbia under her own name.

Like many blues singers, Hunter's life followed a classical pattern. Her greatest revenues were in the heyday of the blues in the 1920s, though unlike some artists, she managed to continue earning a steady income. Black jazz artists often made huge sums of money for a brief period before declining into poverty and obscurity. Hunter, however, managed to escape the fate suffered by so many. She continued to appear in

clubs in the 1930s and during World War II entertained extensively for the USO.

Back in New York following the war, Hunter was living with her mother; they had become quite close. Two years after Laura Hunter died in 1954, with her career on the decline, Hunter quit performing and enrolled in the YWCA's nursing program at 137th Street. "I wanted people to remember me as I was. On top," she said. Hunter had long been a volunteer at the Joint Diseased Hospital in Harlem. For the next 20 years, she was a practicing nurse, but in January 1977 she learned that she was to receive mandatory retirement on her birthday, April 1. She was 82; the hospital thought she was 70. "I loved nursing," she said. "I loved the thought of having to get up and go to work to serve my patients. That was my heartstring, and I had given my all."

On October 10, 1977, Hunter made a comeback at the Cookery in Greenwich Village. "At first she seemed insecure with some of the high notes," wrote Frank Taylor, "but after she was about half-way through it, she was the old pro, at home onstage again. She snapped her fingers, slapped her thighs as if they were tambourines, tossed back her head of gray-black hair tightly pulled into a small bun, and beamed her chocolate-brown eyes at each face in the audience." Her voice was huskier. "My God, I sang like a horse," she said later. Fellow nurses in the audience howled, and the critics were bowled over. Alberta Hunter was an enormous hit, doing television and magazine interviews, negotiating a recording contract with Columbia, making her debut at Carnegie Hall, appearing in *Vogue*, and singing at the Kennedy Center at a ceremony honoring ***Marian Anderson**. Finally at age 89, in 1984, Hunter quit singing because of poor health. She died that October. "That's the truth," she'd say. "I've got it written down. I've got the photos to prove it."

SOURCES:

Herzhaft, Gérard. *Encyclopedia of the Blues*. Translated by Brigitte Debord. Fayetteville, AR: University of Arkansas Press, 1992.

Santelli, Robert. *The Big Book of the Blues. A Biographical Encyclopedia*. NY: Penguin, 1993.

Taylor, Frank C. with Gerald Cook. *Alberta Hunter: A Celebration in Blues*. NY: McGraw-Hill, 1987.

RELATED MEDIA:

Alberta Hunter: Jazz at the Smithsonian (video), Sony, 1982.

Hunter, Clementine (1886–1988)

African-American folk artist. *Born Clementine Reuben near Cloutierville, Louisiana, in December 1886; died near Natchitoches, Louisiana, on January 1, 1988; daughter of Janvier (John) Reuben and Antoinette (Adams) Reuben; briefly attended Catholic elementary school; married Charles Dupree (died 1914); married Emanuel Hunter, in 1924 (died 1944); children: (first marriage) two; (second marriage) five.*

Often referred to as "the black ***Grandma Moses**," Clementine Hunter was self-taught and began painting late in life. She lived most of her life in a small cabin in Natchitoches, Louisiana, far removed from the urban galleries that sold her paintings for hundreds of dollars. Hunter's only indulgence was an upgrade to a house trailer in the 1980s, and the purchase of a nice coffin and mausoleum space.

Hunter was born on a cotton plantation near Cloutierville, Louisiana, in 1886. She attended a local Catholic elementary school only briefly and remained illiterate her entire life. Her family eventually moved to Melrose Plantation near Natchitoches, where Hunter worked in the fields. She was married twice, first to Charles Dupree, with whom she had two children, and then to Emanuel Hunter, with whom she had five. In the late 1920s, Hunter moved into the plantation house to take up full-time domestic duties. At the time, the mistress of Melrose Plantation was **Carmelite "Cammie" Garrett Henry**, whose wide-ranging interests included collecting art.

In 1939, a Frenchman named François Mignon took up residence at the plantation as the curator of Henry's collection. Hunter, then in her 50s, approached Mignon one evening with some discarded paint she had found, and told him she thought she could make a picture of her own if she set her mind to it. He produced an old window shade on which she painted her first picture. Impressed, Mignon continued to supply her with rag-bag supplies—cardboard boxes, paper bags, scraps of wood, and eventually some canvases—anything on which she could work. Hunter became a master at stretching what little oil paint she could muster, often thinning it so much that her some of her finished works resembled watercolors.

Second to Mignon as Hunter's patron was James Register, a writer, artist, and teacher at the University of Oklahoma. After visiting Melrose in the early 1940s, he began sending Hunter cash and art supplies, and in 1944, he secured her a Julius Rosenwald Foundation grant. Both he and Mignon promoted her work, which began to attract attention during the 1950s. Labeled a primitive, Hunter had her earliest solo exhibitions in

1955, at the Delgado Museum (now the New Orleans Museum of Art), and at Northwestern State College, where she was not allowed to view the exhibit with the white patrons but had to slip in after the gallery was closed.

Hunter claimed that she liked to paint from memory and dreams rather than life, and her work is characterized by a flat, representational quality devoid of much detail. Her paintings, which numbered in the thousands, can be categorized into three subject groups: everyday life, religious, and a miscellaneous series of experimental paintings executed in the 1960s. The bold, colorful paintings of the first group comprise the greatest body of the artist's work and portray simple plantation life, with people cooking, doing laundry, tending children, playing games, and participating in festive occasions like weddings, baptisms, and funerals. In this group as well are the African House Murals, a series of nine large plywood panels that were installed in the African House, built on the plantation grounds in 1800. Depicting plantation life along the Cane River, the murals, along with others painted for Chana House and Yucca House, two other buildings at Melrose, were "commissioned" by Mignon, and are considered some of the artist's most important works. The second category of paintings, the religious works, include scenes of the Nativity, the Flight to Egypt, and the Crucifixion, in which Hunter depicts almost all of the figures as black. The work *Cotton Crucifixion,* one of the few paintings that Hunter named, is considered the most provocative of this group. In it, Jesus is portrayed as black, while the thieves are white. At the foot of the cross, black field hands drag large sacks through rows of cotton.

The third group of paintings, the miscellaneous series, represent a departure from the artist's usual work. Created between 1962 and 1963, they comprise an "abstract" series that was influenced by James Register, who permanently settled in Natchitoches in 1962. In an effort to broaden Hunter's scope and test her talent, Register prepared a group of collages from colored advertisements in old magazines and presented them to Hunter to see what they would inspire. "Sometimes the montage would be so difficult, being only a series of color patterns," he explained, "the outlines would have to be traced on the board for her." The resulting 100 or so paintings, with names (probably provided by Register) like *Moon Bird, Chanticleer, Alice in Wonderland, Uncle Tom,* and *Porte Bouquet*, are uncharacteristic in their bright color and patterns, and although Hunter gladly gave up the experiment after two years, it influenced her later work, especially her flower paintings.

During her lifetime, Clementine Hunter had over two dozen solo exhibitions at galleries and museums throughout the United States, most of which she never attended. Seldom involved with the sale of her work, she continued to practically give away her paintings to her neighbors for six dollars apiece. The artist worked up until just weeks before her death. In December 1987, she took to her bed; she died on January 1, 1988, at age 101.

Hunter's work now resides in numerous permanent collections, including those of the Birmingham Museum of Art, the Dallas Museum of Fine Art, the High Museum in Atlanta, and the Louisiana State Museum.

SOURCES:

Bailey, Brooke. *The Remarkable Lives of 100 Women Artists.* Holbrook, MA: Bob Adams, 1994.

Smith, Jessie Carney, ed. *Notable Black American Women.* Detroit, MI: Gale Research, 1992.

Barbara Morgan,
Melrose, Massachusetts

Hunter, Kim (1922—)

***American actress of stage, screen, and television who originated the part of Stella Kowalski in* A Streetcar Named Desire.** *Born Janet Cole on November 12, 1922, in Detroit, Michigan; daughter of Donald Cole (an engineer) and Grace (Lind) Cole (a concert pianist); graduated from Miami Beach Senior High School, Miami Beach, Florida, 1940; studied acting with* **Charmine Lantaff**, *Miami Beach, Florida, 1938–40; a member of Actors Studio from 1948; married William A. Baldwin, on February 11, 1944 (divorced 1946); married Robert Emmett (a writer), on December 20, 1951; children: (first marriage) Kathryn Baldwin; (second marriage) one son.*

Selected theater: made stage debut in title role of Penny Wise *(Miami Woman's Club, Florida, 1939); Broadway debut as Stella Kowalski in* A Streetcar Named Desire *(Ethel Barrymore Theater, 1947); Luba in* Darkness at Noon *(Alvin Theater, New York City, 1951); Ruby Hawes in* The Chase *(Playhouse Theater, New York City, 1952); Karen Wright in the Broadway revival of* The Children's Hour *(Coronet Theater, New York City, 1952); Sylvia Crews in* The Tender Trap *(Longacre Theater, New York City, 1954); appeared with the American Shakespeare Festival (Stratford, Connecticut, summer 1961), as Rosalind in* As You Like It, *the First Witch in* Macbeth, *and as Helen in* Troilus and Cressida*; Julie Sturrock in* Write Me a Murder *(Belasco Theater, New York City, 1961); Miss*

Wilson in Weekend *(Broadhurst Theater, New York City, 1968); Carrie Bishop in* The Penny Wars *(Royale Theater, New York City, 1969); Catherine in* And Miss Reardon Drinks a Little *(national tour, 1971–72); Mary Haines in the Broadway revival of* The Women *(46th Street Theater, New York City, 1973).*

Filmography: The Seventh Victim *(1943);* Tender Comrade *(1944);* A Canterbury Tale *(UK, 1944);* When Strangers Marry *(1944);* You Came Along *(1945);* A Matter of Life and Death *(*Stairway to Heaven, *UK, 1946);* A Streetcar Named Desire *(1951);* Deadline U.S.A. *(1952);* Anything Can Happen *(1952);* Storm Center *(1956);* The Young Stranger *(1957);* Bermuda Affair *(1957);* Money Women and Guns *(1958);* Lilith *(1964);* Planet of the Apes *(1968);* The Swimmer *(1968);* Beneath the Planet of the Apes *(1970);* Escape From the Planet of the Apes *(1971);* Dark August *(1976);* The Kindred *(1987);* Due Occhi diabolici *(*Two Evil Eyes, *It., 1990).*

The daughter of an engineer and a concert pianist, Kim Hunter was born Janet Cole in Detroit, Michigan, in 1922, but moved to Miami after her father's death and her mother's remarriage. She later recalled a lonely childhood, made more tolerable by "acting out" characters from storybooks in front of the mirror. After graduating from high school, where she was featured in plays, she took ingénue roles in a variety of stock companies. An appearance in *Arsenic and Old Lace* at the Pasadena Playhouse brought her to the attention of film producer David O. Selznick, who signed her with Vanguard Films and also changed her name.

After an auspicious screen debut in the quality thriller *The Seventh Victim* (1943), Hunter went on to play in a number of mediocre movies, most on loan to other studios, until English directors Michael Powell and Emeric Pressburger cast her in the English fantasy *A Matter of Life and Death,* which was selected for the first royal command film performance and released as *Stairway to Heaven* (1946) in the United States. In 1995, Columbia, in conjunction with Martin Scorsese and the British Film Institute, would release a restored print of the film. Hunter, who had remained good friends with Powell and Pressburger, was on hand for many of the festivities surrounding the film's restoration.

Hunter's Broadway break came with her return to America and the opportunity to play Stella Kowalski in the Tennessee Williams' drama *A Streetcar Named Desire* (1947). Her portrayal won the praise of the critics, including William Hawkins of the New York *World-Telegram* who thought her "mellow and philosophical as the devoted Stella, who tries to synchronize two impossible loyalties." For her work in *Streetcar,* which ran for two and a half years on Broadway, Hunter won the Donaldson Award (1948) and the Critics Circle Award (1948) for Best Supporting Actress. Elia Kazan, who had directed the play, dubbed Hunter "unique among actresses. She is first a person and second a member of the acting profession." Kazan, who went on to direct the movie version with Marlon Brando and ***Vivien Leigh**, called on Hunter to recreate her role in the film, which was released in 1951. The praise of the critics was once again overwhelming, and Hunter walked away with the 1952 Academy Award for Best Supporting Actress. She also won the Foreign Correspondents Award and a special Achievement Award from *Look* magazine who cited her as "standing out in bold normality among the frenetic characters around her."

Soon after her movie triumph in *Streetcar,* Hunter fell victim to the McCarthy hysteria of the 1950s. Listed in the notorious "Red Channels" as a communist sympathizer, she was blacklisted by the industry for several years. She made movies only sporadically after that, con-

Kim Hunter

centrating instead on stage and television. On Broadway, she was particularly notable as Luba in *Darkness at Noon* (1951) and Karen Wright in *Lillian Hellman's *The Children's Hour* (1952). Her impressive television credits include most of the "playhouse" shows, as well as appearances in such well-known series as "Mannix," "Gunsmoke," "Columbo," "Marcus Welby, M.D.," and "Ironside." Of her later movies, Hunter was particularly proud of the two science-fiction films *Planet of the Apes* (1968) and *Beneath the Planet of the Apes* (1970), although she called the hours in make-up "pure hell."

Kim Hunter's first marriage to William Baldwin ended in divorce in 1946. In 1951, she married writer-director Robert Emmett, and the couple make their home in Greenwich Village, New York. Hunter authored an "autobiographical" cookbook, *Loose in the Kitchen*, in 1975.

SOURCES:

Candee, Marjorie Dent, ed. *Current Biography, 1952*. NY: H.W. Wilson, 1952.

Katz, Ephraim. *The Film Encyclopedia*. NY: HarperCollins, 1994.

McGill Raymond, ed. *Notable Names in the American Theater*. Clifton, NJ: James T. White, 1976.

Tanner, Louise. "Accents and Umlauts," in *Films in Review*. Vol. 46, no. 5–6. July–August, 1995, p. 38.

Barbara Morgan,
Melrose, Massachusetts

Huntingdon, countess of.

See Judith of Normandy (c. 1054–after 1086).
See Adelicia de Warrenne (d. 1178).
See Maude of Chester (1171–1233).
See Margaret (d. 1228).
See Ellen of Wales (d. 1253).
See Hastings, Selina (1707–1791).

Huntington, Anna Hyatt

(1876–1973)

American sculptor and philanthropist, much admired for her animal, garden, fountain, and equestrian statuary, which are seen as a transition between the traditional monuments of the late 19th century and modern abstract sculpture. *Name variations: Anna Vaughn Hyatt; Mrs. Archer M. Huntington. Born Anna Vaughn Hyatt on March 10, 1876, in Cambridge, Massachusetts; died on October 4, 1973, in Redding Ridge, Connecticut; daughter of Audella Beebe Hyatt (an accomplished painter) and Alpheus Hyatt II (a distinguished zoologist and paleontologist); sister of Harriet Hyatt Mayor; attended private school in Cambridge, Massachusetts; studied with sculptor Henry Hudson Kitson, Boston, Massachusetts, in the late 1890s; studied with Herman A. MacNeill and Gutzon Borglum at Art Students League, New York, 1903; self-study of wild animals at the Bronx Zoo; married Archer Milton Huntington (a scholar, poet, and philanthropist), in 1923 (died 1955); no children.*

Selected works: Leo *(bronze lion, Art Institute, Dayton, Ohio, 1908);* Joan of Arc *(bronze, Riverside Drive, New York City, and other worldwide locations, 1915);* Elephants Fighting *(bronze, Carnegie Institute of Pittsburgh, PA, 1917);* Reaching Jaguar *(bronze, 1906) and* Jaguar *(bronze, 1907) both at the Metropolitan Museum of Art, New York;* Diana of the Chase *(bronze, Fogg Museum, Cambridge, MA, 1922);* El Cid Campeador *(bronze, Hispanic Society of America, NYC, among others, 1934);* Cranes Rising *(bronze, Art Institute, Dayton, Ohio, 1934);* Peacocks Fighting *(bronze, University of Michigan, Ann Arbor, MI, 1935–36);* Boabdil *(bas-relief, limestone, Hispanic Society of America, 1935–36);* Don Quixote *(bas-relief, limestone, Hispanic Society of America, 1942);* Torch Bearers *(aluminum, University of Madrid, Spain, 1955);* José Martí *(bronze, Central Park, NYC, 1959);* General Israel Putnam's Escape at Horse Neck *(bronze, Putnam Memorial State Park, Redding, CT, 1969). Work in the collection of Brookgreen Gardens, South Carolina:* Youth Taming the Wild *(limestone, 1927),* Fighting Stallions *(aluminum, 1950),* Mother *(bronze, 1967), among many others. Works are also located in the permanent collections of the Museum of Fine Arts, Boston, MA; Brooklyn Children's Museum, Brooklyn, NY; and the Corcoran Gallery of Art, Washington, D.C., and among more than 200 other museums, private collections, as well as parks and gardens of major cities throughout the world.*

Exhibits: Anna Hyatt Huntington exhibited extensively, across the country and abroad, throughout her life, beginning with a solo show in Boston at age 24 (1900). Major retrospective exhibits: American Academy of Arts and Letters, New York (1936); Palace of the Legion of Honor, San Francisco (1937).

Awards: Paris Salon honorable mention for Reaching Jaguar *and* Jaguar *(1910); France's purple rosette and Panama Pacific International Exposition at San Francisco silver medal, both for* Joan of Arc *(1915); Plastic Club of Philadelphia's Rodin gold medal for* Joan of Arc *(1917); National Academy of Design's Saltus gold medal for* Joan of Arc *(1920) and* Diana of the Chase *(1922); French Legion of Honor for* Joan of Arc *(1922); National Academy of Design's Shaw Memorial Prize for* Bulls Fighting *(1928); Spanish Grand Cross of Alphonso XII for* El Cid Campeador *(1929); American Academy of Arts and*

Letters gold medal for Bulls Fighting *(1930); Syracuse University honorary D.F.A. (1932); American Academy of Arts and Letters gold medal for distinction (1936); Pennsylvania Academy's Widener gold medal for* Greyhounds Playing *(1937); National Sculpture Society's medal of honor (1940); National Sculpture Society's Watrous gold medal for* Don Quixote *and Chi Omega Society's National Achievement Award (1948); Spain's Grand Cross of Isabel the Catholic (1952); Allied Arts of America gold medal of honor for* Nanny and the Twins *(1952); International Institute of Arts and Letters fellowship (1957); National Academy of Design gold medal (1958); Pierpont Morgan Library fellowship. Other honors include honorary vice-president of the National Association of Women Painters and Sculptors; honorary fellow of the National Sculpture Society; member of the National Academy of Design; member of the American Academy of Arts and Letters; corresponding member of the Spanish Academia de Bellas Artes de San Fernando; University of South Carolina, honorary D.F.A.*

Anna Vaughn Hyatt was born in Cambridge, Massachusetts, on March 10, 1876, the third child and younger of two daughters of **Audella Beebe Hyatt** and Alpheus Hyatt II. Her ancestors came to America from England as early as 1629, the Hyatts settling in Maryland and the Beebes in Virginia. Anna Hyatt was raised in a comfortable, intellectually stimulating environment. Her father, a renowned paleontologist at the Massachusetts Institute of Technology and Boston University, was a pupil and friend of Louis Agassiz, the Swiss naturalist. From her father, Anna gained a keen knowledge of animal behavior and physiology, learning to observe the structure of living things with scientific accuracy. Her mother was an accomplished amateur painter who rendered diagrams and illustrations for her husband's books; she encouraged Anna to observe life and draw what she saw. The family had a lasting influence on Anna's learning by stressing the "hands on" approach to nature and animals. Huntington's technical mastery, evident in her monumental equestrian sculptures, was rooted in her early years spent on a family seaside farm in Annisquam, Massachusetts. It was there she developed her love and knowledge of horses and other animals; family lore relates that even as a child she could recognize the distinguishing characteristics of a hundred thoroughbreds. Her nephew A. Hyatt Mayor wrote of his aunt: "[A]s soon as she could crawl she headed for the horse's hooves to examine them. . . . [A]ll her life she understood how to control animals, caressing dangerous dogs without being bitten and breaking colts without breaking her bones." From being a young girl who broke and trained colts for neighbors, she grew to be an expert equestrian.

Anna attended private school in Cambridge with the intention of becoming a concert violinist. At age 19, her future course was altered when she underwent a period of recuperation from nervous exhaustion and turned to clay for recreation. She helped her sister **Harriet Hyatt (Mayor)**, a sculptor, repair a broken foot on a statue. The endeavor proved so successful that Harriet encouraged Anna to collaborate on a sculptural group she was creating, with Harriet doing the human figure and Anna modeling the family's Great Dane as the canine figure. Intrigued, Huntington began to study sculpture with great intensity. Her first studies were with Henry Hudson Kitson of Boston, her sister's teacher. Preferring to learn from nature, she spent time observing and sketching the animals around the farm and at the Bostock's Animal Circus where she gained permission to model the animals (elephants and tigers) at close range.

Anna Hyatt Huntington

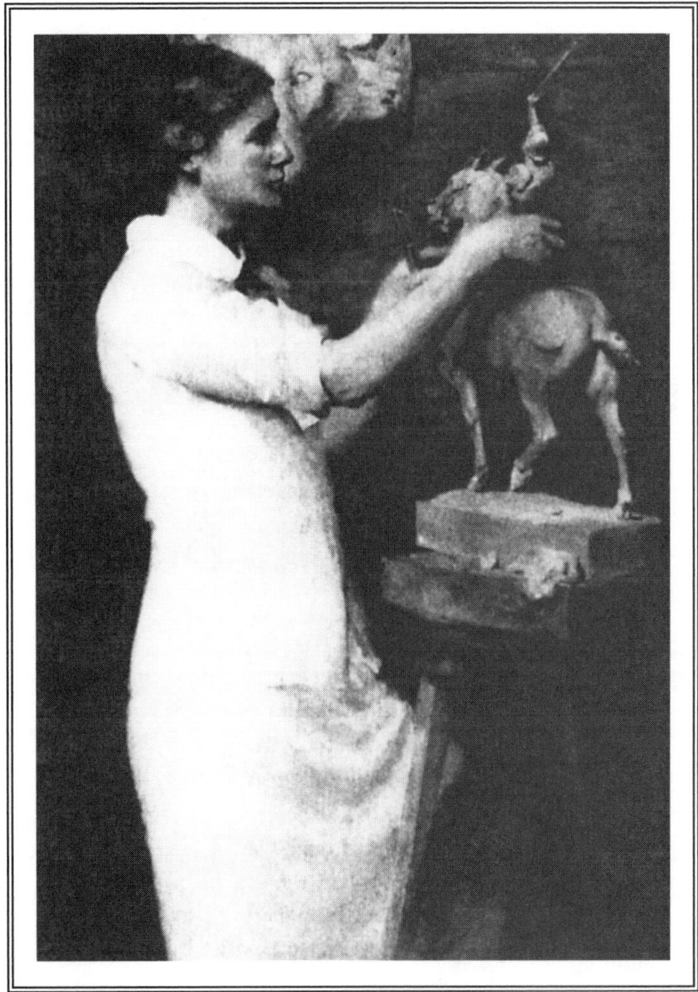

The sisters planned to open an art academy but never carried this through; Harriet's marriage took up most of her time, though she did complete a modest body of work. Huntington went on to an illustrious career. Her first works were commissioned by local Boston patrons, and she showed small pieces in the shop of the Boston jewelers Shreve, Crump and Low. In 1900, she showed 40 pieces at the Boston Art Club, setting a prodigious standard that she followed throughout her career. One of her small bronze animal studies from this show was acquired by the Metropolitan Museum of Art in 1903.

Animals have many moods and to represent them is my joy.

—Anna Hyatt Huntington

In 1903, after her father died, the family moved to New York. Huntington was employed by the Brooklyn Museum for a few years, doing plaster restorations of prehistoric animals. She then studied at the Art Students League under Hermon A. MacNeil and George Gray Barnard, and privately with Gutzon Borglum, designer of the Mount Rushmore monument. In an interview, George Gurney asked Huntington if it was true that she had gained her knowledge of horse modeling from Borglum. "Borglum didn't know anything about horses," she replied. "That's the reason I got kicked out. I must have been conceited. I loved horses and knew everything about them." Her knowledge of the horse's anatomy was so vast that she could render the animals from memory. During her short time at the school, Huntington shared an apartment with two women musicians and another sculptor, **Abastenia Eberle**, with whom she collaborated on a bronze, *Men and Bull* (1903) which was awarded a bronze medal at the Louisiana Purchase Exposition of 1904 in St. Louis. As with her sister, Huntington rendered the animals while Eberle sculpted the human figures. The following year, they again collaborated in the same fashion on *Boy and Goat Playing* (bronze, 1905), which was exhibited at the Gallery of the Society of American Artists. Independent by nature, Huntington preferred to work on her own, becoming a world-renowned animalier in the tradition of the great French artist Barye and other 19th-century equestrian sculptors. In 1905, a *New York Times* reporter came across Huntington, "a tall, young woman in a tailor-made frock and a red-plumed hat," at the Bronx Zoo. With her clay on a high stool, she was doing a study of a bison. Huntington told the reporter that her career was soaring and her commissions were plentiful. When asked whether she would go to Paris, she replied, "Not until I feel strong enough artistically to stand it. One ought to be perfectly independent in one's work and above outside influence . . . before going abroad." Huntington felt Europe had a greater respect for art and the artist, though America was the greater proving ground.

From 1906 to 1910, she studied and worked in France and Italy. In 1908, a pair of bronze life-sized jaguars *Reaching Jaguar* (1906) and *Jaguar* (1907) won an honorable mention at the Paris Salon, the highest international standard for measuring artistic achievement. Her animal sculptures were remarkable for their movement and motion. With her powerful sense of rhythm and design, coupled with the power of her naturalist's observation, she was able to capture the animals' authentic gestures with a sense of empathy. These animal works are considered to be her finest efforts, though some critics relegate her figurative and equestrian works, writes **Charlotte Rubinstein**, to "the heavy-handed academic statues of the official sculptors." Rubinstein posits the contrary view that they belong to a post-1900 school of animal and garden sculpture that serves as a bridge between the earlier grandiose public monuments and the later modern movement. In the early 20th century, many sculptors began to move away from the patriotic public commissions so expressive of civic virtue, a movement exemplified by the use of animals as a metaphor for personal feelings, expressions of mood and attitude. These newer works, smaller and more suitable for purchase by private collectors, gave sculptors the opportunity to explore personal views of life and new concepts of form. Anna Hyatt Huntington, though her powerful equestrian work was relatively academic in the European Beaux Arts tradition, became a part of the new thrust in sculpture due to her rhythmic expressive animal groups, such as *Cranes Rising* (bronze, 1934) and *Peacocks Fighting* (bronze, 1935–36), which showed a decorative art-nouveau quality.

Penny Dunford contends that Huntington's works were never sentimental, but rather she adapted the model to reveal the essential form of the particular animal feeding, resting, and in motion, appearing both singly and in groups. **Eleanor Mellon** finds Huntington's work empathetic. The artist understands the fundamental character of her subjects, renders their inherent beauty and dignity, and depicts vitality and grace, the result of great physical strength completely controlled.

In 1909, Huntington set aside all other commissions and turned to the creation of a full-sized equestrian statue of ***Joan of Arc**, a lifelong dream. Traveling to the towns of Orléans and Rouen in France to immerse herself in the spirit of her subject, she studied ancient fragments of armor and tomb tracings to get an accurate representation of the time. To create the monumental work, she rented the Paris Latin Quarter studio of a 19th-century sculptor because it had doors that made it possible to bring in a horse, a magnificent Percheron she saw in the street, to use as the model of the saint's steed. She then amassed a ton of clay, erected a huge armature, and devoted herself to the task. It was apparent to Huntington that she, like other female artists in the past, would be accused of having men do her work, so she hired only one assistant, a woman, to help her carry out the project. A plaster cast of the work won an honorable mention at the Paris Salon of 1910; it was felt that the male judges doubted she did the work entirely alone, or she would have been awarded a medal.

By 1912, Huntington was one of only 12 women in the United States earning $50,000 a year. Her work was extraordinarily popular, and her commissions kept her busy. When World War I began in Europe, however, Anna put her work aside and retired with her family to their farm at Cape Ann, Massachusetts. Her response to cooperative war efforts on the home front was to accept new responsibilities with energy. Though the studio she had used since childhood was at the farm, Anna devoted herself to dairy farming and gardening, producing no artwork during this time. On Sunday afternoons, she welcomed visitors to the farm. Writers, musicians, and artists such as John Singer Sargent often came to spend the afternoons, setting a pattern for her social life for years to come. Two years later, Huntington returned to her studio in New York City.

That year, she was commissioned to execute the Joan of Arc model in bronze to be placed on Riverside Drive in New York City. The committee for the 500th anniversary of the saint's birth was headed by J. Sanford Saltus of Tiffany and Company, one of Huntington's greatest supporters. She perfected her original conception, studying specific details with the curator of armor at the Metropolitan Museum of Art. Actual stones from the saint's dungeon in Rouen were used in the base. Rather than concentrate on the frailties of the peasant girl Joan, as she was depicted by other artists, Rubinstein relates that Huntington worked to capture the saint's spiritual intensity:

> I thought of her there before her first battle, speaking to her soldiers, holding up the ancient sword. Her wrist is sharply back to show them the hilt, which is in the form of a cross. . . . It was only her mental attitude, only her religious fervor, that could have enabled her to endure so much physically, to march three or four days with almost no sleep. . . . That is how I thought of her, that is how I modeled her.

Rubinstein claims Huntington's own "mental attitude" resembled that of her heroine. After the unveiling in 1915, a time during which the country was in sympathy with the French because of the First World War, the artist was inundated with praise and won the coveted Saltus Medal for Merit from the National Academy of Design in 1920.

Eberle, Abastenia St. Leger (1878–1942)

American sculptor, influenced by the Ash Can School. *Name variations: Abastenia Saint Leger. Born Mary Abastenia St. Leger in Webster City, Louisiana, in 1878; died in 1942; grew up in Canton, Ohio, and Puerto Rico; daughter of a physician; studied in Ohio under Frank Vogan and at the Art Students League, New York City, under Kenyon Cox and George Grey Barnard; also studied in Naples, Italy.*

With a penchant for small bronze sculptures in urban settings, Abastenia Eberle drew many of her subjects from life on New York's Lower East Side: ragpickers, the unemployed, immigrant mothers, and slum children at play. Her works include *The Girl on Roller Skates, Mowgli, Victory* (all housed at the Metropolitan Museum of Art, New York City), *Little Mother* (Art Institute of Chicago), as well as *Dance of the Ghetto Children* and *The White Slave.* A sometime collaborator with ***Anna Hyatt Huntington** when they shared a studio in 1904, Eberle was forced to abandon sculpture in 1919 because of ill health. She was an ardent socialist and suffragist, who once said: "The artist has no right to work as an individualist." She is the "specialized eye of society," who must "see for people, reveal them to themselves." One of her most popular works, *Windy Doorstep* (Worcester Art Museum), was awarded a prize from the National Academy of Design in 1910. The work was rendered at her summer cottage in Woodstock, New York, after she overheard local farmwives discussing the best techniques for sweeping. Notes **Nancy Heller**, the figure "demonstrates Eberle's ability to convey a sense of movement in three dimensions. The breeze whips the woman's skirt to one side as she concentrates intently on her task, eyes down and elbows locked; the fact that the broom extends beyond the sculpture's base also adds to the feeling of brisk motion." Eberle used this technique in many of her other sculptures.

SOURCES:

Heller, Nancy. *Women Artists.* Abbeville Press, 1987.

The *Joan of Arc* is considered a landmark in the history of women sculptors. With her later execution of *El Cid Campeador* (bronze, 1927), as well as her *Joan of Arc,* she would earn the highest honors possible from governments of the U.S., Cuba, and Spain; France awarded her the Chevalier of the Legion of Honor. Replicas of *Joan of Arc* have also been placed in the Garden of the Bishops, in the city of Blois, France, at Gloucester, Massachusetts, and in front of the California Palace of the Legion of Honor in San Francisco. Other notable works of this period are *Diana of the Chase,* which won her a second Saltus gold medal in 1922, and *Youth Taming the Wild* (1933), a romantic vision of man and animal. A bas-relief wall sculpture based on the *Joan of Arc* was erected at the Cathedral of St. John the Divine in New York City.

It was at this time that she served on a committee to plan a sculpture exhibition at the Hispanic Museum, founded by the scholar, poet, and philanthropist Archer Milton Huntington, the adopted son of the railroad magnate Collis Potter Huntington. It was said that wherever Archer put his foot down, a museum sprang up. When they met, he was suffering from depression, having lost his wife to another man. He quickly fell in love with Anna Hyatt and proposed. Anna, who led an active and successful professional lifestyle, was reluctant to change, but when Archer Huntington became extremely ill she relented. In 1923, they surprised everyone by being married without fanfare at her studio. The newlyweds shared many cultural interests and a sense of duty toward their community. A common cause was the Hispanic Museum. Archer was a scholar of Spanish culture, and Anna shared his enthusiasm.

Following her marriage, Huntington was in a position to benefit from her new, more comfortable circumstances, such as working on a scale that was not financially feasible before. Her monumental full-sized and larger-than-life-sized equestrian monuments date from this time. But this asset was in marked contrast to the loss of creative hours due to the entertaining required of her life with the director of many important philanthropies. As the owners of several large estates and a summer camp in northern New York State, the Huntingtons were extremely busy. In 1926, while continuing her hectic social life, helping settle the estate of her husband's mother, and working on her own sculpture, Anna became seriously ill with bronchitis. A year later, she was diagnosed with tuberculosis.

For the next seven years, the Huntingtons' primary cause was the recovery of Anna's health. They traveled to warmer climates, notably the Carolinas. In 1930, they purchased a 6,700-acre tract of land on the South Carolina coast near Charleston, the site of four old plantations, and built a house on the ocean as their winter residence. Without the aid of a landscape architect, Anna laid out a large butterfly-shaped formal garden, with pools and fountains, keeping the rest of the land as a nature preserve of indigenous flora and fauna. Archer Huntington had intended the garden as a display space for Anna's sculptures, but the generous artist included works of her colleagues as well, until the collection grew to 300 pieces. During 1932, Anna recuperated at a sanitarium in Switzerland and spent a long rest period in Arizona. The Huntingtons presented their outdoor museum, called Brookgreen Gardens, to the state of South Carolina that same year to be used as a state park. Brookgreen Gardens is now the largest outdoor garden of academic sculpture in the United States. At the entrance, visitors are greeted by Huntington's *Fighting Stallions,* a huge 17'x14'x7' statue, representative of the work she pioneered using aluminum as a sculptural medium. She felt that the alloy "had a vibrant quality."

As Anna came to share her husband's passion for Spanish culture, the Huntingtons traveled extensively in Spain as part of her recovery from tuberculosis. While there, Huntington dedicated a cast of *El Cid Campeador* at Seville in 1927. For this statue of the 11th-century Spanish hero, she was awarded the Grand Cross of Alphonso XII by the government of Spain, presented personally by the king of Spain in 1929. At the time, she was the only sculptor so honored. A replica was placed on the terrace of the Hispanic Society of America in New York and before the California Palace of the Legion of Honor Museum in San Francisco, where it is a companion piece to her *Joan of Arc.* Though her production was reduced during her illness, she continued to receive widespread recognition. The American Academy of Arts and Letters awarded her the gold medal for distinction in 1930 and held a retrospective exhibition of 171 of her works in 1936.

By 1937, Huntington had found it oppressive to live in the ornate New York City mansion that required so many servants. Convinced that the demands of city living were detrimental to creative work, she persuaded her husband to satisfy her need for a simple, more earthy life by purchasing an estate in Haverstraw, New York, called "Rocas," where Anna had her own zoo. Monkeys, bears, and wolves were among her models. While there, she completed four life-

Great Dane *sculpture by Anna Hyatt Huntington sits at the entrance of her former estate at Brookgreen Gardens, Murrells Inlet, South Carolina.*

sized groups as well as 15 or more smaller pieces. After a few years, the Huntingtons turned "Rocas" over to New York State as a park. With the Second World War looming, the Huntingtons decided to purchase a practical home where farming was possible. In 1940, they bought a wild stretch of 900 acres in Redding Ridge, Connecticut, on a ridge overlooking Long Island Sound. At Stanerigg, they built a stark, 20-room, cement-block house and studio, where Anna maintained a working organic farm and a kennel of around 100 Scottish deerhounds, doing much of the physical labor herself. With five other families, she converted a barn into a cannery to preserve produce from six Victory gardens. She also set up a branch of the Danbury Red Cross at her house so she and her neighbors would not waste precious gasoline traveling to volunteer. Each Sunday, the Huntingtons held "at home" teas attended by intellectuals and dignitaries from across the globe. Anna served tea and discussed science and art with her guests; Archer read from the Koran and long passages from the Spanish writer Cervantes.

Even with her wartime activities, Huntington worked continuously at her sculpture, while her husband published articles, wrote poetry, and engaged in a wide variety of philanthropies. In 1942 and 1943, she produced two major works in bas-relief, *Don Quixote* and *Boabdil,* for the Hispanic Society of America. Besides their continuing support of the Hispanic Society, the Huntingtons were responsible for the founding of 14 museums and the establishment of four public wildlife preserves. When the couple left their Fifth Avenue mansion, they donated it to the National Academy of Design for its headquarters. The philanthropic spirit that permeated their lives had a major impact on the communities in which they lived and worked. A $100,000 gift from the Huntingtons made possible an exhibition of the National Sculpture Society which was accompanied by a catalog that became a major resource about American academic sculpture.

With the advent of modern abstract sculpture, Huntington was disturbed by what she referred to as an "overwhelming flood of degenerate trash drowning sincere and conservative workers in all the arts." Although disappointed that traditional sculpture was giving way to a growing public interest in innovative forms, she continued working in her own style and gained further recognition. In appreciation of her artistic achievements and her unfailing interest in and aid to her fellow sculptors, the National Sculpture Society awarded her a special medal of honor in 1940. Huntington's works were included in the N.Y. State Department of Commerce's color film released in 1950, entitled *New York's Heritage.* In 1952, she was awarded the grand cross of Isabel the Catholic from the government of Spain. Honors would come to her throughout her life, among them a second honorary degree from the University of South Carolina, as well as the designation of honorary vice-president of the National Association of Women Painters and Sculptors and fellow of the National Sculpture Society. A particular honor was being named a corresponding member of the Spanish Academia de Artes de San Fernando, an honor never before given to a woman.

In the spring of 1955, shortly before her husband's death, she completed the symbolic grouping *Torch Bearers.* After his death, Anna Huntington, at age 79, returned with renewed creativity to her art. Over the next two decades, she executed a range of works, from small animal studies to her trademark monumental equestrians, the last five of which she completed at her Stanerigg studio. In 1956, she was commissioned to do an equestrian statue honoring Cuba and chose for her subject the Cuban patriot José Martí; the monument showed the hero falling from his rearing horse at the instant he was hit by Spanish bullets. In 1959, Fidel Castro's unseating of the dictator Fulgencio Batista resulted in pro- and anti-Castro groups rioting in New York at the designated site of the monument at 59th Street at Central Park, so the unveiling was canceled. Years later, in 1965, the statue was erected secretly at dawn. As Huntington's gift to New York City, the statue had a quiet unveiling a few weeks later, attended by the artist and Martí's grandson, actor Cesar Romero.

A 1961 article in *Connecticut Life* described her at 85 as a "woman of vigorous wit and charm who could scamper up a ten-foot ladder to work on her massive sculptures or knock down with her .22 caliber any squirrels molesting the birds on her estate." Her monument to revolutionary-war hero Israel Putnam was completed in 1966, when she was 90. *General Israel Putnam's Escape at Horse Neck* stands on her estate in Connecticut, where a state park was planned at the time of her death in 1973.

The preceding year, Huntington had suffered several dozen small strokes. When she died, at age 97, she left works in progress, but her nephew relates that she was unhappy at the time of her death, convinced she had outlived herself, that her kind of sculpture was superseded and that no one would be interested in it again. Though she was reconciled that she had had her day, she was saddened that it seemed to be over. There is, however, a renewed interest in her style of sculpture, particularly in the work of her contemporary, Augustus Saint Gaudens. The full range of Anna Hyatt Huntington's extraordinary output over a period of 70 years is represented in the collections of more than 200 museums, parks and gardens of major cities throughout the world.

SOURCES:

"Anna Hyatt Huntington," in *Current Biography, 1953.* NY: H.W. Wilson, 1954.

Dunford, Penny. *A Biographical Dictionary of Women Artists in Europe and America since 1850.* Philadelphia, PA: University of Pennsylvania Press, 1989.
Eden, Myrna Garvey. *Energy and Individuality in the Art of Anna Huntington, Sculptor, and Amy Beach, Composer.* Composers of North America, No. 2. Metuchen, NJ: Scarecrow Press, 1987.
"A Giant's Horse for the Asking," in *Connecticut Life.* October 5, 1961.
Gurney, George. *Interview with Anna Hyatt Huntington. March 19, 1970.* Index of American Sculptors, University of Delaware, Newark, Delaware.
Heller, Nancy G. *Women Artists: An Illustrated History.* NY: Abbeville Press, 1987.
Mayor, A. Hyatt. *A Century of American Sculpture: Treasures from Brookgreen Gardens.* NY: Abbeville Press, 1987.
Mellon, Eleanor M. *Anna Hyatt Huntington.* American Sculptors Series 3. NY: W.W. Norton, 1947.
The New York Times (obituary). October 4, 1973.
Rubinstein, Charlotte Streifer. *American Women Artists.* Boston, MA: G.K. Hall, 1982.
———. *American Women Sculptors.* Boston, MA: G.K. Hall, 1990.
Sicherman, Barbara and Carol Hurd Green, eds. *Notable American Women: The Modern Period.* Cambridge, MA: Belknap Press of Harvard University Press, 1980.

COLLECTIONS:

Correspondence, manuscripts, photographs, scrapbooks, diaries, in addition to critical and biographical material, at Syracuse University, Syracuse, New York.

Laurie Twist Binder,
Library Media Specialist, Buffalo Public Schools, Buffalo, New York, and freelance graphic artist and illustrator

Huntington, Lady (1707–1791).

See Hastings, Selina.

Hunton, Addie D. Waites (1875–1943)

African-American activist and Young Women's Christian Association official. *Born Addie Waites in Norfolk, Virginia, on July 11, 1875; died in Brooklyn, New York, on June 21, 1943; eldest of two daughters and a son of Jesse Waites (a businessman) and Adelina (Lawton) Waites; graduated from Girls' Latin School, Boston, Massachusetts; graduated from Spencerian College of Commerce, Philadelphia, Pennsylvania, 1889; married William Alphaeus Hunton (official of the Young Men's Christian Association for Negroes, 1893), on July 19, 1893 (died 1916); children: four; only the two younger, Eunice and William Alphaeus, Jr., lived beyond infancy.*

Born in Norfolk, Virginia, in 1875, Addie Hunton was the daughter of a successful businessman who owned a wholesale oyster and shipping company and was also the co-owner of an amusement park for blacks. Her mother died when she was just a child, and she was reared by a maternal aunt in Boston, where she received most of her education, Upon graduating from Girls' Latin School in Boston and Spencerian College of Commerce in Philadelphia, Hunton went to Normal, Alabama, to teach at State Normal and Agricultural College (later Alabama Agricultural and Mechanical University).

In July 1893, she married William A. Hunton, who had come to Norfolk in 1888 to establish and become secretary of a Young Men's Christian Association for Negro youth. (In 1891, he was selected by the International Committee of the YMCA to direct its work among Southern blacks, and he later became administrative secretary of the Colored Men's Department of the International Committee.) During the early years of her marriage, Hunton worked full time and also served as her husband's secretary, assisting him in many aspects of his YMCA work. After living in Norfolk and Richmond, Virginia, the couple moved to Atlanta, Georgia, in 1899. There, Hunton gave birth to four children, although only the two younger survived infancy. After the Atlanta riot of 1906, fearing for their safety, the family moved to Brooklyn, New York.

Hunton's behind-the-scenes work with the YMCA did not go unnoticed, and in 1907 the National Board of the Young Women's Christian Association (YWCA) appointed her secretary for projects among black students. During the winter of 1907–08, she toured the South and Midwest, conducting a survey for the YWCA. Her pioneering work also included recruiting a number of other black women to work for the YWCA, among them **Eva del Vakia Bowles** and ***Elizabeth Ross Haynes**.

From 1909 to 1910, Hunton took her children to Europe, while her husband, who was now plagued by health problems, continued his work at home. Hunton spent a few months in Switzerland and then traveled to Strassburg, where she took classes at Kaiser Wilhelm University. Upon her return home, she continued her work with the YWCA and enrolled in courses at the College of the City of New York. By 1914, William had grown seriously ill with tuberculosis, and the family moved to Saranac Lake, New York, where they remained until his death in 1916.

When America entered World War I, Hunton, whose children were now grown, volunteered for overseas service with the YMCA and, in 1918, became one of three black women (**Helen Curtis** and **Kathryn Johnson** were the other two) assigned to work with the 200,000 segregated black troops stationed in France. (Later, 16 additional women were included in a group of 100 African-Americans who were sent to France as YMCA workers.) Hunton was first assigned to the Services of Supplies sector at Saint Nazaire. Along with the usual canteen services and movies offered at the YMCA facility, she introduced a literacy course and a Sunday evening discussion program on art, music, and religion, among other subjects. In January 1919, after a bout of influenza and exhaustion, she was transferred to a leave area in southern France, near Aix-les-Bains. There, she helped organize a program of educational, cultural, religious, and athletic activities for the 1,000 African-American troops who arrived weekly for a brief respite from the fighting. In May 1919, she received her most difficult assignment: the military cemetery at Romagne. There, the black soldiers were assigned to find the dead from the battlefield of the Meuse-Argonne and rebury them in the military cemetery. In a book she later co-authored with Kathryn Johnson, *Two Colored Women with the American Expeditionary Forces* (1920), Hunton described the work of the soldiers as "a gruesome, repulsive and unhealthful task, requiring weeks of incessant toil during the long heavy days of summer." She also recounted how the undercurrent of resentment among the soldiers created a constant sense of danger. "Always in those days there was fear of mutiny," she wrote. "We felt most of the time that we were living close to the edge of a smoldering crater."

Returning to the United States in the autumn of 1919, Hunton harbored some bitterness over the racial prejudice she had witnessed during the war, but she soon channeled her anger into positive efforts toward the advancement of her race. She served on the Council on Colored Work of the National Board of the YWCA and was president of the International Council of the Women of Darker Races and of the Empire State Federation of Women's Clubs. Also concerned with women's issues, she became an ardent suffragist and joined the Brooklyn Equal Suffrage League. She was a vice-president and field secretary of the National Association for the Advancement of Colored People (NAACP) and also remained active in the National Association of Colored Women (NACW).

As a member of the executive board of the Women's International League for Peace and Freedom, she was part of a six-woman committee that visited Haiti in 1926 to view the United States occupation. She later wrote a section on race relations for the committee's report, *Occupied Haiti* (1927), which condemned the intervention and advocated restoration of Haiti's independence.

Addie Hunton's last public appearance was at a ceremony honoring outstanding black women at the New York World's Fair in 1939. She died on June 21, 1943, of diabetes, and was buried in Cypress Hills Cemetery in Brooklyn.

SOURCES:

James, Edward T., ed. *Notable American Women, 1607–1950*. Cambridge, MA: The Belknap Press of Harvard University Press, 1971.

Smith, Jessie Carney, ed. *Notable Black American Women*. Detroit, MI: Gale Research, 1992.

Barbara Morgan,
Melrose, Massachusetts

Hunyady, Emese (1967—)

Austrian speedskater. *Born in Hungary in 1967; defected to Austria in 1985; married Thomas Nemeth (an Austrian speedskater).*

Emese Hunyady gave up everything for her dream of winning a speedskating title; originally, her mother had a different plan for her daughter. When Hunyady was five, she was enrolled in a figure-skating program. She hated it. By age ten, she had traded in circles and loops for the speedskating straightaway. In 1984, she represented Hungary at the Sarajevo Olympics, finishing 13th in the 1,500 meters. One year later, in 1985, leaving family and friends behind, Hunyady defected from Hungary to follow her coach Kutas Balint to Austria. She obtained an Austrian passport by entering into an arranged marriage with Austrian speedskater Thomas Nemeth. Five years later, she broke with Balint. "All my life is speedskating," she told a reporter. "For so long a time, for many years, there was only speedskating and nothing else."

In 1992, in Albertville, France, Hunyady took the Olympic bronze medal in the 3,000-meters. In Lillehammer, Norway, in 1994, she was a silver medalist in the 3,000 meters and, against stellar opposition, took the gold medal in the 1,500 meters in 2:2.19, giving Austria its first speedskating gold medal. To do so, she topped the times of ***Bonnie Blair** and ***Gunda Niemann**. After kissing the ice, Hunyady reverted to figure skating, executing twists and turns on her victory lap. The public address announcer decreed: "Marks for artistic impression: 6.0."

Hurd, Dorothy Campbell

(1883–1945)

American golfer. *Name variations: Dorothy I. Campbell. Born Dorothy Iona Campbell on May 6, 1883, in North Berwick, Scotland; killed by a train in Yemassee, North Carolina, on March 20, 1945; married J.B. Hurd, in 1913.*

Won Scottish Ladies' championship (1905, 1906, and 1908); won U.S. Women's Amateur championship (1909 and 1910); won Canadian Amateur Ladies' Open (1910, 1911, and 1912); was first woman to win both the British and U.S. amateur titles in one year (1909).

At the dawn of the 20th century, Dorothy Campbell Hurd was the foremost name in international women's golf. Under her maiden name Dorothy I. Campbell, she was the first woman to win both the British and American titles in one year in 1909, a feat she repeated in 1911. She first came to international attention in Scotland where she won the Scottish Ladies' championship. In 1909, she almost lost the British Ladies' title when she forgot to report the result of the match to the officials, but she retained the title when her oversight was dismissed. In 1909, she was the first British woman to win the U.S. Women's Amateur title. Hurd won 11 major championships, ten between 1905 and 1912. Settling into semi-retirement after her marriage in 1913, she was lured back to tournament golf in the 1920s, winning the U.S. Women's championship in 1924; in 1938, she won the U.S. Women's Senior tournament at age 55. She was inducted into the Golf Hall of Fame, Citizens Savings Hall of Fame Athletic Museum, and Ladies Professional Golfers' Association Hall of Fame. Hurd was killed by a train in 1945, while changing trains in Yemassee, North Carolina.

Karin Haag,
freelance writer, Athens, Georgia

Hurd, Edith Thacher (1910–1997)

Children's book writer who was one of the early figures in the development of children's literature in America. *Name variations: (joint pseudonym with Margaret Wise Brown) Juniper Sage; (nickname) Posey. Born on September 14, 1910, in Kansas City, Missouri; died on January 25, 1997; daughter of John Hamilton and Edith (Gilman) Thacher; Radcliffe College, A.B., 1933; Bank Street College of Education, additional study, 1934; married Clement Hurd (an artist and illustrator), on June 24, 1939 (died 1988); children: John Thacher Hurd (children's book writer and illustrator).*

Taught four years at the Dalton School, New York, N.Y.; worked at the U.S. Office of War Information, San Francisco, California as a news analyst (1942–45).

Selected writings: Hurry, Hurry *(W.R. Scott, 1938, new ed. with illustrations by Clement Hurd, Harper, 1960);* The Wreck of the Wild Wave *(Oxford University Press, 1942);* Jerry, the Jeep *(Lothrop, 1945);* The Galleon from Manila *(Oxford University Press, 1949);* Mr. Shortsleeves' Great Big Store *(Simon & Schuster, 1952);* The Golden Hind *(Crowell, 1960); (illustrated by Lucienne Bloch)* Sandpipers *(Crowell, 1961); (illustrated by Bloch)* Starfish *(Crowell, 1962);* Sailers, Whalers and Steamers *(Lane, 1964);* Who Will Be Mine? *(Golden Gate, 1966); (illustrated by Tony Chen)* The White Horse *(Harper, 1970);* Come With Me to Nursery School *(Coward, 1970); (illustrated by Emily A. McCully)* The Black Dog Who Went into the Woods *(Harper, 1980); (illustrated by McCully)* I Dance in My Red Pajamas *(Harper, 1982); (illustrated by Jennifer Dewey)* Song of the Sea Otter *(Pantheon, 1983); (illustrated by Don Freeman)* Dinosaur, My Darling *(Harper, 1978).*

With husband Clement Hurd as illustrator: Engine, Engine, No. 9 *(Lothrop, 1940);* Sky High *(Lothrop, 1941);* The Annie Moran *(Lothrop, 1942);* Speedy, the Hook and Ladder Truck *(Lothrop, 1942);* Benny the Bulldozer *(Lothrop, 1947);* Toughy and His Trailer Truck *(Lothrop, 1948);* Willy's Farm *(Lothrop, 1949);* Caboose *(Lothrop, 1950);* Old Silversides *(Lothrop, 1951);* St. George's Day in

Edith Thacher Hurd

Williamsburg, Va. *(Colonial Williamsburg, 1952);* Somebody's House *(Lothrop, 1953);* Nino and His Fish *(Lothrop, 1954);* The Devil's Tail: Adventures of a Printer's Apprentice in Early Williamsburg *(Doubleday, 1954);* The Cat from Telegraph Hill *(Lothrop, 1955);* Mr. Charlie's Chicken House *(Lippincott, 1955);* Mr. Charlie's Gas Station *(Lippincott, 1956);* Windy and the Willow Whistle *(Sterling, 1956);* Mary's Scary House *(Sterling, 1956);* It's Snowing *(Sterling, 1957);* Mr. Charlie's Camping Trip *(Lippincott, 1957);* Johnny Littlejohn *(Lothrop, 1957);* Fox in a Box *(Doubleday, 1957);* Mr. Charlie, the Fireman's Friend *(Lippincott, 1958);* The Faraway Christmas: A Story of the Farallon Islands *(Lothrop, 1958);* Mr. Charlie's Pet Shop *(Lippincott, 1959);* Last One Home Is a Green Pig *(Harper, 1959);* Mr. Charlie's Farm *(Lippincott, 1960);* Stop, Stop *(Harper, 1961);* Come and Have Fun *(Harper, 1962);* Christmas Eve *(Harper, 1962);* No Funny Business *(Harper, 1962);* Follow Tomas *(Dial, 1963);* The Day the Sun Danced *(Harper, 1965);* Johnny Lion's Book *(Harper, 1965);* The So-So Cat *(Harper, 1965);* What Whale? Where? *(Harper, 1966); (with son, Thacher Hurd)* Little Dog, Dreaming *(Harper, 1967);* The Blue Heron Tree *(Viking, 1968);* Rain and the Valley *(Coward, 1968);* This Is the Forest *(Coward, 1969);* Johnny Lion's Bad Day *(Harper, 1970);* Catfish *(Viking, 1970);* Wilson's World *(Harper, 1971);* Johnny Lion's Rubber Boots *(Harper, 1972);* Catfish and the Kidnapped Cat *(Harper, 1974);* Look For a Bird *(Harper, 1977);* Under the Lemon Tree *(Little, Brown, 1980); (afterword)* The World Is Round *(North Point Press, 1988).*

"Mother Animal" series; all illustrated by Clement Hurd: The Mother Beaver *(Little, Brown, 1971);* The Mother Deer *(Little, Brown, 1972);* The Mother Whale *(Little, Brown, 1973);* The Mother Owl *(Little, Brown, 1974);* The Mother Kangaroo *(Little, Brown, 1976);* The Mother Chimpanzee *(Little, Brown, 1978).*

With Margaret Wise Brown: Five Little Firemen *(Simon & Schuster, 1948);* Two Little Miners *(Simon & Schuster, 1949);* The Little Fat Policeman *(Simon & Schuster, 1950);* Two Little Gardeners *(Simon & Schuster, 1951);* Seven Little Postmen *(Simon & Schuster, 1952). With Margaret Wise Brown, under joint pseudonym Juniper Sage:* The Man in the Manhole and the Fix-it Men *(W.R. Scott, 1946). Contributor of poetry to* Grade Teacher *and articles to* Horn Book.

Edith Thacher Hurd once described herself as "a Missourian by birth, a New Englander by education, a New Yorker by marriage, and now a happy Californian." She was born in Kansas City in 1910, and, after attending a "wonderfully progressive school" in Missouri where frequent writing assignments evoked stories filled with knights in armor, jousts, and castles (her favorite author was Howard Pyle), she went to a strict boarding school in Switzerland to study for one year. She then moved on to Radcliffe College.

Four years later, diploma in hand, she was greeted with unemployment and the Great Depression. There was little work to be found for an art history major. Instead, Hurd accepted a scholarship to the Bank Street College of Education in New York's Greenwich Village, then taught for four years at the Dalton School in New York City.

"The 1920s were fruitful years for children's literature," noted Hurd, "yet they were devoted to the publication of 'inheritance of great literature,' fairy tales, folk tales, adventure stories, and stories of the fabulous and unreal. Breaking with older narrative forms, experimental writers began to focus directly on the experiences of children and to explore the realm of a child's senses—colors, sounds, smells. Children's emotions and concerns, such as being alone and shy, being lost and being found, became new subjects for writers. I remember well some of these years of explosive creativity, for they led me into the world of children's books and entirely changed my life."

Edith became a member of the Writer's Laboratory at the Bank Street College of Education. Under the guidance of ***Lucy Sprague Mitchell**, the Laboratory was comprised of aspiring writers of books for young children, including ***Margaret Wise Brown** and **Ruth Krauss**. Hurd became deeply involved with their explorations into writing and education as well as the publishing world, especially the nascent Young Scott Books.

Founded in 1938 by **Ethel McCullough Scott**, her brother John McCullough, and her husband William R. Scott, Young Scott Books was sufficiently financed for experimentation. The Scotts, who worked out of an office in the Village and a barn at their summer house in Bennington, Vermont, soon began to publish books that were, writes Hurd, "bold in their child-oriented point of view and unusual in their choice of illustrators and authors."

The Little Fireman by Margaret Wise Brown (1938) established the firm as a leader in innovative children's books, and Brown was asked to join the editorial staff. "I saw a great deal of Margaret, as she was without a doubt the most talented member of the Writer's Laboratory," writes Hurd. "The meetings when 'Brownie' read a new story were delightful, often hilarious, occasions." Working with the Scotts was often an unconventional undertaking. "I remember being invited to their house in North Bennington, Vermont, to spend the night," said Hurd; "the next morning sitting under the tall elm trees, the Scotts, John McCullough and I worked long hours 'rewriting' my first book, *Hurry, Hurry, A story of calamity and woe,* about a babysitter who was always in too much of a hurry." The original *Hurry Hurry* was based on a nurse at the Dalton School. "She was ALWAYS in a dreadful hurry."

Brown suggested that adult authors be queried to write books for children, so letters were sent to Ernest Hemingway, John Steinbeck and ***Gertrude Stein**. Though Hemingway and Steinbeck declined, Stein wrote *The World Is Round*; its illustrator was Clement Hurd. Just before the book's publication, Edith Thacher married Clem Hurd on Cape Cod, Massachusetts, on June 24, 1939. Following the wedding, the couple headed back to New York, where Clem supervised the printing of the Stein book. "I remember that New York was ferociously hot that summer, and we were thankful to head north at last to our little farmhouse in Vermont for a belated honeymoon," writes Hurd.

Through the years, Edith wrote over 75 books, many of which are still in print. From 1959 on, the Hurds worked with their longtime friend and editor ❧▸ **Ursula Nordstrom** at Harper. When Edith died in January 1997, *Publishers Weekly* noted that this signaled "the passing of one of the few remaining early figures in the development of children's literature as we know it." Now over 2,000 children's books are being published each year, and authors and illustrators are recognized as masters in their own right. It is a far cry from the days when, as Edith Hurd once recalled, Bennett Cerf introduced Margaret Wise Brown as a writer of "baby books."

Illustrator Leonard Marcus noted in his tribute to Hurd:

> "Posey," as everyone called her, always seemed a bit amused by the world around her and by herself as part of that world. Yet she also knew exactly what she was about. "Maine is so satisfying," she once said as she watched from the deck of a ferry cruising out among the spruce-and-granite studded islands of Penobscot Bay, "because it looks so much like Maine."

SOURCES:

Junior Literary Guild. March 1980.

Publishers Weekly. February 24, 1997, p. 33.

Stein, Gertrude. *The World Is Round.* Afterword by Edith Thacher Hurd. North Point Press, 1988.

Hurd-Mead, Kate Campbell

(1867–1941)

American physician. *Born April 6, 1867, in Danville, Quebec, Canada; died January 1, 1941, in Haddam, Connecticut; daughter of Edward Payson and Sarah Elizabeth (Campbell) Hurd; educated at the Woman's Medical College of Pennsylvania (in Philadelphia) and the New England Hospital for Women and Children (in Boston) and did postgraduate studies in Paris, Stockholm, London, and Vienna; married William Edward Mead (a college professor), on June 21, 1893.*

Specialized in women's and children's health; participated in and helped found several organizations dedicated to women's and children's health issues; wrote Medical Women of America *(1933) and* A History of Women in Medicine from the Earliest Times to the Beginning of the Nineteenth Century *(1938).*

Kate Campbell Hurd-Mead was born on April 6, 1867, the oldest of three children of Edward Payson Hurd and **Sarah Elizabeth Hurd**. When she was three, her family moved from Quebec, Canada, to her mother's birthplace of Newburyport, Massachusetts, where she attended public school. After her graduation in 1883, she studied with private tutors. Both Kate and her sister, **Mabeth Hurd Paige**, were ambitious in their goals: Mabeth became a distinguished lawyer and a state legislator in Minnesota, and Kate, determined to follow in her father's footsteps, even broke an engagement because her fiancé did not want her to become a doctor. In 1888, she received her M.D. from the Woman's Medical College and then spent a year interning in Boston before going on to postgraduate work in Europe.

Nordstrom, Ursula. *See Brown, Margaret Wise for sidebar.*

In 1890, Hurd returned to the States and began working in Baltimore as the medical director at Bryn Mawr School for girls. This was one of the first schools in America to initiate a health program that was preventative in nature, with such unusual features as physical education and periodic examinations. During this time she also had a private practice. In 1891, Hurd and Dr. **Alice Hall** founded a private charitable institution, the Evening Dispensary for Working Women and Girls of Baltimore City, that was a forerunner in the movement for maternal hygiene and infant well-being. This institution also gave women doctors the opportunity to practice, something that had been lacking before.

After Hurd married William Mead in 1893, they settled in Middletown, Connecticut, where he taught Early English at Wesleyan University. Hurd-Mead was an incorporator of Middlesex County Hospital in 1895 and continued to study and advance women's medicine, eventually specializing in women's and children's diseases. She was organizer of the Middletown District Nurses Association (1900), vice-president of the State Medical Society of Connecticut (1913–1914), organizer of the Medical Women's International Association (1919), president of the American Medical Women's Association (1922–1924), and a financial supporter of the American Women's Hospitals, which backed women physicians in undeveloped regions of the world. From 1907 to 1925, Hurd-Mead served as the consulting gynecologist for Middlesex County Hospital. In 1925, she retired from practice and began to research the history of women in medicine. She spent two years in England at the British Museum Library and then went on to gather information on women physicians in Europe, Asia, and Africa.

In 1929, Hurd-Mead and her husband settled in Haddam, Connecticut, and worked on their writing. *Medical Women in America* was published in 1933, followed in 1938 by *A History of Women in Medicine from the Earliest Times to the Beginning of the Nineteenth Century*. This was the first of a projected trilogy intended to detail the history of women in medicine into the present time, which was left uncompleted when the 73-year-old Hurd-Mead suffered a fatal heart attack while running to help an injured caretaker. She was buried in Middletown. Her vast collection of medical history was bequeathed to the Woman's Medical College of Pennsylvania along with a fund that provided for an annual lecture on the history of women in medicine.

SOURCES:

James, Edward T., ed. *Notable American Women, 1607–1950*. Cambridge, MA: The Belknap Press of Harvard University Press, 1971.

Karina L. Kerr, M.A.,
Ypsilanti, Michigan

Hurrem Sultana (c. 1504–1558).

See Roxelana.

Hurst, Fannie (1889–1968)

American novelist and short-story writer. *Born in Hamilton, Ohio, on October 18, 1889; died in New York City on February 23, 1968; eldest of two daughters of Samuel Hurst (owner of a shoe factory) and Rose (Kopple) Hurst; graduated from Central High School, St. Louis; Washington University, St. Louis, B.A., 1909; married Jacques S. Danielson (a pianist), in 1915 (died 1952); no children.*

Selected writings: (short stories) Just Around the Corner *(1914),* Every Soul Hath Its Song *(1916),* Gaslight Sonatas *(1919),* Humoresque *(1919),* The Vertical City *(1922),* Song of Life *(1927),* Procession *(1929),* We Are Ten *(1937); (nonfiction)* No Food with My Meals *(1935),* Anatomy of Me *(1958); (novels)* Star Dust *(1921),* Lummox *(1923),* Appassionata *(1926),* Mannequin *(1926),* A President is Born *(1928),* Five and Ten *(1929),* Back Street *(1931),* Imitation of Life *(1933),* Anitra's Dance *(1934),* Great Laughter *(1936),* Hands of Veronica *(1937),* Lonely Parade *(1942),* Hallelujah *(1944),* Any Woman *(1950),* The Man with One Head *(1953),* Family! *(1959),* God Must Be Sad *(1961),* Fool—Be Still *(1964); (plays)* Land of the Free *(1917) and* Back Pay *(1921).*

One of the most admired and eagerly awaited writers of the early and mid-20th century, Fannie Hurst is now remembered for her two best-selling novels, *Back Street* (1931) and *Imitation of Life* (1933), both of which were made into popular movies. A total of 32 films were adapted from Hurst's fiction, and she wrote the screenplays for several of them. Her literary output was substantial, including 9 volumes of short stories, 17 novels, 5 plays, a full-length autobiography and autobiographical memoir, and countless nonfiction articles on politics and assorted topics. Often dismissed by critics as sentimental (Harry Salpeter called her "the sob sister of American fiction"), she populated her tales with misfits as well as underdogs, including urban working women. Hurst was also a passionate social activist and an avowed feminist. When she wed Russian-born pianist Jacques Danielson in 1915 (the marriage was not announced until 1920), she retained her maiden name, her own residence, and her own social life, claiming that marriage "should not lessen my capacity for creative work or pull me down into a sedentary state of fatmindedness."

Fannie Hurst was born in Hamilton, Ohio, in 1889, and raised in St. Louis, Missouri, the eldest of two daughters in a middle-class German-Jewish family. Her younger sister Edna died of diphtheria in childhood. Hurst's literary career was foreshadowed by a deluge of teenage essays, stories, and verses, though her early interests also included athletics and dramatics. In 1910, after graduating from Washington University in St. Louis, Hurst left her comfortable home for New York, to do graduate work at Columbia University and pursue her writing career. Her "training for fiction," as she later referred to it, included living in the slums, working variously as a saleswoman, an actress, and a waitress, and traveling to Europe in steerage. Although her first story, "Ain't Life Wonderful," had been published while she was still in college, she subsequently encountered a series of rejections. Finally in 1912, she sold a story, "Power and Horse Power," to *The Saturday Evening Post*; the magazine also took an option on all her future work. In 1914, with the publication of *Just Around the Corner,* a collection of short stories, her career was well under way. She produced four volumes of short stories before venturing into novels.

Hurst wrote for an audience of women, and women, often the victims of social and economic discrimination, are the central characters of her best works, including the novels *Lummox* (1923), the story of an inarticulate servant-girl who barely survives in a callous society, *Back Street* (1931), about the mistress of a married man, and *Imitation of Life* (1933), which focuses on the lives of two mother-daughter pairs, one black and one white. The novel was alternately praised for its sympathetic portrayal of a entrepreneurial black woman and condemned for the character's stereotypical Aunt Jemima occupation.) In each of the novels, the women are victimized not only by societal influences, but by their own passivity, a trait Hurst deplored. Though her characters are often consumed with their need for a man, Hurst believed that women should create their own identities and find a place where they "can give the most service and get the most out of life."

Hurst spoke out for numerous social causes and was active in a number of organizations concerned with social welfare. A friend of ***Eleanor Roosevelt**, she supported labor and New Deal policies. She chaired the Woman's National Housing Commission and the Committee on Workmen's Compensation. She was a member of the National Advisory Committee to the Works Progress Administration (1940–41) and served on the board of directors of the New York Urban League.

She was also active in Zionism and Jewish war relief and, upon her death in 1968, left half of her estate to Brandeis University, a postwar institution established mainly by Jews. In keeping with her feminist views, she worked with a number of organization designed to improve the lot of working women and in groups teaching birth control and human sexuality, including the American Planned Parenthood Federation and the International Planned Parenthood Federation.

Described as "a handsome, dark woman of the opulent type," Hurst, who claimed she slept only four or five hours a night, enjoyed a contented private life. Her husband, who was phobic about public appearances and never fulfilled his potential as a concert pianist, managed her finances and insured her a lifetime of financial security. She resided with a menagerie of animals and, in addition to writing six hours daily, kept a frantic schedule of meetings and speaking engagements. She often traveled alone and maintained a social life quite separate from her husband's, stating that her unconventional marriage kept "the dew on the rose." Indeed, the union endured until Jacques' death in 1952, after which Hurst wrote him a weekly letter, "chattily, not in grief and with no feeling that he knows about it in an afterlife," she noted in her 1958 autobiography *Anatomy of Me*. Reflecting further on her marriage, Hurst explained: "I had very little to bring to Jack in his musical world and actually he dwelt on the periphery of mine. But the alleged desirability of similar interests

did not apply to this perverse marriage of ours. It would seem that our sea of matrimony was full of treacherous archipelagoes. But we sailed it for wonderful years of blue waters, blue sky."

Although many critics of her day labeled Hurst sentimental and "soapy," and never regarded her as a serious writer, others praised her work as vital and sympathetic. No one denies her immense popularity; between 1914 and 1922, the announcement of a new Fannie Hurst story could sell out an issue of *Cosmopolitan* or *The Saturday Evening Post*. "She knew how to tell a story," writes **Susan Koppelman** in *Belles Lettres*. "She created characters who breathed; she captured the reality of a segment of the American population with a seriousness and sympathy that has never been surpassed. An important naturalist, she transferred the meticulous artistry of the 19th-century regionalists to the portrayal of first-generation American urban workers of the early 20th century. She was a great ironist, a great humorist, and as close to a great tragedian as we have seen in this century."

Margery Hurst

SOURCES:

Hurst, Fannie. *Anatomy of Me*. NY: Doubleday, 1958.

Koppelman, Susan. "Fannie Hurst." *Belles Lettres*. Fall 1994.

Kunitz, Stanley, ed. *Twentieth Century Authors*. NY: H.W. Wilson, 1955.

Mainiero, Lina, ed. *American Women Writers From Colonial Times to the Present*. NY: Frederick Ungar, 1980.

McHenry, Robert, ed. *Famous American Women*. NY: Dover, 1983.

Sicherman, Barbara and Carol Hurd Green, eds. *Notable American Women: The Modern Period*. Cambridge, MA: The Belknap Press of Harvard University Press, 1980.

SUGGESTED READING:

Kroeger, Brooke. *Fannie: The Talent for Success of Writer Fannie Hurst*. Times, 1999.

RELATED MEDIA:

Back Street (86 min. film), starring ***Irene Dunne**, John Boles, ***ZaSu Pitts**, directed by John Stahl, screenplay by **Gladys Lohman**, Universal, 1932.

Back Street (89 min. film), starring ***Margaret Sullavan**, Charles Boyer, directed by Robert Stevenson, Universal, 1941.

Back Street (107 min. film), starring ***Susan Hayward**, John Gavin, and **Vera Miles**, directed by Ross Hunter, Universal, 1961.

Imitation of Life (106 min. film), starring ***Claudette Colbert**, ***Louise Beavers**, ***Rochelle Hudson**, and ***Fredi Washington**, directed by John Stahl, Universal, 1934.

Imitation of Life (106 min. film), starring ***Lana Turner**, ***Juanita Moore**, **Sandra Dee**, **Susan Kohner**, and ***Mahalia Jackson**, directed by Douglas Sirk, Universal, 1959.

COLLECTIONS:

Several of Fannie Hurst's notebooks and letters are located at Brandeis University; letters from 1913 to 1942 are held in The Berg Collection, in the New York Public Library.

Barbara Morgan,
Melrose, Massachusetts

Hurst, Margery (1914—)

British business woman who founded the Brook Street Bureau, an international temporary office employment agency. *Born Margery Berney in Southsea, Hampshire, England, in 1914; attended Kilburn High School, London; attended Minerva College and the Royal Academy of Dramatic Art; married an army major, in 1940 (divorced); married Eric Hurst (an attorney), in 1948; children: (first marriage) one daughter; (second marriage) four daughters.*

Self-described as a domineering, unlikable child, Margery Hurst was born in Southsea, Hampshire, England, in 1914, and displayed an early tenacity that would serve her well in later life. After attending Minerva College and spending two years at the Royal Academy of Dramatic Art, she went to work as a typist in her father's building business, progressing quickly to office manager. In September 1940, she married a young army major, and when he was posted overseas, she joined the Women's Auxiliary Territorial Services as a welfare officer. After two years, she suffered a nervous breakdown and returned to civilian life. At age 31, three weeks after the birth of her daughter, she was deserted by her husband and resorted to taking in typing to keep food on the table. With a loan from her father, she subsequently opened an office on Brook Street in London and hired herself out for office work.

Soon faced with more requests than she could handle, Hurst hired a highly trained staff to help her, thus establishing the Brook Street Bureau. From this modest beginning, Brook Street rose to become the largest international secretarial agency in the world, renowned for its original advertising and the high-quality, temporary help it provided. Hurst went on to establish a college for administrative and secretarial studies. In 1962, she received the Pimms Cup for Anglo-American business friendship and, from 1967 to 1970, served on the British National Economic Commission. In 1970, she became one of the first women members of Lloyds Underwriters. Hurst retired as the managing director of Brook Street Bureau in 1976, although she and her second husband, lawyer Eric Hurst, remained co-chairs of the enterprise. Hurst was awarded the OBE in 1976.

SUGGESTED READING:

Hurst, Margery. *No Glass Slipper*. NY: Crown, 1967.

Hurston, Zora Neale (c. 1891–1960)

Anthropologist, novelist, folklorist and the most prolific as well as underrated African-American woman writer during the years 1920 to 1950. *Pronunciation: HERS-ton. Born Zora Neale Hurston on January 7, 1891 (according to one brother and a 1900 census taker) or 1901 (according to her literary biographer and various other sources), in Eatonville, Florida; died at the St. Lucie County Welfare Home on January 28, 1960; interred at the Gardens of Heavenly Rest in Ft. Pierce, Florida; sixth of eight children of Lucy Ann (Potts) Hurston and John Hurston, who migrated to Florida from Alabama after their marriage; completed high school at Morgan Academy in Washington, D.C., then attended Howard University in Washington, D.C. (1923–24) before acquiring a B.A. from Barnard, 1928; married Herbert Sheen, on May 19, 1927 (divorced, July 7, 1931); married Albert Price III, on June 27 1939 (divorced, November 9, 1943); children: none.*

Spent formative years in Eatonville, Florida, the first incorporated all-black town where her father, a carpenter, served as mayor and minister and her mother saw to the needs of eight children; forced to move to Jacksonville to live with a sibling and attend school after mother's death (1904) and father's remarriage; after taking a job as a maid with a traveling theatrical group, ended up in Washington, D.C., where she worked alternately as a waitress and manicurist; saw first story published in the school literary magazine (1924), which precipitated a scholarship to Barnard College (1926); developed an interest in folklore and writing while studying first in Washington and then New York; early literary attempts brought attention from New York art world where she fast became a key member of the famed Harlem Renaissance; fellowships and other support helped her pursue interest in African-American folklore; undertook periodic folklore expeditions throughout the southern U.S. as well as the Caribbean, the material of which she incorporated into her literary and stage ventures (1928–60); held teaching posts for brief periods at Rollins College in Winter Park, Florida, Bethune-Cookman College in Daytona, Florida, and North Carolina College for Negroes (1930s); worked for the WPA (1938–39) and, briefly, as a staff writer for Paramount Studios in California; suffered a decline in publications exacerbated by controversy extending from her political views and personal life (1940); a premature black nationalist, her autobiography, four novels and two books of folklore, together with numerous short stories and critical essays, made her the most prolific if controversial black writer of her time; living variously in New York City and rural Florida towns and on a houseboat or two, struggled to keep poverty at bay and the controversies that hounded her in check; spent last years fending off an intestinal illness that plagued her, and worked alternately as a public school teacher, technical librarian, and maid to support herself; after a stroke sent her to the St. Lucie County Welfare Home, she died, obscure, impoverished and nearly forgotten (January 28, 1960), and lies buried in an uncertainly marked grave at the Gardens of Heavenly Rest in Ft. Pierce, Florida.

*Awards: received two Guggenheim fellowships to collect folklore (1937–38); honorary doctorate from Morgan State (1939); Anisfield-Wolf award for contributing to race relations (*Saturday Review*, 1942); Howard University's Annual Distinguished Alumni Award (March 1943); Bethune-Cookman College Award for Education and Human Relations (May 1956).*

Selected novels: Jonah's Gourd Vine *(Philadelphia, PA: J.B. Lippincott, 1934, reprinted with an in-*

troduction by Larry Neal, 1971); Mules and Men *(Philadelphia, PA: J.B. Lippincott, 1935, reprinted, with an introduction by Darwin Turner, NY: Harper and Row, 1970);* Their Eyes Were Watching God *(Philadelphia, PA: J.B. Lippincott, 1937, reprinted Urbana, IL: University of Illinois Press, 1978);* Tell My Horse *(Philadelphia, PA: J.B. Lippincott, 1938);* Moses, Man of the Mountain *(Philadelphia, PA: J.B. Lippincott, 1939, reprinted, Chatham, NJ: Chatham Bookseller, 1974);* Dust Tracks on a Road *(Philadelphia: J.B. Lippincott, 1942, reprinted, with an introduction by Larry Neal, NY: J.B. Lippincott, 1971);* Seraph on the Suwanee *(NY: Scribner, 1948); (edited by Cheryl Wall)* Zora Neale Hurston: Novels and Stories *(2 vols., Library of America, 1995).*

Selected stories: "John Redding Goes to Sea," in Stylus *(May 1921, pp. 11–22); "Drenched in Light," in* Opportunity *(December 1924, pp. 371–374); "Spunk," in* Opportunity *(June 1925, pp. 171–173, reprinted in* The New Negro, *edited by Alain Locke, NY: Albert and Charles Boni, 1925, pp. 105–111); "Muttsy," in* Opportunity *(August 1926, pp. 246–250); "The Eatonville Anthology," in* Messenger *(September, October and November 1926, pp. 261–262+); "Color Struck: A Play," in* Fire!! *(November 1926, pp. 7–15); "Sweat," in* Fire!! *(November 1926, pp. 40–45); "The First One: A Play" in* Ebony and Topaz *(edited by Charles S. Johnson, NY: National Urban League, 1927, pp. 53–57); "Cudjo's Own Story of the Last African Slaver," in* Journal of Negro History *(October 1927, pp. 648–663); "How It Feels To Be Colored Me," in* World Tomorrow *(May 1928, pp. 215–216); "Hoodoo in America," in* Journal of American Folklore *(October–December 1931, pp. 317–418); "The Gilded Six-Bits," in* Story *(August 1933, pp. 60–70); "Characteristics of Negro Expression," "Conversions and Visions," "Shouting," "The Sermon," "Mother Catherine," "Uncle Monday," "Spirituals and Neo-Spirituals," in* Negro: An Anthology *(edited by* ***Nancy Cunard,** *London: Wishart, 1934); "The Fire and the Cloud," in* Challenge *(September 1934, pp. 10–14); "The 'Pet Negro' System," in* American Mercury *(May 1943, pp. 593–600); "High John De Conqueror," in* American Mercury *(October 1943, pp. 450–458); "Negroes Without Self-Pity," in* American Mercury *(November 1943, pp. 601–603); "The Last Slave Ship," in* American Mercury *(March 1944, pp. 351–358); "My Most Humiliating Jim Crow Experience," in* Negro Digest *(June 1944, pp. 25–26); "Crazy for the Democracy," in* Negro Digest *(December 1945, pp. 45–48); "Conscience of the Court," in* Saturday Evening Post *(March 18, 1950, pp. 22–23, 112–122); "I Saw Negro Votes Peddled," in* American Legion Magazine *(November 1950, pp. 12–13+); "What White Publishers Won't Print," in* Negro Digest *(April 1950, pp. 85–89); "A Negro Voter Sizes Up Taft," in* Saturday Evening Post *(December 8, 1951, pp. 29+).*

The ambiguity surrounding Zora Neale Hurston's birth date seems ominously connected to her uncertain gravesite, a testament both to the elusiveness of fame as well as to the searing certainty of race and sex discrimination. Contemporary critics and writers, like **Mary Helen Washington** and **Alice Walker**, consider Hurston to be the unacknowledged spiritual mother of the many successful African-American women writers from mid-century to the present, and are committed to seeing that her literary achievements get their well-deserved recognition. Indeed, Hurston, who hailed from a remote town in an underdeveloped state, transcended the severe restrictions that early-20th-century America placed on her race and sex to become a key contributor to the black cultural and literary revolution known as the Harlem Renaissance.

The acclaimed "ethnographer" of Eatonville was born in that remote Florida wilderness town with certainty on the 7th of January, and with less certainty, either in 1891 (according to one brother and a 1900 census taker) or 1901 (according to her literary biographer and various other sources). Zora, named by her mother after a neighbor woman, was notoriously misleading on the subject of her age. For a woman who was compelled to plead for money for shoes from her patron in her writing years and to live off welfare in her closing years, this matter of age might seem an odd vanity.

The sixth of eight children of a mulatto father and an educated mother, Zora took well to country living in a large house in the first incorporated all-black town of Eatonville, just five miles away from Orlando. According to literary biographer Robert Hemenway, Zora was an imaginative, intelligent, and adventurous child who was encouraged by her mother **Lucy Ann Hurston** to "jump at de sun" and urged to quell her unseemly ambitions (for a black female) by her father. John Hurston was a formidable man who owned property and provided well for his family despite his philandering ways, until the untimely death of Lucy Ann on September 19, 1904. He remarried shortly thereafter, and Zora's stepmother had little time for Lucy Ann's youngest, elementary-school-age daughter. Zora was sent off to live with an older brother in Jacksonville, Florida, where she learned for the first

Zora
Neale
Hurston

time the unpleasant lesson of what it was like to be black in a white society. When funds dried up, she moved back and forth between Eatonville and Jacksonville, working at times as a maid and pursuing her passion for reading before she landed a position as a "wardrobe girl in a Gilbert and Sullivan repertory company," writes Hemenway. Less than two years later, she left the troupe and found herself in Baltimore, Maryland, enrolled in Morgan Academy, where she completed high school a year later (June of 1918) while living with a minister's family. At this time and for the next several years, she worked alternately as waitress, maid, and manicurist. Although the financial and personal hardships of these schooling years may have portended her later destitution, they also served as a testing ground in the art of survival. Time and time again, Zora Neale Hurston had to fall back on this art.

By 1923, Hurston was enrolled in Howard University, an all-black school in Washington, D.C. She had completed prep school at Howard in 1919, and in 1920 she met her first husband Howard Sheen, a fellow student, jazz pianist, and future doctor. After he went off to medical school at the University of Chicago, they maintained a long-distance relationship and did not marry until 1927. Hurston had her own as yet unshaped aspirations for which she was just setting a course in Washington, despite a checkered scholastic performance. More important, at Howard University Hurston also became involved with the campus literary club and the evening discussion groups at the home of black poet **Georgia Douglas Johnson**. Her first literary success came in 1924 when the campus magazine, the *Stylus,* published Hurston's "John Redding Goes to Sea." The short story combined folklore and fiction and grounded Hurston's inimitable art in Eatonville, Florida, and the cast of black characters and stories that populated it. Her publication and Washington connections brought Hurston to the attention of New York and key proponents and architects of the Harlem Renaissance, most particularly Charles S. Johnson, editor of *Opportunity.* Other successes soon followed. "Drenched in Light" was published in the New York-based *Opportunity* magazine in December of 1924, followed by "Spunk" and a contest-winning play entitled "Color Struck" in 1925. Zora Neale Hurston accepted the prize and an invitation to a dinner in New York City. Her course was set.

Johnson, Georgia Douglas. *See Women of the Harlem Renaissance.*

By 1926–27, Hurston had earned a place in the black literary world as well as a scholarship to exclusive, albeit white, Barnard College. The awards dinner had also introduced her to noted novelist ***Fannie Hurst** who kindly hired Hurston as a secretary, a function for which the fledgling writer and living-room performer-storyteller showed little talent. While Zora enjoyed entertaining her new circle of friends with her wit and lively down-home stories, she was applying herself fervently to the science of anthropology which allowed her, writes Hemenway, "to confront her culture both emotionally and analytically." It must have pleased Hurston to learn that her own lived experience was also an area of legitimate and timely study. By 1927, Zora Neale Hurston—singular black student of Barnard College, personal secretary of a famous novelist, and a published writer herself—welcomed anthropology as a future profession and means of supporting herself. Her hopefulness at this time may have prompted her to marry her long-distance sweetheart, Howard Sheen, on May 19, 1927, in St. Augustine, Florida. But she could not play the role of the traditional wife willing to give up all to follow her husband. She returned to New York and her promising career, and the divorce was finalized on July 7, 1931.

Throughout the 1920s, Zora rode the wave of the Jazz Age in America with its unprecedented freedom and white liberal principles that sparked an interest in black oppression, culture, and history. The National Association for the Advancement of Colored People (NAACP) was born and the "New Negro" was migrating to the North for better jobs and equal opportunities. Black artists and intellectuals led the way, ironically referring to themselves as the "Nigerati." The push for social consciousness and change within this cultural movement was strong, but Hurston, more taken with exploring and valuing the black aesthetic, shied away from social and political agendas in her work and the push to redeem the black race. Besides, she did not necessarily agree that blacks were in need of redemption, a view that stemmed from her largely positive experience growing up in Eatonville, a most unique and independent all-black community.

Hurston saw folklore as a genuine poetry of her people, and she attempted to capture its simplicity, sound, humor, and wisdom in her fictional writing. Her studies in anthropology under Dr. Franz Boas encouraged Hurston to pursue the science or study of folklore, resulting in a lifelong interest in collecting African-American and Caribbean folklore. According to Hemenway, she straddled the respectable and disciplined world of Barnard and the imaginative and liberating world of the writer. Indeed, black folklore served as a bridge between Hurston's racial past and her evolving artist-intellectual self.

After receiving her B.A. degree from Barnard, her success as oral and written bearer of African-American stories led to a grant from the Columbia University anthropology department in 1928, under the direction of Boas. "Anthropology," according to critic **Lillie P. Howard**, "gave Zora the analytical tools for returning to the South and tapping the rich reservoir of material passed around among black folks every day." Other collecting trips followed, subsidized by wealthy white patron **Charlotte Osgood Mason**, who supported ethnic arts as well as other artists like Langston Hughes. Mason also ruled her pet artists with an iron fist, requiring a contract in which Hurston agreed to give Mason any publication rights over all material collected. Hurston was amply supplied with a car and money for travel, but she found herself in the uncomfortable position of having to please "godmother"; Mason's patronage was problematic, notes Hemenway, despite what Hurston referred to as their "psychic bond," and led to "dependency and bitterness."

The demands of the scientific approach also caused Hurston some problems. In one instance, she provided her director with an account of Cudjo Lewis, "only survivor of the last-known slave ship," in a published article entitled "Cudjo's Own Story of the Last African Slaver." Although she had interviewed Lewis herself, Hurston plagiarized most of the information from a previously published account, a fact which remained obscured until well after her death. Hurston was evidently too preoccupied with collecting folklore and hoodoo and planning a black opera with friend and sometime-fellow traveler Langston Hughes. Evidently the rigid documentation requirements of the academic approach did not suit her free-wheeling style. Her lack of discernment in this regard may well have contributed to the later fall-out with Hughes over rights to their mutual theatrical enterprise, "Mule Bone: A Comedy of Negro Life." During a folklore trip through the South in 1928, they had agreed to write and produce a work that would reflect the true nature and spirit of black life, minus the slapstick and patronizing characteristic of its predecessors. At the center of their disagreement was authorship and a secretary whom Hughes wanted to include as a partner, compounded by the possibility of jealousy on Hurston's part. The disagreement resulted in bitter personal conflict, litigation, and controversy, and "Mule Bone" never made it to the stage.

While Hughes broke away from "godmother" Mason, Hurston continued to be financially, and in some ways emotionally, dependent on her until 1932, nearly a year beyond the original contract. In the meantime, Hurston submitted numerous folklore manuscripts, according to biographer Hemenway, only to receive the proverbial rejection letter. Mason did agree to put up a sum of money in early 1932 to help Hurston produce "A Great Day," a well-reviewed musical based on her folklore that later made appearances in Chicago and Florida. Without any source of income, Hurston knocked around New York City, struggling with the fear and uncertainty that accompany unemployment and tenuous artistic projects. She had to hock her own car and radio to get "A Great Day" to the stage and never recouped her losses despite successful performances at the John Golden Theater and the New School of Social Research in New York. Broadway, however, declined to pick up the show, and, her days of patronage over, Hurston accepted a position in the Creative Literature Department at Rollins College of Winter Park, Florida, with the intent of producing a program of black art in concert. Her short-lived appointment did not bring Hurston the professional satisfaction or financial rewards she desired. By the spring of 1932, she returned to Eatonville jobless, scratching around for money to finance basic necessities and recovering from the stomach problems that plagued her throughout her adult life.

> I have been in Sorrow's kitchen and licked out all the pots. Then I have stood on the peaky mountain wrapped in rainbows, with a harp and a sword in my hands.
>
> **—Zora Neale Hurston**

Stress-free Eatonville offered the soothing balm that Hurston needed to heal and reconnect with her muse. A flurry of professional and literary activity followed. After seeing "The Gilded Six-Bits" published in *Story* magazine in 1933, she enjoyed a brief stint as a drama instructor at Bethune-Cookman, an all-black college in Daytona, Florida. But none of her various academic appointments lasted for very long—due in part to a lack of sufficient support and resources—and this one was no exception. By 1932, she had completed work on her collection of field notes begun two years earlier and intended for her first book of folklore, the highly regarded *Of Mules and Men* (1935). Nevertheless, it was *Jonah's Gourd Vine,* an autobiographical novel, that first found a publishing home with Lippincott in 1934. She wrote her first novel on a card table in a one-room house with barely enough money for food, since Lippincott withheld the $200 advance until the completed manuscript was submitted. It took her three months to write, and she had to borrow the money to mail it to the publisher.

Jonah's Gourd Vine paved the way for *Mules and Men.* This collection of folktales, legends, hoodoo practices, and songs cinched Hurston's reputation as an authority on African-American folklore. The narrator functions as both participant and observer, thereby dramatizing the process of collecting folklore and drawing the reader into the experience. Hurston's unique talent was making a foreign experience entertaining and accessible, particularly to a white audience. Black critics later turned this talent against her, claiming that she catered to a white audience. Clearly, Hurston found herself in a Catch-22 position. Her lifelong goal was to make black art and folklore known to the masses, and to do this she had to work with mostly white-owned publishing companies. In addition, unlike many of her black contemporaries, Hurston concerned herself with celebrating black art and life rather than with railing against an unjust white system. Her views and art did not match the tenor of social protest that was so fashionable in the 1930s and early 1940s. As a result, Hurston found herself both out of step and the persistent target of criticism.

Early 1935 was punctuated by a failed love affair with a much younger college student, even as Hurston was negotiating a fellowship with Columbia University in the doctoral program. She had attracted the attention of the Rosenwald Foundation with a variation of "A Great Day"—retitled "Singing Steel"—that was performed in Chicago in November of 1934. Hurston was keen on this popular way of bringing black folk art to the people and of shattering racist myths and stereotypes. But the practical realities of financing combined with her need to earn a living made it impossible for Hurston to continue mounting costly theatrical productions. Both Bethune-Cookman College and Fisk University flirted with Hurston, whose reputation by now was established, with talk of heading a dramatic department. Neither of these prospects materialized, however, leaving Hurston in the precarious position of earning her living with her pen. Nor did the plans with Columbia materialize, partly because of Hurston's own ambivalence as well as the foundation's concerns over Hurston's unorthodox methods and field-study plans.

Opposite page

Zora Neale Hurston

June of 1935 found Hurston living in Belle Glade, Florida, working with a young folklorist involved with collecting black recordings in the South for the Library of Congress. Indeed, one of Hurston's invaluable contributions to the folklore collection was the ease and safety with which she and her white counterparts moved through rural black communities. This year also marked Hurston's final departure from the study of folklore as an academic and scientific inquiry. Instead, the folk materials she gathered so assiduously would serve her art as a writer. Two years later, *Their Eyes Were Watching God,* her finest and most successful novel, was published, appropriately setting forth a black female heroine in search of selfhood and liberation. The years 1936–37 were good ones for Hurston who, while working for the WPA Federal Theater Project, was also awarded two Guggenheim fellowships for another folklore trip to the West Indies, one which extended into the following year and sent Hurston home with her most serious intestinal illness.

After the publication of a third book of folktales, *Tell My Horse,* she went to work for the Florida Federal Writers Project, collecting folklore until 1939 and contributing to a volume called *The New Negro.* Not one to sit still for very long at a desk, Hurston accepted another position teaching and developing a drama department, this time at the North Carolina College for Negroes in Durham. Again pleading lack of resources, she spent most of her time planning to mount a play with Paul Green at Chapel Hill's theater department. Although the play never materialized and the teaching position did not last, another book, *Moses, Man of the Mountain,* was published in 1939, marking a productive era for the struggling writer-folklorist. The same year also saw her second and ultimately unsuccessful foray into marriage with a former WPA colleague, the much younger Albert Price III, on June 27 in Fernadina, Florida. Although the divorce was not final until 1943, the marriage was over long before that, as Hurston's work proved always to be her primary occupation.

At the suggestion of her editor, Hurston reluctantly agreed to write her autobiography in 1941, and to do so she accepted an invitation to stay with **Katherine Mershon**, a wealthy friend living in California. While there, she did some writing for Paramount Studios, and even though her work was interrupted by the devastating attack on Pearl Harbor, Hurston completed the first manuscript of *Dust Tracks on a Road* (1942). The editor reportedly took many liberties with the manuscript, excising some of Hurston's strong anti-military views, among others. But she needed the money and as usual was not in a position to argue with her white employers. Ironically, despite its popularity and positive reviews, this book drew much criticism for its "whitewashing" of the black experience and its appeal to white readers. But always iconoclastic, Hurston nurtured her own vision, refusing to paint a bleak picture of black life which did not match her optimistic view and celebration of black courage, culture, and art.

Dust Tracks proved to be a blend of autobiography and fiction, perhaps because of Hurston's affinity for the "tall tale" combined with her self-protectiveness. Entertaining and engaging, *Dust Tracks* is not the source to consult for the facts of Hurston's life but for the true flavor of her expansive spirit. As it turned out, by 1942 and the time of its publication, Hurston's successful creative productivity had run its course. Why? Certainly, Hurston's continuous struggle with keeping poverty at bay must have taken its toll, along with the lingering effects of her chronic stomach illness and lack of medical care. The controversy and criticism spurred by her unpopular nationalistic views also plagued Hurston, and she often resorted to defending herself in print. But the crowning factor in her professional and personal demise may well be traced to her arrest in New York City in September of 1948 on contrived charges of immoral acts with a ten-year-old boy. A thorough investigation revealed that Hurston's landlord and the mother of the boy acted vindictively against Hurston for giving some unwanted advice on the care of her mildly retarded son. Hurston was out of the country collecting folklore on the dates of the alleged criminal acts, but that did not prevent her arrest or the scandal that followed once the story was picked up by the black newspapers. The experience must have stung Hurston who, having suffered the indignity of the unfair arrest, learned later that it was a black man who peddled the story to the newspapers. Though the court dismissed the charges a year later, the damage to Hurston's life and reputation had already occurred in the press.

Despite her penchant for travel and up until her traumatic arrest in 1948, Hurston spent a good deal of her time during the 1940s living peacefully on houseboats in Florida, cruising along the pristine Halifax River when she was not docked at Daytona. During these tranquil years before the scandal, she planned another collecting trip, this time to the Honduras, but it never panned out. She continued writing with little success, even after being picked up by Scribner's, publishing home of friend and fellow Florida writer ***Marjorie Kinnan Rawlings**. Times got tougher for Hurston when she had no source of income, and the "woman who had tra-

versed the rural South," writes Hemenway, "living in turpentine camps and sawmills, playing jook songs on her guitar while packing a pearl-handled revolver in her purse" suddenly found herself "staring at a bleak future."

After 1948, Hurston resumed living and working but never quite recovered her former ebullient self. While magazines picked up her articles periodically, her full-length works were met with rejection, including a major study she completed on the life of Herod the Great. From 1951 to 1956, she lived reasonably peacefully in a cabin for $20 a month with her two dogs at Eau Gallie, Florida, and "by 1956 Zora was middle-aged and considerably overweight," notes Hemenway, with little money and no energy to earn it. After being expelled by her white landlord, Hurston wandered around Florida from one low-paying job to another—a technical librarian at Patrick Air Force Base, a substitute teacher at Lincoln Park Academy, a contributor to the *Fort Pierce Journal,* a maid for a wealthy woman in Miami—none of which fulfilled her or provided much of an income. The years before her death found her suffering from obesity, ulcers, and the persistent intestinal problems, while living in Fort Pierce, Florida, in a rented green concrete-block house. The landlord, a physician who also took it upon himself to look after Hurston, waived the $10-weekly rent when he perceived the direness of her situation. He could not prevent the stroke she suffered, however, which sent her to the St. Lucie County Welfare home in October of 1959. Refusing to inform family and friends of her impoverished condition, she died virtually alone and penniless from hypertensive heart disease on January 28, 1960. Contributions paid for her burial in a segregated Fort Pierce cemetery. Although she was remembered fondly by some and not so fondly by others, the poor black girl from rural Florida managed to leave an indelible mark on the landscape of African-American folklore and literature. As Lillie Howard put it: "A picaro, she had wandered incessantly, anchoring from time to time but always casting off for farther horizons. She had soared to the skies only to fall back to earth."

In 1973, renowned African-American writer Alice Walker returned to Hurston's home and place of burial, distressed to find that her grave could not be pinpointed with certainty because it lacked a marker. She had one made and placed on the approximate location, and the epitaph she created intends to correct the longstanding wrong done to Hurston's life and work. It reads:

"A Genius of the South"
1901–1960
Novelist, Folklorist, Anthropologist

SOURCES:

Hemenway, Robert E. *Zora Neale Hurston: A Literary Biography.* Foreword by Alice Walker. Chicago, IL: University of Illinois Press, 1977.

Howard, Lillie P. *Zora Neale Hurston.* Boston, MA: Twayne Publishers, 1980.

Hurston, Zora Neal. *Dust Tracks on a Road.* Urbana, IL: University of Illinois Press, 1984.

I Love Myself When I Am Laughing and Then Again When I Am Looking Mean and Impressive: A Zora Neale Hurston Reader. Edited by Alice Walker. NY: The Feminist Press, 1979.

Zora! Zora Neale Hurston: A Woman and Her Community. Compiled and edited by Nathiri. Orlando, FL: Sentinel Communication, 1991.

SUGGESTED READING:

Lyons, Mary E. *Sorrow's Kitchen: The Life of Zora Neale Hurston* (juvenile). NY: Scribner, 1993.

Wall, Cheryl, ed. *Zora Neale Hurston: Novels and Stories.* 2 vols., Library of America, 1995 (complete works of Hurston).

COLLECTIONS:

Zora Neale Hurston Museum in Belle Glade, Florida.

Kathleen A. Waites Lamm,
Professor of English and Women's Studies at Nova Southeastern University in Fort Lauderdale, Florida

Hussey, Ruth (1914—)

***American actress, nominated for an Academy Award for her work in* The Philadelphia Story.** *Name variations: from age 17 until she began acting in movies, used her stepfather's name O'Rourke. Born on October 30, 1914, in Providence, Rhode Island; daughter of George and Julia Hussey: graduated from Classical and Technical High School, Providence, Rhode Island; attended Pembroke Women's College (later Brown University); attended University of Michigan; married Robert Longenecker (talent agent and television executive), on August 9, 1942; children: two sons, one daughter.*

Selected theater: made professional debut as Kay in the touring company of Dead End *(1937); made New York City debut as Mary Mathews in* State of the Union *(Hudson Theater, November 1945); replaced Madeleine Carroll as Agatha Reed in* Goodbye, My Fancy *(Morosco Theater, November 1948); portrayed Julie Cavendish in* The Royal Family *(New York City Center, January 1951).*

Selected filmography: The Big City *(1937);* Madame X *(1937);* Judge Hardy's Children *(1938);* Rich Man, Poor Girl *(1938);* Spring Madness *(1938);* Honolulu *(1939);* Within the Law *(1939);* Maisie *(1939);* Blackmail *(1939);* The Women *(1939);* Fast and Furious *(19139);* Another Thin Man *(1939);* Northwest Passage *(1940);* Susan and God *(1940);*

Ruth Hussey

The Philadelphia Story *(1940);* Flight Command *(1941);* Free and Easy *(1941);* Married Bachelor *(1941);* H. M. Pulham, Esq. *(1941);* Pierre of the Plains *(1942);* Tennessee Johnson *(1943);* Tender Comrade *(1944);* The Uninvited *(1944);* Marine Raiders *(1944);* Bedside Manner *(1945);* I, Jane Doe *(1948);* The Great Gatsby *(1949);* Louisa *(1950);* Mr. Musica *(1950);* That's My Boy *(1951);* Stars and Stripes Forever *(1952);* The Lady Wants Mink *(1953);* The Facts of Life *(1960).*

Born in 1914, Ruth Hussey studied theater in college and was a fashion commentator on the radio in her hometown of Providence, Rhode Island, before heading to New York to pursue a stage career. She supported herself as a Powers model before landing the role of Kay in a touring company of *Dead End* (1937). An MGM talent scout saw her perform in Los Angeles, and although she had not considered the movies, Hussey tested for the studio and won a five-year contract. She had only small roles in her first few films, but by the 1940s had established herself as a second lead, usually playing sophisticated, worldly women. Of her 38 or so film roles, her best was the brittle magazine photographer in *The Philadelphia Story* (1940), for which she was nominated for an Academy Award. Notable among her other films were

H.M. Pulham, Esq. (1941), *The Uninvited* (1944), and *The Great Gatsby* (1949).

Hussey returned to the Broadway stage in 1945, receiving excellent reviews for her performance as the female lead in *State of the Union,* opposite Ralph Bellamy. Three years later, she replaced ***Madeleine Carroll** in *Goodbye, My Fancy,* and in 1951, she starred as Julie Cavendish in the City Center's production of *The Royal Family*. She appeared in films sporadically in the 1950s and also starred on television in such shows as "Climax," "Studio One," and "Alfred Hitchcock Presents." She won an Emmy nomination in 1955 for her performance in the title role of *Craig's Wife* ("Lux Video Theater"). During the 1970s, she was seen in "Marcus Welby, M.D." and "The New Perry Mason."

Hussey, who married television executive Robert Longenecker in 1942, had three children. After the mid-1950s, she spent less time on her acting career and admitted that, although she enjoyed working in films, she never had a lot of actor friends. "My real pals," she said, "were in the make-up department."

SOURCES:

Lamparski, Richard. *Whatever Became of . . . ?* 4th Series. NY: Crown, 1973.

McGill, Raymond, ed. *Notable Names in the American Theater*. Clifton, NJ: James T. White, 1976.

Barbara Morgan,
Melrose, Massachusetts

Husted, Marjorie Child

(c. 1892–1986)

American home economist and businesswoman who helped popularize the image of "Betty Crocker." *Born Marjorie Child in Minneapolis, Minnesota, around 1892; died in 1986; one of the four children of Sampson Reed (a lawyer) and Alice Albert (Webber) Child; graduated from the West High School of Minneapolis; B.A. and B.Ed. from the University of Minnesota, 1913; married K. Wallace Husted, in October 1925.*

Born around 1892, raised in Minneapolis, Minnesota, Marjorie Husted graduated from the University of Minnesota and began her career as secretary to the Infant Welfare Society of Minneapolis. During World War I, she served with the Red Cross, first as director of the information and publicity bureau of the home-service department of the northern division, and later as assistant director of field service in the same division. Following the war, she worked for the Women's Cooperative Alliance until 1923, then secured a job in promotion and marketing with the Creamette Company of Minneapolis. After a year, she moved to the Washburn-Crosby Company, makers of Gold Medal Flour, where she served as a home economics field representative. In 1926, she instituted a home-service department for Washburn-Crosby, with a staff of cooks, nutritionists, and home economics advisers that answered homemaking inquiries from consumers over the signature "Betty Crocker," a name used for that purpose since 1921. In 1928, when the company merged and consolidated into General Mills, Inc., the home-service department was renamed the Betty Crocker Homemaking Service.

For the next 18 years, Husted served as director of the department, helping to transform "Betty Crocker" into the image of the perfect American housewife, an image that became synonymous with General Mills. ***Neysa McMein**, a leading commercial artist of the day, was commissioned to paint a portrait of Betty Crocker, whose likeness and signature was then reproduced on numerous company products. A series of day-time radio shows was launched, bringing the voice of Betty Crocker to the nation's housewives. In 1945, *Fortune Magazine* wrote, "Without much doubt the woman best known to housewives of the U.S., with the exception of Mrs. Roosevelt, is Betty Crocker." A *Business Week* poll, conducted in February 1948, concurred, reporting that "Betty Crocker" was known to 91% of all American housewives, many of whom believed that she was an actual person.

In 1948, Husted was named consultant in advertising, public relations, and home service to General Mills, a position equivalent to a vice presidency at the time. That same year, she served as a consultant to the U.S. Department of Agriculture on food conservation. In 1949, she was honored by the Women's National Press Club in Washington and received the Advertising Woman of the Year Award from the Advertising Federation of America. In 1950, Husted left General Mills to form her own consulting firm, Marjorie Child Husted and Associates. However, "Betty Crocker," with a periodic streamlining of her hairstyle, still survives.

SOURCES:

Current Biography. NY: H.W. Wilson, 1949.

Gutis, Philip S. "Marjorie Husted Dead at 94; Helped Create Betty Crocker," in *The New York Times Biographical Service*. December 1986, pp. 1449–1450.

McHenry, Robert, ed. *Famous American Women*. NY: Dover, 1983.

Hutchinson, Anne (1591–1643)

English-born Puritan, religious leader and teacher, nurse and midwife who resided briefly in the Massa-

chusetts Bay Colony until banished in 1638 following her conviction of heresy. *Name variations: Anne Marbury Hutchinson; Mrs. Hutchinson. Pronunciation: HUTCH-in-sun. Born Anne Marbury around July 17, 1591, in Alford, Lincolnshire, England; died at Pelham Bay settlement, Long Island, during an Indian raid in August or September 1643; daughter of Francis (a spiritual divine) and Bridget (Dryden) Marbury; learned reading, writing, and arithmetic at home from her father; married William Hutchinson, on August 9, 1612; children: Edward (b. 1613), Susanna (b. 1614), Richard (b. 1615), Faith (b. 1617), Bridget (b. 1619), Francis (b. 1620), Elizabeth (b. 1622), William (b. 1623), Samuel (b. 1624), Anne (b. 1626), Mary (b. 1628), Katherine (b. 1630), William (b. 1631), Susanna (b. 1633), Zuriel (b. 1636), and miscarried 16th child in 1637.*

Family moved to London (1605); moved with husband and children to the Massachusetts Bay Colony (1634); tried for heresy (1637); excommunicated, then publicly recanted her religious views (1638); moved to colony on Rhode Island (1638); following continued religious persecution and death of her husband, moved to Long Island to establish settlement at Pelham Bay (1642).

Anne Hutchinson was born into a family of small gentry status in rural Elizabethan England, only three years after the defeat of the Spanish Armada. She grew up in a period that has been characterized as energetic and spontaneous, enthusiastic about meeting life head-on, and even tolerant of moderate religious dissent, but this was largely a propagandistic depiction of late Elizabethan England. The early decades of the 17th century were ones of political and religious tension throughout the country, which prompted much of the emigration to the colonies in America. And while the lives of women at this time have typically been regarded as a constant cycle of pregnancy, birth, and death, these women could, and did, feel persecution on religious grounds as thoroughly as their fathers, husbands, or sons. Just such experience resulted in the moves by Anne Hutchinson and her family from England to Massachusetts Bay Colony, then to Rhode Island and, finally, to Long Island within a span of slightly less than ten years.

Anne's father Francis Marbury was a spiritual English divine who was censured on more than one occasion by the established Church of England. Marbury had strong Puritan leanings, tending to austerity in moral and religious matters, but denied the label of Puritan when he was brought before St. Paul's Consistory Court, London, in 1578. To his personal misfortune, he still continued to preach in the Puritan manner and endured 15 years of enforced silence from preaching. In those years, he was a teacher, and by 1590 he was headmaster of the Grammar School in Alford, Lincolnshire, where all his pupils were boys, since the little education allowed to girls at the time usually occurred within the home.

By 1587, Marbury had married his second wife **Bridget Dryden**, who came from a strongly Puritan family. Anne was their third child, born in July 1591. Marbury was preaching regularly around this time, at the Church of St. Wilfrid in the small market town of Alford. In sermons that stressed his affiliation with the Church of England, he also denounced certain practices and called for improved training and education for its clergy.

Anne grew up in a large family, which eventually included 12 sisters and brothers, as well as two half-sisters; the household was rife with religious discussion, influenced by her father's relatively liberal beliefs. Few records remain from which to reconstruct Anne's childhood years in Alford. In keeping with the status of the Marbury family, she and her sisters probably received some education from their father at home, with emphasis on "necessary" reading, writing, and arithmetic, that was considered practical and appropriate for women in early 17th-century English society. As an elder daughter, along with her half-sisters, Anne also had nursery duties, helping her mother in the care of the younger children, and probably assisting in their delivery.

The development of Anne's conduct, and many of her social attitudes, were heavily influenced by her father. Some biographers maintain that she modeled herself strongly according to his example. For reading materials, she had the Bible (in the Geneva translation) and her father's sermons and writings, at a time when matters of religion were generally fueled by the religious controversy that coincided with the early reign of England's King James I. In 1605, Anne, her parents, and nine siblings moved to London because her father had been appointed to the Church of St. Martin in the Vintry, perhaps as rector. This move, of approximately 140 miles distance, took the girl in her teens from the simple world of rural Lincolnshire into one of unheard-of luxuries that included windowed houses, exotic fruits and plants, and books; it also drew the Marbury family into the larger world of religious nonconformity and political plots.

Religious nonconformists, also known as Protestant dissenters, who declared their disagreement with the doctrines and practices of the Church of England could face penalties ranging from proscription of worship to disqualification from religious office during the reigns of Queen ***Elizabeth I**, and then King James I.

In London, Anne thrived. Her midwifery skills were honed by her attendance at her mother's deliveries of her brothers Thomas and Anthony, in 1606 and 1608, and her sister **Katherine Marbury** in 1610—at a time of increased royal hostility toward women and midwives. From this experience, she began to form her own "rebellious" ideas concerning what she viewed as the inapplicability of the doctrine of original sin to the innocence of newborns; this was at odds with the then-prevalent notion regarding predestination of all souls. Meanwhile, acquaintances and family friends visited the Marbury family during their tenure in London, including William Hutchinson and his father. Textile merchants who made periodic trips from Alford to London, the Hutchinsons stopped by the rectory at St. Martin's whenever they had the opportunity.

In 1611, the death of Francis Marbury meant the loss for Anne of the intellectual companionship and inspirational support she had always enjoyed from him; now the stubborn independence he had always encouraged in her were called upon in support of her grieving mother. Anne became a surrogate parent to her younger siblings, especially her youngest sister Katherine, who could be regarded in some ways as Anne's "first disciple."

At age 21, Anne wed farmer-merchant William Hutchinson and moved with him back to Alford. This marriage has been evaluated variously by her biographers, but most opinions seem to echo the estimation put forward by **Selma Williams**, that this was "one of history's all-time great romances—and, rare for the 17th century, a marriage of equals who respected each other's strengths. Several times during the next three decades, husband and wife would take turns sacrificing everything for the other." Their peers, however, were less generous in their comments on the couple, regarding Anne as dominant and authoritarian while regarding William as weak and wholly controlled by his wife.

Returned to Lincolnshire, Anne Hutchinson's cycle of pregnancy began with the birth and baptism of her first child, Edward, in late May 1613. During her married life, Hutchinson was pregnant, on average, every 15 to 23 months, and throughout a total of 16 pregnancies she relied heavily on piety and prayer to sustain and strengthen her. She was both primary caregiver and health provider for her increasing family. She also supervised the work of the few servants (who were frequently at work in the Hutchinsons' textile shop each morning by six o'clock) and ended the day with supper, followed by prayers and Bible reading. Within Alford, Hutchinson and her family seemed the very picture of respectability and prosperity.

One month before Anne's marriage to William, a new preacher, John Cotton, took over the pulpit of St. Botolph's Church, in the English village of Boston, near Alford. Since there was no preacher in Alford for the next few years, the Hutchinson family made semi-frequent trips to Boston to attend services led by Cotton. During Hutchinson's 1616–17 pregnancy with her fourth child, she experienced a period of "intense mental and spiritual conflict," trying to come to an understanding of her scripturalist interpretation of faith. Cotton's preaching at the time, which increasingly de-emphasized the doctrine that humans were born into a sinful condition, accorded with her "rebelliously Puritan" leanings, as she became less and less interested in ceremonies and rituals. Hutchinson began to follow Cotton's example of holding meetings in her own home, where she would sermonize and discuss personal interpretations and re-interpretations of Scripture with her growing, predominantly female, audience.

In the 1620s, as persecution of nonconformists began to increase, Cotton was harassed by Church of England authorities for his notion of an elite group within his congregation who held a special covenant with God. Coincident with this increase in religious tension was the publication of pamphlets in which the nature of women and the issue of female freedom of behavior were debated. Anne and William had already begun to reflect on the expediency of fleeing religious persecution in England, or of becoming nominal conformists, when the churchman William Laud rose to the office of privy councillor in 1627. Knowing Laud's plans to impose strict religious uniformity, with a particular emphasis on targeting Puritans and the Scots, Hutchinson's sense of anguish and personal crisis was intensified, and Cotton's tenure at St. Botolph's Church became increasingly uncertain. Eventually both Cotton and the Hutchinsons chose to remain in England, but not to conceal their Puritanism, and to work for the purification of the Church and the reformation of the government that they considered urgently necessary.

Anne
Hutchinson

In 1630, following the birth of their 12th child, the Hutchinsons underwent a period of acute personal crisis and grief. In September, their eldest daughter Susanna died within a week of her 16th birthday, and less than a month later 8-year-old Elizabeth died. Illness had prevented Cotton from preaching around that time, and Hutchinson felt the need of more support and inspiration than those around her could provide, especially in the face of accusations that the deaths of her daughters might be a judgment on the parents' sinfulness.

The Lord judgeth not as man judgeth, better to be cast out of the Church than to deny Christ.

—Anne Hutchinson

Laud's persecution of Protestant dissenters continued through the early 1630s, and by 1632 the Hutchinsons were again considering emigration as a means of escape. The death of William's father in the previous year gave the family the money to implement such a decision, and nonconformity charges levied against Cotton only served to strengthen Anne's resolve. The final incentive came when Laud was raised to the office of archbishop of Canterbury, with administrative control of the Church of England. The family decided on New England over Holland and the island of Barbados, and in preparation for departure they tried to become less visible in the village community. Treasured family possessions were given away, and the family business was put in the hands of William's brother John, but then the departure planned for 1633 was delayed because of the advanced stage of Hutchinson's 14th pregnancy. In July of that year, Cotton sailed for New England aboard the *Griffin,* with Hutchinson's oldest son Edward, who was 21, her brother-in-law Edward, and his wife Sarah.

In the summer of 1634, the Hutchinsons finally sailed from England, also aboard the *Griffin,* and arrived in Boston, Massachusetts Bay Colony, on September 18. The Atlantic crossing had been spiritually tumultuous. During the voyage, Hutchinson did not hesitate to voice her hope that New England would mean the end of what she perceived to be "the onerus dictum that women should be seen but never heard." After her announcement to the Reverend Zechariah Symmes that she would lead her own meetings once she was settled in the Colony, and that she held to a covenant of grace rather than the one of works, which was traditionally stressed in Puritan doctrine, she and the misogynistic Puritan preacher developed a mutual dislike of each other. Hutchinson also aroused hostility among others, including William Bartholomew, with her claims of receiving revelations, which contradicted the Puritan, gendered hierarchy. Bartholomew increasingly viewed Hutchinson and her daughter **Faith** as witches, and Reverend Symmes, upon arrival in Boston, advised the Boston church not to accept Hutchinson for membership without first subjecting her to a period of scrutiny. Thus religious controversy had become a significant part of her life by the time Hutchinson first stepped onto New England soil.

Although reunited with her family and her friend Cotton, Hutchinson had many adjustments to make in the strange New World. People around her spoke the same language, but everything from food to living conditions was unfamiliar: people drank water more often than beer, and sweetened foods with maple syrup instead of costly imported sugar. Under the influence of a marked shortage of women in nearly all of the North American colonies, women enjoyed a higher status than their European contemporaries. In early 17th-century colonial Massachusetts, however, marriage was the only acceptable life for women, and those who never married were neither respected nor allowed to exercise any authority over their lives. Women could expect little autonomy in the matter of choosing a potential mate, although they did enjoy some property and contract rights not available in England. Within the Massachusetts colony, however, Protestant dissenter doctrine was firmly opposed to "meddling women," or women who rebelled against their position within political, societal, and religious affairs. Such women were in fact considered subversive to the authority of both church and state.

Initially, Hutchinson and her family seemed valuable additions to the family-based, theocratic farming village of Boston. Small gentry origins gave Hutchinson enhanced social status over what she had known in England, and she had the admiration and regard of colonists whom she nursed through illnesses or helped in the delivery of their babies. She trained her servants well, instructed her children, and in March 1636, at age 44, was delivered of her 15th child. Hutchinson's first two years in the colony were happy ones. People were generally attracted to her, on the basis of her magnetic, forceful personality, as she expressed herself readily and encouraged other women in the village of Boston to do so. Among the colonists who were less kindly disposed toward her, however, were Thomas Dudley and John Winthrop, who was later governor of the colony. Winthrop, in particular, expressed a dislike of "intellectual women."

After a couple of years in Boston, Hutchinson again began to emulate the Reverend Cotton's practice of holding prayer meetings at her house. The gatherings began as a group of five or six women in their late 30s and early 40s who would meet weekly, easing their feelings of loneliness and isolation. Over the months, however, the group increased to an estimated 60 to 80 members, including men as well as women. Then the nature of the gatherings was expanded to include lecture-discussion gatherings on Mondays as well as the original meetings on Thursdays, and Hutchinson found herself rebuked by her friend Cotton for not attending the meetings led by others.

At the core of Hutchinson's religious outlook was a sense of individual initiative, and the worth and responsibility of the person. Boston clergy were initially pleased with her meetings, seeing them as an indication of "a glorious religious revival." But by the autumn of 1636, their concern had begun to shift to her leadership in the meetings. Early in 1637, her brother-in-law John Wheelwright began to preach on the covenants of grace and works; within two months the General Court, meeting in private session, found him guilty of sedition and contempt. By May 1637, opponents to Hutchinson were in political office and ready to act against her.

On August 30, 1637, the first synod ever called in New England, the Newtown Synod, began a nine-day meeting. When it was concluded, 82 of Hutchinson's religious opinions had been found either erroneous or blasphemous. After a two-month delay, Hutchinson faced criminal trial proceedings in Newtown, which was not her town of residence. She received legal counsel neither before nor during the trial and faced as many as 49 inquisitors, with John Winthrop, now governor of the colony, acting as both prosecutor and judge. At the core of the trial proceedings was the question of whether Hutchinson had broken the Fifth Commandment in failing to honor her heavenly Father and his earthly agents, the government of the colony. The inquisitors, led by Winthrop, questioned Hutchinson on her advocacy of a covenant of grace, to which she responded that to "preach a covenant of works for salvation, that is not truth." To these authorities, Hutchinson was presenting herself as a threat to the social and political stability of the colony, on the basis of her claim to leadership as a result of direct revelation from God. Those who desired to give witness on Hutchinson's behalf were bullied into silence, and her husband William was not allowed to testify for her. Hutchinson was being tried not only for her heretical views on matters such as revelation, grace, and predestination, but for her interpretation of the New Testament as preached by Massachusetts Puritan ministers. Personal grievances also came into play, as Governor Winthrop began the hearing with a personalized attack on the accused, condemning her behavior as both ungodly and unfeminine when he referred to her as an "American Jezebel." To her accusers, Hutchinson replied, "If you do condemn me for speaking what in my conscience I know to be truth I must commit myself unto the Lord."

The trial concluded with a sentence of banishment being imposed upon Hutchinson without actually delivering a guilty verdict. It was well into the autumn of 1637, and the court then determined that the weather was too harsh for a woman to leave the colony. She was held under house arrest, with the expectation that she would leave the colony in the spring of 1638. When her 16th pregnancy ended in a miscarriage sometime in the early months of that year, the lost life was rumored to have been "a monster" and the event was seen as an appropriate punishment for her threat to the marital family unit that was the base of Puritan Massachusetts society. In March 1638, Hutchinson made a public recantation of her views, but she had already been excommunicated by the Boston Church.

Hutchinson set out with her husband and children for the colony of Rhode Island, where they settled in the community of Aquidneck. Within a year, she was preaching, which provoked leaders in the Massachusetts colony to send a delegation to Aquidneck in 1640, but they failed to chasten the woman they had banished from their jurisdiction. From this time, she and her followers were declared *antinomians,* or people who refused to follow the moral laws of the Old Testament. In New England, this religious and social movement held particular appeal for women.

In 1642, with the death of William, Hutchinson lost her "beloved husband, best friend, devoted partner." In an effort to deal with her grief as well as continuing persecution directed from the Massachusetts colony, she decided to relocate with the six children still under her care. The beleaguered family set out for Long Island, a Dutch-held colony at the time, where Hutchinson helped to establish a settlement at Pelham Bay. But sometime in August or September of that year, the community came under Indian attack, and Hutchinson and five of her six children were killed. Her youngest daughter, taken into captivity by the attackers, was ransomed by the Dutch years later.

For as long as Puritan authority continued in New England, no written works discussed Anne Hutchinson, in either a positive or a neutral fashion. The first sympathetic account—which portrayed Hutchinson as a woman possessed of "a restless spirit, [and] a questioning mind"—appeared over 30 years after her death, as part of a general revilement of the Puritans and their tenets.

SOURCES:

Abramowitz, Isidore. *The Great Prisoners: The First Anthology of Literature Written in Prison.* Freeport, NY: Books for Libraries Press, 1972.

Battis, Emery. *Saints and Sectaries: Anne Hutchinson and the Antinomian Controversy in the Massachusetts Bay Colony.* Chapel Hill, NC: University of North Carolina Press, 1962.

Koehler, Lyle. "The Case of the American Jezebels: Anne Hutchinson and Female Agitation during the Years of Antinomian Turmoil, 1636–1640," in *William and Mary Quarterly.* 3rd series, Vol. XXXI, no. 1. January 1974, pp. 55–78.

Rugg, Winnifred King. *Unafraid: A Life of Anne Hutchinson.* Boston, MA: Houghton Mifflin, 1930.

Williams, Selma. *Divine Rebel: The Life of Anne Marbury Hutchinson.* NY: Holt, Rinehart and Winston, 1981.

SUGGESTED READING:

Barker-Benfield, Ben. "Anne Hutchinson and the Puritan Attitude toward Women" in *Feminist Studies.* Vol. 1, no. 1. Summer 1972, pp. 65–96.

Evans, Sara M. *Born for Liberty: A History of Women in America.* NY: The Free Press, 1989.

Donna Beaudin,
freelance writer in history, Guelph, Ontario, Canada

Hutchinson, Lucy (1620–post 1675)

English author. *Born 1620 in London, England; died after 1675; daughter of Sir Allen Apsley, lieutenant of the Tower of London, and Lucy St. John; educated by tutors; married John Hutchinson, in 1638 (died 1664); children: eight.*

Known principally for authoring her husband's biography, Memoirs of the Life of Colonel Hutchinson, *which was not published until 1806; also wrote* On the Principles of the Christian Religion, *for her daughter, and* On Theology, *both of which were published in 1817.*

Lucy Hutchinson was born in London in 1620, daughter of Sir Allen Apsley and **Lucy St. John**. According to her autobiography, she learned to read at age four and by age seven was studying music, dance, writing, needlework and language with eight different tutors. She spoke French, Latin, Greek, and Hebrew. After Lucy married John Hutchinson in 1638, they settled near Nottingham where they raised eight children (four girls and four boys), the last of which was born when Lucy was 42 years old. While her children studied, she translated part of Virgil's *Aeneid* and did a verse translation of six books of *De rerum natura* by Lucretius, although her deepening Puritanism later led her to disapprove of such things.

John Hutchinson was a supporter of Parliament during the English Civil War (1642–1646 and 1648–1651) and a colonel in that war. He became the governor of Nottingham Castle during that time and later served as a member of the Long Parliament for Nottinghamshire. In 1649, he was a judge at the trial of Charles I, and one of the signers of the king's death warrant. (Charles I was then publicly beheaded in London.) At the end of the Long Parliament in 1653, the Hutchinsons retired to Owthorpe. Ten years later, John Hutchinson was imprisoned in the Tower of London for his part in the king's execution. Lucy worked to save her husband during his incarceration, but he died of a fever in 1664, four months after being moved to Sandown Castle in Kent. For the next seven years, Lucy Hutchinson worked on his biography to preserve his memory for their children and to lessen her sorrow. Although biased in places, the work is considered one of the most valuable personal accounts of the Civil War—including the active roles women had in it—and of Puritan family life.

Included in the first edition of her memoirs of her husband was a portion of Lucy Hutchinson's autobiography and a poem she had written. The 1885 edition included some of her letters.

Karina L. Kerr, M.A.,
Ypsilanti, Michigan

Hu Tieh (1908–1989).

See Hu Die.

Hutson, Jean (1914–1998)

American library administrator and curator who was chief of the Schomburg Center for Research in Black Culture. *Born Jean Blackwell on September 4, 1914, in Sommerfield, Florida; died on February 4, 1998, in New York City; only child of Paul O. (a farmer) and Sarah (Myers) Blackwell (a school teacher); graduated from Douglass High School, Baltimore, Maryland, 1931; attended the University of Michigan; Barnard College, B.A., 1935; Columbia University School of Library Science, M.A., 1936; married Andy Razaf (a lyricist), in 1939 (divorced 1947); married John Hut-*

son (a librarian), in 1950 (died 1957); children: (second marriage) one daughter, Jean Frances (d. 1992).

Jean Hutson was born in 1914 in Sommerfield, Florida, a small town south of Jacksonville. At age four, she and her mother moved to her grandmother's home in Baltimore, where she received her education. Her father remained in Florida to attend his business but made frequent visits to see his family. Through a babysitter who ran a boardinghouse in Baltimore, Hutson met poet Langston Hughes. The two would maintain a lifelong friendship; he called her "baby sister." It was Hughes who introduced her to many of the leading artists and writers of the time when she journeyed to Harlem as a young girl.

Hutson was class valedictorian at Douglass High School in Baltimore, then attended the University of Michigan. After three years, she transferred to Barnard, where in 1935 she became the second black woman to graduate, the first being ***Zora Neale Hurston**. Hutson went on to receive a degree in library science from Columbia.

She returned home but was denied a job at the public library in Baltimore, because there were no more positions for blacks. She then went to New York, where she was hired as a librarian in the New York City Public Branch Library system. In 1939, Hutson married Andy Razaf, a lyricist who wrote songs for Fats Waller, but the marriage ended in divorce eight years later. (In 1950, she would marry a fellow librarian John Hutson, with whom she would have a daughter, **Jean Frances Hutson**.)

In 1948, Hutson became curator of the Schomburg Collection, named in honor of Arthur Schomburg, a Puerto Rican scholar of African descent who had donated his vast collection of books and documents to the New York Public Library. In 1972, after the Schomburg Collection was renamed the Schomburg Center for Research in Black Culture (New York Public Library), Hutson became chief, a position she held until 1980. Under her strong and capable direction, the library grew from 15,000 to 75,000 volumes and became an internationally recognized center for African-American research and scholarship.

During the integrationist movement of the 1940s and early 1950s, when the need for a separate archive devoted to the black experience was questioned, Hutson staunchly defended the library, and during times of budget crises, she fought to keep it operational, even lobbying the state legislature for funds. She expanded the library's collection of African art by acquiring

paintings by African-American artists and was instrumental in persuading her childhood friend Langston Hughes to donate his papers to the center. Under her administration, the library published its *Dictionary Catalog of the Schomburg Collection* (1962, with supplements in 1967 and 1972), which brought the library worldwide recognition. During her final years with the Schomburg, she was active in fundraising for a new library building, which, to her great pleasure, was under construction by the time of her retirement.

Despite her personal contributions to the Schomburg, Hutson credited much of the library's increasing growth and popularity to the turbulent 1960s. "Of course the Civil Rights movements in the United States and the success of the independence movements in Africa and the Caribbean were the powerful stimulants which brought about the identification of Black Americans with their African heritage and caused the terrific surge of interest in Black Studies. The Schomburg has been in the center of these surging tides."

Hutson lived in Harlem for most of her career and was active in the community, serving on numerous local boards, including the Manhattan Advisory Council of New York and the Urban League. She was also active with the American Library Association, the NAACP, and the National Urban League Guild. After her retirement, she remained in New York City and continued to lecture and consult. Jean Hutson died at Harlem Hospital in 1998, age 83.

SOURCES:

Igus, Toyomi, ed. *Great Women in the Struggle.* NJ: Just Us Books, 1991.

Obituary. *The Day* [New London, Connecticut]. February 2, 1998.

Smith, Jessie Carney, ed. *Notable Black American Women.* Detroit, MI: Gale Research, 1992.

Barbara Morgan,
Melrose, Massachusetts

Hutton, Barbara (1912–1979)

American heiress. *Name variations: (nickname) Bobbie Hutton. Born Barbara Woolworth Hutton on November 14, 1912, in New York City; died on May 11, 1979, in Los Angeles, California; daughter of Franklyn Hutton (a stockbroker) and Edna (Woolworth) Hutton; attended Miss Shinn's School for Girls, in Los Angeles, California; attended Santa Barbara School for Girls, Santa Barbara, California; graduated from Miss Porter's School for Girls, Farmington, Connecticut, 1929; married Prince Alexis Mdivani, on June 22, 1933 (divorced 1935); married Court Haugwitz-Reventlow, a count, in 1935 (divorced 1941); married Cary Grant (an actor), on July 8, 1942 (divorced 1945); married Prince Igor Troubetzkoy, on March 1, 1947 (divorced 1950); married Porfirio Rubirosa (a diplomat), on December 30, 1953 (divorced 1955); married Baron Gottfried von Cramm (a former German tennis ace), on November 8, 1955 (divorced 1960); married Raymond Doan (an artist), on April 7, 1964 (permanently separated 1971); children: (with Count Reventlow) one son, Lance Reventlow (d. 1973).*

Given the facts of her formative years, it is hardly surprising that Barbara Hutton squandered one of America's greatest fortunes, along with her life. She was born in New York City in 1912, the only child of Franklyn Hutton, vice president and partner in his brother's investment firm, The E.F. Hutton Company, and **Edna Woolworth Hutton**, daughter of dime-store magnate Frank Woolworth. Barbara was raised for the most part by nurses and governesses. Her father, a successful broker and notorious philanderer, was scarcely around, and her mother, lonely and revengeful, was driven into her own affair with Bud Bouvier, youngest brother of John Vernon Bouvier, the father of ***Jacqueline Kennedy**. In 1917, Edna Hutton was found dead in her bedroom, probably a suicide, though her death was attributed to a chronic ear disease. According to biographer C. David Heymann, it is widely believed that the family paid off city officials to avoid an investigation into Edna's death. Heymann also claims that despite press coverage that Edna's body was found by a maid, it was in truth discovered by five-year-old Barbara.

Following her mother's death, Hutton was sent to live in the 60-room Long Island mansion of her maternal grandparents, where she played on a velvet-backed rocking horse and dined formally—and in silence—in the enormous Georgian dining room. Hutton had little interaction with her grandmother, **Jennie Creighton Woolworth**, who suffered from premature senile-dementia and spent her days rocking back and forth in a white wicker rocking chair, under the supervision of a medical attendant. Her only family contact was with her grandfather, who called her "princess" and surrounded her with the trappings of royalty. "Woolly was always a little loony, but he was sweet to me," Hutton wrote about the once dynamic tycoon who at 64 was slipping into the paranoia and melancholy that would eventually overcome him. Hutton remained on Long Island until her grandfather's death in 1919, after which her father shuttled her from one relative to another. "She was a wistful, imaginative, lonely child with no family and few friends," said Harrie Hill Page, a longtime acquaintance. Page also recalled that Hutton both hated and feared her father whom she could never please. "He was a cruel and spiteful man. Brilliant in the brokerage business, I suppose, but he had no compassion for anyone, least of all his daughter."

In various private schools in California and New York, Hutton made few friends and spent much of her time alone, writing poetry that revealed her growing ambivalence over her wealth and privilege. "Why should some have all/ And others be without,/ Why should men pretend/ And women have to doubt?" Poetry would continue to be an outlet for Hutton throughout her life. Two of her volumes were privately published: *The Enchanted* (1934) and *The Wayfarer* (1957). She further detailed her life in a series of notebooks, which Heymann found invaluable when writing his 1983 biography of her. "Insofar as it is possible to write the definitive biography of Barbara Hutton," he wrote in the foreword, "it can almost be said that she actually wrote her own."

By age 16, Hutton was living in her own 26-room apartment, decorated with Louis XIV furniture and overseen by a household staff. While outwardly living a fairy-tale existence, her notebooks of the period reveal her fragile self-image and disillusionment. "I long for a friend, somebody to understand me, an intimate with whom to share my innermost thoughts and terrors," she wrote. "Deep down I feel inadequate. I am ugly, fat, awkward. I am also dull. . . . Nobody can ever love me. For my money but not for me. . . . I will always be alone." Years later, Douglas Fairbanks, Jr. would say: "Barbara Hutton lived a fairy-tale existence, a second-rate fairy tale at that. She was like the Cincinnati shopgirl who goes to the movies for the first time, sees a distorted celluloid image of the world, then swallows it hook, line and sinker."

In 1930, following her graduation from the exclusive Miss Porter's School in Farmington, Connecticut, Hutton made her society debut, which included an endless round of parties and culminated in a lavish winter ball at the Ritz-Carlton, with four orchestras, 200 waiters, 2,000 bottles of champagne, 1,000 seven-course midnight suppers, and 1,000 breakfasts. Maurice Chevalier, dressed as Santa Claus, greeted arriving guests, each of whom received a pocket-sized jewelry case containing unmounted diamonds, emeralds, rubies, and sapphires. "It was the night Bobbie became Barbara Hutton—debutante, Glamour Queen, Playgirl of the Western World," remarked one guest.

Hutton's emergence into adulthood not only gave her access to a fortune estimated at well over $28 million, but also marked the beginning of her search for love, a quest that took her through numerous casual affairs, seven marriages and six divorces. Her last marriage would end in a permanent separation, orchestrated by her advisors to keep her from marrying again and risking any more of her fortune. Heymann likens Hutton's failed relationships to "an interlocking series of passion plays, with herself as heroine and the man (or hero) as the unattainable object of her desire. The play endured only as long as the hero remained just out of reach; the moment he capitulated, the moment he revealed his feelings, he was discarded and ultimately replaced."

Among Hutton's husbands were two princes, a count, a baron, an ambassador, an actor, and an artist, each of whom seemingly accepted her wealth as his own, spent it lavishly, and then demanded hefty divorce settlements. Hutton actually purchased a title for her seventh husband, artist Raymond Doan, who was afterwards known as Prince Raymond Doan Vinh Na Champassak. Her second husband, Court Haugwitz-Reventlow, a Danish count with whom she had her only child, was so concerned with Hutton's fortune that he convinced her to sign an "Oath of Renunciation," by which she relinquished her American citizenship, ostensibly to eliminate her tax burden and help preserve her fortune. Of true concern for Reventlow, however, was elimination of the two-thirds U.S. inheritance tax on Hutton's estate in the event of her death. The count subsequently engaged Hutton in a long post-divorce custody battle over their son, Lance Reventlow, who would enjoy a brief career as a race-car driver before his untimely death in a plane crash in 1972. Hutton's third husband was actor Cary Grant.

Her first husband, Alexis Mdivani, is credited with launching her unending battle with anorexia nervosa, although the disorder might have manifested itself even without his help. One doctor called it a cry for the attention she never had as a child. On their wedding night, Mdivani pronounced his bride, who at 5'4" weighed a Rubenesque 148 pounds, too fat, prompting Hutton to embark on a crash diet consisting of nothing but black coffee. Maintaining this regimen for three weeks at a time, she dropped 40 pounds in a few months and established a pattern of fasting and bingeing that would continue throughout her life. While limiting her food intake, Hutton became addicted to cigarettes, alcohol, and barbiturates, often mixing the latter two with dire results. Later, during a bout with digestive disorders, she gave up alcohol and became addicted to Coca-Cola, which she consumed by the caseload.

Besides husbands, Hutton acquired a number of houses (including "Sumiya," a Japanese-style mansion in Cuernavaca, Mexico, and the palace of Sidi Hosni in Tangier), as well as an extraordinary collection of Chinese porcelain, jewelry, and artwork. She also traveled extensively, taking along a small army of help and upwards of 30 pieces of luggage. Although the public denounced Hutton's extravagant lifestyle, particularly during the Depression, it was seemingly fascinated with her comings and goings. The media dogged the heiress and frequently had fun at her expense. "Our felicitations and whatever else may be appropriate to Miss Barbara Hutton, who is spending nobody knows how many millions of American nickels and dimes collected from poor people in America in anticipation of her marriage to a foreigner whose name has slipped our mind," wrote the New York *Daily News*, shortly before

Hutton wed Alexis Mdivani. By 1934, the year that RKO released the film *The Richest Girl in the World,* a comedy loosely based on Hutton's life, she described herself as "the most hated girl in America." Earlier, Hutton had also inspired two hit songs: "Poor Little Rich Girl," by Cole Porter, and "I Found a Million-Dollar Baby (in a Five and Ten Cent Store)," with lyrics by Billy Rose and Mort Dixon. Another crush of publicity surrounded Hutton's second marriage to Court Reventlow, which was announced barely 24 hours after her divorce from Mdivani in 1935. Will Rogers attempted to bring a more balanced view to the event. "Well, a big headline today says Barbara is marrying a count, or a duke or something, and we get all excited and start criticizing as though she was a ward of the people," he wrote in his syndicated column. "It's her money. It's her life. She must pay a tremendous lot of taxes to our government. She deserves some right. Her fortune was made from five- and ten-cent purchases, so nobody got stuck very much. So, if she wants to pick up where the United States Government left off and finance all Europe it's her own business."

Nothing approached the outrage voiced in 1938, when Hutton, at the urging of Reventlow, relinquished her American citizenship and sailed off to Europe. Her departure was viewed as a betrayal of the very country that had provided her fortune, and the heiress was vilified from coast to coast. Walter Winchell took to the airwaves, referring to her as "Society's most outrageous child," while *The New York Times* thought her "Despicable." Reaction to Hutton's renunciation also impacted Woolworth stores in New York. Within two days of her sailing, three stores in New York closed, and 36 others faced a similar plight. Angry employees, who used every opportunity to blame Hutton for their meager paychecks, even wired her at sea: "URGE THAT YOU ORDER MANAGEMENT TO CONCEDE A LIVING WAGE TO THOUSANDS NOW EXISTING ON STARVATION WAGES," read their plea. Hutton did not respond but soon afterwards hired a public relations firm to generate some positive publicity. They began by trumpeting some of Hutton's more magnanimous deeds, including her numerous large contributions to public and private charities. In truth, Hutton was frequently quite generous, although her philanthropy was haphazard. While living in Tangier, Morocco, for example, she donated money to dozens of charitable and philanthropic organizations in the area. She also established a soup kitchen to help feed the impoverished Rifians who arrived in Tangier in 1945 to escape a famine in their native region, and she funded a fellowship program for poor children at the American School there. Hutton also bought expensive gifts for her friends and personal staff, and often made gifts of her own belongings in spontaneous displays of gratitude. What she gave away, however, she soon replaced, collecting expensive art and jewelry as whim dictated. The last of her purchases was a 48-carat, pear-shaped diamond, one of the largest in the world, purchased in 1965 for $400,000.

As she grew older, Hutton began to lose her grasp on reality, much as her grandfather had. In 1968, she was living at Claridge's in London, where she spent most of the time in seclusion. Old friends Derry and **Joan Moore**, found her much changed. "She was very odd by now," said Derry. "In bed she wore all her pearls at once. She retreated into a strange fantasy world, the result of being completely isolated from normal human contact." As time went on, Hutton became more and more reliant on her staff and advisors, some of whom did not have her best interests at heart. Graham Mattison, her long-time lawyer, mismanaged her fortune to the point of depletion, while growing rich himself in the process. Hutton apparently foresaw this coming years before. "Lawyers are the dregs," she once told Cecil Beaton. "Unless you commit mayhem or manslaughter, you're better off without them. They'll only exhaust your money and your patience."

Hutton's final years were marked by the agonizing deterioration of her body and mind, her world reduced to a king-sized bed where she was catered to by nurses and doctors who did little but keep her in a continually drugged state. Among her most frequent visitors in her final years were her cousin, actress ***Dina Merrill**, and Dina's husband, actor Cliff Robertson. Robertson recalled that each time they visited, Hutton was in bed, surrounded by half-empty glasses of Coke and books. "She was definitely alert but you could see her frailness. It was a sad thing," he wrote. "She had a sweet, lost quality, a sensitivity. She also had a strong and determined mind. She was surrounded by sycophants, by people on her payroll. Barbara was a virtual cocoon. She refused to get out of bed." The heiress endured in this state until her death on May 11, 1979, age 66. Only ten mourners attended a simple ceremony for Hutton at Woodlawn Memorial Ceremony, after which she was interred in the Woolworth family mausoleum.

SOURCES:

Heymann, C. David. *Poor Little Rich Girl: The Life and Legend of Barbara Hutton.* Secaucus, NJ: Lyle Stuart, 1983.

SUGGESTED READING:

Jennings, Dean. *Barbara Hutton: A Candid Biography.* NY: Frederick Fell, 1968.

Barbara Morgan,
Melrose, Massachusetts

Hutton, Betty (1921—)

***American actress and singer, best known for her performance in* Annie Get Your Gun.** *Born Betty June Thornburg on February 26, 1921, in Battle Creek, Michigan; youngest of two daughters of Percy Thornburg (a railroad brakeman) and Mabel (Lum) Thornburg; sister of singer Marion Hutton (b. 1919); attended public schools until age 15; married Theodore Briskin (a camera manufacturer), on September 2, 1945 (divorced 1950); married Charles O'Curran (a choreographer), on March 18, 1952 (divorced 1955); married Alan W. Livingston (Capital Records executive), on March 8, 1955 (divorced 1960); married Peter Candoli (a musician), on December 24, 1960 (divorced 1971); children: (first marriage) daughters Lindsay Diane Briskin (b. 1946) and Candice Briskin; (fourth marriage) one daughter Carolyn Candoli.*

Broadway plays: Two for the Show *(1940);* Panama Hattie *(1940);* Fade Out, Fade In *(replacement, 1964);* Annie *(replacement, 1980).*

Selected filmography: The Fleet's In *(1942);* Star Spangled Rhythm *(1942);* Happy Go Lucky *(1943);* Let's Face It *(1943);* The Miracle of Morgan's Creek *(1944);* And the Angels Sing *(1944);* Here Come the Waves *(1944);* Incendiary Blonde *(1945);* Duffy's Tavern *(1945);* The Stork Club *(1945);* Cross My Heart *(1946);* The Perils of Pauline *(1947);* Dream Girl *(1948);* Red Hot and Blue *(1949);* Annie Get Your Gun *(1950);* Let's Dance *(1950); (cameo)* Sailor Beware *(1952);* The Greatest Show on Earth *(1952);* Somebody Loves Me *(1952);* Spring Reunion *(1957).*

Album discography: And the Angels Sing/ Let's Dance *(Caliban 6017);* Annie Get Your Gun *(MGM E-509, MGM E-3227, Metro M/S-548);* Betty Hutton at the Saints and Sinners Ball *(WB 1267);* A Blonde Bombshell *(AEI 2120);* The Fleet's In *(Hollywood Soundstage 405);* Hutton in Hollywood *(Vedette 8702);* Incendiary Blonde *(Amalgamated 238);* Satins and Spurs *(Cap L0547, MPT 4);* Somebody Loves Me *(RCA LPM-3097);* A Square in a Social Circle *(Cap H-256, EMI/Pathé 65521);* Star Spangled Rhythm *(Curtain Calls 100/20, Sandy Hook 2045);* Stork Club *(Caliban 6020).*

With a boundless energy that endeared her to war-weary audiences and made her Paramount's most valuable star, Betty Hutton lit up the screen during the 1940s. Bob Hope once called her "a vitamin pill with legs." Primarily a musical performer who made numerous hit recordings, Hutton also possessed true comedic talent and could even turn in a credible dramatic performance with strong direction. Unfortunately, her manic style masked significant insecurities that ultimately destroyed her career and almost her life.

She was born Betty June Thornburg in Battle Creek, Michigan, in 1921, and was just two years old when her father walked out. "I never had a father," she told Mike Douglas in a 1977 interview. "I was known as a bastard child, which was rough." In order to support Betty and her older sister **Marion Hutton, Mabel Thornburg** moved the children to a Detroit slum, where, after working for a short time in an automobile factory, she decided she could make more money as a bootlegger. Hutton, who credits Mabel with teaching her and Marion to sing, recalled performing songs on the kitchen table while a bunch of strange men stood around drinking bootleg booze. At age 11, she began supplementing her mother's meager income by singing on street corners and in neighborhood speakeasies. Though she later referred to that period in her life as a "nightmare," she would remain devoted to her mother and employ her as her dresser for many years. After Mabel's death in an apartment fire in 1962, Hutton said, "I lived for my mother."

Betty Hutton got her first break at 13, winning a contest to sing with the Vincent Lopez band. After a year, she was making $65 a week and was billed as "America's Number One Jitterbug" because of her madcap, humorous way of selling a song. Hutton stayed with the band for several years, perfecting her "whoop-and-holler" style. In 1939, after a successful 21-week engagement at Billy Rose's Casa Manana night club in New York, Hutton left Lopez for the musical stage, making her Broadway debut in the revue *Two for the Show* (1940). Hutton next undertook a comedy role in *Panama Hattie* (1940), starring ***Ethel Merman**. Through the show's producer Buddy De Sylva, who had left New York to become an executive producer at Paramount Studios in Hollywood, Hutton received a movie contract for *The Fleet's In* (1942), in which her mile-a-minute rendition of "Arthur Murray Taught Me Dancing in a Hurry" brought her immediate visibility. The film was followed by three light-hearted musicals, *Star Spangled Rhythm* (1942), *Happy Go Lucky* (1943), and *Let's Face It* (1943). Even at this early period, Hutton was exhibiting signs of hyperactivity that went far beyond her performances. **Marie Windsor**, who acted with her in *Let's Face It,* recalls, "She was always very popular on the set. Always terribly full of energy. At the time we all thought it was just natural enthusiasm, but in retrospect I think she was a very tense girl."

Hutton's first non-singing role came in the comedy *The Miracle of Morgan's Creek,* the tale of a small-town girl who parties one evening with some soldiers and wakes up the next morning married. John McManus of *PM* called the film "a masterwork of fine casting, excellent characterization and a rare sense of satire, invention, and emotion," and Hutton was acclaimed by critics as "star material." The actress was overwhelmed with new assignments, including *And the Angels Sing* (1944) and *Here Come the Waves* (1944). She lobbied ceaselessly for a role in *Incendiary Blonde* (1945), in which she portrayed nightclub queen ***Texas Guinan** and introduced two songs that would be closely linked to her over the years, "Ragtime Cowboy Joe" and "It Had To Be You." Although the movie received mixed reviews, it was enormously successful.

As her movie career burgeoned, Hutton also performed on the radio and made recordings. In 1943, she was one of the first artists signed by Johnny Mercer for the newly formed Capitol Records. In 1944, she made a series of personal appearances as host of a variety show, and in January 1945 she traveled with a USO unit to entertain troops in the Pacific, covering 50,000 miles in eight weeks. By early 1944, Hutton was receiving some 7,000 fan letters a week from an adoring military. After finishing the film *Duffy's Tavern* (1945), based on Ed Gardner's popular radio program, the actress embarked on another six-week USO tour, but ill health forced her to return to the United States in August.

In September 1945, Hutton, who had reportedly been engaged four times since her arrival in Hollywood, married a young camera manufacturer named Ted Briskin, whom she had met in a Chicago cafe. Briskin wanted her to settle down in Chicago, where his business was based, but Hutton, intent on her career, wanted no part of it; after six months, the couple separated. They soon reconciled, however, and in 1946 had a daughter **Lindsay Diane Briskin**, after which Briskin moved his business to Los Angeles. After several more films, including *The Perils of Pauline* (1947), loosely based on the life of death-defying serial star ***Pearl White**, Hutton gave birth to a second daughter, **Candice Briskin**. Meanwhile, the Briskins lived a frenetic life that included a constant round of parties and a series of moves to some ten houses in five years, each more lavish than the last.

Pivotal in Hutton's career was the role of ***Annie Oakley** in the movie version of *Annie Get Your Gun*. MGM had originally purchased the rights for an unprecedented $700,000, planning to star ***Judy Garland**, but when Garland took ill, Hutton, on loan from Paramount, got her chance. "I think that's God power," Hutton later said. "I didn't wish Judy Garland any harm, but that was my part from the beginning." Hutton threw herself into the demanding role, determined that she would be as good as Garland. The movie was a box-office bonanza and garnered Hutton terrific reviews as well as a *Time* magazine cover. The movie's release, however, coincided with the start of the Briskin-Hutton divorce proceedings and a round of what has been termed manic behavior on the part of the actress, including a whirlwind romance with actor Robert Sterling. There was one brief reconciliation with Briskin before their divorce became final in late 1950.

At 29, Hutton was the top star on the Paramount lot but remained driven by self-doubt and the need to prove herself. After a stint in Korea to entertain troops, and a New Year's Eve performance at the Palace in New York to replace an again-ailing Garland, Hutton returned to Hollywood for her biggest movie to date, *The Greatest Show on Earth* (1952), directed by famed Cecil B. De Mille and co-starring Charlton Heston. The movie was shot on location at the Ringling Brothers, Barnum and Bailey Circus winter quarters in Sarasota, Florida, and Hutton moved her mother and children into one of the local mansions for the duration of the filming. The part required Hutton to train for months on the high wire, during which time she badly injured her arm and had to take painkillers. The film was a blockbuster, winning the Academy Award for Best Picture in 1952. Hutton was at the height of her powers. Then, everything began to go downhill.

During the shooting of her next film, *Somebody Loves Me* (1952), based on the life of vaudeville star ***Blossom Seeley**, Hutton became romantically involved with choreographer Charles O'Curran, though their relationship on the set was stormy. After completing the movie, they eloped to Las Vegas. Shortly afterward, Hutton campaigned to have her new husband signed as the director of her next film, *Topsy and Eva*. When the studio refused, she walked out on her contract, an unpardonable sin. Boycotted by

From the movie Annie Get Your Gun, *starring Betty Hutton.*

every studio in Hollywood, Hutton returned to the nightclub circuit and the recording studio. Plans got under way with O'Curran for a television show called "Satins and Spurs," a western musical à la *Annie Get Your Gun* that ultimately turned into a major disappointment. She was so distraught over its failure that she announced her retirement, telling reporters, "I've got to quit or blow my top. I had to do something to get noticed. I stood on my head, turned cartwheels, yelled, and screamed. I can't take the heartbreak anymore. It's not as glamorous as it seems."

Hutton also announced plans to divorce O'Curran, whom she blamed for the failure of her television show.

Three days after receiving her final divorce decree from O'Curran, Hutton married the newly divorced recording executive Alan Livingston. The couple settled in Hollywood, where Hutton turned her energies to motherhood, caring not only for her own two girls, but Livingston's daughter and ailing son, a hemophiliac. After five months, her ambition to perform resurfaced, and, after a miscarriage, she started work on the small black-and-white movie *Spring Reunion* (1957), in which she played a 35-year-old woman who after years of being dominated by her father falls in love with Dana Andrews. Though considered one of her most sensitive performances, it did not rekindle Hutton's career. By this time, her marriage to Livingston was coming apart, and, in what was becoming an established pattern, she announced plans to divorce, then reconciled several times before making a final break.

In a last-ditch effort to save her career, Hutton next sunk most of her money into the ill-fated television series "Goldie," about a former "showgirl" who becomes the executor of a million-dollar estate and the guardian of three spoiled children. Desperate for success and trusting no one, she tried to do everything herself, with disastrous results. When the first episode aired in October 1959, Hutton told reporters: "You don't know what I've been through the past few weeks. . . . Nobody has been on my side. One day I had to stand with my back to the wall and tell everybody to take their cockamamie ideas and go to hell. I'm not going for the buck with this show. I want to be proud of it. If I'm not proud, then I want to be dead. I don't give a hoot if I don't have a dime at the end of the year." As it turned out, the show was a flop, and Hutton lost a fortune as well as her health. Distraught and down to 90 pounds, she was hospitalized with exhaustion.

Panicked, Hutton was unable to rest and, while still recuperating, accepted a Las Vegas offer which also failed. There was another hasty marriage to jazz trumpeter Pete Candoli in December 1960, and a hectic tour of England the following month in a nightclub act the two put together. After the devastating death of her mother in 1962, Hutton toured in *Gypsy* and, at the end of the year, gave birth to her third daughter, **Carolyn Candoli.** Tours in *Annie Get Your Gun* and *Gentlemen Prefer Blondes* followed, as did a stint replacing **Carol Burnett** in *Fade Out, Fade In* (1964), which turned out to be a week of dropped lines and missed song cues instead of the triumphant return to Broadway it might have been. Afterwards, Hutton retired to a beach house in Laguna, making few appearances for close to two years. (By now, her two older daughters were living with their father.) In 1966, there was an offer to star in two low-budget westerns, but Hutton was not up to the shooting schedule. In 1967, she filed for bankruptcy, declaring, "I've been crucified in this racket, crucified, when I only gave out love. I bought houses, Cadillacs, furs, you name it, for people—even churches for my maids. But when the money went, everyone split." Among Hutton's losses was her fourth husband, who, after a long separation, divorced the actress in 1971. She also had a bitter parting with her sister, Marion. Shattered, Hutton resorted to pills and alcohol, which further destroyed her voice and talent to the point where she could no longer get work. She was forced to give her daughter Carolyn to Candoli and to take up residence in a series of small apartments or with friends.

In April 1974, Hutton had the opportunity to star in a small revival of *Annie Get Your Gun* at a dinner theater outside Boston. Hopelessly out of shape, she prepared rigorously, but the opening night was a disaster. She canceled the rest of her performances and checked into a Boston hospital. There, she met Father Peter Maguire, a Catholic priest who offered her the job of housekeeper in his Portsmouth, Rhode Island rectory. News of this did not reach the public until four months later, when an interview in the weekly diocese newspaper brought a flurry of reporters to the rectory. Headlines announcing Hutton's conversion to Catholicism were accompanied by photographs of her working in the kitchen and pouring coffee for the priests. The publicity provoked 35,000 letters and comedian Joey Adams and restaurateur Arthur Roback held a "Betty Hutton Love-In" at a New York restaurant. The affair raised $10,000 for the actress, who stated emphatically that she was not planning a comeback, and made her way back to the rectory. But pain from her old shoulder injury persisted even after surgery, causing her to rely more and more on pain medication. In December 1975, after suffering a nervous breakdown, she entered a Rhode Island psychiatric center.

After a three-week hospital stay, Hutton wound her way back to Hollywood, where she began to make a few sporadic television appearances, including an episode of "Baretta" and a meandering interview with Mike Douglas, which aired in February 1977. Despite the efforts of well-meaning friends, however, nothing solid materialized for Hutton, and there were trips back to the rectory and additional hospitalizations to help her overcome her addiction to pills.

In the fall of 1980, Hutton returned to Broadway for a three-week replacement stint as Miss Hartigan in the blockbuster *Annie*. Critic Rex Reed wrote glowingly of her in the New York *Daily News*: "She is a seemingly endless fountain of comic exuberance, a one-woman fireworks display that lights up the stage at the Alvin and leaves the audience cheering." Hutton subsequently appeared on the PBS television special "Jukebox Saturday Night," singing some of her old hits, but performing opportunities again faded away. She returned to Rhode Island, where she enrolled at Salve Regina College in Newport. She later joined the faculty there, teaching film and television classes. Mental health problems continued to plague the actress, however, in ensuing years.

SOURCES:

Agan, Patrick. *The Decline and Fall of the Love Goddesses.* Los Angeles, CA: Pinnacle, 1979.

Current Biography 1950. NY: H.W. Wilson, 1950.

Katz, Ephraim. *The Film Encyclopedia.* NY: HarperCollins, 1994.

Parish, James Robert and Michael R. Pitts. *Hollywood Songsters.* NY: Garland, 1991.

Barbara Morgan,
Melrose, Massachusetts

Huxley, Elspeth (1907–1997)

Prolific English writer of nonfiction and fiction who is especially noted for her widely acclaimed books about her experiences in, and the history of, East Africa during the 20th century. *Born Elspeth Josceline Grant on July 23, 1907, in London, England; died in Tetbury, England, in January 1997; daughter of Josceline Grant (an army major and farmer) and Eleanor Lillian (Grosvenor) Grant; attended Reading University, Diploma in Agriculture, 1927; attended Cornell University, 1927–28; married Gervas Huxley (a tea commissioner and writer), on December 12, 1931 (died 1971); children: Charles Grant Huxley (b. February 1944).*

Parents moved to Kenya (1912); joined them (1913); returned to England (1915), sent away to boarding school at Aldeburgh in Suffolk; returned to Kenya (1919); attended Reading University, England (1925–27); studied at Cornell University (1928); worked as assistant press officer for Empire Marketing board, London, England (1929–32); author (1935–97); worked for British Broadcasting Corp. (BBC), London, England, in new department (1941–43), member of general advisory council (1952–59), broadcaster of BBC's "The Critics" program, and on African matters; became a justice of the peace for Wiltshire (1946–77); awarded Commander, Order of the British Empire (1960); served as member, Monckton Advisory Commission on Central Africa (1959–60).

Selected publications: White Man's Country: Lord Delamere and the Making of Kenya *(1935);* Murder on Safari *(1938);* Red Strangers *(1939);* Atlantic Ordeal: The Story of Mary Cornish *(1942);* English Women *(1942);* Settlers of Kenya *(1948);* The Sorcerer's Apprentice: A Journey through East Africa *(1948);* The Walled City *(1949);* Four Guineas: A Journey through West Africa *(1954);* The Flame Trees of Thika: Memories of an African Childhood *(1959);* On the Edge of the Rift: Memories of Kenya *(1962);* Love Among the Daughters: Memories of the Twenties in England and America *(1968);* Livingstone and His African Journeys *(1974);* Florence Nightingale *(1975);* Scott of the Antarctic *(1977);* Nellie: Letters from Africa *(1980);* Out in the Midday Sun: My Kenya *(1985);* Nine Faces of Kenya *(1990).*

In January 1933, at age 26, Elspeth Huxley traveled alone by sea from Marseilles, France, to Mombasa, Kenya. The trip took 19 days. At Port Sudan in the Red Sea, the ship anchored in the harbor and passengers were permitted to go ashore to ride camels and stretch their legs. Unfortunately for Huxley, her hat had blown overboard, and going outside in the tropics without a hat was like visiting the North Pole without a parka. On board was Dr. Roland Burkitt, a surgeon from Ireland who had set up the first private practice in 1911 in Nairobi, Kenya, and who believed ultra-violet rays from the tropical sun to be lethal. The armor against these rays included a wide-brimmed, double-felt sun helmet, known as a *terai*. In her autobiographical work, *Out in the Midday Sun,* written at age 78, Huxley describes how Burkitt reacted to her intentions of going out for a stroll: "[He] was horrified. In his powerful brogue he forecast the direst disasters should I venture hatless ashore—dementia praecox, cardiac failure, renal occlusion, possibly even flat feet. Actinic rays softened the brain, rotted the guts and sapped the moral fibre." She went anyway. On her return to the boat, she met Burkitt and rubbed in the fact that she had suffered no ill effects. Huxley "never wore a sunhat in Africa again."

Elspeth Huxley's entire life was punctuated by breaks with convention. Like the wild animals of Africa, with whom she spent a good portion of her childhood, she was restless, energetic, and peripatetic. This is not surprising considering the family Huxley was born into in London in 1907. Her mother **Nellie Grosvenor Grant** and father Josceline Grant, though both members of the aristocracy, did not live the stodgy, manorial life that has come to be associated with the English elite. Josceline was a wandering adventurer. He had served with The Royal Scots in the Boer War in South Africa and had lost much of his inherited fortune in investments in a diamond mine in Portuguese East Africa (now Mozambique) and in developing a car he and a partner had invented. Josceline loved cars and had participated in the Paris to Madrid race where his chain-driven Mercedes overturned.

Huxley's mother Nellie was also an adventuring entrepreneur who went into business with **Trudie Denman**, buying, training and selling ponies. They broke the wild ponies by strapping a children's pony pannier to the pony's back and placing a child on top. At three years old, Huxley became the chosen guinea pig. In a letter, Nellie describes the pony and Huxley tromping about the training ground: "The pair careered round and round, Elspeth chuckling with delight and poor Nanny Newport rushing and screaming round the perimeter."

Whether [Huxley] is detailing the past and present of friends and relations, describing the death of a fox or Prohibition picnic orgies, she is funny, bawdy, serious, nostalgic and always entertaining.

—Anne Fremantle

When Huxley was five, her parents decided to try their luck in an exciting "new" country that was then the talk of London. British East Africa (now Kenya) had recently been opened up by an "adventurous" railway line. Big game hunting in the interior had already become legendary, and hunters returned to England with stories of wide-open terrain still in pristine condition. The high altitude of much of the territory produced a climate inviting to northern Europeans.

Huxley did not join her parents in Africa for nearly a year. Having stayed behind in England with relatives, she was not to follow until her parents were somewhat established on the 500 acres they had bought 30 miles north of Nairobi near a town later called Thika. Huxley would have none of this forced separation. At age five, she escaped from her nursery at night and set out for Africa with her seven-year-old cousin, Puk. The two collected the bread, butter and cake that Huxley had been saving in a tin beneath the roots of a yew tree, then bedded down for the night in a woods several fields away. A constable discovered them and carried Huxley under his arm back to the nursery.

Huxley's most famous book, *The Flame Trees of Thika,* written in 1959 and later turned into a seven-part "Masterpiece Theater" production airing in 1986, is a semi-autobiographical account of her early years in Africa. "*The Flame Trees of Thika* can well stand comparison with ***Isak Dinesen**'s *Out of Africa,*" wrote Charles Rolo in the *Atlantic Monthly.* Huxley's sequel, *The Mottled Lizard* (1962), picks up the story of Huxley's childhood in Africa. "If one lived to be a hundred," she wrote, "and watched the dawn break and the sun rise over the high veld of Africa every morning, one would never tire of it." Much of her life's work was shaped by these early experiences.

In 1914, the beginning of the Great War put an end to the blissful days in Kenya. Huxley's father joined the King's African Rifles and fought the Germans on several occasions along the border between Kenya and Tanganyika (now Tanzania). In December of that year, he left for England to rejoin his regiment, the Royal Scots. He was wounded in the Battle of Ypres in Belgium in November 1915. A month later, Elspeth and her mother left for England despite the risk of their boat being torpedoed by German submarines. Nellie spent her considerable energy running the Women's Land Army in Wessex while Elspeth was sent off to a girl's boarding school at Aldeburgh in Suffolk. After the freedom and warm climate of Africa, a winter in a boarding school on the coast of East Anglia, when war shortages made heating sources scarce, was like a prison sentence in Siberia. Huxley recalled times when food shortages made her so hungry she ate her toothpaste. During the war, the students watched a Zeppelin crash and burn near Felixstowe. A day or two later, when the school children visited the wreckage, some picked up pieces of the Zeppelin and later made them into brooches. Occasionally during the war, a girl would leave school in tears, having been told of the death of a brother or father. They would return after their brief mourning period and no mention of the loss was ever raised.

In 1919, her parents having already returned to Kenya, Huxley was still interned in Aldeburgh boarding school. Again she was determined to escape to Africa; by now, however, she was old enough to realize she could not do it on her own, so she resolved to make such a nuisance of herself at school that they would be glad to be rid of her. Already interested in horse racing, she set up a book of bets on the Derby. When the authorities found out she was collecting pennies from classmates, she was deemed a source of contamination to the other students and isolated in the sanatorium. Her parents brought Huxley back to Thika rather than find another boarding school. Huxley had won.

In Africa, the coffee plantation the Grants had developed from wild bush was running full gear. Huxley continued her education with lessons from her mother and father and any neighbors who could help. She spent much of her free time hunting in the bush with her .22 rifle. "I was at this time, I regret to say, very bloodthirsty," she writes in *Nellie: Letters from Africa*. "I shot, or shot at, small buck . . . wild pig . . . [and] once, I fear, at a cheetah." Later in life, Huxley renounced all hunting and only shot animals with a camera. She also became a fierce conservationist, joining the National Trust, the Royal Society for Protection of Birds, the World Wildlife Fund, the Rhino Rescue, the Fauna and Flora Preservation Society, and several other groups. In 1984, she collaborated with photographer Hugo van Lawick, ex-husband of ***Jane Goodall**, on the book *The Last Days in Eden,* which records the wildlife of the Serengeti.

In 1922, Nellie Grant's lifelong friend, Trudie Denman, bought the family a 1,000-acre farm near Njoro in the breathtakingly beautiful Rift Valley, 100 miles northeast of Nairobi. Elspeth's father would die in a hospital near this farm 25 years later in 1947. Her mother would live on the farm for 43 years, struggling constantly to make it profitable. Huxley stayed in Kenya until 1925 when she returned to England to complete her education at Reading University, where she received a diploma in agriculture. She would not return to Africa and her parents' farm in the Rift Valley for eight years.

Following Reading, Huxley traveled to the United States where she attended a one-year course in agriculture at Cornell University. She writes perceptively about her college years and 1920s society in England and America in her book *Love Among the Daughters,* published in 1968. Her love of writing began at age 16 when she contributed articles to the East African *Standard* on polo matches. After Cornell, her first job in London was as a press officer for the Empire Marketing Board where she wrote articles for popular newspapers based on the results of recent scientific research.

In 1929, the onset of the Depression threatened her job, and, when she married Gervas Huxley in 1931, she was axed because of the recently instituted Marriage Bar that prohibited married women from serving in the civil service. Gervas Huxley, grandson of Thomas Henry Huxley and first cousin of Julian and Aldous Huxley, also worked for the Empire Marketing Board as head of the publicity division. In 1933, Gervas took a job as the chief commissioner with the Ceylon Association. With the price of tea falling due to over-production, he was put in charge of increasing world demand. His first assignment was a trip to Ceylon (now Sri Lanka) off the coast of India. Elspeth had recently been commissioned to write Lord Delamere's biography and embarked with Gervas from London, but she headed to Kenya to continue her research. Delamere, who died in 1931, had lived for 30 years in Kenya and was one of the central figures in that country's development and government. Huxley's two-volume biography, *White Man's Country: Lord Delamere and the Making of Kenya,* was published in 1935 and remains one of her most important works.

Six months later, Gervas journeyed to Kenya after a side trip to South Africa and an airplane flight during which the pilot lost his way and had to crash-land in the bush. Undaunted, they continued on their scheduled return to London. Their flight, one of the first offered by Imperial Airways, went from Nairobi to Cairo, stopping frequently for fuel and never exceeding 100 miles per hour. They switched to a flying boat to cross the Mediterranean and then to a train in Italy; the planes of the time could not fly high enough to get over the Alps. The trip took six days, with the plane stopping at night.

This was the beginning of extensive travel for the two as Gervas was sent all over the world to begin advertising campaigns in an attempt to boost tea consumption. The couple lived out of a suitcase for the next five years. To pass the time on endless ocean voyages and to avoid playing bridge or shuffleboard, Huxley began writing mysteries. Three of them centered around the American detective Vachell and all took place in Africa. The second of these, *Murder on Safari,* prompted critic Will Cuppy of *Books* (May 29, 1938) to call her "a dangerous rival to ***Agatha Cristie**, ***Mignon G. Eberhart** and other ornaments of the international crime choir." All the novels, though highly entertaining, also show an incisive understanding of African society and a concern with its predicament and future.

In 1937, Huxley returned to Africa to do research for her fictional account of a Kikuyu family dealing with the onslaught of Europeans moving to Africa. To learn all she could about the Kikuyu, an indigenous people living in Kenya, she and her mother lived in a Kikuyu village on the slopes of Mt. Kenya. At one point during their several-months' stay, the inviting challenge of the mountain, at 17,058 the tallest in Kenya, became too much for Huxley's mother. Together with porters, mother and daughter set off to see how high they could climb to see the view. They reached snow-line at about 16,000 feet and, due to inadequate equipment, decided to head back.

The Kikuyu book was published in 1939 as *The Red Strangers*. **Edith Walton** in *The New York Times* (September 10, 1939), describes the work as "a book so richly detailed in its picture of native customs and psychology that it has, despite its author's disclaimers, almost the value of an anthropological study." It is considered one of Huxley's finest works of fiction and brought to the Western world a view of Africa that had rarely been seen. The original publishers, Macmillan, who had also released Huxley's first book, *White Man's Country,* felt that a portion of *Red Strangers,* about female circumcision, was inappropriate for their readership, so they blithely rewrote it. Huxley found the rewrite so ludicrous that she withdrew the book and offered it to Chatto and Windus. They had no problems with the novel in its original form and would remain Huxley's chief publisher.

In 1938, the Huxleys bought a 17th-century farm called Woodfolds in north Wiltshire, England, which they modernized and moved into the following year. At the outbreak of World War II, Huxley became one of Wiltshire's organizers of the Woman's Land Army and in 1941 took a job with the BBC, which lasted until the end of 1943. She resigned from this post when she learned she was pregnant and, in February 1944, gave birth to her son Charles Grant, her only child. Though the Huxleys would continue to travel extensively, the farm in Wiltshire would be their permanent home for over three decades. Elspeth became involved in the small English community she had settled in and in 1946 became a justice of the peace for Wiltshire, a position she held for 31 years.

During the 1940s and 1950s, Huxley wrote prolifically, having her fiction and nonfiction books, primarily on Africa, published almost yearly. She was also busy writing for newspapers and magazines. Now an authority on Africa, in 1959 she became the only female member of the Monckton Advisory Commission on Central Africa, which was appointed by the British government to advise on the future of the Federation of Rhodesia and Nyasaland. In 1962, she was awarded the CBE (Companion of the British Empire) for her services to the country.

In later years, Huxley lost none of the energy and enthusiasm of her youth. She lived in Oaksey and turned her inquiring mind toward that small English village. In 1976, she published a diary of a year in her life titled *Gallipot Eyes: A Wiltshire Diary.* In the 1960s and 1970s, her far-ranging interests led her to write books on philanthropists, immigrants in Britain, modern food production, travel in Australia and, of course, Africa, and explorers, such as *Livingstone and His African Journeys* and *Scott of the Antarctic.*

Nor were the 1980s a quiet decade, with the publication of *Nellie: Letters from Africa* and *Out in the Midday Sun: My Kenya.* In 1990, she published an anthology of writings about Kenya entitled *Nine Faces of Kenya.* The book combined two themes that helped structure and highlight Huxley's life—Africa and literature. She was an expert on the first; the second she created with genuine mastery.

SOURCES:

Huxley, Elspeth. *The Mottled Lizard.* London: Chatto & Windus, 1962.

———. *Nellie: Letters from Africa.* London: Weidenfeld and Nicolson, 1973.

———. *Out in the Midday Sun.* London: Chatto & Windus, 1985.

Huxley, Gervas. *Both Hands.* London: Chatto & Windus, 1970.

Rolo, Charles. *Atlantic Monthly.* Vol. XIII, no. 4. October 1959, p. 113.

SUGGESTED READING:

Huxley, Elspeth. *The Flame Trees of Thika.* London: Chatto & Windus, 1959.

Taylor Harper,
freelance writer in travel and history, Amherst, Massachusetts

Huxley, Julia Arnold (1862–1908)

English educator who was headmistress of Prior's Field. *Name variations: Mrs. Leonard Huxley, Judy Arnold. Born Julia Frances Arnold in 1862; died of cancer on November 30, 1908; granddaughter of the famous headmaster Thomas Arnold of Rugby (1795–1842, an English educator and headmaster of Rugby); daughter of Thomas Arnold (1823–1900), a professor of English literature, and Julia Sorell (1826–1888); sister of* ****Mrs. Humphry Ward*** *(1851–1920); niece of Matthew Arnold (1822–1888), an English poet and critic; attended Oxford High*

*School for Girls; earned a first-class degree in English literature from Somerville College, Oxford, as a home student; married Leonard Huxley (1860–1933), an editor and author who taught at Charterhouse; children: (Noel) Trevenen Huxley (1890–1914); Julian Huxley (1887–1975, a biologist and writer who married *Juliette Huxley; Aldous Huxley (1894–1963, a novelist and critic who married **Maria Nuys Huxley**, then **Laura Archera Huxley**); **Margaret Arnold Huxley** (1896–1979).*

Julia Arnold Huxley was born in 1862, the daughter of Thomas Arnold, a professor of English literature and son of the famous headmaster of Rugby, and **Julia Sorell**. Taking out a bank loan, Julia Huxley founded Prior's Field, a small but significant experimental girls' school in Godalming, Surrey, England, where she was its headmistress.

Huxley, Juliette (1896–1994)

Swiss-born sculptor and writer who was married to Julian Huxley. *Name variations: Lady Huxley. Born Marie Juliette Baillot on December 6, 1896, in Auvernier, Switzerland; died in 1994; only daughter and one of two children of Alphonse Baillot (a building solicitor) and Mélanie Antonia (Ortlieb) Baillot; attended École Supérieure des Jeunes Filles; married Julian Sorell Huxley (1887–1975, a biologist and writer), on March 29, 1919; children: two sons, Anthony and Francis.*

Juliette Huxley was born in 1896 in Auvernier, Switzerland, the daughter of Alphonse Baillot, a building solicitor, and **Mélanie Antonia Baillot**. At age 19, Juliette left for England to find work in order to help pay off an enormous debt the family had incurred when her father's partner absconded with the profits from a joint law practice. Applying for a position as a governess, Juliette was hired by Lady ***Ottoline Morrell** as a companion for Morrell's nine-year-old daughter **Julian Morrell**. For two years, Juliette lived and worked at Garsington Manor, the Morrells' stately home outside Oxford, where Ottoline entertained the lively circle of Bloomsbury writers and artists, among them Bertram Russell, Lytton Strachey, ***Virginia Woolf**, ***Dora Carrington**, ***Vita Sackville-West**, ***Vanessa Bell**, Mark and **Dorothy Gertler**, and the Huxley brothers Aldous and Julian. Juliette married Julian in 1919.

The couple began their married life at Oxford, where Julian had secured a post as a zoology professor, and where Juliette would give birth to the couple's two sons, Anthony and Francis. Julian went on to posts at King's College, at the London Zoo, and, finally, as the first director-general of UNESCO, which took the couple to Paris. With each of her husband's career moves, Juliette met a new cast of fascinating characters, including H.G. Wells, with whom Julian collaborated on *The Science of Life*, and D.H. Lawrence, who rented a chalet next to the Huxleys at Diablerets in the winter of 1927–28, when he was writing *Lady Chatterley's Lover*. Huxley would also travel extensively both with and without her husband, journeying to Africa on several occasions (resulting in the book *Wild Lives of Africa*) and to India, Java, Bali, Thailand, Persia, Syria, Lebanon, and Israel. Following their stint in Paris, the Huxleys returned to London, which served as their home base throughout their later years.

In 1933, when her son was injured in a bicycle accident, Huxley hired the young sculptor and naturalist Alan Best to tutor the boy in clay modeling while he was confined. When Juliette took up clay modeling herself, she realized she had a talent. She subsequently served an apprenticeship at the Central School under John Skeaping and began sculpting in wood. "The deep joy of discovery led me to new perceptions of works of art, to natural forms in their beauty, enriching my life," Juliette wrote in her autobiography *Leaves of the Tulip Tree*.

The Huxley marriage underwent a bumpy period beginning in 1930, when Julian began to explore the world outside the conventional bonds of matrimony and urged his wife to do the same, assuring her that their love and trust in each other would endure. Both partners ultimately engaged in outside relationships; in her autobiography, Juliette writes of two lovers, the second of whom, Jason, disappeared at sea during the war. "It was a liberal exchange, a blessed sharing of new joys," she writes about her affair with Jason, "of new joys, of lazy beaches, silent woods and poetry; a happiness which for a few years nourished me and kept me sane, for it filled the vacant space and healed the wounded heart. I left off my Calvinist shirt and made friends with myself." Among her husband's paramours was 24-year-old ***May Sarton**, who simultaneously became captivated with Juliette, then 39. While May's romance with Julian cooled, her deep love for Juliette endured, though it remained secret. "There was perhaps one week only of physical intimacy" between the women, writes **Susan Sherman**, who edited a volume of Sarton's letters to Juliette. The women corresponded throughout the 1940s, but Juliette broke off the relationship when Sarton threatened to tell Julian. Sarton and

Juliette Huxley

Huxley did not communicate for another 27 years but resumed their correspondence in 1975, following Julian's death.

The Huxleys ultimately reunited. "Marriages crack but some survive; the storm passes," Juliette wrote of the reconciliation. "Much had been uprooted, leaving the ground bare and the trees stripped, ready perhaps for new growth, for different ideas and ways of living. We had come to the place where a choice had to be made." Julian, who suffered several nervous breakdowns in his lifetime, endured another in 1966, which left him in what Juliette describes as a "waste land." He recovered sufficiently to write his memoirs, then had a stroke in 1973. He remained in helpless confusion until his death on February 14, 1975. Juliette survived him by 19 years, dying in 1994, at age 98.

SOURCES:

Huxley, Juliette. *Leaves of the Tulip Tree*. Topsfield, MA: Salem House, 1963.

Publishers Weekly. May 31, 1999.

SUGGESTED READING:

Sherman, Susan, ed. *Letters of May Sarton to Juliette Huxley*, 1999.

Barbara Morgan,
Melrose, Massachusetts

Huxley, Mrs. Leonard (1862–1908).

See Huxley, Julia Arnold.

Huxtable, Ada Louise (1921—)

American architectural critic for* The New York Times *(1963–1981) who won the Pulitzer Prize for distinguished criticism. *Born Ada Louise Landman on March 14, 1921, in New York City; only child of Michael Louis Landman (a physician) and Leah (Rosenthal) Landman; graduated from Wadleigh High School (Manhattan's high school of music and art); Hunter College B.A. (magna cum laude); attended the Institute of Fine Arts at New York University, 1945–1950; married L. Garth Huxtable (an industrial designer), in 1940.*

Born in 1921, Ada Huxtable was raised in New York City, which fostered her acute sense of the urban environment. An only child who was fatherless by age of seven, she spent many solitary hours at the Metropolitan Museum of Art. "If I had not had free access as a child to this museum," she later said, "I would not have developed my interests in art and architecture." After graduating from Wadleigh High School (Manhattan's high school of music and art), she entered Hunter College, where she majored in fine arts and edited the school newspaper. Graduating magna cum laude, she went on to advanced studies in art and architectural history at New York University's Institute of Fine Arts, but quit just short of her degree when her master's thesis topic on Italian architecture was rejected.

In 1946, after a brief stint selling furniture at Bloomingdale's, Huxtable took a position as assistant curator of the department of architecture and design of the Museum of Modern Art. She left in 1950 to accept a Fulbright fellowship for advanced research in architecture and design in Italy. Upon her return in 1952, she organized a touring exhibit on architect Pier Luigi Nervi for the museum and published her first article on Nervi for *Progressive Architecture* (of which she was a contributing editor from 1952 to 1963). Over the next few years, she also produced articles for *Arts Digest, Craft Horizons,* and *Interiors,* as well as for non-professional journals, including *Consumer Reports, Holiday, Horizon,* and *Saturday Review*. Architectural events on the local New York scene also engaged her and were the subject of two books during this period: *Four Walking Tours of Modern Architecture in New York City* (1961) and *Classic New York; Georgian Gentility to Greek Elegance* (1964). Huxtable planned the later book as the first of a six-volume series on the history of New York architecture designed to "open the way to a more general appreciation of a wider range of the city's architecture, and to the kind of preservation that will make the past a proper part of the present and future."

Huxtable's ambitious book project was interrupted by an invitation to join *The New York Times* as a full-time architectural critic, a first-of-its-kind position created on the strength of her frequent and well-received contributions to *The New York Times Magazine*. Huxtable initially turned down the offer. "Most people are bright enough to calculate the angles, about where such a job would lead them," she explained, "but I was just interested in my own work, and was afraid how the job would change my life." However, when the paper threatened to hire someone else for the position, Huxtable reconsidered. She remained with the *Times* for 18 years, advancing to the editorial board in 1973. **Susan Torre**, who discusses Huxtable in *Women in American Architecture,* considers her a powerful influence who "shifted the public's appreciation of architecture from a dignified dilettantism to major concern." **Jane Holtz Kay**, of the *Christian Science Monitor,* referred to Huxtable as "the major person in architecture criticism," adding that "there is no number two." She also credited her with opening up the field to women.

In addition to educating the public, Huxtable used her editorials—or "appraisals," as the *Times* referred to them—to address thoughtless demolition in the name of urban renewal and the deterioration in the quality of public architecture. "You must love a country very much to be as little satisfied with it as she is," wrote Daniel P. Moynihan in the preface to *Will They Ever Finish Bruckner Boulevard?,* a collection of Huxtable's *Times* articles published in 1970. "You must wish very great things for a nation to be so insistent in pointing out how little prepared it is to *do* great things."

Ada Louise Huxtable never shied away from controversy and over the years denounced big-name real-estate developers and land speculators for indiscriminately wiping out historical buildings that link a city to its past. On the other hand, she did not ascribe to preserving old buildings merely as museum pieces. "What preservation is all about," she wrote in 1968, "is the retention and active relationship of the building of the past to the community's functioning present." Huxtable was instrumental in the creation of a Landmarks Preservation Commission for New York City (1965) and also had a hand in saving architectural treasures in other American cities, including the Post Office in St. Louis, the First National Bank of Oregon in Portland, and the Windsor House in Windsor, Vermont.

As a crusader for excellence in the architecture of her own time, Huxtable was critical of some of Manhattan's contemporary offerings, including the New York Hilton Hotel and the

Ada Louise Huxtable

General Motors Building. Some of her more stinging comments were leveled at the Pan Am Building, which she referred to as a "a prime example of a New York specialty: the big, the expedient and the deathlessly ordinary." Huxtable called Washington, D.C.'s Rayburn Building a "national disaster," and her disdain extended to the General Services Administration, which oversees all federal construction in the United States. "It is quite possible that this is the worst building for the most money in the history of construction art," she wrote in March 1965. "It stuns by sheer mass and boring bulk." On the other hand, Huxtable praised the aesthetic values of the Seagram Building (perhaps her favorite), Chase Manhattan Plaza, and the Ford Foundation Building. A staunch defender of the "glass box," she also believes that the skyscraper "is one of the great technological and architectural achievements of our civilization."

Although Huxtable's opinions have come under frequent attack, few find fault with her trenchant, witty, and lively prose style. **Barbara Belford**, in *Brilliant Bylines,* points out that through the use of stylistic devices, Huxtable gently coaxes the casual reader into a critical experience. By way of example she cites the opening to a column on New York's CBS building (March 13, 1966):

> The first observation that one must make about the new CBS headquarters that rises somberly from its sunken plaza at South Avenue and 52nd Street is that it is a building. It is not, like so much of today's large-scale construction, a handy commercial package, a shiny wraparound envelope, a packing case, a box of cards, a trick with mirrors.
>
> It does not look like a cigar lighter, a vending machine, a nutmeg grater. It is a building in the true, classic sense: a complete design in which technology, function and esthetics are conceived and executed integrally for its purpose. As its architect, Eero Saarinen, wanted, this is a building to be looked at above the bottom fifty feet, to be comprehended as a whole.

Torre also points out that Huxtable's pithy descriptions tend to stick, noting that "The Hirshhorn museum in Washington, will forever be the 'biggest marble donut in the world.'"

In 1970, Huxtable received the first Pulitzer Prize for distinguished criticism, and through the years she has been given countless other awards, including over 25 honorary degrees. She left *The New York Times* in 1981, after receiving a MacArthur Foundation "genius grant," which provided a tax-free stipend of $300,000 over five years. Since then, she has produced a book, *The Tall Building Artistically Reconsidered: The Search for a Skyscraper Style* (1985), and a third anthology of her *Times* columns, *Architecture Anyone?* (1985). Earlier collections include *Will They Ever Finish Bruckner Boulevard?* (1970), and *Kicked a Building Lately?* (1976).

Huxtable has been married since 1940 to industrial designer L. Garth Huxtable, whom she met on her first job at Bloomingdale's and with whom she often collaborates. He has taken photographs for her articles, and they designed tableware together for the Four Seasons restaurant in New York. They divide their time between a penthouse apartment in New York and a summer home in Marblehead, Massachusetts. Garth once remarked that his wife's writing style conjures up the image of a large, bony woman in tweeds, although, to the contrary, she is a petite woman (5'2"), who is almost fragile-looking in appearance. Stephen Grover, in an article for the *Wall Street Journal* (November 7, 1972), quoted an architect who had observed her on a building site: "Before you know it, she's got everyone—the builders included—eating out of her hand and telling her everything she wants to know. Then she retreats behind a closed door and out comes this very gutsy critique."

SOURCES:

Belford, Barbara. *Brilliant Bylines.* NY: Columbia University Press, 1986.

Moritz, Charles, ed. *Current Biography 1973.* NY: H.W. Wilson, 1973.

Torre, Susan, ed. *Women in American Architecture.* NY: Whitney Library of Design, 1977.

Barbara Morgan,
Melrose, Massachusetts

Hveger, Ragnhild (1920—)

Danish swimmer. *Born in Denmark on December 10, 1920.*

Broke 42 records at various distances; held world records in the 200-, 400-, 800- and 1,500-meters which stood for 15 years; won the silver medal in the 400-meter freestyle in Olympics Games (1936); elected to the International Swimming Hall of Fame (1966).

The greatest number of world records held by any swimmer, male or female, is 42 (only Arne Borg of Sweden at 32 comes close). Ragnhild Hveger of Denmark accumulated these trophies between 1936 and 1942. When she began swimming in the 1930s, Ragnhild showed great promise. Like so many of her generation, however, her life as well as her athletic career was permanently changed by World War II. In 1936 at the Berlin Games, Ragnhild was only 15 when she won a silver medal in the 400-meter freestyle, losing the gold to Dutch swimmer *Rie Mastenbroek. In 1940, Hveger was 19 and at her peak, but there were no games held from 1936 to 1948 because of the war. She continued to swim, breaking those 42 world records at various distances. From 1938 to 1953, no other swimmer topped Hveger's records in the 200, 400, 800, and 1,500 meters. Though she retired in 1945 and did not try out for the 1948 games, she decided to give the Olympics one last shot in 1952. The 32-year-old swam on the 4th place 4x400-meter relay team and placed 5th in the 400-meter freestyle. Given that few swimmers over 20 compete internationally, her performance was remarkable. Even on that day, no one broke Hveger's world record of 5:00.1 in the 400-meter freestyle.

Karin Loewen Haag,
freelance writer, Athens, Georgia

Hyatt, Anna Vaughn (1876–1973).

See Huntington, Anna Hyatt.

Hycintha Mariscotti (d. 1640).

See Mariscotti, Hycintha.

Hyde, Anne (1638–1671)

Duchess of York and mother of two English queens, Mary II and Anne. *Born on March 12, 1638 (some sources cite 1637), at Cranbourne Lodge in Windsor, Berkshire, England; died on March 31, 1671, at St. James's Palace, London; interred at Westminster Abbey, London; eldest daughter of Sir Edward Hyde (1609–1674), 1st earl of Clarendon, and Frances Aylesbury (1617–1667); married James, duke of York, later James II, king of England (r. 1685–1688), in 1660; children: Charles Stuart (1638–1671); Mary II (1662–1694), queen of England (r. 1689–1694), queen of Scots (r. 1689–1694); James Stuart (1663–1667); Anne (1665–1714), queen of England (r. 1702–1707), queen of Scotland (r. 1702–1707), queen of Britain (r. 1707–1714); Charles (b. 1666, died in infancy); Edgar (b. 1667, died in infancy); Henrietta (1669–1669); Catherine (1671–1671).*

Anne Hyde was born on March 12, 1638, at Cranbourne Lodge in Windsor, Berkshire, the eldest daughter of Sir Edward Hyde, later earl of Clarendon, and **Frances Aylesbury**. Edward Hyde was lord chancellor to King Charles II, who had spent his youth exiled in France. The English Civil War (1642–1649) had wrested the throne from the Stuart family and sent Charles' father, Charles I, to the execution block.

In 1660, Charles II was restored to the English throne. Having already proved his fertility by siring several bastard children, everyone expected that Charles and his queen, *Catherine of Braganza, would provide an heir to the throne. Should Charles die without a legitimate heir, the throne would pass to his younger brother James, duke of York. But James scandalized the court in 1660 when he secretly married Anne Hyde, who had been maid of honor to *Mary of Orange (1631–1660). Although Sir Edward Hyde had faithfully served Charles II, the Hydes were commoners—not suitable royal marriage partners. Edward was "struck to the heart" and offered to send his daughter to the Tower to be executed, but Charles laughed it off. "She would do her husband good," he said.

In quick succession, the duchess of York produced eight children, but only two survived to adulthood. The world took little notice in the years 1662 and 1665 when Anne Hyde gave birth to baby girls, and the new arrivals were swiftly dispatched to the royal nursery. No one would have guessed that they would one day inherit the English throne, for although the children were undeniably of royal blood, they were far removed from the line of Stuart succession.

In accordance with aristocratic childrearing practices of the day, the ladies Mary and Anne were brought up in a royal nursery where they could be groomed in courtly manners and kept secluded from the adults at court. As a result, their relationship with their parents was formal and constrained. Anne referred to her father as "the Duke," or later "the King," and once admitted that she could not recall from memory how her mother had looked. The girls were brought up Protestant under the watchful eye of Lady *Frances Villiers and two Anglican guardians. Therefore, their relationship with their parents became even more distant when Anne Hyde and James converted to Roman Catholicism in 1669.

The ravages of the Civil War had convinced most of the English populace that their monarchs must be members of the Church of England. Since the Test Act (1673) barred non-Anglicans from political and military office, James was dismissed from all government appointments because of his conversion. Political realities dictated that Mary and Anne, against their father's wishes, remain firmly in the hand of their Anglican tutors, where they became fervent defenders of the Protestant faith. After a reasonably happy marriage, Anne Hyde died in 1671, before James had ascended to the throne of England. Many portraits of her were painted by her protegé, Sir Peter Lely.

Hyde, Catherine (1701–1777)

Duchess of Queensberry. *Name variations: Catherine Douglas. Born in 1701; died in 1777; interred at Durisdeer; daughter of Henry Hyde, 4th earl of Clarendon and earl of Rochester, and Jane Leveson-Gower; married Charles Douglas, 3rd duke of Queensbury, on March 10, 1720; children: Henry Douglas (b. 1722), earl of Drumlanrig; Charles Douglas (b. 1726).*

Catherine Hyde was born in 1701, the daughter of Henry Hyde, 4th earl of Clarendon and earl of Rochester, and **Jane Leveson-Gower**, though some think she was the natural daughter of Jane and Lord Carleton. Catherine was a correspondent with Jonathan Swift and a friend to William Congreve, Alexander Pope, James Thomson, Matthew Prior, and William Whitehead.

Hyde, Ida (1857–1945)

American physiologist who developed microtechniques to investigate a single cell. *Born in Davenport, Iowa, on September 8, 1857; died in Berkeley, California, on August 22, 1945; one of four children of Meyer Heidenheimer (a merchant) and Babette (Loewenthal) Heidenheimer; attended the Chicago Athenaeum; attended the University of Illinois, 1881–82; Cornell University, B.S., 1891; attended the University of Strassburg, 1893–95; University of Heidelberg, Ph.D., 1896; never married; no children.*

Noted physiologist Ida Hyde worked 23 years—about the length of her later career as a scientist—just to obtain her education, battling poverty and sex discrimination the entire way. She was born in Davenport, Iowa, in 1857, the daughter of German immigrants who had shortened their name from Heidenheimer to Hyde on arrival in the United States. At age 16, Hyde was apprenticed to a millinery business in Chicago. Determined to continue her education, she attended the Chicago Athenaeum, a school for working students. At age 24, she entered the University of Illinois, but after one year had depleted her finances and was forced to find work. She secured a position teaching in the Chicago public schools, where she remained for the next seven years. It was not until 1888 that she entered Cornell University to once again pursue her education, receiving her undergraduate degree in 1891.

Hyde continued instruction at Bryn Mawr College, where she studied under zoologist Thomas Hunt Morgan (1866–1945) and physiologist Jacques Loeb (1859–1934). In 1893, she was invited to do research at the University of Strassburg, and, with funding from the Association of Collegiate Alumnae (later the American Association of University Women), she was able to accept the offer. At Strassburg, however, she was denied permission to take the Ph.D. examination because of her gender. She transferred to the University of Heidelberg, where she also met with further sex discrimination from noted physiologist Wilhelm Kühne, with whom she wished to study. However, she managed to obtain support from other faculty members and, in 1896, became the first woman to receive a Ph.D. from Heidelberg University. She would later detail her experiences in Germany in the satiric article, "Before Women Were Human Beings." After receiving her degree, Hyde did research at the Heidelberg Table of the Zoological Station, a marine biological lab in Naples. Her experience there interested her in providing a similar opportunity for other women scientists, and she later led the effort to establish the Naples Table Association for Promoting Scientific Research by Women.

Returning to the United States in the fall of 1896, she spent a year as a research fellow at Radcliffe College, working with physiologist William Townsend Porter at the Harvard Medical School, the first woman to do research at that institution. In 1898, she joined the faculty of the University of Kansas as an associate professor of physiology, and in 1905, when a separate department of physiology was established, she was promoted to full professor. In over two decades with the university, Hyde gained an outstanding reputation as a teacher and researcher. In conjunction with her classroom work, she wrote a textbook, *Outlines of Experimental Physiology* (1905), and a laboratory manual, *Laboratory Outlines of Physiology* (1910). Her research was conducted mostly during the summers. She was at the University of Liverpool in the summer of 1904 and spent several subsequent summers at the Marine Biological Laboratory in Woods Hole, Massachusetts. She also managed to further pursue her own education, spending summers between 1908 and 1912 at Rush Medical College in Chicago, and completing nearly all the requirements for an M.D. degree. Retiring from the university in 1922, Hyde returned to the University of Heidelberg for a year to conduct research on the effects of radium.

Hyde's scientific work was broad within her field, including both invertebrates and verte-

Ida Hyde

brates, and dealing with the physiology of the circulatory, respiratory, and nervous systems. Her major contribution was the development of microtechniques by which a single cell could be investigated. The microelectrode that she invented in 1921 is still routinely used in neurophysiology. In recognition of her work, Hyde was the first woman elected to membership in the American Physiological Association.

Throughout her life, Hyde continued to help other women achieve their academic goals, founding scholarships at both Cornell and the University of Kansas and donating $25,000 to establish the Ida H. Hyde Woman's International Fellowship of the American Association of University Women, the organization that had made it possible for her to study in Germany.

After her retirement, Hyde settled in California, living first in San Diego, then Berkeley, where she died of a cerebral hemorrhage in 1945.

SOURCES:

Ogilvie, Marilyn Bailey. *Women in Science*. Cambridge, MA: The MIT Press, 1986.

Sicherman, Barbara and Carol Hurd Green, eds. *Notable American Women: The Modern Period*. Cambridge, MA: The Belknap Press of Harvard University Press, 1980.

Barbara Morgan,
Melrose, Massachusetts

Hyde, Jane (d. 1725)

Countess of Clarendon and Rochester. *Died in 1725; married Henry Hyde, 2nd earl of Rochester, in 1693; children: Henry Hyde (1710–1753), Viscount Cornbury and Baron Hyde, Jacobite MP for Oxford University.*

Jane Hyde was a celebrated beauty and the inspiration for Myra in Matthew Prior's *Judgement of Venus.*

Hyde, Miriam Beatrice (1913—)

Australian composer, pianist, and teacher who composed over 160 works, including a dozen major orchestral pieces. *Born in Adelaide, Australia, on January 15, 1913.*

Won the Sullivan, Farrar and Cobbett prizes for composition at the Royal College of Music; won the Anzac Song prize three times.

Born in Adelaide, Australia, in 1913, Miriam Hyde wrote prolifically throughout her long career. She began studying under her mother before winning an Australian Music Examination Board scholarship at age 12 to Elder Conservatory at Adelaide University. She obtained a diploma in 1931 after studying with William Silver. From 1932 to 1935, Hyde studied at the Royal College of Music as an Elder Scholar. Howard Hadley and Sir Arthur Benjamin taught her piano, while R.O. Morris and Gordon Jacob trained her in composition. She performed two of her Piano Concertos in London with the London Philharmonic conducted by Leslie Heward and the London Symphony conducted by Constant Lambert. When Hyde returned home in 1936, Sir Malcolm Sargent conducted her *Adelaide Overture.* She taught at the Kambala School and became an examiner of music. Winner of many prizes for composition, Hyde wrote extensively, especially for piano. In 1981, she was awarded an OBE.

John Haag,
Athens, Georgia

Hyde, Robin (1906–1939).

See Wilkinson, Iris.

Hyman, Flo (1954–1986)

African-American volleyball player who popularized the sport. *Name variations: Flora Jo. Born Flora Hyman in Inglewood, California, on July 29 (some sources cite July 31), 1954; died in Matsue, Japan, on January 24, 1986; attended the University of Houston.*

Led the American volleyball team to an Olympic silver in the Los Angeles games (1984); honored by the Women's Sports Association with the creation of the annual Flo Hyman Award (1987).

Born in Inglewood, California, in 1954, Flo Hyman rose from obscurity to international acclaim in volleyball, a sport few Americans knew much about. When a sister first encouraged her to join the high school volleyball team in Inglewood, California, Flo was already over six feet tall and growing. Athletically gifted, she soon became one of the nation's top players. Hyman attended the University of Houston where she was a three-time All-American. In 1974, she joined the U.S. national team and in 1976 was named the outstanding collegiate player. By this time, Hyman was 6'5" and, with the help of her coach Arie Selinger, had learned to use her height to tremendous advantage.

America had never been a power in world volleyball. It was not until 1974 that the U.S. Volleyball Association established a training center so that women's and men's teams could train year round, but the women's team failed to qualify for the 1976 Olympics. By 1978, however, the U.S. women's team ranked fifth in the world, a feat for which Flo Hyman was partially responsible. Her leadership was crucial in the 1978 and 1982 World championships. When the U.S. boycotted the Moscow Olympics in 1980, she stayed with the U.S. national team. At this point, Hyman was considered one of the best volleyball players in the world, one of six players to be chosen for the All-World Cup team in 1981.

The American viewing public was finally introduced to volleyball at the 1984 Los Angeles Olympics where Flo Hyman's tall, athletic figure was predominant. The matches received some of the highest television ratings of the Olympics. Millions cheered Flo and her team as they competed with the best in the world. The Americans won a silver, losing to the more powerful Chinese. "We accomplished a lot," said Hyman. "We're proud of our silver medal." In just a decade, Flo Hyman had brought American volleyball from obscurity into the spotlight.

Hyman, who was 30 in 1984 when she retired from the U.S. national team, faced the problem of many women athletes: there were no professional teams in America on which to play. Instead, she signed with the Japanese professional circuit. While on the court in Matsue early in 1986, age 31, Hyman suddenly collapsed and died of a ruptured aorta due to Marfan's syndrome, a genetic disorder. At the time of her death, she was planning to participate in the 1988 Olympics. In 1987, the Women's Sports Association created the Flo Hyman Award in her memory.

SOURCES:

Woolum, Janet. *Outstanding Women Athletes: Who They Are and How They Influenced Sports in America.* Phoenix, Arizona: Oryx Press, 1992.

Karin L. Haag,
freelance writer, Athens, Georgia

Hyman, Libbie Henrietta

(1888–1969)

American zoologist who was an authority on the physiology and morphology of lower invertebrates.
Born on December 6, 1888, in Des Moines, Iowa; died on August 3, 1969, in New York City; only daughter and the third of four children of Joseph Hyman (a tailor) and Sabina (Neumann) Hyman; University of Chicago, B.S., 1910, Ph.D., 1915; never married; no children.

Born in 1888 into a poor immigrant family, Libbie Hyman endured a difficult childhood dominated by her mother. A precocious student, she graduated early as valedictorian of her high school class, then took additional courses in science and German while pasting labels at a Mother's Rolled Oats factory. In 1906, aided by a scholarship, Hyman was able to enter the University of Chicago where she intended to study botany. However, after encountering anti-Semitism in that department, she switched to zoology, receiving her undergraduate degree in 1910. She did her graduate work under the direction of Charles Manning Child and, after receiving her Ph.D. in 1915, stayed on at the university as Child's research assistant and as a laboratory instructor in vertebrate anatomy and elementary zoology. In the course of the next 15 years, Hyman published a number of articles in conjunction with Child's projects, as well as her own *Laboratory Manual for Elementary Zoology* (1919) and *Laboratory Manual for Comparative Vertebrate Anatomy* (1922), both of which became widely used texts.

Libbie Hyman's family had moved to Chicago after her father's death in 1907, and she continued to live at home until her mother's death in 1930. In 1931, she left the university and, with a small income from her books, spent a year exploring scientific centers in Europe. She eventually settled into an apartment in New York and began to write a treatise on the invertebrates, doing much of her research at the library of the American Museum of Natural History. In 1937, the museum made her a research associate, an unsalaried position, but one that provided an office and laboratory space.

Hyman, who was formidable in appearance and manner, was considered something of an oddity among her colleagues. There was a much-circulated rumor about her cigar smoking, though she neither drank nor smoked. Her expertise on the taxonomy and anatomy of the unpopular and unexplored lower invertebrates gained her the respect of scientists in the United States and Europe, who often sent her specimens to identify. With the publication of her comprehensive six-volume encyclopedic survey *The Invertebrates,* published between 1940 and 1967, she won additional stature. Hailed as an astounding scientific achievement, the book is considered a classic and still widely used. In 1960, for her work in zoology, Hyman received the British Royal Society's Gold Medal of the Linnean Society.

Hyman's love of her subject was profound. "I don't like vertebrates," she once pronounced. "It's hard to explain but I just can't get excited about them, never could. I like invertebrates. I don't mean worms particularly, although a worm can be almost anything, including the larva of a beautiful butterfly. But I do like the soft delicate ones, the jellyfishes and corals and the beautiful microscopic organisms." Handicapped by Parkinson's disease during her later years, Hyman was unable to complete additional volumes on arthropods and high mollusks, but she continued to work at the Museum of Natural History until her death in 1969.

SOURCES:

Macksey, Joan and Kenneth Macksey. *The Book of Women's Achievements.* NY: Stein and Day, 1976.

Sicherman, Barbara and Carol Hurd Green, eds. *Notable American Women: The Modern Period.* Cambridge, MA: The Belknap Press of Harvard University Press, 1980.

Barbara Morgan,
Melrose, Massachusetts

Hynde, Chrissie (1951—)

American rock musician and leader of the rock band The Pretenders. *Born on September 7, 1951 in Akron, Ohio; daughter of Bud Hynde (a telephone company employee) and Dee Hynde; attended Kent State University, late 1960s; married Jim Kerr (a rock musician), in 1984 (divorced 1989); married Lucho Brieva (a sculptor), in 1997; children: (with Kinks frontman Ray Davies) Natalie Rae (b. 1983); (with Kerr) Yasmine (b. 1985).*

Chrissie Hynde was born on September 7, 1951, in Akron, Ohio, the second child of Bud and **Dee Hynde**. Her adolescence coincided with the British invasion sparked by the Rolling Stones and the Beatles, and she became enamored of the rock 'n' roll scene. Bored with high school, Hynde spent her youth attending concerts in Cleveland, Ohio, and playing in garage bands. Her career as a rhythm guitarist began when she took up the baritone ukulele at age 16. She began songwriting and practiced her vocals by singing loudly in a closet.

In the late 1960s, Hynde enrolled at Kent State University in Kent, Ohio, as a fine arts major. There she participated in the infamous Kent State antiwar protest during which National Guardsmen shot and killed four students. She dropped out of school and worked a variety of jobs, including a stint waiting tables which she quit because it conflicted with her militant vegetarianism. Eager to become a part of the growing London punk scene, she moved there in 1973 and continued taking low-paying jobs (such as cleaning Keith Richards' house) while trying to break into the music business. Throughout the mid-1970s, Hynde bounced between England, the United States and France, performing with a variety of bands and meeting such punk idols as Johnny Rotten and Sid Vicious of the Sex Pistols, and Mick Jones of the Clash.

In 1978, Hynde got her chance to head a group of her own. Together with the British musicians Pete Farndon, James Honeyman-Scott, and Martin Chambers, she formed the group The Pretenders, named after a song by the Platters. They released their self-titled debut album in 1980 to enormous critical acclaim. Hynde earned much of the praise for the album's success as the principal songwriter, guitarist and gutsy voice behind the blunt lyrics. With the album hitting the top of the charts and the title of "Best New Artists" under their belts (courtesy of the editors of *Rolling Stone* magazine), The Pretenders appeared to be well on their way to stardom.

The early 1980s proved to be rocky for the band, however. Their quick follow-up album, *Pretenders II* (1981), did not match the debut album's power or popularity. In addition to the commercial loss, internal strife and drug abuse resulted in the dismissal of Farndon from the band. Then Honeyman-Scott and Farndon died from drug overdoses in 1982 and 1983, respectively. Hynde managed to hold things together with the addition of two new members, and The Pretenders released their third album, *Learning to Crawl,* in 1984. The title of the album referred both to The Pretenders' struggles as a newly constituted band, and to Hynde's toddler daughter, Natalie Rae (whose father was Ray Davies of the Kinks). The band continued to undergo staff changes over the years, but Hynde remained the center of the group.

Three months after the end of her four-year relationship with Davies, Hynde married Jim Kerr, singer for the Scottish band Simple Minds. A year later, she gave birth to her second daughter, Yasmine. Motherhood did not halt her career: in 1986 The Pretenders released the album *Get Close* and a year later embarked on a world tour.

Another four years passed before the band released the album *Packed!,* although a collection of singles had been produced in 1987. During the hiatus, Hynde and Kerr divorced, and Hynde set up household in London with her two daughters, four cats, and a nanny. During the 1990s, The Pretenders slowed their recording pace even further, waiting until 1995 to produce another album, *Isle of View.* A critically hailed acoustic blend of The Pretenders' music and a string quartet, the album did not sell well. Hynde, never one to let other people's opinions dictate the course of her career, has continued to write the same cutting lyrics and hard-edged guitar riffs that put The Pretenders on the map in the 1970s. Their seventh album, *¡Viva El Amor!,* released in 1999, reflected the South American influence of Hynde's new husband, Colombian sculptor Lucho Brieva. Hynde and Brieva married in 1997 in a low-key ceremony in London.

From the beginning of her career, Hynde has been known for her passion, not only in her

Chrissie Hynde

singing, but also in the causes she supported. She was an animal-rights activist long before it became a popular celebrity cause, and contributed her talents to such worthy endeavors as famine relief for Africa. Despite her impressive body of work and her longstanding career as the queen of no-nonsense rock, Hynde prefers to identify herself more as a "stereotypical middle-aged, divorced cocktail waitress rearing two children in Ohio."

SOURCES:

Current Biography. NY: H.W. Wilson, 1993.

Farber, Jim. "Not Pretending," in *The Day* [New London, CT]. July 2, 1999.

Kevorkian, Kyle. *Newsmakers 1991.* Detroit, MI: Gale Research, 1991.

People Weekly. July 26, 1999, p. 41.

Karina L. Kerr, M.A.,
Ypsilanti, Michigan

Hypatia (c. 375–415)

Alexandrian who became one of the most famous intellectuals of her generation, drawing students from all over the Roman Empire. *Born around 375 CE; died in 415; daughter of Theon (a mathematician and astronomer associated with the Museum of Alexandria).*

Born in Alexandria, Egypt, in 375 or a little earlier, Hypatia was the daughter of Theon, a mathematician and astronomer associated with the Alexandrian Museum. In fact, Theon is the last verified member of that famous institution, founded about 700 years earlier by Ptolemy I, a successor of Alexander the Great and the founder of the dynasty which ruled Egypt until the Romans took direct control of the land in 30 BCE. This Museum was not a repository for art, but rather a think tank where famous artists and intellectuals came to ply their expertise initially under the patronage of the Ptolemies, but eventually under the Romans who allowed the city's administration to underwrite the Museum's expenses. Associated with the Museum—or the "House of the Muses"—was the equally famous Alexandrian Library with a collection numbering about 750,000 volumes (each far more expensive to produce than a modern book, for this was an age well before print). This enormous collection was unparalleled and constituted an intellectual resource of the first magnitude, allowing Alexandria to replace Athens as the cultural center of the Greek world.

Traditionally, to be a member of the Museum was to be a member of a religious fraternity, with the Muses—nine goddesses credited with inspiring the intellectually and artistically gifted—receiving their sacred due. The intellectual responsibilities of Museum associates were minimal, but they were compelled to share the fruits of their labors with their patrons and each other through symposia and publication. Regardless, during Hypatia's lifetime, larger social forces compelled the Museum to change with the times. The 4th century CE was *the* Christian century. When it began, probably no more than ten percent of the population of the Roman Empire were Christians, although these tended to live in cities like Alexandria, in the eastern Mediterranean. However, things began to change drastically when Constantine I the Great legalized Christianity in 312. From that time until Theodosius (Constantine's imperial successor several times removed) essentially outlawed paganism through a series of edicts in 391, the number of Christians multiplied many times. As a result, the culture of the empire became an increasingly Christian one, and many tensions developed as the new Christian majority came head to head with the remnants of the old pagan order. One of these remnants was the Museum. Even though most of the scholars and artists disassociated themselves from the old gods, the establishment was erected around a thoroughly pagan core.

Hypatia was an intellectual prodigy who certainly began her schooling with her father, as her lifelong interests in the fields of mathematics and astronomy indicate. Where she was introduced to a serious study of philosophy, however, is unknown, for her father was not a philosopher. Although Hypatia would later fit well into the neo-Platonic school of Alexandria (which she would head from a very young age), some ancient sources claim that she received her philosophical training at Athens. As enticing as Hypatia visiting Athens may seem, she probably never set foot in Greece. Certainly, Athens had no intellects or resources like those found in Alexandria during the last quarter of the fourth century, for Athens' philosophical heyday was long over by that time. Thus the suggestion that Hypatia studied in Athens probably amounts to no more basis in fact than that the intellectual traditions practiced in Alexandria during Hypatia's lifetime originated in Athens, although Alexandria had replaced Athens as the philosophical center of the Greek world when Hypatia lived.

While still in her 20s, Hypatia developed such a reputation as a mathematician, astronomer, and philosopher that she began to draw students to Alexandria from all over the Roman Empire. Among the mathematical and astronomical works which established Hypatia's reputation were a commentary on Diophantus' *Arithmeticorum* (a work dedicated to algebraic theorems), a revision of *Almagest,* the third book of Ptolemy the astronomer (not to be confused with the kings of Egypt), and a commentary on *Conic Sections*. In the first of these, Hypatia explored the realm of mathematical calculation and ratio without the luxury of Arabic numbers. In the second, Hypatia followed her father's lead in revising Ptolemy's astronomical primer, which had already become the field's standard and would remain so until the Renaissance. Although conceptually flawed, Ptolemy's was one of the greatest scientific tracts of all time. By working within the Ptolemaic tradition, Hypatia accepted its premise of a geocentric (earth centered) universe as opposed to the heliocentric (sun centered) model produced by Aristarchus, another astronomer associated with the Museum in the 3rd century BCE. Hypatia's greatest contribution to Ptolemy's work appears to have been in her use of a sexagesimal system of calculation, the process of computing by 60s, such as 60 minutes, 60 seconds, which was especially well adapted to the task of bringing together Ptolemy's theories of cosmic motion with the observable, orbital motions of astronomical bodies. Of course, since the conception of the physical universe as put forth by Ptolemy was fundamentally wrong, Hypatia's contribution to this conception was more rationalization than good science. Of *Conic Sections,* the final work attested to have been Hypatia's, little can be said. In addition to her contributions to theoretical science, however, she appears to have been an inventor of devices with practical applications. Two such tools are especially noteworthy, the first having been a three-dimensional celestial map and the second a machine to determine the relative specific gravities of different liquids. Hypatia may also have been responsible for adapting an abacus to her sexagesimal system of computation, thus allowing her to be more efficient (and probably faster) in her astronomical calculations.

> [Hypatia was] a person so renowned, her reputation seemed literally incredible.
>
> **—Synesius**

Hypatia's fascination with the heavens stimulated her to become equally intrigued with cosmogony, and the philosophical questions concerning the origins of the universe which cosmogony can generate. Unlike her father, Hypatia began a serious inquiry into the nature of humanity, its purpose, and its relative position in the cosmic hierarchy. As a result, she was drawn to philosophy, and especially to the Plotinian neo-Platonism which in her time was the prominent philosophy of the Museum. It is curious that her metaphysical interests did not lead Hypatia to Christianity, yet it may have been the case that she considered Christianity's intellectual development in her day somewhat crude when compared to the pagan mix of "science" and philosophy such as neo-Platonism had become. One thing seems certain, it was *not* Christianity's tolerance for magic and mysticism which repelled Hypatia, for the philosophical tradition with which she became associated had more than its share of interest in such things. Although the neo-Platonism of Hypatia's world had long had a scientific foundation and a special interest in mathematics, since the time of Plotinus (3rd century CE) those who worked within the philosophical tradition established by Plato also had a profound interest in religious mysticism. Essentially, the neo-Platonists exploited reason as much as possible in the expectation that it would bring them close enough to "Divinity," thereafter permitting the Divinity or "Essence" to be mystically experienced. Although this attitude had been present in Plato—who believed that the material world was in no sense real, and that reality lay entirely in perfect "Forms" which were immaterial and "rediscoverable" by the philosophically inclined through the application of pure reason (and who, if successful, would know the bliss of basking in the glow of the Forms perceived)—after Plotinus, this bias toward mysticism increased.

Plotinus essentially synthesized rationalism in the Platonic mold with his century's growing interest in the afterlife and faith in salvation—a faith which manifested itself in a number of oriental mystery cults, of which Christianity was only one. Plotinus believed that everything which exists is the product of an immaterial and impersonal force that could variously be called "Goodness," the "One," "Beauty," and/or "Truth." To the extent that one is real, or to the extent that one has value, one is united with this Essence. As one approached this Being through the exercise of reason, one became both more real and of greater value. Since this Essence was often characterized as being the source of all "light," enabling anyone who wished to "see," it is easy to understand how Plotinus and his followers became interested in astronomy, for manifestations of the "One" could easily be discovered in the physical reality of the sun and stars. Of course, Plotinian neo-Platonists were not alone in associating the structure of the universe with the very essence of the divine, for many, including the devotees of Mithras, did much the same. What seems to have marked out the tradition to which Hypatia related, however, was its pursuit of mystical understanding through mathematics, for if one could predict what would happen in the cosmos through the language of mathematics, then one (in a very important sense) had reached an understanding of "reality." Numbers are immaterial, immutable and eternal, it was argued. Thus, those who understood mathematics came to understand the only thing which was all of these—that is, the

Hypatia

"One." Without a knowledge of numbers, it was believed that humankind was cut off from that Source of all goodness, and trapped in a changeable cosmos which was not "real," existing but as a pale shadow of the Essence which animates the universe.

Plotinus' philosophy was, of course, considerably more elaborate than can be explored here, but as it was passed on by his student, Porphyry, it came to be intimately linked with the "truths" thought mystically encrypted in the wisdom of ancient pagan religiosity, both Hellenic and Oriental. It was not that this school of thought paid much heed to the rituals associated with traditional pagan religion, for it did not, but it was thought that the mythological traditions associated with age-old cults often contained truths which could supplement scientific discovery and abet one seeking a reunion with the unity of the "One." Thus, respectful of traditional religion, neo-Platonism at the beginning of the 5th century CE was on a collision course with a decreasingly tolerant Christianity, and Hypatia was the most famous contemporary neo-Platonist.

About the year 400, Hypatia became the head of the neo-Platonic school in Alexandria at a very young age for such a prestigious appointment. She was probably no more than 25 when she became perhaps the most influential academic of her world. In her new post, Hypatia had access to the resources of the Museum and Library, although by this time, the religious rituals which had once bound Museum associates together had been discontinued. In her new academic position (or rather, positions), Hypatia drew a civic salary, a very unusual situation at the time for two reasons: first, she was a woman; and second, because she was a staunch pagan in a city of Christians, ruled over by a Christian administration. What her precise responsibilities were to the city of Alexandria are unknown, but it is likely that she was required to educate the young men and women of the city, thus maintaining for the Greeks in Egypt a link with their Hellenic roots. We know that she taught courses in a number of mathematical fields, in astronomy, and in philosophy, in which her fame so extended as to draw students from far and wide. Besides lecturing in the fields of her own research and development, Hypatia also seems to have provided a series of courses in the historical development of philosophy, including introductions to Plato, Aristotle, Pythagoras, Xenophon, the Stoics, the Cynics, and Plotinus. In short, Hypatia was a kind of university professor, although her range was considerably broader than would be expected from a modern-day counterpart. Regardless, her focus, when not pure mathematics or science, was strictly pagan—she seems to have had no interest in Christianity whatsoever, although from personal experience she certainly became familiar with both the development of Christianity and the major Christian theological issues of her day.

Hypatia maintained a high profile throughout Alexandria—so high in fact that her detractors suggested that she was a brazen woman of loose morals. These allegations were almost certainly no more than scurrilous slander, for one—rather coarse—anecdote suggests that she was one intellectual who eschewed the pursuit of physical pleasure. Romantically wooed by one of her students, Hypatia soundly rebuffed his efforts by producing a used sanitary napkin and claiming that what her would-be lover had set his heart upon was no more worth loving than was the napkin. True beauty, goodness, and virtue were not to be found in the fulfillment of physical love, she proclaimed, but only in the pursuit of philosophy and of science.

Whatever eminence Hypatia achieved as an intellectual was equalled by the esteem with which many in Alexandria held her. So valued was her advice that she was consulted about a range of practical issues, some of which were socially volatile. In particular, a prefect (magistrate) of the city of Alexandria, one Orestes, frequently sounded Hypatia out about the ethics of his position and the politics of the moment. It should be noted that this was not only a rapidly changing world with Christianity becoming a social mainstay, it was also a world which cared not at all to separate church from state. In fact, if there was one thing upon which pagans and Christians could agree, it was that no healthy state could function for long without the political structure being active in the appropriate honoring of the gods or God. The only question was, which God or gods? Although virtually everyone at the time held definite opinions about religious issues, not all Christians were convinced that everything associated with the pagan tradition could, or should, be rejected in toto. Such a man apparently was Orestes, who seems to have both valued the wisdom of traditional Hellenism, and to have been willing to use it in his quest to assert his authority over the city of Alexandria's ecclesiastical administration. The ecclesiastical administration was just as anxious to assume many of the prerogatives customarily thought to have been the rightful possessions of the city's civil authorities.

Orestes' primary rival and Hypatia's ultimate nemesis was Cyril. Born about 375, Cyril succeeded his uncle (Theophilus) as the bishop of Alexandria in 412, somewhat after Hypatia had established herself as one of the city's most powerful intellects. Cyril was an orthodox zealot, who took it upon himself both to cleanse Alexandria of all unorthodox thinking and to purge the church everywhere of all heresy. In the latter capacity, once Cyril inherited the See (seat of authority) of Alexandria and thus became Egypt's "first" citizen, he struggled with Nestorius, the patriarch of Constantinople, over a theological issue concerning the nature of Christ. Nestorius maintained that in Jesus a divine being and a human person were united in perfect harmony of deed, but not in the unity of a single individual. This struck Cyril as blatant heresy, and in response he insisted that ***Mary the Virgin** be deemed the "God-bearer" so as to emphasize the total unity of both aspects of her son. The issue escalated over time—probably because of Cyril's and his community's fear that Constantinople would come to be officially recognized as above Alexandria in the emerging hierarchy of the church. Cyril convened a Church Council at Ephesus in 431 which declared Nestorianism a heresy. As a result, Nestorius lost his post and was banished into the Libyan desert, where he continued in his heresy, and from where his brand of Christianity spread to be especially influential throughout central Asia and the Far East.

Cyril was also active closer to home. For example, he closed the churches of the Novatians, a Christian sect which had been deemed heretical. The Novatians believed that, no matter the reason, the church did not have the authority to absolve those who had lapsed from Christianity into paganism, even those who had been threatened with persecution. By the 5th century, this was an old issue, for the Carthaginian Donatus had raised pretty much the same concern as early as 314. Of course, at that time Donatism had been declared Christianity's first official heresy, and steps had been taken to eradicate its notions. Despite the fact that by the 5th century there was no fear of Christians being persecuted by pagans, the objections against one-time apostates (defectors) returning to the church remained alive. The authority of those church officials who had received their commissions in a direct line from those who had previously fallen continued to be questioned by some, splitting the church.

In addition to problems within the church, Cyril was apparently behind an attempt by orthodox Alexandrians to expel the Jewish community of the city. Riots broke out over this issue, for the Jewish community in Alexandria was almost as old as the city itself and was both large and influential. Although no one could pin the Christian riots against the Jews on Cyril, he certainly did nothing to temper the zeal of his parishioners. More than anything else, it was this breakdown in civil order which pitted Orestes—who clearly thought that Cyril had overstepped the bounds of his authority—against Cyril, and, although he clearly consulted her about other issues, prompted Orestes to seek out Hypatia's advice. After much chaos, Orestes gained control of the situation, and Cyril's anti-Semitic faction clearly suffered a setback, while Cyril personally lost face. Although Cyril should not have blamed Hypatia for his temporary defeat, clearly he associated her—a pagan and a woman to boot—with the forces which had frustrated his vision of a Jew-free Alexandria. Hypatia would become a scapegoat, and what followed was gruesome. Whether Cyril actually hired or merely inspired them is unknown, but shortly after Cyril's setback, a group of monks publicly accosted Hypatia. Pulling her from her chariot, they led her into the Caesarium Church where they took an inhuman revenge for her outspoken attacks upon Christianity in general and Cyril in particular. In the church, the monks stripped Hypatia of her clothes, and, taking shells specially honed to a razor-sharpness, they skinned her alive. Such a death, however, was not enough. Thereafter, these paragons of virtue quartered Hypatia and cremated her severed remains. This heinous abuse of one of late antiquity's greatest minds went unpunished. Cyril went on to become recognized, both in the Latin and Greek Orthodox Churches, as a saint.

SOURCES:

Fitzgerald, A. *Letters of Synesius.* Oxford University Press, 1926.

Socrates Scholasticus. *Ecclesiastical History.* Book 7. London: H.B. Bohn, 1853.

SUGGESTED READING:

Dzielska, Maria. *Hypatia of Alexandria.* Translated by F. Lyra. Boston, MA: Harvard University Press, 1995.

Kingsley, Charles. *Hypatia.* 1853.

Quasten, J. "Cyril of Alexandria," in *Patrology.* Vol. 3, 1960, p. 116+.

Waithe, Mary Ellen, *A History of Women Philosophers, 600 B.C.–500 A.D.* Boston, MA: Martinus Nijhoff, 1987.

William Greenwalt,
Associate Professor of Classical History,
Santa Clara University, Santa Clara, California

Iaia (fl. c. 100 BCE)

Ancient Greek painter, mostly of women's portraits. *Pronunciation: ee-EYE-ah. Name variations: Laia; Lala; Laya; Maia; Marcia; Martia. Born at an unknown date in Cyzicus (near present-day Erdek in Turkey, on the Sea of Marmara); never married.*

Painted panels and ivories; executed a large portrait of an old woman on a wooden panel in Naples, and a self-portrait.

No one had a quicker hand than she in painting.

—Pliny the Elder

Of the five women whom Pliny the Elder includes in his discussion of painters in the *Natural History* 35.147, he tells us most about the medium, subjects, quality and technique of Iaia's work. Useful as this information is, it is still ultimately tantalizing. We are told, for example, that Iaia was originally from Cyzicus (a very old Greek colony on the south shore of the Sea of Marmara in present-day Turkey) but that she was active in Rome "during the youth of Marcus Varro," placing her floruit at perhaps 100 BCE. That a talented Greek of this period could find patronage in Rome, by this point virtual master of the Mediterranean and eager to inherit the sophisticated high culture of its Hellenistic subjects, is not surprising. That a woman was able to do so raises many questions about the circumstances of Iaia's education and relocation which are impossible to answer. Unlike several of the other women painters on his list (viz. ***Aristarete**, ***Irene**, and perhaps ***Timarete**), Pliny does not mention Iaia's father's name or profession, so we cannot speculate that she trained in art with him and then followed him to Rome, or know if she established a reputation in Asia Minor before coming to Italy.

Additional interesting facts in Pliny's sketch seem to distinguish Iaia from other male and female artists, yet they too lack the connecting detail of a satisfactory biography. For example, he tells us that Iaia painted mostly portraits of women, and also that she was a lifelong virgin (*perpetua virgo*). We do not know the circumstances that caused her to choose her favorite subject matter, or indeed if this choice had any connection with her marital status in a society in which most free women were expected to marry. Some have speculated that she may have belonged to a priesthood or cult for which chastity was required, but we have no record of any such that fostered artistic members. Nevertheless, glimmers of a personality seem to show around Pliny's description of her skill and success: "No one else had a quicker hand in painting," he says, and he goes on to report on the financial rewards of her talent: "her artistic skill was such that in the prices she obtained she far outdid the most celebrated portrait painters of the same period, Sopolis and Dionysius, whose pictures fill the galleries." While he says nothing explicit of her character, it is tempting to read into this account of her competition with male artists the presence of a healthy ego; Pliny also tells us that she painted (with the assistance of a mirror) a self-portrait, a genre not mentioned often in Classical sources.

Iaia was skilled in the use of the brush, the common implement for painting on panels of wood, linen, and marble. She also used the cestrum, a kind of graver, on ivory, in the imperfectly understood technique of encaustic, which involved applying hot wax varnish to previously applied paint. Unfortunately, like all but one of the known women artists of antiquity (*see entry on ***Helena** for the exception*), nothing of her work or its influence remains. The attention Pliny gave her, however, has not gone unnoticed by subsequent historians of art. It is the allure of her achievements as much as the corrupt text in which they are recorded that is responsible for the numerous speculations from the time of Boccaccio on the true form of her name, which is still uncertain. (*For further background information, see entry on Aristarete.*)

SOURCES AND SUGGESTED READING:

Enciclopedia dell'Arte Antica Classica e Orientiale. S.v. "Timarete." Rome: Instituto della Enciclopedia Italiana, 1958–66.

Paulys Real-Encyclopädie der Classischen Alterumswissenschaft. Edited by Georg Wissowa et al. S.v. "Iaia" by G. Lippold. Stuttgart: J.B. Metzlersche Buchhandlung, 1894—.

RELATED MEDIA:

Saylor, Steven. *Arms of Nemesis: A Novel of Ancient Rome.* NY: Ivy Books, 1992 (Iaia and Olympias appear as completely fabricated but entertaining characters in this historical mystery novel).

Peter H. O'Brien,
Boston University

Ibarbourou, Juana de (1895–1979)

Prizewinning Uruguayan poet who was noted for her path-breaking erotic work. *Name variations: Juana Fernández de Morales; Jeanette de Ibar. Pronunciation: HWA-na day EE-bar-BOO-roo. Born Juana Fernández de Morales on March 8, 1895, in Melo, in the northeastern province of Cerro Largo, Uruguay; died in July 1979; daughter of Vicente Fernández (a Spaniard from Galicia) and Valentina Morales (daughter of a noted Uruguayan politician); attended religious and state schools; married Captain Lucas Ibarbourou, on June 28, 1914; children: one son, Julio César.*

Achieved immediate fame with publication of her first volume of poetry (1919); honored as "Juana de América" (1929); awarded the Grand National Literature Prize of Uruguay (1959).

Major works: Las lenguas de diamante *(The Diamond Tongues, 1919);* Raíz salvaje *(Wild Root, 1922);* La rosa de los vientos *(The Compass Rose, 1930); (prose)* Chico-Carlo *(1945);* Perdida *(Loss, 1950).*

The splendid marble Legislative Palace in Montevideo, Uruguay, was packed to capacity and the assembled guests strained to hear the words of one of Mexico's most noted authors, Alfonso Reyes. "She had taken possession of words," he intoned. "Juana in the North, Juana in the South, in the East, and in the West: everywhere words were displaced. Juana when one said poetry and Juana when one said, woman. Juana everywhere in America where there was a breath." The occasion was the elevation of Juana de Ibarbourou to the lofty position of "Juana of America." The honor was a reflection of her poetry which leaped national boundaries and touched emotions across a continent. It was an award that celebrated the primitive rather than the profound. Juana de Ibarbourou's work was passionate, deliciously irreverent, and heedless of convention and custom.

Born in the northeastern city of Melo in late 19th-century Uruguay, Juana was early exposed to poetry by her father. In 1947, she remembered her childhood and the time spent "under the verdant canopy of trained vines" where her father would recite works by Espronceda and *Rosalia de Castro. "And here it can be said is where my poetic vocation had its genesis." In a biographical sketch, **Dora Isella Russel** notes that Juana's childhood was happy and normal. Indeed, Ibarbourou's autobiographical novel, *Chico-Carlo,* captures a carefree youth: "the moons of my childhood are all full, round, and dazzling. My childhood moon was innocent and full like my own life at that time." The romantic quarters of her moon came later, "when I was still an adolescent and was dreaming about love, suffering, success, and death." Literary critic **Sidonia Carmen Rosenbaum** wrote that she "passed her childhood, and the years of ardent dream-filled adolescence, in those rustic—almost wild—surroundings. They in turn communicated to her all their fragrance and élan." She published her first poems at age seven or eight in the local newspaper of Melo, *El Deber Civico.*

Her first schooling took place in a convent and subsequently in a state school that now bears her name. In both, she was reportedly mischievous and inattentive. Poetry was the only assignment that could focus her attention. At age 19, she fell in love with and married Captain Lucas Ibarbourou; two years later, in 1916, their only son was born. As a military family, they moved frequently, and Juana came to know Rivera, Tacuarembó, Rocha, and Canelones. In the meantime, she was quietly composing the poetry which would launch her into the public eye and establish her reputation.

It was in 1918 that the family moved to the capital, Montevideo, where she sought out the literary editor of the newspaper *La Razón,* Vicente A. Salaverri, and handed him a bundle of poems by Jeanette de Ibar—a pseudonym which Salaverri characterized as "innocent and ridiculous." He received the work with "distrust," according to Rosenbaum, but read them with growing enthusiasm and admiration. As Salaverri said: "She was an Hebraic poetess, of a contagious pantheism and a fragrant sensuality." Some readers agreed and compared her free verse with the erotic lyrics of the Biblical Song of Songs. Juana's poetry attracted an immediate and fervent audience.

Manuel Gálvez, one of Argentina's leading novelists, wrote a prologue to a collection of Juana's poems entitled *Las lenguas de diamante* (Tongues of Diamond) which was published in Buenos Aires in 1919. Such an action on Gálvez' part was extraordinary and gives a good indication of the attractive powers of her verse. The context of the times was also important; 1919 was a most unusual year. World War I had produced a good deal of anxiety in South America, for the relatives of many immigrants to the New World were at war in the Old World. Revolution had brought down the Russia of the tsars and Bolshevik revolution threatened to erupt in the streets of South America's capitals. The poetry of Juana de Ibarbourou was a welcome escape from the state of acute anxiety that gripped many Latin Americans. She was young, fresh, a breath of morning air, a new beginning. With regard to Uruguay, Ibarbourou's popularity also mirrored a spirit of progress and change that characterized the country. The civil wars of the late 19th and early 20th centuries were over, and the nation was in the process of establishing its reputation as the "Switzerland of South America." Uruguay was reestablishing its identity just as Juana de Ibarbourou was establishing hers.

> This primitive love, this constant ardor which youth inspires, and which, she records in pages that breathe the purifying air of nature—and exude its fragrance—is what made her unique, and, in her manner, unsurpassed in Spanish American letters.
>
> **—Sidonia Carmen Rosenbaum**

By all accounts, she was not overwhelmed by her sudden fame and continued to produce poetry for an eager audience. There is no question that her poetry was narcissistic. She contemplates herself and delights in her body. In the words of literary historian Enrique Anderson-Imbert, "Young, spoiled, inviting, she felt in her flesh the power of her beauty." Ventura García Calderón sees in her writing "a miracle of simplicity" and "an ingenuous inventory of Narcissism." In Juana's words, "I am free, healthy, happy, young and brunette." And, in the opinion of Rosenbaum:

> here was a woman ruled not by morals, or conventions, which she dared to overlook—nor even by those yielding, but sheltering barriers that the "timidity" of the sex imposes—but by a primitive urge to be taken simply as one plucks a fruit, picks a flower, or drinks in the refreshing waters of a stream.

Other interpretations reach a bit deeper into the waters and portray Juana de Ibarbourou as a woman who dared to come to terms with the position of a woman in a patriarchal community and society. She was the "defying nymph" who was able to communicate her own feelings of female self-realization, according to **Myriam Díaz-Diocaretz**. In a similar vein, Ibarbourou is now seen as one of the precursors of today's feminist movement. She was a rebel who in her writing broke conventions to give expression to her most private and intimate thoughts.

Ibarbourou was successful in a patriarchal society because she was not perceived as a threat. Most of her readers were content with the innocence and beauty of youth that Juana projected. Beyond her poetry, she enjoyed a reputation as the perfect wife. Unconventional, yet appealing poetry, within the context of a conventional life, assured her a place of esteem in Uruguay and the other Southern Cone countries.

The instant success of *Las lenguas de diamante* was followed in 1920 with *El cántaro fresco* (The Cool Pitcher) and in 1922 with *Raíz salvaje* (Wild Root). The latter reflects confidence and a maturity missing in her earlier poetry. One critic captured the subtle shift in her writing with the phrase, "The clear laughter of Chloe [the rustic beauty] had become the ambiguous, mysterious smile of the Gioconda [Mona Lisa]." In the mid-1920s, Juana turned her attention to education and compiled two anthologies for use in Uruguay's schools. One, entitled *Páginas de literatura contemporánea*, was published in 1924 and included examples of contemporary literature. The other, published in 1927, was a collection of prose poetry called, simply, *Ejemplario* (Examples).

The year 1929 marked the high point of her glory, a year in which her fetishistic admirers demanded that she be honored by the Uruguayan legislature as Juana de América. The ceremonies celebrating her apotheosis may also be seen as a watershed in her life, for Juana's later literary efforts would take a different direction, a direction full of intimations of her mortality.

La rosa de los vientos (The Compass Rose), published in 1930, addresses the passage of years and their effect on Juana de Ibarbourou. With maturity in mind and body, there emerges in her verses a repeated concern with creation and renewal; the fresh and clear images of her earlier work become more obscure. Anderson-Imbert notes that her poetry shows "less feeling and more thinking"; Concha Zardoya sees Juana's work taking a graver and more profound tone, distant and meditative. There is a growing awareness of death. But there is also the defiant sense of triumph over death. For Juana, death becomes transformation rather than annihilation. "Charon: I will be a scandal in your boat" is a poem that chides death yet fails to remove her fear of it.

In the 1930s, Juana's works assumed a deeply religious tone as she sought answers to the vexing problems of mortality. *Los loores de Nuestra Señora* (Praises of Our Lady) and *Estampas de la Biblia* (Bible Scenes), both published in 1934, and a poem about Saint Francis of Assisi which appeared a year later, revealed in the author uneasiness, uncertainty, and anxiety. A deeply spiritual religious quest was indicative of a deeply seated devotion that underlay her pantheism and the pagan qualities of many of her earlier poems.

Still popular in the public eye, Juana continued to win handfuls of medals and honors. In 1938, the three great woman poets of the continent were honored at a grand celebration in Montevideo. ***Gabriela Mistral**, the Chilean poet who would later win a Nobel Prize for Literature, ***Alfonsina Storni**, the frustrated Argentine rebel who was only months away from taking her own life, and Juana de América represented an apogee of collective creativity. Gabriela Mistral said of Juana Ibarbourou's writings: "They are very profound, even though they appear to be so innocent; Nature, daughter of God, and Juana, daughter of Uruguay."

Juana's husband died early in January 1942, and she turned to writing an autobiographical novel of her childhood. *Chico-Carlo* appeared in 1944. While many of the scenes do in fact tell us of Juana's childhood, the novel is so broadly generalized as to be essentially universal. Indeed, Juana told the story of a young Haitian reader who wrote to her with the conviction that in *Chico-Carlo* he found echoes of his own childhood. Juana's childhood, filtered through time, appeared wholly innocent, almost perfect. Its resonance in other countries and cultures was produced by the fact that it related what was good about childhood and triggered nostalgic memories for her readers. An interest in children continued in 1945 with the publication of *Los sueños de Natacha* (Natacha's Dreams), a play for young people.

In 1947, Juana de Ibarbourou received yet another great honor when she was made a member of the Uruguayan Academy of Letters, even though it had been 17 years since the publication of her last truly significant work. That would change with the tragic loss of her mother in 1949. The first poem in *Perdida* (Loss), published in 1950, was entitled "Time." Juana sadly notes the passage of time and, with it, her life. Youth was gone, as was the narcissism and innocence of those days. One critic noted that *Perdida* was her sky, her abyss, her mountain. Melancholy and introspection mark a work that is in many respects a confessional. Juana de Ibarbourou would keep on writing, and those themes would be continued in *Oro y tormenta* in 1956. But *Perdida* in reality completed the final cycle of her most important work. The Union of American Women of New York proclaimed Juana "Woman of the Americas" in 1953, and she won Uruguay's Grand Prize for National Literature, awarded for the first time in 1959. Juana de Ibarbourou died in July 1979.

SOURCES:

Anderson-Imbert, Enrique. *Spanish-American Literature: A History.* 2 vols. 2nd ed. Detroit, MI: Wayne State University Press, 1969.

Díaz-Diocaretz, Myriam. "'I will be a scandal in your boat': Women poets and the tradition," in Susan Bassnett, ed., *Knives and Angels: Women Writers in Latin America.* London: Zed Books, 1990.

Ferro, Hellén. *Historia de la poesía hispanoamericana.* NY: Las Americas Publishing, 1964.

Ibarbourou, Juana de. *Obras completas.* 3rd. ed. (with a biographical sketch by Dora Isella Russel). Madrid: Aguilar, 1968.

Katra, William H. "Uruguay," in David W. Foster, comp. *Handbook of Latin American Literature.* NY: Garland, 1987.

Miller, Beth. ed. *Women in Hispanic Literature: Icons and Fallen Idols.* Berkeley, CA: University of California Press, 1983.

Rosenbaum, Sidonia Carmen. *Modern Women Poets of Spanish America.* NY: Hispanic Institute in the United States, 1945.

Zardoya, Concha. "La muerte en la poesía Femenina Latinoamericana," in *Cuardernos Americanos.* Vol. 71, no. 5, especially pp. 265–270.

SUGGESTED READING:

Franco, Jean. *The Modern Culture of Latin America: Society and the Artist.* Hammondsworth, UK: Penguin, 1970.

Paul B. Goodwin, Jr.,
Professor of History, University of Connecticut, Storrs, Connecticut

Ibárruri, Dolores (1895–1989)

Early Communist activist known as La Pasionaria who, during the Spanish Civil War, became an internationally recognized speaker for the loyalist cause.

Name variations: Dolores Ibarruri; Dolores Ibárruri Gómez; La Pasionaria. Pronunciation: ee-BAR-ru-ree. Born on December 9, 1895, in Gallarta, Spain; died on November 12, 1989, in Madrid, Spain; daughter of Antonio Ibárruri and Dolores Gómez; married Julián Ruíz, in Gallarta, in 1916: children—six, including one set of triplets, but all but two died in infancy or childhood: son Rubén (1921–1942); daughters Esther (1917–1922); Amaya (b. 1923); Amagoya (1923, died young); Azucena (1923–1925); Eva (1928, died young).

Socialist activist in Vizcaya (1918); elected to provincial committee of Spanish Communist Party (1920); became editor, Communist newspaper Mundo Obrero *(Madrid, 1931); elected to Parliament (1936); fled Spain for exile in Soviet Union (1939); became secretary-general of Spanish Communist Party (1944); received Order of Lenin (1965); returned to Spain after 38 years in exile (1977).*

Selected works: Speeches and Articles, 1936–38 *(1938);* The Women Want a People's Peace *(1941);* El único camino *(1962, English translation, 1966);* Memorias de Pasionaria, 1939–1977: Me faltaba España *(1984).*

Dolores Ibárruri

Communist leader and propagandist Dolores Ibárruri Gómez, known to admirers and detractors around the world as La Pasionaria, became one of the most visible symbols of the loyalist cause during the Spanish Civil War (1936–39). Born December 9, 1895, in the iron-mining town of Gallarta, near Bilbao in the northern Basque province of Vizcaya, she was the eighth of eleven children of Antonio Ibárruri and **Dolores Gómez**. A monarchist and devout Catholic, Pasionaria's father worked as a miner all of his life. Prior to their marriage, his wife also had been employed in the mines.

Dolores Ibárruri frequently boasted of her working-class origins, describing herself in her autobiography as "the granddaughter, daughter, wife and sister of miners." However, her family was not as poor as she sometimes claimed, and there is no truth to a once-popular story that as a girl she worked as an itinerant sardine peddler. More fortunate than other miners' children, Ibárruri attended school through the age of 15. Her original ambition was to be a schoolteacher, but when she left school in 1910 she apprenticed for two years to a dressmaker, and for three years after that she worked as a domestic servant and a waitress.

In 1916, "seeking," as she recalled, "liberation from drudgery in other people's homes," Ibárruri married Julián Ruíz (c. 1893–1977), a mineworker and socialist labor organizer from nearby Somorrostro. Together they had six children, including one set of triplets; all but two died in infancy or childhood. Chronic poverty and repeated family tragedies, along with frequent periods of abandonment when Ruíz's political activities took him on the road or landed him in prison, soured Ibárruri on marriage, which she later described as a "joyless, dismal, pain-ridden thralldom." Ibárruri and Ruíz separated in the early 1930s but apparently never divorced.

Though Ibárruri's marriage was unhappy, it represented an important stage in her political and intellectual development. Introduced by Ruíz to working-class politics, she began to read Marxist literature. Because Ibárruri had more formal education than most labor activists, she was soon writing for a local socialist newspaper, *El Minero Vizcaíno* (The Vizcayan Miner). From the beginning, she signed her columns with the pen name La Pasionaria, literally "the passion flower." Because the pseudonym first appeared on an essay published during Holy Week, it was probably a reference to the Passion of Christ. Asked about the choice almost 70 years later in an interview for *The New York Times,* the veteran Communist Party functionary replied, "I can't explain it, except that I was very Catholic."

Dolores Ibárruri's conversion from Catholic schoolgirl to militant revolutionary was absolute and permanent. During a general strike in 1917, she helped to produce dynamite bombs for insurrectionary miners. As it did elsewhere, the October Revolution that year in Russia caused divisions among socialists in Spain, and, when the victorious Bolsheviks established the Communist International (Comintern) at Moscow in 1919, Ibárruri and Ruíz's group at Somorrostro promptly declared its affiliation. In 1920, the couple joined the newly created Spanish Communist Party (Partido Comunista Español), and Ibárruri was elected to the provincial committee for Vizcaya. The following year, the party merged with another Leninist organization to form the Communist Party of Spain (Partido Comunista de España, PCE), in which Ibárruri would continue to occupy leadership roles, both at home and in exile, for the rest of her life.

During the dictatorship of General Miguel Primo de Rivera (1923–1930), Spanish Communists suffered political persecution while wasting much energy in often violent sectarian quarrels with rival working-class organizations, in particular the Spanish Socialist Workers' Party (Partido Socialista Obrero de España, PSOE). Meanwhile, Pasionaria's alliance with PCE Secretary-General José Bullejos brought her increasing preferment within the Communist Party. In 1930, she was named to the central committee and, in 1932, to the political bureau.

The fall of the monarchy and establishment of the Second Republic in 1931 produced major political changes in Spain. Responding to the new régime's openness, the Communists transferred Ibárruri to Madrid to direct the party's women's section and edit its national newspaper, *Mundo Obrero* (Workers' World). Republican authorities, however, proved even less tolerant of her activities than Primo de Rivera. Detained almost immediately upon her arrival in the capital, Pasionaria went to prison for the first of several periods of incarceration. Released in February 1932, she was jailed again in March and held until January 1933.

During her brief interval at liberty in early 1932, Ibárruri attended the PCE's first aboveground congress at Seville, where she managed to get in trouble with her own party. Following current Comintern policy, the Spanish Communists opposed the PSOE-backed government of Manuel Azaña (provisional president, 1931; prime minister, 1931–1933), condemning the socialists for their willingness to collaborate with bourgeois and anarchist parties. In 1932, however, when a rightist military revolt threatened the republic's survival, Pasionaria backed José Bullejos's effort to rally the PCE to its defense. For his deviation, Moscow ordered Bullejos expelled from the party and replaced him as secretary-general with José Díaz, whereupon Ibárruri recanted her error and denounced her former ally and patron. According to historian of the PCE **Joan Estruch**, it was the only time she ever strayed from the party line.

In 1933—the year of Pasionaria's first visit to the Soviet Union to attend a meeting of the Comintern—elections in Spain brought a coalition of rightist parties to power, ousting the PSOE from the government. As elsewhere in Europe, the emergence of fascism in Spain pressured the Communists to modify their previous insistence on sectarian purity. Ibárruri became the national organizer for Women Against War and Fascism, a Communist-led movement which included women of various leftist persuasions. When a socialist-inspired miners' insurrection broke out in 1934 in the northern province of Asturias, only to be brutally put down by the army, Pasionaria and her organization gained international recognition by coordinating the rescue and evacuation of children left orphaned or homeless by the violence. Because Ibárruri's expanding political commitments made it difficult for her to care for her own two children, early in 1935 she sent her son, Rubén Ruíz, and her daughter, **Amaya Ruíz**, to live in the Soviet Union.

> There are so many fantasies about me. I don't know where they all come from.
>
> —Dolores Ibárruri

Ibárruri herself was in Moscow in 1935 for another meeting of the Comintern when the Soviet directors of the international movement announced the Popular Front strategy, an abrupt reversal of previous policy. Placing immediate priority on the defeat of fascism rather than the workers' revolution, the new line called upon Communist parties to form alliances with socialist, bourgeois, and other anti-fascist groups. In elections in Spain in 1936, a PCE-supported coalition ousted the right-wing parties from control of Parliament and established a Popular Front government with Manuel Azaña first as prime minister, then as president (1936–1939). Released after another brief stay in prison, Dolores Ibárruri campaigned for the Popular Front in Asturias, where she was elected to Parliament as a deputy from Oviedo. On that occasion, Pasionaria added to her growing reputation when she intervened in a riot at a local jail by personally releasing the prisoners, many of them miners detained since the 1934 uprising.

Otherwise a troubled and unproductive time, the Second Republic did witness an expansion of opportunities for women in Spanish public life. Dolores Ibárruri was not the first woman to serve in Parliament. Three female deputies—***Clara Campoamor**, ***Victoria Kent**, and ***Margarita Nelken**—had been elected in 1931, even before women received the right to vote, but Ibárruri quickly distinguished herself as a spirited polemicist, engaging in fiery exchanges with leading conservative deputies, among them José María Gil Robles and José Calvo Sotelo. When Calvo Sotelo was shot to death in Madrid on July 13, 1936, rightists accused Pasionaria of having instigated his murder, a charge which she always denied and for which no convincing evidence has ever been presented.

Less than a week after Calvo Sotelo's death, on July 18, civil warfare broke out when army officers in Spanish Morocco declared themselves in rebellion under the leadership of General Francisco Franco. Joined by other generals and supported by various conservative, monarchist, and pro-clerical groups, Franco consolidated his personal control over the insurgency and established his headquarters at Burgos. Franco's Nationalist crusade sought to overthrow not only the Popular Front government, but also the republic itself, and it quickly received military assistance from Adolf Hitler in Germany and Benito Mussolini in Italy, who saw in the insurgent general the promise of a valuable ally in a fascist Spain. Of all the world's non-fascist leaders, only Joseph Stalin of the Soviet Union came openly to the support of the Azaña government.

During the Spanish Civil War (1936–1939), Pasionaria gained her greatest fame as a propagandist. In a radio broadcast the first night of the conflict, she exhorted Madrid's defenders to stand firm against Franco and the Nationalists, vowing dramatically that "they shall not pass!" This stirring phrase was not original with Ibárruri—it has been attributed to France's General Henri-Philippe Pétain at the battle of Verdun in 1916—but, through enthusiastic repetition, it eventually became one of the most familiar slogans of the loyalist cause. Other typical Pasionaria appeals were, "better to die on one's feet than live on one's knees," and "better a hero's widow than a coward's wife." Visiting the front often to bolster troop morale, Ibárruri was active also in recruiting and humanitarian work, and she posed spade in hand for publicity photographs showing her digging trenches for the capital's defense.

A tenacious political in-fighter, Dolores Ibárruri worked to expand the PCE's role within the loyalist coalition. In May 1937, she helped oust Socialist Prime Minister Francisco Largo Caballero and replace him with Juan Negrín, also of the PSOE but more receptive than Largo Caballero to Communist arguments on military and political strategy. In March the following year, Pasionaria helped to bring down Minister of War Indalecio Prieto, whose duties Negrín assumed personally. There is a story that in the Prieto case Ibárruri's motives were as much personal as political. To restrict PCE influence, the socialist war minister had ordered political commissars transferred to regular combat duty at the front, a directive which would have separated Pasionaria from her protégé Francisco Antón, 20 years her junior, with whom she was widely reported to be romantically involved.

Early in 1939, a series of military disasters finally led to the collapse of the republic. Cut off at Elda, near Alicante on the Mediterranean, when news came on March 6 of a coup at Madrid by previously loyal officers, Negrín and what was left of his government decided to flee the country. Escaping aboard one of the last three loyalist aircraft out of nearby Monóvar, Dolores Ibárruri abandoned many friends and supporters to an uncertain fate at the hands of Franco and his vindictive Nationalists, but she always claimed that she agreed to leave only when instructed to do so by the Communist Party. Pasionaria flew first to Algeria, then to Paris, and from there to Moscow. It would be 38 years before she saw her native land again.

Taking up residence in exile in the Soviet capital, Ibárruri was reunited with her children, and ultimately also with Francisco Antón, an arrangement disliked by many of her fellow PCE exiles. In general, Pasionaria adapted well to life under Stalinist rule, but she had to accept the fact that the outbreak of World War II in Europe displaced Spain's future as a matter of concern for her Soviet hosts. Especially after the German invasion in 1941, the defense of the Soviet Union came first. In September 1942, the new conflict cost Dolores Ibárruri dearly when her only son Rubén, who had served briefly in Spain and was now a lieutenant in the Soviet army, was killed at Stalingrad.

Despite her personal loss, Pasionaria continued her propaganda work, broadcasting to audiences at home on Moscow-based Radio Independent Spain (Radio España Independiente, REI), established in 1941. She also rose in the PCE hierarchy, pushing aside the party's ailing and disillusioned Secretary-General José Díaz. Following Díaz's suicide in 1942, Ibárruri asserted her own leadership. In 1944, she became PCE secretary-general, with Soviet approval but without a formal party vote. At the height of Pasionaria's power, she staffed top party positions with her personal adherents, including her reputed lover Antón, her daughter Amaya, and her faithful secretary **Irene Falcón**.

In 1945, expecting the end of World War II to lead quickly to Franco's overthrow, Ibárruri transferred party operations to France. However, the Spanish dictator, who had remained neutral during the global conflict, now took advantage of the emerging Cold War to align himself with the Western powers as a reliable anticommunist. By 1948, with Franco's position stronger than ever, the French authorities grew increasingly inhospitable. Pasionaria returned to the Soviet Union, where complications following surgery for a chronic liver complaint led to months of hospitalization amid concern that she would not live.

During Ibárruri's long illness, Santiago Carrillo emerged as her rival for dominance in the PCE. A Communist youth leader during the civil war, Carrillo was young, ambitious, and tactically gifted. He gradually established control over day-to-day party affairs, and, following Stalin's death in 1953, he won a major victory over Pasionaria by having Francisco Antón expelled from both the political bureau and the central committee. The de-Stalinization campaign launched in 1956 by Soviet Communist Party chair Nikita Khrushchev (1894–1971) enabled Carrillo to consolidate his own authority, based on Moscow's greater tolerance for independence among local Communist parties. In 1960, Ibárruri stepped aside, accepting the honorific post of party president when Carrillo succeeded her as secretary-general.

During the 1960s and 1970s, Pasionaria continued her broadcasting work with REI, which in 1954 had relocated its studios and transmitter to Bucharest, Rumania. Increasingly, she was significant more as a symbolic link with the PCE's past than as a functioning leader. Soviet authorities bestowed upon her many awards and formal recognitions, notably the Lenin Peace Prize in 1964 and the Order of Lenin in 1965. When she was not traveling about the Communist bloc, calling on such leaders as Josip Broz Tito of Yugoslavia, Ho Chi Minh of Vietnam, and Fidel Castro of Cuba, Ibárruri found time to work on her autobiography, the first volume of which was published in 1962 in Spanish, and in 1966 in English. Occasionally, the Soviets employed her as an intermediary in disputes with Communist parties in the Spanish-speaking world. She is reported to have interceded with Castro to keep him aligned with Moscow in the continuing rift with the Chinese Communists, and in 1968 she helped resolve a disagreement with the PCE over its condemnation of the Soviet military intervention that year in Czechoslovakia.

Following the death of Francisco Franco in 1975, a democratic transition began in Spain under a constitutional monarchy headed by King Juan Carlos I. Opposition parties, including the PCE, were legalized, and many exiles were allowed to return. After some hesitation on the new government's part, Dolores Ibárruri received her passport, and on May 13, 1977, she arrived from Moscow to an enthusiastic welcome in Madrid. In the following month's parliamentary elections—the first open elections since the fall of the republic in 1939—voters in Oviedo once again returned Pasionaria as a Communist deputy for Asturias. Much had changed in the 41 years since her last election victory, however. Spain was more modern, more secular, and more prosperous, and the PCE now identified itself with the independent-minded Eurocommunism of the major Communist parties in the West. Also, at 81, Ibárruri was only a thin shadow of the legend that surrounded the almost mythical figure of La Pasionaria.

In delicate health, Dolores Ibárruri left Parliament after only two years, but she continued on as president of the PCE. Accompanied by her longtime friend and personal secretary, Irene Falcón, Pasionaria reported daily to her office at party headquarters in Madrid, but she made few public appearances, in part because PCE leaders preferred not to draw attention to her unfashionable political views. As late as 1983, Ibárruri continued to cite Joseph Stalin as the most memorable Communist leader of her acquaintance, and to describe the Soviet Union as representing for her "what it always has—the possibility of establishing socialism in other countries." Dramatic changes in Moscow beginning in 1985 with the accession of Mikhail Gorbachev further undermined Ibárruri's familiar world, a fact she appeared to acknowledge in February 1988, when she made one of her last speeches. "Life doesn't stop," she told assembled delegates at the PCE's 12th party congress. "Everything moves. Everything changes."

On November 12, 1989, less than a month before her 94th birthday, Dolores Ibárruri died at Madrid following a long illness. Some 50,000 mourners paid their last respects to Pasionaria as she lay in state at PCE headquarters, and her public funeral on November 16 attracted official delegations from approximately 80 countries. Although rich in political symbolism, the passing of Dolores Ibárruri called to mind an observation made two years earlier by Joan Estruch, that as a historical personality Pasionaria had come finally to merit only "the respect due to things of the distant past which lack the capacity to influence the present." In fact, by 1989 the PCE held little appeal for contemporary Spaniards; in elections held the month before Ibárruri's death, the leftist coalition to which the party belonged had won only 9% of the vote. In the end, it was perhaps fortunate for Pasionaria that she did not live to witness the dissolution in 1991 of the Soviet Union itself, to whose service she had devoted seven decades of her life.

SOURCES:

Camino, Jaime. *Intimas conversaciones con La Pasionaria.* Barcelona: Dopesa, 1977.

Darnton, John. "La Pasionaria at 87: Just Embers of Passion Remain," in *The New York Times.* June 24, 1983, p. 2.

Estruch, Joan. "Pasionaria: La verdad de Dolores Ibárruri," in *Historia 16.* (Madrid) No. 118. February 1988, pp. 11–24.

Gutiérrez Alvarez, J. "Dolores Ibárruri, mujer entre hierro y mármol," in *Historia y Vida.* (Barcelona) No. 23, 1990, pp. 4–14.

Ibárruri, Dolores. *Memorias de Pasionaria, 1939–1977: Me faltaba España.* Barcelona: Planeta, 1984.

——. *They Shall Not Pass: The Autobiography of La Pasionaria.* NY: International Publishers, 1966.

SUGGESTED READING:

Carabantes, Andrés and Eusebio Cimorra. *Un mito llamado Pasionaria.* Barcelona: Planeta, 1982.

Mangini, Shirley. *Memories of Resistance: Women's Voices from the Spanish Civil War.* New Haven, CT: Yale University Press, 1995.

Thomas, Hugh. *The Spanish Civil War.* Rev. ed. NY: Touchstone, 1986.

Stephen Webre,
Professor of History, Louisiana Tech University, Ruston, Louisiana

Iceni, queen of.

See Boudica (26/30–60 CE).

Ichikawa Fusae (1893–1981)

Japanese suffragist, feminist, and politician, who was one of the most outstanding women in 20th-century Japan. *Name variations: Ichikawa Fusaye. Pronunciation: ITCH-EE-ka-wa FOO-sa-ae. Born Ichikawa Fusae on May 15, 1893, in Asahi Village, Aichi Prefecture, Japan; died in Tokyo, Japan, in 1981; daughter of Ichikawa Fujikurō (a farmer) and Ichikawa Tatsu; attended public elementary and higher elementary schools, briefly attended Joshi Gakuin (Girls' Academy) in Tokyo, and graduated from Aichi Prefectural Women's Normal School in 1913; never married; no children.*

Taught elementary school (1913–16); was first woman newspaper reporter in Nagoya, Japan (1917–19); moved to Tokyo to become the secretary of the women's section of the Yūaikai (Friendly Society), Japan's first labor organization (1919); founded Shin Fujin Kyōkai (New Woman's Association, 1919–21); networked with women's rights leaders in the U.S. (1921–23); returned to Tokyo, where she worked for the International Labor Organizations (1924–27); founded the Fusen Kakutoku Dōmei (Women's Suffrage League, 1924–40); appointed to the advisory board of the government's organization, Dai Nihon Fujinkai (Greater Japan Women's Association, 1942–44); organized the Sengo Taisaku Fujin Iinkai (Women's Committee on Postwar Countermeasures) to work for women's suffrage (1945); purged by the American occupation (1947–50); served in the House of Councillors (the upper house of the national legislature, 1953–71 and 1974–81).

Publications: (in Japanese) Ichikawa Fusawa no jiden—senzen hen *(The Autobiography of Ichikawa Fusae—The Prewar Period, 1974);* Watakushi no fujin undō *(My Women's Movement, 1972);* Watakushi no seiji shōron *(My Views of Politics, 1972);* Sengo fujikai no dōkō *(Trends of Women's Circles in the Postwar Period, 1969).*

During Ichikawa Fusae's almost 90 years, the status of Japanese women changed dramatically; women progressed from being subordinate to men, in both the private and public sphere, to being their legal equal, and she was one of those most responsible for this change. Remarkably, despite being a militant feminist, at the time of her death in 1981 Ichikawa Fusae was perhaps the most respected politician in Japan.

Born to a farm family at the end of the 19th century, Ichikawa's childhood reflected both the weight of traditions which had oppressed Japanese women and the opportunities which modernization afforded them. As the head of his family, Ichikawa Fujikurō faced no censure for beating his wife; Fusae recalled seeing her mother **Ichikawa Tatsu** whimpering in a corner, unable to defend herself against his blows. But her father was progressive on the issue of education, schooling his daughters, as well as his sons. For this, he tolerated the ridicule of his fellow villagers. Fusae claimed that she was raised to be "bold or aggressive," to ignore conventional propriety—a trait she would exhibit throughout her life.

After attending elementary school, she was briefly enrolled at one of the most progressive girls' schools in Tokyo, Joshi Gakuin (Girls' Academy), whose director, Yajima Kajiko, was an outspoken advocate of women's rights. Between 1909 and 1913, Ichikawa attended public schools of higher education to prepare for what was then the only respectable profession for women—teaching. Following her graduation, she taught girls in a public elementary school. While her own schooling had been pleasant, Ichikawa became critical of the constraints placed upon young women in public schools. "Curiosity and self-consciousness have been ignored in the name of femininity," she complained. "For no reason we are forced to be submissive, to sacrifice ourselves, and to be chaste. . . . We are molded into human beings who lack dignity, are inflexible, and cannot even manage our own lives." Despite the satisfaction she received from earning a salary, Ichikawa quit her teaching job in 1916.

Undoubtedly receiving some pressure to marry, Ichikawa wrote of her confusion:

> Whom should I try to please in this world? Society at large? Women? Myself? If I am prevented from doing what I want to do, I will not have confidence in myself or in my abilities. I know that I will be extremely lonely in the future. Yet, I am most content when I sit alone in my dark room or when I take an evening walk by myself.

Ichikawa Fusae

In the midst of this exploration, Ichikawa became the first woman reporter for the *Nagoya shimbun* (Nagoya News). Working for an editor who advanced women's issues, Ichikawa covered women's organizations and educational opportunities for women. She became restless, however, and moved to Tokyo, hoping to be more intellectually and politically challenged.

Now in her mid-20s, Ichikawa used professional and family contacts to become immersed in the liberal circles of young intellectuals and social activists who were most interested in women's issues. In 1919, she was appointed secretary of the women's section of the Yūaikai (Friendly Society), Japan's first labor organization. Disenchanted, however, with the discrimination against women in the fledgling labor movement, Ichikawa reached the conclusion that "before I worked in a labor movement for women, I would have to work in a woman's movement for male-female equality. Although I tried very hard to raise the position of working women within the federation, I resigned when I realized that the consciousness of Japan's workers was extremely low."

She turned from the labor movement to the women's movement and embarked upon the organizational building which characterized her career. Shortly after arriving in Tokyo, Ichikawa had been introduced to Japan's most prominent feminist, ***Hiratsuka Raichō**, leader of the organization Seito (Bluestockings) and editor of their literary journal. Although Ichikawa was by no means one of the refined, upper-class Tokyo intellectuals with whom Hiratsuka was accustomed to working, the two developed a relationship of mutual respect. Together, in 1919, they launched the Shin Fujin Kyōkai (New Woman's Association), which envisioned a different program for Japanese feminism. In contrast to the Bluestockings, the New Woman's Association sought to organize a broad cross-section of women, for political, rather than cultural purposes.

The group's objective was to achieve equal rights for all women and men. In order to realize their aim, the association set out to obtain a higher standard of education for women, co-education in primary schools, women's suffrage, a revision of laws unfavorable to women, and the protection of motherhood. The association would undertake research on women's issues, convene conferences for women activists, and offer personal consultation for women with problems. Ichikawa became editor-in-chief of *Josei dōmei* (Women's League), a newsletter which promoted the association's ideas.

The story of her life is the modern history of Japanese women in their country's political life. . . . Her dedication made her in her final years the lodestar of all women—even more, an admired and trusted national figure.

—Dorothy Robins-Mowry

Within months, Ichikawa and other association leaders submitted a petition to the Diet (the national legislature), signed by more than 1,500 women, to repeal the section of the Peace Preservation Law which denied women the freedom of assembly. Unless this legislation was revoked, it would be illegal for women to organize and attend political meetings. A second petition, more clearly reflecting the commitments of Hiratsuka than Ichikawa, sought to prohibit men with venereal disease from marrying and to provide women with recourse to divorce husbands with a sexually transmitted disease. The second petition was immediately and overwhelmingly rejected by the Diet because it was not in "accord with the standard of Japanese custom which gave predominance to men over women." Thereafter, association members diligently lobbied the Diet for their initial petition. Hoping to exert pressure, they were conspicuously present in the small women's section of the visitors' gallery where they sat behind wire netting, prompting one woman to say that they "listened to the Diet men quietly, like tiny animals in a cage." They also submitted appeals to Diet members on pink and lavender name cards. The arrest of Ichikawa and Hiratsuka for violation of the Peace Preservation Law at a YMCA meeting was said to have strengthened public support for women's right of assembly. After several failed attempts, the petition was finally approved on February 25, 1922; women had won the legal right to organize and participate in public meetings.

Soon after their victory, the New Woman's Association disbanded. In part, this was the result of an ideological rift within the leadership of the organization. Ichikawa had concluded that Hiratsuka envisioned the association solely as a means of promoting the interests of married women, or, "principle of mothers' rights," while Ichikawa came to identify her own views more clearly with the broader "principle of women's rights."

Disillusioned with this conflict at home, Ichikawa sailed to the United States, where she spent two years meeting with leaders of the women's movement. While there, she discussed labor issues with women trade-union leaders, met with ***Jane Addams** to learn about her federation of women for peace and freedom, and followed the work of ***Carrie Chapman Catt**, who established the League of Women Voters and developed a women's movement for war prevention. Most important, Ichikawa established a lifelong friendship with ***Alice Paul**, who led the radical wing of the U.S. suffrage movement and established the National Women's Party.

From these experiences, Ichikawa drew inspiration and organizational models and returned to Japan in 1924 to what she later termed, "the period of hope," with a focused commitment to work exclusively for Japan's suffrage—the single means by which she thought women's interests might best be served. In personal terms, Ichikawa had a lucrative, fulfilling job in the Tokyo office of the International Labor Organization (ILO), where she investigated women's labor conditions and proposed strategies for improvement. This allowed her to strengthen her credibility with women industrial workers and the leftist organizations which supported them. In organizational terms, Ichikawa established the Fusen Kakutoku Dōmei (Women's Suffrage League), the association most responsible, in the prewar era, for advocating the political rights of women. In 1927, Ichikawa resigned her position from the ILO to work full-time for the League. After the general election of 1928, women's suffrage had become an issue for all political parties, and there was the expectation that with the gradual expansion of the electorate, women would eventually be included.

While Ichikawa sought to bring individuals with different ideological perspectives into the League, her efforts to educate women about political issues were frustrated by criticism from both the right and the left. Conservatives criticized Ichikawa for lacking sensitivity and womanly virtue. "The conservative public opposed women's suffrage," she wrote, "believing that a woman's place was in the family, for the ideal of Japanese womanhood was to be a good wife and mother, and if a woman should have equal rights politically with men, conflicts would probably arise within the family, thereby destroying the traditional family system which had been the center of Japanese life since ancient times." On the left, the communists and socialists were critical of the women's suffrage movement because it did not oppose the political and economic institutions of capitalism. In addition to criticisms from the right and left, Ichikawa suffered from disaffection in her own ranks, as members of the League grew weary of her demands for tireless devotion and personal financial sacrifice for the cause. Ultimately, Ichikawa and the League were unable to capitalize on the apparent momentum of the "period of hope" to achieve women's suffrage.

By the early 1930s, women's suffrage was no longer on the political agenda. Concerned with economic problems associated with the depression and the escalating militarism following the Manchurian Incident in 1931, politicians concluded that the "women problem" could be forgotten. During this time, the rising tide of political crisis forced the women's movement to shift its emphasis from political rights, the tact which Ichikawa had championed, to issues explicitly affecting women's daily lives as housewives and mothers.

In retrospect, there have been questions about Ichikawa's politics during the totalitarian period of the 1930s and 1940s. Certainly, she soft-pedaled her pursuit of the vote for women in favor of more politically acceptable campaigns. In 1933, Ichikawa organized representatives of various non-government women's groups for community-based political activities. This organization, the Tokyo Fujin Shisei Jōka Renmei (Tokyo Women's Alliance for Honest City Government), was designed to involve women in "clean government" activities, including tax reform, opposition to price hikes for home fuel, the decentralization of Tokyo wholesale markets, and efficient garbage collection. In 1934, members of the Women's Suffrage League formed the Bosei Hogo Renmei (Motherhood Protection League) to work for welfare programs for single mothers. Ichikawa saw these campaigns as laboratories for women's political education, in which they would learn to articulate goals and work together to achieve them at the local level, where it was reasoned that government would be responsive to their efforts. While it was a less militant approach to winning women's political rights, it was, nevertheless, a viable alternative to women acting in the role of supplicants, pleading with men to give them their rights.

Despite Ichikawa's efforts to organize women for politically acceptable goals, it became increasingly difficult in the '30s. The government, which sought to organize women for its own purposes, created a number of women's organizations, and expected their members to sacrifice their personal well-being for the good of the country, to uphold the "natural order" of society, to maintain the sanctity of the traditional family, and to support the troops fighting in China.

In the context of national crisis, Ichikawa was determined to remain a critic of the government; but the government's grudging tolerance of Ichikawa changed after the escalation of the war in 1936, when she continued to oppose the war with China. Although they were not physically harmed, women leaders, such as Ichikawa, were subjected to surveillance and police interrogations. In the midst of war, Ichikawa stressed that women must confront the problems of the home front by viewing them from the "women's perspective." In 1937, Ichikawa convinced prominent women from several organizations to join her in establishing the Nihon Fujin Dantai Renmei (Japan Federation of Women's Organizations) to develop programs addressing the problems that women faced during the war: the hardships of women-headed households, the conscription of women laborers, and the shortages of consumer items. In 1938, Ichikawa was one of 30 national figures who recommended that all civilian organizations should encourage their members to engage in practices of civic and personal responsibility, including emperor worship, fiscal restraint in household budgets, personal austerity with respect to appearance, devotion to the well-being of their neighbors, and the judicious disciplining of children. Ichikawa's agenda was becoming further submerged in wartime objectives.

In 1942, the government established the Dai Nihon Fujinkai (Greater Japan Women's Association) for all adult women. War Minister Tōjō Hideki explained that this new organization would be a means of restoring "the fundamental nature of women that has been harmed by Western ideas." Given the organization's objective, Ichikawa was surprised to have been appointed to its advisory board. Later viewed as an illustration of her collaboration with the government during the war, Ichikawa maintained that she remained a critic of the organization (she was the only member of the advisory board to have been fired by the government) while staying politically active because, she later said, "I had been a leader of women and I could not retire abruptly from them. I decided to go with the people, not to encourage the war, but to take care of the people who were made unhappy by the war." Ultimately, the bombing of Tokyo drove Ichikawa from the city to her family's farm where, as was the case with other Japanese, her only objective was survival.

As the war drew to a close, the 30-year campaign for women's political rights had not been successful. The only victory had been the reform of the Peace Preservation Law in 1922, enabling women to organize and participate in political meetings. Women could not, however, join political parties, vote, participate in government, or hold political office. But the American military occupation that followed the war brought about a change in politics which ultimately made these reforms possible. Only ten days after the emperor's surrender, Ichikawa organized the Sengo Taisaku Fujin Iinkai (Women's Committee on Postwar Countermeasures) to work for women's suffrage. This organization maintained that, "suffrage is not something to be granted, but something to be attained by the hands of women themselves." Pressured by the American occupation forces, the Japanese Diet granted women the vote in 1945.

That year, Ichikawa founded the Nihon Fujin Yūkensha Dōmei (Japan League of Women Voters) and the Fusen Kaikan (Women's Suffrage Hall), a research institute designed to increase women's political consciousness. She embarked on an ambitious national tour to promote democratic principles and encourage women's participation in the political process. Ichikawa was, herself, a candidate for the House of Councillors (the upper house of the Diet, the national legislature).

On the verge of what appeared to be the great triumph of her career, Ichikawa was faced with the most painful setback of her life. One month before the first national election held after the war, Ichikawa was purged from public life by American occupation officials. Ironically, the Americans accomplished what the Japanese militarists had never been able to do—they silenced Ichikawa Fusae. Deemed to have been a government collaborator, she was barred from the Women's Suffrage Hall, prohibited from participation in any political activity, and her efforts to publish were censored. Friends and colleagues ceased their contact with her. In effect, prevented from earning a living, Ichikawa returned again to her family's farm where she scratched out an existence by raising vegetables and chickens, while she began writing a history of Japan's women's movement. The purge of Ichikawa Fusae was a tremendous irony; arguably the strongest living advocate for democracy in Japan, and the woman most responsible for women's participation in the political process, was banned from public life. A petition with more than 170,000 signatures protesting Ichikawa's purge was to no avail; the purge was not lifted until 1950.

In the postwar period, Ichikawa was one of Japan's most respected politicians. Beginning in 1953, she was elected to five terms in the House of Councillors; by the 1970s, she was winning the largest percentage of the nationwide vote. One of the keys to her political success was her aversion to political party affiliation. Her success in running as an independent was, in large part, due to the years she devoted to campaigning in the women's movement, but in the postwar period her constituencies expanded to include consumers, peace advocates, and environmentalists.

Ichikawa consistently ran as an anti-establishment candidate, nationally recognized as a critic of political corruption and excessive spending in political campaigns. As president of the Japan League of Women Voters, she urged her membership to be advocates for world peace. A critic of the Japan-U.S. alliance, in 1967 Ichikawa sought an end of the U.S. bombing of North Vietnam and the reversion of Okinawa. On the 25th anniversary of women's suffrage in Japan in 1970, Ichikawa identified peace, pollution, and prices as the most important issues for the women's movement to address. Campaigning on these issues until her death in 1981, Ichikawa laid the foundation for the anti-establishment fervor which swept Japanese politics in the 1980s and 1990s.

SOURCES:

Molony, Kathleen. "One Woman Who Dared: Ichikawa Fusae and the Japanese Women's Suffrage Movement." Ph.D. dissertation, University of Michigan, 1980.

Murray, Patricia. "Ichikawa Fusae and the Lonely Red Carpet," in *Japan Interpreter.* Vol. 10. Autumn 1975, p. 2.

Takeda Kiyoko. "Ichikawa Fusae: Pioneer for Women's Rights in Japan," in *Japan Quarterly.* Vol. 31, p. 4.

Vavich, Dee Ann. "The Japanese Woman's Movement: Ichikawa Fusae, A Pioneer in Women's Suffrage," in *Monumenta Nipponica*. Vol. 22, 1967, pp. 3–4.

SUGGESTED READING:

Robins-Mowry, Dorothy. *The Hidden Sun: Women of Modern Japan*. Boulder, CO: Westview Press, 1983.

Linda L. Johnson,
Professor of History, Concordia College, Moorhead, Minnesota

Ickes, Anna Thompson

(1873–1935)

American politician and reformer. *Name variations: Anna Wilmarth Ickes. Born Anna Wilmarth on January 27, 1873, in Chicago, Illinois; died on August 31, 1935, in Velarde, New Mexico; daughter of Henry Martin Wilmarth (a manufacturer and organizer of the First National Bank) and Mary Jane (Hawes) Wilmarth (1837–1919, a civic and reform leader); educated at private schools, including one in Paris and Miss Hersey's School in Boston, and at the University of Chicago; married historian James Westfall Thompson, in 1879 (divorced 1909); married Harold LeClaire Ickes (a lawyer and later Secretary of the Interior), on September 16, 1911; children (first marriage) Wilmarth Thompson and (adopted) Frances Thompson; children (second marriage): Raymond Wilmarth Ickes and (adopted) Robert Ickes.*

Anna Wilmarth was born in Chicago, Illinois, on January 27, 1873, to Henry Martin Wilmarth, an organizer of the First National Bank, and **Mary Jane Hawes Wilmarth**. The youngest of three daughters, Anna had a strong example for her later reformist endeavors in her mother, who was active in the suffrage movement and charitable organizations. Mary Jane was one of the original trustees of Hull House and, along with ***Jane Addams**, served as a delegate-at-large from Illinois at the 1912 Progressive National Convention.

In 1893, Anna started classes at the year-old University of Chicago, attending for three years before marrying a young instructor there, James Westfall Thompson, in 1897. They had one son and adopted a daughter before divorcing in 1909. At age 38, Anna married Chicago lawyer Harold LeClaire Ickes, a man she had known since her days at the university; together they had one son and adopted another.

Anna Ickes was involved with the Women's Trade Union League, for which her husband was legal counsel, and often posted bail for young women arrested during Chicago strikes. In 1910, she was part of the picket line, with ***Ellen Gates Starr** of Hull House, during the garment workers' strike against Hart, Schaffner, and Marx. Anna and Harold helped form the Progressive Party in Illinois in 1912. After this nascent political party dissolved, they rejoined the Republicans. Neither of the Ickeses were willing to sacrifice their opinions to tow the party line, however; both rebelled at the Republican nomination of Warren G. Harding for president, and Anna campaigned for James M. Cox, the Democratic governor from Ohio.

Anna Ickes' public career took off in 1924 when she was appointed by Governor Len Small to fill a vacancy on the board of trustees for the University of Illinois. Later that year, she ran in the election for the position and won, serving on the board until January of 1929. She also served on boards for the Chicago Home for the Friendless and the Chicago Regional Planning Association during the 1920s.

In 1928, with Harold as her campaign manager, Anna Ickes successfully ran for the state legislature as a Republican. She was reelected handily in 1930 and 1932. During her time in office, she sat on several committees in the lower house, including those on civil service, education, charities and corrections, and industrial affairs. A civic organization that yearly evaluated how well legislators were doing their jobs gave her high ratings.

In 1932, while Anna was running as a Republican, Harold publicly supported Democrat Franklin D. Roosevelt for president instead of Republican Herbert Hoover. This difference in the couple's politics brought some comments from the press. However, Anna, while maintaining her allegiance to the Republican Party, commented that she and her husband had always been independents in politics and that she was "tremendously interested in and enthusiastic over the things that are now being done." Harold Ickes was appointed Secretary of the Interior by Roosevelt in 1933.

Anna spent her days at the family home in Winnetka and in the state capital of Springfield during this period, paying only brief visits to Washington in the role of a Cabinet wife. By 1934, this arrangement had become "too complicated," and Anna did not run for reelection, reportedly at the request of her husband. Instead, she focused her attention on the culture, archaeology, and welfare of Native Americans, issues which had long held her interest. She had previously been a member of the board of the Indian Rights Association of Chicago.

Partly for health reasons, Anna had been spending time each year in New Mexico since the 1920s, studying the culture of the Navajos and Pueblos. Her book *Mesa Land*, published in 1933, was an account of Indian history and amateur anthropology. During a trip to New Mexico in the summer of 1935, Anna Ickes was killed in an automobile accident at the age of 62. She was buried in Memorial Park Cemetery in Evanston, Illinois. Three years later, Harold Ickes married **Jane Dahlman (Ickes)**.

SOURCES:

James, Edward T., ed. *Notable American Women, 1607–1950*. Cambridge, MA: Belknap Press of Harvard University Press, 1971.

Karina L. Kerr, M.A.,
Ypsilanti, Michigan

Ida.

Variant of Ita.

Ida.

Variant of Edith.

Ida de Macon (d. 1224)

Duchess of Lorraine. *Name variations: Ida of Macon. Died in 1224; daughter of Gerard I, count of Macon and Vienne, and* ***Maurette de Salins****, heiress of Salins; married Humbert II de Coligny, around 1170; married Simon II, duke of Lorraine, after 1190.*

Ida of Alsace (c. 1161–1216).

See Ide d'Alsace.

Ida of Austria (d. 1101?)

Margravine of Austria. *Possibly died in 1101; married Leopold II, margrave of Austria (r. 1075–1096); children: Leopold III the Pious of Austria, margrave of Austria (r. 1096–1136, who married *****Agnes of Germany****; he was canonized in 1485).*

In February 1101, two armies set out on Crusade. One was comprised largely of Lombards; the other was French, led by Stephen of Blois, Stephen, bishop of Soissons, and Conrad, constable of Europe. They were followed by William II, count of Nevers, with 15,000 men. "There was also a fourth army," writes **Zoé Oldenbourg** in *The Crusades*, "an extremely large one, estimated at sixty thousand persons including a great many civilian pilgrims, which was led by William IX, Duke of Aquitaine, by Welf IV, Duke of Bavaria, and by the Margravine Ida of Austria, mother of Duke Leopold of Bavaria." On September 15, 1101, surrounded in a battle with the Turks, the fourth army was nearly all slaughtered. William IX and Welf IV narrowly escaped, but Ida "remained on the field of battle and no one ever knew what became of her. She had been one of the most famous beauties of her time." There is some speculation that she was taken prisoner and "ended her days in the harem of Aqsonqor" and had a son Imad ed-din Zengi, a military hero and atabeg of Mosul and Aleppo.

SOURCES:

Oldenbourg, Zoé. *The Crusades*. NY: Pantheon, 1966.

Ida of Boulogne (c. 1161–1216).

See Ide d'Alsace.

Ida of Brabant (1040–1113).

See Ida of Lorraine.

Ida of Ireland (d. 570).

See Ita of Ireland.

Ida of Lorraine (1040–1113)

Saint and countess of Boulogne. *Name variations: Ida of Lower Lorraine; Ida of Brabant. Born in 1040; died in 1113; daughter of Doda and Godfrey II the Bearded, duke of Lower Lorraine (r. 1065–1069); sister of Godfrey III the Hunchback (d. 1076); was the second wife of Eustace II (d. 1093), count of Boulogne (r. around 1057); children: many, including Godfrey, duke of Bouillon and king of Jerusalem (r. 1099–1100); Baldwin I, count of Edessa and king of Jerusalem (r. 1100–1118); Eustace III of Boulogne (who married *****Mary of Atholl*** *[d. 1116]); and possibly a daughter who married Henry IV, king of Germany (though she would not be either of his known wives, *****Bertha of Savoy*** *and *****Adelaide of Kiev****). Eustace II's first wife was Godgifu (c. 1010–c. 1049).*

Ida of Lorraine was born in 1040, the daughter of ***Doda** and Godfrey II the Bearded, duke of Lower Lorraine. At age 17, she married Eustace II, count of Boulogne; both were descendants of Charlemagne. It was a good marriage, though Eustace had first married ***Godgifu** around 1036. Two of Ida's three sons became kings of Jerusalem; a daughter (name unknown) possibly married Henry IV, king of Germany.

Ida of Lorraine was extremely pious; her spiritual counselor St. Anselm, then abbot of Bec, sometimes visited her from Normandy or often wrote uplifting letters. Ida, who gave much of her considerable wealth to charity, enjoyed making fine ornaments for altars. Following the death of her husband in 1093, she sold all her disposable goods to found and endow religious institutions. Ida died in 1113 and was buried at the abbey of Vasconvilliers, near Boulogne. Her feast day is April 13.

Ida of Lorraine (c. 1161–1216).

See Ide d'Alsace.

Ida of Louvain (d. 1260)

Cistercian nun and saint. *Born in Louvain, France; died in 1260.*

Ida of Louvain was a Cistercian nun who died at the abbey of Ramiège in 1260. Her feast day is April 13.

Ida of Lower Lorraine (1040–1113).

See Ida of Lorraine.

Ida of Lower Lorraine (d. 1162)

Noblewoman of Lower Lorraine. *Died on July 27, 1162; daughter of Godfrey I, duke of Lower Lorraine (r. 1106–1139) and *__Ida of Namur__; sister of Godfrey II of Lower Lorraine (d. 1142) and *__Adelicia of Louvain__ (c. 1102–1151, queen of England).*

Ida of Namur

Duchess of Lower Lorraine. *Probably died between 1117 and 1121; daughter of Albert III, count of Namur; first wife of Godfrey I, duke of Lower Lorraine also known as Louvain (r. 1106–1139); children: Godfrey II of Lower Lorraine (d. 1142); *__Adelicia of Louvain__ (c. 1102–1151, queen of England); *__Ida of Lower Lorraine__ (d. 1162). Godfrey I's second wife was *__Clementia__.*

Ida of Nijvel (597–652).

See Ida of Nivelles.

Ida of Nivelles (597–652)

Cistercian nun and queen of the Franks. *Name variations: Blessed Ita, Itta, or Iduberga; Ida of Nijvel; Ida de Nivelles. Born in 597; died in 652; married Pepin I of Landen, mayor of Austrasia (king of the Franks, d. 640); aunt of Saint *__Modesta of Trier__ (d. about 680); children: Gertrude of Nivelles (626–659); *__Begga__ (613–698); Grimoald, mayor of Austrasia (d. 656).*

Following the death of her husband Pepin I, Ida of Nivelles, queen of the Franks, became a nun at the abbey of Nivelles (Belgium) where her daughter ***Gertrude of Nivelles** was abbess. Ida's feast day is May 8.

Ida of Nivelles (d. 1232)

Belgian abbess. *Died in 1232 (some sources cite 1231) at convent of La Ramée, Belgium; never married; no children.*

Few facts are certain about Ida of Nivelles' life. She was given by her parents to the Cistercian convent of La Ramée as a little girl, and remained there her entire life. She was exceptionally well educated at the monastery, and grew up a devout woman who was dedicated to writing and preserving holy works. She eventually became closely identified with the large, busy *scriptorium* (book-production center) of La Ramée, supervising the writing and illustration of manuscripts and performing these functions herself as well. La Ramée produced hundreds of manuscripts a year, for which Ida deserved much of the credit. Ida of Nivelles was a spiritual guide of ***Beatrice of Nazareth** (c. 1200–1268).

Laura York,
Riverside, California

Ida of Saxe-Coburg-Meiningen (1794–1852)

Princess of Saxe-Coburg-Meiningen. *Born on June 25, 1794; died on April 4, 1852; daughter of *__Louise of Hohenlohe-Langenburg__ (1763–1837) and George I (b. 1761), duke of Saxe-Meiningen; married Charles Bernard of Saxe-Weimar (1792–1862); children: __Louise Wilhelmina of Saxe-Weimar__ (1817–1832); William Charles of Saxe-Weimar (b. 1819); Amelia Augusta (1822–1822); Edward (b. 1823); Hermann Henry (b. 1825), prince of Saxe-Weimar; Gustav of Saxe-Weimar (b. 1827); __Anne Amelia of Saxe-Weimar__ (1828–1864); __Amelia Maria da Gloria of Saxe-Weimar__ (1830–1872, who married Henry von Nassau of the Netherlands).*

Ida of Schaumburg-Lippe (1852–1891)

Princess of Reuss. *Name variations: Ida Mathilde Adelheid, princess of Schaumburg-Lippe. Born Ida Matilda Adelaide on July 28, 1852; died on September 28, 1891; daughter of *__Hermine of Waldeck and Pyrmont__ (1827–1910) and Adolphus I Georg, Prince of Schaumburg-Lippe; married Henry 22nd, prince of Reuss, on October 8, 1872; children: six, including*

**Hermine of Reuss (1887–1947, who married Kaiser Wilhelm II).*

Ida of Swabia (d. 986)

***Duchess of Swabia.** Died in 986; daughter of Herman I, duke of Swabia; married Liudolf also known as Ludolf (980–957), duke of Swabia (r. 948–957), in 948; children: Otto I (b. 954), duke of Bavaria; ***Matilda of Essen** (949–1011); and one other daughter.*

Ida Plantagenet (fl. 1175)

***Countess of Norfolk.** Name variations: Isabel Plantagenet. Flourished around 1175; daughter of ***Isabel de Warrenne** (c. 1137–1203) and Hamelin de Warrenne (c. 1129–1202, illegitimate son of Geoffrey of Anjou), 5th earl of Surrey; married Roger Bigod, 2nd earl of Norfolk, one of the 25 sureties of the Magna Carta, and steward of the household of Richard I, king of England; married Robert de Lascy; married Gilbert de Laigle, Lord of Pevensey; children: (first marriage) Hugh Bigod, 3rd earl of Norfolk (r. c. 1200–1225) and earl marshall of England; **Margaret Bigod** (who married Sir John Jeremy); **Margery Bigod** (who married William Hastings, steward to Henry II, king of England); **Alice Bigod** (who married Aubrey IV, 2nd earl of Oxford).*

Jovita Idar

Idar, Jovita (1885–1946)

***Mexican-American journalist, organizer, and educator.** Name variations: Idár. Born Jovita Idar de Juarez in 1885 in Texas; died in 1946.*

The daughter of a Mexican-American newspaper publisher, Jovita Idar was born in 1885 and grew up in South Texas, reaching adulthood during the time of the Mexican Revolution. Like her father, she became a journalist; she also took an active interest in the poverty and racism facing her people. In 1911, Idar helped her father organize the First Mexican Congress, an educational and cultural conference which brought together Mexican-American leaders. Later that same year, she became president of the Mexican Feminist League, which actively opposed lynching, promoted equal rights for women, and fostered education for Mexican-American children. In 1913, Idar also co-founded the White Cross, a group of women who provided medical care for civilians and soldiers from both sides of the Texas-Mexico border.

Apparently fearless when it came to her principles, Idar put herself in harm's way to defend the *El Progreso* newspaper, which in 1914 published an article criticizing President Woodrow Wilson for ordering U.S. troops to the Texas-Mexico border. When the Texas Rangers arrived, armed to the hilt, to close the paper down, Idar defiantly stepped in front of the doorway to keep them out.

In 1917, she moved to San Antonio, where she opened a free kindergarten and edited a Methodist Spanish-language newspaper. Jovita Idar remained active in Mexican-American causes until her death in 1946.

Ide d'Alsace (c. 1161–1216)

***Countess of Boulogne.** Name variations: Ida of Alsace; Ida of Boulogne; Ida of Lorraine; Ide de Lorraine. Born around 1161; died in 1216; reigned from 1173 to 1216; daughter of Marie of Boulogne (d. 1182) and Matthew I (Mattheu d'Alsace), count of Boulogne; sister of ***Maude of Alsace** (1163–c. 1210); married Matthew of Tulli; married Erchard also known as Gerard III of Guelders, count of Guelders; married Berthold, duke of*

Zarengen; married Reinaldo, count of Dammartin; children: Matilda de Dammartin (d. 1258).

Ide d'Alsace was born around 1161, the daughter of ***Marie of Boulogne** and Matthew I. She succeeded her mother as countess of Boulogne in 1173 and ruled until 1216. Her daughter ***Matilda de Dammartin** succeeded her.

Idlibi, 'Ulfah al- (1921—)

Syrian teacher and author. *Name variations: Ulfa al-Idlibi; Ulfat Idlibi. Born in 1921 in Damascus, Syria.*

Selected works: more than 100 stories and four books, including Shamian Stories *(1954),* Farewell, Damascus *(1963),* Damascus, Smile of Sorrow *(released in the U.S. as* Sabriya: A Novel, *1980).*

'Ulfah al-Idlibi was born in 1921 and raised in Damascus, Syria, where she trained to be a teacher. When not educating children, she was a prolific writer, one of Syria's first women to devote the bulk of her writing to short stories. Her realistic, moralistic tone reflects al-Idlibi's belief that stories must have a positive social function. The bulk of her tales explore the lives of Arab women, particularly in Damascus.

Her best-known book is *Damascus, Smile of Sorrow*. Translated by Peter Clark, it was released in paperback in the United States in 1998 by Interlink Publishing Group under the title *Sabriya*. The novel concerns Syria in the 1920s and its national upheaval against the occupying French. It centers around a journal left behind after the suicide of al-Idlibi's protagonist Sabriya who, writes a Kirkus reviewer (May 1, 1997), "finds that her yearnings for political freedom are no more attainable than are love and marriage—the underground 'war' that claims her husband-to-be proves no crueler than the stern patriarchy that demands her devotion to the needs of her aging parents." Though al-Idlibi's matter-of-fact style would be considered less literary in other cultures, it is the standard in Syrian literature, and the author is highly revered.

Crista Martin,
fiction and freelance writer, Boston, Massachusetts

Iduberga (597–652).

See Ida of Nivelles.

Ighodaro, Irene (1916–1995)

Nigerian physician and social reformer. *Born Irene Elizabeth Beatrice Wellesley-Cole in Sierra Leone, Africa, on May 16, 1916; died on November 29, 1995; daughter and one of seven children of Robert Wellesley-Cole (an engineer); attended the Government Model School; graduated from the Annie Walsh Memorial School, Freetown; M.B.B.S. from University of Durham, England; married Samuel Ighodaro (a judge of the High Court of Midwestern Nigeria); children: five; one died in infancy.*

Irene Ighodaro, one of Nigeria's foremost physicians, was born in 1916 in Sierra Leone, a small country on the upper west coast of Africa. The daughter of an engineer, she was raised in relative privilege and encouraged by her father to pursue a medical education. (Irene had originally been interested in the study of languages, but after nursing her mother through a terminal illness, she decided to become a physician.) One of her brothers, also a doctor, financed her education at Durham University in England. After graduating, she married Samuel Ighodaro and moved to Nigeria, where her husband rose to become a justice in the High Court.

Irene Ighodaro

Ighodaro pursued her career while raising and educating a family of five, an accomplishment that would have been impossible, she claimed, without the help of her husband. He was "very broadminded" and believed "in the education of persons (male and female) and the continuous development of the personality." As a result, Irene had "great freedom of movement and action—with his help." Their goals were "the same."

In addition to her private practice, Ighodaro served as chair of the board of management of the University of Benin Teaching Hospital in Benin City, Nigeria, and was a consultant in maternal and child health to the World Health Organization. The author of the book *Baby's First Year*, as well as many articles, she also served as a trustee of the Nigeria Medical Association and as a member of a number of medical advisory committees in western Nigeria. In 1971, she received a professional award establishing her as a Foundation Fellow, with authority to serve as a consultant and examiner in her field. Outside of medicine, Ighodaro was active in both the national and international YWCA, serving also as a member of the YWCA World Executive Committee. In 1958, she was made a Member of the British Empire (MBE).

SOURCES:

Crane, Louise. *Ms. Africa: Profiles of Modern African Women*. Philadelphia, PA: Lippincott, 1973.

Barbara Morgan,
Melrose, Massachusetts

Ihrer, Emma (1857–1911)

***German labor union leader and feminist, one of the first women to head a Social Democratic union in Germany, who served as editor of the journal* Die Gleichheit.** *Born Emma Rother-Faber on January 3, 1857, in Glatz, Silesia, Germany (now Klodzko, Poland); died in Berlin on January 8, 1911.*

Born in Silesia in 1857 into a lower-middle class family (her father was a shoemaker) that was strongly conservative Roman Catholic, Emma Rother-Faber married a pharmacist in the town of Velten but soon tired of this life, moving to Berlin in 1881. Trained as a milliner, she sought work in the ready-made garment industry but quickly discovered the deplorable working conditions in the factories and shops of the German capital. At first, she joined and became active on the board of the Association for Female Manual Workers, but left because of bias. Though the association ran an employment service and provided reading rooms and dining facilities, it was indifferent to the needs of factory working women, favoring instead workers of the middle class. In the early 1880s, labor unions representing factory workers were suppressed by both employers and the police, who invariably sided with the forces of capital against labor. The only political organization to champion the rights of workers, the Socialist Workers' Party (later the Social Democratic Party, or SPD) had been banned on dubious grounds in the late 1870s, and there appeared to be little hope that the living conditions of the working classes would improve at any reasonable point in the future. The masses had numbers in the millions, but the employers and the state had power—legal, military and bureaucratic—on their side.

Despite the danger, Ihrer joined the illegal Socialist Workers' Party in 1881 and was active in efforts to organize Berlin's working women in trade unions. In 1885, she founded the Association for the Representation of the Interests of Female Workers (*Verein zur Vertretung der Arbeiterinnen*), an organization closely allied to the Social Democratic Party, a fact that provided Berlin authorities with the pretext to dissolve it in 1886. Police persecution and harassment did not, however, succeed in breaking Ihrer's spirit. She spread the message of union organization and the ideals of a better society through countless speeches delivered in cities, towns, and villages the length and breadth of the German Reich. By the end of the 1880s, Ihrer had gained the respect of the (male) leadership of the Social Democratic Party and was being viewed as one of the movement's future luminaries.

In July 1889, she went to Paris as a member of the German delegation to participate in the founding congress of the Second International, the new world body of Socialist parties. Back in Berlin later that same year, she served as cofounder and member of the SPD "commission for agitation," a body whose goal was the rapid unionization of female workers. The next year, in November 1890, she was the only woman to serve as a delegate to the founding conference of the SPD Free Trade Union movement. That year saw the end of government repression of the SPD, and, with the new freedom granted to both the party and trade union activities, Ihrer founded and became editor-in-chief of *Die Arbeiterin* (The Woman Worker), the SPD journal for female trade unionists. Under its new title *Die Gleichheit* (Equality), this journal would attract as editors and collaborators some of the most gifted women in the SPD, including ***Clara Zetkin**. In 1893, Ihrer published one of the first books to chronicle the development of women in

German trade unions; it also suggested strategies for future success.

Ihrer's numerous amours sometimes raised eyebrows among the members of the SPD. In an 1891 letter to Karl Kautsky describing Ihrer's activities at the Party conference at Erfurt that year, Karl Marx's former colleague Friedrich Engels noted: "This lady also appears to be very generous with her affections. . . . Her generosity appears also to bring good fortune, in view of the fact that all of her lovers were successful in the most recent elections." In later years, Ihrer settled down with one man, trade-union leader Carl Legien.

Convinced that only the achievement of socialism would bring about the social, economic and personal emancipation of women, Ihrer debated these issues on numerous occasions with middle-class women. In her 1898 book, *The Female Worker in the Class Struggle* (*Die Arbeiterin im Klassenkampf*), she argued for a clear break between bourgeois and proletarian female emancipation. As early as 1895, she had called for a vote in the Reichstag, imperial Germany's Parliament, to decide on granting full civic equality to women. Introduced by the revered leader of the SPD, August Bebel, the resolution went down to defeat. Ihrer grew more militant as time went by. In 1896, along with Zetkin, ***Adelheid Popp**, and ***Eleanor Marx-Aveling**, she issued a statement to the fourth congress of the Socialist International, held that year in London: "For those proletarian women who desire their own liberation, the only place to be is in the ranks of the fighting proletariat, not in the organizations of bourgeois feminists and suffragettes."

Throughout the 1890s and early years of the 20th century, Ihrer was extremely active in various aspects of the German trade-union movement. With each passing year, she was more convinced that Germany's women could only gain full rights if they became union members. By the mid-1890s, she had succeeded in changing the statutes of the Free Trade Unions so that they could both recruit and admit women as full members. Turning socialist theory into practice, in 1901 Ihrer founded a union for women producing artificial flowers, feathers, and dusters. This industry, which had long been fighting a losing battle against industrialization, was located primarily in Berlin, Schleswig, and Saxony. Ihrer faced an uphill climb in attempting to organize workers in this industry, but she was soon publishing *Blumen-Arbeiter* (The Flower Worker), a small monthly journal for union members, and recruiting men as well as women for membership. The work was often seasonal, and union membership fluctuated, but she persisted, and by 1910, the year before her death, the Artificial Flower Makers Union could point to a modest but encouraging growth.

German postage stamp honoring Emma Ihrer.

In 1905, Ihrer entered into a stormy debate that broke out among the Social Democratic intellectuals. In an article published in the ideological journal *Sozialistische Monatshefte* (Socialist Monthly Review), Edmund Fischer argued that Social Democratic advocacy of women's emancipation, long part of the party's agenda, was essentially erroneous in that it went against "the nature of women and of mankind as a whole. It is unnatural, and hence impossible to achieve." Many of the party's leaders, including Ihrer, were infuriated with Fischer's article and responded vehemently. Zetkin published a biting reply in *Die Gleichheit*, and Ihrer, in an article in the *Sozialistische Monatshefte*, heaped scorn on Fischer's idolatry of the notion of "home sweet home," designating such sentimental ideals little more than "a sickness," and categorically dismissing the view that motherhood and childrearing were to be seen as the highest goals for women.

"To be a mother is as little a life's goal as to be a father," wrote Ihrer. "Women can find their life's goal only in general work areas or in solving social tasks that are in the interest of all." For society as a whole, however, she believed that a vast restructuring would be essential so that motherhood and employment could one day be balanced, enabling married women to work and also be successful, nurturing mothers and productive, fulfilled family members. In the new socialist commonwealth of the future, an alternative model would prevail, one that enabled its women to "choose one occupation according to her capabilities and inclinations: she will be either working woman or educator of children or housekeeper, but not all three, as is today's proletarian woman."

In her final years, Ihrer remained a militant defender of the rights of women both within the Social Democratic Party and in the world at large. She died in Berlin on January 8, 1911, much mourned by her colleagues, both men and women. On February 9, 1989, Emma Ihrer was honored by the Federal Republic of Germany when she was depicted on a 5 pfennig postage stamp in the "Women of German History" definitive series.

SOURCES:

Beier, Gerhard. *Schulter an Schulter, Schritt für Schritt: Lebensläufe deutscher Gewerkschafter von August Bebel bis Theodor Thomas.* Cologne: Bund-Verlag, 1983.

Berger, Stefan. "Ihrer, Emma," in A. Thomas Lane, ed. *Biographical Dictionary of European Labor Leaders.* Vol. I. Westport, CT: Greenwood Press, 1995, pp. 441–442.

Dertinger, Antje. *Die bessere Hälfte kämpft um ihr Recht: Über den Anspruch der Frauen auf Erwerb und andere Selbstverständlichkeiten.* Cologne: Bund-Verlag, 1980.

"Emma Ihrer," in *Vorwärts* [Berlin]. January 10, 1911.

Fout, John C., ed. *German Women in the Nineteenth Century: A Social History.* NY: Holmes & Meier, 1984.

Honeycutt, Karen. "Socialism and Feminism in Imperial Germany," in *Signs: Journal of Women in Culture and Society.* Vol. 5, no. 1. Autumn 1979, pp. 30–41.

Ihrer, Emma. *Die Arbeiterinnen im Klassenkampf: Anfänge der Arbeiterinnenbewegung, Ihr Gegensatz zur bürgerlichen Frauenbewegung und ihre nächste Aufgaben.* Hamburg: Verlag der General Kommission der Gewerkschaften, 1898.

Losseff-Tillmanns, Gisela. *Frauenimanzipation und Gewerkschaften.* Wuppertal: Hammer Verlag, 1978.

———, ed. *Frau und Gewerkschaft.* Frankfurt am Main: Fischer Taschenbuch Verlag, 1982.

Quataert, Jean H. *Reluctant Feminists in German Social Democracy, 1885–1917.* Princeton, NJ: Princeton University Press, 1979.

———. "Unequal Partners in an Uneasy Alliance: Women and the Working Class in Imperial Germany," in Marilyn J. Boxer and Jean H. Quataert, eds. *Socialist Women: European Socialist Feminism in the Nineteenth and Early Twentieth Centuries.* NY: Elsevier—North Holland Publishing, 1978, pp. 112–145.

Richebächer, Sabine. *Uns fehlt nur eine Kleinigkeit: Deutsche proletarische Frauenbewegung.* Frankfurt am Main: Fischer Taschenbuch Verlag, 1982.

Riemer, Eleanor, and John C. Fout, eds. *European Women: A Documentary History, 1789–1945.* NY: Schocken Books, 1980.

Schneider, Karl H. "Ihrer, Emma" in Edmund Jacoby, ed. *Lexikon linker Leitfiguren.* Frankfurt am Main: Büchergilde Gutenberg, 1988, pp. 186–187.

Strain, Jaqueline. "Feminism and Political Radicalism in the German Social Democratic Movement, 1890–1914." Ph. D. dissertation, University of California, Berkeley, 1964.

Thönnesen, Werner. *The Emancipation of Women: The Rise and Decline of the Women's Movement in German Social Democracy 1863–1933.* Translated by Joris de Bres. London: Pluto Press Limited, 1973.

John Haag,
Associate Professor of History,
University of Georgia, Athens, Georgia

Ildegarde.

Variant of Hildegarde.

Ildico (fl. 453)

Teutonic princess. *Flourished around 453; married Attila (c. 370/400–453), leader of the Huns, in 453. Attila also married Princess Honoria in 450.*

Around 450, Attila the Hun sent word to the Roman court in Italy claiming the princess ***Honoria** in marriage. His claim was addressed to her brother Valentinian III, although ***Galla Placidia**, their mother, seems to have been the actual regnant. When his claim was rejected out of hand (as he doubtless knew it would be), Attila negotiated with King Gaiseric of the Vandals to secure his flanks in the south, then moved north and west against Western Europe, pillaging, raping and burning a wide swath of destruction west of the Rhine Valley, well into Belgica Secunda. Among the cities laid waste were Reims, Cambrai, Tournai, Metz, Arras, Cologne (Köln) and Trier.

In 453, an aging Attila took another wife. She was young and, according to reports, "comely." Her name was Ildico and she was Hunnish. The wedding took place in a large wooden building and involved a heavy feast with an excessive amount of drinking. Attila was finally able to get to his bedroom, where he collapsed on his bed, lying on his back. He frequently suffered from a bleeding nose, especially after heavy drinking, and it happened then. Unable to rouse himself, he literally drowned in his own blood, his new heavily veiled bride sitting there uncomprehending. When his followers finally discovered the body, it was too late. Ildico was not accused of complicity and the bereaved warriors feasted again, then took the body of their fallen king away and buried him secretly in much the same fashion as other chieftains of that period. The burial site has never been found.

SOURCES:

Brion, Marcel. *Attila, the Scourge of God.* McBride, 1929.

Maenchen-Helfen, Otto J. *The World of the Huns: Studies in their History and Culture.* Edited by Max Knight. University of California Press, 1973.

Thompson, E.A. *A History of Attila and the Huns.* Greenwood Press, 1975 (reprint).

Ileana (1909–1991)

Archduchess of Austria. *Name variations: Ileana Hohenzollern; Mother Alexandra. Born on January 5, 1909, in Bucharest, Rumania; died on January 21, 1991, at St. Elizabeth's Hospital, Youngstown, Ohio; daughter of Ferdinand I, king of Rumania, and* ****Marie of Rumania*** *(1875–1938); married Anthony, archduke of Austria, on July 26, 1931 (divorced 1954); married Dr. Stephen Virgil Issarescu, on June 19, 1954 (divorced 1965); children: (first marriage) Stephen (b. 1932); Marie-Ileana (1933–1959); Alexandra (b. 1935); Dominic (b. 1937); Maria Magdelena (b. 1939); Elizabeth (b. 1942).*

Ileana, the archduchess of Austria, was born in Bucharest, Rumania, in 1909, the daughter of Ferdinand I, the king of Rumania, and ***Marie of Rumania**. In 1931, she married Anthony, archduke of Austria. The marriage was dissolved 23 years later. She then married Stephen Issarescu in 1954. Following her second divorce, Ileana became a nun in the Orthodox faith at the Monastery of the Transfiguration in Ellwood City, Pennsylvania, and took the name Mother Alexandra.

Imagi of Luxemburg (c. 1000–1057)

Countess of Altdorf. *Born around 1000; died on August 21, 1057; daughter of Frederick (c. 965–1019), count of Luxemburg; sister of* ****Ogive of Luxemburg*** *(d. 1030); married Guelph also known as Welf or Wolfard, count of Altdorf and duke of Nether Bavaria, around 1015 (died 1030, some sources cite 1036); children: Guelph or Welf, duke of Carinthia;* ****Cunegunda d'Este*** *(c. 1020–1055).*

Imlay, Fanny (1794–1816).

See Wollstonecraft, Mary for sidebar.

Imlay, Mary (1759–1797).

See Wollstonecraft, Mary.

Imma or Imme.

Variant of Emma.

Immerwahr, Clara (1870–1915)

German chemist, the first German woman to be awarded a doctorate in chemistry, who committed suicide to protest her husband's involvement in the military use of poison gas. *Born in Breslau, Germany (now Wroclaw, Poland), on June 21, 1870; died by her own hand on May 2, 1915; married Fritz Haber (a noted chemist); children: one son, Hermann.*

Clara Immerwahr was born in 1870, the year that marked the final phase of Germany's unification (the first German Reich was officially proclaimed on January 18, 1871). She grew up in a wealthy, highly cultured German-Jewish family, her father having achieved distinction as a chemist. Determined by her late teen years to enter into a scientific career, Clara was unwilling to let institutional discrimination keep her from achieving her goal of becoming a productive research scientist. In 1898, Immerwahr became the first woman in Germany to pass the difficult *Verbandsexamen*, a predoctoral qualifying examination designed to bring higher standards in the training of professional chemists. In 1900, she was awarded her doctorate in physical chemistry, her dissertation being a study of the solubility of metal salts. With her degree, awarded by the University of Breslau with the distinction of magna cum laude, Clara Immerwahr became the first woman to be awarded a doctorate in chemistry at a German university.

After working briefly as research assistant in Clausthal following graduation, in 1901 Immerwahr married Fritz Haber. As gifted in chemistry as his bride, Haber also came from Breslau and could point to a similar family background, having been born into an affluent, assimilated Jewish family (his father ran a successful dye business). Within a year, a son, Hermann, was born to the couple. At first, Immerwahr believed that she would be able to successfully juggle the careers of wife, mother and research chemist, and she collaborated with her husband when he wrote his standard textbook on the thermodynamics of technical gas reactions—a book that he dedicated to her.

Soon it became obvious to Clara that her husband's career came first. Although she was occasionally able to present lectures on such topics of general interest as "Chemistry and Physics in the Household" to women's clubs and adult education classes, she was forced to abandon her plans. Reluctantly, she had to accept the reality that university lectureships were all but unobtainable for women, and that she bore additional burdens because she was Jewish, married and a mother. Her husband, on the other hand, forged ahead with his intention to make his mark on both the world of academia and industry.

By 1908, Haber had been appointed full professor of physical chemistry at the University of Karlsruhe, and in 1911 he became director of the Kaiser Wilhelm Institute for Physical Chemistry and Electrochemistry in Berlin. Along with the directorship, he received a professorial chair at the University of Berlin and membership in the prestigious Prussian Academy of Sciences. Despite the anti-Semitism prevalent in the German Reich of Kaiser Wilhelm II, highly talented individuals of Jewish birth could in fact rise to the top of their professions, but in private many of their colleagues and fellow citizens regarded them as not fully German (to gain full acceptance, Haber had converted to Christianity, but to many both the Habers were still Jews). Certain forms of discrimination remained in place, including a ban on Jews receiving commissions as officers in the Prussian-dominated German Army. In the years immediately preceding World War I, Fritz Haber attempted to establish institutional contacts between his institute and the German military but found himself rebuffed, in part because of anti-Semitism, but also because the mind-set of the military remained largely indifferent and even hostile to science and technology.

In the early years of his scientific career, Fritz Haber made a discovery with immense consequences. In 1909, in a classic experiment using high pressure and a metal catalyst, he was able to make the normally unreactive gas nitrogen combine with hydrogen to form ammonia—something that chemists had been attempting to achieve without success for well over a century. Within four years, the laboratory synthesis of ammonia had been turned into an industrial process that was both practicable and profitable, making possible the extraction of other compounds containing nitrogen that could now be produced in virtually unlimited amounts. These included nitroglycerine and other high explosives for military use. But the same process could also be used to inexpensively produce ammonia fertilizer, thus preventing soil exhaustion.

After less than a decade of marriage, Immerwahr had grown increasingly frustrated and unhappy. "What Fritz has gained in these eight years," she wrote a friend, "I have lost, and what is left of me fills me with profound dissatisfaction."

The start of World War I in August 1914 gave Haber his opportunity to prove his patriotism. His Haber process, perfected by Germany's highly developed chemical industry, now enabled the Fatherland to continue to fight a war that would otherwise have quickly ended when the limited supplies of nitrates for ammunition and explosives as well as agricultural fertilizer ran out. Haber, who had not been able to obtain an officer's commission in peacetime because of the Army's pervasive spirit of anti-Semitism, now became a captain, and soon headed the section in the War Ministry concentrating on gas warfare. In early 1915, he suggested that instead of firing non-lethal irritating gases encased in artillery shells (something the enemy was also experimenting with), another method of chemical warfare be used. His idea, diabolically simple, was to release highly toxic chlorine gas under proper wind conditions, so that it would drift across no man's land and into the enemy's trenches, where it would kill, maim and disable without an artillery bombardment.

Code-named "Disinfection," Haber's experiment in chemical warfare first took place on the western front in the Ypres sector in Belgium on Thursday, April 22, 1915, at just after 1700 hours. Within ten minutes, 6,000 cylinders of chlorine—easily obtained by the military since it was already being produced in electrochemical factories—were released and 150 tons of gas soon was drifting toward the British and French trenches. The defenders were taken completely by surprise, and within minutes the front collapsed. Even hardened military observers were shocked by what they had witnessed: "It was at first impossible for anyone to realize what had actually happened. The smoke and fumes hid everything from sight, and hundreds of men were thrown into a comatose or dying condition, and within an hour the whole position had to be abandoned." Of the 7,000 casualties that day, more than 5,000 died. Although the German forces at first made easy gains of territory, the leadership did not take sufficient advantage of the opportunity on this and other occasions, and the ghastly stalemate of trench warfare would continue for virtually the rest of World War I.

Fritz Haber believed that gas warfare could shorten the war and its suffering as well as make a German victory possible. He hoped that the new form of warfare would break the stalemate, and as a scientist in the service of his nation was untroubled by the moral consequences of the new weaponry. Science, he once said, belonged to humanity in peacetime and to the Fatherland in war. In reality, the attack of April 22, 1915, was followed by countless others which released 125,000 tons of toxic chemicals that resulted in the deaths of at least 100,000 soldiers on both sides of the conflict; at least 1,300,000 combatants were wounded, and many condemned to suffer intense, crippling physical pain for the rest of their lives. By the end of World War I in 1918, all sides in the great conflict were either using poison gas or had massive stockpiles on hand for future use.

For Immerwahr, her husband's enthusiastic dedication to chemical warfare represented the final break. She was horrified by the loss of life and was convinced that the war was bringing about an inhumane application of the uses of science and technology, which for her was meant to advance the cause of humanity. She faulted her husband for choosing to work in a project she believed to be nothing less than "a perversion of the ideals of science." His angry response was to accuse her in front of friends and colleagues of making statements treasonous to the Fatherland.

Having witnessed her husband's metamorphosis from a benefactor of humanity into a weapons scientist, Immerwahr pleaded with him on several occasions to cease working on gas warfare but to no avail. Returning in triumph from the Ypres front to their home in Berlin's elegant suburb of Dahlem, Haber attended a party in his honor the night before he was scheduled to go to the eastern front to supervise a gas attack. Fritz and Clara quarreled, and that same night, May 2, 1915, while he slept with the help of sleeping pills, Immerwahr shot herself fatally with his service revolver. The next morning, Fritz Haber proceeded to his duties at the front. Any notes or letters she may have left behind were destroyed. For the rest of his life, Fritz Haber never discussed any of the details of her death.

By 1917, Haber had transformed the peaceful research facility he ran before the war into a massive research center for tactical military science and technology. He boasted of a staff of 1,500, of which at least 150 researchers in many areas of expertise had been drafted, recruited or reassigned from other military departments to work under him. His total budget was 50 times that of his prewar institute, but his military rank never was higher than that of a captain, while his counterpart in the British Army, like Haber also a professional chemist, became a general. The lingering anti-Semitism of the German military for whom he labored continued to haunt Haber. In 1918, he was awarded the Nobel Prize for his pathbreaking work in ammonia synthesis, but when Haber received his award, the great physicist Ernest Rutherford declined to shake his hand. A few months later, there were calls for Haber's arrest and trial as a war criminal because of the key role he had played in the genesis of gas warfare.

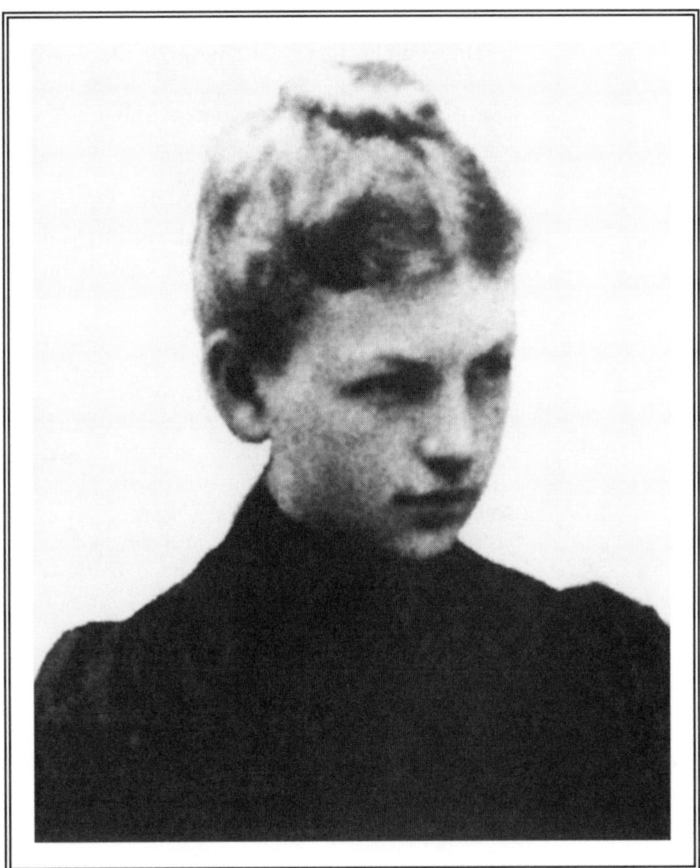

Clara Immerwahr

Fritz Haber remained a major scientific personality in Germany in the Weimar Republic. He remarried, while the memory of Clara Immerwahr faded into obscurity. When the Nazis came to power in 1933, his scientific work for the Fatherland was ignored, and he went into exile, finding refuge in Great Britain. There, too, he was looked upon as a pariah because of his gas warfare activities. Rejected and emotionally shattered, Haber went to Italy to recover his health. On the way, in Switzerland, in January 1934, he died. Many years later, in 1968, when the University of Karlsruhe honored him on the centenary of his birth, the commemorative ceremony was disrupted by students who unfurled a banner reading, *Feier für einen Mörder/Haber = Vater des Gaskriegs* (Celebration for a Murderer/Haber = Father of Gas Warfare).

In the 1970s, the legacy of Clara Immerwahr began to come to the attention of the German public. Historians and activists alike began to investigate this remarkable woman who ended her life in a protest against the desecration of science. Journal articles and a full-length biography by Gerit von Leitner brought Immerwahr's struggles to a generation confronted with the destructive potentialities of science and technology in an age of nuclear, chemical, and biological global mass destruction. A role model for civic courage, she is the subject of Tony Harrison's 1992 play *Square Rounds*. In her honor, the German Section of International Physicians for the Prevention of Nuclear War designated its most prestigious award, the Clara Immerwahr Prize.

SOURCES:

Foelsing, Ulla. *Geniale Beziehungen: Berühmte Paare in der Wissenschaft.* Munich: Verlag C. H. Beck, 1999.

Goran, Morris Herbert. *The Story of Fritz Haber.* Norman: University of Oklahoma Press, 1967.

Haber, L.F. *The Poisonous Cloud: Chemical Warfare in the First World War.* Oxford: Clarendon Press, 1986.

Harrison, Tony. *Square Rounds.* London: Faber and Faber, 1992.

Hervé, Florence, and Ingeborg Nödinger. *Lexikon der Rebellinnen: Von A bis Z.* Dortmund: Edition Ebersbach, 1996.

Johnson, Jeffrey A. *The Kaiser's Chemists: Science and Modernization in Imperial Germany.* Chapel Hill, NC: University of North Carolina Press, 1990.

———. "The Scientist Behind Poison Gas: The Tragedy of the Habers," in *Humanities.* Vol. 17, no. 5. November–December 1996, pp. 25–29.

Lefebure, Victor. *The Riddle of the Rhine: Chemical Strategy in Peace and War.* NY: Chemical Foundation, 1923.

Leitner, Gerit von. *Der Fall Clara Immerwahr: Leben für eine humane Wissenschaft.* Munich: Verlag C.H. Beck, 1993.

McCarthy, Richard D. *The Ultimate Folly: War by Pestilence, Asphyxiation, and Defoliation.* NY: Alfred A. Knopf, 1969.

Mendelssohn, K. *The World of Walther Nernst: The Rise and Fall of German Science 1864–1941.* Pittsburgh: University of Pittsburgh Press, 1973.

Milne, Kirsty. "Top Hat, Tails and Nitrogen," in *Sunday Telegraph* [London]. October 4, 1992, p. 115.

Perutz, M.F. "The Cabinet of Dr. Haber," in *New York Review of Books.* Vol. 43, no. 8. June 20, 1996, pp. 31–32, 34–36.

Press, Newtol. "Haber's Choice, Hobson's Choice, and Biological Warfare," in *Perspectives in Biology and Medicine*, Vol. 29, no. 1. Autumn 1985, pp. 92–108.

Stephan, Inge, Sabine Schilling, and Sigrid Weigel, eds. *Jüdische Kultur und Weiblichkeit in der Moderne.* Cologne, Weimar and Vienna: Verlag Böhlau, 1994.

Stern, Fritz. *Dreams and Delusions: The Drama of German History.* NY: Vintage Books, 1989.

Stoltzenberg, Dietrich. *Fritz Haber, Chemiker, Nobelpreisträger, Deutscher, Jude: Eine Biographie.* Weinheim and NY: VCH Verlag, 1994.

Szöllösi-Janze, Margit. *Fritz Haber 1868–1934: Eine Biographie.* Munich: Verlag C. H. Beck, 1998.

John Haag,
Associate Professor of History,
University of Georgia, Athens, Georgia

Impekoven, Niddy (1904—)

German dancer of the Weimar epoch who combined several styles to become one of the most renowned artists on the periphery of expressionist dance. *Born Luise Antonie Crescentia Impekoven in Berlin, Germany, on November 2, 1904; daughter of Toni Impekoven and Frida (Kobler) Impekoven; children: one daughter.*

In November 1992, Swiss newspapers and German-language dance journals reported the 90th birthday of a virtually forgotten dancer who had once dazzled audiences around the world. For 15 years, Niddy Impekoven had created her own unique style of dance, veering close to the expressionism of the day but never indulging in its emotional excesses. Famous in her own day, she retired in the mid-1930s and by the start of World War II had begun to slip into obscurity.

Born in Berlin in 1904, Niddy Impekoven grew up in an artistic environment, her father Toni enjoying a solid reputation both as an actor and successful playwright. By age three, Niddy's parents noted with approval her spontaneous dancing to any music heard in the house. In 1910, soon after beginning her formal dance training, Niddy made her stage debut in Berlin at a charity performance. Declared a child prodigy, she found herself facing pressure from her parents to prepare for a career as a professional dancer. Soon after her successful debut, the Impekovens moved to Frankfurt am Main, where Niddy continued her studies with Heinrich Kröller (1880–1930), a noted dancer, ballet master and choreographer, whose goal was to fuse classical traditions with modern trends; he succeeded in this, particularly in the works he choreographed for several compositions by Richard Strauss.

After three years of intensive study of classical ballet with Kröller, Impekoven moved to Munich in 1917, where she studied classical gymnastics at the famous Bieberstein Castle School. Her first solo program, presented in 1918 at Berlin's Theater unter den Linden, was designed with the advice of Kröller. The numbers included *Der gefangene Vogel* (The Caged Bird), *Schalk* (Rascal), *Puppentänzen* (Doll Dances), and *Das Leben der Blume* (The Life of Flowers). A war-weary audience was transported into a better world by the artistry of the young girl. The music she chose was invariably classical—Bach, Chopin, Mozart, Schubert and Schumann being among her favorite composers.

Although many contemporary critics felt Impekoven to be unsurpassed in her portrayals of innocent country maidens or in her dances to the music of Mozart, she was also a child of her time. Reflecting her tormented era in German history, she often performed expressionistic works that mirrored the world, including the grotesque *Pretzel Puppen* (Pretzel Dolls). Her multifaceted artistic personality was also revealed in a number of humorous sketches, including *Münchner Kaffeewärmer* (Munich Coffeepot), and several short classically based ballets, among them *Harlekin* and *Pizzicato*.

Emotionally sensitive as well as artistically gifted, Impekoven experienced a crisis in her mid-teen years. The demands of sudden success and pressure from her parents served to trigger severe depression in 1919. She appeared to have given up the will to live and was taken by her parents to recuperate at the Hotel Quellenhof in the spa resort of Bad Ragaz, Switzerland. Losing weight rapidly, she was likely suffering not only from depression but from anorexia nervosa, and her physician as well as her parents and friends became increasingly concerned about her health.

Soon after arriving at Bad Ragaz, Impekoven met the German playwright Reinhard Goering and informed her parents, "Only this person can help me." He, too, was convinced he could cure their daughter. Goering moved into the house where the Impekovens were staying and began his course of treatment, a diet of raw fruits and vegetables, while discouraging any attempts to force Niddy to eat. Within two weeks, she broke her fast and began to recover her health.

Goering then remained secluded in his room for three days, while he meditated and wrote a new drama. He told the Impekovens that *Die Retter* (The Saviors) presented to the world "the kind of love that exists between the little sister (*das Schwesterchen*) and myself." The "little sister" was Impekoven, and Goering, who was married at the time, urged that she consider him her "brother." Though the relationship between the two was platonic and contemplative, years later Goering described his affiliation with the young dancer as one in which they had been able to "converse with each other without speaking. Only then and there and never again did I ever experience anything like this." Recovered, Impekoven returned to her career, but Goering began to send her letters virtually every day. After a while, she decided not to answer each of these, but they continued to arrive even when she spent her next holiday with her grandmother in Switzerland. The suspicious grandmother decided to hide Goering's letters from Niddy, who did not discover them for over three decades. Upon reading them, she learned that the long-unopened missives from Goering to her had in fact been passionate declarations of love.

Throughout the 1920s, Impekoven was acknowledged to be one of the most creative as well as popular dancers in German-speaking Central Europe. She was at home on the stages of Berlin, Munich, Vienna, and Prague, and when the famous Austrian novelist Arthur Schnitzler saw her perform at Vienna's Renaissance Theater in November 1923, he noted in his diary: "Niddy Impekoven: wonderful dancer." She moved in the highest intellectual circles counting as her acquaintances many of the leading artists of the day, including the novelist Thomas Mann. Despite her youth, she was considered an authority on various forms of

Niddy Impekoven

dance and in 1925 served as consultant (along with *Tamara Karsavina) on the film *Wege zur Kraft und Schönheit* (Paths to Strength and Beauty), a documentary calling for a revitalized German national identity after years of war and humiliation. This motion picture, produced by Berlin's Universum (UFA) studios, celebrated sports, exercise techniques, outdoor festivities, and modern-dance forms, while reenacting the sports and outdoor celebrations of Greek and Roman antiquity.

By the early 1930s, Impekoven was an international celebrity, performing in the Far East and the United Kingdom. Her visits to Paris were sensations, with French critics heaping praise on her for her interpretation of the second movement of Beethoven's "Moonlight Sonata." French audiences were delighted with her depiction of a woman of the streets, accompanied by the modernist music of Darius Milhaud. During her visit to London in October 1931, *The Times* reported that her portrayal of "The Life of a Flower" was representative of "the modern school of dancing in which the feet have been dethroned from their old supremacy as the chief means of expression. . . . [I]t is the hands that do most towards the portrayal of the whole process from the opening of the petals to their shrivelling and fall." Furthermore, she was praised for showing "that her command of humour is as great as her command of beauty, and perfectly realized for us how a 'Münchener Kaffeewärmer' [a personified tea-cozy] would dance a waltz, if cosies did dance."

Although only in her 20s, by 1933 Impekoven was considering retiring from the stage. It had been more than two decades since she made her stage debut in 1910 at age six. The Nazi takeover in 1933 also alarmed her. Not only were some of her colleagues now being persecuted and driven from their careers because they were Jewish or politically unreliable, the very future of modern dance in the Third Reich was in jeopardy. Certain aspects of the modern-dance movement, particularly the ones that had cultivated strength, physical beauty and vitality, such as rhythmic gymnastics and mass dance, were seen as a path to a revived German nation and were thus encouraged. The other strand of modern dance during the pre-Nazi Weimar period, which had emphasized often sharp social and political satire, was now characterized as Cultural Bolshevism (*Kulturbolschewismus*) and was outlawed. Although Impekoven had rarely made direct political statements in her art, she was too much an individualist and humanist to be able to co-exist with the demands of Hitler's regime.

During the 1933–34 season, Impekoven gave her farewell appearances in Germany. Soon after, she moved to Switzerland to raise a young daughter and be close to her mother's family. Never interested in teaching, she did not leave behind a specific style of dancing, always having been eclectic and catholic in her tastes. For many years she lived in the city of Basel, eventually moving to Bad Ragaz, the spa resort where she had entranced Reinhard Goering so many decades earlier. Here Niddy Impekoven would celebrate her 90th birthday in November 1994, informing one of her interviewers, "Dancing, that is something I only do once in a while in my dreams."

SOURCES:

"The Arts Theatre Club: A Dance Recital," in *The Times* [London]. October 20, 1931, p. 12.

Braunwarth, Peter Michael, Susanne Pertlik and Reinhard Urbach, eds. *Arthur Schnitzler—Tagebuch 1923–1926*. Vienna: Verlag der Österreichischen Akademie der Wissenschaften, 1995.

Cohen-Stratyner, Barbara Naomi. *Biographical Dictionary of Dance*. NY: Macmillan Publishing/ Schirmer Books, 1982.

Davis, Robert Chapin. *Final Mutiny: Reinhard Goering, His Life and Art*. NY: Peter Lang, 1987.

Diethe, Carol. "The Dance Theme in German Modernism," in *German Life and Letters*. Vol. 44, no. 4. July 1944, pp. 330–352.

Dietrich. "Niddy Impekoven, Tänzerin," *Universum*. No. 37, 1931.

Frentz, Hans. *Niddy Impekoven und ihre Tänze*. Freiburg im Breisgau: Urban-Verlag, 1929.

———. *Weg und Entfaltung Niddy Impekovens*. Leipzig: E. Weibezahl Verlag, 1933.

Grabe, K.G. "Niddy Impekoven," in *Westermanns Monatshefte*. Vol. 149. September 1930, pp. 46–48.

Howe, Dianne S. *Individuality and Expression: The Aesthetics of the New German Dance, 1908–1936*. NY: Peter Lang, 1996.

Impekoven, Niddy. *Die Geschichte eines Wunderkindes*. Zurich: Rotapfel-Verlag AG, 1955.

———. *Werdegang*. Dresden: A. Huhle Verlag, [1922].

Koegler, Horst. *Concise Oxford Dictionary of Ballet*. 2nd ed. London: Oxford University Press, 1987.

Manning, Susan. *Ecstasy and the Demon: Feminism and Nationalism in the Dances of Mary Wigman*. Berkeley, CA: University of California Press, 1993.

Martin, Dorothy Sue. "The Life and Literature of Reinhard Goering: A Study in Contradictions," Ph. D. dissertation, University of Illinois at Urbana-Champaign, 1980.

Menschen der Zeit: Hundert und ein Lichtbildnis wesentlicher Männer und Frauen aus deutscher Gegenwart und jüngster Vergangenheit. Königstein im Taunus and Leipzig: Verlag Karl Robert Langewiesche, 1931.

Moss, Suzan F. "Spinning Through the Weltanschauung: The Effects of the Nazi Regime on the German Modern Dance," Ph. D. dissertation, New York University, 1988.

Müller, Hedwig. "Impekoven, Niddy," in *International Encyclopedia of Dance*. Vol. 3. NY: Oxford University Press, 1998, p. 443.

Pellaton, Ursula. "'Etwas tanzte mich'": Zum neunzigsten Geburtstag von Niddy Impekoven," in *Neue Zürcher Zeitung*. November 2, 1994, p. 46.
———. "Persönlich," *Tanz und Gymnastik*. Vol. 50, no. 4, 1994, pp. 14–16.
———. "'Tanzen, das tue ich nur manchmal noch im Traum': Zum 90. Geburtstag von Niddy Impekoven," in *Ballett-Journal/ Das Tanzarchiv*. Vol. 42, no. 5. December 1994, pp. 34–35.
Prechtl, Robert. "Niddy Impekoven," in *Vossische Zeitung* [Berlin]. October 26, 1919.
Preston-Dunlop, Valerie, and Susanne Lahusen, eds. *Schrifttanz: A View of German Dance in the Weimar Republic*. London and Pennington, NJ: Dance Books, 1990.
Solomon, Janis Little. *Die Kriegsdramen Reinhard Goerings*. Berne: Francke Verlag, 1985.
Sommer, R. "Niddy Impekoven," in *Freiburger Theaterblätter.* 1931–1932, p. 161.
Thomas-Mann-Archiv, Eidgenössische Technische Hochschule, Zurich, Switzerland.
Toepfer, Karl. "Nudity and Modernity in German Dance, 1910–30," in *Journal of the History of Sexuality.* Vol. 3, no. 1. July 1992, pp. 58–108.

COLLECTIONS:

Walter Toscanini Collection of Research Materials in Dance, New York Public Library, Research Division.

John Haag,
Associate Professor of History,
University of Georgia, Athens, Georgia

Ina Maria of Bassewitz-Levitzow (1888–1973)

Countess of Prussia and countess von Ruppin. *Name variations: Ina-Maria. Born on January 27, 1888, in Bristow, Mecklenburg; died on September 17, 1973, in Munich, Germany; daughter of Karl Heinrich, count von Bassewitz-Levetzow, and* ***Margarete Cacilie****, countess von der Schulenburg; married Oscar Charles, prince of Prussia, on July 31, 1914; children: Oscar William (b. 1915); Burchard (b. 19170;* ****Herzeleide*** *(1918–1989); William Charles (b. 1922).*

Inan (fl. c. 800)

Arabian singer whose voice caused more than one caliph of Baghdad to pay tens of thousands in gold to hear her sing her own compositions. *Born and raised in Yamama, Arabia; flourished around 800.*

Inan's life story was similar to many Arabian songstresses. She was a talented slave for whom Harun al-Rashid, the caliph of Baghdad, paid over 30,000 pieces of gold. In modern terms, Inan was very like a top-ranked star signed under contract to a movie mogul. Born and brought up in Yamama, Arabia, she was purchased by Al-Natifi who taught her music. When her fame reached Baghdad, Al-Natifi refused to part with her for less than 30,000 pieces of gold, a price the caliph willingly paid. Harun became deeply infatuated with Inan, causing his wife **Om Jafar**'s great jealousy. Inan might have fared poorly on Harun's death, but the caliph succeeding him gladly paid an equally high price for her services, and she continued to dominate the court with her songs.

John Haag,
Athens, Georgia

Inanna (fl. c. 3000 BCE)

Sumerian composer whose role was similar to St. Cecilia, the patron saint of European music. *Flourished around 3000 BCE; achieved the status of a goddess.*

The central role women have long played in music is demonstrated over and over again by the fact that they were made patrons of this important field of human endeavor in many cultures throughout history. Inanna might be best compared with the patron saint of European music, Saint ***Cecilia**. Women living in Sumeria 3,000 years before Christ were able to be priestesses, businesswomen, and to own property. Their status was higher than would be true in later Mesopotamia, so Inanna's musical talents would not have been considered abnormal in the time in which she lived. She was said to have composed *The Song of Life and Marriage* as well as other Sumerian hymns. These were performed in choral form, probably accompanied by flutes, tambourines and cymbals at ceremonies. Inanna's stature grew with the passage of time, and she was venerated as the goddess of the date palm and eventually as the mother of all creation. She was said to ensure the fertility of the earth. Like St. Cecilia who was also credited with compositions and miracles, Inanna's powers were both creative and mystical.

John Haag,
Athens, Georgia

Inayat-Khan, Noor (1914–1944).

See Khan, Noor Inayat.

Inber, Vera (1890–1972)

Russian poet, writer, and journalist. *Born Vera Mikhaylovna Inber in 1890 in Odessa, Russia; died in 1972; daughter of a publisher and a teacher.*

Selected writings: Bitter Delight *(1917);* Fleeting Words *(1922);* The Goal and the Journey *(1925);* To the Non-Existent Son *(1927); (short story) "Garlic in His Suitcase" (1927); (short story) "Death on the*

Moon" (1928); (travel notes) America in Paris *(1928);* Travel Diary *(1939); (essay) "On Leningrad Children" (1942–43);* Almost Three Years *(1946, about the siege of Leningrad, published in English as* Leningrad Diary*);* Waterway *(1951); (short story) "How I Was Little" (1953);* Inspiration and Mastery *(1957);* April *(1960).*

Vera Inber was born in 1890 in Odessa, Russia, to a publisher father and a mother who taught Russian. Inber visited Western Europe often, and her first work of poetry was published in Paris. Before the Russian Revolution in 1917, she wrote light verse, such as her volume of poetry *Melancholy Wine* (1914), and was influenced by the personal nature of ***Anna Akhmatova**'s works.

In the 1920s, Inber became part of the constructivist movement and applied constructivist technological symbolism and utilitarian theory to her poetry. Much of her work of the 1920s and 1930s dealt with Moscow, the Revolution, and Vladimir Lenin. She also wrote short stories during these years that depicted the clash between old and new Soviet life, as shown in "Nightingale and Rose" (published in *North American Review* in 1924). Memories of Inber's youth found their way into her work, and many of these stories also dealt with children and were often written from a child's perspective. Inber also wrote for the theater, including a verse comedy titled *Mother's Union* (1938), and opera librettos. During World War II, she became a member of the Communist Party and began producing the patriotic works that would bring her renown.

In 1941, she and her husband, a doctor, moved to Leningrad to work during the 900-day siege of the city by the German army. Her poem "Pulkovo Meridian" (1941), in which she details daily life in Leningrad during the siege, won a Stalin Prize in 1946. After the war, Vera Inber continued to live in Leningrad; she died in 1972.

Karina L. Kerr, M.A.,
Ypsilanti, Michigan

Inchbald, Elizabeth (1753–1821)

English novelist, playwright and actress. *Born Elizabeth Simpson on October 15, 1753, near Bury St. Edmunds in Suffolk, England; died at Kensington House, a home for Roman Catholic women, on August 1, 1821; second youngest child of John Simpson (a Roman Catholic farmer at Stanningfield) and Mary (Rushbrook) Simpson; married Joseph Inchbald (an actor), on June 9, 1772 (died 1779).*

Elizabeth Inchbald was born in 1753, near Bury St. Edmunds in Suffolk, England, the second youngest child of John Simpson, a Roman Catholic farmer at Stanningfield, and **Mary Rushbrook Simpson**. Elizabeth's father died when she was eight years old. She and her sisters never enjoyed the advantages of school or regular supervision in their studies, but they seem to have acquired refined tastes at an early age. Ambitious to become an actress, a career for which a speech impediment hardly seemed to qualify her, she applied in vain for an engagement; finally, in 1772, she abruptly left home to seek her fortune in London.

There, to avoid male advances, she impulsively married Joseph Inchbald, an actor more than twice her age, and on September 4 made her debut in Bristol, as Cordelia to his Lear. For several years, she continued to act with her husband in the provinces, eking out a meager existence. Her roles included ***Anne Boleyn**, ***Jane Shore**, Calista, ***Calpurnia**, Lady Anne (***Anne of Warwick**) in *Richard III,* Fanny in *The Clandestine Marriage,* Desdemona, Aspasia in *Tamerlane,* Juliet and Imogen.

Following the death of her husband in 1779, Inchbald continued for some time on the stage; making her first London appearance at Covent Garden as Bellario in *Philaster* on October 3, 1780. Though she remained there for nine years, despite her fair-haired beauty and natural ability for acting, her speech impediment, which had been somewhat cured, still prevented her from enjoying more than moderate success. Her triumph as an author, however, allowed her to retire from the theater in 1789.

Elizabeth Inchbald wrote or adapted 19 plays, and some of them, especially *Wives as They Were and Maids as They Are* (1797), were highly successful. She also wrote *I'll Tell You What* (translated into German, Leipzig, 1798); *Such Things Are* (1788); *The Married Man; The Wedding Day; The Midnight Hour; Everyone has his Fault;* and an adaptation of Kotzebue's *Love's Vows.* Her edited works include a collection from the *British Theatre,* with biographical and critical remarks (25 vols., 1806–09); a *Collection of Farces* (7 vols., 1809); and *The Modern Theatre* (10 vols., 1809). Inchbald's fame, however, rests chiefly on her two novels: *A Simple Story* (1791) and *Nature and Art* (1796). She died at Kensington House on August 1, 1821.

Elizabeth Inchbald had destroyed an autobiography for which she had been offered £1,000 by a publisher; but her *Memoirs,* compiled by J. Boaden, chiefly from her private journal, appeared in 1833 in two volumes. An interesting account of the actress is contained in *Records of a Girlhood* by *Fanny Kemble (1878). Her portrait was painted by Sir Thomas Lawrence.

India, empress of.

See Nur Jahan (1577–1645).
See Mumtaz Mahal (c. 1592–1631).

India, prime minister of.

See Gandhi, Indira (1917–1984).

India, queen of.

See Razia (1211–1240).

India, vicereine of.

See Curzon, Mary Leiter (1870–1906).

Ines or Inés.

Variant of Agnes.

Inescort, Frieda (1900–1976)

Scottish-born actress. *Born Frieda Wightman on June 29, 1900, in Edinburgh, Scotland; died of multiple sclerosis on February 21, 1976, in the Motion Picture Country Hospital where she had been a patient since 1969; daughter of Elaine Inescort (an actress); married Ben Ray Redman (a critic and poet), in 1926 (died 1961); no children.*

Selected films: The Dark Angel *(1935);* The Garden Murder Case *(1936);* The King Steps Out *(1936);* Mary of Scotland *(1936);* Give Me Your Heart *(1936);* Hollywood Boulevard *(1936);* The Great O'Malley *(1937);* Call It a Day *(1937);* Another Dawn *(1937);* Portia on Trial *(1937);* Beauty for the Asking *(1939);* Woman Doctor *(1939);* Tarzan Finds a Son *(1939);* The Zero Hour *(1939);* A Woman Is the Judge *(1939);* Convicted Woman *(1940);* Pride and Prejudice *(1940);* The Letter *(1940);* Father's Son *(1941);* The Trial of Mary Dugan *(1941);* Sunny *(1941);* You'll Never Get Rich *(1941);* Remember the Day *(1941);* The Courtship of Andy Hardy *(1942);* Street of Chance *(1942);* It Comes Up Love *(1943);* The Return of the Vampire *(1943);* Heavenly Days *(1944);* The Judge Steps Out *(1949);* The Underworld Story *(1950);* A Place in the Sun *(1951);* Never Wave at a WAC *(1953);* Casanova's Big Night *(1954);* Foxfire *(1955);* The Eddy Duchin Story *(1956);* Darby's Rangers *(1958);* The Alligator People *(1959);* The Crowded Sky *(1960).*

The daughter of a journalist and the actress **Elaine Inescort**, Frieda Inescort was born in Edinburgh, Scotland, in 1900 and worked in England as a private secretary to Lady ***Nancy Astor** before coming to New York in 1919. After jobs with the National Child Labor Commission and the British Consulate, she made her Broadway debut in *The Truth about Blayds* (1922). Although her mother strongly objected to her acting, Inescort made subsequent appearances in *You and I* (1923) and *Hay Fever* (1925), but did not commit fully to her career until 1926, after her marriage to critic and poet Ben Redman. Following appearances in *Escape* (1927) and *Springtime for Henry* (1931), she headed for Hollywood.

Frieda Inescort

Inescort made her film debut in *Dark Angel* (1935) and appeared regularly through the late 1950s, playing mostly dignified character roles, notably in *Pride and Prejudice* (1940) and *A Place in the Sun* (1951). Steady work and good notices, however, did not spell stardom for the actress who later recognized her 35-year marriage, rather than her career, as her greatest success. Characterized as an unpretentious woman of great humor, Inescort battled multiple sclerosis for many years before succumbing to the disease in 1976.

SOURCES:

Katz, Ephraim. *The Film Encyclopedia.* NY: HarperCollins, 1994.

Lamparski, Richard. *Whatever Became of . . . ?* 4th Series. NY: Crown, 1973.

Barbara Morgan,
Melrose, Massachusetts

Ines de Castro (c. 1320–1355).
See Castro, Inez de.

Ines de la Cruz, Juana (1651–1695).
See Juana Inés de la Cruz.

Ines of Poitou.
See Agnes of Poitou (1024–1077).
See Agnes of Poitou (1052–1078).

Inez.
Variant of Agnes.

Inez de Castro (c. 1320–1355).
See Castro, Inez de.

Inga (fl. 1204)

Queen of Norway. *Flourished around 1204; married Haakon III, king of Norway (r. 1202–1204, killed); children: Haakon IV the Elder (1204–1263), king of Norway (r. 1217–1263).*

Ingebiorge (fl. 1045–1068)

Queen of Scotland. *Name variations: Ingibiorg Finnsdottir. Died before 1070; daughter of Finn Arnasson, jarl of Halland, and* ***Bergliot Halfdansdottir****; married Thorfinn the Black, earl of Orkney, before 1038; became first wife of Malcolm III Canmore, king of Scots, around 1059 (some sources cite 1066); children: (first marriage) Paul I, earl of Orkney; Erlend II, earl of Orkney; (second marriage) Duncan II (1060–1095), king of Scots; Malcolm (d. after 1094); Donald (d. 1085).*

Ingebord.
Variant of Ingeborg.

Ingeborg (c. 1176–1237/38)

Queen of France. *Name variations: Ingeborg of Denmark; Ingeborg Valdemarsdottir; Ingeburge or Ingelburge (French); Ingelborg, Isemburge, Ingibjörg (Danish). Born in Denmark around 1176; died on July 29, around 1237 or 1238 (some sources cite 1236); daughter of Valdemar also known as Waldemar I the Great (1131–1182), king of Denmark (r. 1157–1182) and* ****Sophie of Russia*** *(c. 1140–1198); sister of Canute VI (1163–1202), king of Denmark (r. 1182–1202), and Waldemar II the Victorious (1170–1241), king of Denmark (r. 1202–1241); sister of* ****Richizza of Denmark*** *(d. 1220) and* ****Helen of Denmark*** *(d. 1233); married Philip II Augustus (1165–1223), king of France (r. 1180–1223), on August 14, 1193 (divorced in the eyes of the council of Compiègne in 1193; marriage reinstated in 1213).*

On August 14, 1193, only one day after his marriage at Amiens, Philip II Augustus, king of France, took a sudden aversion to his 18-year-old Danish bride and sought a divorce. He claimed that Ingeborg, who has been described as charming and good-natured, had bewitched him. (Philip was not an ideal husband; he had also threatened to banish his first wife ***Isabella of Hainault**, before she died at age 20.)

For almost 20 years, Philip used every avenue to obtain a declaration of nullity from the Catholic Church. He tried to induce Ingeborg to seek a divorce herself; he forged a genealogical tree to prove that she was too closely related to his first wife; he demanded that Denmark take her back and expelled representatives of the Danish court. The council of Compiègne, a conclave of French bishops, acceded to his wish on November 5, 1193, and Ingeborg was packed off to a monastery near Paris. But when Ingeborg appealed her case to popes Celestine III and Innocent III successively, they took up the defense of the unfortunate queen and declared the dissolution of the marriage had no validity. Meanwhile, the Danish court exerted pressure on the papal court to have her set free. Hearing this, Philip became infuriated, threw Ingeborg into prison in the château of Étampes, and prevented her from corresponding with Denmark.

Philip, then married ***Agnes of Meran** in June 1196. For this, he was excommunicated and his kingdom was just about to be placed under an interdict when Agnes died in 1201. At last, however, in 1213, hoping perhaps to justify, by Ingeborg's hereditary claims, his designs on the throne of England of John I Lackland, Philip was reconciled with Ingeborg, though they never resumed marital relations. She survived him by more than 14 years, passing the greater part of the time in the priory of St. Jean at Corbeil, which she had founded. On good terms with the ensuing French kings, Philip's son and grandson, she lived peacefully, gaining a reputation for kindness, and died highly esteemed in 1237 or 1238.

Ingeborg (d. 1254)

Swedish princess. *Name variations: Ingeborg Ericsdottir. Died in 1254; daughter of* ****Richizza of Denmark*** *(d. 1220) and Eric X, king of Sweden (r. 1208–1216); married Birger of Bjälbo, regent of Sweden, around 1240; children: Waldemar (b. 1243), king of Sweden; Magnus I Ladulas, king of Sweden;* ****Richiza*** *(who married Haakon the Younger, king of Norway); Eric;* ***Christine Birgersdottir*** *(who married Sigge Guttormson);* ***Katherina Birgersdottir*** *(who married Siegfried, prince of Anhalt-Zerbst); Bengt (b. 1254), duke of Finland.*

Ingeborg (d. 1319)

Queen of Denmark. *Name variations: Ingeborg Magnusdottir. Died on August 15, 1319; daughter of ****Hedwig of Holstein*** *(d. 1325) and Magnus I Ladulas, king of Sweden (r. 1275–1290); married Erik or Eric VI Menved (1274–1319), king of Denmark (r. 1286–1319), in June 1296; children: Valdemar or Waldemar; twins Eric and Magnus; and one other son.*

Ingeborg (c. 1300–c. 1360)

Duchess of Südermannland. *Name variations: Ingebjorg, Ingeburga; Ingeborg Haakonsdottir, duchess of Sudermannland. Born around 1300; died after 1360; daughter of Haakon V (b. 1270), king of Norway (r. 1299–1319), and ****Euphemia of Rugen*** *(d. 1312); married Eric Magnusson (son of Magnus I, king of Sweden), duke of Südermannland (r. 1303–1318), on September 29, 1312; married Knud, duke of South Holland, on June 21, 1327; children: (first marriage) Magnus VII (II) Eriksson (1316–1374), king of Norway (r. 1319–1343), king of Sweden (r. 1319–1365); ****Euphemia*** *(1317–c. 1336, who married Albert II, duke of Mecklenburg).*

Early in the 14th century, Norway and Sweden were joined into one kingdom under Magnus Eriksson. Magnus was three years old, and the only available heir, when his grandfather, Norway's King Haakon V, died in 1319. The boy's father, Swedish prince Erik Magnusson, had died in prison at the hands of his uncle, King Berger of Sweden. Thus, when Berger was forced out of his kingdom by dissident nobles, three-year-old Magnus became king of both Norway and Sweden. His mother Ingeborg exerted great influence over the affairs of her son, and her plans to enlarge the combined kingdom included designs on Denmark. But the war she provoked with the Danes proved to be so costly to Norway that a popular noble, Erling Vidkunnsson, was made viceroy and ruled Norway until Magnus Eriksson came of age in 1332.

Ingeborg (1347–1370)

Danish princess. *Name variations: Ingeburga. Born on April 1, 1347; died before June 16, 1370; daughter of Waldemar IV Atterdag, king of Denmark, and ****Helvig of Denmark****; sister of ****Margaret I of Denmark*** *(1353–1412); married Heinrich also known as Hendrik or Henry, duke of Mecklenburg (r. 1379–1383), in 1361; children: ****Marie of Mecklenburg*** *(who married Vratislas of Pomerania).*

Ingeborg Lorentzen (b. 1957).
See Lorentzen, Ingeborg.

Ingeborg of Denmark (c. 1176–1237/38).
See Ingeborg.

Ingeborg of Denmark (d. 1287)

Queen of Norway. *Name variations: Ingeborg Ericsdottir or Eriksdottir. Died in 1287; daughter of ****Jutta of Saxony*** *(d. around 1267) and Erik or Eric IV Ploughpenny (1216–1250), king of Dennmark (r. 1241–1250); married Magnus VI the Law-mender (1238–1280), king of Norway (r. 1263–1280), on September 11, 1261; children: Eric II (b. 1268), king of Norway (r. 1280–1299); Haakon V Longlegs (1270–1319), king of Norway (r. 1299–1319); Olaf (b. 1262); Magnus (b. 1264).*

Ingeborg of Denmark (1878–1958)

Princess of Sweden. *Name variations: Ingeborg Oldenburg; Ingeborg Bernadotte; Ingeborg Charlotte of Denmark. Born on August 21, 1878; died on March 11, 1958; daughter of Frederick VIII, king of Denmark (r. 1906–1212), and ****Louise of Sweden*** *(1851–1926); married Charles of Sweden (1861–1951, son of Oscar II, king of Sweden, and ****Sophia of Nassau****), on August 27, 1897; children: ****Margaretha of Sweden*** *(1899–1977); ****Martha of Sweden*** *(1901–1954, who married the future Olav V, king of Norway); ****Astrid of Sweden*** *(1905–1935, who married Leopold III, king of the Belgians); Carl Gustaf (b. 1911, who renounced the right of succession on July 6, 1937).*

Ingeborg of Novgorod (fl. 1118–1131).
See Ingeborg of Russia.

Ingeborg of Russia (fl. 1118–1131)

Duchess of South Jutland. *Name variations: Ingeborg of Novgorod. Flourished between 1118 and 1131; daughter of ****Christina of Sweden*** *(d. 1122) and Mstislav I (b. 1076), grand prince of Kiev (r. 1125–1132); married Knud or Canute Lavard, duke of South Jutland, around 1118; children: Valdemar also known as Waldemar I the Great (1131–1182), king of Denmark (r. 1157–1182);* ***Margaret Knutsdottir*** *(who married Stig Whiteleather);* ***Kristin of Denmark*** *(who married Magnus IV the Blind, king of Norway, in 1332; he repudiated the marriage in 1133);* ***Katrin Knutsdottir*** *(who married Prizlaw of Obotriten).*

Ingeborg of Sweden (fl. 1070)

Swedish noblewoman. *Flourished around 1070; married Almos, son of Geza I and* ****Synadene of Byzantium*** *(c. 1050–?).*

Ingeborg Oldenburg (1878–1958).

See Ingeborg of Denmark.

Ingeburge.

Variant of Ingeborg.

Ingelberg or Ingelburge.

Variant of Engelberg, Engelberga, or Ingeborg.

Ingelow, Jean (1820–1897)

English poet and novelist. *Name variations: (pseudonym) Orris. Born in Boston, Lincolnshire, at the mouth of the Witham River, England, on March 17, 1820; died in Kensington, England, on July 20, 1897; eldest of 11 children of William Ingelow (a banker) and Jean (Kilgour) Ingelow; never married; no children.*

Selected works: A Rhyming Chronicle of Incidents and Feelings *(1850); (novel)* Allerton and Dreux *(1851);* Poems *(first series, 1863); (juvenile)* Studies for Stories *(1864); (juvenile)* Stories Told to a Child *(1865);* The Story of Doom and Other Poems *(1867); (juvenile)* Mopsa the Fairy *(1869); (novel)* Off the Skelligs *(1872); (novel)* Fated to be Free *(1875); (novel)* Sarah de Berenger *(1879);* Poems *(second series, 1880);* Poems *(third series, 1885);* John Jerome *(1886).*

Describing her early years as "happy, bright, joyous," Jean Ingelow was born in Boston, Lincolnshire, a town at the mouth of the Witham River, England, in 1820, the eldest in a family of 11 children. She grew up in Lincolnshire, Ipswich, and finally London. As an adult, she recalled many details of her childhood, particularly the view of the river from her nursery window, which was a constant source of wonder and inspired her early writings. Educated at home by governesses and tutors, a young Ingelow contributed verses and tales to magazines under the pseudonym of "Orris," but her first (anonymous) volume, *A Rhyming Chronicle of Incidents and Feelings* (1850), did not appear until she was 30. It attracted little attention, although poet Alfred, Lord Tennyson, upon meeting her shortly after its publication, was said to have commented, "I declare, you do the trick better than I do."

Ingelow followed this book of verse with the novel *Allerton and Dreux* (1851), but it was the publication of her collected *Poems* (1863) that raised her to the rank of a popular writer. Notable of the poems in this collection are "Divided," her most acclaimed work, as well as "Song of Seven," "Supper at the Mill," and "High Tide on the Coast of Lincolnshire, 1571," a ballad based on an actual disaster. Many of the poems within the volume, which went through some 30 editions, were set to music and sung in drawing rooms in England and America. Following another popular issue, *The Story of Doom and Other Poems* (1867), Ingelow temporarily gave up verse and turned to novels and short stories, many of the latter intended for children. Her most famous children's book, *Mopsa the Fairy* (1869), is still widely read. Most popular among her novels were *Off the Skelligs* (1872) and *Fated to be Free* (1873), connected stories giving some account of her childhood. She returned to verse with a second series of *Poems*, published in 1880, and a third in 1885.

Ingelow never married. "If I *had* married, I should *not* have written books," she said. Instead, she lived with her brother in Kensington after her parents died. Though shy, she was a woman of candid and courteous manners, reminiscent of a Lady Bountiful from a country parish. She was fearful of being regarded as "literary" or affected and frequently maintained that she was not a great reader. Her large circle of literary friends included ***Christina Rossetti**, ***Jane** and ***Ann Taylor**, as well as her early admirer, Tennyson.

Jean Ingelow's health began to fail in 1896, and she died in her Kensington home on July 20, 1897. English critic George Saintsbury believed, not alone, that Ingelow's reputation could rest on but a single poem: "If we had nothing of Jean Ingelow's but the most remarkable poem entitled 'Divided,'" he wrote after her death, "it would be permissible to suppose the loss, in fact or in might-have-been, of a poetess of almost the highest rank."

SOURCES:

Commire, Anne, ed. *Something About the Author, Vol. 33.* Detroit, MI: Gale Research.

Shattock, Joanne. *The Oxford Guide to British Women Writers.* Oxford and NY: Oxford University Press, 1993.

SUGGESTED READING:

Hickok, K. *Representations of Women: 19th Century British Women's Poetry.*

Peters, M. *Jean Ingelow: Victorian Poetess.*

Barbara Morgan,
Melrose, Massachusetts

Ingerina.

See Eudocia Ingerina.

Ingigerd Haraldsdottir (fl. 1075)

Norwegian noblewoman. *Flourished around 1075; daughter of ****Elizabeth of Kiev*** *and Harald III Haardrada or Haardraada also known as Harald III Hardraade (1015–1066), king of Norway; married Olaf I Hunger, king of Denmark (r. 1086–1095); married Philip, king of Sweden (r. 1112–1118); children: (first marriage) ****Ulfhild of Denmark*** *(died before 1070).*

Ingigerd Olafsdottir (c. 1001–1050)

Princess of Kiev. *Born around 1001 in Sweden; died on February 10, 1050, in Kiev, Ukraine; daughter of Olof or Olaf Sköttkonung or Skötkonung, king of Sweden (r. 994–1022), and ****Astrid of the Obotrites*** *(c. 979–?); sister of Anund Jakob, king of Sweden (r. 1022–1050); married Jaroslav also known as Yaroslav I the Wise (978–1054), prince of Kiev (r. 1019–1054), around 1019; children: Vladimir; Izyaslav also known as Yziaslav I (1025–1078), prince of Kiev (r. 1054–1078); Sviatoslav; Vyacheslav; Igor; Vsevelod I (r. 1078–1093); ****Anne of Kiev*** *(1024–1066, who married Henry I, king of France); ****Anastasia of Russia*** *(c. 1023-died after 1074, who married Andrew I, king of Hungary); ****Elizabeth of Kiev*** *(who married Harald Hardraade); ****Maria of Kiev*** *(d. 1087).*

Ingirid (fl. 1067)

Queen of Norway. *Name variations: Ingirid Svendsdottir. Flourished in 1067; illegitimate daughter of* ***Thora Johnsdottir*** *and Svend II Estridsen (d. 1076), king of Denmark (r. 1047–1074); married Olav the Gentle also known as Olaf III Kyrri (the Peaceful), king of Norway (r. 1066–1093), in 1067.*

Inglis, Elsie Maud (1864–1917)

British physician and surgeon. *Born in Naini Tal, India, in 1864; died at Newcastle Upon Tyne, England, on November 26, 1917; studied medicine at the Edinburgh School of Medicine for Women, the Edinburgh Medical College, and the Glasgow Royal Infirmary.*

Elsie Inglis was born in India in 1864. When her father retired from his job in 1878, the Inglis family returned to Scotland and settled in Edinburgh. Inglis pursued her medical education at the Edinburgh School of Medicine for Women, founded by ***Sophia Jex-Blake**, the Edinburgh Medical College, and the Glasgow Royal Infirmary. After qualifying as a doctor, Inglis was appointed to a teaching post at the New Hospital for Women in London, by its founder ***Elizabeth Garrett Anderson**.

Inglis then returned to Edinburgh and began her practice; she was associated with the Edinburgh Bruntsfield Hospital and Dispensary and also saw private patients. A staunch supporter of women's causes, Inglis was appalled by the lack of facilities for women and the prejudice against women doctors. In response, she established a free maternity hospital for women and children of the city's slums (1901), staffed entirely by women, and also founded the Scottish Women's Suffrage Federation (1906).

At the onset of World War I, Inglis raised money and established the Scottish Field Hospital, which she staffed entirely with women. When the British War Office refused her request for women doctors to serve on the Western front, the Women's Suffrage Federation came to her aid, helping her to organize field hospitals and send them out through the French and Belgian Red Cross. By 1915, the Scottish Women's Hospital Unit had established an Auxiliary Hospital with 200 beds in the 13th-century Royaumont

Elsie Maud Inglis

Abbey. Inglis' team included **Evalina Haverfield**, ***Ishobel Ross**, and ***Cicely Hamilton**.

In April 1915, Inglis began to establish field hospitals in a Serbian unit on the war-torn Balkan front to battle a typhoid epidemic. During the German and Austrian invasion (1915–16), her hospital was captured by the Austrians, and she was imprisoned for a time. British authorities sought the help of American diplomats to negotiate her release.

In August 1916, the London Suffrage Society financed Inglis and 80 women to support Serbian soldiers fighting in Russia. Haverfield was recruited as head of transport. Inglis remained active, serving in Braila, Galatz, and Reni, until the withdrawal of the Serbs in 1917. In her memoirs, ***Florence Farmborough** wrote of a visit with Inglis at the hospital at Podgaytsy. Ishobel Ross also kept a diary of her war-time experiences. "Mrs. Inglis and I went up behind the camp and through the trenches," Ross wrote on February 15, 1917.

> It was so quiet with just the sound of the wind whistling through the tangles of wire. What a terrible sight it was to see the bodies half buried and all the place strewn with

Ingrid of Sweden and Frederick IX

bullets, letter cases, gas masks, empty shells and daggers. We came across a stretch of field telephone too. It took us ages to break up the earth with our spades as the ground was so hard, but we buried as many bodies as we could. We shall have to come back to bury more as it is very tiring work.

Elsie Inglis was taken ill while in Russia and forced to travel back to England. She arrived at Newcastle Upon Tyne on November 25, but local doctors were unable to save her, and she died the following day. During the First World War, Inglis was responsible for 14 medical units serving in France, Serbia, Corsica, Salonika, Rumania, Russia, and Malta. These included doctors, nurses, cooks, ambulance drivers, orderlies, and relief workers. In Edinburgh, her name was commemorated for many years with the Elsie Inglis Maternity Hospital, though it is now closed.

Ingoberge (519–589)

Queen of Paris. *Born in 591; died in 589; married Caribert also spelled Charibert I (521–567), king of Paris (r. 561–567), in 561; children: possibly ****Bertha of Kent*** *(c. 565–c. 616).*

Ingoldsthorp, Isabel

Countess of Northumberland. *Name variations: Isabel Neville. Daughter of Edmund Ingoldsthorp; married John Neville, marquess of Montagu, earl of Northumberland (r. 1461–1471); children: George Neville, duke of Bedford;* ***Elizabeth Neville*** *(Lady Scrope of Masham); ****Margaret Neville*** *(b. 1466); ****Lucy Neville.***

Ingraham, Mary Shotwell (1887–1981)

American founder of the United Service Organizations (USO). *Born in Brooklyn, New York, on January 5, 1887; died in Huntington, Long Island, New York, on April 16, 1981; daughter of Henry Titus Shotwell and Alice Wyman (Gardner) Shotwell; Vassar College, A.B., 1908; Wesleyan University, L.H.D., 1958; Columbia University, L.H.D., 1961; married Henry Andrews Ingraham, on October 28, 1908; children: Mary Alice Ingraham Bunting-Smith (1910–1998); Henry Gardner Ingraham;* ***Winifred Andrews Ingraham*** *(who married Harold L. Warner, Jr.); David Ingraham.*

A 1908 graduate of Vassar College, Mary Ingraham spent her early career with the Brooklyn (New York) Young Women's Christian Association (YWCA), serving as its president from 1922 to 1939, then moving on to serve as president of the national board from 1940 to 1945. Along with ***Dorothy Height** and others, Ingraham was instrumental in bringing about the endorsement of the "Interracial Charter," mandating desegregation, at the 1946 YWCA National Convention.

In 1940, Ingraham founded the United States Organization (USO), which supplied social, recreational, and welfare services to the armed services during World War II. In 1946, in recognition of service to her country, Ingraham was awarded the Medal for Merit by President Harry S. Truman, making her the first woman so honored. She later served as a member of the New York City Board of Higher Education. The USO continued to serve troops during the Korean and Vietnam wars.

Mary Shotwell married Henry Andrews Ingraham in 1908; they had four children. Their daughter ➤ **Mary Ingraham Bunting** was a leading educator and the first woman to serve on the Atomic Energy Commission.

Barbara Morgan,
Melrose, Massachusetts

➤ Bunting, Mary Ingraham (1910–1998)

American educator. *Born in Hartford, Connecticut, on July 10, 1910; died on January 21, 1998; daughter of Mary Shotwell Ingraham (1887–1981) and Henry Andrews Ingraham; Vassar, B.A., 1931; University of Wisconsin, M.A., 1932, Ph.D., 1934; married Henry Bunting, in 1937; children: four.*

Mary Ingraham Bunting was an instructor in biology at Bennington College (1936–37), an instructor in physiology and hygiene at Goucher College (1937–38), a research assistant in the department of bacteriology at Yale (1938–40, 1948–52), a lecturer at Yale (1953–55), a lecturer in the department of botany, Wellesley College (1946–47), dean of Douglass College at Rutgers University (1955–69), president of Radcliffe College in Cambridge, Massachusetts (1960–72), and assistant to the president at Princeton University (1972–75). The Mary Ingraham Bunting Institute of Radcliffe College, a program of the Radcliffe Institutes for Advanced Study, was founded in 1960 as The Radcliffe Institute for Independent Study. The institute is a multidisciplinary research center for women scholars, scientists, artists and writers, and is one of the major centers for advanced study in the United States. Mary Ingraham Bunting died on January 21, 1998.

Ingrid of Sweden (1910—)

Queen of Denmark. *Name variations: Ingrid Bernadotte; Ingrid Victoria of Sweden. Born Ingrid*

Victoria Sophia Louise Margaret on March 28, 1910, at the Royal Palace, in Stockholm, Sweden; only daughter of Gustavus VI Adolphus (1882–1973), king of Sweden (r. 1950–1973), and ****Margaret of Connaught*** *(1882–1920); married Frederick IX (1899– 1972), king of Denmark (r. 1947–1972), on May 24, 1935, at Storkyrkan Cathedral, Stockholm; children: Margrethe II (b. 1940), queen of Denmark (r. 1972—); Benedikte (b. 1944, who married Prince Richard of Sayn-Wittgenstein);* ****Anne-Marie Oldenburg*** *(b. 1946, who married Constantine II, king of Greece).*

Though she was known for her common touch, Ingrid of Sweden was born a princess on March 28, 1910, in Stockholm, the daughter of King Gustavus VI Adolphus and ***Margaret of Connaught**, who was the granddaughter of Queen ***Victoria**. In 1935, Ingrid married Crown Prince Frederick of Denmark, who ascended the throne as King Frederick IX in 1947. During World War II and the occupation of Denmark, Ingrid earned the affection of her people as she broke through the isolation of the royal court and joined the Danes in ordinary pursuits. She could often be seen pushing a baby carriage along the sidewalks of Copenhagen, biking through the streets to make shopping trips, walking her daughters to school. When her husband died in 1972, Ingrid stepped out of the limelight and her daughter ***Margrethe II** became queen. But, as dowager queen, Ingrid remained active well into her late 80s, serving as a patron to dozens of charitable funds. In March of 1997, immediately after being pulled from a burning car, she calmly went out for coffee while her driver put out the flames.

Ingstad, Anne-Stine (c. 1918–1997)

Norwegian archaeologist. *Name variations: Anne Stine Ingstad. Born Anne-Stine Moe in Lillehammer, Norway, around 1918; died in Oslo, Norway, on November 6, 1997; attended University of Oslo, Norway; married Helge Ingstad (an explorer), in 1941; children; one daughter,* ***Benedicta Ingstad.***

Selected writings: Det nye land med de gronne enger *(Oslo, 1975); "The Norse Settlement at L'Anse aux Meadows, Newfoundland: A Preliminary Report from the Excavations, 1961–1968," in* Acta Archaelogica *(Vol. XLI, 1971, pp. 109–154);* The Discovery of a Norse Settlement in America *(NY, 1977);* The Norse Discovery of America, *Vol. 1 (Scandinavian University Press, 1986); (with Helge Ingstad)* The Norse Discovery of America, *Vol. 2 (Scandinavian University Press).*

Born in Lillehammer, Norway, around 1918, Anne-Stine Moe studied archaeology at the University of Oslo and, in 1941, married Helge Ingstad, who had abandoned a successful law career in 1926 to live with and study the Native Peoples (Indians and Eskimos) of northern Canada. Following her marriage, Anne-Stine Ingstad became her husband's companion in adventure and his scientific collaborator. In 1961, the couple retracked a Viking voyage along the northern tip of Newfoundland and, on a site known as L'anse aux Meadows, found conclusive evidence that Vikings had preceded Columbus to North America by 500 years. Although Helge is credited with the discovery, it was Anne-Stine Ingstad who supervised the painstaking excavation to uncover the remains of the 1,000-year-old Viking outpost. Her book *The Norse Discovery of America,* volumes 1 and 2, gives her assessment of the material that came to light during their archaeological expedition. Writes Einar Haugen, professor emeritus of Scandinavian studies at Harvard: "The remarkable discoveries made by Anne-Stine and Helge Ingstad on the northern tip of Newfoundland since 1960 have put an entirely new face on the problem [of the authenticity of the Vinland sagas and the location of Vinland—Newfoundland or New England], which students of the sagas have to take into account."

SOURCES:

Haugen, Einar. "Was Vinland in Newfoundland?," in "Proceedings of the Eighth Viking Congress, Arhus, August 24–31, 1977." Edited by Hans Bekker-Nielsen, Peter Foote, Olaf Olsen. Odense University Press, 1981.

"Obituary," in *The Day* [New London, Connecticut]. November 10, 1997.

Barbara Morgan,
Melrose, Massachusetts

Ingunde (fl. 517)

Queen of the Franks. *Name variations: Ingunda. Flourished around 517; sister of Aregunde; became third wife of Chlothar also known as Clothaire, Clotar, or Lothair I (497–561), king of Soissons and the Franks, around 517; children: Caribert also known as Charibert I (d. 567), king of Paris (r. 561–567); Gontrand also known as Guntram or Gunthram (c. 545–593), king of Orléans and Burgundy (r. 561–593); Sigebert or Sigibert I (535–575), king of Metz (Austrasia, r. 561–575);* ****Clotsinda*** *(who married a Lombard king). Lothair I's first wife was* ****Guntheuca;*** *his second wife was Chunsina; his* *fourth wife was *Aregunde (sister of Ingunde and mother of Chilperic I [523–584], king of Soissons); his fifth wife was *Radegund (518–587); his seventh wife was *Vuldetrade.*

Ino-Anastasia (fl. 575–582).

See Sophia (c. 525–after 600 CE) for sidebar.

Innes, Shane (b. 1956).

See Gould, Shane.

Inshtatheamba (1854–1902).

See La Flesche, Susette.

Inventors

Masters, Sybilla (d. 1720). ***First American inventor to own a patent.*** *Name variations: Sabella or Isabella Masters. Born Sybilla Righton, possibly in Bermuda (date and place of birth unknown); died, possibly in Philadelphia, on August 23, 1720; one of seven children of William Righton (a mariner, merchant, and plantation owner) and Sarah Righton, both Quakers; married Thomas Masters (a planter and prosperous Quaker merchant), between 1693 and 1696 (died 1723); children: Sarah; Mary (Mercy?); Thomas; William (three or perhaps four others died in infancy). British Patents #401 (in 1715) and #403 (in 1716) were issued to her husband on her behalf.*

Knight, Margaret (1838–1914). ***American industrial inventor with at least 23 patents for diverse products including window frames, improvements in engines, machines for cutting shoe soles and machinery for folding and gluing square-bottomed paper bags.*** *Name variations: Mattie Knight. Born on February 14, 1838, in York, Maine; died on October 12, 1914, in Framingham, Massachusetts; interred in the Newton (Massachusetts) Cemetery; daughter of James Knight and Hannah (Teal) Knight; raised in Manchester, New Hampshire, but lived most of her adult life in Framingham; mostly self taught; never married.*

Potts, Mary Florence (c. 1853–?). ***American inventor of the most popular irons ever used.*** *Born Mary Florence Webber around 1853; daughter of a plasterer in Ottumwa, Iowa; married Joseph Potts; children: six. Jointly held one patent for a medical device with her husband; three patents granted to Potts for improvements in sad irons.*

Ryan, Catherine O'Connell (1865–1936). ***American inventor of the self-locking nut and bolt, and holder of six patents which revolutionized joining of tracks for railroads and trolleys.*** *Born Catherine O'Connell on May 26, 1865, in Mayo, Ireland; emigrated to the United States in 1870; married Thomas J. Ryan (operator of a hay and grain business), on May 22, 1882; six children, youngest of whom was attorney Kingsley Ryan who assembled his mother's papers. Holder of six patents for self-locking nuts and bolts.*

Joyner, Marjorie Stewart (1896–1994). ***African-American inventor, entrepreneur, political activist, and philanthropist.*** *Born in Mississippi in 1896; died just after Christmas in 1994; granddaughter of a slave; mother worked as maid; married Robert Joyner, a podiatrist. Received two patents; became a vice president of the Walker Company.*

From door hinges to space vehicles, the work of inventors has shaped life around the world. Inventions are normally protected as "intellectual property" by various types of patents. Utility patents, for example, are granted for "new, useful and not obvious processes, machines, compositions of matter and articles of manufacture" and protect the inventor for 20 years. The United States has been granting patents since 1790. Of the approximately 5,500,000 patents which have been granted since that time roughly 5% include the name of a woman.

This number, however, cannot be taken as an accurate reflection of the number of women who have produced patent-worthy inventions. This is in part because patents are property, like real estate, which can be sold and leased, and there were times and places in the history of the United States when women could not own property; consequently, when a woman created a good idea she might have given it to a father, brother, or husband who then applied for the patent in his own name. Additionally, even once women were permitted to own property, societal norms often suggested that women should be invisible in the worlds of technology and business. (An attorney opposing Catherine O'Connell Ryan's patent-infringement suit remarked that U.S. Steel "shall not encourage any women to exceed their limitations of the kitchen.") This fact also may have led women with new ideas to ask men to apply for the patents. Nonetheless, women patented despite these and other obstacles. Because most of what we know about women inventors of earlier times comes in the form of detailed patents, often little information is available about their personal circumstances.

Sybilla Masters

In a time when machinery and tools had to be brought across the sea or made at home, early American settlers were dependent on their inventiveness for survival. The creativity required to build communities in a land of forests provided women with opportunities to develop talents outside traditional notions of femininity.

We know little about the background of Sybilla Righton Masters, the first American inventor to own a patent. Her father, a mariner and merchant, owned a plantation on the banks of the Delaware River, and most of the family's needs were made on the plantation. She was one of seven children, and, given that she would later invent an improved method for grinding corn, she may have been the one who showed the most interest in mechanical things; thus knowledge may have been passed down to her.

In 1714, Sybilla and her husband, planter Thomas Masters, bought Governor's Mill on the shores of Cohocksink Creek. Since 1700, Pennsylvania colonists had been harnessing its force to turn a wheel to grind Indian corn brought in from the fields. (Falling water has been used since the earliest civilizations as a source of power. Water wheels, made of wood, with wooden buckets, floats or paddles attached to the rim, were used in early America for grinding grain to make flour. They were often located near natural waterfalls or rapidly flowing water like the Cohocksink Creek.) Due to the distance from their mill to customers in Philadelphia, the Masterses needed a way to convince people from town to use their mill rather than closer ones. To this end, Sybilla proposed that they produce a better, finer quality of flour by improving the machinery used in cleaning and processing the grain.

The improvement came in the form of a new technology that she had invented for making "Tuscarora rice." This was a product made from corn that was similar to hominy. The process removed the hull, or outside covering, and ground the corn into powder that could be easily cooked or baked. She combined the old technology of using water wheels to grind grain with a new technology adapted from a technique she learned from the Tuscarora Indians who had come to Pennsylvania in 1713 after losing a great conflict in North Carolina.

In the usual "grist mill" operation, the job of the large water wheel was to turn one heavy millstone on top of another in order to crush and grind grain, such as corn or wheat. Carrying the movement of the water wheel to the top millstone required large oak shafts, stone bearings and wooden gears, as well as pinions and cogwheels to connect the water wheel to the millstone and make the millstone move with the wheel. Sybilla's invention used the same machinery as the old grist mill except, instead of attaching a millstone to the water wheel to grind the corn, she used pestles or mallets which were raised up and down to crush the corn. She had apparently observed the Tuscarora Indian women who, instead of grinding their corn with a flat stone, placed the grain into large bowls and beat it with pestles. Her invention resembled a kind of stamping machine, a mechanical adaptation of the process which the Native Americans did by hand. Power, according to Sybilla Master's invention, could be supplied either by "beasts of burden" like horses or oxen, or by the traditional water wheel.

According to the inventor, the end product was "easy to transport." Sybilla also reported that it was good for treating illnesses such as "consumption" (a common name given to chronic illnesses, especially diseases of the lungs like tuberculosis that caused gradual weakening). It was not unusual at the time to add claims, particularly health claims, to products that were simply improved in texture or taste.

Then as now, it was not enough to have good ideas. To succeed in business, an individual had to protect their rights to profit from inventions. In Sybilla's day, there was no U.S. patent law to keep others from using an inventor's new techniques. There was only English law. Inventors wishing government protection to keep others from using their ideas could apply to King George I for a patent granting protection. This document could be shown if there were any arguments about rights either in the mother country or in the colonies ruled by England.

In addition to inventiveness, Sybilla Masters must have possessed a fair share of courage, confidence and ambition. In 1715, she boarded a ship to cross the ocean with drawings and descriptions of new ideas. After arriving in England, she would have to convince the king's lawyers of the value of her work. She would have to answer many technical questions and prove that she had invented the techniques herself. She came home many months later with British Patent No. 401, granted by the king to Thomas Masters of Pennsylvania for "A New Invencon found out by Sybilla, his Wife, for Cleaning and Curing the Indian Corn Growing in the severall

Colonies in America." Writes **Anne L. Macdonald**, "Even after English King George I acknowledged the critical role that colonist Sybilla Masters played in the development of Pennsylvania's economy by citing her [an] inventor, . . . he nonetheless issued the patent itself to her husband, Thomas Masters."

Sybilla also invented a new way for weaving, staining, and decorating straw hats. In addition to their field and home chores, many women at the time worked as hat makers and seamstresses. Straw hats were the fashion of the day for both sexes. She later received British Patent No. 403, also granted to Thomas on behalf of his wife Sybilla, for "A New Way of Working and Staining in Straw, and the Platt and Leaf of the Palmeta Tree, and covering and Adorning Hatt and Bonnett, in such a Manner as was never before Done or Practised in England or Any of our Plantacons."

The patents the Masterses received gave the couple "full power, sole privilege and authority" to profit from Sybilla's inventions wherever the British ruled. While Sybilla was away, Thomas built a mill in Philadelphia to use the new method of cleaning and drying the grain. On her return, they began a profitable business. Much later, Thomas Masters became one of the early mayors of Philadelphia and a prominent citizen.

Margaret Knight

Called a tomboy as a child due to her preference for tools over dolls, Maggie Knight was not deterred from her inventiveness: "I sighed sometimes because I was not like other girls; but wisely concluded that I couldn't help it and sought further consolation from my tools. I was always making things for my brothers: did they want anything in the line of playthings, they always said, 'Mattie will make them for us.' I was famous for my kites; and my sleds were the envy of all the boys in town."

Child mill-workers, supplied by poor families to add to the family income, were common in some New England towns looking for cheap labor. Knight began working in the Manchester, New Hampshire, cotton mills at the age of nine or ten. While there, she allegedly invented a shuttle restraining device after seeing a worker injured when a sharp, steel-tipped shuttle fell from a loom. There is no record that young Maggie received a patent but safety shuttles were implemented around that time.

In her late teens, Knight learned photography, engraving and upholstery skills as she moved from job to job to support herself. She became interested in the problem of paper bags while working for the Columbia Paper Bag Company in Springfield, Massachusetts. Before the 1870s, customers carried their groceries in net bags, cardboard boxes or wooden boxes. The paper bags in existence were either shaped like envelopes and therefore could not hold much or were flat-bottomed but made by hand, a tedious process. For years men had been trying to design a machine that could make a bag with a flat bottom that could be manufactured inexpensively.

Knight spent many months working out her ideas for a machine that would make a square bottom bag. She made many drawings, tried out the design on a wooden model, and finally had an iron model made to her specifications. A man who had seen her work, Charles F. Annan, beat her to the patent office. She filed a suit against him, claiming that he had copied her idea. During the court battle, Annan and his lawyers tried to convince the court that Knight, being a woman, could not possibly have enough knowledge of machinery to design such a sophisticated machine. Fortunately, many people told the court they had been involved in the various phases of her work, from early discussions, writings, and drawings to the final machine. As a result, she won her case and received her patent in 1870.

That was not the last time Knight would encounter gross gender bias. She and a Newton, Massachusetts, businessman set up the Eastern Paper Bag Company in Hartford, Connecticut, to profit from the machine. When she was invited to help install the machine in the factory where the bags were to be made, the workers would not listen to her advice, convinced that women were incapable of understanding machinery.

With reports that the machine could do the work of 30 humans, Knight's invention, and several later improvements, became hugely popular. Certainly it made square-bottomed paper bags inexpensive to make and use, which changed the way people shopped for groceries and eventually for many other products.

Margaret Knight went on to receive at least 23 patents. Her inventions included internal combustion engines, resilient wheels, machinery for cutting shoe soles, and a window frame and sash. The *Framingham Evening News* (October 13, 1914), one day after her death at age 75, reported that her machinery, which made and folded square-bottom paper bags, was still in use 35 years after the patent was granted. In her obituary, a Boston newspaper referred to Knight as "the woman Edison."

Mary Florence Potts

As a teenager living in Ottumwa, Iowa, Mary Florence Webber grew up in the days before the advent of cotton wash-and-wear clothes (invented by **Ruth Benerito**). Like most girls her age, she probably had to help with the household chores which would have included ironing on Tuesday (because Monday was usually wash day). At 17, she married to Joseph Potts. At 18, she gave birth to a son, the first of six children. At 19, she received the first of her patents.

Just before the modern, electrically heated, iron was invented, pressing devices were made of solid iron from which we get the term "ironing." These devices were called "sad irons" ("sad" is an archaic word for "heavy"). The irons, which were heated on the stove, cooled quickly once removed from the heat and required the user to press down heavily on the material to be smoothed (hence the term pressing). The solid iron base, often attached to an iron handle, caused great discomfort to the hand. Given that the problems of ironing were particularly evident to women who did most of the work, it is not surprising that the solutions often came from female inventors.

> As a child I never cared for things that girls usually do; dolls never possessed any charms for me. . . . the only things I wanted were a jack-knife, a gimlet, and pieces of wood. My friends were horrified.
>
> **—Margaret Knight**

The solid, externally heated iron has gone through a long history of modifications. An early improvement replaced the iron handle with a wooden one. This made "handling" the iron somewhat cooler because the wood did not retain heat as easily; however, while the iron was heating on the stove, the wooden handle sometimes charred, thus weakening the handle's structure. Women often wrapped cloth around their knuckles to protect them from rising heat while ironing. **Julie Dittrich**, who patented one solution to the problem in 1866, proposed a leather heat deflector or shield suspended from a detachable handle. The manufacturer of the **Anna Niffeler** charcoal-heated tailor's iron (design patent, 1868) included a metal heat shield between the handle and the grip.

The most popular sad iron available was the double pointed iron with detachable handle patented by Mary Florence Potts. Manufactured by many companies in the United States, Canada, and Europe, it became the standard of the industry. The body of the Potts iron was cast hollow rather than solid, and the bottom had a thicker layer of iron than the sides. It was filled with material that was a non-conductor of heat, such as plaster of Paris, cement, or clay. Consequently, not as much heat radiated up as from earlier irons. Potts also claimed in her 1870 U.S. patent (reissued in 1880) that her iron held the heat longer so that more articles could be ironed without the need for reheating. Another advantage was its double-pointed shape which allowed for ironing in either direction. Finally, a rounded handle made the tool more comfortable for the wrist.

Mary Potts' masterpiece was the detachable handle patented in 1871 (reissued in 1872 and 1879). She designed a mechanism that permitted the user to place the iron on a hot stove and remove the handle so that it stayed cool. It then became easy to heat several bases at once, pick up the base which was most hot—or one of a different size, more appropriate for the task—and continue to work with the cool handle.

As related in the *Saturday Herald* of Ottumwa, Iowa (May 27, 1899), the inventor had special access to the problems of ironing because "wash day with its sequel of 'ironing' was to Miss Mary, as to many other daughters of Eve, a time of tribulation. That old iron with its solid metal handle, needing always a 'holder,' and then scorching the clothes and scorching the hand was a nuisance."

Because Potts' father was a plasterer, she had knowledge about using plaster to make a mold and about the material's properties. She reasoned that the tool for pressing need not be solid iron, and by using plaster as a core she sought to make the tool cooler on the knuckles. Potts built a plaster mold and asked a local foundry to put a relatively thin layer of iron on the sides and a heavier layer on the bottom, where it was needed to hold the heat and to press the fabric. The *Herald* reports that Mary "would try an experiment":

> A paste board rim was prepared and put around the top of the iron, and then the inclosure filled with plaster paris. That protected the hand from the heat. Then it seemed to her that the shape of the iron could be improved. And lastly the iron handle was disposed and replaced with a wooden, detachable handle. Such was the invention.

Mary and Joseph Potts tried to manufacture and sell the newly patented irons as "Mrs. Potts Iron" attesting to the fact that a woman had invented and tested a product which would be primarily used by women. The effort failed, however, and they filed for bankruptcy. Subsequently they renewed their efforts in Philadelphia where the American Enterprise Company took over the iron's manufacture and distribution. Soon other companies throughout the world were selling the product (or imitations), and it became a huge success. Mrs. Potts irons were manufactured from 1871 until 1951. They were featured at the 1876 American Centennial and became an instant hit.

The Potts irons became so popular that by 1891 special machines were invented that could produce 12,000 to 15,000 semicircular wooden handles in a single day rather than the 300 or 400 handles produced daily with earlier technology. Many men received patents for base and handle adaptations. For example, patents were granted for charcoal, gas, and electrically heated irons, all having Potts' detachable handle. The man who received the charcoal iron patent noted, "The construction and operation of the detachable handle is well known as the Potts sad iron and need not be described more fully." As late as 1920, a design patent was granted to a man for a carved design on Potts' handle.

Potts' inventions were licensed to many companies, and, even after the patents had elapsed, the products continued to be manufactured throughout the world well into the 20th century. Her irons are valued by antique collectors and are still in use in areas of Africa and South America where electricity is not available.

In 1892, Mary and Joseph received a joint patent for a "Remedial or Medical Appliance." The device, which predates electric heating pads, is an early version of a heating pad; it was flexible so as to be comfortable on the body, and was heated externally. Joseph Potts also received a patent for a Spring for Bed Bottom which he assigned to his young wife Mary two months before her sad iron patent was granted. Perhaps Joseph assumed from the start that Mary would be the entrepreneur of the family.

Catherine O'Connell Ryan

Born in Ireland in 1865, Catherine O'Connell came to the United States with her parents in 1870 and married Thomas Ryan just a few days shy of her 17th birthday. Her husband's hay and grain business in St. Paul, Minnesota, was not particularly successful, and as the mother of six children she worked hard to make ends meet. Catherine Ryan became a well-known inventor when her lawsuits to protect her patent rights became national news.

Ryan, without scientific education, found a simple answer to a long-standing problem in the railroad industry. During the 1800s, much money and energy went into keeping the railroad tracks safe for operation. Frequent train and trolley accidents were caused by nuts that had loosened on the bolts which held the rails to the ties. Ryan was strolling along railroad tracks with her husband one day when she noticed that the nuts had come loose from their bolts. She feared that the next train would crash—a frequent occurrence at the time. The assurances she received that railroad men regularly walked the track to tighten the nuts did not quiet her concerns, and during a sleepless night spent worrying about the problem she noticed the way in which her wedding ring was caught behind her knuckle. She instantly envisioned a locking nut. Ryan took her idea to a machine shop, where the nut and bolt were made. In 1904, she received a patent on the idea and then received five more patents for improvements on the self-locking nut and bolt, the last in 1918. Although Ryan lived to see her invention used on trolley tracks as well as railroads throughout the country, she did not profit from the idea that had revolutionized the joining of tracks.

Mary Florence Potts

Ryan was advised to take her blueprints to the U.S. Steel Corporation in New York City, from which practically all railroad equipment was purchased. There she showed the invention to J. Pierpont Morgan in hopes of having him produce it. He kept the designs for two weeks and then told her to go home and manufacture the product herself, claiming it was impractical for U.S. Steel to change all of their production equipment to produce the product.

She returned to Minnesota and formed the Ryan Bolt Manufacturing Co. in hopes of selling the product to the railroads. Ryan soon discovered, however, that Inland Steel Co. of Illinois, a subsidiary of U.S. Steel, was selling the nuts and bolts to the railroads. Ryan's litigation which began in 1916 lasted into the early 1930s and involved such formidable adversaries as U.S. Steel Corporation, Carnegie Steel Company, and Illinois Steel Company. Many attorneys took up her cause and failed, including her youngest son Kingsley Ryan, who studied law especially to defend his mother and women like her. Ultimately, Catherine Ryan ran out of funds and found that she could not fight such giants as Carnegie and Morgan. "The court should recognize that these patents have been stolen from me," she remarked. "I knew and felt that a lone woman would have no chance in court and my friends have so advised me."

In later years, Kingsley Ryan met one of the attorneys for the steel industry. This lawyer admitted that all the steel attorneys knew that Ryan's patents had been infringed but were not permitted to say so because it would be embarrassing to the company and also because U.S. Steel "shall not encourage any women to exceed their limitations of the kitchen."

Marjorie Stewart Joyner

Marjorie Stewart Joyner started as a beautician, moved on to become an inventor and business executive, and dedicated her life to racial and gender equality in Chicago's black community as well as throughout the United States. She was born in Mississippi, the granddaughter of a slave, came to Chicago to be with her divorced mother who had moved north to become a maid. Marjorie married Robert Joyner who became a doctor of podiatry. Early in her career, she worked in a beauty parlor where she was trained to style white women's hair. Her attempt to impress her new mother-in-law, by providing free hair care, ran amuck when the unimpressed woman pointed out that Marjorie knew nothing about styling the hair of African-Americans. Her mother-in-law recommended that she study at one of the Walker schools, a chain which had been developed by Madame *C.J. Walker.

Marjorie Joyner learned quickly the differences involved in working with the hair of blacks and whites. The style of the day for black women was "curling" the hair with various types of straighteners. The process of "curling" or "waving" hair usually included warming a curling iron that looked like pair of dull scissors. The irons were heated in, or on, a stove until electricity became popular, then the irons were heated internally. During a slow, uncomfortable process, each curl had to be set, one curl at a time. A hank of hair was placed in the scissor grip of the iron, then the iron was twirled to create the curl, and each hank had to set for a while.

Joyner reasoned that the process would be more efficient with a group of curling irons hanging from above: each clip could capture a hank of hair and the entire machine could be plugged into an electric outlet, allowing a full head of curls or waves to be set at once. Thus was born Joyner's Permanent Waving Machine. "The object of the invention," said Joyner in her first patent application, "is the construction of a simple and efficient machine that will wave the hair of both white and colored people." The 1928 patent was assigned to the Madame C.J. Walker Manufacturing Company and was used in the entire chain of Walker beauty salons and schools. It became a huge success. Joyner's invention found an unexpected market with white women who wanted to add curl to straight hair, and beauticians serving the much larger white market soon wanted the Joyner Permanent Wave Machine.

Whether one used individual curling irons or the new Permanent Wave Machine, the irons or clips were hot and pinched the scalp, making for an uncomfortable process for the client. In 1929, Joyner patented a Scalp Protector to make the "curling" process more comfortable. This patent was also assigned to the Walker Company, of which Joyner was a member of the Board of the Directors. With a knack for the business, she became vice president of a national chain of 200 Walker beauty colleges. In the 1940s, Joyner founded the United Beauty School Owners and Teachers Association. Her work would be featured as part of a 1987 Smithsonian exhibition. After achieving success as an inventor and entrepreneur, she decided after retirement to return to school to earn a Ph.D. in the humanities.

Marjorie Joyner, along with her mentor Madame C.J. Walker, made a serious impact on the beauty industry. At age 93, she was saluted by *The Washington Post* as the "Grande Dame of Black Beauty Culture." Joyner used her profits to become a generous philanthropist, contributing to African-American societies that served children and the arts. She died just after Christmas in 1994 at the age of 98. Joyner was remembered for her public service, including membership on President Franklin D. Roosevelt's campaign committee and her work with *Mary McLeod Bethune and *Eleanor Roosevelt on issues that concerned women and the African-American community. With clients at her beauty shop including *Billie Holiday, *Lena Horne, *Ethel Waters, *Marian Anderson, and Louis Armstrong, most of all Joyner is remembered for her contributions to the world of beauty.

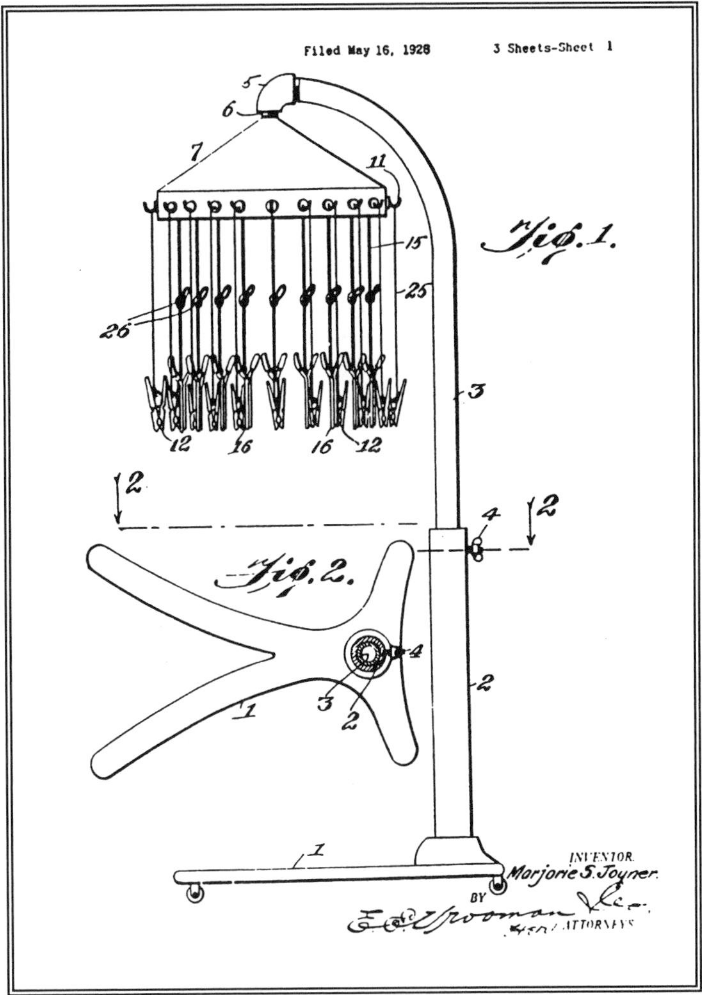

Invention of Marjorie Joyner

SOURCES:

Amram, Fred M.B. "Invention as Problem-Solving: Special Contributions of Female Inventors," in *Bulletin of Science, Technology, and Society.* Vol. 7, 1988.

Beauchamp, Rachelle Sender. "Women Inventors—Becoming a Visible Minority: The Women Inventors Project." Unpublished paper, 1988.

Opposite page
Catherine Ryan

Berney, Esther S. *A Collector's Guide to Pressing Irons and Trivets.* NY: Crown Publishers, no date.
Framingham Evening News. Framingham, MA, October 13, 1914.
Glissman, Edna. Correspondence between 1988 and 1992.
Guide to Northern Liberties. Philadelphia: Northern Liberties Neighbors Association, 1982.
Gunderson, Joan. "Barriers to Invention." Unpublished paper, 1988.
James, Portia P. *The Real McCoy,* Washington, DC: Smithsonian Institution, 1989.
Macdonald, Anne L. *Feminine Ingenuity.* NY: Ballantine Books, 1993.
Mozans, H.J. *Women in Science.* Cambridge, MA: MIT Press, 1974.
Ryan Papers. Owned by Fred M.B. Amram.
Saturday Herald. Ottumwa, Iowa, May 27, 1899.
Showell, Ellen H., and Amram, Fred M.B. *From Indian Corn to Outer Space: Women Invent in America.* Peterborough, NH: Cobblestone Press, 1995.
Stanley, Autumn. *Mothers and Daughters of Invention: A Revised History of Technology.* Metuchen, NJ: Scarecrow Press, 1993.
Swanson, V. "Sad-Irons Invented by Women." Unpublished paper, 1988.
Tolles, Frederick B. "Sybilla Masters," in *Notable American Women, 1607–1950.* Edited by Edward T. James. Cambridge, MA: The Belknap Press of Harvard University, 1971.
U.S. Patent and Trademark Office. *Buttons to Biotech.* Washington, DC: U.S. Department of Commerce, 1990 (and addendum of 1993).
Weimann, Jeanne. *The Fair Women.* Chicago: Academy Chicago, 1981.
Women Inventors to Whom Patents Have Been Granted by the United States Government, 1790 to July 1, 1888. Washington, DC: Government Printing Office, 1888.
Women Inventors to Whom Patents Have Been Granted by the United States Government, July 1, 1888 to October 1, 1892. Washington, DC: Government Printing Office, 1892.
Women Inventors to Whom Patents Have Been Granted by the United States Government, October 1, 1892 to March 1, 1895. Washington, DC: Government Printing Office, 1895.

SUGGESTED READING:

Carroll, Berenice A. "The Politics of 'Originality': Women and the Class System of the Intellect," in *Journal of Women's History,* Vol. 2, no. 2, 1990.
Grist Mills of Early America and Today. Lebanon, PA: Applied Arts Publishers, 1978.
Heilbrun, Carolyn G. *Reinventing Womanhood.* NY: W.W. Norton, 1979.

Fred M.B. Amram,
Professor, General College, University of Minnesota

Inyama, Rosemary (1903—)

Nigerian educator, politician, business tycoon, and community developer who championed the cause of women in Igboland. *Name variations: Mrs. Inyama. Born Rosemary Ike on November 11, 1903, in Arochukwu, Igboland, Nigeria; incapacitated since 1996 due to old age and sickness; daughter of Mazi Okoronkwo Ike (a soldier in the First World War) and Madam Otonahu Ike (who played an instrumental role in the relocation and "cleansing" of the famous* Ibiniukpabi oracle *after the 1901–02 attack on it); married P.K. Inyama (a grade 11 teacher), in 1934; children: Hycientha Inyama Nwauba (consul-general of Nigeria in New York); Nnenna Inyama; Jennifer Inyama; Okoro Inyama.*

Taught in primary schools (1923–35); established a Domestic Science Business Training Center at Ikot Ekpene; dealings in the gold business took her on several business trips to Ghana (1940s–50s); went into trading partnership with 19 women and men across the country, buying and selling foodstuffs; active in Nigeria's politics (1940s–50s); played a key role in community development at Arochukwu; started motherless babies home; honored several times by women's organizations such as the National Council of Women Societies, Nigeria, Imo state branch; incapacitated by advanced age and illness (1996).

The 20th century in Igboland, Nigeria, was characterized by British colonial rule (1891–60), international trade, the Second World War (1939–45), the Great Depression (1929-39), achievement of political independence in 1960, and the Nigerian Civil War (1967–70). Other features on the landscape included the introduction of direct taxation, Christianity, Western education, new technologies, and urbanization. These changes and the Western presence which accompanied them brought new economic opportunities and modern politics to Igboland, and these had an effect on the role and status of Igbo women. One positive result was the opening of new avenues for status enhancement and diversification of women's economic activities. A number of Igbo women who were hitherto subsistence farmers and local petty traders rose to the status of great merchants and traders, acquiring wealth in cash and landed property, taking titles, and investing in their children's education. Literacy spread among some previously illiterate local women, and some women, like Rosemary Inyama, worked as educators of other women.

Igboland was a British possession when Inyama was born on November 11, 1903. She was the first child of Mazi Okoronkwo Ike and Madam **Otonahu Ike** of Igboland's Ujali village, Arochukwu. Her father fought on the side of the British forces during the First World War, and her mother played an instrumental role in the relocation and "cleansing" of the Ibiniukpabi oracle after it was attacked in 1901–02.

Between 1917 and 1922, Rosemary acquired the necessary teaching credentials; she started teaching in 1923. After her marriage to P.K. Inyama (1934), with whom she would have four children, she resigned her teaching position in 1935 unable to effectively combine the family responsibilities with her school work. However, later that same year she established a Domestic Science Business Training Center with two sewing machines and less than £5. Here she taught her apprentices and students—who were mostly young girls, married and unmarried women—home management, including activities such as sewing and bread making. Those in her charge paid fees ranging from ten shillings to £1 depending on the type of skills they were working to acquire and on the duration of the training (usually 3 to 6 months). In 1940, with more than 20 in attendance, Inyama made an average profit of £40 per month from the fees they paid and sales of the center's products.

Due to government regulations, it was not easy to start in the gold business especially as an international trade, but Inyama obtained a government license at Aba in 1942 which authorized her to deal in gold. During the 1940s and 1950s, she made several business trips by steamship to Ghana, where gold was mined, buying up to £3,000 worth of gold in a trip. Then back home in Nigeria a local goldsmith fashioned the raw gold into various designs which Inyama sold to such affluent women as ***Mary Nzimiro** and **Margaret Ekpo**. Rosemary Inyama was one of the first Igbo women to operate bank accounts and did her banking with African Continental Bank in Aba, the town where she conducted most of her business. (She lived, however, in Ikot Ekpene and later Uyo, towns 30 to 40 kilometers from Aba.)

In addition to running the domestic science center and working in the gold trade, Inyama participated in a trading partnership with 19 Nigerian businesswomen and men (14 women and 5 men), dealing in foodstuffs at various times before 1967. The partnership operated between Eastern and Northern Nigeria, buying and selling products such as palm oil and garri (in tins and bags) from the East and selling them in the North, and buying wholesale onions, potatoes, calcium and groundnut oil from the North and selling them in the East. A portion of the annual profits was shared equally among the members at the end of the year, and the remaining sum was put back into the enterprise. The partnership ran a successful business until the Nigerian Civil War ended their efforts in 1967.

Inyama acquired landed property, cars, and a gun for her husband. She also helped in the education of their children, all university graduates. Playing an active part in Nigeria's politics of the 1940s and 1950, she was an energetic member of the NCNC party, women's wing. Inyama took a leading role in organizing women at Ikot Ekpene and Uyo to support and vote for NCNC candidates. Her contemporaries were Mary Nzimiro (Port Harcourt), Margaret Ekpo (Aba), and Mrs. Edede (Calabar). The efforts of these women in mobilizing and organizing the women in Eastern Nigeria enabled the NCNC control of the Eastern regional government and seats in National Assembly.

Rosemary Inyama played her greatest role in community development at Arochukwu where in 1965 she convinced the Aro women to start a motherless babies home. Although disrupted by the civil war, the project was completed after war's end. She also led Aro women to several meetings with the district officers at Arochukwu during which they demanded the improvement of the urban facilities in order to better living conditions.

In 1970, Inyama traveled to the United States on the invitation of her children, one of whom, Hycientha Nwauba, was then consul-general of Nigeria in New York. On Inyama's return in 1974, she was honored by Aro women for the role she played in the improvement of Arochukwu and the betterment of Aro women. On November 28, 1985, she was given a National Certificate by the National Council of Women's Societies, Nigeria, Imo state branch, for having "shown profound love for, and rendered selfless services to the Council for many years."

SOURCES:

Chuku, G.I., "From Petty Traders to International Merchants: A Historical Account of Three Igbo Women of Nigeria in Trade and Commerce, 1886 to 1970," 1998.

———"The Changing Role of Women in Igbo Economy, 1929 to 1985," Ph.D. Dissertation, History Department, University of Nigeria, Nsukka, Nigeria, 1995.

Gloria Ifeoma Chuku, Ph.D.,
Lecturer in History, School of Humanities, Imo State University, Owerri, Imo State, Nigeria

Ioahne (b. 1907).

See Giovanna of Italy.

Iola (1862–1931).

See Wells-Barnett, Ida.

Iolande.

Variant of Yolande.

Iolande Margherita of Italy (b. 1901).
See Yolanda Margherita of Italy.

Iolande of Hungary (1215–1251)

Queen of Aragon. *Name variations: Iolande Arpad; Violante of Hungary; Yolande of Hungary. Born in 1215; died in 1251 (some sources cite 1271); daughter of Andrew II, king of Hungary (r. 1205–1235), and his second wife* ****Yolande de Courtenay*** *(d. 1233); became second wife of James I (1208–1276), king of Aragon (r. 1213–1276), also known as Jaime the Conqueror of Aragon, in 1235; children: Peter III (d. 1285), king of Aragon (r. 1276–1285);* ****Yolande of Aragon*** *(d. 1300, who married Alphonso X, king of Castile and Leon);* ****Isabella of Aragon*** *(1243–1271, who married Philip III, king of France); James II, king of Majorca;* ***Constance of Aragon*** *(d. 1283, who married Manuel of Castile, senor de Villena); Ferran. James I's first wife was* ****Eleanor of Castile*** *(1202–1244).*

Iotti, Nilde (1920–1999)

Italian lawmaker. *Born in Reggio Emilia, Italy, in 1920; died of heart failure on December 3, 1999, in Rome; attended the University of Milan; daughter of a railway worker; lived with Palmiro Togliatti (a Communist Party leader), from around 1948 to 1964 (died 1964); children: (adopted, 1950) Marisa Malagoli Togliatti.*

The first woman to become president of the lower house of Parliament in Italy, Nilde Iotti was born in 1920 in Reggio Emilia, the daughter of a railway worker. Her birthplace was in the center of Italy's "red belt," and Iotti represented the Communist Party throughout her life. She was a literature student at the University of Milan, then served as a Partisan during World War II, before moving to Rome. There, she fell in love with Palmiro Togliatti, Italy's Communist Party leader, but Togliatti was married and divorce was illegal in Italy. Even so, they lived together until Togliatti's death in 1964 and adopted a daughter **Marisa Malagoli Togliatti** in 1950 (Marisa's brother had been killed by police during a strike in Modena).

Iotti was initially elected to the constitutional assembly in 1946, taking part in the "Committee of the 75," a delegation that wrote the first draft for Italy's postwar constitution. During her many years in Parliament, she campaigned to legalize divorce and abortion. For 13 years, from 1979 until 1992, Iotti was second in line to succeed the presidency, while serving as Italy's president of the lower house of Parliament. Known as a faithful member of the central committee of the Communist Party, Iotti's views softened with the collapse of the Berlin Wall. She was among the first to propose abandoning the hammer and sickle and renaming the party "Democrats of the Left." After a long illness, Nilde Iotti resigned from her post in November 1999 and died of heart failure the following month. Her coffin was laid in state in the Italian Parliament, and she was given a state funeral.

Ipp (b. 1909).
See Breslauer, Marianne.

Ippolita (1446–1484)

Queen of Naples. *Name variations: Hippolyta Sforza; Ippolita Sforza. Born in 1446; died on August 20, 1484; daughter of Bianca Maria Visconti (1423–1470) and Francesco Sforza (1401–1466), 4th duke of Milan (r. 1450–1466); married Alfonso of Aragon (1448–1495), duke of Calabria, later known as Alphonso II, king of Naples (r. 1494–1495), on October 10, 1465; children:* ****Isabella of Naples*** *(1470–1524, who married Gian Galeazzo Sforza, duke of Milan); Ferdinand also known as Ferrante II (1469–1496), king of Naples (r. 1495–1496); Piero, prince of Rossano (b. 1472). Alphonso II had a mistress* ***Trogia Gazzela*** *with whom he had two children: Alfonso, prince of Salerno (b. 1481) and* ****Sancha of Aragon*** *(1478–1506).*

Ippolita was born in 1446, the daughter of ***Bianca Maria Visconti** and Francesco Sforza, the 4th duke of Milan. One of the accomplished women of Renaissance Italy, Ippolita once astonished Pope Pius II while he was visiting her father's court by reciting a Latin oration she had composed. She was 12 at the time.

Ippolita (1503–1570).
See Gonzaga, Ippolita.

Ippolita (1535–1563).
See Gonzaga, Ippolita.

Ireland, Patricia (1945—)

American lawyer, social activist, and president of the National Organization for Women (NOW). *Born in Oak Park, Illinois, on October 19, 1945; second of two daughters of James Ireland (a metallurgical engineer) and Joan (Filipak) Ireland; attended DePauw Universi-*

Patricia Ireland

ty, Greencastle, Indiana; graduated from the University of Tennessee, 1966; attended Florida State University, 1972; received law degree from the University of Miami, in 1975; married Donald Anderson (a college student), in 1962 (divorced 1963); married James Humble (an artist and businessman), in 1968; no children.

In 1991, Patricia Ireland succeeded *Molly Yard as the ninth president of the National Organization of Women (NOW), which was founded in 1966 with a mandate to support abortion rights and fight against sexual discrimination in education and employment. As the century ends,

Ireland remains at the organization's helm, having been a driving force in transforming it into the largest and most prominent feminist group in the United States. Given her current status, it is difficult to believe that Ireland once envisioned a conventional future for herself. "I would go on to college. But after that, like my mother before me, I'd get a job for a while, then marry and have children. I would stay at home to raise them and live happily ever after."

The daughter of a metallurgical engineer and a stay-at-home mom, Ireland was born in 1945 in Oak Park, Illinois, and grew up on a farm in Valparaiso, Indiana. When Ireland was four, her older sister Kathy died after a fall from a horse. "I was well into my forties before I started thinking what impact my sister's death had on me," said Ireland. "My strongest defense is always denial." (Ireland's parents subsequently adopted two little girls.) An honor student throughout school, Ireland entered DePauw University at 16, with plans to become a teacher, "because you can be home with your kids after school and take summers off," she later told an interviewer. Shortly into her first semester, she became pregnant and was forced to travel to Japan for a legal abortion, the first of two. In 1962, she married Donald Anderson and transferred with him to the University of Tennessee. The marriage ended after a year, and Ireland went on to graduate with a degree in German. In 1968, she married artist James Humble, and after an unhappy term attending graduate school and teaching German to undergraduates, she and Humble moved to Florida, where she worked as a flight attendant for Pan American Airlines.

Although she had some trepidations about the airline industry—she, too, had winced at the ad, "I'm Cheryl. Fly me."—nothing prepared her for the realities of working as a stewardess. Angered by the daily humiliations she encountered from both passengers and pilots, she began to challenge some of the airline's stipulations, such as those mandating that stewardesses wear girdles, uncomfortable pumps, and makeup. Finally, when the airline's health plan refused to cover dental work for her husband, even though the wives of male employees were covered, she decided to take action. Seeking advice from the Dade County chapter of NOW, who directed her to the Equal Employment Opportunity Commission (EEOC) for further assistance, she was just about to file a legal challenge when the airline suddenly changed its policy in her favor.

Feeling somewhat empowered by that experience, Ireland enrolled in law school at Florida State (she later transferred to the University of Miami), but continued to moonlight as a stewardess to pay expenses. Her frustration resurfaced when she became aware that people treated her with more respect as a law student. "The way I was getting credibility was by moving into a man's job, which is a source of great irritation to me," she told **Donna Minkowitz** of the *Advocate* (December 17, 1991). "I think traditional women's work is undervalued—teaching, health care, social work. That was part of the experience that made me want to be an activist."

While in law school, Ireland served on the *Law Review* and the *Lawyer of the Americas* and also led a successful protest to remove the line, "Land, like a woman, is meant to be possessed," from a textbook. After graduating with high honors in 1975, she worked in corporate law for 12 years, during which time she also did pro-bono work for NOW and assisted corporate clients in establishing affirmative-action programs. As Ireland became more and more committed to women's rights, her involvement with NOW intensified. In 1977, she led her NOW chapter in the fight against entertainer **Anita Bryant**'s anti-gay referendum in Dade County, and in 1982 spearheaded a campaign against Florida State senator Dick Anderson who opposed the Equal Rights Amendment. The following year, she became chair of the Florida chapter of NOW's lesbian rights task force.

By the 1980s, Ireland's political and legal savvy, as well as her accessible personality, had become a great asset to NOW. In 1985, she ran ***Eleanor Smeal**'s successful campaign for the presidency of NOW and in 1987 was elected executive vice-president of the organization on a ticket with septuagenarian Molly Yard as president. Leaving her partnership in the Miami law firm, Ireland moved to Washington, where one of her first projects was to direct NOW's Project Stand Up for Women, a campaign against anti-abortion extremist groups. She also led the organization in opposing right-wing nominations to the Supreme Court and represented NOW at important feminist conferences in the United States and Europe. Yard and Ireland were reelected for a second term in 1989, and when Yard suffered a massive stroke in May 1991, Ireland took over as acting president. In December 1991, she was officially named the organization's president, and has been reelected to the office several times since.

As Ireland accepted the presidency of NOW, a revelation about her personal life set off a flurry of media coverage. Admitting that she had both a husband in Florida and a female companion in Washington, Ireland was unapologetic, stating that both relationships were very important to her. "I'm very comfortable with all that," she told Minkowitz. "I've never hidden how I've lived my life. What I don't like is the idea—with women, I think it's particularly the case—that people try to categorize other people by their sexuality." Ireland is decidedly low-key in both her appearance and public behavior. "It's not smart to make people uncomfortable for reasons apart from the issues," she notes. She sees her husband, who lives in Homestead, Florida, twice a month and refuses to divulge the name of her female companion, for fear that the woman will lose her job if her identity is revealed.

With the controversy behind her, Ireland tackled her first public action, leading a march protesting the nomination of Clarence Thomas as a Supreme Court justice. (In October 1991, law professor **Anita Hill** testified at Thomas' Senate Confirmation Hearings that he had sexually harassed her when they were colleagues at EEOC.) Although NOW was unsuccessful in its attempt to block Thomas's appointment, it did focus the national spotlight on the problem of sexual harassment and brought into focus the need for more female representatives on Capitol Hill. As a result, a record number of women were elected to Congress in 1992. The Thomas debacle also resulted in a three-fold increase in NOW's membership, which had plummeted in 1982, following the defeat of the ERA. "The irony is that the women's movement prospers in adversity," Ireland said. "When things get bad, we get more supporters, more activists, more money, more everything."

Early in her presidency, Ireland also tackled the problem of reuniting competing factions within NOW's membership, particularly the rift between lesbian and non-lesbian members that had grown out of a purge in the early 1970s, during which many lesbians were removed from power in order to eliminate the belief, among some, that all feminists are gay. Although the organization had since made strides in supporting the rights of lesbians, Ireland has stressed that NOW is "not a lesbian rights organization. We're your first full-service organization that has among it four priority issues on lesbian rights." She also took steps to define the organization's role as an advocacy group, of concern since the ouster of former NOW president **Judy Goldsmith** in 1985, after she convinced presidential candidate Walter Mondale to select ***Geraldine Ferraro** as his running mate. Ireland made it quite clear that she had no intention of turning NOW into just another Washington lobbying group. "Nobody is going to give us our rights because they like us or because we're ladylike," she said. "Our role is to be at the cutting edge of controversy."

In the 1990s, Ireland led NOW in a fight against budget cuts proposed by Newt Gingrich and the right-wing Congress, believing that they would jeopardize social programs for women and children. In August 1995, she announced that NOW members had voted to push for a new and expanded ERA. Her future plans include the creation of a television network devoted to feminist issues, the development of a training program for NOW activists, and even the organization of a new political party. Ireland is not one to rest on her laurels, nor does she believe that the fight for sexual equality is anywhere near over. "We must bear in mind . . . that the progress we seek is not inevitable. It will come because we have new energy in our movement."

SOURCES:

Lindop, Laurie. *Champions of Equality.* NY: Henry Holt, 1997.

Moritz, Charles, ed. *Current Biography 1992.* NY: H.W. Wilson, 1992.

Barbara Morgan,
Melrose, Massachusetts

Irene.

Variant of Irina.

Irene (fl. 200 BCE?)

Ancient Greek painter who executed a portrait of a young maiden at Ephesus. *Name variations: Eirene, Yrenes. Pronunciation: ee-RAY-nay. Date and place of birth uncertain; daughter and pupil of the painter Cratinus.*

Irene is the second female painter mentioned by Pliny the Elder in his *Natural History* 35.147-8. All of the few facts we know of her life and career are found in his account; the Greek author Clement of Alexandria also mentions her father Cratinus, a painter of whom we have no other record. Pliny's direct statement that she learned her skill at her father's feet, repeated in the case of ***Aristarete**, is worthy of notice. Pliny mentions just one of her works, saying that she painted "a maiden" (*puellam*) at Eleusis. That this portrait might have had some significance in the rites of the mystery cult of Demeter, an Olympian who may be characterized broadly as an Earth Mother or goddess of corn, seems to be supported by two considerations. First, Eleusis was the ancient center of

Demeter worship. Second, the Latin *puella* translates directly from the Greek *koré*, which was the cultic name of Persephone, Demeter's daughter and a major figure in her myth, found in the *Homeric Hymn to Demeter*.

The next name after Irene in Pliny's list of female artists is ***Calypso.** Both an imperfect text and the fact that this name was usually reserved for immortals has led some to suggest that Calypso (the sea nymph who imprisoned Odysseus on her island for 11 years) is actually the mythical subject of another painting by Irene. If this is true, the three portraits that follow the name Calypso are actually Irene's, making her the author of "An Old Man," "The Juggler Theodorus," and "The Dancer Alcisthenes"—five paintings in all. Further, if this Alcisthenes is identical with a man of the same name mentioned in an extant inscription at Delphi, then we may date Irene's working career to the years around 200 BCE.

I thought her work worthy of some praise, since it is very unusual for women, and is not pursued without a high degree of talent, which is customarily most rare in them.

—Giovanni Boccaccio

Despite the lack of sure information on Irene in the *Natural History*, she (along with ***Timarete** and ***Iaia**) gained the attention of the 14th-century Florentine author Giovanni Boccaccio in his work *On Famous Women*, where he introduces her as "Yrenes." While Boccaccio's presentation of Irene and other ancient women painters adds nothing factual to Pliny and in some places misinterprets him, his discussions are both amusing and indicative of the place of women in the society and historical consciousness of early Renaissance Italy. Further, by imitating Pliny's interest in female artists, Boccaccio helped to make other writers aware of their achievements to such a degree that **Wendy Slatkin** can say, "It would be hard to exaggerate the importance for the subsequent history of women artists of Pliny's brief paragraph about the women artists of antiquity and Boccaccio's elaborations on it." It seems clear, then, that though we possess neither remains of Irene's work nor knowledge of its influence, she has nevertheless exerted some creative force in the history of Western culture. (*For further background information, see entry on Aristarete.*)

SOURCES AND SUGGESTED READING:

Boccaccio, Giovanni. *Tutte le Opere*. Edited by Vittorio Zaccaria. Vol. 10: *De Mulieribus Claris*. 2nd ed. Verona: Arnoldo Mondadori, 1970, pp. 242–245.

"Eirene," in *Allgemeines Lexikon der Bildender Künstler von der Antike bis zur Gegenwart.* Edited by Ulrich Thieme and Felix Becker. Leipzig: W. Engelmann, 1908–50.

"Eirene," in *Enciclopedia dell'Arte Antica Classica e Orientiale.* Rome: Instituto della Enciclopedia Italiana, 1958–66.

Slatkin, Wendy. *Women Artists in History: From Antiquity to the Twentieth Century.* Englewood Cliffs, NJ: Prentice Hall, 1985.

Peter H. O'Brien,
Boston University

Irene (fl. 700s)

Byzantine empress. *Flourished in the 700s; married Anastasius II Artemius, emperor of Byzantium (r. 713–715).*

Irene (c. 1085–1133).

See Anna Comnena for sidebar on Priska-Irene of Hungary.

Irene (fl. late 1100s)

Byzantine princess. *Flourished in the late 1100s; daughter of Alexius III Angelus, Byzantine emperor (r. 1195–1203) and* ***Euphrosyne** *(d. 1203); sister of* ***Anna Angelina** *(d. 1210?) and* ***Eudocia Angelina**; *married Alexius Paleologus; children:* ***Theodora Paleologina** *(who married Andronicus Paleologus).*

Irene (fl. 1310)

Queen of Thessaly. *Flourished around 1310; daughter of Andronicus II (1259–1332), Byzantine emperor (r. 1282–1328) and possibly* ***Irene of Montferrat** *(fl. 1300) or possibly illegitimate; married John II, king of Thessaly (r. 1303–1318). Thessaly was located in the north-easternmost division of ancient Greece.*

Irene (1901–1962)

Hollywood costume designer and entrepreneur. *Name variations: Irene Lentz. Born Irene Lentz on December 8, 1901 (also seen as 1908), in Brookings, South Dakota; died on November 15, 1962; daughter of Emil Lentz (a rancher) and Maude (Watters) Lentz; graduated from Baker High School, Baker, Montana; attended the University of Southern California; graduated from Wolfe School of Design; married Richard Jones, a movie director (died around 1930); married Eliot Gibbons (a screenwriter), in 1936.*

Selected films (alone or in collaboration as costume designer): Flying Down to Rio *(1933);* Merrily We Live *(1937);* Shall We Dance *(1937);* Topper *(1937);* Vivacious Lady *(1938);* Algiers *(1938);* You Can't Take It With You

(1938); Midnight *(1939);* Intermezzo: A Love Story *(1939);* Bachelor Mother *(1939);* Waterloo Bridge *(1940);* Seven Sinners *(1940);* That Uncertain Feeling *(1941);* Bedtime Story *(1941);* To Be or Not to Be *(1942);* Take a Letter *(1942);* Darling *(1942);* The Talk of the Town *(1942);* You Were Never Lovelier *(1942);* The Palm Beach Story *(1942);* Tales of Manhattan *(1942);* Cabin in the Sky *(1943);* The Human Comedy *(1943);* DuBarry Was a Lady *(1943);* Thousands Cheer *(1943);* Madame Curie *(1943);* A Guy Named Joe *(1943);* The Heavenly Body *(1943);* The White Cliffs of Dover *(1944);* Bathing Beauty *(1944);* Gaslight *(1944);* Kismet *(1944);* National Velvet *(1944);* Music for Millions *(1944);* The Picture of Dorian Gray *(1945);* The Clock *(1945);* The Valley of Decision *(1945);* Anchors Aweigh *(1945);* Weekend at the Waldorf *(1945);* Yolanda and the Thief *(1945);* Ziegfeld Follies *(1945);* The Harvey Girls *(1946);* The Postman Always Rings Twice *(1946);* Holiday in Mexico *(1946);* The Dark Mirror *(1946);* Undercurrent *(1946);* Till the Clouds Roll By *(1946);* The Yearling *(1946);* Lady in the Lake *(1947);* The Hucksters *(1947);* Merton of the Movies *(1947);* Song of Love *(1947);* Green Dolphin Street *(1947);* Cass Timberlane *(1947);* B.F.'s Daughter *(1948);* Summer Holiday *(1948);* State of the Union *(1948);* Easter Parade *(1948);* The Barkleys of Broadway *(1949);* Neptune's Daughter *(1949);* The Great Sinner *(1949);* Key to the City *(1950);* Please Believe Me *(1950);* Midnight Lace *(1960);* Lover Come Back *(1961);* A Gathering of Eagles *(1963).*

Costume designer Irene spent the first 16 years of her life far removed from the world of fashion. Born Irene Lentz in 1901 in Brookings, South Dakota, she grew up on a ranch in Montana, and attended school in the nearby town of Baker. Following her graduation from Baker High School, she enrolled at the University of Southern California to prepare for a career as a pianist. Her interest in fashion was piqued when she attended a class at the Wolfe School of Design with a friend. By the end of the first day of class, she had decided to give up music and become a fashion designer.

After completing studies at Wolfe, Irene was persuaded to open a dress shop by her fiancé Dick Jones, a movie director whom she subse-

Irene, holding Liza Minnelli.

quently married. The shop was a success, and its Los Angeles location attracted the business of a number of Hollywood celebrities. (By some accounts, *Lupe Velez was Irene's first important customer; others claim it was *Dolores Del Rio.) Around 1930, following the death of her husband, Irene closed the shop and went to Europe where she studied fashion and dressmaking for a year and a half. Upon her return, she was tapped by an executive of the elite Bullock's Wilshire department store to head up their swanky custom-design salon; it was there that she began designing clothes for motion pictures. In 1942, MGM boss Louis B. Mayer put her under contract to MGM, where she succeeded the renowned Adrian (Gilbert A. Adrian), as executive designer. Mayer also allowed Irene to simultaneously open a business as a wholesale designer, a highly unusual decision for him at the time, as studios discouraged department heads from dividing their loyalties.

Irene remained with MGM throughout the 1940s, dressing the famous figures of ***Hedy Lamarr**, ***Greer Garson**, ***Judy Garland**, ***Lana Turner**, and ***Irene Dunne**. She took pride in turning inexperienced young actresses into "glamorous types" and held to the theory that a woman did not have to have a perfect body to achieve a great look. "It's all in the way she carries herself and walks," she said. "If there is rhythmic music in her movements, it needn't matter that her shoulders are too broad or narrow, her waistline not slim enough; her hips too heavy, her ankles slightly thick." Irene won praise for the naturalness and originality of her designs, particularly her dressmaker suits and figure-revealing gowns. Especially memorable were the all-white outfits she designed for Lana Turner in *The Postman Always Rings Twice* (1946). In 1948, Irene was nominated for an Academy Award for her designs for *B.F.'s Daughter*, which starred ***Barbara Stanwyck**.

After leaving MGM, Irene concentrated on her business, Irene, Inc., financed by 25 department stores throughout the country who held exclusive rights to her designs. Away from her work, the designer hated to "talk shop," although she and her second husband, screenwriter Eliot Gibbons, were part of a large Hollywood circle. Irene frequently accompanied her husband on hunting trips, having learned to shoot as a child. Irene returned to films briefly in the 1960s and was nominated for a second Academy Award for ***Doris Day**'s lavish wardrobe in *Midnight Lace* (1960). Her last movie, *A Gathering of Eagles*, was released in 1963, a year after her death.

SOURCES:

Katz, Ephraim. *The Film Encyclopedia.* NY: HarperCollins, 1994.

Leese, Elizabeth. *Costume Design in the Movies.* NY: Dover, 1991.

Rothe, Anna, ed. *Current Biography.* NY: H.W. Wilson, 1946.

Barbara Morgan,
Melrose, Massachusetts

Irene (c. 1904—)

Greek princess and duchess of Aosta. *Name variations: Princess Irene. Born around 1904; daughter of Constantine I, king of the Hellenes, and* ****Sophie of Prussia*** *(1870–1932); sister of George II (1890–1947), king of Greece (r. 1922–1923, 1935–1947), and* ****Helen of Greece*** *(1896–1982, who married Carol II of Rumania); married the duke of Aosta.*

Irene (b. 1942)

Greek princess. *Born in 1942; daughter of* ****Fredericka*** *(1917–1981), queen of the Hellenes, and Paul I, king of the Hellenes; sister of* ****Sophia of Greece*** *(b. 1938, queen of Spain) and Constantine II, king of Greece (b. 1940; r. 1964–1973).*

Irene (b. 1953)

Rumanian princess. *Name variations: Irene Hohenzollern. Born on February 28, 1953, in Lausanne, Switzerland; daughter of Michael, king of Rumania (r. 1927–1930, 1940–1942), and* ****Anne of Bourbon-Parma*** *(b. 1923); married John Krueger, on December 10, 1983; children: two, including Michael Krueger.*

Irene, Chionia, and Agape of Thessalonica (d. 304)

Sister saints. *Name variations: Irena, Chione and Agape. Died in 304.*

At the time of Diocletian, the crime of being in possession of the Holy Scriptures was punishable by death. When three sisters in Thessalonica—Irene, Chionia, and Agape—were accused of this transgression, they were burned alive in the year 304. Their feast day is April 3.

Irene, Saint.

See Irene of Spain (fl. 300).
See Irene of Santarem (fl. 7th c.).
See Irene of Constantinople (d. around 921).

Irene, Sister (1823–1896)

Roman Catholic Sister of Charity who established the first foundling home in New York City. *Name varia-*

tions: Sister Irene Fitzgibbon. Born Catherine Fitzgibbon in Kensington, London, England, on May 11, 1823; died in New York City on August 14, 1896; attended parish schools in Brooklyn, New York; entered novitiate of Sisters of Charity, 1850.

Born in London, England, in 1823, Catherine Fitzgibbon came to the United States as a child and was raised in Brooklyn, New York, where she attended parish schools. At age 27, she joined the Sisters of Charity, serving as a teacher at St. Peter's Academy in New York City until 1858, when she became mother superior of St. Peter's Convent. During and after the Civil War, when the care of foundling children became a problem in the city, then Archbishop John McCloskey proposed that the Sisters of Charity, under the direction of Sister Irene, establish a home for such children. Until then, the common practice was to place abandoned children in the care of prisoners or residents of the poorhouse. Thus, in October 1869, Sister Irene, with a staff of four sisters, opened the Foundling Asylum, which later became the New York Foundling Hospital. In 1873, the institution was moved to a larger quarters on land donated by the city, and Sister Irene received a state appropriation to help build a new facility.

Sister Irene's compassion and ingenuity were the driving force of the institution. Shortly after the opening of the first home, she organized a group of laywomen to support its work. She took in unwed mothers and encouraged them to keep and care for their babies if at all possible. She also initiated a program of placing children in foster homes when necessary, making provisions for legal adoptions when feasible. As her programs expanded, she established three allied institutions: St. Ann's Maternity Hospital (1880), the Hospital of St. John for Children (1881), and Nazareth Hospital for convalescent children at Spuyten Duyvil, New York City (1881). In 1894, the 25th anniversary of the opening the first foundling home, it was estimated that 26,000 children had been helped. Sister Irene died in 1896.

SOURCES:

McHenry, Robert, ed. *Famous American Women*. NY: Dover, 1983.

Barbara Morgan,
Melrose, Massachusetts

Irene Angela of Byzantium (d. 1208)

Holy Roman empress. *Name variations: Irene of Byzantium. Died on August 27, 1208; daughter of* ****Margaret-Mary of Hungary*** *(c. 1177–?) and Isaac II Angelus, Eastern Roman Emperor (r. 1185–95 and 1203–04); sister of Alexius IV Angelus, Byzantine emperor (r. 1203–1204); married Philip of Swabia (c. 1176–1208), Holy Roman emperor (r. 1198–1208), on May 25, 1197; children:* ****Marie of Swabia*** *(c. 1201–1235);* ****Beatrice of Swabia*** *(1198–1235, who married Otto IV, Holy Roman emperor, and Ferdinand III, king of Castile and Leon); probably* ****Cunigunde of Hohenstaufen*** *(fl. 1215–1230). Philip of Swabia was also married to a daughter of Waldemar I the Great and* ****Sophie of Russia.***

Irene Asen (fl. 1300s)

Empress of Nicaea. *Name variations: Sister Eugenia. Flourished in the 1300s; daughter of Andronicus; married John VI Cantacuzene, emperor of Nicaea (r. 1347–1354); children: Mathew; Manuel;* ****Maria Cantacuzene*** *(who married Nicephorus II of Epirus);* ****Theodora Cantacuzene*** *(who married Orchan);* ****Helena Cantacuzene*** *(who married John V Paleologus). In later years, Irene Asen entered a convent as Sister Eugenia.*

Irene Ducas (c. 1066–1133)

Byzantine empress. *Name variations: Irene Doukas; Irene Doukaina or Ducaena. Born around 1066; died on February 19, 1133; daughter of Marie of Bulgaria (b. 1046) and Andronicus Ducas (a general, known as the traitor of Manzikert); granddaughter of Caesar John Ducas; second wife of Alexius I Comnenus (1048–1118), emperor of Byzantium (r. 1081–1118); children: seven, including Anna Comnena (1083–1153/55); John II Comnenus or Kalojoannes (1088–1143), emperor of Byzantium (r. 1118–1143); Andronicus (killed in battle against the Turks, 1129);* ****Theodora Comnena*** *(fl. 1080s, who married Constantine Angelus);* ****Maria Comnena; *Eudocia Comnena.***

Irene Ducas was born around 1066, the daughter of ***Marie of Bulgaria** (b. 1046) and Andronicus Ducas, a general who was known as the traitor of Manzikert. Irene was the second wife of Alexius I Comnenus, who ruled Byzantium from 1081 until his death in 1118. At first, the marriage was unhappy, for Alexius was infatuated with another: **Maria of Alania.** Eventually, however, the couple became truly devoted to one another and had seven children. Empress Irene often accompanied her husband on campaign and was alert to plots against him. On several occasions, she saved him from danger. When Alexius began to suffer from severe respiratory complaint, Irene would sit up all

Maria of Alania. *See Anna Dalassena for sidebar.*

night with her husband propped in her arms, attempting to ease his breathing.

The best-known period of Irene's life involves an unsuccessful intrigue in which she endeavored to divert the succession from her son John II Comnenus to Nicephorus Bryennius, husband of her first-born daughter ***Anna Comnena**. She failed, however, to persuade Alexius to carry out a coup d'etat with the help of the palace guards. Following Alexius' death in 1118, Irene retired to the convent of Kecharitomene, which she had founded, and ended her life in obscurity, dying there in 1133. Her daughter Anna Comnena would retire there as well, in the company of Anna's daughter Irene.

Irene Emma (b. 1939)

Dutch princess. *Born Irene Emma Elizabeth on August 5, 1939; daughter of* ****Juliana*** *(b. 1909), queen of the Netherlands (r. 1948–1980), and Prince Bernard of Lippe-Biesterfeld; sister of* ****Beatrix*** *(b. 1938), queen of the Netherlands (r. 1980—); married Carlos Hugo, prince of Bourbon-Parma.*

Irene Godunov (d. 1603).

See Godunov, Irene.

Irene Lascaris (fl. 1222–1235)

Nicaean empress. *Name variations: Irene Laskaris. Flourished around 1222–1235; daughter of Anna Angelina (d. 1210?) and Theodore I Lascaris, emperor of Nicaea (r. 1204–1222); married John III Ducas Vatatzes, Nicaean (Byzantine) emperor (r. 1222–1254); children: one son, Theodore II Lascaris, Nicaean emperor (r. 1254–1258).*

Irene Lascaris, daughter of ◂❦ **Anna Angelina** and Theodore I Lascaris, was a young widow when she married John III Vatatzes and shared with him the Byzantine throne, then a government in exile. The marriage was a contented one, despite the fact that Irene was injured in a horseback-riding incident soon after the birth of her only child, Theodore II. She remained an invalid for the rest of her days; her husband was an epileptic.

Irene and John III were exemplary rulers. Because of Irene, the Byzantine court became a center of learning and culture, while John, the greatest of the Nicaean rulers, was a diplomat, warrior, and humanitarian, concerned with establishing schools, hospitals, and libraries. Some years after Irene's death, John married the 12-year-old daughter of Frederick II, ***Constance-Anna of Hohenstaufen**.

❦▸ **Anna Angelina (d. 1210?)**

Nicaean empress. *Died around 1210; daughter of Alexius III Angelus, emperor of Byzantium (r. 1195–1203) and* ****Euphrosyne*** *(d. 1203); married Theodore I Lascaris, emperor of Nicaea (r. 1204–1222); children:* ****Irene Lascaris*** *(who married John III Ducas, Byzantine emperor);* ****Maria Lascaris*** *(who married Bela IV, king of Hungary).*

Irene Lascaris (d. around 1270)

Tsarina of Bulgaria. *Name variations: Irene Laskaris. Died around 1270; daughter of* ****Helen Asen of Bulgaria*** *(d. 1255?) and Theodore II Lascaris, emperor of Nicaea (r. 1254–1258); first wife of Constantine Tich, tsar of Bulgaria (r. 1257–1277).* ****Maria Paleologina*** *was also married to Constantine Tich.*

Irene of Athens (c. 752–803)

First woman to be sole ruler of the Byzantine empire who ruled for ten years, displaying firmness and intelligence, and summoned the council at Nicaea in 787, which formally revived the adoration of images and reunited the Eastern church with that of Rome. *Name variations: Irene the Great; Eirene. Pronunciation: EYE-REE-nee. Born in Athens around 752; died on August 9, 803, on Lesbos; parents unknown, probably noble; grew up an Athenian orphan; married Leo IV the Khazar, Byzantine emperor (r. 775–780), in December 769; children: son, Constantine VI (b. 771), emperor of Byzantium (r. 780–797).*

Regent of and co-emperor with Constantine VI (780–790); organized Seventh Ecumenical Council (Second Council of Nicaea, 787); deposed (790–792); reinstated as co-emperor with Constantine VI (792–797); was sole emperor (797–802); sought as wife by Charlemagne (800); overthrown and exiled (802).

In the middle of the eighth century, Athens was a hotbed of opposition to the policies of the Byzantine emperor Constantine V. For a mixture of political and religious reasons, his father Leo III had begun the policy of banning religious images (icons) of Christ, his disciples and saints, in favor of the symbolism of the cross. The cross signified the empire's strength and prosperity since the time of Constantine the Great. Leo's policy initiated the first wave of iconoclasm in the Eastern Orthodox Church, and it met with strong resistance in Irene's hometown, which tried to break away from the empire along with the rest of Greece. About the time Irene of Athens was born, Constantine V had begun his persecution of the "image worshippers," torturing and martyring monks and nuns, and condoning acts of public humiliation by his armies. This, at least, is the account of later historians who looked favorably upon the use of icons. Whether or not Irene and her family were supporters of the imperial policy, it is likely that her devotion to the images developed when she was young. With this in mind, it is difficult to say why Constantine V chose Irene to marry his eldest son, Leo IV. There may have been many reasons: a sensed need to align the imperial house more closely with mainland Greece rather than the East; a chance to gain firmer control over an unruly area; a gesture of reconciliation toward the empire's icon-loving (iconophile) inhabitants; or even that Leo, who was sickly, would not likely become emperor, so it would have mattered little who his wife was. Another complication is that Irene may have been given the name Irene only when she married, and Irene means "peace."

Leo IV had sworn to continue his father's iconoclastic policy, but when he ascended the throne in 775, he seems to have tolerated the iconophiles. For the first three years of his reign, the abandoned monasteries and nunneries began to fill again, and iconophile monks held high positions in the court. Many historians attribute this period of tolerance to Irene's influence. Nevertheless, in the final year of his reign, Leo began persecuting iconophiles again and, some say, even locked Irene out of their bedroom because she refused to give up some icons she had hidden under her pillow. Leo's premature death brought an end to the first phase of iconoclasm.

In September 780, Irene was made regent and co-emperor with her son Constantine VI who was not yet ten years old. In the words of the chronicler Theophanes: "On September 8 God unexpectedly entrusted the rule to the most pious Irene and her son Constantine, so He could work a miracle through a widow-woman and an orphan child."

Strong-willed and independent, capable of pursuing and holding power herself, Irene was extremely active in administering her own affairs. In her first years, she put down a conspiracy by her brothers-in-law and replaced some rebellious generals who were strong supporters of Leo's and Constantine's later iconoclasm. She replaced the generals with her favorites, who were also iconophiles, and started the process whereby she slowly lost the support of the army. Internal struggles were also weakening the army and the boundaries of the empire.

Irene turned her attention to other matters. In 782, in a bold move, she proposed to betroth ✤▸ **Rotrude**, the daughter of Charlemagne, to her son Constantine. Charlemagne agreed. A tutor was left behind to teach Rotrude Greek and "the customs of the Roman Empire." Irene was forging a link between East and West that could have far-reaching consequences for both halves of the Roman Empire.

In 783, the patriarch, Paul of Cyprus, abdicated and renounced his former vow against the icons. When he died shortly thereafter, Irene had the opportunity to name a new patriarch, one who openly supported the veneration of icons, the learned man Tarasios. Tarasios accepted only on the condition that an ecumenical council be held on the subject of icons. With the possibility of bringing the church back to unity, Irene heartily agreed and issued a call to the bishops of the other three apostolic sees (Rome, Antioch, and Alexandria) to send legations. Though the council began on August 27, 786, it was soon disturbed by the still strongly iconoclastic soldiers, and Irene was unable to hold them back. The soldiers broke up the council and departed.

But Irene, who still wanted the council to meet, retained some of the ambassadors and worked on a plan to sidetrack the empire's army. In the spring of 783, she sent the troops east against some supposed Arab aggression, but when they were safely away she had her men order them to give up their weapons. She then exiled them and their families from the city and forced them to return to their native towns. In May, she again summoned the bishops to Nicaea. On October 11, 787, the Seventh Ecu-

✤▸ **Rotrude** (c. 778–after 839)

Frankish princess. Name variations: *Hrotrud* or *Hrotrude;* (Greek) *Erythro.* Born around 778; died after 839; daughter of Charles I also known as Charlemagne (742–814), king of the Franks (r. 768–814), Holy Roman emperor (r. 800–814), and ***Hildegarde of Swabia** (c. 757–783); sister of ***Gisella of Chelles** (781–814); married Count Rorico, around 800; children: Louis (b. around 800), abbott of St. Denis.*

menical Council was convened by the Patriarch Tarasios with 350 bishops in attendance. The Synod restored the icons and renounced those who had practiced iconoclasm. Irene signed the Synod's decree with her own hand. It was the last Ecumenical Council so recognized by the Orthodox Church.

In 788, for reasons unknown, Irene suddenly decided to break off the engagement of Rotrude and Constantine, then arranged a marriage with a young woman named ◂ **Maria of Amnia**, from Armenia. Constantine seems to have been distressed over this, since he was in love with Rotrude. Being now 17 years old, he felt he should begin to assume more of the imperial duties. But Irene would not yield the reins. She had her name put first on imperial documents. When Constantine formed a conspiracy to oust his mother, Irene learned of the plot and punished all involved. She beat her son and confined him to the palace for several days. She then made the army swear that it would not support her son as ruler as long as she lived. But part of the army had gone to Cyprus to stave off an Arab attack, and when it returned it helped Constantine to power. Irene was deposed in 790 and settled in the palace of Eleutherios in Constantinople.

Constantine ruled as Autokrator for just over a year before he called Irene back. He had engaged in some wars against the Arabs and Bulgars, which he lost, and seems to have been incapable of ruling on his own. In January 792, Irene was acclaimed co-emperor with Constantine, but his name came first on official documents once again. From this time forward, it seems Irene schemed against her son, never forgiving him for ousting her. When a conspiracy was discovered among the palace guards to replace Constantine with his uncle Nicephorus, Irene suggested the punishment. Constantine blinded Nicephorus and another important man, then cut out the tongues of his other four uncles. Theophanes writes: "The punishment took place on a Saturday in August . . . , but not for long did God's avenging justice permit this unjust act. For, five years later, Constantine [would be] blinded by his own mother on a Saturday of the same month."

Constantine now fell in love with a serving woman named ***Theodota** (c. 775-early 800s), but extramarital affairs were harshly condemned by the church. Therefore, in January 795, he forced Maria to become a nun. According to Theophanes: "[H]e hated her because of the insinuations of his mother, who was aiming at the rule: Irene did this to make everyone accuse him." In August of the same year, he made Theodota his wife with the coerced blessing of the patriarch. This caused a great public outcry by the pious, and, in the next year, several prominent religious men broke from communion with Tarasios because he had sanctioned the affair. Constantine reacted with swift punishment for those who opposed him. Irene could now play on negative opinion against Constantine and plot to depose him. On August 15, 797, Constantine was trapped in the Purple Chamber, where he had been born, and on Irene's orders was blinded with the intention of killing him. Now Irene was Autokrator, the first time a woman held the title.

Irene reinstalled her advisors, who had been exiled or silenced by Constantine. But things had changed since she had first assumed power in 780. She was older, there was no pressing religious issue to pursue, and there was no clear heir to the throne. One thing remained the same: she was still unpopular with the military. Once again, Leo IV's brothers conspired for a chance at the throne; once again, they were thwarted. Several patricians positioned themselves so that they or their relatives would become emperor after Irene's death. In March of 799, she put down another conspiracy. In May, she fell ill and thought she would die. Enemies, posing as friends, persuaded her that her favorite eunuch intended to seize power for himself. When Irene recovered, the eunuch convinced her that he had no such intention. The palace was rife with tension and intrigue.

On Christmas day, 800, Charlemagne was crowned emperor of the Romans by Pope Leo III. This act made Charlemagne an equal

---

▸ **Maria of Amnia** (fl. 782)

Byzantine empress. *Name variations: Maria of Armenia. Flourished around 782; first wife of Constantine VI Porphyrogenitus (b. 771), emperor of Byzantium (r. 780–797); children:* ****Euphrosyne*** *(c. 790–c. 840, who married Byzantine emperor Michael II of Amorion).*

The sweet-tempered Maria of Amnia, who grew up in an impoverished household, was the Byzantine Cinderella. She was chosen to be the wife of Constantine VI by winning a beauty contest held by ***Irene of Athens**. Because Maria had been forced on him, Constantine hated his wife. Eventually, he compelled her to withdraw to a nunnery.

with the Byzantine emperor. In Western eyes, that meant that there was only one emperor, since the West did not recognize a woman as emperor. It is not certain how clear this was to Irene and her court. In the East, there seems to have been little problem accepting Irene as a full emperor. But now Charlemagne proposed to marry her. If he were not de facto sole emperor, his marriage to Irene would make him so, since the whole Byzantine Empire would then be under his control. Irene seems to have favored the idea. She had earlier sought to unite East and West, first through the marriage between Rotrude and Constantine. The Ecumenical Council may have been another attempt. The Synod did bring the Eastern and Western churches closer together, but doctrinal differences remained and ultimately split the churches apart in the next century. Why Irene had sought a closer connection between East and West is an even tougher question to answer. It could have been the age-old desire to reunite the empire. It is also possible that all Irene wanted to do was restore the icons to their rightful place in the church. The Western Church supported the use of images. Perhaps she felt a closer connection would help her accomplish that goal. And when it was accomplished, she had canceled the engagement with Rotrude.

But in Constantinople several men were angling for a chance to seize the throne for themselves or their relatives. In 801, Irene waived taxes and reduced import and export duties, which won her great support from the people. Still, the army remained a problem, and the generals were ready to capitalize on it. On October 31, 802, Nicephorus (I), the minister of public finance, seized his opportunity. In an elaborate charade, he lied about an attempted coup by the generals and told the palace guards that Irene had proclaimed him emperor in order to ward off the others. The guards bought the lie and proclaimed him emperor. As the chronicler Theophanes represents it, Nicephorus lied his way through several situations in the next few days and fooled everyone into making him emperor.

Irene promised to go quietly, if Nicephorus would allow her to retreat to the Eleutherios palace. He agreed if she would hand over the imperial treasury to him. She did so but was then exiled to a nunnery on one of the Princes' Islands in the Sea of Marmara. Meanwhile, Charlemagne's envoys were in the city and saw everything. Soon, fearing popular pressure to bring back the beloved Irene, Nicephorus exiled her even further, to Lesbos where she was imprisoned, allowed no visitors, and forced to support herself by spinning. The following year, she died there, on August 9, 803. Her body was moved to the Church of the Holy Apostles in Constantinople later in the 9th century.

A coin depicting Irene of Athens.

Irene of Athens was the first woman to be sole ruler (Autokrator) of the Byzantine empire. Her zeal for the restoration of icons put an end to the most virulent phase of iconoclasm in the Byzantine empire and paved the way for the permanent acceptance of icons in the Orthodox Church. Hated by her political and religious enemies, she was nevertheless adored by the icon-loving Orthodox believers and received favorable treatment from Byzantine historians. Unfortunately, favorable as well as unfavorable accounts provide little insight to her reasoning or motives. Nevertheless, her abiding zeal for the icons is obvious, and her accomplishments in having them readmitted into the Orthodox Church still affect the church. Her dealings with Charlemagne almost united the Eastern and Western empires and might have had a profound effect on the subsequent history of East and West relations.

SOURCES:

Hussey, J.M., ed. *The Cambridge Medieval History, vol. 4: The Byzantine Empire.* Cambridge: Cambridge University Press, 1966.

Jenkins, Romilly. *Byzantium the Imperial Centuries AD 610–1071.* Reprint. Toronto: University of Toronto Press, 1987.

Ostrogorsky, George. *History of the Byzantine State.* New Brunswick, NJ: Rutgers University Press, 1969.

Speck, Paul. *Kaiser Konstantin VI.* Munich: Wilhelm Fink Verlag, 1978.

Treadgold, Warren. *Byzantine Revival 780–842.* Stanford: Stanford University Press, 1988.

Turtledove, Harry, trans. *The Chronicle of Theophanes.* Philadelphia, PA: University of Pennsylvania Press, 1982.

Vasiliev, A.A. *History of the Byzantine Empire.* 2nd ed. Madison: University of Wisconsin Press, 1952.

Robert W. Cape, Jr.,
Assistant Professor of Classics and Director of Gender Studies,
Austin College, Sherman, Texas, and **Sarolta A. Takács**,
Assistant Professor of the Classics,
Harvard University, Cambridge, Massachusetts

Irene of Brunswick (fl. 1300s)

Byzantine (Nicaean) empress. *Name variations: Adelheid of Brunswick; Adelheid-Irene of Brunswick. Flourished in the 1300s; first wife of Andronikos also spelled Andronicus III Paleologus, Byzantine (Nicaean) emperor (r. 1328–1341). Andronicus' second wife was ****Anne of Savoy*** *(c. 1320–1353).*

Irene of Byzantium (d. 1067)

Byzantine princess. *Died in 1067; daughter of Constantine VIII, Byzantine emperor (r. 1025–1028), and possibly ****Helena of Alypia;*** *became first wife of Vsevolod I (1030–1093), grand prince of Kiev (r. 1078–1093), in 1046; children: Vladimir II Monomakh (b. 1053), grand prince of Kiev.*

Irene of Byzantium (fl. 1200s).

See Eulogia Paleologina.

Irene of Constantinople (d. around 921)

Saint. *Name variations: Irene of Chyrsobalanton. Died around 921.*

A Cappadocian, Irene of Constantinople became a nun rather than marry Michael III, emperor of Byzantium. Known as Michael the Drunkard, he went on to marry ***Eudocia Decapolita.** Irene became abbess of the great Chrysobalanton convent in Constantinople, and an important cult flourished around her. She became famous for her prophecies, levitations, and miracles.

Irene of Hesse-Darmstadt (1866–1953)

Princess of Hesse-Darmstadt and granddaughter of Queen Victoria. *Born Irene Louise Mary Anne on July 11, 1866, at Neues Palais, in Darmstadt, Hesse, Germany; died on November 11, 1953, in Hemmelmark, near Eckenford, Schleswig-Holstein, Germany; daughter of ****Alice Maud Mary*** *(1843–1878, daughter of Queen ****Victoria)*** *and Louis IV, grand duke of Hesse-Darmstadt; sister of ****Alexandra Feodorovna*** *(1872–1918); married Henry of Prussia (brother of Kaiser Wilhelm II), on May 24 1888; children: Waldemar (1889–1945); Sigismund (1896–1978); Henry Victor (b. 1900).*

Irene of Hungary (c. 1085–1133).

See Anna Comnena for sidebar on Priska-Irene of Hungary.

Irene of Kiev (fl. 1122)

Princess of Kiev. *Flourished around 1122; daughter of Mstislav I (b. 1076), grand prince of Kiev (r. 1125–1132), and ****Christina of Sweden*** *(d. 1122); married Andronicus (d. 1129), brother of ****Anna Comnena,*** *in 1122.*

Irene of Montferrat (fl. 1300)

Byzantine empress. *Name variations: Yolande-Irene; Yolande of Montferrat; Violante of Montferat or Violante of Montferrat. Born Violante or Yolande; flourished around 1300; daughter of William V the Great, marquis of Montferrat, and ****Isabelle of Cornwall;*** *became second wife of Andronicus II Paleologus (1259–1332), emperor of Nicaea and Byzantine emperor (r. 1282–1328), around 1305; children: John; Teodoro also known as Theodore I (b. 1292), margrave of Montferrat; Demetrius; possibly ****Irene*** *(who married John II of Thessaly); possibly Simonis (who married Milutin).*

Following the death of his young wife ***Anna of Hungary**, Andronicus II Paleologus married the Italian princess Irene of Montferrat, said to be hotheaded. With her marriage, the marquisate of Montferrat in northwest Italy passed to the Palelogi. Though her early married years were happy, Irene became discontented with the fact that Anna of Hungary's son, Michael IX, was heir to the throne while her sons were considered only private citizens. When her husband continued to ignore her pleas to divide imperial territories for each child, Irene turned against him. She eventually left Andronicus and moved to Thessalonica.

Irene of Santarem (fl. 7th c.)

Spanish saint. *Name variations: Irene of Santárem. Flourished during the 7th century; lived at Tomar in Estremadura.*

Much revered in Spain and Portugal, Irene of Santarem lived in the 7th century, during the reign of King Chindaswinth. She was born of nobility, raised for the most part in a convent, and received her later education from a monk from the abbey of Our Lady, who gave her lessons at home.

Living a sequestered life, Irene ventured out only once a year—on the feast of Saint Peter—to pray in church. On one such outing, she was spotted by the noble Britald who was smittened at first sight but knew that his love would be unrequited. In deep despair, Britald's health gave way, and he was expected to die of consumption. Irene, hearing of his plight, visited his bedside, telling him that she had vowed to remain a virgin and promising him that they would meet in Paradise. Heartened by the belief that Irene surely would become his wife had she not promised herself to God, Britald made a speedy recovery.

Meanwhile, Irene's monk from the abbey was also obsessed with her. When he made his passion known, she rebuffed him and gave up her lessons. Steeped in resentment, the monk circulated a rumor that Irene was pregnant. Britald, who believed Irene had lied, was consumed with jealousy and hired an assassin to kill her. Thus, it came to be that Irene was murdered by the thrust of a sword and dumped into the Tagus river, where she was later recovered by the Benedictines near the town of Scalabis. The name of the town was subsequently changed to St. Irene, or Santárem.

Irene of Spain (fl. 300s)

Spanish saint. *Born in Rome in the early days of the 4th century; daughter of Laurentia and a father who later became a priest of the church and was known as S. Lorenzo; sister of the pope St. Damasus I (c. 305–384). Her feast day is February 21.*

Irene of Sulzbach (d. 1161).

See Bertha-Irene of Sulzbach.

Irene of the Khazars (d. 750?)

Byzantine empress. *Born a princess of the Khazar tribe in the Russian steppes; died around 750; first wife of Constantine V Kopronymus, Byzantine emperor (r. 741–775); children: Leo IV the Khazar, Byzantine emperor (r. 775–780, who married ****Irene of Athens****).*

Irene of the Khazars was born a princess of the Khazar tribe in the Russian steppes. The first wife of Constantine V Kopronymus, emperor of Byzantium, she died young while giving birth to Leo IV, heir to the throne.

Irene Paleologina (fl. 1200s).

See Eulogia Paleologina.

Irene Paleologina (fl. 1279–1280)

Tsarina of Bulgaria. *Daughter of Michael VIII Paleologus (1224–1282), emperor of Nicaea (r. 1261–1282), and *Theodora Ducas; sister of Andronicus II (1259–1332), emperor of Nicaea (r. 1282–1328); married Asen III also known as Ivan Asen III, tsar of Bulgaria (r. 1279–1280); children: Andronicus;* ***Maria Asen*** *(who married Roger de Flor).*

Irene the Great (c. 752–803).

See Irene of Athens.

Irfan (fl. mid-800s)

Arabian singer, representing the Persian romantic school of music. *Flourished mid-800s; performed at the court of Caliph al-Mutawakki (r. 847–861).*

Irfan represents the struggle between two forms of music performed in the Arab world. The classical, conservative school of music was represented by the teacher, composer, and theoretician Ishaq al-Mausuli and the songstress ***Oraib**. The innovative romantic Persian school of music was represented by Ibrahim ibn al-Mahdi and the songstress ***Shariyya**.

Since Irfan was a slave of Shariyya, she obviously belonged to the more innovative school. She and her mistress took part in a competition against Oraib and her singers. It was natural for these women to vie for public attention, as songstresses were sought after by caliphs, princes, and wealthy patrons and then, as today, exposure expanded their opportunities. Irfan became attached to the court of Caliph al-Mutawakki and also sang for Abu-l-'Ubais ibn Hamdun. Shariyya may well have freed Irfan, for when she sang at the circumcision festival for al-Mutazz, the son of Caliph al-Mutawakki, she is not recorded as being a slave of Shariyya's. Irfan was obviously a talented singer and composer who performed before the wealthy and powerful, unafraid to practice a new and innovative form of music.

John Haag,
Athens, Georgia

Irina.

Variant of Irene.

Irina (1895–1970)

Princess. *Name variations: Irene Yusupov; Irina Alexandrovna Youssoupoff or Yussoupov; Irina Alexandrovna Romanov or Romanova. Born Irina Alexandrovna Romanova on July 3, 1895; died in 1970; married Felix Yussoupov (1887–1967), count Soumarokov-Elston, in 1914; daughter of* ****Xenia Alexandrovna*** *(1876–1960) and Grand Duke Alexander Michaelovitch (grandson of Nicholas I of Russia).*

Princess Irina, the niece of Tsar Nicholas II, was the sponsor of the notorious Rasputin, a Siberian peasant and self-proclaimed holy man who entered the circle of personal acquaintances surrounding the Russian imperial family sometime after 1905. Tsar Nicholas and especially Empress ***Alexandra Feodorovna** welcomed Rasputin because of the healing powers he supposedly possessed; he seemed to be able to treat the imperial couple's only son, Alexis, who suffered from hemophilia. In 1914, Irina married Felix Yussoupov, count Soumarokov-Elston. Two years later, Felix was among the nobles who poisoned, shot, clubbed and drowned Rasputin in Petrograd.

With the help of ***Fanny Holtzmann,** Princess Irina sued MGM in British courts over that studio's depiction of her as an intimate of Rasputin in *Rasputin and the Empress* (1933). After the well-publicized trial, Irina was awarded $125,000 in damages for the showing of the film in England. Holtzmann then reached a settlement for suits pending in most of the countries where the film was shown, for a sum well into the hundreds of thousands of dollars.

Irine.

Variant of Irina.

Irma of Hohenlohe-Langenburg (1902–1986)

German royal. *Born Irma Helen on July 4, 1902, in Langenburg, Germany; died on March 8, 1986, in Heilbronn, Baden-Wurttemberg, Germany; daughter of* ****Alexandra Saxe-Coburg*** *(1878–1942) and Ernest, 7th prince of Hohenlohe-Langenburg.*

Irmengard (c. 800–851)

Holy Roman empress. *Born around 800; died on March 20, 851; daughter of Hugh, count of Tours; married Lothair also known as Lothar I (795–855), Holy Roman emperor (r. 840–855), in 821; children: Louis II le Jeune also known as Louis II the Child (c. 822–875), Holy Roman emperor (r. 855–875); Lothair or Lothar II (c. 826–869), king of Lorraine;* ****Bertha of Avenay*** *(c. 830–c. 852); Charles the Child (c. 845–863), king of Provence;* ****Rothilde;*** *another daughter (name unknown) married Giselbert, count of Maasgau.*

Irmengard of Hesbain (c. 778–818).

See Ermengarde.

Irmengard of Oettingen

Countess Palatine. *Married Adolph the Simple (1300–1327), count Palatine (r. 1319–1327); children: Rupert II (1335–1398), count Palatine (r. 1390–1398).*

Irmentrude (d. 820)

Countess of Altdorf and founder of the Welf line. *Name variations: Irmentrudis. Died in 820; daughter of* ****Bertha*** *(719–783) and Pepin III the Short, king of the Franks (r. 747–768), mayor of Neustria (r. 741); sister of Charlemagne, king of the Franks (r. 768–814), Holy Roman emperor (r. 800–814); married Isembert, count of Altdorf; children: Welf I.*

Irmentrude, the sister of Charlemagne, married Isembert, count of Altdorf, Swabia. She was the mother of Welf I, founder of both the Italian (Guelf or Guelph) and German branches of that famous family. The younger branch of Welf established itself in Germany and became dukes and duchesses of Brunswick. The British house of Windsor, through the German house of Hanover, descended from this line. Hence, Irmentrude was the direct ancestor of Queen ***Victoria.**

Irmina, Saint (d. 716?).

See joint entry on Adela and Irmina.

Irmingard of Zelle (c. 1200–1260)

Margravine of Baden. *Born around 1200; died on February 24, 1260; daughter of* ***Agnes of Hohen-***

staufen (d. 1204) and Henry, count Palatine of Rhine; married Herman V, margrave of Baden (r. 1190–1243), around 1220; children: Herman VI, margrave of Baden (r. 1243–1250); Rudolf I, margrave of Baden (r. 1243–1288).

Irmtrude.

Variant of Ermentrude.

Irwin, Agnes (1841–1914)

American educator who was the first dean of Radcliffe College. *Born in Washington, D.C., on December 30, 1841; died in Philadelphia, Pennsylvania, on October 16, 1914; the oldest daughter and second of five children of William Wallace Irwin (a Whig lawyer and congressman from Pennsylvania) and Sophia Arabella Dallas (Bache) Irwin (the granddaughter of* ****Sarah Bache****); attended private school in Washington; never married; no children.*

The daughter of a congressional representative and the great-great-granddaughter of Benjamin Franklin and **Deborah Read** on her mother's side, Agnes Irwin grew up in a privileged home. A keenly intelligent youngster, her formal education was supplemented by frequent trips abroad and by her own voracious reading. In 1862, six years after her father's death, Irwin moved with her family to New York, where she took a job as a teacher in a private school. In 1869, she assumed the principalship of the Penn Square Seminary of Philadelphia, after its two principals drowned in a boating accident. She remained there for the next 25 years, earning a reputation as a hard taskmaster who maintained high educational standards. The school was renamed the Agnes Irwin School shortly after her appointment.

In 1894, Irwin was recommended for the post of dean of the newly chartered Radcliffe College, formerly the Society for the Collegiate Instruction of Women, popularly known as the "Harvard Annex." With the endorsement of Harvard's president Charles Eliot and ***Elizabeth Cary Agassiz,** the first president of the fledgling institution, Irwin accepted the position. Turning the Irwin School over to her younger sister, she spent the summer in England observing management techniques at Girton and Newnham (the women's colleges affiliated with Cambridge University) and returned in the fall to assume her new duties. Adopting the "quiet, unaggressive" approach of Agassiz, Irwin spent the early years of her tenure expanding the curriculum of the "sister" institution, which, by 1902, was offering a doctoral program. She raised money for a gymnasium, a library, and an administration building, and worked for the establishment of college-owned residences so as to increase the accessibility of the institution to women throughout the nation. Irwin also established the social policies at Radcliffe, which reflected her Victorian sensibilities and were referred to by a student at the time as "inhibition incarnate." Radcliffe women were not allowed to appear in nearby Harvard Square without hats and gloves, and were forbidden to enter Harvard Yard unless invited by a young man to attend a special function open to women, and then only with a chaperon. On a personal level, however, Irwin was less formidable; students who came to know her spoke of her warmth and sense of humor.

Irwin's relationship with Agassiz was cordial and easy, and as time went on the division of power between the two women grew fuzzy. In 1899, when Agassiz withdrew somewhat from the management of the college to serve as "honorary president," Irwin accepted more responsibilities, becoming, in effect, head of the institution. When the older woman retired in 1903, Irwin was surprised when the trustees bypassed her and selected LeBaron Russell Briggs, dean of the faculty at Harvard, to serve as the new president. Although the choice of Briggs cemented Radcliffe's tie with Harvard, Irwin was disappointed by the snub. Although she stayed on as dean at Radcliffe for another six years, she did not approach her work with the same enthusiasm. Much of her time during her final years at the college was devoted to the Woman's Education Association of Boston, of which she was president from 1901 to 1907.

Read, Deborah. *See Bache, Sarah for sidebar.*

Agnes Irwin left Radcliffe in 1909 and returned to Philadelphia. From 1911 to 1914, she served as the first president of the Head Mistresses' Association of Private Schools. She died of pneumonia in 1914, age 72.

SOURCES:

James, Edward T., ed. *Notable American Women 1607–1950.* Cambridge, MA: The Belknap Press of Harvard University Press, 1971.

McHenry, Robert, ed. *Famous American Women.* NY: Dover, 1983.

Barbara Morgan,
Melrose, Massachusetts

Irwin, Inez Haynes (1873–1970)

American suffragist, novelist and short-story writer. *Born Inez Leonore Haynes in Rio de Janeiro, Brazil, on March 2, 1873; died in Norwell, Massachusetts, on*

September 25, 1970; one of ten children of Gideon Haynes and his second wife Emma Jane (Hopkins) Haynes; graduated from the Bowdoin Grammar School, Boston, 1887; attended the Girls' High School, Boston, 1887–90; graduated from Boston Normal School, 1892; attended Radcliffe College as a special student, 1897–1900; married Rufus Hamilton Gillmore (a newspaper reporter), on August 30, 1897 (divorced around 1913); married William Henry Irwin (a political journalist and biographer of Herbert Hoover), on February 1, 1916.

Selected writings: June Jeopardy *(1908);* Maida's Little Shop *(1910);* Phoebe and Ernest *(1910);* Janey *(1911);* Phoebe, Ernest, and Cupid *(1912);* Angel Island *(1914);* The Ollivant Orphans *(1915);* The Californians *(1916);* The Lady of the Kingdoms *(1917);* The Happy Year *(1919);* The Native Son *(1919);* Maida's Little House *(1921);* Out of the Air *(1921);* The Story of the Woman's Party *(1921);* Gertrude Haviland's Divorce *(1925);* Maida's Little School *(1926);* Gideon *(1927);* P.D.F.R. *(1928);* Confessions of a Businessman's Wife *(1931);* Family Circle *(1931):* Youth Must Laugh *(1932);* Angels and Amazons *(1933);* Strange Harvest *(1934);* Murder Masquerade *(1935);* The Poison Cross *(1936);* Good Manners for Girls *(1937);* A Body Rolled Downstairs *(1938);* Maida's Little Island *(1939);* Maida's Little Camp *(1940);* Many Murders *(1941);* Maida's Little Village *(1942);* Maida's Little Houseboat *(1943);* Maida's Little Theatre *(1946);* The Women Swore Revenge *(1946);* Maida's Little Cabins *(1947);* Maida's Little Zoo *(1949);* Maida's Little Lighthouse *(1951);* Maida's Little Hospital *(n.d.);* Maida's Little Farm *(n.d.);* Maida's Little House Party *(n.d.);* Maida's Little Treasure Hunt *(n.d.);* Maida's Little Tree House *(n.d.).*

Writer and feminist Inez Irwin was born in Rio de Janeiro, Brazil, where her parents had moved from New England to start a coffee business. When the venture failed, they returned to manage several hotels in Boston. Irwin grew up in a large, blended family and even as a child expressed concern about the life of drudgery that awaited her once she reached womanhood. (Her father, a widower, brought five children to his second marriage, which then produced ten more.) In grammar school, after writing a composition on the topic "Should Women Vote?," she became an ardent supporter of women's rights. Following her graduation from Boston Normal School, Irwin taught briefly before her marriage to Rufus Hamilton Gillmore, a newspaper reporter, in 1897. That same year, with Gillmore's encouragement, she entered Radcliffe College as a special student. There Irwin was drawn into the suffrage movement, and in 1900, with ***Maud Wood Park**, she founded the Massachusetts College Equal Suffrage Association, which ultimately expanded into the National College Equal Suffrage League.

In 1900, Irwin and her husband moved to New York where she wrote short stories and magazine articles, and published her first novel, *June Jeopardy* (1908). After a lengthy European tour, Irwin became the fiction editor of Max Eastman's radical periodical *The Masses* and joined the new feminist society Heterodoxy, which put her in contact with many of the notable suffragists of her day. She also met and fell in love with William Henry Irwin, a California journalist who was then managing editor of *McClure's* magazine. She subsequently divorced her husband and, in 1916, married Irwin. Inez shared many professional interests with her new husband and, during World War I, accompanied him to Europe, writing articles from England, France, and Italy for several American magazines.

Returning to New York in 1918, Irwin became involved with the more radical National Woman's Party, serving on its advisory council and as its biographer. Her carefully documented and lively work, *The Story of the Woman's Party* (1921), provides the only written account of the party's activities. Irwin later undertook a more ambitious history, *Angels and Amazons: A Hundred Years of American Women* (1933).

Inez Irwin also continued to write fiction and children's books, the earliest of which included a series about orphaned children; another revolved around a brother and sister. According to **Lynne Masel-Walters** and **Helen Loeb**, Irwin's feminist fiction, written early in her career, has been undeservedly forgotten. In her long novel, *The Lady of the Kingdoms* (1917), Irwin used two heroines, one beautiful and one plain, to "examine the conventional moralities women have been forced into, as well as the unconventional, even 'immoral,' ones women have chosen for themselves." Irwin also wrote two novels dealing with the sensitive subject of divorce: *Gertrude Haviland's Divorce* (1925) and *Gideon* (1927).

Irwin won the O. Henry Memorial Award in 1924 for "The Spring Flight," a short story about William Shakespeare's attempt to overcome writer's block before writing *The Tempest.* During the 1930s and 1940s, her output consisted of murder mysteries and children's books, including the popular "Maida" series, based on her own childhood.

Irwin supported a number of writers' associations, serving as president of the Authors Guild (1925–28) and of the Authors' League of America (1931–33). She was also vice president of the New York chapter of P.E.N. (1941–44). Following the death of her husband in 1948, Irwin retired to the couple's summer home in Scituate, Massachusetts, She died in a nursing home in 1970, at the age of 97.

SOURCES:

Masel-Walters, Lynne, and Helen Loeb. "Inez Irwin," in Mainiero, Lina, ed. *American Women Writers From Colonial Times to the Present.* NY: Frederick Ungar, 1980.

Sicherman, Barbara, and Carol Hurd Green, ed. *Notable American Women: The Modern Period.* Cambridge, MA: The Belknap Press of Harvard University Press, 1980.

Barbara Morgan,
Melrose, Massachusetts

Isaac, Jane (1907–1998).

See West, Dorothy.

Isaac, Joan (fl. 1300s)

Lady of Lorn. *Name variations: Joan de Ergadia. Daughter of Thomas Isaac and* ****Matilda Bruce*** *(d. 1353, daughter of Robert the Bruce); married Ewen de Ergadia, Lord of Lorn; children:* ***Janet de Ergadia.***

Isaacs, Stella (1894–1971)

Influential aid worker in World War II England who organized and ran the women's branch of the civil-defense service. *Name variations: Stella Reading; the Marchioness of Reading; Baroness Swanborough. Born in 1894 in Constantinople (now Istanbul), Turkey; died in 1971; daughter of Charles Charn (one source says Charnaud); married Rufus Isaacs, earl of Reading (later the marquess of Reading), in 1931.*

Red Cross worker during World War I; traveled to India to work in viceroy's office (1925); appointed founding chair of the Women's Volunteer Service for Civil Defense (1938); made Dame of the British Empire (1941); created baroness (1958).

Stella Isaacs, who also held the titles the Dowager Marchioness of Reading and, later, Baroness Swanborough, was born in Constantinople (now Istanbul), Turkey, in 1894. As a child, she suffered from back problems and was kept out of school and tutored at home instead. She was a young woman near the age of 20 when England entered World War I, and she served in the British Red Cross during the conflict. In 1925, she journeyed to India to serve as secretary to the wife of the viceroy of India, **Lady Reading**, who died in 1930. Stella Isaacs then wed the viceroy, also the earl of Reading (later the marquess of Reading) a year after he became a widower. He died in 1935, and she occupied her time by serving on a number of charitable bodies and philanthropic commissions.

Her experience in helping the poor, indigent, and infirm led to the home secretary, Sir Samuel Hoare, asking her to create an organization of women that would help people displaced from their homes as a result of war. This occurred in 1938, as England was foreseeing a possible conflict with Nazi Germany. Though it already had a Civil Defense service from the previous World War, it now was believed that it might not be all that unseemly for women to participate as well. The Women's Volunteer Service (WVS) for Civil Defense, which Isaacs founded, was created to fulfill this mission. Her efforts as chair helped the WVS, as it became known, grow into an organization of a million women by 1942. During the Blitzkrieg (the German Luftwaffe's relentless bombing of London), Isaacs played a great part in coordinating and actively participating in the evacuation of children from cities. The group also lent its energy to a number of other wartime services, such as assisting refugees and providing welfare to the armed forces. After the war, the WVS continued on as helpmates to the elderly and poor and was bestowed with the "royal" designate in 1966. Isaacs chaired it until her death in 1971.

Stella Isaacs' other major involvement was with the British Broadcasting Corporation (BBC) for a period of time after World War II. She was named a governor of the news organization in 1946, and served as vice-chair from 1947 to 1951. For her wartime service, she was named a Dame of the British Empire in 1941 and in 1958 became the first woman life peer as Baroness Swanborough.

SOURCES:

The Dictionary of National Biography. Edited by Lord Blake and C.S. Nicholls. Oxford: Oxford University Press, 1986.

The International Dictionary of Women's Biography. Edited by Jennifer S. Uglow. NY: Continuum, 1985.

Carol Brennan,
Grosse Pointe, Michigan

Isabeau de Lorraine (1410–1453).

See Isabelle of Lorraine.

Isabeau of Bavaria (1371–1435)

Queen of France. *Name variations: Elizabeth of Bavaria; Isabeau of France; Isabel, Isabelle, Isabella. Born around 1371 (some sources cite 1369) in Bavaria; died on September 29 (or 24), 1435, in Paris, France; daughter of Stephen III, duke of Bavaria (r. 1375–1413), and Thaddaea Visconti (d. 1381); married Charles VI (1368–1422), king of France (r. 1380–1422), on July 17, 1385; children: Charles (d. 1386 in infancy); Joan (1388–1390);* ****Isabella of Valois*** *(c. 1389–c. 1410, who married Richard II of England);* ****Joan Valois*** *(1391–1433); Charles (d. 1401);* ****Marie*** *(1393–1438, prioress of Poissy);* ****Michelle Valois*** *(1394–1422); Louis, duke of Guienne (d. 1415); John, duke of Touraine (1398–1417, who married* ****Jacqueline of Hainault****); Catherine of Valois (1401–1437, later queen of England married to Henry V); Charles VII (1403–1461), king of France (r. 1422–1461); Philip (1407–1407).*

Effigy of Isabeau of Bavaria.

Isabeau of Bavaria was one of France's most despised queens. She was a German princess born in 1371, the daughter of Stephen III of Bavaria and ***Thaddaea Visconti.** In 1385, Isabeau married the French king Charles VI as part of a political alliance between Bavaria and France. Isabeau succeeded in the primary duty of a queen, to provide heirs to the throne, by having 12 children with Charles. However, she had the misfortune of marrying the king called "Charles the Mad," who suffered long bouts of insanity for several decades. This caused confusion and intense power struggles at the French court; the queen contributed to these struggles by allegedly having an affair with one of the contenders, Duke Louis of Orleans.

With her husband disabled, Isabeau attempted to administer the government in his name but was largely unsuccessful. However, this failure may have been more due to the chaotic conflicts and wars which were brewing before Charles became incapacitated than through any fault of her own. As regent, Isabeau signed the notorious Treaty of Troyes with the invading English which proved unpopular with the French people; it dispossessed her son Charles and agreed that Henry V of England would succeed Charles as king of France. It also provided for the marriage of Isabeau's daughter ***Catherine of Valois** to King Henry. With this treaty looming over them, the French began to see Isabeau as a curse laid on them, for she had supposedly lost their kingdom to their longtime enemies (although the monarchy did remain in French hands since the Treaty was broken when Charles died).

Much of Isabeau of Bavaria's poor reputation also stemmed from the fact that she was a foreigner; her Bavarian customs and entourage seemed quite bizarre to the French court, and her excessive interest in luxury goods for which she spent great sums of money did not aid her image. On the positive side, Queen Isabeau was recognized as an important patron of artists and writers, among them the celebrated ***Christine de Pizan.** Unpopular and not much mourned, Isabeau died at age 65.

SOURCES:

Anderson, Bonnie S., and Judith P. Zinsser. *A History of Their Own.* Vol. I. NY: Harper & Row, 1988.

Echols, Anne, and Marty Williams. *An Annotated Index of Medieval Women.* NY: Markus Wiener, 1992.

Tuchman, Barbara. *A Distant Mirror: The Calamitous Fourteenth Century.* NY: Ballantine, 1978.

Laura York,
Riverside, California

Isabel.

Variant of Isabella.

Isabel (fl. 1183)

Lady Annandale. *Name variations: Isabel Bruce; Isabel Roos. Flourished around 1183; illegitimate daughter of William I the Lion, king of Scots (r. 11665–1214), and a mistress; married Robert Bruce, 3rd Lord of Annandale, in 1183; married Robert Roos; children: (second marriage) William Roos.*

Isabel (fl. 1225)

Scottish princess and countess of Norfolk. *Name variations: Isabel Dunkeld; Isabel Bigod; Isabella. Flourished around 1225; interred at Church of the Black Friars, London; daughter of William I the Lion (b. 1143), king of Scots, and *****Ermengarde of Beaumont*** *(d. 1234); married Roger Bigod (c. 1212–1270), 4th earl of Norfolk, in May 1225, in Alnwick, Northumberland.*

Isabel (1386–1402)

English noblewoman. *Name variations: Isabel Plantagenet. Born on March 12, 1386; died around April 1402; daughter of Thomas Woodstock, 1st duke of Gloucester, and *****Eleanor de Bohun*** *(1366–1399). Isabel was a nun at Aldgate.*

Isabel (d. around 1410).

See Stewart, Isabel.

Isabel (1409–1484)

Countess of Essex. *Name variations: Isabel Plantagenet. Born in 1409; died on October 2, 1484; interred at Little Easton Church, Essex; daughter of Richard of Conisbrough (c. 1375–1415), 2nd earl of Cambridge (r. 1414–1415), and *****Anne Mortimer*** *(1390–1411); aunt of Edward IV and Richard III, kings of England; married Sir Thomas Grey of Heton, after February 1413 (annulled 1426); married Henry Bourchier (c. 1404–1483), 1st/14th earl of Essex (r. 1461–1483), before April 25, 1426; children: (second marriage) William Bourchier, viscount Bourchier (d. 1483); Henry Bourchier; Humphrey Bourchier, Lord Cornwall; John Bourchier; Thomas Bourchier; Edward Bourchier; Fulke Bourchier; Isabel Bourchier (died young); Hugh Bourchier; Florence Bourchier (d. 1525).*

Isabel (d. 1457?)

Countess of Lennox and duchess of Albany. *Died around 1457; daughter of Duncan, 8th earl of Lennox; married Murdoch Stewart, 2nd duke of Albany, on February 17, 1392; children: Robert Stewart, master of Fife (d. 1421); Walter Stewart of Lennox (d. 1425); Alexander (d. 1425); James (d. 1451); Isabel (who married Walter Buchanan).*

Isabel (1772–1827)

Countess of Sayn-Hachenburg. *Born on April 19, 1772; died on January 6, 1827; married Frederick William, prince of Nassau-Weilburg; children: four, including William, duke of Nassau (1792–1839).*

Isabel, Princess (1846–1921).

See Isabel of Brazil.

Isabel, Princess (1851–1931).

See Isabella II for sidebar on Maria Isabel Francisca.

Isabel, Queen of Portugal (1432–1455).

See Isabel la Paloma.

Isabel, Saint (1207–1231).

See Elizabeth of Hungary.

Isabel, the infanta.

See Isabella II for sidebar on María Isabel Francisca.

Isabel I (1451–1504).

See Isabella I.

Isabel II (1830–1904).

See Isabella II.

Isabel Beaumont (d. 1368).

See Beaumont, Isabel.

Isabel Bruce (c. 1278–1358).

See Bruce, Isabel.

Isabel de Braose (d. 1248?).

See Braose, Isabel de.

Isabel de Clare (c. 1174–1220).

See Clare, Isabel de.

Isabel de Clermont (d. 1465)

Queen of Naples. *Died in 1465; daughter of* **Caterina Orsini** *and Tristan, count of Capertino; became first wife of Ferdinand or Ferrante I (1423–1494), king of Naples (r. 1458–1494), in 1444; children: Alfonso or Alphonso II (1448–1495), king of Naples (r. 1494, abdicated in 1495); *****Leonora of Aragon*** *(1450–1493); Frederick IV (1452–1504), king of Naples (r. 1496–1501, deposed); Giovanni of Naples (1456–1485), cardinal of Tarento; Francesco (1461–1486), duke of Sant'Angelo; *****Beatrice of Naples*** *(1457–1508).*

Isabel de Farnese.

See Farnese, Elizabeth.

Isabel de Gatinais.

See Matilda of Anjou.

Isabel de Limoges (1283–1328)

Duchess of Brittany. *Name variations: Isabel of Limoges. Born in 1283 in Toro; died on July 24, 1328; daughter of Sancho IV, king of Castile and Leon (r. 1284–1296), and* ****Maria de Molina*** *(d. 1321); married Jaime also known as James II the Just, king of Aragon and Sicily, on December 1, 1291 (annulled in 1295); married John III (1276–1341), duke of Brittany (r. 1312–1341), in 1310.*

Isabel de Warrenne (d. before 1147).

See Isabel of Vermandois.

Isabel de Warrenne (c. 1137–1203)

Countess of Surrey. *Name variations: Isabel de Warenne. Born around 1137; died around July 12 or 13, 1203 (some sources cite 1199); buried at Chapter House, Lewes, East Sussex, England; only daughter and heiress of William de Warrenne (1119–1148), 3rd earl of Warrenne and Surrey (r. 1138–1148), and* ****Adela Talvace*** *(d. 1174); married William of Boulogne also known as William de Blois, 4th earl of Warrenne and Surrey (2nd son of King Stephen), in 1148 (died 1159); married Hamelin de Warrenne (c. 1129–1202, illegitimate son of Geoffrey of Anjou), 5th earl of Surrey, in April 1164; children: (second marriage) William de Warrenne (d. 1240), 6th earl of Warrenne and Surrey (r. 1202–1240);* ***Ela Plantagenet*** *(who married Robert Newburn and William FitzWilliam of Sprotborough);* ****Ida Plantagenet*** *(who married Roger Bigod, 2nd earl of Norfolk);* ***Maud Plantagenet*** *(d. around 1212, who married Henry Hastings, Lord Hastings, count of Eu, and Henry d'Estouteville, Lord of Valmont and Rames);* ***Mary de Warrenne*** *(d. after 1208); another daughter (name unknown) associated with John I Lackland, king of England, and gave birth to Richard of Dover, baron of Chilham.*

Isabel de Warrenne (b. 1253)

Queen of Scots. *Name variations: Isabel Balliol; Isabel of Warenne; Isabel de Warren. Born in 1253; death date unknown; daughter of John de Warrenne or Warenne (c. 1231–1304), 7th earl of Warrenne and Surrey, and* ****Alice le Brun*** *(d. 1255); married John Balliol (1249–1315), king of the Scots (r. 1292–1296), before February 7, 1280; children: Edward Balliol (c. 1283–1364), briefly king of Scots (r. 1332–1338); Henry Balliol (d. 1332);* ***Margaret Balliol.***

Isabel de Warrenne (d. 1282)

Countess of Arundel. *Name variations: Isabel de Warren; Isabel of Warenne. Died in 1282; daughter of Maud Marshall (d. 1248) and William de Warrenne, 6th earl of Warrenne and Surrey (r. 1202–1240); married Hugh de Albini, earl of Arundel.*

A patron of the arts, Isabel de Warrenne was the daughter of ***Maud Marshall** and William de Warrenne, 6th earl of Warrenne and Surrey. Matthew Paris dedicated and translated his *La Vie de Saint Edmond, Archeveque de Cantorbery* (*The Life of St. Edmund*) for her. As well, Ralph Bocking dedicated his *Life and Miracles of Richard of Chichester* to her.

Isabel Farnese.

See Farnese, Elizabeth.

Isabel Francisca, Princess (1851–1931).

See Isabella II for sidebar on Maria Isabel Francisca.

Isabel la Paloma (1432–1455)

Queen of Portugal. *Born in 1432; died on December 2, 1455, at Evora; interred at Batalla; daughter of Pedro or Peter of Coimbra, regent of Portugal, and* ****Isabel of Aragon*** *(1409–1443); married Afonso or Alphonso V, king of Portugal (r. 1438–1481), on May 6, 1448; sister of Pedro the Constable also known as Peter the Constable (1429–1466); children: Joao (1451–1455);* ****Joanna*** *(1452–1490), regent of Portugal; Juan also known as John II (1455–1495), king of Portugal (r. 1481–1495).*

Isabel la Paloma, queen of Portugal, who was married to Alphonso V, had strong interests in religion, history and literature. In 1445, she commissioned translations of Ludolph von Sachen's *Vita Christi* and ***Christine de Pizan**'s 1405 *Livre de Trois Vertues* (*The Book of the Three Virtues*). Two years after Isabel's death in 1455, her brother Peter the Constable wrote *Tragédia de la Insigne Reyna Dona Isabel,* a biography of her life. Alphonso's second wife was ***Juana la Beltraneja.**

Isabel Maria (1801–1876).

See Carlota Joaquina for sidebar.

Isabel Neville (1451–1476).

See Neville, Isabel.

Isabel of Angoulême (1186–1246).

See Isabella of Angoulême.

Isabel of Aragon (1271–1336).

See Elizabeth of Portugal.

Isabel of Aragon (1409–1443)

Duchess of Coimbra. *Name variations: Isabel de Aragon; Isabel de Aragón. Born in 1409; died in 1443; daughter of Jaime, count of Urgel; married Pedro or Peter (b. 1392), duke of Coimbra (r. 1439–1549), regent of Portugal, on September 13, 1428; children: Pedro or Peter the Constable (b. 1429) who tried to seize the Aragonese throne in the right of his mother in 1465; John of Coimbra (b. 1431);* ****Isabella la Paloma*** *(1432–1455); Jaime or Jaimes, cardinal of Lisbon (b. 1434); Beatriz (1435–1462, who married Adolf of Cleves); Filippa (1437–1497).*

Isabel of Bar (1410–1453).

See Isabelle of Lorraine.

Isabel of Braganza (1846–1921).

See Isabel of Brazil.

Isabel of Brazil (1846–1921)

Heiress to the throne of Brazil and regent of the empire, who abolished slavery in Brazil. *Name variations: Isabel of Braganza and Orleans (Isabel de Bragança e Orléans); Isabella of Brazil; Princess Royal; Princess Isabel; Condessa or Countess d'Eu; The Redeemer. Born Isabel Cristina Leopoldina Augusta de Bragança on July 29, 1846, in Rio de Janeiro, Brazil; died on November 14, 1921, in the Castle d'Eu, northern France; daughter of Pedro II of Braganza, emperor of Brazil, and Empress Teresa Cristina of Bourbon (1822–1889); married Gastao de Orléans also known as Gaston of Orleans, Conde or Count d'Eu, in Rio de Janeiro, on October 15, 1864; children: Pedro de Alcantara, prince of Grao Pará (b. October 15, 1875); Luis (b. January 26, 1878); Antonio (b. August 9, 1881).*

Regent of the Brazilian Empire (1871–72, 1876–77, and 1887–88); major acts as regent: signed the Free Womb Law (September 28, 1871); signed the Lei Aurea abolishing slavery in Brazil (May 13, 1888).

The role of women in Latin American history as holders of political power and influence has scarcely been explored given the social, cultural, and political constraints placed upon them by Latin American society. The sole exception is Princess Isabel of Brazil. Even this exception, however, continues to be overlooked and her full contribution relegated to the footnotes of history, while her male advisers have received full recognition for the most momentous piece of legislation ever to be implemented in Brazil, the abolition of slavery, for which she was responsible.

> Slavery itself, being an attack against human freedom, is repugnant to me.
>
> —Isabel of Brazil

Princess Isabel, as regent of Brazil, was the only woman to have served as chief of state in Latin America in the 19th century, and to have held immense political power. Her high position did not shield her from the most common stereotypes ascribed to women of her era: feeble mindedness, inherent inability to handle political affairs, easily impressionable, in need of being protected and shielded. Educated to rule the Brazilian Empire, she was barely tolerated by the politicians of the period who could not accept a woman at the helm of the state. A devout Catholic, she was suspected of being influenced by her religion, perhaps by the pope, on the affairs of state. Married to a French prince, it was feared she would govern under the influence of a foreigner. When leading decisively, she was seen as willful. Yet, by all accounts, when she governed Brazil in the absence of her father, she displayed an uncommon ability to govern and learned the role of a ruler without allowing herself to be dominated by politicians. As the heiress to the throne of a country with slavery, she became a quiet abolitionist, and when the moment of decision arrived, she used her position to abolish the institution.

Born in 1846, the second child of Emperor Pedro II and Empress **Teresa Cristina**, Isabel was not in line to ascend to the throne. The heir was Prince Royal Afonso, born in 1845. In the House of Braganza, however, the first-born male rarely survived to assume the throne, and the Brazilian branch was no different. In 1847, Afonso died, and Isabel, 11 months old, became temporarily the heir apparent. In 1848, a second brother, Pedro, was born, but death struck again when the prince died in 1850. Again, Isabel became the heiress to the throne, and in 1850, at age four, she was proclaimed by the General Assembly heir to the throne of Brazil in accordance with the constitution. But gender became an issue. The death of the second male heir was seen as a calamity for the empire. Many consid-

See sidebar on the following page

Teresa Cristina of Bourbon (1822–1889)

Empress of Brazil. *Name variations: Theresa; Thereza Christina of Naples; Teresa Christina Maria; Theresa of Sicily. Born Teresa Cristina Maria on March 14, 1822; died on December 28, 1889, soon after arriving in Portugal, having been exiled from Brazil; daughter of Francis I, king of Naples and Sicily (r. 1825–1830), and* ****Marie Isabella of Spain*** *(1789–1848); sister of* ****Maria Cristina I of Naples*** *(1806–1878), queen of Spain; married Pedro II of Braganza (1825–1891), emperor of Brazil (r. 1831–1889), on September 4, 1843; children: Afonso (1845–1847);* ****Isabel of Brazil*** *(1846–1921);* ***Leopoldine*** *(1847–1871, who married August, prince of Saxe-Coburg-Gotha); Pedro also known as Peter Alfons (1848–1850).*

ered the monarchical system weakened for lacking a male heir, and from the beginning Isabel was not seen with the same favor usually bestowed upon a male heir.

Her education, nevertheless, was planned and directed by Pedro II as if she were male, although combined with disciplines appropriate for females. According to historian Lourenço Luiz Lacombe, in a rigorous schedule under the best tutors available in Brazil, she studied languages—Portuguese, English, German, Italian, French, Greek and Latin—and history, rhetoric, geography, philosophy, political economy, chemistry, mathematics, physics, astronomy, geology, mineralogy, botany, mythology, and history of religions, among other subjects, in addition to the regular curriculum offered to females, of music, dance, drawing, stitching and flower-making, photography, a variety of readings on poetry, pious works and the Bible, and instructive pieces. Examinations were taken in the presence of her parents, tutors, and others. Thus, her education was superior to that given to males and far above that given to females. To supervise her education, Pedro II searched for two years for the ideal governess, finally found in the **Countess de Barral**, a Brazilian living in France, at the court of Louis Philippe I.

Isabel's childhood progressed uneventfully and within a rigid schedule prepared by her father, who prescribed every minute of her day. Social engagements and visits were allowed only on Sundays, holidays, and family birthdays, vacations only once a year. To alleviate such a heavy study schedule, at times she performed in juvenile plays staged in the imperial palace with a few of her childhood friends, and played with dolls, but not much time was left for children's play. According to Lacombe, from this developed one of the features of her adult life: that of maintaining a rigid schedule. At age 14, while her parents were on an official visit to the northern provinces of Brazil, Isabel officially received her first royal guest, archduke Maximilian, the future emperor of Mexico.

As she approached marriageable age, the search for a suitable husband became a matter of state and occupied the attention of Pedro II. The requirements for the ideal candidate were many. He had to be Catholic, since the official religion of Brazil was Catholicism; he had to accept residence in Brazil, then a distant and mostly unknown country far from the glitter of European courts; and he had to have his children born in Brazil. Above all, he had to be willing to accept the position of prince consort, that of a life more in the shadows than in the limelight. Pedro II, himself having been forced to marry without first meeting his bride, added one more requirement, that the future couple should first meet to assure a mutually agreeable marriage. Considerations of a political order had to be heeded also. Political and nationalistic sensitivities eliminated Portuguese princes as candidates. Having been a Portuguese colony, Brazilians feared the possibility that dynastic succession might eventually reunite the two crowns. Religion and the constitution eliminated Protestant candidates. Latent Brazilian xenophobia would certainly be exacerbated by the fear that the future empress of Brazil could fall under the influence of a foreign prince. Eventually, an acceptable candidate was found. On October 15, 1864, Isabel married Gaston d'Orléans, Count d'Eu, son of Louis, duke of Nemours, and ***Victoria of Saxe-Coburg**, grandson of King Louis Philippe I of France. The marriage produced a happy and long-lasting union, but some of the worries raised during the search for an acceptable groom were never fully put to rest, resurfacing periodically, some right after the marriage. Eventually, the Count d'Eu himself became one of the issues in the succession of the Brazilian throne.

In 1865, the couple returned from an extensive honeymoon in Europe to find Brazil immersed in the War of the Triple Alliance against Paraguay. The Count d'Eu, young and in search of military glory, with a previous military career in the Spanish army in Morocco, insisted on leaving for the front. His request caused consternation for many. Isabel, who did not want to run the risk of losing her husband, continuously appealed to her father not to send him to the front. But Pedro II refused to allow his son-in-law to go to war for reasons other than Isabel's pleas.

The newly married couple had not yet assured the succession of the Braganza dynasty in Brazil, and the honorary title of marshal of the Brazilian Army given to the Count d'Eu on the occasion of his marriage to Isabel was a major obstacle should he be allowed to go to the front. It would disrupt the military command structure by placing him above the Brazilian generals conducting the war and placing the Brazilian army in the undesirable position of being led by a foreigner. The count's ensuing behavior, insisting on going to war, constantly petitioning Pedro II, ministers, and generals, perhaps not fully appreciating the delicacy of the situation and of the harm that could be done to Isabel, led the Council of State, the advisory Council of the Monarchy, to examine his request and reject it. The episode laid the groundwork for suspicions that should Isabel assume the Crown, the Count d'Eu would become the power behind the throne. Finally, in 1869, with the war coming to a close and the Brazilian army in Assuncion, the capital of Paraguay, the Count d'Eu assumed the command of the Brazilian forces, whereupon he abolished slavery in Paraguay, an act applauded by Liberals and abolitionists but considered a political error by many in Brazil. Indirectly, it was an implied criticism of slavery in Brazil, a political statement coming from the husband of the heiress of the Brazilian Empire, precisely what a prince consort should avoid. For Conservatives, his act reflected adversely on Isabel, linking her and her husband to abolitionism at a time when the thought of abolishing slavery was seldom uttered.

Isabel assumed the regency for the first time on May 20, 1871, when Pedro II departed for Europe immediately after the end of the War of the Triple Alliance. Her accession to the regency caused much debate and opposition, in part due to her gender, in part due to the unpopularity of her husband, some politicians even suggesting legislation to deny the regency to princesses married to foreigners. Finally, after the Council of State ruled that the constitution assured her accession, she assumed the office in a ceremony that excluded her husband. As regent, Isabel was in constant communication with her father, punctiliously keeping him informed of all affairs of state and asking for suggestions. The first regency was her apprenticeship in government. It coincided with the tenure of the most successful cabinets of the Brazilian Empire, that led by the Visconde de Rio Branco, one of the most talented politicians of the Second Reign, who also served as her mentor. As regent, she presided over the meetings of the Cabinet and of the Council of State where all the matters of state were examined and discussed. As regent, she also signed the Law of Free Womb of 1871, that decreed free all children born of slave mothers. Although the legislation had been developed and introduced to the Parliament under the auspices of her father before she assumed the regency, it fell to her to sign into law the first piece of legislation in the gradual abolition of slavery in Brazil. She returned the reins of government to her father on March 30, 1872, at which time even her critics recognized that she had governed with "justice, prudence, dignity." Twice again, she would be called to be at the head of the government.

As she was being introduced to the art of high government, a campaign began to develop against her, one that resurfaced each time she assumed the regency and that reached its peak in 1888. Among the major complaints was her Catholic faith. In a country where the Church was not present at the high councils of government, and where a crisis had developed over Church and State prerogatives in 1873, she was sought after by Catholics to intercede with her father in favor of the Church. As a result, she began to be labeled as a religious fanatic. Another complaint was Jacobinism, centered on the fact that her husband was a foreigner. Her assertive personality and expansiveness, which some described as willfulness, also caused discomfort among politicians, many of whom, used to the reserved demeanor of Pedro II, were unable to accept orders and judgments from a woman in the highest office. She placed morals and values above compromise, a trait that, in her position of heiress to the throne in a society where women were expected to be subservient, won her the reputation of being headstrong.

Her second regency, from March 26, 1876, to September 26, 1877, passed without major event. With her constitutional right to assume the regency well established, her accession was automatic. As regent, Isabel was far more self-confident, having been left practically on her own by her father, who, during his second trip abroad, communicated neither with Princess Isabel nor with the ministers, which led the ministers to have to work with her, and her to have to make all of the decisions in the government.

Between regencies, Isabel and the Count d'Eu led an active social life of receptions, balls, concerts and feasts. It was at her residence in Rio de Janeiro, not in the imperial palace of Pedro II and Empress Teresa Cristina, known for its austerity and somber atmosphere, that the social life of the Braganza Court took place. A talented musician, Isabel entertained nobility, politicians, diplomats, and commoners in a swirl of gaiety that often times included her parents. A practicing painter, she exhibited three of her works. Above all, she was dedicated to the academic and religious education of her three sons. Throughout her life, Isabel had almost a dislike for the exercise of power, a characteristic that she shared with her father. She would much rather be with her family on long visits to Europe, educating her children, or leading the social life of the Brazilian court. The strong presence of her father, the peace and order of the empire due to his long reign (1840–89) that provided Brazil with an uninterrupted period of stability, might have contributed to her attitude. Or, perhaps, she internalized the attitude of her father, who always displayed a certain degree of detachment from power to the point of being almost fatalistic. But her attitude was not due to the lack of resolve, as her third regency demonstrates.

By 1887, the atmosphere in Brazil had changed. The country was in ferment. The issues of abolitionism and direct elections dominated the political debate, and Pedro II's delicate health required a visit to Europe for medical treatment. Princess Isabel, on a European trip with her husband, was recalled home to assume the regency at a time when the question of abolishing slavery was being pushed by Liberals and abolitionists without the opposition of the northern provinces of Brazil, now with few slaves. Upon touching Brazilian soil, Isabel was enjoined to end slavery. On July 30, 1887, she assumed the regency for the third time. From the beginning, her attitude was different from the previous two regencies. She started by moving into the imperial palace and by setting a heavy schedule for herself.

As the crescendo for abolition increased and the Church joined in the calls for emancipation, Isabel felt that the government should make at least a gesture toward abolition, but the Conservative Cabinet led by the Barao de Cotegipe and installed under Pedro II, resisted taking any step. As she later recounted the events leading to abolition, after a delay Isabel let it be known to the prime minister that the Cabinet could not continue unless it acted on the issue of slavery. As the agitation for immediate abolition increased and the army sent her a memorandum asking to be excused from apprehending fugitive slaves, Isabel decided to ask for the Cabinet's resignation, for in her view it no longer served the interests of the nation. To the contrary, its lack of action was pulling the country into chaos. She perceived clearly that, unless the Crown acted to abolish slavery, slavery would be abolished by other means. The issue was no longer one of political parties or cabinets. Using as a pretext a blunder by the chief of police of Rio de Janeiro, she forced the resignation of the Cotegipe Cabinet, and, going one step further, broke with tradition by naming her choice for the next prime minister, instead of accepting the suggestion of the departing prime minister. Her choice was Joao Alfredo, a well-known abolitionist politician.

Her actions took both Liberals and Conservatives by surprise. By most, used to the long tradition established by Pedro II of alternating political parties in the government, of accepting from the departing prime minister a nomination for the next head of Cabinet, and of impartiality on issues, her actions were construed as an unacceptable exercise of personal power and willfulness in a constitutional government. On the other hand, the entrenched self-interests of slavery were failing to recognize that this time the mood of the country on slavery had changed. Isabel perceived this mood, that the atmosphere of suspense and unrest leading to a clamor for the immediate abolition of slavery could not be contained much longer without serious consequences for the political system. If the Crown did not take the initiative, perhaps a revolution would occur. Since the Crown was still the only national institution to command the necessary prestige and power to act on such a momentous issue, Isabel made the decision of selecting as prime minister a politician willing to form a cabinet for the specific purpose of introducing to the General Assembly legislation to abolish slavery.

By her own account, she had no idea of how precisely the event should occur, preferring to leave the decision to the discretion of her prime minister. One of the proposals circulating was emancipation with a two-year requirement concerning the place of residence of freed slaves, but Prime Minister Joao Alfredo was for immediate abolition, with no qualifications. She learned, from a member of the Cabinet, the precise contents of the project of law to abolish slavery during the inaugural ceremonies of a railway. The project contained two articles, one declaring slavery abolished, the second revoking all laws regarding slavery. On May 10, 1888, the legislation, known as the Lei Aurea, was approved in the Chamber of Deputies, on May 13, in the Senate. Isabel signed it into law on the same day, thus bringing to an end an institution that had survived in Brazil for nearly 300 years. The law provided for no compensation for slave owners.

After signing the Lei Aurea, Isabel's popularity soared. Now called "the Redeemer," she received special recognition from the Catholic Church when Pope Leo XIII sent a special envoy to Rio de Janeiro to present her with the *Rosa de Ouro,* a unique gift of a vase and roses made of gold. But clouds were gathering over the empire. After Pedro II's return from Europe in August 1888, it became clear that he was no longer in condition to rule effectively as he had done for the past 48 years. The possibility of Isabel continuing as regent was discussed but rejected by Pedro II, who reassumed the government immediately. Isabel, however, was not totally removed from the affairs of state, as had been the case in her previous regencies. Given her father's health, she continued to assist him behind the scenes. As his health deteriorated and it became obvious that her reign would soon start, her enemies stepped up their campaign to prevent her from ascending the throne by reviving all the old charges: her Catholicism, abolitionism, and her marriage to a foreigner who not only never stopped being a French prince but also never fully spoke Portuguese without a French accent. Xenophobia against the Count d'Eu was combined with the inherent prejudices against her gender, that women were emotionally weak and impressionable and in need of protection and guidance, awakening fears of Isabel, as queen, being guided behind the scenes by a French prince. As historian Hermes Vieira stated, there were rumors that she was "not emotionally capable of assuming the throne." For others, the decisive manner in which she acted to abolish slavery was a foreboding of the woman about to occupy the throne, an authoritarian and assertive empress.

Yet in retrospect, many of these charges could not be further from the truth. Isabel needed no guidance from her husband in directing the affairs of state. The abolition of slavery was her idea after she correctly read the political and emotional condition of the country, a reality missed both by seasoned politicians, so addicted to the notion of gradual abolition that they still wanted to temporize and extend it for a while longer, and by obdurate Conservatives, bent on derailing any measure bringing slavery to an end. The charges against the Count d'Eu were equally malicious. Although he never lost his French accent, he eventually came to understand the political and social culture of Brazil and made a genuine effort to make contributions in his areas of expertise by being interested in the modernization of the armed forces. On the most important act of Isabel as ruler, the abolition of slavery, despite the well established suspicion that the Count d'Eu would be the power behind the throne, his advice to her was quite conservative. As reported by Hermes Vieira, when Isabel received the draft of the Lei Aurea, she read it to the Count d'Eu, who advised her not to sign, with the admonition: "It is the end of the Monarchy." But Isabel had made up her mind. In a letter penned to her sons in December 1888, Isabel explained the reasons why she decided to abolish slavery, among them, the level of agitation in the country in favor of abolition, the reality of the slaves running away and the impossibility of having the army bringing them back to their owners, the idea that abolition was humanitarian, moral, and supported by the Church, and the fact that the slave owners had had time to prepare themselves for this natural consequence since the law of Free Womb in 1871. With a clear conscience, she decided she could not "fail to act for fear of displeasing a few, or even many," that her obligation was to the motherland, and to clear the throne of this blight. All considered, the idea of abolition finally won her over. Compensation for the owners was never part of her plans. In her view, slave owners, who had refused to free their slaves, had already profited enough and should not be recompensed. Moreover, new taxes would be borne by those who had not profited from slavery. Her decision was political as well as moral.

In the aftermath of abolition, a military crisis led to the overthrow of the monarchy on November 15, 1889. Pedro II refused to take measures that might have averted the fall and, true to his lifelong detachment from power, accepted all the events as a *fait accompli.* Not so Isabel, who wanted action and measures and insisted that her father act until nearly the end. But, barred by precedent from overruling her father, she capitulated. Could events have been different had she continued as regent? Perhaps so. The monarchy still had prestige in Brazil, Isabel still had her supporters, and the military coup was organized by a small clique of Positivists in the army in an action that took most by surprise. The Republican government banished the Braganza family and confiscated all their property in Brazil after offering Pedro II a generous sum to settle in exile, an offer that was rejected by the deposed emperor, leaving the royal family living in exile in France in a state of near poverty. Isabel bore exile and privation with resignation. Only after the death of his father, the duke of Nemours, did the Count d'Eu inherit the castle d'Eu, where he and Isabel lived their last years and where she ended her days.

The Republican government lifted the banishment of the Braganza family in 1920 and allowed the repatriation of the remains of Pedro II and Empress Teresa Cristina. Isabel's delicate health prevented her from accompanying her parents' remains to Brazil, a role fulfilled by the Count d'Eu. Isabel died on November 14, 1921, in the Castle d'Eu. News of her passing was received in Brazil with gestures of respect and reverence and recollections of her role as regent and in abolishing slavery. In recognition, the Republican government ordered the three days of mourning due to a chief of state and repatriation of her remains in a Brazilian man-of-war. In 1971, the remains of Princess Isabel and of the Count d'Eu were finally repatriated to Brazil, receiving full honors in Rio de Janeiro from civil, military, diplomatic, and ecclesiastic authorities before being taken to the city of Petrópolis, where they were laid to rest by the side of the remains of Pedro II and Empress Teresa Cristina. On that occasion, the president of Brazil, having taken into consideration the role of Princess Isabel as regent and her role in ending slavery, granted her the honors of chief of state, and to the Count d'Eu, the honors of commander-in-chief of the Brazilian armed forces for his services in the War of the Triple Alliance, the lack of which had been the source of many of her sorrows. In death, Princess Isabel finally received the recognition that in life had been denied to her, partly as result of the prejudices against women. The same prejudices have prevented a full assessment of her role as a ruler, and of her role in abolishing slavery in Brazil, where she is portrayed as an onlooker rather than as a principal actor in the event.

SOURCES:

Lacombe, Lourenço Luiz. *Isabel, A Princesa Redentora.* Petrópolis: Instituto Histórico de Petrópolis, 1989.

Princess Isabel, Account of the Cotegipe Cabinet and the issue of abolition, December 1888, Doc. 9030, Maço 199, Arquivo do Museu Imperial, Petrópolis. "Notas da Princeza sobre os acontecimentos de Novembro de 1889," Arquivo Particular do Barao de Muritiba, AP 19, Caixa 3, Doc. 13, Arquivo do Museu Imperial, Petrópolis.

Vieira, Hermes. *Princesa Isabel, Uma Vida de Luzes e Sombras.* Sao Paulo: Ediçoes GRD, 1990.

SUGGESTED READING:

Calmon, Pedro. *A Princesa Isabel "A Redentora."* Sao Paulo: Nacional, 1941.

Isabelle, Comtesse de Paris. *Tout m'est Bonheur.* Paris: Roberto Laffont, 1978.

Valadao, Alfredo de Vilhena. *Campanha da Princesa.* Vol. 2. Rio de Janeiro: Leuzinger, 1940.

Lydia M. Garner,
Associate Professor of History,
Southwest Texas State University, San Marcos, Texas

Isabel of Buchan (fl. 1290–1310).

See Isabella of Buchan.

Isabel of Buchan (1296–1358).

See Isabella of France.

Isabel of Castile (1355–1392)

Duchess of York. *Name variations: Isabella. Born in Morales, Spain, in 1355; died on November 23, 1392; daughter of Pedro el Cruel also known as Peter I the Cruel, king of Castile and Leon (r. 1350–1369), and* ****Marie de Padilla*** *(1335–1365); sister of* ****Constance of Castile*** *(1354–1394); married Edmund of Langley (1341–1402), duke of York, in 1372; children: Edward, 2nd duke of York (1372–1415); Richard of York, also known as Richard of Conisbrough, 2nd earl of Cambridge (1376–1415, who married* ****Anne Mortimer****);* ****Constance*** *(c. 1374–1416).*

Isabel of Fife (c. 1332–1389)

Countess of Fife. *Name variations: Isabel Fife; Isabel Macduff; Elizabeth. Acceded as countess of Fife in 1359. Born before 1332; died after August 12, 1389; daughter of Duncan Fife (1285–1353), 10th earl of Fife (r. 1288–1353), and* ****Mary de Monthermer*** *(1298–after 1371); married William Ramsey of Colluthie; married Walter Stewart (d. 1363), after July 22, 1360; married Thomas Bisset of Upsetlington, in 1363; married John de Dunbar.*

Isabel of France (1545–1568).

See Elizabeth of Valois.

Isabel of Gloucester (c. 1167–1217).

See Isabella of Angoulême for sidebar on Avisa of Gloucester.

Isabel of Portugal (1397–1471).

See Isabella of Portugal.

Isabel of Portugal (1428–1496)

Queen-consort of John II of Castile and mother of Isabella I of Castile. *Name variations: Isabella. Born in 1428; died on August 15, 1496, in Arévalo; daughter of Isabella of Braganza (1402–1465) and John of Portugal, grand master of Santiago; became second wife of Juan also known as John II (1404–1454), king of Castile and Leon (r. 1406–1454), on July 22, 1447; children: Isabella I (1451–1504), queen of Castile; Alfonso also known as Alphonso (1453–1468).*

Birth of John II (1406); birth of Isabella I of Castile (1451); execution of Alvaro de Luna (1453);

death of John II and accession of Henry IV (1454); birth of Juana la Beltraneja (1462); death of Alphonso (1468); marriage of Isabella I and Ferdinand of Aragon (1469); death of Henry IV and accession of Isabella I (1474).

In 1428, *__Isabella of Braganza__, wife of Prince John of Portugal, gave birth to a daughter whom she named Isabel. Little is known of Isabel of Portugal's childhood. Her youth coincided with the consolidation of the Portuguese monarchy as the nation began its maritime expansion leading to Portugal's golden age. Meanwhile, widowed John II of Castile began searching for a second wife (his first was *__Maria of Aragon__ [1403–1445]), and his chief minister and constable of Castile, Don Alvaro de Luna, arranged his wedding to Isabel. Luna saw it as a political match, giving Castile a Portuguese counterweight to Aragonese aggression. Isabel and John married on July 22, 1447, in Madrigal de las Altas Torres.

To Luna's consternation, however, Isabel of Portugal quickly became a rival to his power rather than a pawn through which he could continue to control John II. Don Alvaro had provided, in the words of chronicler Mosén Diego de Valera, "the knife that cut off his own head." Luna had been invaluable to John II, helping him dominate the rebellious Castilian aristocracy. But he also tried to dictate the royal couple's domestic arrangements, and the old king found Isabel entrancing. In 1451, she delivered a baby girl, whom the monarchs named Isabella (*__Isabella I__). The birth, however, provoked a prolonged depression in the young mother. Two years later, grown ever more resentful of Luna, the queen persuaded her husband to strip the minister of his power and send him to the scaffold. According to historian **Peggy K. Liss**, "His enemies hailed the Queen as a heroine—another Judith, another Esther, and worthy of comparison to Holy Mary." Luna's death and Isabel's increased popularity strengthened her hand, although it deprived the Castilian monarchy of a powerful albeit self-interested defender. John's reward from Isabel was Alphonso, born on December 17. The king died seven months later, on July 22, 1454.

Henry IV, her stepson by John's first wife Maria of Aragon, began his ill-starred reign. As a dowager in her 20s, Isabel needed to protect the interests of her children, yet protocol insisted that she leave the court. With her son and daughter, Isabel took up residence at Arévalo, west of Segovia, where Henry often held court. Not too long after her arrival there, Henry and one of his courtiers, Pedro de Girón, visited Isabel of Portugal. Girón apparently made some lascivious comments to the widow, which allegedly offended her piety and heightened her depression. Henry and Girón were probably trying to find a way to control Alphonso and Isabel through their mother so they would not become rallying points for factions opposed to Henry's rule. Yet Isabel "closed herself into a dark room, self-condemned to silence, and dominated by such depression that it degenerated into a form of madness," notes Liss. Certainly having to deal with her mother's isolation and mental illness must have helped form the personality of her daughter, Isabella I of Castile.

> Isabel proved to be a strong-minded woman who developed an intense dislike for the constable and soon became one of his most implacable enemies.
>
> —Joseph F. O'Callaghan, ***A History of Medieval Spain***

Meanwhile, dissident nobles soon looked upon the boy Alphonso as a rival to Henry, whose reign became one of the most controversial in Spanish history. Although Henry's first wife *__Blanche of Navarre__ (1424–1464) had no children, allegedly because he was impotent, his second *__Joanna of Portugal__ (1439–1475) became pregnant and gave birth to a daughter in 1462. Alphonso's supporters claimed that a noble at court, Beltrán de la Cueva, had fathered the baby Juana, who became known as *la Beltraneja* (*__Juana la Beltraneja__). Alphonso's partisans nearly deposed Henry IV when the boy Alphonso suddenly died in 1468.

Isabel of Portugal's prolonged insanity made her irrelevant to the unfolding political struggle. Henry's death in 1474 brought her daughter Isabella I to the Castilian throne. Isabella I had already married Ferdinand of Aragon five years earlier, and together they ushered the Spanish kingdoms onto the world stage. Isabel of Portugal lingered in madness at Arévalo until her death in 1496. Her remains were eventually interred in the Carthusian convent of Miraflores at Burgos. Isabella I's own daughter, *__Juana la Loca__ (Juana the Mad), probably inherited a genetic predisposition to mental illness from her grandmother.

SOURCES:

Crónica de don Alvaro de Luna. Madrid: Espasa-Calpe, 1940.

Jaén, Didier Tisdel. *John II of Castile and the Grand Master Alvaro de Luna: a Biography Compiled from the Chronicles of the Reign of King John II of Castile (1405–1454).* Madrid: Castalia, 1978.

Liss, Peggy K. *Isabel the Queen: Life and Times.* NY: Oxford University Press, 1992.

Miller, Townsend. *Henry IV of Castile, 1425–1474.* Philadelphia: Lippincott, 1972.

Valera, Mosén Diego de. *Memorial de diversas hazañas; chrónica de Enrique IV, ordenada por mos en Diego de Valera.* Madrid: Espasa-Calpe, 1941.

Kendall Brown,
Professor of History, Brigham Young University, Provo, Utah

Isabel of Spain (1501–1526).

See Willums, Sigbrit for sidebar on Elisabeth of Habsburg.

Isabel of Urgel (fl. 1065)

Queen of Aragon. *Flourished around 1065; daughter of Armengol III, count of Urgel; married Sancho Ramirez, king of Aragon (1063–1094) and Navarre (1076–1094), around 1065 (divorced in 1071); children: Peter I (1069–1104), king of Aragon and Navarre (r. 1094–1104); possibly Alphonso I (1073–1134), king of Aragon and Navarre (r. 1104–1134); possibly Ramiro II (c. 1075–1157), king of Aragon (r. 1134–1157).*

Isabel of Vermandois (d. before 1147)

Countess of Warrenne and Surrey. *Name variations: Elizabeth of Vermandois; Elizabeth de Crepi or de Crépi; Isabel de Warenne; Isabel de Warrenne. Died before July 1147; daughter of Hugh the Great (b. 1057), count of Vermandois, and* ***Adelaide of Vermandois*** *(d. 1123); married Robert of Meulan, 1st earl of Leicester; married William de Warrenne, 2nd earl of Warrenne and Surrey (r. 1088–1138); children: (first marriage) Waleran of Meulan (b. 1104), earl of Worcester;* ***Isabel Beaumont*** *(c. 1104-d. after 1172); Robert Beaumont, 2nd earl of Leicester; (second marriage) William de Warrenne (1119–1148), 3rd earl of Warrenne and Surrey (r. 1138–1148), a crusader who died in the Holy Land; *****Adelicia de Warrenne*** *(d. 1178);* ***Gundred de Warrenne*** *(d. after 1166, who married Robert de Newburgh, 2nd earl of Warwick, and William de Lancaster, Lord of Kendal); Ralph de Warrenne; Rainald de Warrenne.*

Isabel Plantagenet (c. 1317–c. 1347)

English noblewoman. *Born around 1317; died around 1347; daughter of Henry, earl of Lancaster (r. 1281–1345) and Maud Chaworth (1282–c. 1322).*

Isabel Plantagenet was born around 1317, the daughter of Henry, earl of Lancaster, and ***Maud Chaworth.** Isabel entered a convent in 1337, eventually becoming the abbess of Amesbury.

Isabel Stewart (d. 1494).

See Beaufort, Joan (c. 1410–1445) for sidebar.

Isabella.

Spanish for Elizabeth.

Isabella.

Variant of Isabel.

Isabella (b. 1180)

Noblewoman and poet of France. *Born in 1180 in southern France.*

Isabella was a noblewoman who wrote troubadour poetry during the height of the troubadour period. Unfortunately, almost nothing is known about her. She was born in 1180, possibly in one of the Christian kingdoms in the East. Isabella probably met the troubadour and smith Elias Cairel, with whom she composed tensons, in Italy around 1220. Only one of Isabella's poems has survived, a tenson with Elias, in which the two discuss the love they once had, and analyze what went wrong with their affair; Isabella's voice in this poem is forthright and blunt, telling Elias that he was at fault because he was false and that she now has no use for him.

Laura York,
Riverside, California

Isabella (1206–1251)

Lady Annandale. *Name variations: Isabel or Isobel; Isabel Dunkeld; Isobella le Scot. Born in 1206; died in 1251; interred at Saltre Abbey, Stilton, Gloucester; daughter of *****Maude of Chester*** *(1171–1233) and David Dunkeld, 1st earl of Huntingdon; sister of *****Margaret****, countess of Huntingdon (d. 1228) and *****Ada Dunkeld****; married Robert Bruce (d. 1245), 5th Lord of Annandale, 1209; children: Robert Bruce of Annandale, known as The Competitor (1210–1295);* ***Beatrice Bruce*** *(d. 1276, who married Hugo Neville).*

Isabella (fl. 1219–1269).

See Zabel.

Isabella (d. 1282)

Queen of Beirut. *Died in 1282; eldest daughter of John II of Beirut (d. 1264) and* ***Alice de la Roche*** *of Athens; married Hugh II (d. 1267), child-king of*

Cyprus (r. 1253–1267); married Hamo L'Étranger (Edmund the Foreigner) of England (soon died); married Nicholas L'Aleman; married William Barlais.

As queen of Beirut, Isabella reigned from 1264 to 1282. Her first husband died before the marriage could be consummated; her second husband died soon after the wedding; he had arranged, however, that she be under the protection of Sultan Baibar.

Isabella (1332–1382).

See Philippa of Hainault for sidebar.

Isabella (r. 1398–1412)

Countess of Foix. *Name variations: Isabel or Isabella of Foix. Reigned from 1398 to 1412; daughter of Gaston III Phebus, count of Foix (r. 1343–1391); sister of Matthieu de Castelbon, count of Foix (1391–1398); married Archambaud de Graille; children: at least one son, Jean de Graille, count of Foix.*

Isabella, countess of Foix, was the daughter of Gaston III Phebus, count of Foix. Following the death of her brother Matthieu de Castelbon in 1398, Isabella ruled Foix for the next 14 years, until her own death in 1412.

Isabella, Queen of Spain (1602–1644).

See Elizabeth Valois.

Isabella, Saint (1225–1270).

See Isabelle.

Isabella I (1451–1504)

Queen of Castile, sponsor of Christopher Columbus' voyages of discovery, who is credited, along with her husband King Ferdinand II of Aragon, with the creation of modern unified Spain. *Name variations: Isabel I; Isabella of Spain,; Isabella I of Castile; Isabella the Catholic or Isabel la Católica. Born on April 22, 1451, at Madrigal de las Altas Torres, Spain; died on November 26, 1504, at Medina del Campo, Spain; daughter of Juan also known as John II (1405–1454), king of Castile (r. 1406–1454), and his second wife Isabel of Portugal (1428–1496); married Fernando also known as Ferdinand II, king of Aragon (r. 1479–1516), on October 19, 1469, at Valladolid; children: Isabella of Asturias (1471–1498); Juana la Loca (1479–1555); Maria of Castile (1482–1517); Catherine of Aragon (1485–1536); Juan or John (1478–1497, who married* ****Margaret of Austria*** *[1480–1530]).*

Recognized as heir to throne of Castile (1468); proclaimed queen (1474); established Spanish Inquisition (1480); conquered Granada, expelled Jews, and sponsored Columbus' first voyage (1492).

Born April 22, 1451, at Madrigal de las Altas Torres, near Avila, Isabella was the daughter of King John II of Castile and his second wife, ***Isabel of Portugal**. At her birth, Isabella was second in line for the throne, behind her much older half-brother Henry, a son of John's by his earlier marriage to ***Maria of Aragon** (1403–1445). The birth in 1453 of another male child, Alphonso, moved her a step further away, so it was not expected that she would ever be queen in her own right. When John died in 1454, the older son succeeded him as Henry IV (Enrique IV), and the widowed queen withdrew from court to Arévalo, where she took up residence with her two small children. Stories from the time cast doubt on Isabel of Portugal's emotional stability, but it appears that the royal children enjoyed a comfortable, secure childhood, largely isolated from the pressures of court life. Princess Isabella received little formal education. By all accounts, her schooling was limited to needlework and other domestic skills considered appropriate for high-born women destined only to serve as pawns in dynastic alliances. Intelligent, curious, and an enthusiastic reader, Isabella lamented the gaps in her learning and studied hard to remedy them in later years.

Under Henry IV, Castile experienced almost constant political turmoil. The king himself was known as Henry el Impotente (the Impotent), less because of his ineffectiveness as a ruler than because of his failure to father an heir. Considerable doubt remains regarding Henry's sexual preference, as well as emotional and physiological problems he is said to have had. What appears certain is that his relationships with women were dysfunctional. In 1453, shortly after dissolving his childless marriage to ***Blanche of Navarre**, Henry wed ***Joanna of Portugal**, but for several years this union also remained without issue. Public estimation of Henry's manhood was not high, and it did not help that Queen Joanna was known to have lovers on the side. When in 1461 a daughter was finally born to the royal couple, it was widely repeated that the child's real father was Joanna's favorite, Beltrán de la Cueva. Henry at first claimed the new *infanta*, or princess, whose name was Juana, as his own, but she soon came to be known as ***Juana la Beltraneja**, a mocking reference to her supposed paternity. Doubts about the princess' legitimacy threatened to lead to a disputed succession, the most frightening kind of political crisis in a monarchical system.

During the ensuing decade, civil warfare plagued Castile. Powerful nobles who opposed Henry IV coalesced around his father's two other surviving children, Alphonso and Isabella. In 1465 at Avila, a group of rebels renounced their allegiance to Henry and proclaimed Alphonso as king, although he was only 11 years old. Three years later, the youthful pretender died and his supporters turned to Isabella, but the princess declined to cooperate. Instead, she remained loyal to Henry, demanding as the price of her adherence that he publicly acknowledge her as his legitimate heir. This requirement compelled the king to repudiate the *infanta* Juana la Beltraneja, which he obligingly did in 1468 at Toros de Guisando.

Nature has made no other woman like her.

—Pietro Martire d'Anghiera

Isabella herself was only 17, but her conduct suggests a political maturity, coupled with a shrewdness in judging men and circumstances. Legitimate or not, an unmarried woman by herself would find it difficult to bring Castile's factions under control and rule effectively. Already determined to restore public order and honest government, Isabella recognized her need for a strong husband who could command troops in the field and father children to ensure the succession. Isabella's decision to marry was not an acceptance of the limited procreative role traditionally assigned to royal women. Rather, in the way she went about it, she showed herself to be defiant and independent, a woman who had her own agenda and who knew her own mind. There was no shortage of eligible suitors, including Henry's personal favorite, his brother-in-law King Afonso V of Portugal, but Isabella rejected them all in favor of her own choice, young Ferdinand (II), king of Sicily and heir also to the throne of neighboring Aragon. "It must be he," she is reported to have said, "and no other."

On October 19, 1469, Isabella and Ferdinand were married quietly in a private residence at Valladolid. Although they were second cousins, the bride and groom met for the first time only a few days before the wedding. According to contemporaries, there was an immediate bond between them. Both were young, Ferdinand in fact a year younger than Isabella, and both were reasonably sturdy and attractive. Also, both were intelligent, tough-minded pragmatists. The alliance strengthened Isabella's position at home, but the Aragonese, who were feeling French expansionist pressure to the north, needed it more than she did, a circumstance which allowed her to impose upon Ferdinand a marriage contract limiting his prerogatives to his wife's advantage. Isabella's new husband agreed to reside in Castile and to provide military support to her cause, but he was granted no independent authority in her lands. Official declarations would be issued in both names, but nothing would be done without Isabella's consent, and Ferdinand's rights in Castile would expire upon her death.

Henry IV reacted angrily but indecisively to news of Isabella and Ferdinand's marriage, first reinstating as his heir the *infanta* Juana la Beltraneja, then repudiating her again in order to make peace with his half-sister. On December 11, 1474, Henry died. Isabella was immediately proclaimed queen at Segovia and adherence to her cause spread rapidly across the kingdom. A small group of nobles opposed to the Aragonese connection quickly adopted the cause of the *infanta* Juana and sought assistance from neighboring Portugal in exchange for betrothing the unfortunate nine-year-old to King Afonso V, several decades her senior. Another long period of civil warfare followed. Aided by a Portuguese force, Isabella's opponents enjoyed an early advantage, but in 1476 the tide turned in the queen's favor when Ferdinand defeated Afonso at Toro. In 1479, the Treaty of Alcaçovas brought an end to hostilities and opened the way for Isabella to consolidate her hold on the Castilian throne.

Modern historians differ as to the legality of Isabella's claim, which rested finally on the question of whether or not Juana la Beltraneja was really illegitimate, as contemporaries charged. In any case, the issue was decided not according to justice, but by force of arms, public opinion, and practical exigencies. To Juana's disadvantage was her youth, her dependence upon the Portuguese party, and the damage done by Henry's own repudiation of her. As for Isabella, by the time the war ended, she was 28, politically experienced, and married to a well-liked prince whose family was Castilian in origin, values, and affections. Most important, she had been able to guarantee the succession. The birth in 1471 of a daughter, ***Isabella of Asturias**, and especially in 1478 of a son, Juan, promised political stability in the future. Another factor in Isabella's growing power base was Ferdinand's own accession as king of Aragon upon his father's death in 1479.

With her husband's active collaboration, Isabella took energetic steps to restore public order in Castile, at the same time seeking to consolidate and expand royal authority at the expense of the feudal nobility. In 1476 at the Cortes, or parliament, of Madrigal, the monarchs agreed with the leading municipalities to revive and restructure the old medieval *hermandades*, or town militias, which were now placed under the supervision of a national council dominated by the crown. This effective rural police force cleared the countryside of murderers, robbers, and other violent criminals. In addition, it increased Isabella's influence over the administration of justice at the local level, thereby weakening the traditional aristocracy.

In other measures adopted at Madrigal and later at the Cortes of Toledo (1480), Isabella and Ferdinand sought to curb the power of the great lords by reforming the kingdom's political and administrative structure. The Royal Council, known also as the Council of Castile, became the principal policy-making body for interior affairs. It was staffed largely by university-trained lawyers, whose expertise was necessary to the increasingly complex business of government. Unlike the *grandes*, or members of the high nobility, who had dominated politics in previous reigns, these so-called "new men" had no independent power base of their own. They owed their positions to the monarchs, and, therefore, their loyalty was assured.

Isabella profited from the support of the towns and the "new men," but she did not intend to transfer power to them. The administrative reforms enacted at Toledo also increased royal oversight over municipal affairs, especially through the appointment of *corregidores*, or royal governors, to reside in the kingdom's most important cities. To be able to act autonomously, without restraint or competition, Isabella and Ferdinand required reliable revenues of their own, so that they would not need to request new taxes from the Cortes. To this end, they worked to recover sources of royal income which had been improperly ceded to private parties during the struggle between Henry and Isabella's brother Alphonso. Also, in 1476 Isabella began the process of absorbing into the crown the masterships of the immensely wealthy, but largely independent, military orders of Santiago, Calatrava, and Alcántara. As increased trade and a reformed coinage led to economic expansion, more efficient collection of existing taxes brought even greater returns to the crown. It is estimated that, during the 30 years of Isabella's reign, revenues from taxes increased by 360%. Financial solvency made consultation of the Cortes unnecessary, and between 1483 and 1497 the monarchs did not convene the parliamentary body at all.

Isabella I

Devoutly religious, Isabella believed that it was the duty of Christian rulers to implement God's will on earth. In 1453, when she was still a small child, the Turks had taken Constantinople, an event which reawakened the crusading spirit in Europe. War against infidels was particularly valued in Spain, where Christians had maintained a tense frontier with Islam since the year 711. During the Reconquest, a centuries-long process of southward migration punctuated by periodic outbreaks of warfare, the rulers of what had eventually become Castile and Aragon had gradually recaptured most of the Iberian peninsula. As late as Isabella's reign, however, there was one remaining Muslim stronghold, the kingdom of Granada in the extreme south on the Mediterranean.

With the fall in 1482 of Muslim-held Alhama, Isabella and Ferdinand inaugurated a decade-long campaign to conquer Granada. While her husband took command in the field, the queen mobilized men, arms, and supplies. By necessity and custom, Isabella's role in the struggle was limited to support, but she was frequently at the front with Ferdinand. Her presence is said to have inspired her own soldiers and, on occasion, to have disheartened the enemy, but it also exposed her to great risk. At least twice, she came close to being killed or seriously injured. Castilian forces gradually dismembered the Moorish kingdom, taking in turn such strategic centers as Loja, Málaga, and Baza, and, by the close of 1490, they had settled in outside the city of Granada itself. On January 2, 1492, following a lengthy siege, Granada surrendered, and four days later the king and queen entered the former Muslim capital in triumph.

The fall of Granada marked the recovery of what Isabella believed to be the original patrimony of her distant forebears, the Christian kings of Visigothic Spain, but it was not the limit of her expansionist program. Concerned by recent advances made by the Portuguese in Africa and the Atlantic, as early as 1478 Ferdinand and Isabella had sent an expedition to the Canary Islands to enforce Castilian claims there. Meanwhile, in a more ambitious undertaking, the queen agreed to finance an attempt by the Genoese mariner Christopher Columbus to reach the Indies, that is, the Far East, by sailing westward across the Atlantic. Columbus' October 12, 1492, landfall in the Bahamas opened the way for the establishment of a Castilian empire in the so-called New World.

Castilian ventures in the Atlantic were expected to facilitate access to the riches of Africa and the Orient, but wealth was not the only goal of Isabelline expansionism. Inspired by the Biblical book of the Apocalypse, or Revelations, Isabella shared a current millenarian belief in the imminence of the Second Coming, which must be preceded by the rise of a world emperor who would recover Jerusalem from infidel hands. Given the successful war for Granada, it was easy for Isabella to see herself and Ferdinand, or perhaps one of their descendants, in such a role.

Isabella's fusion of her political agenda with her sense of religious obligation was responsible for two of her most controversial policies, the establishment of the Spanish Inquisition and the expulsion from her realm of the Jews. Long a cultural frontier, Castile had a significant Jewish population, whose members enjoyed great influence, especially as physicians, bankers, and tax gatherers. In the 14th century, outbreaks of anti-Semitic violence led to many baptisms of convenience, and the so-called "new men" were often *conversos*, as Jewish converts to Christianity were called. Also, many noble houses had marriage ties with *converso* families; in fact, Isabella and Ferdinand themselves both had Jewish ancestors. *Conversos* were to be found among the most devout of Christians, but frequent reports of clandestine Judaism in the convert community troubled Isabella, who regarded conformity in matters of belief to be an essential component of the new order of monarchical centralization. To enforce orthodoxy, she and Ferdinand acquired papal authorization to establish Inquisition tribunals, with the provision that, contrary to practice elsewhere in Europe, these courts would be under royal, rather than papal or episcopal, control.

Established first at Seville in 1480, the Spanish Inquisition spread throughout Castile and into Aragon as well, becoming one of the earliest national institutions in Spain. The Inquisition's abuses were notorious. Questioned under torture, defendants were kept ignorant of their accusers' identities. Because the inquisitors were allowed to confiscate the property of convicted persons, corruption was common. Although many of the sentences handed out, such as public penance, were relatively mild, there is a contemporary estimate that, during the 1480s, some 2,000 persons were sentenced, often on flimsy evidence, to death by burning.

The campaign against judaizing *conversos* also brought Castile's remaining Jewish population under Isabella's scrutiny. Convinced that unconverted Jews provided an ever-present bad example to the "new Christians," the queen believed also that the prophecy of the Second Coming required that the Jews disappear as a people before the world empire could emerge. In 1492, shortly after the conquest of Granada, Isabella ordered all the Jews of Castile to accept baptism as Christians or depart the kingdom. Many Jews did convert, but many others chose permanent exile instead. Having been guaranteed religious toleration when Granada surrendered, Castile's Muslims were at first spared similar treatment. Their reprieve was short-lived, however; in 1501, unconverted Muslims were ordered out of Granada, and the following year they were expelled from the rest of Castile as well.

The Spanish Inquisition and the mass deportation of the Jews produced great human suffering, but Isabella's record in religious affairs was not entirely one of bigotry and persecution. Years before state-sponsored church reform became fashionable elsewhere in Christian Europe, the queen recognized the need to improve the quality of the clergy and the discipline of the monastic orders, and to encourage greater spirituality and observance on the part of the laity. Her collaborator in these efforts was her confessor, the ascetic archbishop of Toledo, Cardinal Francisco Jiménez de Cisneros (1436–1517). Largely thanks to Isabella and Cisneros, the Roman Catholic Church cleaned its house in Spain so effectively that, in the 16th century, the Protestant Reformation would have virtually no impact there. In recognition of their many services to the faith, in 1494 Pope Alexander IV awarded Isabella and Ferdinand the title of *los Reyes Católicos,* or the Catholic Monarchs, by which historians still refer to them.

The early 1490s saw Isabella's kingdom in much better shape than she had found it, but the last decade of her life would bring troubles. The Italian Wars (1494–1504), although fought to protect Aragonese dynastic interests against French intrusion, consumed Castilian resources and disheartened the queen, who lamented the expenditure of blood and treasure on war against other Christians, instead of infidels. Also during this period, Isabella experienced several personal tragedies, which had political consequences because stability in a monarchy depended upon the fortunes of the royal family. In Barcelona in December 1492, Ferdinand was almost killed in an assassination attempt, an incident which reminded Isabella of the fragility of the political order in Spain. A greater crisis came in 1497 with the sudden death of the *infante* Juan, the male heir under whom Ferdinand and Isabella had expected Castile and Aragon to be united once and for all. The monarchs' eldest daughter, Isabella of Asturias, now married to King Manuel I of Portugal, was designated as heir, but, while the Castilian Cortes immediately swore allegiance to her, the Aragonese parliament declined to do so, citing a traditional prohibition in that kingdom against female succession.

When Princess Isabella of Asturias herself died in childbirth in 1498, and was followed to the grave two years later by her infant son, the right to inherit in Castile passed to Ferdinand

Columbus standing before Isabella I.

and Isabella's second daughter, Juana. Isabella succeeded this time in extracting acceptance of a female heir from the Aragonese, but the problem of the succession continued to trouble her. Remembered in history as *Juana la Loca, or the Insane, the new heir was emotionally unstable and was also dominated by her husband, Archduke Philip of Burgundy, known as Philip the Fair, whom Isabella did not trust. In 1503, as the queen herself fell seriously ill, possibly of cancer, she attempted in her will to guarantee the continuity of Ferdinand's authority in Castile, a reversal of the terms she had originally insisted upon in their marriage contract.

On November 26, 1504, Isabella died at Medina del Campo and, in compliance with her final wish, was carried to Granada for burial. Preceded in death by two of her children, she foresaw clearly the tragic life to which a third, the unfortunate Juana la Loca, was destined. Of the remaining two princesses, only one, **Maria of Castile**, who, following her sister Isabella of Asturias' death, was married to the widowed Portuguese king and gave birth to many children, enjoyed a relatively contented life. Both personal and political humiliations awaited the youngest daughter, known to history as **Catherine of Aragon**, who in 1509 became the first of the six wives of England's notorious King Henry VIII (1509–1547).

Catherine of Aragon. *See Six Wives of Henry VIII.*

Although the union Isabella and Ferdinand created between Castile and Aragon was at first only a dynastic alliance, under them and their descendants Spain did come increasingly to be thought of as a single, unified power. In more recent times, during the Francisco Franco régime (1939–75), supporters of the dictatorship sought legitimacy in the historical example of the Catholic Monarchs. A movement even emerged proposing Isabella as a candidate for sainthood, but it made little progress because of persistent questions concerning the queen's responsibility for the excesses of the Inquisition and the sufferings of the native inhabitants of the New World.

Isabella the queen is so prominent a figure in history that it is not always easy to catch glimpses of Isabella the woman. By all accounts she was a devoted wife and mother, and, although Ferdinand, true to contemporary standards of princely conduct, was not always faithful to her, it is clear that they respected one another and that, on the whole, their marriage was a good one. United by bonds of genuine affection, as well as of dynastic interest, Isabella and Ferdinand enjoyed a remarkable partnership, successful both as a domestic arrangement and as a political alliance. Always sensitive to her subjects' skepticism regarding women rulers, Isabella deliberately kept Ferdinand on view, so that at times it is difficult for historians to distinguish what in their reign was hers, what was his, and what was theirs. From the beginning, however, Isabella was determined to implement her own vision of Castile's future. She was fiercely protective of her royal prerogatives, and it was she, not Ferdinand, who dictated the terms under which the partners shared authority at all.

Maria of Castile (1482–1517)

Queen of Portugal. *Name variations: Maria of Castile or Marie of Castile; Mary Trastamara. Born on June 29, 1482, in Cordoba; died on March 7, 1517, in Lisbon; daughter of Ferdinand II, king of Aragon, and* ****Isabella I*** *(1451–1504), queen of Castile (r. 1468–1504); became second wife of Miguel also known as Manuel I the Fortunate (1469–1521), king of Portugal (r. 1495–1521), on October 30, 1500; children: Luiz (1506–1555), duke of Beja;* ****Isabella of Portugal*** *(1503–1539);* ****Beatrice of Portugal*** *(1504–1538, who married Charles II of Savoy); Fernando (1507–1534), duke of Guarda; Alfonso (1509–1540), archbishop of Lisbon; Enrique or Henry (1512–1580), cardinal of Portugal; Duarte (b. 1515, who married* ****Isabella of Braganza****); Joao also known as John III, king of Portugal (r. 1521–1557, who married* ****Catherine*** *[1507–1578], sister of Charles V); Maria (1513–1513); Antonio (1516–1516).*

SOURCES:

Elliott, J.H. *Imperial Spain, 1469–1716.* NY: St. Martin's Press, 1964.

Fernández-Armesto, Felipe. *Ferdinand and Isabella.* NY: Taplinger, 1975.

Liss, Peggy K. *Isabel the Queen: Life and Times.* NY: Oxford University Press, 1992.

SUGGESTED READING:

Mariéjol, J.H. *The Spain of Ferdinand and Isabella.* Translated by Benjamin Keen. New Brunswick, NJ: Rutgers University Press, 1961.

Merriman, Roger Bigelow. *The Rise of the Spanish Empire in the Old World and in the New: The Catholic Kings.* Vol. 2. NY: Macmillan, 1918.

Prescott, W.H. *History of the Reign of Ferdinand and Isabella.* Abridged ed. NY: Heritage Press, 1967 (originally published in 1837).

Stephen Webre,
Professor of History, Louisiana Tech University, Ruston, Louisiana

Isabella II (1830–1904)

Queen of Spain from 1833 to 1868, during the nation's difficult transition from absolutism to constitutional monarchy. *Name variations: Isabel II or Maria Isabella Louisa. Born on October 10, 1830, in Madrid, Spain; died on April 9, 1904, in Paris, France;*

eldest surviving daughter born to Ferdinand VII, king of Spain (r. 1813–1833), and his fourth wife, Maria Cristina I of Naples (1806–1878); married Francisco de Asís or Asiz, on October 10, 1846 (died April 17, 1902); children: Ferdinand or Fernando (1850–1850); Maria Isabel Francisca (b. 1851); Maria Cristina (1854–1854); Alfonso or Alphonso XII (1857–1885), king of Spain (r. 1875–1885); Pilar (b. 1861); Maria de la Paz (1862–1946); Eulalia (b. 1864, who married Anthony Bourbon, 5th duke of Galliera).

*Marriage of Ferdinand VII to Maria Cristina of Naples (1829); publication of Pragmatic Sanction (March 29, 1830); birth of Isabella (October 10, 1830); birth of Princess *__Luisa Fernanda__ (January 30, 1832); death of Ferdinand VII (September 29, 1833); Isabella II proclaimed monarch with Maria Cristina as regent (October 24, 1833); onset of first Carlist War against monarchy of Isabella II; end of the first Carlist War (1839); Isabella II declared of age to rule (November 10, 1843); attempted assassination of Isabella II by Angel de la Riva (May 1847); attempted assassination of Isabella II by Franciscan priest Martín Merino (February 2, 1852); birth of Prince Alphonso (November 28, 1857); battle of Alcolea (September 28, 1868); Isabella left for France and exile (September 30, 1868); abdicated in favor of Alphonso (June 25, 1870); Alphonso XII proclaimed king of Spain (December 1874); death of Francisco de Asís (April 17, 1902).*

Born October 10, 1830, to Ferdinand VII of Spain and **Maria Cristina of Naples**, the baby Isabella entered a chaotic world. The French Revolution and subsequent Napoleonic invasion of the Iberian peninsula had unleashed a bitter conflict between Spanish liberals and conservatives. Napoleon forced Ferdinand VII to abdicate in 1808. Lacking a king, patriots resisting the French wrote a liberal constitution in 1812. With the invaders' defeat and Ferdinand's restoration to power, he attempted to return to many aspects of 18th-century royal absolutism. His reactionary behavior was insufficient to please Spain's most ardent conservatives, but it did antagonize the growing middle class. By 1830, political factionalism had torn the nation apart, with political murders, executions, military coups (*pronunciamentos*), and discord.

Isabella was Ferdinand's heir, as he had no surviving children from his three previous marriages to **Maria Antonia of Naples**, **Maria Isabel of Portugal**, and ***Maria Josepha of Saxony.** In fact, he had seemed likely to die without children, and his brother Carlos (Charles, d. 1855) anticipated he would inherit the throne. Maria Cristina's pregnancy threatened his ambitions. Carlos and his followers, among whom were many of the most conservative and proclerical Spaniards, argued that if the baby were a girl, she could not rule. They noted that more than a century earlier, Philip V had made binding on Spain the Salic law, prohibiting women from ruling. Nonetheless, in 1789 Charles IV had secretly rescinded that decree, and on March 29, 1829, Ferdinand made the revocation public.

The Carlists refused to recognize Isabella's claim to the throne when Ferdinand died on September 29, 1833. Nonetheless the Cortes (national assembly) proclaimed Isabella II queen and appointed her mother regent, as Ferdinand's will had stipulated. France, Great Britain, and Portugal recognized her right, but the Vatican and several conservative Catholic nations sided with Carlos. War erupted between the government and Carlists. To preserve Isabella's claim, Maria Cristina decreed the Royal Statute of 1834. This created a Cortes based on ancient tradition and appealed to Moderates and Progressives by establishing a constitutional monarchy. The regent also considered marrying Isabella to Carlos' son, hoping thereby to heal the Carlist breach.

The First Carlist War colored the early years of Isabella's reign and made the monarchy dependent upon a series of generals-turned-politi-

Maria Cristina I of Naples (1806–1878)

Queen and regent of Spain. *Name variations: María Cristina; Maria Cristina of Naples or María Christina I of Naples; Cristina of Naples; Christina of Naples; Marie-Christine of Sicily; Maria Cristina de Borbón or Bourbon. Born in Naples, Italy, on April 27, 1806; died at Havre, France, on August 22 or 23, 1878; daughter of Francis I, king of the Two Sicilies (r. 1825–1830), and *__Marie Isabella of Spain__ (1789–1848); daughter of Francis I, king of the Two Sicilies, and *__Marie Isabella of Spain__ (1789–1848); sister of *__Teresa Cristina of Bourbon__ (1822–1889, empress of Brazil); became fourth wife of Ferdinand VII, king of Spain (r. 1813–1833), on December 11, 1829; secretly married a soldier named Agustín Fernando Muñoz y Sánchez in an irregular ceremony on December 28, 1833; children: (first marriage) *__Isabella II__ (1830–1904) and *__Luisa Fernanda__ (1832–1897); (second marriage) four more. Ferdinand VII's first wife was *__Maria Antonia of Naples__ (1784–1806); his second was *__Maria Isabel of Portugal__ (1797–1818); his third was *__Maria Josepha of Saxony__ (1803–1829).*

Maria Antonia of Naples (1784–1806). *See Maria Carolina for sidebar.*

Maria Isabel of Portugal (1797–1818). *See Carlota Joaquina for sidebar.*

cians. Meanwhile, Maria Cristina failed to provide suitable education or discipline for the young queen. Isabella liked music and had a beautiful singing voice. But she was, in the view of one historian, "indolent, untidy, unkempt, and was ruled by her whims which were always satisfied." This was largely the fault of the adults around her. Martin S.A. Hume, a British observer, recorded that she was a "stoutly built, very precocious girl with full cheeks, a snub nose, and thick sensuous lips, incredibly ignorant but with a great deal of natural shrewdness; in manner somewhat bluff, jovial and outspoken." She also suffered from ichthyosis, or dry scaly skin, which forced her to take periodic medicinal baths at sea resorts.

Maria Cristina did little to build stable, long-lasting support for Isabella. The terms of the regency stipulated that Maria Cristina could not remarry. But within three months of Ferdinand's death she fell in love with a soldier named Agustín Fernando Muñoz y Sánchez and secretly married him in an irregular ceremony. Over the years, she gave birth to four children with Muñoz, none of whom she could publicly recog-

Isabella II

nize. Her behavior set an example for Isabella, whose actions later scandalized public opinion. Maria Cristina's conduct and the continuing political crisis made her increasingly unpopular. She finally abandoned the regency on October 12, 1840, and went to Paris, leaving her ten-year-old daughter under the protection of the first minister, General Baldomero Espartero.

Intrigues, quarrels, and personal ambitions embroiled the government. Hoping to end the turmoil, on November 10, 1843, the Cortes declared Isabella of age, and her personal rule began. Yet she had little preparation for governing, a task which would have bedeviled the most expert politician. For awhile, minister Salustiano Olázaga served as the girl's tutor, and he announced his intention of providing her with an education equivalent to that of Britain's Queen ***Victoria**. In reality, however, he seemed more intent on maintaining her under his influence than preparing Isabella for intellectual and political independence. When ministers and leaders of the Cortes required her opinion on matters of state, she felt inadequate. Her education and training did not help her resolve competing public policies. Perhaps looking for support, she allowed Maria Cristina to return from France, but her mother became one more conservative player in the confusion of Spanish politics.

As Isabella approached puberty, Spanish politicians and foreign governments competed to select a husband for her. The conspiring parties vetoed several potential candidates, leaving Francisco de Asís by default, even though no one thought him appropriate. He was the son of Ferdinand's brother and Maria Cristina's ambitious sister, ***Louisa Carlotta of Naples**. Extremely devout, he posed the danger of siding with the Carlists. Worse still, he was, wrote one historian, "effeminate, believed impotent, and generally thought a homosexual." The better choice would have been his brother Enrique, but he was too liberal to suit the conservatives. Forced to marry Francisco or postpone marriage for several years, Isabella apprehensively agreed to wed him. Queen Victoria reportedly remarked: "The little Queen I pity so much for the poor child dislikes her cousin, and she is said to have consented against her will."

Francisco proved no better a husband than rumor predicted. In her old age, Isabella observed, "What shall I say of a man who on his wedding night wore more lace than I?" They had little in common and often lived apart in different palaces. Francisco occasionally tried to intervene in the government, but neither Isabella nor the politicians tolerated his interference. As her marriage provided no love or companionship, she soon turned to other remedies. The first of her lovers was General Francisco Serrano. Ambitious and cold, he revealed to the public the true nature of Isabella's marriage to Francisco. This drove an even larger wedge between the royal couple, who had never been united in the first place. Her friends advised that she seek an annulment of her marriage. In late 1847, the papal nuncio and General Ramón María Narváez, first minister at the time, managed to work out a superficial reconciliation between the queen and her consort.

> I am convinced that if all the ministers who surrounded her had fulfilled their duties, she would have died occupying the throne, and the fortunes of Spain would have radically changed direction.
>
> **—Natalio Rivas**

Despite her irregular private life, Isabella achieved some popularity for her generosity and love of amusement. On April 23, 1848, she forgave a debt of more than 100,000,000 reales owed her by the state, announcing "The future doesn't matter to me." On other occasions, she donated diamonds to the poor. Once she offered a donation of such outrageous proportions that her minister insisted on putting that many coins on the table. Isabella was amazed by the quantity she had been prepared to give away. Two failed attempts to assassinate her also garnered public sympathy for Isabella. Meanwhile, she spent large amounts on balls, the theater, and other entertainments. "She crammed her existence," wrote one biographer, "with as much amusement as she could." Isabella's scandals alienated many in Madrid, whose proximity to the court made them more aware of her behavior. Outside the capital, however, many Spaniards remained loyal to her as their monarch.

Motherhood sobered her to some extent. On July 11, 1850, she gave birth to a son Fernando, but the infant lived only a few moments. Although Francisco was not the father, to deny his paternity would have meant making himself completely irrelevant. Narváez forced the king-consort to behave as though nothing were amiss, and Francisco began spending more time with Isabella. On December 20, 1851, she gave birth to ▸ **Maria Isabel Francisca**. A young officer, José Ruíz de Arana, was probably the father. Their liaison lasted until late 1856, and he was the first who truly loved her rather than using his relationship with Isabella to enhance his career. In

▸ *See sidebar on the following page*

early 1854, another daughter, Maria Cristina, was born, but she lived only three days. Taking a new lover, captain of engineers Enrique Puigmoltó y Mayáns, she gave birth to Alphonso on November 28, 1857. Isabella was delighted with the crown prince, remarking: "No one in the world could be happier than I at this moment." Three more daughters (**Pilar,** ◆ **Maria de la Paz,** and ***Eulalia**) were born from 1861 to 1864.

Isabella II reigned during a significant restructuring of Spain. With peace restored at the end of the Carlist War, foreign capital flowed in to build railroads, develop mines, and establish a banking system. The nation did not experience general prosperity, but many of the upper and middle classes benefitted. This permitted Moderates and Progressives to reconcile their ideological differences and found the Liberal Union, which temporarily occupied the political center. Some Catholic conservatives refused to join, resentful that the government had sold off Church lands and had refused to re-establish the Inquisition. On the Left, some advocated republicanism, and within the working class were the first stirrings of socialism.

Isabella continued to rely upon the political expertise of generals such as Espartero, Narváez, and Leopoldo O'Donnell. During the regency, such military leaders had protected her monarchy from the Carlists. Later they often provided more effective rule than the civilian politicians. Generals were also necessary to political change. The Spanish political system enabled the governing party to manipulate election results, making it impossible to throw the incumbent party out of office except through a *pronunciamento.* With the Liberal Union, however, such *pronunciamentos* were less common after 1854 and the ministries more stable. Narváez and O'Donnell alternated as her chief ministers between 1854 and 1866, aided by the mid-century economic boom. The decade beginning in 1854 was the best of her reign.

Her troubles began to mount in 1863, despite military victories achieved by the regime in Spanish Morocco. In that year, conservatives engineered O'Donnell's fall and exile, bringing down the Liberal Union and placing the Progressives in the opposition. O'Donnell fell in part because his foreign policy was not sufficiently pro-Vatican. Even so, the constitution of 1856 made Catholicism the state religion, and Spain rejected religious toleration. Isabella's support of the Church sufficed for Pius IX to award her the Golden Rose. Her own pro-Catholic domestic and foreign policies may have derived in part from a sense of guilt over her sexual liaisons. Liberals claimed that **Sor (Sister) Patrocinio,** a shadowy nun who claimed to have the stigmata, controlled the queen. Meanwhile many Spaniards despised Isabella's mother and her soldier-husband Muñoz, who was reportedly venal and meddlesome. Isabella herself had become obese.

By 1866, she faced a crisis. A general European depression sapped Spain. Progressives clamored for power to no avail. Conservatives controlled the electoral machinery, and Isabella refused to call a Progressive ministry. She had grown up in a conservative court and was too pious to feel comfortable with the anti-clerical measures advocated by some Progressives. Two attempted Progressive *pronuncia-*

Maria Isabel Francisca (1851–1931)

Princess of Spain. *Name variations: Princess Isabel, the infanta; Maria Isabel Francisca; Isabella of Spain; countess of Girgenti. Born on December 20, 1851; died on April 23, 1931; daughter of Isabella II (1830–1904), queen of Spain, and probably a young officer, José Ruíz de Arana; tutored by* ****Frances Calderón de la Barca*** *(1804–1882); married Gaetano also known as Caetano de Borbón (1846–1871), count of Girgenti (a distant cousin), on May 13, 1868.*

Because the infanta Maria Isabel Francisca, known as Isabel, was the oldest royal child, and her only brother was weak and chronically ill, it was apparent that she was being educated as the future queen of Spain. In 1868, when the infanta was married, at age 16, to Caetano de Borbón, a distant cousin, a revolution swept through Spain, requiring the royal family to flee into exile in France. Young Isabel, who had developed an almost filial attachment to her former tutor ***Frances Calderón de la Barca,** now wrote from France pleading that Fanny return to her side as confidant, educator, and companion. Isabel's husband had by then developed a severe mental illness (probably acute depression) and was displaying, among other things, suicidal tendencies. In late 1871, despite all efforts, Caetano shot himself to death. While Fanny was consoling the young Isabel in France, Queen ***Isabella II** abdicated the throne of Spain to her—still sickly—son, Alphonso. In 1874, Parliament officially proclaimed him king.

Maria de la Paz (1862–1946)

Spanish princess. *Name variations: María. Born in 1862; died in 1946; daughter of* ****Isabella II*** *(1830–1904), queen of Spain, and Francisco de Asiz or Asis; married Louis Ferdinand of Bavaria (b. 1884).*

mentos failed, one by General Juan Prim, a hero of the fighting in Morocco. Isabella called upon Narváez to crush the dissidents, but his iron fists only added to the discontent. The queen flaunted a new lover, the actor Carlos Marfori. Spain's political elite increasingly saw her as an obstacle to the country's modernization. In April 1868, Narváez died, depriving her of a stalwart defender. In the "September Revolution," Prim, Admiral Juan Bautista Topete, and Isabel's former lover, General Serrano, pronounced against the monarchy. Serrano defeated Isabella's loyalists at the battle of Alcolea on September 28. Two days later, Isabella fled to France when the army refused to defend her further.

Generously received by Napoleon III, Isabella took up residence in Paris, while Prim sought a new monarch for Spain. On June 25, 1870, she abdicated in favor of Alphonso, hoping thereby to save the throne for her son. She also proclaimed her immense relief to be rid of the responsibilities of government. In Spain, however, the Cortes declared a perpetual exclusion of Isabella and her family. Prim and Spain instead turned to Prince Amadeo of Savoy, making him king in late 1870. Amadeo persevered until 1873, when he also abdicated, and Spain then struggled as a republic.

In December 1874, a *pronunciamento* declared in favor of Isabella's son Alphonso XII. Intelligent and well educated, the young king displayed a dignity and sense of responsibility which his mother lacked. She visited Spain occasionally but generally stayed in France, her life "monotonous and uneventful." The king's early death from tuberculosis in 1885 provided no opportunity for Isabella, who lacked any constituency in Spain. Neither did she have any desire to reign again. Instead her heir was succeeded by his posthumous son, Alphonso XIII. In 1902, Francisco de Asís died in anonymity. Two years later, on April 9, Isabella succumbed to influenza in Paris. Her descendants transferred her remains to the Escorial palace outside Madrid and buried her in the royal pantheon, along with Spain's other monarchs.

Isabella II presented Spain with contradictions. She caused scandal yet was generous and pious. As a ruler attempting to moderate from above the partisan disputes of Spanish politics, she remained too partial to the conservatives. Of her affairs and frivolity, notes one author, "innumerable libels, songs, engravings, and every type of defamatory literature were produced; of her positive and real acts of virtue, abnegation, and generosity, little has been written." Her greatest political mistake, according to historian Raymond Carr, "was that by her refusal to admit the Progressives to power she tested their dynastic loyalty too hard and drove them to revolution."

SOURCES:

Angelón, Manuel. *Isabel II: Historia de la reina de España*. Madrid: Librería Española, 1860.

Carr, Raymond. *Spain, 1808–1975*. Oxford: University Press, 1983.

Herr, Richard. *An Historical Essay on Modern Spain*. Berkeley, CA: University of California Press, 1971.

Llorca, Carmén. *Isabel II y su tiempo*. 3 ed. Madrid: Ediciones ISTMO, 1984.

Polnay, Peter de. *A Queen of Spain: Isabel II*. London: Hollis & Carter, 1962.

SUGGESTED READING:

Boetzkes, Ottilie G. *The Little Queen: Isabella II of Spain*. NY: Exposition Press, 1966.

Kendall W. Brown,
Professor of History and chair, Department of History,
Brigham Young University, Provo, Utah

Isabella I of Jerusalem (d. 1205)

Queen of Jerusalem. *Name variations: Isabel I. Reigned from 1192 to 1205; died in 1205; daughter of Amalric I, king of Jerusalem (r. 1162–1174), and* ****Maria Comnena****; half-sister of* ****Sibylla*** *(1160–1190); married Humfred of Turon also known as Humphrey IV, lord of Torun; married Conrad of Montferrat, margrave of Montferrat and king of Jerusalem (r. 1190–1192); married Henry II of Champagne, king of Jerusalem (r. 1192–1197); married Aimery de Lusignan (brother of Guy de Lusignan) also known as Amalric II, king of Jerusalem (r. 1197–1205), king of Cyprus, in 1197; children: (second marriage)* ****Marie of Montferrat*** *(d. 1212); (third marriage)* ****Alice of Champagne*** *(who married her stepbrother Hugh I, king of Cyprus);* ****Isabella of Cyprus*** *(fl. 1230s, who married Henry of Antioch); (fourth marriage)* ****Melisande*** *(who married Bohemund IV of Antioch).*

Isabella II of Jerusalem (1212–1228).

See Yolande of Brienne.

Isabella Capet (fl. 1250)

Queen of Navarre. *Flourished around 1250; daughter of* ****Margaret of Provence*** *(1221–1295) and Louis IX, king of France (r. 1226–1270); sister of Philip III the Bold (1245–1285), king of France (r. 1270–1285); married Teobaldo also known as Theobald II, king of Navarre (r. 1253–1270).*

Isabella Clara Eugenia of Austria (1566–1633)

Spanish ruler of the Netherlands and archduchess of Austria. *Name variations: Infanta Isabella, Archduchess Isabella, Isabella d'Autriche; Isabella Clara of Spain. Born Isabella Clara Eugenia in 1566; died in Brussels in 1633; daughter of Philip II (1527–1598), king of Spain (r. 1544–1598), and Elizabeth of Valois (1545–1568); married Albrecht also known as Albert the Pious, archduke of Austria (governor of the Spanish Netherlands), in 1599.*

Isabella Clara Eugenia of Austria was born in 1566, the daughter of Philip II, king of Spain, and ***Elizabeth of Valois**. When Philip received the low countries in 1598, he passed them along to his daughter Isabella for her dowry. With her husband Albert, she was co-ruler of the Spanish Netherlands from 1598 to 1621; after his death in 1621, she was sole governor. Isabella remained ruler of the Netherlands, as regent for her nephew Philip IV, until her death. Her skill in archery was celebrated in paintings and poems.

Isabella Clara Eugenia of Austria

Isabella de Fortibus (1237–1293).

See Isabella de Redvers.

Isabella de Forz (1237–1293).

See Isabella de Redvers.

Isabella del Balzo (d. 1533)

Queen of Naples. *Died in 1533; married Frederick IV (1452–1504), king of Naples (r. 1496–1501, deposed and died while in prison), in 1487; children: Fernando (b. 1488), duke of Calabria; Alfonso of Naples; Cesare of Naples;* ***Charlotte of Naples*** *(d. 1506, who married Gui XV, count of Laval);* ***Isabel of Naples*** *(d. 1550);* ***Julia of Naples*** *(d. 1542, who married Gian Giorgio, margrave of Montferrat). Frederick's first wife was* ****Anna of Savoy*** *(1455–1480).*

Isabella de Lorraine (1410–1453).

See Isabelle of Lorraine.

Isabella de Redvers (1237–1293)

Countess of Devon and Aumale. *Name variations: Isabella de Fortibus; Isabella de Forz. Born in 1237 in England; died in 1293 in England; daughter of Baldwin de Redvers, 7th earl of Devon, and Amice de Clare; married Count William de Forz of Aumale, around 1249 (died 1260); children: Avelina de Forz (1259–1274), countess of Holderness; and one son.*

An English heiress of great wealth, Isabella de Redvers was born in 1237, the daughter of Baldwin de Redvers, 7th earl of Devon and **Amice de Clare**, a noble Englishwoman. At age 12, Isabella married Count William de Forz of Aumale, a powerful landholder of Yorkshire. Eleven years later, in 1260, William died and left his widow and children extensive properties. Two years later, another death increased Isabella's wealth substantially; this was the death of her only brother, who had succeeded her father as earl of Devon. The earl had no children, and thus all his holdings passed to Isabella, who became countess of Devon as well as countess of Aumale.

Isabella, still a young woman, probably found herself with many ambitious suitors, but she refused to remarry. She was actively involved in the political tensions of her time, a period in which England's barons were conspiring and planning rebellions against King Henry III, under the leadership of Simon de Montfort. Isabella probably sided with her fellow nobles, but played the role of royal supporter on occasions when it would help her preserve her estates. She also spent much of her time in court, suing and being sued over various issues relating to her rights as an overlord and property holder. Isabella even sued her own mother over her rights to her father's property and all the revenues they generated; her mother argued that as the widow of the earl she was due some of that revenue as her own income, but her daughter disagreed. The suit was finally dropped by both sides but only after months of court battles and delays.

Near Isabella's death, the countess became involved in another political matter: the inheritance of her vast estates. She had inherited the entire Isle of Wight from her brother when he died; King Henry III wanted the Isle to be attached to the crown because of its strategic location in the English Channel. When Isabella's only son and heir died, her daughter ❧▸ **Avelina de Forz** became her heir, and King Henry and Isabella married Avelina to one of Henry's sons, Edmund the Crouchback, to assure that the Isle of Wight would remain in royal hands. But then Avelina died childless as well a few years later. In the end, it was on her deathbed in 1293 that Isabella sold the Isle outright to the king for a huge sum of money. A distant cousin inherited the great countess' wealth along with everything else she owned.

SOURCES:

LaBarge, Margaret. *A Small Sound of the Trumpet: Women in Medieval Life.* Boston, MA: Beacon Press, 1986.

Laura York,
Riverside, California

Isabella d'Este (1474–1539).

See joint entry on Este, Beatrice d' and Isabella d'.

Isabella Gonzaga (1474–1539).

See joint entry on Este, Beatrice d' and Isabella d'.

Isabella Leonarda (1620–1704).

See Leonarda, Isabella.

Isabella of Angoulême (1186–1246)

Queen of England. *Name variations: Isabelle d'Angoulême or Angouleme; Isabel of Angoulême. Born in 1186 (some sources cite 1187) in Angoulême; died in 1246 at abbey of Fontevrault, France; daughter of Aymer Taillefer, count of Angoulême, and Alice de Courtenay (d. 1211); married John I Lackland (1166–1216), king of England (r. 1199–1216), in 1200; married Hugh X, count of Lusignan, about 1218; children: (first marriage) Henry III (1206–1272), king of England (r. 1216–1272); Richard (1209–1272), earl of Cornwall, king of the Romans; Joan, queen of Scotland (1210–1238, who married Alexander II of Scotland); ****Isabella of England*** *(1214–1241, who married Frederick II, Holy Roman emperor); Eleanor of Montfort, countess of Leicester (1215–1275, who married the earl of Pembroke and then Simon de Montfort, founder of the English Parliament); (second marriage)* ❧▸ ***Alice le Brun*** *(d. 1255); ****Margaret le Brun*** *(d. 1283); Guy Lusignan; William de Valence, 1st earl of Pembroke (d. 1296).*

Isabella of Angoulême, a French noblewoman, became queen of England. She was born in Angoulême in 1186, the daughter of Aymer Taillefer, count of Angoulême, and ❧▸ **Alice de Courtenay**, French aristocrats who supported the English kings in their struggles against the French monarchy. In 1200, their loyalty was rewarded by the marriage of their 14-year-old daughter Isabella to King John I Lackland, even though Isabella had been previously betrothed to the nobleman Hugh de Lusignan. She was John's second wife; his first was ❧▸ **Avisa of Gloucester**. Isabella had five children with John, who was an intelligent but cruel man; their eldest son became Henry III, and her youngest daughter became ***Eleanor of Montfort**, countess of Leicester. Isabella was, like her husband, ambitious and rather power-hungry.

❧▸ See sidebar on the following page

❧▸ See sidebar on the following page

❧▸ **Avelina de Forz** (1259–1274)

Countess of Holderness. *Born on January 20, 1259; died on November 10, 1274, in Stockwell, England; buried at Westminster Abbey; daughter of William de Forz, 2nd count of Aumale, and ****Isabella de Redvers*** *(1237–1293); married Edmund the Crouchback (c. 1245–1296), 1st earl of Lancaster, on April 9, 1269.*

❧▸ **Alice le Brun** (d. 1255)

Countess of Warrenne and Surrey. *Name variations: Alice de Lusignan. Died on February 9, 1255; daughter of ****Isabella of Angoulême*** *and her second husband Hugh de Lusignan (Isabella's first husband was King John I Lackland); half-sister of Henry III, king of England; married John de Warrenne (1231–1304), 7th earl of Warrenne and Surrey (r. 1240–1304), in August 1247; children: ****Isabel de Warrenne*** *(b. 1253, married John Balliol, king of Scots); ****Eleanor de Warrenne*** *(who married Henry Percy, the 7th baron Percy); William de Warrenne (d. 1286).*

Alice de Courtenay (d. 1211)

Countess of Angoulême. *Name variations: Alice de Courteney. Died around September 14, 1211; daughter of Peter I de Courtenay (c. 1126–1180) and *__Elizabeth of Courtenay__ (d. 1205); married Aymer Taillefer, count of Angoulême; children: *__Isabella of Angoulême__ (second wife of King John I Lackland).*

Avisa of Gloucester (c. 1167–1217)

Queen of England. *Name variations: Avice of Gloucester; Hadwisa; Isabella or Isabelle of Gloucester; Isabelle de Clare. Born around 1167; died in 1217; daughter of William Fitzrobert (d. 1183), 2nd earl of Gloucester, and *__Hawise Beaumont__ (d. 1197); sister of *__Amicia Fitzrobert__ (d. 1225); married Prince John (1166–1216), later John I Lackland, king of England (r. 1199–1216), in 1189 (divorced 1200); married Geoffrey de Mandville, earl of Essex; children: none.*

In 1189, John I Lackland, the future king of England, married his cousin Avisa of Gloucester, to whom he had been betrothed since his tenth year. A decade later, during a royal tour through his southwestern French dominions, however, he decided to marry ***Isabelle of Angoulême**, the 12-year-old daughter of the turbulent count of Angoulême. For this purpose, John coolly arranged for a papal dissolution of his first marriage on grounds that he and Avisa of Gloucester were too closely related. Legend has it that lust got the better of his diplomatic instincts when he made this match—it certainly worsened his relations with Philip II Augustus of France with whom he had been discussing marriage-alliance possibilities.

She aided John with his various struggles to maintain English lands on the Continent and with his own rebellious barons during his troubled reign. Despite the 20 years difference in their ages, John and Isabella seem to have become a close couple, and John usually preferred spending time with his wife to battling his many enemies.

In 1216, John died with the dubious distinction of being England's most unpopular king. He was little mourned except by his children and Isabella, who was devastated by his death. She saw to it that young Henry was put on the throne safely and was surrounded by capable advisors, then returned to her native France. Her daughter ***Joan** had been betrothed to the French noble Hugh de Lusignan, the same man whom Isabella had intended to marry 17 years earlier. Isabella, who seems to have fallen in love with Hugh, quickly broke off his engagement to her daughter. Within a few months, the former queen married her fiancé of childhood.

Although the couple were happy together, this marriage caused problems for the two both in France and England, for former queens were not supposed to remarry without permission of the Parliament. However, the marriage stood, and they remained together for almost 30 years. During the last years of her life, Isabella was caught up in several scandals involving conspiracy against the French king, including allegations that she had paid two cooks to try to poison him. Isabella fled for safety to the abbey of Fontevrault, where she remained in isolation for about a year, dying there at age 60.

SOURCES:

Echols, Anne, and Marty Williams. *An Annotated Index of Medieval Women*. NY: Markus Wiener, 1992.

Kelly, Amy. *Eleanor of Aquitaine and the Four Kings*. Cambridge: Harvard University Press, 1950.

LaBarge, Margaret. *A Small Sound of the Trumpet: Women in Medieval Life*. Boston: Beacon Press, 1986.

Laura York,
Riverside, California

Isabella of Aragon (1243–1271)

Queen of France. *Name variations: Isabel or Isabelle. Born in 1243 (some sources cite 1247); died in 1271; daughter of James I, king of Aragon (r. 1213–1276), and *__Iolande of Hungary__ (1215–1251); became first wife of Philip III the Bold (1245–1285), king of France (r. 1270–1285), in 1262; children: *__Blanche of France__ (c. 1266–1305, who married Rudolf III, king of Bohemia); Philip IV (1268–1214), king of France (r. 1285–1314); Charles I (1270–1325), count of Valois. Philip's second wife was *__Marie of Brabant__ (c. 1260–1321).*

Isabella of Aragon (c. 1300–1330)

Holy Roman empress. *Name variations: Elisabeth or Elizabeth of Aragon, queen of Germany. Born around 1300 or 1302; died on July 2, 1330; married Friedrich also known as Frederick I (III) the Fair of Austria (1289–1330), king of Germany (r. 1314–1322), (co-regent) Holy Roman emperor (r. 1314–1325).*

Isabella of Asturias (1471–1498)

Queen of Portugal. *Name variations: Isabel Trastamara, princess of Asturias. Born on May 31, 1471 (some sources cite 1470), in Duenas; died in childbirth on August 23 or 25, 1498, in Saragosa; daughter of *__Isabella I__ of Castile (1451–1504) and Ferdinand II, king of Aragon (r. 1479–1516); married Prince Afonso also known as Alphonso (1475–1491), heir to the Portuguese throne, on April 18, 1490 (he died from a riding accident shortly thereafter); married Miguel also known as Manuel I the Fortunate (1469–1521),* *king of Portugal (r. 1495–1521), in September or October 1497; children: surviving infant son Miguel (1498–1500) died two years after his mother.*

Isabella of Austria (1503–1539).

See Isabella of Portugal.

Isabella of Austria (1566–1633).

See Isabella Clara Eugenia.

Isabella of Braganza (1402–1465)

Princess of Braganza. *Name variations: Isabel de Barcelos. Born in October 1402; died on October 26, 1465, in Arévalo; daughter of Alphonso, duke of Braganza, and* ***Beatriz Pereira*** *(c. 1380–1412), countess of Barcellos; married Joao or John of Portugal, grand master of Santiago, on November 11, 1424; children: Diego (b. 1426);* ****Isabel of Portugal*** *(1428–1496);* ****Beatrice of Beja*** *(1430–1506); Filippa (b. 1432).*

Isabella of Braganza (1459–1521)

Duchess of Braganza. *Name variations: Isabella of Beja. Born in 1459; died in April 1521; daughter of* ****Beatrice of Beja*** *(1430–1506) and Fernando also known as Ferdinand, duke of Beja and Viseu; married Fernando also known as Ferdinand, duke of Braganza, on September 14, 1472; children: Filippe or Philip (b. 1475), duke of Guimaraes; Jaime or James (1479–1532), duke of Braganza (who married* ****Eleonore de Guzman****); Diniz or Denis (b. 1481); Alfonso or Alphonso (b. around 1482); Margarida (1477–1483); Caterina (1483, died young).*

Isabella of Braganza (1512–1576)

Duchess of Guimaraes. *Name variations: Isabel of Braganza. Born around 1512; died on September 16, 1576, at Villa Vicosa, Evora; married Edward also known as Duarte (1515–1540, son of Manuel I of Portugal and* ****Maria of Castile****), duke of Guimaraes, on April 23, 1537; children:* ****Maria of Portugal*** *(1538–1577), duchess of Parma;* ****Catherine of Portugal*** *(1540–1614); Duarte (1541–1576), duke of Guimaraes.*

Isabella of Brienne (1212–1228).

See Yolande of Brienne.

Isabella of Buchan (fl. 1290–1310)

Scottish royal and countess of Buchan who crowned Robert I, king of Scotland. *Name variations: Isabel. Flourished between 1290 and 1310; daughter of Duncan Fife (1262–1288), 9th earl of Fife (r. 1270–1288), and Joan de Clare (c. 1268–after 1322); sister of Duncan Fife (1285–1351), 10th earl of Fife; married John Comyn, 3rd earl of Buchan (d. 1313?, constable of Scotland).*

Effigy of Isabella of Angoulême.

Isabella of Buchan was born around 1250, the daughter of Duncan Fife, 9th earl of Fife, and ***Joan de Clare**. Isabella's father was murdered by Sir Patrick Abernethy. Isabella, as the countess of Buchan, was a staunch supporter of Robert the Bruce of Scotland, in direct opposition to her husband, John Comyn. Around 1313, after Comyn betrayed an agreement to make Robert the Bruce king, Robert set up a meeting with him at Greyfriar's Church, where Bruce lost his temper and stabbed him; a henchman finished the deed. Earlier, standing in for her brother, the earl of Fife (who was being held prisoner by the British), Isabella had bravely volunteered to crown Robert the Bruce, Robert I, king of Scotland in 1306. To atone for this crime, she was besieged in the castle of Berwick by the English under the leadership of Edward I. When the castle was taken, she was imprisoned for four years in the castle of Roxburgh in a suspended iron

◈ **Bruce, Mary** (fl. 1290–1316)
Scottish royal. *Flourished around 1290 to 1316; died before 1323; daughter of Robert Bruce, earl of Carrick, and* ****Marjorie of Carrick*** *(c. 1254–1292); sister of Robert the Bruce also known as Robert I, king of Scotland (r. 1306–1329); married Neil Campbell of Lochow, around 1312; married Alexander Fraser, in 1316; children: (first marriage) John of Lochow (b. around 1313), earl of Atholl; Dougal; Duncan; (second marriage) John of Touch (b. around 1317); Sir William Fraser (b. around 1318).*

and wooden cage, as was ◈ **Mary Bruce** (a sister of Robert Bruce). Both would survive. Mary's niece ***Margaret Bruce** (1296–1316) narrowly escaped the same fate.

Isabella of Capua (d. 1559).

See Gonzaga, Isabella.

Isabella of Croy-Dulmen (1856–1931)

Archduchess. *Born in Dulmen on February 27, 1856; died in Budapest, Hungary, on September 5, 1931; married Archduke Friedrich (1856–1936); children:* ***Maria Christina*** *(1879–1962);* ***Maria Anna*** *(1882–1940);* ***Gabriele*** *(1887–1954);* ***Isabella*** *(1888–1973);* ***Maria Alice*** *(1893–1962); Albrecht also known as Albert (1897–1955).*

Isabella of Cyprus (fl. 1230s)

Princess of Jerusalem. *Name variations: Isabel. Flourished in the 1230s; daughter of Henry II of Champagne, king of Jerusalem (r. 1192–1197), and* ****Isabella I of Jerusalem*** *(d. 1205); married Henry of Antioch (son of Bohemond IV, prince of Antioch); children: Hugh III, king of Cyprus (r. 1267–1284), king of Jerusalem (r. 1268–1284);* ****Margaret of Antioch-Lusignan*** *(fl. 1283–1291).*

Isabella of Cyprus (fl. 1250s).

Queen of Jerusalem and Cyprus. *Flourished in the 1250s; daughter of Henry I, king of Cyprus (r. 1218–1253) and* ****Plaisance of Antioch*** *(d. 1261); sister of Hugh II, king of Cyprus (r. 1253–1267); married Hugh III, king of Cyprus (r. 1267–1284), king of Jerusalem (r. 1268–1284); children: John I, king of Cyprus (r. 1284–1285); Henry II, king of Cyprus (r. 1285–1324); Amalric of Tyre (d. 1310), governor of Cyprus.*

Isabella of England (1214–1241)

Holy Roman empress. *Name variations: Isabel Plantagenet; Elizabeth, empress of Germany. Born in 1214 in Gloucester, Gloucestershire, England; died on December 1, 1241, in Foggia, Italy; buried in Andria, Sicily; daughter of John I Lackland (1166–1216), king of England (r. 1199–1216), and Isabella of Angoulême (1186–1246); became third wife of Frederick II (b. 1194–1250), Holy Roman emperor (r. 1215–1250), on July 15, 1235 (some sources cite July 20); children: Jordan of Germany (b. 1236); Margaret of Germany (1237–1270, who married Albert of Thuringia); Agnes (1237–1237); Henry of Germany (1238–1253), king of Jerusalem. Frederick II's first wife was* ****Constance of Aragon*** *(d. 1222); his second wife was* ****Yolande of Brienne*** *(1212–1228).*

Isabella of England was born in 1214 in Gloucester, England, the second daughter and fourth child of John I Lackland, king of England, and ***Isabella of Angoulême**. Isabella of England became the third wife of Frederick II, Holy Roman emperor, on July 15, 1235. Her daughter ***Margaret of Germany** was born in February 1237 and, by marriage with Albert, landgrave of Thuringia, became ancestor of the Saxe-Coburg-Gotha house.

Isabella of France (1296–1358)

Queen consort of England who is most famous for her leadership of the rebellion against her husband Edward II (1325–27) and for her short period of power (1327–30) when she and her lover, Roger Mortimer, ruled England in the name of her young son, Edward III. *Name variations: Isabel of Buchan; Isabella the Fair; She-Wolf of France. Born in 1296 (some sources erroneously cite 1292), in Paris, France; died at Hertford castle and thought to be buried at Christ Church, Newgate, London, on August 22, 1358; daughter of Philip IV the Fair (1268–1314), king of France (r. 1285–1314) and Joan I of Navarre (1273–1305); sister of Charles IV, king of France (r. 1322–1328); married Edward II (1284–1327), king of England (r. 1307–1327), on January 25 or 28, 1308; children: Edward of Windsor (1312–1377, later Edward III, king of England, r. 1327–1377, who married Philippa of Hainault); John of Eltham (1316–1336, became earl of Cornwall, 1328); Eleanor of Wood-*

stock (1318–1355), duchess of Guelders; Joan of the Tower (1321–1362), queen of Scotland.

Isabella, princess of France, was born to Philip IV the Fair, king of France, and ***Joan I of Navarre** in 1296. Almost immediately, Isabella became a pawn in international politics. When she was only two, her father entered into negotiations with Edward I Longshanks of England to end the war which had broken out between the two kingdoms in 1294. In 1298, a settlement was reached between the two parties and, in keeping with diplomatic practices of the time, marriages between the two royal houses sealed the final agreement. The English king, Edward I, who had been widowed by the death of his wife ***Eleanor of Castile** in 1290, married Philip IV's half-sister, ***Margaret of France**, and Edward I's son and heir, Edward (II) of Carnarvon, was betrothed to Isabella. The young prince Edward was 15, while his bride-to-be was not yet three.

Although she was betrothed in 1298, Isabella's marriage did not take place until 1308. When he succeeded his father as king in 1307, Edward II acted quickly to fulfill the terms of his prearranged marriage. In January 1308, he jour-

Isabella of France (1296–1358)

neyed to France and did homage to Philip IV for his English possessions in France. With these important and necessary diplomatic formalities completed, Edward and Isabella were married on January 25. At their joint coronation in February, Edward II granted Isabella the counties of Montreuil and Ponthieu as her dower to pay for the personal expenses of her household.

Already accustomed to political life as a result of the time spent at her father's court, the 12-year-old queen quickly began to confront the realities of her husband's court politics and personal behavior. For the first five years of the reign, court diplomacy revolved around the king's charismatic, dominating, and arrogant boyhood friend, Piers Gaveston. As the reign progressed, Edward II showed that he was either unwilling or incapable of restraining himself where Gaveston was concerned. Edward I had recognized Gaveston's hold over his son. Before his death, Edward I banished Gaveston, hoping to avert disaster. The first action Edward II took as king was to recall Gaveston from exile. After Gaveston returned, Edward II elevated him to the earldom of Cornwall and granted Gaveston other lands and privileges.

Gaveston's newfound wealth and his hold over the king's affections gave him unprecedented amounts of political power at the royal court. The English nobility, who resented his rapid rise and hated his arrogance, attempted once again to secure his exile. After tense and protracted political battles with his nobility, Edward II was finally forced to consent to Gaveston's banishment again in late 1311. The exile, however, was short-lived, and Gaveston returned to celebrate Christmas with the king.

Isabella hated Gaveston for usurping much of her position, and she detested the control he wielded over her husband. She apparently made no secret of her feelings but did not openly oppose him at court. Evidence for her attitude can be found as early as 1308, when the queen's relatives who had accompanied her to England for her coronation, returned indignantly to France because "the king loved Gaveston more than his wife." Also in 1308, several monks from West-

Sophie Marceau as Isabella of France, from the movie Braveheart.

minster referred to the queen's hatred of Gaveston in a letter to their colleagues. Around 1311, Thomas of Lancaster, the king's cousin and leader of the aristocratic opposition to Gaveston, wrote to the queen telling her that he would not rest until he had rid her of Gaveston's presence. With or without the queen's active participation, Lancaster made good his word. In June 1312, two Welshmen from his retinue beheaded Gaveston.

Isabella and her husband seem to have improved their relationship in the years after Gaveston's death. The couple rejoiced when their first child, Edward of Windsor (the future Edward III), was born at Windsor on November 13, 1312. Over the next nine years, the queen gave birth to three more children, John of Eltham (1316–1336), ***Eleanor of Woodstock** (1318–1355), and ***Joan of the Tower** (1321–1362). Isabella also gained influence with her husband as she matured. Edward II entrusted her with a mission to France in 1314, and in 1317 he withdrew his own nominee for the bishopric of Durham in favor of her choice. He also furnished her with a household appropriate to her station as royal consort.

Isabella's household contained over 180 persons and constantly moved throughout the kingdom. It was highly organized, staffed by a large number of officials whose duties included collecting her revenues, keeping her accounts, drafting and writing her correspondence, and supervising other functions. This large household, and her own lavish lifestyle, caused her some economic difficulties. Isabella had been bred as royalty and lived as befit a queen; she had expensive habits and tastes. As a result, her expenses frequently outpaced her income. Historian **Hilda Johnstone** has determined that in 1313–14, Isabella's income totaled about 5,600 li., while her expenses amounted to nearly 6,030 li. When the queen mother, Margaret of France, died in 1318, Isabella received some of her mother-in-law's estates, which increased her income. By 1320, Isabella held the county of Ponthieu, estates in North Wales, and lands and castles in 17 other English counties.

In 1322, the relationship between Isabella and Edward II soured noticeably. In that year, Edward defeated Thomas of Lancaster and other opponents and immediately created another dominating influence at court in his new favorite, Hugh Despenser the Younger. In the decade since Gaveston's fall, Isabella had traveled with the king on campaign and gained influence with her husband. After Lancaster's defeat, however, she found herself competing for affection and influence with Despenser, an individual much more dangerous than Gaveston had been. Suspicions about a sexual relationship between the king and Hugh Despenser the Younger mounted, and the relationship between Isabella and Edward deteriorated.

Sensing that his influence was on the rise, Despenser convinced the king that there was a danger of a French invasion and pointed out that Isabella had strong ties to France. Reacting to these charges, in September 1324 the king sequestered his wife's estates. This loss of property severely curtailed Isabella's income and, by extension, her independence and influence. Realizing he had placed Isabella in a desperate position, Despenser pushed for a total victory over the queen. He had his wife ⚘▸ **Eleanor de Clare** appointed as Isabella's housekeeper to spy on the queen and censor all her correspondence, and he was rumored to be in contact with the pope in an effort to annul Isabella's marriage to the king.

Isabella realized that her position was rapidly deteriorating and, in 1325, seized an opportunity to escape the grasping reach of Despenser. Three years earlier, Isabella's brother Charles had become King Charles IV of France. Charles IV had demanded that Edward II come to France and make the oath of homage to him for his lands in France. Edward II balked at Charles IV's demands, and in August 1324 the French king invaded Gascony. Papal officials, who had been unsuccessful mediators between the two parties, suggested that Isabella might be able to succeed in negotiations between England and France where they had failed. Despenser, wary of letting the king slip beyond his influence, agreed with the pope, and Edward II, too, reluctantly agreed. On March 9, 1325, Isabella sailed for France accompanied by members of her household.

Isabella quickly showed that she was a remarkably effective negotiator. Acting as mediator between her brother and her husband, she

⚘▸ **Clare, Eleanor de** (1292–1337)

English noblewoman. *Name variations: Alienor or Eleanor Despenser; Eleanor Zouche. Born in 1292; died in 1337; daughter of Gilbert de Clare, 7th earl of Hertford, 3rd of Gloucester, and* ****Joan of Acre*** *(1272–1307); married Hugh Despenser the Younger, in 1306 (executed, November 24, 1326); married William Zouche, in 1327; children (first marriage)* ***Isabel Despenser;*** *Edward Despenser (d. 1352).*

brought the two sides together in agreement. According to the terms of her settlement, Edward II's French possessions were to be returned to him as soon as he had performed his homage. A French steward would take custody of the duchy until Edward II made his oath. Hugh Despenser, though, feared he might lose his control over the king should Edward be separated from him and go to France to take the oath personally. He persuaded Edward II to invest his heir, Edward of Windsor, with the French lands and send him to France to make the oath in his father's place. Charles IV found this alternative acceptable, and, on September 21, 13-year-old Prince Edward sailed to France to meet with his mother and make the oath of homage to his uncle.

Despenser had erred, and it would cost him his life and the life of his king. He had been able to keep the king in England but had misjudged the queen and her abilities, and Isabella quickly took full advantage of Despenser's mistake. In France, a circle of English nobles disaffected with Hugh Despenser's influence and power had collected around the queen. When Prince Edward arrived in France, this group took control of the heir to the throne and refused to return him to England. When the queen and her son did not return, Edward II began to worry. He sent letters to his wife pleading with her, but she responded openly that she would not return to England as long as her enemy Hugh Despenser was there. Isabella had made a decision. She told Charles IV that her marriage with Edward II had been broken and that she would live as a widow until Despenser had been removed.

News of Isabella's response spread, accompanied by rumors of impending invasion. Edward II and Despenser finally realized their exposed position and began to react. Isabella, however, found herself faced with a daunting task. Despenser was widely hated in England, and she would have little trouble raising support to unseat him, but she had created difficulties for herself in France. Among the circle of disaffected English nobles who joined her at the French court was an erstwhile rebel, Roger Mortimer of Wigmore. At some point, Mortimer and Isabella became lovers—the origins and timing of the affair are unclear. Rumors of the affair between Mortimer and the queen, though, spread quickly throughout Europe. Charles IV received complaints about the scandalous behavior of his sister from no less than the pope. Incensed at her adultery, he withdrew his support from her and made it clear that she should leave his court.

In fear of being returned to England, the conspirators left France and traveled to Hainault, where they were received by William II, count of Holland, Hainault, and Zeeland. At William's court, Isabella and her followers gained a sympathetic ear—for a price. Isabella, always the intriguer and negotiator, persuaded the count of Hainault to give her military support for her invasion. In return, William II obtained the marriage of his daughter ***Philippa of Hainault** (1314–1369) to the young Prince Edward. With the agreement concluded, the rebels set sail for England from Dordrecht on September 23, 1326.

The queen, Mortimer, and their small band of followers landed at Orwell, Suffolk, the next day and began their advance. Opposition to the rebels melted as Isabella's forces marched towards London. As the rebels approached, Hugh Despenser and the king panicked and their own support in London evaporated. They fled west, where the bulk of Despenser's land lay and where Edward's support was strongest. Mortimer and the queen followed. They captured Despenser's father, the earl of Winchester, at Bristol and executed him. They captured the king and the younger Despenser at Neath Abbey shortly afterwards. On November 24, Despenser was "tried" and executed. Though Isabella and her followers had removed Despenser from the scene, they refused to return power to Edward II. They turned rebellion into revolution by deposing a lawfully crowned king, an action that had never before been taken in England. Isabella had her husband imprisoned and, on January 25, 1327, forced him to abdicate his throne in favor of his son, Edward of Windsor, who succeeded to the throne as Edward III. Because the new king was only 14 years of age, his mother and her lover assumed control of the government as regents and ruled England in his name until he should come of age.

Isabella and Mortimer had capitalized on the English nobility's hatred of Edward II's mismanagement and Despenser's tyranny to take control of the government. Much of the nobility's hatred of Despenser had been spurred by his domination of the king and the greed he had shown in his drive to accumulate ever more land and wealth. The new government meted out some rewards to its adherents, but Isabella and Mortimer quickly showed themselves to be just as grasping and ambitious as Despenser had been. They confiscated the lands of their enemies and, instead of redistributing them to their associates and allies, began to accumulate huge blocks of wealth that easily rivaled Despenser's at his height. Isabella's dower of 4,500 li. was not only restored to her, it was increased significantly by seizing confiscated lands until her income was a staggering 13,333 li. a year. Mortimer regained his family estates and added a huge block of lands that had belonged to Despenser and other rebels until he was the most powerful man in Wales. In 1328, he created and assumed the title earl of March, a presumption of nobility which further aggravated his relations with English magnates.

When the nobility realized that they had not rid themselves of tyranny but only changed the tyrants, Isabella and Mortimer quickly began to lose their base of popular support. The suspicious death of Edward II in Berkeley Castle in late 1327, an unpopular peace treaty which recognized the independence of Scotland, and the scandal and unchecked greed of the queen and her lover cast ominous shadows over the ruling partnership. Influential nobles such as Henry of Lancaster and Thomas Wake, who had supported the invasion in 1326, began to distance themselves from the regents, who reacted brutally to any hint of disloyalty or disaffection.

One of those most disaffected with the actions and ambitions of the queen and her lover was the young king himself, Edward III. In March 1330, Mortimer designed a trap to catch Edward III's uncle, Edmund, earl of Kent, in a treasonous plot. Mortimer circulated rumors that Edward II was still alive, and Kent, filled with guilt at his role in his half-brother's deposition, took the bait Mortimer's agents dangled before him and made arrangements to free Edward II. At a parliament held at Winchester, Isabella and Mortimer presented the evidence of Kent's actions and had him convicted of treason. The earl was sentenced to death and executed without any regard for the royal blood that coursed through his veins.

After the Winchester Parliament, Edward III decided the situation had deteriorated far enough, and he quite rightly judged himself to be in personal danger. A small circle of intimate friends gathered around the tall, charismatic young king to plot the overthrow of his mother and her paramour. In June 1330, Edward III's position was strengthened immeasurably when his queen, Philippa, gave birth to their first son, Edward of Woodstock (the future Edward, the Black Prince), and thereby secured the succession. Isabella and Mortimer clearly fretted about these developments and moved to neutralize any erosion of their position.

In late summer 1330, the regents moved the court to Nottingham and called for a parliament to meet there in October. Edward III and his friends, led by a cleric named Richard de Bury and William Montague, a young knight who had been raised with Edward III, began to work for the overthrow of the regency and the personal assumption of government by the young king. Through intrigues that would have made Isabella proud, Edward III gained the blessing of the pope for his intended coup. When Parliament met at Nottingham in October, the small group of conspirators was ready to act.

Late on the night of Friday, October 19, William Montague and a handful of his men entered a secret passage into Nottingham castle. They emerged into the keep and joined the king, who was waiting for them there. The conspirators then burst into Mortimer's chamber and, after a short melee in which two of Mortimer's bodyguards were killed, arrested him, trundled him out of the castle through the secret passageway, and sent him to London to be imprisoned in the Tower. The queen, hearing the fight, realized what was happening and cried out to her son in fear from her chamber, "Have pity on gentle Mortimer!" Her pleas fell on unsympathetic ears.

The next morning, Edward III assumed complete control of the government. He declared that his mother and Mortimer had been guilty of maladministration, that the regency was ended, and that he would govern for himself in the future. The reign of Isabella and Mortimer had ended; Mortimer was executed for treason a month later. The king was more lenient with his mother, however, and forbade any mention of her role in the events of 1327–30 in the charges brought against Mortimer. Nonetheless, he knew his mother too well to allow her to continue to play a prominent part in political life. He placed her in honorable confinement at Castle Rising and forced her to surrender much of what she had taken while in power, reducing her income to 3,000 li.

Isabella lived for another 28 years after her defeat in the palace coup d'etat of 1330. She still seems to have been given to extravagance, for her presence at Castle Rising proved to be a steady burden on the citizens of Lynn, who complained that they were being ruined by demands of the queen mother's lifestyle. Despite her earlier behavior, throughout her life Edward III continued to visit her—at least twice a year—and often sent her letters and presents. She amused herself with hawking, reading romances, and collecting religious relics. Eventually, she was allowed to travel more freely, appear at court, and was even considered for diplomatic missions to France. In 1348, it was proposed that she mediate a peace between England and France; and in May 1354, the pope asked her to intercede with her son for the release of the duke of Brittany. Shortly before her death, she became a nun and entered the Order of the Poor Clares. She died at Hertford castle, in 1358, and was buried in the Franciscan church at Newgate.

SOURCES:

Annales Londoniensis: Chronicles of the Reigns of Edward I and Edward II. Edited by William Stubbs. Rolls Series. Vol. 76, no. 1. London, 1882 (Latin).

Annales Paulini: Chronicles of the Reigns of Edward I and Edward II. Edited by William Stubbs. Rolls Series. Vol. 76, no. 1. London, 1882 (Latin).

Gesta Edwardi de Carnarvan: Chronicles of the Reigns of Edward I and Edward II. Edited by William Stubbs. Rolls Series. Vol. 76, no. 1. London, 1882 (Latin).

Vita Edwardi Secundi. Edited by N. Denholm-Young. London, 1957 (Latin, with English translation).

SUGGESTED READING:

Johnstone, Hilda. "Isabella, The She-wolf of France," in *History.* Vol. 21, 1936–37.

McKisack, May. *The Fourteenth Century, 1307–1399.* Oxford, 1959 (especially chap. 3, "Reaction and Revolution").

Packe, Michael. *King Edward III.* Edited by L.C.B. Seaman. London. 1983.

RELATED MEDIA:

Braveheart (fictionalized account of English-Scottish wars), starring Mel Gibson as William Wallace, Patrick McGoohan as Edward I Longshanks, and **Sophie Marceau** as Isabella of France; produced by Paramount, 1995.

Douglas C. Jansen, Ph.D.
in Medieval History, University of Texas, Austin, Texas

Isabella of France (c. 1389–c. 1410).

See Isabella of Valois.

Isabella of Gloucester (c. 1167–1217).

See Isabella of Angoulême for sidebar on Avisa of Gloucester.

Isabella of Guise (1900—)

Countess of Harcourt. *Name variations: Isabella de Guise; Isabella Murat. Born on November 27, 1900; daughter of ****Isabella of Orleans*** *(b. 1878) and John (1874–1940), duke of Guise; married Bruno, count of Harcourt, on September 15, 1923; married Prince Pierre Murat, on July 12, 1934.*

Isabella of Hainault (1170–1190)

Queen of France. *Name variations: Isabel; Elizabeth of Hainault or Hainaut. Born at Lille in 1170; died in childbirth in 1190; daughter of Baldwin V, count of Hainault, and ****Margaret of Alsace*** *(c. 1135–1194, sister of Philip of Alsace); married Philip II Augustus (1165–1223), king of France (r. 1180–1223), in 1180; children: Louis VIII (1187–1226), king of France (r. 1223–1226).*

During the first decade of his reign as king of France, Philip II Augustus began to solidify his position by marriage alliances and by pitting various feudal factions against one another. In 1180, he married Isabella of Hainault, the daughter of a count from one of the important Flemish feudal territories. Isabella was crowned at St. Denis on May 29. Through her dowry, Philip gained the northern French county of Artois and claims to other cities and areas to the north such as Amiens. Though Isabella received extravagant praise from certain chroniclers, she failed to win the affections of Philip, who, in 1184, while waging a war against Flanders, was angered at seeing her father support the opposing side and called a council at Sens for the purpose of nullifying the marriage. In 1187, Isabella of Hainault gave Philip a son and heir, the future Louis VIII. She died in childbirth in 1190 and was buried in the church of Notre Dame in Paris.

SUGGESTED READING:

Baldwin, John W. *The Government of Philip Augustus.* University of California Press, 1986.

Davidson, Robert. *Philip II August von Frankreich und Ingeborg.* Stuttgart, 1888.

Levron, Jacques. *Philippe Auguste.* Librarie Academique, 1979.

Isabella of Mar (d. 1296)

Queen of Scotland. *Name variations: Isabel; Isobel of Mar. Died in 1296; daughter of Donald, 6th earl of Mar, and ****Helen*** *(fl. 1275, possibly daughter of Llywelyn the Great); became first wife of Robert I the Bruce, king of Scotland (r. 1306–1329), around 1295; children: ****Margaret Bruce*** *(1296–1316). Robert I's second wife was ****Elizabeth de Burgh*** *(d. 1327).*

Isabella of Naples (1470–1524).

See joint entry on Este, Beatrice d' and Isabella d' for sidebar.

Isabella of Orleans (1848–1919).

See Maria Isabella.

Isabella of Orleans (b. 1878)

Duchess of Guise. *Name variations: Isabella d'Orleans. Born on May 7, 1878; daughter of ****Maria Is-***

*abella (1848–1919) and Louis Philippe (1838–1894), count of Paris; married Jean also known as John (1874–1940), duke of Guise, on October 30, 1899; children: **Isabella of Guise* (b. 1900); **Françoise of Guise* (1902–1953); **Anne of Guise** (b. 1906, who married Amadeus, duke of Aosta); Henry (b. 1908), count of Paris.*

Isabella of Orleans (b. 1911)

***Countess of Paris.** Name variations: Isabelle d'Orléans; Isabella d'Eu. Born on August 13, 1911; daughter of Pedro de Alcántra, prince of Grao Para, and **Elizabeth Dobrzenska** (b. 1875); married Henry (b. 1908), count of Paris, on April 8, 1931; children: **Isabella of Guise** (b. 1932); Henry of Clermont (b. 1933, who married *Maria Theresa of Wurttemberg); **Helene of Guise** (b. 1934); François (b. 1935); Michael and James (b. 1941); Thibaut (b. 1948).*

Isabella of Parma (1692–1766).

See Farnese, Elizabeth.

Isabella of Parma (1741–1763)

***Princess of Parma.** Born on December 31, 1741, in Buen Retiro near Madrid, Spain; died on November 27, 1763, in Vienna; daughter of ***Louise Elizabeth** (1727–1759) and Philip de Bourbon (1720–1765, duke of Parma and son of Elizabeth Farnese); became first wife of Joseph II (1741–1790), emperor of Austria (r. 1780–1790), Holy Roman emperor (r. 1765–1790), on October 6, 1760; his second wife was ***Maria Josepha of Bavaria** (1739–1767).*

Isabella of Poland (1519–1559)

***Queen of Hungary.** Name variations: Izabella Szapolyai. Born in 1519; died in 1559; daughter of ***Bona Sforza** (1493–1557) and Zygmunt I Stary also known as Sigismund I the Elder (1467–1548), king of Poland (r. 1506–1548); married Jan Zapolya also known as John Zapolya (1457–1540), king of Hungary (r. 1526–1540); children: John (II) Sigismund Zapolya, king of Hungary (r. 1540–1571).*

Isabella of Portugal (1271–1336).

See Elizabeth of Portugal.

Isabella of Portugal (1397–1471)

***Duchess of Burgundy.** Name variations: Isabel of Portugal. Born on February 21, 1397, in Evora; died on December 17, 1471 (some sources cite 1472 or 1473), in Nieppe; interred in Dijon; daughter of Joao I also known as John I of Aviz (1357–1433), king of Portugal (sometimes called the Bastard and the Great, r. 1385–1433) and Philippa of Lancaster (1359–1415, who was the daughter of John of Gaunt); sister of Prince Henry the Navigator and Edward I, king of Spain; became third wife of Philip the Good (1396–1467), duke of Burgundy (r. 1419–1467), on January 10, 1430; children: Charles the Bold (1433–1477), duke of Burgundy (r. 1467–1477). Philip the Good's first wife was ***Michelle Valois** (1394–1422); his second wife was ***Bonne of Artois** (d. 1425).*

Isabella of Portugal was born in Evora in 1397, the daughter of John I of Aviz, king of Portugal, and ***Philippa of Lancaster.** Through the patronage of Isabella, the exiled Portuguese established a foothold in the Burgundian court of her husband Philip the Good, duke of Burgundy.

Isabella of Portugal (1503–1539)

***Holy Roman empress who governed as regent of Spain during her husband's prolonged absences from the peninsula.** Name variations: Isabel of Portugal; Isabella of Austria. Born on October 24, 1503, in Lisbon; died on May 1, 1539, in Toledo; daughter of Manuel I the Fortunate (1469–1521), king of Portugal (r. 1495–1521), and his second wife Maria of Castile (1482–1517); married Charles V (1500–1558), king of Spain (r. 1516–1556), king of the Romans (r. 1519–1530), Holy Roman Emperor (r. 1519–1558), on March 10, 1526; children: Philip II (b. 1527), king of Spain (r. 1556–1598), king of Portugal as Philip I (r. 1580–1598); Joanna of Austria (1535–1573), Fernando; Marie of Austria (1528–1603).*

Birth of Charles V (1500); death of Isabella the Catholic (1504); death of Ferdinand of Aragon (1516); Charles V became king of Spain (1517); Luther launches the Reformation (1517); Charles elected Holy Roman Emperor (1519); Francis I defeated and captured by Charles V's forces at Pavia (1526); Treaty of Madrid (1526); sack of Rome by Charles V's army (1527); Schmalkaldic League formed by German protestants (1532); abdication of Charles V in favor of Philip II (1556); death of Charles V (1558).

The daughter of Manuel I of Portugal and his second wife, Queen **Maria of Castile,** Isabella of Portugal was born in Lisbon on October 24, 1503. Her mother, a daughter of the Spanish monarchs, Ferdinand and ***Isabella I,**

Maria of Castile* *(1482–1517).
See Isabella I of Castile for sidebar.

was "very honest, devout, and charitable" and punished her children "when they deserved it without pardoning any of them." She also inculcated ambition and religious piety in Isabella and her sisters. According to Maria of Castile's will, they were to either marry kings or become nuns. When the princess was 14, her mother died, at which point Manuel gave Isabella her mother's properties plus the income from Viseo and Torres Vedras.

Isabella of Portugal was renowned for her beauty and reportedly was determined to marry only the greatest king of Christian Europe. That her father Manuel I proposed her marriage to Charles V, king of Spain and Holy Roman Emperor, must have pleased her immensely, for Charles was the foremost ruler in Christendom. Even more satisfying was Charles's response. In fact, Charles needed to wed for political reasons. Whereas Charles had been raised in Burgundy, his Spanish subjects insisted that he marry someone from the Iberian peninsula and that his heir be raised in Spain. The only delay in the engagement stemmed from the size of the dowry that Charles demanded. He was desperate for money to help finance his political ventures in Central Europe. Eventually Manuel agreed to provide 900,000 ducats, and Charles and Isabella were betrothed. Charles wasted no time in securing a papal dispensation (Isabella's mother was Charles' aunt, making the royal couple first cousins). He intended to wed and then leave his bride as regent to govern Spain while he went to Central Europe to deal with political and religious troubles there. They married on March 10, 1526, in Seville.

A woman of regal dignity, strong character and profound religiosity.

—Peter Pierson

Writes historian Roger B. Merriman, "The Emperor was more fortunate in his marriage than he knew; for besides the financial and political advantages, he had the additional satisfaction of falling in love with his wife." Isabella seems to have entranced the emperor, and he tarried with her longer than anticipated. They honeymooned for several months in Granada. Her first pregnancy brought the birth on May 21, 1527, in Valladolid of the much-desired heir, the future Philip II. Altogether she had three children who survived to adulthood: Philip II, **Marie of Austria**, and ***Joanna of Austria**. Charles did not leave Spain until July 1529.

Marie of Austria. *See Elisabeth of Habsburg for sidebar.*

As Charles had planned, he appointed Isabella regent and governor of Spain during his absence from the peninsula. She attended meetings of the governing councils and consulted with the ministers. As time passed, Isabella took a more active role in the policy-making process, suggesting her own solutions rather than merely accepting the advisors' recommendations. Charles considered her deliberations "very prudent and well thought out." She actively participated in the negotiations of marital alliances between the French and Spanish royal families, concerned that her own young children not be forced to wed the much older offspring of Francis I. During those years, she and the court traveled from city to city, moving in part to avoid exposure to epidemics.

Marriage to Charles was not easy, despite the mutual affection the royal couple shared. His first absence lasted from 1529 to April 1533. For two years, he remained in Spain, only to depart again in December 1536. Although he came back briefly in 1538, he left almost immediately, returning in November 1539. She wrote him regularly but often spent months without letters from Charles. During one of the emperor's long absences, complications from childbirth claimed her life on May 1, 1539 in Toledo. There is also speculation that she may have suffered from consumption, and its debilitating effects hastened her death. A contemporary described Isabella not long before her death: "The Empress is the greatest pity in the world; she is so thin as to not resemble a person." Nonetheless, during her 13 years of marriage to Charles V, according to historian J.H. Elliott, Isabella proved herself "the perfect Empress, a magnificently regal figure."

Charles V felt her loss greatly. In his later years, he spent hours contemplating Titian's portrait of her. He also ordered her body transported to Granada for entombment near his parents. The Marquis of Lombay accompanied the cortege with instructions to identify the corpse on arrival in Granada. Decomposition had so disfigured it, however, that he could not recognize Isabella. He was allegedly so horrified at what death had done to her beauty that he became a Jesuit, gaining fame as San Francisco de Borja. Two decades after Isabella died, her husband breathed his last. He succumbed clutching the same crucifix held by his beloved wife on her death bed.

SOURCES:

Elliott, J.H. *Imperial Spain, 1469–1716.* NY: Penguin, 1990.

March, José María. *Niñez y juventud de Felipe II; documentos inéditors sobre su educación civil, literaria y religiosa y su iniciación al gobierno (1527–1547).* 2 vols. Madrid: Ministerio de Asuntos Exteriores, 1941–1942.

Mazarío Coleto, María del Carmen. *Isabel de Portugal: emperatriz y reina de España.* Madrid: Consejo Superior de Investigaciones Científicas, 1951.

Mexía, Pedro. *Historia del Emperador Carlos V.* Madrid: Espasa-Calpe, 1945.

Vales y Failde, Francisco Javier. *La Emperatriz Isabel.* Madrid: M. Aguilar, 1917.

Kendall W. Brown,
Professor of History, Brigham Young University, Provo, Utah

Isabella of Portugal (1797–1818).

See Carlota Joaquina for sidebar on Maria Isabel of Portugal.

Isabella of Spain (1451–1504).

See Isabella I.

Isabella of Spain (1830–1904).

See Isabella II.

Isabella of Valois (1389–c. 1410)

Queen of England. *Name variations: Isabella de France; Isabella of France; Isabel Valois. Born on November 9, 1389, in Paris, France; died in childbirth on September 13, 1410 (some sources cite 1409), in Blois, Anjou, France; buried at the Church of the Celestines, in Paris, around 1624; second daughter of Charles VI the Mad, king of France (r. 1380–1422), and* ****Isabeau of Bavaria*** *(1371–1435); became second wife of Richard II (1367–1400), king of England (r. 1377–1399), on October 31, 1396; became first wife of Charles Valois (1391–1465), duke of Orléans and count of Angoulême, on June 29, 1406; children: (second marriage) one daughter Jeanne de Orléans (c. 1410–1432, who married Jean II d'Alencon).*

Became child bride of the king of England (1396) who was deposed and imprisoned three years later; led rebel army against husband's foes, but was unsuccessful; returned to France; wed her cousin (1406).

Isabella of Valois was known as the Little Queen, for she was still a child when she arrived in England to become the wife of its king. She was born in Paris in 1389, second daughter of the French king, Charles VI the Mad, and Queen ***Isabeau of Bavaria.** Arranged marriages among Europe's contentious royal families were common at the time, and it was hoped that the latest conflict, in an ongoing series of battles between England and France that became known as the Hundred Years' War, would be resolved by the marital alliance of Isabella to Richard II, king of England and ruler of the House of York.

Isabella of Valois was only seven when she wed Richard II at the English-controlled port of Calais (now France) on October 31, 1396. A year later, she was crowned queen in Westminster Abbey; allegedly, several people died in the crush to get a glimpse of the famous young bride. Richard II was by then around 30 years of age, and the pair did not live together. Isabella instead grew up in Windsor Castle, where her husband visited her and brought gifts. There was conflict within his extended royal family, however, and the throne was coveted by his cousins in the House of Lancaster. It is said that Richard II's last gift to Isabella was a dog to be her companion throughout her upcoming hardships, of which she was probably unaware; soon afterward, his cousin, Henry of Bolingbroke, deposed him and took the throne as Henry IV.

Isabella never saw her husband again after that last visit. He was imprisoned, and she, barely entering her teens, was moved to Sunninghill along with her court. Factions loyal to Richard II saw her as a valuable ally, however, and told her that he had escaped, and that she should lead an army of rebels to victory against the House of Lancaster and Henry IV. She complied, but the mayor of a town called Cirencester was loyal to the Lancasters, and informed Henry IV of the plot against him. Isabella's two cohorts, the earls of Kent and Salisbury, were executed for their role in the insurgency; she was lucky to be judged too immature, and little actual threat, to be charged with any crime.

Isabella was, however, still an attraction as a royal spouse, and Henry IV wished to marry her to his son who was near her own age. That boy would become Henry V, and also the inspiration for the "Prince Hal" in Shakespearean drama. To Isabella, however, the idea was abhorrent, and she refused to cooperate or even speak at court. She assumed Richard II was dead, which was indeed true by 1400; he had either been murdered or had died after a self-imposed hunger strike while imprisoned at Pontefract Castle. Isabella's family in France campaigned for her return, but Henry IV would not allow it for several years. Eventually she was allowed to leave England, and was married to her cousin, Charles Valois, the duke of Orléans and count of Angoulême, on June 29, 1406. Supposedly, the marriage was against her wishes, and she cried throughout the ceremony. Isabella died after giving birth to a daughter in September of 1410 (one source cites 1409 as her date of death), in Blois, Anjou, France. She was either 20 or 21 years of age. Later her husband fought "Prince Hal" at the infamous Battle of Agincourt in 1415. Charles Valois lost the battle, however, and was imprisoned in the Tower of London for

25 years, where he wrote poetry. Isabella of Valois is buried in Paris.

Carol Brennan,
Grosse Pointe, Michigan

Isabella the Catholic (1451–1504).

See Isabella I.

Isabelle (1225–1270)

French princess and saint. *Name variations: Isabel; Saint Isabelle; Blessed Isabelle. Born in March in 1225; died in 1270; daughter of Blanche of Castile (1188–1252) and Louis VIII, king of France (r. 1223–1226); sister of Saint Louis IX (1214–1270), king of France (r. 1226–1270).*

Daughter of ***Blanche of Castile** and King Louis VIII of France, Saint Isabelle was born in 1225, the youngest sister of Saint Louis IX. From an early age, Isabelle studied natural history, medicine, logic, Eastern languages, and Latin, along with the scriptures. She was known for her piety. Her brother Louis often delighted in disclosing that Isabelle was once so deep in prayer that she hardly knew her bed was being made up with her in it.

At age ten, the young princess was betrothed to the son of the count of Angoulême. Not long after, while the French court was at Saint-Germain, Isabelle grew dangerously ill, "as a result of mortifications." A holy person, brought to her bedside, prophesied that she would recover and give her life to God. Her brother Louis broke off the betrothal with 10,000 silver francs.

Then Frederick II, Holy Roman emperor, proposed that she marry his son Conrad (IV), heir to his empire. When Pope Innocent IV championed the request, Isabelle told the pope that she would rather be last in the ranks of the Lord's virgins than first in the world as empress.

In 1258, she founded the abbey of Longchamp, opposite Mount Valerian, on the right bank of the Seine. The convent, comprised of 60 nuns, mostly from the court circle, followed the rule of St. ***Clare of Assisi**. Though Pope Urban IV moderated the rule as much as possible, Isabelle was too ill to follow the routine. Instead, she lived within the convent walls for the last ten years of her life without taking her vows, repairing clothes for the poor. She died, age 46, lying on a bed of straw. Her feast day is February 22.

Isabelle d'Autriche (1554–1592).

See Elisabeth of Habsburg.

Isabelle d'Autriche (1566–1633).

See Isabella Clara Eugenia of Austria.

Isabelle de Clare (c. 1167–1217).

See Isabella of Angoulême for sidebar on Avisa of Gloucester.

Isabelle of Austria (1554–1592).

See Elisabeth of Habsburg.

Isabelle of Bavaria (1371–1435).

See Isabeau of Bavaria.

Isabelle of Bourbon (d. 1465).

See Mary of Burgundy for sidebar.

Isabelle of Cornwall

Marquise of Montferrat. *Married William V the Great, marquis of Montferrat; children:* ***Irene of Montferrat** *(who married Andronicus II Paleologus, emperor of Nicaea, r. 1282–1328); possibly* **Beatrix of Montferrat** *(who married Andre [Guigues] VI, dauphin de Viennois).*

Isabelle of France (1349–1372)

French princess. *Name variations: Isabella de France; Isabella or Isabelle of Valois. Born in 1349; died in 1372; daughter of Jean or John II the Good (1319–1364), king of France (r. 1350–1364), and Bona of Bohemia (1315–1349); sister of Charles V (1337–1380), king of France (r. 1364–1380), and* ***Jane of France** *(1343–1373), queen of Navarre; married John Galeas Visconti also known as Giangaleazzo or Gian Galeazzo Visconti (1351–1402), lord of Milan (r. 1378–1402), duke of Milan (r. 1396–1402), in 1364; children: a son who died young; Valentina Visconti (1366–1408); and two others.*

Isabelle of France was born in 1349, the daughter of John II the Good, king of France, and ***Bona of Bohemia**. Because of the costs incurred during the Hundred Years' War, John II was desperately in need of funds when Galeazzo II, lord of Milan, offered to pay 100,000 florins in order that the king's daughter might marry his son. Thus, in 1364, 14-year-old Isabelle of France married 12-year-old Gian Galeazzo, the future duke of Milan. Their first son was born two years later, but he died in childhood. Isabelle had three other children, but her daughter ***Valentina Visconti** was the only child to survive. Isabelle died in 1372, age 22, following the birth of her fourth child. Gian Galeazzo's second wife was his cousin *Catherine Visconti. He also had many illegitimate children: including son Gabriele Maria Visconti with **Agnese Mantegazza** and possibly two other sons with a woman named **Lusotta**.

Isabelle of Gloucester (c. 1167–1217).

See Isabella of Angoulême for sidebar on Avisa of Gloucester.

Isabelle of Lorraine (1410–1453)

***Queen of Naples.** Name variations: Isabel, Isabella, Isabelle or Isabeau de Lorraine; Isabel of Bar. Born around 1410 in Lorraine, France; died in 1453 in Anjou; daughter of Charles II, duke of Lorraine, and Margaret of Bavaria; married René I the Good (1408–1480), duke of Lorraine and Bar, duke of Provence, duke of Anjou and Guise, and later king of Naples; children: John II (1424–1470), duke of Calabria; Margaret of Anjou (1429–1482); ***Yolande of Vaudemont** (1428–1483, who married Frederick of Vaudemont).*

Isabelle of Lorraine was a bold French duchess and military leader. She was born around 1410, the daughter of Charles II, duke of Lorraine, and **Margaret of Bavaria**. Isabelle married René I the Good, duke of Anjou, as a young woman, and was the mother of ***Margaret of Anjou**. Like many educated noblewomen of her age, Isabelle patronized the arts and helped endow several colleges. When a rival noble kidnapped her husband, Isabelle gathered an army from among her vassals. She rode at its head and was responsible for gaining her husband's release. She also served as René's regent after he conquered Sicily, and held the title of queen of Naples. A year after Isabelle's death in 1453, René married ***Jeanne de Laval** (d. 1498).

Laura York,
Riverside, California

Isabelle of Savoy (d. 1383)

***Duchess of Bourbon.** Name variations: Isabelle of Valois; Isabella de Valois. Died on August 26, 1383 (some sources cite 1388); daughter of Charles I, count of Valois, and ***Mahaut de Chatillon** (d. 1358); married Pierre or Peter I (1311–1356), duke of Bourbon (r. 1342–1356), on January 25, 1336; children: ***Jeanne de Bourbon** (1338–1378, who married Charles V, king of France); ***Blanche of Bourbon** (c. 1338–1361, who married Peter the Cruel, king of Castile and León).*

Isabelle of Valois (d. 1383).

See Isabelle of Savoy.

Isakova, Maria (1920—)

***Soviet skater.** Born in Khlynovka, Soviet Union, in 1920; married; children: at least one daughter.*

Won the Women's World championships (1948, 1949, 1950).

Maria Isakova began her athletic career participating in track and field in school; she soon switched to ice skating. At 16, she was a member of the Dynamo Club. She attended Kirov Physical Training College, then moved to Moscow during the early years of World War II and attended the Stalin Central Institute of Physical Culture. Isakova won the women's world speed-skating championships thrice in succession and broke the USSR record for 1,000 meters at 1:41.2 in 1947. Sadly, women's speed-skating did not become an Olympic event until 1960.

Isberge (c. 753–807).

See Gisela.

Iscah

***Biblical woman.** Daughter of Haran; sister of Milcah and Lot.*

Ise (877–940)

***Japanese court woman, known as Lady Ise, who was considered one of the most accomplished poets of her time.** Name variations: Lady Ise. Pronunciation: EE-say. Born in 877 (some sources cite 875) in an unknown location; real name is not known (Ise was the Japanese province of which her father was once governor); died in 940 (some sources cite 938) in an unknown location, although most likely the capital, Kyoto; daughter of Fujiwara no Tsugikage, governor of Ise and, later, Yamamoto; lover of Prince Atsuyoshi; concubine of the Emperor Uda; children: (with Prince Atsuyoshi) daughter Nakatsukasa (a poet); (with Uda) Prince Yuki-Akari.*

Lady Ise ranks with another woman poet, ***Ono no Komachi**, as the most accomplished poet of 9th–10th century Japan. She was born in 877, the daughter of Fujiwara no Tsugikage, the governor of Ise and, later, of Yamamoto. She was the lover of Prince Atsuyoshi and then the concubine of the Emperor Uda. Ise is thought to have entered the service of Empress *Onshi, consort of Emperor Uda, around 892.

Lady Ise was one of a larger group of Japanese women writers of this time, whose prominence is said to be unparalleled in world literature. More than 500 of Ise's poems were compiled in various anthologies. Her poetry was characterized by wit and her love poems reflected great passion. "If only the resemblance/ Of my fleshy body," she wrote, "As the fields/ Withered dry by weather/ Meant that the way we both are seared by fire/ Would bring me also the waited spring."

SOURCES:

Brower, Robert H., and Earl Miner. *Japanese Court Poetry.* Stanford, CA: Stanford University Press. 1961.

Linda L. Johnson,
Professor of History, Concordia College, Moorhead, Minnesota

Iselda, Lady (fl. 12th c.)

Provençal troubadour. *Flourished in the 12th century in Provence.*

Iselda was a Provençal troubadour about whom very little is clear. She was one of the writers of an unusual *tenson* with two other women, ***Alais** and **Carenza**. Possibly Iselda and Alais were considering becoming nuns, for they ask Carenza if she recommends marriage, which she emphatically does not. This humorous anti-marriage poem is the only known work written by Iselda.

Laura York,
Riverside, California

Iseut de Capio (1140–?)

French noblewoman and poet. *Born in 1140 in southern France.*

A troubadour in southern France during the height of the troubadour period, Iseut de Capio's family background is unknown. She was probably from the town of Les Chapelins, in the southeast corner of modern France. Only one of her poems still survives; it is a *tenson*, or dialogue, written with another female troubadour, ***Almucs de Castelnau.** In the poem, Iseut asks Almucs to act more kindly to a dying knight or to at least let him receive the sacraments before his death; Almucs, who resents the knight for his discourteous behavior towards her, refuses to forgive him unless Iseut can get him to repent his actions.

Laura York,
Riverside, California

Isitt, Adeline Genée (1878–1970).

See Genée, Adeline.

Isobel.

Variant of Isabel.

Isom, Mary Frances (1865–1920)

American librarian. *Born Mary Frances Isom on February 27, 1865, in Nashville, Tennessee; died on April 15, 1920, in Portland, Oregon; daughter of John Franklin Isom, a surgeon, and Frances A. (Walter) Isom; educated at Cleveland public schools, Wellesley College, and the Pratt Institute Library School in Brooklyn, New York; never married; children: (adopted daughter) Berenice Langdon.*

Born the only child of John Franklin Isom, a prominent surgeon, and **Frances Isom** on February 27, 1865, Mary Isom grew up in Cleveland, Ohio, where she attended public schools. Her start at Wellesley College in 1883 came to halt because of ill health, and she devoted herself to keeping house for her father after the death of her mother in 1891. His death in 1898 left her temporarily unmoored until ***Josephine Rathbone**, an old friend and a faculty member at Pratt Institute Library School, encouraged Isom to enroll at Pratt. Isom graduated in 1900, then moved to Portland, Oregon, in 1901 to catalog the John Wilson Collection at the Library Association, then a private library.

In 1902, Isom became the librarian there, and, in accordance with the stipulations of the institution's donor, the library was transformed from a private subscription library to a free public one. Within a year, great changes had been made, including a new registration system, a children's department, and larger reference services. The library had also expanded to serve the county as well as the city. In less than six years, Isom helped set up three branches and eleven reading rooms around the county. Books were also being taken to schools, stores, fire stations, and grange halls.

In 1905, Isom played a crucial role, along with board member Winslow B. Ayer, in getting legislation passed that established the Oregon State Library Commission. That same year, she helped convince **Cornelia Marvin** to leave her job as secretary of the Wisconsin Library Commission and take over the development of Oregon's public libraries.

The period from 1911 to 1913 saw the necessity for seven large permanent branches to meet the growing needs of the Portland area, and Isom played an important part in the procurement of Carnegie funds that allowed these branches to be established. Working closely with architect Albert E. Doyle, Isom also was instrumental in the building of the new Multnomah County Public Library.

During World War I, Isom helped to organize libraries in army and lumber camps throughout Oregon and Washington. She also accepted a request, despite ill health, from the American Library Association to organize hospital libraries in France. She spent six months on this task and returned home in poorer health. However, she did not want to stop her activities and so remained involved by phone and letters until her death of cancer at the age of 55 on April 15, 1920.

SOURCES:

James, Edward T., ed. *Notable American Women 1607–1950.* Cambridge, MA: The Belknap Press of Harvard University Press, 1971.

McHenry, Robert, ed. *Famous American Women.* NY: Dover, 1983.

Karina L. Kerr, M.A.,
Ypsilanti, Michigan

Israels, Belle Lindner (1877–1933).

See Moskowitz, Belle.

Ita.

Variant of Ida.

Ita of Ireland (d. 570)

Irish princess and saint. *Name variations: Saint Ida of Ireland; Ite; Mida; Mary of Munster. Born near Drum, County Waterford, birth date unknown; baptized Dorothy or Deirdre; died at Killeedy around 569 or 570 in Limerick, Ireland; said to have been of royal descent; never married; no children.*

Next to Saint ***Bridget** (c. 453–c. 524), Saint Ita was the most revered Irish holy woman. She was baptized Dorothy or Deirdre, but gained the name Ita much later, a name which means thirst in Gaelic, from her thirst for divine love. She was descended from the royal house of Ireland, and raised by parents who had accepted Christianity. Encouraged by her parents to pursue a religious life, she took the veil as a girl and eventually founded a community of women at Killeedy (Cill Íde) near Newcastle West, County Limerick. Soon the community was officially established as an abbey, and Ita became its leader; legend has it that St. Brendan attended her school. Ita was highly regarded as an intelligent, learned, and wise woman, and was often consulted by peasants and nobles alike on personal matters. The holy woman was credited with several miracles and with the ability to see the future. Ita corresponded with many of the leaders of the early Christian church and was greatly mourned at her death. She was soon canonized. Her Feast Day is January 15.

SOURCES:

Dunbar, Agnes. *Dictionary of Saintly Women, vol. I.* London: G. Bell and Sons, 1904.

Laura York,
Riverside, California

Ita of Nivelles (597–652).

See Ida of Nivelles.

Italy, queen of.

See Bertha of Toulouse (fl. late 700s).
See Cunegunde (fl. 800s).
See Engelberga (c. 840–890).
See Bertha of Swabia (fl. 900s).
See Marie Adelaide of Austria (1822–1855).
See Margaret of Savoy (1851–1926).
See Elena of Montenegro (1873–1952).
See Marie José of Belgium (b. 1906).

Italys, Alice (d. after 1326).

See Hayles, Alice.

Ite.

Variant of Ida.

Iti (c. 2563–2424 BCE)

Egyptian singer, believed to be the first songstress chronicled in the annals of history. *Lived around the time of the reign of Neferefre, 2563–2424 BCE.*

Like many ancient Egyptians, Iti's tomb as well as numerous references to her in writing and in pictures document her celebrity during her lifetime. Hers is a beautiful grave near the Chefren (Khafren) pyramids in the Necropolis of Giza. She performed during the reign of Pharaoh Neferefre (2563–2424). Iti is also depicted in the Necropolis of Saqqarah which was part of Memphis, the former capital of Ancient Egypt. A noble Egyptian had Iti's picture put in his tomb wishing to enjoy her music in the next life as well as to memorialize her art. In this tomb, Iti holds one hand to her ear and makes a cheironomic sign with the other to signal her accompanist as to which note she wishes played. In this depiction, Iti is accompanied by the harpist, Hekenu. Iti is the first chronicled songstress in Egyptian history. The careful records left in her memory document the importance of Iti and women like her throughout history.

John Haag,
Athens, Georgia

Itkina, Maria (1932—)

Russian runner. *Born in 1932.*

Won the 200-meter race at the European championships (1954); won the 400-meter race at the European championships (1958, 1962).

The first 400-meter specialist and the first to successfully combine the 400 meter and the 200 meter, Maria Itkina was a formidable competitor from 1952 to 1962, winning three European titles. In 1960, with the 400 meter still absent from the Olympic agenda, Itkina had to run in the 200, placing fourth. (In both 1956 and 1960, her team placed fourth in the 4x100 meter relay.) The 400-meter race was first introduced as an Olympic event in 1964 in Tokyo. By that time, Itkina was 32. She placed fifth.

Itta.

Variant of Ita or Ida.

Iturbi, Amparo (1898–1969)

Spanish pianist who performed on concert stages throughout the world and was widely known as a teacher. *Born in Valencia, Spain, on March 12, 1898; died in Beverly Hills, California, on April 21, 1969; one of four children of Ricardo Iturbi (a piano tuner) and Teresa (Baguena) Iturbi; sister of José Iturbi (1895–1980).*

Born in Valencia, Spain, on March 12, 1898, Amparo Iturbi had a distinguished career as an international concert pianist. In 1925, she gave her first important concert outside Spain at the Salle Gaveau in Paris. She was first heard in America on May 2, 1937, when she performed the Haydn Piano Concerto for CBS radio. Two months later, she performed the Mozart Concerto for Two Pianos with her equally gifted brother, José Iturbi, at Lewisohn Stadium. Though she was somewhat overshadowed by her brother, Amparo Iturbi was an accomplished musician and stylish performer. As a teacher, she trained a number of excellent artists including Bruce Sutherland. She died in Beverly Hills, California, in 1969.

John Haag,
Athens, Georgia

Iulia.

Variant of Julia.

Iulia Balbilla (fl. 130 CE).

See Balbilla.

Iurevskaia, Princess (1847–1922).

See Dolgorukova, Ekaterina.

Ivanovna, Anna (1693–1740).

See Anna Ivanovna.

Ivanovskaia, Praskovia (1853–1935)

Revolutionary and terrorist who was involved in two of the most sensational political assassinations in Russian history. *Name variations: P.S. Voloshenko; Praskovya Ivanovskaya. Pronunciation: E-van-OFF-sky-ya. Born Praskovia Semenovna Ivanovskaia in 1853 in Sokovnina, Russia; died in the Soviet Union in 1935; daughter of Semen Ivanov (a village priest); educated at church boarding school in Tula until 1871; attended Alarchin courses in St. Petersburg, 1773–76; married I.F.(?) Voloshenko; no children.*

Was involved in the "to the people" movement and other Populist enterprises (1876–79); was a member of Narodnaia Volia (1880–82), with special responsibility for running the party's illegal printing presses; arrested (1882), tried (1883) and sentenced to hard labor for life in Siberia; escaped (1903); was a member of Combat Organization of the Socialist Revolutionary Party (1903–05); participated in the election campaign to the First State Duma (1906).

Selected writings: "Avtobiografiia" (Autobiography), in Entsiklopedicheskii slovar', *vol. XL (1927), pp. 151–163 (reprinted in* Deiateli SSSR i revoliutsionnogo dvizheniia Rossii *[Personalities of the USSR and the Revolutionary Movement in Russia], Moscow, 1989).*

On April 3, 1883, Praskovia Ivanovskaia was sentenced to death by hanging for "striking a blow at the heart of the state" when she assisted in the assassination of Tsar Alexander II. Like many other young Russians, both male and female, she had been actively involved in "going to the people" during the 1870s and had joined the terrorist group Narodnaia Volia (the People's Will) in 1880. Perhaps because her assignment had been to run the organization's illegal printing press, rather than actually throwing the bombs which killed the tsar on March 1, 1881, her sentence was eventually reduced to a life of hard labor in eastern Siberia. After 20 years of confinement and exile, she escaped in 1903 and resumed terrorist activity as a member of the Socialist Revolutionary Party in St. Petersburg.

"My childhood was one of neglect and grim poverty," Ivanovskaia wrote in 1925. "We grew up like weeds in the field, without the slightest supervision." Shortly after Praskovia's birth in

1853 in a small village in Tula Province, her mother had died. Her father, Semen Ivanov, was a parish priest who showed little interest in the upbringing of his six children. He did, however, become the close friend of M.A. Bodisko who as a young officer had taken part in the Decembrist Revolt of 1825 and now was living on a nearby estate. Through Bodisko's generosity, Praskovia and one of her sisters were able to enroll in a church boarding school for girls in Tula where "the wave of new ideas of the sixties found their way to us, penetrating the stone walls of our cloister." Many of these ideas were contained in illegal books and journals supplied by her revolutionary brother and which became the resources for a radical study circle organized at the school. After the police discovered the library, Ivanovskaia was arrested and threatened with dire consequences by the school's rector if she continued along the same path as her brother. "To reject the influence of good books," she wrote later:

> the books that gave us a taste for a larger, brighter life, and that put us on guard against the stifling, humdrum existence around us—that was equivalent to suicide! The sense that there was a better way to live had gradually become part of our souls. And not only through reading—we felt it whenever we looked at the injustice all around us, at the downtrodden, benumbed masses. Our souls pined for truth and justice.

Women of Ivanovskaia's generation were barred from seeking "truth" through attending Russian universities. They could, however, audit the Alarchin non-degree courses offered in St. Petersburg. Praskovia enrolled in these in 1873 and thus spent the next three years in the Russian capital supplementing her meager education, joining study circles with other women of radical persuasion, and deepening her commitment to social change. In 1876, she was offered a teaching position by a liberal *zemstvo* but chose instead to "labor 'in union with the people'" by living and working among the lower classes and perhaps infusing them with her own new-found ideals concerning agrarian socialism. She spent several months in a rope factory in Odessa, the summer of 1876 as a peasant on a Ukrainian estate, and a short time as a cobbler's apprentice in Nikolaev. Even though she did not initially join a revolutionary organization, she considered herself a Narodnik or Populist and participated in several attempts to free fellow Populists from prison. She also helped organize the first armed demonstration in Russian history in Odessa in 1878, and she spent three months in a tsarist jail for her convictions.

In 1880, Ivanovskaia returned to St. Petersburg as an experienced revolutionary and joined Narodnaia Volia—the Populist terrorist organization dedicated to the assassination of Alexander II. She was assigned the job of maintaining the organization's illegal printing press and running off thousands of copies of revolutionary leaflets. It was dangerous but boring work without the glamour associated with throwing bombs or the prestige of writing articles and pamphlets. In some respects, it was considered "women's work" by the leadership; Ivanovskaia did it well and without complaint. As one of the leaders, ***Vera Figner**, recalled, she was a woman with "an attractive face in the purely Russian style and a voice of marvelous timbre; her warmth, simplicity, and sensitivity charmed everyone with whom she came into contact."

Praskovia Ivanovskaia

The successful assassination of Alexander II in March 1881 did not bring the results Narodnaia Volia had wanted. The peasant masses remained apathetic, the new tsar was opposed to further reforms, and the police arrested most of the leading revolutionaries. Ivanovskaia was one of the few to escape, at least temporarily. She went first to Moscow and then was sent to Vitebsk to help assemble a new printing press. In September 1882, the police caught up with her. The next spring she was one of the defendants in the "Trial of the Seventeen"—all members of Narodnaia Volia involved in the tsar's assassination. While she avoided the gallows, she did not escape the horrors of confinement in Siberia. In her correspondence she gives:

> a picture of a small part of our life in these penal tombs, which shattered the lives of thousands of ardent young people, turning human beings into the living dead. . . . The Kara prison most resembles a tumble-down stable. The dampness and cold are ferocious; there's no heat at all in the cells, only two stoves in the corridor. The cell doors are kept open day and night—otherwise we would freeze to death. . . . Willy-nilly, people swiftly decay in the tomb that is Kara. There

is an inescapable feeling that for many of us, life is irrevocably over; still, one must marvel at the spiritual courage with which we all endure our slow deaths.

By striking a blow at the heart of the state, the party had cried aloud, not only to our compatriots but to the whole world as well: "Russia and the Russian people need political freedom. We need the complete liberation of our country!"

—Praskovia Ivanovskaia (1925)

In 1898, Ivanovskaia was finally released from Kara prison but forced to live in exile elsewhere in eastern Siberia. Five years later, at the age of 50, she escaped and made her way back to St. Petersburg where she joined the Combat Organization of the Socialist Revolutionary Party (SR). In 1904, she played a support role in the organization's sensational assassination of V.K. Plehve, the despised minister of the interior. "The conclusion of this affair," she wrote in her brief autobiography, "gave me some satisfaction—finally the man who had taken so many victims had been brought to his inevitable end, so universally desired." In the early days of the unsuccessful 1905 Revolution, she again was involved in SR assassination plots against the tsarist regime. On March 16, however, before these plans could come to fruition, she and most of the Combat Organization were arrested. After seven months of detention, she was released in accordance with the general amnesty which accompanied the granting of the October Manifesto. Ivanovskaia then moved to Saratov Province where she participated in the 1906 election campaign to the First State Duma or parliament. In 1907, the local police finally sought to arrest her for fleeing Siberia four years earlier. Her autobiography recalls that as they approached the front of her house "I left by the back door." She also walked off the pages of history. We know only that she died in 1935 at the age of 82 in the Soviet Union.

SOURCES:

Engel, Barbara Alpern, and Clifford N. Rosenthal, eds. and trans. *Five Sisters Against the Tsar*. NY: Alfred A. Knopf, 1975 (the quotations used above come from the translated excerpts of Ivanovskaia's autobiography and letters found in this volume).

Ivanovskaia, P.S. "Avtobiografiia," in *Entsiklopedicheskii slovar'*. Vol. XL, 1927, pp. 151–163.

R.C. Elwood,
Professor of History, Carleton University, Ottawa, Canada

Ivers, Alice (1851–1930).

See Tubbs, Alice.

Ivetta.

Variant of Ivette, Joveta, and Yvette.

Ivetta of Huy (1158–1228)

Belgian anchoress. *Name variations: Ivette of Huy; Jutta of Huy; Yvette of Huy. Born in 1158 in Huy, Belgium; died in 1228 in Belgium; daughter of nobles; married; children: three.*

A holy woman of the Low Countries, Ivetta of Huy was born into a noble Belgian family in 1158. Her early life is obscure; her parents forced her to wed at age 13, and she was widowed at 18 with three sons to support. Ivetta wanted to pursue a religious life but had to fight against her parents' wish that she remarry; finally she convinced a local bishop to help her. It is not clear with whom she left her children, but Ivetta did penance for her sins by serving in a leper hospital in Huy. After a few years, she decided that to reach her true calling she needed to enclose herself as a recluse, or anchoress. She received the necessary permissions and had a cell built next to the leper hospital.

Ivetta of Huy spent more than four decades in her cell, which consisted of two small rooms with a window so that she could consult with visitors and those seeking guidance. Her piety made her famous in that area, and eventually a community of other religious men and women grew up around her, its members attracted by the idea of living in an informal setting without taking vows but devoting themselves to serving others. Ivetta became the indirect leader of this community, giving spiritual guidance and counseling the brothers and sisters, but not taking responsibility for their material well-being, as a regular abbess or prioress did. Among her other accomplishments, she worked to set up inns for the protection of travelers on pilgrimage and distributed all of her substantial property and money to the poor of Huy. Her feast day is January 13.

Laura York,
Riverside, California

Ivey, Jean Eichelberger (1923—)

American composer. *Born in Washington, D.C., on July 3, 1923; daughter of Joseph S. Eichelberger (editor of an anti-feminist newspaper) and Elizabeth (Pfeffer) Eichelberger; earned her Bachelor of Arts from Trinity College on full scholarship in 1944; Master's Degree in music from Peabody Conservatory in 1946; second Master's at Eastman School of Music; awarded Doctorate of Philosophy at the University of Toronto* *in 1972; among her teachers were Claudio Arrau, Pasquale Tallarico,* ***Katherine Bacon****, and Herbert Elwell.*

Taught at the Peabody Conservatory, Trinity College, Catholic University in Washington, and College Misericordia; became a leader in electronic composition and was founder-director of the Peabody Electronic Music Studio.

Composing and conducting are two of the last male bastions, though women are steadily making inroads into these fields. Jean Eichelberger Ivey battled this prejudice not only in the field of music but also in academia where women were less likely to be awarded tenure, foundation grants, performance opportunities, and commercial recordings. Much of the time, Ivey made her living as a teacher of piano, organ, and theory while she was composing. While teaching, she continued to compose for orchestra, chamber ensembles, chorus, solos, and electronic music. In 1968, she was the only woman composer represented at the Eastman-Rochester American Music Festival. Her electronic music, *Continuous Form,* has been played many times, especially during station breaks on Channel 13 in New York City and on WGBH Channel 2 in Boston, both educational stations. The playing of her music in short intervals gained her a wide audience.

Ivey had mixed feelings about her reputation in electronic music: "My favorite medium is voice. It was mainly a historical accident that my electronic music tended to be featured in the late sixties and early seventies in connection with the Peabody studio. I prefer not to be too identified with electronic music." In fact most of her compositions were written for traditional instruments. Some, like *Testament of Eve,* offer a startling opportunity to rethink the myth of the Garden of Eden from a woman's perspective.

SOURCES:

Block, Adrienne Fried, and Carol Neuls-Bates, compilers and eds. *Women in American Music: A Bibliography of Music and Literature.* Westport, CT: Greenwood Press, 1979.

Cohen, Aaron I. *International Encyclopedia of Women Composers.* 2 vols. NY: Books & Music (USA), 1987.

SUGGESTED READING:

Ivey, Jean Eichelberger, and Pauline Oliveros. "The Composer as Teacher," in *Peabody Conservatory Alumni Bulletin.* Vol. XIV, no. 1, 1974.

———. *Observations by Composers.* Ed. by Elliott Schwartz. Praeger, 1973.

RELATED MEDIA:

"A Woman Is . . . ," a film about Jean Eichelberger Ivey, 1973.

COLLECTIONS:

An interview at the Yale University Music Library; thesis at Eastman School of Music, Sibley Music Library.

John Haag,
Athens, Georgia

Ivinskaya, Olga (1912–1995)

Russian magazine editor. *Name variations: Olga Ivinskaia. Born in Russia in 1912; died in Moscow on September 8, 1995; buried in Moscow; lived with Boris Pasternak (1890–1960); married twice; children: two, including Dmitri Vinogradov.*

The character Lara in Boris Pasternak's Nobel Prize-winning *Doctor Zhivago*, played by **Julie Christie** in the 1965 movie, was inspired by Olga Ivinskaya. Born in Russia in 1912, she was a magazine editor for a Moscow literary journal. She was jailed twice, spending more than eight years in Soviet prison camps because of her anti-Soviet activities related to her 14-year affair with Pasternak. Pasternak, an anti-Stalinist writer, was very much out of favor with the Soviet regime. (Throughout their relationship, however, Pasternak never left his second wife **Zinaida Nikolaevna Pasternak**.)

When Olga met Boris in 1946, she was 34, he was 56. Each had been married twice and had two children. In love even before they met, she once told her mother that seeing Pasternak at a recital had been like "communing with God." While in prison the first time because of her association with him, in 1949 Ivinskaya miscar-

Olga Ivinskaya

ried their child. In 1958, when the Communist Party attacked *Doctor Zhivago* and refused to let Pasternak accept a Nobel Prize for Literature, the couple contemplated double suicide. They were still together when he died two years later.

Olga was then sentenced to eight more years in a labor camp. "She paid dearly for it all," said her son, Dmitri Vinogradov, "but even just before her death she said she had no regrets. She would live that life again and again. She loved him as a man, whether he was a poet or not." Ivinskaya wrote about her life with Pasternak in the book *A Captive of Time,* published in 1978, and letters between Ivinskaya and Pasternak survive. *Doctor Zhivago* was not published in Russia until 1988; the movie was not released there until 1994.

SUGGESTED READING:

Ivinskaya, Olga. *A Captive of Time* (also titled *A Prisoner of Time*), 1978.

"Olga Ivinskaya, 83, Pasternak Muse for 'Zhivago'," in *The New York Times Biographical Service.* September 1995, p. 1351.

"Undying Love," in *People Weekly.* December 2, 1996.

RELATED MEDIA:

Doctor Zhivago (197 min. film), starring Julie Christie, Omar Sharif, Tom Courtenay, Rod Steiger, Alec Guinness, Ralph Richardson, **Rita Tushingham, Geraldine Chaplin,** and ***Siobhan McKenna,** screenplay by Robert Bolt, directed by David Lean, MGM, 1965.

Maria Ivogün

Ivogün, Maria (1891–1987)

Hungarian coloratura soprano. *Name variations: Maria Ivogun. Born Ilse Kempner on November 18, 1891, in Budapest, Hungary; died on October 2, 1987, in Beatenberg, Lake Thun; daughter of the singer* ***Ida von Günther****; studied with Schlemmer-Ambros in Vienna and with Schöner in Munich; married Karl Erb (a tenor), in 1921 (divorced 1932); married Michael Raucheisen (her accompanist), in 1933.*

Made debut at the Bavarian Court Opera (1913), Berlin State Opera (1925), and Covent Garden (1927); taught at the Vienna Academy of Music and the Berlin Hochschule für Musik.

Maria Ivogün was born Ilse Kempner in Budapest, Hungary, in 1891. She devised her stage name from her mother's maiden name—**Ida von Günther**. Singing came naturally to Ivogün as her mother was also a vocalist. After studies at the Vienna Music Academy and in Munich, Ivogün appeared at the Bavarian Court Opera where she would perform from 1913 to 1925, often under the baton of Bruno Walter. When Walter went to Berlin to conduct opera, she followed him and eventually appeared at both the Stätische Oper and the Staatsoper. Her most famous role was Zerbinetta in *Ariadne auf Naxos* by Strauss; the composer claimed Ivogün was "unique and without rival." Her recordings were limited but she made enough acoustical and electrical transcriptions to demonstrate what an accomplished singer she was. Her recordings show an ease of production but a lack of force and energy on the high notes. In 1933, Ivogün married the noted accompanist Michael Raucheisen with whom she established an extensive recital career after retiring from the opera stage in 1932. A favorite at Salzburg and Covent Garden, she never appeared at the Met. Ivogün became a teacher and is best remembered for her pupil, ***Elisabeth Schwarzkopf.**

John Haag,
Athens, Georgia

Izabel or Izabella.

Variant of Isabel or Isabella.

Izumi Shikibu (c. 975–c. 1027)

***Japanese poet who wrote the fictionalized diary* Izumi shikibu nikki.** *Born around 975 CE; died, possibly around 1027 CE; married Tachibana no Michisada (divorced); married Fujiwara no Yasumasa (958–1036); children: (first marriage) daughter Koshikibu no naishi (a poet who served Empress Shoshi and died young).*

Izumi Shikibu served Empress ➤ **Shoshi,** like her friend ***Murasaki Shikibu,** and was known for her extramarital affairs with Prince Tametaka and Prince Atsumichi which resulted in the eventual dissolution of her first marriage. Two hundred and forty of Izumi Shikibu's poems are represented in imperial anthologies. Izumi Shikibu carried on a "fascinating correspondence," wrote Lady Murasaki. "She does have a rather unsavory side to her character but has a genius for tossing off letters with ease and can make the most banal statement sound special. Her poems are quite delightful." When Izumi Shikibu received a note for her daughter **Koshikibu no naishi** who had recently died at age 26, she wrote: "This name of hers,/ Not buried together with her,/ And not decaying,/ Underneath the moss, oh/ Seeing it brings such sorrow!"

◄ **Shoshi.** *See Murasaki Shikibu for sidebar.*

ACKNOWLEDGMENTS

Photographs and illustrations appearing in *Women in World History, Volume 7,* were received from the following sources:

Courtesy of the AFL-CIO, **p. 541**; Photo by Marion Allen, **p. 577**; Courtesy of the Amateur Speedskating Union, **pp. 208, 439**; Courtesy of Fred M.B. Amram, **pp. 678–679**; Courtesy of Harriet Horne Arrington, **p. 475**; Painting by Bermejo, 1493, **p. 713**; Photos by Marcus Blechman, **pp. 87, 561**; Courtesy of the Library of the Boston Atheneum, **p. 603**; © Brooksfilms, Ltd., 1980, **p. 319**; Photo by Robin Carson, **p. 395**; Courtesy of Columbia Pictures, **pp. 112, 406**; Photo by Edward Cronenweth, **p. 479**; Courtesy of the *Daily Worker,* **p. 640**; Photo by De Baron, 1934, **p. 425**; © Editions du Seuill (Paris), photo by Ulf Anderson, **p. 141**; Courtesy of David Zadig, the *Episcopal Times,* **p. 8**; Courtesy of Font Memorial Library (Columbus, Mississippi), **p. 115**; Painting by Chester Harding, **p. 83**; Courtesy of Beth Heiden, **p. 156**; Courtesy of Heinemann Educational Publishers (Oxford, England), **p. 125**; Courtesy of Susan Hockaday, **p. 361**; Courtesy of Moorland-Spingarn Research Center, Howard University (Washington, D.C.), **p. 15**; Courtesy of the Hummel Museum and Art Gallery (New Braunfels, Texas), **p. 559**; Courtesy of the University of Illinois at Urbana-Champaign, **p. 119**; © The Imogen Cunningham Trust, 1978, 1996, **p. 419**; Courtesy of the International Museum of Photography at the George Eastman House, **p. 589**;Courtesy of International Swimming Hall of Fame **p. 415**; Photo by Ray Jones, **p. 47**; Courtesy of the Kenneth Spencer Research Library, University of Kansas, **p. 626**: Courtesy of Karl Lagerfeld, **p. 6**; Photo by Leopold (Munich, Germany), **p. 744**; Courtesy of the Library of Congress, **pp. 63, 88, 267, 343, 469, 517, 593, 597**; Courtesy of the Marine Biological Labratory Library (Woods Hole, Massachusetts), **p. 44**; © Merchant-Ivory, photo by Seth Rubin, **p. 197**; Courtesy of Metro-Goldwyn-Mayer, **p. 438** (photo by Ruth Harriet Louise), **p. 613**; Photo by Carl Mydans, **p. 293**; Photo by Nadar, **p. 718**; Courtesy of the National Organization of Women, **p. 683**; Courtesy of the National Portrait Gallery (London), **p. 367**; © New World Picture, **p. 551**; Courtesy of the Oregon Historical Society, **p. 452**; © Paramount Pictures, 1995, **p. 728**; © Paramount Pictures and Miramax Films, 1999, **p. 297**; Courtesy of the Schlesinger Library, Radcliffe College, **pp. 211, 373, 502**; Photo by A.L. Schafer, **p. 109**; Courtesy of the National Portrait Gallery, Smithsonian Institution, photo by Clara E. Sipprell, **p. 377**; Courtesy of the Sports Museum of Finland, **p. 37**; Courtesy of Square Haskins Photo (Dallas, Texas), **p. 547**; Courtesy of the Nationalgalerie, Staatliche Museen Preussischer, Kulturbesitz (Berlin), **p. 357**; Courtesy of the Hoover Institution Archives, Stanford University, **p. 457**; Courtesy of the Records of the Women's International League for Peace and Freedom, Swarthmore College, **p. 281**; Courtesy of the Institute of Texan Cultures, **p. 652**; Courtesy of the Nettie Lee Benson Latin American Collection, University of Texas at Austin, **p. 256**; Courtesy of Twentieth Century-Fox, **p. 76**, © 1967, **p. 234**, © 1949, **p. 413**; Courtesy of the U.S. House of Representatives. **pp. 146, 289, 430, 437, 533**; Courtesy of the U.S. Senate Historical Office, **pp. 81, 564**; Courtesy of Underwood & Underwood, **p. 653**; Courtesy of UNICEF/5261, photo by John Isaac, **p. 229**; Courtesy of the Unisys Corporation, **p. 470**; Courtesy of United Artists, 1951, **p. 241**; Painting by Anthony van Dyke, **p. 219**; Courtesy of Marianne Horney Von Eckardt, **p. 489**; © Warner Bros., **p. 553**; Courtesy of Warner Bros. Records, Inc., **p. 630**; Courtesy of the Archives of Labor and Urban Affairs, Wayne State University (Detroit, Michigan), **p. 539**.